Lecture Notes of the Institute for Computer Sciences, Social Informatics and Telecommunications Engineering

198

More information about this series at http://www.springer.com/series/8197

Lecture Notes of the Institute for Computer Sciences, Social Informatics and Telecommunications Engineering

198

More information about this series at http://www.springer.com/series/8197

Robert Deng · Jian Weng
Kui Ren · Vinod Yegneswaran (Eds.)

Security and Privacy in Communication Networks

12th International Conference, SecureComm 2016
Guangzhou, China, October 10–12, 2016
Proceedings

 Springer

Editors
Robert Deng
Singapore Management University
Singapore
Singapore

Jian Weng
Jinan University
Guangzhou, Guangdong
China

Kui Ren
University at Buffalo
Buffalo, NY
USA

Vinod Yegneswaran
SRI International
Menlo Park, CA
USA

ISSN 1867-8211   ISSN 1867-822X   (electronic)
Lecture Notes of the Institute for Computer Sciences, Social Informatics
and Telecommunications Engineering
ISBN 978-3-319-59607-5   ISBN 978-3-319-59608-2   (eBook)
DOI 10.1007/978-3-319-59608-2

Library of Congress Control Number: 2017943011

Printed on acid-free paper

This Springer imprint is published by Springer Nature
The registered company is Springer International Publishing AG
The registered company address is: Gewerbestrasse 11, 6330 Cham, Switzerland

Preface

The 12th EAI International Conference on Security and Privacy in Communication Networks (SecureComm) was held during October 10–12, 2016, in the beautiful city of Guangzhou, China. SecureComm 2016, one of the premier conferences in cyber security, was the first EAI-supported conference organized in Southern China. It provided an opportunity for researchers, technologists, and industry specialists in cyber security to meet and exchange ideas and information.

We were honored to have hosted keynote speeches by Dr. Moti Yung and Dr. Guofei Gu. The conference program included technical papers selected through peer reviews by the Program Committee members, invited talks, special sessions, industrial presentations, and student demo sessions. Out of a total number of 137 submissions, 30 were selected as full papers and 25 as poster papers.

We would like to thank many people for having worked hard to make SecureComm 2016 a success. First, we would like to thank the EAI, especially Prof. Imrich Chlamtac of EAI, for their strong support of this conference. We thank the members of the conference committees and the reviewers for their dedicated and passionate work. In particular, we thank the Program Committee co-chairs, Dr. Kui Ren and Dr. Vinod Yegneswaran, for their leadership in putting up such a wonderful program. We also thank Ms. Anna Horvathova and Ms. Ivana Allen of EAI and Ms. Xiujie Huang of Jinan University for their hard work and dedication in taking great care of the conference organization. We are grateful to all the authors who submitted papers to the conference, for none of this would have happened without their valuable contributions. We also thank our sponsors for their financial support: Jinan University and Create-Net. Without the extremely generous support of EAI, this conference could not have taken place. Last but not least, we thank the Steering Committee of SecureComm for having invited us to serve as the general chairs of SecureComm 2016.

We hope you enjoy the proceedings of SECURECOMM 2016 as much as we enjoyed the conference.

April 2017

Robert Deng
Jian Weng

Organization

Steering Committee

Imrich Chlamtac	University of Trento, CREATE-NET, Italy
Guofei Gu (Co-chair)	Texas A&M University, USA
Krishna Moorthy Sivalingam	IIT Madras, India
Peng Liu	Pennsylvania State University, USA
Z. Morley Mao	University of Michigan, USA
Xiaofeng Wang	Indiana University Bloomington, USA
Vinod Yegneswaran	SRI International, USA

General Co-chairs

Robert Deng	Singapore Management University, Singapore
Jian Weng	Jinan University, Guangzhou, China

TPC Co-chairs

Kui Ren	SUNY Buffalo, USA
Vinod Yegneswaran	SRI International, USA

Local Chair

Liang Gu	Jinan University and Yale University, USA

Publications Chair

Xiaodong Lin	University of Ontario Institute of Technology, Canada

Workshop Co-chairs

Aziz Mohaisen	SUNY Buffalo, USA
Songqing Chen	George Mason University, USA

Panels Co-chairs

Danfeng Yao	Virginia Tech, USA
Roberto Di Pietro	University of Rome III, Italy

Publicity and Social Media Co-chairs

Weili Han   Fudan University, China
Rongxing Lu   Nanyang Technological University, Singapore
Marina Blanton   University of Notre Dame, USA
Ruggero Donida Labati   University of Milan, Italy

Web Chair

Cong Wang   City University of Hong Kong, SAR China

Sponsorship and Exhibits Chair

Yongdong Wu   Institute for Infocomm Research, Singapore

Conference Coordinator

Anna Horvathova   European Alliance for Innovation

Technical Program Committee

Elisa Bertino   Purdue University, USA
Yinzhi Cao   Lehigh University, USA
Neha Chachra   Facebook, USA
Kai Chen   Chinese Academy of Sciences, China
Yan Chen   Northwestern University, USA
Sherman S.M. Chow   Chinese University of Hong Kong, SAR China
Jun Dai   California State University, Sacramento, USA
Mohan Dhawan   IBM Research, India
Birhanu Eshete   University of Illinois at Chicago, USA
Debin Gao   Singapore Management University, Singapore
Ryan Gerdes   Utah State University, USA
Yier Jin   The University of Central Florida, USA
Murat Kantarcioglu   University of Texas at Dallas, USA
Yingjiu Li   Singapore Management University, Singapore
Xiaodong Lin   University of Ontario Institute of Technology, Canada
Zhiqiang Lin   University of Texas at Dallas, USA
Yao Liu   University of South Florida, USA
Zhe Liu   University of Waterloo, Canada
Long Lu   Stony Brook University, USA
Rongxing Lu   Nanyang Technological University, Singapore
Aziz Mohaisen   SUNY Buffalo, USA
Goutam Paul   Indian Statistical Institute, India
Pierangela Samarati   Università degli Studi di Milano, Italy
Seungwon Shin   KAIST, Korea
Kapil Singh   IBM T.J. Watson Research Center, USA

Anna Squicciarini	The Pennsylvania State University, USA
Kun Sun	College of William and Mary, USA
Eugene Vasserman	Kansas State University, USA
Shobha Venkataraman	AT&T Labs Research, USA
Cong Wang	City University of Hong Kong, SAR China
Haining Wang	University of Delaware, USA
Qian Wang	Wuhan University, China
Nicholas Weaver	International Computer Science Institute, USA
Mengjun Xie	University of Arkansas at Little Rock, USA
Danfeng Yao	Virginia Tech, USA
Fareed Zaffar	Lahore University of Management Sciences, Pakistan
Bingsheng Zhang	University of Lancaster, UK
Junjie Zhang	Wright State University, USA
Kehuan Zhang	Chinese University of Hong Kong, SAR China
Yinqian Zhang	The Ohio State University, USA
Sheng Zhong	Nanjing University, China
Yongbin Zhou	Chinese Academy of Sciences, China
Sencun Zhu	The Pennsylvania State University, USA
Cliff Zou	University of Central Florida, USA

Contents

Web Security and Privacy

System Security

Mobile Security II

Hardware Security

Poster Session

Mobile Security I

AppShield: Enabling Multi-entity Access Control Cross Platforms for Mobile App Management

Zhengyang Qu[1]([✉]), Guanyu Guo[2], Zhengyue Shao[2], Vaibhav Rastogi[3], Yan Chen[1], Hao Chen[4], and Wangjun Hong[1]

[1] Northwestern University, Evanston, IL 60208, USA
{zhengyangqu2017,wangjunhong2015}@u.northwestern.edu,
ychen@northwestern.edu
[2] Zhejiang University, Hangzhou, China
{guanyuguo,szylover}@zju.edu.cn
[3] University of Wisconsin, Madison, WI 53706, USA
vrastogi@wisc.edu
[4] University of California, Davis, CA 95616, USA
hchen@ucdavis.edu

Abstract. Bring-your-own-device (BYOD) is getting popular. Diverse personal devices are used to access enterprise resources, and deployment of the solutions with customized operating system (OS) dependency will thus be restricted. Moreover, device utilization for both business and personal purposes creates new threats involving leakage of sensitive data. As for functionalities, a BYOD solution should isolate an arbitrary number of entities, such as those relating to business and personal uses and provide fine-grained access control on multi-entity management. Existing BYOD solutions lack in these aspects; we propose a system, called APP-SHIELD, which supports multi-entity management and role-based access control with file-level granularity, apart from local data sharing/isolation. APPSHIELD includes (1) application rewriting framework for Android apps, which builds Mobile Application Management (MAM) features into app automatically with complete mediation, (2) cross-platform proxy-based data access mechanism, which can enforce arbitrary access control policies. The fully functional controller with data proxy is implemented for both Android and iOS. APPSHIELD allows for enterprise policy management without modifying device OS. The evaluation shows that APP-SHIELD is successful at policy enforcement and is reliable. It induces little impact on application's performance and size, for example, our app rewriting introduces less than 5% code size increment in over 95% apps in our evaluation.

1 Introduction

Bring your own device (BYOD) enterprise policies have been growing in popularity. Employees use their personal devices to access an enterprise's proprietary resources. According to the survey by RCR Wireless News in 2015 [1], 85% of respondents indicated BYOD was incorporated into their organization's current

© ICST Institute for Computer Sciences, Social Informatics and Telecommunications Engineering 2017
R. Deng et al. (Eds.): SecureComm 2016, LNICST 198, pp. 3–23, 2017.
DOI: 10.1007/978-3-319-59608-2_1

telecom offering. The popularity of BYOD represents both an opportunity and a challenge. On the one hand, it boosts productivity and reduces the cost of dedicated devices. On the other hand, using the same device for both business and personal activities incurs new security threats, such as data exfiltration and revenue loss due to lost devices, employee job hopping, and malware. For example, considering the threat of malware alone, both Android and iOS have been reported to be affected by malware or low-reputation content [16,19,30]. Used in a BYOD setting, infected devices could threaten the confidentiality and integrity of business data. The concept of Mobile Application Management (MAM) is thus proposed to secure the BYOD utilization. Specifically, MAM solutions are the software and services that control access to enterprise resources at the mobile application level.

Android and iOS have discretionary access control to isolate data among apps. Regarding data sharing, Android provides the world read-/writable external storage, and iOS maintains a similar directory /Documents/Inbox/. The system default data sharing/isolation mechanisms are insufficient for the complicated scenario of BYOD, given the numerous inter-app information flows from various entities. We also investigate existing BYOD commercial solutions (in Sect. 3.1), studies on information flow control [25,31–33,42] and application virtualization/sandboxing [21,29,43]. The following issues are not addressed.

- **Portability.** Many existing studies have been proposed to secure privileged resources in the enterprise environment [29,37], but they are rarely adopted by vendors. Users have to get the customized firmware in deploying the security extension on their devices; this may not be possible because most devices have locked boot loaders and even in cases where this is technically possible, users may lack the right skills. The fragmentation issue of Android is another dominant factor that hinders the solutions with customized OS dependency from deploying in large scale. A recent report [8] showed 599 distinct Android brands with 11,868 distinct devices in 2013 and 18,796 distinct devices in 2014. Moreover, each of Android OS versions 2.3, 4.0, 4.1, 4.2, 4.4 has more than 10% of the worldwide market share. A solid MAM solution should not have any OS-specific requirement, e.g. version, firmware, to bolster the portability.
- **Multi-entity management.** Given a device, parallel data access control among application sets of various business entities is essential in the scenario of external business partner collaboration. For example, when a consulting company works closely with multiple clients simultaneously, it requires privileged data from those companies. The data sharing within each company's application set should be orthogonal. Existing BYOD solutions cannot address this issue because they only support bisecting the apps on device into the personal set and the business set.
- **Role-based access control (RBAC).** Role-based access control (RBAC) [36–38] associate permissions with roles and users are made members of roles. It eases access management and is especially beneficial to large organizations like financial and medical institutions.

While some operating systems (such as Android 5.0 and above) offer multi-account based management, the approach is not as flexible and lacks multi-entity management and RBAC support. We believe a BYOD solution should provide greater flexibility to enterprise policy administrators with respect to these aspects.

- **Fine-grained access control.** More stringent privacy laws have recently imposed new levels of confidentiality on health care and insurance companies, and financial institutions. Existing solutions do not have the policy enforcement flexible enough to secure high-credential data. In a solid solution, the data access among apps is controlled at a file level. For example, a user can share normal attachments received via email to `Dropbox`, but for a patent document with high-credential, any file sharing app's access can be blocked.

To resolve these problems in existing MAM solutions, we take the approach of application rewriting and provide it in a fully implemented prototype APP-SHIELD with the consideration of portability, which is able to enforce arbitrary access control policies with no dependency of OS. APPSHIELD includes two parts: (1) application rewriting framework for Android platform, which builds MAM features into an app, (2) cross platform proxy-based data access mechanism, which is able to enforce arbitrary access control policies.

The application rewriting framework automatically converts a personal app to the business version with almost no developer support. Specifically, the application using APPSHIELD does not need to be developed in a certain way w.r.t storing/accessing documents. We hook into the `libc` [6] to capture all file system system-call related calls and those relevant to Android content provider [7]. This design enables APPSHIELD to achieve complete mediation. APPSHIELD protects privileged data access through the stealth channels: (1) native code, (2) dynamic code loading [34], and (3) Java reflection. The interposed low-level system calls can reliably intercept the privileged data request from the application level in all these scenarios. While we provide our proxy-based data access mechanism for both platforms, the application rewriting is available for Android only due to the closed-source nature of iOS. Nonetheless, with a little developer support (such as using an "APPSHIELD" SDK), it is possible to provide iOS support.

The proxy-based data access mechanism is implemented within a controller application. Then we transparently proxy the data requests through our own controller that manages the applications' file-system-level data, content provider data and enforces access control policies. Apart from portability, the novel design of decoupling policy enforcement from OS also brings the benefit of cross platform. With the idea of data request proxy, we implement the fully functional controller application on iOS platform.

The APPSHIELD Android app[1] has been released on both Google Play in North America, and Myapp in China. Our contributions are:

- We design a proxy-based data access mechanism that does not need OS support to enforce arbitrary access control policies, including those like

---

[1] https://play.google.com/store/apps/details?id=com.webshield.appshield&hl=en.

MAC/SELinux [39] also. It is easily extended to other platforms, which is implemented on both Android and iOS.

- We investigate applying our proxy-based data access mechanism to Android MAM. The system prototype supports the configuration/enforcement of four types of security policies. *File isolation.* The privileged files of business apps are isolated from personal apps. *Multi-entity management & RBAC.* Apps can be divided into an arbitrary number of logical sets. It is further utilized in modeling RBAC, with orthogonal intra-set data access and multicast security policy update. Although we are not the first to apply RBAC to Android platform [36,37], we propose a novel design without OS modification to boost portability. *Fine-grained file access control.* To provide special protection on high-credential data, the access control policy could be defined at file-level granularity. *Content provider isolation.* Other than managing the privileged structured data in system content provider, the data requests from the business apps are redirected to a private mirror content provider. For example, the business contacts are hidden from the personal apps.
- Our evaluation shows that APPSHIELD has low overhead in memory, runtime, and package size and that it can reliably rewrite a large number of apps.

The remainder of this paper is organized as follows. Section 2 presents a brief background. Next, we cover the problem statement and APPSHIELD design in detail in Sect. 3, followed by the implementation aspects in Sect. 4. Section 5 deals with the evaluation of APPSHIELD. We have the relevant discussion and related work in Sects. 6 and 7. Finally, we conclude our work in Sect. 8.

2   Background and Threat Model

Background. Android apps are implemented in Java, which is compiled down to Dalvik bytecode. It is also possible to use native code in apps. Android runtime environment enforces the sandbox mechanism to separate running apps. An app is assigned a unique user identifier (UID), by which the Linux kernel enforces discretionary access control (DAC) on low-level resources. Specifically, each app holds a private directory to keep the data in the internal storage, which cannot be accessed by any other app. The middleware further offers a permission system [9]. An app is granted permissions during installation. Apart from the pre-defined permissions guarding the system services, an app can define its customized permissions to restrict the access to their own components: *Activities, Services, Content Providers* [7], and *Broadcast Receivers.* Android includes content providers to control the access to a structured set of data.

3 types of MAM solutions have been proposed for BYOD.

- *Application Rewriting.* This approach inserts management hooks into existing Android apps. It has the advantages that it requires no developer collaboration and that it is independent of the OS version. However, it fails on apps that have been protected by anti-decompilation techniques.

- *Software Development Kit (SDK).* MAM vendors provide software development kits (SDK) for developers to incorporate into their apps. This approach has the disadvantage that developers must build and distribute two versions of the same app, and users' choice of business apps is limited to the markets.
- *OS Modification.* MAM features are directly built into the OS, so it neither requires developer collaboration nor can be defeated by anti-decompilation. However, since it relies on OS customization, the portability is limited.

In the case of application rewriting, third-party BYOD services are deployed with enterprise mobile marketplace. The client company selects useful general app, and BYOD vendor generates the enterprise version. Application rewriting requests reverse-engineering the personal app. With developer's cooperation in an enterprise setting, the developers can be asked not to apply anti-decompilation techniques, and either the developer's certificate or the unique certificate generated by BYOD vendor can be used to sign the business app under the agreement. Thus, app update can be easily managed in a timely manner.

Permissions are associated with roles, and users are made members of appropriate roles. Compared with the traditional group-based access control that only involves a set of users, using the role concept to bridge the user set and the permission set largely simplifies management of permissions and brings extra semantics in access control, which is valuable in the scenario of MAM.

Threat Model. On the device, both personal apps and business apps are installed. The personal apps may contain malware, which is able to access and leak the privileged data to untrusted servers. Moreover, for the data owned by an enterprise, other companies are motivated to track it.

OS level protection sacrifices the portability. Considering Android fragmentation, a solution without portability cannot fulfill the needs of BYOD, where employees utilize their diverse personal smartphones for business usage also. We agree that our defenses can be compromised if a device is rooted. Root is however too strong a threat model. Only hardware or hypervisor-based solutions can ensure defense against superuser attacks. OS-level defenses remain vulnerable. Furthermore, a lot of modern devices are not rootable by any known means, meaning our defenses can offer complete protection.

3 System Design

3.1 Problem Statement

Security Model. The security model of AppShield is depicted in Fig. 1. An employee may install both personal and business apps on her device. A personal app may be any app that the user wishes to install, including possibly malicious apps. The business app, however, is issued by the IT administrator, who grants business apps as follows. First, he selects any off-the-shelf app from a mobile marketplace that is useful for his organization and submits the request to the BYOD vendor. Then, BYOD provider vets it using existing malware detection

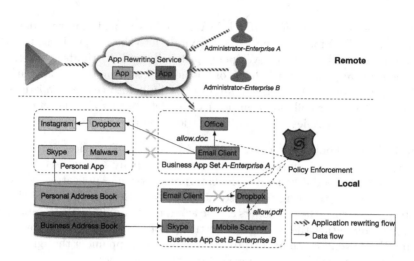

Fig. 1. Security model

systems, such as [20, 26, 35]. Finally, the app is converted into business version and deployed in the enterprise mobile application marketplace after getting the agreement from the application developer.

Personal apps share data by existing mechanisms, such as content provider and public external storage, on Android. For example, Instagram posts the photos managed by Dropbox. Business apps share corporate data using the mechanisms provided by APPSHIELD. APPSHIELD manages a secure space where all the business data are maintained and security policies can be dynamically configured and enforced at file-level granularity as the tuple:

$$Policy = (\text{App\_S}, \text{Obj}, \text{App\_R}, \text{D}), \tag{1}$$

where App_S and App_R are the apps to share and receive the data, Obj is the object to be shared, and D is the decision made. When the Office app, for example, opens a document "allow.doc" from the business Email Client, APP-SHIELD validates the identity of the Office app, verifies against the security policy, opens the attachment file, and provides the business version of Office with the file descriptor of the opened file, whereas the app Dropbox could not access the file "deny.doc" owned by Email Client due to the policy violation.

As for multi-entity management, business apps from different companies installed on a device can be classified into various logic sets by the IT administrator. Given the flexibility and simplicity of management, RBAC is introduced to model the capabilities assigned to the user through the user-role review phase. Specifically, in Fig. 1, the business app set A represents that a user is assigned the role holding the permissions to check the email and edit attached enterprise document belonging to enterprise A. The business app set B grants higher privilege to the user and allows the access to the address book and scanned document shared via the cloud service of enterprise B.

Table 1. Comparison with existing MAM solutions

Method	System	Isolation	Multi-entity management	RBAC	Granularity	Sharing	Portability
Rewriting	**AppShield**	**Sandbox**	**Yes**	**Yes**	**File-level dynamic**	**Local**	High
	AirWatch [2]	Sandbox	No	Yes	Static	Online	
	Mocana [15]	Sandbox	No	No	Static	Online	
SDK	Good [13]	Sandbox	No	No	Coarse dynamic	Online	High
	Citrix [12]	Sandbox & Encryption	No	Yes	Static	Local	
	AirWatch	Sandbox	No	Yes	Static	Online	
OS modification	Android L	DAC	No	No	Coarse dynamic	Local	Low

System Overview. Our system is organized into two parts: (1) an application rewriting framework for Android platform as the back-end that converts a personal app from mobile markets to a hardened business version by injecting MAM functionalities; (2) a front-end mobile app for both Android and iOS platforms that enforces the security policies with our proxy-based data access mechanism.

Table 1 lists existing MAM solutions on corporate data isolation/sharing and access control. The leading MAM vendors, except Citrix [12], fail to support local privileged data sharing, which requires the network connection and reduces the usability. Given the lack of fine-grained access control, these solutions are not able to provide special care of data with high-credential. All of the existing MAM solutions listed in Table 1 only bisect apps into the business set and the personal set. APPSHIELD supports classifying the installed apps into an arbitrary number of groups, which enables multi-entity management. Some current BYOD systems provide RBAC support, but they deploy the access control module on the server side handled by their own administrators, which is not feasible in managing the data from multiple companies on the same device due to the lack of communication channel among IT administrators. Our solution jointly considers role modeling and multi-entity management.

To our best knowledge, Bring Android to work [11] deployed on Android 5.0 and above is closest to our framework but it still fails to satisfy all the requirements listed in Sect. 1. This system is implemented at the operating system level. It divides the external storage into two directories: `/storage/emulated/0/` for personal apps and `/storage/emulated/10/` for business apps. The two versions of an app run with different UIDs. The data in one directory is only publicly accessible and shareable by apps from the corresponding set.

On Android L, we found that enterprise data could be shared among them without proper regulation. Because Android L only enforces DAC at the root directories of the two application sets, the fundamental data sharing mechanism of authorized apps remains the same with general personal apps. When a privileged file is shared via file system, it goes through the public storage that is readable by other business apps, and the only difference is that data exchange is in the business root directory. It is not capable of setting up multiple business application sets, and thus neither the multi-entity management nor the fine-grained access control is supported.

Given our radically different design and methodology from existing studies, we summarize the following challenges:

- **Lack of OS support.** The existing Android storage mechanism can only support either data isolation by private internal storage or data sharing by the system-wide read-/writable external storage or by content providers. Previous work, such as TrustDroid [28,43], Maxoid [42], Aquifer [31], and DR BACA [37], need to modify Android middleware to achieve the domain-level data isolation or permission regulation, which strongly reduces the portability. Thus, it is non-trivial to enable allocating a selective set of apps privileged data access permission without OS modification and root privilege.
- **Diversity of data access behavior.** Developers could utilize a diverse set of methods to access privileged data. We need to abstract the data access behavior to completely enforce the data isolation/sharing policies.
- **Performance penalty.** Some previous studies employ virtualization-based approaches to provide isolation between private and corporate domains [22]. Such methods do not scale well on the resource-constrained mobile device. Moreover, deep virtualization reduces the battery lifetime given the duplication of complete OS.

3.2   Application Rewriting Framework

The developer can either call the OS API based on the framework interface written in Java or directly invoke the native libraries. All the OS-level API invocations go through libc, which then makes system calls into the kernel. The libc layer provides us with a reliable point that abstracts all the complex high-level data access requests. Overwriting the entries in the global offset table (GOT) during the dynamic linking procedure allows us to inject our hooks to monitor the app's data access behavior and enforce our security policies. Details of this application rewriting method were discussed in Aurasium [41]. We do not claim the application rewriting design as our contribution, but rather our investigation on its usage in data access control.

Android apps are distributed in APK, which is a JAR archive including compiled Java source files in Dalvik bytecode, compiled manifest file, resources such as layout, images, and native libraries. We first unpack the APK file and decompile the dex bytecode to an intermediate representation (IR) smali [17] to enable our modification on bytecode. Our rewriting modifies 3 parts of application:

- **Native code.** We implement our customized system call hooks in C/C++ to monitor the privacy-sensitive behavior, such as open() and rename() for file access and ioctl() for data exchange via the content provider. Java code cannot modify process memory space, so we include the native code to overwrite the GOT with the address of our detour hooks whenever any ELF file is loaded. Moreover, business apps have frequent communication with

APPSHIELD, which includes information such as the identifier of business app to enforce security policies, and we thus implement the communication via the socket in the native layer for the latency performance.

- **Manifest file.** Android OS has the process `zygote` to initialize all the apps. When an app is running, its runtime environment is established. To enable GOT overwriting in ELF file, we modify the Manifest file to wrap the target app with our preprocess procedure. Specifically, we inject a service into the app that invokes the native code to modify the GOTs of all the loaded ELFs, and the preprocess procedure is configured in the parent class of the whole target app to guarantee it is running in the middle of `zygote` initialization and the start of the app. Moreover, APPSHIELD front-end app manages the security policy repository set by the IT administrator and enforces the security policies that grant the app the access to privileged data. Thus, we need to declare the *Activities* in the manifest file, which are injected into the target app's bytecode to popup UI message about the violation of secure policies. Regarding the data sharing/isolation of content provider, we create a mirror content provider in the private internal storage of APPSHIELD and guard it with a special permission. Therefore, if a business app needs access to this content provider, it must declare this permission in the Manifest file.

- **Bytecode.** We modify the bytecode to configure the preprocess procedure in the parent class of the app. For example, `class A` is the child class of `class B` whose parent class is `android.app.Application` [4]. Then we replace the parent class of `class B` with our injected service. The *Activities* showing UI message are written in Java, compiled and converted to Dalvik bytecode.

We then compile the IR into the rewritten version of bytecode and repack the app into an APK file. An app needs to be signed, but rewriting invalidates its original signature, and APPSHIELD cannot sign the rewritten app using its original private key. The signature is mainly used for identifying the developer. Moreover, app updates require the new version of each app to be signed with the same private key as the old version. APPSHIELD can achieve these functions by signing apps originally signed with same keys with same (but new) keys.

APPSHIELD is deployed as a remote service and generates a random private key to sign each business app. When the app is installed, the client side APPSHIELD keeps the mapping from the package name to its signature, which is used to differentiate business apps and personal apps. Due to the physical isolation of signature generation and the one-to-one mapping of original keys to new keys, it is difficult for an attacker to create a malicious app with the same signature as that of a legitimate business app to launch the privilege escalation attack. Our remote service can manage app update in the same way as mobile markets.

3.3   Proxy-Based Data Access Mechanism

Figure 2 illustrates our proxy-based data access mechanism. In Android, any operation on privileged data via file system and content provider goes through our customized low-level system calls. The injected bytecode collects the context

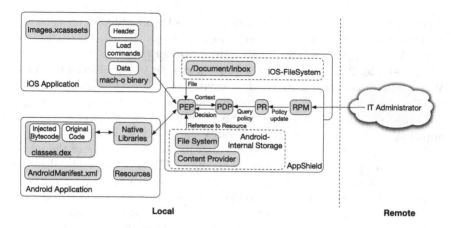

Fig. 2. Proxy-based data access mechanism

of the operation, such as the package name, signature, and data properties. The context is then sent to the **Policy Enforcement Point (PEP)**, which is implemented as a *Service* in AppShield and can be accessed by other apps through the socket in the native layer. On iOS platform, the request of file operation carrying the app's identity and target file object is sent to PEP, which is implemented as a handler. The **Policy Decision Point (PDP)** decides whether the operation is allowed based on the context from PEP and the query results from the **Policy Repository (PR)** that could be remotely updated by IT administrator via **Remote Policy Manager (RPM)**.

Android. AppShield virtually maintains a file system and content providers in its internal storage. If data sharing is allowed, AppShield generates a reference to the data, which is granted to the business app. The business app indirectly operates on privileged data based on the reference to avoid creating duplicated data for the sake of performance, security, and synchronization. Data isolation is achieved, because the file system and the content provider are privately stored in the internal storage, and PDP validates whether the app requesting data operation is a business one; if so, application identity is further verified against security policy set.

File-system. Wherever the original app stores the data, such as public external storage and privately accessible space, AppShield redirects the file operations from business apps to its own internal storage. We need to hook the following system calls:

- **open(), creat().** As an app invokes these two system calls, AppShield invokes the original system calls with a modified file path in the internal storage of AppShield and passes the flags and modes with a returned file descriptor.

- **rename(), mkdir(), remove().** The file paths in the parameters of these system calls are replaced with the business file paths in its internal storage.
- **stat(), lstat().** APPSHIELD first gets a file descriptor to the business file in its internal storage and then invokes the `fstat()` to fetch the file status.

Content Provider. Content providers manage the access to a structured set of data, which is identified by URI [10]. Our proxy-based data access mechanism on content provider goes as follows:

- **Mirror content provider.** The core of content provider is the *SQLite* database. APPSHIELD duplicates the target content provider with the same schema and table definition in its private internal storage. APPSHIELD guards the mirror content provider with a special permission.
- **System call ioctl().** This is the main system call through which all binder IPCs are sent. By interposing on this system call, APPSHIELD replaces the URIs to the original content provider with the URIs to the mirror content provider to redirect the data operation. Using context in this system call, APPSHIELD validates who initiates the operations on the content provider, and the PDP module decides whether to allow the access. The malicious app thus cannot operate on the mirror content provider by the overwriting URI and permission declaration.

iOS. Given the closed source iOS, it is difficult to have the rewriting framework inject the MAM features into general iOS apps without developer support. However, we easily extend our proxy-based data access mechanism on iOS platform and implement the APPSHIELD iOS client in `Swift`, which manages the virtual file system in its private space. The business app, which owns the privileged file, could *create* and *update* privileged file by sending it to APPSHIELD's directory `Documents/Inbox/`. At the same time, APPSHIELD records the mapping between the app's identity and the file object, which is expressed as App_S and Obj in Eq. 1. The "Open-in management" feature, introduced from iOS 7 [14], allows APPSHIELD to control which app the device uses to open a file. Thus, when an app App_R attempts to operate on the privileged file, APPSHIELD validates the request against the policies in PR.

3.4   Security Policy

File Isolation. The file-related operations from personal apps to business apps are strictly prohibited. All the files owned by business apps are kept in the internal storage of APPSHIELD client app, which is invisible to all the other apps. When an app initializes the file operation request, the package name bound with its signature are sent to APPSHIELD, which verifies whether it is a business app against the record in a database. It is extremely challenging to evade this security check because it requires the attacker to get the mapping relation between package name to app signature, which is constructed on the remote server side and securely stored in the private space of APPSHIELD client side.

Multi-entity Management and RBAC. Given the business apps from different companies, IT administrators can set up multiple app sets, where the union of the apps set's functionalities represents the permissions granted to this role (set). After a business app is pushed and installed on the device, it is assigned to a business app set following the configuration made by IT administrators, which can be dynamically adjusted on-the-fly. Once the business identity of the app requesting file access App_R is verified, APPSHIELD would further check whether there is an app set including both the owner of the target file App_S and App_R. If the two apps are not grouped into the same set, the file operation will be denied, which thus guarantees the orthogonal data access among roles. The example is illustrated in Fig. 3a and b, where one app set includes email client Outlook, document editor Docs to Go, and another set consists of the app Quickoffice. When Quickoffice tries to open the file *allow.doc* as an attachment in Outlook, the request is denied because the policy maintains the parallel access among different roles.

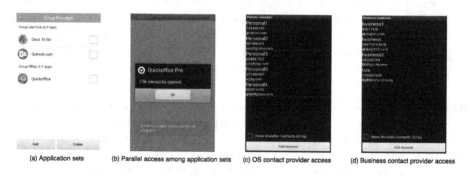

(a) Application sets   (b) Parallel access among application sets   (c) OS contact provider access   (d) Business contact provider access

Fig. 3. Multi-entity management, RBAC & Content provider isolation

Fine-Grained File Access Control. Android Lollipop allows all the requests across the business apps. In contrast, APPSHIELD's file sharing is managed at file-level granularity for the apps in the same set. Given the sender app App_S, the receiver app App_R, and the file object Obj, APPSHIELD checks the corresponding security policy in its repository, whose default value is Allow. This mechanism enables more flexible access control in protecting the high confidential file.

Content Provider Isolation. Business app conducts operations on the mirror content provider. If the app's identity is verified, the cursor of the mirror content provider will be returned, or APPSHIELD will assign the app with the reference to the system content provider. This design guarantees the isolated operation on data in system default content provider and business privileged content provider. Note the example app in Fig. 3c and d, with the behavior of accessing the system's address book, the enterprise app fetches the business contacts in mirror content provider.

4   Implementation

We leverage the existing open source tools `apktool` [3] to unpack, decompile, and repack the app. We implement our customized system calls in C/C++. The open source tool AXML [5] allows us to modify the Manifest file at ease. The activities used to popup warning message are implemented in Java and those `.class` files are converted to bytecode using `dx` included in Android build tools. We also implement a script in `Python` to rewrite the bytecode in IR.

Android has 3 system content providers: contact provider, SMS provider, and calendar provider. The proxy-based data access mechanism is currently implemented on the contact provider. The calendar provider and SMS provider could be extended easily with small engineering efforts. For the content providers of third-party apps, our solution interposes on the system call `ioctl()` and blocks the operation when the app managing the content provider and the app accessing the data are from different sets.

5   Evaluation

We evaluated APPSHIELD on a Samsung Galaxy Nexus with 4.3 Jelly Bean and an iPhone 5 s with iOS 8.1.1.

5.1   Security Policy Enforcement

We selected 50 apps from Google Play to evaluate the effectiveness of our proxy-based data access mechanism. These apps have common business functions, such as email, file-sharing, document editing/viewing, and contact management, which were classified into two sets by the type of sensitive data operation: (1) 35 file-related apps, and (2) 15 contact provider-related apps.

We first used APPSHIELD to convert these 50 apps to business versions. Then we manually interacted with these apps. Only one app can not be rewritten due to its obfuscation, which crashed the reverse engineering toolchain during unpacking, decoding, and repacking. One app crashed after rewriting. Even if we just decompiled and repacked the app without any code modification or injection, this app still crashed, which is probably attributed to the usage of repackage-detection techniques, e.g. integrity verification.

We then tested each file-related app against three security policies. Specifically, whether the file owned by the business app was isolated from personal apps and business apps from another group; whether the request from other business apps in the same group can be allowed and blocked according to the configuration. The results are listed in Table 2. Two apps cannot enforce the security policies regarding multi-entity management and fine-grained access control. After investigating the reason through application reverse-engineering, we found that these two apps looked up files with the path starting with "/./sdcard", which was not considered when being converted to paths in the private space of APPSHIELD and thus the business files cannot be located.

Table 2. 35 File-related applications

Package name	Isolation	Multi-entity management & RBAC	File-level granularity
com.pixatel.apps.filemgr	√	√	√
cn.wps.moffice_eng	√	√	√
com.aor.droidedit	√	√	√
com.dataviz.docstogo	√	√	√
net.appositedesigns.fileexplorer	√	√	√
com.ImaginationUnlimited.instaframe	√	√	√
com.joodioapps.DocToPdf	√	√	√
com.lyrebirdstudio.mirror	√	√	√
com.mail.emails	√	√	√
com.majedev.superbeam	√	√	√
com.microsoft.skydrive	√	√	√
com.outlook.Z7	√	√	√
com.outthinking.textonpic	√	√	√
org.devgiant.project.zipfileextracter	√	√	√
com.sketchpicture.pictutreeffect	√	√	√
com.taxaly.noteme	√	√	√
com.thomasgravina.pdfscanner	√	√	√
com.ToDoReminder.gen	√	√	√
com.youthhr.phonto	√	√	√
cz.awk.android.docconv	√	√	√
joa.zipper.editor	√	√	√
jp.ne.shira.csv.viewer	√	√	√
net.daum.android.solmail	√	√	√
com.acr.sdfilemanager	√	√	√
com.sapparray.docmgr	√	√	√
com.jellydog.freereader	√	√	√
com.olivephone.office	√	√	√
vn.esse.WordToText	√	×	×
couchDev.tools.DocxParser	√	×	×
com.qo.android.am3	√	√	√
com.probcomp.filexplorer	√	√	√
com.seeke.pdfreader	Crash		
com.topnet999.android.filemanager	√	√	√
com.nimblesoft.filemanager	√	√	√
com.infraware.office.link	Cannot rewrite		
Succeed	33/35	31/35	31/35

Table 3. 15 Contact provider-related applications

Package name	Isolation
com.appyown.contactsbackuprestore	√
com.globile.mycontactbackup	√
com.idea.backup.smscontacts	√
com.ijinshan.kbackup	√
com.mofinity.ui	√
com.payneservices.LifeReminders	×
com.tos.contact	√
net.IntouchApp	√
com.actimust.simplecontacts	√
com.netqin.contactbackup	√
no.uia.android.backupcontacts	√
com.xuecs.ContactHelper	√
digiteria.backup	√
nexg.contactbackup	√
com.brainworks.contacts.cuteblue	√
Succeed	14/15

The 15 contact provider-related apps were evaluated on content provider isolation. We checked whether each app loaded data from the system contact provider before rewriting and from the mirror contact provider as the business version. The results are abstracted in Table 3. One app failed in policy enforcement. Unlike the normal case where app loaded the address book data from contact provider, this app indirectly used Intent to start the system contact manager app. Our solution does not have the control over system apps.

Across the 120 times of policy enforcement (3 for each file-related app, 1 for each contact provider-related app), our mechanism achieves the success rate 109/120 (90.8%). The general reason for the failure is that our implementation does not consider developer's specific pattern of API invocation. e.g., the path of the privileged file.

5.2   Reliability

For the test on the reliability of AppShield, we picked top 250 apps by popularity on Google Play in September 2015 within the following categories: Business, Finance, Medical, and Productivity. We used AppShield to convert these 1000 apps to their business versions, and then automatically ran the apps using the UI/Application Exerciser Monkey [18]. The results are shown in Table 4.

12 apps failed during rewriting because their obfuscation crashed the reverse engineering tools apktool in unpacking, decoding, and repacking. While we

Table 4. Large-scale evaluation on 1000 applications

Total apps	Succeed	Cannot be rewritten	Crashed
1000	953(95.3%)	12(1.2%)	35(3.5%)

acknowledge that APPSHIELD cannot reliably rewrite apps with anti-reverse engineering techniques, our large-scale test shows that the percentage of these apps is still low. Also, developers are actively improving the reverse engineering tools that APPSHIELD relies on. For the 35 rewritten apps that crashed during execution, we ran their original versions and found 29 of them also crashed, which clearly were not caused by APPSHIELD. To investigate the reasons why the remaining 6 rewritten apps crashed while their original versions did not, we just unpacked and repacked them without modifying their code or data, and found all of them still crashed after repacking. We hypothesize that they might use anti-repacking techniques, such as signature validation. We performed these tests on real-world apps without developer support. In an enterprise MAM situation, however, it is reasonable to assume that the MAM provider can work with the developers so as to enable successful rewriting of their apps. Developers have strong incentive to work with MAM providers as this allows their apps to be used across entire enterprises.

5.3   Impact of Application Rewriting

Latency. We evaluated APPSHIELD's performance by both *micro-benchmark* and *macro-benchmark*. We implemented a test app that opens files and loads data from contact provider. Moreover, we developed an iOS app that can delegate the permission of accessing its private files to a selective set of apps. Given the closed nature of iOS, we could not modify the invocation of low-level system calls and hence cannot build an application rewriting framework. For evaluation, we implemented the proxy-based data access mechanism inside the app. Even though our rewriting framework is not cross platform, our proxy-based data access mechanism is. We expect that with reasonable developer support, our solution is still feasible on iOS platform.

- **Micro-benchmark.** We conducted a stress test with 1000 data access operations to investigate the latency introduced by APPSHIELD. First, we recorded the accumulated time spent on getting the file descriptor on Android and getting the file contents from the iOS APPSHIELD client with and without our security policies enforced. Because we cannot dig into low-level system calls of closed-source iOS, we measured the time of loading file contents on that platform. We also measured the total time of fetching the cursor, which is a reference to the content provider. Only the operations that we benchmarked contain the latency introduced by APPSHIELD for policy enforcement, and the further operations on data remained the same with the unmodified app. The results are listed in Table 5. In the worst case, APPSHIELD introduced an overall latency of 0.202 s on Android file system during 1000 operations, because acquiring each file descriptor involves one round of IPC with APP-SHIELD. For the performance on iOS, APPSHIELD introduced a latency of 0.176 s. APPSHIELD introduced a latency of 1.711 s when getting the cursor of a content provider. Since IPC is the dominant factor in the latency and has a fixed cost, the relative latency decreases, as the original operation takes longer.

- **Macro-benchmark.** We asked one user to manually load data via the file system and contact provider on the smartphone. We recorded the time from when the user started to access the data until when she closed the app after the data was fully rendered on screen. The user performed a series of data access operations for 5 times with and without APPSHIELD. Table 5 shows the average of time. APPSHIELD introduced a latency of 52 ms, 110 ms, and 126 ms in data operations on Android file system, iOS file system, and Android content provider, respectively. Such latency is barely perceptible. Although user experience on application response might not be accurate to the order of millisecond and there is a slight difference in each round of manual operation, we try our best to simulate user's daily usage manner.

Memory Consumption and Code Size. Figure 4 shows the cumulative distribution function (CDF) of the overhead in memory usage and code size caused by rewriting. To eliminate the side effect of Android garbage collection when calculating memory usage, we used the tool dumpsys in Android Debug Bridge (adb) to get the maximal memory usage during the execution of an app. To eliminate the side effect of compression during app packing, when calculating code size, we sum up the customized native libraries, Manifest file, and bytecode.

APPSHIELD's rewriting introduced less than 5% code size increment in over 95% apps, and more than 85% apps incurred the memory usage overhead less than 60%. The average overhead was 8049.1KiB in memory usage and 121.2KiB in code size. Our system hooks into the low-level system calls, and the dynamic linking naturally supports the efficient memory utilization by avoiding code duplication. Moreover, we add our customized system calls, and the classes for UI notification just once rather than inlining them at every point where the original app accesses privileged data.

Table 5. Runtime latency introduced by APPSHIELD

	File system				Content provider	
	Android		iOS		Android	
	Original	APPSHIELD	Original	APPSHIELD	Original	APPSHIELD
Micro-benchmark×1000 (s)	0.180	0.382	0.171	0.347	7.303	9.014
Macro-benchmark (s)	1.472	1.524	1.643	1.753	1.068	1.194

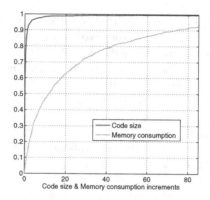

Fig. 4. Code size & memory usage overhead (CDF)

6   Discussion

APPSHIELD does have some limitations because of its current implementation. Our rewriting mechanism involves unpacking the APK file and decompiling the dex bytecode to IR. App developers sometimes use anti-reverse engineering techniques to crash decompilation tools to protect their intellectual property. Moreover, when the IT administrators conduct the security verification on the apps to be selected as business ones, the obfuscated app may challenge the correctness of the verification. However, our large-scale evaluation shows that the percentage of these apps is low. Moreover, the app developer could be asked not to apply such tools, where tiny developer support is needed. Developers are often willing to work with enterprises as this offers them a large high-payoff user base.

Another limitation is that it depends on hooking on the dynamically-linked libc. Any system call invoked not via the system libc, such as by using a statically-linked libc, will bypass our hooking mechanism. The chance of this happening is very low, and can be detected statically. Regarding the iOS platform, it is extremely hard to automatically rewrite apps and hook those system calls, given its closed-source nature. However, the proxy-based data access mechanism is cross-platform, which is implemented as a client iOS app leveraging the "Open-in management" feature.

7   Related Work

Virtualization and Sandboxing. L4Android [29] combines the L4Linux and Google modifications of Linux kernel to enable executing Android OS on top of a microkernel. Running multiple Android OS instances in parallel on the same device enables the complete isolation but has high performance penalty. TrustDroid [43] addresses the performance issues. It introduces the logical domain isolation approach, where two single domains are considered and isolation is enforced as a data flow property between the logical domains without running each domain as a single virtual machine. Boxify [21] constructs virtual sandboxes to secure Android apps, but the decision on which app to be isolated relies on manual identification. We model the data access control problem in the scenario of MAM, and app identity is classified by its business/personal purpose. These approaches fail to consider the data-sharing problem to give a fine-granulated control that grants a selective set of apps the access to privileged data.

Rewriting. Davis et al. [24] rewrite the Dalvik bytecode to allow interposing on security sensitive APIs. Retroskeleton [23] supports the retrofit of app's behaviors by static and dynamic method interposition. These approaches are based on the high-level API interposition, and thus, they cannot completely enforce the security policies across all layers of Android framework. Aurasium [41] adopts the design most similar to us that provides reference monitor capabilities by repackaging Android apps to use a customized version of libc. APPSHIELD extends the usage of this application rewriting technique with the proxy-based data access mechanism to achieve data access control, and multi-entity management. Similarly, ASM [27] provides a programmable interface for API hooking, which can also be leveraged to implement user-level access control.

RBAC. Vaidya et al. [40] propose RoleMiner to assist automatic role construction following a learning approach. Previous studies mostly focus on the general modeling of RBAC. Rohrer et al. [36,37] further investigate the specific RBAC problem when using Android device in sensitive environment, such as finance and health, but the mechanism involves the modification of system middleware and lacks a system prototype to be evaluated.

8   Conclusion

In this paper, we present the proxy-based data access mechanism, which can enforce arbitrary access control policies. Given the critical issues of MAM, our prototype system APPSHIELD achieves multi-entity management and RBAC at file-level granularity, apart from privileged data isolation from personal apps and corporate data sharing across business apps. We implement it on both Android and iOS platforms to demonstrate its cross platform property. Our design has neither dependency on OS nor the root privilege, which thus has good portability. APPSHIELD is successful at policy enforcement with low latency and is reliable.

Acknowledgments. We thank our reviewers for their valuable comments. This paper was made possible by the National Natural Science Foundation of China under Grant No. 61472209, by the U.S. National Science Foundation under Grant CNS-1408790. The statements made herein are solely the responsibility of the authors.

References

1. Predictions: The year of BYOD management (2016). http://www.rcrwireless.com/20160129/opinion/2016-predictions-the-year-of-byod-management-tag10
2. AirWatch: Enterprise Mobility Management. http://www.air-watch.com/
3. Android-apktool: A tool for reengineering Android apk files. http://code.google.com/p/android-apktool/
4. Android application class. http://developer.android.com/reference/android/app/Application.html
5. Android binary XML file parser. https://github.com/xgouchet/AXML
6. Android bionic. https://android.googlesource.com/platform/bionic/
7. Android content provider. http://developer.android.com/guide/topics/providers/content-providers.html
8. Android fragmentation report august 2014 - opensignal. http://opensignal.com/reports/2014/android-fragmentation/
9. Android manifest permission. http://developer.android.com/reference/android/Manifest.permission.html
10. Android Uri. http://developer.android.com/reference/android/net/Uri.html
11. Bring Android to Work. http://www.android.com/it/preview/
12. Citrix. https://www.citrix.com/
13. Good Technology. https://www1.good.com/
14. iOS Open-in management. http://searchmobilecomputing.techtarget.com/tip/Open-in-management-helps-secure-iOS-data
15. Mocana - Strong and Usable Security. https://www.mocana.com/
16. Significant iPhone and iPad malware threats will emerge (2015). http://www.ibtimes.co.uk/significant-iphone-ipad-malware-threats-will-emerge-2015-1490577
17. Smali: An assembler/disassembler for Android's dex format. http://code.google.com/p/smali/
18. UI/Application exerciser Monkey. http://developer.android.com/tools/help/monkey.html
19. What You Need to Know About iOS Malware XcodeGhost. http://www.macrumors.com/2015/09/20/xcodeghost-chinese-malware-faq/
20. Arp, D., Spreitzenbarth, M., Hübner, M., Gascon, H., Rieck, K., Siemens, C.: Drebin: effective and explainable detection of android malware in your pocket. In: Proceedings of NDSS (2014)
21. Backes, M., Bugiel, S., Hammer, C., Schranz, O., Von Styp-Rekowsky, P.: Boxify: Full-fledged app sandboxing for stock android. In: Proceedings USENIX Security (2015)
22. Barr, K., Bungale, P., Deasy, S., Gyuris, V., Hung, P., Newell, C., Tuch, H., Zoppis, B.: The VMware mobile virtualization platform: is that a hypervisor in your pocket? ACM SIGOPS Operating Syst. Rev. **44**(4), 124–135 (2010)
23. Davis, B., Chen, H.: Retroskeleton: Retrofitting android apps. In: ACM MobiSys (2013)
24. Davis, B., Sanders, B., Khodaverdian, A., Chen, H.: I-ARM-Droid: a rewriting framework for in-app reference monitors for android applications. In: IEEE MoST (2012)
25. Enck, W., Gilbert, P., Chun, B., Cox, L., Jung, J., McDaniel, P., Sheth, A.: Taintdroid: an information-flow tracking system for realtime privacy monitoring on smartphones. In: USENIX OSDI (2010)

26. Grace, M., Zhou, Y., Zhang, Q., Zou, S., Jiang, X.: Riskranker: scalable and accurate zero-day android malware detection. In: ACM MobiSys (2012)
27. Heuser, S., Nadkarni, A., Enck, W., Sadeghi, A.-R.: ASM: a programmable interface for extending android security. In: Proceedings USENIX Security (2014)
28. Kodeswaran, P., Nandakumar, V., Kapoor, S., Kamaraju, P., Joshi, A., Mukherjea, S.: Securing enterprise data on smartphones using run time information flow control. In: IEEE MDM (2012)
29. Lange, M., Liebergeld, S., Lackorzynski, A., Warg, A., Peter, M.: L4Android: a generic operating system framework for secure smartphones. In: ACM SPSM (2011)
30. Lever, C., Antonakakis, M., Reaves, B., Traynor, P., Lee, W.: The core of the matter: Analyzing malicious traffic in cellular carriers. In: NDSS (2013)
31. Nadkarni, A., Enck, W.: Preventing accidental data disclosure in modern operating systems. In: ACM CCS (2013)
32. Nauman, M., Khan, S., Zhang, X.: Apex: extending android permission model and enforcement with user-defined runtime constraints. In: ACM ASIACCS (2010)
33. Ongtang, M., Butler, K., McDaniel, P.: Porscha: policy oriented secure content handling in android. In: ACM ACSAC (2010)
34. Poeplau, S., Fratantonio, Y., Bianchi, A., Kruegel, C., Vigna, G.: Execute this! analyzing unsafe and malicious dynamic code loading in android applications. In: NDSS (2014)
35. Rastogi, V., Chen, Y., Jiang, X.: Droidchameleon: evaluating android anti-malware against transformation attacks. In: ACM ASIACCS (2013)
36. Rohrer, F., Feleke, N., Zhang, Y., Nimley, K., Chitkushev, L., Zlateva, T.: Android security analysis and protection in finance and healthcare. Comput. Sci. Educ. Comput. Sci. 8(1), 80–89 (2012). Boston University MET
37. Rohrer, F., Zhang, Y., Chitkushev, L., Zlateva, T.: DR BACA: dynamic role based access control for android. In: ACM ACSAC (2013)
38. Sandhu, R.S., Coyne, E.J., Feinstein, H.L., Youman, C.E.: Role-based access control models. Comput. 29(2), 38–47 (1996)
39. Smalley, S., Craig, R.: Security enhanced (SE) android: Bringing flexible MAC to android. In: NDSS (2013)
40. Vaidya, J., Atluri, V., Warner, J.: RoleMiner: mining roles using subset enumeration. In: ACM CCS (2006)
41. Xu, R., Saïdi, H., Anderson, R.: Aurasium: practical policy enforcement for android applications. In: USENIX Security Symposium, pp. 539–552 (2012)
42. Xu, Y., Witchel, E.: Maxoid: transparently confining mobile applications with custom views of state. In: ACM EuroSys (2015)
43. Zhao, Z., Osono, F.C.C.: Trustdroid: preventing the use of smartphones for information leaking in corporate networks through the used of static analysis taint tracking. In: IEEE MALWARE (2012)

H-Binder: A Hardened Binder Framework on Android Systems

Dong Shen[1], Zhangkai Zhang[1], Xhua Ding[2], Zhoujun Li[1]([✉]), and Robert Deng[2]

[1] School of Computer Science and Engineering, Beihang University, Beijing 100191, China
{dongshen,lizj}@buaa.edu.cn, zhangzhangkai315@gmail.com
[2] School of Information Systems, Singapore Management University, Singapore, Singapore
{xhding,robertdeng}@smu.edu.sg

Abstract. The Binder framework is at the core of Android systems due to its fundamental role for interprocess communications. Applications use the Binder to perform high level tasks such as accessing location information. The importance of the Binder makes it an attractive target for attackers. Rootkits on Android platforms can arbitrarily access any Binder transaction data and therefore have system-wide security impact. In this paper, we propose *H-Binder* to secure the Binder IPC channel between two applications. It runs transparently with Android and COTS applications without making changes on their binaries. In this work, we design a bare-metal ARM hypervisor with a tiny code base at runtime. The hypervisor interposes on the main steps of a Binder transaction by leveraging ARM hardware virtualization techniques. It protects secrecy and integrity of the Binder transaction data. We have implemented a prototype of the H-Binder hypervisor and tested its performance. The experiment results show that H-Binder incurs an insignificant overhead to the applications.

Keywords: Android · Binder · Virtualization · ARM · System security · Hypervisor

1 Introduction

Android is designed with an object-oriented philosophy where a variety of built-in system applications (named as *managers* by Android) are abstracted as objects and tasked to manage system-wide resources, such as display and network I/O. User applications such as games and m-banking apps usually do not directly access system resources like their counterparts on a PC. To access system resources or to distribute data, applications heavily utilize interprocess communication (IPC) to remotely call other objects' methods. The Linux kernel in the Android system offers the Binder mechanism [28] as the main avenue for IPC transactions. Functionality-wise, the centerpiece of Android's Binder framework

© ICST Institute for Computer Sciences, Social Informatics and Telecommunications Engineering 2017
R. Deng et al. (Eds.): SecureComm 2016, LNICST 198, pp. 24–43, 2017.
DOI: 10.1007/978-3-319-59608-2_2

is its Binder driver residing in the kernel, although a large portion of code is in user space for marshaling the data.

Of the similar consequence of a rogue router attacking networking applications, a malware with kernel privilege can attack the Binder-based interprocess communications. Recent attacks [4,24,34] have demonstrated the feasibility and easiness of reading and manipulating the Binder transaction data, including keyboard inputs, SMS messages. Note that the Binder IPC is also sometimes used for an application's internal data exchanges. For instance, an m-banking app's user-interface thread may use the Binder to forward the transaction amount to its processing thread. The usage of the Binder could be transparent to the app developer. As shown in [4], an app using HTTPS for its Internet communications does not send out ciphertext directly. Instead, its plaintext data is firstly forwarded to Android's Network Manager through the Binder channel. In short, the corrupted Binder framework is a single point of failure of system security because the rootkit can easily read/write *all* applications' transaction data by accessing their memory buffers, without applying any sophisticated tricks. Most existing schemes of secure Binder transactions [5,30,35] focus on application-level protection, which cannot deal with rootkit attacks.

In this paper, we design a tiny trustworthy hypervisor called *H-Binder* with a small trusted computing base (TCB) to protect sensitive Binder transaction data against the rootkit on the ARM platform. H-Binder interposes on the Binder transactions to ensure the secrecy and integrity of the transaction data against the rootkit's malicious accesses.

H-Binder functions transparently to the Linux kernel, Android middleware and COTS applications without any modification on their binary codes. It can smoothly work in tandem with other virtualization based schemes [9,10,20,36] to harden the platform's security such as data protection in the kernel. To the best of our knowledge, H-Binder is the first work on Binder security against the rootkit. We have built a proof of concept of H-Binder and evaluated its performance. The results show that it is practical to use H-Binder on mobile phones to protect critical Binder transactions.

ORGANIZATION. In the next section, we explain the background of Android Binder framework and recent virtualization techniques introduced to ARM processors. In Sect. 3, we present an overview of H-Binder including the security problem, the threat model and the challenges. We present two building blocks of H-Binder in Sect. 4 and the details of H-Binder workflow in Sect. 5. A report on H-Binder implementation and performance evaluation is in Sect. 6. We then present related work in Sect. 7 and a conclusion in Sect. 8.

2   Background

We explain below the background information of Android's Binder framework and the virtualization techniques on ARM platforms.

2.1   The Binder Framework

The Android platform is designed with an object oriented style with a wide range of system manager applications managing various resources and providing capabilities for user applications. The Binder IPC is the primary channel for user applications to interact and collaborate with system services or among themselves to carry out their intended tasks. For instance, a user application needs to interact with Android's LocationManager to access the mobile phone's location data.

A Binder transaction follows the traditional client-server model. In a typical scenario, it involves three parties: a thread of a resource manager app acting as a server, a thread of a user app as a client, and the Binder driver in the kernel. To facilitate applications to engage in a Binder transaction, Android's ServiceManager works as a registry service for user apps to look up a registered service provider. In a high level view, the client and server thread interact in a Binder transaction with the following steps. Note that the server has a pool of worker threads in sleeping mode waiting for processing the requests.

(1) To request the service from a service thread, the client thread issues a blocking *ioctl* system call through which it issues a command to the Binder driver.
(2) The Binder driver saves the client thread information, locates the intended server's sleeping worker thread, and wakes it up to handle the request.
(3) The wakened worker thread immediately processes the request and issues an *ioctl* system call to return the reply to the Binder driver.
(4) The Binder driver uses the information saved in step 2 to locate the client thread, wakes it up and passes the data to it.

One of the most critical data structures in the Binder framework is the `binder_transaction_data` (as depicted in Fig. 1) which is passed by the user-space threads to the Binder driver as one of the parameters of *ioctl*. The shadowed boxes are those bytes which are not changed by an honest kernel. In essence, `code` specifies the method for the receiving app to execute, while the buffer pointed to by `data.ptr.buffer` stores the parameters and objects needed by that remote method with length `data_size`. For ease of reference, we collectively call the bytes in the shadowed boxes as *transaction raw data* throughout the paper. As shown later, we are concerned with the integrity of the transaction raw data and secrecy of bytes pointed to by `data.ptr.buffer`.

It is necessary to highlight how a client application looks up and identifies the service application it intends to engage, because it is relevant to authentication issues of a Binder transaction. The lookup procedure is also a Binder transaction.

The `target` field in Fig. 1 is a *local* handler passed to the Binder driver to specify the intended destination. To look up a service application, the client sets `target` as 0 in a Binder request containing a text string. The Binder driver forwards this lookup request to Android's ServiceManager which then returns a handler to the client. Therefore, to engage with the service application, the client sets its `target` with the handler in its Binder request.

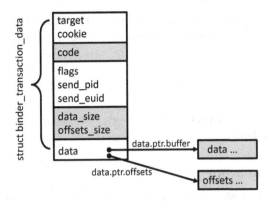

Fig. 1. Binder_transaction_data. The shadowed regions refer to the Binder transaction raw data which are the actual payload of a Binder communication.

2.2   Hardware Virtualization on ARM Processor

The recent ARMv7-A [1] architecture introduces hardware-assisted virtualization on ARM processors as an architectural extension. Different from x86 hardware virtualization where the CPU runs in the root mode (for the hypervisor) or the non-root mode (for the guest), ARM's hardware virtualization introduces a new privilege mode called the hyp mode for the hypervisor, which has a higher privilege level, i.e., Privilege Level 2 (or PL2 for short), than the svc mode used by the kernel.

When the CPU runs in the hyp mode, it accesses not only to those general registers and banked registers, but also to a set of new mode-specific registers including the Hyp Configuration Register (HCR) and the Hyp Syndrome Register (HSR). The former is used to configure the types of exceptions to be trapped into the hypervisor. For example, when HCR's Trap General Exception (TGE) bit is set to 0×1, the supervisor call exception will be trapped to the hypervisor, which allows the hypervisor to intercept system calls from user space. HSR records the information about the exceptions trapping to the hypervisor. The Exception Class (EC) bits HSR[31:26] indicate the cause of the trap, e.g., 0×12 for a hypervisor call.

The HVC instruction can be used to enter into the hyp mode from the svc mode by raising a hypervisor call exception. After handling the call, the hypervisor uses the ERET instruction to switch the mode and returns to the next instruction following the HVC instruction. All exceptions trapping to the hyp mode use the exception vector at offset 0×14 of the hypervisor vector table.

Similar to memory virtualization on x86 platforms, ARM virtualization also supports two-stage address mapping for the virtual machine (VM). A virtual address (VA) in both usr and svc modes in the non-secure world is mapped to an intermediate physical address (IPA) by the Stage-1 page table managed by the kernel. Then, the IPA is mapped to the physical address (PA) by the Stage-2 page table managed by the hypervisor and is beyond the kernel's control. Therefore, the hypervisor can control the attribute bits in the Stage-2 page table entries (PTEs) to regulate memory accesses from the VM for interception and isolation purposes.

3 Overview

This section presents an overview of our work. We begin with the explanation of the security problems.

3.1 The Problem Scope

Our aim is to protect the secrecy and integrity of sensitive transaction data transmitted between two Android applications through the Binder IPC. We consider the following adversary model and design restrictions.

Adversary Model. We consider rootkits whose attacks are targeted at the Linux kernel, e.g., reading and writing arbitrary kernel objects and manipulating the kernel's control flow. For instance, a rootkit can start its attack on Binder transactions by locating the global kernel object called `binder_context_mgr_node` which contains a pointer pointing to an array of buffers used for each Binder transaction.

CAVEAT. Out of several reasons, we do *not* consider rootkits that directly reads/writes an application's user space data and tampers with its control flow. Firstly, most rootkits do not target a specific application because it is less cost-effective to attack user space. It requires non-significant semantic knowledge of the victim application (e.g., the source code) while the damage is limited to the victim. Secondly, attacking on the kernel objects is much more catastrophic as it impacts all applications. Lastly, user-space protection techniques have been proposed on x86 platforms. Systems like Overshadow [9], InkTag [20], TrustPath [36], AppShield [11] can be exported to the ARM platform to cope with the user space security problem. The systems can run in tandem with H-Binder for the full protections. We do not attempt to re-invent the wheel.

Design Restriction. We restrict our design from modifying the existing Linux kernel, Android middleware or the applications. It is also refrained from changing the existing Binder framework, including the protocol and the syntax of relevant data objects. This is mainly due to compatibility concern.

CAVEAT. Under the design restriction above, the Binder data integrity protection only prevents rootkits from modifying the Binder data sent by applications. It does not deal with forgery. A rootkit can always inject its own Binder data to an application. Any countermeasure requires changes on either the application code or the Binder framework.

3.2 Challenges

The security problems described above present several challenges. Firstly, H-Binder should not incur significant overhead to the mobile phone. Since mobile phones are power constrained, this requirement is especially more critical than a secure system on desktop computers. Therefore, the hypervisor should only interpose on system call for Binder transactions, instead of all system calls. Unfortunately, the current ARM virtualization technology does not have the ability to filter out system calls.

Secondly, the interposition on Binder transactions should be at the thread level rather than in the process level, because Android apps are multi-threaded. A process level interposition may stall all running threads no matter whether they are relevant to the security, and therefore downgrades the performance of the application.

Another challenge is the transparency and compatibility to the COTS Android system and applications. It precludes any changes to the present Binder framework, including the IPC protocol and the data structures. A tentative way to protect Binder IPC is to follow the SSL style on communication protection. Namely, the Binder client and server run a key exchange protocol (possibly mediated by a trusted party) and then exchange their encrypted Binder requests and replies. We do not opt for this method because it requires non-negligible changes not only on the Android runtime, but also the applications' code.

3.3   Our Contributions

The rest of the paper presents our proposed solution to the aforementioned problems. In a nutshell, our work makes the following contributions.

- We propose two novel techniques which can be used in hypervisors, i.e., selective system call issuance interception and thread-level system call return interception. These techniques can be used in H-Binder and in other hypervisors as well.
- We propose H-Binder, a security system running in the hyp mode that protects the Binder transactions to ensure the transaction raw data's integrity and secrecy. H-Binder is fully compatible and transparent to Android and its applications without requiring any changes on their codes.
- We build a prototype of H-Binder and evaluate the performance and compatibility with off-the-shelf applications.

4   H-Binder Building Blocks

In the following, we first introduce two novel techniques used as building blocks for H-Binder, i.e., selective interception for system call issuance and thread-level interception for system call return. We then present the details of H-Binder workflow.

4.1   Selective Interception for System Call Issuance

With ARM virtualization extensions, the system calls can be easily trapped to the hypervisor by setting HCR.TGE bit to 0×1. Nonetheless, it traps *all* system calls from user space, which takes a significant performance toll on the whole system. To avoid unnecessary traps, H-Binder does not set HCR.TGE bit. Instead, it securely places a hook in the kernel which notifies the hypervisor on selected system calls according to the system call number and the issuing process. Unrelated calls are passed to the kernel directly.

Normal System Call Trap to Svc Mode. The system call trap from the usr mode to the svc mode is triggered by the SVC instruction. The exception vector addresses are stored in a vector page shown in Fig. 2 where the base address __vectors_start is set according to the 13th bit of the System Control Register (SCTLR), i.e. SCTLR.V bit.

```
1    __vectors_start:
2        b  vector_rst
3        b  vector_und
4        ldr pc, __vectors_start+0x1000
5        b  vector_pabt
6        ...
```

Fig. 2. Exception vectors stored in the vector page at either 0×00000000 or 0×FFFF0000 based on SCTLR.V bit.

An SVC instruction causes the Program Counter (PC) to jump to Line 4 in Fig. 2. As a result, the hardware loads PC with the content stored at __vectors_start+0×1000, which is exactly the address of the kernel's SVC handler. Thus, the control flow jumps to the SVC handler which then responds to the system call.

System Call Hook. We use a hook to filter out unrelated system calls as depicted in Fig. 3. When H-Binder protection starts (at secure boot up or triggered by a hypervisor call at runtime), the hypervisor writes the hook code into a reserved memory page in kernel space. It then places the entry address of the hook into __vectors_start+0×1000. As a result, whenever a system call is invoked in the user space, the hardware passes the control to the hook code instead of the kernel's handler. The hook code examines the system call number in R7 and the value of the Translation Table Base Register 0 (TTBR0)[1] which allows the hypervisor to check the identity of the issuer process. For instance, if it is *ioctl* issued by a concerned process, the hook issues a hypervisor call to the hypervisor. When the control returns from the hypervisor, the hook passes the control back to the original handler.

---

[1] In ARM architecture, TTBR0 points to the translation tables used by the current running user process and the Translation Table Base Register 1 (TTBR1) points to the translation tables used by the kernel.

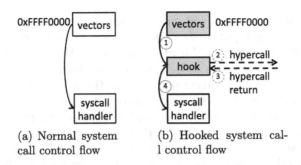

(a) Normal system call control flow   (b) Hooked system call control flow

Fig. 3. Illustration of hooking the system call control flow where the shadowed boxes refer to pages that are read-only to the kernel and whose addresses cannot be changed. Step 2 and 3 are executed when the intercepted system call needs to be trapped.

Hook Protection. A rootkit may tamper with the physical addresses of the vector page or the hook page to bypass the interception. For this purpose, the hypervisor freezes the control flow path from the vector page to the hook code, in the sense that (1) the physical addresses of the vector page and the hook code page cannot be remapped by the kernel; (2) the code and data in both pages cannot be altered by the kernel. For this purpose, the hypervisor takes the following steps before placing the hook code page.

1. Set the Trap Virtual Memory (TVM) bit of HCR to 0×1 in order to intercept the kernel's write access to SCTLR and the Translation Table Base Register 1 (TTBR1) so that the hypervisor blocks all changes to SCTLR.V bit and TTBR1.
2. It traverses from the root of the Stage-1 page table pointed by TTBR1 to the page table page pointing to the vector page which resides at 0×00000000 or $0\times$FFFF0000 depending on the SCTLR.V bit. Set all pages on this path as *read-only* by configuring the Stage-2 page table. In this way, any attempt to remap the physical address of the vector page is then trapped and blocked by the hypervisor.
3. It traverses from the root of the Stage-1 page table pointed by TTBR1 to the page table page pointing to the hook code page. In the same fashion as the previous step, an update on any page on this path is not allowed if it affects the mapping of the hook code.
4. The hypervisor sets both the vector page and the hook code page as read-only so that the kernel cannot tamper with their contents.

Therefore, when a system call is invoked, the hardware always locates the vector page and the hook page at their predefined addresses. Moreover, since both pages are read-only, the correct hook code is executed as expected.

4.2 Thread-Level Interception for System Call Return

A thread expecting the Binder transaction data sleeps after issuing an *ioctl* system call. When the data arrives, the kernel completes the system call invocation by waking up the thread.

Unlike system call issuance, system call return does not throw out any exception. Hence we need to inject an exception in order to intercept the event. The challenge is how to generate a thread-specific event. It is a common practice for Android applications to use a dedicated worker thread for handling Binder transactions. Process-level interception affects all threads of the application and is not a good choice. For instance, setting a code page as non-executable introduces a page fault for all threads attempting to fetch instructions from this page, because the application's code (data) sections are shared among threads.

Our proposed method is based on the fact that threads do not share their stacks. The underlying idea is to manipulate the relevant thread's user space stack so that a stack operation after system call return is trapped to the hypervisor.

The first step is to map an empty physical memory page into the target application's heap. This page, named as *vault page* is to introduce the needed exception. The application is in fact not aware of its vault page and never uses it. The hypervisor sets the vault page *inaccessible* by configuring the Stage-2 page table, in order to block any access and to introduce the page fault for system call return. Note that the vault page must be mapped to the application's virtual address space. Otherwise, the exception it incurs is trapped to the kernel instead of the hypervisor.

Next, when the system call for receiving data is issued, the hypervisor intercepts it using the technique described previously. The hypervisor saves the thread's SP_usr into the hypervisor space, and then sets SP_usr to point to the application's vault page. The stack manipulation does not affect the kernel's execution because both the system call parameters and the return address are passed to the kernel through registers.

Lastly, when the system call returns upon data arrival, the thread returns from the svc mode to the usr mode. The user space stack is then used to resume user space execution. Since SP_usr points to the inaccessible page, a stack popup operation triggers a page fault exception and is trapped to the hypervisor.

5   The H-Binder Workflow

To facilitate the description of H-Binder, we present the basic idea and details of H-Binder.

5.1   The Approach

While it is straightforward to encipher the Binder raw data for a sending application, it is challenging to perform decryption securely. Without a rigorous checking of the recipient's identity, the improper decryption may reveal the plaintext to an imposter application. Therefore, the issues of data confidentiality and entity authentication are mingled together. It is difficult to authenticate the recipient thread because of the semantic gap faced by the hypervisor. The actual destination of the Binder transaction data is determined by the Binder driver at runtime, instead of by the user threads. A rootkit can tamper with the data used by the Binder driver, and as a result, the driver delivers the transaction data to an imposter.

In a nutshell, the H-Binder scheme uses the building blocks introduced in Sect. 4 to interpose on each of the four Binder steps. After a step is intercepted, the hypervisor either saves or restores the data, depending whether it is to send or to receive the data. Nonetheless, the interception is transaction-agnostic in the sense that the intercepted data does not exhibit its relation to other events or any specific Binder transaction. Hence, the hypervisor has to trace the Binder transaction data flows in order to restore the data properly, including the lookup transaction. In specific, when a client issues a Binder request, the hypervisor saves the data and replaces it with a random number as an ID which is different from the existing entries. When the request arrives at the server end, the corresponding client's request is restored by checking the received request's ID. Therefore, when the server's worker thread replies, the hypervisor knows exactly its intended destination. When the reply arrives at the client end, the hypervisor checks whether the present application is the intended thread.

5.2 Details

We elaborate the details of H-Binder by explaining its protection over a Binder transaction between a user app and a resource manager app.

Initialization. When a user app is launched, an untrusted kernel module allocates a vault page whose virtual address is passed to the hypervisor. The hypervisor configures the Stage-2 page table to set the vault page *inaccessible*. It saves into the hypervisor space a pair $\langle ttbr, addr \rangle$ representing TTBR0 data and the vault page's physical address, respectively. This page is used to intercept system call return as described in Sect. 4.2 and save the Binder data.

The hypervisor also maintains a Service Table whose entries pair a service description with the TTBR0 value of the corresponding system service application, e.g., LocationManager. For each user application, the hypervisor also maintains a Handler Table whose entries pair a handler with the corresponding service's TTBR0. A user application's Handler Table is initialized with an entry $\langle 0, ttbr^* \rangle$ where $ttbr^*$ is the TTBR0 used by ServiceManager.

The hypervisor creates the *Transaction Table* shown in Table 1 to save data related to every Binder transactions such that each intercepted event can be linked to a Binder transaction. In this table, *ClientID* is set as the client application's TTBR0 which points to the root of its page table. *SApp* identifies the server app by using its TTBR0 value while *SThread* identifies the server's worker thread by using the virtual address of its stack base. *ReqID* and *AckID* save the ID of the request and reply as their respective identifiers. *State* records the present transaction states.

Table 1. The format of the transaction table

ClientID	SApp	SThread	ReqID	AckID	State
0×96206f40	0×960b4280	0×76ef2000	0×47aa6d75	0×b0aacdf4	2
...	...	...	...	...	...

Runtime. The H-Binder hypervisor interposes on all four steps of a Binder transaction by using the building blocks priorly described. The workflow of H-Binder proceeds in four phases as depicted in Fig. 4 wherein a user app requests data from a manager app through a Binder IPC channel.

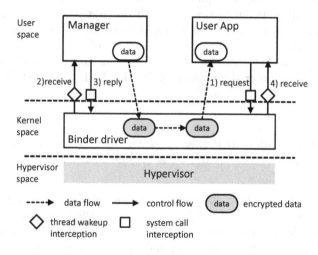

Fig. 4. Overview of H-Binder work flow.

Phase 1: User App Sending Request. Using techniques in Sect. 4.1, the hypervisor intercepts the user app's *ioctl* call right after it traps to the kernel. If the second parameter of *ioctl* is BINDER_WRITE_READ, the hypervisor locates the binder_transaction_data structure via the third parameter. Then it executes the following steps:

(1) It saves the request data in the client's vault page and replaces it with a random number which is different from the ReqID entries in the Transaction Table.
(2) It inserts to the Transaction Table a new record T, where T.ClientID is the current value of TTBR0; T.ReqID is the generated random number in the first step; T.State is set to 0 to indicate that a request is sent out. Based on the target of the intercepted Binder structure, the hypervisor looks up the client app's Handler Table to retrieve the corresponding TTBR0 and assigns it to T.SApp. (An error is returned if no matching record is found in the Handler Table.) All other fields of the new entry are set as NULL.

Phase 2: Manager Receiving Request. When the request is delivered by the Binder driver to the manager app, the manager's worker thread is wakened up to handle it. Using techniques in Sect. 4.2, the control is trapped to the hypervisor before the request is processed further by the thread. The hypervisor first checks data integrity and verifies whether the intercepted app is an imposter. It executes the following steps:

(1) It looks up the Transaction Table for a record with a matching record T such that T.ReqID equals to the request data.
(2) If no matching record is found or T.State is not 0, it drops this request and returns an error to the manager because the incoming request's integrity is compromised.
(3) To check whether the intercepted app is legitimate for receiving the request, it compares T.SApp with the present TTBR0. If they do not match, an exception is thrown out. Otherwise, it loads the data from the client's vault page to recover its original Binder request, saves T.SThread with SP_usr&0×FFFFE000 to record the worker thread's identity, and lastly set T.State to 1 to indicate that the request is received by the server.

Phase 3: Manager Sending Reply. After handling the user app's request, the manager's worker thread returns a reply to the user app. Using the hook in Sect. 4.1, the thread's *ioctl* is trapped to the hypervisor which then performs the following steps:

(1) It looks up the Transaction Table for a matching record T such that T.SThread equals to the present worker thread's stack base address. If no matching record is found, it drops the reply and returns an error indicating that the reply is not associated with any previously checked Binder request. Otherwise, it goes to the next step.
(2) It checks whether T.State is 1. If not, it drops the reply and returns an error indicating inconsistent states. Otherwise, it goes to the next step.
(3) It saves the data pointed to by data.ptr.buffer in Binder_transaction_ data structure in the vault page, and replaces it with a random number which is different from the AckID entries in the Transaction Table. It then updates T by assigning T.AckID with the generated random number and setting T.State to 2.

Phase 4: User App Receiving Reply. When the Binder driver delivers the manager's reply to the user app, it wakes up the user's blocked thread described in Phase 1. Using the techniques in Sect. 4.2, the control is trapped to the hypervisor before the thread processes the reply. Similar to Phase 2, the hypervisor checks both data integrity and the recipient app's authenticity before restoring the data. It runs the following steps:

(1) It looks up the Transaction Table to find a matching record T such that T.AckID equals to the reply data. If no matching record is found, it discards the reply as its integrity is compromised and returns an error. Otherwise, it proceeds to the next step.

(2) It checks whether the present TTBR0 is the same as T.ClientID and whether T.State is 2. If either one fails, it returns an error because the present application is not the intended destination of the reply.

(3) It loads the data from the server's vault page, deletes T from the Transaction Table, and passes the control back to the user app. If T.SApp refers to ServiceManager, the hypervisor obtains the handler from the data and updates the Handler Table of the client app. Note that if a suitable permission model is in place, the hypervisor can also enforce the access control policies before restoring data.

5.3   Security Analysis

We provide an informal analysis to explain how the Binder transaction is protected. The analysis begins with recipient authenticity which is the premise of proper Binder data protection.

Recipient Authenticity. Recipient authenticity is about whether a Binder transaction request/reply is delivered to the intended destination. For the flow from the client to the server, the hypervisor extracts the intended recipient's identity when the request is sent out and verifies the recipient's identity by checking its TTBR0 value when the request is delivered. Note that the rootkit's attack on an app's handler only leads to denial-of-service and cannot be used for impersonation.

For the return trip from the server to the client, the hypervisor verifies the recipient's identity by tracking the transactions flows using the Transaction Table. Specifically, for the matching record T, T.ReqID links Phase 1 and Phase 2, and T.SThread links Phase 2 and 3, while T.AckID links Phase 3 and 4. In this way, the hypervisor has sufficient knowledge to decide the intended recipient for a Binder reply from the server app.

Application Data Integrity and Secrecy. The rootkit's attack on the Binder data is neutralized by the data replacement used by the hypervisor. The sensitive data in the Binder_transaction_data structure is replaced before it is passed to kernel space in a system call issuance. As shown in Phase 2 and 4, a restoring is only performed after a successful authentication of the recipient app. Therefore, only the intended applications can access those data.

Binder data integrity is ensured by T.ReqID and T.AckID. A fraudulent Binder request is detected in Phase 2 and 4 before the recipient app processes it. The transaction's state stored in T.State is used to detect replay attacks which show inconsistence.

CAVEAT. The security of H-Binder hypervisor can be protected by the hardware. The hyp mode is transparent to the system so that the rootkits don't know the existence of the hypervisor. Furthermore, the small TCB can reduce the probability of vulnerability.

6 Implementation and Performance Evaluation

We have implemented a prototype of H-Binder running in the hyp mode. The runtime TCB of H-Binder only consists of 1,813 SLOC (1,144 lines of C code and 669 lines of asm code).

The experimental environment is Linux Ubuntu 14.04 on a PC with an Intel(R) Core(TM) i7-4790 CPU @3.6 GHz processor and 16 GB main memory. In this platform, we run ARM FastModels [3] with FVP which emulates a mobile phone with a Cortex-A15 × 1 processor. The H-Binder hypervisor runs in the emulated phone as a bare-metal hypervisor. On top of the hypervisor, it runs Android 4.1 with a Linux kernel 3.9.0-rc3+. Due to the emulation, we do not measure the absolute time in our experiments. Instead, we use the CPU cycles to evaluate H-Binder performance.

6.1 Component Cost of H-Binder

The overall time overhead incurred by H-Binder is the sum of the CPU time for context switches due to the hypervisor interceptions or hypervisor calls and the CPU time spent by the hypervisor's execution. To evaluate the former cost, we measure the turnaround time of an empty hypcall which causes the CPU to enter to the hyp mode and return immediately. Our experiments show that the average cost for a round-trip mode switch cycle in a hypervisor call is about 96 cycles in our environment.

We also measure the CPU time spent in each of the four phases described in Sect. 5. The average CPU cycles spent in each of the phases are listed in Table 2 where the transaction involves 100 bytes returned by the server application. In general, the hypervisor spends 854 CPU cycles for involving in sending the Binder data, and spends 630 cycles for involving in receiving the Binder data.

Table 2. The number of CPU cycles spent in four phases of a Binder transaction, where the Binder request has 48 bytes and the Binder reply has 100 bytes

Phase 1	Phase 2	Phase 3	Phase 4
712	607	996	654

As shown in Sect. 5, a Binder IPC upon H-Binder involves 4 traps into the hypervisor. Therefore, the overall H-Binder cost for protecting a Binder based IPC is the sum of mode switch costs and the hypervisor's processing time, which amounts to 3, 353 CPU cycles. For a mobile phone with 1 GHz CPU frequency, the time latency for one Binder transaction is about 3.4 µs, which is very tiny.

Note that the system call hook has negligible performance overhead as it only adds few instructions in the existing system call handler.

6.2   Application Level Performance Evaluation

To measure the performance impact of H-Binder on Android applications using the Binder, we measure the time spent for completing a task, e.g., to acquire the current location. We use the open-source application *RMaps*[2] as the client requesting for the mobile phone's location data. The program is instrumented to count the CPU cycles for invoking the LocationManager's `getLastKnownLocation()` function which runs Binder transactions with Android's LocationManager. We conduct the experiment in three different environments: the native Android, the Android running inside the host domain of KVM, and the Android running on the H-Binder hypervisor. Note that all three environments are hosted by ARM FastModels emulation. The results are presented in Table 3 below.

Table 3. Turnaround time (in CPU cycles) needed to obtain the location in different settings

	Android	KVM	H-Binder
Read location	68,577	69,929	77,344
Overhead	–	1,352	8,767

It shows that H-Binder incurs about 9,000 CPU cycles to get the location more than in Android. This relative overhead does not affect the whole application's performance because the absolute time delay is insignificant. For a mobile phone with 1 GHz CPU frequency, the time latency incurred by H-Binder is less than 9 µs. Note that the physical location is normally obtained in every one second or every three meters the device has moved. Therefore, supposing that the phone is on a running car moving with the speed of 15 m/s, the shortest time interval of location update is 67 ms. The latency of 9 µs is only around 0.01% compared to the time interval of location update. Hence the delay caused by H-Binder does not affect the location software's performance. The delay is also imperceptible for human users as the shortest time interval a human perceives is roughly between 50 ms to 150 ms [29].

CAVEAT. Our selective system call interception technique in Sect. 4.1 allows for performance isolation since those unrelated system calls are not intercepted and their performance is not affected by H-Binder. It can be further extended to select the critical applications and service to protect.

6.3   Time Cost for Different Sizes of Transferred Data

We then analyze how the size of the transferred data affects the overhead. We implement two Android applications using Binder IPC to transfer data

---

[2] https://github.com/ramnathv/rMaps.

between them. One app registers itself to Android's ServiceManager as the service providers while the other acts as a client. We vary the size of the data the server application returns and evaluate the turnaround time of getting the data, including the time spent for the Binder channel setup. Table 4 reports the experiment results in three different platforms.

Table 4. A whole binder transaction time in CPU cycles with different sizes of transferred data

# of Bytes	Android	With KVM	H-Binder
4	94,848	94,932	95,170 (0.3%)
8	95,070	95,178	95,781 (0.7%)
12	95,670	95,900	96,812 (1.2%)
20	96,070	96,318	96,960 (0.9%)
40	97,196	97,579	102,871 (5.8%)
80	100,349	100,743	107,118 (6.7%)
200	109,219	109,631	118,508 (8.5%)
400	120,875	121,353	130,496 (8.0%)

It shows that the time cost grows with the size growing. The main overhead is incurred by H-Binder's protection. As the size of data is not very large when the data is transferred in the Binder directly, the overhead of H-Binder in a whole Binder transaction will be less than 9%.

7   Related Work

Xen [6] is one of the earliest open source hypervisors initially developed for x86 platforms. Based on the Xen hypervisor, Hwang et al. proposed and implemented Xen-on-ARM [22] for the ARM architecture. Xen-on-ARM is a para-virtualization hypervisor and requires modifications to the kernel, as it is built on ARMv4/v5 which does not offer virtualization extension. From ARMv7 onwards, virtualization extension was introduced to support hardware virtualization on ARM architecture [1]. The first hypervisor using ARM virtualization extension was proposed in [31]. EmbeddedXen presents a new virtualization framework tailored to various ARM-based embedded systems [27]. ARMvisor [15] provides system virtualization for ARM, and KVM/ARM [13] is the first full system ARM virtualization solution that can run unmodified operating system on ARM multicore hardware. KVM/ARM has been integrated to the Linux kernel as a Linux ARM hypervisor.

H-Binder addresses the security of the Binder framework. A brief study on the technical details of Binder mechanism and its security weaknesses was described in [26]. More recent attacks [4] presented in the Black Hat conference further demonstrated the cruciality of Binder security. It is shown in [4] that a malware which controls the Binder framework by attacking the *ioctl* system call can access and manipulate a variety of sensitive data, including keystrokes, in-app data, and SMS messages. ComDroid [12] proposes a tool to detect the vulnerabilities in Binder transaction, but it can't provide a runtime protection. AppFence [21] is built based on TaintDroid [16], using dynamic taint analysis to track the spread of the taint data. H-Binder can combine with this method to get stronger ability. However, TaintDroid can only protect the sensitive data while H-Binder can also protect the RPC with the Binder transactions.

The protection of Binder transactions has a direct impact on Android's access control mechanism. Some fine-grained access control mechanism [8,25,32] are proposed for diverse security and privacy policies. Android has a systematic permission model to control how applications access sensitive devices and data stores [33]. Most sensitive resource accesses are through the Binder framework where the data is returned or through call-backs by the resource manager app. The manager app typically checks the permission of the requesting apps before offering the service. Nonetheless, malicious apps without proper permissions may bypass the permission check by launching the permission re-delegation attacks [19]. In [17], Felt et al. analyzed different kinds of permission re-delegation attacks and proposed some possible ways to address this problem. Their method is to reduce the privileges of callee. In [7], Bugiel et al. also proposed a solution for a system-centric and policy-driven runtime monitoring of communication channels between applications at multiple layers in the inspiration of QUIRE [14] and a tool called Woodpecker [18] is developed to employ inter-procedural data flow analysis. The ways above are faced to the usr mode of Android. If the binder driver is hijacked by attackers, two data buffers will be changed which will lead to the leakage of some sensitive data. While H-Binder is faced to untrusted kernel, the encryption will keep the security of the sensitive information.

In a broader sense, H-Binder is related to Android's malware defense. Copper-Droid [30] and VetDroid [35] leverage system call analysis and Binder transaction analysis to detect the application behavior. While Scippa [5] uses a call chain to get provenance information to implement the defense of the attack in Binder transaction. Cells [2] provides a virtualization architecture for enabling multiple virtual smartphones to run in an isolated secure manner. Nonetheless, neither of these systems can deal with kernel space attacks. To the attacks towards kernel space, many of them are against kernel interfaces like system call interface [23]. Attackers will hijack the system call handlers to let the kernel execute the attackers' instructions. H-Binder may not block all these attacks, but it can protect the sensitive data from being leaked as the data will be encrypted before entering the svc mode.

8   Conclusion

We have proposed H-Binder which leverages the recent ARM hardware virtualization techniques to secure Binder transactions in Android platforms. H-Binder ensures secrecy and integrity of the sensitive data transported between two application threads interacting via Binder IPC. The H-Binder hypervisor intercepts the critical system calls from target applications and protects their data by using replacement techniques against attacks from rootkit. We have implemented a prototype of H-Binder on ARM FastModels. Our experiments show that the overhead incurred by H-Binder is not significant. Our future work is to prevent malicious code residing in the Android framework from attacking Binder transactions.

Acknowledgment. This research work is supported in part by the Singapore National Research Foundation under the NCR Award Number NRF2014NCR-NCR001-012, the National Natural Science Foundation of China under grants (Nos. 61170189, 61370126, 61672081), the National High Technology Research and Development Program of China under grant No. 2015AA016004, and Beijing Advanced Innovation Center for Imaging Technology (No. BAICIT-2016001).

References

1. Architecture Reference Manual (ARMv7-A and ARMv7-R edition). ARM DDI C (2008)
2. Andrus, J., Dall, C., Hof, A.V., Laadan, O., Nieh, J.: Cells: a virtual mobile smartphone architecture. In: 23rd ACM Symposium on Operating Systems Principles, pp. 173–187. ACM (2011)
3. Fast Models - ARM. http://www.arm.com/products/tools/models/fast-models/
4. Artenstein, N., Revivo, I.: Man in the Binder: He Who Controls IPC, Controls the Droid. Black Hat (2014)
5. Backes, M., Bugiel, S., Gerling, S.: Scippa: system-centric IPC provenance on android. In: 30th Annual Computer Security Applications Conference, pp. 36–45. ACM (2014)
6. Barham, P., Dragovic, B., Fraser, K., Hand, S., Harris, T., Ho, A., et al.: Xen and the art of virtualization. ACM SIGOPS Oper. Syst. Rev. **37**(5), 164–177 (2003)
7. Bugiel, S., Davi, L., Dmitrienko, A., Fischer, T., Sadeghi, A.R., Shastry, B.: Towards taming privilege-escalation attacks on android. In: 19th Annual Network and Distributed System Security Symposium, pp. 346–360 (2012)
8. Bugiel, S., Heuser, S., Sadeghi, A.R.: Flexible and fine-grained mandatory access control on android for diverse security and privacy policies. In: 22nd USENIX Security Symposium, pp. 131–146 (2013)
9. Chen, X., Garfinkel, T., Lewis, E.C., Subrahmanyam, P., Waldspurger, C.A., Boneh, D., et al.: Overshadow: a virtualization-based approach to retrofitting protection in commodity operating systems. ACM SIGPLAN Not. **36**(1), 2–13 (2008)
10. Cheng, Y., Ding, X., Deng, R.H.: DriverGuard: a fine-grained protection on I/O flows. In: Atluri, V., Diaz, C. (eds.) ESORICS 2011. LNCS, vol. 6879, pp. 227–244. Springer, Heidelberg (2011). doi:10.1007/978-3-642-23822-2_13
11. Cheng, Y., Ding, X., Deng, R.H.: Efficient virtualization-based application protection against untrusted operating system. In: 10th ACM Symposium on Information, Computer and Communications Security, pp. 345–356. ACM (2015)
12. Chin, E., Felt, A.P., Greenwood, K., Wagner, D.: Analyzing inter-application communication in android. In: 9th International Conference on Mobile Systems, Applications, and Services, pp. 239–252. ACM (2011)

13. Dall, C., Nieh, J.: KVM/ARM: the design and implementation of the linux ARM hypervisor. ACM SIGPLAN Not. **49**(4), 333–348. ACM (2014)
14. Dietz, M., Shekhar, S., Pisetsky, Y., Shu, A., Wallach, D.S.: QUIRE: Lightweight Provenance for Smart Phone Operating Systems. USENIX Security Symposium (2011)
15. Ding, J.H., Lin, C.J., Chang, P.H., Tsang, C.H., Hsu, W.C., Chung, Y.C.: ARMvisor: system virtualization for ARM. In: Proceedings of the Ottawa Linux Symposium, pp. 93–107 (2012)
16. Enck, W., Gilbert, P., Han, S., Tendulkar, V., Chun, B.G., Cox, L.P., et al.: Taintdroid: an information flow tracking system for real-time privacy monitoring on smartphones. ACM Trans. Comput. Syst. **32**(2), 99–106 (2014)
17. Felt, A.P., Wang, H.J., Moshchuk, A., Hanna, S., Chin, E.: Permission redelegation: attacks and defenses. USENIX Secur. Symp. **6**, 12–16 (2011)
18. Grace, M.C., Zhou, Y., Wang, Z., Jiang, X.: Systematic detection of capability leaks in stock android smartphones. In: 19th Annual Network and Distributed System Security Symposium (2012)
19. Hardy, N.: The confused deputy: (or Why capabilities might have been invented). ACM SIGOPS Oper. Syst. Rev. **22**(4), 36–38 (1988)
20. Hofmann, O.S., Kim, S., Dunn, A.M., Lee, M.Z., Witchel, E.: Inktag: secure applications on an untrusted operating system. ACM SIGARCH Comput. Archit. News **41**(1), 265–278. ACM (2013)
21. Hornyack, P., Han, S., Jung, J., Schechter, S., Wetherall, D.: These aren't the droids you're looking for: retrofitting android to protect data from imperious applications. In: 18th ACM Conference on Computer and Communications Security, pp. 639–652. ACM (2011)
22. Hwang, J.Y., Suh, S.B., Heo, S.K., Park, C.J., Ryu, J.M., Park, S.Y., Kim, C.R.: Xen on ARM: system virtualization using Xen hypervisor for ARM-based secure mobile phones. In: 5th IEEE Consumer Communications and Networking Conference, pp. 257–261. IEEE (2008)
23. Lee, H.C., Kim, C.H., Yi, J.H.: Experimenting with system and Libc call interception attacks on ARM-based linux kernel. In: Proceedings of the 2011 ACM Symposium on Applied Computing, pp. 631–632. ACM (2011)
24. Li, W.X., Wang, J.B., Mu, D.J., Yuan, Y.: Survey on Android Rootkit. Microprocessors (2011)
25. Roesner, F., Kohno, T., Moshchuk, A., Parno, B., Wang, H.J., Cowan, C.: User-driven access control: rethinking permission granting in modern operating systems. In: 33rd IEEE Security and Privacy, pp. 224–238. IEEE (2012)
26. Rosa, T.: Android binder security note: on passing binder through another binder (2011)
27. Rossier, D.: EmbeddedXEN: A Revisited Architecture of the Xen Hypervisor to Support ARM-Based Embedded Virtualization. White Paper, Switzerland (2012)
28. Schreiber, T.: Android binder-android interprocess communication. Seminar thesis, Ruhr-Universität Bochum (2011)
29. Shneiderman, B.: Designing the User Interface: Strategies for Effective Human-Computer Interaction. Pearson Education, India (2010)
30. Tam, K., Khan, S.J., Fattori, A., Cavallaro, L.: CopperDroid: automatic reconstruction of android malware behaviors. In: 22nd Annual Network and Distributed System Security Symposium (2015)
31. Varanasi, P., Heiser, G.: Hardware-supported virtualization on ARM. In: 2nd Asia-Pacific Workshop on Systems (2011)

32. Wang, Y., Hariharan, S., Zhao, C., Liu, J., Du, W.: Compac: enforce component-level access control in android. In: 4th ACM Conference on Data and Application Security and Privacy, pp. 25–36. ACM (2014)
33. Wei, X., Gomez, L., Neamtiu, I., Faloutsos, M.: Permission evolution in the android ecosystem. In: 28th Annual Computer Security Applications Conference, pp. 31–40. ACM (2012)
34. You, D.H., Noh, B.N.: Android platform based linux kernel rootkit. In: 6th International Conference on Malicious and Unwanted Software, pp. 79–87. IEEE (2011)
35. Zhang, Y., Yang, M., Xu, B., Yang, Z., Gu, G., Ning, P., et al.: Vetting undesirable behaviors in android apps with permission use analysis. In: 2013 ACM SIGSAC Conference on Computer and Communications Security, pp. 611–622. ACM (2013)
36. Zhou, Z., Gligor, V.D., Newsome, J., McCune, J.M.: Building verifiable trusted path on commodity x86 computers. In: 33rd IEEE Symposium on Security and Privacy, pp. 616–630. IEEE (2012)

Exploiting Android System Services Through Bypassing Service Helpers

Yacong Gu[1], Yao Cheng[3], Lingyun Ying[1,2(✉)], Yemian Lu[1], Qi Li[4],
and Purui Su[1,2]

[1] Institute of Software, Chinese Academy of Sciences, Beijing, China
{guyacong,luyemian,yly,supurui}@tca.iscas.ac.cn
[2] University of Chinese Academy of Sciences, Beijing, China
[3] Singapore Management University, Singapore, Singapore
ycheng@smu.edu.sg
[4] Graduate School at Shenzhen, Tsinghua University, Shenzhen, China
qi.li@sz.tsinghua.edu.cn

Abstract. Android allows applications to communicate with *system service* via *system service helper* so that applications can use various functions wrapped in the system services. Meanwhile, system services leverage the service helpers to enforce security mechanisms, e.g. input parameter validation, to protect themselves against attacks. However, service helpers can be easily bypassed, which poses severe security and privacy threats to system services, e.g., privilege escalation, function execution without users' interactions, system service crash, and DoS attacks. In this paper, we perform the first systematic study on such vulnerabilities and investigate their impacts. We develop a tool to analyze all system services in the newly released Android system. Among the 104 system services and over 3,400 system service methods in the system, we discover 22 vulnerable service interfaces that can be exploited to launch real-world attacks. Furthermore, we implement and construct attacks to demonstrate the impacts of these vulnerabilities. In particular, by utilizing these vulnerabilities, these attacks result in implicit user fingerprint authentication in background, NFC data retrieval in background, Bluetooth service crash, and Android system crash.

Keywords: Android · System services · Service helpers · Vulnerabilities

1 Introduction

One of the most salient features in Android is that it wraps various functions in its *system services*, such as telephony, notification, and clipboard, so that different applications ("apps") can easily access these functions through inter-process communication (IPC). Normally, apps use these system services via *system service helper*. In order to protect system services, service helpers provide various security mechanisms so as to protect the system services, e.g., validating input

© ICST Institute for Computer Sciences, Social Informatics and Telecommunications Engineering 2017
R. Deng et al. (Eds.): SecureComm 2016, LNICST 198, pp. 44–62, 2017.
DOI: 10.1007/978-3-319-59608-2_3

parameters against service crash, checking callers' status against user authentication in background, identifying and handling duplicated requests against unnecessary resource consumption, and passing callers' identities (IDs) to allow system services to authenticate the callers.

However, we find that these mechanisms can be easily bypassed, which incurs serious security problems. For example, as shown in Fig. 1, `FingerprintManager`, i.e., the service helper of system service `FingerprintService`, automatically obtains a caller's identity (i.e., the app's package name) and passes it to `FingerprintService` so that the service could enforce particular restrictions based on the caller's identity. Unfortunately, a malicious app can bypass the service helper and directly feed fake ID to `FingerprintService`. Therefore, the system service will directly accept the fake ID without any authentication. As we observed, the vulnerabilities of bypassing service helpers can incur privilege escalation, automatic function execution without user interaction, system service crash, and Denial-of-Service (DoS) attacks. Therefore, it is necessary to systematically study such vulnerabilities and their impacts, which has not yet been well studied in the literature.

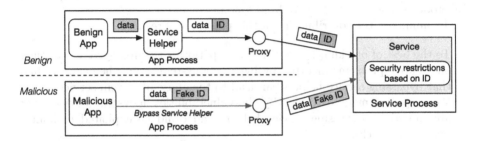

Fig. 1. A benign app interacts with a system service through the corresponding service helper which automatically collects the caller's identity and passes it to the system service. However, a malicious app can bypass the service helper, and directly feed a fake identity to the system service.

In this paper, we perform a systematic study on the above security breaches related to service helper bypass. The root cause of the breaches is that system services assume correct execution of security mechanisms in the corresponding service helpers that actually can be bypassed. In order to find out all vulnerable IPC methods in system services that can be exploited because of service helper bypass, we develop a four-step approach to identify IPC methods that do not enforce security mechanisms corresponding to that in the service helpers. Firstly, we enumerate all system services as well as their IPC methods in the Android source code. Secondly, we identify the corresponding service helper classes for each of the services. Here, we need to consider internal and hidden APIs which can be invoked by third-party apps through Java reflection. By scrutinizing the source code, we extend Android SDK and define service helpers as the classes in the extended SDK that can access system services via IPC methods.

The extended SDK includes all APIs accessible to third-party apps. Thirdly, after obtaining system services and their helpers, we identify the presence of security mechanisms for each method in two categories of classes, i.e., system services and the corresponding service helpers, by applying static analysis. Since service helpers run in the same process with the calling apps, while services do not, we cannot use the same method to identify the mechanisms in these two classes. To address this issue, we extract and compare code features of security mechanisms in the system services and the corresponding service helpers so as to obtain the difference in the security mechanisms. Finally, vulnerabilities are detected if system services do not enforce security mechanisms that are enabled in the corresponding service helpers.

We study the vulnerabilities in the Android 6.0.1. We find 22 vulnerabilities in system services resulted from bypassing service helpers that can be exploited by third-party apps to launch real-world attacks. We have submitted all vulnerabilities to Android Security Team and got confirmed by multiple Android Bug IDs. To demonstrate the impacts of the vulnerabilities, we exploit several representative vulnerabilities by constructing real-world attacks that lead to user fingerprint authentication in background, NFC data retrieval in background, Bluetooth service crash, and Android system crash.

In summary, the contributions of this paper are three-fold.

- To the best of our knowledge, this paper performs the first systematic study on security problems incurred by bypassing system service helpers. We find that bypassing service helpers can lead to the abuse of system services.
- We propose a method to identify the vulnerabilities in system services that are caused by bypassing service helpers and could be exploited to launch real-work attacks.
- We identify 22 vulnerabilities in total in Android 6.0.1, all of which are confirmed by Android Security Team. Moreover, we construct several malicious apps to exploit the vulnerabilities to illustrate the impacts of the vulnerabilities.

2   Background

In this section, we briefly review system services and service helpers, and the security mechanisms enabled in service helpers.

2.1   System Service vs. Service Helper

System services encapsulate essential functions in Android and compose significant parts of Android Open Source Project (AOSP) [1]. Two representatives of the functions in the form of system service are Near Field Communication (NFC) service and notification service. Usually, system services run as system processes and are registered in the *service manager* which serves as a service information center. Apps that intend to use a system service can query available services in the service manager, and then obtain the service proxy object through which functions in the system service can be used.

Service helpers enabled in Android SDK provide interfaces of functions in the system services for apps so that apps can easily use the functions, e.g., service helpers can automatically feed in parameters for functions in the system services. Most of system services that can be accessed by third-party apps are with one or more service helpers. In order to protect system services, the corresponding service helpers also use some security mechanisms to validate the requests from apps before issuing an IPC call to the system services.

A data flow of accessing system service is shown in Fig. 1. Since service helpers run in the same process with the calling app, an app directly calls the service helper within its own process. The service helper acquires the corresponding service proxy from the service manager, and then sends the request to the service proxy that is responsible for communicating with the target service via IPC calls so as to execute the system functions. The detailed communication procedures between services and the corresponding service proxies are defined by Android Interface Definition Language (AIDL) [2].

2.2 Security Mechanisms in Service Helpers

In order to ensure security, reliability, and efficiency of system services, service helpers include the following mechanisms. First of all, they enable the fail-fast principle [3] to ensure system reliability. As providing direct interfaces to apps, service helpers should detect failures as early as possible. We find that service helpers validate parameters and the caller's status to prevent service failures incurred by wrong parameters and status. Secondly, service helpers automatically collect data required by the system services, e.g., passing caller's identity, which reduces the risk incurred by passing invalid parameters to services. Meanwhile, they decrease the number of parameters that apps need to feed in. Lastly, service helpers help the system services to deal with duplicated requests that waste the service resources. Now we use four examples to illustrate the typical protection enabled by service helpers to protect the system services.

Validating Input Parameters. Parameter validation is one of the most important security mechanisms. For example, `BluetoothHealth`, the helper of the system service `BluetoothHealthService`, checks in `BluetoothHealth.registerAppConfiguration` `(String name, int dataType, ...)` to verify whether the first string parameter is non-null. It will send the remote request to `HealthService` via its service proxy only if the parameter is not empty.

Validating Callers' Status. Some Android system services may be allowed to be used only when the callers are currently active in the foreground. Service helpers provide such assistance to verify caller's status. One example is `NfcAdapter`, which is the helper of system service `NfcService`, verifies a caller's status in `NfcAdapter.enableForegroundDispatch()`. If the caller is not currently active in the foreground, the registration request for using NFC listeners will be rejected.

Passing Callers' Identities. System services need to verify various identity information of the callers (see Sect. 3.3.1), such as caller's `uid`, which can be achieved by interacting with `Binder` [4]. For other information, such as package name, system services rely on their helpers to collect. For instance, in the notification service, the first parameter of `NotificationManagerService.` `enqueueToast` `(String pkg, ITransientNotification callback, int duration)` is collected by one of its helpers `Toast`. Note that, such information delivery is transparent to apps because it is automatically performed by service helpers.

Constraining Duplicated Requests. There may exist multiple IPC requests from an app to a system service during the app's lifetime. IPC requests will consume the limited system resources, such as memories, CPU time, and file descriptors. Therefore, if a system service accepts all duplicated requests, the limited resources may be exhausted. In order to prevent resource being exhausted by duplicated requests, service helpers handle duplicated calls locally and mitigate the impacts. Service helpers use two strategies to constrain duplicated requests. For resource requests, service helpers restrict the number of calls that an app can issue. If the number of duplicated calls exceeds a threshold, which can be treated as abnormal or unnecessary, the following calls will be ignored locally. While for requests of registering listeners, service helpers initiate an IPC call to the remote system service only under receipt of the first request from the app. For instance, an app can get a notification when the clipboard changes by registering a listener to the system service `ClipboardService`. `ClipboardManager`, which is the service helper of `ClipboardService`, only registers the service once to get such listener after receiving the first request. After that, `ClipboardManager` maintains a local listener queue. Any duplicated requests of registering listeners afterwards will be only added to this queue locally. When the clipboard changes, `ClipboardService` notifies its helper `ClipboardManager` of the change. Then, `ClipboardManager` notifies all the listeners in its local queue. Thereby, system services only allocate resources for one request from the app, but still can notify the app when there is any update.

Unfortunately, these mechanisms can be easily bypassed if a malicious app directly invokes methods in system services instead of that in the service helpers. In this paper, we will focus on the vulnerabilities incurred by bypassing service helpers and the consequent impacts on the system services.

3   Identifying Vulnerabilities

In this section, we present an approach to systemically studying the vulnerabilities caused by bypassing service helpers.

3.1   Overview

The main idea of our approach is to find out whether the security mechanisms enforced by system services are consistent with that in their service helpers.

Fig. 2. Overview of our approach.

If they are not consistent, we regard it as a potential vulnerability that may be exploited through bypassing the service helper. For each potential vulnerability, we need to manually confirm it since not all potential vulnerabilities can be exploited. Following this, our study based on the source code of Android composes of four steps as shown in Fig. 2.

Firstly, we identify all system services as well as their IPC methods that can be accessed by third-party apps. We need to consider the services both in framework layer and native layer. We leverage service manager, in which all services are registered, as choke points to obtain all system services. We obtain IPC methods for most services that can be extracted from the AIDL files. Note that, a small portion of services (i.e., five system services) do not have their public IPC methods in the AIDL files. We manually extract their IPC methods.

Secondly, for each service, we need to find out its service helper class(es). We extend Android SDK to define service helpers as the classes that request services via IPC methods and can be accessed by third-party apps. We associate system services with their service helpers in the method level. If a service helper method includes an IPC call to invoke a remote service method, we treat these two methods as a pair. Here, we need to take all APIs into consideration, including the internal and hidden ones that can be invoked by third-party apps using Java reflection.

Thirdly, we examine the presence of security mechanisms in both system services and service helpers. We extract the code features of different security mechanisms. In this step, we need to detect the presence of security mechanisms in system services and their helper classes separately due to their differences.

Finally, potential vulnerabilities are detected by comparing whether the security mechanisms in the method pairs are consistent. If they do not match, it means that the service includes a potential risk of being exploited by bypassing service helpers and the inside security mechanisms. We manually confirm the vulnerabilities by launching real attacks.

There are two major challenges to identify all vulnerabilities. Firstly, it is not easy to find out all service helper classes. The internal and hidden APIs [5] that can be invoked by third-party apps through Java reflection are not included in the official Android SDK. If we intend to find out all service helper classes that third-party apps access, we need to consider all APIs. Secondly, it is difficult to identify security mechanisms in system service methods and the corresponding service helper methods. The security mechanisms in service helpers and the system services are implemented with different methods, in particular, service helpers run in the same processes with the caller app, whereas system services run in a separate system process. Therefore, we cannot directly compare the source code of security mechanisms in system services and their corresponding service helpers.

3.2   Enumerating Service Helper Classes

We show how to find service helper classes for various system services. Since the standard Android SDK does not include the internal and hidden APIs that can be invoked by third-party apps through Java reflection, we cannot directly enumerate all the APIs. To address this, we extend Android SDK to define service helpers as the classes that can use the corresponding system services via IPC methods. Internal APIs are located in `com.android.internal` package which is available in the `framework.jar` file on real Android device, while hidden APIs are located in `android.jar` file with `@hide` javadoc attribute. We merge the `android.jar` file and the `framework.jar` file to generate the *extended* SDK which includes all APIs that can be directly accessed by third-party apps.

We use Soot [6] to automatically analyze all classes in the extended SDK. One class is treated as a service helper as long as it invokes an IPC method of a system service by using one or more methods. If an identified class is a nested class, an inner class, a local class or an anonymous class, the top level enclosing class is considered as the service helper class. We further associate the service helper method with the service IPC method, and these methods compose a method pair that will be used to analyze security mechanisms in a later subsection.

3.3   Detecting Security Mechanisms

We identify the presence of security mechanisms in these methods by constructing a call graph and detecting their code features in the graph. We construct call graphs to express the relationships inside system services and service helpers and that between them. The call graphs are constructed by using Soot on the method level according to system services and service helpers. Moreover, we use PScout [7] to parse indirect dependency, e.g., *Message Handler* invokes different methods to handle messages according to the message content, so as to construct complete call graphs. Note that, in order to allow our approach to work with the latest Android 6.0, we also adopt the new compiling strategy in Android 6.0. Since Android 6.0, AOSP adopts a new Java Android Compiler Kit (Jack) toolchain [8] to generate `.jack` and `.dex` files as build targets. Since PScout uses `.jar` files as default input, we need to convert `.dex` files to `.jar` files by using `dex2jar` tool [9].

3.3.1   Identify Security Mechanisms in Service Helpers

We use different methods to identify the presence of the four types of security mechanisms in service helpers, separately.

Identifying Parameter Validation. We adopt `def-use` analysis [10] to identify the parameter validation mechanisms. `Def-use` analysis links each variable definition with that is referred, which can be used to identify if the variable, i.e., an input parameter, is referred in a validation process. Firstly, we check whether input parameters of a method are used in boolean expressions or whether they are used in other methods that return boolean values. Secondly, if the parameters are indeed related to boolean values, we further verify whether the boolean values are used in conditional statements, which contain statements with early returns or thrown exceptions. If these two conditions are met, the method includes input parameter validation.

Identifying Caller Status Validation. For the caller status validation, it is similar to the input parameter validation from the perspective of code features. We can identify caller status validation by analyzing APIs that return callers' status and verifying if these APIs are used in conditional statements.

Identifying the Process of Passing Caller's Identity. Apps provide different types of identities. As we observed, there are seven types of identity information in Android, i.e., package name, uid (i.e., linux user identifier), pid (i.e., linux process identifier), gid (i.e., linux group identifier), tid (i.e., linux thread identifier), ppid (i.e., linux parent process identifier), and UserHandle (i.e., representing a user in Android that supports multiple users). Each of them can be obtained by calling relevant methods that are summarized in Table 1. If there is any method included in a service helper method before an IPC method of the target service in the call graph, there is a high possibility that this service helper will pass a caller's identity to its service.

Identifying the Constraint of Duplicated Requests. In order to prevent resource consumption incurred by duplicated requests from apps, service helpers

Table 1. Methods used by service helpers to obtain caller's identity.

Identity type	Method
Package name	Context.getPackageName()
	Context.getBasePackageName()
	Context.getOpPackageName()
UID	Process.myUid()
	Process.getUidForPid()
	Context.getUserId()
PID	Process.myPid()
	Process.getPids()
	Process.getPidsForCommands()
GID	Process.getGidForName()
	Process.getProcessGroup()
PPID	Process.myPpid()
	Process.getParentPid()
TID	Process.myTid()
UserHandle	Process.myUserHandle()

adopt two ways to constrain the number of duplicated requests delivered to the system services according to the type of requested resources (see Sect. 2.2). The first approach is to restrict the number of requests that an app can issue to request resources. If the total number of requests exceeds a threshold, the following requests would be ignored. To identify the existence of this approach, we search all methods in service helpers to locate the conditional statements where the conditions are with constant integer expressions. If such conditional statement is located after the entry of the corresponding service helper and before the IPC calls to the service in the call graph, there is a high probability that the statement is used to check duplicated requests, which is similar to input parameter validation. Therefore, we can use a similar method to further confirm the detected mechanisms.

The second approach is to constrict the number of duplicated requests to register listeners. Usually, a service helper method accepts a listener as its parameter, and saves the listener to a local list. For example, the service helper method, `EthernetManager.addListener(Listener listener)` saves the parameter listener to `ArrayList <Listener> mListeners`. If it is the first registration request, the helper will register in the remote service via IPC. Otherwise, the service helper method only adds the request's listener to the local list. When the service helper receives the update from the service, it dispatches the update to all the listener maintained in that list. We capture the mechanism by identifying the code maintaining the listener lists.

3.3.2 Identifying Security Mechanisms in System Services

The idea of identifying security mechanisms in service helpers can be used to identify the security mechanisms enforced in system services. However, we cannot directly adopt the methods in Sect. 3.3.1 to system services because of the difference between systems services and service helpers.

Firstly, service helpers run in the same process with the caller while services do not. Service helpers can directly obtain the caller's identity via methods in Table 1. However, system services need different APIs to obtain the information about the caller and check the caller's properties, since they run in system processes which are separate from the caller processes. For instance, system services use `Binder.getCallingUid()` and `Binder.getCallingPid()` to obtain the callers' identities instead of the methods listed in Table 1. Secondly, system services need to validate app identities and verify whether the calling app is privileged to perform sensitive operations, which is not required in the service helpers. Fortunately, we find that system services heavily rely on the functions provided by `AppOpsService` to perform validation. For example, `AppOpsService.checkPackage(int uid, String packageName)` checks whether the input package name actually belongs to the given uid, and `AppOpsService.checkOperation(int code, int uid, String packageName)` checks whether the uid has the privilege to perform the sensitive operation indicated by the code. We can use these key methods to

Table 2. Methods used by services to obtain and check identity.

Function	Method
Get caller's UID	Binder.getCallingUid()
Get caller's PID	Binder.getCallingPid()
Get caller's UserHandle	Binder.getCallingUserHandle()
Check package name	AppOpsService.checkPackage()
Check operation	AppOpsService.checkOperation()

identify the process of verifying identities in system services. These key methods in system services are listed in Table 2.

3.3.3 Detect Possible Vulnerabilities

The final step is to examine whether the security mechanisms are consistent in the method pairs we identified in Sect. 3.2, i.e., the service method and the corresponding service helper method. The examination is straightforward and can be automated in most cases. Taking parameter validation as an example, we separately form the parameters validated in each party of the method pair into two sets. The parameters validated in the service method are denoted as set S, and those in the service helper method are denoted as set H. If S is *not* the superset of H, which means the helper checks more parameters than the service, the parameters p, which belongs to H but does not belong to S, may be abused with illegal values. For the processes of dealing with duplicated calls which are few in numbers (9 methods of 7 system helpers), we manually verify the enforcement consistency within the pairs.

4 Vulnerability Results

We develop a tool based on the methodology in Sect. 3, and apply it to analyze the latest AOSP 6.0.1. This section firstly summarizes our experimental findings, including the vulnerabilities related to the four types of security mechanisms in service helpers. Then, we construct real-world attacks exploiting representative vulnerabilities.

4.1 Vulnerability Summary

In the extended SDK containing 8130 classes, we find out 158 service helper classes. Among these service helpers, there are 86 cases where the helper passes caller's identity to the service. Also, these helpers classes include 227 methods that validate input parameters, six methods that verify caller's status, and nine methods that handle duplicated requests. Among these service helpers, as shown in Table 3, we capture 22 vulnerabilities, which can lead to privilege escalation, bypass of user interactions, service crash, or Android system soft reboot. All these

Table 3. Summary of vulnerabilities resulted from bypassing service helpers.

Service helper	Vulnerable service method	Security implication	Type
Toast	enqueueToast	Soft reboot	Fake identity
NotificationManager	setNotificationPolicy	Privilege escalation	Fake Identity
	getNotificationPolicy		
	setInterruptionFilter		
FingerprintManager	authenticate	Privilege escalation	Fake identity
	cancelAuthentication		
	getEnrolledFingerprints		
	hasEnrolledFingerprints		
	isHardwareDetected		
MediaBrowser	addSubscription	DoS	Illegal parameter
	removeSubscription		
BluetoothHealth	registerAppConfiguration	DoS	Illegal parameter
NfcAdapter	enableForegroundDispatch	Bypass of user interaction requirements	Fake status
ClipboardManager	addPrimaryClipChangedListener	Soft reboot	IPC flooding
AccessibilityManager	addClient	Soft reboot	IPC flooding
LauncherApps	addOnAppsChangedListener	Soft reboot	IPC flooding
TvInputManager	registerCallback	Soft reboot	IPC flooding
EthernetManager	addListener	Soft reboot	IPC flooding
WifiManager	WifiLock.acquire	Soft reboot	IPC flooding
	MulticastLock.acquire		
LocationManager	addGpsMeasurementsListener	Soft reboot	IPC flooding
	addGpsNavigationMessageListener		

vulnerabilities have been confirmed by Android Security Team and assigned with different Android Bug IDs. We describe the vulnerabilities in the following.

Vulnerabilities Caused by Passing Fake Identity. We find 19 inconsistent method pairs that are identified in 86 cases where service helpers pass the callers' identities to the services. That is, 19 service methods receive callers' identities from the corresponding service helpers but fail to verify the authenticity of the received identities as the service helpers do. We manually verify whether all of them can be exploited. Our verification shows that nine out of the 19 inconsistent method pairs can be used to launch real-world attacks. The rest 10 methods are not vulnerable to the fake identity attacks. Among them, five methods are protected by high level permissions (i.e., `signature` and `signatureOrSystem` levels) and cannot be granted to third-party apps, such as `StatusBarManager.setIcon()`, and the other five methods do not incur security issues, such as `BackupManager.dataChanged()`.

One vulnerability is abuse of `enqueueToast()` in notification service, which can lead to system reboot. Malicious apps will be regarded as one of the system apps by passing a fake package name "android" and can exhaust the system resources. The other eight vulnerabilities are in the `notification` service and the `fingerprint` service, which will result in the privilege escalation. A real-world attack to `fingerprint` service is illustrated in Sect. 4.2.1.

Vulnerabilities Caused by Passing Illegal Parameter. We find out 227 service helper methods validating their input parameters. Among these service helper methods and their corresponding service IPC methods, 51 method pairs are inconsistent in validating the input parameters. These methods may be exploited. After manual verification, three methods are identified to be vulnerable, i.e., they can be exploited to crash their services.

The reason most of inconsistent method pairs are secure is that Android automatically adds handle code for some common exceptions when generating Java classes from AIDL. The six most common exceptions are well handled in the system services defined by AIDL, including `BadParcelableException`, `IllegalArgumentException`, `IllegalStateException`, `NullPointer Exception`, `SecurityException`, and `NetworkOnMainThreadException` [11]. For other exceptions, it re-throws them as `RuntimeExceptions`. The exceptions thrown by system service IPC methods are caught by the Binder framework. The Binder framework then passes the exception to the IPC caller through `Parcel.writeException()` so that the caller could handle these exceptions in its own process. Therefore, if the exception triggered by illegal parameters occurs inside the service IPC methods, it would be handled well and not crash the service. However, if the parameter is used outside the service IPC methods, such as being used in asynchronous handler or stored for later access, it may lead to security issues due to the failure of handling exceptions. These three vulnerabilities in `MediaBrowserService` and `HealthService` are due to such failure in handling exceptions. In Sect. 4.2.3, we construct a real-world attack to illustrate the process of crashing Bluetooth service by passing illegal parameters.

Vulnerabilities Caused by Invoking IPC with Fake Status. We find that six service helper methods check the caller's status. One of them lacks the validation of the caller's status in its corresponding service method, i.e., `NfcService`. It bypasses user interaction to access function without user initiation or user permission, we will show such a case in Sect. 4.2.2 that an app can retrieve NFC data in background.

Vulnerabilities Caused by IPC Flooding. We identify nine methods in service helpers that handle duplicated requests which can be bypassed. These helper methods firstly check whether the current request is a duplicated one. These methods handle duplicated requests either by processing the requests locally (but not delivering them to the services) or restricting the number of the requests that can be delivered to the services. However, as we point out, these methods can be easily bypassed by directly using the methods in the corresponding services. A malicious app can abusively invoke corresponding service via IPC without any restriction. A large number of IPC calls would lead to Android resource exhaustion, which can further cause the system reboot. An attack leading to Android soft reboot will be described in Sect. 4.2.1.

4.2   Real-World Attacks

In this section, we demonstrate the impacts of several representative vulnerabilities by constructing real-world attacks to exploit these vulnerabilities.

4.2.1   User Fingerprint Authentication in Background

The FingerprintService provides functions related to user fingerprint authentication. We discover that there are five vulnerable methods in Fingerprint Service which all result in the privilege escalation by passing fake identify. The functions include fingerprint authentication (authenticate() and cancelAuthentication()), accessing the information about the enrolled fingerprints of a particular user (getEnrolledFingerprints() and hasEnrolled Fingerprints), and determining if the fingerprint sensor is present and functional on the current device (isHardwareDetected()).

Take FingerprintService.authenticate() as an example, the helper class of FingerprintService, i.e., FingerprintManager, is responsible for automatically collecting and passing the caller's package name to FingerprintService. FingerprintService.authenticate() is used to authenticate a given fingerprint. As shown in Listing 1, in authenticate(), it verifies whether the caller is allowed to use fingerprint based on received package name (Line 2). In canUseFingerprint(), it evaluates whether the caller is the current user or profile (Line 12), whether App Ops allows the operation (Line 14), and whether the caller is currently in the foreground (Line 16). Note that if the caller's package name is of KeyguardService, the caller is always allowed to use the fingerprint, and above restrictions could be bypassed (Line 10). Unfortunately, authenticate() never verify the authenticity of received package name. A malicious app can bypass the service helper to directly feed the KeyguardService's package name to the service method FingerprintService.authenticate(). In this case, a malicious app can circumvent these three restrictions in canUseFingerprint(). This vulnerability is confirmed with Bug ID AndroidID-29324069.

```
1  public void authenticate(/* other parameters */, String pkgName) {
2      if (!canUseFingerprint(pkgName, true)) {
3          Slog.v(TAG, "authenticate(): reject " + pkgName);
4          return;
5      }
6      ....
7  }
8  boolean canUseFingerprint(String pkgName, boolean foregroundOnly) {
9      checkPermission(USE_FINGERPRINT);
10     if (pkgName.equals(mKeyguardPackage))
11         return true; // Keyguard is always allowed
12     if (!isCurrentUserOrProfile(UserHandle.getCallingUserId()))
13         return false;
14     if (mAppOps.noteOp(OP_USE_FINGERPRINT, uid, pkgName) != MODE_ALLOWED)
15         return false;
16     if (foregroundOnly && !isForegroundActivity(uid, pid))
17         return false;
18     return true;
19 }
```

Listing 1: Code snippet in FingerprintService.java

(All code we present in this section has been simplified for brevity).

4.2.2 NFC Data Retrieval in Background

The NfcService provides NFC operations such as reading data from a close NFC tag. The service helper of NfcService checks the app's status by its method, i.e., NfcAdapter.enableForegroundDispatch(), so that only the app currently running in the foreground could register NFC listeners (see Listing 2). It is a rational design that the activity currently in the foreground should be the preferential destination for new coming NFC events. However, a malicious app could directly call service proxy method INfcAdapter.enableForegroundDispatch() to register an NFC listener. This is different from passing fake identities. There is no need to feed a fake status as the status is not passed to the service side. The NFC service does not verify whether the app is indeed in the foreground. In this case, the malicious app in the background can successfully register NFC listeners. When an NFC tag approaches the device, the malicious app in the background can read data on the NFC tag which may lead to user privacy leakage. We have reported this vulnerability to Android Security Team. It is tracked with AndroidID-28300969 with moderate severity level.

```
1   /**
2    This method must be called from the main thread,
3    and only when the activity is in the foreground (resumed).
4   */
5   void enableForegroundDispatch(Activity aty, /* other paramters */) {
6       if (!aty.isResumed()) {
7           throw new IllegalStateException("Foreground dispatch can only be
              ↪ enabled " + "when your activity is resumed");
8       }
9       sService.setForegroundDispatch(intent, filters, parcel);
10  }
```

Listing 2: Code in NfcAdapter.java, the helper class of NFC service.

4.2.3 Bluetooth Service Crash

The HealthService service, which provides health-related Bluetooth service, contains a vulnerability that can be exploited by passing illegal parameters. The method pairs, i.e., the service helper method BluetoothHealth. registerAppConfiguraton(String name, int dataType...) and the corresponding service method HealthService.BluetoothHealthBinder.register AppConfiguration(String name, int dataType...), do not use the same method to validate parameters. The helper method checks the "name" parameter to make sure it is not null, whereas the service method does not. The service does not use the value of "name" parameter immediately in the IPC method. Instead, it stores the value and uses it in BluetoothHealthApp Configuration.equals(). In BluetoothHealthAppConfiguration.equals(), it assumes config.getName(), that returns the value of "name", can never be null as shown in Listing 3. When a malicious app bypasses the service helper and registers a config with null-value in "name" parameter, there would be a NullPointerExcetion in BluetoothHealthAppConfiguration. equals(). Unfortunately, this method fails to handle the exception, and hence the HealthService crashes. This vulnerability is acknowledged by Android Security Team, and tracked as AndroidID-28271086.

```
1   public boolean equals(Object o) {
2       if (o instanceof BluetoothHealthAppConfiguration) {
3           BluetoothHealthAppConfiguration config = o;
4           // config.getName() can never be NULL
5           return mName.equals(config.getName()) && ... ;
6       }
7       return false;
8   }
```

Listing 3: Code snippet in BluetoothHealthAppConfiguration.java. The possible reason is that Google engineers assume that mName should never be NULL since it is validated in its corresponding helper class.

4.2.4   Android System Crash

This is an attack related to restriction on duplicated requests. The helper class associated with Wi-Fi service is WifiManager. An app can acquire Wi-Fi lock to prevent Wi-Fi to go in stand-by. This is done by calling WifiManager.WifiLock.acquire(). The source code is shown in Listing . This method examines whether the current request exceeds the maximum lock number that an app can acquire. If it detects that the current request has exceeded the threshold, it would release the lock immediately. We can see from the comments in AOSP that the restriction here is to "prevent apps from creating a ridiculous number of locks and crashing the system by overflowing the global ref table." However, a malicious app can easily bypass such restriction in the service helper by directly issuing requests to Wi-Fi service via the service proxy, i.e., IWifiManager.acquireWifiLock(). A large number of IPC calls would overflow the reference table, and lead to the crash of Wi-Fi service and then the reboot of Android. This vulnerability is tracked as AndroidID-27596394.

```
1   /* Maximum number of active locks we allow.
2    * This limit was added to prevent apps from creating a ridiculous number of
      ↪ locks and crashing the system by overflowing the global ref table.
3    */
4   private static final int MAX_ACTIVE_LOCKS = 50;
5   .....
6   public void acquire() {
7       mService.acquireMulticastLock(mBinder, mTag);
8       if (mActiveLockCount >= MAX_ACTIVE_LOCKS) {
9           mService.releaseWifiLock(mBinder)
10          throw new Exception("Exceeded maximum number of wifi locks");
11      }
12      ...
13  }
```

Listing 4: Code snippet in WifiManager.java.

5 Discussion

5.1 Lessons Learned

Service helpers play an important role in assisting both app developers (for easy app development) and services (for security verification). Unfortunately, we show that the use of the service helpers could be manipulated. In a manipulated process, service helpers can be bypassed. It means all the security mechanisms would be in vain. We have identified that there are indeed a large number of such vulnerabilities (Sect. 4). These vulnerabilities can lead to privilege escalation, bypass of user interaction requirements, service crash, and Android system soft reboot.

All vulnerabilities discussed in our paper are incurred by that security mechanisms in service helpers are bypassed. Since Android cannot guarantee a control flow to the service is initiated by a service helper, to completely prevent the attacks, an intuitive solution is to let services enforce the same security mechanisms as that in the corresponding service helpers, i.e., verifying callers' identities, verifying callers' status, validating input parameters, or constraining duplicated requests.

5.2 Limitations

False Negatives. Even though we have detected a series of vulnerabilities caused by the bypass of service helpers, we have to admit that there may be more such vulnerabilities to be uncovered. There are two factors leading to false negatives. One factor is that we do not consider the sequence of check and use. In our approach, we examine whether the service enforces the same security mechanisms as the service helper does. We assume that as long as there are the same enforcements in services, the adversary cannot abuse the service even though (s)he can bypass its service helpers. However, some defective services may perform sensitive operations before the security checking, e.g., using the parameter before the validation. In this case, the early use may lead to potential risks even with the presence of the same verifications in services. Another factor is that some services invoke native code using JNI, which is a small portion of the service code [5]. We do not study on these native code in our analysis, which also results in false negatives. We leave the analysis on services with JNI native code as future works.

Manual Work. Our approach is mostly automated, but still involves some manual works. The manual works are used in three processes. The first one is to identify the IPC methods that are not defined by AIDL. Fortunately, there are only five such services implementing their own IPC methods without AIDL. The second manual work is to examine whether the process of dealing with duplicated request are consistent in method pairs. There are nine pairs in total that need to be manually verified. The third one is to verify whether the experimental results can indeed be exploited to launch real-world attacks. It is also necessary to investigate the impacts of the vulnerabilities by verifying if they can be exploited.

6 Related Work

Vulnerabilities in Android have been extensively studied, including private data leakage [12–16], privilege escalation [17–21] and component hijacking [22–25]. In this section, we only summarize and compare with the existing studies closely related to ours.

Android System Service Security. There have been only a few works [5, 26,27] on the security of system services, despite the significant part they take in Android framework and the important role they play in Android. Huang et al. [26] discover a design flaw in the concurrency control of Android system services. They notice that Android system services often use the lock mechanism to protect critical sections or synchronized methods. If an application takes a lock for a long time, other services sharing the same lock would freeze, and then the watchdog thread would force Android to reboot. Shao et al. [5] find out that there are multiple execution paths leading to the same system service function but with inconsistent privilege requirement. Malicious apps can escalate their privileges or even perform DoS attacks by redirecting their requests to the paths with less enforced permissions. Different from the study only on the service side, our work focuses on investigating the impacts of bypassing service helpers by studying the security mechanisms in both services and service helpers. Another related work [27] examines the input validation in system services using fuzzing. They have identified several DoS attacks due to the lack of proper input validation in system services. Parts of our work is related to the input validation of system services. The identity collected by the service helper and the parameters prepared by the developer are passed to the service as its input. Our relevant findings in Sects. 4.2.1 and 4.2.3 reveal more vulnerabilities in the parameter validation which are missed in their detection. These studies are unable to discover the vulnerabilities since they can be exploited by constructing special parameters. For example, the `FingerprintService` service can be exploited if the input parameter is set to be the package name of `KeyguardService` (see Sect. 4.2.1). However, it is not easy for fuzzing to construct the parameters so as to effectively find this vulnerability.

Static Analysis in Android. Static analysis is one of the most effective ways to analyze the vulnerabilities in both Android systems and apps. Based on static analysis, there have been various researches on malware detection [28–30], library security [31], repackaging detection [32,33], component security [25], system service security [5,26], and permission specification [7]. Static analysis tools [6,34,35] also have been proposed to solve different problems. The two [5,26] closely related to our work both use static analysis. The difference is that our study focuses on the security breaches related to bypassing service helpers. Moreover, since static analysis cannot accurately reflect the precise situations in runtime, the analysis results may not be accurate. In our paper, we verifies the found vulnerabilities by constructing real-world attacks.

7 Conclusion

To our best knowledge, our study is the first systemic study on security problems of bypassing service helper of various Android system services. We point out that system services face the risk of being abused via bypassing the security mechanisms in service helpers. In order to identify such vulnerabilities and demonstrate the impacts of vulnerabilities, we develop a tool to analyze the system services in the latest AOSP. The experimental results reveal 22 vulnerabilities that can be used to launch real-world attacks.

Acknowledgments. This work was partially supported by the National Natural Science Foundation of China under grants 61572278, 61502468, 61502469 and 61572483, the National Key R&D Program of China under grant 2016YFB0800102, and the National Basic Research Program of China (973 Program) under grant 2012CB315804.

References

1. Android open source project. https://android.googlesource.com/
2. Android interface definition language. https://goo.gl/UFrnT3
3. Gray, J.: Why do computers stop and what can be done about it? In: Symposium on Reliability in Distributed Software and Database Systems (1986)
4. Android API reference: Binder. https://goo.gl/w2fXFH
5. Shao, Y., Chen, Q.A., Mao, Z.M., Ott, J., Qian, Z.: Kratos: discovering inconsistent security policy enforcement in the android framework. In: Proceedings of the 23rd NDSS (2016)
6. Soot. https://sable.github.io/soot/
7. Au, K.W.Y., Zhou, Y.F., Huang, Z., Lie, D.: Pscout: analyzing the android permission specification. In: Proceedings of the 19th CCS (2012)
8. Compling with jack. https://goo.gl/o9RYX8
9. Dex2jar. https://goo.gl/skfQLl
10. Aho, A.V., Sethi, R., Ullman, J.D.: Compilers, Principles, Techniques, and Tools. Addison Wesley, Boston (1986)
11. Android API reference: Parcel.writeexception(). https://goo.gl/7zuXuR
12. Rasthofer, S., Arzt, S., Bodden, E.: A machine-learning approach for classifying and categorizing android sources and sinks. In: Proceedings of the 21st NDSS (2014)
13. Cai, L., Chen, H.: Touchlogger: inferring keystrokes on touch screen from smartphone motion. In: Proceedings of the 6th HotSec (2011)
14. Xu, Z., Bai, K., Zhu, S.: Taplogger: inferring user inputs on smartphone touchscreens using on-board motion sensors. In: Proceedings of the Fifth WISEC (2012)
15. Aviv, A.J., Sapp, B., Blaze, M., Smith, J.M.: Practicality of accelerometer side channels on smartphones. In: Proceedings of the 28th ACSAC (2012)
16. Cheng, Y., Ying, L., Jiao, S., Su, P., Feng, D.: Bind your phone number with caution: automated user profiling through address book matching on smartphone. In: Proceedings of the 8th ASIACCS (2013)
17. Bugiel, S., Davi, L., Dmitrienko, A., Fischer, T., Sadeghi, A.-R., Shastry, B.: Towards taming privilege-escalation attacks on android. In: Proceedings of the 19th NDSS (2012)

18. Bugiel, S., Davi, L., Dmitrienko, A., Fischer, T., Sadeghi, A.-R.: Xmandroid: a new android evolution to mitigate privilege escalation attacks. Technische Universität Darmstadt, Technical Report TR-2011-04 (2011)
19. Felt, A.P., Wang, H.J., Moshchuk, A., Hanna, S., Chin, E.: Permission re-delegation: attacks and defenses. In: Proceedings of the 20th USENIX Security (2011)
20. Davi, L., Dmitrienko, A., Sadeghi, A.-R., Winandy, M.: Privilege escalation attacks on android. In: Burmester, M., Tsudik, G., Magliveras, S., Ilić, I. (eds.) ISC 2010. LNCS, vol. 6531, pp. 346–360. Springer, Heidelberg (2011). doi:10.1007/978-3-642-18178-8_30
21. Dietz, M., Shekhar, S., Pisetsky, Y., Shu, A., Wallach, D.S.: Quire: lightweight provenance for smart phone operating systems. In: Proceedings of the 20th USENIX Security (2011)
22. Zhou, Y., Jiang, X.: Detecting passive content leaks and pollution in android applications. In: Proceedings of the 20th NDSS (2013)
23. Bianchi, A., Corbetta, J., Invernizzi, L., Fratantonio, Y., Kruegel, C., Vigna, G.: What the app is that? Deception and countermeasures in the android user interface. In: Proceedings of 36th IEEE Security and Privacy (2015)
24. Chin, E., Felt, A.P., Greenwood, K., Wagner, D.: Analyzing inter-application communication in android. In: Proceedings of the 9th MobiSys (2011)
25. Lu, L., Li, Z., Wu, Z., Lee, W., Jiang, G.: Chex: statically vetting android apps for component hijacking vulnerabilities. In: Proceedings of the 19th CCS (2012)
26. Huang, H., Zhu, S., Chen, K., Liu, P.: From system services freezing to system server shutdown in android: all you need is a loop in an app. In: Proceedings of the 22nd CCS (2015)
27. Cao, C., Gao, N., Liu, P., Xiang, J.: Towards analyzing the input validation vulnerabilities associated with android system services. In: Proceedings of the 31st ACSAC (2015)
28. Enck, W., Ongtang, M., McDaniel, P.: On lightweight mobile phone application certification. In: Proceedings of the 16th CCS (2009)
29. Fuchs, A.P., Chaudhuri, A., Foster, J.S.: Scandroid: automated security certification of android (2009)
30. Grace, M., Zhou, Y., Zhang, Q., Zou, S., Jiang, X.: Riskranker: scalable and accurate zero-day android malware detection. In: Proceedings of the 10th MobiSys (2012)
31. Grace, M.C., Zhou, W., Jiang, X., Sadeghi, A.-R.: Unsafe exposure analysis of mobile in-app advertisements. In: Proceedings of the Fifth WISEC (2012)
32. Zhou, W., Zhou, Y., Jiang, X., Ning, P.: Detecting repackaged smartphone applications in third-party android marketplaces. In: Proceedings of the Second CODASPY (2012)
33. Hanna, S., Huang, L., Wu, E., Li, S., Chen, C., Song, D.: Juxtapp: a scalable system for detecting code reuse among android applications. In: Flegel, U., Markatos, E., Robertson, W. (eds.) DIMVA 2012. LNCS, vol. 7591, pp. 62–81. Springer, Heidelberg (2013). doi:10.1007/978-3-642-37300-8_4
34. Androguard. http://code.google.com/p/androguard
35. Androbugs. http://www.androbugs.com

Secure Keyboards Against Motion Based Keystroke Inference Attack

Shaoyong Du, Yue Gao, Jingyu Hua, and Sheng Zhong$^{(\boxtimes)}$

State Key Laboratory for Novel Software Technology,
Department of Computer Science and Technology,
Nanjing University, Nanjing, China
shaoyong.du.cs@gmail.com, njucsmoon@gmail.com,
{huajingyu,zhongsheng}@nju.edu.cn

Abstract. Nowadays, attackers seek various covert channels to access the users' privacy on the mobile devices. Recent research has demonstrated that the built-in motion sensors can be exploited to monitor the users' screen taps and infer what they have typed. This paper presents several practical and convenient countermeasures against this attack in terms of the soft keyboard. We find that this attack is sensitive to the motion noise of the mobile device and the layout variation of the soft keyboard. We, thus, present two kinds of countermeasures against this attack by introducing vibration noise in sensor readings and dynamics in the keyboard layout, respectively. We implement these countermeasures on Android platform and recruit 20 volunteers to evaluate these countermeasures' effectiveness and usability on both the smartphones and tablets. The results show that the proposed countermeasures can effectively reduce the attackers' keystroke inference accuracy without significantly hurting the typing efficiency.

Keywords: Keystroke inference attack · Motion sensor · Mobile device · Countermeasure · Soft keyboard

1 Introduction

The mobile devices' popularity makes themselves become one of the key targets of the attackers. To collect the users' privacy on the mobile devices, the attackers seek various covert channels, for example, the on-board sensors. It has been demonstrated that the cameras [9], gyroscopes [12], microphones [16,19] and ambient-light sensors [21] all can be used directly to exhibit the users' sensitive information.

Recent research [1,2,4,5,8,14,17,23] has demonstrated that the motion sensors can be utilized to record the user's screen taps so as to further infer what the

This work was supported in part by the Jiangsu Province Double Innovation Talent Program and in part by the National Natural Science Foundation of China under Grant NSFC-61300235, Grant NSFC-61321491, Grant NSFC-61402223, and Grant NSFC-61425024.

user has typed on the soft keyboard, which is called the motion based keystroke inference attack (MoBaKIA attack). It is first proposed by Cai *et al.* in [4] and they give a detailed presentation about it in [5]. Owusu *et al.* have proved that it is possible to infer the 6-character passwords in as few as 4.5 trails with the accelerometer readings [17]. Meanwhile, it can also get high accuracy on inferring English words on both the smartphone and tablet [14]. Aviv *et al.* enhance MoBaKIA attack with the polynomial fitting and signal processing techniques, making it possible to infer 40% of the patterns and 20% of the PINs within 5 attempts when users are walking [2]. A real Android Trojan application about MoBaKIA attack, TapLogger [23], has been implemented by Xu *et al.*

Nowadays, besides the standard soft keyboard, the users can utilize a variety of novel soft keyboards in the mobile application market, such as Swype[1] and Dynamic Keyboard[2], to type something on the mobile devices. Despite the innovative user experience provided, these soft keyboards pay little attention to defending against the covert channel attacks on the mobile devices, for example, MoBaKIA attack. They are still vulnerable to MoBaKIA attack, since the operations on them depend heavily on the entered content, which can be recorded by the motion sensors.

Prior work [2,14,17,23] has presented some countermeasures on MoBaKIA attack such as reducing the sampling rate, requiring specific permission on the motion sensors and so on, but they leave these countermeasures alone without any further implementation or evaluation. Some researchers attempt to provide a dynamic, flexible and fine-grained control on the access to the motion sensors [3,6,7,13,18,22,24]. However, these countermeasures are highly specified, which are implemented on the specific operating systems and require the alterations on the Android framework as well as the Linux kernel that can only be done by *ROOT*. With rooted Android, the users will encounter some practical problems, such as invalidating warranty and causing update issues[3]. As a result, these countermeasures cannot be widely applied to current Android versions.

To make the countermeasures more practical, a number of researchers seek to defend against MoBaKIA attack on the application layer in terms of keyboard [10,11,15,25–27], instead of security framework. Since these keyboards are much different from the standard keyboard, the users have to spend much longer time to learn about them and be more concentrative when they type.

In this paper, we take both the countermeasure's effectiveness and usability into account, and propose some practical and convenient countermeasures against MoBaKIA attack in terms of keyboard.

When we analyze the process of launching MoBaKIA attack, we have the following two observations:

I. *MoBaKIA attack is sensitive to the shaking noise of the mobile device.* When the motion data are used to infer the typed content, the motion noise of the

---

[1] https://play.google.com/store/apps/details?id=com.nuance.swype.trial.

[2] https://play.google.com/store/apps/details?id=com.alastairbreeze.dynamickey board&hl=en.

[3] http://betanews.com/2013/10/01/5-reasons-not-to-root-android/.

mobile device has a great influence on the inference result. For example, the shaking caused by the user's movement usually has a greater influence on the mobile device's state than just tapping the screen, which makes it more difficult to infer the typed content [23].

II. *MoBaKIA attack relies on the fixed screen area and constant layout of the soft keyboard.* It is the soft keyboard's fixed position and constant layout that enable MoBaKIA attack to infer the content that the user has typed with high accuracy [4]. Therefore, the fixed mappings from the keys to their screen locations are very critical to MoBaKIA attack. We can try to break these fixed mappings by dynamically modifying the soft keyboard's layout.

Our countermeasures against MoBaKIA attack are just based on these two observations. In this paper, we make the following contributions:

1. Driven by the first observation, we propose our first kind of countermeasures that we take advantage of the vibrator in the mobile device to add noise to the motion sensor readings. We make a detailed analysis of the vibration noise in terms of correlation and frequency spectrum, and we find that it can be difficult for the attackers to remove this noise.
2. Based on the second observation, we propose the second kind of countermeasures, which defends against MoBaKIA attack through dynamically modifying the layout of the keyboard. We make use of the entropy theory to analyze and select the modification strategies. Meanwhile, we present several effective strategies to reduce the side effects on the usability.
3. Based on Google's sample soft keyboard project, we implement these countermeasures and evaluate their effectiveness and usability on both the smartphones and tablets. With the experiment conducted among 20 volunteers and more than 90,000 keystrokes collected, we can see that the proposed countermeasures can effectively reduce the attackers' keystroke inference accuracy without significantly affecting the typing efficiency.

As for the soft keyboard, it can be unavoidable to sacrifice some usability to protect the user's privacy. We try our best to keep the soft keyboard's usability while modifying it. What is more, we do not want to persuade the users to use our countermeasures all the time. It depends on the specific contexts. When the users type their account numbers, passwords and other sensitive information, it could be acceptable for them to sacrifice the usability to protect their private information. At other time, they can still use the standard keyboard without any modification.

The rest of this paper is organized as follows. We start our work with the realization of MoBaKIA attack in Sect. 2. In Sects. 3 and 4, we give a detailed description of our two kinds of countermeasures against MoBaKIA attack respectively. We present our experiments and evaluations of these countermeasures in Sect. 5. We show the related work in Sect. 6. In Sect. 7, we conclude the whole paper.

2   MoBaKIA Attack Introduction

MoBaKIA attack can be considered as a problem of classification, and it can be divided into two stages: training stage and inferring stage. Through a well-designed malicious application (e.g., a mobile game application), the attacker can collect the labeled motion data sequences, which have been associated with the accurate touched areas on the mobile device. And then, the attacker builds the classifiers with these labeled motion data sequences. When the malicious application runs in the background, it stealthily accesses the motion data sequences when the user types something on the mobile device. With these unlabeled motion data sequences, the attacker can infer the original content that the user has typed.

To make an evaluation of our countermeasures' effectiveness, we implement and launch MoBaKIA attack on Android platform first:

Step 1. **Motion sensor selection:** We use the accelerometer and orientation sensor, which are utilized in prior work [2,4,5,14,17,23], to launch this attack.

Step 2. **Configuration of motion sensor:** To get a detailed presentation about the touch event, we set the sensor's receiving rate to the fastest one, 100 Hz.

Step 3. **Touch event extraction:** We record the exact time when a key is pressed and released so that we can easily locate the touch event in the motion data.

Step 4. **Feature selection:** Following the prior work [14,17], we extract both time domain and frequency domain features from the motion data.

Step 5. **Classifier selection:** Different classification algorithms' effect on MoBaKIA attack has been compared by Owusu *et al.* in [17] and they have claimed that the Random Forest classification algorithm has the best effect, so in this paper we adopt the Random Forest classification algorithm.

In the following parts, we will give a detailed description about our countermeasures which are based on the observations presented in Sect. 1. In this paper, we only focus on the alphabetic soft keyboard. Other soft keyboards can utilize the same strategies.

3   Countermeasure Based on Observation I

The prior work [23] has pointed out that MoBaKIA attack is sensitive to the motion noise of the mobile device. Based on this point, we can add some noise to the motion data before they are delivered to the registered *SensorListeners*. There are two measures to add noise. The first one is to modify the real sensor data by the programs. Raghavan *et al.* in [18] propose to add Gaussian noise to the acceleration data when the soft keyboard is activated. However, it requires the modifications of current operating systems, contradictive to our intention. The second one is to dynamically change the state of the mobile device. It can depend on the users to make extra motion when they operate the mobile devices, which can be inconvenient for the users. A more convenient way is to utilize the vibrator in the mobile device. Once a key is pressed, the vibrator is started. In Fig. 1, we can see that the noise produced by the vibrator can absolutely disturb the motion sensor readings. In this part, we mainly consider the accelerometer's readings, since the vibration noise has the similar influence on the other motion sensors' readings, according to our observation.

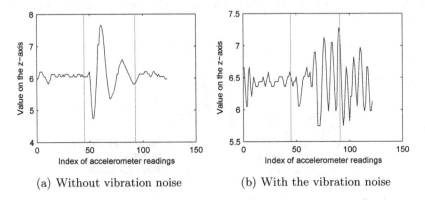

(a) Without vibration noise   (b) With the vibration noise

Fig. 1. Comparison of the accelerometer readings on the z-axis with the key "U" typed (The blue lines mark the time when the touch events start and stop.) (Color figure online)

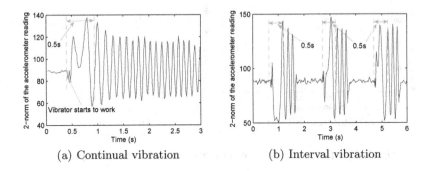

(a) Continual vibration   (b) Interval vibration

Fig. 2. Vibration noise analysis

Before fully utilizing the vibration noise, we start with an investigation to learn about the features of the vibration noise. In Fig. 2(a), we can see that the noise is periodic when the vibrator keeps working for some time, except for the first 0.5 s when the vibrator starts to work. Our extra experiments' result in Fig. 2(b) validates our observation. Based on our observation, we can see that the correlation coefficient of the vibration noise in the first 0.5 s each time follows the uniform distribution over $[-1, 1]$, making it hard to filter out this kind of noise. With 27,307 touch events collected, we obtain the average touching time which is just 0.48 s, shorter than 0.5 s. Therefore, we can take advantage of the irregular vibration noise in the first 0.5 s to disturb the original motion data about the touch events. Moreover, with the spectral analysis, we can see that the frequency spectrum of the vibration noise in Fig. 3(a) is much similar to that of the touch events in Fig. 3(b). Therefore, even with the band-pass filter, it is still difficult to remove the vibration noise from the motion sensor readings.

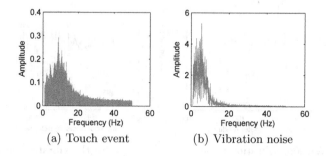

(a) Touch event   (b) Vibration noise

Fig. 3. Spectral analysis of the touch event and the vibration noise

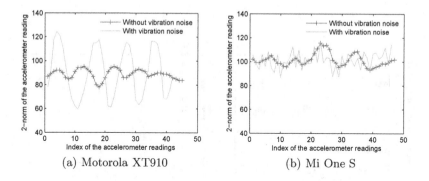

(a) Motorola XT910   (b) Mi One S

Fig. 4. Comparison of the touch events with different smartphones

Now, we test the vibration noise on different smartphones to gain the further insights about it. We find that it highly relies on the smartphones, which can be classified into two categories. To make a brief presentation about them, we take the representative one from each category in this part. Compared with the motion data without noise, some of the noise, in Fig. 4(a), can be strong enough to disturb the original motion data, while some of them, in Fig. 4(b), cannot. Moreover, with the spectral analysis of the touch events with different smartphones' vibration noise in Fig. 5, we can see that some vibration noise's

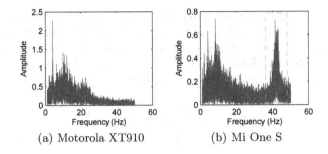

Fig. 5. Spectral analysis of the touch events with different smartphones' vibration noise (Mi One S vibration noises frequency is marked by the red dash rectangle.) (Color figure online)

frequency in Fig. 5(b) is so high that it can be filtered out by the band-pass filter, when compared with the touch events' frequency in Fig. 3(a). Therefore, this countermeasure's effect heavily depends on the smartphones. In the next section, we introduce some countermeasures that can be used on the whole smartphones.

4   Countermeasures Based on Observation II

The soft keyboard's fixed position on the screen and constant layout establish the fixed relations between letter keys and screen locations, which makes it possible to infer the typed information with the motion data. Therefore, we can dynamically adjust the keyboard's layout to break the fixed relations so as to increase the difficulty of MoBaKIA attack. Before we describe our detailed schemes, we first present the principle guiding our design.

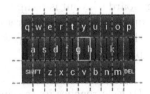

Fig. 6. The standard soft keyboard layout

Fig. 7. Randomize the layout without improvement

In the standard soft keyboard in Fig. 6, there are a total of 28 keys. We represent them by $k_1, k_2, \cdots, k_{28}$. If the user taps on k_i, a classifier may falsely recognize it as a different key based on the eavesdropped motion data. We denote by P_{ij} the probability that the tapped key k_i is falsely recognized as k_j. To break the fixed layout of the keyboard, we aim to find a randomization strategy to dynamically change the representing letter of each key. Supposing that after applying this strategy, the probability that k_i represents letter l_j is $Q_{k_i l_j}$. Note that the value of P_{ij} is determined by the locations of k_i and k_j, which have nothing to do with the randomization of the representing letters. Taking the inference error into consideration, if the classifier claims that the user has tapped on k_j in the last tapping event, the probability that letter l_s is entered is

$$P_{k_j \to l_s} = \sum_{i=1}^{i=28} (P_{ij} \times Q_{k_i l_s}). \tag{1}$$

The values of $P_{k_j \to l_s}$ for $s = 1, 2, \cdots, 28$ can be regarded as the probability distribution of a stochastic event, which is denoted by E_{k_j}. Then, the entropy of this event is

$$H(E_{k_j}) = - \sum_{s=1}^{s=28} (P_{k_j \to l_s} \times log(P_{k_j l_s})). \tag{2}$$

As we know that a greater entropy indicates that the stochastic event is more difficult to predict. Thus, we can claim that the greater the value of $H(E_{k_j})$ is, the more difficult it is for the attacker to predict which letter has been typed when the MoBaKIA attack classifier infers that k_j has been tapped on. Therefore, we should find a randomization strategy of the letter keys to maximize $H(E_{k_j})$ for each i for security. Usability has a great influence on the users' acceptance of these strategies. Therefore, when we design these strategies, we take full consideration of the usability and try to make the strategies user-friendly by following users' typing habits.

4.1   Completely Randomize the Layout

When we want to dynamically adjust the keyboard's layout, the most direct way is to completely randomize it. However, when the keyboard's layout is completely randomized, it makes it difficult for the user to pick up the target key. Therefore, in this part, besides the basic strategy to randomize the layout, we come up with some improved strategies to accelerate the user's typing speed.

Basic Strategy. According to the entropy theory, $H(E_{k_j})$ reaches its maximal value when $P_{k_j \to l_s} = 1/28$ for all $s = 1, 2, \cdots, 28$. We can easily prove that this condition is satisfied when $\forall i$, $Q_{k_i l_1} = Q_{k_i l_2} = \cdots = Q_{k_i l_{28}} = 1/28$, which means that the letters are completely randomly distributed to the keys. Therefore, our first countermeasure follows this observation and completely randomizes the layout of the alphabet keyboard as shown in Fig. 7. Note that our randomization does not include "Shift" and "Del" keys. When this strategy is applied, once a touched screen area is identified, the attacker can predict nothing but randomly select one letter to report. The probability that one input letter is inferred correctly is *3.85%* ($\frac{1}{26}$). This is the best strategy as for security. Nevertheless, this solution may make it difficult for the user to find out the target letter, slowing

(a) Decentralized   (b) Centralized

Fig. 8. Randomize the layout with improvement (keys marked with the white dash rectangles are the keys with high probabilities to be pressed.)

Fig. 9. Randomly resize the keys

down the typing speed. In our opinion, it can be acceptable for the users when they are typing very sensitive information on the screens such as bank accounts and passwords.

Improved Strategies. To provide a comprehensive and acceptable protection on the typed content no matter whether it is sensitive or not, we need to work further on the basic strategy to improve its usability. With the occurrence frequencies of words and the letter sequence entered by the user, we can predict the next letters with some probability and highlight them so as to speed up typing. The first improvement that we make is to resize the letter keys according to the probabilities that they are going to be pressed with. The higher probability the letter key is going to be pressed, the larger its size will be made. Once the user types one letter, we follow the basic strategy to randomize the letter keys' positions and then resize each key according to the associated probability. It keeps the basic strategy's effectiveness. Figure 8(a) shows the soft keyboard when the letter key "A" is touched. However, the predicted letter keys are decentralized, which is still hard for the user to find out his target letter key. Therefore, we can add an additional step to move the predicted letter keys with high probabilities to the center of the soft keyboard so that the user can pick up his desired letter key more easily. The initial keyboard's layout is just as the one of the basic strategy. With more letters typed, the attacker still can learn nothing since he cannot build a robust classifier, in advance, to infer the associated letters, except for random guess. Therefore, this improved strategy still keeps the basic strategy's effectiveness. Figure 8(b) shows the soft keyboard when the letter key "A" is touched in this case. To make the countermeasures not only effective in resisting MoBaKIA attack but also user-friendly, we should consider more information, such as the keys' proximate relations.

4.2   Randomly Resize the Keys

Randomly resizing the keys can adjust the soft keyboard's layout as well as keep the proximate relations between the keys in some degree in Fig. 9. Therefore, we treat it as one of the promising strategies, but we should pay attention to its side effects such as it can be difficult for the user to touch the key accurately and it may be impossible to present the whole soft keyboard on the screen. With the minimum key size considered, we resize the keys. We firstly randomize the keys' width in each row and guarantee that they cover the whole space in the horizontal direction. And then, we modify the keys' height in each row. When we modify the keys' width and height, we also adjust the keys' positions to avoid the block between the keys. Based on the remained space in the vertical direction, we randomly modify all the keys' y-coordinate values in the first row so that all the keys are randomly shifted in the vertical direction.

4.3   Heuristically Adjust the Layout

The neglect of the users' habits formed on the standard soft keyboard leads to the bad user experience. To guarantee the usability of the soft keyboard, we focus our attention on the users' habits. In Sect. 4.2, we randomly resize each key. It keeps the proximate relations between the keys in some degree. However, when the user tries to type the key with the small size, he may accidentally type the key nearby instead of it. It is just because of the key's small size. In this part, we still adjust the keyboard's layout, but we adjust the keys' positions in the local areas around their original positions, following some specific regulations. Based on the entropy theory discussed in Sect. 4, it is easy to see that the larger the key's adjustment area is, the larger the key's entropy value is. Driven by this observation, we come up with the following strategies:

H1. *Shift each column within a random distance.* We make uniform modification of the whole letter keys' height so that the original 3 rows in Fig. 6 are divided into 6 rows. In this way, each column can be shifted within a random distance in the vertical direction in Fig. 10(a).

H2. *Randomize the row order.* We just randomly resort the three rows each time a key is pressed just as shown in Fig. 10(b).

H3. *Randomize the keys within a local area.* We dynamically take the four keys nearby as a group, and randomly rearrange them among these four positions, as shown in Fig. 10(c).

H4. *Randomly shift the keys in each row.* We randomly select a constant for each row and all the keys in the same row are moved with the randomly selected constant in a circle, just as shown in Fig. 10(d).

We can see that there can be various heuristic strategies to adjust the soft keyboard's layout and we just enumerate some of them. However, we want to find a representative one among them. Now we give analysis about the effectiveness of the above schemes based on the entropy theory that we described earlier.

We first divide the keyboard area into a grid of 3×10 *cells* as shown in Fig. 6. Each cell represents a key (i.e., the minimal recognizable area that we consider in this analysis). For simplicity, we think that the keystroke inference accuracy reaches 100%, i.e., $P_{ii} = 1$ and $P_{ij} = 0$ $(i \neq j)$. We take the key $k_{example}$ highlighted in Fig. 6 as an example to compare the effectiveness of different schemes.

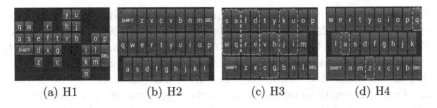

| (a) H1 | (b) H2 | (c) H3 | (d) H4 |

Fig. 10. Heuristic strategies ((c) is a moment that the keys marked within the white dash rectangles are randomly rearranged. The keys marked with the white dash rectangles in (d) are the first keys in each row in the standard soft keyboard.)

We first consider the strategy H1 shown in Fig. 10(a). In this scheme, if $k_{example}$ is considered to be tapped on, the input letter has three possibilities: "Y", "H", and "V". We can derive that $Q_{k_{example}Y} = 1/3$, $Q_{k_{example}H} = 1/3$ and $Q_{k_{example}V} = 1/3$. Therefore, according to Eq. 2, the entropy value is $H(k_{example}) = -3 \times \frac{1}{3}log\frac{1}{3} = 1.58$. Similarly, we can compute $H(k_{example})$ with the other heuristic strategies H2–H4, which are equal to 1.92, 2.50, and 3.17, respectively. We can see that H4 have the largest entropy value, so we choose H4 as the representative of the heuristic strategies and make further evaluation on it in the following section.

5   Experiment and Evaluation

From the aforementioned countermeasures, we select the representative ones and implement them on Android platform to evaluate their effectiveness and usability. For simplicity, we index all these countermeasures as Table 1. We use *BASIC*, the standard soft keyboard without any modification, as a baseline to make comparison with other countermeasures.

Table 1. Indexed countermeasures

Index	Countermeasure
BASIC	The standard soft keyboard without modification
C1	Add noise with the vibrator
C2	Randomize the layout without improvement
C3	Randomize the layout with improvement decentralized
C4	Randomize the layout with improvement centralized
C5	Randomly resize the keys
C6	Randomly shift the keys in each row

1. **Participants:** We recruit 20 volunteers (10 males, 10 females), whose average age is *24.50 years old*, to make evaluations of all these countermeasures on both the smartphones and tablets.

2. **Test Devices:** We conduct our experiments on 5 different smartphones (*Motorola XT910, Mi One S, Mi 2, Samsung Galaxy SII* and *Samsung Galaxy S4*) and 2 different tablets (*Samsung GT-N8000* and *Huawei MediaPad 10*).
3. **Further Illustrations:** During the experiments, the participants sit when they are typing and all the devices are kept in portrait mode. We do not have any further restrictions on the participants' typing manners so that they can follow their own habits to keep the mobile device and type the content on it.

5.1   Effectiveness

Settings. As our purpose in this paper is to resist MoBaKIA attack, we evaluate the countermeasures' effectiveness at first. Prior work [1,2,4,14,17,23] focuses on the keystroke inference accuracy, since it can directly affect the target key's rank among the candidates, which has a significant influence on the number of attempts needed to correctly infer the whole content. Therefore, we also focus on the keystroke inference accuracy when we evaluate these countermeasures' effectiveness.

We require the participants to touch the keys one by one ("*A*" → "*B*" → "*C*" → ... → "*Z*") in each round and go on for about 10 rounds with each countermeasure. With the captured motion data, we build the personal keystroke inference models for each participant and make *K-fold cross validations* ($K=10$), which are used in prior work [1,2,5,14,17], to obtain the inference accuracy on each key with each countermeasure.

We do not take *C3* and *C4* into account in this subsection, as they are just made to improve the usability of *C2*, which does not work in this experiment. Just as we have talked in Sect. 3, *C1*'s effect highly depends on the mobile devices, in this part, we only evaluate it on the mobile devices whose vibration noise can be similar to that in Figs. 4(a) and 5(a).

Effectiveness on Smartphone. We firstly conduct the effectiveness evaluation on the smartphones. Before we begin to evaluate these countermeasures, we deploy *BASIC* at first to show MoBaKIA attack's keystroke inference accuracy without any countermeasures. Following the steps presented in Sect. 2, we obtain the result in Fig. 11(a), similar to the result of Owusu *et al.* in [17]. We can see that the inference accuracy of the letter keys varies, which is mainly because of the keys' positions in the soft keyboard. The average inference accuracy is *40.84%*.

Compared with the average keystroke inference accuracy obtained without any countermeasures, all the average keystroke inference accuracies are reduced in Fig. 12 when we apply our countermeasures. We can see that *C1* does have some influence on the keystroke inference accuracy. However, since we do not have any restrictions on the participants' typing manners, *C1*'s effect varies among the participants, which leads to the inconspicuous reducing on the average keystroke inference accuracy. Although *C1*'s effect is not very significant, under some conditions it can be still effective to defend against MoBaKIA attack as it

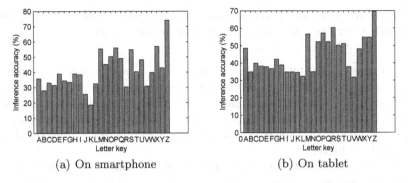

(a) On smartphone   (b) On tablet

Fig. 11. Keystroke inference accuracy of standard soft keyboard

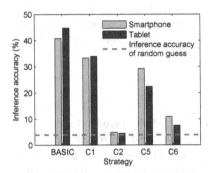

Fig. 12. Comparison of average inference accuracies on smartphone and tablet in the real scenario (*C3* and *C4* are excluded since they do not work when the keys are pressed one by one, "*A*" → "*B*" → ... → "*Z*".)

Fig. 13. Comparison of the average time of typing one letter between *BASIC* and *C1*

makes it hard to detect when a type starts and stops when the user types some information continually.

Among these countermeasures, *C2* is the most effective one to defend against MoBaKIA attack, as it reduces the average inference accuracy to about *3.85%*, the inference accuracy of random guess. Just as we have talked above, it may cost the user a much longer time to pick up the target letter key. If the content that is going to be typed is sensitive, it can be acceptable for the user in consideration of security. The second candidate is *C6*. Compared with *C2*, it preserves some proximate relations on the standard soft keyboard, but it may not be as effective as the first one, since it just reduces the accuracy to *10.89%*. We can see that *C5* does have some influence on the keystroke inference accuracy, but its influence is not very significant. It is mainly because that when we dynamically modify the keys' size, the majority of the keys' position do not change dramatically.

Therefore, each letter key is still located in a fixed area, compared with *C6* in which each letter key can appear at 7 possible areas at least.

Effectiveness on Tablet. Besides the smartphones, we also make an evaluation on the tablets. The process on the tablets is the same as that on the smartphones. With *BASIC*, we obtain the original keystroke inference accuracy as shown in Fig. 11(b). The average value is *44.82%*. The evaluation result of the proposed countermeasures on the tablets is also presented in Fig. 12, from which the similar result can be achieved.

Comparing the evaluation results on the smartphones and tablets, we can see that the average keystroke inference accuracy of *BASIC* on the tablets is higher than that on the smartphones, which is mainly because that the key's size on the tablets is larger than that on the smartphones, making it easier to infer the target key, just as Owusu *et al.* state in [17]. It is also the keyboard's larger display area on the tablets that makes *C2*, *C5* and *C6* more effective on the tablets, as the key's variation that can be made is much larger on the tablets than on the smartphones.

5.2   Usability

When we make some modifications of the soft keyboard's layout, we need to take the usability into account. In this paper, we pay attention to the time cost to type. In Fig. 13, we can see that *C1* does not introduce extra time when compared with *BASIC*. Therefore, in this part, we do not take *C1* into account and just list time statistics on *BASIC* and the countermeasures that modify the keyboard's layout.

Table 2. Application scenarios

Index	Scenario
S1	Entering account numbers and passwords
S2	Writing SMSes and making phone calls
S3	On-line chatting through the mobile social network Apps
S4	Posting and replying on the social networks
S5	Sending E-mails
S6	Searching through the Internet

We start our evaluation with a survey, which fully considers the application scenarios in Table 2. It is about the keyboard's popular application scenarios as well as the sensitive information that the participants consider. There are 132 participants (96 males and 36 females, the average age of which is 22.27 years old) taking part in this investigation. The obtained result is presented in Fig. 14.

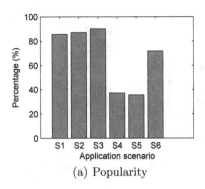
(a) Popularity

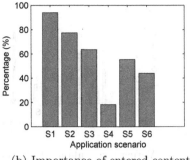
(b) Importance of entered content

Fig. 14. Voting results about the keyboard's application scenarios in Table 2

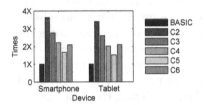

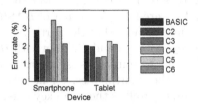

Fig. 15. Average typing time cost of different keyboards, compared with *BASIC*

Fig. 16. Typing error with different keyboards

In Fig. 2(a), we can see that the top 3 popular scenarios are *S3*, *S2* and *S1*. Under these scenarios, it is common that the content cannot be too long to type at one time. In this way, we design 10 sentences for testing, the average length of which is 11 words (about 56 letters per sentence, except for the blanks). 20 participants use the devices that we provide for testing. Considering their familiarity with the keyboard as well as the content to be typed, which can have some influence on the time cost to type, we demand them to repeatedly type the sentence for 6 times with each countermeasure, and then we calculate and compare the average typing time. We take into account the time that they spend on correcting the mistakes that they accidentally made. The detailed result is presented in Fig. 15. *C2* is very effective to defend against MoBaKIA attack, but it costs the longest time to enter which is about 3.63X times longer than that cost by *BASIC* in Fig. 15 on smartphones, so it can be applied only when users are entering some sensitive information such as account numbers and passwords. With the improvement on usability, in Fig. 15, *C4* can reduce the time to be only about 2.21X times of that with *BASIC*. In this way, no matter what the users enter, they can choose *C4* that not only can resist MoBaKIA attack but also does not cost too much time. However, if users think that the content to be entered is long but not so sensitive, they can also select other secure strategies instead, like *C5*.

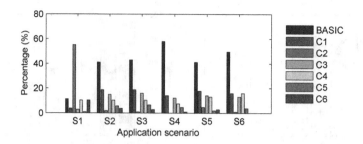

Fig. 17. Voting result about the keyboards over different application scenarios

What is more, we can see that the error rate that the participants tap the wrong keys by mistake varies over the keyboards in Fig. 16. The error rates of $C2$ and $C3$ are lower than that of $BASIC$, on both the smartphones and tablets. It is mainly because that the participants need to spend more time searching the target keys with $C2$ and $C3$ than with $BASIC$. $C5$ has the higher error rate than $BASIC$, due to some keys' small size that cannot be accurately tapped by the users. On the smartphones, $C4$ has the highest error rate, since the centralized target keys as well as the small key size lead to the users typing the wrong letters frequently.

We conduct a further survey on the countermeasures' adoption in different scenarios with the 132 participants. However, in this part, only 107 participants' feedbacks are analyzed since there are 25 participants who do not take MoBaKIA attack seriously and persist in using current keyboard on the whole scenarios. The obtained result is presented in Fig. 17. Comparing it with Fig. 14, we can see that the more sensitive the content to enter is, the more effective secure strategy they will choose. Under $S1$, 88.79% participants tend to adopt some countermeasures to defend against MoBaKIA attack and 55.14% participants directly select $C2$ to protect their sensitive information at the cost of usability. Moreover, over the whole application scenarios, at least 40% participants tend to adopt some defenses against MoBaKIA attack. In fact, these countermeasures can be set to switch automatically based on the importance of the content to be typed and so is the refreshing rate to modify the soft keyboard's layout, which can further improve our countermeasures' usability as well as keep the effectiveness in defending against MoBaKIA attack.

6   Related Work

The keyboard based countermeasure can be widely applied to current Android versions, so it has attracted many researchers' attention. Making use of the dragging, dropping and tapping action, Kwon *et al.* propose Drag-and-Type [10], to improve the typing accuracy. To defend against MoBaKIA attack, they propose to randomize the keyboard layout based on their basic method. Furthermore, they propose a rolling image visual keyboard, RIK [15], to fully utilize dragging and dropping actions to enter, which can effectively counter with MoBaKIA attack. CoverPad [25] introduces *variants* that are randomly generated and only can be seen by the users when they enter the sensitive information to build a random mapping between the entering keys and the target keys so as to defend against MoBaKIA attack. PassWindow [26] guarantees the security of PIN with a moving grid-configured window over a virtual keypad. To defend against MoBaKIA attack, the rear camera is utilized to imitate the touch events instead of touching on the screen. This kind of keyboards is much different from the standard keyboard, so the users need to spend much longer time to learn about them and be more concentrative when they type.

Yue *et al.* in [27] propose Privacy Enhancing Keyboard (PEK), randomly shuffling the keys and introducing the Brownian motion, respectively. Chu *et al.* propose *para-randomized keyboard* with MoBaKIA attack considered when designing TrustUI [11]. While both PEK and *para-randomized keyboard* can be utilized to defend against MoBaKIA attack, the researchers do not pay much attention to the further improvement on usability.

The most similar work is what Song *et al.* do in [20]. They propose two kinds of defenses: reducing the accuracy of accelerometer readings with a kernel modification that sets their square sum to a constant value, and completely randomizing keyboard layout. Much different from their work, we make a deep investigation on the vibrator's effect on defending against MoBaKIA attack. What is more, when we randomize the keyboard layout, we apply the entropy theory to guide our design and analyze the proposed countermeasures' effectiveness. Meanwhile, we try our best to improve the countermeasures' usability.

7   Conclusion

In this paper, we are engaged in the practical countermeasures against MoBaKIA attack. In our opinion, it is the motion data without noise as well as the fixed screen area and constant layout of soft keyboard that provide the opportunity to launch this attack, based on which, we propose our countermeasures. We evaluate them on Android platform in terms of effectiveness and usability. The result shows that while all the countermeasures have some influence on the keystroke inference accuracy, some of them can reduce the keystroke inference accuracy of MoBaKIA attack without significantly hurting the typing efficiency.

References

1. Al-Haiqi, A., Ismail, M., Nordin, R.: On the best sensor for keystrokes inference attack on android. Procedia Technol. **11**, 989–995 (2013)
2. Aviv, A.J., Sapp, B., Blaze, M., Smith, J.M.: Practicality of accelerometer side channels on smartphones. In: Proceedings of the 28th Annual Computer Security Applications Conference, pp. 41–50. ACM (2012)
3. Bugiel, S., Heuser, S., Sadeghi, A.R.: Flexible and fine-grained mandatory access control on android for diverse security and privacy policies. In: Presented as Part of the 22nd USENIX Security Symposium (USENIX Security 2013), pp. 131–146 (2013)

4. Cai, L., Chen, H.: Touchlogger: inferring keystrokes on touch screen from smartphone motion. HotSec **11**, 9–9 (2011)
5. Cai, L., Chen, H.: On the practicality of motion based keystroke inference attack. In: Katzenbeisser, S., Weippl, E., Camp, L.J., Volkamer, M., Reiter, M., Zhang, X. (eds.) Trust 2012. LNCS, vol. 7344, pp. 273–290. Springer, Heidelberg (2012). doi:10.1007/978-3-642-30921-2_16
6. Cappos, J., Wang, L., Weiss, R., Yang, Y., Zhuang, Y.: Blursense: dynamic fine-grained access control for smartphone privacy. In: 2014 IEEE Sensors Applications Symposium (SAS), pp. 329–332. IEEE (2014)
7. Chakraborty, S., Shen, C., Raghavan, K.R., Shoukry, Y., Millar, M., Srivastava, M.: ipShield: a framework for enforcing context-aware privacy. In: 11th USENIX Symposium on Networked Systems Design and Implementation (NSDI 2014), pp. 143–156 (2014)
8. Damopoulos, D., Kambourakis, G., Gritzalis, S.: From keyloggers to touchloggers: take the rough with the smooth. Comput. Secur. **32**, 102–114 (2013)
9. Fiebig, T., Krissler, J., Hänsch, R.: Security impact of high resolution smartphone cameras. In: 8th USENIX Workshop on Offensive Technologies (WOOT 2014) (2014)
10. Kwon, T., Na, S., Park, S.H.: Drag-and-type: a new method for typing with virtual keyboards on small touchscreens. IEEE Trans. Consum. Electron. **60**(1), 99–106 (2014)
11. Li, W., Ma, M., Han, J., Xia, Y., Zang, B., Chu, C.K., Li, T.: Building trusted path on untrusted device drivers for mobile devices. In: Proceedings of 5th Asia-Pacific Workshop on Systems, p. 8. ACM (2014)
12. Michalevsky, Y., Boneh, D., Nakibly, G.: Gyrophone: recognizing speech from gyroscope signals. In: 23rd USENIX Security Symposium (USENIX Security 2014), pp. 1053–1067 (2014)
13. Miettinen, M., Heuser, S., Kronz, W., Sadeghi, A.R., Asokan, N.: Conxsense: automated context classification for context-aware access control. In: Proceedings of the 9th ACM Symposium on Information, Computer and Communications Security, pp. 293–304. ACM (2014)
14. Miluzzo, E., Varshavsky, A., Balakrishnan, S., Choudhury, R.R.: Tapprints: your finger taps have fingerprints. In: Proceedings of the 10th International Conference on Mobile Systems, Applications, and Services, pp. 323–336. ACM (2012)
15. Na, S., Kwon, T.: Rik: a virtual keyboard resilient to spyware in smartphones. In: IEEE International Conference on Consumer Electronics (ICCE), pp. 10–13 (2014)
16. Narain, S., Sanatinia, A., Noubir, G.: Single-stroke language-agnostic keylogging using stereo-microphones and domain specific machine learning. In: Proceedings of the 2014 ACM Conference on Security and Privacy in Wireless & Mobile Networks, pp. 201–212. ACM (2014)
17. Owusu, E., Han, J., Das, S., Perrig, A., Zhang, J.: Accessory: password inference using accelerometers on smartphones. In: Proceedings of the Twelfth Workshop on Mobile Computing Systems & Applications, p. 9. ACM (2012)
18. Raghavan, K.R., Chakraborty, S., Srivastava, M., Teague, H.: Override: a mobile privacy framework for context-driven perturbation and synthesis of sensor data streams. In: Proceedings of the Third International Workshop on Sensing Applications on Mobile Phones, p. 2. ACM (2012)
19. Schlegel, R., Zhang, K., Zhou, X.Y., Intwala, M., Kapadia, A., Wang, X.: Soundcomber: a stealthy and context-aware sound Trojan for smartphones. In: NDSS, vol. 11, pp. 17–33 (2011)

20. Song, Y., Kukreti, M., Rawat, R., Hengartner, U.: Two novel defenses against motion-based keystroke inference attacks. arXiv preprint arXiv:1410.7746 (2014)
21. Spreitzer, R.: Pin skimming: exploiting the ambient-light sensor in mobile devices. In: Proceedings of the 4th ACM Workshop on Security and Privacy in Smartphones & Mobile Devices, pp. 51–62. ACM (2014)
22. Tong, T., Evans, D.: Guardroid: a trusted path for password entry. In: Proceedings of Mobile Security Technologies (MoST) (2013)
23. Xu, Z., Bai, K., Zhu, S.: Taplogger: inferring user inputs on smartphone touch-screens using on-board motion sensors. In: Proceedings of the Fifth ACM Conference on Security and Privacy in Wireless and Mobile Networks, pp. 113–124. ACM (2012)
24. Xu, Z., Zhu, S.: Semadroid: a privacy-aware sensor management framework for smartphones. In: Proceedings of the 5th ACM Conference on Data and Application Security and Privacy, pp. 61–72. ACM (2015)
25. Yan, Q., Han, J., Li, Y., Zhou, J., Deng, R.H.: Leakage-resilient password entry: challenges, design, and evaluation. Comput. Secur. **48**, 196–211 (2015)
26. Yi, H., Piao, Y., Yi, J.H.: Touch logger resistant mobile authentication scheme using multimodal sensors. In: Jeong, H.Y., S. Obaidat, M., Yen, N.Y., Park, S.H. (eds.) CSA 2013. LNEE, vol. 279, pp. 19–26. Springer, Heidelberg (2014). doi:10.1007/978-3-642-41674-3_4
27. Yue, Q., Ling, Z., Liu, B., Fu, X., Zhao, W.: Blind recognition of touched keys: attack and countermeasures. arXiv preprint arXiv:1403.4829 (2014)

Network Security

Cloud-Based Privacy-Preserving Parking Navigation Through Vehicular Communications

Jianbing Ni[1], Kuan Zhang[1], Xiaodong Lin[2], Yong Yu[3]([✉]),
and Xuemin (Sherman) Shen[1]

[1] Department of Electrical and Computer Engineering,
University of Waterloo, Waterloo, ON N2L 3G1, Canada
{j25ni,k52zhang,sshen}@uwaterloo.ca
[2] Faculty of Business and Information Technology,
University of Ontario Institute of Technology, Oshawa, ON L1H 7K4, Canada
xiaodong.lin@uoit.ca
[3] School of Computer Science and Engineering,
University of Electronic Science and Technology of China, Chengdu 611731, China
yuyong@uestc.edu.cn

Abstract. Finding a vacant parking space in a congested area, such as shopping mall, airport, etc., is always time-consuming and frustrating for drivers. Real-time parking information can avoid vehicles being cruising on the roads. However, when the drivers are acquiring parking information, their privacy is inevitable to be disclosed. In this paper, to minimize drivers' hassle and preserve drivers' privacy, we propose CPARN, a Cloud-based Privacy-preserving pARking Navigation system through vehicular communications, in which a cloud server guides drivers to vacant parking spaces close to their desired destinations without exposing the privacy of drivers, including drivers' identities, references and routes. Specifically, CPARN allows drivers to query vacant parking spaces in an anonymous manner to a cloud server that maintains the parking information, and retrieve the protected navigation responses from the roadside units when the vehicles are passing through. CPARN has the advantage that it is unnecessary for a vehicle to keep connected with the queried roadside unit to ensure the retrievability of the navigation result, such that the navigation retrieving probability can be significantly improved. Performance evaluation through extensive simulations demonstrates the efficiency and practicality of CPARN.

Keywords: Vehicular ad hoc networks (VANETs) · Parking navigation · Privacy preservation · Vehicular communications

1   Introduction

With the large number of vehicles in metropolises, parking in a congested area, e.g., downtown, shopping mall, particularly in peak hours, has become

Y. Yu—This work is supported by the Fundamental Research Funds for the Central Universities under Grant ZYGX2015J059, ZYGX2014J062.

a conflicting and confusing issue for a number of drivers [1]. It is common for vehicles to cruise among parking lots or circle within a large parking lot for an accessible parking spot. In crowded area, such vehicles cause an average 30% of the traffic on the road [2]. This situation becomes worse in some developing countries, such as China and India, where the number of the parking facilities is not sufficient for private vehicles. The extra traffic leads to significant social problems, such as traffic congestions, fuel waste, air pollution and vehicle accidents. Although traditional navigation systems, e.g., Google map and on-board navigation systems, can assist to locate parking garages, drivers may still worry about whether there is available parking space when they arrive, specifically in peak hours and congested area. Parking guidance information systems [3,4] can broadcast the availability of parking spaces at some specific spots or on the Internet. However, the former method may increase the traffic pressure around these spots, and the latter approach is unrecommended since it is dangerous for the drivers to use mobile devices when driving.

Recently, vehicular ad hoc networks (VANETs) become increasingly popular in both industry and academia [5,6]. In VANET, each vehicle, equipped with an onboard unit (OBU) device, is allowed to communicate with other vehicles nearby, e.g., vehicle-to-vehicle (V2V) communications, and with roadside units (RSUs), i.e., vehicle-to-roadside (V2R) communications [7,8]. VANET-based parking navigation systems can provide real-time parking navigation services for drivers on roads. By means of the widely deployed vehicular communication infrastructure, the vehicles can use OBUs to acquire the real-time parking information. Specifically, a vehicle can query the available parking space near the destination through the nearby RSUs and obtain the up-to-date information to find the accessible parking lot. Such a parking navigation system has the advantage that the driver can conveniently enjoy real-time parking navigation services and reach available parking space within short time and low fuel cost.

However, security and privacy issues are preliminary concerns for drivers in VANETs, since the infrastructure is confronted with various malicious attacks. If these issues cannot be well addressed, it is impossible for drivers to adopt the parking navigation services. To prevent attackers from submitting invalid queries to the RSUs, registration is necessary for the navigation services. The drivers must be authenticated to make sure that they are the registers, such that it is feasible for detecting a fabricated vehicle, which pretends a legal vehicle to enjoy free services. Besides, to ensure the trustworthiness of the interactions, all messages sent by vehicles and RSUs must be signed to guarantee that they are not polluted or forged by the attackers. Confidentiality of queries and responses is another security issue for VANET-based parking navigation systems. A driver does not want other drivers nearby to learn the destination by eavesdropping on the queries. Furthermore, the navigation response should not be shared with all vehicles nearby if this service is charged; otherwise, the vehicles can enjoy free parking navigation services, in case they have the same destination with the querying vehicle.

Location privacy is another concern for drivers, and there have been numerous controversies due to the track exposure [9,10]. For example, some navigation applications, offered by Google and Apple, collect drivers' locations and destinations [11], which may reveal sensitive information about the drivers' personal lives. In VANET-based parking navigation systems, the OBUs on vehicles frequently communicate with RSUs to query and receive the parking information. The vehicle's location is inevitable to be exposed, which is tightly related to the driver however. An attacker can learn the routes of vehicles and predict the location of drivers at a specific time, and even identify the references, health condition, social and political affiliations based on the visiting frequency of specific places. Moreover, the disclosure of vehicles' location may bring significant convenience for car thieves, since the thieves may trace the vehicles several days before action and prefer to steal cars parking in quiet places [12]. Therefore, location privacy is a must to be preserved for the wide acceptance of navigation service to the public. One common approach of location privacy leakage-resilient is to keep the drivers anonymous using pseudonyms or anonymous credentials. As a result, no attacker can identify the identities of drivers or link navigation messages to reconstruct the route of a specific driver. Nevertheless, once the drivers' identities are preserved, it is impossible to return the navigation responses to the target vehicles. To address the contradiction between identity privacy preservation and navigation responses retrievability, Chim et al. [13] require the vehicle to keep the connection alive with the RSU after sending the navigation query until it successfully obtains the reply, which is quite challenging in reality, particularly, when the vehicle moves at a pretty high speed. As a result, the successful delivery probability of navigation responses is limited. In addition, full anonymity is not perfect because a vehicle may launch a denial-of-service attack by sending a large number of queries to the RSUs in a short period of time. The misbehaving drivers should be traced when necessary.

In this paper, we propose a Cloud-based Privacy-preserving pARking Navigation (CPARN) system by integrating vehicular communications and a cloud server, which provides navigation service to assist drivers to find available parking spots efficiently. In specific, a driver can query a vacant parking spot by submitting his/her current location and desired destination to the cloud server. Then, the server automatically searches for an available parking lot close to the destination and vacant parking spots in the recommended lot using the real-time parking information outsourced by parking lots. Finally, the server returns the navigation response to the driver through RSUs on the way to his/her destination. This is reasonable because most of drivers use GPS, so that the driving direction to a destination from an area can be predicted. As a result, the RSUs that the driver will pass through can also be determined, and thereby receive the navigation response successfully. The contributions of this paper are four-fold:

- We propose CPARN based on VANETs to achieve parking navigation for drivers. With the parking navigation offered by the cloud server, a vehicle can quickly find a vacant parking space close to the desired destination. The gasoline and the time wasted on searching for parking spaces can be reduced.
- CPARN achieves conditional privacy preservation for drivers by utilizing anonymous credentials. Specifically, an authenticated vehicle sends the

parking navigation query to the cloud server without exposing the real identity. Meanwhile, a trusted authority can trace the identity of a misbehaving vehicle.

- We propose a novel approach to improve navigation retrieving probability in anonymous vehicular communications. We do not require the vehicle to communicate with the same RSU in the query and response procedures. Instead, the driver can send parking navigation query to the cloud server through a nearby RSU, and search and retrieve the response from the RSUs built on the driving routes. In this case, the communication delay is tolerable, and the probability that vehicles can retrieve the navigation responses successfully can be dramatically improved. Note that the new method is still suitable for the situation where the response of the query is returned rapidly, and thus, the vehicle can retrieve the navigation response from the queried RSU.
- We discuss the security features and evaluate the performance of CPARN. The extensive simulations demonstrate that the system is efficient and practical.

The remainder of this paper is organized as follows. In Sect. 2, we formalize system model, threat model and security goals. In Sect. 3, we propose the CPARN system, followed by security discussion in Sect. 4, and the performance evaluation in Sect. 5, respectively. We review the related work in Sect. 6 and conclude our paper in Sect. 7.

2   Problem Statement

In this section, we state the problem by formalizing the system and threat models, and identify the security goals.

2.1   System Model

We consider the system model of the parking navigation service, which consists of a trusted authority (TA), a cloud, parking lots, a large number of vehicles and some RSUs.

- *TA.* The TA is a trusted party, whose responsibility is to generate the public key certificates for all the entities in the system, and to trace the identities of vehicles when necessary.
- *Cloud.* The cloud, which consists of a server and connected RSUs, can provide two types of services. One service is offering the real-time parking data storage for the parking lots in a specific area; the other is providing the parking navigation for drivers by using the maintaining real-time parking data. For example, the red points in Fig. 1(a) are parking lots around CN tower, and the cloud stores the parking data for these lots and navigates for the drivers whose destination is CN tower.
- *Parking Lots.* Parking lots offer parking spots to vehicles. To manage the parking spaces and charge the parking fee, parking lots record the real-time occupancy of each parking space, and outsource their data to the cloud to reduce the cost of data management and maintenance.

- *Vehicles.* Each vehicle is equipped with an irreplaceable and temper-proof OBU, which provides the capacity to communicate with the nearby vehicles and the RSUs. OBUs can also execute some simple computations and have a small amount of read-only memory.
- *RSUs.* RSUs are deployed on the road, which can communicate with each other and with vehicles driving through. They can also interact with the cloud and the TA via the Internet. Each RSU is resource in rich, indicating that it has enough storage space to maintain the navigation responses and computational capacity to perform the cryptographic operations.

Figure 1(b) shows the system model of parking navigation service. Firstly, the cloud server, vehicles and RSUs generate the public-secret key pairs and register the public key certificates at TA, respectively. The cloud offers parking data storage service to parking lots and the parking lots outsource their real-time parking data to the cloud through the Internet. As there is no security and privacy issues for the parking lots, the data storage service is beyond our work. To make fully use of the real-time parking data, the cloud provides parking navigation for drivers. To participate the parking navigation service, each vehicle needs to register at the cloud server and obtain an anonymous credential to access the service. The parking navigation consists of two phases: querying and retrieving. In the querying phase, a vehicle firstly generates and sends a parking query to the nearby RSU (Step 1). Upon receiving a query, the RSU forwards it to the cloud server (Step 2). The cloud server recommends an accessible parking lot to the vehicle according to the real-time parking information and the desired destination of the vehicle. In the retrieving phase, the cloud server firstly sends the navigation response to the RSUs located on the roads that the querying vehicle may drive through (Step 1). The RSUs store the navigation responses on a navigation table temporarily after receiving the messages from the cloud server. When the vehicle enters the coverage area of an RSU, it sends a retrieving query to the RSU (Step 2). Upon receiving the retrieving query from a vehicle, the RSU searches the navigation response and returns it to the vehicle if the RSU is maintaining the response; otherwise, the RSU returns failure and the vehicle tries to retrieve the response from the next RSU (Step 3).

2.2 Threat Models

The threats may be from internal and external attackers. The external attackers may compromise the cloud server and RSUs to steal sensitive information about drivers. The eavesdroppers can listen on the communication channels and capture the transmitting messages to analyze driver's references. Internal threats come from the curious employees in cloud or drivers who want to learn more information about other drivers. Therefore, the whole infrastructure is confronted with a variety of security threats and no entity can be fully-trusted except the TA. Although the cloud server has to follow the regulations and agreements that are agreed with the vehicles, it is also interested in drivers' privacy and eager to mine private knowledge from the parking navigation queries.

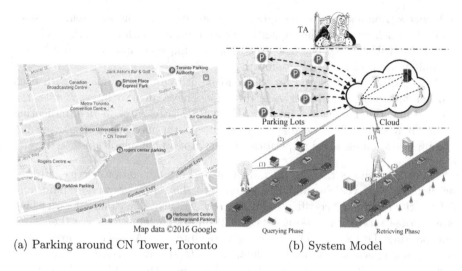

(a) Parking around CN Tower, Toronto   (b) System Model

Fig. 1. System model of CPARN

The vehicles may be compromised and launch some attacks to the cloud server, e.g., denial-of-service attack, impersonation attack and replay attack. Besides, they are also curious about the driving routes of the nearby drivers. The RSUs may also be compromised and the attackers can obtain the navigation messages maintained on storage devices. The RSUs are interested in the drivers' privacy and try to learn information by analyzing the forwarding data, e.g., navigation queries and navigation responses.

2.3 Security Goals

We aim to construct a system, which can provide real-time parking navigation, to achieve the following security goals:

- Service Authentication. A vehicle should be authenticated before submitting the parking navigation query, such that no attacker can impersonate a registered vehicle to enjoy free navigation service if the service is charged.
- Message Authentication and Integrity. The cloud server, the RSUs and the vehicles should ensure that the sent messages, including the navigation queries and responses, would not be polluted or forged by attackers. Thus, the receivers can believe the genuine of the messages.
- Identity Privacy Preservation. The identities of the drivers should be well-protected against the cloud server, the RSUs and other vehicles during the parking navigation procedure. Moreover, given two navigation queries, neither the cloud server nor the RSUs can identify whether these queries are sent by the same vehicle.
- Confidentiality. The contents of a navigation query and the corresponding response should be confidential to the vehicles nearby, the RSUs and the

eavesdroppers. Even the compromised RSUs cannot learn any knowledge about the navigation queries and responses.

- Traceability. The TA can trace the real identities of the vehicles who submit the parking navigation queries to the cloud server. Furthermore, to prevent the denial-of-service attack, the identity of the vehicle who submits more than two different parking navigation queries in a time period, e.g., one second, can be recovered by the cloud server.

3 The CPARN System

In this section, we demonstrate the preliminaries and describe CPARN in detail.

3.1 Preliminaries

If S is a non-empty set, $s \in_R S$ denotes s is randomly chosen from S. $(\mathbb{G}_1, \mathbb{G}_2, \mathbb{G}_T)$ is a set of cyclic groups of the same prime order p. $\hat{e} : \mathbb{G}_1 \times \mathbb{G}_2 \to \mathbb{G}_T$ is type 3 bilinear pairing [14], in which $\mathbb{G}_1 \neq \mathbb{G}_2$ and there is no efficiently computable homomorphism between $\mathbb{G}_1$ and $\mathbb{G}_2$ in either direction.

PS Signature. The PS signature is proposed by Pointcheval and Sanders [14], which has the same features as the CL signature [15], but is more efficient than the CL signature due to the advantage of using type 3 pairing. The existential unforgeability of the PS signature under chosen message attacks can be reduced to the modified LRSW Assumption 2 [14].

Let $\hat{g}$ be a generator of $\mathbb{G}_2$. The secret key of the signer is $(x, y_1, \cdots, y_r) \in_R \mathbb{Z}_p^{r+1}$ and the public key is $(\widehat{X}, \widehat{Y}_1, \cdots, \widehat{Y}_r) \leftarrow (\hat{g}^x, \hat{g}^{y_1}, \cdots, \hat{g}^{y_r})$. A signature on multi-block messages $(m_1, \cdots, m_r) \in \mathbb{Z}_p^r$ is $\sigma = (\sigma_1, \sigma_2) = (h, h^{x+\sum_{j=1}^r y_j m_j})$, where h is randomly chosen from $\mathbb{G}_1 \setminus 1_{\mathbb{G}_1}$. The signature σ can be verified publicly as $\sigma_1 \neq \mathbb{G}_1 \setminus 1_{\mathbb{G}_1}$ and $\hat{e}(\sigma_1, \widehat{X} \prod_{j=1}^r \widehat{Y}_j^{m_j}) = \hat{e}(\sigma_2, \hat{g})$.

3.2 The CPARN System

Our proposed CPARN consists of five phases: system setup, vehicle registration, navigation querying, response retrieving and vehicle tracing. The details of the CPARN are described as follows.

System Setup. Let $\mathbb{G}_1$, $\mathbb{G}_2$ and $\mathbb{G}_T$ be three cyclic groups of the same large prime order p. Suppose that $\mathbb{G}_1$, $\mathbb{G}_2$ and $\mathbb{G}_T$ are equipped with type 3 pairing, that is, $\hat{e} : \mathbb{G}_1 \times \mathbb{G}_2 \to \mathbb{G}_T$. g is a generator of the group $\mathbb{G}_1$ with $g \neq 1_{\mathbb{G}_1}$, and $\hat{g}, \hat{g}_0$ are two generators of the group $\mathbb{G}_2$ with $\hat{g} \neq \hat{g}_0 \neq 1_{\mathbb{G}_2}$. Define a collision-resistant hash function $\mathcal{H} : \{0,1\}^* \to \mathbb{Z}_p$. $\mathcal{C} = AES_{ENC}(\mathcal{K}, \mathcal{M})$ and $\mathcal{M} = AES_{DES}(\mathcal{K}, \mathcal{C})$ denote the encryption and decryption algorithms of AES scheme, respectively. The TA chooses $(x, x_1) \in_R \mathbb{Z}_p^2$ and computes $\widehat{X} = \hat{g}^x$, $\widehat{X}_1 = \hat{g}^{x_1}$. The secret key of the TA is (x, x_1) and the public key is $(g, \hat{g}, \widehat{X}, \widehat{X}_1)$.

The cloud server randomly chooses $(y, y_1, y_2, y_3) \in_R \mathbb{Z}_p^4$ and computes

$$(Y, Y_1, Y_2, Y_3, \widehat{Y}, \widehat{Y}_1, \widehat{Y}_2, \widehat{Y}_3) \leftarrow (g^y, g^{y_1}, g^{y_2}, g^{y_3}, \hat{g}^y, \hat{g}^{y_1}, \hat{g}^{y_2}, \hat{g}^{y_3}).$$

The secret key of the cloud server is (y, y_1, y_2, y_3, Y), and the public key is $(Y_1, Y_2, Y_3, \widehat{Y}, \widehat{Y}_1, \widehat{Y}_2, \widehat{Y}_3)$.

Each RSU has a unique number RID associated with its location. The RSU chooses a random number $z \in_R \mathbb{Z}_p$ as its secret key and computes $Z = g^z$ as its public key. In addition, the RSU defines three Bloom filters. BF_K is a (m, n, k, H)-Bloom filter, CBF_K is a (m, n, k, H, λ)-counting Bloom filter and VBF_K is a variant of the Bloom filter. In these Bloom filters, k hash functions $h_l \in H$ are defined as $h_l : \mathbb{G}_1 \rightarrow \mathbb{Z}_m$, for $1 \leq l \leq k$. The difference between VBF_K and the traditional Bloom filter is that instead of using an array of bits to represent the set membership in Bloom filter, VBF_K uses an array of γ-bit strings to indicate the storage addresses of the navigation messages. Every storage address S is divided into k shares of γ-bit, $S_1, S_2, \cdots, S_k$, using the XOR-based secret sharing scheme, and each share is stored on one index in VBF_K according to the hash values of the input. Initially, the array in BF_K, the counters in CBF_K and the strings in VBF_K are set to be zero.

Each vehicle has a unique identity VID. To register on the TA, a vehicle chooses two random $(v, v') \in_R \mathbb{Z}_p^2$ and computes

$$(V, \widehat{V}, \widehat{V}', \widehat{V}_0) \leftarrow (g^v, \widehat{X}_1^v \widehat{X}^{v'}, \hat{g}^{v'}, \widehat{X}_1^v).$$

It sends $(VID, V, \widehat{V}, \widehat{V}')$ to the TA, along with the zero-knowledge proof:

$$\mathcal{PK}_1 = \{(v, v') : V = g^v \wedge \widehat{V} = \widehat{X}_1^v \widehat{X}^{v'} \wedge \widehat{V}' = \hat{g}^{v'}\}.$$

The TA firstly computes $\widehat{V}_1 = \widehat{V}/\widehat{V}'^x$. Then, the TA verifies the validity of the proof $\mathcal{PK}_1$ and checks the equation $\hat{e}(V, \widehat{X}_1) = \hat{e}(g, \widehat{V}_1)$. If either is invalid, the TA returns failure and aborts. Otherwise, the TA generates a random $w \in_R \mathbb{Z}_p$ to calculate

$$(B_1, B_2, B_3) \leftarrow (g^w, (g^x V^{x_1})^w, \hat{e}(B_1, \widehat{X}_1)).$$

(B_1, B_2) is a valid PS signature on v and B_3 is a pre-computed item that allows the vehicle to avoid the bilinear pairing computation during the signing procedure. Finally, the TA returns (VID, B_1, B_2, B_3) to the vehicle through secure channel and stores $(VID, V, \widehat{V}_1)$ in a secret database. Upon getting the response, the vehicle sets its secret key as $(v, \widehat{V}_0, B_1, B_2)$ and the corresponding public key as (V, B_3). The key pair is stored in the read-only memory of the OBU.

Vehicle Registration. To enjoy the parking navigation service, a vehicle should register on the cloud server to obtain an anonymous credential. The vehicle with an identity VID selects two random $(t, s) \in_R \mathbb{Z}_p^2$ to compute $C = g^t Y_1^{VID} Y_2^s Y_3^v$, and sends (VID, C, V) to the cloud server, along with the zero-knowledge proof:

$$\mathcal{PK}_2 = \{(t, s, v) : C = g^t Y_1^{VID} Y_2^s Y_3^v \wedge V = g^v\}.$$

When the cloud server receives the message, it checks the validity of $\mathcal{PK}_2$. If it is invalid, the cloud server returns failure and aborts; otherwise, it chooses a random $u \in_R \mathbb{Z}_p$ to compute

$$(A_1, A_2) \leftarrow (g^u, (YC)^u).$$

Then, the cloud server returns (A_1, A_2) to the vehicle through secure channel and stores (VID, C, V, A_1, A_2) in its database. The vehicle checks

$$\hat{e}(A_1, \widehat{Y})\hat{e}(A_1, \hat{g}^t \widehat{Y}_1^{VID} \widehat{Y}_2^s \widehat{Y}_3^v) \stackrel{?}{=} \hat{e}(A_2, \hat{g}).$$

If yes, the vehicle calculates $A_3 = A_2/A_1^t$, and obtains the anonymous credential $AC = (A_1, A_3)$. Finally, it stores (AC, s) in the read-only memory of the OBU.

Navigation Querying. When a vehicle with the identity VID and the anonymous credential AC is on the road, the driver submits a parking navigation query to the cloud server to find a vacant parking space close to the desired destination. The vehicle generates the basic query information, including the destination $DEST$, current location CL, acceptable price range AP, current time t_1, expected arrival time t_2, expiration time t_3, etc., and performs the following steps to generate a parking navigation query:

- Pick a random $\kappa \in_R \mathbb{Z}_p$ to compute a temporary session key $U = \hat{g}^\kappa$ and calculate $L = \mathcal{H}(DEST, CL, AP, t_1, t_2, t_3, N)$ and $T = \hat{g}^{vt_1} \hat{g}_0^{Ls}$, where N is a random number chosen from $\mathbb{Z}_p$.
- Choose two random $(\alpha, \beta) \in_R \mathbb{Z}_p^2$ to compute $AC' = (A_1', A_3') = (A_1^\alpha, A_3 A_1^\beta)^\alpha$ and generate a zero-knowledge proof as

$$\mathcal{SPK} \left\{ \begin{array}{c} (VID, v, s, \kappa, \beta) : \hat{e}(A_3', \hat{g}) = \hat{e}(A_1', \widehat{Y})\hat{e}(A_1', \widehat{Y}_1^{VID} \widehat{Y}_2^s \widehat{Y}_3^v)(A_1', \hat{g})^\beta \\ \wedge U = g^\kappa \\ \wedge T = \hat{g}^{vt_1} \hat{g}_0^{Ls} \end{array} \right\} (N).$$

- Encrypt $(DEST, CL, AP, t_2, t_3)$ by selecting two random $r \in_R \mathbb{Z}_p$ and $r_1 \in \mathbb{G}_1$, and computing $c_1 = g^r$, $c_2 = r_1 Y_1^r$, and $c_3 = AES_{ENC}(r_1, DEST\|CL\|AP\|t_2\|t_3)$.
- Randomise (B_1, B_2, B_3) by selecting two random $(r', r'') \in_R \mathbb{Z}_p^2$ and computing

$$(\widetilde{B}_1, \widetilde{B}_2, \widetilde{B}_3) \leftarrow (B_1^{r'}, B_2^{r'}, B_3^{r'r''}),$$

calculate $c = \mathcal{H}(\widetilde{B}_1, \widetilde{B}_2, \widetilde{B}_3, N, t_1, U, T, AC', \mathcal{SPK}, c_1, c_2, c_3)$, $\tau = r'' + cv$, and output $(\widetilde{B}_1, \widetilde{B}_2, c, \tau)$ as a signature.

Finally, the vehicle stores (U, κ) on the OBU and sends the query $Q = (N, t_1, U, T, AC', \mathcal{SPK}, c_1, c_2, c_3, \widetilde{B}_1, \widetilde{B}_2, c, \tau)$ to the nearby RSU, if it is in the coverage area of an RSU. Otherwise, the vehicle can send Q to the nearby vehicles, and they deliver the query Q to RSUs via delay-tolerant V2V communications. When the vehicle enters the coverage area of an RSU, it sends Q to the RSU again.

When an RSU with RID receives a query Q from a vehicle, it verifies the validity of the signature $(\widetilde{B}_1, \widetilde{B}_2, c, \tau)$ by computing $B = \hat{e}(\widetilde{B}_1, \widehat{X}^c)\hat{e}(\widetilde{B}_2, \hat{g}^{-c}) \; \hat{e}(\widetilde{B}_1, \widehat{X}_1^\tau)$ and checking whether $c \overset{?}{=} \mathcal{H}(\widetilde{B}_1, \widetilde{B}_2, B, N,$ $t_1, U, T, AC', \mathcal{SPK}, c_1, c_2, c_3)$ holds. If it is invalid, the RSU broadcasts failure and requests the vehicle to re-transmit the query. Otherwise, the RSU checks whether the new query Q has the same tag T with a received query. If yes, it ignores Q. Otherwise, the RSU generates a signature on Q by selecting a random $r_2 \in_R \mathbb{Z}_p$ and computing

$$B_r = g^{r_2}, \quad c_r = \mathcal{H}(RID, Q, B_r), \quad \tau_r = r_2 + zc_r.$$

Finally, the RSU sends (RID, Q, B_r, τ_r) to the cloud server.

When the cloud server receives the query (RID, Q, B_r, τ_r), it verifies the validity of the signature of the RSU by computing $c_r' = \mathcal{H}(RID, Q, B_r)$ and checking the equation $B_r Z^{c_r'} \overset{?}{=} g^{\tau_r}$. If it does not hold, the server returns failure and requests the RSU to re-transmit the query. Otherwise, the server checks whether the tag T in Q is equal to the one in a received query. If yes, the server ignores this query. Otherwise, the server checks the validity of the signature $(\widetilde{B}_1, \widetilde{B}_2, c, \tau)$ and $\mathcal{SPK}$. If either is invalid, the server sends the query Q to the TA and aborts. Otherwise, the server decrypts (c_1, c_2, c_3) to obtain $DEST||CL||AP||t_2||t_3$ as $r_1 = c_2/c_1^{y_1}$, $DEST||CL||AP||t_2||t_3 = AES_{DEC}(r_1, c_3)$. If the query is expired, the server aborts; otherwise, it searches an accessible parking lot for the vehicle according to the destination $DEST$, the current location CL, acceptable price range AP, the expected arrival time t_2 and the real-time data of parking lots.

Response Retrieving. The cloud server firstly generates a navigation response RES, including the location of accessible parking lot, the number of vacant parking spots, the parking price. To prevent the response from being obtained by unregistered vehicles, the server picks two random values $k_1 \in_R \mathbb{Z}_p$, $k_2 \in_R \mathbb{G}_1$ and computes $s_1 = g^{k_1}$, $s_2 = k_2 U^{k_1}$, $s_3 = AES_{ENC}(k_2, RES)$ and $K = U^{y_1}$. Then, to prevent attackers from corrupting the response, the server generates a signature by selecting a random value $k_3 \in_R \mathbb{Z}_p$ to compute $\sigma_1 = g^{k_3}$, $\sigma_2 = \mathcal{H}(t_3, K, s_1, s_2, s_3, \sigma_1)$ and $\sigma_3 = k_3 + y_1\sigma_2$. After that, the cloud server predicts the current location of the vehicle according to the destination and the previous location, and determines $\mathcal{R}$, the set of RSUs that the vehicle would drive through. Finally, the cloud server sends the navigation message $R = (t_3, K, s_1, s_2, s_3, \sigma_1, \sigma_3)$ to the RSUs in $\mathcal{R}$. If the parking information of the recommended parking lot changes, the server generates a new navigation message R^* and sends it to the RSUs in $\mathcal{R}$ in the same way described above.

Upon receiving the message R from the cloud server, each RSU in $\mathcal{R}$ computes $\sigma_2' = \mathcal{H}(t_3, K, s_1, s_2, s_3, \sigma_1)$ and verifies the signature (σ_1, σ_3) as $\sigma_1 Y_1^{\sigma_2'} \overset{?}{=} g^{\sigma_3}$. If it does not hold, the RSU returns failure and requests the server to re-transmit the navigation message. Otherwise, as shown in Fig. 2, the RSU performs the following steps to store the navigation message:

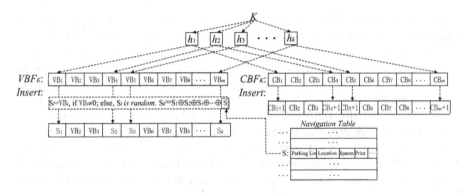

Fig. 2. Insert operation for the RSU.

- Insert K into the counting Bloom filter CBF_K. Specifically, for each $1 \leq l \leq k$, the counter $CB_{h_l(K)}$ increases by one and the rest counters keep the same.
- Store R on the navigation table and obtain the storage address S.
- Insert S into the Bloom filter VBF_K. Firstly, the RSU splits S into k shares of γ-bit, $S_1, S_2, \cdots, S_k$, using the XOR-based secret sharing scheme. If the location on the index $h_l(K)$ of VBF_K has been occupied, the RSU reuses the string $VB_{h_l(K)}$, that is, S_l is fixed to be $VB_{h_l(K)}$, where $l \in \{1, \cdots, k-1\}$; otherwise, S_l is a random γ-bit string. The last string S_k is set to be $S_k = S \oplus S_1 \oplus S_2 \oplus \cdots \oplus S_{k-1}$. Note that the probability that all the locations in VBF_K have been occupied when an address S inserts, is equal to the false positive probability of a Bloom filter. Then, the RSU sets $VB_{h_l(K)}$ to be S_l, for each $1 \leq l \leq k$.

When the vehicle enters the coverage area of an RSU^* with RID^* and (z^*, Z^*), it queries whether the parking navigation message R exists on the RSU^*. Firstly, the vehicle reads (U, κ) from the memory of the OBU device and computes $K^* = \widehat{Y}_1^\kappa$. Then, the vehicle chooses $(u_1, u_2) \in_R \mathbb{Z}_p^2$ to calculate

$$(C_1, C_2, C_3) \leftarrow (B_1^{u_1}, B_2^{u_1}, B_3^{u_1 u_2}),$$
$$\beta_1 = \mathcal{H}(C_1, C_2, C_3, K^*, \tilde{t}),$$
$$\tau_1 = u_2 + \beta_1 v,$$

where $\tilde{t}$ is the current time used to resist the replay attack. Finally, the vehicle sends the retrieving query $(K^*, C_1, C_2, \beta_1, \tau_1, \tilde{t})$ to the RSU^* to retrieve the response of the navigation query.

Upon receiving $(K^*, C_1, C_2, \beta_1, \tau_1, \tilde{t})$, the RSU^* verifies the signature $(C_1, C_2, \beta_1, \tau_1)$ by computing $C_3' = \hat{e}(C_1, \widehat{X}^{\beta_1})\hat{e}(C_2, \hat{g}^{-\beta_1})\hat{e}(C_1, \widehat{X}_1^{\tau_1})$ and checking whether $\beta_1 = \mathcal{H}(C_1, C_2, C_3', K^*, \tilde{t})$ holds. If not, the RSU^* returns failure and requests the vehicle to re-send the message. Otherwise, the RSU^* checks whether all counters in CBF_K on the locations $h_1(K^*), \cdots h_k(K^*)$ are nonzero. If one of them is zero, the RSU^* returns failure to the vehicle and aborts. Otherwise, it recovers the storage address S by computing $S = VB_{h_1(K^*)} \oplus VB_{h_2(K^*)} \oplus \cdots \oplus VB_{h_k(K^*)}$ and finds the navigation message R directly according the storage address S. Then, the RSU* picks a random $r_3 \in_R \mathbb{Z}_p$ to compute $\sigma_1^* = g^{r_3}$, $\sigma_2^* = \mathcal{H}(RID^*, R, \sigma_1^*)$ and $\sigma_3^* = r_3 + z^* \sigma_2^*$. After that, the RSU* returns $(RID^*, R, \sigma_1^*, \sigma_3^*)$ to the vehicle and broadcasts a Bloom filter BF_{K^*} to other RSUs, in which $BF_{K^*}[h_l(K^*)] = 1$ for $1 \leq l \leq k$, and the other bits in the array are zero. Finally, the RSU* performs the deletion operation to remove K^* from CBF_K and delete S in VBF_K. Specifically, the counters in CBF_K on the indices $h_l(K^*)$ for $1 \leq l \leq k$ decrease by one, and the shares of S in VBF_K are removed if the corresponding counters in CBF_K are set to be zero. In addition, if the stored response is expired or an RSU receives a broadcasted BF_{K^*}, the RSU performs deletion operation by deleting the expired or retrieved navigation message and updating the Bloom filters, CBF_K and VBF_K.

If the vehicle receives failure from the RSU*, it can send the retrieving query to other RSUs. Otherwise, the vehicle obtains $(RID^*, R, \sigma_1^*, \sigma_3^*)$. The vehicle checks the validity of the signature (σ_1^*, σ_3^*) by computing $\sigma_4^* = \mathcal{H}(RID^*, R, \sigma_1^*)$ and verifying whether $\sigma_1^*(Z^*)^{\sigma_4^*} = g^{\sigma_3^*}$ holds. If not, the vehicle returns failure and requests the RSU to re-transmit the message. Otherwise, the vehicle calculates $\sigma_4 = \mathcal{H}(t_3, K, s_1, s_2, s_3, \sigma_1)$ and verifies whether $\sigma_1 Y_1^{\sigma_4} = g^{\sigma_3}$ holds. If not, the vehicle sends the message R to the TA for complaint. Otherwise, the vehicle computes $k_2 = s_2/s_1^\kappa$ and recovers the navigation response $RES = AES_{DEC}(k_2, s_3)$. Finally, the vehicle can find a vacant parking space according to the parking navigation response. When the vehicle is driving through other RSUs, it would still send the retrieving query to the nearby RSU to check whether the navigation message is updated and retrieve the latest response.

Vehicle Tracing. The vehicle tracing consists of two phases: the cloud server tracing and the TA tracing. In the cloud server tracing phase, the cloud server can recover the identity of a vehicle who submits two different navigation queries in the same time period, which is detected as the denial-of-service attacks. Having two queries Q_1 and Q_2, the cloud server obtains $(DEST, CL, AP, t_1, t_2, t_3, N, T)$ from Q_1 and $(\overline{DEST}, \overline{CL}, \overline{AP}, \bar{t}_1, \bar{t}_2, \bar{t}_3, \overline{N}, \overline{T})$ from Q_2, respectively. To trace the identity of the vehicle, the server computes $L = \mathcal{H}(DEST, CL, AP, t_1, t_2, t_3, N)$, $\overline{L} = \mathcal{H}(\overline{DEST}, \overline{CL}, \overline{AP}, \bar{t}_1, \bar{t}_2, \bar{t}_3, \overline{N})$, and $\hat{g}^v = (\frac{T^{\overline{L}}}{\overline{T}^L})^{\frac{1}{t_1(\overline{L}-L)}}$. Then, the cloud server tests $\hat{e}(g, \hat{g}^v) = \hat{e}(V, \hat{g})$ to find the misbehaving vehicle.

In the TA tracing phase, the TA uses the vehicle's signature $(\widetilde{B}_1, \widetilde{B}_2, c, \tau)$ to trace the identity of the vehicle. The TA checks whether $\hat{e}(\widetilde{B}_2, \hat{g}) = \hat{e}(\widetilde{B}_1, \widehat{X})$ $\hat{e}(\widetilde{B}_1, \widehat{V}_1)$ holds or not, until it gets a match.

4   Security Discussion

In this section, we demonstrate that our CPARN meets all security and privacy goals described in Sect. 2.3.

Service Authentication: Each vehicle is delegated with an anonymous credential AC by the cloud server in vehicle registration phase, which is used to access the parking navigation service. To query an available parking spot, the vehicle firstly proves the possession of AC and then sends the navigation query to the cloud server. Therefore, only the vehicles having the anonymous credentials can enjoy this service if the credentials cannot be forged. To generate the credentials for vehicles, the cloud server uses its secret key to sign the commitments of the vehicles to generate a blind signature. Now we show that the unforgeability of the blind signature (A_1, A_3) can be reduced to the modified LRSW Assumption 1 [14]. The credential AC satisfies $A_1 = g^u$, $A_3 = (Yg^tY_1^{VID}Y_2^sY_3^v)^u/g^{ut} = (YY_1^{VID}Y_2^sY_3^v)^u$, which is a valid PS signature on message (VID, s, v). However, the blind signature has the public parameters (Y_1, Y_2, Y_3) compared with the PS signature. Thus, the security of the blind signature can be reduced to the modified LRSW Assumption 1, while the unforgeability of PS signature depends on the modified LRSW Assumption 2 [14]. Therefore, if the modified LRSW Assumption 1 holds, it is impossible for the attackers to forge the anonymous credentials.

Messages Authentication and Integrity: We utilize signature schemes to ensure that all messages sent by authenticated entities cannot be polluted or forged by attackers. The interactions between the cloud server and the RSUs are authenticated using the Schnorr signature scheme, as well as the messages sent by the RSUs to vehicles. Since the Schnorr signature is proved secure under the discrete logarithm assumption, the authentication and integrity of the messages are satisfied. The queries are signed by the vehicles using a randomized secret key, which is a valid PS signature [14] distributed by the TA. Since the PS signature is unforgeable if the modified LRSW Assumption 2 holds, no attacker can forge the secret key (B_1, B_2) and further generate the signatures on vehicles' queries. Therefore, all the exchanged messages between the cloud server and vehicles are authenticated and intact.

Identity Privacy Preservation: We discuss the identity privacy preservation from two aspects. Firstly, in the navigation querying phase, the identities of vehicles cannot be disclosed to the attackers and the curious entities, including the cloud server, RSUs and other vehicles. To prove the possession of the credential AC, the vehicle utilizes the zero-knowledge proof $\mathcal{SPK}$ to show its qualification to enjoy the service, without exposing the identity VID or (V, B_3). The signature on the query $(\widetilde{B}_1, \widetilde{B}_2, c, \tau)$ also does not reveal any information about vehicle's identity, since $\widetilde{B}_1, \widetilde{B}_2$ are randomized and only the TA's public key is required to verify the signature. In addition, although the tag T includes vehicle's secret key v, an attacker cannot identify the vehicle's identity or link two tags to the same vehicle, unless the DDH assumption in $\mathbb{G}_2$ does not hold. Specifically, if there exists an adversary $\mathcal{A}$ that can identify an honest vehicle out of two challenging vehicles, we show how to construct a simulator $\mathcal{S}$ to solve an instance of the Decisional Diffie-Hellman (DDH) problem in $\mathbb{G}_2$. That is, given $G, G_1, G_2, G_3 \in \mathbb{G}_2$, $\mathcal{S}$ can tell whether there exists (ω_1, ω_2), such that $G_1 = G^{\omega_1}, G_2 = G^{\omega_2}, G_3 = G^{\omega_1\omega_2}$.

We use the security model due to Au et al. [15] to formalize the adversary's capacity and the anonymity goal.

$\mathcal{S}$ generates the system parameters and sets $\hat{g} = G$, $\hat{g}_0 = G_1$. $\mathcal{S}$ chooses two vehicles (VID_0, g^{v_0}) and (VID_1, g^{v_1}), where $v_0, v_1 \in_R \mathbb{Z}_p$ and sends them to $\mathcal{A}$. $\mathcal{S}$ simulates the registration phase acting as the authority and the cloud server. $\mathcal{S}$ interacts with $\mathcal{A}$ on behalf of the vehicles VID_0 and VID_1 in the following interactions.

$\mathcal{S}$ honestly acts as VID_0 to answer the parking navigation query. For VID_1, $\mathcal{S}$ randomly picks $\kappa, v, s, t_1, L \in_R \mathbb{Z}_p$ to compute $U = G^{\kappa}$, $T = G^{vt_1}G_1^{Ls}$, generates $(c_1, c_2, c_3, AC', \widetilde{B}_1, \widetilde{B}_2, c, \tau)$, and simulates the zero-knowledge proof $\mathcal{SPK}$ to interact with $\mathcal{A}$.

$\mathcal{S}$ chooses a random $\beta \in \{0,1\}$. If $\beta = 0$, $\mathcal{S}$ honestly generates a navigation query; otherwise, $\mathcal{S}$ chooses $\kappa^*, v^*, t_1^*, L^* \in_R \mathbb{Z}_p$ to compute $U^* = G^{\kappa^*}$, $T^* = G^{v^*t_1^*}G_3^{L^*}$, and generates $(c_1^*, c_2^*, c_3^*, AC^*, \widetilde{B}_1^*, \widetilde{B}_2^*, c^*, \tau^*)$. $\mathcal{S}$ simulates the zero-knowledge proof $\mathcal{SPK}^*$ and sends them to $\mathcal{A}$. It is easy to see that the simulation is perfect if $log_G G_3 = log_G G_1 \cdot log_G G_2$. Otherwise, it contains no information about VID_0 and VID_1.

Finally, $\mathcal{A}$ returns β'. If $\beta' = \beta$, $\mathcal{S}$ confirms that there exists (ω_1, ω_2), such that $G_1 = G^{\omega_1}, G_2 = G^{\omega_2}, G_3 = G^{\omega_1\omega_2}$. Thus, $\mathcal{S}$ resolves the DDH problem [16] in $\mathbb{G}_2$.

Secondly, in the response retrieving phase, the identities of vehicles are protected against other entities. Specifically, the retrieving query $(K^*, C_1, C_2, \beta_1, \tau_1, \tilde{t})$ sent by the vehicle contains no information about the identity. K^* is a result of Diffie-Hellman agreement, which can be viewed as a random value, and $(C_1, C_2, \beta_1, \tau_1)$ is a signature that only the TA' public key is required for verification. Therefore, our CPARN meets the goal of identity privacy preservation.

Confidentiality: For the navigation queries and responses, we adopt the AES encryption scheme to encrypt them and the Elgamal encryption scheme to securely transmit the symmetric keys to receivers. Specifically, $DEST\|CL\|AP\|t_2\| t_3$ is protected by a random symmetric key r_1, which is encrypted by the public key of the cloud server to generate (c_1, c_2). Thus, the cloud server can decrypt (c_1, c_2) to obtain the random key r_1 and further recover the navigation query. In terms of the navigation response RES, a random symmetric key k_2 is chosen to encrypt RES and k_2 is encrypted by the vehicle's temporary public key U using the Elgamal encryption scheme. Since the AES encryption and Elgamal encryption are deemed to be secure, the navigation queries and responses are well-protected against the curious vehicles, RSUs and eavesdroppers.

Traceability: The cloud server traces a vehicle's identity successfully if it finds a match of the equation $\hat{e}(g, \hat{g}^v) = \hat{e}(V, \hat{g})$, where $\hat{g}^v = (\frac{T^L}{\hat{g}^L})^{\frac{1}{t_1(L-L)}}$. As the information $(DEST, CL, AP, t_2, t_3)$ is required to compute L, which can be obtained by decrypting (c_1, c_2, c_3) using the secret key of the cloud server, only the cloud server can trace the identity of the vehicle, who sends more than one navigation queries in a time period. The TA can recover the vehicle's identity by checking the equation $\hat{e}(\widetilde{B}_2, \hat{g}) = \hat{e}(\widetilde{B}_1, \widehat{X})\hat{e}(\widetilde{B}_1, \widehat{V}_1)$. Here $\widehat{V}_1$ is only known by the TA, so that only the TA can recover the vehicle's identity from its signatures.

In summary, CPARN achieves service authentication, message authentication and integrity, identity privacy preservation, confidentiality and traceability, simultaneously.

5 Performance Evaluation

In this section, we evaluate the performance of our CPARN in terms of the computational and communication overheads.

5.1 Computational Overhead

We firstly evaluate the computational overhead of vehicles. By counting the number of the scalar multiplication in $\mathbb{G}_1$ or $\mathbb{G}_2$, AES encryption/decryption, exponentiation in $\mathbb{G}_T$ and bilinear pairing required in each phase, we show the efficiency of CPARN. Other operations, e.g., point addition, integer multiplication, are not resource-consuming compared with the scalar multiplication and bilinear pairing operations. We use T_{SM}, T_{AES}, T_{Exp}, T_p to denote the running time of the scalar multiplication in $\mathbb{G}_1$ or $\mathbb{G}_2$, AES encryption or decryption, exponentiation in $\mathbb{G}_T$ and bilinear pairing operations for vehicles, respectively. We compare our CPARN with VSPN [13] and show the comparison results in Table 1. Since the bilinear pairing operation in querying phase can be precomputed with the aid of the cloud server, there is no bilinear pairing operation in querying and retrieving phases in CPARN, which are frequently performed by the vehicles to enjoy the parking navigation service. The retrieving phase in CPARN is much more efficient than that in VSPN, although the querying phase in CPARN costs a little more time than that in VSPN.

Table 1. Computational burden of vehicles

Phases	CPARN	VSPN
System setup	$8T_{SM}$	$3T_{SM} + T_p + T_{AES}$
Vehicle registration	$13T_{SM} + 3T_p$	$6T_{SM} + T_{AES}$
Navigation querying	$14T_{SM} + 4(T_p) + T_{AES} + 4T_{Exp}$	$T_{SM} + T_{AES}$
Response retrieving	$9T_{SM}$	$4\nu T_p$

$^*\nu$ is the number of RSUs that relay the navigation query in VSPN.

We also run these operations on HUAWEI MT2-L01 smartphone with Kirin 910 CPU and 1250M memory. The operation system is Android 4.2.2 and the toolset is Android NDK r8d with MIRACL 5.6.1 library [17]. The parameter p is approximately 160 bits and the elliptic curve is defined as $y = x^3 + 1$ over

Table 2. Computational burden of RSUs

Phases	CPARN	VSPN
Vehicle registration	0	$2T_p + 3T_{SM} + T_{AES}$
Navigation querying	$3T_p + 4T_{SM}$	$2T_p + T_{SM} + T_{AES}$
Response retrieving	$3T_p + 8T_{SM}$	T_{SM}

$\mathbb{F}_q$, where q is 512 bits. The scalar multiplication operation and AES encryption/decryption operation takes 3.609 ms and 0.023 ms, respectively. The executing time of the exponentiation operation in $\mathbb{G}_T$ and bilinear pairing operation is 0.001 ms and 56.201 ms. Thus, the rough running time of vehicles in system setup and registration phases is 28.869 ms and 215.518 ms, respectively. A vehicle should perform approximately 54.197 ms and 32.478 ms to generate a navigation query and obtain the response.

As for computational overhead of RSUs, we show the comparison results of CPARN and VSPN in Table 2. Our CPARN needs more bilinear pairing operations than VSPN in both querying and retrieving phases. However, these pairing operations in CPARN come from the verification of the vehicle's signature, which is used to ensure the integrity of the messages sent by vehicles, while Chim et al. VSPN [13] does not achieve this security requirement.

5.2 Communication Overhead

We show the communication overhead of CPARN among vehicles, RSUs and the cloud server. The parameters are set the same as those in the simulation. To find a vacant parking space, the vehicle sends the parking navigation query Q, which is $5216 + |N| + |DEST| + |CL| + |AP| + |t_1| + |t_2| + |t_3|$ bits, to the nearby RSU, where $|N|, |DEST|, |CL|, |AP|, |t_1|, |t_2|, |t_3|$ denote the binary length of $N, DEST, CL, AP, t_1, t_2, t_3$, respectively. Then, the RSU appends a 672-bit Schnorr signature to Q and forwards them to the cloud server. The cloud server generates the message R with binary length of $1696 + |t_3| + |RES|$ bits, where $|RES|$ denotes the binary length of RES. After that, the vehicle sends $(K^*, C_1, C_2, \beta_1, \tau_1)$ to the RSU*, which is of the length $1856 + |\tilde{t}|$ bits, where $|\tilde{t}|$ denotes the binary length of $\tilde{t}$. If the navigation message R is stored on RSU*, it returns $(RID^*, R, \sigma_1^*, \sigma_3^*)$ to the vehicle, which is $2368 + |RID^*| + |t_3| + |RES|$ bits, where $|RID^*|$ denotes the binary length of RID^*.

To compare the communication overhead of CPARN and VSPN in the response retrieving phase, we assume the length of navigation response RES in CPARN is equal to that in VSPN and $|RID^*| = |t_3| = 160$ bits. The comparison results are shown in Fig. 3. The communication overhead of vehicles is constant in our CPARN, while the overhead increases linearly with respect to the number of RSUs in VSPN.

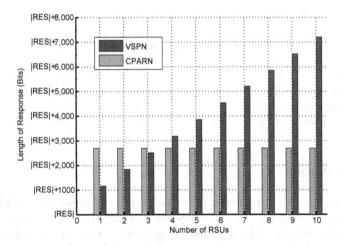

Fig. 3. Communication cost for vehicles.

6   Related Work

Some works [1,13,18,19] have been proposed to achieve privacy-preserving navigation based on VANETs recently. However, the differences between their protocols and ours are significant, as shown in Table 3. Lu et al. [1] presented an intelligent privacy-preserving parking scheme that uses three RSUs to localize the vehicles and assist them to find vacant parking spaces in a large parking lot. While this scheme is of small scale that covers vehicles parking lot. Chim et al. [13] proposed a VANET-based secure and privacy-preserving navigation scheme, in which the online road information collected by RSUs is utilized to guide the drivers to desired destinations in a distributed manner. However, this scheme suffers from inside attack since a system master key is shared among all vehicles. Therefore, Cho et al. [18] developed an improved privacy-preserving navigation protocol to eliminate the system master secret distribution. Consequently, Sur et al. [19] demonstrated that the protocols [13,18] are constructed under the assumption that all RSUs are trusted, and they cannot provide non-transferability of anonymous credentials, i.e., a vehicle can share its credential with others illegitimately. To overcome these weakness, they proposed a secure navigation protocol from one-time credential pseudonymous certificates and proof of knowledge. Different from the existing work, we remove the strong assumption that the querying vehicle can hold the alive connection with the RSU, and allow the vehicle to retrieve the navigation response from the RSUs driving through.

Table 3. Comparison of five navigation protocols

	Lu et al. [1]	Chim et al. [13]	Cho et al. [18]	Sur et al. [19]	CPARN
Privacy preserving	√	√	√	√	√
Cover large scale	X	√	√	√	√
Untrusted RSUs	X	X	X	√	√
Multi-time pseudonym	√	√	√	X	√
No alive connection	X	X	X	X	√

7   Conclusions

In this paper, we have proposed a cloud-based privacy-preserving parking navigation system in VANETs to find accessible parking spots for vehicles. Specifically, a vehicle can query the available parking space to a centralized server and retrieve the result without exposing any sensitive information about the driver. We have presented a novel method to improve the navigation retrieving probability for anonymous vehicular communications under the assumption that the connection between the vehicle and the RSU is difficult to be hold due to the high mobility of the vehicle. Through the security discussion, we have shown that the proposed system meets all the security and privacy goals, and demonstrated its efficiency and practicality for implementation in performance evaluation. For the future work, we will design a privacy-preserving navigation system based on mobile crowdsensing and VANETs to achieve real-time navigation for drivers.

References

1. Lu, R., Lin, X., Zhu, H., Shen, X.: An intelligent secure and privacy-preserving parking scheme through vehicular communications. IEEE Trans. Veh. Technol. **59**(6), 2772–2784 (2010)
2. Vacancy, N.: Park slope's parking problem. http://www.transalt.org/news/releases
3. Thompsona, R.G., Takadab, K., Kobayakawa, S.: Optimisation of parking guidance and information systems display configurations. Transp. Res. Part C Emerg. Tech. **9**(1), 69–85 (2001)
4. Parking guidance and driver information. http://www.ssspl.org/uploads/Products/Pdf/ParkingGuidancesystem.pdf
5. Lin, X., Sun, X., Ho, P.-H., Shen, X.: GSIS: A Secure and Privacy-Preserving Protocol for Vehicular Communications. IEEE Trans. Veh. Technol. **56**(6), 3442–3456 (2007)
6. Lu, R., Lin, X., Luan, T.H., Liang, X., Shen, X.: Pseudonym changing at social spots: an effective strategy for location privacy in VANETs. IEEE Trans. Veh. Technol. **61**(1), 86–96 (2012)
7. Lu, R., Lin, X., Zhu, H., Ho, P.-H., Shen, X.: ECPP: efficient conditional privacy preservation protocol for secure vehicular communications. In: IEEE INFOCOM 2008, Phoenix, AZ, USA, pp. 1903–1911. IEEE Society (2008)
8. Pereira, P.R., Casaca, A., Rodrigues, J.J., Soares, V.N., Triay, J., Cervelló-Pastor, C.: From delay-tolerant networks to vehicular delay-tolerant networks. IEEE Commun. Surv. Tutor. **14**(4), 1166–1182 (2012)

9. Apple, Google collcet user data. http://www.wsj.com/articles
10. How Apple tracks your location without consent, and why it matters. http://arstechnica.com/apple/2011/04
11. Wu, D.J., Zimmerman, J., Planul, J., Mitchell, J.C.: Privacy-preserving shortest path computation. In: NDSS 2016, San Diego, California, USA (2016)
12. Things car thieves know that you do not. http://abcnews.go.com/Business/things-car-thieves/story?id=20938096
13. Chim, T., Yiu, S., Hui, L.C., Li, V.O.: VSPN: VANET-based secure and privacy-preserving navigation. IEEE Trans. Comput. **63**(2), 510–524 (2014)
14. Pointcheval, D., Sanders, O.: Short randomizable signatures. In: Sako, K. (ed.) CT-RSA 2016. LNCS, vol. 9610, pp. 111–126. Springer, Cham (2016). doi:10.1007/978-3-319-29485-8_7
15. Au, M.H., Liu, J.K., Fang, J., Jiang, Z.L., Susilo, W., Zhou, J.: A new payment system for enhancing location privacy of electric vehicles. IEEE Trans. Veh. Technol. **63**(1), 3–17 (2014)
16. Boneh, D., Boyen, X.: Short signatures without random oracles. In: Cachin, C., Camenisch, J.L. (eds.) EUROCRYPT 2004. LNCS, vol. 3027, pp. 56–73. Springer, Heidelberg (2004). doi:10.1007/978-3-540-24676-3_4
17. Multiprecision integer and rational arithmetic C/C++ library.http://www.freshports.org/math/miracl/
18. Cho, W., Park, Y., Sur, C., Rhee, K.H.: An improved privacy-preserving navigation protocol in VANETs. J. Wirel. Mob. Netw. Ubiquit. Comput. Dependable Appl. **4**(4), 80–92 (2013)
19. Sur, C., Park, Y., Rhee, K.H.: An efficient and secure navigation protocol based on vehicular cloud. Int. J. Comput. Math **93**(2), 325–344 (2016)

TruSDN: Bootstrapping Trust in Cloud Network Infrastructure

Nicolae Paladi[(✉)] and Christian Gehrmann

SICS Swedish ICT, Stockholm, Sweden
{nicolae,chrisg}@sics.se

Abstract. Software-Defined Networking (SDN) is a novel architectural model for cloud network infrastructure, improving resource utilization, scalability and administration. SDN deployments increasingly rely on virtual switches executing on commodity operating systems with large code bases, which are prime targets for adversaries attacking the network infrastructure. We describe and implement TruSDN, a framework for bootstrapping trust in SDN infrastructure using Intel Software Guard Extensions (SGX), allowing to securely deploy SDN components and protect communication between network endpoints. We introduce *ephemeral flow-specific pre-shared keys* and propose a novel defense against *cuckoo attacks* on SGX enclaves. TruSDN is secure under a powerful adversary model, with a minor performance overhead.

Keywords: Software Defined Networking · Trust · Integrity · Virtual switches

1 Introduction

Renewed and widespread interest in virtualization – along with proliferation of cloud computing – has spurred a series of innovations, allowing cloud service providers to deliver on-demand compute, storage and network resources for highly dynamic workloads. Consequently, more hardware and virtual components are added to already large networks, complicating network management. To help address this, SDN emerged as a novel network architecture model. Separation of the *data* and *control* planes is its core principle, allowing network operators to implement high-level configuration goals by interacting with a single *network controller*, rather than configuring discrete network components. The controller applies the configuration to the *network edge*, i.e. to its global view of the data plane [11]. Data and control plane separation in SDN challenges network infrastructure security best practices evolved in the decades since packet-switched digital network communication gained popularity [16, 22].

In the cloud infrastructure model, SDN allows tenants to configure complex topologies with rich network functionality, managed by a network controller. The availability of a global view of the data plane enables advanced controller capabilities – from pre-calculating optimized traffic routing to managing applications that replace hardware middleboxes. However, these capabilities also make the controller a valuable attack target: once compromised, it yields the adversary complete control over the network [27]. The global view itself is security sensitive: an adversary capable of

© ICST Institute for Computer Sciences, Social Informatics and Telecommunications Engineering 2017
R. Deng et al. (Eds.): SecureComm 2016, LNICST 198, pp. 104–124, 2017.
DOI: 10.1007/978-3-319-59608-2_6

impersonating network components may distort a controller's global view and influence network-wide routing policies [13].

Virtual switches are another category of security sensitive components in SDN deployments. They execute on commodity operating systems (OS) and are often assigned the same trust level and privileges as hardware switches – specialized network components with compact embedded software [28] or application specific integrated circuits. Commodity OS are likely to contain security flaws which can be exploited to compromise virtual switches. For example, their configuration can be modified to disobey the protocol, breach network isolation and reroute traffic to a malicious destination or compromise other network edge elements through lateral attacks. Such risks are accentuated by the extensive control a cloud provider has over the infrastructure of its tenants.

Security and isolation of tenant infrastructure can be strengthened by confining select SDN components to trusted execution environments (TEE) and attesting their integrity before provisioning security-sensitive data. TEEs with strong security guarantees can be built using SGX, a set of recently introduced extensions to the x86 instruction set architecture and related hardware [1, 18]. Earlier work used SGX to protect computation in cloud environments, by executing modified OS instances in SGX enclaves [2] or a data processing framework in a set of SGX enclaves [33]. However, while both of the above efforts *highlighted* the need to secure network communication, they did not *address* it.

1.1 Contribution

This paper makes the following contributions:

- We present TruSDN, a framework to bootstrap trust in SDN infrastructure.
- We introduce flow-specific pre-shared keys for communication protection.
- We propose a defense against cuckoo attacks [23], based on properties of the enhanced privacy ID (EPID) scheme [4] used for remote enclave attestation.
- We describe the implementation and a performance evaluation of TruSDN.

1.2 Organization

We introduce the system model in Sect. 2, describe the adversary model in Sect. 3 and the design of TruSDN in Sect. 4. In Sect. 5 we provide a security analysis, describe the prototype implementation and performance evaluation in Sect. 6 and review the related work in Sect. 7. We discuss future work in Sect. 8 and conclude in Sect. 9.

2 System Model

In this section we describe the SDN architectural model and the SDN deployment layers. Furthermore, we describe the use of TEEs based on Intel SGX.

2.1   Software Defined Networking

In this paper we target SDN in infrastructure cloud deployments. The system model follows the architecture presented in [5] and depicted in Fig. 1.

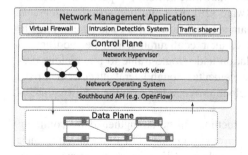
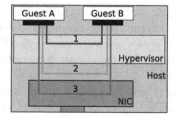

Fig. 1. The SDN architectural model.

Fig. 2. Communication paths between collocated endpoints: (1) virtual switch; (2) host-local, e.g. native bridging; (3) virtual queues in the NIC.

The *data plane* includes hardware and software switch implementations. *Software switching* is used in cloud deployments due to its scalability and configuration flexibility. Figure 2 illustrates the software switching approaches for communication between two collocated endpoints. In a typical switch implementation, its kernel-space component is optimized for forwarding performance, lacks decision logic and only forwards packets matching rules in its *forwarding information base* (FIB) [20]. The FIB comprises packet forwarding rules deployed to satisfy network administrator goals. Mismatching packets are discarded or redirected to the *control plane* through the *southbound API*. While the data plane uses complementary functionality of both virtual and physical switches, the role of the latter is often reduced to routing IP-tunneled traffic between hypervisors [25]. In this paper we do *not* address control of hardware switches and traffic routing between hosts; we assume that the physical network provides uniform capacity across hosts, based on e.g. equal-cost multi-path routing [14], such that if multiple equal-cost routes to the same destination exist, they can be discovered and used to provide load balancing among redundant paths. Overlay networks – e.g. VLANs or GRE [10] – are used for communication between endpoints. In this work, we focus exclusively on software switching and use the term "switch" to denote a virtual, software implementation. We refer to hardware switch implementations as "hardware switches".

In the *control plane*, high-level network operator goals are translated into discrete routing policies based on the *global network view*, i.e. a graph representation of the virtual network topology. The main component of a control plane is the *network controller*, which we define as follows:

Definition 1. *Network Controller (NC) is a logically centralized component that manages network communication in a given deployment by updating the FIB with* *specific forwarding rules. The NC compiles forwarding rules based on three inputs: the dynamic global network view, the high-level configuration goals of the network operator, and the output of the network management applications.*

The NC is typically implemented as part of a logically centralized *network OS*, which builds and maintains the global network view and may include a *network hypervisor*, to multiplex network resources among distinct virtual network deployments.

Southbound API is a set of vendor-agnostic instructions for communication between data and control planes. It is often limited to flow-based traffic control of the data plane, with management done through a configuration database [25].

Network operators use *network management applications* (NMAs), e.g. fire walls, traffic shapers, etc., to configure the network using high-level commands.

2.2 Deployment Layers

We next describe the deployment layers of SDN infrastructure (Fig. 3).

The *hardware layer* includes infrastructure for data transfer, processing and storage and is comprised of network hardware (including hardware switches and communication channels), hardware server platforms and data storage.

The *infrastructure layer* includes software components for virtualization and resource provisioning to infrastructure users, referred to as *tenants*. For network resources, this layer includes the network hypervisor, which creates *network slices* by multiplexing physical network infrastructure between tenants. Infrastructure providers expose a *slice* (i.e. a quota) of network resources to the tenants.

The *service layer* includes components controlled by tenants. Network components operated by tenants are grouped into *network domains*, comprising the virtual network

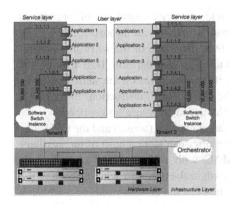

Fig. 3. Deployment layers.

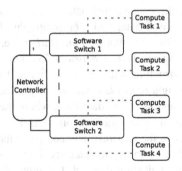

Fig. 4. Logical communication segments: α: between the NC and switches; β: among the switches on each host; γ between host-local switches and network endpoints.

resources and topologies that logically belong to the same organizational unit and network slice, and perform related tasks or provide a common service. The *network hypervisor* ensures that a tenant's control plane can only control switches in its own slice. Within their slice, tenants have exhaustive creation, destruction and configuration privileges over components, such as instances of switches, the NC, NMAs and network domains. We define three *logical* communication segments (Fig. 4): between the network controller and switches (α segments); among the switches on each host (β segments); between host-local switches and network endpoints (γ segments).

The *user layer* includes endpoint consumers of network services, e.g. virtualization guests, containers and applications in a network domain.

2.3   Trusted Execution Environments

The proposed solution relies on TEEs that *both* provide strong isolation and allow remote code and data integrity attestation. Such a TEE can be created using Intel SGX enclaves (introduced in [1, 18]) during OS runtime and relies for its security on a trusted computing base (TCB) of code and data loaded at build time, processor firmware and processor hardware. At build time, the CPU measures the loaded code, data and memory page layout. At initialization time, the CPU produces a final measurement, after which the enclave becomes immutable and cannot be externally modified. The CPU maintains the measurement throughout the enclave's lifetime to later assert the integrity of the enclave contents. Processor firmware is the root of trust (ROT) of an enclave. It prevents access to the enclave's memory segment by either the platform OS, other enclaves, or other external agents. Enclaves operate in a separate memory region inaccessible to non-enclave processes, called the enclave page cache (EPC). Multiple mutually distrusting enclaves can operate on the platform. The processor enforces separation of memory access among enclaves based on the layout in the *EPC map*. Program execution within an enclave is transparent to both the underlying OS and other enclaves.

Remote attestation allows an enclave to provide integrity guarantees of its contents [1]. For this, the platform produces an attestation assertion with information about the identity of the enclave and details of its state (e.g. the mode of the software environment, associated data, and a cryptographic binding to the platform TCB making the assertion). For *intra-platform attestation* (i.e. between enclaves on the same platform), the reporting enclave (*reporter*) invokes the EREPORT instruction to create a REPORT structure with the assertion and calculate a message authentication code (MAC), using a *report key*, known only to the target enclave (*target*) and the CPU. The structure contains a user data field, where the reporter can store a hash of the auxiliary data provided. The target recomputes the MAC with its report key to verify the authenticity of the structure, and compares the hash in the user data with the hash of the auxiliary data, to verify its integrity. Enclaves then use the auxiliary data to establish a secure communication channel. For *inter-platform attestation* the remote verifier first sends a challenge to the enclave platform, where the challenge is complemented with the indentity of a *quoting enclave* (QE) and forwarded to the reporter, which appends the challenge response to the REPORT and attests itself to the QE. The QE verifies the structure, signs it with a platform-specific key using the *enhanced privacy ID group signature scheme* (EPID) [4] and returns it to the verifier, to check the authenticity of the signature and the report itself [1]. The use of the EPID scheme is part of the SGX implementation and allows to maintain the privacy of the platform which hosts the enclave.

3 Adversary Model

We now describe the adopted adversary model, as well as the core security assumptions on which we base our design. The adversary model we adopt can be described by the capabilities of the adversary at the *network* and *platform* levels respectively (overview in Table 1).

Table 1. Summary of the *Adv* capabilities in relation to the adversary model.

Type	Network	Platform
Included	Intercept, record, forge, drop, Replay messages; Analyze the traffic patterns; Disrupt or degrade network connectivity; Launch topology poisoning attacks	Control non-processor hardware; Control software stack OS, hypervisor; Pause execution; Deploy arbitrary software components; "Cuckoo attack": Forward function calls to compromised SGX enclaves; Return arbitrary values to system calls
Not included, mitigations known		Side-channels: cache-collision, Controlled channel; Attacks on shielded execution;
Excplicitly excluded	Denial-of-Service (DoS) attacks	Side-channels: power analysis; DoS attacks

3.1 Network Infrastructure

For SDN infrastructure, we adopt the adversary model introduced in [7] and extended with SDN-specific attack vectors in [22]. We assume a powerful adversary (*Adv*), which controls the cloud deployment network infrastructure; it can intercept, record, forge, drop and replay any message on the network, and is only limited by the constraints of the employed cryptographic methods. Particularly, the *Adv* may forge messages that do not match any of the rules installed in the FIB. Furthermore the *Adv* may create own instances of switches and launch Sybil attacks [8] and launch other types of topology poisoning attacks [13] to distort the global network view. Finally, *Adv* can store arbitrary quantities of intercepted communication and attempt its decryption with encryption keys intercepted or leaked at a later point. It can analyze the traffic patterns in the network through passive probing and may disrupt or degrade network connectivity to achieve its goals. We explicitly exclude Denial-of-Service attacks on the SDN infrastructure.

3.2 Platform

For platform security, we consider a powerful adversary, similar to [2, 33], that may control the entire software stack in the cloud provider's infrastructure.

On the hardware level, we assume the processor is correctly implemented and remains uncompromised; furthermore, we assume a reliable and secure source of random numbers (which can be provided by the CPU). Adv has full control over the remaining hardware, including memory, I/O devices, periferials, etc. Similarly, Adv fully controls the software stack, including the platform OS and the hypervisor. This implies that Adv may pause indefinitely the execution of the code in the TEE and return arbitrary values in response to OS system calls. However, a deployment orchestrator and NC execute under tenant control, on a fully trusted platform and software stack. We exclude side-channel attacks. While some side-channel attacks – e.g. timing, cache-collision, controlled channel attacks – can be mitigated through software modification [36], preventing other side-channel attacks – such as power analysis – requires hardware modifications. An Adv with advanced capabilities may leverage its full control over the OS to utilize the class of known attacks on shielded execution; while we do not address such attacks, they have known countermeasures [2, 6].

SGX, similar to other trusted computing solutions, is vulnerable to *cuckoo attacks* [23]. In one attack scenario, malware on the target platform forwards the messages intended for the *local* SGX enclave (SGX_L^E) to a remote enclave under Adv's physical control (*malicious* enclave, SGX_M^E). Having physical access to SGX_M^E, Adv can apply hardware attacks to violate its security guarantees. As a result, Adv controls all communication between the verifier and SGX_L^E, with access to an oracle that provides all of the answers a benign SGX^E would, but without its expected security properties.

Briefly, the adversary model for platform security largely matches the remote administrator capabilities of an infrastructure cloud provider.

4 Solution Description

In this section we present TruSDN, a framework for bootstrapping trust in SDN deployments. Its goal is to allow tenants to securely deploy computing tasks and create virtualized network infrastructure deployments, given the adversary model defined in Sect. 3. To satisfy this goal, the framework must satisfy the following set of requirements:

- *Authentication:* communication in the domain must the authenticated, and a secure enrollment mechanism for data plane components must be in place.
- *Topology integrity:* the NC must be protected from network components that attempt to distort the global network view.
- *Component integrity:* integrity of switches must be attested prior to enrollment and the cryptographic material required for their network access must be protected with a hardware ROT.
- *Confidentiality protection of domain secrets:* network domain secrets – such as VPN session keys – should not be revealed to the Adv.

- *Protected network communication:* network communication in the tenant domain must be confidentiality and integrity protected.

4.1 TruSDN Overview

We begin by introducing the building blocks of TruSDN (Fig. 5).

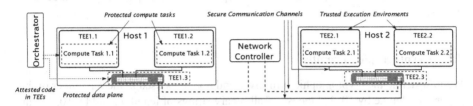

Fig. 5. Illustration of core building blocks of TruSDN.

Trusted Execution Environments: TruSDN uses TEEs that guarantee secure execution in the given adversary model, assuming the CPU and executed code are correctly implemented.

Protected Compute Tasks: Security sensitive compute tasks (CT) are deployed in TEEs. Such tasks include all operations that tenants aim to protect from the $\mathcal{A}dv$. However, CTs rely on the untrusted OS for I/O and support functionality.

Protected Data Plane: Switches are deployed in TEEs – they route traffic between CTs according to forwarding rules communicated through secure channels and maintained in the FIB. The FIB of the switches, and the key material necessary to establish the secure channels are stored in TEEs.

Attested code in TEEs: An orchestrator under tenant control attests the TEEs during network infrastructure deployment, to ensure integrity of the deployed code and data before keys or key material are provisioned to the respective TEE.

In a typical deployment scenario, the tenant invokes an orchestrator to deploy a switch *bootstrap application* on the hosts in the tenant's domain. The bootstrap application invokes a host-local SGX driver to build an SGX enclave containing a switch. Next, the orchestrator attests the created enclave (as described in Sect. 2.3) prior to enrolling the switch with the NC. The orchestrator uses the enclave's public key from the attestation quote to securely transfer the enclave-specific integrity and confidentiality protection session keys used to establish a protected communication channel between the NC and the TEE. Finally, the NC communicates any remaining security-sensitive payload to the created TEE, e.g. the initial FIB. Next, CTs are deployed in TEEs on the host and the switch forwards packets between the CTs, matching them against the rules in the FIB. Mismatching packets are forwarded to the NC, which may update the FIB with new rules. For clarity, we assume the orchestrator and NC are collocated on a platform under tenant control and view both as a single component, further referred to as "NC".

Secure Communication: TruSDN protects the communication between CTs, between switches and the NC, as well as among the switches, in the above adversary model. Communication security is ensured using confidentiality and integrity protection keys provisioned to authenticated network components and endpoints executing in TEEs. Furthermore, TruSDN leverages SDN principles to introduce a novel mechanism – per-flow communication protection using ephemeral flow-specific pre-shared keys (PSKs).

4.2   Cryptographic Primitives

We now define the cryptographic primitives and notations used in the remainder of this paper. We denote by $\{0, 1\}^n$ the set of all binary strings of length n, and by $\{0, 1\}^*$ the set of all finite binary strings. In a set U, we refer to the ith element as u_i, and use the following notation for cryptographic operations:

- Given an arbitrary message $m \in \{0, 1\}^*$, we denote by $c = \mathsf{Enc}(K, m)$ a symmetric encryption of m using the secret key $K \in \{0, 1\}^*$. The corresponding symmetric decryption operation is $m = \mathsf{Dec}(K, c) = \mathsf{Dec}(K, \mathsf{Enc}(K, m))$.
- We denote by pk/sk a public/private key pair for a public key encryption scheme. We denote by $c = \mathsf{Enc}_{\mathsf{pk}}(m)$ the encryption of message m with the public key pk, and the decryption by $m = \mathsf{Dec}_{\mathsf{sk}}(c) = \mathsf{Dec}_{\mathsf{sk}}(\mathsf{Enc}_{\mathsf{pk}}(m))$.
- We denote a digital signature over a message m by $\sigma = \mathsf{Sign}_{\mathsf{sk}}(m)$ and the corresponding verification of a digital signature by $v = \mathsf{Verify}_{\mathsf{pk}}(m, \sigma)$, where $v = 1$ if the signature is valid and $v = 0$ otherwise.
- We denote a Message Authentication Code (MAC) using a secret key K over a message m by $\mu = \mathsf{MAC}(K, m)$.

We next describe key sharing and communication protection mechanisms on the identified logical segments. Table 2 summarizes the keys used by TruSDN.

4.3   SDN Trust Bootstrapping and Secure Communication

The first step in deploying a TruSDN infrastructure is to launch a set of trusted switches for connectivity and topology building. The NC requests the creation of switch enclaves to deploy switches in TEEs on hosts in its domain. Switches are deployed based on parameters provided by the NC in plaintext (application code and configuration). Next, the NC *attests* the integrity of switch enclaves and only *enrolls* the successfully attested ones (Fig. 6). A TEE E_i is attested following the protocol introduced in [1]. With TruSDN however, the reporter generates an enclave-specific public-private keypair and submits its public key EK_i^{pk} along with the attestation data; a hash of the public key is stored in the user data field. The switch enclave is only enrolled to the global network view if its reported state matches the one expected by NC.

Table 2. Summary of keys used in the TruSDN framework.

Key	Created by	Access	Usage
K_i^α	NC	NC, switch	Enclave-specific session, segment α
K_j^β	NC	NC, switch	Domain-specific session, segment β
K'	NC	NC, switch	Ephemeral session key
K''	NC	NC, switch	Ephemeral MAC key
EK_i^{pk}	Switch	Public	Public key of the switch enclave
EK_i^{sk}	Switch	Switch	Private key of the switch enclave
CK_i^{pk}	CT	Public	Public key of the compute task
CK_i^{sk}	CT	CT	Private key of the compute task
QE^{pk}	Vendor	Public	Public key of the quoting enclave
QE^{sk}	Vendor	Vendor, QE	Private key of the quoting enclave
SK_{ij}^γ	NC	NC, CT_i, CT_j	Ephemeral flow-specific pre-shared key

Having attested enclave E_i, NC communicates an **Enrollmentmessage** (Table 3) with the enclave-specific pre-shared key K_i^α and domain-specific preshared key K_j^β, encrypted with an ephemeral key K_i'. Switches within a domain use K_j^β to protect communication on β segments. The *NC* appends a MAC of the message calculated with K_i'' and encrypts the keys K_i', K_i'' with EK_i^{pk}.

Table 3. Enrollment message sent by the NC upon switch enrollment.

$m = \text{Enc}(K_i', (K_i^\alpha, K_j^\beta))$	$\mu = \text{MAC}(K_i'', m)$	$\text{Enc}(EK_i^{pk}, (K_i', K_i''))$

Once switches are deployed and enrolled, tenants may configure the network topology using the NC to update the switch FIBs. Communication on α segments – e.g. FIB updates or unmatched packets forwarded to the NC – is protected using the session key K_i^α (e.g. using TLS [9]), which never leaves the TEE.

Similarly, a secure channel is established among the switches within the same domain, using the pre-shared key K_j^β, to protect communication between switches on different hosts (e.g. TEEs 1.2 and 2.3 in Fig. 5). K_j^β never leaves the TEEs, has a limited validity time and is periodically redeployed by the NC. On β segments, traffic may traverse multiple hardware switches, forwarded to the host over tunnels deployed on top of a standard routing protocol (e.g. [14]).

Next, the tenant may deploy CTs in TEEs and attest their integrity using the very same scheme and principles as for the switch deployment described above. The CTs and the network controller use the **Enrollment message** to establish a secure communication channel (e.g. TLS).

Once the NC has deployed and attested the TEEs with switches and CTs, intra-host communication (i.e. between two CT enclaves on the same host) is straightforward

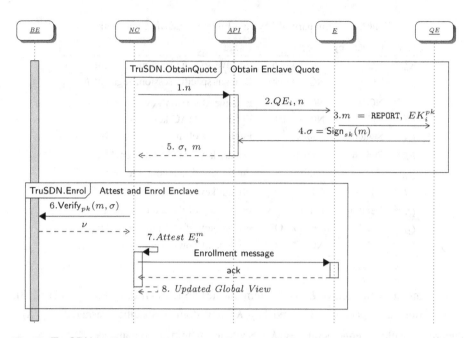

Fig. 6. TruSDN enclave attestation and enrollment: (1.) Random nonce n is (2.) supplemented with the host QE identity; (3.) Quote m produced by the enclave is (4.) signed by the QE. (6.) The verifier checks the signature of the QE, (7.) attests the integrity of the enclave and (8.) only enrolls the enclave upon success. BE: back-end.

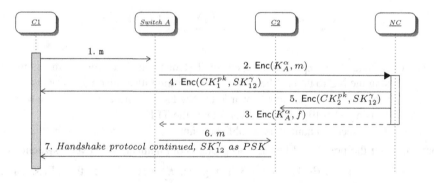

Fig. 7. Intra-host communication with TruSDN.

(Fig. 7): when a packet m sent from C1 (e.g. a TLS ClientHello message) reaches the local host *switch A*, it attempts to match m against a FIB entry; if no suitable flow rule f is present, the switch forwards $\mathsf{Enc}(K_A^\alpha, m)$ to NC, which processes the packet, generates and deploys on the CTs C1, C2 a flow-specific pre-shared key SK_{12}^γ and finally updates the switch FIB with f, after which steps 2 and 3 are ignored; once the FIB is updated, the switch forwards m to C2, which continues the message exchange and uses SK_{12}^{γ} to protect the communication with C1, using e.g. TLS with a PSK ciphersuite [9].

Communication between CTs C1 and C3 deployed on distinct hosts is similar, with the only notable difference that the NC updates the FIB of the local switches on both hosts where C1, C3 are deployed.

In the above scenarios TruSDN leverages two aspects of the SDN model – **(1)** the deployment has a central authority (the NC) and **(2)** the first packet of a flow is forwarded to the central authority – to deliver on demand ephemeral PSKs to communication endpoints. This allows to relax the need for high-quality entropy being available to CTs (a known issue in virtualized environments [30]). Furthermore, this approach ensures communication security without compromising packet visibility – having control over the keys used to protect communication between the CTs allows the NC to maintain fine-grained insight into the traffic.

4.4   Preventing Cuckoo Attacks

To prevent cuckoo attacks [23], we propose a solution that leverages cryptographic properties of the EPID scheme used by the QE [4] and the *SIGn and Message Authentication* (SIGMA) protocol [35], which are both part of the Intel SGX implementation. The EPID scheme supports two signature modes: *fully anonymous mode* – the verifier cannot associate a given signature with a particular member of the group; *pseudo-anonymous mode* – the verifier can determine whether it has verified the platform previously. The unlinkability property distinguished in the two modes depends on the chosen *base*. A signature includes a pseudonym B^f where B is the base chosen for a signature and revealed during the signature; f is unique per member and private. For a *random base* R, the pseudonym is R^f – in this case the signatures are unlinkable. For a *name base*, the pseudonym is N^f where N is the name of the verifier – in this case the signatures remain unlinkable for *different* verifiers, while signatures with a common N can be linked. For privacy reasons, the EPID scheme currently implemented in Intel SGX accepts *name base* pseudonyms only from verifiers authorized by the EPID authority [31], which is done by provisioning qualified verifiers with an X.509 certificate – e.g. an intermediate certification authority (CA) certificate – signed by the EPID authority acting as root CA.

We propose the following algorithm to prevent cuckoo attacks. At deployment time, the EPID authority issues, to an authorized verifier V_P, an intermediate CA verifier certificate for the platforms in the cloud provider's data center. Next, V_P attests its platforms following the SIGMA protocol and publishes a list of resulting platform EPID signatures and the signature name base, B_P^N. To guard against cuckoo attacks, tenants first request V_P to issue an X.509 certificate and enable them to become *authorized verifiers*. Next, tenants choose the same pseudonym base B_P^N (and a private f), follow the SIGMA protocol, and verify that the resulting signature is linkable to a signature in the published list. The cloud provider has multiple tools to protect platform privacy and prevent untrusted tenants from fingerprinting the platform infrastructure, e.g. limiting the validity of issued certificates, changing the name base, etc.

Considering that the EPID scheme is currently not implemented in the SGX emulation software we used for prototyping, we intend to describe the implementation of the above algorithm in a follow-up report.

5 Security Analysis

In this section we analyze the security properties of the proposed framework in the adversary model described in Sect. 3. On the network level, many of the Adv capabilities are thwarted by first authenticating the switches deployed on the data plane, as well as the network edge (i.e. the compute tasks that generate or receive the network traffic), in combination with confidentiality and integrity protection of the traffic on the three identified segments. Authenticating the network components prevents topology poisoning attacks (a countermeasure mentioned in [13]), while confidentiality and integrity protection of all of the network traffic in the deployment prevents the Adv from either learning the contents of the exchanged packets or successfully forging packets. The Adv may in this case still intercept and record messages. However, collecting encrypted traffic does not yield the Adv any more information about the contents of the exchanged packets. Similarly, the Adv does not gain an advantage by simply dropping or replaying messages, since these actions would at most simply reduce the channel capacity (as would the ability of the Adv to disrupt network connectivity). Finally, the proposed framework does not prevent the Adv analyzing the traffic patterns and does not prevent it from fingerprinting the components of the deployment, making it vulnerable to rule scanning and denial of service attacks. While the goals of TruSDN did not include this, such traffic analysis could be prevented using anti-fingerprinting techniques, as proposed in [3].

On the platform level, the security of the proposed framework relies to a large extent on the security properties of Intel SGX enclaves. This allows to protect the execution of switches and network edge components deployed in TEEs from the capabilities of an Adv controlling non-processor hardware, the software stack of the OS and the hypervisor. Similarly, pausing execution of switches executing in TEEs, while possible, would have no further effect than degrading network connectivity, already discussed above. While the Adv may attempt to deploy own arbitrary components on the data plane or the network edge in order to launch Sybill attacks, the integrity of such components would not be successfully attested, unless they are identical to legitimate components, which are assumed to be executing correctly – rendering Sybill behavior impossible. The Adv is prevented from launching cuckoo attacks by enabling tenants to verify the platforms, as described in Sect. 4.4. As presented in Table 1, several relevant classes of attacks are not addressed by TruSDN, but have known mitigations, namely cache-collision, controlled channel and attacks on shielded execution (addressed in [33, 36]). The capability of the Adv to return arbitrary values to system calls, while not addressed in this work, can be mitigated by a validation component as described in [2].

6   Implementation and Evaluation

We now describe the implementation and evaluation of TruSDN.

6.1   TruSDN Implementation

The TruSDN prototype deployment follows the design presented in Sect. 4 and is illustrated in Fig. 8. *Host 1* and *Host 2* are instances of Ubuntu OS 15.04. In each instance, we deployed Linux Containers[1], similarly based on Ubuntu OS 15.04. Containers create an environment with own process and network space, implemented using *namespaces*, with a distinct user ID, network stack, mount points, file systems, processes, inter-process communication, and hostname. We chose containers to facilitate prototype implementation, using their lightweight process isolation. Containers are part of the untrusted OS and this implementation choice is orthogonal to the security of TruSDN. Compute tasks are deployed in TEEs created using SGX enclaves (Fig. 8): *enclaves* E1, E2, E4, E5 are placed respectively within containers C1, C2, C3, C4. The switches are deployed in TEEs created using SGX enclaves (enclaves E3, E6 in Fig. 8).

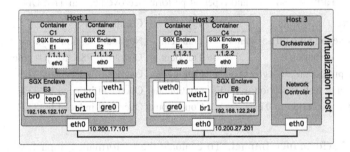

Fig. 8. Prototype deployment of TruSDN

Considering that platforms with hardware and software support for SGX were not publicly available at the time of writing, we used *OpenSGX* [15] to emulate the TEEs. It is a software SGX emulator and a platform for SGX development, implemented using binary translation of QEMU and emulating Intel SGX hardware components at instruction level. It includes emulated hardware and OS components, enclave program loader, the OpenSGX user libraries, debugging and performance monitoring support. The emulator allows to implement, debug, and evaluate SGX applications, but does not support binary compatibility with Intel SGX. Furthermore, OpenSGX does not implement all instructions, e.g. debugging instructions. While OpenSGX does not provide security gurantees, it allows us to obtain performance estimates for the proposed approach. We used *mbedTLS*[2] v1.3.11 (distributed with the emulator) for

---

[1] Linux Containers Project Website: https://linuxcontainers.org/.

[2] mbed TLS project website https://tls.mbed.org/.

attestation of the SGX enclaves. We used OpenSSL v1.0.2d (distributed with the emulator) to set up protected communication channels between the CT enclaves and the local switches, and among switches within the same domain.

An SDN network controller is deployed in a third instance (*Host 3*). We used the *Ryu*[3] SDN framework, due to its flexibility and versatile APIs.

6.2   TruSDN Evaluation

We now analyze the performance impact, present evaluation results and discuss aspects that cannot be measured with the current prototype.

Sources of Performance Impact. TruSDN introduces several potential sources of performance impact (Table 4). We distinguish between *transient* performance overhead, which occurs occasionally (e.g. TLS key negotiation) and *continuous* performance overhead, present throughout the infrastructure operation. We *do not* consider the one-time cost of infrastructure deployment, e.g. provisioning the software, attesting TEEs and enrolling the components.

Table 4. Sources and types of performance overhead in TruSDN

Source	Type	Clarification
TLS negotiation all segments	Transient	Negotiate session keys for TLS
PSK distribution	Transient	Distribute PSK for γ segments
TLS protection all segments	Continuous	Overhead induced by TLS
Compute task execution in TEEs	Continuous	Overhead induced by TEE
Switch execution in TEEs	Continuous	Overhead induced by TEE

Measured Performance Impact. To evaluate the performance impact, we measured the footprint of establishing TLS sessions on α and γ segments. We used *iperf*, *openssl s_time* and an own Ryu application (Table 5).

TLS overhead on the α segment: We measured the round-trip latency of packets sent in plaintext and with TLS, over 1000 tests, each request sending messages of 100 bytes with the 80 bit OpenFlow header. Furthermore, we measured the data transfer rates for plaintext and TLS communication. Use of TLS increased total transfer time by 14.2% and reduced the transfer rate by 15.98%.

Delay on γ segment: As mentioned above, the first packet of the flow is intercepted by the switch and forwarded to the NC in a packet in message [24]. At this point the NC processes the flow and installs a flow rule on the switch. TruSDN *extends* this procedure by generating and distributing to the communicating CTs a pre-shared key, to be used for communication protection. Since this must be done prior to both forwarding the message to the destination CT and installing the flow rule, generating and

---

[3] Ryu SDN framework: https://osrg.github.io/ryu/.

Table 5. Summary of performance evaluation of TruSDN

Data	Minimum	Maximum	Mean	Median	Std dev
Total transfer time, ms	0.4	1.1	0.66	0.7	0.07
Total transfer time w. TruSDN, ms	0.5	7.1	0.8	0.8	0.22
TruSDN overhead, **total transfer time**			**21.2%**	**14.2%**	
Transfer rate, bytes per second	1225	2095	1595	1583	98.07
Transfer rate w. TruSDN, bytes per second	919	1589	1338	1330	64.86
TruSDN overhead, **transfer rate**			**16.11%**	**15.98%**	
First packet latency γ	1.53	6.50	3.48	3.38	0.42
First packet latency γ w. TruSDN	3.35	10.7	5.37	5.14	0.93
TruSDN overhead, **first packet latency**			**54.31%**	**52.07%**	
TLS handshake, ms	36.53	77.72	67.97	67.48	7.42
TLS handshake w. TruSDN, ms	52.35	76.44	67.15	66.53	3.93
TruSDN overhead, **TLS handshake**			**−2.21%**	**−2.41%**	
Key generation NC, ms	0.11	0.51	0.178	0.16	0.04
Key distribution γ, ms	0.37	1.06	0.54	0.53	0.08
Key total γ, ms	0.50	1.30	0.71	0.7	0.11

distributing the PSK would normally delay the installation of the flow rule and increase the latency of the *first* packet (all subsequent packets are forwarded according to the flow rule). To measure the introduced delay, we have sequentially established 1000 TLS sessions between compute tasks C1 and C2 (according to Fig. 8). After each TLS session, we flushed the installed flow rules (with ovs-ofctl del-flows br0), which resulted in a packet in message upon each new session. The latency of the first packet is shown in Fig. 9, and compared against the latency of a first packet without the TruSDN extension.

The induced delay is primarily caused by two operations performed by the NC: *generating* a 256-bit PSK and distributing it to the CTs. Figure 10 displays a fine-grained picture of the induced delay. Key generation lasted on average 0.178 ms, while key distribution on average 0.54 ms (Table 5). We remind that the test environment is fully virtualized and posit that overhead of key generation can be reduced in a production environment, either by using pre-generated keys or with specialized hardware (e.g. crypto processors). In our tests, the duration of establishing a TLS session with ephemeral flow-specific pre-shared keys using the PSK-AES256-CBC-SHA cipher suite was 2.41% *less* compared to the use of e.g. ECDH-RSA-AES128-SHA256. Thus, TruSDN enables flexible use of pre-shared keys, which in turn reduces the duration of the TLS handshake, by avoiding expensive public key cryptographic

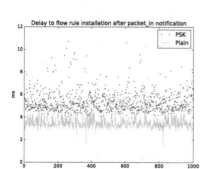

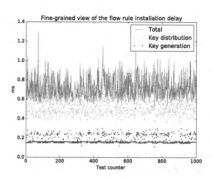

Fig. 9. Coarse-grained view

Fig. 10. Fine-grained view

operations [17]. Moreover, it reduces the CPU utilization for key derivation in CTs, at the cost of a minimal flow rule installation delay. The above approach may be applicable to other protocols. For example, none of the differences between the datagram TLS (DTLS) and TLS protocols specified in [29] indicate that the above approach is incompatible with DTLS. We leave further investigation for future work.

Unmeasured Performance Overhead. Implementing TEEs with OpenSGX limits the level of detail when it comes to performance evaluation, since: **(a)** the OpenSGX emulator *is not* binary compatible with Intel SGX [15]; **(b)** in its current version[4] and unlike Intel's description of SGX [1], OpenSGX has yet to implement support multithreaded applications[5]. Thus, a fully accurate measurement on TruSDN performance cannot be done until Intel SGX hardware and software is made available. However, we believe our experiments yield a fair picture of the expected performance impact.

7 Related Work

Adversary models: Kreutz et al. presented a list of attack vectors in SDN [16] (forged traffic flows, vulnerabilities in switches and NCs, lack of trust establishment mechanisms, etc.). However, only part of the described attack vectors are exclusively relevant to SDN networks and no specific solutions are proposed. Work in [22] introduced an adversary model, attack vectors, and security requirements towards multi-tenant SDN infrastructure, highlighting the need to limit the effect of NC vulnerabilities, protect internal SDN communication, verify integrity of SDN components prior to enrollment, and enforce policy and quota isolation. TruSDN addresses several of the attack vectors described in [16, 22].

Secure SDN controllers: The "NOX" network OS [11] presents NMAs with a centralized programming model, allowing to operate with higher-level abstractions and apply graph processing algorithms to compute paths. It consists of several controller

---

[4] Commit e0713c7 on https://github.com/sslab-gatech/opensgx.

[5] Issue #34 on https://github.com/sslab-gatech/opensgx/issues/34.

processes which use the global view for network management decisions and update switch FIBs over the OpenFlow API [19]. FortNOX [26] extends NOX with role-based authorization (RBA) and enforcement of security constraints. It translates high-level threats into flow rules to handle suspicious traffic as well as detects rule conflicts, resolves them depending on the authorization of the rule requestor and enforces least privilege authorization. Neither NOX nor FortNOX address malicious network components and Sybill attacks, addressed by TruSDN. "Rosemary" NOS [34] uses NMA sandboxing to improve network resilience, by launching each NMA in a separate process context with access to the required libraries, along with a resource monitor to supervise NMA compliance. It does not address data plane security; TruSDN complements it and creates a foundation for trusted deployment of a secure NOS. Topo-Guard [13] detects network topology poisoning and mitigates this through port property management, network edge probing and verification of topology updates. TruSDN complements this by verifying the *integrity* of switches prior to enrollment into the topology.

Software Guard Extensions: SGX was introduced in [18] with a description of the software model, extensions to the x86 ISA and hardware modifications for isolated execution; work in [1] described CPU based attestation. SGX-based solutions in a cloud setting are first described in [2, 33]. "Haven" [2] is a modified version of Windows 8 OS ported to an SGX enclave, evaluated with Apache Web Server and SQL Server using synthetic data sets. It includes a mechanism to protect the enclave from a malicious kernel and a semantically secure data store protecting data and file metadata confidentiality against malicious hosts. TruSDN protects network communication for a similar adversary model. While we deploy compute tasks in SGX enclave-based TEEs, the work in [2] is largely complementary, and similar "Haven"-like OSs could be used.

"VC3" [33] is a Map-Reduce deployment using SGX enclaves. *Map* and *reduce* functions are compiled into private (encrypted) code and public code implementing key exchange and job execution protocols. Code is initialized in enclaves and attested by the users. Public code performs the key exchange, decrypts the private code and runs the job execution protocol. To defend against cuckoo attacks, *cloud quoting enclaves* are created on *each* platform in the cloud provider data centers, to "countersign" quotes produced by the QE. The approach is largely complementary to protecting communication between CTs with TruSDN. However, the proposed defense against cuckoo attacks increases the complexity of the attestation protocol and does not prevent $\mathcal{A}dv$ from exploiting a compromised cloud QE outside of the physically secure datacenter perimeter. Instead, the approach described in Sect. 4.4 leverages the cryptographic properties of EPID scheme, without modifying the attestation protocol.

8 Future Work

Along with security guarantees, the use of Intel SGX imposes limitations on TruSDN. Further performance evaluation may be done once software and hardware support for Intel SGX becomes available; moreover, we note several security limitations.

Controlled-channel attacks [36] are a novel type of side-channel attacks allowing the OS to extract data from protected applications. They were successfully applied to "Haven" [2] and TruSDN could also be vulnerable; however, we explicitly excluded such attacks from the adversary model. Known mitigations are: rewriting applications to decouple memory access patterns from sensitive data, prohibiting paging by the OS, or obfuscating memory access patterns [36]. Another limitation stems from the reliance on the platform vendor, which could leak $QE^{sk,}$ to create a "deniable back-door" and allow *person-in-the-middle* attacks on attestation [32]. This challenge remains unaddressed.

In future work we aim to integrate TruSDN with other approaches to cloud infrastructure security, such as in [21], to provide a complete framework for secure cloud infrastructure deployments in the given adversarial model.

9 Conclusion

We described, implemented and evaluated TruSDN – a framework for bootstrapping trust in SDN infrastructure. It isolates network endpoints and switches in SGX enclaves, remotely attests their integrity, and establishes secure communication channels. We leveraged the principles of SDN to introduce *ephemeral flow-specific PSK* distributed at flow creation, which reduce the overhead of key derivation and reduce the total time to establish protected channels, at the cost of a minor delay in the flow rule installation. Finally, we leveraged the properties of the EPID scheme to propose an improved approach to prevent cuckoo attacks.

Acknowledgements. This research has been performed within 5G-ENSURE project (www.5GEnsure.eu) and received funding from the European Union's Horizon 2020 research and innovation programme under grant agreements No. 671562 and No. 644814.

References

1. Anati, I., Gueron, S., Johnson, S., Scarlata, V.: Innovative technology for CPU based attestation and sealing. In: Proceedings of the 2nd International Workshop on Hardware and Architectural Support for Security and Privacy, p. 10. ACM (2013)
2. Baumann, A., Peinado, M., Hunt, G.: Shielding applications from an untrusted cloud with Haven. In: USENIX Symposium on Operating Systems Design and Implementation (OSDI) (2014)
3. Bifulco, R., Cui, H., Karame, G.O., Klaedtke, F.: Fingerprinting software-defined networks. In: 2015 IEEE 23rd International Conference on Network Protocols (ICNP), pp. 453–459, November 2015
4. Brickell, E., Li, J.: Enhanced privacy ID: a direct anonymous attestation scheme with enhanced revocation capabilities. IEEE Trans. Dependable Secure Comput. 9(3), 345–360 (2012)
5. Casado, M., Foster, N., Guha, A.: Abstractions for software-defined networks. Commun. ACM 57(10), 86–95 (2014)

6. Checkoway, S., Shacham, H.: Iago attacks: why the system call API is a bad untrusted RPC interface. SIGARCH Comput. Archit. News **41**(1), 253–264 (2013). http://doi.acm.org/10.1145/2490301.2451145

7. Dolev, D., Yao, A.C.: On the security of public key protocols. IEEE Trans. Inf. Theor. **29**(2), 198–208 (1983)

8. Douceur, J.R.: The sybil attack. In: Druschel, P., Kaashoek, F., Rowstron, A. (eds.) IPTPS 2002. LNCS, vol. 2429, pp. 251–260. Springer, Heidelberg (2002). doi:10.1007/3-540-45748-8_24

9. Eronen, P., Tschofenig, H.: Pre-shared key ciphersuites for transport layer security (TLS). Technical report, RFC 4279, December 2005

10. Farinacci, D., Traina, P., Hanks, S., Li, T.: Generic routing encapsulation (GRE). In: IETF (2000). tools.ietf.org/html/rfc2784

11. Gude, N., Koponen, T., Pettit, J., Pfaff, B., Casado, M., McKeown, N., Shenker, S.: NOX: towards an operating system for networks. ACM SIGCOMM Comput. Commun. Rev. **38** (3), 105–110 (2008)

12. Hoekstra, M.: Using innovative instructions to create trustworthy software solutions. In: Proceedings of the 2nd International Workshop on Hardware and Architectural Support for Security and Privacy, p. 10. ACM (2013)

13. Hong, S., Xu, L., Wang, H., Gu, G.: Poisoning network visibility in software - defined networks: new attacks and countermeasures. In: Proceedings of the Network and Distributed System Security Symposium (NDSS) (2015)

14. Hopps, C.: Analysis of an Equal-Cost Multi-Path Algorithm. In: IETF (2000). tools.ietf.org/html/rfc2992

15. Jain, P., Desai, S., Kim, S., Shih, M.W., Lee, J., Choi, C., Shin, Y., Kim, T., Kang, B.B., Han, D.: OpenSGX: an open platform for SGX research. In: Proceedings of the Network and Distributed System Security Symposium (NDSS) (2016)

16. Kreutz, D., Ramos, F., Verissimo, P.: Towards secure and dependable software- defined networks. In: Proceedings of the Second ACM SIGCOMM Workshop on Hot Topics in Software Defined Networking, pp. 55–60. ACM (2013)

17. Kuo, F.C., Tschofenig, H., Meyer, F., Fu, X.: Comparison studies between pre-shared and public key exchange mechanisms for transport layer security. In: INFOCOM 2006. 25th IEEE International Conference on Computer Communications. Proceedings, pp. 1–6. IEEE (2006)

18. McKeen, F., Alexandrovich, I., Berenzon, A., Rozas, C.V., Shafi, H., Shanbhogue, V., Savagaonkar, U.R.: Innovative instructions and software model for isolated execution. In: Proceedings of the 2nd International Workshop on Hardware and Architectural Support for Security and Privacy, pp. 1–1. ACM (2013)

19. McKeown, N., Anderson, T., Balakrishnan, H., Parulkar, G., Peterson, L., Rexford, J., Shenker, S., Turner, J.: OpenFlow: enabling innovation in campus networks. ACM SIGCOMM Comput. Commun. Rev. **38**(2), 69–74 (2008)

20. Nadeau, T.D., Gray, K.: SDN: Software Defined Networks. O'Reilly Media Inc., Sebastopol (2013)

21. Paladi, N., Gehrmann, C., Michalas, A.: Providing user security guarantees in public infrastructure clouds. IEEE Trans. Cloud Comput. **PP**(99), 1 (2016)

22. Paladi, N., Gehrmann, C.: Towards secure multi-tenant virtualized networks. In: 2015 IEEE Trustcom/BigDataSE/ISPA, vol. 1, pp. 1180–1185. IEEE (2015)

23. Parno, B.: Bootstrapping trust in a "trusted" platform. In: HotSec (2008)

24. Pfaff, B., Lantz, B., Heller, B., et al.: OpenFlow switch specification, version 1.3.0. Open Networking Foundation (2012)

25. Pfaff, B., Pettit, J., Koponen, T., Jackson, E.J., Zhou, A., Rajahalme, J., Gross, J., Wang, A., Stringer, J., Shelar, P., et al.: The design and implementation of Open vSwitch. In: 12th USENIX Symposium on Networked Systems Design and Implementation (2015)
26. Porras, P., Shin, S., Yegneswaran, V., Fong, M., Tyson, M., Gu, G.: A security enforcement kernel for OpenFlow networks. In: Proceedings of the First Workshop on Hot Topics in Software Defined Networks, pp. 121–126. ACM (2012)
27. Porras, P., Cheung, S., Fong, M., Skinner, K., Yegneswaran, V.: Securing the software-defined network control layer. In: Proceedings of the Network and Distributed System Security Symposium (NDSS) (2015)
28. Qazi, Z.A., Tu, C.C., Chiang, L., Miao, R., Sekar, V., Yu, M.: SIMPLE-fying middlebox policy enforcement using SDN. ACM SIGCOMM Comput. Commun. Rev. **43**, 27–38 (2013). ACM
29. Rescorla, E., Modadugu, N.: RFC6347–datagram transport layer security version 1.2. IETF (2012) tools.ietf.org/html/rfc6347
30. Ristenpart, T., Yilek, S.: When good randomness goes bad: virtual machine reset vulnerabilities and hedging deployed cryptography. In: NDSS (2010)
31. Ruan, X.: Safeguarding the Future of Computing with Intel Embedded Security and Management Engine, 1st edn. Apress, Berkely (2014)
32. Rutkowska, J.: Thoughts on Intel's upcoming Software Guard Extensions (Part 2) (2013). http://theinvisiblethings.blogspot.de/2013/09/thoughts-on-intels-upcoming-software.html. Accessed Mar 2016
33. Schuster, F., Costa, M., Fournet, C., Gkantsidis, C., Peinado, M., Mainar-Ruiz, G., Russinovich, M.: VC3: Trustworthy data analytics in the cloud using SGX. In: 2015 IEEE Symposium on Security and Privacy (SP), pp. 38–54, May 2015
34. Shin, S., Song, Y., Lee, T., Lee, S., Chung, J., Porras, P., Yegneswaran, V., Noh, J., Kang, B.B.: Rosemary: a robust, secure, and high-performance network operating system. In: Proceedings of the 2014 ACM SIGSAC Conference on Computer and Communications Security, pp. 78–89. ACM (2014)
35. Walker, J., Li, J.: Key exchange with anonymous authentication using DAA-SIGMA protocol. In: Chen, L., Yung, M. (eds.) INTRUST 2010. LNCS, vol. 6802, pp. 108–127. Springer, Heidelberg (2011). doi:10.1007/978-3-642-25283-9_8
36. Xu, Y., Cui, W., Peinado, M.: Controlled-channel attacks: deterministic side channels for untrusted operating systems. In: 2015 IEEE Symposium on Security and Privacy (SP), pp. 640–656. IEEE (2015)

Key Update at Train Stations:
Two-Layer Dynamic Key Update Scheme
for Secure Train Communications

Sang-Yoon Chang[1,2]($\boxtimes$), Shaoying Cai[3], Hwajeong Seo[3], and Yih-Chun Hu[1,4]

[1] Advanced Digital Sciences Center, Singapore, Singapore
[2] University of Colorado Colorado Springs, Colorado Springs, CO, USA
schang2@uccs.edu
[3] Institute for Infocomm Research, A*STAR, Singapore, Singapore
[4] University of Illinois at Urbana-Champaign, Urbana, IL, USA

Abstract. Modern train systems adopt communication-based train control (CBTC), which uses wireless communications to better monitor and control the train operations. Despite the well-studied security issues in wireless networking in information technology applications, security implementations in trains have been lagging; many train systems rely on security by obscurity and forgo well-established security practices such as key updates. To secure train systems against increasingly evolving and persistent attackers and mitigate key breach (which can occur due to misuse of the key), we build a key update scheme, *Key Update at Train Stations* (KUTS), that leverages the inherent physical aspects of train operations (mobility/infrastructure-asymmetry between the stations and the trains and the operational differences when the trains are at stations and between the stations). Furthermore, by incorporating separation of key chain and use and on the entities providing the key seeds, KUTS protects the key seeds for future updates against the breach of the current key and is both key-collision irrelevant (thwarting known collision-based threats on one-way random functions) and system-compromise resilient (protecting the key secrecy even when the train system is compromised). We theoretically analyze KUTS's effectiveness, security strength, and security properties. We also implement KUTS on various computing devices to study the performance overhead.

1 Introduction

Communication-based train control (CBTC) uses wireless communication to deliver operational-control messages from the train to the track-side antenna, which in turn relays the message to the operational control center (OCC) via wired connection, and vice versa. In addition to being lightweight in infrastructure and better supporting the mobility of the trains, CBTC enables finer granularity for the train vehicle's location sensing (which is a key parameter for train control) than the traditional fixed-block technology (which uses discrete railway-track segments for train localization). Consequentially, because CBTC enables

© ICST Institute for Computer Sciences, Social Informatics and Telecommunications Engineering 2017
R. Deng et al. (Eds.): SecureComm 2016, LNICST 198, pp. 125–143, 2017.
DOI: 10.1007/978-3-319-59608-2_7

greater customer transport efficiency (e.g., enabling more trains to get packed per distance during busy hours), train operators have increasingly deployed CBTC for train systems.

While safety issues have been well-studied in train systems (some measures of which can also mitigate communication availability issues) because of the physical consequences of failure, security in general has not garnered much attention from the train system integrators and operators. They, instead, largely rely on security by obscurity and that the protocols are confidential and proprietary. While this does increase the barrier for security breach, especially for the type of system that is not readily accessible by the public (e.g., unlike computers or cars, not many people own/operate a train), history has shown that such approach is insufficient against motivated and persistent cyber-attackers, e.g., Stuxnet malware discovered in 2010. The security-by-obscurity approach is further challenged by the recent push to make the train systems interoperable across European nations, which will involve effort to unify and standardize the practice/design and thus make the information more obtainable [1]. Previous failures in train systems, e.g., whether accidental [2] or playful [3], demonstrate vulnerabilities in train systems and let us wonder how much more of an impact sophisticated attackers can make on train operations. Also, the recent high-profile security incidents in car applications that allowed remote (Internet-connected) attackers to take control of car operations [4–7] are alarming to train operators as well because while the wireless channels breached during these incidents deliver allegedly non-critical communications, e.g., software updates, the trains use them for critical CBTC messages that directly control the train operations. Only recently, there has been concerted effort into begin addressing security for train communication systems [8–10].

To address the security gap of train communications, we study key management within the train communication systems, which is a fundamental building block of many secure communication protocols and practice. Given an initial seed acting as a root of trust, we design a key update protocol, so that the key remains fresh and secret. Our work not only makes the key breach significantly harder but also limits the impact of such breach to the current key.

Our solution takes advantage of the unique physical aspects that are inherent in train applications. In specific, trains transport people in two phases: *at stations*, the human customers embark or get off of the train vehicle, and *between stations*, the train vehicle moves from one point to another to transport passengers and goods. Because the train at stations is static or moving much more slowly and because the station contains more infrastructure, stations provide a more tightly controlled environment for trains; CBTC implementations to track the train vehicle locations also focus more on the latter periods when the trains are travelling between the stations because such period generally presents greater challenges (less resources/equipment along the rail tracks, more exposure to the public wild, mobility of the train, and so on). We also align our scheme to these two phases and update the key when the train is at the station and use the key when the trains are between the stations, time-interleaving the key update and its use. We thus call our scheme *key update at train stations* (KUTS); however, KUTS does not need to be implemented at all physical stations but only a subset of the stations (*KUTS stations*).

KUTS is based on one-way functions that generate pseudo-randomness. However, it defeats the known output-collision-based threats on one-way functions that significantly reduce the entropy (key strength) by introducing a two-layer approach for updating the KUTS keys; the separation between the two layers (one for the key seeds/chain and the other for the keys being used) also protect the future keys even when the currently used keys (for CBTC operations) are compromised. Furthermore, KUTS uses key seeds from both the train and the station (which are logically separate from each other) to increase resilience against train-system compromise.

The rest of the paper is organized as follows. Section 2 describes related work while Sect. 3.1 provides an overview of the train system, focusing on the part that is relevant to our work. We build the corresponding system and threat models in Sects. 3.2 and 3.3, respectively. KUTS scheme (the key update and the key failure detection) is described in Sect. 4, and we theoretically analyze its security effectiveness and properties in Sect. 5. Furthermore, KUTS is implemented and its efficiency and effectiveness analyzed in Sect. 6. Lastly, we conclude our work in Sect. 7.

2   Related Work

As discussed in Sect. 1, security developments in train networks has lagged other fields in computer security and has largely focus on wireless availability, e.g., [1,10,11]. We study an orthogonal problem of key exchange, a critical building block on which many security protocols in the digital domain rely. In related work, Lopez and Aguado [12] sketch an improvement of the European Rail Traffic Management System (ERTMS)'s outdated PKI system, which was designed in the 1990s. Separately, Hartong et al. [13] also proposes key management requirements for train systems. Our work also studies key management but, in contrast to prior work studying broader aspects of key management, we focus on improving the security by introducing updates and dynamism on the keys (with the update cycle synchronized with the physical train operations of periodic station visits).

Our work is inspired by path authentication work in computer security. Path authentication provides assurance that the object of the mechanism went through a specific path by having the relaying entities (along that path) interact with the object. It is used in the contexts of network routing [14–16] and device manufacturing/supply-chain [17–20] to identify the path and avoid the tampering of the object. Although our work is similar in the sense that the relaying nodes (stations) are stationary and help with the authentication via interactions with the moving objects (trains), KUTS is fundamentally different because the train's mobility trajectory is defined by the railway tracks and its route pre-established by the OCC while the stations have fixed geographical locations and are interwoven with many aspects of the train operations. In other words, while the objective of path authentication in supply-chain and network-routing is to ensure that the object travels through a path, the travel path actually serves as a source of assurance in KUTS, as it is difficult to make the train diverge from the path defined by the railway tracks.

KUTS uses two layers of pseudo-random generators (hash chains). Prior work also adopt multiple layers of hashing, but the schemes are in different contexts and the different layers are for orthogonality purpose, for example, multicast source authentication work by Challal et al. [21] uses different layers for redundancy control and chooses one layer from multiple layers for execution, and Fredman et al. designed a scheme for efficient data lookup [22] that has different layers to describe orthogonal dimensions of the pointer. In contrast, KUTS uses multiple layers for greater security, and the layers are sequentially executed to generate the key update. On the other hand, our cryptographic construction shares greater similarity with Ohkubo et al.'s use of two-layer hash chains for RFID privacy [23]; their work aims to achieve forward security (preventing backward tracking, so that the breach does not enable an attacker to trace the data back through past events). However, in contrast to their work, we protect both the future and the past keys from the key breach by separating the keys being used for CBTC and the key seeds used for updates; furthermore, our construction also involves multiple independent parties distributing the key seeds to build resiliency against system compromise and is thus more complex. The use of such cryptographic constructions in resource-constrained RFID tags shows great promise that the overhead will be even more marginal for train applications, as train-borne devices has much less hardware constraints and requirements.

Our instantiation of KUTS uses SHA-256 hash for the pseudo-random generator. To put the attacker's cost in perspective, we discuss SHA-256's use in bitcoins and bitcoin mining in Sects. 4.2 and 6.2.

3   Train System Model

3.1   The Application System

Trains are designed to transport people from one geographical point to another. And to provide the customers with more options for the geographical points for their departure/arrival, trains operate on pre-established and fixed stations, which are where the customers ride or get off the train. The stations are connected with railway tracks, on which the trains operate and move, and thus the train operational trajectories are fixed/limited and clearly defined by the railway tracks. We make use of these physical aspects, e.g., the trains visit and stop at the more controlled environment of stations, to build security in the cyber-domain; for example, it is difficult for an attacker to physically take the train and have it diverge from the railway tracks.

In CBTC, the operational control center (OCC) is actively involved in the real-time control of all the trains on the line. However, since the centralized OCC controls many spatially distributed trains, it uses networking to communicate

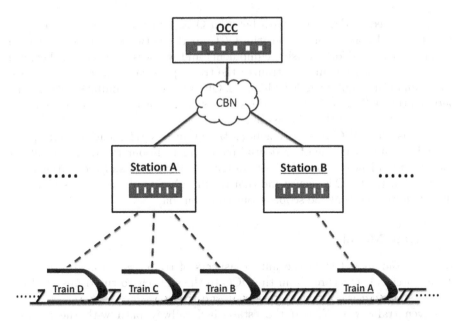

Fig. 1. CBTC communication architecture. CBN stands for communication backbone network, and the solid/dotted line represent wired/wireless connectivity, respectively.

with the trains; the OCC communicates its operational control messages, and the trains report their statuses to the OCC. OCC thus has a central view of the train line and know the time schedules/itineraries of the train operations and the train vehicles' locations at any given time, which can also be used for safety (e.g., train collision avoidance) and better traffic management. To enable real-time monitoring and control, the OCC and the trains communicate periodically; the protocol has failed if the expected messages do not arrive in a timely manner or if any of the channels conflict with each other and result in inconsistency (train systems rely on redundancy for many logical operations), which events can trigger fail-safe. Any deviation resulting in inconsistency will be detected, regardless of the failure source or the cause, and we build on such protocols to develop a failure-detection scheme in the endhosts's (OCC's and trains's) perspectives in Sect. 4.3.

Train operations rely more heavily on CBTC between stations than at stations, as discussed in Sect. 1, because of the following reasons. First, train's location (which is the most important sensing factor for CBTC) changes in faster pace than at stations, requiring greater amount of information exchange between the individual train and the OCC. Second, there are greater resources for train sensing at stations, enabling tighter and more precise control of the train operations; for example, as the train enters the stations, a dense sequential array of trackside beacons (operating independently to CBTC) are deployed for better alignment of the platform screen doors for passenger boarding.

As depicted in Fig. 1, the path between OCC and the trains are comprised of both wired connections (from the OCC to the network switches and then to the stations and/or trackside equipment) and wireless connections (between the stations/trackside and the trains); the trains physically move over long distances and thus require wireless channels. Often acting as a communication relay between the OCC and the trains, the stations also incorporate control, e.g., control booth to oversee the on-site operations.

Because the OCC primarily acts as the brain in CBTC-based train operations, it assumes the role of credential management in our work. Specifically, it allocates the identities and the roots of trust to the trains and the stations. We assume that the OCC is secure and that the initial roots of trust are established; OCC failure is beyond the scope of our contribution.

3.2   Train Model

We build our model from the unique aspects of train system operations, i.e., the hierarchical structure (from the OCC to the stations to the trains) and the mobile/static nature of trains/stations, respectively.

Given trains $i \in T$ and the established railway path with the stations $j \in S$ (with S being a vector set with the elements in a particular order), we model the train system discussed in Sect. 3.1 and the host connectivity with a graph. Figure 2 shows a sample snapshot of the connectivity graph with

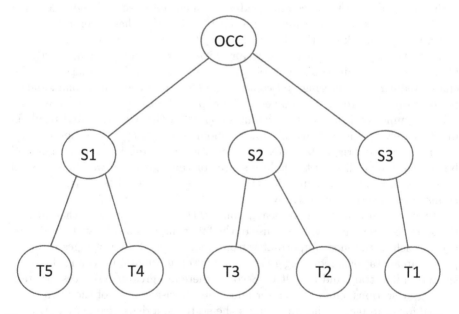

Fig. 2. A sample graph with three KUTS stations and five trains on the line. The nodes indicate the hosts involved in KUTS (with S being stations and T being trains), and the edges indicate logical KUTS interactions.

three KUTS stations and five trains on the line, i.e., $\mathcal{S} = \{S1, S2, S3\}$ and $\mathcal{T} = \{T1, T2, T3, T4, T5\}$. Only the hosts that are involved in KUTS - the OCC, KUTS stations, and trains - are represented in the graph, and not all physical train stations (where the passengers embark/debark the trains) need to be involved in KUTS[1]. Henceforth, we define *stations* to mean KUTS stations, and not the rest of the train stations irrelevant to KUTS. S nodes correspond to stations and T to trains, and the edges indicate the current connectivity. The lowest row with trains are mobile, thus making the graph dynamic in time, while the two upper rows are stationary. The indices correspond to time where the trains travel from left to right. For example, T1 is the first train, T2 the second train, and so on. Similarly, S1 is the first station that the trains encounter, S2 the second, and so on. In the figure, for example, T1 passed S1 and S2 and is currently either stationed at S3 or just passed S3 enroute to the next station. Our model applies generally to the train-line topology, e.g., for a line that is a loop with 5 stations, the same physical station can be captured by incrementing j for every train cycle (so that the physical station owns all the indices of j modulo 5 and enables that the station's keys be unique per train cycle) and can be straightforwardly adapted for multiple train-route cases (as long as there is a countably finite sets of stations and trains and the OCC knows each of the train's routes); in fact, KUTS is largely described in each of the train's view in Sect. 4, e.g., station j corresponds to the j-th station that a train encounters.

As described in Sect. 3.1, the OCC distributes keys to the stations and the trains, and the trains use those keys to secure their communications to/from the stations and the OCC. The stations' key seeds are denoted k^j while the trains' key seeds are k_j^i where j and i are, respectively, the station index and train index as described previously; the presence of the subscript indicates whether it is train's key seed (subscript present) or station's key seed (subscript absent). The subscript for train key seeds corresponds to time and gets incremented when the train passes KUTS stations, i.e., j in k_j^i corresponds to the last station that the train stopped. For example, for Fig. 2, T1 currently passed S3 and thus uses k_3^1 to drive the key chain. As the initial root-of-trust, the OCC also distributes k_0^i to train i. KUTS provides a key update scheme given k^j, $\forall j \in \mathcal{S}$ and k_0^i, $\forall i \in \mathcal{T}$. In other words, given a train i and its initial seed k_0^i, KUTS computes k_j^i (when passing the station j), which afterward is used to generate the keys that are used for securing train communication protocols. Section 4 discusses KUTS in greater details.

3.3   Threat Model

As in other key-establishment work, we consider attackers whose objectives are to learn the key. In addition to the traditional threat model of attackers residing outside of the train system, we consider any attackers but the OCC (the

---

[1] The choice of KUTS stations is a design parameter which has a tradeoff between security strength and complexity/computation and is beyond the scope of this paper. Section 5 provides analyses and insights that can be helpful in making such design choices.

trusted authority, as discussed in Sect. 3.1) and the corresponding train (who owns the set of keys). The attackers do not have control over or did not compromise the hosts depicted in Fig. 2 (the logical entities that govern KUTS), but they can physically reside within the train infrastructure system, e.g., the station-trackside relay/switch or the parts of the station irrelevant to KUTS intelligence are within the scope of our attacker model. Such attackers can also conduct active attacks and disrupt the KUTS by diverging from the protocol, e.g., drop the KUTS exchange or relay incorrect keys; we develop a detection countermeasure for such active threats in Sect. 4.3. Such insider compromise (where attackers breached parts of the system) is increasingly being considered in critical infrastructure security, such as in the car vehicular networking (multiple credential authorities collaborating with each other for vehicular credential management system) [24] and in device and chip manufacturing (split manufacturing) [25,26].

4   KUTS Scheme

We build our scheme on the model described in Sect. 3.2 and, using the jth station's key seed (k^j) and train i's initial key seed (k_0^i), describe KUTS which updates the key for dynamic key establishment. The key updates are generated on the train when it is at the KUTS stations (OCC, keeping track of the trains' locations, also separately update the key using KUTS) and used while the train is moving between the stations, which provides well-defined time-separation between the key updates and use. We use well-established cryptographic tools, e.g., one-way functions, for the key update in Sect. 4.2 and describe the key failure detection in Sect. 4.3. But first, we define the contribution scope of KUTS in Sect. 4.1.

4.1   KUTS Contribution Scope

Our contribution lies in establishing the keys between the OCC and trains for CBTC, but not in *how* to use those keys to secure the communications. How to use the keys for secure networking depends on the threat model and the corresponding threat vectors, on which the security measure focuses, and such developments are widely studied in computer security. For example, the keys can generate digital signatures for communication integrity; the keys can be used for message encryption for confidentiality; the keys can drive randomization to thwart network reconnaissance or wireless denial-of-service attacks; and so on. Our work thus serves as a building block to secure communication against attackers in various scopes (whether they compromised the network and are physically residing within the train network, e.g., switch, or have access to the wireless link between the train and the station). Our analyses for KUTS in Sect. 5 also supports such generality in key use and attacker scope.

We focus on key updates given a key infrastructure with key seeds distributed a priori, as discussed in Sect. 3.2. While key updates in other contexts, such

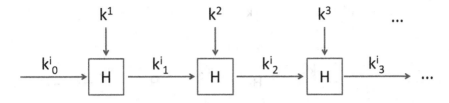

(a) KUTS key-chain update

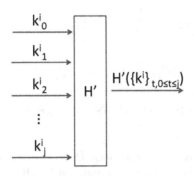

(b) KUTS key generation

Fig. 3. KUTS scheme for train i

as those discussed in Sect. 2, are either time-dependent (periodic updates with regular time intervals) or event-based (triggered by an event), KUTS update is space-dependent (updates at the stations) and uses the train's pre-established route (defined by the railway tracks and publicly announced).

4.2   KUTS Update and Key Generation

OCC, as the trusted authority, knows all the keys. For any $i \in \mathcal{T}$ and $j \in \mathcal{S}$, the station j knows its own key seed k^j and shares it to train i upon the arrival of the expected train i. Train i takes its current key seed k^i_{j-1} and the station's key seed k^j to update its key seed to k^i_j. Only k^j is communicated, and the other keys (e.g., k^i_{j-1} and its history) are locally stored within the train and the OCC; the computations are also performed locally. We design KUTS to provide such an update and, for scalability, keep the train's key seeds k^i_j, $\forall j \in \mathcal{S}$ the same size.

KUTS uses two cryptographic one-way functions, H and H'. H is used for key seed update and to drive the one-way chain, while H' is used for generating the key that will be actually used for CBTC. In other words,

$$H : (k^i_{j-1}, k^j) \rightarrow k^i_j \tag{1}$$

$$H' : \{k^i_t\}_{0 \le t \le j} \rightarrow H'(\{k^i_t\}_{0 \le t \le j}) \tag{2}$$

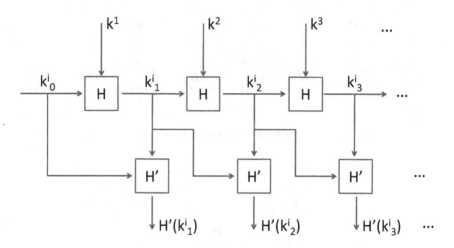

Fig. 4. Our KUTS instantiation

As cryptographic one-way functions, both H and H' are easy to compute but difficult to reverse, i.e., given $H(x)$ for some x, it is difficult to find that x. Also, as discussed in Sect. 5.1, KUTS is not sensitive to collision and is not subject to many collision-based attacks on one-way computations.

Figure 3(a) describes KUTS's key seed updates using H. For any $i \in T$ and $j \in S$, train i receives k^j when it is stopped at station j (the upper row of key seeds), then it uses H to compute k_j^i from k^j and k_{j-1}^i (the lower row of key seeds). Afterward, as described in Fig. 3(b), it uses $\{k_t^i\}_{0 \le t \le j}$ to compute $H'(\{k_t^i\}_{0 \le t \le j})$; the weight can be controlled for the input seeds of $\{k_t^i\}_{0 \le t \le j}$; for example, our instantiation described in Fig. 4 uses only k_j^i and k_{j-1}^i at station j. $H'(\{k_t^i\}_{0 \le t \le j})$ is used as a key for secure CBTC operations, i.e., k_j^i are not designed to be directly used. Introducing additional complexity of H' protects the security of the key chain, as discussed in Sect. 5.1.

We build an instantiation of KUTS, described in Fig. 4, to analyze the efficiency and the overhead in Sect. 6. In particular, we use SHA-256 hashes for both H and H' with input size of 512 bits. We use SHA-256 because it is quick (as we will see in Sect. 6.1) and is computationally infeasible to reverse the computation. Since we use a 512-bit-long inputs for H and H', the input for H is a concatenation of k^j and k_{j-1}^i, and the input for H' is a concatenation of k_{j-1}^i and k_j^i.

Like KUTS, bit-coins use one-way hash chains driven by SHA-256. However, KUTS is fundamentally different from bit-coin mining in the following three aspects. First, the upcoming bit-coin blocks are generated by solving the reverse of Hash or finding collisions, while KUTS is given the inputs and compute the Hash in the forward-direction to generate the key updates. Second, while the bit-coin hash blocks, once solved, are publicly advertised, KUTS-output keys are sensitive and are designed to be protected from adversaries. Third, a realistic adversary (even for a particularly persistent one) against train systems is significantly less computationally capable than the combined effort of bit-coin miners, as bit-coin miners are a global network of machines with some individual miners investing millions of dollars (even with such massive-scale distributed network, each SHA-256-based bit-coin block gets solved roughly in every ten minutes by design).

4.3 Detection of Key Failure

KUTS key update *failure* occurs when the OCC and the train do not agree on the key, and the failure event can happen because of the fault on the train side (e.g., receiving the station's key seeds and computing the updates) or the fault on the station side (e.g., transferring the station's seeds to the trains). KUTS detection uses the following aspects of the train communication infrastructure: it is hierarchical with OCC communicating with the stations and the stations communicating with the trains and vice versa, as described in Fig. 2; it is also dynamic with the trains moving from one station to another; and the trains' operations (and their KUTS key uses) are orthogonal to each other.

KUTS detects key-update failures (e.g., an outdated/incorrect key is used) when two or more distinct failure events are observed, where the *distinctness* of failure events come from different connectivity edges (relayed from different stations in the OCC view) or from the same edge but with different train/time instances (where time instances are according to j updates in any of the train's view, e.g., any train on the station's child branch leaves or enters). The distinctness is required because the key update relies on the cooperation with the stations and needs to distinguish between the protocol failure on the station and that on the train. This limits the failure event to one occurrence until another distinct failure event is observed, which can trigger further investigation on the node that has repeatedly caused failures. In the case of an update failure event (and before the second event occurs), the train involved in the failure uses the key before the failed update, and proceeds with the key for KUTS once it arrives the next station; OCC keeps track of this to leave a record of key failures.

For example, in Fig. 2, suppose the OCC senses a KUTS failure event when the communication got relayed from S2 and originated from T4. However, since it does not know whether the failure is from S2 or T4, it waits until T4 moves to S3 or until T5 enters S2. If T4 is misbehaving, then a failure event will occur on S3 or any other future stations that T4 will encounter; if S2 is the one misbehaving, then another failure event will occur for T5 or any of the later trains. After the first observation of the failure (with k_2^4), T4 and the OCC use the key that they agreed on before T4 arrived at S2 (k_1^4) before arriving to S3 and, upon arriving in S3, updates the new key with $H(k_1^4, k^3)$.

5 Security Analyses

We analyze the KUTS scheme in this section. While Sect. 5.1 derives security properties from the KUTS design, Sect. 5.2 theoretically analyzes the security strength.

5.1 Security Properties

KUTS is designed carefully to have the following properties that will be useful in securing the train communications. In addition to being scalable (because the key sizes remain the same for all updates) and enabling detection of misbehaving insider station or train (as described in Sect. 4.3), it is interwound with the established physical operations of the trains, insensitive to key collisions (defending some known attacks on hash algorithms), and robust to compromise. We discuss about these properties in greater details in this section.

Established and Publicly Known Trajectory of Train Operations. KUTS uses the established operational trajectory/path of the trains as a source of security assurance. Because the path is clearly defined by the railway tracks and many users involved in the operation (the train-borne customers, the train-borne logic, the stations, the OCC, and so on) a priori agreed on the path, it is difficult to change the train's operational path during CBTC (i.e., when KUTS keys are used). For example, in contrast to the path authentication work in packet routing and supply chains discussed in Sect. 2, it is challenging to make the train physically diverge from the railway tracks, re-route it without any of the entities noticing, or stop it in between stations and engage the train with KUTS; not only do the trains themselves also keep track of their own locations relative to the stations, e.g., by using odometry and/or beacons, but there are also additional redundant mechanisms to check whether the train is at a station, e.g., more capable and densely populated sensors enable higher precisions on train sensing and better alignment with the platform screen doors.

Two-Layer Approach for Collision Irrelevance. KUTS introducing two distinct hash computations (H using the key seeds and H' using the outputs of H) provides the following security properties. First, collision-based attacks on KUTS-output keys do not breach the security of the KUTS key chain because of the separation of the two hashes, as finding a collision of one hash does not also yield a collision in the other hash. As it is generally easier to find a collision than the exact hash input, this property makes KUTS more secure and thwarts many collision-based threats that has been studied to break hash algorithms. Thus, for many one-way functions, e.g., SHA-256 hash that we used in our instantiation implementation, the state-of-the-art attackers are forced to resort to brute-force. Second, it enables the additional protection of key seeds, as the key seeds are separate from H' and are not directly used to generate the keys that are actually being used for train communications. We investigate this further in Sect. 5.2.

Two-Seed Approach for Compromise Resilience. In addition to separating the key chain from the CBTC-driving keys, the train's key seed and the station's key seed are independent and originate from separate entities. Therefore, even if either of them gets compromised (which by itself is a difficult task, as the train key seed is stored and computed inside the train vehicle with no need for networking, and there is a mature set of digital cryptography techniques that can be used to ensure confidentiality of the train-station exchange for the station's seed, e.g., using the current before-update key), the entropy for the other key seed still holds against the attacker. Section 5.2 investigates this property further against varying attacker capabilities.

5.2   Security Strength Analyses

We analyze the security strength of KUTS, against an attacker whose goal is to learn the key as described in Sect. 3.3, and use the metric of entropy which quantifies how random the value is against an unauthorized attacker [27,28] to abstract away from the key length and other implementation details (and the corresponding information leakage). The *entropy* of a discrete random value α, whose sample size is $\mathcal{S}$, is $\mathcal{H}(\alpha)$, and $\mathcal{H}(\alpha) = -\sum_{i \in \mathcal{S}} \Pr_i \log(\Pr_i)$ where $\Pr_i$ is the probability of i occurring; if the logarithm is base-2, then $\mathcal{H}(\alpha)$ is in bits. The entropy $\mathcal{H}$ becomes additive across independent random values. For example, if α is a sequence of independent uniformly-distributed bits (standard practice for digital keys) that are n bits long, then $\Pr[\alpha = \gamma] = \frac{1}{2^{\mathcal{H}(\alpha)}} = \frac{1}{2^n}$, $\forall \gamma \in \mathcal{S}$, and it takes the attacker $2^{\mathcal{H}(\alpha)-1} = 2^{n-1}$ trials to guess the correct α in expectation.

Definition 1. Given any function f, y_f is the entropy of the output of f, and x_f is the entropy of the input of f. In other words, if $\beta = f(\alpha)$, $y_f = \mathcal{H}(\beta)$ and $x_f = \mathcal{H}(\alpha)$.

In our instantiation, $x_f > y_f$ for both $f = H$ and $f = H'$, because both H and H' compress information (lossy) and have longer inputs than outputs. We initially assume that the keys, both k_j^i and k^j, $\forall j \in \mathcal{S}$, $\forall i \in \mathcal{T}$, are secure. However, we take a step-by-step approach to introduce stronger threat scenarios (under our threat model in Sect. 3.3) to break the assumption and show that KUTS still remains secure and the key random; the rest of the section is organized in the increasing order of attacker capability/difficulty. Through this analysis, we highlight the effectiveness of the separation and provide insights helpful for choosing the parameters for KUTS, such as the key seed length.

General Security Strength of KUTS. For static keys, the attacker only needs to breach the key that is being used for the train networking, and the entropy is $y_{H'}$.

In contrast, KUTS dynamically updates the keys. Because it separates the key chain and the key used for CBTC, as described in Sect. 5.1, and the computations are done locally within the KUTS machines, the attacker needs to jointly attack H and H' (as H is beyond H'), and the cost of doing so is x_H. For example, against our implementation instantiation described in Fig. 4, $x_H = \mathcal{H}(k_{j-1}^i, k^j) = \mathcal{H}(k_{j-1}^i) + \mathcal{H}(k^j)$ where the last equality comes from k_{j-1}^i and k^j being independent to each other. KUTS key chain remains secure if x_H is positive, because the *exact* input is required and KUTS is irrelevant to hash collisions; in fact, the following paragraphs study when parts of KUTS is compromised, starting from when H' is breached and $y_{H'} = 0$.

Outsider Attacker Breaching H'

Depending on the use of the KUTS-driven CBTC keys (H') and the computational capability of an attacker, the attacker can learn H'. Suppose this happens and $y_{H'} = 0$. If static keys were used, the key is compromised, and the attacker has access to the CBTC communications.

On the other hand, against KUTS dynamic keys, the attack is mitigated and its breach impact is limited to the following key update, as the rest of the KUTS is still secure, e.g., $x_{H'} = \mathcal{H}(k_j^i, k^j) > 0$ for our instantiation, because H' is a one-way function and is not injective, i.e., many-to-one mapping. Section 4.3 also provides a fall-back mechanism against temporarily compromised keys.

Infrastructure Compromise and Breaching k^j

An insider attacker who compromised the train infrastructure can learn k^j, for example, by attacking the key exchange between the station-side KUTS machine and the train. In cases where a capable insider attacker breaches the key k^j, i.e., $\mathcal{H}(k^j) = 0$, KUTS still remains secure because of the randomness in k_{j-1}^i and $x_H = \mathcal{H}(k_{j-1}^i) > 0$.

Train Compromise and Breaching k_{j-1}^i

It is difficult to compromise k_{j-1}^i because this key does not leave the train's KUTS engine, which also performs the local computations for KUTS updates. Nevertheless, even if k_{j-1}^i is compromised and $\mathcal{H}(k_{j-1}^i) = 0$, $x_H = \mathcal{H}(k^j) > 0$ and the security strength depends on k^j.

6   Implementation Analyses

To estimate the computational overhead, we implement KUTS on three machines: *i7* (Intel i7 64-bit processor at 2.5 GHz, 16 GB RAM, Mac OS), *i5* (Intel i5 64-bit processor at 1.6 GHz, 16 GB RAM, Linux OS), and *AVR* (Atmel AVR 8-bit microcontroller at 8 MHz, 4 KB RAM). i7 and i5 machines are widely used for general-purpose computers, and AVR microcontrollers are playing greater roles in modern computing as more devices and applications, especially those constrained in resource, require logic and connectivity to realize Internet of Things (IoT); even with the processing-limited AVR and no effort to optimize, KUTS overhead is marginal as discussed in Sect. 6.2. SHA-256-based hash algorithms (for KUTS H and H') are adapted from OpenSSL, which provides a commercial-grade open-source library, widely adopted on modern-day Internet and other digital transactions.

6.1   Computational Overhead from Hashing

Figure 5(a) and (b) show the average processing overhead of computing a hash, respectively, in clock cycles and in seconds while varying the hash input size. Both i7 and i5 use 64-bit processors and have comparable processing overhead in clock cycles (e.g., i5 is slightly more efficient, requiring 3–10% less number of

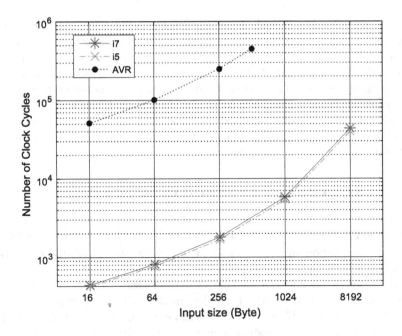

(a) Computation overhead in clock cycles

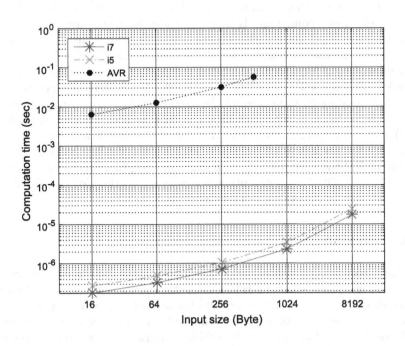

(b) Computation overhead in time

Fig. 5. KUTS hash computation overhead

clock cycles to compute a hash depending on the input size), and the primary difference between i7 and i5 in seconds is derived from the clock frequency. On the other hand, the AVR significantly requires greater overhead in both clock cycles and seconds; it requires 118–150 times more clock cycles than i5, depending on the hash input size, and 114–139 times greater than i7. The difference becomes even greater in seconds due to the processing frequency difference; AVR at least takes 3.578×10^4 times longer than i7, and the difference in computational time becomes greater than four orders of magnitude. We leverage these measurements to estimate the cost of KUTS in Sect. 6.2.

6.2   KUTS Cost Analysis Between Train and Attacker

As described in Sect. 4.2, to implement KUTS, we use SHA-256 for both H and H', and the input for H is a concatenation of k^j and k^i_{j-1} while the input for H' is a concatenation of k^i_{j-1} and k^i_j. Thus, we focus on 512-bit or 64-Byte inputs. For KUTS, the overhead is dominated by the two hash computations of H and H' (the overhead from memory-based processing, i.e., read/write of the bit registry, is relatively minor). For a legitimate train, the computation takes $2 \times 326.9 = 653.8$ ns for i7, $2 \times 482.4 = 964.8$ ns for i5, and $2 \times 12.57 = 25.14$ ms for AVR. Even if the train system requires the security measure to be entirely modular to the rest of the system and uses the AVR microcontroller, the KUTS processing time overhead (of less than 3% of a second) is dominated by the time spent at the trains with customer and physical-operation-related delays (which are in the order of seconds) and is thus acceptable for deployment.

On the other hand, the attacker cannot access the hash chain and, not having the inputs of the hash, need to resort to brute-force, as described in Sect. 5.1. For example, in our implementation using the most capable i7, the attacker cost to break KUTS is $2 \times 2^{512-1} \times 326.9$ ns $= 1.409 \times 10^{140}$ years in expectation. In contrast, depending on the design of the train operations, our key updates can occur in the order of minutes (for urban metros) or hours (for rural inter-city trains). Our result corroborates with the general belief that SHA is secure enough (KUTS is also insensitive to collisions) and is thus widely used for security-sensitive digital transactions such as finance and crypto-currency (as discussed in Sect. 4.2); it will take a computing power as big as the globally distributed network of bit-coin miners to compete with the KUTS updates.

7   Conclusion

To achieve secure key establishment for train-to-infrastructure networking, we develop a key update scheme KUTS that mitigates the key breach by limiting the breach impact to the current key and builds resiliency against system compromise. KUTS design is tightly interwound with the inherent train applications (the hierarchical architecture for the vehicle-to-infrastructure CBTC communications and the differences in physical operations at and between stations, which lead to the logical separation of KUTS key update and use). We also provide a temporary fall-back mechanism and a detection scheme, which can be used to trigger a failure-response mechanism. We build KUTS based on the state-of-the-art pseudo-random generator function (SHA-256 in our instantiation) and analyze its security strength and properties while keeping the security overhead marginal (a small fraction of a second per KUTS operation).

Acknowledgments. This work was supported by the National Research Foundation (NRF), Prime Ministers Office, Singapore, under its National Cybersecurity R&D Programme (Award No. NRF2014NCR-NCR001-31) and administered by the National Cybersecurity R&D Directorate and by the Human-Centered Cyber-physical Systems Programme at the Advanced Digital Sciences Center from Singapore's Agency for Science, Technology and Research (A*STAR).

References

1. Heddebaut, M., Mili, S., Sodoyer, D., Jacob, E., Aguado, M., Zamalloa, C.P., Lopez, I., Deniau, V.: Towards a resilient railway communication network against electromagnetic attacks. In: TRA - Transport Research Arena, France, p. 10p, April 2014. https://hal.archives-ouvertes.fr/hal-01061258

2. He, H.: Passenger wi-fi freezes third Shenzhen metro train in a week. South China Morning Post. http://www.scmp.com/news/china/article/1078165/passenger-wi-fi-freezes-third-shenzhen-metro-train-week

3. Squatriglia, C.: Polish teen hacks his citys trams, chaos ensues. Wired. http://www.wired.com/2008/01/polish-teen-hac/

4. Greenber, A.: Hackers remotely kill a jeep on the highwaywith me in it. Wired. http://www.wired.com/2015/07/hackers-remotely-kill-jeep-highway/

5. Finkle, J., Woodall, B.: Researcher says can hack GM's OnStar app, open vehicle, start engine, Reuters. http://www.reuters.com/article/2015/07/30/us-gm-hacking-idUSKCN0Q42FI20150730

6. Foster, I., Prudhomme, A., Koscher, K., Savage, S.: Fast and vulnerable: a story of telematic failures. In: 9th USENIX Workshop on Offensive Technologies (WOOT 2015). USENIX Association, Washington, D.C., August 2015. http://blogs.usenix.org/conference/woot15/workshop-program/presentation/foster

7. Checkoway, S., McCoy, D., Kantor, B., Anderson, D., Shacham, H., Savage, S., Koscher, K., Czeskis, A., Roesner, F., Kohno, T.: Comprehensive experimental analyses of automotive attack surfaces. In: Proceedings of the 20th USENIX Conference on Security, SEC 2011, p. 6. USENIX Association, Berkeley (2011). http://dl.acm.org/citation.cfm?id=2028067.2028073

8. American Public Transportation Association (APTA): Securing control and communications systems in rail transmit environments, part II: Defining a security zone architecture for rail transit and protecting critical zones, Recommended Practice, ATPA-SS-CCS-RP-002-13 (2013)

9. American Public Transportation Association (APTA): Cybersecurity considerations for public transit, Recommended Practice, ATPA-SS-ECS-RP-001-14 (2014)

10. Deniau, V.: Overview of the European project security of railways in Europe against electromagnetic attacks (secret). IEEE Electromagn. Compat. Mag. **3**(4), 80–85 (2014)

11. Chang, S.-Y., Tran, B.A.N., Hu, Y.-C., Jones, D.L.: Jamming with power boost: leaky waveguide vulnerability in train systems. In: 2015 IEEE 21st International Conference on Parallel and Distributed Systems (ICPADS), pp. 37–43, December 2015

12. Lopez, I., Aguado, M.: Cyber security analysis of the european train control system. IEEE Commun. Mag. **53**(10), 110–116 (2015)

13. Hartong, M., Goel, R., Wijesekera, D.: Key management requirements for positive train control communications security. In: Proceedings of the 2006 IEEE/ASME Joint Rail Conference, pp. 253–262, April 2006

14. Reiter, M., Stubblebine, S.: Resilient authentication using path independence. IEEE Trans. Comput. **47**(12), 1351–1362 (1998)

15. Zhao, M., Smith, S.W., Nicol, D.M.: Aggregated path authentication for efficient BGP security. In: Proceedings of the 12th ACM Conference on Computer and Communications Security, CCS 2005, pp. 128–138. ACM, New York (2005). http://doi.acm.org/10.1145/1102120.1102139

16. Kim, T.H.-J., Basescu, C., Jia, L., Lee, S.B., Hu, Y.-C., Perrig, A.: Lightweight source authentication and path validation. In: Proceedings of the 2014 ACM Conference on SIGCOMM, SIGCOMM 2014, pp. 271–282. ACM, New York (2014). http://doi.acm.org/10.1145/2619239.2626323

17. Blass, E.-O., Elkhiyaoui, K., Molva, R.: Tracker: security and privacy for RFID-based supply chains. In: 18th Annual Network and Distributed System Security Symposium NDSS 2011, 6–9 February 2011, San Diego, CA, USA (2011). http://www.eurecom.fr/publication/3233. Accessed Feb 2011

18. Elkhiyaoui, K., Blass, E.-O., Molva, R.: CHECKER: on-site checking in RFID-based supply chains. In: Proceedings of the Fifth ACM Conference on Security and Privacy in Wireless and Mobile Networks, WISEC 2012, pp. 173–184. ACM, New York (2012). http://doi.acm.org/10.1145/2185448.2185471

19. Cai, S., Li, Y., Zhao, Y.: Distributed path authentication for dynamic RFID-enabled supply chains. In: Gritzalis, D., Furnell, S., Theoharidou, M. (eds.) Information Security and Privacy Research. SEC 2012. IFIPAICT, vol. 376, pp. 501–512. Springer, Heidelberg (2012)

20. Cai, S., Deng, R.H., Li, Y., Zhao, Y.: A new framework for privacy of RFID path authentication. In: Bao, F., Samarati, P., Zhou, J. (eds.) ACNS 2012. LNCS, vol. 7341, pp. 473–488. Springer, Heidelberg (2012). doi:10.1007/978-3-642-31284-7_28

21. Challal, Y., Bouabdallah, A., Hinard, Y.: Efficient multicast source authentication using layered hash-chaining scheme. In: 29th Annual IEEE International Conference on Local Computer Networks, pp. 411–412, November 2004

22. Fredman, M.L., Komlós, J., Szemerédi, E.: Storing a sparse table with 0(1) worst case access time. J. ACM **31**(3), 538–544 (1984). http://doi.acm.org/10.1145/828.1884

23. Ohkubo, M., Suzuki, K., Kinoshita, S.: Cryptographic approach to "privacy-friendly" tags. In: RFID Privacy Workshop (2003)

24. Whyte, W., Weimerskirch, A., Kumar, V., Hehn, T.: A security credential management system for V2V communications. In: Vehicular Networking Conference (VNC), pp. 1–8. IEEE, December 2013

25. Rajendran, J., Sinanoglu, O., Karri, R.: Is split manufacturing secure? In: Design, Automation Test in Europe Conference Exhibition (DATE), pp. 1259–1264, March 2013

26. Imeson, F., Emtenan, A., Garg, S., Tripunitara, M.: Securing computer hardware using 3D integrated circuit (IC) technology, split manufacturing for obfuscation. In: Presented as Part of the 22nd USENIX Security Symposium (USENIX Security 2013), pp. 495–510. USENIX, Washington, D.C. (2013). https://www.usenix.org/conference/usenixsecurity13/technical-sessions/presentation/imeson

27. Shannon, C.E.: A mathematical theory of communication. Bell Syst. Tech. J. **27**(3), 379–423 (1948). http://dx.doi.org/10.1002/j.1538-7305.1948.tb01338.x

28. Shannon, C.E.: Communication theory of secrecy systems. Bell Syst. Tech. J. **28**(4), 656–715 (1949)

Faulty Node Repair and Dynamically Spawned Black Hole Search

Wei Shi[1(✉)], Mengfei Peng[2], Jean-Pierre Corriveau[3],
and William Lee Croft[3]

[1] School of Information Technology, Carleton University, Ottawa, Canada
wei.shi@carleton.ca
[2] Aurora Technology Development Inc., Toronto, Canada
mengfei@auroratd.com
[3] School of Computer Science, Carleton University, Ottawa, Canada
jeanpier@scs.carleton.ca, LeeCroft@cmail.carleton.ca

Abstract. New threats to networks are constantly arising. This justifies protecting network assets and mitigating the risk associated with attacks. In a distributed environment, researchers aim, in particular, at eliminating faulty network entities. More specifically, much research has been conducted on locating a single static black hole, which is defined as a network site whose existence is known a priori and that disposes of any incoming data without leaving any trace of this occurrence. However, the prevalence of faulty nodes requires an algorithm able to (a) identify faulty nodes that can be repaired without human intervention and (b) locate black holes, which are taken to be faulty nodes whose repair does require human intervention. In this paper, we consider a specific attack model that involves multiple faulty nodes that can be repaired by mobile software agents, as well as a virus v that can infect a previously repaired faulty node and turn it into a black hole. We refer to the task of repairing multiple faulty nodes and pointing out the location of the black hole as the *Faulty Node Repair and Dynamically Spawned Black Hole Search*. We first analyze the attack model we put forth. We then explain (a) how to identify whether a node is either (1) a normal node or (2) a repairable faulty node or (3) the black hole that has been infected by virus v during the search/repair process and, (b) how to perform the correct relevant actions. These two steps constitute a complex task, which, we explain, significantly differs from the traditional *Black Hole Search*. We continue by proposing an algorithm to solve this problem in an asynchronous ring network with only one whiteboard (which resides in a node called the *homebase*). We prove the correctness of our solution and analyze its complexity by both theoretical analysis and experiment evaluation. We conclude that, using our proposed algorithm, $b + 4$ agents can repair all faulty nodes and locate the black hole infected by a virus v within finite time. Our algorithm works even when the number of faulty nodes b is unknown a priori.

Keywords: Faulty node repair · Black hole search · Mobile agent

© ICST Institute for Computer Sciences, Social Informatics and Telecommunications Engineering 2017
R. Deng et al. (Eds.): SecureComm 2016, LNICST 198, pp. 144–162, 2017.
DOI: 10.1007/978-3-319-59608-2_8

1   Introduction

Over the past few years, as cloud-based services have become prevalent, so has the need for effective diagnosis of all-too-frequent network anomalies and faults. As cloud servers involving multiple data centers are usually geographically dispersed (thus not physically coupled), locating a network fault physically may be expensive and difficult, if not impossible. Using software agents to locate and/or repair network faults becomes a reasonable solution and thus has attracted the attention of researchers, especially in distributed computing [31]. Many types of faults exist in a network, such as black holes (e.g., [9, 15, 19]), repairable black holes (e.g., [8, 12]), faulty agents (e.g., [5, 23]), etc. Among these, a *black hole* is a severe and pervasive problem. A black hole models a computer that is accidentally off-line or a network site in which a resident process (e.g., an unknowingly-installed virus) deletes any visiting agents or incoming data upon their arrival without leaving any observable trace [16].

In practice, many computer faults/virus cannot be completely removed by anti-virus software: After a repair, a previously infected node may still be more vulnerable than the ones that have never been infected, and can be easily reinfected. For instance, a hacker injects into a computer host a virus that can delete any incoming data and that may later be removed by an anti-virus agent. However, after repair, an unknown vulnerability remains on that host and it enables the hacker's next attack. Indeed, with fast spreading worms mentioned in [33] (such as W32/CodeRed, Linux/Slapper, W32/Blaster or Solaris/Sadmind), a host can be exploited only if the system has a vulnerability known a priori. Such virus behaviour is commonly referred to as *vulnerability dependency*. More generally, in cloud computing, the term vulnerability refers to the flaws in a system that allow an attack to be successful [25]. The vulnerability security issue has been widely discussed in research works such as [1, 6, 24].

Cooper *et al.* [8] first introduced a type of weaker black hole, which he called a *hole*, that eliminates any incoming data but can be repaired by the first encountering agent. Assuming vulnerability dependency, the hacker can then inject an even more powerful virus and turn this repaired host into a genuine (i.e., unrepairable without human intervention) black hole at some point in the future. Our work originates in that attack model. A black hole is still taken to be a node that is not repairable without human intervention. But to avoid any ambiguity around the term "hole", we will refer to a node with abnormalities that can be repaired by a software agent as a *faulty node* (rather than a hole). In this paper, we introduce the *Faulty Node Repair and Dynamically Spawned Black Hole Search problem* (*repair and search problem* for brevity).

In our new attack model, there are multiple faulty nodes. Each such node eliminates any incoming data and can be repaired upon being visited by an antivirus agent who, in effect, "dies" at the end of this repair. That is, following Cooper [8], we assume there is a cost for repairing a fault, namely, the repairing agent is unable to continue exploring the network. Furthermore, we assume that when multiple antivirus agents simultaneously enter a faulty node, they all die at the end of the repair.[1]. We assume this worst

---

[1] This is the worst case scenario, which we use to calculate, later in the paper, the theoretical maximum number of agents sacrificed to solve the problem.

case scenario for the design of our solution to the proposed repair and search problem. Obviously, fewer agents are required in less damaging cases.

In our attack model, a faulty node, once repaired, behaves like a normal one but remains vulnerable and can be infected again after attacked by what we call a *gray virus*. A *gray virus* (*GV* for brevity) is a piece of malicious software that can infect a repaired node (due to the latter's vulnerability) by residing in it and turning it into a black hole. In this paper, we consider what we call a one-stop *GV*, that is, a virus that permanently resides in the node it infects and thus cannot harm other nodes. (More generally, a *multi-stop gray virus* can infect multiple repaired nodes.) A *GV* is taken to have no destructive power on a normal node or link. Here, we consider a single one-stop *GV* that infects a single faulty node. That is, we consider searching for a single black hole. (More generally, there could be multiple black holes resulting from one or more multistop *GV s*.) Furthermore, in this paper, we specifically study the search and repair problem in an asynchronous ring network.

The solution we propose for this version of the repair and search problem uses a team of *mobile agents* to repair all faulty nodes and locate the single black hole (by marking the edges leading to it). These agents have limited computing capabilities and bounded storage. They all obey an identical set of behavioural rules (referred to as the "protocol"), and can move from a node to a neighbouring node. Also, these agents are anonymous (i.e., do not have distinct identifiers) and autonomous (i.e., each has its own computing and bounded memory capabilities). Such characteristics are systematically adopted for the traditional black hole location problem in computer networks.

Contrary to the traditional black hole search [32], in which all agents start in a network knowing a priori that there is one and only one black hole, in our proposed new attack model, a repaired faulty node can be infected again and turned into a black hole at any point in time (regardless of the agents traversing the network and trying to repair faulty nodes). That is, at what time a node becomes the black hole is unpredictable. Additionally, this unpredictable black hole may coexist with multiple faulty nodes. This drastically changes the nature of the black hole search problem in asynchronous networks. That is, the possible scenarios we must consider are significantly more complex than those associated with traditional black hole search. Let us briefly elaborate. To locate a black hole in traditional black hole search in an asynchronous network, there is a commonly used technique called *cautious walk*: a first agent has to leave a "mark" indicating a potential danger (e.g. a token or a whiteboard message) in its current node before it moves along a link potentially leading to the black hole. When a second agent sees this mark, it does not go to visit the same potentially dangerous node. This technique is used to minimize the loss of mobile agents. The cautious walk technique points to the fact that the only mechanism used to terminate a traditional black hole search algorithm is to let at least one agent survive and successfully traverse the entire network except one node. This only *unexplored* (i.e. never been visited by any agent) node is then declared to be the black hole. But when there are multiple faulty nodes in the network, even when more sophisticated communications between agents are available, none of the existing black hole search algorithms solve the repair and search problem. This is because, in these algorithms, there is no mechanism to distinguish a black hole from a faulty node. Consequently, given a faulty node would be treated the same way as the black hole, no agent is able to successfully explore $(n - 1)$ nodes and survive.

2 Related Work

The problem of finding the most efficient solution (with respect to time and minimum number of agents required) for the black hole search is studied in an edge-labeled undirected synchronous network using 2 co-located agents using the *face-to-face* communication model in [9–11, 26, 27]. Czyzowicz *et al.* [10] show any efficient solution is NP-hard, and propose a 9.3-approximation algorithm for it. Klasing *et al.* [27] prove that this problem is not a polynomial- time approximation within any constant factor less than $\frac{389}{388}$ (unless P = NP), and give a 6-approximation algorithm. Czyzowicz *et al.* present a $\frac{5}{3}$ -approximation algorithm in an arbitrary tree without a map in [9]. Furthermore, Klasing *et al.* [26] provide a $3\frac{3}{8}$ -approximation algorithm for an arbitrary network with the help of a network map.

The black hole search problem in an asynchronous network is much more complex and more significant in practice. Dobrev *et al.* [20] introduce an algorithm to locate the black hole in an un-oriented ring network with dispersed agents in $O(kn + n\log n)$ moves. For some other common interconnection networks, Dobrev *et al.* [13] present a general strategy to locate the black hole in $O(n)$ moves by using 2 co-located agents. Shi *et al.* [32] prove that 2 co-located agents, each with $O(1)$ tokens, can locate the black hole in $\Theta(n)$ moves for hyper- cube, torus and complete networks. Moreover, for an arbitrary unknown network graph with known n, Dobrev *et al.* [14] present an algorithm using $\Delta + 1$ agents, one token per agent and $O(\Delta^2 M^2 n^7)$ moves to locate the black hole. Here, M is the total number of edges of the graph. In an arbitrary network, Dobrev *et al.* [17] prove that in the whiteboard model, the black hole search problem can be solved with $\Delta + 1$ agents in $\Theta(n^2)$ moves without network maps. Balamohan *et al.* [3] prove that in an unknown graph with a constant number of agents, at least $\Delta + 2$ agents and at least 3 tokens are necessary in total to locate the black hole, where Δ is the maximum node degree.

Multiple black hole search (MBHS for brevity) problem has been studied by Cooper *et al.* [7] in synchronous networks. Later, the same authors [8] present solutions to the multiple repairable black holes (faulty nodes) problem. D'Emidio *et al.* [12] study the same problem under the same condition as [8] with a change of one assumption: if more than one agent enters the same faulty node at the same time, all agents die. Flocchini *et al.* tackle the MBHS problem via a *subway model* in [21]. The authors use carriers (the subway trains) to transport agents (the passengers) from node to node (subway stops), and the black holes no longer affect the carriers and can only eliminate the agents. After assuming that the graph is strongly connected after all black holes have been removed, Kosowski *et al.* [28] study a synchronous network with arbitrary size, while Flocchini *et al.* [22] study the MBHS problem with asynchronous dispersed agents.

Cai *et al.* [5] study a network decontamination problem with a black virus, which is related to both black hole search and intruder capture problems. The authors define a black virus as a dangerous process that is initially resident in the network. A black virus behaves like a moving black hole that can destroy any arriving agent and can move from node to node. However, unlike a black hole that cannot be repaired or destroyed, a black virus can be eliminated when it enters into a node with an anti-viral agent. Luccio *et al.* [30] consider a mobile agents rendezvous problem in spite of a malicious agent, which is similar to [18], which rendezvouses agents in a ring in spite of a black hole. While a malicious agent in [30] can only block other agents from visiting its resident node and can move in the network at arbitrary speed, a black hole in [30] can delete all visiting agents but it cannot move. Královič *et al.* [29] research a periodic data retrieval problem using a whiteboard in asynchronous ring networks with a malicious host. The malicious host can manipulate the agent by storing and copying it and releasing the replica later to confuse other agents, or by killing an agent. Bampas *et al.* [4] improve this result by showing that at least 4 agents are required when the malicious host is a gray hole, which can choose to behave as a black hole or as a safe node, and 5 agents are necessary when the whiteboard on the malicious host is unreliable.

3 Premises

In this section, we present our assumptions for the solution we propose for the *Faulty Node Repair and Dynamically Spawned Black Hole Search problem* in an asynchronous ring network.

Let $G = (E, V)$ denote an edge-labeled undirected ring network, where E is the set of edges, V is the set of network nodes and n ($n = |V|$) denotes the number of nodes in G. $(u, v) \in E$ represents the link from u to v, where $u \in V$ and $v \in V$ and u to v are neighbouring nodes. The links and nodes in the network enforce a FIFO rule, that is, mobile agents cannot overtake each other when traveling in the same direction over the same link or node. Without this assumption, systematical termination of a repair and search algorithm with minimal number of agents cannot be guaranteed.

Let $\mathcal{A}$ denote a group of k ($k \geq 2$) identical mobile agents initially waking up in the same node referred to as their *homebase (hb)*. This *homebase* is assumed to be safe in the ring network: it is neither faulty nor a black hole. These agents have limited computing capabilities and bounded storage[2], obey the same set of behavioural rules (the "protocol"), and can move from node to node via neighbouring nodes. We make no assumptions on the amount of time required by an agent's actions (e.g., computation or movement, etc.) except that it is finite. Thus, the agents are *asynchronous*. Also, these agents are anonymous (i.e., have no ID) and know the topology of the network in which they reside. Most importantly, these agents have no knowledge of the number of faulty nodes.

We let $V_f \subseteq V$ denote the static, i.e., fixed a priori set of b ($b < n$) faulty nodes. Once a faulty node has been repaired, it is referred to as a *repaired node*. We

---

[2] Minimal storage just sufficient to keep track of the number of moves an agent has performed during each exploration of a new node.

emphasize that, unlike a normal node, a repaired node can be infected by a *GV* and turn into a black hole.

We postulate that a *whiteboard* [16] (i.e., shared memory) in the *hb* offers the *only* means of communication between agents. This whiteboard in *hb* can be accessed by agents in *fair mutual exclusion* [2].

We assume the network is an un-oriented ring, that is, there is no agreement on a common *sense of direction* among the agents [16]. However, using the whiteboard in *hb*, all agents shall be able to agree on what corresponds to the clockwise direction (also referred to as the left direction) and the counterclockwise direction (also referred to as the right direction) of the ring. In order to ease the understanding of the algorithm description, N_0, N_1, ... N_{n-1} are used to label the nodes of the ring sequentially using the left direction starting from the *hb*. Such labelling is only used for explanation and algorithm proof purpose; it is not required by our algorithm per se.

Observation 1. *When a repaired node gets reinfected by a GV only after all faulty nodes have been repaired, the Repair and Search problem becomes a faulty node repair problem followed by a single black hole search problem for which all possible locations of the black hole are known a priori since only repaired nodes can be reinfected.*

In this special case, the proposed problem becomes easier to solve than a traditional single black hole search problem. Consequently, this special case is of no interest here. That is, in this paper, we are only interested in studying the scenario in which a one-stop *GV* may infect a repaired node before the last faulty node is repaired. As previously mentioned, in contrast with the traditional black hole search, it is the coexistence of a black hole with at least one faulty node that makes the *Repair and Search* problem complex. We present a solution to this challenging problem in the next section.

4   Algorithm and Solutions

4.1   General Description

The status of each node in a network can be either "faulty" or "repaired" or "black hole" or "normal" or "unknown". The general goal of each agent is to explore a new node (we call it a status *unknown* node or just *unknown* node) and update the whiteboard upon returning to the *hb*. During this exploration, an agent may die after repairing a faulty node, or in a black hole or survive and successfully return to the *hb* and restart the procedure of exploring a new node. This new exploration and checking the whiteboard get repeated until all nodes' status are marked as either a repaired node, or a black hole or a normal node. In order to prevent multiple agents die in the same faulty node or black hole, we develop a status marking process as part of agents' protocol to execute. The following paragraph and Tables 1 and 2 explain such a process:

Upon an agent A wakes up at hb, it initializes the whiteboard as shown in Table 1. All nodes are *unknown* nodes. Agent A puts a *leaving* mark (?) in the cell of First Agent for node N_1, and then goes to visit node N_1. Upon its arrival, agent A returns to hb immediately. Once A returns to hb, agent A changes the leaving mark to a *returned* mark ($\sqrt{}$) (Table 2 shows an example).

Table 1. Homebase whiteboard initial state

Node list	First agent	Second agent	Third agent	Fourth agent	Repaired node list
N_1					
...					
N_{i-1}					
N_i					
...					
N_{n-j}					
N_{n-j+1}					
...					
N_{n-1}					

Table 2. An example of how agents indicate their status.

Node list	First agent	Second agent
N_1	$\sqrt{}(l)$	
N_2	$\times$	$\sqrt{}(l)$
...		
N_i	$?(l)$	$?(l)$
...		
N_{n-2}	$?(r)$	
N_{n-1}	$\sqrt{}(r)$	$?(r)$

By repeating this process, agent A explores nodes $N_2, N_3, \cdots, N_i$. Other agents such as B may wake up any time during A's exploration. When B sees a leaving mark for node N_i. Agent B goes to node N_i to confirm the status of node N_i. B puts a leaving mark under Second Agent column on node N_i. Upon its arrival, agent B returns to hb immediately and changes the leaving mark into a returned mark. By the time agent B returns, agent A may have returned (i.e. A's mark is changed from leaving to returned), which means node N_i is not a faulty node. Otherwise, agent B concludes that agent A has died after repairing a faulty node N_i. In this situation, B will change the *leaving* mark (?) of A into a *died* mark ($\times$) (see Scenario S5 in Table 3) and mark N_i as a repaired node under the Repaired Node List column.

While agents A and B are out exploring in the left direction, other agents C and D may wake up. C and D immediately start exploring the ring in the right direction to visit node $N_{n-1}, N_{n-2}, ..., N_{n-j}$. This mechanism is designed to avoid unnecessary loss of agents (i.e. the black hole has already appeared, sending agents to the same direction will lead to agent loss). As long as there is one unknown node showed in the whiteboard, a newly

Table 3. Agents leaving and returning to the homebase scenarios as marked on the whiteboard.

Scenarios	First agent	Second agent	Targeted node is	No. of status unknown agents
S1	? (*l/r*)		Unknown	1
S2	√ (*l/r*)		Safe	0
S3	? (*l/r*)	? (*l/r*)	Unknown	2
S4	√ (*l/r*)	? (*l/r*)	Safe	1
S5	×	√ (*l/r*)	Repaired node	0 (1 died)
S6	√ (*l/r*)	√ (*l/r*)	Safe	0

?: a status unknown agent that left to explore a node.

×: an agent died either in a black hole or after repairing a faulty node.

√: an agent that has returned to *hb*

awake agent will not go to the direction, in which there are already 2 agents. Furthermore, as long as the ring has one unknown nodes and 4 agents are currently exploring a new node, a newly waking up agent will just wait at *hb* until at least 1 of the 4 agents returns. This mechanism is used to minimize the total agent moves, that is to minimize the network traffic. The details are described in Procedure *New Node Exploration* (Subsect. 4.2).

When an agent sees that there is only one unknown node left in the network, it starts executing Procedure *Find the Meeting Node*. Eventually 2 agents enter the last unknown node from the left direction and 2 agents from the right one. If one of these 4 agents, say agent E dies in the black hole (just appeared) on its way to check the last unknown node, this last unknown node is not a black hole. Hence, at least 1 out of the 4 agents left to explore the last unknown node can return to the *hb* successfully. If the last unexplored node is the black hole, we need a mechanism to make sure at least one agent is able to safely return to the *hb* and concludes that the last unexplored node. This mechanism is described in Procedure *Find the Meeting Node* (Subsect. 4.3) and Procedure *Double Check* (Algorithm 3).

4.2   Procedure New Node Exploration

Whenever an agent returns to *hb*, it scans the whiteboard. It goes through the node list from the top to the bottom. The agent may find a node to be: *unexplored*, that is a node that has never been visited by any agent, namely, no mark on the whiteboard (i.e. the row of the node in Table 1 is empty); or *repaired*, that is a node that has a √ under the Second Agent column and a × mark under the First Agent column (i.e. the Second Agent returned but the first one did not. See Scenario S5 in Table 3); or *safe*, that is a non-faulty node that has a √ under the First Agent column (i.e. the First Agent has returned. See Scenario S2, S4 and S6 in Table 3); or *unknown*, that is a node that has a ? under under the First Agent column or both First and Second Agent columns. (i.e. both agents have left but no agent ever returned. See Scenarios S1 and S3 in Table 3). The status of a node is considered to be *known* if it is either *safe* or *repaired*.

While scanning the nodes list in the whiteboard, an agent A counts the number pd_l of ?(*l*) if there is any unexplored node. It determines the next step accordingly.

If A cannot find an unexplored node, the agent will finish searching the whole list and execute Procedure Find The Meeting Node. When at most one agent has left in the left direction ($pd_l < 2$), agent A leaves in the left direction to visit an unexplored node or confirm the status of an unknown node. When $pd_l = 2$, the agent counts the number pd_r of ?(r). If $pd_r < 2$, agent A leaves in the right direction. When 2 agents are out in each direction ($pd_l = 2\&pd_r = 2$), agent A has to wait at hb until one returns. If node N_i is the last unexplored node, once N_i is explored, it becomes a *meeting node*, that is the last unexplored node in the network.

4.3   Procedure Find the Meeting Node

When an agent A cannot find an unexplored node in the whiteboard, it executes Procedure Double Check if there are no more unknown nodes. Otherwise, A counts the number of status unknown agents pd in the entire list and executes the following:

1. When $pd > 4$, A waits at hb.
2. When $pd = 4$ and the 4 status unknown agents are not on the same node, A waits at hb.
3. When $pd = 4$ and the 4 status unknown agents are marked on the same node, A starts Procedure Double Check immediately.
4. When $pd < 4$ and there are no nodes in Scenario S1: a. If all status unknown agents are not on the same node, A waits at hb; b. If all status unknown agents are on the same node, A goes to that node.

Algorithm 1. NEW NODE EXPLORATION

1: initialize the whiteboard to Table 1
2: **loop**
3:     **if** an unexplored node N_i is found **then**
4:         count the number pd_l of status unknown agents out in the left direction ?(l)
5:     **else if** no unexplored node is found **then**
6:         execute FIND THE MEETING NODE
7:     **end if**
8:     **if** $pd_l = 0$ **then**
9:         go to node N_i
10:     **else if** $pd_l = 1$ and node N_{i-1} is in Scenario S1 **then**
11:         go to node N_{i-1}
12:     **else if** $pd_l = 1$ and node N_{i-1} is in Scenario S4 **then**
13:         go to node N_i
14:     **else if** $pd = 2$ **then**
15:         count the number pd_r of ?(r)
16:         leave in the right direction when $pd_r < 2$, otherwise wait at hb
17:     **end if**
18:     upon arriving, return to hb immediately, then change own ?(l/r) into $\sqrt{}(l/r)$
19:     **if** the current agent is the Second Agent and the First Agent is ? **then**
20:         change the ? of the First Agent to ×
21:     **end if**
22: **end loop**

---

5. When $pd < 4$ and there are one/two nodes in Scenario S1, A goes to a node which can be reached without passing through a status unknown agent, otherwise, A waits at hb until one returns.

If A returns to hb from a node with 4 status unknown agents, it marks this node as the "Last" node.

4.4 Procedure "Double Check"

As detailed in Procedure Find the Meeting Node, an agent A will only start executing Procedure Double Check when A sees that all nodes' statuses are known (either safe or repaired) or all nodes' statuses are known save for one. In this latter scenario, according to line 10 in Procedure Find the Meeting Node, four ?s are on that node.

Agent A continues this task by marking all repaired nodes in Table 1. A then searches the Third Agent column:

1. If there are 2 status unknown agents in this column, A wait at hb until one of them returns;
2. If there is only 1 status unknown agent, A searches this column from top to bottom until it finds an empty cell. If the empty cell is above the status unknown agent, A puts a $?(l)$ in the cell, and then goes to the node. Otherwise A leaves in the right direction after putting down a $?(r)$. A returns to hb immediately after visiting this node. It changes the ? to a $\sqrt{}$.

Algorithm 2. FIND THE MEETING NODE

```
 1: loop
 2:     count the number of status unknown agents pd
 3:     if every node is known to be safe or repaired then
 4:         execute Double Check
 5:     end if
 6:     if pd > 4 or pd = 4 and the 4 ? are not on the same node  then
 7:         wait at hb
 8:     else if pd = 4 and the 4 status unknown agents are on the same node  then
 9:         execute Double Check
10:     else if pd < 4 and no node is in Scenario S1 then
11:         if  all status unknown agents are not on the same node then
12:             wait at hb
13:         else if all status unknown agents are on the same node  then
14:             go to this node, and ensure 2 agents from the left direction and 2 from
                    the right
15:         end if
16:     else if pd < 4 and one/more than one node is in Scenario S1  then
17:         go to a reachable node in Scenario S1, otherwise wait at hb
18:     end if
19:     upon arriving, return to hb
20:     if hb is reached and the cell of the Third Agent for the same node is ? then
21:         change the third ?(l/r) into ×, mark this node "Last"
22:     end if
23: end loop
```

---

3. If there is only 1 status unknown agent and no empty cell in the Third Agent column, the node with the only status unknown agent is the black hole.

5   Theoretical Correctness and Complexity Analysis

Lemma 1. *There can be no more than 4 status unknown agents co-exist in the network as long as at least one node has not been marked on the whiteboard by any agent. At least 1 of these 4 agents will return to hb.*

Proof. In the homebase *hb*, as long as an agent *A* can find an unexplored node in the node list, it always needs to explore a new node (by executing Procedure New Node Exploration) before it executes any other procedure.

An agent *A* always searches the node list starting from the top first, if at most one agent have left in the left direction, *A* will also leave in the left direction. Otherwise it searches the node list starting from the bottom. Hence, there will never be more than 2 status unknown agents leaving in the left direction. Similarly, when *A* searches from bottom to top of the node list, *A* leaves in the right direction if at most one agent has left in the right direction. If *A* finds 2 agents have left in both left and right directions, *A* will wait at *hb* until Table 1 is changed by a returned agent (see Line 16 in Procedure New Node Exploration). Consequently, there will never be an occasion in which any agent will leave *hb* when there are two ?s on each side of it. Hence, there cannot be more than 4 status unknown agents as long as at least one node is unexplored.

Algorithm 3. DOUBLE CHECK

 1: search the repaired node list
 2: **if** the list is blank **then**
 3:     mark all repaired nodes in the list
 4: **end if**
 5: **while** the black hole has not been located **do**
 6:     search the Third Agent column
 7:     **if** there are 2 ? in this column **then**
 8:         wait at *hb* until an agent returns
 9:     **else if** there is 1 ? in this column **then**
10:         search this column from top to bottom until an empty cell is found
11:         **if** the empty cell is above the ? **then**
12:             go left to the node, upon arriving, return to *hb* immediately
13:         **else if** the empty cell is below the ? **then**
14:             search this column from top to bottom until an empty cell is found, go to the node
15:         **else if** an empty cell cannot be found **then**
16:             the black hole is determined to be the node with ?
17:         **end if**
18:     **else if** there is no ? in this column **then**
19:         search this column from top to bottom until an empty cell is found, go to the node
20:     **end if**
21: **end while**
22: ALGORITHM TERMINATES

We now prove that at least 1 of these 4 agents will return to *hb* eventually. It is trivial to observe that all the explored nodes are in one or two consecutive sections in a ring: when there is no unexplored node remaining in the ring, all explored nodes are in one consecutive section; otherwise, the two sections of explored nodes are separated at each end by the *hb* and a consecutive section of unexplored nodes. We call these two sections the left part and the right part. When there are 4 status unknown agents in the network, it can only be the case that 2 are in the left part and 2 in the right part. According to our assumptions, we know that once the black hole appears, it can only exist either in the left part, or in the right part.

Clearly if the black hole has not appeared yet, the two second-agents (1 on each side) in both parts will return to *hb* traversing through the section of the ring with consecutive explored nodes while the two first-agents (1 on each side) may die if the last unexplored node happens to be a faulty node. If the black hole appears in the left part, the second-agent in the right part will return successfully and the two agents in the left part die in the black hole. Similarly, if the black hole is in the right part, the second-agent in the left part will return while the other three die. In summary, no matter when the black hole appears and no matter where the black hole is, in the process of exploring the last an unexplored node, at least 1 of the 4 status unknown agents will return to the *hb*.

Lemma 2. *At most 5 status unknown agents coexist during the time the at least node is being explored. At least 1 of these 5 status unknown agents will return to hb.*

Proof. When the last unexplored node is being explored, according to Procedure New Node Exploration lines 16, only when there are fewer than 4 status unknown agents coexist in the network, a newly waking up agent will decide accordingly to go to the last unexplored node. After this agent has left, there are no more unexplored nodes in Table 1 and 4 status unknown agents exist in the ring at this moment. Furthermore, according to Procedure Find The Meeting Node lines 4 and 7, Procedure Double Check can be executed when either all nodes' statuses are known or when 4 status unknown agents are exploring the same node. This latter case is where the fifth agent is needed in the network. In all other cases, a newly waking up agent waits at *hb*.

If this last node is not a black hole, none of the 4 agents can return. According to Procedure Double Check a new agent enters the network. It goes to check each node as the fifth status unknown agent in the network. It conclude that the last node is the black hole according to Line 16 in Procedure Double Check. If this last node is not a black hole, the fifth Agent may die stepping into a black hole that just appeared. However, the two other agents that successfully explored the last unexplored node should return to the *hb* successfully. Eventually one of the two will die in the black hole while the other one survive after Therefore, at least 1 of the 5 status unknown agents will return to *hb*.

Lemma 3. *All faulty nodes will be repaired within finite time.*

Proof. If a faulty node N_x has not been repaired, its status shown in the whiteboard in *hb* must be either unexplored or unknown, that is the exploring agent either died after repairing a faulty node or in a back hole or has not returned to *hb* yet. If N_x is unexplored, according to Lines 4, 9 and 11 in Procedure New Node Exploration, an agent will explore N_x and any other unexplored node before it executing the procedure that can lead to the termination of the algorithm.

If N_x is a status unknown node, it can be either in Scenario S1 or S3. When N_x is in Scenario S1, according to Lines 11 and 13 in Procedure New Node Exploration, it is either the case that the First Agent returns to hb after exploring N_x and marks this node safe in the whiteboard; or a Second Agent will explore N_x and consequently change the marking in the whiteboard into Scenario S3.

When N_x is in Scenario S3, it may become S4-safe, S5-repaired, S6-safe, or stay S3-unknown. As proven in Lemma 1, at most 2 nodes may be in Scenario S3. When 2 nodes are in Scenario S3, at least one agent will return to hb, since there is only one black hole. This returning agent will change one of the two Scenario S3 nodes. Consequently, at most 1 node remains in Scenario S3.

For this last unknown node, a third and a fourth agent will go to this node according to Line 14 in Procedure Find the Meeting Node. As proven in Lemma 2, as long as this node is not a black hole, one of the 4 agents will return to hb. If this node is the black hole, it must have been a repaired node first. Therefore, we conclude that all faulty nodes will be repaired within finite time.

Lemma 4. *Procedure Double Check locates the black hole correctly.*

Proof. Procedure Double Check gets executed in two only conditions: (1) all nodes have known status, (2) only one node is unknown and it has 4 status unknown agents. In the former case, according to Line 12 and 14 in Procedure Double Check, each new agent or a newly returned (to hb) agent simply leaves to check each node one by one, and the last repaired node that has no agent returned is the black hole. In the latter case, a Fifth Agent is needed to continue the Double Check. As previously proven in Lemma 2, at least 1 of these 5 status unknown agents will return to hb. If the returning agent is this Fifth Agent, it will continue checking another node until it returns to hb and notices that there is only one repaired node with no agent has returned. If the returning agent is one of the 4 agents that were marked on the last status unknown node, according to Line 1st:line:Meet8 in Procedure Find the Meeting Node, the status of this unknown node becomes known and is marked "Last". Consequently, this latter case is turned into the former case, and the black hole is located.

Lemma 5. *Minimally $b + 2$ agents are necessary to repair all faulty nodes and locate the black hole in an asynchronous ring network.*

Proof. Since there are b faulty nodes in the ring network and 1 agent can only repair 1 faulty node, b agents are needed. To distinguish the black hole from the repaired nodes, at least one agent has to enter the black hole and die, thus, $b + 1$ agents are required. To report the locations of the faulty nodes and the black hole, at least 1 agent has to survive, hence, $b + 2$ agents are necessary.

Lemma 6. $b + 4$ *agents suffice to repair all faulty nodes and locate the black hole in a ring network using only one whiteboard in the homebase.*

Proof. To repair $b - 1$ faulty nodes, $b - 1$ agents are necessary and sufficient. In the worst case, the last unknown node is the black hole and all 4 status unknown agents die in it, and one more agent is needed to perform the Procedure Double Check. All other cases are proven in Lemma 2: at least 1 of these 5 agents will return to hb and locate the black hole. Therefore, $b + 4$ agents suffice.

Lemma 7. *In an arbitrary ring that contains b faulty nodes and a one-stop GV, b + 2 agents are necessary to repair all faulty nodes and locate the black hole.*

Proof. b agents are required to repair all b faulty nodes and 1 extra agent has to die in the black hole in order to locate it, while 1 agent needs to survive and report. Therefore, $b + 2$ agents are necessary to repair all faulty nodes and locate the black hole.

Lemma 8. *All faulty nodes can be repaired and the black hole can be located within O (n^2) moves.*

Proof. In the worst case, the b faulty nodes are the nodes from N_{n-1} to N_{n-b} and each node in the ring has been visited by 2 agents in Procedure New Node Exploration. Therefore, it costs $2 * 2 * (1 + 2+3 + 4 + \cdots + (n - 1)) = 2(n - 1)(n - 2)$ moves. The last unknown node may be explored by 4 agents in Procedure Find the Meeting Node. Hence, at most $4 * 2(n - 1)$ moves are performed. In Procedure Double Check, each node needs to be visited again which costs $2(n - 1)(n - 2)$ moves. In total, $4 * (n - 1)(n - 2) + 4 * 2(n - 1) = O(n^2)$ moves are needed.

Theorem 1. *Algorithm Dynamically Spawned Black Hole Search (DSBHS) can repair all faulty nodes and locate the black hole with b + 4 co-located agents in $O(n^2)$ moves using only one whiteboard in the homebase.*

6 Verifying Correctness and Complexity Using Simulation

In this section, we present the experimental results obtained from a series of Java simulations of the proposed algorithm. The experiment is done in a ring network with only one whiteboard in the homebase node which can only be accessed when the agents are in the homebase. All agents start from this homebase and execute the same protocol as described above. For the number of faulty nodes, we use a variable (*faulty posb*) to present the possibility that whether or not a node in the experimental network is faulty. This possibility varies between 20% to 40%. Thus, at the beginning of the exploration, the agents do not know the number of faulty nodes or their locations. In addition to the possibility of a node is faulty or normal, we assign a probability that dictates how likely a repaired node becomes a black hole. The dynamically generated location of a black hole is used to simulate the behaviour of the *GV* that is it can infected a repaired node at any time before the last repaired node is found.

To make the implementation more realistic, the distance of each link between two neighbouring nodes are randomly assigned to simulate an asynchronous network; that is, the time an agent spends on a link is unpredictable but finite. The implementation has a task scheduler, which will wake up a sleeping agent after a random amount of time. This is used to simulate the behaviours of agents that sleeps unpredictable amount of time in an asynchronous network.

Our simulation is executed in networks consist of number of nodes vary from 20 to 100. The execution of a simulation is considered to be successful if the location of the black hole and faulty nodes are correctly marked on the homebase whiteboard. Otherwise, the simulation is counted as a failure. For each successful simulation, we count the total number of moves that are used to repair all faulty nodes and locate the black hole. All data is calculated from 100 independent successful runs of each setting with random generated faulty nodes and a black hole. For each *faulty posb* = 20%, 30%, 40% and n = 20, 30, 40, ..., 90, 100, we provide 100 independent runs which are 2700 runs in total. In each setting, only 100 times executions are necessary in order to obtain 100 independent successful runs. All results show that $b + 4$ agents are sufficient to finish the repair and search task. Additionally, there is a 14.8% possibility that the task can be finished using only $b + 3$ agents or fewer.

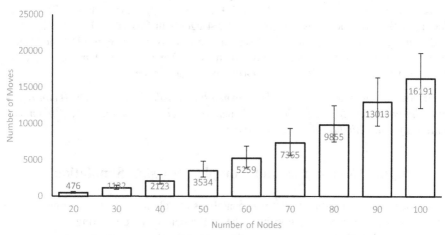

Fig. 1. The Relationship between Number of Moves and Nodes

Figure 1 illustrates the average move results as well as the lower and upper bound of the total number of moves for each setting. Results confirm that $O(n^2)$ moves suffice to repair all faulty nodes and locate the black hole in all simulations. It is obvious (as confirmed in Fig. 1) that the larger the network is, the more moves are necessary for the task to complete.

We further analyze whether the number of faulty nodes will affect the number of moves. Figures 2 and 3 show that as the number of faulty nodes increases, the total number of moves also has a slight increase. However, the same as above mentioned, the increase is not continuous and obvious. Thus, we conclude the number of faulty nodes does not have a direct relation to the total number of moves performed by the team of agents.

The theoretical analysis and simulation results both prove that, all faulty nodes can be repaired and the black hole can be located with $b + 4$ agents in $O(n^2)$ moves using only one whiteboard in the homebase. Furthermore, this simulation study further prove

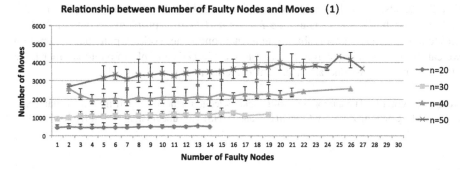

Fig. 2. The Relationship between number of moves and faulty nodes (20 to 50-node networks)

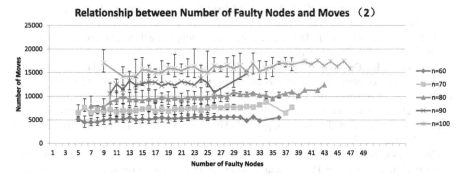

Fig. 3. The Relationship between number of moves and faulty nodes (60 to 100-node networks)

the correctness of the algorithm. It should be noticed that, our algorithm requires no knowledge of the number b of faulty nodes a priori.

7 Conclusion and Future Work

In this paper, we first present a new attack model containing both faulty nodes and a gray virus that may infect a repaired faulty node at an arbitrary point in time. We then propose a solution to the *Faulty Node Repair and Dynamically Spawned Black Hole Search problem* with only one whiteboard in an asynchronous ring network with the presence of a *GV*. This drastic network behaviour change significantly increases the difficulty and complexity of the solution to the traditional black hole search containing a single static black hole, whose existence must be known before the search starts. After the proof of algorithm correctness and complexity analysis, we conclude that $b + 4$ agents can repair all faulty nodes as well as locate the black hole that is infected by a one-stop *GV*.

A *GV* that can move from node to node, therefore infect multiple repaired nodes is not discussed in this paper and is a direction that should be explored in the future. It is important to notice that in an asynchronous network, the *GV* may move much faster than the agents. From the agents' view point, it could appear that all the repaired nodes appear to be black holes. Thus, the *Repair and Search* problem becomes a MBHS problem and remains unsolvable in an asynchronous network. A potential assumption we can bring into the equation is that a moveable *GV* can only move to another node after deleting at least one agent instead of being able to move freely.

Acknowledgment. The authors gratefully acknowledge financial support from the Natural Sciences and Engineering Research Council of Canada (NSERC) under Grant No. GPIN-2015-05390.

References

1. Almorsy, M., Grundy, J., and Müller, I.: An analysis of the cloud computing security problem. In: Proceedings of APSEC 2010 Cloud Workshop, Sydney, Australia, 30th Nov (2010)
2. Anderson, J.H., Kim, Y.-J., Herman, T.: Shared-memory mutual ex- clusion: major research trends since 1986. Distrib. Comput. **16**(2–3), 75–110 (2003)
3. Balamohan, B., Dobrev, S., Flocchini, P., Santoro, N.: Exploring an unknown dangerous graph with a constant number of tokens. Theor. Comput. Sci. **610**, 169–181 (2014)
4. Bampas, E., Leonardos, N., Markou, E., Pagourtzis, A., Petrolia, M.: Improved periodic data retrieval in asynchronous rings with a faulty host. In: Halldórsson, Magnús M. (ed.) SIROCCO 2014. LNCS, vol. 8576, pp. 355–370. Springer, Cham (2014). doi:10.1007/978-3-319-09620-9_27
5. Cai, J., Flocchini, P., Santoro, N.: Network decontamination from a black virus. In: 2013 IEEE 27th International Parallel and Distributed Processing Symposium Workshops and PhD Forum (IPDPSW), pp. 696–705. IEEE (2013)
6. Chow, R., Golle, P., Jakobsson, M., Shi, E., Staddon, J., Masuoka, R., Molina, J.: Controlling data in the cloud: outsourcing computation without outsourcing control. In: Proceedings of the 2009 ACM workshop on Cloud computing security, pp. 85–90. ACM (2009)
7. Cooper, C., Klasing, R., Radzik, T.: Searching for black-hole faults in a network using multiple agents. In: Shvartsman, M.M.A.A. (ed.) OPODIS 2006. LNCS, vol. 4305, pp. 320–332. Springer, Heidelberg (2006). doi:10.1007/11945529_23
8. Cooper, C., Klasing, R., Radzik, T.: Locating and repairing faults in a network with mobile agents. Theor. Comput. Sci. **411**(14–15), 1638–1647 (2010)
9. Czyzowicz, J., Kowalski, D., Markou, E., Pelc, A.: Searching for a black hole in tree networks. In: Higashino, T. (ed.) OPODIS 2004. LNCS, vol. 3544, pp. 67–80. Springer, Heidelberg (2005). doi:10.1007/11516798_5
10. Czyzowicz, J., Kowalski, D., Markou, E., Pelc, A.: Complexity of searching for a black hole. Fundamenta Informaticae **71**(2–3), 229–242 (2006)
11. Czyzowicz, J., Kowalski, D., Markou, E., Pelc, A.: Searching for a black hole in synchronous tree networks. Comb. Probab. Comput. **16**(4), 595–619 (2007)
12. D'Emidio, M., Frigioni, D., Navarra, A.: Exploring and making safe dangerous networks using mobile entities. In: Cichoń, J., Gębala, M., Klonowski, M. (eds.) ADHOC-NOW 2013. LNCS, vol. 7960, pp. 136–147. Springer, Heidelberg (2013). doi:10.1007/978-3-642-39247-4_12

13. Dobrev, S., Flocchini, P., Kralovic, R., Prencipe, G., Ruzicka, P., Santoro, N.: Black hole search by mobile agents in hypercubes and related networks. In: OPODIS, vol. 3, pp. 169–180 (2002)

14. Dobrev, S., Flocchini, P., Královič, R., Santoro, N.: Exploring an unknown graph to locate a black hole using tokens. In: Navarro, G., Bertossi, L., Kohayakawa, Y. (eds.) TCS 2006. IIFIP, vol. 209, pp. 131–150. Springer, Boston, MA (2006). doi:10.1007/978-0-387-34735-6_14

15. Dobrev, S., Flocchini, P., Královič, R., Santoro, N.: Exploring an unknown dangerous graph using tokens. Theor. Comput. Sci. **472**, 28–45 (2013)

16. Dobrev, S., Flocchini, P., Prencipe, G., Santoro, N.: Mobile search for a black hole in an anonymous ring. In: Welch, J. (ed.) DISC 2001. LNCS, vol. 2180, pp. 166–179. Springer, Heidelberg (2001). doi:10.1007/3-540-45414-4_12

17. Dobrev, S., Flocchini, P., Prencipe, G., Santoro, N.: Searching for a black hole in arbitrary networks: optimal mobile agent protocols. In: Proceedings of the Twenty-first Annual Symposium on Principles of Distributed Computing, NY, USA, PODC 2002, pp. 153–162. ACM, New York (2002)

18. Dobrev, S., Flocchini, P., Prencipe, G., Santoro, N.: Multiple agents rendezvous in a ring in spite of a black hole. In: Papatriantafilou, M., Hunel, P. (eds.) OPODIS 2003. LNCS, vol. 3144, pp. 34–46. Springer, Heidelberg (2004). doi:10.1007/978-3-540-27860-3_6

19. Dobrev, S., Flocchini, P., Santoro, N.: Improved bounds for optimal black hole search with a network map. In: Královič, R., Sýkora, O. (eds.) SIROCCO 2004. LNCS, vol. 3104, pp. 111–122. Springer, Heidelberg (2004). doi:10.1007/978-3-540-27796-5_11

20. Dobrev, S., Santoro, N., Shi, W.: Locating a black hole in an un-oriented ring using tokens: the case of scattered agents. In: Kermarrec, A.-M., Bougé, L., Priol, T. (eds.) Euro-Par 2007. LNCS, vol. 4641, pp. 608–617. Springer, Heidelberg (2007). doi:10.1007/978-3-540-74466-5_64

21. Flocchini, P., Kellett, M., Mason, Peter C., Santoro, N.: Mapping an unfriendly subway system. In: Boldi, P., Gargano, L. (eds.) FUN 2010. LNCS, vol. 6099, pp. 190–201. Springer, Heidelberg (2010). doi:10.1007/978-3-642-13122-6_20

22. Flocchini, P., Kellett, M., Mason, Peter C., Santoro, N.: Fault-tolerant exploration of an unknown dangerous graph by scattered agents. In: Richa, Andréa W., Scheideler, C. (eds.) SSS 2012. LNCS, vol. 7596, pp. 299–313. Springer, Heidelberg (2012). doi:10.1007/978-3-642-33536-5_30

23. Flocchini, P., Luccio, F.L., Song, L.X.: Size optimal strategies for capturing an intruder in mesh networks. In: Communications in Computing, pp. 200–206 (2005)

24. Grobauer, B., Walloschek, T., Stocker, E.: Understanding cloud computing vulnerabilities. IEEE Secur. Priv. **9**(2), 50–57 (2011)

25. Hashizume, K., Rosado, D.G., Fernández-Medina, E., Fernandez, E.B.: An analysis of security issues for cloud computing. J. Internet Serv. Appl. **4**(1), 1–13 (2013)

26. Klasing, R., Markou, E., Radzik, T., Sarracco, F.: Hardness and approximation results for black hole search in arbitrary networks. Theor. Comput. Sci. **384**(2), 201–221 (2007)

27. Klasing, R., Markou, E., Radzik, T., Sarracco, F.: Approximation bounds for black hole search problems. Networks **52**(4), 216–226 (2008)

28. Kosowski, A., Navarra, A., Pinotti, Cristina M.: Synchronization helps robots to detect black holes in directed graphs. In: Abdelzaher, T., Raynal, M., Santoro, N. (eds.) OPODIS 2009. LNCS, vol. 5923, pp. 86–98. Springer, Heidelberg (2009). doi:10.1007/978-3-642-10877-8_9

29. Královič, R., Miklík, S.: Periodic data retrieval problem in rings containing a malicious host. In: Patt-Shamir, B., Ekim, T. (eds.) SIROCCO 2010. LNCS, vol. 6058, pp. 157–167. Springer, Heidelberg (2010). doi:10.1007/978-3-642-13284-1_13

30. Luccio, F.L., Markou, E.: Mobile agents rendezvous in spite of a malicious agent (2014). arXiv:1410.4772
31. Peng, M., Shi, W., Corriveau, J.-P., Pazzi, R., Wang, Y.: Black hole search in computer networks: state-of-the-art, challenges and future directions. J. Parallel Distrib. Comput. **88**, 1–15 (2016)
32. Shi, W., Garcia-Alfaro, J., Corriveau, J.-P.: Searching for a black hole in interconnected networks using mobile agents and tokens. J. Parallel Distrib. Comput. **74**(1), 1945–1958 (2014)
33. Szor, P.: The Art of Computer Virus Research and Defense. Pearson Education, New Jersey (2005)

Applied Cryptography

Attribute-Based Encryption
with Granular Revocation

Hui Cui, Robert H. Deng[(✉)], Xuhua Ding, and Yingjiu Li

Secure Mobile Centre, School of Information Systems,
Singapore Management University, Singapore, Singapore
{hcui,robertdeng,xhding,yjli}@smu.edu.sg

Abstract. Attribute-based encryption (ABE) enables an access control mechanism over encrypted data by specifying access policies over attributes associated with private keys or ciphertexts, which is a promising solution to protect data privacy in cloud storage services. As an encryption system that involves many data users whose attributes might change over time, it is essential to provide a mechanism to selectively revoke data users' attributes in an ABE system. However, most of the previous revocable ABE schemes consider how to disable revoked data users to access (newly) encrypted data in the system, and there are few of them that can be used to revoke one or more attributes of a data user while keeping this user active in the system. Due to this observation, in this paper, we focus on designing ABE schemes supporting selective revocation, i.e., a data user's attributes can be selectively revoked, which we call ABE with granular revocation (ABE-GR). Our idea is to utilize the key separation technique, such that for any data user, key elements corresponding to his/her attributes are generated separately but are linkable to each other. To begin with, we give a basic ABE-GR scheme to accomplish selective revocation using the binary tree data structure. Then, to further improve the efficiency, we present a server-aided ABE-GR scheme, where an untrusted server is introduced to the system to mitigate data users' workloads during the key update phase. Both of the ABE-GR constructions are formally proved to be secure under our defined security model.

Keywords: Granular revocation · ABE · Efficiency · Cloud storage

1 Introduction

Attribute-based encryption (ABE) [21] provides a promising solution to preserve data privacy in a scenario (e.g., cloud storage services [23]) where data users are identified by their attributes (or credentials), and data owners want to share their data according to some policy based on the attributes of data users. In a ciphertext-policy ABE (CP-ABE) system, each data user is given a private attribute-key reflecting his/her attributes generated by the attribute authority (AA), and each data owner specifies an access policy to the message over a set of attributes[1]. A data user will be able to decrypt

---

[1] There are two complimentary forms of ABE: CP-ABE and key-policy ABE (KP-ABE). In a KP-ABE system, the situation is reversed that the keys are associated with the access policies and the ciphertexts are associated with the attributes. In the rest of this paper, unless otherwise specified, what we talk about is CP-ABE.

© ICST Institute for Computer Sciences, Social Informatics and Telecommunications Engineering 2017
R. Deng et al. (Eds.): SecureComm 2016, LNICST 198, pp. 165–181, 2017.
DOI: 10.1007/978-3-319-59608-2_9

a ciphertext if and only if the attributes ascribed to his/her private attribute-key satisfy the access policy (or access structure) associated with the ciphertext. Though ABE favorably solves the problem arising in the situations where different users with different attributes are given access to different levels of the encrypted data, it fails to address the issue of dynamic credentials where the attributes of every data user change with time. This challenge motivates the study of revocation mechanisms [1], where a periodical key update process disables revoked data users to update their decryption keys to decrypt newly encrypted data.

In terms of attribute-based setting, user revocation is divided into indirect revocation and direct revocation [1]. Regarding indirect revocation, one solution is to ask data users to periodically renew their private attribute-keys [7], but this requires the update key size to be $O(N - R)$ group elements where N is the number of all users and R is the number of revoked users. To reduce the cost of key update from linear to logarithmic $\left(\text{i.e.,} O\left(R \log\left(\frac{N}{R}\right)\right)\right)$, Boldyreva, Goyal and Kumar [5] put forth a revocation methodology by combining the fuzzy IBE scheme [21] with the binary tree data structure [18] where the AA publicly broadcasts the key update information for each time period, but only non-revoked data users can update their decryption keys to decrypt a newly generated ciphertext. In direct revocation [1, 2], data owners possess a current revocation list, and specify the revocation list directly when running the encrypting algorithm so that user revocation can be done instantly without requiring the key update phase as in the indirect method[2]. There are also constructions (e.g., [25]) that delegate the direct revocation ability to a semi-trusted server who cannot collude with the data users, where the server helps data users with decryption but terminates the decryption operation for any revoked data user.

Since an attribute-based encryption system might involve a large number of data users whose attributes change over time, it is desirable to build an attribute-based encryption scheme that the credentials possessed by data users can be selectively revoked. However, most of the previous revocable ABE systems [1, 2, 5, 20, 25] only consider efficient user revocation to prevent revoked data users from accessing the encrypted data, and there is little attention on how to independently revoke one or more attributes from a data user, i.e., selective revocation on attributes. Due to this observation, in this paper, we focus on the design of efficient and revocable attribute-based encryption schemes where the attributes possessed by each data user can be selectively revoked via a periodical key update phase, which we call attribute-based encryption with granular revocation (ABE-GR). Notice that ABE-GR can achieve user revocation by revoking all credentials possessed by a data user.

---

[2] Note that direct revocation can be done immediately without the key update process which asks for the communication from the AA to all the non-revoked users over all the time periods, but it requires all the data owners to keep the current revocation list. This makes the system impurely attribute-based, since data owners in the attribute-based setting create ciphertext based only on attributes without caring revocation. In this paper, unless otherwise specified, the revocation mechanism we talk about is indirect revocation.

1.1   Our Contributions

We describe the system architecture of an ABE-GR scheme in Fig. 1-(a). In an ABE-GR system, each data user's key is divided into three parts: private user-key (with a corresponding public user-key), private attribute-keys (associated with different attributes) and public key update information, from the latter two of which a data user can extract a decryption key. The AA, who keeps the master private key and publishes the public parameter, is responsible for the distribution of personalized pairs of public and private user-keys and private attribute-keys. In addition, the AA regularly posts the public key update information. Each data owner encrypts a message under an access structure and a time period using the public parameter. To decrypt a newly generated ciphertext, a data user needs to possess a pair of public and private user-keys as well as a decryption key on the current time period satisfying the access policy of this ciphertext. The key challenge in building an ABE-GR scheme is to prevent a data user from using his/her revoked attributes to decrypt any newly generated ciphertext. Traditionally, in an ABE scheme, each attribute possessed by a data user corresponds to one element in his/her private attribute-key, and these key elements are tied together through a random value. In order to support granular revocation in ABE, we need a technique to enable different key components on different attributes to be created separately but linkable to each other. Thanks to the key separation technique in distributed ABE [17] where the task of the single AA is split across multiple AAs and each attribute is controlled by one specific AA, we can equip an ABE scheme with a similar technique but under a single AA. Thus, each key component associated with the corresponding attribute will be created separately, but they still bind together due to the sharing of the same identification information (i.e., the public user-key) which is unique to each data user. As a result, we build an ABE-GR scheme by combining an ABE scheme with the key separation technique in distributed ABE [17]. To reduce the size of key update for the AA from linear to logarithmic in the number of users, we apply the binary tree data structure [18] in the algorithms of our ABE-GR scheme. Details about this ABE-GR scheme, which we will refer to as a basic ABE-GR scheme, is given in Sect. 4.

As alluded in [19], binary tree data structure [18] is useful in alleviating the workload of the AA, but it could not mitigate the workload of each data user who needs to periodically update the decryption key. Is it possible to fix the keys stored by data users such that they are not required to frequently update their decryption keys while without affecting the revocation? To give an affirmative answer to this question, we bring in an untrusted server[3] to the basic ABE-GR system to mitigate the workloads of data users. We depict the system architecture in Fig. 1-(b), which involves four entities: an AA, data owners, data users, and a server. Different from that in the basic ABE-GR construction, the public and private user-key pair is divided into a pair of public and private user-user-keys and a pair of public and private authority-user-keys, of which the

---

[3] The server is untrusted in the sense that it honestly follows the protocol but without holding any secret information (i.e., it may collude with data users). Besides, all operations done by the server can be performed by anyone, including data users (i.e., any dishonest behaviour from the server can be easily detected).

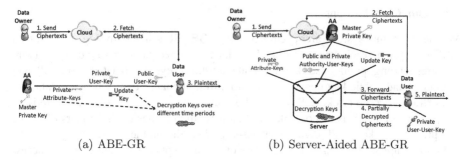

(a) ABE-GR   (b) Server-Aided ABE-GR

Fig. 1. System architectures of ABE-GR (left) and server-aided ABE-GR (right).

former is generated by each data user himself/herself[4] and the latter is extracted by the AA based on the public user-user-key. The server is given the public and private authority-user-keys and private attribute-keys of data users as well as the key update information. A data user fetches a ciphertext from the cloud, and sends it to the server for partial decryption. For any non-revoked user, from the private attribute-keys and key update information, the server can generate a collection of decryption keys (associated with a set of attributes), which, combining with the public and private authority-user-keys, can partially decrypt a ciphertext forwarded by this user if his/her non-revoked attributes satisfy the access structure ascribed to the ciphertext. A data user can obtain the plaintext by decrypting the partially decrypted ciphertext using his/her self-generated private user-user-key. This does not compromise the security, because the public user-user-key is embedded in the private authority-user-key, the server cannot fully unwrap the ciphertext without the private user-user-key. A detailed description of the construction is presented in Sect. 4.

Since both our constructions are built on an ABE scheme that is selectively secure [17, 24], where the adversary has to commit the challenge access structure in advance, we can only achieve selective security in our ABE-GR schemes. Note that the techniques can be applied to fully secure ABE schemes (e.g., [20]) to obtain fully secure (server-aided) ABE-GR schemes.

1.2 Related Work

Revocable IBE. With regard to revocable IBE, Boneh and Franklin [7] suggested that users periodically renew their private keys, but this method has a disadvantage in that it requires all users to regularly contact the key generation centre (KGC) to obtain new private keys, and thus a secure channel must be established between the KGC and each user for such transactions. Hanaoka et al. [10] presented a convenient methodology for users to periodically renew their private keys without communicating with the KGC by making the KGC publicly post the key update information. However, as each user in

---

[4] This pair of user-user-keys can also be generated by the AA, but this requires a secure channel between each data user and the AA for private key distribution.

this case needs to posses a tamper-resistant hardware device, the solution is very cumbersome. Boldyreva, Goyal and Kumar [5] put forth an efficient revocable IBE scheme to reduce the size of key update from linear to logarithmic, but it asks all non-revoked users to regularly update their decryption keys. To address the revocation issue in a better way, revocation with a third party [3, 6, 9, 13, 15, 16, 19] has been introduced, in which a semi-trusted[5] (or untrusted) third party is assigned to share the decryption capability with all users and help them the ciphertext decryption. Once an identity is revoked, the mediator immediately terminates decrypting the ciphertext for this user.

Revocable ABE. Regarding user revocation in ABE, there are two revocation mechanisms [1, 8]: direct revocation and indirect revocation. Considering the former, in which each data owner keeps a current revocation list, and directly specify the revocation list when encrypting, there are schemes in [2, 11, 14]. In addition, Yang et al. [25] put forward an approach by assigning a semi-trusted server to share the decryption capability with data users such that when a data user is revoked, the server stops the decryption for the user. Regarding the latter, which we intend to achieve in this paper, Boldyreva, Goyal and Kumar [5] proposed a revocable KP-ABE scheme where the AA indirectly achieves the revocation by disabling revoked users to update their keys. Later, based on the same technique adopted in [5], Attrapadung and Imai [1] gave a hybrid revocable KP-ABE scheme under selective security model which allows a data owner to select the revocation mode (direct or indirect) when performing encryption. Sahai, Seyalioglu and Waters [20] showed a generic way to build ABE schemes that support dynamic credentials, where the AA indirectly accomplishes revocation by stopping updating the keys for revoked users. Cui and Deng [8] proposed two indirectly revocable and decentralized ABE schemes in the composite-order groups where the AA'role is split over multiple AAs.

1.3 Organization

The remainder of this paper is organized as follows. In Sect. 2, we briefly review the relevant notions and definitions to be used in this paper. In Sect. 3, after describing the framework for ABE-GR, we present its security model. In Sect. 4, we present two concrete constructions of ABE-GR, and provably reduce their security. In addition, we compare our ABE-GR schemes with previous revocable ABE schemes in Sect. 4. We conclude the paper in Sect. 5.

2 Preliminaries

In this section, we review some basic cryptographic notions and definitions that are to be used in this paper.

---

[5] In this paper, unless otherwise specified, "semi-trusted" means that the corresponding entity is disallowed to collude with the malicious data users.

2.1 Bilinear Pairings and Complexity Assumptions

Let p be a prime number, and G be a group of order p that is generated from g. We define $\hat{e} : G \times G \to G_1$ to be a bilinear map if it has two properties [7].

- Bilinear: for all $g \in G$, and $a, b \in Z_p$, we have $\hat{e}(g^a, g^b) = \hat{e}(g, g)^{ab}$.
- Non-degenerate: $\hat{e}(g, g) \neq 1$.

We say that G is a bilinear group if the group operation in G is efficiently computable and there exists a group G_1 and an efficiently computable bilinear map $\hat{e} : G \times G \to G_1$ as above.

Decisional Parallel Bilinear Diffie-Hellman Exponent Assumption [24]. The decisional q-parallel bilinear Diffie-Hellman exponent (BDHE) problem is that for any probabilistic polynomial-time (PPT) algorithm, given

$$\overrightarrow{y} = \begin{matrix} \forall j \in [1, q] \\ \forall 1 \leq j, k \leq q, k \neq j \end{matrix} \quad \begin{matrix} g, g^\mu, g^a, \ldots, g^{a^q}, g^{a^{q+2}}, \ldots, g^{a^{2q}}, \\ g^{\mu \cdot b_j}, g^{a/b_j}, \ldots, g^{a^q/b_j}, g^{a^{q+2}/b_j}, \ldots, g^{a^{2q}/b_j}, \\ g^{a \cdot \mu \cdot b_k / b_j}, \ldots, g^{a^q \cdot \mu \cdot b_k / b_j}, \end{matrix}$$

it is difficult to distinguish $\left(\overrightarrow{y}, \hat{e}(g, g)^{a^{q+1}\mu} \right)$ from $\left(\overrightarrow{y}, Z \right)$, where $g \in G, Z \in G_1, a, \mu, b_1, \ldots, b_q \in Z_p$ are chosen independently and uniformly at random.

2.2 Access Structures and Linear Secret Sharing

Definition 1 (*Access Structure* [12, 24]). *Let $\{P_1, \ldots, P_n\}$ be a set of parties. A collection $\mathbb{A} \subseteq 2^{\{P_1, \ldots, P_n\}}$ is monotone if $\forall B, C : if B \in \mathbb{A}$ and $B \subseteq C$, then $C \subseteq \mathbb{A}$ A monotone access structure is a monotone collection $\mathbb{A}$ of non-empty subsets of $\{P_1, \ldots, P_n\}$, i.e., $\mathbb{A} \subseteq 2^{\{P_1, \ldots, P_n\}} \setminus \{\emptyset\}$. The sets in $\mathbb{A}$ are called the authorized sets, and the sets not in $\mathbb{A}$ are called the unauthorized sets.*

Definition 2 (*Linear Secret Sharing Schemes (LSSS)* [12, 24]). *Let P be a set of parties. Let $\mathbb{M}$ be a matrix of size $l \times n$ (l rows and n columns). Let $\rho : \{1, \ldots, l\} \to P$ be a function mapping a row to a party for labeling. A secret sharing scheme Π over a set of parties P is a linear secret-sharing scheme over Z_p if*

1. *The shares for each party form a vector over Z_p.*
2. *There exists an $l \times n$ matrix $\mathbb{M}$ named the share-generating matrix for Π. For $x = 1, \ldots, l$, the x-th row of matrix $\mathbb{M}$ is labeled by a party $\rho(i)$ for $\rho : \{1, \ldots, l\} \to P$ being a function mapping a row to a party for labeling. Considering that the column vector $\overrightarrow{v} = (\mu, r_2, \ldots, r_n)$ with $\mu \in Z_p$ being the secret to be shared and $r_2, \ldots, r_n \in Z_p$, then $\mathbb{M}\overrightarrow{v}$ is the vector of l shares of the secret μ according to Π. The share $(\mathbb{M}\overrightarrow{v})_i$ belongs to party $\rho(i)$.*

It has been concluded in [12] that every LSSS enjoys a property called linear reconstruction. Assume that Π is an LSSS for an access structure A. Denote $\mathbf{A}$ as an authorized set, and $I \subseteq \{1, \ldots, l\}$ as $I = \{i | \rho(i) \in \mathbf{A}\}$. Then the vector $(1, 0, \ldots, 0)$ is in the span of rows of matrix $\mathbb{M}$ indexed by I, and there exist constants $\{w_i \in Z_p\}_{i \in I}$ such that, for any valid shares $\{v_i\}$ of a secret μ according to Π, $\sum_{i \in I} w_i v_i = \mu$ holds. These constants $\{w_i\}$ can be found in polynomial time depending on the size of the share-generating matrix $\mathbb{M}$ [4].

Boolean Formulas [12]. An access policies can be described in a monotonic boolean formula as well. An LSSS access structure is more general, and can be derived from a representation as a boolean formula. There are generic techniques to transfer any monotonic boolean formula into an LSSS matrix. An boolean formula can be represented as an access tree with the interior nodes being AND and OR gates and the leaf nodes corresponding to attributes. Note that the number of rows in the corresponding LSSS matrix is the same as the number of leaf nodes in the access tree.

2.3   Terminologies on Binary Tree

We follow the definitions about the binary tree in [5, 19]. Denote BT as a binary tree with N leaves representing N users, and **root** as the root node of the tree BT. Let Path (θ) be the set of nodes on the path from θ to **root** (which includes both θ and **root**) if θ is a leaf node. Let θ_l and θ_r be left and right child of θ if θ is a non-leaf node. Assume that nodes in the tree are uniquely encoded as strings, and the tree is defined by all descriptions of its nodes. There is an algorithm KUNodes defined to calculate the minimal set of nodes for which the key update needs to be published so that only non-revoked users at a time period t can decrypt ciphertexts, which works by firstly marking all the ancestors of the revoked nodes as revoked, and then outputting all the non-revoked children of revoked nodes. Formally, the KUNodes algorithm takes a binary tree BT, a revocation list rl and a time period t as the input, and outputs a set of nodes, the minimal set of nodes in BT, such that none of the nodes in rl with the corresponding time period at or before t (users revoked at or before t) have any ancestor (or, themselves) in the set, and all other leaf nodes (corresponding to non-revoked users) have exactly one ancestor (or, themselves) in the set.

KUNodes (BT, rl, t)
$X, Y \leftarrow \varnothing$.
$\forall (\theta_i, t_i) \in rl$, if $t_i \leq t$, then add Path(θ_i) to X.
$\forall x \in X$, if $x_l \notin X$, then add x_l to Y; if $x_r \notin X$, then add x_r to Y.
If $Y = \varnothing$, then add **root** to Y.
Return Y.

3   System Architecture and Security Definition

We describe the system architecture and formal security definition of attribute-based encryption with granular revocation in this section.

3.1 Framework

An ABE-GR scheme involves three entities: attribute authority (AA), data owners and data users, where the algorithms run by these parties are described as follows.

- GSetup(1^λ) $\rightarrow$ (*par*, *msk*). Taking a security parameter λ as the input, this algorithm, run by the AA, outputs the public parameter *par* and the master private key *msk*.

- ASetup(*par*, A_i) $\rightarrow$ (PK_{A_i}, SK_{A_i}, rl_i, st_i). Taking the public parameter *par* and an attribute A_i as the input, this algorithm, run by the AA, outputs a public key PK_{A_i} a private key SK_{A_i} an initially empty revocation list rl_i and a state st_i.

- UserKG(*par*, *msk*, *id*) $\rightarrow$ (sk_{id}, pk_{id}). Taking the public parameter *par*, the master private key *msk* and an identity *id* as the input, this algorithm, run by the AA, outputs a private user-key sk_{id} and a public user-key pk_{id} for user *id*.

- PrivKG(*par*, SK_{A_i}, pk_{id}, st_i) $\rightarrow$ (pk_{id}^{Ai}, st_i). Taking the public parameter *par*, the private key SK_{A_i} a pubic user-key pk_{id} and a state st_i as the input, this algorithm, run by the AA, outputs a private attribute-key pk_{id}^{Ai} and an updated state st_i for user *id* possessing an attribute A_i.

- TKeyUp(*par*, SK_{A_i}, *t*, rl_i, st_i) $\rightarrow$ ($ku_t^{(i)}$, st_i). Taking the public parameter *par*, the private key SK_{A_i} a time period *t*, a revocation list rl_i and a state st_i as the input, this algorithm, run by the AA, outputs the key update information $ku_t^{(i)}$ and an updated state st_i.

- DecKG(*par*, $pk_{id}^{A_i}$, $tku_t^{(i)}$) $\rightarrow$ $dk_{id,t}^{(i)}$. Taking the public parameter *par*, a private attribute-key $pk_{id}^{A_i}$ and the key update information $tku_t^{(i)}$ as the input, this algorithm, run by each data user, outputs a decryption key $dk_{id,t}^{(i)}$ for used *id* at time period *t*.

- Encrypt(*par*, $(\mathbb{M}, \rho)$, *t*, $\{PK_{A_i}\}$, *M*) $\rightarrow$ CT. Taking the public parameter *par*, an access structure $(\mathbb{M}, \rho)$, a time period *t*, a set of public keys $\{PK_{A_i}\}$ for relevant attributes and a message *M* as the input, this algorithm, run by each data owner, outputs a ciphertext CT (will be stored to the cloud).

- Decrypt(*par*, pk_{id}, sk_{id}, $\{dk_{id,t}^{(i)}\}$, CT) $\rightarrow$ $M/\perp$. Taking the public parameter *par*, a public user-key pk_{id}, a private user-key sk_{id}, a collection of decryption keys $\{dk_{id,t}^{(i)}\}$ of the same *id* and a ciphertext CT as the input, this algorithm, run by each data user, outputs a message *M* if the attribute set $\{A_i\}$ satisfies the access matrix associated with the ciphertext or a failure symbol $\perp$.

- Revoke(*id*, A_i, *t*, rl_i, st_i) $\rightarrow$ rl_i. Taking an attribute A_i of identity *id* to be revoked, a time period *t*, a revocation list rl_i and a state st_i as the input, this algorithm, run by the AA, outputs an updated revocation list rl_i.

Note that in order to create public and private keys, private attribute-keys, key update information and decryption keys corresponding to multiple attributes, the corresponding algorithms ASetup, PrivKG, TKeyUp and DecKG are extended to take in many attributes by running the "single attribute" version once for each attribute.

For the correctness of an ABE-GR scheme, we require that for any security parameter λ and any message *M* (in the message space), if the data user is not revoked at time period t (in the space of time periods), and if all entities follow the above algorithms as described, then Decrypt $(par, sk_{id}, \{dk_{id,t}^{(i)}\}, CT) = M$ if $\{dk_{id,t}^{(i)}\}$ is a set of decryption keys for the same identity id over a set of attributes satisfying the access structure of the ciphertext CT.

3.2 Security Definition

Below we describe the security game between an adversary algorithm $\mathcal{A}$ and a challenger algorithm $\mathcal{B}$ as indistinguishability under chosen plaintext attacks (IND-CPA security) for an ABE-GR scheme.

- Setup. Algorithm $\mathcal{B}$ runs the GSetup algorithm, sends algorithm $\mathcal{A}$ the public parameter par and keeps the master private key msk. Also, it runs the ASetup algorithm, keeps the private keys $\{SK_{A_i}\}$, initially empty revocation lists $\{rl_i\}$ and states $\{st_i\}$ and sends the public keys $\{PK_{A_i}\}$ to algorithm $\mathcal{A}$.
- Phase 1. Algorithm $\mathcal{A}$ adaptively issues queries to the following oracles.

  1. Private-User-Key oracle. Algorithm $\mathcal{A}$ issues a private user-key query to algorithm $\mathcal{B}$ on an identity id, and algorithm $\mathcal{B}$ returns sk_{id} by running UserKG(par, msk, id), and adds (id, pk_{id}) to the user list.
  2. Private-Attribute-Key oracle. Algorithm $\mathcal{A}$ issues a public attribute-key query to algorithm $\mathcal{B}$ on an identity id with an attribute set $\{A_i\}$, and algorithm $\mathcal{B}$ returns $\{pk_{id}^{A_i}\}$ by running UserKG(par, msk, id) (if id does not exist in the user list), PrivKG $(par, SK_{A_i}, pk_{id}, st_i)$ for each A_i of id.
  3. Key-Update oracle. Algorithm $\mathcal{A}$ issues a key update query to algorithm $\mathcal{B}$ on a time period t, and algorithm $\mathcal{B}$ returns $\{tku_t^{(i)}\}$ by running TKeyUp $(par, SK_{A_i}, t, rl_i, st_i)$ for each A_i.
  4. Decryption-Key oracle. Algorithm $\mathcal{A}$ issues a decryption key query to algorithm $\mathcal{B}$ on a time period t and an identity id with an attribute set $\{A_i\}$, and algorithm $\mathcal{B}$ returns $\{dk_{id,t}^{(i)}\}$ by running UserKG(par, msk, id) (if id does not exist in the user list), PrivKG $(par, SK_{A_i}, pk_{id}, st_i)$, TKeyUp $(par, SK_{A_i}, t, rl_i, st_i)$, DecKG $(par, pk_{id}^{A_i}, tku_t^{(i)})$ on each A_i of id. Notice that queries on a time period t that has not been issued to the Key-Update oracle cannot be issued to this oracle.
  5. Revocation oracle. Algorithm $\mathcal{A}$ issues a revocation query to algorithm $\mathcal{B}$ on an attribute A_i of identity id and a time period t, and algorithm $\mathcal{B}$ runs Revoke(id, t, rl_i, st_i) and outputs an updated revocation list rl_i. If a key update query has been issued on a time period t, this oracle cannot be queried on t.

- Challenge. Let $I_{\mathbb{M}^*,\rho^*} = \{\mathcal{I}_1, \ldots \mathcal{I}_\chi\}$ be a set of minimum subsets of attributes satisfying $(\mathbb{M}^*, \rho^*)$. Algorithm $\mathcal{A}$ outputs two messages M_0^* and M_1^* of the same size, an access structure $(\mathbb{M}^*, \rho^*)$ and a time period t^* following the constraint that for each id, if algorithm $\mathcal{A}$ asks for a collection of private attribute-keys on an attribute set covering an $\mathcal{I}_j \in I_{\mathbb{M}^*,\rho^*}$ $(j \in [1, \chi])$ then (1) the revocation oracle must be queried on some tuple (id, t, A_i) where t happens at or before t^* and $A_i \in \mathcal{I}_j (j \in [1, \chi])$, and (2) the Decryption-Key oracle cannot be queried on $(id, t,$

$\{A_i\})$ for any $t = t^*$ and $\mathcal{I}_j \subseteq \{A_i\} (j \in [1, \chi])$. Algorithm $\mathcal{B}$ randomly chooses $\gamma \in \{0, 1\}^*$, runs Encrypt $(par, (\mathbb{M}^*, \rho^*), \{PK_{Ai}\}, t^*, M_\gamma^*)$ to obtain the challenge ciphertext CT^*, and sends CT^* to algorithm $\mathcal{A}$.

- Phase 2. Following the restriction defined in the Challenge phase, algorithm $\mathcal{A}$ continues issuing queries to algorithm $\mathcal{B}$ as that in Phase 1.
- Guess. Algorithm $\mathcal{A}$ makes a guess γ' for γ. It wins the game if $\gamma' = \gamma$.

Algorithm $\mathcal{A}$'s advantage in the above game is defined to be $\Pr[\gamma = \gamma'] - 1/2$. An ABE-GR scheme is said to be IND-CPA secure under the defined security model if all PPT adversaries have at most a negligible advantage in the security parameter λ λ. In addition, an ABE-GR scheme is said to be selectively IND-CPA secure if an Init stage where algorithm $\mathcal{A}$ commits to the challenge access structure (M^*, ρ^*) which it attempts to attack is added before the Setup phase.

Remarks. Note that the above security definition is different from those in previous revocable ABE schemes. The definitions in [1, 8, 20] did not consider a realistic threat called decryption key exposure attacks [22][6], while the above model allows an additional Decryption-Key oracle to resist such attacks so that no information of the plaintext is revealed from a ciphertext even if all (short-term) decryption keys of different time periods are exposed.

4   Attribute-Based Encryption with Granular Revocation

In this section, we present two ABE-GR constructions and their security analysis. Also, we compare them with several existing revocable ABE schemes.

4.1   Basic Construction

Let the attribute space be Z_p, the time space be Z_p, and the message space be G_1. The basic attribute-based encryption scheme supporting granular revocation is composed of the following algorithms, which is built upon the CP-ABE scheme presented in [24].

- GSetup. On input a security parameter λ, it randomly chooses a group G of a prime order p with $g \in G$ being the generator, and defines a bilinear map $\hat{e} : G \times G \to G_1$ Additionally, it randomly chooses $u, h \in G$, $a, \alpha \in Z_p$, and defines a function $F(y) = u^y h$ to map an element y in Z_p to an element in G. The public parameter is $par = (g, g^a, u, h, \hat{e}(g, g)^\alpha)$. The master private key is $msk = \alpha$.
- ASetup. On input the public parameter par and an attribute A_i, it randomly chooses $\alpha_i \in Z_p$, and computes $PK_{A_i} = g^{\alpha_i}$. Let rl_i be an empty list storing revoked users and BT_i be a binary tree with at least N leaf nodes. It outputs the public key PK_{A_i} along with rl_i and st_i where st_i is a state which is set to be BT_i, and keeps α_i as the private key SK_{A_i}.

---

[6] This does not affect the security of these schemes, because such attacks are not covered by their security models.

- **UserKG.** On input the public parameter par, the master private key msk and an identity id, it randomly chooses $\beta \in Z_p$, and outputs a private user-key $sk_{id} = g^{\alpha}(g^{a})^{\beta}$ and a public user-key $pk_{id} = g^{\beta}$.
- **PrivKG.** On input the public parameter par, a private key SK_{A_i} a public user-key pk_{id} and a state st_i, it firstly chooses an undefined leaf node $\theta^{(i)}$ from the binary tree BT_i, and stores id in this node. Then, for each node $x^{(i)} \in \text{Path}(\theta^{(i)})$, it runs as follows.

   1. It obtains $g_{i,x}$ from the node $x^{(i)}$. If $x^{(i)}$ is undefined, it randomly chooses $g_{i,x} \in G$, and computes $P_x^{(i)} = (g^{\beta}/g_{i,x})^{\alpha_i}$. It stores $g_{i,x}$ in the node $x^{(i)}$.
   2. It outputs the private attribute-key $pk_{id}^{A_i} = \{x^{(i)}, P_x^{(i)}\}_{x^{(i)} \in \text{path}(\theta^{(i)})}$, and an updated state st_i.

- **TKeyUp.** On input the public parameter par, a private key SK_{A_i} a time period t, a revocation list rl_i and a state BT_i, for all $x^{(i)} \in \text{KUNodes}(BT_i, rl_i, t)$, it gets $g_{i,x}$[7] from the node x. Then, it randomly chooses $s_{i,x} \in Z_p$, and computes $Q_{x,1}^{(i)} = g_{i,x}^{\alpha_i} \cdot F(t)^{s_{i,x}}$, $Q_{x,2}^{(i)} = g^{s_{i,x}}$. It outputs $ku_t^{(i)} = \{x^{(i)}, Q_{x,1}^{(i)}, Q_{x,2}^{(i)}\}_{x^{(i)} \in \text{KUNodes}(BT_i, rl_i, t)}$ as the key update information.
- **DecKG.** On input the public parameter par, a private attribute-key $pk_{id}^{A_i}$ and the key update information $tku_t^{(i)}$ as the input, it parses each $pk_{id}^{A_i}$ as $\{x^{(i)}, P_x^{(i)}\}_{x^{(i)} \in I, tku_t^{(i)}}$ as $\{x^{(i)}, Q_{x,1}^{(i)}, Q_{x,2}^{(i)}\}_{x^{(i)} \in J}$ for some set of nodes $I = \text{Path}(\theta^{(i)}), J = \text{KUNodes}(BT_i, rl_i, t)$. If $I \cap J = \emptyset$, it returns $\perp$. Otherwise, for any $x^{(i)} \in I \cap J$, it randomly chooses $s'_{i,x} \in Z_p$, and computes

$$dk_1^{(i)} = P_x^{(i)} \cdot Q_{x,1}^{(i)} \cdot F(t)^{s'_{i,x}} = pk_{id}^{\alpha_i} \cdot F(t)^{s_{i,x} + s'_{i,x}},$$
$$dk_2^{(i)} = Q_{x,2}^{(i)} \cdot g^{s'_{i,x}} = g^{s_{i,x} + s'_{i,x}}.$$

  It outputs the decryption key $dk_{id,t}^{(i)} = (dk_1^{(i)}, dk_2^{(i)})$.
- **Encrypt.** On input the public parameter par, an LSSS access structure $(\mathbb{M}, \rho)$ with $\mathbb{M}$ being an $l \times n$ matrix, a set of public keys $\{PK_{A_i}\}$ for relevant attributes, a time period t and a message M, it randomly chooses a vector $\overrightarrow{v} = (\mu, y_2, \ldots, y_n)^{\perp} \in Z_p^n$ (these values will be used to share the encryption exponent μ). For $i = 1$ to l, it calculates $v_i = \mathbb{M}_i \cdot \overrightarrow{v}$ where $\mathbb{M}_i$ is the i-th row of $\mathbb{M}$. Also, it randomly chooses $\mu, \mu_1, \ldots, \mu_k \in Z_p$, and computes

$$C_0 = \hat{e}(g,g)^{\alpha\mu} \cdot M, \quad C_2^{(i)} = (g^a)^{v_i} \cdot (PK_{\rho(i)})^{-\mu_i},$$
$$C_1 = g^{\mu}, \quad C_3^{(i)} = g^{\mu_i}, \quad C_4^{(i)} = F(t)^{\mu_i}.$$

- It outputs the ciphertext $CT = ((\mathbb{M}, \rho), t, C_0, C_1, \{C_2^{(i)}, C_3^{(i)}, C_4^{(i)}\}_{i \in [i,l]})$.

---

[7] Here $g_{i,x}$ is always predefined in the PrivKG algorithm.

– Decrypt. On input the public parameter *par*, a public user-key pk_{id}, a private user-key sk_{id}, a set of decryption keys $\{dk_{id,t}^{(i)}\}$ and a ciphertext CT, it computes

$$\frac{\hat{e}(C_1, sk_{id}) \prod_{i \in I} \hat{e}(C_4^{(i)}, dk_2^{(i)})}{(\prod_{i \in I} \hat{e}(C_2^{(i)}, pk_{id}) \hat{e}(C_3^{(i)}, dk_1^{(i)}))^{w_i}} = \hat{e}(g, g)^{\alpha\mu},$$

and then cancels out this value from C_0 to obtain the plaintext M. Suppose that $\{A_i\}$ associated with $\{pk_{id}^{A_i}\}$ satisfies the access structure $(\mathbb{M}, \rho)$. Let I be defined as $I = \{i : \rho(i) \in \{A_i\}\}$. Denote $\{w_i \in Z_p\}_{i \in I}$ as a set of constants such that if $\{v_i\}$ are valid shares of any secret μ according to $\mathbb{M}$, then $\sum_{i \in I} w_i v_i = \mu$.

– Revoke. On input an attribute A_i of identity *id*, a time period t, a revocation list rl_i and a state st_i, for all the nodes $x^{(i)}$ associated with identity *id*, it adds $(x^{(i)}, t)$ to rl_i, and outputs the updated rl_i.

Theorem 1. *Under the decisional q-parallel BDHE assumption, the above basic ABE-GR scheme is selectively IND-CPA secure.*

Proof. In the proof, it is assumed that if an adversary has issued a private user-key query on an identity *id*, and a private attribute-key query on attributes $\{A_i\}$ of this identity *id* satisfying the challenge access structure $(\mathbb{M}^*, \rho^*)$, then at least one attribute in each set of minimum attributes satisfying $(\mathbb{M}^*, \rho^*)$ of this identity *id* is revoked at or before the challenge time period t^*. We detail the proof in the full version of this paper due to the space limit[8].

4.2 Construction with Improved Efficiency

The main drawback in our previous construction lies in that all non-revokes data users need to periodically update their decryption keys. To remove such cumbersome workloads from data users, we give another ABE-GR scheme, which we call a server-aided ABE-GR scheme. Our method is to introduce an untrusted server to the basic ABE-GR scheme such that the server will help data users with the workloads in key update stage. The algorithms of our server-aided ABE-GR scheme mostly follow those in the basic ABE-GR scheme except with two differences.

– Firstly, the user-key generation algorithm is replaced by two algorithms, where one is run by each data user himself/herself called UUserKG, and the other one is run by the AA called AUserKG. The UUserKG algorithm outputs a public and private user-user-key pair. On input a public user-user-key and the master private key of the AA, the AUserKG algorithm outputs a public and private authority-user-key pair and publicly transmits them to the server.

– Secondly, the decryption algorithm is divided into two parts, of which one is run by the server called SDecrypt using the public and private authority user-keys and decryption key, and the other one is run the data user called UDecrypt with the

---

[8] Please contact the author for the full version.

private user-user-key. The SDecrypt algorithm takes a ciphertext as the input, and outputs a partially decrypted ciphertext. The UDecrypt algorithm takes a partially decrypted ciphertext as the input, and outputs the plaintext.

Assume that for each data user, the server keeps a list of tuples (identity, attributes, public and private authority-user-keys, a set of private attribute-keys), i.e., $(id, \{A_i\}, (pk_{id}, sk_{id}), \{pk_{id}^{A_i}\})$. We detail the concrete construction as follows.

- GSetup. The same as that in the basic ABE-GR construction.
- ASetup. The same as that in the basic ABE-GR construction.
- UUserKG. The data user id randomly chooses $\tau \in Z_p$, and outputs a public and private user-user-key pair $(pk_{id}', sk_{id}') = (g^\tau, \tau)$.
- AUserKG. The AA randomly chooses $\beta \in Z_p$, and outputs a private and public authority-user-key pair $(sk_{id}, pk_{id}) = ((pk_{id}')^\alpha (g^a)^\beta, g^\beta)$. The AA will publicly send (sk_{id}, pk_{id}) to the server.
- PrivKG. The same as that in the basic ABE-GR construction. The AA will publicly send $pk_{id}^{A_i}$ to the server.
- TKeyUp. The same as that in the basic ABE-GR construction. The AA will publicly send $ku_t^{(i)}$ to the server.
- DecKG. The same as that in the basic ABE-GR construction except that it is run by the server rather than the data user.
- Encrypt. The same as that in the basic ABE-GR construction.
- SDecrypt. Given the private authority-user-key and decryption key, the server computes

$$C_0' = \frac{\hat{e}(C_1, sk_{id}) \prod_{i \in I} \hat{e}(C_4^{(i)}, dk_2^{(i)})}{(\prod_{i \in I} \hat{e}(C_2^{(i)}, pk_{id})\hat{e}(C_3^{(i)}, dk_1^{(i)}))^{w_i}} = \hat{e}(pk_{id}', g)^{\alpha\mu},$$

and sends $CT' = (id, C_0, C_0')$ to the data user.
- UDecrypt. The data user computes $M = C_0/(C_0')^{\frac{1}{\tau}}$ using the private user-user-key.
- Revoke. The same as that in the basic ABE-GR construction.

Remarks. It is worth noticing that the server-aided ABE-GR scheme has an edge over the basic ABE-GR one in both storage and computation overheads. Firstly, each data user in the server-aided ABE-GR construction only needs to keep one short private key, while in the basic ABE-GR one each data user keeps a private key of large size (depending on the size of attribute sets he/she owns and the total number of data users allowed in the system). Secondly, each data user in the server-aided ABE-GR system only needs to perform one exponentiation and no pairing computation to decrypt a ciphertext, while in the basic ABE-GR one each data user needs to perform many exponentiation and pairing computations. Thirdly, there is no secure channel required in the server-aided ABE-GR scheme for private key transmission, but the AA in the basic ABE-GR one needs to send the private user-key and attribute-keys to each data user via a secure channel.

Theorem 2. *Under the decisional q-parallel BDHE assumption, the above server aided ABE-GR scheme is selectively IND-CPA secure.*

Proof. In the proof, it is assumed that if an adversary has issued a private user- user-key query, a private authority-user-key query, and a private attribute-key on attributes $\{A_i\}$ satisfying the challenge access structure $(\mathbb{M}^*, \rho^*)$ on an identity id, then at least one attribute in each set of minimum attributes satisfying $(\mathbb{M}^*, \rho^*)$ of this identity id is revoked at or before the challenge time period t^*. The proof is similar to that in Theorem 1, and we detail it in the full version of this paper due to the space limit.

4.3 System Analysis

To the best of our knowledge, besides the result in this paper, [1, 5, 20, 25] are also about constructions on revocable ABE from the bilinear maps in the prime-order groups. This paper aims to achieve granular revocation in CP-ABE such that the AA can selectively revoke specific attributes of data users. The KP-ABE scheme with indirect user revocation is proposed in [5] where the AA enables the revocation by disallowing revoked users to update their keys. In [1], a KP-ABE scheme with hybrid user revocation is raised in which a data owner can select to use either direct or indirect revocation mode when encrypting a message. A generic way to build ABE schemes supporting dynamic credentials is elaborated in [20], in which the AA indirectly accomplishes user revocation by preventing revoked data users from updating their keys. In [25], a semi-trusted server is assigned to share the decryption capability with data users such that the server can indirectly revoke a data user by stopping helping this data user with decryption.

Denote "NA" by the meaning of not-applicable. Let R be the number of revoked users, N be the number of all data users, l be the number of attributes presented in the

Table 1. Comparison of properties among revocable ABE (RABE) schemes

	RABE in [5]	RABE in [1]	RABE in [25]	RABE in [20]	Basic ABE-GR	Server-aided ABE-GR
Revocation mode	Indirect	Indirect & direct	Direct	Indirect	Indirect	Indirect
Selective revocation	No	No	No	No	Yes	Yes
Type of ABE	KP-ABE	KP-ABE	CP-ABE	KP-ABE & CP-ABE	CP-ABE	CP-ABE
Key exposure Resistance	No	No	No	No	Yes	Yes
Secure channel	Yes	Yes	Yes	Yes	Yes	No
Server	NA	NA	Semi-trust	NA	NA	Untrust
Size of key updates	$O(R\log(\frac{N}{R}))$	$O(R\log(\frac{N}{R}))$	NA	$O(R\log(\frac{N}{R}))$	$O(m\,R \cdot \log(\frac{N}{R}))$	$O(m\,R \cdot \log(\frac{N}{R}))$
Size of key stored by user	$O(l\log N)$	$O(l\log N)$	$O(1)$	$O(l\log N)$ & $O(k\log N)$	$O(k\log N)$	$O(1)$
Data user's computation overhead	$\geq 2(E+P)$	$\geq 3E+4P$	E	$\geq E+P$	$\geq E+4P$	E

access structure, k be the size of attribute set possed by each data user, and m be the maximum size allowed for k. In Table 1, we compare our revocable systems with the revocable ABE constructions in [1, 5, 20, 25], where "E" and "P" denote the calculation of exponentiation and pairing, respectively. It is straightforward to see that our notion of ABE-GR is the first that achieves selective revocation while preserving desirable properties in terms of both security and efficiency. Additionally, our server-aided ABE-GR scheme greatly reduces the storage and computation overhead incurred to each data user with the help of an untrusted server.

5 Conclusions

In this paper, we introduced a notion called attribute-based encryption with granular revocation (ABE-GR) to achieve selective revocation, where each data user's attributes (or credentials) can be selectively revoked. To our knowledge, there are few works on such a revocation mechanism, and most of the existing revocable ABE schemes aim to revoke a data user from the system such that a revoked data user will become underprivileged to all (newly) encrypted data in the system. Motivated by the key separation technique in distributed ABE [17] where one single AA's workload is split across several AAs and each AA is responsible for at least one specific attribute, we equipped a normal ABE system with a similar technique such that each data user's attribute-keys are composed of key elements (corresponding to different attributes) generated separately but essentially linkable to each other. Thus, each data user's attributes can be selectively revoked by the AA, and a data user can be revoked from the system by separately revoking all of his/her attributes. After the description of security model for SR-ABE, we presented a basic construction of ABE-GR, which utilizes the binary tree data structure to reduce the workload of the AA. Then, we further improved the efficiency by introducing an untrusted server to the proposed ABE-GR scheme to help data users with the workloads incurred in key update and decryption, which we call server-aided ABE-GR. In addition, we formally proved the security of our ABE-GR and server-aided ABE-GR schemes, and compared them with other concrete constructions of revocable ABE that are related to our work.

Acknowledgements. This research work is supported by the Singapore National Research Foundation under the NCR Award Number NRF2014NCR-NCR001-012.

References

1. Attrapadung, N., Imai, H.: Attribute-based encryption supporting direct/indirect revocation modes. In: Parker, M.G. (ed.) IMACC 2009. LNCS, vol. 5921, pp. 278–300. Springer, Heidelberg (2009). doi:10.1007/978-3-642-10868-6_17
2. Attrapadung, N., Imai, H.: Conjunctive broadcast and attribute-based encryption. In: Shacham, H., Waters, B. (eds.) Pairing 2009. LNCS, vol. 5671, pp. 248–265. Springer, Heidelberg (2009). doi:10.1007/978-3-642-03298-1_16

3. Baek, J., Zheng, Y.: Identity-based threshold decryption. In: Bao, F., Deng, R., Zhou, J. (eds.) PKC 2004. LNCS, vol. 2947, pp. 262–276. Springer, Heidelberg (2004). doi:10. 1007/978-3-540-24632-9_19

4. Beimel, A.: Secure schemes for secret sharing and key distribution. Ph.D. thesis, Israel Institute of Technology, June 1996

5. Boldyreva, A., Goyal, V., Kumar, V.: Identity-based encryption with efficient revocation. In: Proceedings of the 2008 ACM Conference on Computer and Communications Security, CCS 2008, Alexandria, Virginia, USA, 27–31 October 2008, pp. 417–426. ACM (2008)

6. Boneh, D., Ding, X., Tsudik, G., Wong, C.: A method for fast revocation of public key certificates and security capabilities. In: 10th USENIX Security Symposium, Washington, D.C., USA, 13–17 August 2001. USENIX (2001)

7. Boneh, D., Franklin, M.: Identity-based encryption from the weil pairing. In: Kilian, J. (ed.) CRYPTO 2001. LNCS, vol. 2139, pp. 213–229. Springer, Heidelberg (2001). doi:10.1007/ 3-540-44647-8_13

8. Cui, H., Deng, R.H.: Revocable and decentralized attribute-based encryption. Comput. J. **59** (8), 1220–1235 (2016). doi:10.1093/comjnl/bxw007

9. Ding, X., Tsudik, G.: Simple identity-based cryptography with mediated RSA. In: Joye, M. (ed.) CT-RSA 2003. LNCS, vol. 2612, pp. 193–210. Springer, Heidelberg (2003). doi:10. 1007/3-540-36563-X_13

10. Hanaoka, Y., Hanaoka, G., Shikata, J., Imai, H.: Identity-based hierarchical strongly key-insulated encryption and its application. In: Roy, B. (ed.) ASIACRYPT 2005. LNCS, vol. 3788, pp. 495–514. Springer, Heidelberg (2005). doi:10.1007/11593447_27

11. Horváth, M.: Attribute-based encryption optimized for cloud computing. In: Italiano, Giuseppe F., Margaria-Steffen, T., Pokorný, J., Quisquater, J.-J., Wattenhofer, R. (eds.) SOFSEM 2015. LNCS, vol. 8939, pp. 566–577. Springer, Heidelberg (2015). doi:10.1007/ 978-3-662-46078-8_47

12. Lewko, A., Waters, B.: Decentralizing attribute-based encryption. In: Paterson, Kenneth G. (ed.) EUROCRYPT 2011. LNCS, vol. 6632, pp. 568–588. Springer, Heidelberg (2011). doi:10.1007/978-3-642-20465-4_31

13. Li, J., Li, J., Chen, X., Jia, C., Lou, W.: Identity-based encryption with outsourced revocation in cloud computing. IEEE Trans. Comput. **64**(2), 425–437 (2015)

14. Li, Q., Xiong, H., Zhang, F.: Broadcast revocation scheme in composite-order bilinear group and its application to attribute-based encryption. IJSN **8**(1), 1–12 (2013)

15. Liang, K., Liu, Joseph K., Wong, Duncan S., Susilo, W.: An efficient cloud-based revocable identity-based proxy re-encryption scheme for public clouds data sharing. In: Kutyłowski, M., Vaidya, J. (eds.) ESORICS 2014. LNCS, vol. 8712, pp. 257–272. Springer, Cham (2014). doi:10.1007/978-3-319-11203-9_15

16. Libert, B., Quisquater, J.: Efficient revocation and threshold pairing based cryptosystems. In: Proceedings of the Twenty-Second ACM Symposium on Principles of Distributed Computing, PODC 2003, Boston, Massachusetts, USA, 13–16 July 2003, pp. 163–171. ACM (2003)

17. Müller, S., Katzenbeisser, S., Eckert, C.: Distributed attribute-based encryption. In: Lee, P.J., Cheon, J.H. (eds.) ICISC 2008. LNCS, vol. 5461, pp. 20–36. Springer, Heidelberg (2009). doi:10.1007/978-3-642-00730-9_2

18. Naor, D., Naor, M., Lotspiech, J.: Revocation and tracing schemes for stateless receivers. In: Kilian, J. (ed.) CRYPTO 2001. LNCS, vol. 2139, pp. 41–62. Springer, Heidelberg (2001). doi:10.1007/3-540-44647-8_3

19. Qin, B., Deng, R.H., Li, Y., Liu, S.: Server-aided revocable identity-based encryption. In: Pernul, G., Ryan, P.Y.A., Weippl, E. (eds.) ESORICS 2015. LNCS, vol. 9326, pp. 286–304. Springer, Cham (2015). doi:10.1007/978-3-319-24174-6_15

20. Sahai, A., Seyalioglu, H., Waters, B.: Dynamic credentials and ciphertext delegation for attribute-based encryption. In: Safavi-Naini, R., Canetti, R. (eds.) CRYPTO 2012. LNCS, vol. 7417, pp. 199–217. Springer, Heidelberg (2012). doi:10.1007/978-3-642-32009-5_13

21. Sahai, A., Waters, B.: Fuzzy identity-based encryption. In: Cramer, R. (ed.) EUROCRYPT 2005. LNCS, vol. 3494, pp. 457–473. Springer, Heidelberg (2005). doi:10.1007/11426639_27

22. Seo, J.H., Emura, K.: Revocable identity-based encryption revisited: security model and construction. In: Kurosawa, K., Hanaoka, G. (eds.) PKC 2013. LNCS, vol. 7778, pp. 216–234. Springer, Heidelberg (2013). doi:10.1007/978-3-642-36362-7_14

23. Wan, Z., Liu, J., Deng, R.H.: HASBE: a hierarchical attribute-based solution for flexible and scalable access control in cloud computing. IEEE Trans. Inf. Forensics Secur. 7(2), 743–754 (2012)

24. Waters, B.: Ciphertext-policy attribute-based encryption: an expressive, efficient, and provably secure realization. In: Catalano, D., Fazio, N., Gennaro, R., Nicolosi, A. (eds.) PKC 2011. LNCS, vol. 6571, pp. 53–70. Springer, Heidelberg (2011). doi:10.1007/978-3-642-19379-8_4

25. Yang, Y., Ding, X., Lu, H., Wan, Z., Zhou, J.: Achieving revocable fine-grained cryptographic access control over cloud data. In: Desmedt, Y. (ed.) ISC 2013. LNCS, vol. 7807, pp. 293–308. Springer, Cham (2015). doi:10.1007/978-3-319-27659-5_21

Tokenisation Blacklisting Using Linkable Group Signatures

Assad Umar[✉], Iakovos Gurulian, Keith Mayes,
and Konstantinos Markantonakis

Information Security Group, Royal Holloway, University of London,
Egham, Surrey TW20 0EX, UK
{Assad.Umar.2011,Iakovos.Gurulian.2014,Keith.Mayes,
K.Markantonakis}@rhul.ac.uk

Abstract. Payment cards make use of a Primary Account Number (PAN) that is normally used by merchants to uniquely identify users, and if necessary to deny users service by blacklisting. However, tokenisation is a technique whereby the PAN is replaced by a temporary equivalent, for use in mobile devices that emulate payment cards, but with reduced attack resistance. This paper outlines how tokenised payments contradict the process of blacklisting in open transport systems. We propose the use of a linkable group signature to link different transactions by a user regardless of the variable token. This allows the transport operator to check if a user's signature is linked to a previous dishonest transaction in the blacklist, while still maintaining the anonymity of the user.

1 Introduction

Card payments rely on the high levels of security and tamper-resistance provided by the chip embedded in the bank card. The chip provides secure storage for sensitive credentials such as the Primary Account Number (PAN) [1], as well as performing cryptographic operations. More recently, the use of contactless payments has risen significantly. There are now more than 81 million contactless bank cards on issue in the UK alone [2]. Contactless payments are quick and typically do not require cardholder verification, which makes them suitable for low value transactions. This opens up new use-cases for contactless payments such as transport. Major Transport Operators (TrOs) such as Transport for London (TfL) and the Utah Transit Authority (UTA) have moved from using proprietary smart card solutions exclusively, to accepting contactless credit/debit bank cards already in the user's possession. This model is generally referred to as the *'Open Ticketing Model'*. In open ticketing, the TrO typically relies on the PAN of the user, to determine the points of entry and exit that make up a complete journey.

In addition, by already having the infrastructure (terminals) to accept contactless bank cards, TrOs can also accept payments by Near Field Communication (NFC)-enabled devices with minimal or no changes. This is because both contactless cards and NFC devices comply with the ISO/IEC 14443 standards [3]. In fact, a terminal sees an NFC device in *card emulation mode* as if it were a

© ICST Institute for Computer Sciences, Social Informatics and Telecommunications Engineering 2017
R. Deng et al. (Eds.): SecureComm 2016, LNICST 198, pp. 182–198, 2017.
DOI: 10.1007/978-3-319-59608-2_10

regular contactless card. In this paper we focus on NFC device-based payments in transport.

Traditionally, an NFC device in card emulation mode relies on the Secure Element (SE) for enhanced security. It was envisaged that the host Operating System (OS) cannot guarantee the levels of security required by applications such as payment and transport. The SE is a small hardware tamper-resistant chip similar to the chip in a bank card in terms of functionality. The SE is typically embedded in the device, but could also be realised using the SIM card or an external memory card. The NFC controller routes messages received from a terminal to an application in the SE. The SE is tightly controlled by the Original Equipment Manufacturer (OEM) or by the Mobile Network Operator (MNO) in the case of a SIM card. This means only they can dictate who can provision an application on the SE and will usually charge a fee to do so. This adds an extra cost to NFC-based payments and adds to the complexity of the ecosystem.

However, *Host-based Card Emulation* (HCE) offers a drastic alternative to card emulation with an SE. HCE was first introduced by Cyanogenmod [4] and more notably by Google on Android 4.4 (KitKat) [5] onwards. It lets an application on the OS emulate a smart card. The NFC controller here routes messages directly to the application, bypassing the SE. Therefore security is traded for flexibility, because the guarantees of hardware-backed security are lost.

Different techniques have been proposed to manage the risks of HCE's reliance on software and make it acceptably secure for payments. More details on HCE and the feasibility of these approaches, as well their pros and cons can be found in [6,7]. Of significance to this paper is *tokenisation*. The idea of tokenisation is to replace the PAN in the user's device with a surrogate value that has a shorter life-span than the original PAN.

1.1   Problem Statement

The PAN has evolved from being just an account reference of the user. Merchants, in this case TrOs, rely on the PAN as a static value to uniquely identify users, and consequently blacklist them [8,9]. However, in the case of tokenised payments, it is paradoxical for a merchant to rely on a non-static token for blacklisting. We highlight how tokenised payments in transport call into question the ability to blacklist dishonest users on the transport network. This variability in 'identity' exposes the TrO to attacks similar to the Sybil attack [10]. This is a potential problem for both academic proposals and real life implementations that rely on a static value to identify or distinguish users.

1.2   Proposed Solution

In this paper, we ue linkable group digital signatures to propose a solution to the blacklisting problem [11,12]. Linkable signatures have a property that lets a verifier link the signatures of a user on different messages, anonymously. We rely on the 'linkability' property to blacklist dishonest users, regardless of their non-static token. We also exploit the anonymity provided by the linkable signature, which is an important requirement for transport ticketing systems. 'Dishonest user' in this paper refers to a user travelling with no funds in the account, or an attacker using a stolen or compromised device. We are able to blacklist users regardless of their short-lived tokens while maintaining user anonymity. We test the feasibility of our solution by implementing it on an NFC mobile device.

1.3 Related Work

The work in [13] evaluates open ticketing using TfL and the Chicago Transit Authority (CTA) as case studies. The author mainly focused on the theoretical aspects of adoption, such as the issue of unbanked riders. In [14], linkable group signatures were used to detect the double usage of tickets; however, their proposal was based on a closed model and tickets were purchased well before the travel. To the best of our knowledge, the only academic open ticketing proposal is [15]. The authors proposed the use of bank cards and, specifically, using the PAN to identify users. However, the authors rely on Certificate Revocation List (CRL) to blacklist dishonest users. We shall discuss the problems with using CRLs below.

2 Transport Ticketing Systems

Transport ticketing systems can be classified into two broad categories: closed and open ticketing systems. Closed ticketing systems are proprietary systems that are typically 'card/device centric'; i.e. the card holds the logic, tickets, transaction value and other accounting related data used in the calculation of fares. In this model, the TrO is essentially its own 'bank'. Notable examples are the London Oyster card and the Hong Kong Octopus card. However, this paper focuses on the open ticketing systems described in more detail below.

2.1 Open Ticketing Systems

Open systems rely on the well established global payment infrastructure. This means users can make travel payments with contactless cards, mobile applications issued by the bank cards, or even digital wallets. Therefore the TrO in this model accepts payments like any other merchant. The TrO saves the cost of issuing the cards and managing the card system. It is considered that almost 10% of revenue generated on the London transport network goes to managing the Oyster card system [16].

Open ticketing can be realised in different ways. To that effect, the UK Cards Association (UKCA)[1] has designed a framework that outlines three contactless ticketing models as agreed by the card and transit industries [17]. This paper focuses on the 'Aggregated Pay As You Go' model. In this model, the payment device is used multiple times and the price is not known at the beginning of the

---

[1] "The UK Cards Association is the trade body for the card payments industry in the UK, representing financial institutions which act as card issuers and acquirers".

journey. Each usage of the device in a day is acknowledged and later aggregated at the back-office to determine the fare to be charged; and subsequently request for payments from the user's bank through the payment network. It is important to highlight the concept of *delayed authorisation* of payments as it forms the basis upon which the aggregated pay as you go model relies.

In delayed authorisation, instead of requesting authorisation for every transaction as usual, the TrO only acknowledges the usage of the user's device at various points on the transport network (also known as a *TAP*) and sends the TAPs to the back-office. At the back office, all TAPs by the same user are aggregated at the end of the day. And only then does the TrO request for authorisation of funds. The apparent risk here is that a dishonest user can travel with no funds in the account since authorisation is not done at the time of travel. We refer to this as the *'first time travel risk'*. Currently, this risk is negotiated and accepted between the TrO and the bank issuers [17].

2.2 Blacklisting in Transport Ticketing

With over £200 million lost by UK transport operators in revenue due to dishonest users [18], blacklisting is an essential requirement for ticketing systems. Blacklisting becomes even more important for systems that rely on delayed authorisation due to first time travel risk. This gives the TrO monetary incentives to deny the user travel until outstanding payments and possibly fines are settled. Therefore, a blacklisting solution must be able to uniquely identify a dishonest user and subsequently deny travel. In open ticketing, the two unique values that could potentially be used for blacklisting are the user's public keys through CRLs, or the PAN. Earlier solutions [15] have relied on CRLs. However, the use of CRLs for real life implementations has its challenges, the distribution of CRLs to merchants faces problems of efficiency. Furthermore, due to the strict timing requirements of transport ticketing systems, the look-up times of CRLs may prove to be too high. Also, with a huge number of transactions, it is impossible to update CRLs in an efficient way. More on CRLs can be found in [19].

2.3 EMV Payment Tokenisation

Tokenisation replaces the PAN with a short-lived surrogate value referred to as a 'token' [20]. The idea is to eliminate sensitive cardholder information, specifically the PAN, from the payment device as well as merchant terminals and replace it with a token. If the device is compromised, the token will be of minimal importance as it is only valid for a short time. EMVCo[2] has released a specification on the use of tokenisation for mobile payments [20].

EMVco introduces a new entity to the existing payment network known as the Token Service Provider (TSP). The TSP is responsible for generating, issuing,

---

[2] EMVCo, made up of six members; American Express, Discover, JCB, MasterCard, UnionPay, and Visa, facilitates worldwide interoperability and acceptance of secure payment transactions.

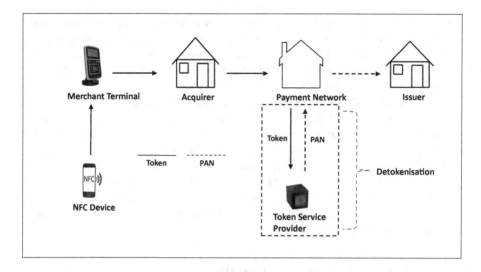

Fig. 1. Diagram showing the transaction flow of a tokenised payment

and provisioning payment tokens to legitimate token requests. The TSP is also responsible for maintaining the PAN-token mapping in the token vault, as well as *detokenisation*, i.e. the translation of tokens back to PANs for legitimate requests. Figure 1 shows the transaction flow in an EMV tokenised transaction. Methods of verifying the legitimacy of these requests, the token generation methods, and the way in which these tokens are provisioned to the device are out of the scope of this paper. We assume tokens will be generated and provisioned using global best practices. Also the validity period of tokens is out of scope; the amount of time for which a token is valid should be determined based on the perceived risk level.

3   Linkable Group Digital Signatures

Group signatures as first proposed by Chaum in [21] allow any member of a particular group to generate signatures anonymously. The verifier gets cryptographic assurances that a legitimate member of the group signed the message without revealing the signer's identity.

Group signatures with different properties have been proposed in the literature. In this paper, we use the linkable group signature first proposed in [12] (referred to as a list signature) and standardised by ISO/IEC in [11]. In its original construction, it supports the linking of signatures provided they were signed using the same linking tag. In [12] a time frame was used as the linking tag, allowing the linking of all signatures generated by a user within a given time frame. However, [11] shows the linking tag can also be any random value, as long as it is constant. This signature also supports revocation; it supports both private key revocation and verifier blacklist revocation. In the section below, we give an overview of the processes involved in this signature. For a detailed outline of the process and mathematical proofs, please refer to [11,12].

3.1   Intractability Solutions

Strong RSA Assumption. First introduced in [22]; Let p' and q' be two distinct primes of equal length such that: $p = 2p' + 1$ and $q = 2q' + 1$ are also primes. The multiplicative group of quadratic residues modulo n denoted by $QR(n)$, is a cyclic group of order $p'q'$. Where $n = pq$, and is referred to as safe RSA modulus.

Decision Diffie-Hellman Assumption (DDH). Let g be the generator of a finite cyclic group G. The DDH assumption for group G states that it is hard to distinguish the DDH tuple: (g^x, g^y, g^{xy}) from random triples (g^x, g^y, g^z), for a random (x, y, z) modulo the order of group G.

In general, the DDH problem can also be constructed for arbitrary finite abelian groups. Therefore, if $G = QR(n)$, then G has composite order. If the group composition of G is known, then the DDH problem in G is reduced to the DDH problem in the components of G.

Table 1. Notations and meanings

Notation	Meaning
T_k	Token generated from the PAN
t_{nt}	Timestamp at the point of entry
t_{xt}	Timestamp at the point of exit
R_n	Random nonce
$s\,t\,n_{id}$	Unique train station identity
Sig_x	Linkable signature with key x
bsn	Linking base
T_4	Linking tag
A, e, x	Signature key
G_{pk}	Group public key = (n, a, a_0, g, h, b)
G_{mk}	Group membership issuing key = (p', q')
$CHALL$	$\{t_{nt}/t_{xt}\|\|R_n\|\|s\,t\,n_{id}\}$
TAP	$\{t_{nt}/t_{xt}\|\|R_n\|\|s\,t\,n_{id}\|\|T_k\|\|T_4\}$

3.2   Phases

Below we describe the phases involved in a linkable group signature. We maintain the notations used in [11] and their meanings are given in Table 1 above.

1. **Key Generation Phase:** The key generation is made up of two parts: Setup phase and the group membership issuing phase. In the setup phase, the group manager creates the group public parameter, G_{pk}, and G_{mk}. The group membership issuing process is a protocol run between the group manager and a

group member to create a unique signature key (A, e, x), where (x) is the private key and (A, e) is the group membership certificate for each group member. We assume the presence of a secure channel between the group manager and the group member.

(a) Setup Phase: We assume the existence of two hash functions H: $\{0,1\}^* \rightarrow \{0,1\}^k$ and $H_\Gamma : \{0,1\} \rightarrow \{0,1\}^{2lp}$. The group manager chooses the group public parameters: $(l_p, k, l_x, l_e, l_E, l_X, \epsilon)$. The group manager also chooses random generators: (a, a_0, g, h, b) of QR(n). $G_{pk} = (n, a, a_0, g, h, b)$ and $G_{mk} = (p', q')$

(b) Group Membership Issuing Phase: At the end of this phase, the member knows a random $x \in [0, 2^{l_x} - 1]$ and the group manager knows a^x mod n and nothing more. Then the group manager chooses a random prime $e \in [2^{lE} - 2^{le} + 1]$ and computes $A = (a_0 C_2)^{d1}$ mod n where $C_2 = a^x$ mod n and $d_1 = 1/e$ mod n. The group manager sends A and e to the member. The member checks that $A^e = a_0 a^x$ mod n. The group member signature key is (A, e, x) and x is the private key.

2. **Signing Phase:** The signature process takes as input; the (G_{pk}), the group member signature key (A, e, x), a *linking base (bsn)* and the message to be signed and outputs a linkable signature Sig_x.

Algorithm 1. Signing

1: Compute f $= (H_\Gamma(bsn))^2$ (mod n)
2: Chooses random integers: $w_1, w_2, w_3 \in [0, 2^{2lp} - 1]$
3: Compute: $T_1 = Ab^{w1}$ (mod n),
$\quad\quad\quad\quad T_2 = g^{w1}h^{w2}$ (mod n),
$\quad\quad\quad\quad T_3 = g^e h^{w3}$ (mod n),
$\quad\quad\quad\quad T_4 = f^x$ (mod n).
4: Choose random integers:
$\quad\quad\quad\quad r_1 \in [0, 2^{\epsilon(le+k)} - 1]$,
$\quad\quad\quad\quad r_2 \in [0, 2^{\epsilon(lx+k)} - 1]$,
$\quad\quad\quad\quad r_3, r_4, r_5 \in [0, 2^{\epsilon(lp+k)} - 1]$
5: Choose random integers: $r_9, r_{10} \in [0, 2^{\epsilon(2lp+le+k)} - 1]$
6: Compute: $d_1 = T_1^{r1}/(a^{r2}b^{r9})$ (mod n)
$\quad\quad\quad\quad d_2 = T_2^{r1}/(g^{r9}h^{r10})$ (mod n)
$\quad\quad\quad\quad d_3 = g^{r3}h^{r4}$ (mod n)
$\quad\quad\quad\quad d_4 = g^{r1}h^{r5}$ (mod n)
$\quad\quad\quad\quad d_5 = f^{r2}$ (mod n)
7: Compute:
$\quad\quad\quad\quad$ c $= H(a||a_0||g||h||T_1||T_2||T_3||T_4||d_1||...d_5||m)$
$\quad\quad\quad\quad s_1 = r_1 - c(e - 2^{lE}), s_2 = r_2 - c(x - 2^{lX})$,
$\quad\quad\quad\quad s_3 = r_3 - cw_1, s_4 = r_4 - cw_2$,
$\quad\quad\quad\quad s_5 = r_5 - cw_3, s_9 = r_9 - cew_1$,
$\quad\quad\quad\quad s_{10} = r_{10} - cew_2$
8: Set the signature as:
$\quad\quad\quad\quad Sig_x = (c, s_1, s_2, s_3, s_4, s_5, s_9, s_{10}, T_1, T_2, T_3, T_4)$

---

3. **Verification Phase:** The verification process takes as input a message, bsn, a linkable signature Sig_x, and G_{pk} corresponding to the group of the signer. It returns 1 if the signature is *VALID*, else it returns 0.

Algorithm 2. Verification

1: Compute:
$$f = H_\Gamma(bsn))^2 \pmod{n}$$
$$t_1 = a_0^c T_1^{s1-cl'}/(a^{s2-cL}b^{s9}) \pmod{n} \text{ where } l' = 2^{lE} \text{ and } \quad L = 2^{lX}$$
$$t_2 = T_2^{s1-cl'}/(g^{s9}h^{s10}) \pmod{n} \text{ where } l' = 2^{lE}$$
$$t_3 = T_2^c g^{s3} h^{s4} \pmod{n}$$
$$t_4 = T_3^c g^{s1-cl'} h^{s5} \pmod{n} \text{ where } l' = 2^{lE}$$
$$t_5 = T_4^c f^{s2-cL} \pmod{n} \text{ where } L = 2^{lX}$$

2: Compute:
$$c' = \mathrm{H}(a\|a_0\|g\|h\|T_1\|T_2\|T_3\|T_4\|d_1\|d_2\|d_3\|d_4\|d_5\|m)$$

3: If

$$c' = c, s_1 \in [-2^{le+k}, 2^{\epsilon(le+k)} - 1],$$
$$s_2 \in [-2^{lx+k}, 2^{\epsilon(lx+k)} - 1],$$
$$s_3 \in [-2^{2lp+k}, 2^{\epsilon(2lp+k)} - 1],$$
$$s_4 \in [-2^{2lp+k}, 2^{\epsilon(2lp+k)} - 1],$$
$$s_5 \in [-2^{2lp+k}, 2^{\epsilon(2lp+k)} - 1],$$
$$s_9 \in [-2^{2lp+le+k}, 2^{\epsilon(2lp+le+k)} - 1],$$
$$s_{10} \in [-2^{lp+le+k}, 2^{\epsilon(2lp+le+k)} - 1] \text{ return 1 (valid signature) else return}$$
0 (invalid signature)

---

4. **Linking Phase:** The linking process takes two valid linkable signatures and determines if they are linked, i.e. if they were signed by the same user.

Algorithm 3. Linking

Takes two **valid** linkable signatures:
$(c, s_1, s_2, s_3, s_4, s_5, s_9, s_{10}, T_1, T_2, T_3, T_4)$ and
$(c', s_1', s_2', s_3', s_4', s_5', s_9', s_{10'}, T_1', T_2', T_3', T_4'))$ If $T_4 = T_4'$ output 1 *i.e* they are linked, otherwise 0

---

5. **Revocation Phase:** The original construction of the signature supports two types of revocation: *Private Key Revocation* and *Verifier Blacklist Revocation*. In this paper we focus on the latter. In verifier blacklist revocation, the verifier generates a blacklist using T_4. So if the verifier needs to blacklist a dishonest signer, the signer's T_4 is added to the blacklist. Therefore the verifier can check if future signatures by the same signer are revoked by checking as follows: for each $T_{4'}$, check $T_{4'} \neq T_4$. If any of the checks fail, output 0 (revoked), else, output 1 (valid).

4 Transport Ticketing Requirements and Adversary Model

Transport ticketing systems have both functional and security requirements. A general survey of electronic ticketing requirements can be found in [23]. Open ticketing models however, have fewer requirements than closed systems because most of the logic and fare calculation is moved to the back-office. We outline the requirements below. We also explain the capabilities and motivations of a determined adversary.

4.1 Adversary Model

The motivation for an adversary here is to abuse the 'first time travel risk' mentioned in Sect. 2.1 above, by maliciously evading detection on the blacklist. The adversary could either be an attacker in possession of a stolen device, or a legitimate user trying to cheat the system. A determined attacker will try to avoid the blacklisting mechanism by producing a signature with a fake linking tag. According to the described Adversary model, we list the presumptive capabilities of the attacker below:

1. The attacker cannot break the linkable signature algorithm used in this paper.
2. The attacker is active, and can generate fake tokens and linking tags.
3. The attacker has access to the payment device, as well as a legitimate signing key.

4.2 Functional Requirements

1. Offline Verification: It should be possible to validate offline, if the user is allowed to travel. This is because network connectivity cannot be guaranteed in some areas such as underground stations. Connecting to a back-end will also introduce latency to the overall transaction speed.
2. Efficiency: Transport ticketing systems should be very efficient in terms of passenger throughput. Therefore they are required to produce transaction speeds of 300–500 ms from the time the user taps the device to the time the terminal grants or rejects access.

4.3 Security Requirements

1. Integrity: It should be possible to verify if a wrong ticketing credential is used. There should also be cryptographic evidence binding the user's transaction to a location at a particular time.
2. Anonymity: Although more of a privacy concern, the identity of the users of a transport system must not be revealed.
3. Exculpability: It should be impossible for any entity, including the group manager to falsely accuse a user of making a transaction at an entry or exit point on the transport network.

4. Blacklistability: It should be possible to build a blacklist of dishonest users (or compromised devices), and be able to deny them further usage of the transport network.

5 Proposed Model

In this section, we outline the general architecture of our proposed model. We define the entities involved, as well as the roles played by each entity. We also highlight the general assumptions made which are necessary for our proposed model.

We propose an open transport ticketing model which relies on EMV tokens provisioned to NFC devices. The protocol makes use of linkable digital signatures. Linkable digital signatures provide security features suitable for open transport ticketing models. By correctly verifying a user's signature, the TrO has assurance that the user belongs to a known group. More importantly for this paper, we use linkable signatures to solve the problem of blacklisting in tokenised payments. In case of a dishonest user, the TrO is able to link the signatures of the user on different tokens, while maintaining the anonymity of the user. Figure 2 shows the sequence of messages exchanged in the proposed protocol.

5.1 Assumptions

1. The transport application, and credentials including cryptographic material, shall be provisioned to the user's device using secure best practices such as using GlobalPlatform.

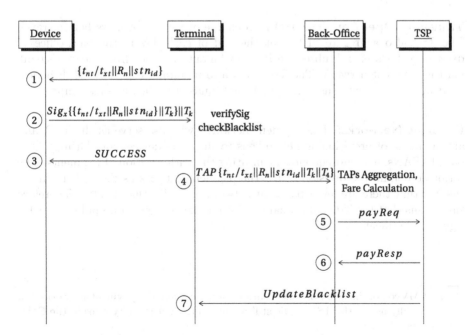

Fig. 2. Sequence diagram showing the protocol of the proposed solution

2. The payment networks act as TSPs, and shall subject users to necessary identification and verification (ID&V) prior to issuing new tokens.
3. Each user is part of a group of users depending on their payment network. For example, all MasterCard users are part of the same group.
4. The validity of the token in this paper is at least seven days.
5. We assume the maximum security features available via the platform/OS will be in place to store tokens, keys, and other cryptographic material. Therefore, in reality, the validity of the token will be based on the perceived residual risk.
6. The user is in possession of an NFC device with a payment application used for regular tokenised payments such as retail.
7. There is mutual trust between the TrO and the rest of the EMV ecosystem, and the terminals will be provided with the group public keys of the payment network.
8. Each train station has entry and exit gates, equipped with a terminal and a turnstile to grant or deny entry.

5.2   Entities

Below we describe the functions of the entities that make up the architecture of the proposed model.

User: A user in this context will already have a bank account and possibly a bank card. The user also has a NFC-enabled mobile device as well as a payment application provisioned to the device.

Transport Operator: The TrO is in charge of validating users before travel. The TrO also aggregates TAPs at the end of each day in the back-office to determine the fare, and subsequently apply for authorisation from the user's bank via the payment network. The TrO shall also maintain a blacklist of dishonest users in cases where the user has insufficient funds or in the case of a compromise.

Payment Networks: The payment networks will also serve as the TSP, and are in charge of provisioning new tokens to the users device, translating tokens back to PANs, and subsequently facilitating the authorisation of payments. The rationale behind the decision to use the payment network as the TSP is due to the fact that there are fewer payment networks globally, than banks[3]. Therefore this means that the TrO's terminal will have to keep a few group public keys for signature verification.

---

[3] The EMVco specification on tokenisation indicates that the payment networks can additionally act as the TSP, while still maintaining their primary roles in the EMV ecosystem.

5.3   Phases

Our solution is divided into 4 phases: the *setup phase, validation phase, accounting phase* and the *blacklisting phase.* The specifics of the accounting phase are out of the scope of this paper. It is however important to mention as it precedes the blacklisting phase.

Setup Phase: This phase is executed between a user and the payment network. A user initiates this phase by opting to use the payment application on his device for transport payments. They both engage in an ID&V process to verify the user's identity and bank account, and check if the user's has any outstanding transport fares. The process is terminated if any of the checks fail. Otherwise they go through the key generation process as explained in Sect. 3.2. In the end, the user will have a unique signature key; (A, e, x), a token (T_k), and a TrO-specific (bsn). We assume the TSPs group public keys to be well known and are provided to the TrOs well before hand.

Validation Phase: This phase is illustrated in Fig. 2. We see that a user taps the device on a terminal at a train station, the terminal sends a challenge to the user. Challenge includes; timestamp (t_X), random nonce (R_n) and the station ID $(st\,n_{id})$. User concatenates the token (T_k) to the challenge, and signs as explained in the signing phase in Sect. 3.2, using the (bsn) of the TrO. (t_x) could either be (t_{nt}) or (t_{xt}) for entry and exit gates respectively. The user concatenates (T_k) to the signed message and sends to the terminal. The terminal verifies the signature using (G_{pk}) as outlined in verification phase in Sect. 3.2. If the signature is valid, the terminal checks to see if the user's (T_4) is included in the blacklist. If it doesn't correspond with any (T_4) on the blacklist, the user is allowed to travel otherwise the user is denied travel. Afterwards, the terminal records a TAP. A TAP includes the challenge signed by the user, the users (T_k), and the amount to be charged which is determined in the *accounting phase* below. The blacklist check is only needed at the entry gates.

Accounting Phase: This is a back-office process where $TAPs$ of all users for the day are aggregated to determine the fare to be paid by the user. The TrO sends a payment request (payReq), which includes the (T_k) and the amount to be charged, to the payment network for authorisation[4].

Blacklisting Phase: This phase only becomes necessary in cases where an authorisation fails due to insufficient funds in the user's account. The TSP sends a *transaction decline* message to the TrO. The TrO then puts the users T_4 in its blacklist database and updates the terminals at the stations with the latest blacklist entries. A user's device can also be put in the blacklist in the case of compromise or a lost device.

---

[4] The payment network, acting as the TSP, translates the token back to a real PAN and authorisation is processed as per normal EMV flow.

5.4   Proof of Concept

A proof of concept was developed to test the feasibility of our proposal and also analyse it against the requirements mentioned in Sect. 4. A HCE-based Android application was installed on an NFC device for the digital signature implementation. We adapted an implementation of the digital signature in [24] which was part of an analysis of group signatures on mobile devices [25]. For the terminal, we had a Java application using the smartcard I/O Application Programming Interface (API) running on a PC; this acts as the terminal at a train station (Table 2).

Table 2. Devices used in proof of concept

Device	Manufacturer	Operating system	RAM
Phone (Nexus 5)	LG Electronics	Android 5.1.1 (Lollipop)	2 GB
Laptop	Dell	Windows 10	8 GB
Reader	ACS (ACR1281U)	N/A	N/A

5.5   Lessons Learned/Considerations

Support for extended Application Protocol Data Unit (APDUs)[5] on NFC devices is still not as extensive as smart cards. Therefore most NFC devices can only send normal APDUs with a maximum length of 256 bytes. We realised this is a software-based restriction rather than the NFC controller's inability to handle bigger messages. Due to the size of the signature in our protocol, we modified the Android source to allow the device to send back the signature in one APDU, rather than in chunks.

Sending a substantial amount of data over the NFC channel may not always be efficient. Due to the size of the signature we used, we realised the time cost of compressing the message and decompressing at the terminal's side is trivial. We found the *BZip2* compression algorithm to be the most efficient.

Most of the parts of the signature can be precomputed; that is those parts that do not depend on the challenge from the reader.

5.6   Performance Analysis

The total size of $Sig_x\{\{t_{nt}/t_{xt}||R_n||s\,t\,n_{id}\}\,||T_k\}||T_k$ is 3536 bytes, with a 512 bit key, plus additional 15 bytes for concatenating the token to the signature in plain text. This is compressed to 1617 bytes, providing 45.7% compression.

We took average timings of individual processes, as well as the total time it takes the full protocol to run over 100 iterations. The mobile device takes

---

[5] Application Protocol Data Unit is the unit of communication between a device and a reader. APDUs are specified in ISO/IEC 7816 be.

an average of 9.92 ms to sign the challenge received from the reader and also compress the signature. The *Round Trip Time* (RTT), i.e. the time from when the reader sends the challenge to when it receives the response, takes on average 420.75 ms. We refer to this as *CHALL*. It is important to note that about 90% of the RTT is spent on the NFC communication link. The signature verification on the terminal side, including decompression of the received data, takes 20.5 ms on average. The whole protocol takes on average 451.17 ms.

For performance measurements of checking the blacklist, we rely on a comparative study of Database Management Systems (DBMS) in [26]. Each DBMS was populated with 1,000,000 records, and the timings for a *'select'* query for each was taken. The select query emulates the look up of a user's (T_4) from a blacklist database. SQL Server was the fastest and took 18ms, while the slowest was Oracle and took 23 ms. These projections show that the delay introduced by searching a blacklisting is trivial and therefore, our protocol still runs within the accepted transaction time range for transport usage.

Table 3. Table showing transaction times in milliseconds (ms)

	CHALL	Sign	Verify	Full protocol
Average	420.75	9.92	20.5	451.17
Min	405.55	7.65	17.32	430.45
Max	445.63	10.65	23.75	480.03

5.7   Requirements Analysis

We analyse our proposal against both the security and functional requirements mentioned in Sect. 4.3 above. Our model meets the *offline verification* requirement because the terminal is able to verify a signature, as well as run the blacklisting function offline, i.e. without connecting to a back-office or relying on a third party. The protocol, as shown in Table 3 above, is within the acceptable transaction speed range, as stipulated by the *efficiency* requirement. It is worth noting that, currently, NFC devices in HCE only operate at the lowest NFC data rate of 106 kbps[6]. We found out this limitation is also a software limitation and not the NFC controller's inability to operate at higher data rates. Therefore at higher rates, our solution is expected to be much faster.

In terms of security, for a signature verified to be valid, it is computationally hard for anyone except the group manager to reveal the identity of the actual signer. In the random oracle model, the proof of knowledge that is part of the signature can be proven in statistically zero knowledge. Also trying to identify a particular signer with certificate (A, e) requires the adversary to know if $log_b T_1/A, log_g T_2$, and $log_g T_3/g^e$ are equal. This is assumed to be infeasible

---

[6] NFC supports data rate of 106, 212, 424, and 848 kbps.

under the decisional Diffie-Hellman assumption. Therefore our protocol meets the *anonymity* requirement.

As shown in the key generation phase in Sect. 3.2, the group manager does not learn any new information about the user's private key (x), and at the end of the phase, the group manager only learns a^x. Also, because (T1, T2 and T3) represent an unconditional binding commitments to $(A$ and $e)$. This implies that if the factorization of n is feasible, the group signature is a proof of knowledge of the discrete logarithm of $A/a0$ [27]. Therefore no entity, including the transport operator and the payment network – acting as the group manager, can sign a message on behalf of a user as computing discrete logarithm is assumed to be infeasible. Therefore our protocol thereby meets the *exculpability* requirement because a user cannot be framed for a false transaction.

In addition, *integrity* is achieved because it is not possible for anyone without access to the private key (x) to generate a valid signature. Secondly, the TrO is able to verify that the signed message includes the correct challenge it had sent, thereby cryptographically linking the user to that point on the transport network at that particular time. Hence creating the 'TAP'.

User *blacklisting* is achieved because a legitimate user cannot avoid detection on the blacklist by forging a false linking base. (T_4) is linked with (T_1) through the proof of knowledge and also the private key x. In addition, a legitimate user cannot repeatedly cheat the system by signing on a rogue token with a legitimate credential, because after the first payment request is declined, the TrO can blacklist the user with the corresponding (T_4).

6   Conclusion and Future Work

In this paper, we have looked at how a security solution – tokenisation, affects the unique identification of users in certain scenarios. In particular, we have highlighted how this calls into question user blacklisting in transport ticketing. We have shown how linkable group signatures can be used to link two transactions regardless of the changing token. This concept is used to create a blacklist of dishonest users.

We have also shown the feasibility of our solution by building a proof-of-concept which is analysed against the outlined requirements. Our solution can also be used in use-cases outside ticketing that rely on the static nature of PANs. For example, in retail to link different transactions of a user (with different tokens) for loyalty and promotional purposes.

As future work, we plan to investigate more efficient methods of achieving linkability while maintaining anonymity. We also plan to further improve the security of our proposed solution by implementing it on a Trusted Execution Environment (TEE).

References

1. Identification cards - Identification of issuers - Part 1: Numbering system. ISO/IEC 7812-1. Standard, International Organization for Standardization, Geneva, CH (2015)
2. The UKCARDS Association. Card expenditure statistics, January
3. International Organization for Standardization (ISO). Identification cards - Contactless integrated circuit cards - Proximity cards (2008)
4. Yeager, D.: Added NFC Reader support for two new tag types: ISO PCD type A and ISO PCD type B (2012)
5. Android Developer Guide. Host-based Card Emulation. https://developer.android. com/guide/topics/connectivity/nfc/hce.html
6. MNFCC-14002: Host Card Emulation (HCE) 101, SmartCardAlliance, Technical report MNFCC-14002, August 2004. http://www.smartcardalliance.org/ downloads/HCE-101-WP-FINAL-081114-clean.pdf
7. Umar, A., Mayes, K., Markantonakis, K.: Performance variation in host-based card emulation compared to a hardware security element. In: Mobile and Secure Services (MOBISECSERV), pp. 1–6, February 2015. doi:10.1109/MOBISECSERV. 2015.7072872
8. Radu, C.: Implementing Electronic Card Payment Systems. Artech House Computer Security Series. Artech House, USA (2003)
9. Samsung Pay Will Transform the Mobile Wallet Experience. Standard, Samsung Electronics Co. Ltd. (2016)
10. Douceur, J.R.: The sybil attack. In: Druschel, P., Kaashoek, F., Rowstron, A. (eds.) IPTPS 2002. LNCS, vol. 2429, pp. 251–260. Springer, Heidelberg (2002). doi:10. 1007/3-540-45748-8_24
11. Information technology - Security techniques - Anonymous digital signatures. Standard, International Organization for Standardization, Geneva, CH (2013)
12. Canard, S., Schoenmakers, B., Stam, M., Traoré, J.: List Signature Schemes, vol. 154, pp. 189–201. Elsevier Science Publishers B.V., Amsterdam (2006)
13. Brakewood, C.E.: Contactless Prepaid and Bankcards in Transit Fare Collection Systems, June 2010
14. Arfaoui, G., Dabosville, G., Gambs, S., Lacharme, P., Lalande, J.-F.: A Privacy-Preserving NFC Mobile Pass for Transport Systems, vol. 2, p. e4 (2014)
15. Ekberg, J.-E., Tamrakar, S.: Mass transit ticketing with NFC mobile phones. In: Chen, L., Yung, M., Zhu, L. (eds.) INTRUST 2011. LNCS, vol. 7222, pp. 48–65. Springer, Heidelberg (2012). doi:10.1007/978-3-642-32298-3_4
16. Transport Committee: The Future of Ticketing. Greater London Authority (2011)
17. Krikorian-Slade, B., Burholt, N.M.A.: Contactless Transit Framework. Standard and Cards Association, UK (2016)
18. Annual Fraud Indicator: Report. University of Portsmouth, Centre for Counter Fraud Studies, Portsmouth, England (2016)
19. Gentry, C.: Certificate-based encryption and the certificate revocation problem. In: Biham, E. (ed.) EUROCRYPT 2003. LNCS, vol. 2656, pp. 272–293. Springer, Heidelberg (2003). doi:10.1007/3-540-39200-9_17
20. EMV Payment Tokenisation Specification. Standard (2014)
21. Brands, S., Chaum, D.: Distance-bounding protocols. In: Helleseth, T. (ed.) EUROCRYPT 1993. LNCS, vol. 765, pp. 344–359. Springer, Heidelberg (1994). doi:10. 1007/3-540-48285-7_30

22. Barić, N., Pfitzmann, B.: Collision-free accumulators and fail-stop signature schemes without trees. In: Fumy, W. (ed.) EUROCRYPT 1997. LNCS, vol. 1233, pp. 480–494. Springer, Heidelberg (1997). doi:10.1007/3-540-69053-0_33
23. Mut-Puigserver, M., Magdalena Payeras-Capellí, M., Ferrer-Gomila, J.-L., Vives-Guasch, A., Castellí-Roca, J.: A Survey of Electronic Ticketing Applied to Transport, vol. 31, pp. 925–939. Elsevier Advanced Technology Publications, Oxford (2012)
24. Potzmader, K.: ISO20008-2.2 Group Signature Scheme Evaluation on Mobile Devices (2013)
25. Potzmader, K., Winter, J., Hein, D., Hanser, C., Teufl, P., Chen, L.: Group Signatures on Mobile Devices: Practical Experiences, pp. 47–64 (2013)
26. Bassil, Y.: A comparative study on the performance of the top DBMS systems (2012). abs/1205.2889
27. Ateniese, G., Camenisch, J., Joye, M., Tsudik, G.: A Practical and Provably Secure Coalition-Resistant Group Signature Scheme, pp. 255–270. Springer, London (2000)

Privacy-Preserving Multi-pattern Matching

Tao Zhang, Xiuhua Wang, and Sherman S.M. Chow[✉]

Department of Information Engineering,
The Chinese University of Hong Kong, Sha Tin, N.T., Hong Kong
{zt112,wx015,sherman}@ie.cuhk.edu.hk

Abstract. Multi-pattern matching compares a large set of patterns against a given query string, which has wide application in various domains such as bio-informatics and intrusion detection. This paper presents a privacy-preserving multi-pattern matching system which processes an encrypted query string over an encrypted pattern set. Our construction is a symmetric-key system based on Aho-Corasick automaton. The computation complexity is the same as the basic automaton in the base case, and within a multiplicative cost in the length of the longest pattern in general.

Keywords: Multi-pattern matching · Symmetric searchable encryption

1 Introduction

Storage service witnesses an increasing popularity for satisfying different needs. Some cloud services also provide applications which perform computation over the outsourced data. However, the data is often sensitive. The users may not fully trust the well behaviour of the cloud. A natural solution for the client is to encrypt the data and outsource the ciphertexts instead. Without the key, one learns nothing about the plaintext. The cloud thus cannot perform any useful function over the data. For example, one may want to apply multi-pattern search over the emails or network traffic for virus scanning or intrusion detection.

Chase and Shen [6] propose a queryable encryption scheme for substring queries based on suffix trees. It can find all occurrences of a query string p as a substring of an outsourced string s. This is like the dual of the multi-pattern search problem — a set of pattern is outsourced and the query is a string for checking which pattern appears at which position of the string.

This paper studies multi-pattern matching over encrypted pattern sets and encrypted query. Given a large pattern set M where each pattern consists of the characters from an alphabet set Σ, the multi-pattern matching algorithm can locate all the patterns from M which appear in a query string q (also consisting of the characters in Σ). This allows the owner of a large set of patterns to outsource the set to a cloud server. At the same time, the data owner can allow any client to make queries to this encrypted pattern set. The cloud server is deterred from learning the pattern or the query. Multi-pattern matching is one of the key technologies for string analysis, and has found application in bioinformatics, business analytics, natural language processing, web search engines, *etc.*

© ICST Institute for Computer Sciences, Social Informatics and Telecommunications Engineering 2017
R. Deng et al. (Eds.): SecureComm 2016, LNICST 198, pp. 199–218, 2017.
DOI: 10.1007/978-3-319-59608-2_11

1.1 Related Work

Searchable Encryption and Structured Encryption. Symmetric searchable encryption (SSE) [7] is a symmetric-key encryption scheme which allows any server hosting the ciphertexts to search over them. The search requires a token generated by the client who holds the symmetric-key. The server is usually considered honest-but-curious, except in special schemes such as verifiable SSE proposed by Kurosawa and Ohtaki [10]. In a typical SSE, the server can easily know which parts of the memory have been accessed when the same memory block is accessed again. The security definition of SSE acknowledged the leakage of information about the plaintext due to a query, such as access pattern.

Most of the existing schemes aim to locate where the keyword query is in the outsourced files, if exists. Some SSE schemes support search beyond the basic keyword equality testing. For example, Cash *et al.* [4] proposed an efficient construction for searches involving multiple keywords. Generally speaking, exact keyword search and pattern matching are quite different. A recent scheme by Wang *et al.* [13] uses locality sensitive hash (LSH) with other techniques to achieve fuzzy search. Yet, LSH is for hashing similar keywords to the same output, but is not applicable for pattern matching in general.

Our privacy-preserving multi-pattern matching scheme falls in the scope of structured encryption [5,11]. Structured encryption is a generalization of SSE, which protects the data privacy while preserving the functionality in the original data structure. However, existing instantiations [5,11] only support data structures which are not readily extensible for our multi-pattern matching problem.

Secure Two-Party Computation of Pattern Matching. Pattern matching and other text processing has been studied in the context of secure two-party computation [3,8,9,12]. The motivation is to protect sensitive data such as DNA records from the client. In other words, the client has no knowledge about the data on the server, and should not obtain extra knowledge beyond each query. In contrast, our setting assumes the client knows and prepares the data to be outsourced to the server. It partially explains why efficient query is possible.

Authenticated Multi-pattern Matching. Recently, Zhou *et al.* [14] proposed an authenticated but not privacy-preserving solution for Aho-Corasick automaton [2]. Their scheme use dynamic accumulator (*e.g.*, [1]) to ensure the authenticity of the query result, which features constant-size proof. However, when the data stored on the server is encrypted, it is unclear how to follow their technique and generate accumulator for different nodes dynamically during a query. Instead, our proposed scheme uses symmetric-key encryption for authentication.

1.2 Our Contribution

We propose the first multi-pattern matching algorithm on encrypted pattern which is secure against malicious adversaries. Our scheme is based on

Aho-Corasick automaton (AC automaton) [2] and benefits from its efficiency. The computation complexity is $O(n+m)$ in the best case (the same as the plain AC-automaton with direct *fail* pointers), or $O(n \cdot d)$ in the worst case, where n is the length of the query string, m is the number of matched patterns, and d is the length of the longest pattern. The communication complexity is proportional to the computation complexity, as both are proportional to the nodes processed.

2 Preliminaries

This section reviews the pattern matching algorithm and some cryptographic primitives used in our proposed system.

2.1 Trie

Trie, also known as prefix tree or radix tree, is a $|\Sigma|$-ary tree for storing a large amount of strings formed by characters from the alphabet Σ. Each path from the root to a node represents a string, which is a common prefix of the strings represented by its succeeding (child) nodes. Every string in a trie can be represented by a path from the root to a node, and this path represents a common prefix of some strings. The root node denotes a null string. Any other node represents a prefix that is created by appending the character of the incoming edge, to the prefix that its parent node represents.

Figure 1 shows a sample trie. A trie $\mathcal{T}$ is setup by adding the patterns to it one by one. We traverse $\mathcal{T}$ from the root with respect to the character sequence of a pattern string. During the traversal, the current node may not have an outgoing edge which represents the next character in the string. In such cases, we add a new edge, from the current node to a new child node, to denote this missing character. The node identifier is its timestamp of insertion. We continue the traversal until the current node is the *end of the pattern*. We then mark it as a *gray* ending node, *e.g.*, node 4. Trie can reduce storage by merging all the common prefixes. The dashed and dotted edges (representing *fail* and *sp* pointers respectively) will be used by the AC automaton.

Searching on a trie is performed in a depth-first manner by sequentially taking one character from the query each time. If there is an outgoing edge for the character, it moves along it. If the outgoing edge for the next character does not exist or the query ends on a non-ending node, the search fails.

2.2 Aho-Corasick String Matching Algorithm

A naïve and costly way of multi-pattern matching is to enumerate all the patterns. Aho-Corasick algorithm [2] (AC automaton) is a pattern matching algorithm based on the trie structure which aims to guarantee the correctness without explicitly processing the patterns one by one. Multi-pattern matching algorithm can locate all the pattern occurrences in the query text by checking if the pattern is a prefix of any suffix of the text. The major idea is to sort all the prefixes of the query string (*e.g.*, "otear") from short to long (*e.g.*, "o", "ot", "ote", "otea", "otear"), then find all the suffixes which are in the pattern set for each prefix (*e.g.*, "tea" and "a" for "otea"). Correctness is guaranteed by conceptually covering all the suffixes.

For the searching process, the automaton traverses the trie from the root according to the query string, except for the following two special treatments.

The AC automaton adds *fail* pointers to the trie for quick traversal when mismatch happens, *i.e.*, if a node does not have an outgoing edge for a character c, it must have a *fail* pointer pointing at a node to which the searcher should go since that represents a suffix of the current node. Specifically, consider the string denoted by the path from the root to a node v, if there exists another path which denotes a suffix of it, and the last node on this path has a child node w denoting the character c, then *fail* pointer for c of node v points at w. If there is no such suffix on the trie, the *fail* pointer for c of node v points at the root.

In Fig. 1, *fail* pointers are shown as dashed edges. For example, consider node 8, it has one *fail* pointer for 'n' pointing at node 5, and one for 'r' pointing at node 3. Note that a null string is always a suffix, we omit the *fail* pointers pointing at the root or the second level nodes because there are too many of them (*e.g.*, *fail* pointers pointing at nodes 1, 4, 6 for 'e', 'a', 't', respectively are omitted). Step 5 in Table 1 is an example of quick traversal via *fail* pointers.

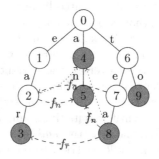

Fig. 1. AC automaton with pattern set {"ear", "a", "an", "tea", "to"}

When the traversal returns to the root via a *fail* pointer, it gives up the current character and moves to the next character in the query string. Step 1 in Table 1 gives an example, which removes 'o' and starts processing 't'.

The second special treatment is the suffix pattern (*sp*) pointers. They are shown as dotted edges in Fig. 1. For a node (may not storing a pattern) which the traversal path from the root to it gives the string s, its *sp* pointer points to an ending node (except itself) which denotes the longest suffix of s in the pattern set. In this way, we can *efficiently output* all the matched patterns for a given query by backtracing along *sp* pointers until the root is reached. (See Step 4 in Table 1 as an example.) Since all the suffixes corresponding to a particular node were accessed, backtracing guarantees that any results will not be missed even though the traversal is processing a particular path.

Table 1. Matching Flow for "otear"

Step	Prefix	Suffix	Movement	Action
1	"o"	""	$0 \to 0$	The root has no edge for 'o', and its *fail* pointer for 'o' points at the root itself, so stay at the root, and the character in the query to be processed is now 't"
2	"ot"	"t"	$0 \to 6$	The root has an edge for 't', move to Node 6
3	"ote"	"te"	$5 \to 7$	Node 6 has an edge 'e', move to Node 7
4	"otea"	"tea"	$7 \to 8$	Node 7 has an edge 'a', move to Node 8. Output **"tea"** as it is an ending node. Also output **"a"**, because Node 4 is linked by the *sp* pointer of Node 8
5	"otear"	"ear"	$8 \to 3$	Node 8 has no edge 'r', use *fail* pointer f_r to jump to Node 3. Output **"ear"** as it is an ending node. Node 3 has no *sp/fail* pointer, so search ends

Each node v stores a set of pointers for its child nodes $\{w_c\}_{c \in \Sigma}$, *fail* pointers, and its *sp* pointer. We require the total number of the child edges and the *fail* pointers of each node is exactly the size of the alphabet $|\Sigma|$, which is a constant. Every nodes thus look the same in this regard which helps us to achieve privacy.

Efficiency. We omit the factor of $|\Sigma|$ in our analysis since it is a small constant for all alphabetic scripts such as English, French, *etc.* Let N denote the number of patterns stored by $\mathcal{T}$, and ℓ is the average pattern length. For setup, the time complexity is $O(N\ell)$, including constructing the trie, the *fail* pointers and the *sp* pointers for each node of the trie. The storage size is also $O(N\ell)$.

Searching accesses $O(n + m)$ nodes where n is for traversal, and m is for outputting result including backtracing.

2.3 Cryptographic Building Blocks

Symmetric-Key Encryption (SKE). An SKE $\Pi = (\mathsf{Gen}, \mathsf{Enc}, \mathsf{Dec})$ consists of the following three probabilistic polynomial-time (PPT) algorithms:

- $K \leftarrow \mathsf{Gen}(1^\lambda)$: this algorithm takes the security parameter λ and outputs a secret key K of length determined by λ.
- $CT \leftarrow \mathsf{Enc}_K(M)$: this algorithm takes a key K and a message M, outputs a ciphertext CT.
- $(M, \bot) \leftarrow \mathsf{Dec}_K(CT)$: this algorithm takes a key K and a ciphertext CT, outputs a message M, or the symbol $\bot$ indicating CT is invalid.

We require the following security properties for symmetric encryption:

- *Correctness* requires $\mathsf{Dec}_K(\mathsf{Enc}_K(M)) = M$ with probability of 1 for all K and M.

- *CPA (chosen-plaintext attack) security* requires that for any PPT adversary who can adaptively query an encryption oracle, the ciphertexts reveal no information about plaintexts (other than their lengths).
- *Ciphertext integrity* requires that given accesses to an encryption oracle, all PPT adversaries cannot construct a new ciphertext (not output by the encryption oracle) that decrypts successfully. We say that a symmetric encryption scheme is *authenticated* if it has both CPA security and ciphertext integrity.
- *Key hiding* (also known as *which-key concealing*) requires that given two encryption oracles, all PPT adversaries cannot tell whether they encrypt using the same key or different keys.

Pseudorandom Function (PRF) Family. A PRF $F : \{0,1\}^\lambda \times \{0,1\}^* \to \{0,1\}^*$ is a family of functions with efficient evaluation. The output of a PRF is computationally indistinguishable from a uniform distribution over the range of F.

2.4 Queryable Encryption

We borrow the notion of queryable encryption introduced by Chase and Shen [6] to model our privacy-preserving multi-pattern matching scheme.

Definition 1 (Queryable Encryption). For message space $\mathbb{M}$, query space $\mathbb{Q}$, and result space $\mathbb{R}$, we define a *queryable encryption scheme* which supports query functionality $\mathcal{F} : \mathbb{M} \times \mathbb{Q} \to \mathbb{R}$ by the PPT algorithms/protocols below.

- $\mathsf{Gen}(1^\lambda) \to \mathsf{sk}$: this algorithm takes a security parameter λ as an input and outputs a secret key sk.
- $\mathsf{Enc}(\mathsf{sk}, M) \to CT$: this algorithm takes a secret key sk and a plaintext message $M \in \mathbb{M}$ as inputs and outputs a ciphertext CT.
- $\mathsf{Query}((\mathsf{sk}, q), CT)$: this is an interactive query protocol between a client and a server. The client input is a secret key sk and a query $q \in \mathbb{Q}$. During the interaction, the client generates a query token to be sent to the server. The server input is a ciphertext CT. The server interacts with the client by receiving query tokens and returning intermediate results. The final output of the client is a query result $R \in \mathbb{R}$. The server has no final output.

Correctness of queryable encryption requires, for all $\lambda \in \mathbb{N}$, $q \in \mathbb{Q}$, $M \in \mathbb{M}$, let $\mathsf{sk} \leftarrow \mathsf{Gen}(1^\lambda)$, $CT \leftarrow \mathsf{Enc}(\mathsf{sk}, M)$, and $R \leftarrow \mathsf{Query}(\mathsf{sk}, q, CT)$, we have that $\Pr[R = \mathcal{F}(M, q)] = 1 - \mathsf{negl}(\lambda)$, where $\mathsf{negl}(\lambda)$ is a *negligible* function of λ.

The security definition of a queryable encryption is parameterized by two leakage functions $\mathcal{L}_1$ and $\mathcal{L}_2$. $\mathcal{L}_1$ denotes the information about the message leaked by the ciphertext. For any j, $\mathcal{L}_2(M, Q_1, \cdots, Q_j)$ denotes the information about the message and all queries made so far that is leaked by the j-th query.

We allow the adversary to be arbitrarily malicious in the protocol. Thus we require that a malicious server either produces the correct output or will be detected. This definition guarantees both privacy and correctness. We recall the definition of security against $(\mathcal{L}_1, \mathcal{L}_2)$-chosen query attack (CQA2) [6].

Definition 2 (Malicious $(\mathcal{L}_1, \mathcal{L}_2)$-CQA2 security). Let $\mathcal{E}$ = (Gen, Enc, Query) be a queryable encryption scheme for message space $\mathbb{M}$, query space $\mathbb{Q}$, result space $\mathbb{R}$, and query functionality $\mathcal{F} : \mathbb{M} \times \mathbb{Q} \to \mathbb{R}$. We define the following experiments for leakage functions $\mathcal{L}_1$ and $\mathcal{L}_2$, adversary $\mathcal{A}$, and simulator $\mathcal{S}$:

- **Real$_{\mathcal{E},\mathcal{A}}(\lambda)$:** The challenger uses $\mathsf{Gen}(1^\lambda)$ to output a secret key K. The adversary $\mathcal{A}$ outputs a message M. The challenger runs $CT \leftarrow \mathsf{Enc}(K, M)$ and sends CT to the adversary. The challenger adaptively makes a polynomial number of queries $Q_1, \cdots, Q_t$. The challenger plays the role of client in the query protocol with input (K, Q_i) and sends the output to adversary. Finally, $\mathcal{A}$ outputs a bit b.
- **Ideal$_{\mathcal{E},\mathcal{A},\mathcal{S}}(\lambda)$:** The adversary outputs a message M. Given $\mathcal{L}_1(M)$, the simulator $\mathcal{S}$ outputs CT. The adversary adaptively makes a polynomial number of queries $Q_1, \cdots, Q_t$. For each query Q_i, the simulator is given $\mathcal{L}_2(M, Q_1, \cdots, Q_i)$ and interacts with the adversary. Then the simulator produces a flag f_i. If $f_i = \bot$, then the challenger sends $\bot$ to $\mathcal{A}$. Otherwise it outputs $\mathcal{F}(M, Q_i)$. Finally, $\mathcal{A}$ outputs a bit b.

We say that $\mathcal{E}$ is $(\mathcal{L}_1, \mathcal{L}_2)$-CQA2 secure against malicious adversaries if, for all PPT adversaries $\mathcal{A}$, there exists a simulator $\mathcal{S}$ such that:

$$|\Pr[\mathbf{Real}_{\mathcal{E},\mathcal{A}}(\lambda) = 1] - \Pr[\mathbf{Ideal}_{\mathcal{E},\mathcal{A},\mathcal{S}}(\lambda) = 1]| \leq \mathsf{negl}(\lambda).$$

3   Privacy-Preserving Multi-pattern Matching Solution

We first give some intuitions about how to process the AC-automaton for preserving its privacy, then we present the details of our construction.

3.1   Modified AC-automaton

To preserve privacy, we need to hide as much structure as possible. We should allow the recovery of the pointers only when needed. A straightforward approach which works on encrypted trie requires a high number of interactions. It can be as much as the number of traversal steps since the client cannot predict ahead the path of traversal, especially for *fail* or *sp* pointers. Here, we describe how to preprocess the AC-automaton for hiding all the pointers, and encrypt both the query string and the trie, while keeping communication complexity in mind.

Matching the Encrypted Query and the Encrypted Trie. A straightforward way to let the server query over the encrypted trie is to process each character in the query one by one. Our scheme instead generates a sequence of substrings of length $d + 1$ from the query, *i.e.*, one character longer than the longest pattern. We can thus reduce the interaction rounds from $O(n)$ to $O(\frac{n}{d})$ in the best case.

The client prepares the query token by encrypting the query substrings as a series of ciphertexts. The server uses the pre-computed keys stored in the trie to try decrypting them. The keys are pre-computed by the data owner in the following way. For each node, the data owner derives its *address in the dictionary* and a symmetric key to be stored in its parent node by using two PRFs, both taking as input the string denoted by the path from the root to this node.

During the traversal, if there exists a key which can successfully decrypt the given ciphertext, which happens when the string corresponding to the node matches the sub-string corresponding to the query token, the server can locate the next node with the address obtained from the decryption. Otherwise, the client and the server rely on the *fail* pointer to continue searching.

Handling the *fail* Pointers. Recall that if there is a mismatch happens while searching on the current path, the traversal follows the *fail* pointer which indicates a node to go. When this happens, we say that the search triggers a *fail event*. As described in the previous part, a query is divided into substrings. A fail event ends the current substring at the fail position, and starts the next substring at this fail position. The node pointed at by the *fail* pointer is the *entrance node* for continuing the next query substring.

Whenever a fail event happens, the client can always know the string denoted by the path from the root to the entrance node, when given the level of this node. The reason is that this string is a suffix string of the current substring. The current node indicates the ending position and the level of the next entrance node indicates the length of this suffix string. With this suffix string, the client can compute and send to the server the address of this entrance node (recall how the address in the dictionary is computed from the previous part).

Instead of storing the *fail* pointer directly, a node stores a tuple (c, L_c), denoting that a *fail* pointer for the character c points at a node at level L_c. The client finds the entry for the first mismatching character to get the level of the next entrance node, and recovers the *fail* pointer on spot during the search.

One could omit the *fail* pointers which point to the root. However, this approach leaks the number of fail pointers. Instead, each node stores an entry for every character in the alphabet (*e.g.*, by setting $L_c = -1$ for a child edge denoting c which is not a *fail* pointer). The overhead is reasonable for a small alphabet size.

Handling the *sp* Pointers. Consider the string denoted by the path from the root to current node, recall that the *sp* pointer indicates its longest suffix which is in the pattern set. Instead of storing the *sp* pointers, each node stores all the suffix patterns of a node (located by tracing recursively through the *sp* pointers until the root) with its own pattern. This modification reduces the number of steps during the search to $O(n)$ where n is the length of the query, but increases the server storage to $O(N\ell)$. The maximum number of suffix patterns a node has is the same as the height d of $\mathcal{T}$. We can hide the number by additionally storing at most d dummy patterns for each node. To reduce the storage, we store an encryption of the pattern identities instead of the actual strings.

Handling Malicious Servers. We allow the server to be malicious (returning tampered messages) instead of just being honest-but-curious. We use authenticated symmetric-key encryption such that the client (decryptor) can check the authenticity of the ciphertext returned by the server.

For a node in the trie, the data owner encrypts the information of the path of this node, its child node, its fail pointers, and its patterns. Modification of the path requires the server to modify the encrypted information of one or more nodes. For deletion of any nodes, the server needs to return the ciphertext stored on the parent node of the node it wants to delete, but that is also authenticated. In these ways, any malicious tampering of servers can be detected.

3.2 Our Proposed Construction

Our scheme requires a PRF $F : \{0,1\}^\lambda \times \{0,1\}^* \to \{0,1\}^\lambda$, and an authenticated, key-hiding, CPA-secure symmetric-key encryption scheme $\Pi = (\mathsf{Gen}, \mathsf{Enc}, \mathsf{Dec})$ where $\Pi.\mathsf{Gen}$ outputs a λ-bit key. Table 2 lists the major notations. Below we describe the three algorithms/protocols Gen, Enc, and Query of our scheme.

Table 2. Notations

N	The number of all patterns on the trie $\mathcal{T}$
d	The height of $\mathcal{T}$ and the length of the longest pattern
ℓ	The average pattern length
m	The number of matched patterns
w_c	A child node of v that the edge between v and w_c denotes the character c
L_c	The level of the node w_c pointed at by the *fail* pointer for character c
w_{sp}	A node linked by the *sp* pointer of v
p_v	The string denoted by the path from the root to the node v
p_{root}	A special symbol denoting a "null" string corresponding to the string of the root
$\mathcal{P}$	The set of patterns stored in a node
$\mathcal{N}$	The set of decryption keys (f_c for character c) for locating next nodes
$\mathcal{F}$	The set storing the character of the *fail* pointer and the level of the node it points at
$\mathcal{O}$	The set of search results sent from the server to the client
n	The length of the query string q
q^η	The η-th substring of q (division of q into substrings is done in a specific way)
q_i^η	The i-th character in the η-th substring q^η
Σ	The alphabet
Σ_v	The set of characters corresponding to the existing child edges of node v
Σ_{fail}	The set of characters corresponding to the non-existing child edges of v

$\mathsf{Gen}(1^\lambda) \to \mathsf{sk}$. The data owner randomly chooses $K_D, K_1, K_2 \xleftarrow{\$} \{0,1\}^\lambda$, and sets $\mathsf{sk} = (K_D, K_1, K_2)$.

Enc(sk, M) → CT. Based on the plaintext pattern set M, the data owner sets up the AC-automation $\mathcal{T}$. The data owner encrypts each node of the resulting $\mathcal{T}$ in a specific way (to be detailed below), and stores the encrypted structure as address/value pairs in a dictionary D on the server. Note that the data owner also stores the height d of $\mathcal{T}$ locally. Algorithm 1 shows the pseudocode. Below we explain the pseudocode and illustrate it with an example.

Algorithm 1. Encrypting the pattern set M with the secret key sk

---

1: **procedure** Enc(sk, M)
2:     Setup AC-automaton $\mathcal{T}$ to store the pattern set M
3:     Initialize a dictionary D and a queue Q
4:     Q.enqueue($root$) // first enqueue the root of $\mathcal{T}$
5:     **while** Q is not empty **do**
6:         $v := Q$.dequeue()
7:         $v.\mathcal{P} := \emptyset;\ v.\mathcal{F} := \emptyset;\ v.\mathcal{N} := \emptyset;$
8:         $(\{w_c\}_{c \in \Sigma_v \cup \Sigma_{fail}}, w_{sp}) \leftarrow v$
9:         **if** p_v is a pattern **then** $v.\mathcal{P} := \{p_v\}$
10:        **if** v has a suffix pattern pointer sp **then** $v.\mathcal{P} := v.\mathcal{P} \cup v.w_{sp}.\mathcal{P}$
11:        **for all** $c \in \Sigma$ **do**
12:            $v.\mathcal{N} := v.\mathcal{N} \cup \{F_{K_2}(p_v \| c)\}$
13:            $v.\mathcal{F} := v.\mathcal{F} \cup \{(c, (c \in \Sigma_{fail}\ ?\ L_c : -1)\}$
14:        **end for**
15:        $addr_v := F_{K_1}(p_v)$
16:        $C_v := \Pi.\mathsf{Enc}_{K_D}((addr_v, v.\mathcal{P}, v.\mathcal{F}, v.\mathcal{N}))$
17:        $D[addr_v] := (v.\mathcal{N}, C_v)$
18:        **for all** $c \in \Sigma_v$ **do**
19:            Q.enqueue(w_c) //child node w of v
20:        **end for**
21:    **end while**
22:    Output: D
23: **end procedure**

For each node v in the trie setup by the AC-automaton, we define three sets.

1. Set $\mathcal{P}$ stores the pattern of v and all its suffixes which are also patterns.
2. Set $\mathcal{F}$ stores all the *fail* pointers including those pointing at the root or the child nodes of the root (at level 2). Each entry is in the form of (c, L_c):
   - c is the next character in the query which cannot be reached.
   - L_c is the level of the node that the *fail* pointer for c points to.
   If a character $c \in \Sigma_v$, then the entry $(c, -1)$ is stored to make sure that $|\mathcal{F}| = |\Sigma|$.
3. Set $\mathcal{N}$ stores a set of decryption keys used for decrypting the address of next node. For next node w_c, the key is $F_{K_2}(p_{w_c})$ where p_{w_c} denotes the path from the root to node w_c. No matter whether there exists an outgoing edge for the character c, $\mathcal{N}$ contains an entry for all character c in the alphabet.

The client encrypts $(\mathsf{addr}_v = F_{K_1}(p_v), \mathcal{P}, \mathcal{F}, \mathcal{N})$ as C_v under key K_D, and stores the value $(\mathcal{N}, C_v)$ at address addr_v of dictionary D, i.e., $D[\mathsf{addr}_v] = (\mathcal{N}, C_v)$.

Consider the example in Fig. 1. Suppose the alphabet is $\{$a, e, n, o, r, t$\}$. The pattern set is $\{P_1 = \text{"ear"}, P_2 = \text{"a"}, P_3 = \text{"an"}, P_4 = \text{"tea"}, P_5 = \text{"to"}\}$. For node 8, $p_8 = \text{"tea"}$ as the traversal from the root passes through edges marked with 't', 'e', 'a'. It has fail pointers marked with 'n' and 'r' in particular (fail pointers for 'a', "e', 'o', 't' are not drawn in Fig. 1), i.e.,

- $\mathcal{P} = \{P_4, P_2\}$, $\mathcal{F} = \{(a,2), (e,2), (n,3), (o,1), (r,4), (t,2)\}$.
- $\mathcal{N} = \{F_{K_2}(\text{"teaa"}), F_{K_2}(\text{"teae"}), F_{K_2}(\text{"tean"}), \cdots, F_{K_2}(\text{"teat"})\}$, in which all of them are never re-used in the trie as node 8 has no next (child) node.
- $D[\mathsf{addr}_8] = (\mathcal{N}, \Pi.\mathsf{Enc}_{K_D}(\mathsf{addr}_8, \mathcal{P}, \mathcal{F}, \mathcal{N}))$, where $\mathsf{addr}_8 = F_{K_1}(\text{'tea'})$.

The client also stores locally that $\mathcal{T}$ is of height 3. We do not model it as secret state information kept by the client since it is difficult to protect its secrecy unless the client adds many dummy entries and occasionally issues dummy requests.

$\mathsf{Query}(sk, q, CT) \to \mathcal{R}$. This protocol contains two parts: $\mathsf{query}_{\mathsf{client}}()$ (Algorithm 2) on client side, and $\mathsf{query}_{\mathsf{server}}()$ (Algorithm 3) on server side. These two algorithms interactively compute search result $\mathcal{R}$ as the client private output.

The client runs $\mathsf{query}_{\mathsf{client}}()$ with the input of the secret key sk from the data owner, and a query string $q \in \Sigma^n$ where n can be an arbitrary integer. We separate the query string twice instead of processing the entire q at one shot.

The first separation, from line 5 to line 10 of Algorithm 2, is to protect the access sequence for a long query string. We divide the query string q of length n into overlapping sub-query strings $\{q^\eta\}$ of length randomly chosen from the range $[d+1, n-1]$, where d is the length of the longest pattern (a state information kept at the client side). Setting the maximum length to $n-1$ means q is divided into at least 2 sub-query strings when $|q| > d$. If $|q| \leq d$, there will be only one sub-query string which is q itself. We also randomly permute the order of these sub-query strings. We make the overlap to be exactly of length d. The overlap ensures that the division and the order permutation do not affect the match result. Any duplication caused by the overlapping part can be eliminated since the results correspond to not only the matched pattern but also the matched position in the entire query q. Other than duplicate elimination, one can treat each sub-query string as an independent query.

The second separation is for constructing the substrings dynamically for each communication round. Each sub-query string is separated into substrings of length $d+1$. If the total length of the rest of the query is not long enough, the client appends randomly chosen characters (denoted by $c_{\mathsf{pad},j}$ where j denotes the position of the padded character) to the end. The corresponding matching results will be discarded. The length of $d+1$ ensures that every interaction will raise a transition via a fail pointer, so the server is able to send back all the matched results.

For a substring from position i to $i+d$ of a sub-query string q^η, if i is beyond the length of q^η, the client proceeds to search for another unprocessed sub-query. Otherwise, the client performs the following steps to generate the query ciphertexts:

1. The client computes $\mathsf{ind}_j = F_{K_1}(q_i^\eta \cdots q_{i+j-1}^\eta)$ as the search index and $K_j^* = F_{K_2}(q_i^\eta \cdots q_{i+j-1}^\eta)$ as the search key, for the j-th substring $q_i \cdots q_{i+j-1}$ (where $j \in [1, d+1]$) of the query string.
2. The client encrypts ind_j using K_j^* as $T_j \leftarrow \Pi.\mathsf{Enc}_{K_j^*}(\mathsf{ind}_j)$.
3. If the remaining query length is less than $d+1$, the client continues to pad random character c_{pad} and generate T_j for $j \in [|q^\eta| + 1, d+1]$.
4. The client sends $(\mathsf{entrance}, \{T_j\}_{j=1}^{d+1})$ to the server where $\mathsf{entrance}$ is the starting entry for searching in D. This $\mathsf{entrance}$ is either $F_{K_1}(p_{root})$ (the address for the root where the input for pseudo-random function F is null string) or decided by the previous communication in the same sub-query string q^η. The latter case will be elaborated later.

To illustrate, suppose the client queries for "otear", $i.e.$, $n = 5$. Recall that the client stores locally the height of tree $d = 3$. The range is $[3 + 1, 5 - 1]$, the length of sub-query string can only be 4. Thus the sub-query strings after first separation are "otea" and "tear". Suppose "tear" is permuted as the first, the second separation first picks a substring of length $3 + 1$ from it, which is "tear" itself in this case and nothing remains.

Then the client performs the second separation and processes in the first round of the query and sends $Q = \{\mathsf{entrance} = F_{K_1}(p_{root}), T_t, T_e, T_a, T_r\}$ to the server. For example, $\mathsf{ind}_t = F_{K_1}("t")$, $K_t^* = F_{K_2}("t")$, $\mathsf{ind}_r = F_{K_1}("tear")$, $K_r^* = F_{K_2}("tear")$, $T_t = \Pi.\mathsf{Enc}_{K_t^*}(\mathsf{ind}_t)$, and $T_r = \Pi.\mathsf{Enc}_{K_r^*}(\mathsf{ind}_r)$.

Once received Q, the server runs $\mathsf{query}_{\mathsf{server}}(\mathsf{entrance}, \{T_j\}_{j=1}^{d+1})$.

1. The server sets $\mathsf{addr} = \mathsf{entrance}$ and locates the entry $(\mathcal{N}, C_v) \leftarrow D[\mathsf{addr}]$.
2. The server adds the ciphertext C_v as the value of entry $D[\mathsf{addr}]$ and add the tuple $(0, C_v)$ to the response set $\mathcal{O}$ which 0 is the current position in this sub-query. The server tries $\mathsf{addr}_j \leftarrow \Pi.\mathsf{Dec}_{f_c}(T_j)$ for all $f_c \in \mathcal{N}$ of the node at $\mathsf{entrance}$ where $j = 1$. If there exists f_c which successfully decrypts T_1, updates $\mathsf{addr} = \mathsf{ind}_j$ and repeats the process for $j \in [2, d+1]$; otherwise, breaks the iteration.

Algorithm 2. Part of the Query protocol executed by the Client for querying q

---

1: **procedure** $\mathsf{query}_{\mathsf{client}}(\mathsf{sk}, q)$
2:     $\mathcal{R} := \emptyset$
3:     Parse $q = q_1 q_2 \cdots q_n$
4:     $i := 1, \mathsf{cnt} := 0$ // i is the starting position of the cnt-th sub-query string
5:     **while** $(i \leq \max(n - d, 1)) \vee (i > 0)$ **do** // divide q into sub-query strings
6:         $\mathsf{cnt} := \mathsf{cnt} + 1$
7:         $n_{\mathsf{cnt}} \xleftarrow{\$} [d+1, n-1]$
8:         $n_{\mathsf{cnt}} := \min(n_{\mathsf{cnt}}, n - i + 1)$ // to set the length of the last sub-query string
9:         $q^{\mathsf{cnt}} := q_i q_{i+1} \cdots q_{i+n_{\mathsf{cnt}}-1}$
10:        $i := i + n_{\mathsf{cnt}} - d$ // to ensure the overlapping length is d
11:    **end while**
12:    $\zeta := \mathsf{cnt}$ // the number of sub-query strings
13:    Choose a random permutation $P : [\zeta] \rightarrow [\zeta]$

```
14:    for all η' = 1 to ζ do
15:        η ← P(η') // {q^η}_{η=1}^ζ is the set of sub-query strings after permutation
16:        i := 1
17:        entrance := F_{K_1}(p_{root})
18:        while i ≤ |q^η| do
19:            for all j = i to min(i + d, |q^η|) do
20:                ind_j := F_{K_1}(q_i^η q_{i+1}^η ··· q_j^η);   K_j^* := F_{K_2}(q_i^η q_{i+1}^η ··· q_j^η);
21:                T_j := Π.Enc_{K_j^*}(ind_j)
22:            end for
23:            if |q^η| < d + i then // pad the substrings to be of the same length d + 1
24:                for all j = |q^η| + 1 to i + d do
25:                    c_{pad,j} ←^$ Σ
26:                    ind_j := F_{K_1}(q^η c_{pad,|q^η|+1} ··· c_{pad,j})
27:                    K_j^* := F_{K_2}(q^η c_{pad,|q^η|+1} ··· c_{pad,j})
28:                    T_j := Π.Enc_{K_j^*}(ind_j)
29:                end for
30:            end if
31:            Client sends Q := (entrance, T_i, T_{i+1}, ··· , T_{i+d}) to the server
32:            Client receives the response O
33:            {(k, C_{k,v})}_{k=0}^{n'} ← O
34:            n* = min(n', |q^η| − i + 1) // the ending position without padding
35:            for all k = 0 to n* do
36:                (addr_k, P_k, F_k, N_k) ← Π.Dec_{K_D}(C_{k,v})
37:                if decryption in the above line returns ⊥ then abort
38:                i' := k + i
39:                if (k > 0 ∧ ind_{i'} ≠ addr_k) then abort
40:                if (⊥ ← Π.Dec_{f_c}(T_{i'}), ∀f_c ∈ N_k) then abort
41:                pos := Σ_{j=1}^{η'−1} |q^j| + k + i − 1
42:                for all p ∈ P_k do
43:                    if (pos, p) ∉ R then R := R ∪ {(pos, p)}
44:                end for
45:            end for
46:            L := L_{q_{i+n*}^η} − 1, where L_{q_{i+n*}^η} is from F_{n*} for character q_{i+n*}^η
47:            if L == 0 then // fail pointer points to root
48:                i := i + n* + 1
49:                entrance := F_{K_1}(p_{root})
50:            else if L > 0 then // fail pointer does not point to root
51:                i := i + n*
52:                entrance := F_{K_1}(q_{i−L+1}^η ··· q_i^η)
53:            else // invalid L value or the response set is incomplete
54:                resend Q to the server or abort
55:            end if
56:        end while
57:    end for
58:    Output: R
59: end procedure
```

Algorithm 3. Part of the Query protocol executed by the Server

1: **procedure** query$_{\text{server}}(Q)$
2:    Parse $(\text{entrance}, T_1, T_2, \cdots, T_{d+1}) \leftarrow Q$
3:    $v := (\mathcal{N}, C_v) \leftarrow D[\text{entrance}]$
4:    Initialize an empty set $\mathcal{O}$
5:    $\mathcal{O} := \mathcal{O} \cup \{(0, C_v)\}$
6:    **for all** $i = 1$ to $d + 1$ **do**
7:        **for all** $f_c \in v.\mathcal{N}$ **do**
8:            $\text{addr}_c \leftarrow \Pi.\text{Dec}_{f_c}(T_i)$
9:            **if** $\text{addr}_c \neq \perp$ **then**
10:               $v := (\mathcal{N}, C_v) \leftarrow D[\text{addr}_c]$
11:               $\mathcal{O} := \mathcal{O} \cup \{(i, C_v)\}$ // i is the occurring position of C_v
12:               break // quit the inner loop once the matching character c is found
13:           **end if**
14:       **end for**
15:       **if** $\text{addr}_c == \perp, \forall f_c \in \mathcal{N}$ **then**
16:           break // quit the outer loop once the query string "disconnected"
17:       **end if**
18:   **end for**
19:   Output: $\mathcal{O}$ // send $\mathcal{O}$ to the client
20: **end procedure**

---

3. When the server has iterated all the $d + 1$ items or the iteration was broken due to failing in decryption for all $f_c \in \mathcal{N}$, the server sends the set $\mathcal{O}$ to the client as the result for this interaction.

To illustrate, the server can use $F_{K_2}(\text{"t"})$ in $\mathcal{N}$ of the root to decrypt $T_t = \Pi.\text{Enc}_{K_t^*}(\text{ind}_t)$, and get $\text{ind}_t = F_{K_1}(\text{"t"})$, which is the address of node 6. Similarly, $\mathcal{N}$ of node 6 has a key to decrypt $T_e = \Pi.\text{Enc}_{F_{K_2}}(\text{"te"})(\text{ind}_e)$ for address of node 7, and $\mathcal{N}$ of node 7 has a key to decrypt T_a for address of node 8. Once the search reaches address $\text{addr} = \text{ind}_a$ (node 8), decryption leads to $\text{ind}_r = F_{K_1}(\text{"tear"})$ but D has no corresponding entry at this index since there exists no path for "tear" in the trie (or node 8 which corresponds to "tea" has no child pointer of 'r'). The server returns $\mathcal{O}$.

The client continues executing query$_{\text{client}}()$ after it gets $\mathcal{O} = \{(k, C_{k,v})\}_{k=1}^{n'}$ of size at most d for the last interaction starting at position i. The client then recovers the ending position in the query string where the pattern occurs as $\text{pos} := \sum_{j=1}^{\eta'-1} |q^j| + k + i - 1$, where η' is the number of sub-queries processed so far. This position can be further used to eliminate duplications.

The client first checks whether the size of the received sequence exceeds the query length. If $n' \leq |q^\eta| - i + 1$, the received items T_j correspond to characters within the query for all $j \in [1, n']$. In this case, $n^* = n'$ is the number of valid responses. Otherwise, the items T_j for $j \in [|q^\eta| - i + 2, n']$ correspond to the padded random characters. In this case, $n^* = |q^\eta| - i + 1$ is the size of valid response items. The client decrypts all $C_{k,v}$ to get $(\text{addr}_k, \mathcal{P}_k, \mathcal{F}_k, \mathcal{N}_k)$ for $k \in [0, n^*]$, where the tuple for $k = 0$ corresponds to the entrance. If any decryption returns $\perp$ or $\mathsf{addr}_k \neq \mathsf{ind}_k$ for any k, the client concludes that the server misbehaved and aborts the execution. The client adds the patterns along with their occurring position pos to the result set $\mathcal{R}$.

After obtained the item $(q_{i+n^*}^{\eta}, L_{q_{i+n^*}^{\eta}})$ from $\mathcal{F}_{n^*}$ where $q_{i+n^*}^{\eta}$ is the first mismatched character in the current substring, the client can get the depth of the parent node for the character $q_{i+n^*}^{\eta}$ linked by this *fail* pointer via $L = L_{q_{i+n^*}^{\eta}} - 1$. The client generates the starting position for the next substring as follows.

- If $L = 0$, the *fail* pointer points at the root of $\mathcal{T}$. There is no match for the $(i+n^*)$-th character in the current sub-query string. There is no pattern whose prefix is also a suffix of the string from the first to the $(i+n^*)$-th character of this sub-query string. The client needs to skip the character q_{i+n^*} by setting the next substring starting at position $i + n^* + 1$ and $\mathsf{entrance} = F_{K_1}(p_{root})$.
- If $L > 0$, we should find the next node at level $L_{q_{i+n^*}^{\eta}} > 1$. The client sets this node as the entrance by $\mathsf{entrance} = F_{K_1}(q_{i+n^*-L+1}^{\eta} \cdots q_{i+n^*}^{\eta})$. The *fail* pointer of the last matched node is q_{i+n^*}. Hence the next substring starts searching at position $i + n^*$ of the current sub-query string.
- If $L < 0$, which means that there exists a child node for the last tuple in $\mathcal{O}$. By construction L is a positive number and hence an invalid value is returned. It means the obtained response set is incomplete. The client can try resend the query for current substring to the server, or the client simply aborts and issues a complaint against the server.

The client and the server iteratively proceed with the substrings in the above way. When the client finishes querying all the substrings and sub-query strings q^{η} for a query q, it outputs $\mathcal{R}$.

In our example, after received the response set for the first interaction, the client generates the second round of query as follows.

1. The client reaches the last matched item $(\mathsf{addr}_8, \mathcal{P}, \mathcal{F}, \mathcal{N})$. The client finds that there is a fail pointer ('r', 4) in $\mathcal{F}$ for the mismatching character "r" of the last matched item. The client traces back $4 - 1 = 3$ characters from 'r' to get the starting position of the path the *fail* pointer pointing at and the substring "ear".
2. The client generates the new $\mathsf{entrance}$ for the second round of query where $\mathsf{entrance} = F_{K_1}(\text{"ear"})$. This is exactly the address for node 3. As the former interaction has searched for a substring of "tea", the second substring for sub-query string "tear" is generated as 'r'. The client pads this string with randomly chosen $c_{\mathsf{pad},j}$ until it has the length of 4. Then the client generates the ciphertexts for these padding characters.
3. The client sends new $Q = \{\mathsf{entrance}, T_{c_{\mathsf{pad},1}}, \cdots, T_{c_{\mathsf{pad},4}}\}$ to the server.

After the server receives Q it directly locates the address for 'r' through the new $\mathsf{entrance}$ and adds the tuple $(0, C_r)$ into the new $\mathcal{O}$ set, where 0 is the occurrence position of 'r' in this substring and C_r is the ciphertext of the entry for 'r'. It continues the search until a fail event happens and then sends back the new response set.

During the second separation, the pattern query of sub-query string "tear" can be finished in two rounds of interaction. However, if the sub-query string is long, the interactions will increase accordingly.

After querying all the substrings in sub-query string "tear", the client can get back the patterns and their occurrence from the result set, and delete those patterns matched by padding characters. The client can perform the query for the second sub-query string "otea" with the same method.

Finally, we remark that the result for a sub-query string is constructed by performing all its interactions in a right sequence, but the result for a query is constructed by combining all the results of its sub-query strings regardless of the order. As long as the substrings for one sub-query string are queried in the right order, mixing the substrings from different sub-query strings or even from different queries during communication will not affect the matching results. The client can switch among different sub-query strings q^{η} of the same query q, or switch among multiple different queries while interacting with the server, and still get the correct answer for each query. The randomized sub-query string order and the mixing of substrings can further hide the information of the queries and the dictionary. The server can only learn the sequence of nodes hit by a substring, but not the sequence of nodes for a whole query.

3.3 Complexity Analysis

We discuss the complexity of our schemes in this section, and further discuss the feasibility to parallelize the schemes.

Encryption. The computational complexity for AC automaton setup is $O(N\ell)$, which is the total length of all the patterns. The data hiding for the small alphabet case accesses every node on the trie once in a breadth-first manner. The number of nodes does not exceed $N\ell$, so the total complexity is $O(N\ell)$. For each node, at most $|\Sigma| + 1$ PRF evaluations (1 for each character and 1 for the dictionary address) and 1 encryption are performed. So Enc contains $N\ell \cdot (|\Sigma|+1)$ PRF evaluations and $N\ell$ encryption operations.

The storage for the original AC automaton is $N\ell|\Sigma|$. After we remove sp pointers, and store all the patterns hit by the node, including the patterns traced via sp, on every node, the average storage of a node is increased by a multiplicative factor of d. We require $|\Sigma|$ to be a small constant, or we cannot use this implementation of *fail* pointers (as described in Sect. 2.2). The storage complexity is thus $O(N\ell d)$.

Query. We first divide the query string into sub-query strings which overlap with the adjacent substrings for length at most d. In the worst case, all the sub-query strings are of the length $d+1$. In this case, each sub-query string only contains one substring. We have n sub-query strings. For each sub-query string, considering that *fail* event happens for each character, then there will be $O(d)$ generation of T_j for each sub-query. Hence, the worst case complexity is $O(n \cdot d)$. The original query computational complexity of the AC automaton is $O(n+m)$, where the worst case is also $n + m$.

As our algorithm stores the suffix pattern set in each node instead of using an *sp* pointer to trace the suffix patterns, the number of steps is further reduced to $O(n)$, where the worst case is also n. At each step, the server performs at most $|\Sigma|$ decryptions; and the client performs 1 encryption, 1 decryption, and 2 PRF evaluations. The best case computational complexity remains to be $O(n)$. In the worst case, the server performs at most $n \cdot |\Sigma|$ decryptions while every step requires $|\Sigma|$ decryptions. In our scheme, dividing one sub-query string into several substrings of length $(d + 1)$ introduces extra computation overhead. The worst case computational complexity is increased to $O(n \cdot d)$ for the client in the case that each step triggers a *fail* event, as each substring involves $d + 1$ encryptions. The time complexity on for the server remains the same. This case is the same as that the sub-query strings are of length $d + 1$, which is discussed previously.

Similar to the computational complexity, the communication bandwidth between the server and the client is $O(n)$ for the best case, and $O(n \cdot d)$ for the worst case. The number of interactions for the best case is $O(\frac{n}{d})$, while for the worst case is $O(n)$.

3.4   Security

Due to page limitation, we informally define the leakage of our scheme and outline some important parts of its security proof. We first define the information leakage $\mathcal{L}_1$ and $\mathcal{L}_2$. $\mathcal{L}_1(D)$ contains:

- the number of nodes in $\mathcal{T}$,
- the height of $\mathcal{T}$ which is d.

$\mathcal{L}_2(D, Q)$ contains:

- the sequence of entries $(\mathsf{entrance}, \mathsf{addr}_1, \mathsf{addr}_2, \cdots, \mathsf{addr}_{fail})$ in D hit by each substring Q^i including the $\mathsf{entrance}$ entries and the *fail* positions,
- the distribution of *fail* events.

The queries $Q^i \in \mathbf{Q}$ are substrings of length $d + 1$, and may be from different queries or different divisions of the same query. The substrings in the set $\mathbf{Q}$ and the corresponding result from the actual server are given to the simulator $\mathcal{S}$ to perform the simulation. This information is leaked to $\mathcal{S}$ by eavesdropping. By our design, the server cannot tell whether two substrings Q^i, Q^j are from the same query or not, where $i \neq j$. $\mathcal{S}$ uses the leaked information from the previous queries in $\mathbf{Q}$ to answer the adversary's query in **Query** phase.

Theorem 1. *The privacy-preserving multi-pattern matching scheme satisfies malicious $(\mathcal{L}_1, \mathcal{L}_2)$-CQA2 security under the random oracle model, if F is a PRF, and Π is an authenticated, key-hiding, symmetric-key encryption scheme.*

Proof. We show that our scheme only leaks $\mathcal{L}_1, \mathcal{L}_2$ by showing that no PPT adversary $\mathcal{A}$ can distinguish an interaction with the real client from one with a simulator $\mathcal{S}$ which is only given the leakages.

Encryption. $\mathcal{S}$ chooses a secret key $K_D \xleftarrow{\$} \{0,1\}^\lambda$, and sets up the dictionary D with the number of entries matching the number of nodes according to $\mathcal{L}_1(D)$. For each entry i, $\mathcal{S}$ randomly chooses $f_{i,c} \xleftarrow{\$} \{0,1\}^\lambda$ for $c \in \Sigma$, and sets $D[f_{i,1}] = (\{f_{i,c}\}_{c \in \Sigma}, C_i)$ where $f_{i,1} \xleftarrow{\$} \{0,1\}^\lambda$ and $C_i = \Pi.\mathsf{Enc}_{K_D}(0, \emptyset_p, \emptyset_{fail}, \emptyset_f)$.

$\mathcal{S}$ maintains two lists R_1, R_2. R_1 stores the visited items in D. For a queried sub-query Q^i, at the j-th position, the string $p_{i,j}$ is the string denoted by the path from the root to the current node. If this is the first time $p_{i,j}$ appears, $\mathcal{S}$ randomly picks an item with address addr in D, and sets $R_1[i,j] = \mathsf{addr}$. R_2 stores the status of each node and its child nodes. $R_2[\mathsf{addr}] = (K^*, \mathsf{flag}, \{\mathsf{flag}_c\}_{c \in \Sigma})$. $\mathsf{flag}, \{\mathsf{flag}_c\}_{c \in \Sigma}$ are the status of the nodes on the simulated trie indicating whether the nodes or their child nodes are accessed by the previous queries. The initial values of flag and flag_c are all 0, indicating that the node denoted by addr and its child node corresponding to the character c are all unvisited. If addr is chosen as the item for $p_{i,j}$ in the substring Q^i at the j-th step, $\mathcal{S}$ finds $\mathsf{addr} = R_1[(i,j)]$, sets $R_2[\mathsf{addr}].\mathsf{flag} = 1$, picks a character c where $R_2[R_1[(i,j-1)]].\mathsf{flag}_c = 0$, sets it to 1, and sets $R_2[\mathsf{addr}].K^* = D[R_1[(i,j-1)]] \cdot f_c$. If a *fail* event occurs at the position j, $\mathcal{S}$ will stop the process.

Query. For a new incoming substring $Q' = (\mathsf{entrance}, T_1, \cdots, T_{d+1})$, $\mathcal{S}$ first checks $\mathcal{L}_2(D, Q)$ for an entrance. If Q' has a common entrance with any one of the substrings in Q, $\mathcal{S}$ uses this entrance, otherwise, $\mathcal{S}$ randomly chooses an entry in D (no matter visited or not), updates it as visited, and updates R_1, R_2 accordingly.

At the j-th step of the substring Q', $\mathcal{S}$ checks $\mathcal{L}_2(D, Q)$ for a common prefix string p_j. If $\mathcal{S}$ finds an item $p_{i,j}$ which equals p_j, which means this prefix string p_j has been visited by the previous substrings Q^i, $\mathcal{S}$ sets $\mathsf{ind}_j = R_1[(i,j)]$ and $K_j^* = R_2[F_{K_1}(p_j)].K^*$, and computes $T_j = \Pi.\mathsf{Enc}_{K_j^*}(\mathsf{ind}_j)$. If $p_{i,j}$ found from $\mathbf{Q}$ which equals p_j has triggered a *fail* event, or $j = d+1$, $\mathcal{S}$ generates the rest of T_j with randomly chosen ind_j and K_j^*. Otherwise, if p_j is not a common prefix or common *fail* event for any substrings in Q, $\mathcal{S}$ first flips a coin according to the distribution of *fail* event, and proceed with the following two cases:

- If $\mathcal{S}$ decides that p_j is not a *fail* event, it randomly chooses an item addr in D, updates R_1 and R_2, and computes T_j as described previously.
- Otherwise, it generates the rest of T_j with randomly chosen ind_j and K_j^*.

When a *fail* event occurs or the index $d+1$ is reached, $\mathcal{S}$ sends Q' to $\mathcal{A}$. $\mathcal{A}$ then follows the process in the real scheme to return $\mathcal{O}' = \{k, C_k\}_{k=0}^{n'}$ to $\mathcal{S}$. $\mathcal{S}$ checks whether the returned C_k is the same as the ciphertext stored in $D[\mathsf{ind}_j]$. If not, $\mathcal{S}$ aborts the simulation and concludes that $\mathcal{A}$ returns wrong response.

Here, we show that the real scheme (Game 0) and the simulation above (Game 5) are indistinguishable from $\mathcal{A}$'s view through the transitions below.

Game 0. This game is the real scheme. $\mathcal{A}$ chooses a series of substrings (not necessarily from the same query), and interacts with $\mathcal{S}$ to obtain the outputs from $\mathcal{S}$.

Game 1. This game is the same as Game 0, except that F_{K_1} and F_{K_2} are replaced with two random oracles. $\mathcal{S}$ keeps records of the evaluation of F_{K_1} and F_{K_2} in two tables. Game 0 and Game 1 are indistinguishable due to the pseudorandomness of F.

Game 2. This game is the same as Game 1, except that $\mathcal{S}$ decides whether to output $\perp$ by checking whether the returned ciphertext $C_{k,v}$ equals the one stored in D for each $k \in [1, n']$ instead of decrypting $C_{k,v}$. Game 1 and Game 2 are indistinguishable due to the authenticity (ciphertext integrity) of Π.

Game 3. This game is the same as Game 2, except that

- C_v encrypts two empty sets instead of the real pattern set and the real *fail* information set for each node;
- T_j encrypts randomly chosen ind for $j \geq i$ if *fail* event occurs at position i.

Game 2 and Game 3 are indistinguishable due to the CPA-security of Π.

Game 4. This game is the same as Game 3, except that T_j is generated with randomly chosen symmetric key K^* for $j \geq i$ if *fail* event occurs at position i. Game 3 and Game 4 are indistinguishable due to the key-hiding property of Π.

Game 5. This game is the same as Game 4, except that $\mathcal{S}$ simulates the scheme without the real pattern set or the real substrings. This is easily achieved, because from Game 1 to Game 4, $\mathcal{S}$ has gradually replaced all the parts related to the pattern set or the substrings with either randomness or the information from $\mathcal{L}_1(D)$ and $\mathcal{L}_2(D, Q)$. Game 5 is actually the simulation described previously, and is indistinguishable with Game 4.

Hence, $\mathcal{S}$ can successfully simulate the scheme with only the information leakage provided by $\mathcal{L}_1$ and $\mathcal{L}_2$, if F is a PRF, and Π is an authenticated, key-hiding, symmetric-key encryption scheme. $\qquad\qquad\qquad\qquad\qquad\qquad\qquad\square$

4   Conclusion

In this paper, we propose the first privacy-preserving multi-pattern matching scheme. The previous privacy-preserving searching schemes can only support searching for one pattern at a time. Our scheme enables the feature to search for multiple target patterns simultaneously. A data owner can outsource the storage of a large pattern set and the computation of the searching. Our scheme protects the privacy of both the queried string and the target pattern set. The client does not need to download any data other than the matching result in the process. Our design considers the adversary to be malicious. The client can catch any dishonest behavior of the cloud server during the pattern matching process.

Our scheme is a symmetric-key scheme in which the data owner needs to share the secret key with the clients who need to use the multi-pattern matching service. It is also interesting to design a public-key scheme.

Acknowledgement. We thank for the helpful discussions with Russell W.F. Lai, Jiafan Wang, Yongjun Zhao, and Zhe Zhou.

Sherman S.M. Chow is supported in part by General Research Fund Grant No. 14201914 and the Early Career Award from Research Grants Council, Hong Kong; and Huawei Innovation Research Program (HIRP) 2015.

References

1. Acar, T., Chow, S.S.M., Nguyen, L.: Accumulators and U-Prove revocation. In: Financial Cryptography, pp. 189–196 (2013)
2. Aho, A.V., Corasick, M.J.: Efficient string matching: an aid to bibliographic search. Commun. ACM **18**(6), 333–340 (1975)
3. Baron, J., Defrawy, K., Minkovich, K., Ostrovsky, R., Tressler, E.: 5PM: secure pattern matching. In: Visconti, I., Prisco, R. (eds.) SCN 2012. LNCS, vol. 7485, pp. 222–240. Springer, Heidelberg (2012). doi:10.1007/978-3-642-32928-9_13
4. Cash, D., Jarecki, S., Jutla, C., Krawczyk, H., Roşu, M.-C., Steiner, M.: Highly-scalable searchable symmetric encryption with support for boolean queries. In: Canetti, R., Garay, J.A. (eds.) CRYPTO 2013. LNCS, vol. 8042, pp. 353–373. Springer, Heidelberg (2013). doi:10.1007/978-3-642-40041-4_20
5. Chase, M., Kamara, S.: Structured encryption and controlled disclosure. In: Abe, M. (ed.) ASIACRYPT 2010. LNCS, vol. 6477, pp. 577–594. Springer, Heidelberg (2010). doi:10.1007/978-3-642-17373-8_33
6. Chase, M., Shen, E.: Substring-searchable symmetric encryption. PoPETs **2015**(2), 263–281 (2015)
7. Curtmola, R., Garay, J.A., Kamara, S., Ostrovsky, R.: Searchable symmetric encryption: improved definitions and efficient constructions. In: Proceedings of the 13th ACM Conference on Computer and Communications Security, CCS 2006, Alexandria, VA, USA, 30 October–3 November 2006, pp. 79–88 (2006)
8. Hazay, C., Lindell, Y.: Efficient protocols for set intersection and pattern matching with security against malicious and covert adversaries. J. Cryptol. **23**(3), 422–456 (2010)
9. Katz, J., Malka, L.: Secure text processing with applications to private DNA matching. In: Proceedings of the 17th ACM Conference on Computer and Communications Security, CCS 2010, Chicago, Illinois, USA, 4–8 October 2010, pp. 485–492 (2010)
10. Kurosawa, K., Ohtaki, Y.: UC-secure searchable symmetric encryption. In: Keromytis, A.D. (ed.) FC 2012. LNCS, vol. 7397, pp. 285–298. Springer, Heidelberg (2012). doi:10.1007/978-3-642-32946-3_21
11. Lai, R.W.F., Chow, S.S.M.: Structured encryption with non-interactive updates and parallel traversal. In: 35th IEEE International Conference on Distributed Computing Systems, ICDCS 2015, Columbus, OH, USA, 29 June–2 July 2015, pp. 776–777 (2015)
12. Mohassel, P., Niksefat, S., Sadeghian, S., Sadeghiyan, B.: An efficient protocol for oblivious DFA evaluation and applications. In: Dunkelman, O. (ed.) CT-RSA 2012. LNCS, vol. 7178, pp. 398–415. Springer, Heidelberg (2012). doi:10.1007/978-3-642-27954-6_25
13. Wang, Q., He, M., Du, M., Chow, S.S.M., Lai, R.W.F., Zou, Q.: Searchable encryption over feature-rich data. IEEE Trans. Dependable Secure Comput. (2016)
14. Zhou, Z., Zhang, T., Chow, S.S.M., Zhang, Y., Zhang, K.: Efficient authenticated multi-pattern matching. In: Proceedings of the 11th ACM on Asia Conference on Computer and Communications Security, AsiaCCS 2016, Xi'an, China, 30 May–3 June 2016, pp. 593–604 (2016)

Parallel and Dynamic Structured Encryption

Russell W.F. Lai and Sherman S.M. Chow[(✉)]

Department of Information Engineering,
The Chinese University of Hong Kong, Sha Tin, N.T., Hong Kong
{russell,sherman}@ie.cuhk.edu.hk

Abstract. We design a searchable symmetric encryption scheme for structured data which supports dynamic updates and parallel computation. The abstract data type supported by our scheme not only can represent the usual keyword-file search but also other data type such as graph structure. Unlike previous parallelizable schemes, search complexity of our scheme is optimal, namely, linear in the number of matches divided by the number of processors. Moreover, previous parallel and dynamic schemes require an interactive update protocol to minimize the leakage caused by the updates. It is thus a major technical challenge to mandate non-interactive updates. While achieving multiple requirements simultaneously, our scheme leverages a simple tree structure. Our scheme is secure against adaptive chosen query attack. We also evaluate the efficiency of our scheme with synthetic data (of higher edge density) and real-life data for the application of online social network where connections among users are represented by graphs.

Keywords: Searchable symmetric encryption · Structured encryption · Non-interactive · Dynamic · Parallel · Graph encryption

1 Introduction

In searchable symmetric encryption (SSE), the key used for encryption has an additional capability of generating a *search token*, with which the encrypted content can be queried efficiently without leaking the plaintext data. A common application of SSE is to outsource the storage of a set of documents to an untrusted server. The ability to search is especially critical to mobile devices where transmission speed and storage space are usually limited.

Structured Encryption. Since the seminal work of Song *et al.* [11], many SSE schemes focus on keyword search over files. Later schemes extended the query type to more complex keyword searches, such as range search [13], similarity

---

Sherman S.M. Chow is supported in part by General Research Fund Grant No. 14201914 and the Early Career Award from Research Grants Council, Hong Kong; and Huawei Innovation Research Program (HIRP) 2015 (Proj. No. YB2015110147). We thank Chen Change Loy and Multimedia Lab, Dept. of Information Engineering, CUHK for their computational resources we used for some of our initial experiments.

© ICST Institute for Computer Sciences, Social Informatics and Telecommunications Engineering 2017
R. Deng et al. (Eds.): SecureComm 2016, LNICST 198, pp. 219–238, 2017.
DOI: 10.1007/978-3-319-59608-2_12

search [14], *etc.* Chase and Kamara [1] generalize SSE to *structured encryption* for supporting queries over arbitrary structured data.

Leakage. Ideally, an SSE scheme should satisfy two security requirements: (1) the encrypted database does not reveal any information about the plaintext, and (2) the tokens for adaptively issued queries and updates do not reveal any further information beyond the query results. Typically, SSE schemes often reveal the access and search pattern [2,3]. Yet they are *non-interactive*, which means that the client only needs to delegate the search token and needs not to provide further help for any subsequent searches. There are *interactive* solutions like oblivious RAM [4] which can hide the access pattern, yet at the cost of efficiency.

Beyond access and search patterns, other information about the plaintext could be leaked to the server. This information can be precisely defined by a set of leakage functions [1,2,7]. Informally, we say that an SSE scheme is secure against adaptive chosen query attack (CQA2), a generalization of adaptive chosen keyword attack (CKA2) [2], if any adversary issuing a polynomial number of queries adaptively cannot distinguish a real SSE scheme from one simulated with the knowledge of the leakages. Note that the adversaries for different schemes (of different efficiency) are often given different sets of leakage functions.

Existing Parallel and Dynamic SSE. SSE schemes proposed by Kamara *et al.* [7], Kamara and Papamanthou [6], and Hahn and Kerschbaum [5] (denoted by KPR, KP, and HK respectively) support *dynamic* updates of files, *i.e.*, files can be added or removed. This can be done via the help of an *update token*. A recent SSE scheme proposed by Stefanov *et al.* [12] (denoted by SPS) can update individual (keyword, file) pairs dynamically, but is unable to directly remove a file, *i.e.*, the client needs to manually remove all the (keyword, file) pairs for the unwanted file.

Supporting update poses more challenges in preventing leakage. For supporting efficient dynamic updates, early work (*e.g.*, KPR [7]) made compromise in allowing more leakage when compared with some prior static SSE schemes. Moreover, KPR uses linked list as its internal data structure which is inherently sequential, making the scheme not parallelizable and less practical to be used in parallel computing architecture.

Recent parallel and dynamic schemes (KP [6] and SPS [12]) made the trade-off by requiring *interaction* between the data owner and the server in *every updates* to minimize leakage. These schemes adopt different design principles in addressing the same problem. From a high-level point of view, KP employs a simple and direct approach which passes the data structure maintenance problem incurred by the update back to the owner. On the other hand, SPS relies on an interactive cryptographic protocol known as oblivious sorting. One can view these two schemes as adopting approaches at two ends of a spectrum. The former method requires the data owner to locally decrypt the relevant part of the data structure, and upload again an encryption of them after maintenance for keeping the parallel efficiency. The use of oblivious sorting requires *local storage* at the client side (apart from the private key) and makes the resulting scheme relatively heavyweight. In short, both approaches require quite a large amount of communication and work at the client side. These schemes also store redundant information which required to be traversed during a search, thus the full power of parallel computation diminishes. In more details, KP stores the actual data only in the leaf nodes of a tree and SPS firstly creates a "Delete" node during deletion rather than actually removing the data.

HK uses a simplistic approach for handling data dynamic by exploiting the leakage incurred from the first search on any keyword. While the majority of the existing SSE schemes required a pre-computed inverted index, HK simply stores the encrypted files as sequences of encrypted keywords in the database, and creates a simple inverted index on the fly using the leaked access pattern. Therefore, adding and deleting files in HK are as easy as adding or removing the corresponding sequence of encrypted keywords as a whole, and updating the rather small inverted index. Subsequent search can be easily parallelized as the inverted index is stored in plaintext. However, as the search history becomes longer, the inverted index becomes larger which slows down the addition and deletion algorithms.

To summarize, it is fair to say that designing SSE with a desirable trade-off between functionality, security, and efficiency is a challenging problem.

Our Contribution. We propose a searchable symmetric encryption scheme RBT which supports dynamic updates and parallel computation. In summary, our scheme makes technical contributions in two dimensions.

First, we extend structured encryption for dynamic abstract data type which allows updates to both the data space and the query space. Specifically, RBT allows updates to individual (query, data) pairs. This requires a more fine-grained access control over the encrypted database. Under this abstraction, RBT allows deletion of data which automatically deletes all (query, data) pairs related to the piece of data in question. To the best of our knowledge, our scheme is the first to support both types of updates. In addition to returning all data related to a given query, our scheme also supports meta-query to check if a (query, data) pair exists in the database, *i.e.*, that the query is related to the data. This contribution will be presented in Sect. 2. We will illustrate the applicability of this abstract data type, particularly to representing connections in online social network, in Sect. 2.2.

Second, in the premise of parallel SSE, we aim at the optimal search complexity linear in the number of matches divided by the number of processors, simultaneously ensuring that searches only leak search and access patterns, while minimizing the leakages during updates. This will be presented in Sect. 4. Despite making the above improvements, our scheme leverages a simple randomized binary tree (hence the name RBT) to achieve non-interactive queries and updates.

Finally, we show that our scheme is secure against adaptive chosen query attack, and demonstrate its performance in Sect. 5 using both synthetic data for general scenarios and real-life data for online social networks.

Performance Comparison. We compare our scheme with KPR, KP, and SPS and HK in Table 1. Yet, we remark that it is a simplified discussion due to the differences in leakages (of different data-structures), the interaction

Table 1. The search complexities of KPR, KP, SPS, HK, and RBT (m, N, and p denote the number of matches, number of all files/data, and number of processors resp.)

Scheme	Search complexity
KPR	$O(m)$
KP	$O(m/p) \log N$ ($\because$ storing data only in leaf nodes)
SPS	$O(m/p) \log^3 N$ ($\because$ rebuild mechanism)
HK	$O(N/p)$ (first time, $\because$ no pre-built inverted index)
	$O(m/p)$ (subsequent search)
RBT	$O(m/p)$

requirements, *etc.* In particular, during updates, KPR leaks local information; RBT leaks the affected sub-trees' traversal information μ_t (Table 2); KP and SPS leak nothing by interaction (throwing back the update-task to the client and performing interactive oblivious-updates respectively) as we explained.

2   Our Dynamic Abstract Data Type

2.1   Definition

We extend the definition of static data type by Chase and Kamara [1] to dynamic data type. A dynamic abstract data type $\mathcal{T}$ is defined by a data space $\mathcal{D}$ with a query operation Query : $\mathcal{D} \times \mathcal{Q} \rightarrow \mathcal{R}$ and an update operation Update : $\mathcal{D} \times \mathcal{U} \rightarrow \mathcal{D}$, where $\mathcal{Q}$ is the query space, $\mathcal{R}$ is the response space, and $\mathcal{U}$ is the update space.

As in most of the other SSE schemes, the responses to the queries are prepared during encryption. Without loss of generality, we let a data structure δ of type $\mathcal{T}$ and size parameter (M, N) to have the following structure:

- Data set: $\delta \subset \delta^* = \{(q_i, r_j)\}_{i=1, j=1}^{M, N} \in \mathcal{D}$
- Query space: $\mathcal{Q}(\delta) = \{q : \exists r \text{ s.t. } (q, r) \in \delta\}$
- Response space: $\mathcal{R}(\delta) = \{r : \exists q \text{ s.t. } (q, r) \in \delta\}$
- Update space: $\mathcal{U}(\delta) = \{(\text{"Add"}, d) : d \in \delta^* \setminus \delta\} \cup \{(\text{"Del"}, d) : d \in \delta\}$

where q_i is a query, r_j is a piece of data corresponding to a query, and δ^* is considered to be the largest possible collection of data. The operations Query and Update are defined in the natural way. This representation expresses each of the possible query-response pairs as a data item.

It can be useful to check if a certain pair of query and response exists. We therefore build extra "meta-queries" based on the normal query-response pairs. Concretely, we extend the query space to $\mathcal{Q}' = \mathcal{Q} \cup \delta$ and the response space to $\mathcal{R}' = \mathcal{R} \cup \{\text{true}, \text{false}\}$. The query operation is also extended so that, given a "meta-query" $d = (q, r)$, it checks if (q, r) is in the data set. If so, it returns true. Otherwise, it returns false. The update operation is extended in the natural way.

2.2   Instantiating Our Abstract Data Type

To illustrate the generality and flexibility of our abstract data type, we show how it covers (the common) searches for keyword in files, and other common data types considered in existing structured encryption of Chase and Kamara [1].

For keyword search, each keyword is encoded as a query, all the files containing a certain keyword are the corresponding responses. Via the meta-query, our data type further supports the query for checking if a certain keyword exists in a particular file, which minimizes the unnecessary traversal (and leakage) of other files containing the same keyword.

For lookup queries on matrix-structured data (e.g., pixel-based images) [1], we just encode the matrix data (e.g., the colors in different models like RGB and CMYK) as the responses. There can be various instantiations according to the specific needs of the application, e.g., one may assign (the index of) a row as the query and all the responses as the entries of that row, or one may assign a multi-dimension index (e.g., (row, column) pair in a 2D matrix) as the query, and our list of responses allow storing more than one data item in a single (indexed) entry. Looking ahead, with the dual structure storing both (query, response) and (response, query) pairs, our schemes can be extended to support transpose-related operations on matrices natively.

Finally, for graph, one natural representation is to assign nodes with outgoing edges as queries, and those with incoming edges as responses. The existing structured encryption [1] scheme supports neighbor queries and adjacency queries. Neighbor queries return all the nodes adjacent to a given node i. It is apparent that i will be the query and the adjacent nodes are all stored as its response. For queries to check if two nodes are adjacent, it can be easily supported by our meta-query. As mentioned in the original application [1], this allows us to support controlled disclosure of friendship graphs of a social network, for example.

3   Cryptography Background

3.1   Basic Notations

Let λ be the security parameter. All sets and other parameters depend on λ implicitly. $\{0,1\}^n$ denotes the set of all binary strings of length n. $\{0,1\}^*$ denotes the set of all finite length binary strings. $\mathbf{0}$ denotes the λ-bit string with all zeros. $\mathbf{0}_k$ denotes k consecutive zero strings $\mathbf{0}$. ϕ denotes the empty set. If X is a set, $x \leftarrow X$ denotes the sampling of an element x uniformly from X. If A is an algorithm, $x \leftarrow A$ means that x is the output of A. "$\oplus$" denotes the bit-wise exclusive OR (XOR) operation. If $x, y \in \{0,1\}^n$, $|y|$ denotes the length of y, i.e., n; and $x \oplus= y$ denotes $x = x \oplus y$, i.e., assigning $x \oplus y$ as the new value of variable x. ";" denotes string concatenation.

3.2   Pseudorandom Functions and Symmetric-Key Encryption

Pseudorandom functions (PRFs), informally, is a class of polynomial-time computable function family such that no polynomial-time adversary can distinguish between a randomly chosen function among this family and a truly random function (whose outputs are sampled uniformly and independently at random), with a significant advantage relative to the security parameter. Each PRF takes a secret key and an input. The secret key serves as an index to determine which function in the family to use.

To build a symmetric-key encryption scheme with computational security, one can use a PRF to output the mask to be XOR-ed with the message. Note that the input of the PRF should be unique to ensure security.

3.3   Dynamic Symmetric Structured Encryption

We combine and simplify existing definitions of dynamic SSE and (static) structured encryption to dynamic structured encryption for our abstract data type defined in Sect. 2. The standard security notion of SSE designed for keyword search over files is the notion of security against adaptive chosen keyword attack (CKA2). Below we generalize it to the notion of security against adaptive chosen query attack (CQA2) for structured encryption. For modeling the security of our dynamic structured encryption, we also extend dynamic CKA2 and (static) CQA2 security [1,7] to dynamic CQA2.

Definition 1. *Let T be a dynamic abstract data type with query operation* Query : $\mathcal{D} \times \mathcal{Q} \to \mathcal{R}$ *and update operation* Update : $\mathcal{D} \times \mathcal{U} \to \mathcal{D}$. *A dynamic symmetric-key structured encryption scheme for T is a tuple of six probabilistic polynomial-time algorithms* DSSE = (Gen, Enc, QryTkn, Qry, UdtTkn, Udt):

- $K \leftarrow$ Gen(1^λ): *The key generation algorithm inputs a security parameter λ and outputs a secret key K.*
- $\gamma \leftarrow$ Enc(K, δ): *The encryption algorithm inputs a secret key K and a data structure δ of type T. It outputs an encrypted data structure γ.*
- $\tau_q \leftarrow$ QryTkn(K, q): *The query token generation algorithm inputs a secret key K and a query $q \in \mathcal{Q}$. It outputs a query token τ_q.*
- $\mathcal{R} \leftarrow$ Qry(τ_q, γ): *The query algorithm inputs a query token τ_q and an encrypted data structure γ. It outputs a sequence of identifiers $\mathcal{R}$.*
- $\tau_u \leftarrow$ UdtTkn(K, u): *The update token generation algorithm inputs a secret key K and an update $u \in \mathcal{U}$. It outputs an update token τ_u.*
- $\gamma' \leftarrow$ Udt(τ_u, γ): *The update algorithm inputs an update token τ_u and an encrypted data structure γ. It outputs a new encrypted data structure γ'.*

We say that DSSE is correct if for all $\lambda \in \mathbb{N}$, for all K output by Gen(1^λ), for all $\delta \in \mathcal{D}$, for all γ output by Enc(K, δ), for all sequences of queries and updates, the queries always return the correct sequences of identifiers of the responses from δ matching to the queries.

Definition 2 *(Dynamic CQA2-security). Let* DSSE *be a structured encryption scheme as defined in Definition 1. Consider two probabilistic experiments, where $\mathcal{A}$ is a stateful adversary, $\mathcal{S}$ is a stateful simulator, and $\mathcal{L}_e$, $\mathcal{L}_q$, $\mathcal{L}_u$ are stateful leakage algorithms:*

- **Real$_\mathcal{A}(1^\lambda)$**: *the challenger runs* DSSE *with the input data structure δ specified by $\mathcal{A}$. $\mathcal{A}$ returns a bit b that is output by the experiment.*
- **Ideal$_{\mathcal{A},\mathcal{S}}(1^\lambda)$**: *$\mathcal{A}$ outputs δ. Given $\mathcal{L}_e(\delta)$, $\mathcal{S}$ generates and sends γ to $\mathcal{A}$. $\mathcal{A}$ makes a polynomial number of adaptive updates u and queries q. For queries, $\mathcal{S}$ is given $\mathcal{L}_q(\delta, q)$. It returns a query token τ_q and a response R. For updates, $\mathcal{S}$ is given $\mathcal{L}_u(\delta, u)$. It returns an update token τ_u and an encrypted data structure γ. Finally, $\mathcal{A}$ returns a bit b that is output by the experiment.*

We say that DSSE *is $(\mathcal{L}_e, \mathcal{L}_q, \mathcal{L}_u)$-secure against adaptive dynamic chosen-query attacks if for all* PPT *adversaries $\mathcal{A}$, there exists a* PPT *simulator $\mathcal{S}$ such that*

$$|\Pr[\mathbf{Real}_\mathcal{A}(1^\lambda) = 1] - \Pr[\mathbf{Ideal}_{\mathcal{A},\mathcal{S}}(1^\lambda) = 1]| \leq \mathsf{negl}(\lambda).$$

4   DSSE from Random Binary Tree

Our goal is to construct a dynamic SSE scheme for structured data, such that: (1) the computation complexity of the server during queries is optimal up to a constant time overhead, and (2) updates are non-interactive. Our solution is to represent the response spaces using random binary search trees. We use the concept of normal and dual nodes to support updates like KPR [7]. For any *data* $(q, r) \in \delta$, there are a normal node and a dual node storing (q, r) which is indexed by q and r respectively.

4.1   Intuition

Take keyword search over files as an example. All keyword-file pairs are prepared; and an index is built where the pairs with the same keyword are grouped into sets. Searching for a keyword (or making a query q) is then equivalent to traversing through a set (of responses $\{r : (q, r) \in \delta\}$). Yet, the server can only traverse the set upon receipt of the corresponding token; otherwise, it can identify all (encrypted) responses to a specific (unknown) query by traversing a set.

To delete a file, the server needs to retrieve all the keywords associated with it. Hence, one can consider it as "file search over keywords" instead of keyword search over files. This explains the role played by the set of dual nodes.

The simplest method to represent either kind of set is to use a linked list, as adopted in, for example, KPR. Yet traversing a linked list is inherently sequential. Another way is to use binary trees (*e.g.*, KP). While traversing a binary tree can be parallelized, updating a binary tree requires balancing or the tree will eventually degenerate to a linked list. However, balancing a tree often requires finding a suitable "replacement" node which can be at a branch "faraway" from the position where the modification was originally made. Reaching this node requires traversal and hence the client needs to leak sufficient secret to the server. To avoid balancing the tree explicitly, we use binary search trees with random addresses as their search keys [10].

4.2 High-Level Description

We first describe our scheme RBT in high-level. This part emphasizes on the encryption and decryption part, in particular, how to use different kinds of keys in the tokens (listed in Table 3) to retrieve the information stored in each cell (listed in Table 2).

(a) Setup: RBT consists of dictionaries I and A, where I is an index pointing to some cell of A, and the cells of A are connected in random binary trees. For each data $(q; r) \in \delta$, query $q \in \mathcal{Q}(\delta)$, and response $r \in \mathcal{R}(\delta)$, a *normal node* and a *dual node* are created and stored at *random* addresses in A. Each node stores multiple types of information labeled as μ_s, μ_t, μ_d, and μ_a as explained in Table 2. This information is masked by XOR-ing with a pseudo-random function (PRF) output computed from a key and the randomness stored in μ_a of the node. The keys for masking each type of information are listed in Table 3.

The dictionary I maps an index to a masked address of A, where the index and the mask are computed by applying PRFs to the corresponding data, query, or response. The *normal nodes* in A correspond to the data $(q, \cdot)$. Data corresponding to the same q are connected in a random binary search tree using random addresses as their *search keys*. Similarly, the *dual nodes* correspond to the data $(\cdot, r)$ and response r are connected in a random binary search tree. Figure 1 shows a toy-example of an encrypted database. Since our binary search trees use random addresses as their search keys, the trees are roughly balanced even after a sequence of insertion and deletion [10], hence expect no balancing.

Table 2. The information stored in an array cell of RBT, with subscript in boldface in the description: μ_t of a node stores the traversal keys of its children, which thus grants the access to all μ_t down its sub-tree

Info.	Description
μ_s	The response r to be returned upon **search** query corresponding to the data $(q; r)$
μ_t	The addresses of the parent and children nodes, and the **traversal** keys of the children nodes used for traversal during queries *and* updates
μ_d	The address and **traversal** key of the **d**ual node used for delete updates *only*
μ_a	The randomness used (in PRF to derive the key) for masking the above

Table 3. The keys required for masking the information stored in an array cell: S, T_b and D_b are PRFs where b is the type (0:normal; or 1:dual) of the node

Info	Key
μ_s of all $(q; \cdot)$	The search key $S(q)$
μ_t of $(q; r)$	The traversal key $T_b(q; r)$
μ_d of $(q; r)$	The dual key $D_0(\hat{q})$ or $D_1(\hat{r})$

As in KPR [7], one reason for storing a dual structure is to support the deletion of queries and responses. For example, to delete a response r', all nodes corresponding to r', namely $\{(q, r') \in \delta\}$, must also be removed from the database. The dual structure provides a mechanism for updating each (q, r) which belongs to different trees.

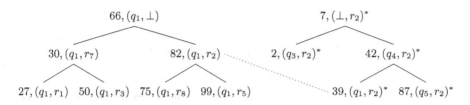

Fig. 1. Setup: Tree for q_1 and dual tree for r_2; Searching q_1 returns $r_1, r_7, r_3, r_8, r_2, r_5$ (in-order traversal based on the randomly assigned addresses $27, 30, 50, 66, 75, 82, 99$)

(b) Queries: μ_t of a node is masked using a traversal key stored in its parent node. So, to query q, the client computes and sends the following to the server: the index (in I), the index mask (to unmask the entry in I), the search key (to unmask μ_s and get back response r of a node), and the traversal key of q.

In more details, by unmasking the appropriate index of I, the server locates the root node of q, and traverses down by unlocking the traversal key of the children nodes iteratively. Parallel traversal is done by traversing both the left and right sub-trees of a node simultaneously. Upon arrival at a node, it uses the search key to unmask μ_s. The response to client contains all μ_s obtained during traversal.

(c) Meta-Queries: For meta-query (q, r), the client only sends the index and the index mask to the server (while the search key and traversal key are replaced by random strings). This means that the server is able to locate the node corresponding to (q, r), but cannot obtain the μ_s stored nor traverse down the sub-tree. Nevertheless, the server performs the same operations as for (normal) queries and returns the "unmasked" μ_s if a node is located. The client interprets the response as false if the server returns the empty set ϕ, or true otherwise.

(d) Add and Link Updates: The server creates a new node to be inserted under a random address in A. Adding a new query q or response r are considered to be *Add* updates, while adding a new data $d = (q, r)$ is a *Link* update.

For the *Add* update, the new node for q or r serves as the root node. For the *Link* update, node d is inserted into the tree corresponding to query q. To do this, the update token includes the traversal key of the root node, so that the server can use it to unmask the traversal keys of its children, traverse down the tree, and update the tree linkage. The same procedure is then repeated for adding the dual node of d. Figure 2 shows an example of a "Link" update.

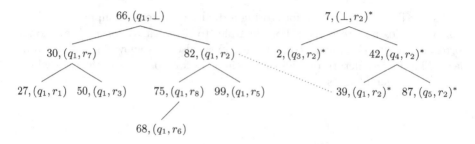

Fig. 2. Adding (q_1, r_6) to address 68

(e) Unlink Updates: Deleting $d = (q, r)$ from the database is considered to be an *Unlink* update. The server looks up I and locates the normal node for d in A, traverses down the sub-tree using the traversal key $T_b(d)$ to find the right-most left-sibling (or left-most right-sibling), and replaces the target node with the sibling. The same procedure is repeated for removing the dual node of d. Figure 3 shows an example of an "Unlink" update.

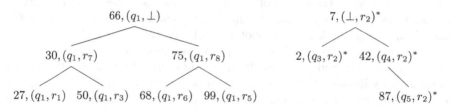

Fig. 3. Removing (q_1, r_2) from address 82 (replaced by (q_1, r_8) in address 75) and $(q_1, r_2)^*$ in address 39

(f) Delete Updates: To delete a response r, the server traverses the dual tree corresponding to r and delete all the dual nodes down the tree. Each dual of the dual nodes, which is a normal node, is also deleted from the corresponding normal tree. Parallel deletion is possible by deleting the left and right sub-trees simultaneously. Similar procedures can be done to delete a query q.

4.3   Concrete Construction

Now we give the details in how to construct our RBT scheme, according to the high-level description explained in the last sub-section. This part will be especially helpful for those who want to implement or possibly optimize our scheme. Recall that in last sub-section we have explained the encryption/decryption part of RBT. The rest is mostly about tree traversal and addition/deletion of nodes, which should be simple to understand for any computer scientists. While conceptually simple, writing down the actual steps in algorithm require a careful management of the pointers involved in (possibly more than one kinds of) the tree. Readers who are interested in its security can go straight to Sect. 4.4, or the performance evaluation in Sect. 5 which also explains part of the codes below and their sub-routines in Appendix A.

Let δ be a data structure of type $\mathcal{T}$ of size parameter (M, N) as defined in Sect. 2. Let $*$ be a special symbol denoting an empty string. Let $\mathcal{F} = \{\{F_b, G_b, T_b, D_b\}_{b \in \{0,1\}}, S\}$ be a set of PRFs such that for each $f \in \mathcal{F}$, $f : \{0,1\}^\lambda \times \{0,1\}^* \to \{0,1\}^\lambda$. Let $H_s : \{0,1\}^\lambda \times \{0,1\}^* \to \{0,1\}^\lambda$, $H_t : \{0,1\}^\lambda \times \{0,1\}^* \to \{0,1\}^{5\lambda}$, and $H_d : \{0,1\}^\lambda \times \{0,1\}^* \to \{0,1\}^{2\lambda}$ be another three PRFs to be modeled as random oracles. All PRFs use different keys. For brevity, we will not specify the key each time we use a PRF.

Our scheme RBT = (Gen, Enc, QryTkn, Qry, UdtTkn, Udt, Dec) is defined as follows, and the sub-routines QryTrav, Ins, Del, DelTrav, and replc are defined in Appendix A.

Algorithm $K \leftarrow$ Gen(1^λ):

1: Generate λ-bit random strings as keys of each PRF
2: Output K which includes all the generated keys

Algorithm $\gamma \leftarrow$ Enc(K, δ):

1: Initialize empty dictionaries I and A
2: Set $\gamma = (I, A)$
3: **for all** $d = (q; r) \in \delta$ **do**
4:     **if** $\hat{q} = (q; *)$ is not added **then**
5:         Run $\tau_u \leftarrow$ UdtTkn$(K, ($"Add"$, (\hat{q})))$
6:         Run $\gamma \leftarrow$ Udt(τ_u, γ)
7:     **end if**
8:     **if** $\hat{r} = (*; r)$ is not added **then**
9:         Run $\tau_u \leftarrow$ UdtTkn$(K, ($"Add"$, (\hat{r})))$
10:       Run $\gamma \leftarrow$ Udt(τ_u, γ)
11:    **end if**
12:   Run $\tau_u \leftarrow$ UdtTkn$(K, ($"Add"$, d))$
13:   Run $\gamma \leftarrow$ Udt(τ_u, γ)
14: **end for**
15: Return γ

Algorithm $\tau_q \leftarrow$ QryTkn(K, d):

1: Parse d as (q, r)
2: **if** $r = *$ **then**
3:     Return $\tau_q = (F_0(d), G_0(d), T_0(d), S(d))$
4: **else**
5:     Return $\tau_q = (F_b(d), G_b(d), t, s)$, where $b \leftarrow \{0,1\}$ and $t, s \leftarrow \{0,1\}^\lambda$
6: **end if**

Algorithm $\mathcal{R} \leftarrow$ Qry(τ_q, γ):

1: Parse γ as (I, A) and τ_q as $(\tau_1, \tau_2, \tau_3, \tau_4)$
2: Abort if τ_1 is not in I

3: Retrieve addr $= I[\tau_1] \oplus \tau_2$
4: Run $\mathcal{R} \leftarrow$ QryTrav(addr, τ_3, τ_4)
5: Return $\mathcal{R}$

Algorithm $\tau_u \leftarrow$ UdtTkn($K, (mode, d)$):
1: Parse d as (q, r)
2: **if** $mode =$ "Add" and ($q = *$ or $r = *$) **then**
3:     Set $b = (q = *)$
4:     Set $\overline{\mu_s} \leftarrow \{0,1\}^\lambda$
5:     Set $\overline{\mu_t} = H_t(T_b(d), r_t)$
6:     Set $\overline{\mu_d} \leftarrow \{0,1\}^{2\lambda}$
7:     Set $\mu_a = (r_s, r_t, r_d) \leftarrow \{0,1\}^{3\lambda}$
8:     Set $\tau_u = (\text{"Add"}, F_b(d), G_b(d), (\overline{\mu_s}, \overline{\mu_t}, \overline{\mu_d}, \mu_a))$
9: **else if** $mode =$ "Add", $q \neq *$ and $r \neq *$ **then**
10:     Set $\mu_a = (r_s, r_t, r_d) \leftarrow \{0,1\}^{3\lambda}$
11:     Set $\mu_a' = (r_s', r_t', r_d') \leftarrow \{0,1\}^{3\lambda}$
12:     Set $\overline{\mu_s} = r \oplus H_s(S(\hat{q}), r_s)$.
13:     Set $\overline{\mu_s'} \leftarrow \{0,1\}^\lambda$
14:     Set $\overline{\mu_t} = H_t(T_0(d), r_t)$
15:     Set $\overline{\mu_t'} = H_t(T_1(d), r_t')$
16:     Set $\overline{\mu_d} = (0, T_1(d)) \oplus H_d(D_0(d), r_d)$
17:     Set $\overline{\mu_d'} = (0, T_0(d)) \oplus H_d(D_1(d), r_d')$
18:     Set

$$\tau_u = (\text{"Link"},$$
$$F_0(\hat{q}), G_0(\hat{q}), T_0(\hat{q}), F_0(d), G_0(d), T_0(d),$$
$$F_1(\hat{r}), G_1(\hat{r}), T_1(\hat{r}), F_1(d), G_1(d), T_1(d),$$
$$(\overline{\mu_s}, \overline{\mu_t}, \overline{\mu_d}, \mu_a), (\overline{\mu_s'}, \overline{\mu_t'}, \overline{\mu_d'}, \mu_a'))$$

19: **else if** $mode =$ "Del" and ($q = *$ or $r = *$) **then**
20:     Set $b = (q = *)$
21:     Set $\tau_u = (\text{"Del"}, F_b(d), G_b(d), T_b(d), D_b(d))$
22: **else if** $mode =$ "Del", $q \neq *$ and $r \neq *$ **then**
23:     Set $\tau_u =$

$$(\text{"Unlink"}, F_0(d), G_0(d), T_0(d), F_1(d), G_1(d), T_1(d))$$

24: **else**
25:     Set $\tau_u = \bot$
26: **end if**
27: Return τ_u

Algorithm $\gamma' \leftarrow$ Udt(τ_u, γ):
1: Parse γ as (I, A) and τ_u as $(mode, \tau_1, \tau_2, \ldots)$
2: **if** $mode =$ "Add" **then**
3:     Recall that

$$\tau_u = (\text{"Add"}, F_b(d), G_b(d), (\overline{\mu_s}, \overline{\mu_t}, \overline{\mu_d}, \mu_a))$$

```
 4:     Abort if τ₁ or τ₄ is in I
 5:     repeat
 6:         Sample root ← {0,1}^λ
 7:     until A[root] is free
 8:     Set I[τ₁] = root ⊕ τ₂
 9:     Set A[root] = τ₃
10: else if mode = "Link" then
11:     Recall that
```

$$\tau_u = (\text{"Link"},$$
$$F_0(\hat{q}), G_0(\hat{q}), T_0(\hat{q}), F_0(d), G_0(d), T_0(d),$$
$$F_1(\hat{r}), G_1(\hat{r}), T_1(\hat{r}), F_1(d), G_1(d), T_1(d),$$
$$(\overline{\mu_s}, \overline{\mu_t}, \overline{\mu_d}, \mu_a), (\overline{\mu_s}', \overline{\mu_t}', \overline{\mu_d}', \mu_a'))$$

```
12:     Abort if τ₁ or τ₇ is not in I
13:     Set root_q = I[τ₁] ⊕ τ₂
14:     Set root_r = I[τ₇] ⊕ τ₈
15:     repeat
16:         Sample tgt, dual ← {0,1}^λ
17:     until A[tgt] and A[dual] are free
18:     Set I[τ₄] = tgt ⊕ τ₅ and I[τ₁₀] = dual ⊕ τ₁₁
19:     Set A[tgt] = τ₁₃ and A[dual] = τ₁₄
20:     Set A[tgt].μ̄_d.dual ⊕= dual
21:     Set A[dual].μ̄_d.dual ⊕= tgt
22:     Run A ← Ins(root_q, τ₃, tgt, τ₆)
23:     Run A ← Ins(root_r, τ₉, dual, τ₁₂)
24: else if mode = "Del" then
25:     Recall that
```

$$\tau_u = (\text{"Del"}, F_b(d), G_b(d), T_b(d), D_b(d))$$

```
26:     Abort if τ₁ is not in I
27:     Set root = I[τ₁] ⊕ τ₂
28:     Run A ← DelTrav(root, τ₃, τ₄)
29: else if mode = "Unlink" then
30:     Recall that
```

$$\tau_u = (\text{"Unlink"}, F_0(d), G_0(d), T_0(d), F_1(d), G_1(d), T_1(d))$$

```
31:     Set tgt = I[τ₁] ⊕ τ₂
32:     Set dual = I[τ₄] ⊕ τ₆
33:     Run A ← Del(tgt, τ₃)
34:     Run A ← Del(dual, τ₆)
35: end if
36: Set γ = (I, A)
37: Return γ
```

4.4   Security Analysis

We follow the existing framework [7] which describes the security of SSE schemes against an honest-but-curious server by a set of leakage functions $(\mathcal{L}_e, \mathcal{L}_q, \mathcal{L}_u)$ for encryption, queries, and updates respectively. RBT leaks information about the internal data structure when performing updates on the tree structure. Its security is asserted in Theorem 1 while the details of $(\mathcal{L}_e, \mathcal{L}_q, \mathcal{L}_u)$ are specified in its proof. The proof can be found in Appendix B.

Theorem 1. *The dynamic searchable symmetric encryption scheme on structured data presented above is $(\mathcal{L}_e, \mathcal{L}_q, \mathcal{L}_u)$-secure against adaptive dynamic chosen-query attacks in the random oracle model.*

5   Efficiency Evaluation

5.1   Complexities Analysis

Let p be the number of processors and m be the number of data related to a given query q or response r. It is easy to see from Qry algorithm that (after Line 1–3 which takes $O(1)$ time) it just applies QryTrav to traverse from the root of a tree. The algorithm QryTrav (after Line 4–8 which recovers the key for unwrapping the two child pointers in particular) just applies QryTrav to traverse the tree recursively. So the query complexity of our scheme is optimal, namely $O(m/p)$.

The update algorithm Udt encapsulates different modes of updates, namely, "Add", "Link", "Unlink", and "Delete". For "Add" update, which just samples a free address (Line 5–7) and masks them (Line 8–9) from the corresponding keys in the update token (Line 3), is constant time. "Link" and "Unlink" updates have complexity $O(\log m)$. Here we just explain "Link". Similar to "Add', it firstly parses the update token (Line 11). From there, the root addresses for q and r are obtained (Line 13–14). To insert the new node, it samples a target address (tgt) for storing the node itself and dual for storing its dual (Line 15–17), sets them up (*e.g.*, masking) appropriately (Line 18–21), and eventually calls Ins (Line 22–23) for locating the actual place to insert into an existing tree. Ins then calls itself recursively if needed just like the traversal in QryTrav. The longest traversal happens when it is inserted at the leaves level of the tree having m nodes, hence the complexity is $O(\log m)$.

Finally, "Delete" mode of update, *i.e.*, DelTrav, traverses the tree to find the node to be deleted similar to Qry. This traversal can be done in parallel, results in a complexity of $O(m/p)$. The sub-routine Del in DelTrav performs the actual deletion. It updates the pointers related to the normal node and the dual node accordingly after finding the replacement node, which is in $O(1)$ time. The step of finding replacement node via Replc simply traverses a tree which can be done in $O(\log m)$ time. To summarize, the complexity of the whole DelTrav algorithm is $O(m/p)$.

5.2 Experiments on Implementations

To demonstrate the applicability of RBT, we consider a privacy-preserving version of decentralized social networks where user connections are represented by graphs. The connections between users are encrypted by RBT, and are searchable by the users possessing search tokens delegated by the host. As described in Sect. 2.2, our scheme naturally supports "friends of friends" and "are Alice and Bob friends" types of queries.

To evaluate the performance of our scheme we implemented RBT in C++ using Crypto++ 5.6.2 library for cryptographic primitives and Intel Threading Building Blocks 4.2 Update 3 library for multi-threading. All PRFs are implemented by HMAC-SHA256. All computations were performed locally in memory (without network transfer). A distinctive feature of RBT over existing schemes is that it supports non-interactive parallel queries and updates. Computations are sequential unless specified.

The experiments were conducted on a machine with Intel Core i5-4590 at 3.50 GHz and 8.00 GB of memory running Windows 8.1. In each experiment, we used RBT to encrypt a set of synthetic data or real-life data. For real-life data, we used a graph [9] representing some Facebook social circles with 4039

Table 4. Timing for RBT ("//" denotes parallel computation)

Type	Synthetic	Synthetic	Facebook
M	500	1000	4039
N	500	1000	4039
$|\delta|$	125,000	500,000	176,468
Density	50%	50%	1.08%
Enc	88 s	451 s	110 s
QryTkn (Normal)	15 μs	17 μs	15 μs
QryTkn (Meta)	12 μs	12 μs	12 μs
Qry (Meta)	420 μs	1173 μs	5 μs
Qry (Normal, //)	39 μs	101 μs	59 μs
Qry (Normal)	64 μs	168 μs	94 μs
UdtTkn (Add)	122 μs	121 μs	121 μs
UdtTkn (Link)	139 μs	137 μs	141 μs
UdtTkn (Delete)	14 μs	20 μs	12 μs
UdtTkn (Unlink)	11 μs	11 μs	12 μs
Udt (Add)	577 μs	780 μs	453 μs
Udt (Delete, //)	29 ms	89 ms	5 ms
Udt (Delete)	38 ms	133 ms	9 ms
Udt (Link)	582 μs	783 μs	472 μs
Udt (Unlink)	360 μs	566 μs	353 μs

nodes and 88,234 undirected (*i.e.*, 176,468 directed) edges. The edge density is relatively small for this set of data. Hence, we also perform experiments on synthetic data which better model other application scenarios. The synthetic data contains graphs with 500 and 1000 nodes respectively with 50% of edge density.

The timing for encryption, "Add" updates, and "Link" updates, are computed by taking the average time needed for the respective operations for building the encrypted database from scratch. The timing for queries, "Delete" updates, and "Link" updates are computed by taking the average time needed for 100 times of the respective operations selected at random. For the timing of normal queries, the values are further divided by the number of responses returned by each query.

Our implementations were hardly optimized, yet the results show the moderate efficiency of our scheme; in particular, parallel computation effectively reduces the time for queries and especially for deletion (Table 4).

6   Conclusion

Searchable symmetric encryption (SSE) has been extensively studied in recent years. One can view the researches on designing SSE as finding a desirable trade-off between functionalities, security, and efficiency. As shown in the literature, devising an SSE scheme which simultaneously achieves a number of desirable properties across these three domains is not an easy task. In this paper, we presented an SSE scheme on structured data supporting parallel traversal. Our aim is to achieve optimal query efficiency while minimizing leakage and communication incurred by the updates.

The abstract data type supported by our SSE scheme can represent queries over many common structured data. In particular, we consider an online social network such as Facebook. The connections between users can be represented by graphs, and common types of queries such as "friends of Alice" and "are Alice and Bob friends" can be represented by neighbor and adjacency queries respectively, which naturally correspond to the normal and meta queries over our abstract data type.

Moreover, we demonstrated the practicality of our scheme by evaluating its efficiency against both real-life graph data of online social network, and synthetic data for graphs in general. We believe our work makes an important step in advancing the field of SSE.

A   Sub-routines in Our Construction

To make our scheme easier to understand, we modularize a number of operations for traversal during a query, insertion, and (the traversal needed for) deletion. Specifically, now we give the details of the operations[1] performed in the sub-routines QryTrav, Ins, Del, DelTrav, and Replc. Algorithms QryTrav and DelTrav

---

[1] Our poster [8] suggested a preliminary idea of using tree structure, but gave no details on the actual construction.

are invoked by Qry and "Del" mode of Udt respectively to traverse the binary search trees. They are identical to ordinary tree traversal algorithms except that the addresses of the children nodes need to be unmasked by using the traversal key. Due to the nature of tree traversal, QryTrav and DelTrav are parallelizable.

Algorithm $\mathcal{R} \leftarrow$ QryTrav(tgt, tkey, k_{srch}):

1: **if** $A[\text{tgt}]$ is free **then**
2:      Return ϕ
3: **end if**
4: Compute $h_0 = H_s(k_{\mathsf{srch}}, A[\text{tgt}].\mu_{\mathsf{a}}.r_s)$
5: Compute $h_1 = H_t(\text{tkey}, A[\text{tgt}].\mu_{\mathsf{a}}.r_t)$
6: Compute $\mu_s = A[\text{tgt}].\overline{\mu_s} \oplus h_0$
7: Compute $\mu_t = A[\text{tgt}].\overline{\mu_t} \oplus h_1$
8: Parse μ_t as $(\text{prt}, \text{chd}_0, k_0, \text{chd}_1, k_1)$
9: Set $\mathcal{R}_0 \leftarrow$ QryTrav($\text{chd}_0, k_0, k_{\mathsf{srch}}$)
10: Set $\mathcal{R}_1 \leftarrow$ QryTrav($\text{chd}_1, k_1, k_{\mathsf{srch}}$)
11: Return $\mathcal{R} = \mathcal{R}_0 \cup \mathcal{R}_1 \cup \{\mu_s\}$

Algorithm $A' \leftarrow$ DelTrav(tgt, tkey, dkey):

1: **if** $A[\text{tgt}]$ is free **then**
2:      Return A
3: **end if**
4: Compute $h_1 = H_t(\text{tkey}, A[\text{tgt}].\mu_{\mathsf{a}}.r_t)$
5: Compute $h_2 = H_d(\text{dkey}, A[\text{tgt}].\mu_{\mathsf{a}}.r_d)$
6: Compute $\mu_t = A[\text{tgt}].\overline{\mu_t} \oplus h_1$
7: Compute $\mu_d = A[\text{tgt}].\overline{\mu_d} \oplus h_2$
8: Parse μ_t as $(\text{prt}, \text{chd}_0, k_0, \text{chd}_1, k_1)$
9: Parse μ_d as (dual, k_D)
10: Run $A \leftarrow$ Del(dual, k_D)
11: Run $A \leftarrow$ DelTrav($\text{chd}_0, k_0, \text{dkey}$)
12: Run $A \leftarrow$ DelTrav($\text{chd}_1, k_1, \text{dkey}$)
13: Remove tgt from A
14: Return A

Ins is identical to an ordinary tree insertion algorithm except that it uses the traversal key to unmask the addresses of the children. Note that Ins determines the position of the insertion based on the address, which is chosen at random.

Algorithm $A' \leftarrow$ Ins(root, $\text{tkey}_{\mathsf{root}}$, tgt, $\text{tkey}_{\mathsf{tgt}}$):

1: Compute $h_1 = H_t(\text{tkey}_{\mathsf{root}}, A[\text{root}].\mu_{\mathsf{a}}.r_t)$
2: Compute $\mu_t = A[\text{root}].\overline{\mu_t} \oplus h_1$
3: Parse μ_t as $(\text{prt}, \text{chd}_0, k_0, \text{chd}_1, k_1)$
4: Set $b = (\text{addr} > \text{root})$
5: **if** $\text{chd}_b = 0$ **then**
6:      Set $A[\text{root}].\overline{\mu_t}.\text{chd}_b \oplus= \text{tgt}$
7:      Set $A[\text{root}].\overline{\mu_t}.k_b \oplus= \text{tkey}_{\mathsf{tgt}}$
8:      Set $A[\text{tgt}].\overline{\mu_t}.\text{prt} \oplus= \text{root}$

9: **else**
10:     Run $A \leftarrow \mathsf{Ins}(\mathsf{chd}_b, \mathsf{k}_b, \mathsf{tgt}, \mathsf{tkey}_{\mathsf{tgt}})$
11: **end if**
12: Output A

Del is identical to an ordinary tree deletion algorithm except that it uses the traversal key to unmask the addresses of the children nodes, and uses the dual key to unmask the addresses of the dual node. It also truly deletes the target node by updating its children and parent to point to the replacement node, instead of just copying the values as in some tree deletion algorithms, or just marked as "deletion pending" which requires housekeeping later. The replacement node is either the right-most left-sibling or the left-most right-sibling of the tree, computed using the algorithm Replc.

Algorithm $A' \leftarrow \mathsf{Del}(\mathsf{tgt}, \mathsf{tkey}_{\mathsf{tgt}})$:

1: **if** $A[\mathsf{tgt}]$ is free **then**
2:     Return A
3: **end if**
4: Compute $h_1 = H_t(\mathsf{tkey}_{\mathsf{tgt}}, A[\mathsf{tgt}].\mu_a.r_t)$
5: Compute $\mu_t = A[\mathsf{tgt}].\overline{\mu_t} \oplus h_1$
6: Parse μ_t as $(\mathsf{prt}, \mathsf{chd}_0, \mathsf{k}_0, \mathsf{chd}_1, \mathsf{k}_1)$
   ▷ Updating Replacement Node and its Neighbors
7: Sample $b \leftarrow \{0, 1\}$
8: Compute $\Delta \leftarrow \mathsf{replc}(b, \mathsf{chd}_b, \mathsf{k}_b)$
9: Parse Δ as $(\mathsf{replc}, \mathsf{tkey}_{\mathsf{replc}}, \mu_t')$
10: Parse μ_t' as $(\mathsf{prt}', \mathsf{chd}_0', \mathsf{k}_0', \mathsf{chd}_1', \mathsf{k}_1')$
11: Set $A[\mathsf{prt}'].\overline{\mu_t}.\mathsf{chd}_{1-b} \oplus= \mathsf{replc} \oplus \mathsf{chd}_b'$
12: Set $A[\mathsf{prt}'].\overline{\mu_t}.\mathsf{k}_{1-b} \oplus= \mathsf{tkey}_{\mathsf{replc}} \oplus \mathsf{k}_b'$
13: Set $A[\mathsf{chd}_b'].\overline{\mu_t}.\mathsf{prt} \oplus= \mathsf{replc} \oplus \mathsf{prt}'$
14: Set $A[\mathsf{replc}].\overline{\mu_t}.\mathsf{prt} \oplus= \mathsf{prt}' \oplus \mathsf{prt}$
15: Set $A[\mathsf{replc}].\overline{\mu_t}.\mathsf{chd}_0 \oplus= \mathsf{chd}_0' \oplus \mathsf{chd}_0$
16: Set $A[\mathsf{replc}].\overline{\mu_t}.\mathsf{k}_0 \oplus= \mathsf{k}_0' \oplus \mathsf{k}_0$
17: Set $A[\mathsf{replc}].\overline{\mu_t}.\mathsf{chd}_1 \oplus= \mathsf{chd}_1' \oplus \mathsf{chd}_1$
18: Set $A[\mathsf{replc}].\overline{\mu_t}.\mathsf{k}_1 \oplus= \mathsf{k}_1' \oplus \mathsf{k}_1$
   ▷ Updating Target Node and its Neighbors
19: Set $b = (\mathsf{tgt} > \mathsf{prt})$
20: Set $A[\mathsf{prt}].\overline{\mu_t}.\mathsf{chd}_b \oplus= \mathsf{tgt} \oplus \mathsf{replc}$
21: Set $A[\mathsf{prt}].\overline{\mu_t}.\mathsf{k}_b \oplus= \mathsf{tkey}_{\mathsf{tgt}} \oplus \mathsf{tkey}_{\mathsf{replc}}$
22: Set $A[\mathsf{chd}_0].\overline{\mu_t}.\mathsf{prt} \oplus= \mathsf{tgt} \oplus \mathsf{replc}$
23: Set $A[\mathsf{chd}_1].\overline{\mu_t}.\mathsf{prt} \oplus= \mathsf{tgt} \oplus \mathsf{replc}$
24: Remove tgt from A
25: Return A

Algorithm $(\mathsf{replc}, \mathsf{tkey}_{\mathsf{replc}}, \mu_t) \leftarrow \mathsf{Replc}(b, \mathsf{tgt}, \mathsf{tkey}_{\mathsf{tgt}})$:

1: **if** $A[\mathsf{tgt}]$ is free **then**
2:     Return $(\mathsf{tgt}, \mathsf{tkey}_{\mathsf{tgt}}, \mathbf{0}_5)$
3: **end if**

4: Compute $h_1 = H_t(\mathsf{tkey}_{\mathsf{tgt}}, A[\mathsf{tgt}].\mu_{\mathsf{a}}.r_t)$
5: Compute $\mu_{\mathsf{t}} = A[\mathsf{tgt}].\overline{\mu_{\mathsf{t}}} \oplus h_1$
6: Parse μ_{t} as $(\mathsf{prt}, \mathsf{chd}_0, \mathsf{k}_0, \mathsf{chd}_1, \mathsf{k}_1)$
7: **if** $A[\mathsf{chd}_{1-b}]$ is free **then**
8:    Return $(\mathsf{tgt}, \mathsf{tkey}_{\mathsf{tgt}}, \mu_{\mathsf{t}})$
9: **else**
10:    Return $\mathsf{replc}(b, \mathsf{chd}_{1-b}, \mathsf{k}_{1-b})$
11: **end if**

B   Security Proof

Proof (of Theorem 1). The leakage of our scheme is implied by the capability of the search keys skey, traversal key tkey, and dual keys dkey. Initially, with the encrypted database, $\mathcal{L}_e$ leaks the size of itself, namely $|\mathcal{Q}| + |\mathcal{R}| + 2|\delta|$. Suppose each of the $|\mathcal{Q}| + |\mathcal{R}| + 2|\delta|$ nodes has a unique identifier. $\mathcal{L}_q$ leaks upon a query q the access pattern, or precisely all μ_{s} stored in the normal nodes corresponding to $(q; \cdot)$. It also leaks the identifiers of these nodes. $\mathcal{L}_u$ leaks upon an update the type of the update. In addition, a "Link" update for $d = (q; r)$ leaks the identifiers of the normal nodes for $(q; \cdot)$, and the identifiers of the dual nodes for $(\cdot; r)$; an "Unlink" update for $d = (q; r)$ leaks the identifiers of the normal nodes for $(q; \cdot)$ under the sub-tree rooted at the normal node for $(q; r)$, and the identifiers of the dual nodes for $(\cdot; r)$ under the sub-tree rooted at the dual node for $(q; r)$; a "Delete" update for $(q; *)$ (resp. $(*; r)$) leaks the identifiers of the normal (resp. dual) nodes for $(q; *)$ (resp. $(*; r)$), as well the identifiers of the corresponding dual (resp. normal) nodes of these nodes.

To prove the security of our scheme, we need to construct a simulator $\mathcal{S}$ which interacts with an adversary $\mathcal{A}$ in the experiment $\mathbf{Ideal}_{\mathcal{A}, \mathcal{S}}(1^\lambda)$ defined in Definition 2. Due to space limitation, we provide the essential idea here, but remark that the simulation is straightforward given the set of leakage functions and follows the same structure of existing proofs [2,6,7].

The simulator simulates the encrypted database by random dictionaries of appropriate sizes given by the leakage function $\mathcal{L}_e$. It simulates all PRF by random functions, and all random oracles (RO) by maintaining and programming the corresponding tables.

For each query/update, the respective leakage ($\mathcal{L}_q/\mathcal{L}_u$) reveals the identifiers of some of the nodes stored in A. The simulator programs the corresponding RO (*e.g.*, H_s and H_t for queries) such that on input the corresponding simulated key (*e.g.*, skey) and randomness (*e.g.*, r_s) stored in μ_{a} of the entry, it produces the suitable mask.

Finally, for answering the random oracle queries, it checks whether the answer for this query to the random oracle is programmed to some particular value. If so, it outputs the programmed value. Otherwise, it outputs a random value. The only possibility that an adversary can distinguish the simulated database from the real database is when it queries the random oracle for a valid pair of (key, randomness), while the corresponding information is not yet revealed in any queries or updates. However, since all simulated keys are produced by random functions, the probability of having such collision is negligible.   □

References

1. Chase, M., Kamara, S.: Structured encryption and controlled disclosure. In: Abe, M. (ed.) ASIACRYPT 2010. LNCS, vol. 6477, pp. 577–594. Springer, Heidelberg (2010). doi:10.1007/978-3-642-17373-8_33
2. Curtmola, R., Garay, J.A., Kamara, S., Ostrovsky, R., Encryption, S.S.: Improved definitions and efficient constructions. J. Comput. Secur. **19**(5), 895–934 (2011)
3. Goh, E.-J.: Secure Indexes. Cryptology ePrint Archive, Report 2003/216
4. Goldreich, O., Ostrovsky, R.: Software protection and simulation on oblivious RAMs. J. ACM **43**(3), 431–473 (1996)
5. Hahn, F., Kerschbaum, F.: Searchable encryption with secure and efficient updates. In: ACM Conference on Computer and Communications Security (CCS), pp. 310–320 (2014)
6. Kamara, S., Papamanthou, C.: Parallel and dynamic searchable symmetric encryption. In: Financial Cryptography, pp. 258–274 (2013)
7. Kamara, S., Papamanthou, C., Roeder, T.: Dynamic searchable symmetric encryption. In: ACM Conference on Computer and Communications Security (CCS), pp. 965–976 (2012)
8. Lai, R., Chow, S.: Structured encryption with non-interactive updates and parallel traversal. In: IEEE International Conference on Distributed Computing Systems (ICDCS), pp. 776–777 (2015)
9. Leskovec, J., Krevl, A., Datasets, S.: Stanford Large Network Dataset Collection, June 2014. http://snap.stanford.edu/data
10. Reed, B.A.: The height of a random binary search tree. J. ACM **50**(3), 306–332 (2003)
11. Song, D.X., Wagner, D., Perrig, A.: Practical techniques for searches on encrypted data. In: IEEE Symposium on Security and Privacy, pp. 44–55 (2000)
12. Stefanov, E., Papamanthou, C., Shi, E.: Practical dynamic searchable encryption with small leakage. In: NDSS (2014)
13. Wang, B., Hou, Y., Li, M., Wang, H., Li, H.: Maple: scalable multi-dimensional range search over encrypted cloud data with tree-based index. In: ASIACCS, pp. 111–122 (2014)
14. Wang, Q., He, M., Du, M., Chow, S.S.M., Lai, R.W.F., Zou, Q.: Searchable encryption over feature-rich data. IEEE Trans. Depend. Secure Comput. (to appear). doi:10.1109/TDSC.2016.2593444

ATCS Workshop - Session 1

Secure IoT Using Weighted Signed Graphs

Pinaki Sarkar[1(✉)] and Morshed Uddin Chowdhury[2]

[1] Department of Computer Science and Automation,
Indian Institute of Science, Bangalore, Karnataka, India
pinakisark@csa.iisc.ernet.in
[2] School of Information Technology, Deakin University,
Burwood Campus, Burwood, VIC, Australia
morshed.chowdhury@deakin.edu.au

Abstract. Key management has always remained a challenging problem for the entire security community. Standard practice in modern times is to agree on symmetric keys using public key protocols. However, public key protocols use heavy computations; rendering them inappropriate for application to low cost devices of Internet of Things (IoT). This led to proposals of various key management strategies for low cost networks; a prominent discovery being key predistribution technique for Wireless Sensor Network (WSN)–a prototype of IoT. Such schemes require several communicating nodes to share the same cryptographic key. This leads to interesting (combinatorial) graphical models and related optimality problems, that get intense for hierarchical architecture. Most protocols meant for hierarchical (low cost) networks employ separate designs for individual levels and/or clusters. Consequently only local optimal values can be computed. We develop a single universal platform using weighted signed graph (WSG) that designs the entire network for a hierarchical setup. This model can be used as itself or clubbed with a key predistribution scheme (KPS) to enhance the latter's security when applied to a WSN. After generic presentation, we combine our universal model with prominent KPS to facilitate comparative study with existing protocols.

Keywords: IoT · WSN · Weighted Signed Graph · Key management · Smart attacks

1 Introduction

Internet of Things (IoT) is a sophisticated concept that aims to connect our world more than we ever thought possible. IoT employs various types of devices to gather information about physical surroundings, process them and communicate these data intelligently among themselves before sending feedback to an end user. Since devices can be resource constrained and are expected to exchange large volumes of data, communication and storage overheads should be minimized. Prominent applications of IoT are smart homes, smart cities, smart grids, smart water networks, vehicular networks, peer-to-peer (P2P) networks, agriculture, health-care, etc.

Wireless Sensor Networks (WSN) are nice prototype of IoT. They are regarded as revolutionary information gathering systems owing to their easy deployment and

© ICST Institute for Computer Sciences, Social Informatics and Telecommunications Engineering 2017
R. Deng et al. (Eds.): SecureComm 2016, LNICST 198, pp. 241–256, 2017.
DOI: 10.1007/978-3-319-59608-2_13

flexible topology. They consists of numerous low-cost identically resource starved wireless devices (sensors or nodes) that deal with sensitive IoT data. WSN finds wide-scale applications in military and scientific arenas (listed above) where security is a premium.

Due to resource constraints in constituent sensors, symmetric key cryptosystems (SKC) are preferred over a public key setup in such networks. SKC schemes requires both sender and receiver to possess same encryption-decryption key before message exchange. This is achievable by various techniques; key predistribution being preferred due to cost effective implementation. Ideally any key predistribution schemes (KPS) should have small key-rings, and yet support large number of nodes with appreciable resiliency, scalability and communication probability (or connectivity). However, renowned scientists proved the impossibility of constructing a 'perfect KPS' that meet all these criteria [17, 18, 21]. This motivated proposals of several designs that are robust for specific purpose(s). We try to unify them under a single banner after investigation.

Employing a hierarchy with certain powerful special nodes is perhaps wiser and more practical approach for IoT. An extensive literature survey reveals that all prominent hierarchical schemes [1–4, 10, 23, 25–28] try to glue local and global graphs quite artificially. We try to give a more natural description of the local and global models of any hierarchical network using an uniform banner of Weighted Signed Graph (WSG) and thereby demonstrate the impact on various aspect of such networks. To date, to the best of our knowledge, no scheme represents an hierarchical structure by a single (deterministic) model though there have been some elegant trials [2, 4, 26, 27].

1.1   Motivation and Plan of Work

A critical challenge encountered while designing secure protocols for low cost IoT networks like WSN is to ensure secure communication between two nodes that are not in each other's communication range. Priors works use intermediate users who gets access to these communications in clear text. Our work ascertain that these communications remain protected by use of two different cryptosytems possessing separate keys. This concept is set out in Sect. 6 while applying of our WSG model to low cost networks.

KPS involves preloading of symmetric cryptographic keys before deployment and establishing them immediately after deployment. Use of unique association of keys to their ids that are transmitted in open during key establishment ensure that actual keys are not revealed; though the network graph becomes public. A node's secondary id (set of key ids or their unique function–node ids [25]) is extra information that gets hidden during adaptation of our WSG model. These converted private information of individual nodes are used during key establishment to hide the network graph from an adversary.

This helps to eradicate selective node attack or smart attack. Refer to Sect. 2.

Ruj and Pal [23] state that random graph models are well suited for 'scalability' and 'resilience'. Thereby they try to justify their random designs based on preferential attachment models with degree bounds. Unfortunately, all designs of [23] suffers from highly skewed load distribution, poor connectivity and resiliency; and hence, are inappropriate for IoT applications. Interestingly, renowned researchers [17, 18, 21, 25] report that deterministic schemes possess advantages like predictable connectivity, resilience, scalability etc., which occurs with certain probability in random ones.

Sensitive IoT applications require protocols to yield connected networks (thereby reduce hops; so attacks). So we opt deterministic protocols for security applications in IoT networks, despite most them having restricted scaling operations. Our WSG model can supports large number of such scaling operations (not unrestricted, though), as demonstrated in Sect. 4.3.

2 Basic Concepts and Definitions

Design of our graphical model requires formalizing of fundamental notions, like hierarchical WSN–various connectivity radii and neighbors; two types of network graphs– global and local for individual clusters; hence respective keys; security models.

- **Hierarchical WSN (HWSN):** A standard method to incorporate an hierarchy in these networks is to inject special (purpose) devices. They are relatively more resourceful than an ordinary sensor; however, much weaker than any Base Station (BS). Such devices are generally called Cluster Heads (CH) or Gateway Nodes (GN). Some authors also term them as super nodes [3] or agents [1, 25].
- **Radius of communication:** of a device is the maximum of the distances that it can transmit and/or receive messages from other devices. This maximum distance, denoted by r_{device}, and is varied for different type of entities. The identical sensors have the least value 'r_{node}'; while any BS has the highest communication radius. The communication radius for any CH (assumed identical for all) is usually greater than the identical nodes, however, less than the BS(s). Since any designer's target is to increase network connectivity, we focus on r_{node} and simply denote as r.
- **Neighboring devices or Neighbors:** two devices with *same* r_{device} are neighbors if they are within communication radius of each other. In case $r_{device_1} < r_{device_2}$ for two devices $device_1$ (say a node) and $device_2$ (say a CH) and distance between $device_1$ and $device_2$ is greater than r_{device_1} but less than r_{device_2}, then $device_1$ is a neighbor of $device_2$ but not otherwise. Providing security to such communication that often happens among varied type of IoT devices is a major challenge.

  More critical challenge is to secure communication of two low power devices that are not neighbors. Priors works usually use intermediate users who gets to see these communications in clear text. Our work ensure that these communications remain protected by recursive use of two different keys of independent cryptosytems.[1]
- **Global, Local graphs, respective keys:** Our model has two types of graphs–global (network) graph and local (cluster) graphs. Any device will be treated as vertex and a link between two devices as an edge between them. For the same pair of vertex,

---

[1] Use of double encryption requires careful implementation. For instance, double encryption with two smartly chosen AES − 128 keys may enhance the security level by 1.5 times. That is, from 120 − BIT security to approximately 180 − BIT against any present day adversary.

there may be multiple edges–exactly one local and others, global (if any, see Sect. 3). These graphs are used to employ independent cryptosystems; hence respective (complementary sets) of keys. Refer to footnote 1 (above).

- **Local graphs:** are 'in-cluster' or 'local' graphs for individual cluster that depicts the key sharing between devices of a given cluster. A generic construction presented in Sect. 3 denotes the edges of these graphs by negative sign for consistency. Here we assume that all the nodes in a cluster are in each other's communication radius.
- **Global graph and key sharing:** Our weighted signed graph can simultaneously model a complete network. This owes to the fact that the graphical representations supports any number of links (weights) and assigns signs. We exploit the positive sign to denote secure links for pairs of nodes that share a common key, globally. Due to limited memory of any sensor and large sized network, single key must be shared by multiple nodes to assure desired (high) level of (secure) connectivity.
- **Secure communication:** between a pair of entities is assured if their communication is secured by some *shared* cryptographic key, either local or global (or both).

Sharing of global (network) keys leads to a certain weakness in any protocol, specially considering that IoT networks are vulnerable to device compromise. We consider the robustness of our networks against two such attacks, as described below:[2]

- **Random node compromise:** may lead to partial disclosure key-rings of existing devices; thereby restrict the use of links that were secured by these keys. A system's resilience against such an attack may be measured by a standard metric, viz., *fail(s)* which estimates the ratio of links broken of non-compromised nodes to the remaining number of links in the network after random compromise of s nodes.
- **Smart Attack [22] or Selective Node Capture Attack [25]:** Essentially in this type of attack, an attacker tries to break communications of two specific nodes by selectively capturing other node(s) that share the same key(s) being used for communications of the former nodes. This happens because sharing of (global) keys usually leads to exchange of *(unencrypted) key ids* during key establishment. This reveals the *global key sharing graph*. This key sharing knowledge may aid an adversary in selectively (or smartly) targeting specific nodes that share key(s) with the communicating nodes. All existing works, for instance [5, 7–14, 16–19, 21–25, 28, 29] are prone to this attack. Readers are referred to [22] for a more technical definition.

3 Graphical Model and Its Representation

We use weighted signed graph to design an entire hierarchical network. Enumerate each ordinary network user (node for a WSN) by a specific *id (node id./node no.)*. Special purpose users (CHs for a WSN) are separately enumerated. Their enumeration is prefixed with specific number of 0's denoting their height above the node level. The following convention are adapted while defining our local and global graphs:

---

[2] This can be best analyzed by employing a particular KPS as a candidate for our global graph.

- Denote a *link* between two specific entities of the global (distributed) graph as: **(lower entity no.)(e)(higher entity no.)**. In most case, we will only have **(lower node no.)(e)(higher node no.)**. This is because we do not allow hierarchical communication using global keys. This will make our model have wide-spread applicability to any distributed system. Such networks employ a fixed cryptosystem with single type of key; for instance, application of KPS in WSN.
- *Local graphs* have two types of entities, viz several lower level devices (nodes/CHs) and an upper level user (corresponding CH/BS). So we need to define separate links for distinct type of connections:
- *Local graph links or simply local links* that involve *user at different level* shall be denoted by: **(−)(lower level entity no.)(e)(higher level entity no.)**. Resultant local links triplet for a CH at penultimate level (one level above ordinary node level) and its CH at two level above node level is: $-(0)(CH\ no.)(e)(0)(0)(CH\ no.)$; while that of a node and its CH (one level above the level of this ordinary node) is: $-(node\ no.)(e)(0)(CH\ no.)$. Specifically, connectivity link between any Node i under its CH A is denoted by $-ie0A$. Here '−ve' implies local link.
- *Local links* involving *same level* entities are denoted by: **(−)(lower entity no.)(e)(higher entity no.)**. We use ordering of node id (or CH id) due to global network to ensure unique representation of this link and '−ve' sign implies local link.[3]
- *Local link* between *CH A* and *CH B* is denoted by $-0Ae0B$ whenever $A < B$. '−ve' denotes that this edge is due to local graph at cluster head level. Convention prefix of '0' symbolizes that these CHs are hierarchically one level above nodes.

These definition have canonical generalization for (corresponding) users higher up in the hierarchy. Parenthesis are used for clarity of representation and shall be dropped later when there is no ambiguity. That is, for consistency entities in each hierarchical level adds a 0's to the prefix of the already available representation of the links. The following example clarifies the concept:

1. Suppose we want global link between nodes 2 and 5, then their edge or link is represented by: **(2)(e)(5)** or simply **2e5**.
2. various local links between various devices are as below:

   - Same level local link between nodes 7 and 3 is represented by: **−(3)(e)(7)** or simply **−3e7**. Figure 1 depicts the scenario pictorially.
   - Connectivity link between a node (say, 2) and its cluster head (CH 1) is $-2e01$.
   - link between CH 2 and CH 1 is $-01e02$. Observe order of representation in each.

Parallel edges/links: occur between a pair of nodes when they simultaneously possess both local and global connectivity links. Evidently, they must be in the *same cluster* (refer to Fig. 1) and share a global key. One edge (global link) will thus be represented by a *positive ('+')* sign and another edge (local link) will have *negative ('−')* sign. Since the local graphs results in less key sharing (in fact, pairwise key sharing in most cases), using this local key may provide optimal security. In case, pairwise key sharing

---

[3] Usually node ids are positive number (like KPS applications). Therefore 0 or negative numbers are not used for global links. So we make extensive use of 0 and −ve sign for our local graph.

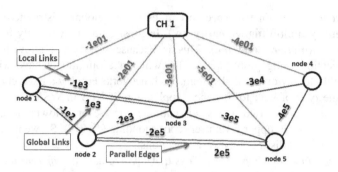

Fig. 1. Connectivity between nodes of same cluster: parallel edges

is not assured by the local graphs (storage factor), use of hash of both the local and global keys may give ideal resilience (up to security of underlying cryptosystem).

Suppose, for simplicity, that nodes with *ids* 2 and 5 belong to same cluster and share both global and local link. Thus there will be *two* parallel edges or links connecting these two nodes. The global link will be denoted by $2e5$, while the local edge/link will be represented by $-2e5$. Note the difference in sign. We propose use of the local link, i.e. $-2e5$ in case this is achieved pairwise; else use hash (shared local keys‖global key).

Sharing of multiple global keys is another case of occurrence of parallel links between a pair of nodes. An example of this situation is to consider the global graph to be a KPS design [24] where each pair of nodes share a minimum of 4 keys. This will give rise to a minimum of 4 global key links. In such multiple key sharing cases, a standard method [11] is to use hash of all the shared keys to effective obtain one global link.

4   Design of Key Management Scheme

We propose a key management scheme that may find suitable applications in Internet of Things (IoT). Primary focus is on low cost networks–WSN being a prototype. Basic devices in such low cost IoT networks are resources starved; example ordinary nodes of a WSN. This imposes certain restrictions while designing key management schemes for such low cost networks; forcing us to opt for key predistribution strategies. So we aim to apply our weighted signed graph design to a key predistribution scheme and ensure enhanced security with minimum strain on ordinary devices. This upper bounds the key storage in individual devices (*key-ring*) and imposes a degree bound on each of them.

4.1 Keyrings and Degree Bound on Devices

Most key management protocols for IoT [1, 3, 5–14, 16–19, 21–25, 28, 29], distributed or hierarchical, allow intermediate entities to access communication of non-neighboring devices in clear text. This is because either there was single global graph model (example, any KPS) or in case of two distinct graphical models (in-cluster and global), their application did not complement each other. Thereby simultaneous use of two separate cryptosystem and hence repeated encryption was prohibited. Though some odd schemes like [2, 4, 26, 27] uses repeated encryption, their constructions are actually super-imposition of three local graphs and a global. All existing protocols can now be visualized as subgraphs of our WSG applied to individual schemes. By nature, WSG permits titanic pliability and can support wide range of designs for arbitrary networks; however constraints of devices of particular application platform may compel additional restrictions.

Bearing in mind the constraints in resource of ordinary devices of a low cost IoT network, we propose applications of weighted signed graphs with degree bound $(WSG - DB)$ to design security model for such networks. For this, a bound is first fixed on the maximum number of keys k a node can have and the maximum number r of nodes on the cycle of each key; thereby fixing the degree of each device and the maximum degree (d_{max}) that the graph can have. We primarily try to assume a reasonable (uniform) bound for d_{max} of ordinary nodes as their resources are at premium; whereas the value of d_{max} may be much greater for relatively resourceful (fewer) CHs. For the sake of simplicity of computation, let every ordinary device have k_{user} keys and each key cycle be r so that $d_{max} = d_{user} = rk_{user}$. It is easy to see that a node's maximum degree $d_{max} = d_{user} = rk_{user}$ is obtained in case any two pair of nodes intersect in exactly one local and/or global key. While combining with a suitable KPS, this optimality condition may be exploited. Observe that r is also assumed same, and not individual cycles (r_l and r_g) of local and global keys for simplicity.

4.2 Distribution of Local and Global Keys

WSG gives enormous flexibilities and can support wide range of designs; a particular hierarchical one meant for resource constraint IoT (for instance, WSN) networks is being discussed here. For a given user, let $k_{l_{user}} :=$ number of keys preallocated for its local (in-cluster) connections and $k_{g_{user}} :=$ keys for a node's links due to the global graph (say a KPS). Evidently, $k_{user} := k_{l_{user}} + k_{g_{user}}$. For practical applications (to be discussed in Sect. 6), we assume $k_{l_{user}} = k_{g_{user}} \implies k_{user} = 2k_{l_{user}} = 2k_{g_{user}} (= k, \text{say})$. To overcome storage problem, we preallocate as many local keys $(\frac{k}{2})$ as global; so that an upper bound is $\frac{d_{max}}{2r}$ for each node.

Establishment of global keys using their unique *ids* is the essence of any key pre-distribution and leads to interesting combinatorial graph problems. Whereas, local keys need not be established as the number of nodes per clusters is orders less than that in entire network (see Sect. 5 below). Local keys can be used to secure key establishment of global keys (set out in Sect. 6). These keys can also form independent (hierarchical) key predistribution systems themselves; but best effects occur when combined with keys of a global graph like a KPS. Our applications assume $r_l = 2$ during initial deployment, that is, local graphs for every cluster yield a pairwise key distribution.

4.3 Scalability: Addition of Nodes and/or CHs

Topology of most IoT networks is fast changing due to frequent node movements, addition, deletion and/or compromise. Our WSG model supports both deletion and addition of users. Deletion of users in our model is fairly simple–just delete remaining network's edges corresponding to all the keys exposed due to comprise of device(s).[4] Addition of users may increase r values of existing users. Generally r_g is fixed; so effectively the increment may occur in r_l. Employing $WSG - DB$ concept during scaling operations aids in enhancing our existing design as is briefed in Sect. 4.3.

Local graph induced by our $WSG - DB$ allows the network graph to expand with the addition of every extra vertex (node or CH). This is achieved by assigning all inherited global edges and required local edges needed for this new vertex. Addition of new nodes in existing clusters imply setting up new local links with existing nodes and their CH.

Injection of moderate number of ordinary users and barely a few super users may perhaps be managed by repeated use of same local key(s) to connect several users; thereby increasing r_l. Of course we assume that r_g is fixed for all ordinary users including the new comers. Further, assume that k_{user} is also fixed. Therefore the overall degree bound d_{max} of the network implies an upper bound on r_l. Though the global graph is restrictive in its growth (due to fixed $k_{g_{user}}, r_g$), the above scaling strategy results in better scalability for the combined model. Figure 2 explains the scenario graphically. This overcomes the problem of storage cost for devices even during scaling.

Enormous increment of nodes may lead to huge network growth. This can be tackled by new cluster formation via local graphs. These links are governed by the rules defined in Sect. 3. The incoming nodes and CH are injected with all required keys by the BS to connect with its concerned CH. Cluster-wise deployment may ensure proper cluster formation. In case of any 'misplaced node', a key rescheduling technique, set out in Algorithm 1 of Sect. 5, may be invoked to ensure secure communication of this node.

5   Deployment of Nodes and Cluster Heads

We suggest a cluster-wise deployment, i.e. deploy the nodes with their respective CH. Desired cluster formation should result in most cases. Standard methods of *challenge and response* [14, Sect. 2.1] using cluster wise broadcast keys may be adapted to check correctness of deployment, i.e., proper cluster formation. Evidently, instead of totally

---

[4] We have to rely on standard intrusion prevention system and/or traitor protocols like [15, 20] for updated information about compromised nodes to facilitate their deletion.

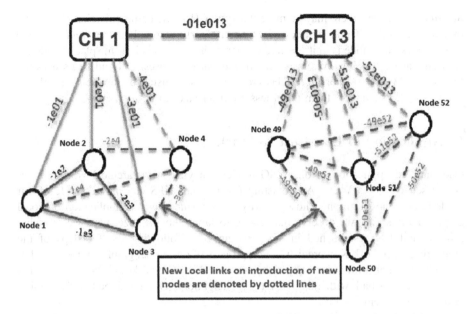

Fig. 2. Communication of (distant) Nodes N_i, N_j of different clusters using local keys

random deployment, we are proposing *group-wise* or *locally* random deployment of the nodes and respective CH according to the local graph. However their exact positions are still unknown. This implies that *local keys for correctly deployed nodes need not be established* and can be directly utilized; for instance an application may be to establish global keys (with large cycles r_g). However, in an unlikely event of a node falling out of their cluster, we adopt the below described key rescheduling technique:

BS generates and preallocates in each node and CH a *global re-scheduling key* (**rsk**$_{user}$). They are used for the specific purpose of cluster formation during initial deployment and subsequent key refreshment as described in Algorithm 1. These keys are temporary and recursive in the sense that: (i) a fresh set of such keys are generated and transferred to all existing as well as in-coming nodes and CH using existing **rsk**$_{user}$ keys that are (ii) thrashed soon afterwards during every round of key establishment. As such, there is exactly one such key in every node at any given point of time barring short-lived periods of key refreshment when there are exactly two such. Correspondingly there are $O(N)rsk_{user}$ keys in the BS (since number of CHs is orders less than number of nodes = N). We do not require such keys to be share between CHs and nodes.

Recursive use of rsk_{user} keys expands the local graphs; thereby profound network scaling occurs (see Sect. 4.3). Further, their use adapts our model to *dynamic environment*. For any significant movement of an user (from its initial cluster into another), we perform a fresh 'key rescheduling' process by treating this node as 'misplaced node'.[5]

---

[5] These processes will be detailed in extended version of this work.

Remark 1. At times, there may be more than one CH in the communication radius of a (misplaced) node. If one of these CHs can properly respond to the *challenge and response* test, this node is in its desired cluster. Otherwise, this is a 'misplaced node'. It uses Global Positioning System (GPS) to find out the closest CH and treats it as the 'new' CH. In case two or more CHs are at minimum distance from this 'misplaced node', we choose any of them (with lesser cluster size) to be its (new) CH.

6 Application to Low-Cost Networks

One standard application of our WSG model can yield a hierarchical key predistribution scheme for a WSN. Any existing (distributed) KPS can play the role of our (underlying) 'global graph' whose security gets enhanced by the application of 'local graph'. To this end, we observe that owing to large network size, keys were predistributed and later established in any existing KPS following the footsteps of the pioneering work [14]. Key predistribution process of our global graph can be treated in a similar manner with secure key establishment due to local keys.[6] We assume that cluster size is small with all nodes being neighbors. Our combined WSG design achieves improvements in:

---

1 Each user i sends a challenge text to their respective CH A (see Remark 1) encrypted using (intended) preloaded local (broadcast) key K_o;

2 **if** *CH A is able to correctly decrypt the challenge,* **then**

3   CH A concludes K_o is shared local key with user i;

4   and broadcasts: "User i is correctly placed.";

  end

5 **else if** *CH A is unable to respond correctly to the challenge,* **then**

6   CH A broadcasts this 'location error of user i';

7   CH A_0, intended CH of user i receives this broadcast by CH A (like others);

8   CH A_0 verifies information by *challenge and response* and confirms to BS;

9   CH A_0 uses the link $-0A_0e0A$, $-0A_0e00BS$ to securely transmit K_o to CH A and BS (for escrow);

10   Meanwhile, on hearing CH A's broadcast user i encrypts K_o with the key rsk_i that it uniquely shares with the BS;

11   This encryption is routed to the BS via CH A (CH A is unable to decrypt);

12   BS decrypts this encrypted K_o using rsk_i;

13   BS generates a fresh of key K_n for CH A and user i;

14   Sends K_n to CH A and user i after encrypting with rsk_A and rsk_i respectively;

15   User i and CH A computes fresh shared (local) key as: $K_n \oplus K_o$;

  end

16 A fresh set of 'global rescheduling keys' rsk_{user} are generated;

17 All the old rsk_{user} keys are revoked immediately afterwards.;

Algorithm 1. Key Rescheduling Protocol For 'Misplaced Nodes'.

---

[6] Represent global links as (*lower node no.*)(k_i)(*higher node no.*) for $1 \leq i \leq v$; $k_1, k_2, k_3, \cdots k_v$ are all the keys of selected KPS. This automatically captures the (regular) degree ($r_{KPS} = r_g$) of concerned KPS. Refer to [18, Sect. 2] for this definition of r_{KPS}, where it is denoted as r.

Key Establishment Protocol (KEP) of any existing KPS uses unencrypted transmission of (global) key *ids*. This process reveals the network (key) graph to an eavesdropper and induces *smart attacks*. Introduction of the '*local keys*' facilitates transmission of encrypted key ids during '*(global) key establishment phases*' (of our combined KPS); and so, restricts an attacker from equating the *unencrypted key ids*. As a result, an attacker need to break the underlying cryptosystem meant for the local graphs to trace the '*(global) key sharing graph*' of combined networks; unlike previous works. Hence, this novel key establishment technique results in eradication of the pertinent weakness of '*selective node attacks*' or '*smart attacks*', generically prevalent in most existing KPS [5–11, 13, 14, 16–19, 21, 22, 24, 28, 29].[7]

Message Exchange of any existing KPS involves the following steps:

- for neighboring sensors that share a common key (traced during key establishment), a message to be transmitted is encrypt with that common key.[8] Sender node then transmits this encrypted message via wireless channels. Only those receivers who posses the shared keys can decrypt this encryption to recover original text.
- direct encrypted communication is forbidden for sensors that do share any common key or are not in communication radius of each other. An alternate (path key) strategy of routing though other nodes is suggested. This brings in extra complexity of tracing optimized secure path, which is a major challenge for any KPS.

Our WSG based combined model outperforms existing KPS due to supplementary cryptosystem arising from the local graphs. '*Local keys*' may provide unique direct connectivity between nodes and CH of the same cluster; specially during initial deployment. This results in *ideal security* in terms of key distribution; that is, here the system's security depends solely on the underlying (KPS) cryptosystem. Local keys can independently links two nodes i and j of different clusters by use three local links as below:

- local link $-(ie0A)$ between the sender node i and its CH A;
- local link $-(0Ae0B)$ between respective CH A, B of sender and receiver nodes;
- local link $-je0B$ between the receiver node and its CH B.[9]

In case 'misplaced nodes' do not have any shared global key with its (new) neighbors, above process ensures that it is still securely connected to the network. This problem that every node, even misplaced ones, remain securely connected to the network is a challenging one and not many KPS provide adequate solution like we just did.

---

[7] Of course the use of local keys here requires proper cluster formation to ensure desired inter- cluster connectivity. One plausible way to obtain the desired cluster formation is to deploy the nodes and their Cluster Heads in a locally (uniform) random or group-wise random fashion. This assures proper cluster formation in most cases. In a rare event of 'misplaced node', we propose implementation of Key Rescheduling Protocol, described in Algorithm 1.

[8] In the event of (same set of) multiple keys shared between a pair of nodes, a standard method [11] is to concatenate all of these keys and use hash of this concatenated key.

[9] These communications make use of (fixed) publicly available addresses (like MAC or I.P. or email ids) of users (here nodes). Observe that these primary addresses are independent of the created secondary *node ids* [24, 26, 27] used during (global) key establishment.

Local connectivity defined above suffers from 'one point' attacks on the CH, though such an attack may be practically harder to mount on a handful of CH. Previous works generally assume considerable trust on CH and even nodes as message meant for distant nodes are routed via intermediate CH/nodes who can see these message in clear text. To be on safer side, we use an alternate trick of recursive encryption-decryption (maintaining orders) for distant nodes that possess a shared global key; described below:

- a sender (node i) encrypts the message twice; (i) first with the global key shared with intended recipient(s); and (ii) second with local key shared with its parent CH A. Sends the doubly encrypted message to its CH A using the link $-ie0A$ (remember recipient(s) are beyond communication range).
- Sender's parent CH A opens the outer encryption and puts on another encryption using the key shared with recipient's parent CH B. Sends this double encrypted message to recipient's CH B via $-0Ae0B$.
- Receiver's parent CH B opens the outer encryption and puts on another encryption using local key shared with recipient node j and sends to recipient via link $-0Be\,j$.
- Intended recipient node j has both the required local and global keys to decrypt the repeated encryption. Recursive decryption of this doubly encrypted message by: (i) first by the shared local key with its parent CH B and (ii) then the global key shared with sender node i reveals the clear text message.

Figure 2 represents these inter-cluster communications pictorially where Node i communicates with Node j with the KPS link $ie\,j$ (positive sign). This is the only step in our work that involves double encryption and results in highly enhanced network security.

7 Resiliency of Combined Model: Theoretical Analysis

Though most works concerning hierarchy in WSN restricts an attacker from compromising special nodes (CH), we think this assumption is rather strong. We give more power to an adversary. Consider a weaker assumption that an adversary can comprise CH but such captures are relatively harder as compared to compromising nodes. From this section onwards, the symbol 's' will represent number (no.) of nodes compromised, and the symbol 't' is reserved for number of CHs captured in penultimate tier (just above the level of ordinary nodes). So our attack models assumes $s \gg t$.

Resiliency of existing KPS are measured by a standard metric '$fail(s)$' that denotes the ratio of links broken after compromise of s nodes to the total links in remaining network. Formally:

$$fail(s) = \frac{\text{number of links broken of non−compromised nodes due to capture of s nodes}}{\text{total number of links in after compromise of s nodes}}.$$

Evidently, most KPS [6, 7, 16–19, 21] try to minimize this '$fail(s)$' values for their respective schemes. We canonically extend this definition to $fail(s,t)$ as below:

Definition 1. *For the combined (Weighted Signed Graph) system, define fail(s,t) to be*

$$= \frac{number\ of\ global\ links\ broken\ due\ to\ capture\ of\ s\ nodes\ and\ t\ (CH)}{total\ number\ of\ KPS\ links\ in\ after\ compromise\ of\ s\ nodes}.$$

Remark 2. We do not consider links broken in our newly constructed local graphs. Focus is on global (KPS) links since the corresponding keys are shared between many nodes; whereas local keys are uniquely shared (at least initially). Details of scaling effects on resilience of local graphs will be presented in extended version of our work.

Though it is difficult to have an estimate of the exact value of *fail(s,t)* when 's' nodes and '*t*' CHs of a WSN are captured, we can compute an estimated upper bound of *fail(s,t)* of the combined design for a particular chosen KPS scheme.

Theorem 1. *Suppose s nodes of the chosen KPS t out of the original c CHs in the last tier of the combined network are captured. Then an upper bound of* fail(s,t) *is*

$$\frac{t}{c} \times fail(s),$$

where fail(s) *is the resiliency of chosen KPS due to the capture of s nodes.*

Proof. Special nodes (like CH for WSN) of the local graphs enable repeated encryption of messages using unique local keys (at least initially). Messages being transmitted always remain encrypted and only the outer encryption of these double encrypted on messages are decrypted and re-encrypted (by different keys). Removal of a CH means that the nodes of that cluster operate with only global keys; so that, extra security due to our WSG model gets negated for nodes of this cluster. Of course, capture of all c CHs at the penultimate level of the hierarchy eradicates every additional security imparted due to the local graphs of WSG model. This (latter) unlikely event reduces the security of this compromised combined system to that of underlying KPS.

Under the standard assumption that nodes are uniformly distributed under their CH in individual clusters, we conclude resilience upon capture of a CH, $fail(s,t) = \frac{fail(s,t)}{c}$. So when t CHs out of total c CHs at penultimate level are compromised, resiliency metric $fail(s,t) = \frac{fail(s,t)}{c}$. Thus, our desired result is achieved. $\square$

7.1   Simulation Results: Comparative Study

We select $TD(k, p)$ deign of Lee and Stinson [18] with $k = p$ as underlying KPS of our combined model; i.e., KPS based on $TD(k, p)$ designs our global graph. From here on, by combined protocol, we shall refer to this combination of KPS [18] as global graph and pairwise local graphs (due to negative signs). This combined system has been used to conducted simulations with $s = 100, 200, ..., 1000$ and $t = \frac{s}{25}$ under hypothetical conditions that replicate real life scenarios. Results obtained were compared with some prominent existing schemes [11, 13, 14, 18, 25, 28]. Each network is assumed to have roughly $N \approx 10000$ nodes and stated connectivity probability p_c. These results

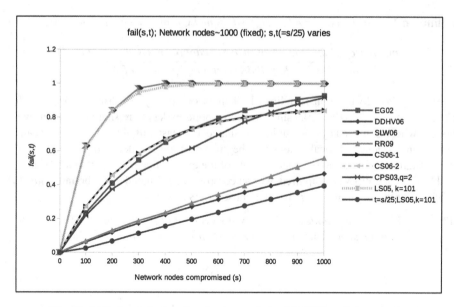

Fig. 3. fail(s,t) comparison for almost equal sized (10000 nodes) networks

presented in Fig. 3 help in visualizing the improvements achieved when our combined scheme is compared with KPS having following set of parameters:

1. Lee and Stinson (LS05) (distributed) scheme [18]: $p = 101$, $k = 101$, $p_c = 0.99$ and $N = 10201$;
2. Proposed combined scheme: $p = 101$, $k_{TD} = 202$, $t = \frac{s}{25}$, $p_c = 1$ and $N = 11040$;
3. Chakrabarti and Seberry (hierarchical) schemes [10] with 25 nodes compromised per cluster ($s_{cluster} = 25$) and CH compromised = (4% of nodes compromised of entire network) $t = 4, 8, ..., 40$:
   (a) CS06-1 where both tiers are based on symmetric BIBD [7] (construction extended over F_{p^z}); parameter: $p^z = 11, 9$ for node and CH levels respectively. Therefore, key-rings of nodes: = $k_{nodes} = 12$ and key-rings of CH: = $k_{CH} = 10$ and $N = 133 * 91 = 12103$;
   (b) CS06-2 uses [18] for lower tier, extended symmetric BIBD [7] for upper; parameter: $p^z = 11, 9$ for node and CH levels respectively. Therefore, $k_{nodes} = 11$ with $k_{CH} = 10$ and $N = 121 * 91 = 11011$;
4. Simonova et al. (SLW06) (location aware) scheme [28]: $k = 16$, $p = 11$, $m = 2$, $N = 12100$ over $TD(k, p)$ KPS [18] with $k = 4$, $p11$, so that $p_c = 0.363$;
5. Ruj and Roy (RR09) (hierarchical) scheme [25]: $n = 143$, $k = 12$, $N = 16093$.
6. Eschenauer and Gligor (EG02) (distributed) scheme [14]: $k = 263$, $p_c = 0.5$, $N = 10000$.
7. Chan et al. (CPS03) q-composite (distributed) scheme [11]: $q = 2$, $k = 263$, $p_c = 0.5$, $N = 10000$.
8. Du et al. (DDHV06) (location aware) scheme [13]: $k = 67$, $p_c = 0.5$ and $N = 10000$;

8 Conclusion and Future Work

This paper proposes a universal design to model any hierarchical graph. This design is based on Weighted Signed Graph (WSG). Such a model is particularly useful in designing key management schemes for low cost networks. As an application, we select any popular key predistribution scheme (KPS) that are particularly useful in resource starved environment of WSN–a prototype of IoT. Comparative study of a fixed KPS as the global (inter cluster) graph with a pairwise local (intra cluster) graph establishes the superior performance of our scheme with prominent existing schemes.

Due to page limits, we leave detailed study of scalability (thanks to local/cluster graph) of combined network for the extended version of this paper. We shall analyze the side effects of scalability on resiliency for fully connected resultant networks.

References

1. Bag, S.: A new key predistribution scheme for grid-group deployment of wireless sensor networks. Ad Hoc Sens. Wirel. Netw. **27**(3–4), 313–329 (2015)
2. Bag, S., Dhar, A., Sarkar, P.: 100% connectivity for location aware code based KPD in Clustered WSN: Merging Blocks. In: Information Security Conference (ISC) 2012, Passau, Germany, pp. 136–150 (2012)
3. Bag, S., Roy, B.K.: A new key predistribution scheme for general and grid-group deployment of wireless sensor networks. EURASIP J. Wirel. Commun. Networking **2013**, 145 (2013)
4. Bag, S., Saha, A., Sarkar, P.: Highly resilient key predistribution scheme using transversal designs and reed muller codes for wireless sensor network. In: Wyld, D.C., Wozniak, M., Chaki, N., Meghanathan, N., Nagamalai, D. (eds.) CNSA 2011. CCIS, vol. 196, pp. 344–355. Springer, Heidelberg (2011). doi:10.1007/978-3-642-22540-6_33
5. Banihashemian, S., Ghaemi Bafghi, A., Yaghmaee Moghaddam, M.H.: Centralized key management scheme in wireless sensor networks. Wirel. Pers. Commun. **60**(3), 463–474 (2011)
6. Bose, M., Dey, A., Mukerjee, R.: Key predistribution schemes for distributed sensor networks via block designs. Des. Codes Cryptogr. **67**(1), 111–136 (2013)
7. Çamtepe, S.A., Yener, B.: Combinatorial design of key distribution mechanisms for wireless sensor networks. In: ESORICS 2004, French Riviera, France, pp. 293–308, 13–15 September 2004
8. Chakrabarti, D., Maitra, S., Roy, B.: A key pre-distribution scheme for wireless sensor networks: merging blocks in combinatorial design. In: Zhou, J., Lopez, J., Deng, R.H., Bao, F. (eds.) ISC 2005. LNCS, vol. 3650, pp. 89–103. Springer, Heidelberg (2005). doi:10.1007/11556992_7
9. Chakrabarti, D., Maitra, S., Roy, B.K.: A key pre-distribution scheme for wireless sensor networks: merging blocks in combinatorial design. Int. J. Inf. Sec. **5**(2), 105–114 (2006)
10. Chakrabarti, D., Seberry, J.: Combinatorial structures for design of wireless sensor networks. In: Zhou, J., Yung, M., Bao, F. (eds.) ACNS 2006. LNCS, vol. 3989, pp. 365–374. Springer, Heidelberg (2006). doi:10.1007/11767480_25
11. Chan, H., Perrig, A., Song, D.: Random key predistribution schemes for sensor networks. In: IEEE Symposium on Security and Privacy, pp. 197–213. IEEE Computer Society (2003)

12. Dhar, A., Sarkar, P.: Full communication in a wireless sensor network by merging blocks of a key predistribution using reed solomon codes. In: CCSAE, pp. 389–400 (2011)
13. Du, W., Deng, J., Han, Y.S., Varshney, P.K.: A key predistribution scheme for sensor networks using deployment knowledge. IEEE Trans. Dependable Sec. Comput. 3(1), 62–77 (2006)
14. Eschenauer, L., Gligor, V.D.: A key-management scheme for distributed sensor networks. In: ACM Conference on Computer and Communications Security, pp. 41–47 (2002)
15. Fiat, A., Tassa, T.: Dynamic traitor tracing. J. Cryptology 14(3), 211–223 (2001)
16. Henry, K., Paterson, M.B., Stinson, D.R.: Practical approaches to varying network size in combinatorial key predistribution schemes. In: Lange, T., Lauter, K., Lisoněk, P. (eds.) SAC 2013. LNCS, vol. 8282, pp. 89–117. Springer, Heidelberg (2014). doi:10.1007/978-3-662-43414-7_5
17. Lee, J., Stinson, D.R.: On the construction of practical key predistribution schemes for distributed sensor networks using combinatorial designs. ACM Trans. Inf. Syst. Secur. 11(2), 1–35 (2008)
18. Lee, J., Stinson, D.R.: A combinatorial approach to key predistribution for distributed sensor networks. In: IEEE Wireless Communications and Networking Conference WCNC 2005, New Orleans, USA, pp. 1200–1205, 13–17 March 2005. Invited Paper
19. Martin, K.M., Paterson, M.B., Stinson, D.R.: Key predistribution for homogeneous wireless sensor networks with group deployment of nodes. TOSN 7(2) (2010)
20. Newman, R.: Computer Security: Protecting Digital Resources. Jones & Bartlett Learning, Sudbury (2009)
21. Paterson, M.B., Stinson, D.R.: A unified approach to combinatorial key predistribution schemes for sensor networks. Des. Codes Cryptogr. 71(3), 433–457 (2014)
22. Pietro, R.D., Mancini, L.V., Mei, A.: Energy efficient node-to-node authentication and communication confidentiality in wireless sensor networks. Wirel. Netw. 12(6), 709–721 (2006)
23. Ruj, S., Pal, A.: Preferential attachment model with degree bound and its application to key predistribution in WSN. In: 30th IEEE International Conference on Advanced Information Networking and Applications, AINA 2016, Crans-Montana, Switzerland, 23–25 March 2016, pp. 677–683 (2016)
24. Ruj, S., Roy, B.: Key predistribution using partially balanced designs in wireless sensor networks. In: Stojmenovic, I., Thulasiram, R.K., Yang, L.T., Jia, W., Guo, M., Mello, R.F. (eds.) ISPA 2007. LNCS, vol. 4742, pp. 431–445. Springer, Heidelberg (2007). doi:10.1007/978-3-540-74742-0_40
25. Ruj, S., Roy, B.K.: Key predistribution using combinatorial designs for grid-group deployment scheme in wireless sensor networks. TOSN 6(1), 4:1–4:28 (2009)
26. Sarkar, P., Saha, A.: Security enhanced communication in wireless sensor networks using reed-muller codes and partially balanced incomplete block designs. JoC 2(1), 23–30 (2011)
27. Sarkar, P., Saha, A., Chowdhury, M.U.: Secure connectivity model in Wireless Sensor Networks (WSN) using first order Reed-Muller codes. In: MASS, pp. 507–512 (2010)
28. Simonova, K., Ling, A.C.H., Wang, X.S.: Location-aware key predistribution scheme for wide area wireless sensor networks. In: ACM Workshop on Security of Ad Hoc and Sensor Networks (SASN 2006), Alexandria, VA, USA, 30 October 2006, pp. 157–168 (2006)
29. Zhou, L., Ni, J., Ravishankar, C.V.: Supporting secure communication and data collection in mobile sensor networks. In: 25th IEEE International Conference on Computer Communications, Joint Conference of the IEEE Computer and Communications Societies, INFOCOM 2006, 23–29 April 2006, Barcelona, Catalunya, Spain (2006)

A Multi-protocol Security Framework
to Support Internet of Things

Biplob R. Ray[1], Morshed U. Chowdhury[2]($\boxtimes$), and Jemal H. Abawajy[2]

[1] School of Engineering and Technology,
CQ University, Rockhampton, Australia
b.ray@cqu.edu.au
[2] School of Information Technology, Deakin University, Burwood, Australia
{muc,Jemal}@deakin.edu.au

Abstract. In this paper we are proposing a multi-protocol security framework for sensors and actuators used in Internet of Things (IoT). This is to make sure that IoT security framework is capable of accommodating a number of secure communication protocols to support diverse need of IoT systems. The proposed framework will extend scope of combining common security functionalities like mutual authentication, malware injection of all integrated secure communication protocols and will make these services universally available to them. The IoT provision requires all diverse actuators and sensor networks connected together. The aim of the proposed security framework is to secure this connected diverse networks universally with least amount of performance tradeoff.

Keywords: IoT · Framework · Security · Multi-protocol · Sensors and actuators

1 Introduction

While securing a system like IoT, security provision needs a mechanism to accommodate more than one security protocols to ensure security and business needs of the system. A framework with multi-protocol adaptation capability will be appropriate to provide security for diverse networked system like IoT [1]. Furthermore, the IoT security systems have to ensure that redundant security services are not repeatedly executed for the system by multi-protocols. As an example, an ownership protocol [2] implemented mutual authentication to an actuator and then immediately the same system executed tracking protocol [3] which require to execute mutual authentication too. In this case the duplication of mutual authentication is not required as long as earlier one is still valid. A system like IoT needs to stop execution of this redundant security services to make system scalable.

A number of work identified in literature that worked to provide security framework for IoT. Among them, the proposed framework by Ray et al. [1] have attempted to integrate multiple security protocols. However, none of the existing protocols have a working process that allows a unified framework to integrate security protocols therefore they can be used universally. This gives us a rational to develop a unified security framework which is capable to adapt multi-protocol and eliminate duplicate

© ICST Institute for Computer Sciences, Social Informatics and Telecommunications Engineering 2017
R. Deng et al. (Eds.): SecureComm 2016, LNICST 198, pp. 257–270, 2017.
DOI: 10.1007/978-3-319-59608-2_14

security services for the system. In our work we have extended the framework from [1] to achieve two things:

- Multiple security protocol adaption with in the same framework
- Elimination of redundant security service execution for the system.

The rest of the paper is organized as follow: in Sect. 2 we detail the relevant existing work and the system model used in this paper. The proposed framework and techniques are detailed in Sect. 3. The working process and computational details of the required techniques for the framework are detailed in Subsects. 3.2 and 3.3. Finally in Sect. 4 we conclude our paper.

2 Background

To allow seamless connectivity of global objects, multiple administrative domains need to work together collaboratively. The IoT system must have a security mechanism that are well accepted (universal) [1, 4] by all administrative domains. This prompts the need of a security framework that offers unification for smoother integration of diverse networked systems. Moreover, it also needs to offer scalability, security and adaptability to make it usable with IoT. In Subsect. 2.1, we have presented existing research and development on security framework, secure and scalable identification techniques, universal security clearance to reduce security trade-off. The system model used in this paper is detailed in Subsect. 2.2.

2.1   Literature Review

The security risks poses by sensors and actuators systems is a serious concern [2, 4] for IoT deployment. To make security assurance acceptable by all involved entities in IoT, the sensors and actuators system need to offer stronger security with easily deployable universal security framework. However not much work has been done to address this issue. We have identify three sensors and actuators security related frameworks proposed in [4, 7, 8]. In [7], Konidala et al. have proposed a security framework for RFID-based applications in smart home environment. This framework was designed to protect consumer privacy in application level but it does not provide any guideline to protect communication between reader and objects. It has proposed the use of HTTPS to secure communication between mobile device and RFID backend server in application layer. The smart home is a micro part of the IoT system.

Dong Seong et al. [4] have proposed a framework to achieve universal authentication and authorization for RFID multi-domain System. The work in this paper [4] can be considered the pioneer work to address security requirements for sensors and actuators in the context of IoT. This paper [4] also acknowledged a need of a universal security framework to address security of sensors and actuators systems. However, the work is focused to achieve authentication and authorization only and did not consider other security properties required to be protected in the context of IoT. Lim et al. [8] have proposed a cross- layer framework to address privacy of IoT system. The paper

[8] has stated that traceability of sensors and actuators is a multi-layer problem, and called for a multi-layer solution to address the problem appropriately. Their privacy protection framework works in physical and MAC layer for protection from traceability [8]. This work used randomized bit encoding scheme to mitigate 'same-bit' problem, and proposed a more secure system model that can protect the unique identifier of actuator autuators against disclosure to eavesdroppers and unauthorized interrogators.

Most recently, Cisco has announced a flagship Cisco IoT System which has 6 layers: Network Connectivity, Fog Computing, Security, Data Analytics, Management with Automation and Application Enablement Platform [9]. The security layer of this system has four sub-layers: authentication, authorization, network enforced policy and inherent security analysis [9]. The Cisco IoT system aims to address security through network- powered technology. Using this system, devices connecting to the network will take advantage of the inherent security that the network provides (rather than trying to ensure security at the device level) [9]. It left users privacy on the hand of effective processes and policies of the organization. The security of Cisco IoT system does not ensure device level security which is one of the crucial concerns for ubiquities computing. Inclusion of the security layer in Cisco IoT system clearly justify that there is a serious need of security protection for IoT systems. However their security solution does not address requirements of IoT systems such as openness, unification, device level security protection. Most importantly, Cisco security layer considered security of the IoT ecosystem but forgot the security at individual IoT domain, device and business service level.

Ray et al. proposed a security framework in [1] to combine multi-protocol in a framework. This framework is the most relevant work in the literature which aims to support diverse system for IoT. However, it doesn't have any scope to adapt a new protocol in it. In addition it does not show how a client and master reader communicate with each other within the system.

In this paper we extend the work from [1] and address the following:

- Multiple security protocol adaption with in the same framework
- Elimination of redundant security service execution for the system.

2.2   System Model

In this section, we present an IoT system model where our proposed multiprotocol framework can be used to secure the system. Our adapted IoT system for FP is shown in Fig. 1. As illustrated in Fig. 1, the system is connecting diverse actuator systems to ensure a global information network for objects. Each system of the IoT controlled by different administrative domains with a common system structure as shown in zoomed view in Fig. 1. This common system architecture has a master reader which coordinates all other readers (client readers) of the system. The master reader is responsible to represent the entire system to another system.

As illustrated in Fig. 1, the system model's master readers are communicating over Internet cloud. The authorized client readers will be able to execute the mutual authentication and exchange information of the object according to the need of the

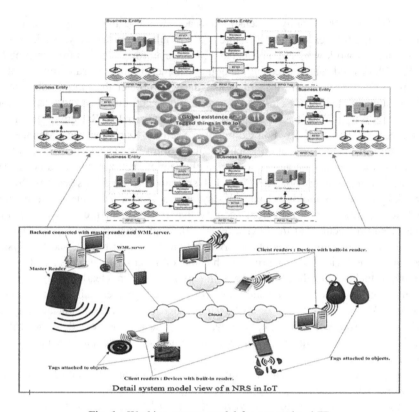

Fig. 1. Working system model for our updated FP

system. However, this information need to be transported to other system via master readers. The developed framework will have a client module in client readers to support the master module of master readers.

The client and master module of the framework coordinate each other to ensure security protection of the IoT system. It uses Security Check Handoff (SCH) to dynamically choose security services required for an object based on system's business requirement. To illustrate the workflow of the system better, we have reading process using our proposed framework in an IoT system illustrated in Fig. 2. As we can see in Fig. 2, master reader of a system can presents it to another system with in IoT network. It also contribute mainly in systems security management.

3 Proposed Framework and Techniques

In this section, we state our improved framework that will be the holistic unified security solutions for IoT. This is followed by the SCH technique to support improved framework. We also detail the working process of improved mutual authentication. We will only state detail of our improvement over contributions in [1].

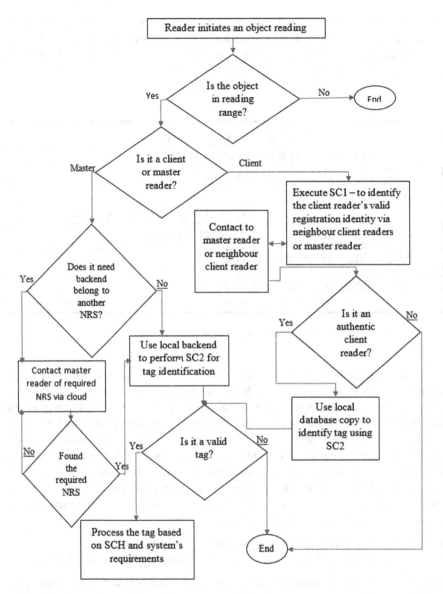

Fig. 2. A generic workflow of our system model that uses our proposed framework

3.1 The Framework

The updated framework is illustrated in Fig. 3. This framework is extending common services to all the required security protocols by adapting them in a unified framework. The framework has adapted System Components (SC) 1 to 4 from [1]. The functionality of each of these SCs will be same as detailed in contribution [1]. The execution of SC1, SC2 and SC4 ensures mutual authentication between readers and actuators in the system domain to safeguard the system. The SC3 is a simple malware command checking layer that stop actuators to pass malicious command to the back-end. To integrate a security protocol for specific security requirement we add a new layer name integration layer. We present detail about the integration layer (SC_I^i) below.

Security Framework (SF)	
SC1- Reader (RID) identification stage	
SC2- Tag (TID) identification stage	
SC_I^i – Integration layer	

	SC_I^1	Ownership transferring protocol
	SC_I^2	Tracker protocol

SC3 – Malware detection stage
SC4 – Mutual authentication stage

Fig. 3. The unified proposed framework

System Component $I(SC_I^i)$: is integration layer that accommodates additional security services that are specific to a business need. Our work integrates two business needs and their specific security services as shown in Fig. 3. Each sub-layer of integration layer SC_I is identified by a unique i value as superscript that makes the presenting symbol of this layer (SC_I^i). The i value is a sequential number for each integrated security protocol that uniquely identify the service of the integration sub-layers. An IoT system can add integration sub-layers based on their need. It can also dynamically choose which sub-layer to run for a particular execution using our updated SCH. However, security protocols need to satisfy two simple requirements below to be added to an integration sub-layer of SF.

- They have to support universal operation.
- They should not duplicate security services provided by SF in SC1 to SC4

The number of security protocols to be integrated in integration layer depend of system's requirements and need. This unified framework assumes that the system will have a list of authentic readers in backend along with actuators information. The integration layer manages the implementation of these integrated security protocols using SCH that is explained in the following sub-section.

3.2 SCH to Support the SF

In this section, we will present our improved SCH to work with our new integration layer. The SCH is the technique which not only provide faster security clearance but also provide a mechanism to manage system components of SF. It coordinates and provides security services based on system's security and business need. The updated SCH has two system bits and identify bits to accommodate integration layer as illustrated in Fig. 3.

The security clearance bit type identify the security clearance status of the actuators. The integration bit type specify the integration requirement for the tag by the system.

The last SCH bits (Identity bits) only required if integration bit is "ON". The identity bits used to pass the identification value of the specific integration protocol requested to be executed by the system. The proposed SCH only allow one integration protocol to be executed by a specific execution at a time. We present the discussion below to comprehend different possible SCH bits combination a system might need in FP executions.

Let us first consider two system bits (security clearance bit and integration bit) so $SCH_b|_{size}(b_T) = 2\,bits$ where security clearance bit control security related system components (SC1, SC2, SC3 and SC4) and integration bit controls integration layer (SC_i^i) system components. Each bit has two states $ON(1)$ and $OFF(0)$ makes four maximum combinations when $SCH_b|_{size}(b_T) = 2\,bits$ as detailed below

- If $SCH_b = 0(OFF)0(OFF)$
  - In this situation security clearance bit is $0(OFF)$, the actuator is not subject to security clearance (need to execute SC 1 and SC 4). All actuator s will have its initial security clearance value is $0(OFF)$.
  - As integration bit is $0(OFF)$, the FP system does not require to execute any integrated protocol for the actuator.
- If $SCH_b = 1(ON)0(OFF)$
  - In this case security clearance bit is $1(ON)$, the actuator is subject to faster security clearance (need to pass SC 1 to SC 2). In most cases, after its initial identification the actuator sets its security clearance bit $1(ON)$.
  - However as the integration bit is $0(OFF)$, the FP system does not require to execute any integrated security protocols for the actuator.
- If $SCH_b = 1(ON)1(ON)$
  - In this event the security clearance bit is $1(ON)$ and also the integration bit is $1(ON)$ Therefore the actuator is subject to faster security clearance (need to pass SC 1 to SC2 only) and the FP system require to execute an integrated security protocol from its sub-layer. The selection of the integrated protocol will be based on identification bits of the SCH.
- If $SCH_b = 0(OFF)1(ON)$
  - Here the security clearance bit is $0(OFF)$, the actuator is not subject to security clearance (need to execute SC 1 and SC 4). This is ideal initial condition of the actuator.
  - However, the integration bit is $1(ON)$ therefore FP system require to execute an integrated security protocol from the listed protocols of its sublayer.

The identification of the integration layers protocols will be represented using superscripted i value of the integrated protocol. For an example, if the SCH value for an actuator is $SCH = 1110$ then the system can conclude that the actuator's security clearance and integration bits both are in *ON* state. The system also can extract that the identification value that is 10 bits which is equivalent of decimal value 2. This means system should run integration protocol with superscripted i value 2.

The working process of the new SCH is illustrated in Fig. 4 which shows that if integration bit is *OFF* then identification bits are excluded from SCH to make it moderated size value. We store the random position value and SCH value in the backend to ensure intruders will not be able to exploit the system.

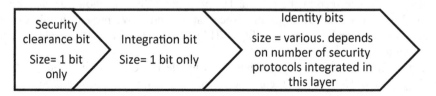

Fig. 4. Components of SCH

The SCH bit works as a bond of this framework to hold all the layers together and provide a means to dynamically execute system components based on systems status, requirement and security need.

3.3   Working Process of SF

This section detail working procedure of our proposed unified framework. The updated SCH is an integral part of the framework as it supports the framework to achieve its objectives. The framework works as a black-box so rest of the techniques used in the framework can be replace by an updated one if required. Similarly, the security protocols adapted in integration sub-layer can be also replaced by an updated one, if required. A new sub-layer can also be added to accommodate a new security protocol as required by the system (Fig. 5).

In the discussion of this section our proposed SF is supported by

- Improved SCH from Subsect. 3.2.
- Reader/actuators identification and mutual authentication techniques detailed in [1].

The SF uses 96 bits frame formats illustrated in Fig. 6 to detail its process. The frames have 5 bits header which carry information about the type of packet. There is a End of a Header (EH) field that is one bit equivalent null non-writeable space to separate header from payload. The payload portion carry actual data that is required to execute relevant operations.

The frame always has a CRC-32 value to handle error in transmission.

The five bits header information will represent type of packet based on their "*ON*" bits that is 1. The detail of each "*ON*" bits shown below:

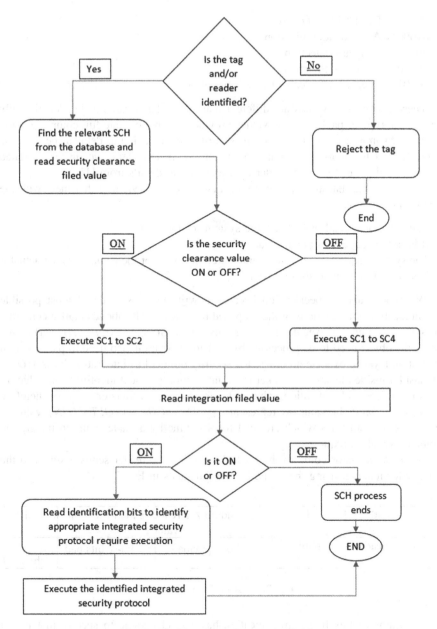

Fig. 5. Working flow of the updated SCH

Header	EH	Payload	CRC
5 bits	Null bit	90 bits	32 bits

Fig. 6. Generic FP frame format

10000 = Reader identification
01000 = Actuator identification
00100 = Malware detection
00010 = Mutual authentication
00001 = Integration layer's protocol execution

These packet type values are different than SCH status value as header bits only identify the type of packet. These values provide a degree of state full communication by keeping some state information of the security clearance. Let us detail a specific case to understand the working mechanism of our SF better. Here, we discuss updated details only that need to be consider in association to details from [1].

Let us assume that an object came to a client reader's vicinity that meet with the specification below:

- The actuator is read by the specific system for first time.
- It is in the range of a client reader.
- The system require to execute an integrated protocol for the actuator as the actuator is subject to an ownership transfer.

We choose above specification because it will allow us to detail most possible communication combinations of the proposed framework. The above detail specify that the system require to execute a SCH status where $SCH_b = 0(OFF)1(ON)[1_2]$ that means the object need to be processed by SC1 to SC4 and it also need to pass through integration layer to execute an integrated security protocol as integration bit is $1(ON)$. The last bit inside the square bracket is the integration protocol identification value. In this specific case, identification value is 1_{10} for ownership transfer protocol therefore SCH_b holds value 1_2 value to represent 1_{10}. The $SCH_b = 0(OFF)1(ON)$ value is default for all actuator s which are read for first time by a reader with an integration protocol execution request.

When the actuator come to the reader's vicinity, the reader sends a signal to the actuator for reading, using the frame format illustrates in Fig. 7.

11000	EH	Randomized reader's identification value		CRC
5 bits header	Null bit	l bits payload	90- l bits pad	32 bits

Fig. 7. First FP frame format

The frame of this first communication has a header value to specify that it is a reader and actuator identification packet. The frame has a randomized reader identification value that occupies 90 bits or less. If the l bits payload is lesser than 90 bits then a randomized padding value will be used.

The actuator then respond with a frame as illustrates in Fig. 8 below. In this frame actuators transport a 16 bits randomized actuator set value, a read count value of 10 bits and 64 bits hash value.

11000	EH	Randomized Actuator set value	Read count value	A hash value	CRC
5 bits header	Null bit	16 bits	10 bits	64 bits	32 bits
		90 bits payload			32 bits

Fig. 8. Second FP frame format

The system at this point initiate reader and actuator identification process.

As the actuator is read by a client reader of the system, it requires to send a communication to the master reader or neighbor client reader for authorization by sending randomized actuator set value and reader's identification. If the client reader is registered and authorized to process the actuator then the master reader will allow the client reader to do the rest of the process.

If the actuator is read by the client reader for second time then it execute the actuator identification process by itself without requiring authorization from anyone else. The whitelist of registered reader is used to check the reader's registration. The neighbor client readers are those who have a trusted relation with the respective client readers and registered. The communication process of this client reader's validation is illustrated in Fig. 9.

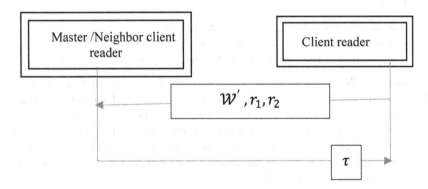

Fig. 9. Verify identity of a client reader to eliminate rogue readers

11000	EH	Token value	A hash value	unused	CRC
5 bits header	Null bit	16 bits	64 bits	10 bits	32 bits
			90 bits payload		32 bits

Fig. 10. SC4 FP frame format

Let r_2 be the randomized reader ID, $r_h = (h)(r_2)$ is the hashed value of r_2 protect RR_{DB} from disclosure, W' be the randomized actuator set value and r_l is a l bit random number that is used to randomize readers ID and actuator set value. The client reader sends W', r_l *and* r_h values to master reader/neighbor client reader to validate itself. The master reader then verify the readers ID using its registered client reader's white list and validity actuator set value W.

$$h(r_2) \overset{?}{==} h(RR_{DB} \oplus r_1) \tag{1}$$

If Eq. (1) returns true and actuator set value W is within the valid range, the master reader sends client reader a random success token τ which is calculated using Eq. (2).

$$\tau = W \oplus RC'_T \tag{2}$$

In our updated SF, the client reader use this token value in mutual authentication stage to verify itself. If master reader cannot find reader ID in registered reader's database then it reject all communication from the reader.

After receiving the token τ, the valid client reader use actuator identification technique from [1] to identify the actuator. If the actuator ID is valid then it retrieve SCH value from the database. In our case this system is reading the actuator for first time and it requires to execute the ownership transferring process therefore the SCH value of the actuator will be $SCH_b = 011$. The detail of each bit of SCH_b value is shown below

0_2 = the actuator is not subject to security check handoff
1_2 = The actuator need to execute a integration layer protocl
$1_2 = 1_{10}$ = the actuator requres to execute the first integration layer protocol.

Based on SCH_b values, the reader execute SC3 for the actuator to identify any malicious command in the values transmitted by the actuator. If actuator's transmitted values are clean then it executes the mutual authentication process in SC4.

Otherwise it rejects all the communicated information. In addition to mutual authentication process detailed in [1], the client reader also send τ to validate its own identify. The new frame format of the communication of SC4 is illustrated in Fig. 10 which is an updated version of Fig. 11.

As we can see in Fig. 11, we are transmitting a token code and a hash value.

Because of this new token value, our updated mutual authentication process is shown in Fig. 11. As illustrated in Fig. 11, the master or a neighbour client reader send the verification token τ to the reader. The reader send this in its communication along with r_4 that constitute SC4 (mutual authentication) of the framework and protocol details in [1]. The actuator executed Eq. (4) of Fig. 11 to verify the identity of the reader before executing Eq. (5) as illustrated in Fig. 11. The token code and hash value let the actuator verify the validity of the reader. These values also let the actuator update its read count information and actuator ID, if required.

At the end of the successful execution of SC4, the actuator wait for a communication from it's current owner to execute ownership transfer protocol as specified in

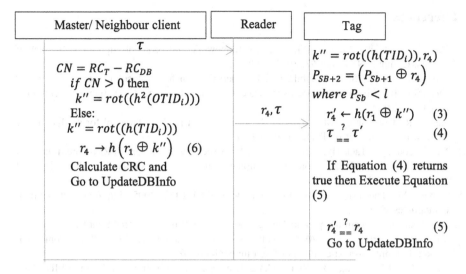

Fig. 11. Updated mutual authentication process for SC4

SCH which follow the execution detail discussed in [1]. The execution cycle remains incomplete until the ownership transfer is done. During this incomplete stage, the actuator does not communicate with any other owner except the one just executed mutual verification. The actuator gets back to normal state as soon as it finishes it's ownership transfer (Complete execution cycle) as specified in *SCH* value. The overall process flow of our unified framework is illustrated in Fig. 2.

4   Conclusion

In this paper, we proposed a security framework to ensure there is a scope for security protocols adaptation. The integrity layer of the protocol can adapt any number of security services and protocols to support the entire system. Our proposed holistic unified framework in this chapter is built on enhanced SC4 and SCH detailed in this paper. These improvements are done to ensure that our framework is ready to support unified security service requirements of IoT. The IoT has many administratively controlled domains as a result universality and unification of security and business services are crucial to increase acceptance of uses. This chapter detailed working process of our enhanced SF and updated packet formats required to achieve objectives of our study. The solutions proposed in this study are simple and can work with existing hardware. This study also considered the constraint of the actuator s computational capability to ensure high implacability of the SF.

References

1. Ray, B.R., et al.: Scalable RFID security framework and protocol supporting Internet of Things. Comput. Networks **67**, 89–103 (2014)
2. Ray, B.R., et al.: Secure mobile RFID ownership transfer protocol to cover all transfer scenarios. In: 7th International Conference on Computing and Convergence Technology (ICCCT) (2012)
3. Ray, B.R., Chowdhury, M., Abawajy, J.: Secure object tracking protocol for the Internet of Things. IEEE Internet of Things J. **PP**(99), 1
4. Dong Seong, K., Taek-Hyun, S., Jong Sou, P.: A security framework in RFID multi- domain system. In: 2007 ARES Second International Conference on Availability, Reliability and Security, pp. 1227–1234 (2007)
5. Roberti, M.: The history of RFID technology. RFID J. LLC (2005). http://www.rfidjournal.com/articles/view?1338
6. MacBean, N.: 'Electronic pickpocketing' looms as next threat in credit card fraud, police, security experts say (2014). http://www.abc.net.au/news/2014-05-30/electronic-pickpocketing-looms-as-next-credit-card-fraud-threat/5486806
7. Konidala, D.M., Kim, D., Yeun, C.Y., Lee, B.: Security framework for RFID-based applications in smart home environment. JIPS **7**(1), 111–120 (2011)
8. Lim, T.-L., Li, T., Yeo, S.-L.: A cross-layer framework for privacy enhancement in RFID systems. Pervasive Mob. Comput. **4**(6), 889–905 (2008)
9. Wang, et al.: New Cisco Internet of Things (IoT) System Provides a Foundation for the Transformation of Industries (2015). http://www.marketwatch.com/story/new-cisco-internet-of-things-iot-system-provides-a-foundation-for-the-transformation-of-industries-2015-06-29

Tinder Me Softly – How Safe Are You *Really* on Tinder?

Mark Carman[1] and Kim-Kwang Raymond Choo[1,2(✉)]

[1] School of Information Technology and Mathematical Sciences,
University of South Australia, Adelaide, Australia
carmd006@mymail.unisa.edu.au,
raymond.choo@fulbrightmail.org
[2] Department of Information Systems and Cyber Security,
University of Texas at San Antonio, San Antonio, USA

Abstract. There are known privacy concerns with the use of Tinder, a popular dating app. In this paper, we examine previous attacks on Tinder that have not been documented academically. We also documented the Tinder network API in order to test the previous attacks in a live environment. Although our testing revealed accurate user location data, which was the crux of the prior attacks, has since been patched; we were able to: associate a Facebook profile with a Tinder account due to their shared information, see Facebook pages a user had liked or was a member of, as well as gather user images, which Tinder sends via plain HTTP, for a reverse image search. We also demonstrated the potential for a less accurate location attack that takes into account Tinder's updated security.

Keywords: Tinder privacy risks · Dating app risks · Geo-social privacy risks · Mobile app security

1 Introduction

Tinder is a mobile application (i.e. an "app") that provides a matchmaking service, which has facilitated over 10 billion matches [1]. Tinder's defining quirk is that matchmaking only occurs between users that are geographically close, and messaging is only allowed between users that encounter and "like" each other through the matchmaking process, which also provides only a single chance to like or pass on each match. Once matched, users are able to freely message each other to chat or to arrange real-world meetings for friendship, dating, or, as identified in popular culture - for casual relationships called "hook-ups" [2].

Privacy has always been a concern with geo-social apps [3, 4]. Tinder and many other dating apps allow users to vet each other before agreeing to meet. However, because Tinder is also a geo-social app, it has an inherent privacy flaw: geo-social apps need to collect location information about their users in order to function. By examining the output of the app, as well as manipulating the input, it is possible that the app might leak personal information about its users. As a trivial example, if you move away from another user until the app no longer considers them nearby, you now know the other user is outside the cut-off distance of the app.

© ICST Institute for Computer Sciences, Social Informatics and Telecommunications Engineering 2017
R. Deng et al. (Eds.): SecureComm 2016, LNICST 198, pp. 271–286, 2017.
DOI: 10.1007/978-3-319-59608-2_15

While rigorous academic research on Tinder has been limited, Tinder is certainly in the public consciousness. The latter is unsurprising, as Tinder attracts thousands of news and blog posts, millions of users, and billions of swipes. While many stories deal with the social aspects and implications of Tinder and related apps, such as discussions on hook-up culture, there are significantly fewer that deal with privacy and security issues surrounding Tinder. Of these, the most crucial involved attacks that were able to obtain the GPS data and Facebook ID of a Tinder user. These attacks provided the motivation for our research. While Tinder has since reportedly patched these vulnerabilities, there is still a question about whether fundamental geo-location information could be exploited to recreate the effects of some of the attacks.

In this paper, we examine and document the network protocol of Tinder to determine what sort of data travels between the Tinder app and the Tinder servers. We then examined how this data might be manipulated to affect the privacy and security of Tinder users. We also conducted tests using Tinder data and our proposed methods in a live environment to get a glimpse at possible real world implications.

2 Background and Related Work

2.1 Background

Tinder is a free mobile app for both Android and iOS devices, with 50–100 million installs on Android devices alone, at the time of this research [5]. Tinder requires a Facebook account, and uses Facebook permissions when a user creates an account to give Tinder access to their list of friends, photos, and biographical information (e.g. name, age, interests, education, and employment).

Once connected through Facebook, Tinder allows a user to customise their profile from the Facebook entries collected. This includes setting the primary image displayed during matchmaking, as well as up to 5 additional images for their profile. Employment and current academic education are also able to be selected. First name and age are also included on a user's Tinder profile, but are only editable through their Facebook account. In addition to Facebook-sourced information, Tinder allows a user to select their gender, enter a 500 character biography, and connect to an Instagram account.

The ephemeral nature of Tinder's matchmaking comes from the "stack" of potential matches displayed to a user on the main Tinder screen. This stack is a set of recommendations based on a user's age, gender, and distance preferences, as well as Tinder's matchmaking algorithm which includes various hidden parameters, such as "desirability" [6]. For each match in the stack, the user is able to either "pass", "like", or "super like" the prospective match by swiping left, right, and up, respectively.

The profiles themselves are displayed as a stack of cards. While there are superficial differences between the Android and iOS versions, the content of the profiles is the same for both versions. Initially the primary profile picture, first name, and age are displayed, along with buttons to pass, like, super like, and "rewind". Rewind is a feature only available for paying Tinder users, and allows the user to undo a swipe action made immediately prior. Tapping on the profile picture brings up additional information – this includes employment or education information, city, distance between users, photos from a connected Instagram account, if applicable, as well as scrollable slides of up to 5 other images the user has uploaded. Any shared interests, which are Facebook pages both users have liked, as well as shared Facebook friends, are also displayed (Fig. 1).

Fig. 1. A de-identified example of a Tinder user card. Initial view on left, truncated detailed view on right (Source: http://orzzzz.com/find-out-what-tinder-really-is-before-you-rush-to-join-it. html; Last accessed: 20/07/2016)

Passing or liking a profile removes them from the stack and the next card in the stack is displayed. Once a match has been removed from the stack, it is ostensibly gone forever. However, circumstances such as creating a new account would reset matches.

Liking a profile initially does nothing. However, if the like is reciprocated at any point, Tinder displays a match notification. This then enables messaging between the two users. This is the only time messaging is enabled between users. Once messaging is enabled, users are able to freely message each other through the Tinder app, enabling the ability to continue the conversation, move to a different medium, or setup an off-line meeting for friendship, dating, or a hook-up. Messaging is predominantly text-based, although a partnership with the company GIPHY in 2016 means users can now search and send preselected, "expressive", video images [7]. Either party is able to un-match at any stage, which revokes the ability to send messages (Fig. 2).

A super like is functionally similar to a like, but displays a blue background, a short message, and a star-icon to your potential match when they view your card in their stack. This may seem trivial at first glance, but with messaging disabled between unmatched users, a super like is the only way to signal that you have seen and enjoyed another user's profile. Super likes are limited to 1 per day [8] (Fig. 3).

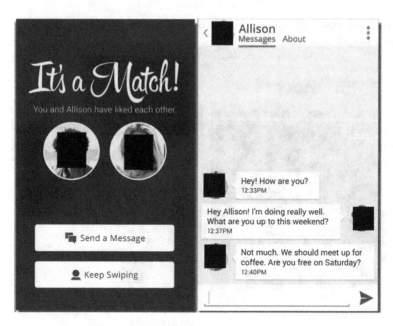

Fig. 2. An example Match taking place (Source: Google App Store Tinder page, https://play. google.com/store/apps/details?id=com.tinder; Last accessed 05/07/2016)

Fig. 3. An example of a super like indication. (Source: http://blog.gotinder.com/updated-introducing-super-like-a-new-type-of-swipe/; Last accessed 23/07/2016)

2.2   Previous Work

As stated earlier, existing technical research on Tinder is lacking. For example, in the earliest and most dangerous exploit (described more fully below), the only information we could find was obtained from social commentary websites and social media, due to Tinder's infancy at the time. Eventually we came across a news article displaying emails sent to Tinder by the creator of the attack, disclosing its details [9]. Tinder eventually claimed they had fixed these vulnerabilities, but only after a week without reply lead the attacker to go public with his story [9]. Because the vulnerability was only publicly known for a day, and the only evidence of it consisted of emails to and from Tinder (rather than a well-documented formal disclosure), there was no way to verify the correctness of the claims made. However, given that the server no longer returned the location data when we tested it - see Fig. 4, and the fact that details of the attack were reported on several social news websites, this attack appears to be authentic.

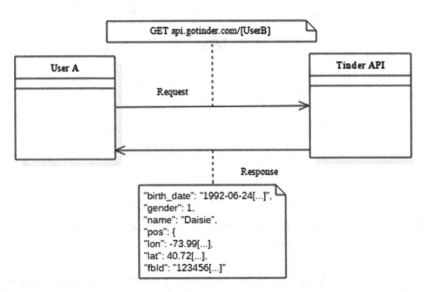

Fig. 4. The first major Tinder attack. GPS and Facebook ID data were returned when getting a user profile

The attack as described was completely straightforward. When the Tinder Application Programming Interface (API) requested a user profile (which the app does to display its profile stack), the API returned extra information. Unfortunately, this extra information was in the form of exact GPS co-ordinates, and a Facebook ID, which the attacker was able to read by examining the network traffic. GPS co-ordinates could obviously then be used to compromise the location of the user. Furthermore, a Facebook ID allowed the attacker to obtain the Facebook profile of the user, which generally contains more personal information than Tinder displays, which may escalate the attack in other ways.

Several months after the attack described above was fixed, a second attack, using a more novel approach was described. While exact GPS co-ordinates were no longer available, the response from the Tinder API included a very accurate distance between two users [10]. The author of this attack utilised this by creating three fake profiles and trilateration to determine the exact location of the user (see Fig. 5). Trilateration is essentially the projection of three circles with radii set to the respective distances reported by Tinder, and then seeing the point where all the circles intersect. Again, the write-up was posted on a security blog (rather than a formal publication), and included a tool, explanation, and video on how to locate your own Tinder account [10].

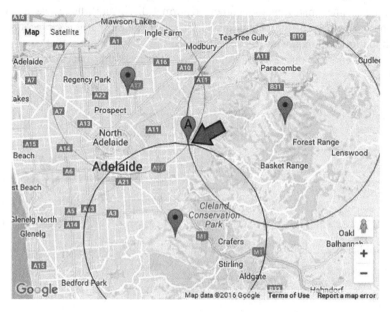

Fig. 5. Visualising an example trilateration attack. Point 'A' (University of South Australia) is the point where all three circles intersect

Such vulnerability motivated this research. Tinder also fixed this vulnerability and now only provides approximate numbers in its API. However, we question whether this is sufficient to keeps users safe.

While there have been two major security concerns for Tinder, there have also been a considerable amount of effort invested into gaming the Tinder system. From basic bots that automatically swipe right to give a "like" on every profile to maximise the chance of getting a match [11, 12], to a much smarter bot that learns what facial features you find attractive based on your swipe history, and can even automate conversation openers [13]. Other bots have a financial rather than romantic or sexual interest at heart, where they pretend to be a highly attractive user that sends spam messages to any matches it can make [14]. While Tinder has not implemented any changes that directly target bots, a March 2015 update [15] limited the number of swipes free users had per day, which significantly reduced the effectiveness of these mass swiping bots. Paid users retained unlimited swipes.

The aim of this study is to determine if there are still privacy concerns when using Tinder.

Specifically, we investigated whether Tinder now prevents the type of attacks previously conducted, and whether other, more subtle attacks, were possible - particularly associated with the following: GPS location, personal user data and social media connections. In order to do this, we used tools to understand how the Tinder API worked and then used that information to examine the quality of Tinder's security, and to propose attacks.

3 Experiment Design

A client device (Table 1) was connected to Tinder to document its API. To accomplish this, all of the network traffic from the client device was captured using a proxy, and then documented. Once the API was well understood, we then replicated the phone's functionality by developing a specialised Tinder bot. The areas of the API we focussed on understanding and attempting to exploit were:

- GPS location of users
- Personal user data (Birthday, name, pictures, etc.)
- Social media connections

Table 1. Client device details

Make	Model	OS	Tinder version
Motorola	Moto E	Android 4.4.4	Tinder 4.5.2

3.1 Server Set-up

To properly capture the traffic from the Tinder application, a server was required to analyse the network traffic from our client device. We chose a pre-packaged software tool called Charles for this task because it was available for many different platforms, was easy to use, and was able to analyse HTTPS traffic from the client. Because Tinder uses HTTPS, which is encrypted, we needed to use Charles as a man-in-the-middle proxy between the client phone and the Tinder API server (see Fig. 6; similar to the approach in [16]). This set-up allows the proxy to pretend to be the server to the client and the client to the server, allowing decryption for both. Further, we used the same server machine to run our eventual bot, which was developed in C#.

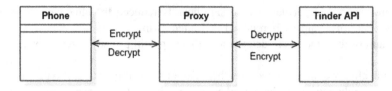

Fig. 6. Proxy setup with proxy in between the client device and the Tinder server

3.2   Client Set-up

To set-up our client, we first installed Tinder 4.5.2 on the client device. Next, we set our Charles server as the phone's internet proxy using the Wi-Fi settings page in Android, which allows us to examine HTTP traffic on the Charles server. To allow us to examine SSL traffic, we needed to generate a root Charles Certificate Authority Certificate. A Certificate Authority is a trusted authority able to sign and distribute SSL certificates, which is required to decrypt and re-encrypt the traffic from our phone to forward to the Tinder server. After generating this certificate on the Charles computer, we added the certificate as a Certificate Authority through the Android security settings. With both the client and the server correctly configured, we then used Tinder in a normal fashion on the phone for a few minutes while recording all the network traffic through Charles.

4   Findings

4.1   API Testing

To map the API, we used a client device as described above and performed some typical user actions, such as logging in, viewing profiles, "liking" a user, and "passing" on a user. From these actions, we collated and tested a list of endpoints as described below.

Authentication. Authentication is the first step when connecting to the Tinder API. Other than the authentication (auth) endpoint, all requests to Tinder end-points require the X-Auth-Token ("Tinder Token") to be sent as a header in the request in the form of:

```
X-Auth-Token:   xxxxxxxx-xxxx-4xxx-yxxx-xxxxxxxxxxxx*
```

* x is a hexadecimal digit, 4 is the literal number, and y is a character from the set {8, 9, a, b}.

If the Tinder token is not supplied, then Tinder returns a "401 Unauthorized" error message. Once the Tinder token has been set, requests can be made to all the other Tinder endpoints. Further, the Tinder token is the *one and only* object Tinder uses for verification, for all requests, following the initial authentication.

To receive a valid Tinder token, a user requires their Facebook ID as well as an appropriate Facebook token (as distinct from a Tinder token). The Facebook token is generated by authenticating with Facebook through Tinder. The exact mechanics of Facebook authentication are out of the scope of this paper, and can be found on Facebook's developer site [17]. Additionally, Tinder requires other headers to be set which mimic a real phone's request. This includes any valid user agent, for example:

```
User-Agent: Tinder Android Version 4.5.2
```

In addition, the content type must also be set. This is in the form of:

```
Content-Type: application/json
```

We then used cURL[1] to create a valid Tinder authentication request:

```
curl -k -v -X POST -H "Content-Type: application/json"
-H "User-Agent: Tinder Android Version 4.5.2"
https://api.gotinder.com/auth  --data
"{"facebook_token": "[Token]*", "locale": "en",
"facebook_id": "[ID]* "}"
```

* Actual Facebook token and ID has been redacted for privacy reasons.

While the auth response also returned the authenticating user's complete profile information, our interest was the "token" field, which we set as our Tinder token. As the Tinder token is the only thing required to access Tinder's endpoints, we examined it more closely: if the token was predictable, then impersonating users would be possible by accessing the endpoints with other valid tokens. Having another user's token is extremely problematic because much of the authenticated user's information is available by accessing the profile end-point through:

```
curl -k -v -X GET -H "Content-Type: application/json" -
H "User-Agent: Tinder Android Version 4.5.2" -H ``X-
Auth-Token: xxxxxxxx-xxxx-4xxx-yxxx-xxxxxxxxxxxx''
https://api.gotinder.com/profile
```

As you can see, this request only requires a valid Tinder token, and returns personal information including Facebook ID, date of birth, and exact GPS co-ordinates.

The tokens themselves are Version 4 UUID tokens and the document which defines them states:

"Do not assume that UUIDs are hard to guess; they should not be used as security capabilities (identifiers whose mere possession grants access), for example. A predictable random number source will exacerbate the situation [18]".

While we personally found no problems with Tinder's usage of UUIDs, a theoretical attack, which would require intimate knowledge of a predictable random generator in use by Tinder, does exist. In essence, the attacker would first authenticate using their own account. Then, they would retrieve their randomly generated token, and

---

[1] cURL is a command-line utility to send and retrieve data over the Internet. Detailed documentation on history and usage is available at: http://linux.about.com/od/commands/l/blcmdl1_curl.htm (last accessed: 20/07/2016).

then use that token in the weak random number generator to generate the next valid token in the sequence. The attacker could then access the profile of, and see personal information of, the person who logged after them.

Testing HTTPS. One of the more basic things we wanted to check was that all sensitive traffic to Tinder was being sent over HTTPS. HTTP, which is not encrypted, is extremely vulnerable to man-in-the-middle attacks, as well as packet sniffing. Our examination revealed all traffic, except images, were sent over HTTPS (Fig. 7).

Fig. 7. Left: images.gotinder.com is not transmitted over HTTPS. Right: Tinder ID is visible in path of image URL (pixilated for privacy)

Pictures sent over plain HTTP can be intercepted through the methods mentioned above. We also found that a user's Tinder ID was transmitted in the path of the image, the relevance of which will become apparent when we discuss attacks further below. In addition, we found that the first image requested after authenticating was always the authenticated user. Being able to view images of people is not a security problem by itself, however users' belief that they are anonymous until they choose otherwise, may mean that they are prone to using more compromising images on Tinder. For example, there was an incident involving a married Canadian politician alleged to have made a Tinder account linked to his official campaign Facebook page [19]. Compounding this, users *could* be identified by using their image in a reverse image search. However, in our testing, this did not happen because most large web-crawlers respect Facebook's rules which disallow user profile crawling [20]. Should a user re-use their Tinder images elsewhere on the web, such as on other social media or dating websites, the probability for a successful reverse image search does increase. Further, if a user has an Instagram account connected, this again increases the chance that a user's image will be indexed on a search engine.

Setting Location. Setting the user's location was one of the potential privacy problems we wanted to investigate. While the previous trilateration attack involved creating fake accounts [10]: physically moving a phone to all of these locations would have proven extremely time consuming. Indeed, most location-based attacks are only made feasible by being able to freely and rapidly adjust the attacker's location until ideal conditions are found. This is to say, being able to freely change your own location is a security concern. We found that adjusting your location through Tinder's API was trivial, as it can be accomplished through the following command:

```
curl -k -v -X POST -H "Content-Type: application/json"
-H "User-Agent: Tinder Android Version 4.5.2" -H "X-
Auth-Token:  xxxxxxxx-xxxx-4xxx-yxxx-xxxxxxxxxxxx"
https://api.gotinder.com/user/ping --data "{'lat': 0.0*,
'lon': 0.0* }"
```

* A valid latitude and longitude are obviously required here.

As can been seen above, unlike some other geo-social apps, such as Mitalk or LOVOO [4], Tinder does not use checksums or signatures to validate the location it receives. Further, while Tinder does reject very small and very large changes to location, small changes can be accomplished by performing them in two opposed larger moves. Furthermore, very large changes can be performed by sending no location changes for a few minutes, and *then* sending the large change. We believe this behaviour is to accommodate users who turn off their phones and catch a plane, for example; otherwise these users may become permanently out of sync with Tinder.

4.2 Validating Previous Attacks

Now that all of the Tinder endpoints could be accessed, we wanted to verify that all of the old attacks that we examined earlier were actually patched, and no longer functional. The simplest method to test the first major vulnerability, which leaked exact user GPS data and Facebook ID, was to request a user's card and examine the results. We used a cURL command to accomplish this, in the form of:

```
curl -k -v -X GET -H "Content-Type: application/json" -
H "User-Agent: Tinder Android Version 4.5.2" -H "X-
Auth-Token:  xxxxxxxx-xxxx-4xxx-yxxx-xxxxxxxxxxxx"
https://api.gotinder.com/user/00000000000000000000000000*
```

* Substitution of dummy 0's with a valid Tinder ID is required.

Our response from Tinder is presented in Fig. 8:

As can been seen from Fig. 9, we confirmed that GPS co-ordinates and Facebook IDs are no longer being sent by Tinder. Furthermore, the distance returned is now a whole number, rounded to the nearest mile, rather than the exact distance we saw in the original trilateration attack [10]. However, we also wanted to test whether the distance returned was still accurate under specific circumstances, for example, if the distance was simply rounded to the nearest integer, gradually moving away from the target until the distance switched between two integers would give you exactly half the distance between those two integers, which you could then use as a point to conduct a

bio: ""
birth_date: "31/07/1989 9:37:01 AM"
gender: 0
name: "Mark"
ping_time: "10/07/2016 9:50:58 PM"
▷ photos
jobs
▲ schools
    ▲ [0]
        name: "University of South Australia"
        id: "38078347904"
    id: "56a5a⬚⬚⬚⬚⬚⬚⬚⬚⬚⬚⬚⬚"
distance_mi: 14

Fig. 8. Partial response from Tinder server to a user GET request. The Tinder ID field has been pixilated for privacy reasons

trilateration attack. We developed a program to try and accomplish this, which is detailed in the next section.

4.3   New Attacks

Identifying Facebook users. Our first attack came from noticing that an "ID" field is sent with some of Facebook "groups" data. As an example, examination of the information presented in Fig. 8 shows that ID "38078347904" was sent for our school details at University of South Australia. We then used this ID to visit the Facebook page for that group, and found everyone who liked the page. In this example, the URL would be:

```
https://www.facebook.com/search/38078347904/likers
```

Since we know that all Tinder users have a Facebook account and Tinder sources both name and photos from Facebook - we manually examined the list produced by the Facebook search until we found a user with a matching first name and similar image. We also had some success simply Googling the user's first name, along with their place of schooling, job, and any relevant bio data provided by Tinder. Although extremely basic, this attack did allow us to connect Tinder users and their Facebook accounts, which we consider a privacy problem. Also remember, that the only piece of information required for this attack to work is a Tinder ID, which, if you recall from our findings in Fig. 8, is sent as plain text and is not encrypted.

Location attack. We wanted to propose and test a new version of the previous trilateration attack. We developed a program that retrieved a Tinder ID from our matchmaking list and then moved our profile away slightly. We then requested the user's profile using their Tinder ID again and looked at whether Tinder reported their distance had changed. We picked 3 points, and did several refining passes on each to dial in the accuracy. The next figure demonstrates one of our results.

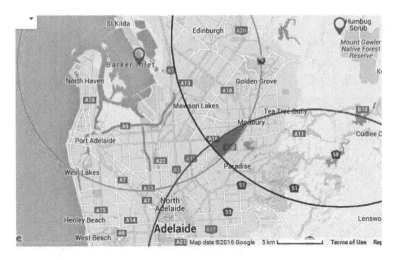

Fig. 9. Attempting our own trilateration when the reported distance changed from one whole number to the next produced a large 3–4 km² area of uncertainty (shaded orange). (Color figure online)

We tested several things, such as treating the integer returned as the floor, ceiling, as well as different rounding points – nothing seemed to produce anything more accurate than Fig. 9.

If the distance measured was not an accurate representation of the actual distance, then what was it? To test this we used two fake accounts, and had one "orbit" the other at a set distance as reported by Tinder. To do this, we used a reverse Haversine function that moved a set distance along a defined bearing. Again, we used several refining passes at our chosendistance (11 miles) so the point captured was exactly when Tinder changed from reporting 10 miles to 11 miles.

```
set bearingRads, set d //the bearing in radians to move
along, and the distance in metres to move

set φ1 //the latitude of the starting point in radians

set λ1 //the longitude of the starting point in radians

set R = 6371008 // average radius of the Earth

φ2 = Asin(Sin(φ1) * Cos(d / R) + Cos(φ1) * Sin(d / R) *
Cos(bearingRads))

λ2 = λ1 + Atan2(Sin(bearingRads) * Sin(d / R) *
Cos(φ1), Cos(d / R) - Sin(φ1) * Sin(φ2))

φ2 = toDegrees(φ2), λ2 = (toDegrees(λ2) + 540)%360-180
```

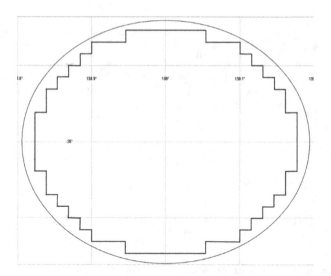

Fig. 10. Outer circle: an 11 mile (All of Tinder's internal representations of distance are in miles, which we have opted to keep for the sake of clarity) radius circle projected around a point. Inner shape: An 11 mile radius "circle" projected around the same point according to Tinder. Actual distance of inner shape to centre point ranged between 9.4883 and 10.6578 miles.

The function described above, looped over 360° produced the following:

From Fig. 10, it became obvious that Tinder has reduced accuracy in their distance calculation. We believe accurate GPS co-ordinates are being "snapped" to a less accurate grid which is then used for distance calculations performed by Tinder and displayed to the user.

If indeed the accuracy is being reduced at some stage of the process, it makes it extremely difficult, if not impossible to recover it.

While we were unable to perform an effective practical attack on the location of the user, we would like to propose the possibility of a further attack. Unfortunately, we were not able to determine if this attack would work, because pre-computing the Tinder grid over the internet was an extremely slow process, taking hours to get results within even one degree of accuracy. An attacker with considerable time, however, may gain success.

This attack would involve accurately precomputing the grid for Tinder (Fig. 11). The attacker would pick a GPS point, and move until they are snapped onto part of the pre- computed distance grid. Then, the attacker would manoeuvre to the very corner of the section they were in This would be Point 1. The attacker would then move to the left or right to find the reciprocal point on the other half of the grid. This would be Point 2. By measuring the distance from Point 1 to Point 2, and using a pre-computed table of distances, the attacker would now know which part of the grid they were on and be able to determine the bearing to the target centre point.

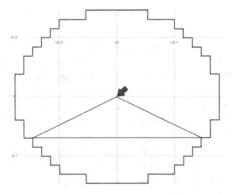

Fig. 11. An attack against the Tinder grid. This is an example 11 mile grid

Armed with two points, one distance, and two angles, the attacker could use trigonometry to find the final point, being the target (arrow on Fig. 11).

While this attack would only able to reveal which grid the target had snapped to, the grids appear to be $1/6^{th}$ of 0.1 degree of latitude or longitude at their most accurate. This equates to a square of roughly 2.8 km^2 (in South Australia), which is more accurate than the 3–4 km^2 identified in Fig. 9. Furthermore, it is unknown whether these grids are static, or whether their shape or accuracy can change.

5   Conclusion and Future Work

After significant probing we found that all known, significant, prior attacks on Tinder were no longer functional. We did find a number of security issues where Tinder has not followed best practice, including solely relying on UUID tokens for authentication, not properly validating location updates from users, sending user images over HTTPS, and including the Tinder ID in the user image path.

In terms of practical attacks, we found we were able to connect a Facebook profile to a Tinder account due to the shared information between them, the possibility of their images appearing on a search, as well as Tinder leaking the ID of certain Facebook groups the user was in. However, this attack was not consistent, required significant manual work, and depended on various luck factors such as Google indexing the right Facebook profile, or the user posting a Tinder image on the web.

For a location attack, we were able to get a rough location (3–4 km^2) using existing methods. We proposed a slightly more accurate attack (~ 2.8 km^2) using new methods, based on our belief that Tinder is now using grid snapping to remove exact user co-ordinates from calculations. However, owing to the apparent extremely inefficient pre- calculations required, we were unable to complete the attack ourselves.

Future work includes extending the research to grid-based attacks to speed up the attacks, and to attempt a practical application.

References

1. Tinder. https://www.gotinder.com/press. Last accessed: 20 July 2016
2. Russel, S., Kissick, D.: Is Tinder really creating a 'dating apocalypse'? https://www.theguardian.com/technology/2015/aug/16/tinder-app-creating-dating-apocalypse-twitter-storm. Last accessed: 20 July 2016
3. Farnden, J., Martini, B., Choo, K-K.R.: Privacy risks in mobile dating apps. In: 21st AMCIS 2015 (2015). http://aisel.aisnet.org/cgi/viewcontent.cgi?article=1427&context=amcis2015. Last accessed: 21 July 2016
4. Zhao, S., Luo, X., Bai, B., Ma, X., Zou, W., Qiu, X., Au, M.H.: I know where you all are! exploiting mobile social apps for large-scale location privacy probing. In: Liu, J.K.K., Steinfeld, R. (eds.) ACISP 2016. LNCS, vol. 9722, pp. 3–19. Springer, Cham (2016). doi:10.1007/978-3-319-40253-6_1
5. Tinder on Google Play Store. https://play.google.com/store/apps/details?id=com.tinder. Last accessed: 17 July 2016
6. I found out my internal Tinder rating and now I wish I hadn't. https://www.fastcompany.com/3054871/whats-your-tinder-score-inside-the-apps-internal-ranking-system. Last accessed: 20 July 2016
7. Official Tinder Blog – Giphy Announcement. http://blog.gotinder.com/say-more-with-tinders-new-messaging-features/. Last accessed: 20 July 2016
8. Official Tinder Blog – Super Like Announcement. http://blog.gotinder.com/updated-introducing-super-like-a-new-type-of-swipe/. Last accessed: 21 July 2016
9. Tinder Privacy Breach. http://qz.com/107739/tinders-privacy-breach-lasted-much-longer-than-the-company-claimed/. Last accessed: 20 July 2016
10. Trilateration attack on any Tinder user. http://blog.includesecurity.com/2014/02/how-i-was-able-to-track-location-of-any.html. Last accessed: 20 July 2016
11. Tinder Bot "Bonfire". https://www.tinderliker.com/. Last accessed: 20 July 2016
12. Tinder Bot "Auto Liker". http://tinderautoliker.com/. Last accessed: 20 July 2016
13. Tinder Bot with EigenFaces. http://crockpotveggies.com/2015/02/09/automating-tinder-with-eigenfaces.html. Last accessed: 20 July 2016
14. Official Symantec Blog – Tinder Spam. http://www.symantec.com/connect/blogs/tinder-spam-year-later-spammers-still-flirting-mobile-dating-app. Last accessed: 20 July 2016
15. Official Tinder Blog – Limited Swipe Announcement. http://blog.gotinder.com/keeping-tinder-real/. Last accessed: 20 July 2016
16. D'Orazio, C., Choo, K.-K.R.: An adversary model to evaluate DRM protection of video contents on iOS devices. Comput. Secur. **56**, 94–110 (2016)
17. Facebook Developer Site – Access Tokens. https://developers.facebook.com/docs/facebook-login/access-tokens/. Last accessed: 20 July 2016
18. A Universally Unique IDentifier (UUID) URN Namespace. https://tools.ietf.org/html/rfc4122. Last accessed: 20 July 2016
19. Married Politician on Tinder. http://www.news1130.com/2015/01/12/married-lower-mainland-federal-politician-appears-on-dating-app-tinder/. Last accessed: 20 July 2016
20. Facebook Robots File. https://www.facebook.com/robots.txt. Last accessed: 20 July 2016

Biometric Authentication
Using Facial Recognition

Mozammel Chowdhury[1(✉)], Junbin Gao[2], and Rafiqul Islam[1]

[1] School of Computing & Mathematics,
Charles Sturt University, Bathurst, Australia
{mochowdhury,mislam}@csu.edu.au
[2] Discipline of Business Analytics,
The University of Sydney Business School, Sydney, Australia
junbin.gao@sydney.edu.au

Abstract. Biometric authentication has been gaining popularity for providing privacy and security in many applications including secure access control, surveillance systems, user identification and many more. This research proposes a robust scheme for biometric authentication by analyzing and interpreting facial image using a neural network. Human face has become as the key attribute for biometric authentication over the recent years due to its uniqueness and robustness. Our system focuses on efficient detection and recognition of user's face for precise authentication. The facial features of a user are compared with a face database in order to perform matching for authentication and authorization. The proposed system estimates the face by analyzing skin color components in the facial image. The facial edge features are then extracted from the detected face skeleton. A neural network is employed and trained with the extracted edge features to recognize the user face by comparing with the facial database. Once the user is identified, authentication is granted. Experimental evaluation demonstrates that our proposed system provides better performance meeting accuracy requirements and less computation time.

Keywords: Biometric authentication · Secure access control · Surveillance system · Facial recognition

1 Introduction

Biometric authentication has become very popular nowadays in security and privacy preserving applications such as, access control, surveillance system, visa processing, border checking and so on. Biometric authentication is a technique that relies on the unique biometric characteristics of individuals to verify user identity for secure access to electronic devices or systems [1]. Biometric features such as, fingerprint, face, facial components, palm print, hand geometry, iris, retina, gait and voice are common form of key attributes in biometric authentication [2]. In recent years, human faces are widely used as the most distinctive key attributes for biometric authentication due to their uniqueness, robustness, availability, accessibility and acceptability characteristics [3].

© ICST Institute for Computer Sciences, Social Informatics and Telecommunications Engineering 2017
R. Deng et al. (Eds.): SecureComm 2016, LNICST 198, pp. 287–295, 2017.
DOI: 10.1007/978-3-319-59608-2_16

User authentication is crucial in secure access control that provides the safety and security of any system. User authentication is traditionally performed based on the following arrangements: (a) something that the user knows (such as, a PIN, a password) or (b) something that the user holds (typically a key, a token, a smart card, a badge, or a passport). These traditional methods for the user authentication have deficiencies that restrict their applicability in security systems. Traditional methods are based on properties that can be forgotten, disclosed, lost or stolen. Passwords often are easily accessible to colleagues and even occasional visitors and users tend to pass their tokens to or share their passwords with their colleagues to make their work easier. Biometric authentication or simply biometrics, on the other hand, authenticates users properly and reliably [4]. Biometric characteristics are unique and not duplicable or transferable. Biometric authentication identifies and authorizes a person based on the physiological or behavioral characteristics such as a fingerprint, an iris pattern, face or a voice sample [5].

The interest of doing research on biometrics is very significant due to its immense importance in the privacy and security community. This paper aims to develop an efficient scheme for biometric authentication based on facial recognition using a neural network. The system works with visual and geometrical information of the user's face in an image and detects the face skeleton using the similarity measure of the colour components of the image in the YC_bC_r colour space. Once the face is detected, the edge features of the face skeleton are then extracted and fed into the neural network to teach the network in order to identify the user face. Once the user is identified by facial recognition, authentication is granted to access the secure system. The proposed technique can treat images with different lighting conditions and complex backgrounds.

The rest of the paper is organized as follows. In Sect. 2, we present an overview of facial recognition. Section 3 demonstrates the architecture of our proposed facial recognition system. Experimental results are reported in Sect. 4. Finally, Sect. 5 concludes the paper.

2   Facial Recognition

Human face plays an important role in person recognition in vision-based surveillance system. Facial recognition is a technique for automatically identifying or verifying a person from an image or a video frame. Compared with other biometrics, face recognition has the potential to recognize uncooperative subjects in a non-intrusive manner. It has now become the most common and widely used means of biometric identification [6].

Facial recognition technology has been developed based on two arrangements: facial metrics and eigenfaces [7]. Facial metrics relies on the measurement of the facial features such as, eyes, nose, mouth. Eigenfaces refers to an appearance-based approach to face recognition that seeks to capture the variation in a collection of face images and use this information to encode and compare images of individual faces in a holistic (as opposed to feature-based) manner. In the facial recognition technique, the system captures the face image of the user by a camera or sensor and extracts the features from the face. The features are then compared with one which is stored in a face database, and if there is a match, the user's face is identified.

The face recognition process generally consists of the following steps. The initial task of facial recognition is to locate the face within the image sequence. Then the detected face block is normalized and extracted. The facial features are then extracted from the selected face block. Finally, the face is recognized.

A tremendous amount of research works have been done for automatic detection and recognition of human face over the last couple of decades [8, 9]. To name a few, good surveys exist for illumination invariant face recognition [10], face recognition across pose [11–13], video-based face recognition [14], and heterogeneous face recognition [15], face recognition using multi-scale Local Binary Patterns (LBP) [16], Locally linear regression based face recognition [17], and face recognition based on Dual-Cross Patterns (DCP) features [18].

Facial recognition techniques mentioned above have some deficiencies. The dependency on the light, resolution and facial expression reduces the accuracy of the facial recognition. We therefore, have employed facial edge features in recognition process which are independent of the variation of pose and illumination.

3   Proposed System Architecture

The general architecture of the proposed biometric authentication scheme is shown in Fig. 1. The scheme comprises of the following steps: (i) Pre-processing of the face image, (ii) Face detection, (iii) Facial features extraction, (iv) Feature matching, (v) Face identification, and (vi) Authentication.

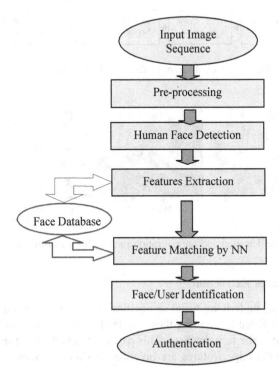

Fig. 1. Architecture of the proposed biometric authentication system.

3.1 Preprocessing of the Face Images

In computer vision systems, there may be significant amount of noise in the captured images. We therefore, employ a fuzzy median filtering technique [19] for refining the facial images corrupted by noise. This filter employs fuzzy rules for deciding the gray level of the pixels within a window in the image.

3.2 Face Detection

The most important part of the facial recognition is detecting the face in the image. Face detection is concerned with determining the part of an image which contains face. Several techniques have been developed for face detection in last couple of years, which includes: geometric modeling, genetic approach, neural network, principal component analysis, color analysis and so on [20–26].

In this paper, we have employed a fast and robust face detection technique based on skin color segmentation [27]. The face skeleton is detected from the largest connected area of the skin color segmented image. The method considers the frontal view of the face in color scale image. The detected face image is normalized and cropped with a dimension of 180×160 pixels. The steps of the face detection method are demonstrated in Fig. 2. The outcomes of face detection and normalization process are shown in Fig. 3.

Fig. 2. Block diagram of the face detection method.

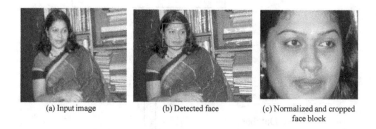

(a) Input image   (b) Detected face   (c) Normalized and cropped
                                                            face block

Fig. 3. Face detection and normalization process for a real image sequence.

3.3 Facial Features Extraction

One of the key tasks underlying facial recognition is the features extraction. Once the face is detected, the facial features are then extracted from this face block for matching with the one stored in the face database. This paper extracts the edge features from the face region, since the edge features are invariant to pose variation and illumination changes. The extracted facial edge features are then fed into a back propagation neural network (BPNN) to train the network for recognizing the face.

Edge or gradient histogram corresponds to the spatial distribution of the edge features in the image. The gradient of an image $f(x, y)$ can be expressed by,

$$\nabla f = \begin{bmatrix} \frac{\partial f}{\partial x} \\ \frac{\partial f}{\partial y} \end{bmatrix} = \begin{bmatrix} G_x \\ G_y \end{bmatrix} \tag{1}$$

where $G_x = \frac{\partial f}{\partial x}$ is the gradient in x direction, and
$G_y = \frac{\partial f}{\partial y}$ is the gradient in y direction.

The gradient direction can be calculated by the formula:

$$\theta = \tan^{-1}\begin{bmatrix} G_y \\ G_x \end{bmatrix} \tag{2}$$

We use Sobel edge detector to extract the edge features from the images. Figure 4 shows the edge features extracted from the face image.

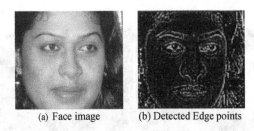

(a) Face image   (b) Detected Edge points

Fig. 4. Facial edge features extraction.

3.4   Facial Recognition with Neural Network

Facial recognition is achieved by employing a backpropagation neural network. The architecture of the neural network is illustrated in Fig. 5.

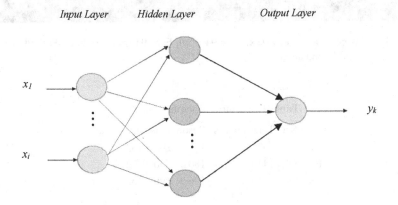

Fig. 5. Architecture of the back propagation neural network.

The nodes in the input layer receive the edge features. In this network, the layers are connected with each other through their neurons with specific weights. The input signals transmit from left to right directions while the error signals propagate from right towards left. Back propagation algorithm presents a training sample to the neural network and compares the obtained output to the desired output of that sample. It calculates the error in each output neuron. The BPNN adjusts the weights of each neuron for minimizing the error value. The minimum error margin is set to 0.001 for experimental evaluation.

4 Experimental Evaluation

In order to evaluate the effectiveness of the proposed method, experiments have been carried out for real images at different illumination conditions. We have performed experiments on three different face databases (Face 94, Face 95 and Face 96) of the University of Essex [29–31] with different poses and illuminations. Figure 6 demonstrates some sample images of these face databases. The features of the face databases are summarized in Table 1.

Fig. 6. Face image database of Essex: Face 94 (top), Face 95 (middle), Face 96 (bottom) with different poses and illuminations.

Table 1. Features of the face databases

Data Set	Total Images	Resolutions	Individuals
Face 94	3078	180 × 200	153
Face 95	1440	180 × 200	72
Face 96	3016	196 × 196	152

Experiments are carried out on a computer with 2.2 GHz Intel Core i5 processor and 4 GB RAM. The algorithm has been implemented using Visual C ++. Half of the images of the each face database are used as a training dataset and the remaining images are used as probe images in the recognition test. The extracted facial edge features are used to train the neural network.

We have performed experiments to compare our proposed algorithm with other existing methods including, principal component analysis (PCA) [11], Gabor [28], LBP [16], and DCP [18]. The results as furnished in the Fig. 7 and Fig. 8.

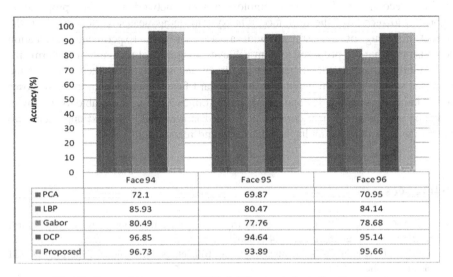

	Face 94	Face 95	Face 96
■ PCA	72.1	69.87	70.95
■ LBP	85.93	80.47	84.14
■ Gabor	80.49	77.76	78.68
■ DCP	96.85	94.64	95.14
▨ Proposed	96.73	93.89	95.66

Fig. 7. Recognition accuracy (%) of different methods for three datasets

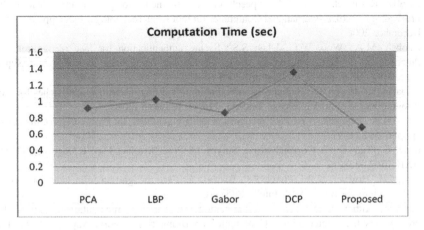

Fig. 8. Computation time for different recognition methods.

Experimental results demonstrate that our approach achieves almost similar recognition accuracy comparable to the state-of-the art method, while taking significant less amount of computation time. We believe that our method can be applicable in real time commercial environment where computational efficiency is a major concern.

5 Conclusion

In this paper we propose an effective and robust biometric authentication scheme based on facial recognition. The scheme employs a neural network with back propagation algorithm to recognize the user face. The system authenticates a user based on the correct matching of his/her face with a face database. Experimental evaluation demonstrates that the proposed system achieves a significant recognition performance with fulfillment of a tradeoff between accuracy and speed. The effectiveness of the proposed system has been justified using standard face databases with different poses and illuminations in complex and simple backgrounds. Our system is able to employ in real time applications where computation speed is a crucial. Our next approach is to extend the algorithm for multi-face detection and recognition.

References

1. Jain, A.K., Ross, A., Pankanti, S.: Biometrics: a tool for information security. IEEE Trans. Inf. Forensics Secur. **1**(2), 125–144 (2006)
2. Ahmed, I.T.: Continuous Authentication Using Biometrics: Data, Models, and Metrics. IGI Global, Hershey (2012)
3. Park, U., Jain, A.K.: Face matching and retrieval using soft biometrics. IEEE Trans. Inf. Forensics Secur. **5**(3), 406–415 (2010)
4. Kar, B., Kartik, B., Dutta, P.K.: Speech and face biometric for person authentication. In: Proceedings of IEEE International Conference on Industrial Technology, India, pp. 391–396, December 2006
5. Dabbah, M.A., Woo, W.L., Dlay, S.S.: Secure authentication for face recognition. In: Proceedings of IEEE Symposium on Computational Intelligence in Image and Signal Processing, USA, pp. 121–126, April 2007
6. Gopalan, R., Jacobs, D.: Comparing and combining lighting insensitive approaches for face recognition. Comput. Vis. Image Underst. **114**(1), 135–145 (2010)
7. Turk, M.A., Pentland, A.P.: Face recognition using eigenfaces. In: Proceedings of the IEEE, pp. 586–591 (1991)
8. Ding, C., Tao, D.: A Comprehensive Survey on Pose-Invariant Face Recognition (2015) arXiv:1502.04383v2
9. Barr, J.R., Bowyer, K.W., Flynn, P.J., Biswas, S.: Face recognition from video: a review. Int. J. Pattern Recognit. Artif. Intell. **26**(5) (2012)
10. Zou, X., Kittler, J., Messer, K.: Illumination invariant face recognition: a survey. In: Proceedings IEEE International Conferenfce on Biometrics, Theory, Appl. Syst., pp 1–8 (2007)
11. Zhang, H., Zhang, Y., Huang, T.S.: Pose-robust face recognition via sparse representation. Pattern Recogn. **46**(5), 1511–1521 (2013)

12. Zhang, X., Gao, Y.: Face recognition across pose: A review. Pattern Recogn. **42**(11), 2876–2896 (2009)
13. Zhang, Y., Shao, M., Wong, E.K., Fu, Y.: Random faces guided sparse many-to-one encoder for pose-invariant face recognition. In: Proceedings IEEE International Conference on Computer Vision, pp. 2416–2423 (2013)
14. Beveridge, R., Zhang, H., Draper, B., et al.: Report on the fg 2015 video person recognition evaluation. In: Proceedings IEEE International Conference on Automatic Face and Gesture Recognition (2015)
15. Ouyang, S., Hospedales, T., Song, Y.Z., Li, X.: A survey on heterogeneous face recognition: sketch, infrared, 3D and low resolution (2014). arXiv preprint: arXiv:14095114
16. Chen, D., Cao, X., Wen, F., Sun, J.: Blessing of dimensionality: high-dimensional feature and its efficient compression for face verification. In: Proceedings IEEE Conference on Computer Vision Pattern Recognition, pp. 3025–3032 (2013)
17. Chai, X., Shan, S., Chen, X., Gao, W.: Locally linear regression for pose-invariant face recognition. IEEE Trans. Image Process. **16**(7), 1716–1725 (2007)
18. Ding, C., Choi, J., Tao, D., Davis, L.S.: Multi-directional multi-level dual-cross patterns for robust face recognition, August 2015. arXiv:1401.5311v2
19. Satter, A.K.M.Z., Chowdhury, M.M.H.: A Fuzzy algorithm for de-noising of corrupted images. Int. J. Comput. Inf. Syst. (IJCSI) **6**(4), 15–17 (2013). Silicon Valley Publishers (SVP), United Kingdom
20. Li, H., Lin, Z., Shen, X., Brandt, J., Hua, G.: A convolutional neural network cascade for face detection. In: CVPR 2015, pp. 5325–5334
21. Uddin, J., Mondal, A.M., Chowdhury, M.M.H., Bhuiyan, M.A.: Face detection using genetic algorithm. In: Proceedings of 6th International Conference on Computer and Information Technology, Dhaka, Bangladesh, pp. 41–46, December 2003
22. Shinn-Ying, H., Hui-Ling, H.: Facial modeling from an uncalibrated face image using a coarse-to-fine genetic algorithm. Pattern Recogn. **34**(8), 1015–1031 (2001)
23. Kukenys, I., McCane, B.: Support vector machines for human face detection. In: Proceedings of the New Zealand Computer Science Research Student Conference (2008)
24. Viola, P., Jones, M.: Fast and robust classification using asymmetric AdaBoost and a detector cascade. Adv. Neural Inf. Process. Syst. **2**, 1311–1318 (2002)
25. Heisele, B., Serre, T., Poggio, T.: A component-based framework for face detection and identification. Int. J. Comput. Vision **74**(2), 167–181 (2007)
26. Talele, K.T., Kadam, S., Tikare, A.: Efficient face detection using Adaboost. In: IJCA Proceedings of International Conference in Computational Intelligence (2012)
27. Chowdhury, M., Gao, J., Islam, R.: Human detection and localization in secure access control by analysing facial features. In: Proceedings of IEEE Conference on Industrial Electronics and Applications (ICIEA), China, June 2016
28. Khatun, A., Bhuiyan, M.A.: Neural network based face recognition with gabor filters. IJCSNS Int. J. Comput. Sci. Netw. Secur. **11**(1), 71–76 (2011)
29. Face Recognition Data. University of Essex, UK, Face 94. http://cswww.essex.ac.uk/mv/allfaces/faces94.html
30. Face Recognition Data. University of Essex, UK, Face 95. http://cswww.essex.ac.uk/mv/allfaces/faces95.html
31. Face Recognition Data. University of Essex, UK, Face 96. http://cswww.essex.ac.uk/mv/allfaces/faces96.html

Platform as a Service (PaaS) in Public Cloud: Challenges and Mitigating Strategy

Fidel Ikundi$^{(\boxtimes)}$, Rafiqul Islam, and Peter White

School of Computing and Mathematics,
Charles Sturt University, Bathurst, Australia
ikundif@yahoo.fr, {mislam,pewhite}@csu.edu.au

Abstract. Cloud computing is geared towards the effective and efficient use of computational resources and it has been making a big revolution in the field of information technology by reducing capital investment. It delivers computing as a service, that enables effective utilization of computational resources, rather than, a product, for a fraction of the cost. This paper explores key security issues associated with PaaS and proposed mitigating strategies are provided. These security challenges slow down the adoption of PaaS. Mitigating these security issues could increase PaaS adoption. This paper focuses on the security issues associated with Platform as a Service (PaaS) offering on a public cloud platform and provides various mitigating techniques to address these security issues. If properly implemented, we could realize an increase in PaaS adoption.

Keywords: PaaS · Cloud computing · Security

1 Introduction

Cloud computing is a concept that provides economic outsourcing of computational resources and qualified maintenance [8]. Various kinds of computational resources are shared through simple interfaces via high-capacity networks [12]. Despite the many benefits of cloud computing, such as better utilization of resources and less time taken in deploying new services, the sharing of resources in a PaaS platform has security challenges. These challenges range from access control issues to privacy awareness. Ubiquitously shared and distributed resources bring a new series of security problems that professionals in information technology need to address.

Eliminating this security challenges will speed up PaaS adoption and increase its usage. An increase in PaaS usage leads to better utilization of computational resources. It will also shorten time to deploy new services, speeds up technology adaptation, as well as carbon footprint [1].

Cloud computing has four deployment models [5]. These deployment models are:

- Public cloud – provides shared resources to a community of users
- Private cloud – provides services which are controlled and exclusive to the user
- Hybrid cloud – provides the ability to move workloads between private and public platforms

© ICST Institute for Computer Sciences, Social Informatics and Telecommunications Engineering 2017
R. Deng et al. (Eds.): SecureComm 2016, LNICST 198, pp. 296–304, 2017.
DOI: 10.1007/978-3-319-59608-2_17

- Community cloud – provisioned for organizations with shared concerns Similarly, cloud computing has three service delivery models [5]. These models are:
- Software as a Service (SaaS) – consumed as a service only for the applications needed
- Platform as a Service (PaaS) – provides the core hosting operating system and optional building block services that allow users to run their own applications
- Infrastructure as a Service (IaaS) – outsource the elements of infrastructure like virtualization, storage, networking and load balancers.

PaaS plays a significant role in a cloud environment because it brings customs software development to the cloud. Moreover, PaaS provides an environment for users to run applications. Examples of PaaS services includes SharePoint or MSSQL server on Azure. PaaS is defined as "the capability provided to the consumer to deploy onto the cloud infrastructure consumer-created or acquired applications created using programming languages and tools supported by the provider" [5]. PaaS will drive demand for cloud computing as desktop operating systems and development tools drove the demand for PCs in the 1990s. "PaaS consumers employ the tools and execution resources provided by cloud providers to develop, test, deploy and manage the operation of PaaS applications hosted in a cloud environment. PaaS consumers can be application developers who design and implement application software; application testers who run and test applications hosted in a cloud-based environment; or, application developers who publish applications into the cloud. PaaS consumers can be billed according to the number of PaaS users; the processing, storage and network resources consumed by the PaaS application; and the duration of the platform usage" [5].

PaaS is not a single technology. It is a collection of related services used in creating and deploying software on a cloud platform. PaaS brings challenges along with its many benefits, like all new technologies. Getting to PaaS success requires understanding what can get in the way of its fullest realization. While some PaaS challenges are organizational, others are technical in nature. However, these challenges do not exist in a vacuum. They exist in an organizational specific setting. Depending on an organizational potential PaaS users and choice of PaaS technology, they will encounter different types of the major PaaS challenges.

Concerns about cloud security are not new, however, PaaS could increase risk exposure. The cloud tends to blur the security perimeter in general because with PaaS, an organization's business extends to multi-tenant servers in unknown geographic locations. If a PaaS application connects to other enterprise systems, it could become a "route" for improper access and potential vulnerability. Connections between cloud-based applications built on PaaS and other enterprise systems present security, operational and governance challenges. The paas-based software is inherently service-oriented. It has the ability to call on application programming interfaces (APIs) exposed on numerous systems. These include APIs that use Simple Object Access Protocol (SOAP) as well as the increasingly popular Representational State Transfer (REST). Without adequate controls, systems can be exposed through APIs along with the business processes they support. Of course, few organizations simply leave an API totally open to the world. However, the difference in development and change cycles between legacy systems and PaaS software can lead to challenges because the legacy system cannot keep up with new PaaS features. If external users can access internal business process through APIs that are out of sync, that can cause operational and compliance difficulties. Alternatively, if an API is not available because a change in the PaaS solution has broken the connection, that is also bad for business.

In this paper, we will focus on the key characteristics of a PaaS platform, security risks associated with a PaaS environment and proposed mitigation strategy.

2 Key Characteristics of PaaS

PaaS offering is widely being adopted in the business world; as a result, it is gaining rapid growth. This growth is bringing broad changes across the information technology sector. PaaS vendors are contemplating how to take the opportunity to this new expanding market and many developers are moving towards PaaS application development. Moreover, the increase in PaaS application consumption and development is driving the need for a platform technology built specifically to support the PaaS market. Below are some of the attributes behind the PaaS market expansion:

- **Multi-tenant architecture**

A PaaS platform has to be multi-tenanted. A multi-tenant platform is one that uses common computing resources including hardware, operating system, application code and a single underlying database with a shared schema to support multiple customers simultaneously.

- **Customizable/Programmable User Interface**

A PaaS platform must provide the capability to construct highly flexible user interfaces through a simple "drag & drop" methodology that permits the creation and configuration of UI components [2]. This "drag & drop" capability allows the creation of new layers quickly and easily without requiring much custom coding.

- **Unlimited Database Customizations**

The core of many applications is data persistence. Therefore, a key characteristic of PaaS is facilitating the creation, configuration, and deployment of persistent objects without requiring programming knowledge. So, a PaaS platform must have the capability to support the construction of objects, the definition of relationships between the objects and the configuration of advanced data behavior all from within the comfort of the Web browser via a "point and click" declarative concept.

- **Robust Workflow engine/capabilities**

The objective of a business process execution through process automation is vital to establish any business application in the business world. A PaaS offering should be able to offer a business-logic engine that can support the definition of workflow processes and the specification of business rules to engender process automation [8]. A workflow process defines the different stages a business object flows through, during its life cycle.

- **Granular control over security/sharing (permissions model)**

The PaaS offering should provide a flexible access control system that allows detailed control over what users of the SaaS application can see and the data each user can access. Definition of access from the application level (including tabs, menus, objects, views, charts, reports and workflow actions) to the individual field level should be possible. Defining an access control model should be possible through the creation of groups and roles and the assignment of users to groups or roles. For complex large-scale implementations, the ability to define which features and data each user can access should be available so users can be segmented across common organizational structures to provide fine-grained access to data/application features.

- **Flexible "services-enabled" integration model**

PaaS facilitates the rapid construction of applications in the cloud by providing foundational elements, such as data persistence and workflow capabilities that are essential to the creation of any business application. However, given the complex IT environments that permeate most enterprises today, the PaaS offering should leverage Service Oriented Architecture (SOA) principles to enable seamless integration of cloud application data and functionality residing in the cloud platform with other on-premise/on-demand systems and applications [8].

3 Challenges of PaaS

In the PaaS environment, the user objects are spread over the host. This could make it easier for objects to gain access to resources. In order to mitigate such risk, the objects will need to be protected from malicious providers.

PaaS is in a multi-tenant environment. This implies the environment is shared with other customers. Accessing a network in a shared environment brings challenges, such as access control and secure communication. However, access control and secure communication are not the only concerns in a multi-tenancy environment.

In the cloud environment, software and hardware resources from different vendors are integrated for efficient use. This integration of computing resources may bring about security challenges because the security setting of each computing resource may be different [12]. Similarly, each resource that is shared in a shared platform is a communication channel [11]. This could lead to a potential communication leakage.

Below are some of the challenges encountered in PaaS in a public cloud and strategies to mitigate the challenges.

- **Lack of interoperability**

The pooling of resources could eventually end up causing security vulnerabilities if access to the resources is not controlled. A security setting for a particular resource could lead to a breach to another. For example, Jones is authorized to access a file named "Passive" but mistakenly gained access to a secret file named "PASSIVE". "Interoperability can be maintained by providing common interfaces to objects for resource access" [8]. However, in order to control access to a PaaS platform, resource interfaces should be designed carefully.

- **Vulnerable hosts**

  The idea of sharing the same platform in the cloud by multiple users has been around for a long time [6]. In recent times, this concept is still widely used. A multi-tenancy environment is made up of objects and hosts. These hosts and objects need protection.

  However, if this protection fails, an attacker could gain access to both the resources of the hosts and tenant objects as well. This protection can be achieved by evaluating resource access request from each object on the host. TCB is a solution for hosts' vulnerability.

- **Vulnerable objects**

An object in a PaaS environment can either be compromised when a service provider accesses a user's object residing in the hosts, a user may attack another users' object in the same hosts or an attack by a third party. A service provider needs access to an object to execute the object. An object cannot be executed only when it is stored in the cloud.

- **Access control**

Access to remote entities must be controlled to keep network communication confidential. Some of the common attacks in a cloud-based environment are; phishing attacks, brute force attacks, and password reset attacks. Authentication, authorization, and traceability are the major concepts of access control. Solutions such as two-factor authentication (smart cards and biometric mechanisms) could protect against such attacks.

3.1 Proposed Mitigating Strategies

Lack of interoperability and vulnerable hosts can be mitigated by the use of trusted computing base (TCB). On the other hand, the risks posed by vulnerable objects can be mitigated by protecting the sensitive parts of the objects with encryption.

- TCB is a secure collection of executable code and configuration files. It is assumed to be secure because it is thoroughly analyzed for vulnerabilities before installing as a layer over the operating system. It provides standardized application programming interface (API) for the user objects. The principle of minimizing TCB is a widely accepted solution for a secure solution [6]. Interoperability is achieved when TCB is installed on every host and resource assignments are accessed via TCB. Every request assignment is checked by TCB, thus, preventing any possible attack from objects to hosts.
- Encrypting the objects to protect the integrity and privacy of a user object while the object is on the host is the responsibility of the service provider. The consumer trusts that the objects are protected. However, if a host is breached or the provider is malicious, the object could be read, rendered inaccessible, modified or deleted. Symmetric and asymmetric encryption schemes, hashing and signatures could be used to protect the content in an object. This could prevent the content in an object

from being accessed. Key storage is very important in a PaaS environment in a public cloud. Users' keys should be stored in an encapsulated key storage field according to their access roles. Encryption should be applied on the keys themselves for added security (Tables 1 and 2).

Table 1. Challenges and solutions to breaching an object's security.

Challenge	Proposed solution
Lack of interoperability	Use trusted computing base (TCB)
Vulnerable host	Use TCB
Vulnerable object	Encrypt objects Use hashing schemes Use signatures Implement access controls policies encrypt key storage

Table 2. Network access challenges and proposed solution

Network challenge	Proposed solution
Confidentiality	• Use transport layer security (TLS) • Implement access control policies
Authentication	• Use TLS • Implement access control policies
Authorization	• Use policy enforcement points (PEPs) • Implement access control policies
Traceability	• Keep records of events • Users should monitor their applications • Users should audit their data

3.2 Broad Network Access and Measured Services Challenges

There are some basic requirements for securing a network communication. The confidentiality of communications over a network channel must be guaranteed and remote users must be authenticated for a secure network access. Authentication, authorization, confidentiality, and traceability are the backbone of access control.

- **Authentication**

This is a process in which credentials are compared with what is stored on file during an interaction. Authentication is a method of identifying who is requesting or attempting access.

- **Authorization**

Authorization is the method of granting access to specified resources. This is another form of access control. When attempting to gain access to an object in a PaaS environment, authorization will definitely allow only the authenticated individual with the correct authorization to access the object. The object will be compromised if authorization mechanisms are not in place. Objects in a PaaS public cloud are not stable. They are constantly migrating and the host could also be reconfigured, it may be possible that a reconfiguration may change or degrade the access policy.

In a PaaS environment, hosts are very intelligent because they have to know each object's specific policy. This will enable the host to apply the specific policy to an individual object.

- **Confidentiality**

The notion that communication over a network channel needs to be confidential is one of the most important roles of a network security professional. In a PaaS platform, the users will need to communicate with the objects. This communication could be intercepted and sensitive information could be stolen from the host. As a result, it is vital to implement security in the communication.

- **Traceability**

This access control method can be realized by keeping records of all occurrences on the platform. The stakeholder in the cloud would like to know what is actually going on. Stakeholders are actually billed on usage, so as a result, they will like to monitor and audit any access to their data. These records are actually kept in logging systems. These systems should be protected and secured.

3.2.1   Proposed Mitigating Strategies

By using a transport layer security (TLS) we can achieve access control mechanisms in a PaaS environment. Access control policies can be enclosed in similar objects. This will enable an easy distribution and customization. "Authorization is applied on the hosts with the help of policy enforcement points (PEPs) with respect to the encapsulated access control policies" [10]. To trace events that happen in the cloud environment, a logging protocol is introduced.

- **Transport Layer Security (TLS)**

Confidential channels can be formed through TLS to prevent eavesdropping and for secure authentication [11]. While the object is being accessed, it is recommended to have mutual authentication in place, so as to avoid a man-in-the-middle attack [9].

- **Policy Enforcement Points (PEPs)**

PEP is software used to read and manage the encapsulated access control policies embedded in the objects. During the decision-making process, PEPs of the host must behave according to the undeniable logging protocol [10]. PEPs are normally tied to the hosts. The PEP will read the object's access control policies and consequently decides if the connection will be established.

- **Undeniable Logging Protocol**

In this protocol, malicious activities are detected and exposed to the parties concerned. This protocol helps in investigating incidents that occur in a PaaS environment in the public cloud. There is an online bulletin board that helps to ensure that the logs cached by this protocol have not been tampered with. The bulletin board is a public write-only storage. If a related party needs access, they will send an access request. However, the request is not sent directly to the related party but through the bulletin board. So the bulletin board logs the activities of both parties.

4 Privacy Awareness Challenges

For a user to be authenticated, the user will need to provide very specific information. For example, if an employee of a company wants to access the company's printer, using his or her personal laptop, the printer will refuse access.

However, if the employee is using a work laptop, access will be granted. When accessing devices or materials through the Internet, users should be careful not to provide too much information because their privacy may be compromised [13]. Proxy certificates can help to reduce the risk of revealing excess attributes [7]. When using privacy aware authentication with a proxy certificate, the following will need to be met:

- More attributes must not be requested by the host and the object than the attributes that they need. "If more attributes than required is requested, the only practical solution is negotiating the service terms" [7].
- With the assistance of a trusted third party, the credentials should be easy to configure.

5 Service Continuity and Fault-Tolerance Challenges

Service interruption is not new in a networked platform. Attacks such as distributed denial of service (DDoS) can compromise the systems in a network and makes the network stop. If there are any network issues in a PaaS environment, the contents of the objects may be modified or even completely wiped out by a malicious attacker. "Byzantine quorum approach is adopted to obtain fault-tolerance and service continuity under these circumstances" [4]. In the Byzantine quorum approach, "any subset of all hosts that resides the copies of the same object forms a quorum" [3]. We can determine a copy of the object where the number of hosts is enough. As a result of that, in the byzantine quorum system, any modification of the object will be detected.

6 Conclusion

PaaS technologies have the potential to accelerate software development while reinventing how IT supports the development process. With PaaS, developers are tempted to take shortcuts and release applications without considering important security factors. There has to be a balance between the need for speed and sensible planning and controls. Many software tools are available to coordinate and control the PaaS development process. PaaS success is an organizational issue. However, the technology itself can only do so much to bring about the kind of collaboration that will make PaaS an effective mode of software development. However, PaaS infrastructure will deliver best results when security challenges are understood and mitigation strategies implemented. Moreover, operational plans have to align with security.

In this paper, we have designed some strategies in which a PaaS offering in the public cloud could be rendered secure. Some security challenges, such as resource pooling and rapid elasticity, broadband network access and measured services, privacy awareness issues, service continuity and fault-tolerance challenges have been investigated and proposed strategies to mitigate the above security challenges discussed.

References

1. Brunette, G.: Platform as a service offering. J. Cloud Comput. **10**(3), 17–21 (2015)
2. Dijk, M., Juels, A.: Attributes of platform as a service offering. J. Cloud Comput. **17**(4), 20–23 (2015)
3. Gallagher, M.: Understanding platform as a service models. J. Inf. Technol. **18**(4), 33–37 (2015)
4. Kaufmann, M.: Data security in the world of cloud computing. J. Secur. Priv. **9**(2), 54–63 (2015)
5. Mell, P., Grance, T.: The NIST definition of cloud computing. http://nvlpubs.nist.gov/nistpubs/Legacy/SP/nistspecialpublication800-145.pdf. Accessed 25 Mar 2016
6. Momm, C.: The principle of minimizing TCB (2014). https://mommconrad.com/threats/multitenancyplatformsv1.0.pdf. Accessed 21 Mar 2016
7. Natis, Y.: Research on platform as a service. J. Cloud Comput. Secur. **10**(1), 11–16 (2015)
8. Osvik, D., Shamir, A.: The concept of cloud computing. J. Inf. Technol. **12**(3), 26–29 (2015)
9. Percival, C.: Securing the transport layer. p. 25. The New York Times. http://www.nytimes.com. Accessed 20 Jan 2015
10. Saltzer, J.: Protection and the control of information sharing. In: ACM Conference on Information Sharing and Protection, vol. 6, no. 2, pp. 11–15 (2014)
11. Shacham, H., Savage, S.: Exploring information leakage in third-party commute clouds. J. Cloud Comput. **9**(1), 13–17 (2015)
12. Subashini, S., Kavitha, V.: Shared resources in the cloud. J. Netw. Comput. Appl. **14**(2), 27–29 (2015)
13. Takabi, H., Joshi, D.: Security and privacy challenge in cloud computing environments. J. Cloud Comput. Secur. **23**(1), 66–72 (2015)

ATCS Workshop - Session 2

Architecture Support for Controllable VMI on Untrusted Cloud

Jiangyong Shi$^{(\boxtimes)}$ and Yuexiang Yang

National University of Defense Technology, Changsha, China
{shijiangyong,yyx}@nudt.edu.cn

Abstract. This paper combines architecture isolation with latest Intel SGX technology to make a controllable virtual machine introspection architecture on untrusted cloud. The main goal of SGX is to protect important applications from being attacked by untrusted OS, while the main goal of VMI is to protect OS from being attacked by untrusted applications. So it seems like contradictory, but actually they are complementary. By combining SGX and VMI, we can both monitoring the behavior of untrusted applications and preventing sensitive applications from being monitored. This is very practical in public cloud, as the cloud server provider is untrusted, but we still rely on its resource to provide computing. As far as we know, this is the first proposal to implement security monitor in an untrusted cloud with the help of trusted hardware. Preliminary security analysis and performance evaluation show that our architecture can ensure the confidentiality and integrity of the VM hosted on untrusted cloud server while providing VMI services with less than 20% overhead.

Keywords: VMI · SGX · Enclave · Untrusted cloud · Security design · Privacy

1 Introduction

Virtual Machine Introspection (VMI) [1] has been evolved over the last decade. While it indeed improved the security of VMs by stealthily monitoring the execution of VMs of different tenants, it also has the risk of privacy invasion, especially when the cloud server is untrusted. The condition of cloud service provider (CSP) being untrusted includes: (1) The CSP itself abuse of privileges. Even though large CSP companies such as Amazon and Microsoft have good reputation in information area, they might still collect users' data and behavior using techniques including VMI in order to better provide service or coordinate with the investigate demand of the government. Besides, internal staff who is vicious or act as a spy might intentionally leave backdoors or manipulate the privileges to steal users' data or break VM integrity. (2) The cloud server being attacked. This is especially true when a malicious or compromised VM escapes the constraint of VMM and breaks the isolation between VMs. When that happens, the

© ICST Institute for Computer Sciences, Social Informatics and Telecommunications Engineering 2017
R. Deng et al. (Eds.): SecureComm 2016, LNICST 198, pp. 307–316, 2017.
DOI: 10.1007/978-3-319-59608-2_18

attackers can either shutdown the VM on the same physical machine to cause deny of service attack, or steal sensitive information of other VMs by VMI. As the VMM is a privilege layer below the VMs and CSP takes control of all the VMMs, these two situations are hard to prevent by the users.

To change that, we investigate the hardware routine to control VMM's access to resources of VMs. The resources a VM owns include disk, memory and network packet. The network flow can be protected through security protocol such as SSL. The disk can be encrypted using full disk encryption (FDE) technique. The most difficult to protect is volatile storage including memory and CPU state due to several reasons. Firstly, volatile storage is frequently read and wrote which makes encryption extremely performance costing. Secondly, multiple VMs' share of the same physical memory space and frequently memory scheduling make it hard to define the memory range to protect. While virtualization provides good memory isolation between different VMs, it doesn't consider the VMM being malicious. So the VMM can arbitrarily manipulate the physical memory space to intercept sensitive data or inject malicious code, including VMI operations.

Based on the analysis, we propose a controllable VMI architecture based on existing hardware feature and new hardware enhancement technology. Our architecture can provide VMI as a service based on the users' requirements, while in the same time prevent the VMM from monitoring the VM without the permit of the user.

The organization of the paper is as follows. Relate works with VM and VMM isolation are discussed in Sect. 2. To make our work more clear, the trusted model of our architecture is described in Sect. 3, followed by our architecture design in Sect. 4. The detailed implementation of our architecture is described in Sect. 5. Sections 6 and 7 analyze the security and performance of our architecture. Lastly, a short conclusion is drawn in Sect. 8.

2   Related Work

CryptVMI [2] proposes an encrypted VMI framework to prevent cloud manager from forging VMI requests and intercepting VMI results. Even though it considers the problem of cloud manager being malicious, it assumes that the VMM is secure and trusted, which is not always true as we discussed in the introduction part. In order to control VMM's access to memory of VMs, we need to re-design the hardware architecture to support memory isolation between VMs and VMM. Related researches include HyperWall [3], HyperCoffer [4] and Intel SGX [5].

HyperWall designs a confidentiality and integrity protection (CIP) architecture to protect the VM memory from being tampered by VMM [3]. The architecture uses resource isolation (focusing on the memory of the virtual machines), as opposed to cryptographic isolation, to implement hypervisor secure virtualization. The architecture includes modification of hardware, hypervisor and VM, such as new instructions and registers to CPU, new procedure for updating memory mapping, and new random number generators. By isolating memory of VM and VMM, it can successfully prevent VMM from tampering with VM memory. However, this also adds challenge to VMI, as VMI requires mapping the VM memory to where VMI applications are deployed. HyperWall scrubs any memory pages that are freed and prevents them from being shared, which disables most VMI applications that relied on memory sharing.

Compared with HyperWall, HyperCoffer has less effect on hypervisor as it adds another separate layer called VM-shim to cooperate with the secure CPU [4]. The security of VM-shim is ensured by combining each VM-shim with VM to reduce the impact on TCB. Besides, it uses hardware encryption and integrity checking to protect the data of VM memory and disk, which can defend both VMM attack and hardware attack. However, it still needs the cooperation of VM OS and hypervisor to work. Besides, as the hypervisor is authorized part of the data access according to the type of VMEXIT, it is still possible to attack the VM. Moreover, encryption of the VM memory disabled VMI tools, which is a loss to security.

Both HyperWall and HyperCoffer aim at protecting the whole VM from being accessed by VMM, however, this would add difficulties to management of VMs as VMM is the main management layer. Besides, all-VM encryption and integrity checking add high performance cost and are inflexible. To overcome these disadvantages, Intel proposed new protection architecture named Intel Software Guard Extension (SGX) in its sixth generation processor Skylake. SGX is designed to protect the memory of applications, instead of all-VMs, from being tampered and snooped by VMM without the acknowledgement of the VM user. As it is application granularity, SGX is more flexible than HyperWall and HyperCoffer. Besides, only encryption specific application memory brings lower performance cost. Applications based on SGX include Haven [6], VC3 [7] and M2R [8], most of which aim at providing a new protection of the existing sensitive and vulnerable applications.

However, SGX only can protect the ring 3 applications from being accessed by ring 0 software, including OS kernel and VMM. SGX cannot protect kernel-level security applications, such as AV and Firewall, while these tools must run in kernel mode to monitor other programs.

Our core idea is to put VMI-applications into a disjunctive VM (VMI Server) and prevent VMM from being able to read or write other VMs' memory. If VMM is able to map memory addresses of the introspected VM, it might map the VM memory to its own address space so as to read or write its contents, which must be prevented in un-trusted cloud. The details will be discussed in Sect. 5.

3   Trusted Model

We assume the cloud service provider and the cloud server to be untrusted. This indicates following potential threats to cloud users' VM security and privacy:

1. The delivery of the VMI requests might be intercepted by CSP, and they might use the intercepted data to replay the VMI requests. The CSP might also forge VMI requests to get the state of the VM.

2. The VMM might arbitrarily access the physical memory of the user's VM and use VMI to get sensitive information. As VMM has higher privilege than the VM, it is hard to prevent by traditional cloud architecture.
3. The result of the VMI operations might be intercepted by VMM, as the results would finally be sent via physical network which is controlled by VMM.

To counter these threats, our proposed architecture use following methods:

1. The VMI operations need the participation of the CSP, but only to locate the position of the cloud server to which the VM locates, which requires only the User-ID and VM-ID. The VMI command is encrypted by a user key and always kept secret to CSP.
2. The memory access of the VM is strictly controlled by a hardware access control list located in physical memory and protected by CPU. The memory to store the ACL table is initialized before the VMM launches and only accessible to the CPU.
3. The VMI results are encrypted using a CPU key and only the user can decrypt it.

The trust root of our architecture is the new designed CPU, which reserves a part of physical memory to store ACL and control the access to VM memory, and provides a remote control mechanism for the user to adjust the policy of ACL.

4   Architecture

To overcome the limits of HyperWall, we propose a new controllable VMI architecture based on hardware support. The core idea is to separate the memory of VMM and VM by similar solutions with HyperWall, and enable VMI access to VM memory by stripping VMI from VMM to a separate VM and authorize the VMI VM to access target VM memory when there is a request from cloud user. The VMI Server can be kept reliable by trust initialization and persist integrity monitoring. Our architecture is shown in Fig. 1.

The main process of our architecture consists of the following steps.

1. The user sends its VMI request to cloud manager. The request is a 3-tuple consists of User-ID, VM-ID and VMI command, with the command encrypted using a public key EKvm and can only decrypted by server CPU with private key DKvm. The command is a set of security related instructions, such as process list and network connection list.
2. After receiving the request of user, the cloud manager will look up the corresponding relationship between (User-ID, VM-ID) and physical machine, thus locating the physical machine where the VM is. Then the cloud manager sending the request to the physical machine.
3. On receiving VMI request from cloud server, the physical CPU adjusts the ACL to enable VMI server's access to the VM's memory and decrypted the VMI request.

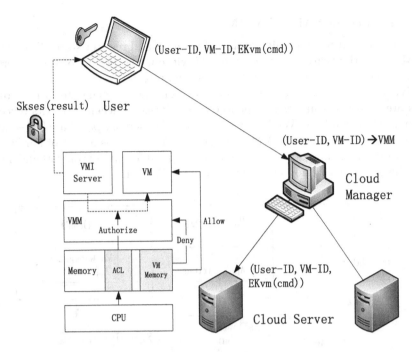

Fig. 1. Architecture of controllable VMI (VMI as a service)

4. On receiving plaintext request, the VMI server would look up the ACL list to see if the vm belongs to the user and executes the VMI command. Then encrypt the result and return it to the user. As the result is encrypted using a session key (SKses), the VMM or CSP cannot decrypt it.

5. There would be a counter calculating the fails of VMI requests on user side as the CSP might just discard the VMI requests or results. So if there are too many failures, the user can stop the execution of the VM. Another counter exists in the server side recording the number of VMI requests and is sent to user with the VMI results. So if there are any forged VMI requests, the user can discover it through the change of the counter.

5 Implementation

Our architecture mainly consists of three parts, including the memory isolation of VM and VMM, the VMI control mechanism and the establishment of secret communication channel. We will discuss them in the following parts. To disallow memory sharing between VMM and VMs, we proposed an memory isolation mechanism in Sect. 5.1. To enable and control VMI Server's access to the VM memory, we designed our access control list (ACL) which will be discussed in Sect. 5.2. And to enable secure communication between the VMI Server and the user, we enhanced the secure communication channel of HyperWall in Sect. 5.3.

5.1 Isolation of VM and VMM

The context VMI need mainly consists of memory and register state. To prevent VMM from arbitrarily introspect the VM without the permit of the owner of the VM, memory and register state should be protected.

Hyperwall encrypts the general purpose registers and generates a hash over the state so as to ensure its confidentiality and integrity when VM exits (except for that of hypercall) [3]. While to memory, a VM's memory pages are locked and protected by CPU when the VM is initialized. And there is a part of hardware-only accessible memory to store the CIP table (used for access control) and TEC table (used for attestation and logging) of the VM memory.

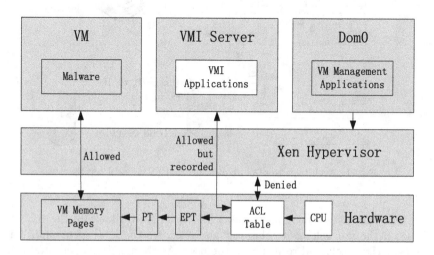

Fig. 2. Memory Isolation of VM and VMM

To disable VMM access to VM memory while in the same time keep the ability of introspecting a VM, we use the disjunctive VMI model proposed in [9]. The core idea is to move the VMI applications from VMM to a separate VM so as to reduce the size of TCB. The security of VM where VMI applications are deployed can be ensured by varies of methods, including security boot and integrity checking based on TPM, minimal kernel design to reduce the attack surface and even the latest Intel SGX to protect VMI applications from being tampered. By using SGX to execute VMI applications in enclaves, we can isolate the VMI application from being accessed by the kernel and other applications of the same VMI server. As shown in Fig. 2, and the others being untrusted. The CPU is the root of the trust chain and the trust relationship is controlled and transmitted by the ACL table.

5.2 VMI Control Mechanism

HyperWall control the access of VM memory by CIP table. To enable VMM access the VM memory, we just need to remove the HD (Hypervisor Deny)

Protection bit of the corresponding pages. Different from HyperWall, HyperCoffer adjust the policy of VM-shim to authorize access to its memory. By using *raw_ld* and *raw_st* instructions, the VMM can directly load the VM memory. Both the method of HyperWall and HyperCoffer will break the isolation again and give the VMM opportunity to subvert the VM and that's why we use a disjunctive VMI model as discussed in above section.

We use a tailored access control method of HyperWall to implement the access control of VMI requests. To enable VMI server access the VM memory, we add a ID (introspection deny) option to the protection field of the ACL. To enable users' attestation to the VMI actions, we add a counter field to the ACL table, which is used to record the VMI times.

Table 1. Fields in ACL table

Fields	Content	Length
MA	Machine address	48 bit
GPA	Guest physical address	48 bit
VMID	VM identifier, generated by CPU when VM is created	8 bit
In-use	Controls whether the page is usable	1 bit
Protection	Controls whether the page is accessible by VMM or VMI server	2 bit
Counts	Record the times of this page being accessed by VMI server	21 bit

The detailed component of VMI access control list (ACL) is shown in Table 1. The VMI Server deploys VMI applications in Enclave which are protected by SGX from the VMM or other applications and kernel of the VMI Server. After the hardware receive the VMI requests, it will enable memory share with VMI Server by removing the ID protection, then deliver the requests to the VMI Server. When the VMI requests arrive at VMI Server, the VMI applications parses the requests and maps the memory pages of the introspected VM to its own memory space. After that, the VMI applications are able to read the VM memory and extract the security related information. After the VMI operations, the counter field of the VM pages in ACL will increase. The VMI results and the counter are encrypted and sent back to user via secret communication channel, which will be discussed in detail in the following section. The user can compare the counter to verify that the VMI Server has introspect the VM as he/her requires, instead of arbitrarily introspecting the VM without the permit of the user.

5.3 Secret Communication Channel

HyperCoffer provides no secure communication routine between the user and VM. So we just discuss and improve the method of HyperWall. The keys we used during secret communication channel building are listed in Table 2.

Table 2. Keys in secure remote communication

Key	Function
SK_{cpu}	Encrypt other keys, enclave memory. Sign VMI and attestation results
(EK_{vm}, DK_{vm})	Public-private key pair used to build secure communication between user and VM
$Cert$	Certificate of CPU, issued by hardware manufactory, can verify the signature's validity of SKcpu
SK_{ses}	Session key, used to encrypt communication between user and VM

Secret communication channel is essential in securely transferring information between remote users and the VMI server. As the VMM can intercept these communications, it might suffer MITM attack. To counter this threat, user's data is send to VM via public-private key pair (EK_{vm}, DK_{vm}) so as to defend against MITM attack. The key pair is generated during VM initialization and the public key EK_{vm} is signed by CPU with its key SK_{cpu}, user verifies the sign using CPU's certificate to make sure the EK_{vm} is coming from the VM, which is very similar to SSL protocol.

HyperWall states that the user can establish secret channel using the EK_{vm}. However, as the VMM can intercept the EK_{vm} during the above handshake process, it can forge VMI requests and decrypt communication which is encrypted using DK_{vm}. So we cannot directly use DK_{vm} to encrypt the result data. Instead we add another modification to the process of HyperWall. After getting EK_{vm}, the user generates a session key and encrypts it with EK_{vm}, then send it to VMI server. After the VM server get that, they can establish secret channel using the session key. As the session key changes whenever a new VMI request is made, the VMM is unable to execute replay attack.

6   Security Analysis

Isolation is ensured by architecture support. We setup different separated memory regions for VMM and VMs, while keeping a ACL table to enable VMI server with necessary access to VMs' memory. This ACL table is controlled by CPU, thus disabling VMM from tampering or snooping on it.

The confidentiality of VMI applications is ensured by moving them into enclaves, which is provided by Intel SGX feature. This can disable the possible vulnerabilities of the VMI server which might affect the VMI applications as it might be compromised by an attacker. The confidentiality of communications is ensured using a modified SSL protocol. This can disable the VMM from replaying the VMI requests or snooping the VMI results.

Integrity is measured when the VM is created and can be attested in the runtime by user. The details are the same with HyperWall, so we will not discussed them again as our main job is to enable VMI in untrusted cloud, instead of integrity protecting.

Availability is not a goal of our architecture. Anyhow, availability is what the cloud provides, without it there is no chance for the survival of the CSP.

7   Performance Evaluation

The main additional performance cost by our architecture is introduced by SGX encryption and ACL of memory. The encryption cost of SGX MEE (memory encryption engine) is evaluated by Intel, which is between 2.2% to 12%, with average 5.5% for SPECINT 2006 test [10].

As the ACL of memory happens only during VMI operations, VM creation, interruption and termination, it will have little impact on the overall CPU performance during VM running. As our ACL mechanism is similar to that of Hyperwall, the access overhead is similar too. In the worst case, it would introduce 36% additional memory accesses during hypervisor boot, but it will only introduce less than 15% additional memory during the whole life cycle of VMs [3].

However, our architecture will cost more memory (DRAM) space to store the ACL table than Hyperwall. Each ACL entry is 14 bytes large as shown in Table 1, for a physical server with 32 GB memory and 4 KB page size, there would need $32\,GB/4\,KB * 14\,byte = 112\,MB$ space to store the ACL, compared with 4MB of Hyperwall [3]. As the DRAM is cheap enough, this storage cost is affordable.

Overall, our architecture will introduce less than 20% additional overhead to enable VMI operations while in the same time enforce access control from VMM to VMs. The practical performance cost depends on the type of VMI applications and VMI frequencies.

8   Conclusion

We designed a controllable VMI architecture on untrusted cloud. Relative works either totally prevent the VMI operations when the cloud is untrusted or enable VMI operations when the cloud is trusted. In fact, with new hardware support such as SGX, we are able to trust the VMI applications while distrust the VMM layer. Besides, we use our former proposed disjunctive VMI model [9] to provide VMI as a service.

We integrated SGX into HyperWall, so as to accomplish a two layer security. The first layer is the isolation provided by architecture support of VM memory and VMM memory, thus disabling VMM from introspecting VM. The second layer is the isolation between VMI applications and other components of the VMI server, including the OS kernel and other applications. The second layer is used to protect the key security tools from being tampered by malware on the same VM, which is often the case when there are system vulnerabilities.

We modified HyperWall to better support controllable VMI and audit. We add two key fields, ID and count, with the former one controls whether a page is able to be accessed by a VMI server, the later one records the introspection behavior so as to provide attestation to user. We enhanced the original secure communication channel by introducing an additional session key which is randomly changed during each VMI requests, thus disabling forged VMI requests or replay attacks by VMM.

9   Future Work

As Sect. 7 analyzes, the overhead is mainly caused by two aspects, namely encryption and decryption of enclave memory, and ACL policy enforcement. However, implementation and quantitative performance analysis are still needed to further evaluate our architecture's performance in practical usage. Because of the lack of open source simulation tool for this comprehensive architecture, we need to further investigate similar works and modify related simulators to analysis our work in quantity.

References

1. Garfinkel, T., Rosenblum, M., et al.: A virtual machine introspection based architecture for intrusion detection. In: NDSS, vol. 3, pp. 191–206 (2003)
2. Yao, F., Campbell, R.H.: CryptVMI: encrypted virtual machine introspection in the cloud. In: 2014 IEEE 7th International Conference on Cloud Computing (CLOUD), pp. 977–978. IEEE (2014)
3. Szefer, J., Lee, R.B.: Hardware-enhanced security for cloud computing. In: Jajodia, S., Kant, K., Samarati, P., Singhal, A., Swarup, V., Wang, C. (eds.) Secure Cloud Computing, pp. 57–76. Springer, Heidelberg (2014)
4. Xia, Y., Liu, Y., Chen, H.: Architecture support for guest-transparent vm protection from untrusted hypervisor and physical attacks. In: 2013 IEEE 19th International Symposium on High Performance Computer Architecture (HPCA2013), pp. 246–257. IEEE (2013)
5. Anati, I., Gueron, S., Johnson, S., Scarlata, V.: Innovative technology for CPU based attestation and sealing. In: Proceedings of the 2nd International Workshop on Hardware and Architectural Support for Security and Privacy, p. 10 (2013)
6. Baumann, A., Peinado, M., Hunt, G.: Shielding applications from an untrusted cloud with haven. In: USENIX Symposium on Operating Systems Design and Implementation (OSDI) (2014)
7. Schuster, F., Costa, M., Fournet, C., Gkantsidis, C., Peinado, M., Mainar-Ruiz, G., Russinovich, M.: VC3: Trustworthy data analytics in the cloud using SGX (2015)
8. Dinh, A., Saxena, P., Chang, E.-C., Ooi, B.C., Zhang, C.: M2R: Enabling stronger privacy in mapreduce computation. In: 24th USENIX Security Symposium (USENIX Security 2015), Washington, DC (2015)
9. Shi, J., Yang, Y., Li, C.: A disjunctive VMI model based on XSM. In: The Fifth International Symposium on Cloud and Service Computing (2015)
10. Gueron, S.: A memory encryption engine suitable for general purpose processors, Cryptology ePrint Archive, Report 2016/204 (2016). http://eprint.iacr.org/2016/204

IacCE: Extended Taint Path Guided Dynamic Analysis of Android Inter-App Data Leakage

Tianjun Wu$^{(\boxtimes)}$ and Yuexiang Yang

College of Computer, National University of Defense Technology,
Changsha 410073, China
{wutianjun08,yyx}@nudt.edu.cn

Abstract. There exists a need for overall security analysis of a set of apps. We demonstrate IacCE, a tool implementing our approach that applies concolic execution on combined apps guided by extended Inter-App taint paths. Furthermore, we replay the event-and-input generated by concolic execution on the original app set, to monitor the actual data-leakage behavior. To our knowledge, we are the first to apply concolic execution for dynamic analysis of Inter-App communications.

Keywords: Inter-App communication · Android application · Dynamic analysis · Concolic execution · Static taint analysis

1 Introduction

Android is by far the most ubiquitous mobile operating system, and we are witnessing a surge in the adoption of Android applications (also called *apps*). The situation for app security is severe, due to the weakness of the permission system and the programming model. The Inter-Component communication model for instance, which is used as an efficient data-exchange mechanism for loosely-coupled apps, might be misused to leak private data outside the device without user consent.

There are growing efforts for analyzing Android apps, aimed at discovering such safety issues as malware behavior and application vulnerabilities. Static app analysis tools, such as the static taint analysis tool FlowDroid [4], can efficiently analyze all the code in the application, but they are inherently imprecise as there may be behavior misses or falsely behavior report. Dynamic analysis tools, such as TaintDroid [29], avoid those shortcomings, but are relatively slow as they have to run the code, and are inherently incomplete as they can only tell the behavior that they execute [18–20].

Despite those researches on single app security, there are few tools for Inter-App vulnerability analysis. Literature [3] performed an investigation on 500 apps from Google Play [24], F-Droid [25], Bazaar [26], and MalGenome [27]. It found that only 32 percent of acquired permissions are necessary for API calls and averagely each app has about two unchecked but used permissions. This incurs a vulnerable path from the exported interface of the app component to the API use, which can be exploited by the interaction of the app with other apps. Issues related to this kind of vulnerability already exist, such as collusion attacks and privilege escalation chaining [28]. The need for overall security analysis of a set of apps exists.

© ICST Institute for Computer Sciences, Social Informatics and Telecommunications Engineering 2017
R. Deng et al. (Eds.): SecureComm 2016, LNICST 198, pp. 317–333, 2017.
DOI: 10.1007/978-3-319-59608-2_19

Thus, in this paper, we propose the first tool named "IacCE" (analyzing Inter-App Communications using Concolic Execution) that dynamically analyze Inter-App data leakage by combining static taint analysis and cocolic execution. We first apply static Inter-App data-flow analysis on the combined app of the app set, then generate inputs and events to execute sensitive Inter-App paths by extended-taint-path guided concolic execution, finally dynamically verify the leakage by executing apps in the app set with those generated inputs and events.

The contribution of this paper is three fold. First, to our knowledge, we are the first to apply concolic execution for dynamic analysis of Inter-App communications. Our combination of static taint analysis and concolic execution achieves higher precision and recall than state-of-the-art tools. Second, we developed IacCE, an open-source tool for Inter-Component and Inter-App dynamic analysis. Third, we compose a benchmark based on DroidBench [22] and ICC-Bench [23] for better assessment of Inter-Component and Inter-App analyzers with 77 apps.

2 Background

Android Basis. Android defines four types of app component, i.e., *Activity* (defining user interface), *Service* (performing background processing), *ContentProvider* (managing database), and *BroadcastReceiver* (receiving Inter-App broadcast messages). There are discontinuities within a component, which are used to drive apps with runtime *events* (system events or user interactions) and *life-cycle callbacks* (state transition of an app) from Android framework, besides the traditional input form of *data inputs*. Android provides specific methods, for triggering Inter-Component communications (*ICC*) and Inter-App communications (*IAC*). These methods are called with *Intent*, which specifies the *action, category, mimetype, data*, etc. Intent can be either *explicit* or *implicit* by define the receiver component or not. Components determine which Intent to receive by specifying an *Intent Filter*. Android permission system identifies the privileges of an app in the manifest file.

Static Taint Analysis. Static taint analysis starts at a sensitive source (location get by *getLastKnownLocation()*, for instance) and then tracks the sensitive data through the app until it reaches a sensitive sink (e.g. the *sendTextMessage()* API) [4]. It gives precise information about which data may be leaked.

Concolic Execution. *Concolic* (concrete + symbolic) *execution* (or dynamic symbolic execution) uses a combination of concrete and symbolic execution to analyze how input values flow through a program as it executes, and uses this analysis to identify other inputs that can result in alternative execution behaviors [10]. It traces symbolic registers at each conditional statement in order to build path conditions for specific execution traces. After collecting path constraints, a constraint solver is used for solving them and the result is just the program input we desire.

3 Motivating Example

To motivate and illustrate our approach, consider the app set "SWE" (SendSMS, WriteFile, and Echoer) in Fig. 1, which leaks data through Inter-App communication. The apps are inspired those used by IccTA [1] and DidFail [2], but further contain several challenging issues for existing static analysis methods as described in [3].

```
(A)
public class SendSMS extends Activity {
    protected void onCreate(Bundle savedInstanceState) {
        ...
        Button b = (Button) findViewById(R.id.b);
        b.setOnClickListener(new OnClickListener(){
            public void onClick(View v) {
                Intent i = new Intent(Intent.ACTION_SEND);
                i.setType("text/plain");
                String uid = (TelephonyManager)
getSystemService(Context.TELEPHONY_SERVICE).getDeviceId();// SRC
                StringBuilder sb = new StringBuilder();
                sb.append("secret");
                sb.append("1");// SRC
                i.putExtra(sb.toString(), uid);
                this.startActivityForResult(i, 0);// SNK
            }
        });
    }
    protected void onActivityResult(int rq, int rs, Intent i) {
        ...
        String msg = i.getExtras().getString("secret1");// SRC
        SmsManager.getDefault().sendTextMessage("10086",, msg,,);// SNK
        ...
    }
}
```

```
(C)
public class Echoer extends Activity {
    protected void onCreate(Bundle savedInstanceState) {
        ...
        Button b = (Button) findViewById(R.id.b);
        b.setOnClickListener(new OnClickListener(){
            public void onClick(View v) {
                // check emul
                if (!android.os.Build.BOARD.contains("goldfish")) {
                    Intent i = getIntent();// SRC
                    this.setResult(0, i);// SNK
                }
            }
        });
    }
}
```

```
(B)
public class WriteFile extends Activity {
    protected void onCreate(Bundle savedInstanceState) {
        ...
        Button b = (Button) findViewById(R.id.b);
        b.setOnClickListener(new OnClickListener(){
            public void onClick(View v) {
                Intent i = new Intent(Intent.ACTION_SEND);
                i.setType("text/plain");
                String curl.oc = (LocationManager)
this.act.getSystemService(Context.LOCATION_SERVICE).getLastKnownLoc
ation(LocationManager.GPS_PROVIDER).toString();
                i.putExtra("secret2", curl.oc);
                this.startActivityForResult(i, 0);// SNK
            }
        });
    }
    protected void onActivityResult(int rq, int rs, Intent i) {
        StringBuilder sb = new StringBuilder();
        sb.append("secret");
        sb.append("2");
        String sinkData = data.getExtras().getString(sb.toString());// SRC
        FileOutputStream outputStream;
        ...
        // check perm
        if (checkCallingPermission("android.permission.WRITE_EXTE
RNAL_STORAGE")==PackageManager.PERMISSION_GRANTED) {
            outputStream.write(sinkData.getBytes());// SNK
        }
    }
}
```

Fig. 1. Code snippets of the app set SWE.

The SendSMS app get device's id by calling the sensitive API *getDeviceId()*, and sends the private data to other apps for returned results using the implicit Intent call *startActivityForResult()*. Once some app receives the Intent (as long as the Intent matches its Intent Filter) and replies with exactly the received Intent by calling *setResult()*, the Echoer app for instance, the callback method *onActivityResult()* of SendSMS will be called by Android SDK. This method sends replied data outwards in SMS message by calling the sensitive API *sendTextMessage()*. Note that Android framework requires the SendSMS app declare *READ_PHONE_STATE* and *SEND_SMS* permissions to use those two sensitive APIs, while the Intent receiver app Echoer need none of such declarations. It is similar for the WriteFile app.

Neither SendSMS nor WriteFile can leak private data independently. They rely on Echoer to pass on those data to avoid merely intra-component data flows.

We further add the challenging *stateful operations* in SWE. For example, the field of the Intent that SendSMS sends out contains a key constructed by StringBuilder. This method appends "*1*" to the string "*secrete*". When SendSMS receives the echoed Intent, it only sends out the data specified by the key "*secrete1*" in SMS.

We also include *runtime conditional execution*. For instance, WriteFile checks permission declared by the caller component, and it won't write files if the caller does not have the permission to access SD card. Echoer, for another instance, won't send sensitive data via SMS when resided in an emulator, thus circumventing detection.

4   Analysis Method

The workflow of IacCE can be depicted as Fig. 2, which proceeds as follows.

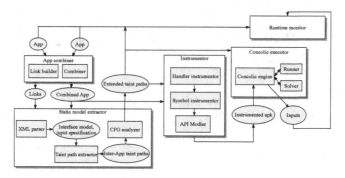

Fig. 2. Overview of IacCE.

- App combination: The apps under analysis are analyzed for IAC/ICC links and are combined as a single app.
- Static model extraction: We extract interface model, input specifications, control flow graph, and sensitive Inter-App paths. We further extend taint paths with implicit-control-flow-dependent event-chains.
- Instrumentation: The combined apk file will be instrumented for Android life-cycle entry points, event handlers, symbolic registers, register-related assignments along the extended taint paths, and user-specified external APIs.
- Concolic execution: It executes the instrumented app in emulator, performs symbolic tracing, and generate app inputs.
- Runtime monitoring: A simple dynamic monitor is implemented by running and observing the original apps with inputs generated by concolic executor.

4.1   App Combination

The first phase of IacCE builds links and combines apps in the set.

(1) ICC link exaction: An ICC link [1] is used to link two components in which the source component contains an ICC method m that holds explicit/implicit Intent information to access the target component C. Our extraction includes identifying ICC methods and Intent information, identifying target components by parsing the Intent

Filters statically declared in manifest file or dynamically defined in Java bytecode, and finally matching ICC methods with target components according to [5].

(2) App combination: In order to perform Inter-App analysis, we combine multiple Android apps to a single app in a naïve way, by extracting components and UI layout files of each app and repacking them into one apk file. This combination eases instrumentation and concolic execution of the apps, because we can consider the apps as a whole without the need of dynamically coordinating them.

4.2   Static Model Extraction

This phase produces following models.

(1) The interface model: It provides information about all input fields, as well as information about the Android IPC message (i.e., Intent) handled by Activities. All Android components contained in the app and Intent information can be decided by parsing the manifest file. Input fields can be obtained from the layout XML files.

(2) The Inter-App taint paths: Those paths cross app-boundaries before combination. They are computed by performing taint flow analysis on the connected app code. Blindly execution of all possible program paths is boring, and instructions which transmit sensitive information are better places which deserve our focus.

Before path extraction, we need to do some connection. Each ICC method call will be replaced with an instantiation of the target component with the appropriate Intent. And a dummyMain method will be generated for each component where all the life-cycle and callback methods are modeled.

After specifying sensitive source-and-sink APIs, we can then apply static taint flow analysis to find out all those Inter-App taint paths. For more details please refer to [1].

(3) The extended taint paths:

Firstly, we add supportive method calls to the paths. Taint paths only contain taint-data transmitting instructions, which may be not able to execute all by themselves. For the example shown in Fig. 3, the taint path we get is {*getDevId*, i1} => {*sendSMS*, i2}. We need additionally include callers of *getDevId()* and *sendSMS()*, that is, *onCreate()* and *onResume()* for *getDevId()*, and *onClick(b2)* for *sendSMS()*.

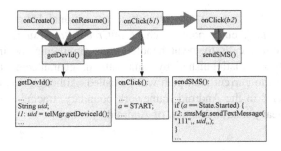

Fig. 3. Example of taint path extension. (Color figure online)

Secondly, we consider supportive event-chain extension, which is inspired by [9]. We examine implicit-control-flow dependent events with regard to the branch conditions of those extracted taint paths, for which we here only consider channels of static fields. Other channels such as file system and network should be future works. We say two events are dependent when the field read by one event is previous written by the other. For each dependency, we added a directed edge. As shown in Fig. 3, the event handler *onClick(b2)* contains a branch condition that depends on the global variable *a*. The require value *START* for *a* is set by the event handler *onClick(b1)*. Thus, the taint path will additionally include the edge {onClick(*b1*),} => {onClick(*b2*),}, where *b1* and *b2* are two distinct button instances.

The extended taint path for the example in Fig. 3 is depicted in red bold line.

4.3   Java Bytecode Instrumentation

The app is mostly executed normally, while only some variables have to be traced symbolically. To achieve this, instrumentation is needed, as illustrated by Fig. 4.

```
public class MainActivity extends Activity {
...
    protected void onCreate(android.os.Bundle)
    {
        Expression _sym_tmp_1 = null, $r2$sym, $z0$sym;
        MainActivity $r0 := @this: MainActivity;
        Button1Listener $r1 = new Button1Listener;
        ...
        a3targs$symargs = argpop(0, 0, 2);
        $r2$sym = models.strVar$sym;// Modeling user-specified external APIs or fields
        String $r2 = strVar;
        $r2 = getSolution_string("$X$sym_sample_vars__java_lang_String_strVar");// Injecting solutions
        $z0$sym = _contains($r2$sym, null, $r2, "pwd");// Symbolizing registers
        boolean $z0 = $r2.contains("pwd");
        _sym_tmp_1 = $z0$sym;
        if $z0 == 0 goto label1;// Symbolizing path conditions
        assume(_sym_tmp_1, 0, 0);
        .../* SNK API */
    label1:
        assume(_sym_tmp_1, 0, 1);
        goto label2;
    label2:
        View $r3 = new View($r0.getApplicationContext());
        $r1.onClick($r3);// Inserting calls to event handlers
        return;
    }
}
```

Fig. 4. A sample code after instrumentation. Method summaries are simplified for reading.

(1) Inserting calls to event handlers: It is an optional heuristic to instrument component's default entry point, such as *onCreate()/onResume()* of Activity, to allowing for direct calls to event handlers thus simulating the injection of raw events. Events are distinguished by taint-path id, guaranteeing that only event handlers related to current taint path will be called. Although it is more general to inject raw events in the Android framework boundary, tracing the extra injection path require heavy instrumentation of Android system.

(2) Symbolizing registers, assignments and path conditions: This prepares for symbolic tracing, dumping path conditions, and overwriting registers with solutions at runtime. We need instrument registers, assignments and path conditions with their symbolic counterparts. However, we do not instrument all these occurrences in the app, rather than limit to those on the extended taint paths. We symbolically trace input-tainted variables within components as well as through Intent bundles.

(3) Modeling user-specified external APIs or fields: We specify user inputs such as UI text field according to the interface model we get in the static model extraction phase, to enable symbolic tracing of them. Besides, the target app might call external APIs or fields which may be hard to be symbolized. We model those user-specified APIs or fields by replacing the actual API methods with stub methods which return certain concrete values or even symbolic variable.

(4) Injecting solutions: After constraint solver find a solution, we replace each symbolic register or model w.r.t. the r-value of the original assignment with its corresponding solution. This is done by inserting method calls in the form of *getSolution_Xxx(String symVarName)*, where *"Xxx"* is a certain variable type.

4.4 Concolic Execution

We run and symbolically trace the instrumented combined app in Android emulators. Our extended-taint-path (ETP, for short) guided concolic execution iteratively does following procedures as depicted in Algorithm 1.

For each ETP, we first generate symbolic model/input configuration according to interface model which specifies user inputs. Secondly, the emulator's environment is cleaned and the instrumented combined apk is installed. Thirdly, we determine the default entry component by finding the root's containing component for each ETP. And then we start the component via am-start command. Fourthly, the solutions to inputs and modeled APIs will be injected into symbolic registers in the instrumented app[*]. When execution deviates from the intended taint path by branching to the wrong basic block, we dump conditions over symbolic registers in a path condition[*], negate the last clause of the path condition[*1], and then feed the resulted path constraint to a SMT solver for a new solution of concrete register values leading to execution of the intended basic block. Iterate above steps until we hit the sink API for each taint path.

Note that our concolic execution is enforced only along the ETP, which avoids the notorious problem of path explosion and drives execution only along data-transmitting paths.

---

[1] These steps marked with the superscript "*" will be done by the instrumented app itself, rather than by the concolic engine.

Algorithm 1. ETP guided concolic execution
Input: ETP:extended taint paths, IM:interface model APK:instrumented combined apk,
Output: In:data inputs, Ev:event inputs
1 model ← getInputAndModel(IM)
2 i ← 0
3 **foreach** path **in** EPT.getPaths() **do**
4 **do**
5   In[i] ← {}, Ev[i] ← {}
6   clean()
7   install(APK)
8   entry ← getEntry(ETP)
9   startComponent(entry)
10   path ← EPT.getNextPath()
11   Ev[i].add(path.getHandlers())
12   In[i].add(getSolution(model))
13 **while** !isSnkHit()
14 i ← i+1
15**end**
16**return** In,Ev

4.5   Runtime Monitoring

Although we can just directly observe the behavior of the instrumented combined app, we should further ensure that discovered Inter-App data leaks do happen for the original apps. What is more, vendors often do not expect that data-leak issues rendered by analyst are merely related to a modified or combined version of the original app set.

```
# start entry component
adb shell am start -n app1/app1.MainActivity

# tap button1
Tap(248.0,351.0)
UserWait(4000)

# set GPS
adb -s emulator-5554 emu geo fix 121.420413 31.215345

# tap button 2
Tap(279.0,493.0)
UserWait(4000)

# send sms
adb shell am start -a android.intent.action.SENDTO -d
sms:10086 --es sms_body "secrete" --es exit_on_sent true

# press sender key to submit
adb shell input keyevent 66
```

Fig. 5. An example of Monkey scripts and am commands.

We inject events and inputs through Android Debug Bridge (adb) [11], step by step along each extended taint path, without any repacking of the original apps.

Firstly, according to the triggering order of events and inputs along the path, we generate a script for each path which contains directly injectable events. For instance, it can be a Monkey script [12] for UI events according to their location on the screen, or may be a list of the Activity Manager tool (am) [13] commands for system events according to their concrete types and the solutions to event parameters. Note that as the resolution and size of emulator's screen is fully under control, we can statically determine the location of UI widgets according to their layout files. The mixed scripts and commands shown in Fig. 5 is an example of a test that we generate.

Then, we replay UI events and system events on the original app set, by means of separate mechanisms. Raw UI events are injected directly to the emulator using the monkeyrunner tool [12]. System events are triggered using am. Specifically, we need to send an explicit Intent by am to launch the entry component of the current taint path.

Text inputs are regarded as the combination of UI events. For example, when injecting a text-input solution to an editable text widget, we generate such sequence of events as tapping the editable text widget, typing each character of the solution string by tap the corresponding soft/hard key, and typing the submitting soft/hard key.

For those modeled environment-dependent APIs or fields which cannot be directly injected, such as emulator checkers or timing bombs, we set them with the solution we get from the SMT solver facilitated by Android InstrumentationTestRunner [14].

Finally, by observing the triggered behavior for each taint paths, we can confirm the existence of data-leakage in our original app set.

5   Implementation Details

5.1   IC3 and AppCombiner

The ICC links are built by IC3 [16] and stored in database for further analysis of Inter-Component/Inter-App taint paths. ApkCombiner [17] takes all apps in the target app set as input, and outputs a combined app.

5.2   IccTA (Modified)

We use IccTA [1] to extract the Inter-App taint paths. To seamlessly integrate the static analysis process with concolic executor, we modify IccTA to store paths in the global *ArrayList* structure resided in the main entry of instrumentor. Along with that, we extract interface model and extend taint paths, thus avoiding preparing Soot [15] structures in memory for many times.

5.3   Instrumentor

We borrow ConDroid's [8] instrumentation utility, which in fact is inherited from Acteve [8]. For methods along the extended taint paths, we implement path-sensitive event-handler instrumentation, symbolic tracing of various variable types, input symbolization, and Android SDK and third-party libraries instrumentation.

5.4   Concolic Executor

We used Acteve [8] as our concolic execution engine. Extended-taint-path guided execution is already guaranteed by our customized instrumentation, while more works are involved to determine the entry component of the combined app, and to store event-and-input sequence for runtime replaying.

When encountering input-related objects which require complex instantiation, such as strings created by StringBuilder and intent data contained in Bundle, we symbolically trace them by modeling the instantiation operations of the data structure.

When those complex objects are not input-related, to avoid missing *true positive*, just add paths from intent with complex key to receiver. We are not worried about the might resulted *false positive*, as we can directly observing whether those paths actually leak data in the runtime monitor.

We integrate the string-constraint solving via z3-str SMT solver, by referring to the code of ConDroid [6] which introduces a back-tracing procedure for semantically richer solutions to registers of boolean type.

5.5   Runtime Monitor

For runtime monitor, we write a generator of Monkey scripts and am commands. It reads path information and solutions from concolic executor. We replay events and inputs contained in those scripts and commands, and observe the dynamic behavior of the whole app set.

6   Experimental Evaluation

In the following subsections, we evaluate how IacCE can be used to automatically drive sensitive data transmission, how IacCE compares with existing tools, and what capabilities IacCE has to analyze real-world apps.

6.1   Case Study: The SWE App Set

To demonstrate its capabilities in practice, we first evaluate IacCE on the SWE example described in Sect. 3. IacCE analyzes the set as follows.

- *Inter-App taint analysis*

    Two Inter-App taint paths will be extracted for the combined app. Methods containing instructions along those two paths are *SendSMS$1.onClick(View) => Echoer $1.onClick(View) => SendSMS.onActivityResult(int,int,Intent)* and *WriteFile$1. onClick(View) => Echoer$1.onClick(View) => WriteFile.onActivityResult(int,int, Intent)*.

- *Extending Inter-App taint paths*

    Supportive life-cycle handlers are added. As there exists none static-field-related event dependency, no extra extension is needed.

- *Instrumentation for event-handler calls*

Take SendSMS for example. The invocation *"ocl.onClick(view);"* is inserted at the end of *SendSMS.onCreate(Bundle)*, where *ocl* is an anonymous instance of *OnClickListener* and *view* is created according to the app context.

- *Symbolization, symbolic tracing, and solution injection*

The API/field *android.os.Build.BOARD* is path-condition related. It is modeled and to be symbolic traced during concolic execution. Every statement along taint paths will be instrumented to have its symbolic counterpart. A solution will overwrite the variable storing *BOARD*, when there is any. The instrumented code is similar to that of Fig. 4. For each path, concolic executor iteratively performs following steps until hitting the sink APIs. Just take the first path as example:

- *Concolic execution*

We perform concrete execution of the combined app along with the symbolic tracing of the modeled *BOARD* field. As with an emulator, the branch condition in Echoer will not be taken. The path constraint *"not (Contains Xsym_an-droid_os_Build__java_lang_String_BOARD "goldfish")"* is dumped as the sink API is not hit.

- *Solving path consraints*

The SMT solver find a solution string, say *"abc"*, which is injected into the variable storing the value retrieved from the *BOARD* field.

- *Hitting the sink API*

As there is no other symbolic-variable related branch on the Inter-App taint path, the sink *sendTextMessage("10086",,msg,)* is hit in the second run of concolic execution. The iteration for the first path will then stop.

Since no symbolic-variable related branch exists for the second path, concolic execution degrades to simple concrete execution. As no relative permission granted, the branch checking the permission of Echoer in WriteFile is not taken. Thus, the sink *write(sinkData.getBytes())* will never be hit, and the leakage implied by the second taint path does not happen.

- *Replaying inputs and monitoring data-leakage*

All apps in SWE are installed in a fresh emulator. We launch the root component of the first path, i.e., SendSMS, by running an am command that sends to it an explicit starting Intent. The UI events, i.e., successive taps on the buttons, are injected via a Monkey script. The field *BOARD* is set as the solved string *"abc"*. A message containing device id is observed to be sent, and we confirm the first path as Inter-App data-leaking.

6.2 Comparison with Existing Tools

Subject Apps. We choose two benchmarks, one contains **40** apps from DroidBench [22], ICC-Bench [23], and the SWE app set; the other with **77** apps is an improved version of the first one. DroidBench and ICC-Bench are frequently used as ground truth to evaluate data-leakage analyzers. DroidBench has lately added 3 app sets for evaluating IAC analyzers. As these naïve apps are initially composed for static analysis, no branches appear on any data-flow paths. Therefore, we duplicate those apps (except SWE) into two groups, and each sensitive-API call in those apps is enclosed by an additional branch condition. The resulted apps along with SWE comprise our second benchmark. All added branch conditions in one group are satisfiable, while those in the other group cannot be satisfied at runtime.

As IAC and ICC are essentially the same, we also evaluate the efficacy of existing analyzers on ICC leaks.

We compare IacCE with three existing tools: FlowDroid, IccTA, and ConDroid. We manually match the Intra-Component results of FlowDroid to report ICC leaks, just like [1] did. As with ConDroid, we add support for other components besides Activity and instrumentation of explicit intent call to enable ICC analysis, which are all described in the paper [7] while not implemented in the provided source code. We guide ConDroid with taint flows analyzed by IccTA instead of targeted call graph. COVERT is not considered as it does not perform data-leakage analysis.

For each tool on the first benchmark, each precision is 27.4%, 93.9%, 100%, and 100%, and each recall is 60.6%, 93.9%, 48.5%, and 100%.[2] The result on the second benchmark is detailedly given in Table 1.

(a) FlowDroid misses lots of ICC flows and all IAC leakages, as it cannot produce precise data-flow traces, even in the case where the components are within a single app. *(b)* ConDroid, as a dynamic methodology, reports no false positive. However, it misses a large number of leakages as it does not solve the problem of symbolically tracing implicit ICC Intents, not to mention those explicit and implicit IAC Intents. *(c)* IccTA performs well on the first benchmark of simple apps. The precision sharply degrades on the second benchmark, due to the inefficacy of static analysis for determining whether those added branch conditions on taint paths will be satisfied at runtime. *(d)* IacCE achieves higher precision and recall. It reports no false positive as it dynamically observes the execution of apps. And it does not miss any leakages as it performs conservative static taint path extraction for complicated state-full operations. **However, the 100% result does not mean IacCE always detect exactly all leaks for any app set, as will be described in Sect.** 7.

---

[2] Due to space limitation as well as the relative incapability of evaluating dynamic tools experienced by this benchmark, the result is not included in the paper.

Table 1. Experimental results on the second benchmark. For each app (or app set) and tool, indication of explicit or implicit ICC/IAC, true positive (TP), false positive (FP), and false negative (FN) are listed. Precision (TP/(TP + FP)) and recall (TP/(TP + FN)) are mesmerized.

App name	Explicit?	FlowDroid	IccTA	ConDroid	IacCE
DroidBench (Extended)					
startActivity1	Y	TP, FP(3)	TP, FP	TP	TP
startActivity2	Y	TP, FP(9)	TP, FP	TP	TP
startActivity3	Y	TP, FP(65)	TP, FP	TP	TP
startActivity4	N	FP(4)	–	–	–
startActivity5	N	FP(4)	–	–	–
startActivity6	Y	FP(4)	–	–	–
startActivity7	Y	FP(4)	FP(2)	–	–
startActivityForResult1	Y	TP, FP	TP, FP	TP	TP
startActivityForResult2	Y	TP, FP	TP, FP	TP	TP
startActivityForResult3	Y	TP, FP(3)	TP, FP	TP	TP
startActivityForResult4	Y	TP(2), FP(4)	TP(2), FP(2)	TP(2)	TP(2)
startService1	Y	TP, FP(3)	TP, FP	TP	TP
startService2	Y	TP, FP(3)	TP, FP	TP	TP
bindService1	Y	TP, FP(3)	TP, FP	TP	TP
bindService2	Y	FN	TP, FP	TP	TP
bindService3	Y	FN	TP, FP	TP	TP
bindService4	Y	TP, FP(3), FN	TP(2), FP(2)	TP(2)	TP(2)
sendBroadcast1	N	TP, FP(3)	TP, FP	FN	TP
insert1	N	FN	TP, FP	FN	TP
delete1	N	FN	TP, FP	FN	TP
update1	N	FN	TP, FP	FN	TP
query1	N	FN	TP, FP	FN	TP
startActivity1_src,snk	N	FN	TP, FP	FN	TP
startService1_src,snk	N	FN	TP, FP	FN	TP
sendBroadcast1_src,snk	N	FN	TP, FP	FN	TP
ICC-Bench (extended)					
Explicit1	Y	TP, FP	TP, FP	TP	TP
Implicit1	N	TP, FP	TP, FP	FN	TP
Implicit2	N	TP, FP	TP, FP	FN	TP
Implicit3	N	TP, FP	TP, FP	FN	TP
Implicit4	N	TP, FP	TP, FP	FN	TP
Implicit5	N	TP, FP(3)	TP, FP	FN	TP
Implicit6	N	TP, FP	TP, FP	FN	TP
DynRegister1	N	FN	TP, FP	FN	TP
DynRegister2	N	FN	FN	FN	TP
SWE					
SendSMS,Echoer,WriteFile	N	FN	FP, FN	FN	TP

(continued)

Table 1. (*continued*)

App name	Explicit?	FlowDroid	IccTA	ConDroid	IacCE
Summary					
TP		20	31	16	32
FP		126	34	0	0
FN		13	2	17	0
Precision		13.7%	47.7%	100%	100%
Recall		60.6%	93.9%	48.5%	100%

6.3   Application to Real-World Apps

Although IacCE is only a prototype by far, we successfully dynamically confirm (or eliminate false positives) several suspicious real-world leakages reported by previous static analyzers [1, 3]. Those apps are crawled from Google Play [24] and F-Droid [25].

We here describe an example of our findings. *Ermete SMS* is reported by COVERT to be vulnerable to privilege escalation if it is installed along with *Binaural beats therapy* [3]. In that case, Binaural beats therapy, designed for relaxation, creativity and many other desirable mental states and is without WRITE_SMS permission, sends an Intent with SEND action and text/plain payload data to Ermete SMS, a free web-based text messaging application that has WRITE_SMS permission.

The authors of COVERT, however, had to manually review them to confirm the vulnerability. Rather, IacCE dynamically checks the vulnerability and find it is a false positive as Ermete SMS acctually does not receive the Intent sent by the former app due to Intent field mismatching.

We further compose a malicious app which leaks location through an Intent deliberately constructed to be receivable by Ermete SMS. In this case, IacCE verified that the Inter-App data leakage does take place.

7   Discussion and Limitations

Here are some sources of unsoundness and imprecision of IacCE.

> *(1) Complex object symbolization.* Objects which require complex initialization are difficult to symbolize and trace for symbolic execution. Although concolic execution already elevates this by concretely executing none relevant part of code and only symbolizing a rather small part, there are situations where symbolization of complex object is necessary. Presently, we tackle this problem by modeling some of the most frequently used Android complex objects.
>
> *(2) Native code, reflection and dynamic loading.* Both commercial apps and malicious apps are starting to use native codes, reflection, dynamic loading, and other tricks to hide their real business logic to avoid being analyzed. This is a common issue for all existing static and dynamic analysis tools. Although researchers are trying to solve this, none satisfying solutions are available.
>
> *(3) Remote procedure calls (RPC).* Besides Intent-based ICC/IAC, apps also can communicate through remote procedure calls. The latter induces method-invocation

interaction using stubs which are automatically generated by specifying component interface described in Android's Interface Definition Language (AIDL). RPC is less used than Intent. We plan to support RPC in the future.

8 Related Work

FlowDroid [4] is a state-of-the-art open-source tool for intra-component static taint analysis. It is context-, flow-, object-, and field-sensitive and Android app lifecycle-aware. However, it is confined to single components.

Didfail [2] and IccTA [1] are state-of-the-art tools for statically detecting Android ICC leaks, all based on FlowDroid. IccTA achieves better precision and recall than Didfail. It extracts the ICC links and then modifies the Jimple code of apps to directly connect the components to enable data-flow analysis between components. It then uses FlowDroid to perform high precise intra-component taint analysis and builds a complete control-flow graph of the whole Android application. IccTA allows propagating the context (e.g., the value of Intents) between Android components.

TaintDroid [29] is probably the most prominent tool for dynamic analysis of Android apps. It dynamically traces data leaks occurred during the execution of apps by applying dynamic taint analysis. Such tools are not suited for fully automated analysis since they require user interaction to drive execution of the apps.

AppIntent [6], ConDroid [7] and IntelliDroid [9], however, successfully tackles the problem of automate input generation. They use concolic execution for dynamic analysis of apps. AppIntent identifies paths which incur information leaks and performs concolic execution only on those paths. The notion of event space proposed by AppIntent is incomplete, as it only take method-call like control flow into account. ConDroid is a directed concolic analyzer for dynamic code loading in Android apps. Similar to AppIntent, it performs directed concolic execution. IntelliDroid [7] further extract event dependency according to path conditions to generate event chains.

Only quite recently, tools have emerged for IAC analysis. COVERT [3], one of such tools, detects Inter-App vulnerabilities with static model checking. It mainly performs call graph analysis for privilege escalation vulnerability rather than flow analysis for information leakage. Also, it inherits the drawbacks of static analysis.

9 Conclusion

We proposed a tool for dynamic analysis of Inter-App data leakage. It performs concolic execution guided by extended taint paths extracted by static taint analysis, and then dynamically observe and confirm whether the leakage happens at runtime. Future works include conducting tests on more real-world apps, and analyzing other types of vulnerabilities by applying model checking.

Acknowledgements. The authors would like to thank the reviewers for their detailed reviews and constructive comments, which have helped to improve the quality of this paper. This work was supported by the National Natural Science Foundation of China under Grants No. 61170286, No. 61202486.

References

1. Li, L., Bartel, A., Bissyandé, T.F., Klein, J., Traon, Y.L., Arzt, S.: IccTA: detecting inter-component privacy leaks in android apps. In: International Conference on Software Engineering, pp. 280–291 (2015)
2. Klieber, W., Flynn, L., Bhosale, A., Jia, L., Bauer, L.: Android taint flow analysis for app sets. In: International Workshop on the State of the Art in Java Program Analysis, pp. 1–6 (2014)
3. Bagheri, H., Sadeghi, A., Garcia, J., Malek, S.: Covert: compositional analysis of android inter-app permission leakage. IEEE Trans. Softw. Eng. 41(6), 6–37 (2015)
4. Arzt, S., Rasthofer, S., Fritz, C.: FlowDroid. ACM SIGPLAN Not. 49(6), 259–269 (2014)
5. Android documentation. http://developer.android.com/guide/components/intents-filters. html#Resolution
6. Yang, Z., Yang, M., Zhang, Y.: AppIntent: analyzing sensitive data transmission in android for privacy leakage detection. In: ACM SIGSAC Conference on Computer & Communications Security, pp. 1043–1054 (2013)
7. Schutte, J., Fedler, R., Titze, D.: ConDroid: targeted dynamic analysis of android applications. In: IEEE Conference on Advanced Information Networking and Applications, pp. 571–578 (2015)
8. Anand, S., Naik, M., Harrold, M.J.: Automated concolic testing of smartphone apps. In: International Symposium on the Foundations of Software Engineering, pp. 1–11 (2012)
9. Wong, M.Y.Y.: Targeted dynamic analysis for android malware. Dissertations & Theses Gradworks (2015)
10. Schwartz, E.J., Avgerinos, T., Brumley, D.: All you ever wanted to know about dynamic taint analysis and forward symbolic execution (but might have been afraid to ask). In: IEEE Symposium on Security and Privacy, vol. 7, pp. 317–331 (2010)
11. Android Debug Bridge. http://developer.android.com/tools/help/adb.html
12. UI/Application Exerciser Monkey. http://developer.android.com/tools/help/monkey.html
13. Android Activity Manager. http://developer.android.com/android/app/ActivityManager.html
14. Android instrumentationtestrunner. http://developer.android.com/reference/android/test/ InstrumentationTestRunner.html
15. Soot analysis framework. http://www.sable.mcgill.ca/soot/
16. IC3. https://github.com/siis/ic3
17. ApkCombiner. https://github.com/lilicoding/ApkCombiner
18. He, J., Yang, Y.X., Qiao, Y.: Accurate classification of P2P traffic by clustering flows. China Commun. 10(11), 42–51 (2013)
19. Zhang, Z.N., Li, D.S., Wu, K.: VMThunder: fast provisioning of large-scale virtual machine clusters. IEEE Trans. Parallel Distrib. Syst. 25(12), 3328–3338 (2014)
20. Zhang, Z.N., Li, D.S., Wu, K.: Large-scale virtual machines provisioning in clouds: challenges and approaches. Front. Comput. Sci. 10(1), 2–18 (2016)
21. Kirat, D., Vigna, G., Kruegel, C.: Barecloud: bare-metal analysis-based evasive malware detection. Malware Detection (2014)
22. DroidBench Benchmarks. https://github.com/secure-software-engineering/DroidBench
23. ICC-Bench. https://github.com/fgwei/ICC-Bench
24. Google play market. http://play.google.com/store/apps/
25. F-Droid. https://f-droid.org/
26. Bazaar. https://cafebazaar.ir/
27. MalGenome. http://www.malgenomeproject.org

28. Felt, A.P., Chin, E., Hanna, S., Song, D., Wagner, D.: Android permissions demystified. In: ACM Conference on Computer and Communications Security, pp. 627–638 (2011)
29. Enck, W., Gilbert, P., Chun, B.G., Cox, L. P., Jung, J., McDaniel, P., Sheth, A.N.: Taintdroid: an information-flow tracking system for realtime privacy monitoring on smartphones. In: USENIX Conference on Operating Systems Design and Implementation, pp. 1–6 (2010)

A Multi-layer Model to Detect Spam Email at Client Side

Kamini (Simi) Bajaj[(✉)]

School of Computing, Engineering and Mathematics,
Western Sydney University, Parramatta, Australia
k.bajaj@westernsydney.edu.au

Abstract. A solution to spam emails remains elusive despite over a decade long research efforts on spam filtering. Among different spam detection mechanisms that have been proposed, Naïve Bayesian Content Filtering has been very popular and has attained a reasonable level of success. SpamBayes is one such content filtering spam detection tool based on Naïve Bayesian classification using textual features. It is easy to deceive the learning techniques focusing only on textual attributes. Hence, in this paper we propose a multi-layer model that imposes, on top of SpamBayes, a second layer of non-textual filtering that exploits alternative machine learning techniques. This multi-layer model improves the accuracy of classification and eliminates the grey email into spam and ham emails. The experimental results of this model are quite encouraging.

Keywords: SpamBayes · Client based email filtering · Email spam · Content filtering · Supervised learning

1 Introduction

Spam exists in various forms such as spam email, web spam [1, 2], spam SMS [3, 4], and social spam [5]. Oxford dictionary defines spam as irrelevant messages sent on the internet to a large number of recipients.

The spam emails in any user's inbox has taken many forms such as phishing, image spam, DOS attacks, and malware distribution. It has impacted users and organizations from simple annoyance, loss of productivity, loss of personal information, system crashes to financial losses. Spam has varied from 36–95% [6–10] in more than a decade, the highest being 96% in 2010 [11] when this problem was at its peak and has reduced to about 53% in April–June 2015 [12, 13].

Though email is a form of communication for most these days, majority of the email traffic comes from business emails which account for over 116 billion emails sent and received per day [14] in 2015. This trend is going to continue and emails remain predominant form of communication in the business world [14]. Therefore, at least 58 billion emails sent and received daily are spam. For more than a decade efforts have been put into controlling the issue of spam. Various solutions such as blacklists, white lists, grey lists, content filtering, AIS (Artificial Immune Systems) filtering, reputation based filtering, content filtering (at mail server and email client) techniques have been

© ICST Institute for Computer Sciences, Social Informatics and Telecommunications Engineering 2017
R. Deng et al. (Eds.): SecureComm 2016, LNICST 198, pp. 334–349, 2017.
DOI: 10.1007/978-3-319-59608-2_20

suggested [15–23], however the statistics above indicate that the issue is still ongoing and the area is open to further research.

Among the above mentioned techniques, machine learning techniques [24–26] have gained a reasonable amount of success and popularity in content filtering [27] both at mail server and client side. When applying filtering solutions at mail server, it is important to consider the following two points. Firstly, the filtering is being applied to all the emails being received on behalf of email users of the organization. Secondly, the same email may be spam to one user and not spam to some other user. Therefore, if the level of filtering at server side is very stringent, it would lead to a high number of false positives (FP: legitimate emails tagged/classified as spam by the filter). FP causes loss of important information. On the other hand if filtering at server side is too relaxed it would lead to high number of false negatives (FN: spam email that is classified/tagged as legitimate email) which is a source of annoyance for the user. Hence, another level of filtering at client's end should be applied. In summary, server side mail filtering is not enough to classify incoming emails correctly, and client side filtering is essential. Many tools, both open source and commercial exist as an add-on to give another level of filtering at the client side. The major focus of these tools is to filter spam email that escapes the mail server filter. For this research, we are focusing on client level filtering that is at an optimum level of accuracy to reduce FP and FN. Earlier experiments have found that training this tool with user preferred training data reduces the FN in user inbox by 86% [28].

Since Naïve Bayesian Content Filtering has been very popular and achieved some level of success [22, 29–32], we explored Naïve Bayesian implementation. Many open source tools based on Naïve Bayesian classification techniques exist; one of the existing tools called SpamBayes was chosen to analyze the performance at client level filtering. SpamBayes classifies emails using text features into three categories: spam, ham and unsures. Unsure is an email that lies between the threshold values called the grey area and is not clearly classified as spam or ham. It contains features that belong to both spam and ham. From now on, we would refer to unsures as grey in this paper. An example spam email that SpamBayes would successfully classify is given in Fig. 1. It would be able to identify the words such as 'information', '$2 million', '1–800' as spam words and classify the email a spam.

```
Subject: re : information requested
hi , name is john ' m 27 years old . was able $ 2 million
working home , 'd share did . please few moments busy life
listen short message tell ! call listen , 1-800 - 764-6203
change life !
```

Fig. 1. Sample spam email with text features

Spammers keep innovating new ways to deceive the filters. The content of the spam has evolved to contain more than just words such as links, numeric digits, special characters etc. Most of these features are non-textual as shown in the sample spam (Fig. 2) and would not be identified by SpamBayes or any textual based filtering

```
Subject: free promotional offer
' ' own 100 % free web site site : http : / / 000000138 .
0000127 . 000044 . 00000005 . cearth . . ca / users /
freewebsites / * * * charge * * * * * commitment * * * *
* * problem * * * opportunity s33kers internet m@rketers
small lagre site is . s1te linked thousands web sites ?
amazing site . . . http : / / 000000000138. 000027 . 44 . 5
. cearth . . ca / users / freewebsites / * * * charge * * *
* * * commitment * * * * * problem * * * is truly going
site century ! * * * * * * * * * * * * * * * * * * * * * *
please excuse intrusion . one fr33 offer mailing * * * *
* * * * * * *
```

Fig. 2. Sample spam with non-text features

mechanism. Therefore, as suggested in [33], to improve the performance of SpamBayes we decided to introduce non-textual features.

The introduction of non-textual features is also testified by the Spam Reports published by Kaspersky labs for Quarter 2, 2015 [12] which highlighted the variation in features identified in spam emails that spammers are using to deceive the filtering solutions. These features listed are modified IP addresses, presence of upper case and lower case letters, special characters, use of number symbols, mis-spelt words, and number of links used to go to spam resources. In order to identify potential non-textual features, we analyzed the spam datasets and identified list of potential non-textual features. Subsequently to select the optimal non-textual features, we ran the program and observed the performance on the test set using F1 score and selected the features that gave high performance.

We explored the possibility to change the token type, size and thresholds in SpamBayes. To analyze the performance of the tool, we conducted further experiments to monitor its performance with various thresholds, token types (unigrams, bigrams and trigrams) and token sizes (15 to 25000 for different token types) which is elaborated in Sect. 2.2. We found that the overall performance would not substantially improve by increasing token type and size. Thresholds can be modified by the user as per need in SpamBayes.

In this paper we propose a multi-layer model that firstly builds an attribute set using many non-text features (Table 3) along with text features as a frequency matrix as shown in Fig. 3. Various non-text features such as number of link symbols, number of mis-spelt words, over use of numeric characters provide significant information about emails.

The aim of the model is to increase user productivity by not losing important emails as FP in greys and spam. This model eliminates unsures by classifying them as spam or ham. It also removes any FP by verifying the emails identified as spam in the junk folder. This model is based on CART, SVM, k nearest neighbor and Logistic regression machine learning techniques that have been used for spam categorization and classification [34, 35]. It has been tested with 10 datasets and results show that it has achieved 99+ % correct classification, with FP is as low as 0% to highest being 0.8%, at the max averaging at 0.3–0.4%.

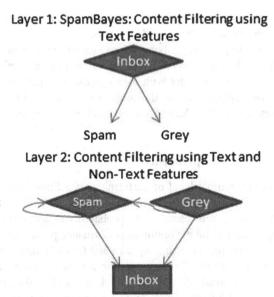

Fig. 3. Flowchart showing 2 layer filtering process

The paper is structured as follows. Section 2 introduces Spam Bayes in Subsect. 2.1 followed by performance testing of SpamBayes using various token types, max-discriminators (token sizes) and thresholds in Subsect. 2.2. Results of SpamBayes experiments are reported in Sect. 2.3 along with the discussion justifying the need for a model to improve the performance of SpamBayes. Section 3 focuses on the multi-layer model and its integration with SpamBayes framework to eliminate greys from Spam-Bayes with the acceptable level of FP and FN. The experimental results to validate the model are reported in Sect. 4 followed by conclusion and future work in Sect. 5. In this paper, we would refer to spam email as spam and a legitimate email as ham.

2   Spambayes Performance Testing

2.1   SpamBayes

SpamBayes[1] is an open source content filtering tool that classifies emails on the basis of Naïve Bayesian techniques and can be installed as an add-on to the users email client such as Microsoft outlook. It builds the learning model from the training data and classifies the new incoming emails into three categories-spam, ham and grey (unsure). To classify an email, SpamBayes selects 150 significant unigram (single word) tokens called max_discriminators from the header and body of an email and calculates the total spam score of the email. It uses the default threshold of 0.15 and 0.9 to classify

---

[1] http://spambayes.sourceforge.net.

emails. In SpamBayes manager a user can change the settings of thresholds such as ham and spam cut offs to suit their individual needs.

Readers are referred to [28] that elaborates background, training model and learning method of SpamBayes. Training data plays an important role in training the classifier. Our experiments on training the filter with user specific data [28] indicated that such training improves the performance of the tool. We noted similar trend during the experiments conducted while conducting this research as elaborated in Sect. 2.3.

2.2 Performance Testing Experiments

With an aim to find the optimal level of performance for SpamBayes, we conducted experiments using various datasets. As mentioned in Sect. 2.1, SpamBayes uses unigrams with 150 significant tokens based on the probability of occurrence of a particular token in the training data. To find the optimum performance parameters for SpamBayes we decided to conduct experiments using bigrams and trigrams with varying thresholds (Table 1) and tokens sizes (Table 2). Since getting access to live data is difficult, we decided to use publically available spam email datasets. The datasets chosen were Lingspam [36], PU1 [37], ENRON (divided into 6 preprocessed datasets since ENRON is very large dataset) [38], and CSDMC2010 SPAM corpus[2] available at csmining website. We also used dataset published at the Text REtrieval conference 2007 (TREC2007[3]), by University of Waterloo, Canada. In all, we used 10 datasets to conduct the experiments.

Table 1. Various thresholds

Ham cut-off	0.5	0.15	0.2	0.3	0.8
Spam cut-off	0.5	0.9	.9	0.8	0.6

Table 2. Various token sizes (max discriminators) used for 3 token types

Unigram	Bigrams	Trigrams
15	150	150
50	500	500
75	5000	5000
150	10000	10000
200	20000	20000
	25000	25000

Naïve Bayesian classification considers tokens as independent to each other; however correlations are possible between various tokens in an email. To identify these correlations we considered creating a correlation matrix. Since the size of matrix would

---

[2] http://www.csmining.org/index.php/spam-email-datasets-.html.

[3] http://plg.uwaterloo.ca/~gvcormac/treccorpus07/.

become very large, consume large amount of memory, and make the classifier performance very slow, we decided to consider the correlations between neighboring tokens by using bigrams and trigrams.

Bigrams are created only with neighbouring tokens. For example, if a, b and c are the three tokens then bigrams are ab, bc, a, b, and c. The frequencies of bigrams are calculated as the number of times they appeared in spam and ham emails. Trigrams are created in a similar manner. Subsequently, all tokens (normal, bigrams or trigrams) are sorted by their importance and only first max_discriminators are taken for calculating the score of an email.

We divided each dataset randomly in a 70–30 ratio; 70% used for training and 30% used for testing. For each parameter set, we ran 20 iterations randomly selecting emails for training and testing. For example, for unigrams, token size 15 and thresholds as 0.5–0.5 for spam and ham cut off, 20 iterations for each dataset was conducted with emails selected randomly allocated into the pool of training and testing set for each iteration. Results were recorded and averaged for FP, FN and Grey rates along with the time taken to process for every parameter set. There were totals 85 parameter sets −25 for unigrams, 30 each for bigrams and trigrams.

2.3   Results and Discussion – Spam Bayes

Initial results indicated inconsistent behavior among various datasets. The value of FP, FN and grey varied for all 5 datasets. Different data sets have different optimum values for cutoffs and max discriminators. This may mean that each data set is a bit different since data sets belong to different times, probably have different styles of both spam and ham emails belonging to different authors and spam designs.

In this light, we can conclude that training data set has great impact on choice of parameters of a classification [28]. So we decided to run experiments with mix of data from all of the datasets and record the results. Mixed dataset namely, data from all the datasets that are messages belonging to different persons, involving different authors, styles, written in different times, showing different notions of what is spam, etc., thus preventing the classifier to "find the rule" for classification.

From the results for unigrams for mixed dataset shown in Fig. 4, it is evident that amount of greys are high, implying unacceptable loss of important emails.

The performance of the tool was monitored based on reduction in FP and FN verses the time it takes to achieve these values of FP and FN. Though we found that using bigrams with higher token sizes improved the performance of the tool with thresholds of .4 and .6, it was taking longer to process. Increasing the number of tokens (max_discriminators) didn't contribute much to the performance of the classifier as shown in Fig. 5.

Hence, we conclude that though the values of unsures was high for the default thresholds of .15 and .9 contributing to more FP and FN for default 150 token size, the scores were comparable for unigrams, bigrams and trigrams as shown in Fig. 4. Therefore, we decided to focus on improving the performance of SpamBayes for unigrams with token size of 150.

It is known that merely increasing the number of features does not necessarily (and usually does not) provide better models in machine learning. This is verified by the

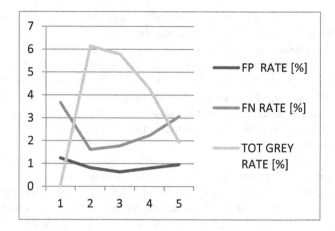

Fig. 4. Rates for unigrams for mixed dataset

results obtained from our experiments. The trick is to find only a few most important features. Hence, there is a need to find the optimum text features and to consider the non-text features to be added to SpamBayes as stated in [33].

3 Multi-layer Model - A Hybrid Classifier

3.1 Definitions

3.1.1 Text Features

Text Features help user make sense of what they are reading. It generally comprises of the actual text in the document that contributes towards user understanding the content and context of the document. They are the building block of the document that enhances the comprehension.

3.1.2 Non-text Features

Non-text features contribute to the information about the document such as the size and structure of the document. It also includes the features such as illustrations, labels, subtitles, table of contents, glossary, maps, index, comparisons etc. as shown in Fig. 6. In case of emails non-text information would include date and time of an email, subject field, hyperlinks, numeric digits, word count, use of special characters, etc. (Fig. 6).

3.1.3 Machine Learning Techniques

CART. Classification And Regression Trees (CART) algorithm is a supervised learning techniques for prediction, and classification. It constructs decision trees based upon attributes that belong to predefined classes from a collection of training data. For CART to construct these regression trees, we must define the list of attributes and the number of classes as an outcome. It then uses the training data with assigned classes to construct the rules via the decision trees. These decision trees are then used to classify new data into the said classes defined.

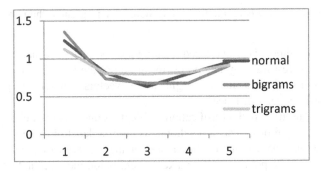

Fig. 5. Results for three token types for 150 max_discriminators for mixed dataset

Fig. 6. Non Fiction Text Features for a document

For our case the attributes defined are text as well as non-text attributes are defined in Sect. 3.1.2 and the classes are spam and ham. The training data is the data used to train SpamBayes and for experiments purpose the datasets listed in Sect. 2.2.

SVM. Support vector machines [34] (SVMs) are a set of supervised learning methods used for classification, regression and detection. Unlike normal classification methods, SVM uses a subset of training points called support vectors and finds a boundary that has maximum margin by solving an optimization problem. In SVM, we tried to find a hyperplane in an n-dimensional space defined by the attributes of the emails in the training data. One side of this hyper plane is spam emails and other side is ham emails. Since support vector machine are effective not only in high dimensional spaces, but also effective in cases where number of dimensions is greater than the number of samples.

knn. *k*-nearest neighbors is a supervised learning method that, as its name suggest, uses the labels of k-nearest training data points to figure out the label of the test data point under consideration. Once again we imagine all the vectors as points in a space and the distance being Euclidean distance.

KNN can be used for both classification and regression. In case of classification, we take the majority vote of k-nearest neighbors to find the label of a test data point. For regression, we take the average of the values for the k-nearest of a point to find the response for a new test point. In order make the regression more accurate, the response of the nearer neighbors is given more weight compared to the farther points. Usually, the weight given to points decrease inversely with their distance from the test point.

Logistic Regression. Logistic regression is a common classification technique used in situations where there is not much need to be very deterministic about the predictions made.

It works by maximizing likelihood, i.e. maximizing P[y|X] where X is the feature matrix each row of which is a feature vector and y is the vector of labels, one element for each row in X. We train the model such that it learns the probability distribution of the labels over the set of attributes.

Logistic regression is called regression even though we use it for classification because we try to approximate a real continuous function in this case. This function is the probability of getting a label; let's say the label 'spam', given a feature vector of an email. Since the probability function is continuous and real as opposed to discrete, it's called logistic regression.

Training a model for logistic regression involves defining an error measure. An error is a value whose magnitude tells us how far we are from the learned model that would predict correctly on the training data.

Once we have defined the error measure, the problem of learning the model is translated into an optimization problem wherein we have to reduce the error measure while changing the variables that it depends upon.

An example of error measure is that of likelihood, i.e. how likely are we to generate the training responses from the training features.

3.2   Multi-layer-Model

The proposed multi-layer model, a hybrid classifier is based on supervised alternative machine learning techniques applied to the features selected using text and non-text components of the email. This classifier carries out supervised learning, extracts text as well as non-text features from training data and applies that learning to detect and classify new email documents.

The emails that arrive at the email client are first filtered by the mail server. The filtering mechanism at the mail server marks an incoming email as ham, sends it to the Inbox or as spam, and sends to the Junk Mail. Some other work has gone into this area of adaptive, multi-stage learning systems to filter email spam using a variety of machine learning techniques [18, 39] but none of them provide 2 layer filtering at the client side. SpamBayes provides a layer (Layer 1) of filtering that reclassifies the emails in Inbox and Junk mail as spam, ham and grey, landing ham in Inbox, greys in Junk Suspect and spam in Spam Folder. The proposed multi-layer model applies yet another layer (Layer 2) of filtering as shown in Fig. 3, to the greys as well as spam classified by SpamBayes to increase the precision and accuracy of classification since both would contain FP and FN and the aim is to reduce FP. It is very important that this model achieves a high level of performance (correct classification of spam and ham or least FP). To ensure this we analyzed the data sets to carefully identify the features that provide correct classification. The following sub-sections explain the selection of text and non-text features and how they were combined to build the multi-layer model.

Text Features

To extract text features from the training data, bag-of-words approach has been applied to transforms data into numerical features that can be used for machine learning techniques. Term frequency-inverse document frequency (tf-idf) has been applied to this bag of words. To do so tf-idf reflects the importance of each word related to a document in the training documents. The value of tf-idf increases proportionally to number of times a word appears in the document, but is offset by the frequency of the word in the corpus, which helps to adjust for the fact that some words appear more frequently in general in the training documents.

This gives us sparse Document-Term Matrix with a huge number of columns. To apply machine learning algorithm to such a matrix, we have to filter these columns. We tried different methods such as sparse LSA, mutual information and chi-square test for filtering and found that chi-square test works well. Using this method we filter 1000–2000 columns of the document-term matrix which is then used as feature for classification.

Non-text Features

To extract non-text features, analysis of the selected datasets was conducted to identify the possible list of attributes. To select the correct features cross validation of manual analysis was done with classifier. The right feature is the feature that helps the classifier to improve its performance i.e. if we run the classifier without feature and the F1-score is $F\_without$ and then run it with feature and the score is F_with, then the feature is the "right" feature if $F\_with > F\_without$ with statistical significance. This corresponds to suggestions made in [33]. Features set containing non-text features was developed as given in Table 3.

For combining features, we used a statistical non-parametric learning technique called Gradient Boosting Regression Trees classifier that gives the highest score. It's one of the strongest methods in machine learning for classification. After extracting the features from training data and combining them using Gradient boosting, we tested the performance using F-1 score.

Once the features extraction is completed, the model then uses those features as attributes for classification. The model contains methods such as CART, Support vector machine (SVM), k-Nearest Neighbor and Logistic Regression. These methods utilize the decision boundaries that they identify from the training data and apply for classification. The detailed description of how these methods are applied has been provided

Table 3. List of non-text attributes

0: email header and body lengths,
1: number of abnormal symbols,
2: number of numeric characters,
3: number of punctuation symbols,
4: number of links symbols,
5: 'number of keywords',
6: number of keyword 'unsubscribe'
7: 'send time in 8:00:00–18:59:59,
8: length of subject field,
9: mis-spelt word count
10: similar to abnormal words
11: maximum run length of capitals
12: average run length of capitals

in Sect. 3.1. Each of these methods individually classifies the email spam and greys classified by Spam Bayes into clear spam and ham. The multi-layer model further uses rules on these classifications to predict an email as spam or ham. The rules are defined by the following voting system to classify an email document:

[all four methods agree]: outcome is the agreed classification decision
[Three methods agree]: outcome is the agreed classification decision
[Two methods agree]: outcome is Ham. This outcome has been chosen with an aim to reduce FP as some degree of FN is acceptable whereas FP is not acceptable.

3.3 SpamBayes Framework with Multi-layer Model

Since SpamBayes results in classification of emails into three categories, we apply the multi-layer model to the emails tagged as greys and spam. The rationale behind doing this has been explained in Sect. 2. The integration of the multi-layer model – a hybrid classifier to SpamBayes aims to eliminate greys category from the outcome classification Fig. 7.

4 Experiments and Results - Multi Layer Model

The experiments were conducted to test the multi-layer model at two levels. At the first level, we conducted experiments to test the performance of the multi-later model using the datasets and at the second level after integrating the multi-layer model with SpamBayes in order to classify the greys and reclassify the 'spams' moved to the junk folder by the SpamBayes. The model was tested with same 10 datasets as mentioned in Sect. 2.2 to measure the performance in terms of FP and FN. Once a satisfactory level of performance was achieved with the multi-layer model on its own, the integrated SpamBayes Framework (Fig. 7) was tested with the same set of 10 datasets.

The performance of new SpamBayes framework was measured with respect to % of ham, greys and FP in SpamBayes.

The results showed that the multi-layer model improves the performance of SpamBayes by reducing the overall % of FP to less than 0.2. This means that model is performing at 99.8% which is very encouraging improvement (Table 4).

Table 4. Comparison of SpamBayes and multi-layer model showing % of FP, FN and greys

Dataset name	Percentage of	SpamBayes %	Multi-layer model %
CSDMC2010	FP	0	0
	FN	0	1.2
	Ham greys	1.01	0
ENRON1	FP	1.3	0.9
	FN	0	2.3
	Ham greys	5.1	0
ENRON2	FP	0	0.2
	FN	0.1	2
	Ham greys	0.8	0
ENRON3	FP	0.1	0.06
	FN	0.1	4.6
	Ham greys	1.2	0
ENRON4	FP	0.1	0.2
	FN	0.3	0.9
	Ham greys	0.2	0
ENRON5	FP	0.1	0.4
	FN	0.2	0.3
	Ham greys	0.8	0
ENRON6	FP	0.2	0.6
	FN	0.3	0.7
	Ham greys	1.3	0
Lingspam	FP	0	0.1
	FN	0	1.4
	Ham greys	1.7	0
PU1	FP	0.9	0.3
	FN	0	5.4
	Ham greys	4.8	
TREC07	FP	0	0
	FN	2.9	2.9
	Ham greys	0	

We also calculated the % improvement for each of the datasets for overall FP which includes ham greys in SpamBayes that contributes towards FP. Figure 8 below shows the percentage improvement multi-layer model bring to SpamBayes for each dataset.

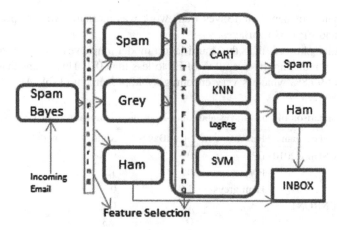

Fig. 7. Multi-layer model integrated with Spam Bayes

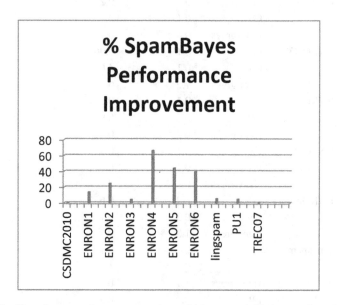

Fig. 8. % performance improvement the multi-layer model brings to SpamBayes

5   Conclusion and Future Work

Spam is an annoying and causes financial damage to organizations and individual users. This paper focused on supervised machine learning techniques based ensemble and its implementation via an open source tool called SpamBayes. As a base point we tested the performance of SpamBayes with various parameters such as different settings for thresholds and token size as well as the characteristics of feature sets such as unigrams, bigrams and trigrams of different sizes ranging from 75 to 20000 and noted that there is room for improvement. SpamBayes classifies a new email as spam, ham or grey. Greys leave an area that user has to manually classify to eliminate the false positives and false negatives. Results reported showed that for optimum parameters that give the least amount of FP and FN, the size of greys needs to be reduced. A multi-layer model was proposed to eliminate the greys from SpamBayes. This model applied to SpamBayes framework was tested and results are reported. We would like to further compare these results of multi-layer model to some other models against the same datasets.

We believe the application of this multi-layer can also be applied for social network analysis. In our future work, we would like to extend the application of this multi-layer model to social networks such as Twitter, Facebook and alike.

References

1. Wang, D., Irani, D., Pu, C.: A social-spam detection framework. In: Proceedings of the 8th Annual Collaboration, Electronic Messaging, Anti-Abuse and Spam Conference 2011, pp. 46–54. ACM, Perth (2011)
2. Bo, L., et al.: Filtering spam in social tagging system with dynamic behavior analysis. In: International Conference on Advances in Social Network Analysis and Mining, ASONAM 2009 (2009)
3. Wang, C., et al.: A behavior-based SMS antispam system. IBM J. Res. Develop. **54**(6) (2010)
4. Europe, M.: AdaptiveMobile launches anti-spam app for operators. News Analysis (2011)
5. Heymann, P., Koutrika, G., Garcia-Molina, H.: Fighting spam on social web sites: a survey of approaches and future challenges. IEEE Internet Comput. **11**(6), 36–45 (2007)
6. Clifford, M., et al.: Miracle cures and toner cartridges: finding solutions to the spam problem. In: 19th Annual Computer Security Applications Conference (ACSAC 2003) (2003)
7. Jung, J., Emil, S.: An empirical study of spam traffic and the use of DNS black lists. In: Internet Measurement Conference, Taormina, Italy (2004)
8. Jaeyeon, J., Emil, S.: An empirical study of spam traffic and the use of DNS black lists. In: Proceedings of the 4th ACM SIGCOMM Conference on Internet Measurement 2004. ACM, Taormina (2004)
9. Leavitt, N.: Vendors fight spam's sudden rise. Computer **40**(3), 16–19 (2007)
10. Mikko, S., Carl, S.: Effective anti spam strategies in companies: an international study. In: 39th Hawaiia International Conference on System Sciences. IEEE (2006)
11. Gina Spam statistics of third-quarter 2010. Panda Security Report (2010)
12. Shcherbakova, T., Vergelis, M., Demidova, N.: Spam and phishing in Q2 2015. Quarterly Spam Reports (2015)
13. Symantec, Symantec Intelligence Report: July 2015, p. 19, July 2015
14. Levenstein, J.: Email statistics report, 2013–2017. In: Radicati, S. (ed.) Reports. Radicate Group Inc.: 1900 Embarcadero Road, Suite 206, Palo Alto, CA 94303 (2013)
15. Meyer, T.A., Whateley, B.: SpamBayes: effective open-source, Bayesian based, email classification system. In: First Conference on Email and Anti-Spam (CEAS), Mountain View, CA (2004)
16. Pelletier, L., Almhana, J., Choulakian, V.: Adaptive filtering of spam. In: Proceedings of the Second Annual Conference on Communication Networks and Services Research (2004)
17. Saito, T.: Anti-spam system: another way of preventing spam. In: Proceedings of the Sixteenth International Workshop on Database and Expert Systems Applications (2005)

18. Yan, Z., Mulekar, M.S., Nerellapalli, P.: Adaptive spam filtering using dynamic feature space. In: 17th IEEE International Conference on Tools with Artificial Intelligence, ICTAI 2005 (2005)

19. Lai, C.-C.: An empirical study of three machine learning methods for spam filtering. Knowl. Based Syst. **20**(3), 249–254 (2007)

20. Youn, S., McLeod, D.: A comparative study for email classification. In: Elleithy, K. (ed.) Advances and Innovations in Systems, Computing Sciences and Software Engineering, pp. 387–391. Springer, Netherlands (2007)

21. Karthika Renuka, D., et al.: Spam classification based on supervised learning using machine learning techniques. In: International Conference on Process Automation, Control and Computing (PACC 2011) (2011)

22. Zhang, Y., Yang, X., Liu, Y.: Improvement and optimization of spam text filtering system. In: 2nd International Conference on Computer Science and Network Technology (ICCSNT 2012) (2012)

23. Sarafijanovic, S., Le Boudec, J.-Y.: Artificial immune system for collaborative spam filtering

24. Krasnogor, N., et al. (eds.): Nature Inspired Cooperative Strategies for Optimization (NICSO 2007), pp. 39–51. Springer, Berlin (2008)

25. Balakumar, M., Vaidehi, V.: Ontology based classification and categorization of email. In: International Conference on Signal Processing, Communications and Networking, ICSCN 2008 (2008)

26. Chih-Chin, L., Ming-Chi, T.: An empirical performance comparison of machine learning methods for spam e-mail categorization. In: Fourth International Conference on Hybrid Intelligent Systems, HIS 2004 (2004)

27. Caruana, G., Li, M.: A survey of emerging approaches to spam filtering. ACM Comput. Surv. **44**(2), 1–27 (2012)

28. Blanzieri, E., Bryl, A.: A survey of learning-based techniques of email spam filtering. Artif. Intell. Rev. **29**(1), 63–92 (2008)

29. Bajaj, K., Pieprzyk, J.: A case study of user-level spam filtering. In: Proceedings of the Twelfth Australasian Information Security Conference, vol. 1492014, pp. 67–75. Australian Computer Society, Inc., Auckland

30. Wu, J., Deng, T.: Research in anti-spam method based on bayesian filtering. In: Pacific-Asia Workshop on Computational Intelligence and Industrial Application (PACIIA 2008), pp. 887–891 (2008)

31. Wei, Z., et al.: Active learning based spam filtering method. In: 2010 8th World Congress on Intelligent Control and Automation (WCICA) (2010)

32. Hu, Y., Zhang, C.: An improved bayesian algorithm for filtering spam e-mail. In: 2011 2nd International Symposium on Intelligence Information Processing and Trusted Computing (IPTC) (2011)

33. Seibel, P.: Practical: a spam filter. In: Practical Common Lisp, pp. 291–309 (2005)

34. Bajaj, S.K., Pieprzyk, J.: Can we CAN the email spam. In: 2013 Fourth Cybercrime and Trustworthy Computing Workshop (CTC) (2013)

35. Drucker, H., Donghui, W., Vapnik, V.N.: Support vector machines for spam categorization. IEEE Trans. Neural Netw. **10**(5), 1048–1054 (1999)

36. Chao, X., Yiming, Z.: Transductive support vector machine for personal inboxes spam categorization. In: International Conference on Computational Intelligence and Security Workshops, CISW 2007 (2007)

37. Androutsopoulos, J.K., Chandrinos, K.V., Paliouras, G., Spyropoulos, C.D.: An evaluation of naive bayesian anti-spam filtering. In: 11th European Conference on Machine Learning, Barcelona, Spain (2000)

38. Androutsopoulos, J.K., Chandrinos, K.V., Spyropoulos, C.D.: An experimental comparison of naive bayesian and keyword-based anti-spam filtering with personal e-mail messages. In: 23rd Annual International ACM SIGIR Conference on Research and Development in Information Retrieval (SIGIR 2000), Athens, Greece (2000)
39. Metsis, V., Androutsopoulos, I., Paliouras, G.: Spam filtering with naive bayes—which naive bayes? In: 3rd Conference on Email and Anti-Spam (CEAS 2006), Mountain View, CA, USA (2006)
40. Islam, M.R., Wanlei, Z., Chowdhury, M.U.: Email categorization using (2 + 1)-tier classification algorithms. In: Seventh IEEE/ACIS International Conference on Computer and Information Science, 2008. ICIS 2008 (2008)

Cloud Security

Access Control Management
for Secure Cloud Storage

Enrico Bacis[1], Sabrina De Capitani di Vimercati[2], Sara Foresti[2],
Stefano Paraboschi[1(✉)], Marco Rosa[1(✉)], and Pierangela Samarati[2]

[1] Università degli Studi di Bergamo, Bergamo, Italy
{enrico.bacis,stefano.paraboschi,marco.rosa}@unibg.it
[2] Università degli Studi di Milano, Milan, Italy
{sabrina.decapitani,sara.foresti,pierangela.samarati}@unimi.it

Abstract. With the widespread success and adoption of cloud-based
solutions, we are witnessing an ever increasing reliance on external
providers for storing and managing data. This evolution is greatly facilitated by the availability of solutions - typically based on encryption
- ensuring the confidentiality of externally outsourced data against the
storing provider itself. Selective application of encryption (i.e., with different keys depending on the authorizations holding on data) provides a
convenient approach to access control policy enforcement. Effective realization of such policy-based encryption entails addressing several problems related to key management, access control enforcement, and authorization revocation, while ensuring efficiency of access and deployment
with current technology. We present the design and implementation of
an approach to realize policy-based encryption for enforcing access control in OpenStack Swift. We also report experimental results evaluating
and comparing different implementation choices of our approach.

1 Introduction

Cloud technology is increasingly becoming a central component for storing or
processing data. Such growing adoption and success of cloud-based solutions
is due to the considerable obvious benefits they provide in terms of reliability,
scalability, elasticity, efficiency, and economic cost. This adoption would further
accelerate in the presence of robust solutions guaranteeing effective control by
data owners over the data they outsource to cloud service providers.

A promising solution for providing data protection and maintaining control
in the hand of data owners is encryption, with data encrypted before being outsourced to the external cloud service provider. The first obvious benefit of using
encryption when outsourcing data is that data are kept unknown to the provider
hosting them. Also, encryption provides the ability to realize an approach where
the evaluation of the policy and user authentication are separate from the management of the physical access to the data. This also ensures the protection of
data confidentiality against adversaries who may have access to the physical

© ICST Institute for Computer Sciences, Social Informatics and Telecommunications Engineering 2017
R. Deng et al. (Eds.): SecureComm 2016, LNICST 198, pp. 353–372, 2017.
DOI: 10.1007/978-3-319-59608-2_21

representation or who may be able to subvert an access control service managed by the cloud service provider. Another important benefit provided by data encryption is that it enables effective enforcement of access control. In fact, data can be encrypted with different keys, depending on the authorizations holding on them, and keys shared with users according to authorization (*policy-based encryption* [7]). This policy-based encryption translates the access control policy into an equivalent *encryption policy* which provides self-protection and effective access control enforcement on the outsourced data.

One of the complicating aspects in the management of policy-based encryption relates to the enforcement of possible changes to the access control policy, and in particular revocation of authorizations. When resource maintenance is decoupled from access control thanks to the use of encryption, revocation cannot be simply managed by dropping access to the encryption key (as done in other scenarios). The revoked user can, in fact, have maintained local copies of the keys, and if the layer of protection is not refreshed, the user could still be able to pass the encryption wrap and access objects for which she does not have authorization anymore. On the other hand, changing the key and re-encrypting objects affected by revocation would entail download and re-upload operations by owners, which could become cumbersome and affect the performance of the system. The solution that was proposed to this problem in [7] assumes the introduction of *over-encryption*, based on the application by the server of an additional layer of encryption (operating on the object already encrypted by the data owner) with a key not accessible by the revoked user, thus adapting the encryption on objects to the new state of the access control policy.

Policy-based encryption for providing self-enforcement of the access control policy and over-encryption for supporting policy changes result particularly appealing and promising. However, their integration and deployment in available cloud storage systems requires addressing several problems, including: the support for co-existence of several data owners in a single system, the realization of key management solutions to enable users to access keys used for objects for which they have authorizations, and the implementation of policy-based encryption and over-encryption functionality with services supported by the cloud service providers. In this paper, we investigate all these issues and illustrate the realization of policy-based encryption and over-encryption in the context of OpenStack Swift. OpenStack [16] represents today the reference platform for the cloud [19], and is receiving significant attention by the industrial community, and Swift is the OpenStack's object storage system. Swift exhibits features that are shared by most object storage solutions for the cloud, like Amazon S3. In this paper, we illustrate how policy-based encryption can be realized building on the OpenStack Swift module. We also investigate how policy changes can be enforced implementing over-encryption in Swift. For over-encryption, in particular, we investigate different implementation alternatives, which can be suitable for different scenarios, depending on the frequency of access requests and policy changes. The contribution of the paper is therefore twofold. First, it provides an effective design and implementation of policy-based encryption and over-encryption, which can be adopted by others and see immediate deployment in current cloud storage solutions. Second, our extensive experimental evaluation of different design choices can provide precious observations for such adoption, enabling the tuning of the implementation depending on the characteristics of the considered scenario.

Outline. The remainder of this paper is organized as follows. Section 2 describes some basic concepts as well as the scenario and the problem considered. Section 3 illustrates how policy-based encryption can be realized in Swift. Section 4 shows how policy changes can be enforced and describes different options for the implementation of over-encryption. Section 5 presents experimental results. Section 6 discusses related work. Finally, Sect. 7 presents our conclusions.

2   Basic Concepts

We consider a scenario where users wish to outsource data to an external cloud service provider (CSP) and selectively share their data with others. Different data (owned by the same user) may be accessible by different sets of users. Every data owner has an access control policy specifying authorizations on her data.

We assume that the CSP is based on the OpenStack framework, which includes the Swift module, an object storage service allowing users to store and access data in the form of *objects* (i.e., each resource, such as a file, uploaded on Swift is an object). Swift organizes objects in *containers*, which are user-defined storage areas containing sets of objects. Containers are organized in *tenants*, which are sets of containers. Each tenant is usually assigned to an organization. Swift enforces discretionary access control restrictions over the objects it stores by associating a read access control list and a write access control list with each container and tenant in the system. These access control lists identify the users who can read and write the container/tenant. To enforce access control restrictions, Swift relies on *Keystone* for users authentication. Keystone is an OpenStack component acting as identity server, which provides a central directory of users mapped to the OpenStack services they can access.

We assume the cloud service provider to be *honest-but-curious*, that is, trusted to correctly manage the data (i.e., trustworthy) but not trusted for accessing the content of objects. Consistently with our focus on data confidentiality, in this paper we are concerned with the representation and enforcement of an access control policy regulating read access to objects. We note however that our approach can be extended to the consideration of write authorizations [5]. In the following, $acl(o)$ denotes the read access control list of object o and $\mathcal{A}_u$ is the set of read access control lists defined by user u for her objects. Figure 1(a) illustrates an example of authorization policy defined by user Alice. In this example, we assume that there are three users, Alice (A), Bob (B), and Dave (D), and four objects (o_1, o_2, o_3, and o_4) owned by Alice. In the matrix in Fig. 1(a), entry $[u, o]$ has value 1 if u is authorized to read o (i.e., $u \in acl(o_i)$) and 0 if u is not authorized to read o (i.e., $u \notin acl(o_i)$).

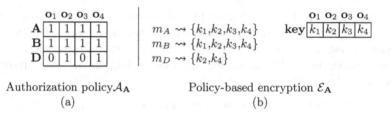

Fig. 1. An example of authorization policy defined by user Alice (a) and corresponding policy-based encryption (b)

Our work is based on the policy-based encryption and over-encryption approach proposed in [7,8], and aims at their representation and enforcement with Swift, which also require some re-definition and adjustment of these concepts. Essentially, each user is associated with a symmetric key, and each object is encrypted using a symmetric key that depends on the access control policy. Keys are organized in such a way that a user u can derive (via public tokens), all and only the keys of the objects o_i she is authorized to access (i.e., $u \in acl(o_i)$). Policy updates, which would require re-encryption of an object, are enforced by super-imposing a second layer of encryption on the encrypted object itself. Every object can then have a first layer of encryption (*BEL, Base Encryption Layer*) imposed by the data owner for protecting the confidentiality of the data from unauthorized users as well as from the CSP, and a second layer of encryption (*SEL, Surface Encryption Layer*) applied by the CSP for protecting the object from users who are not be authorized to access the object but who might know the underlying BEL key. A user will be able to access an object only if she knows both the SEL key and the BEL key with which the object is encrypted. In the following, we use notation $\mathcal{E}_u$ to denote the policy-based encryption equivalent to the authorization policy $\mathcal{A}_u$ defined by user u. Figure 1(b) illustrates the policy-based encryption equivalent to the authorization policy in Fig. 1(a). In this figure, keys m_A, m_B, m_D are the symmetric keys of the users and keys k_1, k_2, k_3, k_4 are the symmetric keys used to encrypt the objects. Notation $m_x \leadsto k_y$ represents the fact that key k_y is derivable from key m_x. In the remaining sections, we first describe how a policy-based encryption can be realized in Swift (Sect. 3), and then illustrate how to enforce policy updates (Sect. 4).

3   Access Control Enforcement in Swift

Our approach translates the authorization policy defined by a user into a policy-based encryption that relies on the use of different keys and ad-hoc structures supporting the client-based Swift encryption. In this section, we describe such keys and ad-hoc structures (which are stored as traditional Swift objects), and then illustrate how policy-based encryption can be implemented.

3.1 Keys and User-Based Repositories

Our approach is based on the definition and management of different keys. There are (symmetric) keys associated with objects for objects' encryption (enforcing the self-protection mentioned in the introduction). Also, each user is associated with a (symmetric) key as well as with two pairs of asymmetric keys to support identity management and signature, respectively. Finally, authorizations are realized by encrypting object keys with user keys. This allows users to retrieve the key of objects they are authorized to access, providing the same functionality that public-tokens provided in [7,8].

We describe the different keys and their characteristics and functionality in the following.

Data Encryption Key (DEK) k_i. Every object o_i is protected by symmetric encryption using a DEK k_i. Each DEK k_i has a given size, is associated with an encryption algorithm, and has an identifier, denoted $id(k_i)$, that identifies the key among all the keys used in the system.

Master Encryption Key (MEK) m_u. Every user u has a personal symmetric master encryption key m_u. The knowledge of this key permits to access, directly or indirectly, all the objects that user u is authorized to see. Given the user identity loss that would derive from a compromise of the MEK, it is assumed that the user keeps the MEK only on the client-side, never exposing it to the server or to other users.

User encryption key pair $\langle p_u, s_u \rangle$. Each user u is associated with an asymmetric key pair $\langle p_u, s_u \rangle$ for encryption (our implementation adopts RSA). As we show later on, the availability of asymmetric cryptography supports the realization of a cooperative cloud storage service, where each user may make her objects available to other users. Note that in most application domains, the correspondence between a user identity and a public key is supported by certificates issued by a trusted Certification Authority. Swift can instead benefit from the availability of Keystone, which already centralizes the management of user identities, and the public key is assumed to be available in the user profile managed by Keystone.

User signing key pair $\langle sp_u, ss_u \rangle$. Each user u is associated with an asymmetric key pair $\langle sp_u, ss_u \rangle$ for signing messages (our implementation adopts EC-DSA). The reason for having a signing key pair is that it is common in security systems to separate the encrypting and signing identities. This improves security and flexibility, giving the option to use a dedicated cryptographic technique for each function. Signatures are used to guarantee the integrity of objects and of the information that users adopt for deriving the DEKs. Like for asymmetric encryption, the public key for signatures is also stored in the Keystone profile of users.

Key Encryption Key (KEK). A KEK is at the basis of the mechanism that translates the access control policy defined by a user into an equivalent policy-based encryption. Intuitively, a KEK is the encryption of a DEK that a user can extract using a secret (key) that only she knows. For each container that a user is authorized to access, there is therefore a KEK that the user can decrypt to obtain the DEK used for encrypting the objects in the container. As we will see in the following sub-section, there are two variants of KEKs, depending on the cryptographic technique used to protect them: symmetric KEKs, encrypted with the MEKs of users, and asymmetric KEKs, encrypted with the public keys of users. The KEKs that allow a user u to derive the keys of the objects she is authorized to access are stored in a user-based repository, denoted $\mathcal{R}_u$. Each KEK is characterized by the following information: a KEK identifier, the identifier of the protection key, the identifier of the encrypted key, a timestamp, the identifier of the creator (only for asymmetric KEKs), an authentication code, and the encrypted key. The authentication code is used to verify the integrity of a KEK and is generated with the symmetric key of the user who creates the KEK (in case of symmetric KEK) or with the private signing key of the creator (in case of asymmetric encryption). Functions are available that allow the user to extract from her repository the KEK associated with a given protected key identifier.

The identifier of the DEK used to protect an object is maintained in the descriptor of the object itself. Such a piece of information is needed, whenever a user accesses an object, to retrieve the right KEK that allows the user to derive the corresponding DEK. Analogously, the descriptor of a container includes the identifier of the key to be used to encrypt the objects that will be inserted in the container. At initialization time, the key identifier in the descriptor of the objects stored in a container coincides with the key identifier in the container descriptor. As we will discuss in Sect. 4, due to policy changes, the key associated with a container may change and objects in the container may still be protected with a previous container key.

3.2   Policy-Based Encryption

All users in the system can define an access control policy for the objects they own. We now describe how the authorization policy $\mathcal{A}_u$ defined by user u is translated into an equivalent policy-based encryption $\mathcal{E}_u$ using the keys illustrated in the previous section.

User u creates as many containers $C_1, \ldots, C_m$ as needed and, for each of them, creates a DEK k_i, $i = 1, \ldots, m$, using a robust source of entropy. Consistently with Swift working, we assume that all objects in a container have the same acl. User u then encrypts all objects in a container C_i with the DEK k_i of the container and stores them in C_i, which will have therefore the same acl for all the objects in it. Each DEK k_i is encrypted with the MEK m_u of the user who created the container and the resulting KEK is stored in the user's repository $\mathcal{R}_u$. For each user u_j in the acl corresponding to container C_i, user u encrypts DEK k_i with u_j's public key p_{u_j} and signs it using ss_u, thus producing an asymmetric KEK usable by u_j. This KEK is stored in u_j's repository $\mathcal{R}_{u_j}$.

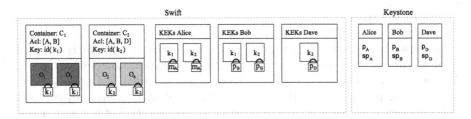

Fig. 2. Policy-based encryption $\mathcal{E}_A$ equivalent to the authorization policy $\mathcal{A}_A$ in Fig. 1(a)

Example 1. Consider the authorization policy of Alice in Fig. 1(a). Figure 2 shows how this policy is translated into an equivalent policy-based encryption. Alice creates two containers C_1 and C_2 and stores objects o_1 and o_3 both encrypted with key k_1 in C_1, objects o_2 and o_4 both encrypted with k_2 in C_2. She then creates her KEKs as well as the KEKs that Bob and Dave can use to access the objects for which they are authorized. In particular, Alice encrypts DEKs k_1 and k_2 with her MEK m_A and stores the resulting KEKs in her repository $\mathcal{R}_A$. Then, she encrypts DEK k_1 with Bob's public key p_B and DEK k_2 with public keys p_B and p_D of Bob and Dave, respectively. The resulting KEKs are stored in repositories $\mathcal{R}_B$ and $\mathcal{R}_D$, respectively. The figure also illustrates the profiles of Alice, Bob, and Dave managed by Keystone. These profiles contain the public keys of the users.

When a user u_j wishes to access an object o_l, the object descriptor is first accessed to retrieve the identifier of the DEK used to encrypt o_l. This identifier is then used to retrieve the corresponding KEK from repository $\mathcal{R}_{u_j}$ and then derive the DEK k_l. Derivation will require user u_j either to use her own MEK m_{u_j} (for symmetric KEK), or to apply the private encryption key s_{u_j} (for asymmetric KEK). To improve the efficiency of the subsequent accesses to the key and simplify the procedure, once a DEK provided by another user is extracted from an asymmetric KEK, the KEK is replaced in the repository by a symmetric KEK built using the user own MEK. For instance, suppose that Bob requires access to object o_1. Bob first retrieves from the descriptor of object o_1 the identifier $id(k_1)$ of DEK k_1. Then, it retrieves from $\mathcal{R}_B$ the corresponding KEK, decrypts it using his private key s_B and uses the retrieved DEK for decrypting o_1. Furthermore, Bob replaces the original asymmetric KEK with a symmetric KEK obtained by encrypting k_1 with his master key m_B.

When a new object o_l is inserted into a container C_i, user u retrieves the descriptor of the container and looks for the identifier $id(k_i)$ of the corresponding DEK k_i. The user will then look in her repository $\mathcal{R}_u$ for the KEK associated with $id(k_i)$ and will extract the corresponding DEK. The DEK will be used to encrypt object o_l that will be given to Swift and DEK $id(k_i)$ will be inserted into the object descriptor. For instance, suppose that Alice inserts a new object o_5 in C_2. Since the DEK associated with C_2 is k_2, Alice encrypts o_5 with k_2, inserts $id(k_2)$ in the descriptor of o_5, and stores the encrypted version of o_5 in C_2.

4 Policy Updates

Since the authorization policy regulating access to objects in Swift is enforced through a policy-based encryption, every time the authorization policy changes, also the encryption policy needs to be re-arranged accordingly. Updates to the authorization policy include the insertion and deletion of users, objects, and authorizations. The insertion of a user requires the generation of her master key, user encryption key pair, and signing key pair, and the insertion of her public keys in Keystone. The removal of a user requires only the removal from Keystone of her public (encryption and signing) keys. The removal of an object instead requires its deletion from the container including it. We then focus on granting and revoking authorizations, and on the insertion of new objects. For simplicity, but without loss of generality, we consider policy updates that involve a single user u_i and a single container C (the extension to a set of users and of containers is immediate).

In the remainder of this section, we first illustrate how policy updates can be realized, and then discuss different alternatives for the practical implementation in Swift of the over-encryption requested for their enforcement.

4.1 Enforcement of Policy Updates

We now illustrate how granting and revoking authorizations as well as the insertion of a new object with its authorization policy can be enforced. Recall that authorization policies operate at the granularity of container. Then, grant and revoke operations modify the set of users authorized to access a container C, and hence all the objects that it stores. Also, the insertion of an object in a container implies that it inherits the container acl.

Grant authorization. If user u grants u_i access to container C (and hence to the content of all its objects), she simply needs to create an (asymmetric) KEK enabling u_i to derive the DEK k of the container and to store it in the repository $\mathcal{R}_{u_i}$ of user u_i. For instance, with reference to the authorization policy in Fig. 1(a), to grant Dave access to container C_1, Alice needs to create a KEK enabling Dave to derive k_1.

Revoke authorization. If user u revokes from u_i access to container C (and hence to all its objects), it is not sufficient to delete the KEK that allows u_i to derive the DEK k of the container, as the revoked user u_i may have accessed the KEK before being revoked and may have locally stored its value. A straightforward approach to revoke user u_i access to container C consists in replacing the DEK of the container with a new key k_{new}. However, this would require the owner u of the container to download from the server all the objects in C, decrypt them with the original DEK k, encrypt them with the new DEK k_{new}, and then re-upload the encrypted objects, together with the KEKs necessary to authorized users to derive k_{new}. This would cause a significant performance and economic cost to user u. To limit such an overhead, we adopt over-encryption (Sect. 2). Hence, when a user u revokes from another user u_i the authorization

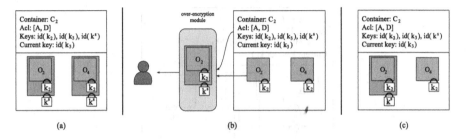

Fig. 3. An example of implementation of a revoke operation using immediate (a), on-the-fly (b), and opportunistic (c) over-encryption

to access the objects in a container C, u updates C's acl and asks the storing server to over-encrypt the objects in C with a SEL key k^s that only non-revoked users can derive. Each container is then associated with a DEK k at the BEL enforcing the initial authorization policy, and possibly also with a DEK k^s at the SEL enforcing revocations. Also, there is a KEK for each user initially authorized for C enabling her to compute k, and a KEK for each non-revoked user enabling her to compute k^s. For instance, consider the authorization policy in Fig. 1(a), and assume that Alice wants to revoke from Bob the access to C_2. As illustrated in Fig. 3(a), objects o_2 and o_4 are over-encrypted with a SEL key k^s. Also, the KEK enabling Bob to compute k_2 is dropped from $\mathcal{R}_B$, while the KEKs enabling Alice and Dave to compute k^s are created and inserted into $\mathcal{R}_A$ and $\mathcal{R}_D$, respectively.

Insert object. When a new object o_j is inserted into a container C, the object inherits the acl of the container. To enforce such an authorization policy, the object owner u can simply decide to encrypt o_j in the same way as the objects already in the container. However, if the authorization policy regulating access to the container has already been modified, this would require to encrypt o_j with both the DEK at the BEL k and the DEK at the SEL k^s associated with the container. Since the policy of object o_j has never been updated, the adoption of the SEL might be an overdo. We therefore propose to adopt a new DEK k_{new} at the BEL to protect objects that are inserted into a container on which revoke operations had been applied. As a consequence of the revoke operation (and the new acl associated with the container), a new DEK BEL key (and the corresponding KEKs) corresponding to the new acl is generated for the container, and used for objects that will be inserted into the container after the revoke operation. While for existing objects over-encryption is needed to guarantee protection from the revoked user, new objects can be encrypted with the new key known only to the users actually authorized for them. To enable non-revoked users to derive the new (current) key of the container, an (asymmetric) KEK enabling them to derive the new key is added to their repositories. Consider, as an example, container C_2 illustrated in Fig. 3(a), which is encrypted with k_2 at the BEL and with k^s at the SEL because of the revoke of Bob. Assume now that Alice needs to insert a new object o_5 into C_2. Object o_5 will be encrypted at the

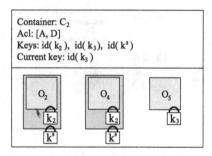

Fig. 4. An example of insertion of an object into an over-encrypted container

BEL with key k_3, generated when Bob has been revoked access to C_2 (together with the KEKs enabling Alice and Dave to compute k_3 from their own private key). Figure 4 illustrates the content of container C_2 after the insertion of o_5.

4.2 Implementation of Over-Encryption

The implementation of over-encryption for the enforcement of revoke operations in Swift can operate in different ways, depending on the time at which SEL encryption is applied, which can be: materialized at policy update time (*immediate*), performed at access time (*on-the-fly*), or performed at the first access and then materialized for subsequent accesses (*opportunistic*). In the following, we elaborate on each of these strategies.

Immediate Over-Encryption. The storing server applies over-encryption when a user revokes the authorization over container C to a user u_i. Immediate over-encryption requires the user to define, at policy update time: the SEL DEK k^s necessary to protect the objects in the revoked container C, and the KEKs necessary to authorized users (and to the server) to derive k^s. Also, the objects in container C will be over-encrypted. The server will then immediately read from the storage the objects in C, re-encrypt their content (possibly removing SEL encryption), and write the over-encrypted objects back to the storage. Hence, immediately after the policy update, the objects in C are stored encrypted with two encryption layers. Every time a user needs to access an object in C, the server will simply return the stored version of the requested object. Figure 3(a) illustrates container C_2 in Fig. 2 after Bob has been revoked access to C_2, when adopting immediate over-encryption.

Immediate over-encryption causes a considerable cost at policy update time, which is however significantly lower than the cost that would be paid if over-encryption is not used. The advantage of immediate over-encryption lays in its simplicity in the management of **get** requests by clients, because objects will be returned by the server as they are stored. This approach can be an interesting option in scenarios where policy updates are extremely rare and the overall size of objects is modest.

On-the-fly Over-Encryption. The storing server applies over-encryption on-the-fly, that is, every time a user accesses an object. Then, even if the owner of the container asks the server to over-encrypt the objects in C, the server only keeps track of this request, but it does not re-encrypt stored objects. When a user needs to access an object in C, the server possibly over-encrypts the object before returning it to the user. Figure 3(b) illustrates the adoption of on-the-fly over-encryption when Alice accesses object o_2, after Bob has been revoked access to container C_2 in Fig. 2. As it is visible from the figure, the server over-encrypts o_2 with k^s, which can be computed by Alice and Dave but not by Bob, before sending the object to the requesting user.

When adopting on-the-fly over-encryption, keys can be managed according to the following two strategies.

- *Static key generation*: the owner of the container defines, at revoke time, the SEL DEK k^s necessary to protect the objects in the revoked container C, and the KEKs necessary to non-revoked users (and to the server) to derive k^s.
- *Dynamic key generation*: the server generates a fresh SEL DEK k^s for every get request involving an object in the revoked container C. Also, it creates and makes available to the requesting user a KEK enabling her to derive k^s. At revoke time, the owner of the container only needs to communicate to the server the container C subject to the revoke operation and the revoked user.

In terms of performance, if the same user makes repeated requests for objects in the same container (i.e., protected with the same DEK), dynamic key generation may require a greater amount of work. On the other hand, if the number of requests for the objects in a container is significantly lower than the number of KEKs produced by the static approach for the same container, the dynamic approach is more efficient. The profile of key management for the two alternatives presents significant differences, but key management operations exhibit negligible computational and I/O costs compared to the management of the objects themselves. This is the reason why in the experiments (Sect. 5), focusing on the overall object management cost, we do not distinguish between static and dynamic key generation.

The advantage of on-the-fly over-encryption is that over-encryption is applied only when needed. However, if an object is asked multiple times during a period when the policy is stable, the server will incur a higher cost than immediate over-encryption, due to the multiple applications of encryption on the same object. On-the-fly over-encryption can then be an interesting option in scenarios where the ratio between accesses and revoke operations is low.

Opportunistic Over-Encryption. This approach aims at combining the advantages of both immediate over-encryption and on-the-fly over-encryption. It presents a similarity with the *Copy-On-Write* approach commonly used by operating systems to improve the efficiency of copying operations. Analogously to the immediate approach, opportunistic over-encryption requires the owner, when a user is revoked access to a container, to define both the SEL DEK k^s necessary to protect the objects in the revoked container C, and the KEKs necessary to authorized users (and to the server) to derive k^s. Similarly to the on-the-fly approach, the server over-encrypts an object o_j in the revoked container C only when it is first accessed. However, instead of discarding it, the result of over-encryption is written back to storage for future accesses.

The management of opportunistic over-encryption is more complicated than the approaches illustrated above. In fact, after multiple policy updates and object insertions, a container may include objects associated with different BEL and SEL keys. Therefore, the object descriptor must specify also its state (i.e., not over-encrypted, over-encrypted with the most up-to-date SEL key, over-encrypted with an old SEL key). When a user needs to access an object o_j, the server first checks its descriptor. If o_j is protected only at BEL and it has been subject to a revoke operation, the server derives the most recent SEL key and over-encrypts o_j on-the-fly, storing then the result. If o_j is protected also at the SEL with the most up-to-date key (or it is encrypted only at the BEL and no revoke operation affected the container), it is returned to the requesting user. Finally, if o_j is protected at the SEL with an outdated key (e.g., because another revoke operation has been performed after o_j has been last accessed), the server decrypts o_j with the old SEL key, re-encrypts it with the new one, and stores the result. Note that KEKs enabling to derive old SEL keys can be dropped from repositories only when no object is protected with those keys. Figure 3(c) illustrates container C_2 in Fig. 2 after Bob has been revoked access to C_2 and Alice has accessed object o_2. As it is visible from the figure, object o_2 is protected at both the BEL and SEL, while o_4 is encrypted only at the BEL as it has not been accessed yet.

The critical advantage of opportunistic over-encryption is that it shows good adaptability to a variety of scenarios. In some peculiar combinations of policy update frequency, size of data collection, and access profile by clients, the other solutions may be preferable. However, based on our experimental results, we expect that this solution will be preferred in the majority of scenarios.

5   Experimental Results

We discuss the experimental results performed for evaluating the practical applicability of our proposal. We performed different series of experiments aimed at evaluating the following aspects:

- the benefits of the use of over-encryption compared to a system where policy changes are enforced by the client downloading, re-encrypting, and re-uploading the objects involved (Sect. 5.1);
- the performance of the immediate, on-the-fly, and opportunistic options (Sect. 5.2);
- the performance of a batch and a streaming option for the execution of encryption by the server (Sect. 5.3);
- the performance at the client-side for the removal of the two encryption layers for over-encrypted objects (Sect. 5.4).

The experiments were executed on two PCs with Linux Ubuntu 16.04, 16 GB RAM, 4-core i7 CPU, 256 GB SSD disk. The client and the server were connected with a 100 Mb/s network channel.

5.1   Comparison Between Client Re-Encryption and Over-Encryption

We compare different options of over-encryption with a scenario where a policy update on a container is enforced by the data owner through the download, re-encryption and upload of the whole container. For this set of experiments, we consider a container with 1000 files of size 1 MB. Client side re-encryption does not require server work (except for the download and upload request, which are the same in every scenario) and is necessary only for revocations.

Figure 5 compares the overall time required for the management of a policy update followed by a number of get requests. The line on top corresponds to the configuration without over-encryption. In the lower part, we have the lines that describe the time required when using over-encryption, considering the on-the-fly approach and the opportunistic approach with uniform distribution of access requests (corresponding to $\alpha = 1$). We also report the time exhibited by the management of a sequence of direct get requests, where no encryption is applied to the objects. The graph shows that the lower lines are all one near to the other, proving that over-encryption has a small overhead.

5.2   Analysis of Over-Encryption Approaches

We compare the performance of immediate, on-the-fly, and opportunistic approaches. For this set of experiments, we consider a container with 100 files of size 1 MB. We focus on the time required for the processing on the server module, without considering the time required for the transfer of data across the network. This permits to focus on the component that is most influenced by these options (the network is typically a bottleneck and it hides the difference

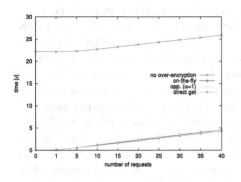

Fig. 5. Overhead of all the solutions

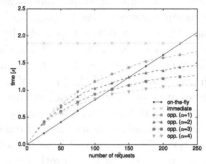

Fig. 6. Cumulative server work with different over-encryption approaches

between the approaches, as shown in Fig. 5). Figure 6 reports the cumulated execution time associated with a sequence of requests, for the three over-encryption approaches.

The immediate option requires, at policy update time, to read all the objects in the container, possibly decrypt them, and encrypt and write them back. This creates an immediate overhead at policy update, before the first request. Subsequent requests do not require a specific processing by this module, which manages the get requests with a direct mapping to the retrieval of the over-encrypted representation of the object. Figure 6 represents the immediate approach with a horizontal line.

The on-the-fly option requires to apply SEL encryption on every returned object. The cost is then identical for all the requests. Figure 6 shows that the on-the-fly option is associated with a constant growth.

For the opportunistic approach, the cost depends on the number of files in the container that are accessed more than once. When an object is accessed for the first time after the policy update, the server will have to encrypt it at the SEL level and then save its new representation. This adds to the encryption cost the cost for the storage of the new version. Subsequent requests for the same object will be managed as a simple get of the over-encrypted representation of the object. The frequency of repeated accesses has then an impact on the efficiency of this approach. In our experiments, we therefore consider request profiles associated with power law distributions [11] with varying values for the α parameter, from 1 to 4. A value of α equal to 1 corresponds to a uniform distribution, where all the requests have an equal probability of asking any of the objects in the container; increasing values of α lead to an increasingly skewed distribution of requests. The analysis shows that for the first requests the cost associated with the opportunistic approach is greater than that of the on-the-fly approach. As requests continue to be executed, the opportunistic approach becomes increasingly more efficient compared to the on-the-fly approach. The advantage increases as the profile becomes more unbalanced. The worst case is represented by the uniform distribution, which still becomes more efficient after 180 requests.

From this experimental analysis we conclude that the choice of the over-encryption approach has to consider a few aspects. In terms of pure performance, the opportunistic approach always dominates the immediate approach. The choice between the on-the-fly and the opportunistic approach has to evaluate the frequency of policy updates, the number of access requests generated between each policy update, and the profile of access requests. For scenarios where policy updates are relatively frequent compared to the frequency of access requests, and the profile is uniform, the on-the-fly approach can be the most efficient solution. In these scenarios, a choice should be made between the static and dynamic key generation. This choice will have to take into account design and configuration aspects, with the static generation requiring a greater upfront processing, but then more efficient computation, and the dynamic generation minimizing setup costs, but requiring a DEK and a KEK creation for every access request. In domains with a profile opposite to that leading to the on-the-fly approach, the opportunistic approach can prove to be the best option.

In addition to performance, there are design and security requirements that may have an impact on the choice. In terms of design, the opportunistic approach requires a more complex procedure, whereas the immediate and on-the-fly approaches both map to a simpler implementation. With respect to security, the immediate approach (for all the objects) and the opportunistic approach (for objects that have already been accessed since the last update) offer greater protection, because a revoked user who may have access to the Swift storage infrastructure would not be able to access the plaintext of the objects, whereas in the on-the-fly approach such an attack would succeed for a revoked user. System administrators will then have to make a choice based on the consideration of a number of parameters. Our expectation is that in most scenarios administrators will select the opportunistic approach.

5.3   Streaming and Batch Encryption

We performed a set of experiments aimed at comparing the execution time of a number of **get** requests when two different kinds of encryptions are used by the server: *Streaming* and *Batch*. They both use the AES-CTR encryption mode. Streaming encryption makes use of the WSGI structure of the Swift servers, and it consists in encrypting every chunk of the file as it is obtained from the proxy server. On the contrary, Batch encryption consists in encrypting the whole file after it is returned from the proxy server and before it is sent to the client. In these experiments, files of the same size are inserted into a container, which has the total size of 1 GB. We studied the benchmark of Streaming and Batch encryption applied to the on-the-fly approach against the direct **get** call that does not apply any encryption.

As it is visible from Fig. 7, compared to the direct **get** call, Streaming encryption adds an overhead between 1% and 3%, whereas Batch encryption adds an overhead between 7% and 15%. It is then clear that Streaming encryption is more efficient, both because of shorter response times and because it has a lower memory usage, since it does not have to load the entire object in RAM before encrypting it. Note that the encryption of the chunks could also be parallelized, further reducing the overhead compared to the direct **get** call.

5.4   Application of Two Encryption Layers

When over-encryption is used, the client has to decrypt the downloaded objects twice, using the same encryption algorithm with two distinct keys. The simplest approach for the implementation of these two decryptions consists in first removing the SEL layer on the full object and then removing the BEL layer. Such an approach is not the most efficient option, because the portion of the object that has been SEL-decrypted (and still BEL-encrypted) will have to either be temporarily stored in RAM or on mass memory. This is similar to the analysis

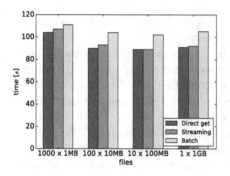

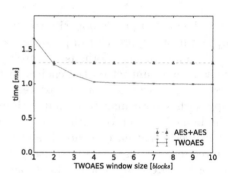

Fig. 7. Comparison of the overhead caused by Streaming and Batch on-the-fly approaches with respect to the direct get call

Fig. 8. BEL+SEL encryption performance on a 1MB file using two subsequent AES invocations and TWOAES

	without AES-NI			with AES-NI		
	ECB	CBC	CTR	ECB	CBC	CTR
128 bits	253 MB/s	215 MB/s	154 MB/s	1857 MB/s	408 MB/s	284 MB/s
256 bits	192 MB/s	170 MB/s	133 MB/s	1301 MB/s	336 MB/s	248 MB/s

Fig. 9. AES encryption rate for the modes *ECB*, *CBC*, and *CTR* using the *pycrypto* library without and with AES-NI

for Streaming and Batch encryption for the server, where Streaming encryption proves to be more efficient.

We started from these considerations and investigated the joint application of SEL and BEL decryptions. We were also interested in evaluating the performance profile of decryption on the client and in evaluating the impact of the hardware support offered for the execution of cryptographic functions. In particular, we verified the impact of the AES-NI (Intel AES New Instruction set) instructions available on Intel processors. A first set of experiments, reported in Fig. 9, showed that the encryption performance of AES-NI compared to an AES software implementation (we used the one available in OpenSSL) is around 7 times faster.

We then focused on the application of two decryptions. Our expectation was that the consecutive application of a SEL decryption and BEL decryption on the same block would have produced a benefit, as it would have avoided to pay the penalty of a transfer outside the CPU cache of the data. As shown in Fig. 8, where AES-NI instructions were used, we instead observed that the performance of the interleaved decryption depends on the number of consecutive blocks processed with each key. The worst performance is observed when after each block there is a switch of encryption key. Further investigation allowed us to verify that

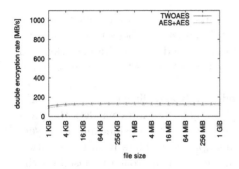

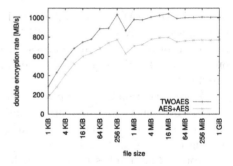

Fig. 10. Re-encryption using AES   **Fig. 11.** Re-encryption using AES-NI

the source of this behavior was an optimization by the C compiler that avoided to execute a write to the registers storing the key value when no changes had occurred to the key since the previous execution. When the switch from the application of the SEL decryption to the BEL decryption occurs after a number of blocks, the cost of the key setup is amortized over a number of blocks, but the blocks remain in the CPU cache after the first decryption and the second decryption becomes more efficient.

We then compared the execution times for the (a) serial application of SEL and BEL decryption (a full SEL decryption, followed by a full BEL decryption) and (b) interleaved SEL and BEL decryption, with the application of the two decryptions 8 blocks at a time. Figures 10 and 11 report the results of these experiments when not using AES-NI and when using AES-NI, respectively. The greater performance of hardware-accelerated AES emphasizes the impact that the CPU/RAM interface has on performance. Figure 10 indeed shows that the difference between the two approaches when hardware acceleration is not used is limited. Figure 11 shows that the 20% benefit observed is persistent across objects with a variety of sizes.

This approach is then the one that has to be applied whenever two layers of decryption have to be removed. It is also important to note that the throughput that can be obtained in the application of two decryptions (a few GB/s) is orders of magnitude greater than the bandwidth available for the network connections between a client and the Swift provider. This confirms the applicability of over-encryption in this scenario.

6 Related Work

The design of encryption techniques for data stored in the cloud is a large research area, with a considerable variety of topics and proposals. A significant amount of work has been dedicated to the design of techniques that support the efficient search and retrieval of encrypted data (e.g., [18]). Techniques have been designed that let the data be available only to users with specific properties (e.g., ABE [4,12]). Another important line of research focuses on protecting access privacy (e.g., [9,10,17]). In this paper, we focus the analysis on over-encryption, on the approaches for existing cloud storage frameworks, and on proposals for the sharing of large client-encrypted objects (instead of structured data).

Over-encryption has been proposed to effectively and efficiently enforce policy updates over encrypted outsourced data [7,8]. This solution considers the presence of a single data owner, and it has been extended to consider multiple users owning (and willing to share) data [6]. This approach differs from the solution we proposed as it relies on Diffie-Hellman, while our approach is based on the definition of symmetric and asymmetric KEKs. Also, these proposals consider a generic resource management scenario, with no specific connection to existing cloud frameworks. Over-encryption has also been considered in [3] in conjunction with a novel approach called Mix&Slice. In this context, over-encryption does not involve a whole resource but only a fragment of it.

Several proposals have contributed to the design of solutions for the protection of outsourced data with reference to current cloud frameworks. In [2], OpenStack security issues are extensively analyzed. The confidentiality of objects stored in Swift is considered as a significant aspect, but no specific technical solution is presented. A subsequent work by the same authors [1] describes an approach for the encryption of objects in Swift. In [14] another approach for server-side encryption is presented, with the goal of protecting "data at rest" (i.e., an approach for making the object representation on storage devices protected against physical accesses). In these approaches, keys are never seen by clients and they do not consider the support for container acls. Then, they do not have to look at the management of the encryption policy and its evolution.

A number of proposals have considered the application of encryption on the client-side. In [20], a service is presented that maps a file system to an encrypted representation on Amazon S3. The proposal does not support the sharing of files among distinct users and acls are not considered. In [13], an architecture for sharing encrypted objects outsourced to a cloud provider is presented. Revocation is considered as important and difficult and the proposed solution enforces it by limiting access to encryption keys for revoked users. In [21], an extensive architecture for the management of a cloud-based data sharing system is proposed. Resources are protected with keys that are consistent with the policy and significant attention is paid to revocation. The approach used is based on proxy re-encryption and lazy re-encryption. Proxy re-encryption relies on expensive cryptographic techniques that allow a server to convert a representation of a resource encrypted with a key to one associated with a different key, without letting the server executing the transformation be able to access the plaintext of the resource. Proxy re-encryption supports expressive encryption schemes, which allow attribute-based selection. Over-encryption uses standard symmetric encryption, which does not support those features but exhibits better performance. Lazy re-encryption shares some features with our opportunistic over-encryption approach, as it saves on re-encryptions by applying them only after an access request is made to the object, but the motivation is different. The advantage of lazy re-encryption is due to the ability to avoid re-encryptions for resources that are not accessed between a number of policy updates. The same benefit is also valid in our opportunistic approach, but in those scenarios our on-the-fly approach can be preferable.

The OpenStack Swift community is making a significant effort toward the introduction of object encryption in Swift [15]. The support is offered for the server side, aiming at protecting data at rest. We are monitoring this development and are confident that our solution can be easily adapted to leverage their implementation, extending it with our over-encryption techniques.

7 Conclusions

The design of techniques able to enforce confidentiality of outsourced data has the potential to greatly accelerate the rate of adoption of cloud storage, leading it to become the standard approach for the management of any kind of data. Local storage and traditional file systems would then only play the role of a cache that speeds up access to data, but persistence would be guaranteed by cloud providers. The realization of this vision requires to integrate the security techniques developed by the research community with existing cloud solutions.

The work presented in this paper goes in this direction and shows that this integration has to consider several aspects. Our proposal offers then a contribution for the most used open-source cloud storage solution, but the approaches that have been considered for Swift have a clear immediate application also to other domains.

Acknowledgements. This work was supported in part by the EC within the H2020 under grant agreement 644579 (ESCUDO-CLOUD) and within the FP7 under grant agreement 312797 (ABC4EU).

References

1. Albaroodi, H., Manickam, S., Anbar, M.: A proposed framework for outsourcing and secure encrypted data on OpenStack object storage (Swift). J. Comput. Sci. **11**(3), 590–597 (2015)
2. Albaroodi, H., Manickam, S., Singh, P.: Critical review of OpenStack security: Issues and weaknesses. J. Comput. Sci. **10**(1), 23–33 (2014)
3. Bacis, E., De Capitani di Vimercati, S., Foresti, S., Paraboschi, S., Rosa, M., Samarati, P.: Mix&Slice: Efficient access revocation in the cloud. In: Proceedings of CCS, Vienna, Austria, October 2016
4. Chow, S.S.M.: A framework of multi-authority attribute-based encryption with outsourcing and revocation. In: Proceedings of SACMAT, Shanghai, China, June 2016
5. De Capitani di Vimercati, S., Foresti, S., Jajodia, S., Livraga, G., Paraboschi, S., Samarati, P.: Enforcing dynamic write privileges in data outsourcing. Comput. Secur. **39**, 47–63 (2013)

6. De Capitani di Vimercati, S., Foresti, S., Jajodia, S., Paraboschi, S., Pelosi, G., Samarati, P.: Encryption-based policy enforcement for cloud storage. In: Proceedings of SPCC, Genova, Italy, June 2010

7. De Capitani di Vimercati, S., Foresti, S., Jajodia, S., Paraboschi, S., Samarati, P.: Over-encryption: Management of access control evolution on outsourced data. In: Proceedings of VLDB, Vienna, Austria, September 2007

8. De Capitani di Vimercati, S., Foresti, S., Jajodia, S., Paraboschi, S., Samarati, P.: Encryption policies for regulating access to outsourced data. ACM TODS 35(2), 12:1–12:46 (2010)

9. De Capitani di Vimercati, S., Foresti, S., Paraboschi, S., Pelosi, G., Samarati, P.: Efficient and private access to outsourced data. In: Proceedings of ICDCS, Minneapolis, USA, June 2011

10. De Capitani di Vimercati, S., Foresti, S., Paraboschi, S., Pelosi, G., Samarati, P.: Shuffle index: Efficient and private access to outsourced data. ACM TOS 11(4), 19:1–19:55 (2015)

11. Easley, D., Kleinberg, J.: Networks, Crowds, and Markets: Reasoning About a Highly Connected World. Cambridge University Press, New York (2010)

12. Goyal, V., Pandey, O., Sahai, A., Waters, B.: Attribute-based encryption for fine-grained access control of encrypted data. In: Proceedings of ACM CCS, Alexandria, USA, October–November 2006

13. Kaaniche, N., Laurent, M., El Barbori, M.: Cloudasec: a novel public-key based framework to handle data sharing security in clouds. In: Proceedings of SECRYPT, Vienna, Austria, August 2014

14. Kang, S., Veeravalli, B., Aung, K.M.M.: ESPRESSO: An encryption as a service for cloud storage systems. In: Sperotto, A., Doyen, G., Latré, S., Charalambides, M., Stiller, B. (eds.) AIMS 2014. LNCS, vol. 8508, pp. 15–28. Springer, Heidelberg (2014). doi:10.1007/978-3-662-43862-6_2

15. Richling, J., Cole, A.: At-rest encryption. http://specs.openstack.org/openstack/swift-specs/specs/in_progress/at_rest_encryption.html

16. Sefraoui, O., Aissaoui, M., Eleuldj, M.: OpenStack: Toward an open-source solution for cloud computing. IJCA 55(3), 38–42 (2012)

17. Stefanov, E., van Dijk, M., Shi, E., Fletcher, C., Ren, L., Yu, X., Devadas, S.: Path ORAM: An extremely simple oblivious RAM protocol. In: Proceedings of ACM CCS, Berlin, Germany, November 2013

18. Wang, C., Cao, N., Ren, K., Lou, W.: Enabling secure and efficient ranked keyword search over outsourced cloud data. IEEE TPDS 23(8), 1467–1479 (2012)

19. Wen, X., Gu, G., Li, Q., Gao, Y., Zhang, X.: Comparison of open-source cloud management platforms: OpenStack and OpenNebula. In: Proceedings of FSKD, Sichuan, China, May 2012

20. Yao, J., Chen, S., Nepal, S., Levy, D., Zic, J.: Truststore: making Amazon S3 trustworthy with services composition. In: Proceedings of CCGrid, Melbourne, Australia, May 2010

21. Yu, S., Wang, C., Ren, K., Lou, W.: Achieving secure, scalable, and fine-grained data access control in cloud computing. In: Proceedings of INFOCOM, San Diego, USA, March 2010

Attribution of Economic Denial of Sustainability Attacks in Public Clouds

Mohammad Karami and Songqing Chen[✉]

Department of Computer Science, George Mason University, Fairfax, VA, USA
{mkarami, sqchen}@gmu.edu

Abstract. The cloud pricing model leaves cloud consumers vulnerable to Economic Denial of Sustainability (EDoS) attacks. In this type of attacks, an adversary first identifies web resources with high levels of cloud resource consumption, and then uses a botnet of compromised hosts to make fraudulent requests to these costly web resources. The attacker's goal is to disrupt the economical sustainability of the victim by inflicting cost through fraudulent consumption of billable cloud resources.

In this paper, we propose two different Markov-based models to profile the behavior of legitimate users in terms of their resource consumption and to detect malicious sources engaged in fraudulent use of cloud resources. Our experimental evaluation results demonstrate the effectiveness of the proposed attribution methodology for identifying malicious sources participating in EDoS attacks.

Keywords: Economic Denial of Sustainability · EDoS detection · Markov chain · Hidden semi Markov model

1 Introduction

As a new paradigm, cloud computing is reshaping the entire information technology industry. Cloud service providers enable their consumers to access shared computing resources in a flexible way without the need for upfront investment on infrastructure, platform, and software. Although the adoption of cloud computing has experienced significant growth in recent years, some concerns regarding the unique features of cloud computing environments have hindered its broader adoption. Security and privacy concerns in particular are frequently ranked as one of the top reasons why some organizations are reluctant to adopt cloud computing [5, 26, 27].

The understanding and mitigation of security and privacy risks of the public cloud computing model has been an active area of research in recent years. The research efforts, however, have been primarily focused on protecting the confidentiality and integrity of sensitive data processed in public cloud environments as well as ensuring the continuous availability of cloud services for their intended users [23]. Very little attention has been paid to security threats targeting the cost model of consumers running their services on the public cloud [11].

Services running on public clouds are vulnerable to fraudulent resource consumption attacks aiming at increasing the financial burden of the victim service.

© ICST Institute for Computer Sciences, Social Informatics and Telecommunications Engineering 2017
R. Deng et al. (Eds.): SecureComm 2016, LNICST 198, pp. 373–391, 2017.
DOI: 10.1007/978-3-319-59608-2_22

This is enabled by exploiting the utility-based pricing model of the cloud where consumers are charged for the actual consumption of computing resources such as CPU cycles, RAM, bandwidth, and storage [14].

An adversary can conveniently rent a botnet [24] consisting of thousands of bot machines to incur artificial cost to a victim service. The target of the attack will have to pay for the cost of fraudulent resource consumption resulted from requests made by bot clients. By keeping the rate of fraudulent requests made by individual bots low to mimic the behavior of legitimate users, and intelligently focusing on requests that are most costly in terms of resource consumption, an attacker can sustain the attack over an extended period of time and maximize the effectiveness of the attack.

In practice, any device with an Internet connection is capable of launching an EDoS attack. The attacker can simply instrument the device to send HTTP GET requests to the victim service at the highest rate possible. This is basically the method used in application layer DDoS attacks where the attacker's goal is to render a targeted service unavailable to its intended users by overwhelming victim's resources. However, this will very quickly result in a significant deviation from the request rate of normal users and this artifact can be used for detecting and blocking the offending source [6, 15, 30].

In this paper, we focus on an adversarial scenario in which the attacker's goal is to increase the financial burden of the victim. This attack is also refereed to as Fraudulent Resource Consumption (FRC) attack by some researchers in the literature [11, 14]. In a recent empirical study, Wang et al. [29] show how practical EDoS attacks can be launched by abusing popular third-party services provided by companies such as Google, Facebook, etc.

In this paper, we assume that the attacker is intelligent in the sense that she makes requests that are resource-intensive resulting in higher costs for the victim. To be effective, an EDoS attack needs to be stealthy and remain undetected for an extended period of time (e.g., weeks or months). To this end, not only that malicious requests must not cause any noticeable degradation of service quality, but also the quantity of requests made by malicious sources should not be significantly different from those of legitimate users. Although high-rate DDoS attacks with the intention of overwhelming resources of a victim hosted on a public cloud can increase the resource consumption cost for the victim, in our threat model we assume that targets are properly protected against such attacks and we instead only focus on addressing low-rate and stealth EDoS attacks.

As malicious clients participating in a stealth EDoS attack make requests in a similar rate as legitimate users, this type of attacks can be challenging to detect and mitigate. In this paper, we present a method for detecting stealth EDoS attackers by directly assigning a cost to each user request in proportion to the resources consumed to serve that request.

The proposed methodology is based on statistical anomaly detection. First, we process web server logs to identify the sequence of requests made by each individual user over a predefined period of time. Next, according to the amount of resources consumed to serve each request, a relative cost value is assigned to each request. The result is a dataset consisting of a sequence of request costs for each of the legitimate users in the processed web access logs. The sequence of request costs for each user is considered as a random or stochastic process and this data is used to construct two different Markov-based models to capture the behavior of users in terms of the cost they incur to a service over time. We use sequence of request costs collected for normal users as training data to estimate the model parameters. Once the parameters are estimated, at the detection phase, the abnormality of a newly observed sequence of request costs is tested against the trained model to identify malicious sources participating in an EDoS attack.

We use real-world web access logs of about a month from an academic website to experimentally evaluate the effectiveness of the proposed method. Experimental results are presented for the two Markov-based detection methods that we propose, a simple Markov chain model, and a more complex Hidden semi-Markov Model (HsMM). The experimental results show that our proposed detection methods are very effective in differentiating normal users and malicious users participating in EDoS attacks. While most of previously proposed methods require a malicious source to make significantly more requests than legitimate users to be effective, our proposed attribution methodology can successfully detect malicious sources that try to remain undetected by making only a few resource-intensive requests.

The remainder of this paper is structured as follows. We begin with a discussion on the exploitation of the cloud pricing model that motivates this work. Related work is discussed in Sect. 3. Section 4 presents a brief background on Markov chains and HsMM as well as our proposed Markov-based methods for identifying malicious sources participating in EDoS attacks. The details of experiments designed to validate the proposed methodology and their results are presented in Sect. 5. Finally, discussion and conclusion remarks are presented in Sects. 6 and 7, respectively.

2 Exploitation of the Utility-Based Pricing Model

The cloud computing technology provides many attractive benefits such as avoiding the need for upfront spendings on computing infrastructure, improved manageability, security, and elasticity to businesses of various sizes. While the flexibility of the "pay-as-you-go" pricing model adopted by cloud service providers can be beneficial to cloud consumers, it leaves them vulnerable to financial risks imposed by EDoS attacks [11, 14].

To launch an EDoS attack, all an attacker needs to do is to simply send seemingly legitimate requests to a victim service to make it consume cloud resources for which the victim will have to pay for the cost. If the attacker is able to enforce significant fraudulent resource consumption over an extended period of time, the economical sustainability of the victim service could be threatened.

In an EDoS attack, the attack target can be a website or web applications hosted on a third party public cloud and we assume that attack targets predominantly serve public content accessible to all Internet users.

Unlike Distributed Denial of Service (DDoS) attacks, an EDoS attack is not meant to cause availability issues or noticeable degradation of service quality for the users of a target service. To be effective, an EDoS attack needs to be stealthy and remain undetected over an extended period of time (e.g., weeks or months). To remain undetected, a wise attacker will want to keep the rate of fraudulent requests low to blend them into the noise of legitimate requests, while trying to focus on requests resulting in high levels of cloud resource consumption to achieve the objective of the attack.

As documented in recent studies, DDoS-for-hire services can be readily located and rented on underground black markets [4, 16, 17]. These abusive services are often supported by botnets consisting of tens of thousands of compromised hosts and offer both network layer and application layer attacks [28]. With the availability of DDoS-for-hire services, an attacker does not need to be capable of building a supporting attack infrastructure.

The potential impact of an EDoS attack can be best quantified by examining a hypothetical attack on a service hosted on a real public cloud service provider. In the sequel, we consider a hypothetical attack on a victim service hosted on Amazon's Elastic Compute Cloud (EC2) platform. Although cloud consumers are billed for various cloud resources including computing, network, and storage resources, for simplicity, this work only focuses on data transferred from the cloud environment to the Internet to serve received requests. Table 1 shows the cost of outgoing data transfer for Amazon's EC2 platform [3].

Table 1. Amazon EC2 outgoing data transfer pricing as of February 2016.

Traffic volume	Cost
First 1 GB /month	$0.00 Per GB
Up to 10 TB/month	$0.09 Per GB
Next 40 TB/month	$0.085 Per GB
Next 100 TB/month	$0.07 Per GB
Next 350 TB/month	$0.05 Per GB

According to the HTTP Archive [2], which regularly measures the Alexa top 10,000 websites [1], the average page size was 2,225 KB for the homepage of the top 10,000 websites visited in January 2016. However, many websites host a number of much larger web resources such as videos or large compressed files that an attacker can focus on to maximize the cost of resource consumption for a victim operating on a public cloud. For the purpose of our hypothetical EDoS attack, we assume the average size of web resources requested by malicious bots participating in the attack to be 100 MB.

At the rate of only 100 requests per month which is too low to raise any red flags, a single bot would consume about 10 GB of outgoing bandwidth and the monthly bill will increase by 90¢. Sending requests with the same characteristics as the single bot scenario from 1000 bots will approximately cost the victim $900 per month. The inflicted cost grows linearly by increasing the request rate, requesting larger files, or employing more malicious bots. For instance, by locating and requesting files that are 1 GB in size, the fraudulent resource consumption cost of the previous EDoS attack scenario will escalate to about $9000 per month. As seen from the hypothetical attack scenarios, the resource consumption cost accumulated over time can impose an important financial burden to public cloud consumers, especially small businesses.

As individual bots show no trace of excessive request rates, most of existing detection schemes that look for a large number of requests in a short period of time [15, 22] will not succeed at detecting the described hypothetical attack.

It is worth noting that leasing a botnet to carry out an EDoS attack will be a cost factor that an attacker would need to take into consideration. However, due to the fact that only a very small fraction of resources available to a compromised host are actually required to make a few requests at a very low rate, the cost of accessing a botnet can be significantly reduced for an attacker by renting nondedicated botnets shared with other cybercriminals using the bots for various purposes. According to Huang et al. [10], using the pay-per-install marketplace, an attacker can gain access to 1000 compromised machines for as low as $10.

3 Related Work

So far there are only a few studies in the literature directly concerning the issue of EDoS attacks.

Khor and Nakao [18] propose a mitigation mechanism based on cryptographic puzzles to dissuade clients from submitting fraudulent requests. The basic idea of their proposed scheme called self-verifying Proof of Work (sPoW) is to require clients to present a proof of work before a protected service commits its resources to serve clients' requests. When a client first requests a resource, it receives a "crypto-puzzle" from sPoW that mediates all communications between clients and the protected service. The puzzle contains encrypted information necessary to reach the intended service such as the IP address and port number as well as a partial encryption key with k bits concealed. The client will have to spend its resources to discover the encryption key by brute forcing the k concealed bits so that it can decrypt the information necessary to contact the requested service.

However, sPoW or any other solution based on the "crypto-puzzle" approach [21] are more relevant when malicious sources are sending requests at a high rate to a target service. In an intelligent and stealth EDoS attack, malicious clients can afford to solve the puzzles to submit only a few well-crafted, resource intensive requests and succeed at adding financial burden to a victim service protected by sPoW.

Sqalli et al. propose a mitigation scheme called EDoS-Shield to address the issue of EDoS attacks in cloud environments [25]. The main idea of EDoS-Shield is to detect whether an incoming request is initiated by a legitimate user or by an automated source. EDoS-Shield depends on CAPTCHA tests to verify the source of requests. The proposed architecture consists of virtual firewalls (VF) and verifier nodes (V-Nodes) that are deployed as virtual machines in the cloud. The V-Nodes are responsible for verification of request sources, and VF nodes are implemented to decide if incoming packets should be forwarded or dropped based on the verification results received from the V-nodes. One weakness of the EDoS-Shield mitigation scheme has to do with the cost of additional cloud resources required for deploying the verifier nodes and the virtual firewalls. But, more importantly, this approach requires all users to be verified and research studies suggest that CAPTCHA tests could be annoying for some users and even a certain portion of legitimate users may not be able to solve them [7]. In addition, some existing CAPTCHA tests have been shown to be vulnerable to automated attacks [8], and recently inexpensive CAPTCHA solving services backed by crowd sourced human labor can be used to effectively defeat the protection purpose of CAPTCHA tests [20].

In [12] the authors use a number of statistical self-similarity metrics including Zipf's law, and Spearman's Footrule distance to detect the occurrence of FRC attacks. The proposed detection mechanism only looks at the aggregate pattern of user requests and does not deal with identification of individual malicious sources participating in an attack. In contrast, our proposed method is concerned with identification of malicious sources exhibiting a similar behavior as legitimate users in terms of request rates, but focusing on resource-intensive requests to maximize the cost for the victim service.

Idziorek and Tannian propose a method that attempts to model the behavior of individual users based on the number of requests per session generated by each user over a fixed period of time [11]. A pause of 900 or more seconds between consecutive requests from the same user is used as the criterion to group user requests into web sessions. The premise is that malicious users generating sessions with a random number of requests would be sufficiently different from the profile of normal users, so that an entropy-based detection method could be used to identify malicious sources. This method is based on the assumption of malicious users making more requests/web sessions than legitimate users. However, as mentioned earlier, an intelligent attacker does not necessarily need to make malicious sources to send more requests than legitimate users to succeed. By focusing on web resources that are expensive in terms of resource consumption, malicious sources with similar request rates as legitimate users can be still effective.

In [13], the authors propose a methodology for identifying malicious sources trying to inflate the utility bill of a victim by making fraudulent requests. The proposed methodology combines four different usage metrics including the number of sessions, the number of requests, and the average number of requests per session. For the last usage metric, the overall request frequency distribution of documents hosted on a website is computed, and the requests made by individual users are compared against this distribution. To evaluate a user, a probability score is calculated for each of the four metrics and then an overall average probability is computed. The more deviation observed from the normal usage, the higher would be the probability score and the more likely the user would be a malicious client. Again, this model is heavily influenced by the quantity of requests made by individual users, and it will not be effective for detecting malicious users making a small number of high cost requests. As we will show in Sect. 5, our proposed method is able to detect both malicious sources making an anomalous number of random requests, as well as more subtle malicious sources with a request rate similar to that of legitimate users but focusing on requests that are more costly for the victim.

4 The Proposed Markov-Based Models for Detecting Sources Participating in an EDoS Attack

In this study, our goal is to build an anomaly detection system to identify malicious sources participating in EDoS attacks. In this section we introduce our proposed detection methodology and describe our formulation of detecting malicious sources participating in an EDoS attack using two different Markov-based models.

Most web requests are for HTML documents that are meant to be rendered, and displayed by a user browser. These requests are typically followed shortly by several subsequent HTTP GET requests to fetch objects such as images, scripts, and CSS files embedded in the main requested document. The requests can also be for downloading objects such as binary files over HTTP. Web servers can be configured to log the details of all user requests including the IP address of the requesting host, the requested document, the type of request (GET, POST, etc.), and the size of data transferred to serve the request. Although all the HTTP request types cause resource consumption on the server side, to simplify our experimentations, we only focus on HTTP GET requests in our work.

Proportional to the amount of data transferred to serve a request, a relative cost value can be calculated and assigned to each request. Based on the data size of various requests, one can decide on a small number of buckets to represent different cost values to be associated with user requests. We will see an example of this in Sect. 5 where we use cost values from 1 to 5 for requests in our dataset.

Using collected web server logs, requests made by each individual user during a specific period of time can be identified and mapped to request cost values. The result would be a sequence of request cost values for each user. We assume that individual users (both legitimate and malicious) can be uniquely identified by their IP addresses. Using browser fingerprinting techniques [9] can be a potential solution for cases where some users can not be reliably identified by their IP addresses.

The sequence of request costs from individual users during a specific period of time can be considered as a discrete-time stochastic process and a Markov-based model can be used to describe the behavior of users in terms of the cost they incur to a service over time. A much simpler approach to distinguish between legitimate and malicious users would be to calculate the sum of request costs per user over a predefined period of time and apply a threshold value to identify users exceeding the threshold as malicious. However, as we will show in Sect. 5, such a naive approach will result in high false positive rates where legitimate users are incorrectly identified as malicious.

We use requests made by legitimate users to estimate the parameters of the Markov model and then use the trained model to compute the likelihood of new request cost sequences generated by users. The request cost sequences generated by malicious users would be different from legitimate users and this will result in much smaller likelihood values than those of legitimate users. As we will show in Sect. 5, using the right threshold likelihood value, legitimate users and malicious users can be effectively distinguished.

In this paper, we propose and evaluate the detection performance for two different Markov-based models. The first one is a simple Markov chain model in which the observed request costs are considered as the states of the Markov chain. We also evaluate a HsMM which has more complexity and computational cost but can outperform the simple Markov chain model for detecting low rate attacks focusing on high cost requests. In our HsMM, the request cost values are the observable outputs and the hidden states represent different levels of resource consumption by users. The models that we propose and evaluate are both discrete-time and the discrete points in time correspond to user requests as recorded in the web access logs. In the subsequent subsections, we give a brief background on the theory of Markov chains and HsMM and briefly discuss the process of learning model parameters using training data.

4.1   Markov Chain Model

A Markov chain models the state of a system with a random variable taking states from a finite state space as the time passes. Given the current state of a Markov chain denoted as st, the state of the chain at time $t + 1$ will only depend on s_t. In a stationary Markov chain, the state transition probabilities are assumed to be constant and independent of time. Consider a Markov chain model with M states denoted as $S = \{s_1, s_2, ..., s_M\}$. A Markov chain model can then be specified by its parameters as $\lambda = (\{\pi_m\}, \{a_{mn}\})$ where:

- $\pi_m \equiv \Pr[s_1 = m]$ is the initial state probability distribution. s_t denotes the state taken by the model at time t and $m \in S$. The sum of initial state probabilities adds up to 1 ($\Sigma_m \pi_m = 1$).
- $a_{mn} \equiv \Pr[s_t = n | s_{t-1} = m]$ is the state transition probability for $m, n \in S$, satisfying $\Sigma_n a_{mn} = 1$.

Given the model parameters, the probability of a particular sequence of states $s_1, s_2, ..., s_T$ to be taken by the model is computed as follows:

$$P(s_1, s_2, \ldots s_T) = \pi s_1 \sum_{t=2}^{T} a_{s_{t-1} s_t}$$

The initial state probability distribution and the state transition probability matrix can be readily learned from historical observations of the system states. These two model parameters can be learned using the formulas below [19]:

$$a_{mn} = \frac{N_{mn}}{N_m}$$

$$\pi_m = \frac{N_m}{N}$$

where:

- N_{mn} is the number of observed direct transitions from state m to state n.
- N_m is the number of observations where the Markov chain is in state m.
- N is the total number of observations.

In our context, we process web access logs to compute the sequence of request costs for normal users and then use this data to learn the parameters of a Markov chain model representing the resource consumption behavior of normal users. At the detection phase, newly observed sequences of request costs are analyzed to compute the likelihood of those sequences being supported by the trained Markov chain model. The resource consumption behavior of users participating in EDoS attacks would be different from that of normal users and the requests from these users are therefore expected to receive low likelihood of support when analyzed by the trained model.

4.2 Hidden Semi-Markov Model

A hidden Markov model (HMM) is a Markov model in which the states of the system being modeled are not directly observable (hidden). HsMM extends the traditional HMM by allowing states to have variable durations [31]. The duration of a state represents the number of observations made while in that state. Consider a HsMM with M states denoted as $S = \{s_1, s_2, ..., s_M\}$. A HsMM can be specified by its parameters as $\lambda = (\{\pi_m\}, \{a_{mn}\}, \{b_m(k)\}, \{p_m(d)\})$ where:

- $\pi_m \equiv \Pr[s_1 = m]$ is the initial state probability distribution. s_t denotes the state taken by the model at time t and $m \in S$. The sum of initial state probabilities adds up to 1 ($\Sigma_m \pi_m = 1$).
- $a_{mn} \equiv \Pr[s_t = n | s_{t-1} = m]$ is the state transition probability for $m, n \in S$, satisfying $\Sigma_n a_{mn} = 1$.
- $b_m(k) \equiv \Pr[o_t = k | s_t = m]$, for $m \in S$, $k \in \{1, ..., K\}$ is the state output distribution. The observable output at t is denoted by o_t and k is the index into the observable output set with cardinality K. The output distribution satisfies $\Sigma_k b_m(k) = 1$.
- $p_m(d) \equiv \Pr[\tau_t = d | s_t = m]$ is the state residual time distribution, for $m \in S$, $d \in 1, ..., D$. D represents the maximum interval between any consecutive state transitions and the residual time distribution satisfies $\Sigma_d p_m(d) = 1$.

Then, if at time t, the pair process (s_t, τ_t) takes on the value (m, d), where $d >= 1$, the semi-markov chain will remain in state m until time $t + d - 1$ and will transit to the next state at time $t + d$. The states themselves are not directly observable. The observables are a sequence of observations $O = (o_1, ..., o_T)$. The notation o_a^b represents the observation sequence from time a to time b and conditional independence of observed outputs is assumed so that $b_m(o_a^b) = \Pi_{t=a}^b b_m(o_t)$ The model parameters are initially estimated and are then updated as new observations o_t are collected. This process is known as parameter reestimation and it can be done by following the forward and backward algorithm proposed by Yu and Kobayashi [32]. The forward and backward variables are defined as follows:

$$\alpha_t(m, d) \equiv \Pr[o_1^t, (s_t, \tau_t) = (m, d) | \lambda]$$
$$\beta_t(m, d) \equiv \Pr[o_{t+1}^T, (s_t, \tau_t) = (m, d) | \lambda]$$

which can be recursively computed by forward and backward algorithms. Next, the three following joint probabilities are defined that can be expressed and computed in terms of the model parameters and the forward and backward variables defined above. These probabilities are used to readily derive the reestimation formulas to update the model parameters after collecting new observation sequences.

$$\varsigma_t(m, n) \equiv \Pr[o_1^T, s_{t-1} = m, s_t = n | \lambda]$$
$$\eta_t(m, n) \equiv \Pr[o_1^T, s_{t-1} \neq m, s_t = m, \tau_t = d | \lambda]$$
$$\gamma_t(m) \equiv \Pr[o_1^T, s_t = m, | \lambda]$$

Now, using the joint probabilities defined above, the model parameters can be reestimated by the following formulas:

$$\hat{\pi}_m = \gamma_1(m) / \sum_{m=1}^{M} \gamma_1(m)$$

$$\hat{a}_{mn} = \sum_{t=1}^{T} \varsigma_t(m, n) / \sum_{t=1}^{T} \sum_{n=1}^{M} \varsigma_t(m, n)$$

$$\hat{b}_m(k) = \sum_{t:o_t=k} \gamma_t(m) / \sum_{k} \sum_{t:o_t=k} \gamma_t(m)$$

$$\hat{p}_m(d) = \sum_{t=1}^{T} \eta_t(m, d) / \sum_{t=1}^{T} \sum_{d=1}^{D} \eta_t(m, d)$$

The model parameters are reestimated for each observation and after processing all observation sequences, the trained model can be used to compute the likelihood of a new observation sequence by the following formula:

$$\Pr[o_1^T | \lambda] = \sum_{m} \sum_{d} \Pr[o_1^T, (s_T, \tau_T) = (m, d) | \lambda]$$
$$= \sum_{m} \sum_{d} \alpha_T(m, d)$$

For our HsMM, the request cost values are the observable outputs and the hidden states represent different levels of resource consumption by users. In our implemented model, we use 5 hidden states where the model is always initialized in the first state. Also, in our model a transition can only happen from a lower state to a higher state.

Similar to the Markov chain model, we use requests made by legitimate users to estimate the parameters of the HsMM and then use the trained model to compute the likelihood of new request cost sequences generated by users. The request cost sequences generated by malicious users would be different from legitimate users and this will result in much lower likelihood values than those of legitimate users. As we will show in the next section, using the right threshold likelihood value, legitimate users and malicious users can be effectively distinguished.

5   Experimental Evaluation

We conduct experiments to evaluate the effectiveness of the proposed method for detecting malicious sources engaged in fraudulent use of cloud resources. This section provides a description of our experiments and presents the obtained results.

5.1   Dataset Description

Our experiments are based on request logs from a university department's public web server collected over 32 days from Nov 8, 2015 to Dec 9, 2015. We use the rules below to filter out requests that are irrelevant for our purpose:

- Requests that are not HTTP GET.
- HTTP GET requests with a response code other than 200 (OK).
- Requests with a user agent string indicating access from a non-user entity (e.g., Googlebot, wget, etc.).
- Request sources making requests using 10 or more different user agent strings. This is to remove aggregate request sources such as NAT boxes or web proxies making requests on behalf of their clients. About 90% of all request sources in the dataset only use a single user agent string.
- The access logs are split into two 16-day periods. We only include requests from users making at least 3 requests in one of the 16-day periods.

A request for an HTML document and the subsequent requests for fetching objects embedded in the same HTML document are combined and treated as a single request. Table 2 presents a summary of the normal dataset used for training and testing the proposed methodology.

Table 2. Summary of the normal experimental dataset.

Metric	Train dataset	Normal test dataset
Number of days	16	16
Total number of unique users	4,933	5,252
Total number of requests	36,466	36,474
Avg number of requests per user	7.39	6.94

To generate the normal training dataset, requests in the first half of the logs are grouped based on the request source, and then, proportional to the amount of data transferred to serve the requests, they are mapped to relative cost values. The same process is applied to the requests in the second period of the logs to generate the test dataset representing users with normal resource usage behavior. Based on our observation of the user requests in the dataset, we choose to use the values from 1 to 5 to represent the relative cost of user requests. Thus, the final dataset is a sequence of request costs ranging from 1 to 5 in value for each user. Table 3 summarizes the mapping from the request size to relative cost values and the distribution of requests in terms of their cost values in our dataset.

Although in our experiments we use an observation window of 16 days to profile the behavior of normal users and the same observation period is used for detection of malicious users, the proposed methodology is only sensitive to the resource usage pattern of users and is not restricted to a specific observation period.

Table 3. Mapping of request sizes to relative cost values.

Request size	Relative cost	Percentage of requests
< 500 KB	1	86.7
$\geq$ 500 KB and < 5 MB	2	11.4
$\geq$ 5 MB and < 50 MB	3	1.9
$\geq$ 50 MB and < 500 MB	4	0.1
$\geq$ 500 MB	5	5.4e−03

5.2   Attack Scenarios

To conduct an EDoS attack, an attacker needs to specify the behavior of individual bots by defining the request rate and the requested resources in term of their resource consumption cost. By varying these two parameters, various attack strategies that an attacker is likely to adopt can be constructed and the effectiveness of the proposed detection methodology can be evaluated for those attack strategies. We first consider attack strategies where the attacker focuses on making requests that result in high levels of resource consumption. For these attack strategies we assume that the attacker has a prior knowledge about the rate of requests made by legitimate users, and uses this knowledge to avoid suspicions by making requests with similar rates as legitimate users.

In sequel, we briefly describe a number of various attack scenarios that we use to generate synthetic malicious request sequences to evaluate the performance of the proposed attribution methodology. These attack scenarios are ordered in a decreasing order of attack effectiveness from the attacker's perspective. For the attack scenarios listed below the number of requests made by individual malicious sources is normally distributed with parameters $\mu = 7$ and $\sigma = 2$ which means the number of requests made by malicious users are not significantly different from those of legitimate users. The lengths of malicious request sequences drawn for this normal distribution is shared by all of the attack scenarios.

– **Scenario 1 (S1)**: All malicious requests have a cost of 5.
– **Scenario 2 (S2)**: All malicious requests have a cost of 4 or 5.
– **Scenario 3 (S3)**: The request cost is 5 for 75% of malicious requests. The cost for the remaining 25% of requests is uniformly distributed between 1 and 4.
– **Scenario 4 (S4)**: 75% of malicious requests have a cost of 4 or 5. The cost for the remaining 25% of requests is uniformly distributed between 1 and 3.
– **Scenario 5 (S5)**: The request cost is 5 for 50% of malicious requests. The cost for the remaining 50% of requests is uniformly distributed between 1 and 4.
– **Scenario 6 (S6)**: 50% of malicious requests have a cost of 4 or 5. The cost for the remaining 50% of requests is uniformly distributed between 1 and 3.

5.3   Experimental Results

For each attack scenario, we generate a dataset of malicious requests according to the description of that attack scenario. Each test dataset consists of generated malicious request sequences, combined with the request sequences from the normal test dataset. The normal test dataset is the same for all attack scenarios. Also, in our experiments, each test dataset contains the same number of normal and malicious sources (5,252). False Positive Rate (FPR), and False Negative Rate (FNR) are the metrics used for performance evaluation of the proposed attribution methodology under various attack scenarios. These metrics are briefly described in the following:

- **FPR**: The percentage of request sequences generated by legitimate users classified as malicious. Keeping the FPR under a low threshold is very important. Otherwise, legitimate users will be denied access to the protected service.
- **FNR**: The percentage of malicious request sequences generated by sources participating in an EDoS attack scenario not detected by the proposed method. Unlike an Intrusion Detection System (IDS) where it is very crucial not to miss any intrusions, because a single missed intrusion can result in system compromise, in our context, missed malicious sequences would only cause some billable fraudulent resource consumption.

For each attack scenario, the trained model is used for computing the log likelihood for all request sequences in the test dataset of that attack scenario. In general, the request sequences from legitimate users which are similar to the data used for training the model are expected to receive higher log likelihood values. On the other hand, malicious request sequences representing a resource consumption behavior dissimilar to that of legitimate users are expected to be assigned lower log likelihood values. Once the log likelihoods are computed for all request sequences, the detection performance can be evaluated for different threshold values.

Table 4 shows experimental detection results for the attack scenarios based on the strategy of focusing on high cost requests using the simple Markov chain model. Table 5 shows the results for the same attack scenarios using the HsMM. The results are presented for several different threshold values to demonstrate the trade-off between higher false positive rates and lower false negative rates and vice versa. For each threshold value, the resulting FPR and the FNR for each of the six attack scenarios are presented. As shown, both models can achieve low FPRs for reasonable FNRs. The HsMM however consistently outperforms the simple Markov chain model for the same FPR value.

For instance for a FPR of 0.67%, the FNR is 0.00% for the first attack scenario when the HsMM is used. This means that for a small FPR, all sources generating malicious requests according to the description of the first attack scenario (S1) are successfully detected. In comparison, the simple Markov chain Model produces a FNR of 7.24% for the attack scenario and the same FPR. In our experiments, the last attack scenario (S6) is the most challenging to detect as it is more similar to requests from legitimate users. But even for this attack scenario, for a FPR of 0.51%, still close to 70% of malicious request sequences are successfully detected using the HsMM.

Table 4. Experimental results for the Markov chain model for the attack strategy of focusing on high cost requests.

Threshold	FPR (%)	Attack scenario FNR (%)					
		S1	S2	S3	S4	S5	S6
−20	2.32	0.00	2.55	0.97	5.79	5.14	13.58
−25	1.35	0.00	6.32	2.30	10.68	8.87	22.51
−30	0.91	0.00	7.81	3.77	14.58	13.40	31.51
−35	0.67	7.24	16.85	11.23	25.08	22.37	43.01
−40	0.46	7.24	21.63	13.08	31.70	28.64	52.36
−45	0.29	16.28	28.66	22.43	42.25	37.93	63.06

Table 5. Experimental results for the HsMM for the attack strategy of focusing on high cost requests.

Threshold	FPR (%)	Attack scenario FNR (%)					
		S1	S2	S3	S4	S5	S6
−15	2.32	0.00	0.00	0.44	1.64	2.76	7.52
−20	1.26	0.00	2.57	2.02	5.62	6.84	15.69
−25	0.67	0.00	2.57	3.56	8.95	10.68	23.67
−30	0.51	7.24	9.04	10.95	16.70	20.13	33.80
−35	0.36	7.24	11.18	15.19	23.38	28.87	45.35
−40	0.21	16.28	18.55	23.59	33.45	38.42	57.60

It should be noted that the undetected malicious sequences are usually comprised of fewer requests compared to the successfully detected malicious sequences. For instance, when applying a threshold value of −25 for the attack scenario S5 using the HsMM, about 10% of malicious users are not identified as malicious. The average number of requests for these undetected malicious users is 3.98 versus 7.23 for the detected malicious users. This implies that the undetected malicious request sequences are less effective in terms of fraudulent resource consumption and the more effective malicious request sequences that are more aggressive in nature run higher risk of detection.

In our experiments, the FPRs are resulted by legitimate users in the test dataset generating significantly more requests than the other legitimate users. For instance, when applying a threshold value of −25 for the HsMM, 35 legitimate users out of 5252 users are incorrectly identified as malicious. On average, each of these 35 users generates 72 requests. In comparison, the overall average number of requests for all legitimate users is only 7. Longer request sequences result in lower log likelihood values and therefore legitimate users generating a large number of requests contribute to some undesirable false positives. Sometimes a given website may have legitimate users that use the website in unusual ways. If unusual request patterns are expected from specific users, false positives can be avoided by ignoring requests from these known users. In our experiments, the legitimate users with an abnormally large number of requests are incorrectly identified as malicious.

Comparison with the naive detection approach: as mentioned previously, a naive detection approach based solely on the cumulative sum of request costs will suffer high positive rates. As a concrete example, to achieve a FNR of 0.00% for the S1 attack scenario, the naive approach will need to identify all users with a cumulative sum of request costs of 15 or more as malicious. This however will result in a very high FPR of 9.96% making this approach inapplicable in practice. In contrast, as shown in Tables 4 and 5, using the proposed attribution methodology, for the S1 attack scenario all malicious users can be successfully detected with FPRs less than 1%.

Table 6. Experimental results for the Markov chain model for the attack strategy of focusing on high number of requests.

Threshold	FPR (%)	Number of requests per source FNR (%)					
		50	60	70	80	90	100
−20	2.32	3.77	0.72	0.00	0.00	0.00	0.00
−25	1.35	17.02	3.41	0.32	0.00	0.00	0.00
−30	0.91	42.19	14.38	3.24	0.32	0.02	0.00
−35	0.67	67.82	34.22	12.20	2.65	0.30	0.02
−40	0.46	86.27	59.12	29.86	10.45	2.21	0.49
−45	0.29	95.00	79.38	51.71	25.46	8.85	2.70

Table 7. Experimental results for the HsMM for the attack strategy of focusing on high number of requests.

Threshold	FPR (%)	Number of requests per source FNR (%)					
		50	60	70	80	90	100
−15	2.32	6.51	2.11	0.76	0.15	0.02	0.00
−20	1.26	23.42	10.66	3.27	0.74	0.23	0.06
−25	0.67	49.58	20.91	9.69	4.23	1.52	0.74
−30	0.51	82.77	51.79	25.32	10.62	4.09	2.04
−35	0.36	94.94	79.59	54.72	24.68	12.32	6.78
−40	0.21	98.19	92.90	79.99	53.98	27.88	13.23

As evidenced by the obtained experimental results, attacks based on the strategy of focusing on requests with high resource consumption costs can not go undetected. The alternative for an attacker would be to attempt making requests with a similar distribution of request costs as legitimate users, but in larger quantities to increase the amount of fraudulently consumed resources.

Tables 6 and 7 show experimental detection results for the attack strategy where the attacker focuses on making larger numbers of requests that have the same distribution of request costs as legitimate users. FNRs are reported for various number of requests per source and the same threshold and FPRs as the previous experiments. As expected, malicious users are more likely to be detected when making higher number of requests. For instance, when malicious clients are making 70 requests, for a FPR of 0.67%, more than 90% of malicious sources are successfully detected by the HsMM. For the experiments involving long sequences of malicious requests, the performance of the two models are comparable and none of them consistently outperforms the other model for the same FPR value. However, when the number of requests per source is 80 or more, the simple Markov chain model seems to produce lower FNRs.

It should be noted that from the standpoint of an EDoS attacker, regular requests not causing high levels of resource consumption are not very helpful and this attack strategy only makes sense when malicious sources are able to make a significant number of regular requests and manage to remain undetected.

6   Discussion

The proposed EDoS attribution methodology directly considers the cost of user requests as the metric to model the behavior of individual users. This makes it very challenging for malicious users involved in an EDoS attack to be effective in terms of fraudulent consumption of billable cloud resources and at the same time managing to remain undetected. As demonstrated experimentally, malicious users exhibiting anomalous resource consumption behavior can be quickly identified and prevented after making only a small number of suspicious requests. An attacker can attempt to optimize the requests made by individual participating bots by learning and mimicking the request pattern of top legitimate users in terms of higher usage footprint. However, it is unlikely for an attacker to be able to access historical data on requests of legitimate users or intercept communications to collect such data to optimize the behavior of participating bots. Even assuming the lack of such restrictions, applying such optimized request patterns can still significantly limit the effectiveness of the participating bots. An attacker can try to compensate for the limited utility of individual bots by employing a much larger botnet. However, larger botnets could be very difficult to locate, rent and operate and may not be practical in practice.

The proposed EDoS attribution methodology only relies on resource usage footprint of users for detecting malicious sources. For future work, we plan to incorporate other aspects of user behavior to further improve detection of malicious sources participating in EDoS attacks. For instance, the popularity of requested documents can be computed for each request cost bucket, and this can be considered when computing the likelihood of observed request sequences. In general, attackers are not expected to know the distribution of document popularity on victim websites. Focusing on requests involving documents with the highest resource consumption can result in deviation from the normal document popularity distribution and this additional metric can help to improve the detection performance.

7 Conclusion

The consumers of public cloud services are charged for computing resources that they use. This pricing model exposes the cloud consumers to EDoS attacks where the adversary seeks to increase the financial burden of the victim service by making fraudulent requests that result in high consumption of billable resources.

We have presented a Markov-based anomaly detection scheme to profile the behavior of legitimate users in terms of their resource consumption. To detect users participating in an EDoS attack, the likelihood of request sequences generated by individual clients during a specific period of time is computed by the trained model. Users with likelihood values smaller than a threshold are identified as malicious. The effectiveness of the proposed attribution methodology for identifying malicious sources engaged in fraudulent use of cloud resources has been demonstrated using experimental evaluations for various attack scenarios. While most of previously proposed methods are only effective when malicious sources make significantly more requests than legitimate users, our proposed method is able to detect both malicious sources making an anomalous number of random requests, as well as more subtle malicious sources with a request rate similar to that of legitimate users but focusing on requests that are more costly for the victim.

Acknowledgements. We would like to thank anonymous reviewers for their comments. This work was supported in part by an ARO grant W911NF-15-1-0262 and a NSF grant CNS-1524462.

References

1. Alexa. http://www.alexa.com/
2. Http archive. http://httparchive.org/interesting.php?a=All&l=Jan%2015%202016
3. Amazon ec2 pricing (2016). https://aws.amazon.com/ec2/pricing/
4. Alomari, E., Manickam, S., Gupta, B., Karuppayah, S., Alfaris, R.: Botnet-based distributed denial of service (DDoS) attacks on web servers: classification and art. *arXiv preprint* arXiv: 1208.0403 (2012)
5. Armbrust, M., Fox, A., Griffith, R., Joseph, A.D., Katz, R., Konwinski, A., Lee, G., Patterson, D., Rabkin, A., Stoica, I., et al.: A view of cloud computing. Commun. ACM **53**(4), 50–58 (2010)
6. Beitollahi, H., Deconinck, G.: Tackling application-layer DDoS attacks. Procedia Comput. Sci. **10**, 432–441 (2012)
7. Bursztein, E., Bethard, S., Fabry, C., Mitchell, J.C., Jurafsky, D.: How good are humans at solving captchas? A large scale evaluation. In: 2010 IEEE Symposium on Security and Privacy (SP), pp. 399–413. IEEE (2010)
8. Bursztein, E., Martin, M., Mitchell, J.: Text-based captcha strengths and weaknesses. In: Proceedings of the 18th ACM Conference on Computer and Communications Security, pp. 125–138. ACM (2011)
9. Eckersley, P.: How unique is your web browser? In: Atallah, M.J., Hopper, N.J. (eds.) PETS 2010. LNCS, vol. 6205, pp. 1–18. Springer, Heidelberg (2010). doi:10.1007/978-3-642-14527-8_1

10. Thomas, K., Huang, D., Wang, D., Bursztein, E., Grier, C., Holt, T.J., Kruegel, C., McCoy, D., Savage, S., Vigna, G.: Framing dependencies introduced by underground commoditization. In: Proceedings of the 14th Annual Workshop on the Economics of Information Security (2015), Netherlands, June 22–23 (2015)
11. Idziorek, J., Tannian, M.: Exploiting cloud utility models for profit and ruin. In: 2011 IEEE International Conference on Cloud Computing (CLOUD), pp. 33–40. IEEE (2011)
12. Idziorek, J., Tannian, M., Jacobson, D.: Detecting fraudulent use of cloud resources. In: Proceedings of the 3rd ACM Workshop on Cloud Computing Security Workshop, pp. 61–72. ACM (2011)
13. Idziorek, J., Tannian, M., Jacobson, D.: Attribution of fraudulent resource consumption in the cloud. In: 2012 IEEE 5th International Conference on Cloud Computing (CLOUD), pp. 99–106. IEEE (2012)
14. Idziorek, J., Tannian, M.F., Jacobson, D.: The insecurity of cloud utility models. IT Prof. **2**, 22–27 (2013)
15. Jung, J., Krishnamurthy, B., Rabinovich, M.: Flash crowds and denial of service attacks: characterization and implications for CDNs and web sites. In: Proceedings of the 11th International Conference on World Wide Web, pp. 293–304. ACM (2002)
16. Karami, M., McCoy, D.: Understanding the emerging threat of DDoS-as-a-service. In: Proceedings of the USENIX Workshop on Large-Scale Exploits and Emergent Threats (2013)
17. Karami, M., Park, Y., McCoy, D.: Stress testing the booters: understanding and undermining the business of DDoS services. In: Proceedings of the World Wide Web Conference (WWW) (2016)
18. Khor, S.H., Nakao, A.: sPoW: on-demand cloud-based eDDOS mitigation mechanism. In: HotDep (Fifth Workshop on Hot Topics in System Dependability) (2009)
19. Mitchell, T.M.: Machine Learning, vol. 45, p. 995. McGraw-Hill, Burr Ridge (1997)
20. Motoyama, M., Levchenko, K., Kanich, C., McCoy, D., Voelker, G.M., Savage, S.: Re: Captchas-understanding captcha-solving services in an economic context. In: USENIX Security Symposium, vol. 10, p. 3 (2010)
21. Naresh Kumar, M., Sujatha, P., Kalva, V., Nagori, R., Katukojwala, K., Kumar, M.: Mitigating economic denial of sustainability (edos) in cloud computing using in-cloud scrubber service. In: 2012 Fourth International Conference on Computational Intelligence and Communication Networks (CICN), pp. 535–539. IEEE (2012)
22. Oikonomou, G., Mirkovic, J.: Modeling human behavior for defense against flash-crowd attacks. In: IEEE International Conference on Communications, ICC 2009, pp. 1–6. IEEE (2009)
23. Ryan, M.D.: Cloud computing security: the scientific challenge, and a survey of solutions. J. Syst. Softw. **86**(9), 2263–2268 (2013)
24. Sood, A.K., Enbody, R.J.: Crimeware-as-a-service—a survey of commoditized crimeware in the underground market. Int. J. Crit. Infrastruct. Prot. **6**(1), 28–38 (2013)
25. Sqalli, M.H., Al-Haidari, F., Salah, K.: Edos-shield-a two-steps mitigation technique against edos attacks in cloud computing. In: 2011 Fourth IEEE International Conference on Utility and Cloud Computing (UCC), pp. 49–56. IEEE (2011)
26. Subashini, S., Kavitha, V.: A survey on security issues in service delivery models of cloud computing. J. Netw. Comput. Appl. **34**(1), 1–11 (2011)
27. Takabi, H., Joshi, J.B., Ahn, G.-J.: Security and privacy challenges in cloud computing environments. IEEE Secur. Priv. **6**, 24–31 (2010)

28. Thing, V.L., Sloman, M., Dulay, N.: A Survey of Bots Used for Distributed Denial of Service Attacks. In: Venter, H., Eloff, M., Labuschagne, L., Eloff, J., Solms, R. (eds.) SEC 2007. IFIP, vol. 232, pp. 229–240. Springer, Boston, MA (2007). doi:10.1007/978-0-387-72367-9_20

29. Wang, H., Xi, Z., Li, F., Chen, S.: Abusing public third-party services for EDoS attacks. In: 10th USENIX Workshop on Offensive Technologies (WOOT 2016) (2016)

30. Wen, S., Jia, W., Zhou, W., Zhou, W., Xu, C.: Cald: surviving various application-layer DDoS attacks that mimic flash crowd. In: 2010 4th International Conference on Network and System Security (NSS), pp. 247–254. IEEE (2010)

31. Yu, S.-Z.: Hidden semi-Markov models. Artif. Intell. **174**(2), 215–243 (2010)

32. Yu, S.-Z., Kobayashi, H.: An efficient forward-backward algorithm for an explicit-duration hidden Markov model. IEEE Sig. Process. Lett. **10**(1), 11–14 (2003)

A Secure and Fast Dispersal Storage Scheme Based on the Learning with Errors Problem

Ling Yang[1,2,3], Fuyang Fang[1,2,3], Xianhui Lu[1,2(✉)], Wen-Tao Zhu[1,2],
Qiongxiao Wang[1,2], Shen Yan[1,2,3], and Shiran Pan[1,2,3]

[1] State Key Laboratory of Information Security,
Institute of Information Engineering, Chinese Academy of Sciences, Beijing, China
{yangling,fangfuyang,luxianhui,wangqiongxiao,yanshen,
panshiran}@iie.ac.cn, wtzhu@ieee.org
[2] Data Assurance and Communication Security Research Center,
Chinese Academy of Sciences, Beijing, China
[3] University of Chinese Academy of Sciences, Beijing, China

Abstract. Data confidentiality and availability are of primary concern in data storage. Dispersal storage schemes achieve these two security properties by transforming the data into multiple codewords and dispersing them across multiple storage servers. Existing schemes achieve confidentiality and availability by various cryptographic and coding algorithms, but only under the assumption that an adversary cannot obtain more than a certain number of codewords. Meanwhile existing schemes are designed for storing archives. In this paper, we propose a novel dispersal storage scheme based on the learning with errors problem, known as storage with errors (SWE). SWE can resist even more powerful adversaries. Besides, SWE favorably supports dynamic data operations that are both efficient and secure, which is more practical for cloud storage. Furthermore, SWE achieves security at relatively low computational overhead, but the same storage cost compared with the state of the art. We also develop a prototype to validate and evaluate SWE. Analysis and experiments show that with proper configurations, SWE outperforms existing schemes in encoding/decoding speed.

Keywords: Dispersal storage · Data confidentiality · Data availability · Dynamic data operations · The learning with errors problem

1 Introduction

Data is wealth for both individuals and companies. Guaranteeing data confidentiality and availability are of primary concern in data storage [1–3]. Because of

This work was supported by the National 973 Program of China under Grant 2014CB340603, and the Strategic Priority Research Program of Chinese Academy of Sciences under Grant XDA06010702. This work was also supported by the National Natural Science Foundation of China under Grants 61272479, 61272040, and 61572495.

© ICST Institute for Computer Sciences, Social Informatics and Telecommunications Engineering 2017
R. Deng et al. (Eds.): SecureComm 2016, LNICST 198, pp. 392–411, 2017.
DOI: 10.1007/978-3-319-59608-2_23

vulnerabilities in storage software, unreliability of disk drives and so on, storing data in users' personal computers cannot absolutely guarantee data confidentiality and availability [4]. Thus more and more users resort to cloud storage. However, cloud storage still cannot absolutely guarantee confidentiality and availability [5]. Amazon S3 suffered seven-hour downtime in 2008 [6]. Facebook leaked users' contact information in 2013 [7]. iCloud leaked users' private information in 2014 [8]. All similar incidents lead users to focus on designing storage systems which can provide data confidentiality and availability [3]. Dispersal storage schemes are techniques to guarantee these two security properties.

Existing dispersal storage schemes are (k, n) threshold schemes, where k is the threshold [3]. In these schemes, data is transformed into n related codewords. Then the codewords are stored in separate storage servers, which belong to different administrative and physical domains. Meanwhile, storage servers can belong to either the same service provider or (more favorably) different providers, respectively. Even if $(n - k)$ out of the n codewords are corrupted or completely unavailable, the data can still be recovered. With fewer than k out of the n codewords, no information of the data can be obtained.

In POTSHARDS [9], Shamir's secret sharing algorithm [10] is used as the dispersal scheme. Shamir's algorithm [10] achieves *information-theoretical security*. However, the storage overhead of Shamir's algorithm is n times of the data, and the encoding time linearly grows with $n \times k$ [3]. Compared with Shamir's algorithm, Rabin's IDA [11] improves encoding/decoding speed, and saves storage overhead. However, data confidentiality of Rabin's IDA is far less. SSMS [12] provides a *computationally secure* dispersal scheme. As far as we know, AONT-RS [3] is the best scheme that achieves balance between confidentiality and data processing performance. Meanwhile, data integrity of AONT-RS is protected.

Existing schemes [3, 10–12] achieves a different level of data confidentiality with different performance and storage overhead. However, existing schemes still suffer several problems. First, existing schemes achieve data confidentiality under the assumption that an adversary cannot obtain more than $(k - 1)$ out of the n codewords. However, this assumption is unsuitable for some dispersal storage scenarios, such as a user setting one login password for all storage servers, public cloud storage, etc. In those scenarios, an adversary can easily obtain k out of the n codewords and then recover users' data. Second, existing schemes [3, 10, 12] are designed for storing archives or static data. In these schemes, while executing dynamic operations, users are required to download and decode corresponding codewords, which is inefficient. However, data is frequently updated by users, especially in cloud storage [13, 14]. Thus, existing schemes may be unsuitable for many storage scenarios.

In this paper, we propose a novel computationally secure dispersal storage scheme based on the learning with errors (LWE) problem [15], called storage with errors (SWE). To the best of our knowledge, SWE is the first work that applies LWE into dispersal storage schemes. The key idea of SWE is reforming LWE to meet the requirements of dispersal storage. Then we set the secret information in LWE to be the stored data. After the data is processed, we can utilize k

out of the n codewords to recover the data, which guarantees data availability. The hardness of LWE guarantees data confidentiality. Meanwhile, the number theoretic transform is applied to optimize arithmetic operations in SWE.

The merits of SWE are three-fold: **(i)** Analysis shows that under our assumptions, SWE with the same storage as the state of the art, achieves higher confidentiality than existing schemes. In SWE, even though an adversary obtains all the codewords, it still cannot recover the data. **(ii)** As SWE has the *additive homomorphic* property and each column of the codeword is independent of others, SWE favorably supports efficient and secure dynamic data operations (i.e., modifying, deleting, and appending). **(iii)** With proper configurations, SWE outperforms the state of the art in encoding/decoding speed.

The rest of this paper is organized as follows. Technical background is introduced in Sect. 2. We then present preliminaries in Sect. 3. We detail design and analysis of SWE in Sects. 4 and 5, respectively. Experiments and evaluations are shown in Sect. 6. Section 7 presents the conclusion.

2   Technical Background

2.1   Dispersal Algorithms

In (k, n) threshold dispersal storage schemes, $\frac{n-k}{n}$ represents the *fault-tolerance ability* (i.e., even though any $(n - k)$ out of the n codewords are corrupted or completely unavailable, the data can still be recovered). The key part of dispersal schemes shown in Fig. 1 is also called the *dispersal algorithm* (DA). Here, G is the dispersal or generator matrix, which is an $n \times k$ integer matrix. G is public. $\mathbf{d}$ is the data vector with k elements. $\mathbf{c}$ is the codeword vector with n elements, and $\mathbf{c} = \mathbf{G} \times \mathbf{d}$. Elements of $\mathbf{d}$ or $\mathbf{c}$ are integers. Each element of $\mathbf{c}$ is stored in a different storage server. Thus even if $(n - k)$ storage servers are out of service, $\mathbf{d}$ can still be reconstructed. Because of the distributed property of

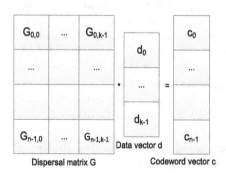

Fig. 1. The key part of dispersal schemes.

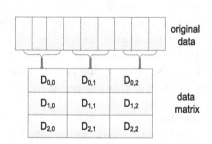

Fig. 2. An example of generating data matrix from original data.

storage servers, dispersal storage schemes can survive from non-security-related events (e.g., power failure, water damage).

The dispersal matrix $\mathbf{G}$ should satisfy that any k rows of $\mathbf{G}$ can constitute an invertible matrix. Thus we can reconstruct $\mathbf{d}$ from any k intact codewords. When reconstructing $\mathbf{d}$, if the i-th codeword is chosen, the i-th row of $\mathbf{G}$ should be chosen. Let $\mathbf{c}'$ be the vector which has k codewords, $\mathbf{G}'$ be the corresponding $k \times k$ sub-matrix of $\mathbf{G}$. Then the invertible matrix of $\mathbf{G}'$ multiplies $\mathbf{c}'$ yield $\mathbf{d}$.

2.2 The Learning with Errors (LWE) Problem

The learning with errors (LWE) problem is a generalization of the famous "learning parity with noise" problem to larger modulus. The most attractive feature of LWE is the connection of worst-to-average-case [15–18]. LWE has two forms [15]: *search-LWE* and *decision-LWE*. We apply *search-LWE* in SWE.

Definition 1. (search-LWE[15]). Let $n, k \geq 1$ be integers, q be an integer and $q = q(k) \geq 2$, χ be a distribution which can be Gaussian-like distribution or uniform distribution on $\mathcal{Z}_q$, and $\mathbf{x} \in \mathcal{Z}_q^k$ be the secret information. We donate by $\mathcal{L}_{x,\chi}^k$ the probability distribution on $\mathcal{Z}_q^{n \times k} \times \mathcal{Z}_q^n$ obtained by choosing $\mathbf{A} \in \mathcal{Z}_q^{n \times k}$ uniformly at random, choosing the "noise" or errors vector $\mathbf{e} \in \mathcal{Z}_q^n$ according to χ^n, and returning $(\mathbf{A}, \mathbf{Ax} + \mathbf{e}) = (\mathbf{A}, \mathbf{c}) \in \mathcal{Z}_q^{n \times k} \times \mathcal{Z}_q^n$. search-LWE is the problem of recovering $\mathbf{x}$ from $(\mathbf{A}, \mathbf{c}) \in \mathcal{Z}_q^{n \times k} \times \mathcal{Z}_q^n$ sampled according to $\mathcal{L}_{x,\chi}^k$.

Döttling et al. [16] give the first work that applies uniform error-distribution (i.e., error-distribution is $\mathcal{U}[-r, r]$) to LWE. This work proves that instances of LWE with uniform errors are as hard as lattice problems. Furthermore, the result of [16] shows that the *matrix-version of LWE* (i.e., $A \in \mathcal{Z}_q^{n \times k}$, $X \in \mathcal{Z}_q^{k \times l}$, and $E \in \mathcal{U}[-r, r]^{n \times l}$) is also hard.

2.3 Related Work

Next, we introduce some dispersal storage schemes that are most related to our work, which are summarized in Table 1.

Shamir's algorithm [10] can guarantee information-theoretic security of data. However, the storage overhead of Shamir's algorithm is n times of the data. Besides, encoding/decoding speed of Shamir's algorithm is slow. Compared with Shamir's algorithm, SWE improves data processing performance, and reduces storage overhead.

In Rabin's IDA [11], the *non-systematic erasure code* (e.g., the dispersal matrix is the Vandermonde matrix [19]) is applied to disperse data to achieve availability. Rabin's IDA saves time and reduces storage overhead to n/k times of the data. However, data confidentiality of Rabin's IDA is far less and would be unacceptable in many storage scenarios [3]. Compared with Rabin's IDA, SWE achieves higher confidentiality.

In SSMS [12], a symmetric cryptographic algorithm is applied to encrypt data. Then the ciphertext is dispersed using a erasure code. The key used in the

Table 1. Comparison with existing schemes. "IS" represents information-theoretical security. "CS" represents computational security. "b" represents data size.

Schemes	Security	Techniques	Storage
Shamir's algorithm [10]	IS	Shamir's secret sharing	nb
Rabin's IDA [11]	IS	Non-systematic erasure code	$\frac{nb}{k}$
SSMS [12]	CS	Encryption algorithms & non-systematic erasure codes	$\frac{nb}{k}$
AONT-RS [3]	CS	AONT & systematic Reed-Solomon code	$\frac{nb}{k}$
SWE	CS	LWE	$\frac{nb}{k}$

cryptographic algorithm is dispersed using Shamir's algorithm. Bessani et al. [20] apply the idea of SSMS to propose the first cloud-of-clouds storage application.

AONT-RS [3] is the backbone dispersal algorithm of a well-known storage company, Cleversafe. In AONT-RS, a variant of All-Or-Nothing Transform (AONT) is applied to achieve confidentiality. Meanwhile, the *systematic Reed-Solomon code* (RS) [19] (i.e., the first k rows of the dispersal matrix compose a $k \times k$ identity matrix) is applied to achieve availability. Besides, an extra word, "canary", which has a known and fixed value, is applied to check integrity of the data when it is decoded. SSMS, Rabin's IDA, and AONT-RS have approximate the same storage overhead. Compared with AONT-RS, SWE with proper configurations is faster than AONT-RS in encoding/decoding speed.

Furthermore existing schemes [3,10–12] guarantee data confidentiality under the assumption that an adversary cannot obtain more than $(k - 1)$ out of n codewords. However, SWE can guarantee data confidentiality even though an adversary obtains all the codewords. Besides, SWE favorably supports efficient and secure dynamic data operations, which is more practical in cloud storage.

3 Preliminaries

3.1 Notation

- $\mathcal{Z}_q$: The mathematic structure of group. q is a prime.
- $x \leftarrow \mathcal{Y}$: x is independently, randomly, and uniformly chosen from the distribution or set $\mathcal{Y}$.
- **A**: The dispersal matrix of SWE which is an $n \times k$ integer matrix. $\mathbf{A}_{i,j} \leftarrow \mathcal{Z}_q$.
- **D**: The data matrix which represents the data to be stored. D is a $k \times l$ integer matrix. $\mathbf{D} \in \mathcal{Z}_q^{k \times l}$.
- $f(s,r)$: The pseudorandom function whose inputs are s and r. Each outputs of $f(s,r)$ is independently, randomly, and uniformly chosen from the uniform distribution $\mathcal{U}[-r,r]$.
- **E**: The error matrix of SWE. which is just like the matrix **E** in LWE. **E** is generated by using $f(s,r)$ and thus $\mathbf{E}_{i,j} \leftarrow \mathcal{U}[-r,r]$.

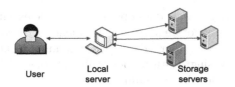

Fig. 3. The system model of SWE.

- **C**: The codewords matrix which is the result of $(\mathbf{A} \times \mathbf{D} + \mathbf{E}) \bmod q$.
- q_x: The prime which is the smallest prime bigger than 2^x. For examples, $q_{2048} = 2^{2048} + 981$, $q_{1024} = 2^{1024} + 643$, $q_{768} = 2^{768} + 183$, and so on.

3.2 System Model and Design Goals

Figure 3 shows the system model of SWE. There are three entities in SWE: user, local server, and storage server.

- User: An entity that applies SWE to store data. A user can be a person, a proxy, a storage gateway and so on.
- Local server: Each user has its own local server and stores s, r, q, n, k, l, $\mathbf{A}$, and so on in it. Among these, only s should be securely stored. Users calculate $\mathbf{C}$, recover $\mathbf{D}$, execute dynamic operations and so on local servers.
- Storage server: An entity which provides storage and computing service. All codewords $\mathbf{C}$ are stored in storage servers. Different storage servers belong to different administrative and physical domains. Storage servers can belong to either the same service provider or different providers, respectively.

We assume that storage servers are honest but curious. Thus, storage servers should honestly execute the operations which are authorized by users. However, storage servers may pry into users' data. Meanwhile, an adversary can obtain all the codewords, but it cannot obtain s which is kept secret by users.

Existing schemes guarantee data confidentiality under the assumptions that an adversary cannot obtain more than $(k-1)$ out of the n codewords, and storage servers will not pry into users' data. However, in practical storage scenarios, data may be stored in public clouds. A user may set one login password for all storage servers. Moreover, storage vendors may collude to pry into users' data. In those scenarios, obtaining more than $(k-1)$ out of the n codewords is feasible for an adversary. As long as an adversary obtains k out of the n codewords, it can recover users' data. Hence, our assumptions are more practical than those of existing schemes.

Based on the above assumptions, we design SWE with the following goals.

- Data confidentiality: SWE can guarantee that even if an adversary obtains all the codewords, it still cannot recover users' data.
- Data availability: SWE can guarantee that even if any $(n-k)$ out of the n codewords are corrupted or unavailable, the data can still be reconstructed.

- Efficient and secure dynamic data operations: While executing dynamic data operations, users are not required to download or decode codewords. An adversary cannot recover users' data from dynamic operations.
- Efficient data processing: With proper configurations, SWE outperforms the state of the art in encoding/decoding speed.

4   A New Dispersal Scheme: SWE

Existing schemes [3,10–12] achieve confidentiality under the assumption that an adversary cannot obtain more than $(k - 1)$ out of the n codewords. Some schemes achieve high confidentiality but require too many storage and computational costs. Although some schemes reduce storage and improve encoding/decoding speed, these schemes achieve relatively weak confidentiality. Meanwhile, existing schemes are designed for archives storage, which is inefficient in dynamic operations. Meanwhile, trivial applying those schemes in dynamic data operations also leak users' data information. To deal with these limitations, we propose a novel dispersal storage scheme, SWE. SWE can achieve higher confidentiality, availability, and fast encoding/decoding speed. Meanwhile, SWE favorably supports efficient and secure dynamic data operations.

4.1   The Basic Scheme

Technical highlights: In order to build a secure and efficient dispersal storage scheme, we reform LWE and make it meet the requirements of dispersal storage. We use the *matrix-version of LWE* (i.e., $\mathbf{A} \in \mathcal{Z}_q^{n \times k}$, $\mathbf{X} \in \mathcal{Z}_q^{k \times l}$, and $\mathbf{E} \in \mathcal{U}[-r, r]^{n \times l}$) [16] to construct SWE. We consider $\mathbf{X}$ in LWE to be the data matrix $\mathbf{D}$, $\mathbf{A}$ to be the dispersal matrix, and the result of $(\mathbf{A} \times \mathbf{D} + \mathbf{E}) \bmod q$ to be the codewords $\mathbf{C}$. Because of the hardness of LWE, it is difficult for an adversary to recover $\mathbf{D}$ by obtaining $\mathbf{A}$, $\mathbf{C}$, r, and q. As $\mathbf{A}$ is an $n \times k$ matrix and $n > k$, we can use any k rows of $\mathbf{C}$ to recover $\mathbf{D}$ and thus SWE achieves availability. We also use uniform errors (i.e., $\mathbf{E}_{i,j} \leftarrow \mathcal{U}[-r, r]$), small dimension $\mathbf{A}$, exponential r and q, and the number theoretic transform and its inverse to build the secure and efficient scheme.

We do not simply use erasure codes and a stream cypher to generate $\mathbf{E}$ to build a computationally secure dispersal scheme. Because such trivial method requires that $\mathbf{E}_{i,j}$ is no shorter than $(\mathbf{A} \times \mathbf{D})_{i,j}$. Obviously, the bit size $\log r$ of $\mathbf{E}_{i,j}$ in LWE is shorter than the bit size $\log q$ of $(\mathbf{A} \times \mathbf{D})_{i,j}$, which saves the time of generating $\mathbf{E}$.

SWE consists of three phases: **(i)** setup, **(ii)** computing the codewords, called *encoding*, and **(iii)** recovering the data, called *decoding*.

4.1.1   Setup
During setup, proper parameters of SWE should be chosen. Then, the dispersal matrix $\mathbf{A}$, the data matrix $\mathbf{D}$, and the error matrix $\mathbf{E}$ are generated.

Table 2. Examples of parameters in LWE and SWE.

Schemes	k	q	r
LWE	200	2^{35}	2^{15}
SWE	10	q_{768}	$\lceil \sqrt{q_{768}} \rceil$

Choose parameters: As $\mathbf{A} \in \mathcal{Z}_q^{n \times k}$ and $\mathbf{E} \in \mathcal{U}[-r, r]^{n \times l}$ is generated by using $f(s, r)$, parameters n, k, q, r, and s should be chosen. Arbitrarily setting parameters of SWE will lead to an insecure dispersal scheme. Directly applying common parameters of LWE into SWE may not be able to achieve data availability or efficient encoding/decoding. Thus, when users choose parameters of SWE, both security and performance should be taken into consideration.

$\frac{n-k}{n}$ represents the fault-tolerance ability. Larger $\frac{n-k}{n}$ means higher availability and more storage overhead. For SWE, the storage overhead of $\mathbf{C}$ is $\frac{n}{k}$ times of that of $\mathbf{D}$. However, higher fault-tolerance also means that an adversary needs to compromise fewer storage servers to recover users' data, which leads to relatively weaker security. Therefore users should set $\frac{n-k}{n}$ according to the demand of availability and security.

Common instances of LWE such as LWE shown in Table 2 cannot satisfy that any k rows of $\mathbf{A}$ can constitute an invertible matrix. Therefore, we cannot use any k out of the n codewords to reconstruct the data and thus SWE cannot guarantee data availability. However, if q is a large integer, randomly generating $\mathbf{A}$ can meet the demand of the dispersal matrix. Besides, in order to compute multiplicative inverse numbers in decoding, users should set q to be a prime too. Thus, q should be a large prime in SWE.

Meanwhile, r and s also affect the security of SWE. If r and s are too small, an adversary can easily recover $\mathbf{E}$ by brute force attacks, and then recover the data. Hence the probability of successful guessing r and s should be negligible. In SWE, $r = \lceil \sqrt{q} \rceil$. s is a random string, whose length is longer than 256 bits.

Directly increasing q and r of common instances of LWE can develop secure dispersal schemes, but these schemes are inefficient and thus impractical. Such inefficient schemes cannot be applied to performance-sensitive large data storage scenarios. For the sake of security and high-performance, we should set n and k to be small integers such as the example shown in Table 2.

After proper parameters are chosen, $\mathbf{A}$, $\mathbf{D}$, and $\mathbf{E}$ are generated as follows.

Generate A: $\mathbf{A}_{i,j} \leftarrow \mathcal{Z}_q$. In SWE, as the smallest q is q_{768}, any k rows of $\mathbf{A}$ can constitute an invertible matrix.

Theorem 1. *If q is a large prime, $\mathbf{A} \in \mathcal{Z}_q^{n \times k}$ and $n > k$, then any k rows of $\mathbf{A}$ constitute an invertible matrix.*

Proof. We calculate the invertibility probability of a $k \times k$ sub-matrix of $A \in \mathcal{Z}_q^{n \times k}$. Specifically, the first vector of A can be any nonzero vector, of which there are $q^k - 1$ (i.e., $q^k - q^0$) choices. The second vector can be chosen from $q^k - q^1$, etc. Hence, the number of ways to choose vectors of A is

$$(q^k - q^0)(q^k - q^1)...(q^k - q^{n-1}) = \prod_{i=1}^{n}(q^k - q^{i-1}).$$

So, the probability that any $k \times k$ sub-matrix of A is invertible is

$$\frac{\prod_{i=1}^{n}(q^k - q^{i-1})}{q^{nk}} = \prod_{i=1}^{n}(1 - q^{i-1-k}) < 1 - \frac{1}{q}.$$

As q is a large prime, the invertibility probability is extremely close to 1. Therefore, we always suppose that any k rows of A constitute an invertible matrix.   □

Generate D: $\mathbf{D} \in \mathcal{Z}_q^{k \times l}$ is generated from the original data. Because of $q = q_x$, each element of $\mathbf{D}$ is transformed from corresponding x bits of the data. For example, if $q = q_{1024}$, $\mathbf{D}_{i,j}$ is transformed from corresponding 1024 bits of the original data. Users generate the first column of $\mathbf{D}$, then the second column and so on. Figure 2 illustrates an example of generating $\mathbf{D}$. If the last column of $\mathbf{D}$ has fewer than k elements, the remaining elements can be filled with 0. For the sake of confidentiality, if the entropy of $\mathbf{D}_{i,j}$ is too low, users can add some random bits in $\mathbf{D}_{i,j}$.

Generate E: In order to build an efficient scheme, we apply uniform errors rather than Gaussian errors in SWE. $\mathbf{E}$ is generated by using $f(s, r)$ and thus $\mathbf{E}_{i,j} \leftarrow \mathcal{U}[-r, r]$. For the sake of confidentiality, when encoding different data matrices, users should apply $f(\cdot)$ to generate new errors matrices. The same inputs of $f(\cdot)$ can generate the same $\mathbf{E}$.

In practical, $\mathbf{A}$, n, k, q, and r can be public. $\mathbf{E}$ should be kept secret. However, users do not need to securely store $\mathbf{E}$ in their local servers. As $\mathbf{E}$ is generated by using $f(s, r)$, only s should be kept secret. In practical, if a user does not want to securely store s, the user can assign a unique identifier to each of its data files, called *file-id*. Then the user chooses a strong password. Subsequently the user combines the password and the *file-id* of corresponding $\mathbf{D}$ as inputs of a pseudorandom function. The output of the pseudorandom function is s. Thus even if the user stores many files, the user only needs to remember the password.

In many storage scenarios (e.g., cloud storage), securing storage of encryption keys (e.g., s in SWE) is not a notoriously difficult problem. In these scenarios, we do not want to keep secret of data for a very long lifetimes or periods of decades (actually, we intend to design a storage system for dynamic data). Thus, an adversary cannot recover users' data by waiting for cryptanalysis techniques to catch up the encryption algorithm. Meanwhile, storing s or encryption keys in a user's local server also saves the storage overhead compared with AONT-RS and SSMS.

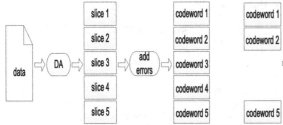 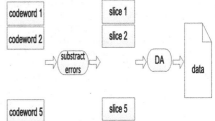

Fig. 4. An example of encoding in SWE.

Fig. 5. An example of decoding in SWE.

4.1.2 Encoding

After $\mathbf{A}$, $\mathbf{D}$, and $\mathbf{E}$ are generated, encoding is calculating $(\mathbf{A} \times \mathbf{D} + \mathbf{E}) \bmod q$ to get the codewords $\mathbf{C}$. Figure 4 shows an example of encoding, where $n = 5$, $k = 3$. Specifically, $\mathbf{C}_{i,j} = (\sum_{x=0}^{k-1} \mathbf{A}_{i,x} \times \mathbf{D}_{x,j} + \mathbf{E}_{i,j}) \bmod q$.

As $\mathbf{A}_{i,j}$ and $\mathbf{D}_{i,j}$ are all large integers, the complexity of conventional multiplication is $O(m^2)$, where $m = max\{|\mathbf{A}_{i,j}|, |\mathbf{D}_{i,j}|\}/w$ ($|\cdot|$ represents the length of $\cdot$ and w is the data bus width). The number theoretic transform can reduce the complexity to $O(m \log m)$. So, when implementing SWE, we use the number theoretic transform and its inverse to optimize encoding/decoding speed.

After generating $\mathbf{C}$, users should store $\mathbf{C}$ in distributed storage servers based on their storage strategies. For example, if $n = 4$, $k = 3$, and $l = 5$, a user stores the four rows of $\mathbf{C}$ in Amazon S3, Windows Azure, Cleversafe, and Oceanstore, respectively. Even if one of the cloud storage is out of service, the user can recover $\mathbf{D}$ using the remaining codewords. SWE can also be used to protect data avoiding suffering vendor lock-in [21]. Furthermore, users can take full advantage of physically distributed storage servers to achieve better service (e.g., achieving codewords from nearer storage servers reduces downloading time).

4.1.3 Decoding

As any k rows of $\mathbf{A}$ can constitute an invertible matrix, we can recover the data $\mathbf{D}$ using any k intact out of the n codewords. Decoding is recovering $\mathbf{D}$ using k intact out of the n codewords of $\mathbf{C}$, the corresponding sub-matrix of $\mathbf{A}$, and the corresponding sub-matrix of $\mathbf{E}$. Figure 5 shows an example of decoding, where $n = 5$ and $k = 3$. A user downloads $\mathbf{C}_{0,0}$, $\mathbf{C}_{1,0}$, and $\mathbf{C}_{4,0}$ from storage servers. The user generates $\mathbf{E}_{0,0}$, $\mathbf{E}_{1,0}$, and $\mathbf{E}_{4,0}$ by using $f(s,r)$. Then, the user solves the following liner congruential equations with single modulus q to recover $\mathbf{D}$.

$$\begin{cases} (\mathbf{A}_{0,0}\mathbf{D}_{0,0} + \mathbf{A}_{0,1}\mathbf{D}_{1,0} + \mathbf{A}_{0,2}\mathbf{D}_{2,0} + \mathbf{E}_{0,0}) \bmod q = \mathbf{C}_{0,0} \\ (\mathbf{A}_{1,0}\mathbf{D}_{0,0} + \mathbf{A}_{1,1}\mathbf{D}_{1,0} + \mathbf{A}_{1,2}\mathbf{D}_{2,0} + \mathbf{E}_{1,0}) \bmod q = \mathbf{C}_{1,0} \\ (\mathbf{A}_{4,0}\mathbf{D}_{0,0} + \mathbf{A}_{4,1}\mathbf{D}_{1,0} + \mathbf{A}_{4,2}\mathbf{D}_{2,0} + \mathbf{E}_{4,0}) \bmod q = \mathbf{C}_{4,0} \end{cases} .$$

Table 3. The procedure of modifying data in SWE.

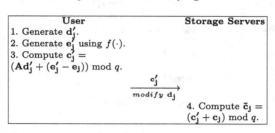

If the user applies the Gaussian elimination to solve the above equations, it can recover $\mathbf{D}$, but this method is inefficient. In SWE, we store the invertible sub-matrix of $\mathbf{A}$ corresponding to commonly used codewords in local servers, $\hat{\mathbf{A}}$. Let $\tilde{\mathbf{C}}$ be the codewords, $\tilde{\mathbf{E}}$ be the corresponding sub-matrix of $\mathbf{E}$. Thus, decoding is calculating $\mathbf{D}_{i,j} = (\sum_{x=0}^{k-1} \hat{\mathbf{A}}_{i,x} \times (\tilde{\mathbf{C}}_{x,j} - \tilde{\mathbf{E}}_{i,j})) \bmod q$.

Integrity checking: In AONT-RS, an extra word of data, "canary", which has a fixed value, allows users check the integrity of the data when it is decoded. In SWE, users do not need to add such a fixed value word. In SWE, users only need to retrieve $(k + 1)$ codewords and execute two times of decoding using different k codewords. If the two decoding results are the same, the data is intact and thus we check the integrity of the data.

4.2 Support for Dynamic Operations

So far, we assume that users' data is static. However, data is frequently updated by users especially in cloud storage scenarios [13,14]. Therefore, the investigations on dynamic data operations are also of paramount importance.

When a user changes a file, we suppose the user changes the *file-id* to a new one. Then the user combines the new *file-id* and its password as s'. Then the user utilizes $f(s', r)$ generating $\mathbf{e}'$. If the entropy of the data in dynamic operations is low, for the sake of confidentiality, the user can add some random bits in it. Then the user execute corresponding dynamic operations.

Modifying: Suppose that a user wants to modify $\mathbf{D}_{i,j}$ to $\mathbf{D}_{i,j} + m$. The user only needs to modify the $(j + 1)$-th column of $\mathbf{C}$. Let $\mathbf{d_j}$ be the $(j + 1)$-th column of $\mathbf{D}$, $\mathbf{c_j}$ be the $(j + 1)$-th column of $\mathbf{C}$, and $\mathbf{e_j}$ be the $(j + 1)$-th column of $\mathbf{E}$. Table 3 illustrates the operations. Specifically, **(i)** The user generates the new vector $\mathbf{d'_j}$ in which the $(i + 1)$-th element is m and other elements are 0. **(ii)** The user utilizes $f(s', r)$ to generate the error vector $\mathbf{e'_j}$. **(iii)** The user calculates $\mathbf{c'_j} = (\mathbf{A} \times \mathbf{d'_j} + (\mathbf{e'_j} - \mathbf{e_j})) \bmod q$. **(iv)** The user stores elements of $\mathbf{c'_j}$ to corresponding storage servers and authorizes storage vendors to do the addition operation. **(v)** Storage vendors compute $\tilde{c}_j = (\mathbf{c'_j} + \mathbf{c_j}) \bmod q$.

As an adversary cannot reconstruct $\mathbf{e'_j} - \mathbf{e_j}$, it cannot recover $\mathbf{D}$ or $\mathbf{d'_j}$ from $\mathbf{c'_j}$ and $\tilde{c}_j$. When decoding, the user can recover $\mathbf{D}_{i,j} + m$ with $\mathbf{A}$, $\mathbf{e'_j}$, and $\tilde{c}_j$. Subtraction and multiplication can use the same way mentioned above.

Deleting: This operation can be divided into two groups: **(i)** Deleting a whole column of **D**. As each column of the codewords **C** is independent of others, users only need to delete the column of **C** corresponding to the column of the deleted data. **(ii)** Deleting some elements of **D** in a column. Users apply the modifying operation by setting deleted numbers to corresponding positions.

Appending: When users want to append data to **D**, they do not need to change the codewords of **D**. They should generate the new data matrix **D′** which is transformed from the appending data. Then they generate the new error matrix **E′** using $f(\cdot)$, and then they encode **D′** to get the corresponding codewords **C′**. At last, users store **C′** to corresponding storage servers.

In a word, SWE favorably supports efficient and secure dynamic data operations. The reasons are as follows. **(i)** As SWE has the *additive homomorphic* property, the addition of **C** equals the addition of **D**. Therefore, users are not required to download or decode **C** while executing dynamic data operations. **(ii)** Each column of **C** is independent of others. Therefore, users only need to change the columns of **C** corresponding to the changed columns of **D**. **(iii)** If **C′** is the codeword generated in dynamic operations and **C** is the original codewords, an adversary cannot recover users' data from **C′** or **C** due to the hardness of LWE.

5   Scheme Analysis

In this section, we analyze SWE and comparable schemes form confidentiality, availability, and performance. As SSMS [12] does not specify a dispersal or encryption algorithm, we do not include it for the comparison.

5.1   Confidentiality

In SWE, we assume that different storage servers belong to different administrative and physical domains. Storage servers are honest but curious. An adversary can obtain all n codewords, except for s. We consider the attacking scenario that an adversary possesses some codewords and wants to verify whether the data that it encodes matches some predetermined value. Furthermore, if an adversary can verify that one element of **D** matches, then the adversary can be assured that the rest matches. Although this scenario is generous, many realistic attacking scenarios can be reduced to this one [3].

Shamir's algorithm [10]: If an adversary obtains k codewords, it can recover the data by solving the k liner equations. If an adversary obtains fewer than k codewords, it cannot discover any information of the data. Suppose that **d** is the data whose length is w bits. Each codewords is no shorter than w bits. If an adversary obtains $(k-1)$ codewords, it has to enumerate 2^w times to generate the k-th codewords. Every possible value of **d** is equal. Thus, Shamir's algorithm achieves information theoretic security.

Rabin's IDA [11]: In this dispersal scheme, the data is dispersed by the *non-systematic Reed-Solomon code*. Specifically, $c = G \times d$, where **G** is the Vandermonde matrix and is public. Hence, there is no randomness in the codewords.

Even if an adversary obtains one element of **c**, it can find some information of **d** by verifying that a codeword has a predetermined value.

AONT-RS [3]: The variant of AONT (i.e., the AONT utilizes AES-256 as "generator" and SHA-256 as "hash function") is applied in AONT-RS to guarantee data confidentiality. If an adversary obtains k codewords, it can compute the hash of encrypted data, h. Since the last element of the AONT package is $key \oplus h$, the adversary can recover the encryption key by computing $key \oplus h \oplus h$. Then the data can be recovered. If an adversary obtains fewer than k codewords, in order to find some information of the data, it has to enumerate 2^{256} times.

SWE: We analyze the confidentiality of SWE by using the brute force attack and the Arora-Ge algorithm [22].

(i) *Scenario 1: An adversary knows $f(\cdot)$ (i.e., the function of generating errors* **e***).* We utilize the brute force attack to analyze the confidentiality of SWE. If an adversary obtains k codewords, it has to figure out s to recover the data **d**. Let z be the length of s. Hence, the adversary has to enumerate 2^z times to recover **d**. In SWE, s is longer than 256 bits. If an adversary obtains fewer than k codewords, it cannot find any information of **d**. For example, an adversary obtains $(k - 1)$ codewords. In order to recover **d**, it has to enumerate at least $2^{z+q_{768}}$ times.

(ii) *Scenario 2: An adversary does not know $f(\cdot)$.* As different users can utilize different pseudorandom generators to implement $f(\cdot)$ as long as $e_{i,j} \leftarrow \mathcal{U}[-r, r]$, $f(\cdot)$ can be kept secret. Therefore, this storage scenario is common in practical. In this scenario, we utilize both the brute force attack and the Arora-Ge algorithm [22] to analyze the confidentiality of SWE.

(ii-A) The brute force attack: We consider this attack in two cases. The first case is to enumerate **e** to recover **d** for an adversary obtaining k codewords. In SWE, an adversary has to enumerate $(2r + 1)^n$ times. If an adversary obtains fewer than k codewords, it cannot discover any information of **d**. There is another exhaustive search method [23] for solving **d**, however, the method needs more than $2k$ codewords to transform the LWE instances to norm form of LWE. In the second case, the entropy of errors **e** is determined by s and the total complexity of brute force attack is 2^z times, where z is the length of s. Compared with the above two cases, we set the r is enough large to make that the complexity of brute force attack is at least 2^z. In our scheme, the smallest r is $\lceil \sqrt{q_{768}} \rceil$, which satisfies the requirement.

(ii-B) The Arora-Ge algorithm: The idea of Arora-Ge [22] is generating a nonlinear errors-free system of equations from LWE samples. We adapt the results of Arora-Ge from LWE with Gaussian errors to LWE with uniform errors. If an adversary has the computational power as the Arora-Ge algorithm, the time of recovering the data is $k^{O(r)}$. However this method needs $\mathcal{O}(k^{2r+1})$ codewords.

Theorem 2. *Assume that $r > 0$, $(\mathbf{A}, \mathbf{A}\mathbf{d} + \mathbf{e}) = (\mathbf{A}, \mathbf{c}) \in \mathcal{Z}_q^{n \times k} \times \mathcal{Z}_q^n$, and the uniform distribution of errors is $\mathcal{U}[-r, r]$, then the time complexity of the Arora-Ge algorithm is $k^{O(r)}$.*

Proof. The polynomial generated in the Arora-Ge can be $P(x) = X \prod_{i=1}^{r}(X-i)$. Assume that $q > (2r+1)n$ and $1 \leq n \leq \binom{k+1}{2}$, and generate $f_1, ..., f_n$, where $f_l = P(c_l - \sum_{j=1}^{k} x_j \mathbf{A}_{j,l})$. $f_1^H, ..., f_n^H$ are linearly independent with probability larger than $1 - \frac{(2r+1)n}{q}$ according to Schwartz-Zippel-Demillo-Lipton Lemma [22]. $P(\cdot)$ is monomials polynomial and has degree $D_{AG} \leq 2r+1$. Then the time complexity of Arora-Ge algorithm is $k^{O(D_{AG})} = k^{O(r)}$.   □

There are other algorithms which can assess *concrete hardness* of LWE such as BKW and other algorithms developed from BKW [23]. However, these algorithms are designed for standard instances of LWE with large k and relatively small q such as the example shown in Table 2. Contrary to LWE, SWE has relatively small k and large q. Meanwhile, BKW work in the assumption that an adversary can query oracle polynomial times. However, in dispersal storage scenarios, an adversary can obtain at most n codewords. Thus BKW is unsuitable for assessing the confidentiality of SWE.

From the above analysis, we can see that SWE achieves higher confidentiality than existing schemes under our assumptions. Although SWE has small k and exponential q, it still can guarantee data confidentiality. Furthermore, q and r are important to the confidentiality of SWE. When selecting parameters of SWE, we should set q to be large integers.

5.2 Availability

SWE and many existing schemes, such as Shamir's algorithm [10], Rabin's IDA [11], AONT-RS [3], etc., can guarantee data availability even though $(n-k)$ out of the n codewords are corrupted or completely unavailable. Therefore, larger $\frac{n-k}{n}$ means higher availability. However, larger $\frac{n-k}{n}$ also means more storage overhead and relatively lower security (i.e., an adversary needs to compromise fewer storage servers to reconstruct the data).

With the same data availability, the storage overhead of SWE is the same as the state of the art. For example, the data is $10\,\text{MB}$, $k = 3$, and $n = 5$. For Shamir's algorithm, as each codewords has the same length as the original data, the storage overhead is $5 \times 10 = 50\,\text{MB}$. For SWE, Rabin's IDA, and AONT-RS, $\mathbf{C}_{i,j}$ has the same length as $\mathbf{D}_{i,j}$. Thus SWE, Rabin's IDA, and AONT-RS require approximately the same storage overhead, $\frac{5}{3} \times 10 \approx 16.7\,\text{MB}$.

5.3 Performance

We suppose that the data $\mathbf{D}$ is $4\,\text{KB}$, $k = 6$, and $n = 12$. As multiplication is the most time consuming operation, we use the number of multiplications as the metric for comparing various algorithms.

Shamir's algorithm: To apply Shamir's algorithm, we divide $\mathbf{D}$ into 4096 bytes, $d_0, ..., d_{4095}$. Each of the 12 slices, $S_0, ..., S_{11}$, is composed of 4096 bytes, $s_{i,0}, ..., s_{i,4095}$. $s_{i,j}$ is a function of d_j and $r_{j,x}$. Specifically,

$$s_{i,j} = d_j \otimes \sum_{x=1}^{5} (i+1)^x \times r_{j,x},$$

where $r_{j,x}$ is a random byte. The arithmetic is over *Galois Field*, $GF(2^8)$. The number of multiplications is $12 \times 5 \times 4096 = 245760$.

Rabin's IDA: With Rabin's IDA, we append 2 bytes to **D**, and divide it into 6×683 bytes, $d_{0,0}, ..., d_{5,682}$. Subsequently, we calculate the 12×683 codewords using the *non-systematic Reed-Solomon coding*. Specifically,

$$c_{i,j} = \sum_{x=0}^{5} (i+1)^x \times d_{x,j}.$$

The arithmetic is over $GF(2^8)$. Therefore, the number of multiplications is $12 \times 6 \times 683 = 49176$.

AONT-RS: With AONT-RS, we utilize AES-256 as "generator" and SHA-256 as "hash function" in its AONT phase. We use the *systematic (6, 12) Reed-Solomon code* over $GF(2^8)$ in its RS phase. We divide **D** into 256 128-bit elements, $d_0, ..., d_{255}$. Then we add 128-bit "canary", d_{256}. We choose *key* to be 256 random bits and compute $c_i = d_i \oplus E(key, i+1)$. Next, we calculate $h = H(c_0, ..., c_{256})$. Subsequently, we set $c_{257} = h \oplus key$. As with the RS phase, we add 2 bytes and then divide the 4146 bytes into 6×691 bytes slices, which are also the first 6×691 codewords. Subsequently we calculate the last 6×691 codewords over $GF(2^8)$. AES-256 calls 14 times of the rounds function. Each rounds function of AES-256 equals six times of exclusive-or. We consider each rounds function of AES-256 to be six times of multiplication. The rounds function of SHA-256 has 64 iterations, and each input calls one time of the rounds function [24]. We consider each iteration in the rounds function of SHA-256 to be one time of multiplication. Thus the number of multiplications in AONT phase is $14 \times 257 \times 6 + 64 \times 257 = 38036$. The number of multiplications in RS phase is $6 \times 6 \times 691 = 24876$. The number of multiplications in AONT-RS is $38036 + 24876 = 62913$.

SWE: With SWE, when $k = 6$ and $n = 12$, the corresponding $q = q_{1024}$. Thus the arithmetic is over $GF(q_{1024})$. We append 4096 bits to **D**, and divide it into 6×6 1024-bit elements, $d_{0,0}, ..., d_{5,5}$. Next, we calculate 12×6 codewords

$$c_{i,j} = \sum_{x=0}^{5} a_{i,x} \times d_{x,j} + e_{i,j},$$

where $a_{i,j} \leftarrow \mathcal{Z}_q$. Suppose that SWE is implemented on a 64-bit machine. We use the number theoretic transform (NTT) and its inverse (INTT) to optimize the multiplication. Specifically,

$$a_{i,x} \times d_{x,j} = \text{INTT}(\text{NTT}(\hat{a}_{i,x}) \odot \text{NTT}(\hat{d}_{x,j})),$$

where $\odot$ donates point-wise multiplication, $\hat{a}_{i,x}$ is the polynomial corresponding to $a_{i,x}$, and $\hat{d}_{i,x}$ is the polynomial corresponding to $d_{i,x}$. The length of NTT or INTT is $m = 1025 \div 64 \approx 17$. We consider NTT and INTT to be $m \log_{10} m$ times of multiplication. Thus the number of multiplications is $12 \times 6 \times 6 \times (3 \times 17 \log_{10} 17 + 17) \approx 34454$.

From the above analysis, we can see that with those parameters, SWE outperforms Rabin's IDA, AONT-RS, and Shamir's algorithm. Shamir's algorithm is the slowest scheme among the four schemes. Although AONT-RS employs the *systematic Reed-Solomon code* [3] to eliminate the need to encode the first 6×691 codewords, the AONT phase is time consuming. The experiment results in the following section also demonstrate the above analysis.

6 Experiments and Evaluations

In order to validate SWE and obtain optimal parameters for SWE, we build the prototype of SWE. The experiments are conducted on a 64-bit machine with an Intel (R) Core (TM) i7-4790 processor (4 cores) at 3.6 GHZ with 4 GB RAM. We use Ubuntu 14.04 LTS as the operating system. We use NTL-9.3.0 and GMP-5.1.3 [25] as the tools for the number theory. We build the prototype of AONT-RS using OpenSSL-1.0.2f and Jerasure-1.2 [26]. SWE, AONT-RS, and Shamir's algorithm are implemented using C language and a single thread. The following experiment results are averaged from 50 experiments.

6.1 Performance Tuning

If we implement SWE with parameters only satisfying the hardness of LWE, data confidentiality can be guaranteed, but encoding/decoding speed may be slow. Therefore, in order to validate SWE and choose optimal parameters for SWE, we build the prototype of SWE and do the following experiments.

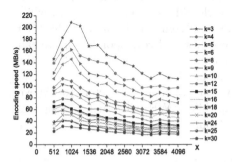

Fig. 6. Encoding speed of SWE varying with k and q_x.

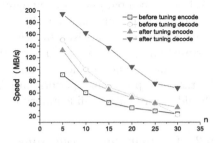

Fig. 7. Comparison data processing performance of SWE before and after optimizing parameters, where $k/n = 3/5$.

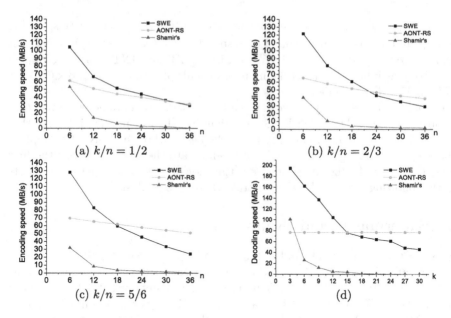

Fig. 8. Comparison of encoding/decoding speed, where (a)–(c) are for encoding and (d) is for decoding.

In this experiment, $\mathbf{A} \in \mathcal{Z}_q^{k \times k}$, $q = q_x$, q changes from q_{512} to q_{4096}, and $r = \lceil \sqrt{q} \rceil$. Figure 6 illustrates encoding speed of SWE varying with k and q_x. The results show that: **(i)** When $3 \leq k \leq 6$, the optimal q is q_{1024} (i.e., achieves fastest speed). **(ii)** When $6 < k \leq 30$, the optimal q is q_{768}.

After performance tuning, we do the experiment of comparison data processing performance of SWE, where $k/n = 3/5$ and $r = \lceil \sqrt{q} \rceil$. Before tuning SWE, $q = q_{2048}$. After tuning SWE, when $3 \leq k \leq 6$, $q = q_{1024}$, and when $6 < k \leq 18$, $q = q_{768}$. Figure 7 illustrates the results. The results show that: **(i)** k and n affect performance heavily. In practical, we should use smaller k and n, while SWE with such parameters should guarantee availability and confidentiality. **(ii)** q also affects performance heavily. With proper k and corresponding q, we can build a more efficient dispersal scheme. **(iii)** When encoding speed is high, the corresponding decoding speed is relatively high.

In a word, when implementing SWE, we should tune parameters to achieve better data processing performance. Meanwhile, SWE with such parameters should satisfy data confidentiality and availability.

6.2   Comparison on Encoding and Decoding

In this section, we evaluate performance of SWE and comparable schemes. Rabin's IDA [11] cannot guarantee data confidentiality. SSMS [12] does not specify a dispersal or encryption algorithm. Therefore, we do not compare SWE with Rabin's IDA or SSMS. Shamir's algorithm [10] achieves availability and high confidentiality. As far as we know, AONT-RS [3] is the best scheme that achieves balance between confidentiality and data processing performance. Thus, we compare SWE with Shamir's algorithm and AONT-RS in encoding/decoding speed. In AONT-RS, AES-256 and SHA-256 are applied in its AONT phase.

Encoding: We measure the encoding speed of SWE, Shamir's algorithm and AONT-RS. For SWE, $r = \lceil \sqrt{q} \rceil$, when $3 \leq k \leq 6$, $q = q_{1024}$, and when $6 < k \leq 30$, $q = q_{768}$. Figure 8 (a), (b) and (c) exhibit the encoding comparison results, where $k/n = 1/2$, $k/n = 2/3$, and $k/n = 5/6$, respectively. The results show that: **(i)** When $6 \leq n \leq 30$ and $k/n = 1/2$, SWE outperforms AONT-RS in encoding speed. **(ii)** When $6 \leq n \leq 18$ and $k/n = 2/3$, the encoding speed of SWE is faster than that of AONT-RS. **(iii)** When $6 \leq n \leq 12$ and $k/n = 5/6$, SWE performs better than AONT-RS in encoding speed. **(iv)** Among all the experiments, SWE outperforms Shamir's algorithm in encoding speed.

Decoding: We also measure the decoding speed of SWE, Shamir's algorithm, and AONT-RS. In this experiment, the parameters of SWE are the same as the parameters used in the encoding speed comparison. As the decoding speed of SWE or Shamir's algorithm depends on k (i.e., solve k equations), we only mention k in Fig. 8 (d). The results in Fig. 8 (d) show that: **(i)** As k and n grow, the decoding speed of SWE reduces heavily. The smaller is k, the higher is the decoding speed of SWE. **(ii)** When $k \leq 15$, the decoding speed of SWE is faster than that of AONT-RS. **(iii)** Among all the experiments, SWE outperforms Shamir's algorithm in decoding speed. **(iv)** As the *systematic Reed-Solomon code* is applied to disperse data in AONT-RS, if the codewords are obtained from the first k rows, decoding only involves the AONT phase. Thus, decoding speed of AONT-RS mentioned in Fig. 8 (d) is the best result. For AONT-RS, if there are some codewords which are not obtained from the first k rows, decoding involves both the AONT and Reed-Solomon decoding operations. Hence decoding speed of AONT-RS will be slower than the results mentioned in Fig. 8 (d), and as k and n grow, decoding speed of AONT-RS will reduce heavily.

Resch and Plank [3] suggest that in practical storage scenarios, n should always be smaller than 16. From the experiment results, we can see that with common configuration (i.e., $n \leq 16$), SWE outperforms AONT-RS and Shamir's algorithm in encoding/decoding speed.

Large k and n (e.g., $k = 200$, $n = 240$) lead to slow encoding/decoding speed. However, SWE with such a configuration is resistant to attacks from a quantum computer, which is capable of solving the *generalized discrete Fourier transform problems* [27]. When k and n are large, we can also use many well-established algorithms [28] to optimize matrices operations and thus improve encoding/decoding speed of SWE. However, such algorithms [28] are not efficient for AONT-RS, as the time consuming phase of AONT-RS is the AONT phase. In a word, when setting configurations for SWE, we should make trade-offs between data processing performance, confidentiality, and availability.

7 Conclusion

In this paper, we have proposed a secure and fast dispersal storage scheme, known as SWE. By applying the reformed LWE to SWE, even if an adversary obtains all the codewords, SWE can still guarantee data confidentiality. Theoretical analysis shows that under our assumptions, SWE achieves higher confidentiality than existing schemes, but still at the same storage cost with the state of the art. Furthermore, SWE favorably supports secure and efficient dynamic data operations, where users are not required to download or decode corresponding codewords, and no data information is leaked. Analysis and experiment results also show that with proper configurations, SWE outperforms the state of the art in encoding/decoding speed.

Based on our work, the hardness of LWE with small k, exponential q, and uniform errors can be further investigated. We hope an efficient reduction from the standard LWE to such variant of LWE can be given. Furthermore, efficient and secure dynamic data integrity auditing can be investigated based on SWE. These further investigations will allow us to build a securer and more efficient dispersal storage scheme.

References

1. Ciriani, V., De Capitani di Vimercati, S., Foresti, S., Jajodia, S., Paraboschi, S., Samarati, P.: Keep a few: outsourcing data while maintaining confidentiality. In: Backes, M., Ning, P. (eds.) ESORICS 2009. LNCS, vol. 5789, pp. 440–455. Springer, Heidelberg (2009). doi:10.1007/978-3-642-04444-1_27
2. Samarati, P., Di Vimercati, S.D.C.: Data protection in outsourcing scenarios: issues and directions. In: Proceedings of the 5th ACM Symposium on Information, Computer and Communications Security, pp. 1–14. ACM (2010)
3. Resch, J.K., Plank, J.S.: AONT-RS: blending security and performance in dispersed storage systems. In: Proceedings of the 9th USENIX Conference on File and Storage Technologies, pp. 229–240 (2011)
4. Bairavasundaram, L.N., Arpaci-Dusseau, A.C., Arpaci-Dusseau, R.H., Goodson, G.R., Schroeder, B.: An analysis of data corruption in the storage stack. ACM Trans. Storage (TOS) 4(3), 8 (2008)
5. Ab Rahman, N.H., Choo, K.K.R.: A survey of information security incident handling in the cloud. Comput. Secur. 49, 45–69 (2015)
6. Amazon S3 availability event: July 20, 2008 (2008). http://status.aws.amazon.com/s3-20080720.html
7. Experts say Facebook leak of 6 million users data might be bigger than we thought (2013). http://www.huffingtonpost.com/2013/06/27/facebook-leak-data_n_3510100.html
8. iCloud leaks of celebrity photos (2014). https://en.wikipedia.org/wiki/ICloud_leaks_of_celebrity_photos
9. Storer, M.W., Greenan, K.M., Miller, E.L., Voruganti, K.: POTSHARDS–a secure, recoverable, long-term archival storage system. ACM Trans. Storage (TOS) 5(2), 5 (2009)
10. Shamir, A.: How to share a secret. Commun. ACM 22(11), 612–613 (1979)

11. Rabin, M.O.: Efficient dispersal of information for security, load balancing, fault tolerance. J. ACM (JACM) **36**(2), 335–348 (1989)
12. Krawczyk, H.: Secret sharing made short. In: Stinson, D.R. (ed.) CRYPTO 1993. LNCS, vol. 773, pp. 136–146. Springer, Heidelberg (1994). doi:10.1007/3-540-48329-2_12
13. Erway, C.C., Küpçü, A., Papamanthou, C., Tamassia, R.: Dynamic provable data possession. ACM Trans. Inf. Syst. Secur. (TISSEC) **17**(4), 15 (2015)
14. Dong, X., Jiadi, Y., Luo, Y., Chen, Y., Xue, G., Li, M.: Achieving an effective, scalable and privacy-preserving data sharing service in cloud computing. Comput. Secur. **42**, 151–164 (2014)
15. Regev, O.: On lattices, learning with errors, random linear codes, and cryptography. J. ACM (JACM) **56**(6), 34 (2009)
16. Döttling, N., Müller-Quade, J.: Lossy codes and a new variant of the learning-with-errors problem. In: Johansson, T., Nguyen, P.Q. (eds.) EUROCRYPT 2013. LNCS, vol. 7881, pp. 18–34. Springer, Heidelberg (2013). doi:10.1007/978-3-642-38348-9_2
17. Brakerski, Z., Langlois, A., Peikert, C., Regev, O., Stehlé, D.: Classical hardness of learning with errors. In: Proceedings of the 45th Annual ACM Symposium on Theory of Computing, pp. 575–584. ACM (2013)
18. Micciancio, D., Peikert, C.: Trapdoors for lattices: simpler, tighter, faster, smaller. In: Pointcheval, D., Johansson, T. (eds.) EUROCRYPT 2012. LNCS, vol. 7237, pp. 700–718. Springer, Heidelberg (2012). doi:10.1007/978-3-642-29011-4_41
19. Reed, I.S., Solomon, G.: Polynomial codes over certain finite fields. J. Soc. Ind. Appl. Math. **8**(2), 300–304 (1960)
20. Bessani, A., Correia, M., Quaresma, B., André, F., Sousa, P.: DepSky: dependable and secure storage in a cloud-of-clouds. ACM Trans. Storage (TOS) **9**(4), 12 (2013)
21. Abu-Libdeh, H., Princehouse, L., Weatherspoon, H.: RACS: a case for cloud storage diversity. In: Proceedings of the 1st ACM Symposium on Cloud Computing, pp. 229–240. ACM (2010)
22. Arora, S., Ge, R.: Learning parities with structured noise. Electron. Colloquium Comput. Complex. **17**, 66 (2010)
23. Albrecht, M.R., Player, R., Scott, S.: On the concrete hardness of learning with errors. J. Math. Cryptology **9**(3), 169–203 (2015)
24. New instructions supporting the secure hash algorithm on Intel architecture processors (2013). https://software.intel.com/en-us/articles/intel-sha-extensions
25. NTL: A library for doing number theory (2015). http://www.shoup.net/ntl/
26. Plank, J.S., Simmerman, S., Schuman, C.D.: Jerasure: a library in c/c++ facilitating erasure coding for storage applications-version 1.2. Technical report. Citeseer (2008)
27. Curty, M.: Quantum cryptography: know your enemy. Nat. Phys. **10**(7), 479–480 (2014)
28. Drevet, C.É., Islam, M.N., Schost, É.: Optimization techniques for small matrix multiplication. Theor. Comput. Sci. **412**(22), 2219–2236 (2011)

ase-PoW: A Proof of Ownership Mechanism for Cloud Deduplication in Hierarchical Environments

Lorena González-Manzano[1($\boxtimes$)], Jose Maria de Fuentes[1],
and Kim-Kwang Raymond Choo[2]

[1] University Carlos III of Madrid, Leganés, Spain
{lgmanzan,jfuentes}@inf.uc3m.es
[2] Department of Information Systems and Cyber Security,
University of Texas at San Antonio, San Antonio, USA
raymond.choo@fulbrightmail.org

Abstract. Proof-of-Ownership (PoW) can be an effective deduplication technique to reduce storage requirements, by providing cloud storage servers the capability to guarantee that clients only upload and download files that they are in possession of. In this paper, we propose an attribute symmetric encryption PoW scheme (ase-PoW) for hierarchical environments such as corporations, in which (1) the external cloud service provider is honest-but-curious and (2) there is a flexible access control in place to ensure only users with the right privilege can access sensitive files. This is, to the best of our knowledge, the first such scheme and it is built upon the ce-PoW scheme of González-Manzano and Orfila (2015). ase-PoW outperforms ce-PoW in thaact it does not suffer from content-guessing attacks, it reduces client storage needs and computational workload.

Keywords: Deduplication technique · Proof of Ownership · Symmetric encryption · Access control

1 Introduction

Cloud storage services are increasingly popular with both individual and organizational users[1]. This is, perhaps, unsurprising due to the wide range of cloud storage solutions offering significant or unlimited amount of storage to individual users and organizations such as educational institutions [1,2]. Cloud storage has also attracted the attention of researchers [3] such as forensics [4–6], security and privacy [7–9], in addition to designing efficient and effective storage solutions. For example, deduplication techniques have been the subject of recent research focus due to their potential in significant reduction of cloud storage requirements.

---

[1] http://www.computerweekly.com/opinion/Time-to-outsource-data-storage and
http://www.lima.co.uk/blog/3-reasons-why-businesses-choose-to-outsource-their-data-storage/; last accessed 10 May 2016.

© ICST Institute for Computer Sciences, Social Informatics and Telecommunications Engineering 2017
R. Deng et al. (Eds.): SecureComm 2016, LNICST 198, pp. 412–428, 2017.
DOI: 10.1007/978-3-319-59608-2_24

Specifically, the deployment of deduplication techniques allows cloud servers to store only a single copy of the uploaded data together with the list of owners, thus, significantly reducing the storage requirements [10].

There are two main security challenges faced in deploying deduplication techniques in a hierarchical context, namely file access control and data leakage prevention. In the former, it is critical to ensure that only authorized users are granted access to the file. Let us consider a naive deduplication scheme, where a client sends a file identifier to the cloud and if it is already stored, then the server assumes that the client owns the file. However, this allows an attacker (including another malicious client) who only knows a file identifier but does not have the file to gain access to the file (e.g. by "colluding" with the file owner such as compromising the device of the file owner using malware). Proof of Ownership (PoW) scheme has been shown to be a viable solution against such an attack. PoW schemes, first introduced by Halevi *et al.* [11], guarantee that clients are in possession of the uploaded files, by presenting a proof of file ownership that can only be established when the file is available to the clients. Under a security parameter, a PoW is assumed to be secure even when an adversary knows part of the file [12]. Several PoW schemes extending the work of Halevi et al. have been proposed in the literature. For example, Di Pietro et al. [12] propose the s-PoW scheme designed to enhance client-side efficiency, Blasco et al. [13] present the bf-PoW scheme designed to achieve flexibility and scalability, and González-Manzano et al. [14] propose the ce-PoW scheme designed to deal with honest-but-curious servers and to achieve efficiency. In a hierarchical deployment, deduplication also needs to ensure that users have rights to access the data and a number of proposals have been presented in this regard [15–21]. Such requirement is also referred to as authorized deduplication [19]. However, existing proposals generally impose a significant burden on the cloud server or do not necessarily ensure that users own the file.

In the data leakage prevention scenario, given that data storage is outsourced, cloud servers are assumed to be honest-but-curious. Such servers honestly execute the proposed scheme but they may attempt to learn the stored content. To mitigate such threats, previous attempts have focused on encrypting the files. We observe that current solutions generally use symmetric encryption, due to the need to ensure that the result of the encryption of a same file remains the same in order to allow deduplication. The most common approach is to apply the Convergent Encryption (CE) scheme [16], where files are encrypted using their content as a key [22]. However, CE suffers from a number of limitations including content guessing attacks (i.e. malicious clients are able to discover the plaintext content) [14,16]. There is no known PoW solution that provides both file access control and data leakage prevention. This is the gap that this paper seeks to contribute to.

We present the Attribute Symmetric Encryption Proof of Ownership scheme (hereafter referred to as ase-PoW), which extends the ce-PoW scheme presented in [14]. Specifically, we include a lightweight access control procedure that does not impose any burden on the cloud server and our proposed scheme is designed to withstand content guessing attacks. To ensure that the scheme can be deployed in a hierarchical application, access control is achieved through encryption where the keys are linked to user attributes. Thus, only users with a given attribute (say belonging to a particular department, e.g. human resources) can access (and further deduplicate) the corresponding file (e.g. employees' contracts). We then demonstrate that ase-PoW outperforms ce-PoW, in terms of both storage and client efficiency.

The structure of the paper is as follows. Section 2 reviews the ce-PoW scheme. Section 3 describes the proposed scheme ase-PoW. We demonstrate the security and utility of the proposed scheme in Sects. 4 and 5. Related work is discussed in Sect. 6. Finally, Sect. 7 concludes the paper and outlines future research directions.

2   Revisiting the ce-PoW Scheme

The ce-PoW scheme [14] is an efficient PoW scheme designed for an environment involving honest-but-curious servers. In the scheme, files are encrypted using Convergent Encryption (CE) where the encryption key is the file itself, and proof of ownership is achieved by requesting from clients some CE-encrypted chunks. Specifically, let $\mathcal{H}_1 : \{0,1\}^* \rightarrow \{0,1\}^n$ and $\mathcal{H}_2 : \{0,1\}^B \rightarrow \{0,1\}^l$ cryptographic hash functions, where B and l represent the chunk size and the token size respectively; and n is a positive integer. There are two phases in the ce-PoW scheme, namely:

– **Initialization**: The client sends the file size to the server, which responds with the number of chunks the file should be split into. Then, the client convergently encrypts each chunk, computes $\mathcal{H}_2$ over each encrypted chunk and finally, computes $\mathcal{H}_1$ over the resulting hashes obtaining h_c. Both h_c and the encrypted chunks are then sent to the server. The server will compute h_c from the received encrypted chunks and verify whether the computed result is the same as the received data to avoid poisoning attacks. If the verification returns true, then the server creates an array storing three structures, namely: one structure to store the list of owners, one structure to maintain a list of challenges, and another one to store the responses to the challenges.
– **Challenge**: The server receives a h_c value. If h_c entry is not found, then the server requests the client to upload the file size; thus, reverting to the initialization phase. If an entry for h_c exists, then the server loads in memory the first unused challenge together with the corresponding responses, prior to sending the challenge to the "claiming" client. The client then computes the response token for each of the J chunk indices and sends the array of response tokens to the server. Subsequently, the server checks whether the received tokens match the stored tokens. If the check returns true, then the server labels the PoW as successful and assigns the file to the client. Otherwise, the client is considered to have failed the PoW.

This scheme is proven to be secure under the bounded leakage setting, in which a limited portion of a file may be leaked (i.e. 64 MB) but the file owner is able to prove the possession of such a file in a secure manner [11].

However, the ce-PoW scheme suffers from two main weaknesses.

1. Due to the use of convergent encryption, the scheme is vulnerable to the inherent content-guessing attacks.
2. Due to the need to store decryption keys (i.e. chunk hashes) on the client devices in order to decrypt downloaded files, the number of keys stored by any client corresponds to the file size for files smaller than 64 MB and 5% of the file size for files larger than 64 MB. This is an unrealistic requirement, particularly for client devices such as smart phones.

3 Attribute Symmetric Encryption Proof of Ownership Scheme

In this section, we present an overview of the system, the threat model and the goals of the proposed scheme, prior to describing the scheme.

3.1 System Overview

To explain how ase-PoW can be implemented in practice, let us consider the following use case.

Use Case. A University consists of Departments (D_i) divided into Groups (G_i), which work in different Projects (P_i). Members of a given G_i may work in different P_i. In addition, each P_i has a G_i who is the designated leader. Users involved in D_i, G_i and P_i have their own attributes and thus, they have corresponding keys.

For simplicity, we now assume that there are two departments, D_1 and D_2 (Fig. 1). The former is composed by G_1 and G_2, which manage a pair of projects, P_1 and P_2. G_1 and G_2 are leaders of P_1 and P_2 respectively. In D_2, there is only one group, G_3, which is the leader of P_3. Moreover, G_1 takes part in P_2 and G_2 is involved in P_3.

In terms of managing files f_1 and f_2 of P_3, there are two main steps, namely: encryption and deduplication. For encryption, let us assume that f_1 needs to be accessible only to users involved in P_3 whereas f_2 can only be accessed by G_2 members working on P_3. Thus, f_1 is symmetrically encrypted with K_{P_3} while f_2 is also symmetrically encrypted with K_{f_2} which is created encrypting K_{G_2} with K_{P_3}.

For deduplication, we will now focus our discussion on f_1. At first, one of the users involved in P_3 uploads f_1 after encryption, together with its digest h_c (recall Sect. 2). It must be noted that h_c is used by the server to identify f_1 in subsequent uploads. Then, the server prepares three data structures, namely one to store the list of owners, another to keep a list of challenges, and the third for their expected responses. Thus, at the time other client tries to upload f_1,

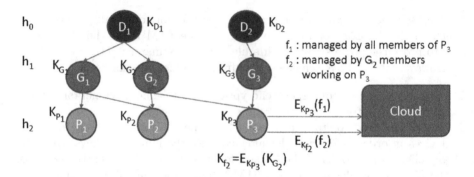

Fig. 1. An example use case

the server requests a set of challenges. If such challenges are provided as per specification, it is assumed that f_1 is owned by this client and the client will be added to the list of owners.

3.2   Entities

In ase-PoW, three entities are identified. First, the **client** is the entity that holds the file to be deduplicated. Each client is a user of a hierarchical organizations, i.e. a corporation, that belongs to one or more of its areas, i.e. departments. He performs the PoW to the storage server, which is in charge of keeping all files. For each file, the **server** manages data structures that contain the identities of clients which are allowed to access to the file and the challenges to be satisfied in the PoW, as it will be explained later. Apart from the client and the server an **Attribute Certificate Service (ACS)** is introduced. It is responsible for managing which users belong to each department over time. As such, ACS grants or revokes the permission to access to confidential files, once a user joins or leaves an area.

3.3   Threat Model

The adversary is assumed to be an attacker who attempts to download a file he does not possess, via the following means:

– **Content-guessing attack** where attackers intercept interchanged PoW challenges and try to guess their content.
– **Collusion attack** in which the legitimate file owner colludes with a malicious client (an adversary $\tilde{C}$) leaking part of the file content. In [14], a PoW scheme works on the assumption that the exchange of information is not interactively performed along the PoW challenge, in addition to the assumption that 64 MB is sufficiently large to discourage collusion [11].

3.4   Goals

A total of six goals are considered in this proposal. The first three goals focus on security, namely: goals one and two capture the scenario where an adversary seeking to download a file he does not own, and the third goal deals with access control. The remaining set of goals capture the performance requirements, namely: minimizing bandwidth, memory consumption and storage space. Specifically, the goals of this proposal are as follows:

Security: an adversary $\tilde{C}$, who does not possess a complete file f, has a negligible advantage in succeeding in a PoW given a security parameter κ.

Collusion resistance: an adversary $\tilde{C}$, who does not possess a complete file f, must exchange a minimum amount S_{min} of information with the legitimate owner of f to be successful in the PoW. According to Halevi et al. [11] S_{min} is set to 64 MB.

Simple fine-grained access control: the encryption, apart from providing confidentiality, should allow the management of access control without involving the cloud server in the access control management process and without requiring the involvement of additional tasks for the client and the server. Besides, it should be as fine-grained as possible, thus allowing the specification of different encryption policies.

Bandwidth efficiency: the number of exchanged bytes between client and server along a PoW execution should be minimized.

Server space efficiency: in a PoW, the server should load in memory a small piece of information independent of the input file size.

Client space efficiency: regardless of the use of cryptography, clients have to store as few keys as possible. In addition, the number of stored keys should be independent of file sizes.

3.5   The Proposed Scheme

The scheme builds on the scheme presented in [14], and the key differences are the use of symmetric encryption on the chunks and the enforcement of access control.

To carry out cryptographic computations, ase-PoW leverages on the hierarchical structure of organizations as well as the existence of ACS. In particular, belonging to each organizational unit (say Department or Group) or working on a given Project implies that each user holds an attribute. Each attribute is linked to a key provided by ACS. Thus, when a user requests the attestation of attributes, ACS verifies such attributes and provides keys accordingly.

In this scheme, there are two phases – see Fig. 2. In the **Initialization phase**, the client firstly requests keys to ACS and symmetric keys are delivered when the client possesses the right attributes. Then, the client requests the upload of a file sending the digest of the encrypted file h_c to the server. Once the server verifies the file is not already stored (h_c not stored), the client sends the file size and the server provides the amount of chunks the file should be split into. The

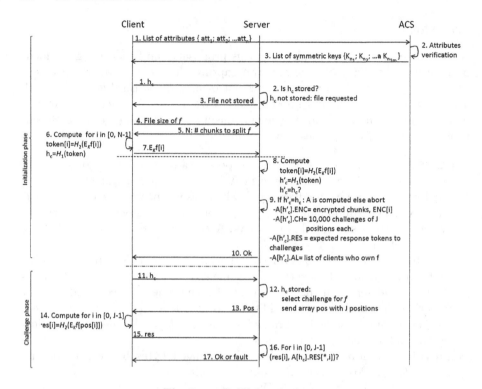

Fig. 2. ase-PoW description.

client symmetrically encrypts each file chunk applying keys provided by ACS (Algorithm 1). In case multiple keys are at stake, each chunk is symmetrically encrypted with a key (K_S). Such key is formed by a recursive encryption of the set of keys that are found in the path from f_i to the highest group of corporate members that need access to it. Thus, let a and b the levels in which f_i and the said group are located, respectively. The encryption key is then formed by $K_S = E_{K_a}(...(E_{K_{b-1}}(K_b)))$. Note that if $a = b$, then no recursive encryption is needed since the file is already accessible to the smallest group of members. After encryption, each encrypted chunk of file f is denoted as $E_{K_S}f[i]$. In last place, the encrypted file is sent to the server which initializes an array $\mathcal{A}$ where h_c is the lookup key - $\mathcal{A}[h_c].ENC$ contains encrypted file chunks, $\mathcal{A}[h_c].CH$ stores 10,000 challenges (with J random positions each), $\mathcal{A}[h_c].RES$ keeps the expected response tokens that correspond to the challenges and $\mathcal{A}[h_c].AL$ contains a list of identifiers of clients who own f (Algorithm 2).

In the **Challenge phase**, when a stored file is requested because h_c sent by the client matches with the one stored in the server, the client encrypts requested file chunks and performs a digest $\mathcal{H}_2$ over it until complete the requested challenge (Algorithm 3). As aforementioned, the encryption may involve creating K_S recursively. Finally, the PoW will be passed or not according to the verification

---

Algorithm 1. First client upload at client side

Input: Number of chunks N, a file f and encryption key(s) K_j in the encryption order $\{1;...;j\}$
Output: Hash h_c of the symmetrically encrypted file chunks; and symmetric encrypted chunks $E_{K_j}f[i]$ or $E_{K_j}(...(E_{K_1}f[i]))$
for $i \leftarrow 0$ **to** $N-1$ **do**
  $|$ $token[i] \leftarrow [\mathcal{H}_2(E_{K_N}f[i])$ or $\mathcal{H}_2(E_{K_j}(...(E_{K_1}f[i]))))]$;
end
$h_c \leftarrow \mathcal{H}_1(token)$;
return h_c and $E_{K_j}f[i]$ or $E_{K_j}(...(E_{K_1}f[i]))$;

Algorithm 2. First client upload in ase-PoW. Server side (analogous to ce-PoW [14] except for the encryption procedure)

Input: Encrypted chunks $ENC[i] = E_{K_S}f[i]$ and h_c uploaded by client $\mathcal{C}$.
Output: The entry $\mathcal{A}[h_c]$
for $i \leftarrow 0$ **to** $N-1$ **do**
  Compute array $token$ from received $ENC[i]$
  $token[i] \leftarrow \mathcal{H}_2(ENC[i])$;
end
$h_c \leftarrow \mathcal{H}_1(token)$;
if $\neg Match(h_c, \mathcal{H}_1(token))$ **then**
  $|$ **return** $\perp$;
end
Store 10,000 random challenges CH with J indexes each
for $x \leftarrow 0$ **to** 9999 **do**
  for $y \leftarrow 0$ **to** $J-1$ **do**
    $|$ $pos[y] \leftarrow PRF(seed)$; $CH[x,y] \leftarrow pos[y]$; $RES[x,y] \leftarrow token[pos[y]]$;
  end
end
$\mathcal{A}[h_c].ENC \leftarrow ENC$; $\mathcal{A}[h_c].CH \leftarrow CH$; $\mathcal{A}[h_c].RES \leftarrow RES$; $\mathcal{A}[h_c].AL \leftarrow \{id(\mathcal{C})\}$;
return $\mathcal{A}[h_c]$;

---

the server performs comparing the received responses (res) with the stored ones ($\mathcal{A}[h_c].RES$) (Algorithm 4).

4 Security Analysis

We now demonstrate that the ase-PoW scheme achieves the first three goals described in Sect. 3.4, and the remaining goals will be addressed in Sect. 5.

4.1 Security

The security analysis of ase-PoW is based on ce-PoW [14] and builds on the earlier proofs of Di Pietro et al. [12] and Blasco et al. [13]. The adversary is

Algorithm 3. Challenge phase at client side

Input: A file f, an array pos of J indexes and encryption key(s) K_j in the
encryption order $\{1,...,j\}$
Output: An array res of J response tokens
for $i \leftarrow 0$ *to* $J - 1$ do
$\quad | \quad res[i] \leftarrow [\mathcal{H}_2(E_{K_j} f[i])$ *or* $\mathcal{H}_2(E_{K_j}(...(E_{K_1} f[i])))]$;
end
return res;

Algorithm 4. Challenge phase in ase-PoW. Server side. (Analogous to
ce-PoW [14])

Input: h_c of a file f; two arrays pos and res of J indexes and client response
tokens, respectively
Output: The outcome of the challenge
for $i \leftarrow 0$ *to* $J - 1$ do
$\quad$ if $\neg Match(res[i], \mathcal{A}[h_c].RES[*, i]))$ then
$\quad\quad | \quad$ return $\bot$;
$\quad$ end
end
$\mathcal{A}[h_c].AL \leftarrow \mathcal{A}[h_c].AL \bigcup\{id(\mathcal{C})\}$;
return $\top$;

challenged on J independent chunk positions where the probability of success is:

$$P(succ) = P(tok_i)^J = (p + 0.5^l(1 - p))^J, \tag{1}$$

where p is the probability that a malicious client $\tilde{\mathcal{C}}$ knows part of the file; thus,
able to perform a collusion or a content guessing attack.
From Eq. 1, a lowerbound for J is derived which ensures $P(succ) \leq 2^\kappa$, where κ
is the security parameter, as

$$J \geq \frac{\kappa \ln 2}{(1 - p)(1 - (0.5^l))} \tag{2}$$

In this regard, the first goal of ase-PoW, *security*, is satisfied when Eq. 2
holds under parameter κ. Moreover, the second requirement, *collusion resis-tance* involves ensuring that a legitimate client $\mathcal{C}$ does not exchange S_{min} bytes
with a malicious client $\tilde{\mathcal{C}}$ to allow the malicious client to run a successful PoW
for an unknown file. Considering that chunks are managed, there are $\frac{F}{B}$ tokens
in a file f of size F of chunks of size B, the token length l can be set as:

$$l \geq S_{min} \frac{B}{F} \tag{3}$$

The third security goal, *simple access control*, is also achieved. Access control is
enforced by the fact that the ownership of attributes becomes a key to access
files. Just an ACS is introduced to deliver keys once attributes are attested and
it does not have any active role in the deduplication process. In addition, fine

grained access control is achieved due to the use of recursive encryptions. They can be compared with the encryption of files with attributes (keys) concatenated with AND operators, meaning that different encryption policies can be applied.

Apart from the previous issues, ase-PoW tackles the content-guessing attack. In contrast to [12,13] which do not apply encryption and to [14] which applies CE, a symmetric encryption scheme is applied herein. It ensures encrypted chunks are independent of files entropy, thus preventing this attack. Indeed, even if files were obtained by attackers they could not be decrypted.

4.2 Complexity

We now evaluate the complexity of ase-PoW with that of Di Pietro et al. [12], Blasco et al. [13] and González-Manzano et al. [14]. In particular, the evaluations (see Table 1) focus on client and server computation and I/O, server memory usage, bandwidth, and number of used keys (if required).

We remark that ase-PoW complexity differs from ce-PoW in a critical aspect, namely: the number of keys managed by the client. Particularly, in ase-PoW, client computation involves a symmetric encryption scheme based on a chosen number of recursive encryptions (n_{re}) in relation to owned attributes. As a result, the client only needs to manage up to n_{re} keys, regardless of the number of files under deduplication. In ce-PoW, the client needs to store all chunk hashes of every file deduplicated, as these hashes are the file-specific decryption key. This may be up to 5% the file size, e.g. 50 MB for 1 GB files. Thus, ase-PoW reduces the storage space needed in the client to allow deduplication.

The comparisons between ase-PoW and s-PoW and bf-PoW are similar to those with ce-PoW. It is clear that client and server computations involve less complexity in s-PoW and bf-PoW than in the other schemes, since there is no encryption involved. The bandwidth requirement is also noticeably lower in s-PoW and bf-PoW, as in ase-PoW and ce-PoW J tokens are sent to the server. However, neither s-Pow nor bf-PoW protect against honest-but-curious servers. Thus, striking a balance between security and efficiency is expected. The remaining set of features can be considered similar among all studied schemes.

5   Performance Evaluation

We now present the findings of our evaluations, based on the settings described in [14]. Specifically, ase-PoW is evaluated against bf-PoW [13] and ce-PoW [14]. We did not evaluate our proposal against s-PoW [12] because it has been shown that ce-PoW outperforms s-PoW.

All schemes were implemented in C++ using OpenSSL as a cryptographic library. AES in counter mode and SHA-1 are the two main operations. As in [14], $\mathcal{H}_1$ and $\mathcal{H}_2$ are based on SHA-1 being $\mathcal{H}_2$ applied over encrypted chunks extending the length of the hash to l through the use of the stream cipher RC4.

To ensure a fair evaluation, we used the parameters defined in [13,14], namely: the security parameter is set to $\kappa = 66$; $S_{min} = 64$ MB, the size of tokens (l) is

Table 1. Complexity comparative summary. Applied symbols are taken from Sect. 4

	s-PoW [12]	bf-PoW [13]	ce-PoW	ase-PoW [14]
Client computation	$O(F) \cdot hash$	$O(F) \cdot hash$	$O(B) \cdot CE \cdot hash \cdot hash$	$O(B) \cdot Sym. \cdot n_{re} \cdot hash$
Client I/O	$O(F)$	$O(F)$	$O(F)$	$O(F)$
Server init computation	$O(F) \cdot hash$	$O(F) \cdot hash$	$O(B) \cdot hash \cdot hash$	$O(B) \cdot hash$
Server regular computation	$O(n \cdot \kappa) \cdot PRF$	$O\left(\frac{l \cdot \kappa \cdot (log 1/p_f)}{p_f}\right) \cdot hash$	$O(n \cdot l \cdot \kappa) \cdot PRNG$	$O(n \cdot l \cdot \kappa) \cdot PRNG$
Server init I/O	$O(F)$	$O(F)$	$O(F)$	$O(F)$
Server regular I/O	$O(n \cdot \kappa)$	$O(0)$	$O(0)$	$O(0)$
Server memory usage	$O(n \cdot \kappa)$	$O\left(\frac{log(1/p_f)}{l}\right)$	$O(n \cdot l \cdot \kappa)$	$O(n \cdot l \cdot \kappa)$
Bandwidth	$O(\kappa)$	$O\left(\frac{l \cdot \kappa}{p_f}\right)$	$O(l \cdot \kappa)$	$O(l \cdot \kappa)$
# stored keys	–	–	up to 5% file size	$\mid att \mid$

Table 2. Chunk sizes (B) in bytes, computed from the file size, the token size and S_{min}

l(B)	File size (MB)									
	4	8	16	32	64	128	256	512	1024	2048
16	16	16	16	16	16	32	64	128	256	512
64	64	64	64	64	64	128	256	512	1024	2048
256	256	256	256	256	256	512	1024	2048	4096	8192
1024	1024	1024	1024	1024	1024	2048	4096	8192	16384	32768

set to {16, 64, 256,1024} bytes, the probability (p) that an adversary knows a chunk of a file is set to {0.3; 0.5; 0.75; 0.95} and that key size is 256B. According to these values and Eq. 2, the number of requested challenges (J) corresponds to {65, 91, 182, 914}. Similarly, considering the said values of l, S_{min} and the input file size, the size of chunks (B) is according to Eq. 3 – see Table 2.

The experiments were performed on a AMD Athlon(tm) II x2 220 processor with 4 GB of RAM. Input files were randomly generated and their sizes ranged from 4 MB to 2 GB doubling the size at each step.

The client side computation is studied in the following section. Server side computation of ase-PoW is similar to that of ce-PoW since the server tasks remain unaltered. Then, server side computation in ase-PoW (and ce-PoW) is comparable with that of bf-PoW (see [14]).

On the client side, the most relevant issue to consider is the time taken (in clock cycles units) to compute challenges. First of all, the time taken to create the chunk encryption key were computed, resulting in 12262 clock cycles when there were 7 keys (6 recursive encryptions) and 18743 clock cycles when there were 11 keys (10 recursive encryptions). These values are considered negligible relative to the remaining part of the scheme. Then, to present a worst case

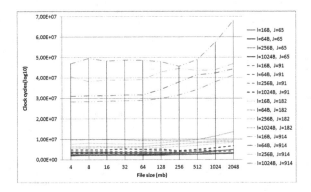

Fig. 3. Client response creation clock cycles for $J = \{65,91,182,914\}$ challenges and 11 keys.

analysis, the computation of challenges considering 11 keys was studied. Results are depicted in Fig. 3. We concluded that:

- The time remains constant regardless of the number of requested challenges, namely for J = 65 and J = 91. As expected, the time increases when more challenges are computed, specially for J = 914.
- The time also remains constant regardless of the file and chunk size when $l < 64$B. In case of higher l, e.g. $l = 1024$ B, the time increases between files of 512 MB and 2 GB but it is just particularly noticeable for J = 914, and to a lesser extent for J = 182.

Figure 4 describes the evaluation findings of bf-PoW, ce-PoW and ase-PoW when there were 11 keys, and it is clear that bf-PoW has the best performance. This is because in bf-PoW, a token is computed for each J chunk index through a hash function. However, performance of bf-PoW is comparable with ase-PoW for $l = 1024$ b and bf-PoW does not protect against honest-but-curious servers. On the other hand, ase-PoW outperforms ce-Pow in all cases. In ce-PoW, a hash per encrypted chunk is computed which increases the computation time. By contrast, ase-PoW symmetrically encrypts chunks and though the chunk encryption key may involve several recursive encryptions, findings demonstrate that the time to compute this key is negligible in comparison with the rest of the process.

6   Related Work

Deduplication, such as PoW schemes, has been the subject of research focus [11–14,23]. For example, the PoW schemes in [15,17,24–27] are designed to work with honest-but-curious servers. Due to the use of CE in many existing PoW schemes such as [16,17,22,25,26], these schemes are not secure against content analysis attacks as previously discussed [16]. A number of proposals to avoid such pitfalls has also been proposed in recent years. For example, in [27], files are

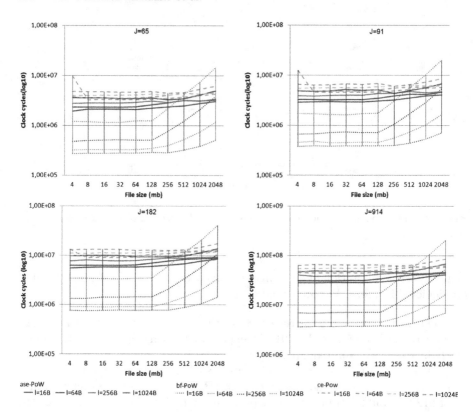

Fig. 4. Client response creation clock cycles for $J = \{65,91,182,914\}$ challenges and 11 keys.

asymmetrically encrypted and decryption keys are interchanged among clients. The proposed approach in [24] involves an identity provider designed to prevent sybil attacks, and an indexing server to prevent data leakage.

The significant amount of data managed by cloud servers necessitates the implementation of access control solutions, as this will allow servers the capability to determine whether a requesting client has the appropriate access rights. Attribute based encryption (ABE) is one commonly used method to achieve fine grained access control in the cloud [28–31], where files are encrypted under a set of attributes and decrypted by a key with the right attribute policy [28]. However, deduplication is not considered in these works which is unsurprisingly since ABE is a non-deterministic encryption scheme and therefore, cannot be applied to this context.

Table 3 compares the proposed ase-PoW scheme and other similar deduplication and access control schemes, based on the use of a PoW scheme, security against honest-but-curious servers, involvement of third parties, theoretical security analysis, search of bandwidth, server and client side space efficiency, and empirical performance analysis.

Table 3. Comparative summary

Proposals	PoW scheme	Honest-but-curious servers	Third parties	Theoretical security analysis	Bandwidth efficiency	Server space efficiency	Client space efficiency	Empirical analysis
[15]	√	Not specified Public keys used	Intermediator	–	–	–	–	–
[16]	–		Metadata manager, additional server	–	–	–	–	√
[17, 21]	√*	Message-lock encrypt	Key server	–	√	–	–	√
[19]	√*	Convergent encryption	Private	–	–	–	–	–
[20]	–	Convergent encryption	Multiple servers	–	–	–	–	√
[18]	–	Convergent encryption	Distributed key server	–	–	–	–	√
[32]	√	–	Auditor	√	–	–	–	–
ase-PoW	√	Symmetric encryption	Attribute certification server	√	√	√	√	√

*: mentioned but not applied

It is clear that access control and deduplication require additional entities and additional management tasks. In [16], for example, a metadata manager enforces key management and handles deduplication. In [17,21], there exists a key server per group of clients which is in charge of key management and helps in the deduplication process. In [20], the Dekey scheme shares encryption keys among clients via distributed key servers. The SecDep scheme in [18] involves multiple key servers, which are also tasked with deduplication. In [32], an auditor verifies the integrity of data in the cloud.

There are only a small number of proposals using a PoW scheme while managing deduplication and access control [15,17,19,21]. Although [15,17,21] mention the use of PoW, no concrete details are provided. In [19], an intermediator becomes the PoW verifier.

Shin et al. [32] appears to be the only work that provides a security analysis and no other studies examine server and client space efficiency. With the exception of [15], key storage is externalized to additional servers, relieving clients from the burden of managing and storing keys. Bandwidth efficiency is considered only in [17,21], and just some schemes do an empirical analysis [16–18,20,21].

In summary, it is clear that achieving both effective and secure PoW and access control management for deduplication in the presence of honest-but-curious servers is an understudied topic.

7   Conclusion

Cloud storage is a trend that is unlikely to go away anytime soon, and one of the key challenges is to reduce storage requirements. Deduplication schemes are a viable solution, and in this paper, we present the Attribute Symmetric Encryption Proof of Ownership (ase-PoW) scheme. The scheme is based on recursively and symmetrically encrypting file chunks to prove the possession of files. We demonstrate the security of the scheme, as well as the utility of the scheme using empirical analysis. Specifically, we show that ase-PoW is efficient and has better performance compared with similar schemes in the literature (e.g. outperforms ce-PoW, and ase-PoW has the benefit of having a constant computation time for file types when $l < 64\,\text{B}$).

Future work includes enhancing access control expressiveness, and combining deduplication and Proof of Works [33] and Remote Data Possession Checking [34] in an environment with untrusted cloud servers. Moreover, simple fine-grained access control is achieved in this work but the development of a more complex access control management scheme, e.g. [30], is the following step.

Acknowledgments. This work was partially supported by the MINECO grant TIN2013-46469-R (SPINY: Security and Privacy in the Internet of You) and the CAM grant S2013/ICE-3095 CIBERDINE-CM (CIBERDINE: Cybersecurity, Data, and Risks) funded by Madrid Autonomous Community and co-funded by European funds. L. González and J.M. de Fuentes were also supported by the Programa de Ayudas para la Movilidad of Carlos III University of Madrid, Spain.

References

1. Girardi, R.: New drive for education with unlimited storage (2014). http://google.umich.edu/tech-updates/newdriveforeducationwithunlimitedstorage
2. Quick, D., Choo, K.-K.R.: Impacts of increasing volume of digital forensic data: a survey and future research challenges. Digit. Invest. **11**(4), 273–294 (2014)
3. Zissis, D., Lekkas, D.: Addressing cloud computing security issues. Future Gener. Comput. Syst. **28**(3), 583–592 (2012)
4. Martini, B., Choo, K.-K.R.: Cloud storage forensics: owncloud as a case study. Digit. Invest. **10**(4), 287–299 (2013)
5. Quick, D., Martini, B., Choo, K.-K.R.: Cloud Storage Forensics. Syngress Publishing/Elsevier, Waltham (2013)
6. Quick, D., Choo, K.-K.R.: Dropbox analysis: data remnants on user machines. Digit. Invest. **10**(1), 3–18 (2013)
7. Li, L., Lu, R., Choo, K.-K.R., Datta, A., Shao, J.: Privacy-preserving outsourced association rule mining on vertically partitioned databases. IEEE Trans. Inf. Forensics Secur. **11**(8), 1 (2016)
8. Liu, X., Choo, K., Deng, R., Lu, R., Weng, J.: Efficient and privacy-preserving outsourced calculation of rational numbers. IEEE Trans. Dependable Secure Comput. **PP**(99), 1–14 (2016)
9. Liu, X., Deng, R.H., Choo, K.-K.R., Weng, J.: An efficient privacy-preserving outsourced calculation toolkits with multiple keys. IEEE Trans. Inf. Forensics Secur. **11**(11), 2401–2414 (2016)

10. Harnik, D., Pinkas, B., Shulman-Peleg, A.: Side channels in cloud services: deduplication in cloud storage. IEEE Secur. Priv. **8**(6), 40–47 (2010)
11. Halevi, S., Harnik, D., Pinkas, B., Shulman-Peleg, A.: Proofs of ownership in remote storage systems. In: Proceedings of the 18th ACM Conference on Computer and Communications Security, pp. 491–500. ACM (2011)
12. Di Pietro, R., Sorniotti, A.: Boosting efficiency and security in proof of ownership for deduplication. In: Proceedings of the 7th ACM Symposium on Information, Computer and Communications Security, pp. 81–82. ACM (2012)
13. Blasco, J., Orfila, A., Pietro, R.D., Sorniotti, A.: A tunable proof of ownership scheme for deduplication using bloom filters. In: Proceedings of the IEEE Conference on Communications and Network Security, CNS (2014)
14. González-Manzano, L., Orfila, A.: An efficient confidentiality-preserving proof of ownership for deduplication. J. Netw. Comput. Appl. **50**, 49–59 (2015)
15. Jin, X., Wei, L., Yu, M., Yu, N., Sun, J.: Anonymous deduplication of encrypted data with proof of ownership in cloud storage. In: Proceedings of the 13th IEEE/CIC International Conference on Communications in China (ICCC), pp. 224–229 (2013)
16. Puzio, P., Molva, R., Önen, M., Loureiro, S.: Block-level de-duplication with encrypted data. Open J. Cloud Comput. (OJCC) **1**(1), 10–18 (2014)
17. Bellare, M., Keelveedhi, S., Ristenpart, T.: Dupless: server-aided encryption for deduplicated storage. In: Proceedings of the 22nd USENIX Conference on Security, pp. 179–194. USENIX Association (2013)
18. Zhou, Y., Feng, D., Xia, W., Fu, M., Huang, F., Zhang, Y., Li, C.: Secdep: a user-aware efficient fine-grained secure deduplication scheme with multi-level key management. In: 2015 31st Symposium on Mass Storage Systems and Technologies (MSST), pp. 1–14 (2015)
19. Li, J., Li, Y.K., Chen, X., Lee, P.P., Lou, W.: A hybrid cloud approach for secure authorized deduplication. IEEE Trans. Parallel Distrib. Syst. **26**(5), 1206–1216 (2015)
20. Naresh, V., Kumar, G.: A novel secure deduplication implementation with efficient and reliable. Int. J. Innov. Technol. **3**(6), 1001–1006 (2015)
21. Miao, M., Wang, J., Li, H., Chen, X.: Secure Multi-server-Aided Data Deduplication in Cloud Computing. Elsevier, Amsterdam (2015)
22. Storer, M.W., Greenan, K., Long, D.D., Miller, E.L.: Secure data deduplication. In: Proceedings of the 4th ACM International Workshop on Storage Security and Survivability, pp. 1–10. ACM (2008)
23. Arbour, F.M., Reker, M.M.: System and method for exporting data directly from deduplication storage to non-deduplication storage. US Patent Application 11/731,178, 30 March 2007
24. Stanek, J., Sorniotti, A., Androulaki, E., Kencl, L.: A secure data deduplication scheme for cloud storage. Technical report, IBM (2013)
25. Xu, J., Zhou, J.: Leakage resilient proofs of ownership in cloud storage, revisited. In: Boureanu, I., Owesarski, P., Vaudenay, S. (eds.) ACNS 2014. LNCS, vol. 8479, pp. 97–115. Springer, Cham (2014). doi:10.1007/978-3-319-07536-5_7
26. Li, J., Chen, X., Li, M., Li, J., Lee, P., Lou, W.: Secure deduplication with efficient and reliable convergent key management. IEEE Trans. Parallel Distrib. Syst. **25**(6), 1615–1625 (2014)
27. Ng, W.K., Wen, Y., Zhu, H.: Private data deduplication protocols in cloud storage. In: Proceedings of the 27th Annual ACM Symposium on Applied Computing, SAC 2012, pp. 441–446. ACM (2012)

28. Yu, S., Wang, C., Ren, K., Lou, W.: Achieving secure, scalable, and fine-grained data access control in cloud computing. In: INFOCOM, 2010 Proceedings IEEE, pp. 1–9. IEEE (2010)

29. Wang, G., Liu, Q., Wu, J.: Hierarchical attribute-based encryption for fine-grained access control in cloud storage services. In: Proceedings of the 17th ACM Conference on Computer and Communications Security, pp. 735–737. ACM (2010)

30. Chow, S.S.: A framework of multi-authority attribute-based encryption with outsourcing and revocation. In: Proceedings of the 21st ACM on Symposium on Access Control Models and Technologies, pp. 215–226. ACM (2016)

31. Yang, Y., Liu, J.K., Liang, K., Choo, K.-K.R., Zhou, J.: Extended proxy-assisted approach: achieving revocable fine-grained encryption of cloud data. In: Pernul, G., Ryan, P.Y.A., Weippl, E. (eds.) ESORICS 2015. LNCS, vol. 9327, pp. 146–166. Springer, Cham (2015). doi:10.1007/978-3-319-24177-7_8

32. Shin, Y., Koo, D., Hur, J., Yun, J.: Secure proof of storage with deduplication for cloud storage systems. Multimedia Tools Appl. 1–16 (2015)

33. Laurie, B., Clayton, R.: "Proof-of-work" proves not to work; version 0.2. In: Workshop on Economics and Information, Security (2004)

34. Chen, L.: Using algebraic signatures to check data possession in cloud storage. Future Gener. Comput. Syst. 29(7), 1709–1715 (2013)

Web Security and Privacy

Website Forensic Investigation
to Identify Evidence and Impact of Compromise

Yuta Takata[1,2]([✉]), Mitsuaki Akiyama[1], Takeshi Yagi[1], Takeshi Yada[1],
and Shigeki Goto[2]

[1] NTT Secure Platform Laboratories, Tokyo, Japan
{takata.yuta,akiyama.mitsuaki,yagi.takeshi,yada.takeshi}@lab.ntt.co.jp
[2] Waseda University, Shinjuku, Japan
goto@goto.info.waseda.ac.jp

Abstract. Compromised websites that redirect users to malicious websites are often used by attackers to distribute malware. These attackers compromise popular websites and integrate them into a drive-by download attack scheme to lure unsuspecting users to malicious websites. An incident response organization such as a CSIRT contributes to preventing the spread of malware infection by analyzing compromised websites reported by users and sending abuse reports with detected URLs to webmasters. However, these abuse reports with only URLs are not sufficient to clean up the websites; therefore, webmasters cannot respond appropriately to such reports. In addition, it is difficult to analyze malicious websites across different client environments, i.e., a CSIRT and a webmaster, because these websites change behavior depending on the client environment. To expedite compromised website clean-up, it is important to provide fine-grained information such as the precise position of compromised web content, malicious URL relations, and the target range of client environments. In this paper, we propose a method of constructing a redirection graph with context, such as which web content redirects to which malicious websites. Our system with the proposed method analyzes a website in a multi-client environment to identify which client environment is exposed to threats. We evaluated our system using crawling datasets of approximately 2,000 compromised websites. As a result, our system successfully identified compromised web content and malicious URL relations, and the amount of web content and the number of URLs to be analyzed were sufficient for incident responders by 0.8% and 15.0%, respectively. Furthermore, it can also identify the target range of client environments in 30.4% of websites and a vulnerability that has been used in malicious websites by leveraging target information. This fine-grained information identified with our system would dramatically make the daily work of incident responders more efficient.

Keywords: Compromised website · Drive-by download · Redirection graph

© ICST Institute for Computer Sciences, Social Informatics and Telecommunications Engineering 2017
R. Deng et al. (Eds.): SecureComm 2016, LNICST 198, pp. 431–453, 2017.
DOI: 10.1007/978-3-319-59608-2_25

1   Introduction

Attackers redirect many unsuspecting users to malicious websites by compromising popular websites and integrating them into a drive-by download attack scheme. One security vendor reported that approximately 67% of malicious websites originated from compromised websites [1]. For example, Darkleech attacks exploiting vulnerable Apache modules had successfully compromised a large amount of websites; over 40,000 domains and IP addresses by May 2013, including 15,000 that month alone [2]. This means that even attentive users will be exposed to drive-by malware infections if high-reputation websites are compromised. An incident response organization such as a CSIRT (Computer Security Incident Response Team) contributes to preventing the spread of malware infection by patrolling the Web and warning users. As part of the patrol, the organization re-analyzes compromised websites reported by users, identifies evidence of malicious websites, and shares this information [3]. This shared information is important for cleaning up compromised websites by reporting abuse to webmasters. Abuse reporting has been conducted as a national project and as a security service that contributes to cleaning up compromised websites by re-analyzing URLs shared from various security vendors [4] and security products [5]. However, attackers build a redirection chain to evade analysis as well as to dynamically and selectively inflict malware on targeted users [6,7]. On compromised websites, attackers can prevent any disclosure of malicious content by injecting only redirection code that leads to malicious websites, not exploit code or malware. This redirection chain also allows attackers to use cloaking techniques to launch drive-by downloads depending on the user's client environment and makes it difficult to analyze [8,9]. Therefore, to mitigate these anti-analysis techniques and expedite the clean-up of compromised websites, it is important to identify the evidence and impact of compromise. Identifying evidence that a website has been compromised, such as the precise position of compromised web content and malicious URL relations in a redirection chain, contributes to shortening the incident response time and increasing clean-up rates. Identifying the impact of a compromised website, such as the target range of client environments and information of vulnerability abused in malicious websites, contributes to shortening the re-analysis time in addition to accelerating security updates to users of the targeted client environments. Li et al. reported that it is important to give more detailed diagnostic information, such as injected content, to webmasters because they lack sufficient expertise to clean up their websites [5]. They also found that the most challenging incident type relates to redirect attacks where websites become cloaked gateways.

To identify the evidence and impact of compromise, we propose a method of constructing a redirection graph by tracing redirection chains and JavaScript executions on websites. After extracting a malicious path, which is a redirection path to a malicious URL, our method identifies the web content that is the origin of the redirection, i.e., compromised web content, by traversing backwards along the malicious path. Our system with the proposed method accesses a website using a multi-client environment to identify targeted client environments.

This environment detects the differences of redirected URLs using these multiple analysis results while minimizing the number of environment profiles by designing them on the basis of known vulnerability information. To the best our knowledge, our system is the first tool for *website forensics* that can automatically identify the evidence and impact of compromise on the basis of useful forensic artifacts, e.g., packet capture data or website data. Specifically, this system can reveal which from web content does a redirection originate, which URLs are associated with attacks, and which client environment is exposed to threats. This fine-grained information would provide practical directions to CSIRTs/security vendors for prompt incident response and expedite compromised website clean-up.

In summary, we make the following contributions.

- Our system successfully identified the precise position of compromised web content and malicious URL relations. As a result, the amount of web content and the number of URLs to be analyzed were sufficient for incident responders by 0.8% and 15.0%, respectively.
- We show that our system can automatically identify client-dependent redirections and the target range of client environments in 30.4% of websites. Using target range information, we can also identify a vulnerability that has been used in malicious websites.

The rest of this paper is structured as follows. In Sect. 2, we provide an overview of compromised website response and explain problems in conventional methods. We introduce our proposed method for addressing the challenges in Sect. 3. In Sect. 4, we explain an experiment conducted to evaluate our method and discuss case studies on our findings in Sect. 5. We discuss the limitations of our method in Sect. 6 and review related work in Sect. 7. We conclude the paper in Sect. 8.

2 Overview of Compromised Website Response

Most of the techniques used by attackers on compromised websites are injections of redirection code to malicious URLs rather than of exploit code or malware. Therefore, identifying web content that is the origin of redirection (redirection origin) is important in the analysis of compromised websites. However, attackers use various anti-analysis techniques to evade a defender's analysis and detection. In this section, we explain web compromise and anti-analysis techniques. We also provide an overview of compromised website response by CSIRTs/security vendors and explain problems in conventional methods.

2.1 Web Compromise Technique

Attackers use redirect code injections using HTML tags or JavaScript to compromise websites.

HTML-Based Compromise. HTML-based compromises inject the redirection code of the `iframe` and `script` tags. These HTML tags are mainly injected into unusual positions in the Document Object Model (DOM) tree such as outside an `html` tag or `body` tag. In the case of an `iframe` tag, many redirections occur without a user being aware by injecting the tag in an invisible state on the browser. A `script` tag is also used in combination with the following JavaScript-based compromise. However, since these tags are directly written in an HTML file, it is easy to analyze them and find the redirection origin.

JavaScript-Based Compromise. JavaScript-based compromises execute code that dynamically generates the above-mentioned HTML tags (`iframe` and `script` tags) using `document.write`, `innerHTML`, and `appendChild` (DOM API code). A `location` object that redirects to a different URL is also injected, but the user is aware of the automatic redirection because it explicitly switches the browser frame to a different URL. Therefore, it is rare to use a `location` object as a first step. JavaScript-based compromises can target various web content, e.g., that enclosed by a `script` tag and that of a URL that is loaded by a `script` tag. The DOM API code and code separation make it difficult to analyze JavaScript. In addition, attackers utilize obfuscation techniques, as described in the next section, on JavaScript to conceal the redirection origin.

2.2   Anti-analysis Technique

In most cases, attackers leverage various existing web techniques, such as code obfuscation, redirection chains, and browser fingerprinting, to protect their own malicious content against the inspections of CSIRTs/security vendors.

Code Obfuscation. Code obfuscation is generally used for code protection and code minimization. For example, obfuscated JavaScript is de-obfuscated by string manipulation functions, and this de-obfuscated string is executed as JavaScript code by functions such as `eval`, `setInterval`, and `setTimeout`. Malicious websites try to prevent analysis by using complicated obfuscation techniques combined with compression techniques[1], cryptographic techniques, and browser-specific functions.

Redirection Chain. Drive-by download attacks redirect users of a landing website (landing URL) to malicious websites (exploit URL) via multiple websites (redirection URL). When a client accesses an exploit URL, an attack code that exploits the vulnerabilities of the web browser and/or its plugins is executed and forces the client to download and install malware from a website (malware distribution URL) [6]. This redirection chain is composed of HTTP 3XX in addition to HTML tags and JavaScript. Attackers abuse compromised popular websites and web search results as landing URLs to lure unsuspecting

---

[1] D. Edwards, "/packer/," http://dean.edwards.name/packer/.

users by constructing an inter-domain redirection chain to malicious URLs [10]. Therefore, they only have to inject redirection code rather than exploit code or malware for website compromises and can prevent any disclosure of malicious content. Moreover, multiple redirection stages contribute to reducing the operation cost of attacks since compromised websites under a chain can be integrated into a different malware campaign by changing only the redirection URLs.

Browser Fingerprint. Browser fingerprinting, which is a method of profiling the environment of a client, i.e., browser and browser plugin, is generally used for user tracking and distributing web content according to the environment. Attackers leverage browser fingerprinting to target clients by redirecting an exploitable user to a malicious URL on the basis of the client's fingerprint. This technique, called "cloaking," is also abused for circumventing the detection of CSIRTs/security vendors by redirecting them to a benign URL [8].

2.3 Problems in Conventional Methods for Compromised Website Response

An incident response organization, such as a CSIRT, constantly patrols whether websites that are under their own organization and hosting services have been compromised, i.e., the active crawls in Fig. 1 ①–③. Such organization also re-analyzes compromised websites that are reported by general public users and sends abuse reports with the detected URL to webmasters after confirming the reproducibility of attacks, i.e., the reactive crawls in Fig. 1 ①–⑤ [3]. However, in many cases, an abuse report with only URLs generated in this way is not sufficient to clean up compromised websites; therefore, webmasters cannot respond appropriately to the report with just URLs. Moreover, malicious websites cannot always be detected due to cloaking. Therefore, to create detailed abuse reports and increase clean-up rates, the following information is required.

- **Redirection origin:** Identifying a fine-grained redirection origin as evidence that a website has been compromised, such as which web content redirects to which malicious website, is important for webmasters when cleaning up compromised web content precisely. Thus, we must handle complicated obfuscations and redirection chains.
- **Targeted client environments:** Identifying targeted client environments as the impact of a compromised website, such as which versions of browsers

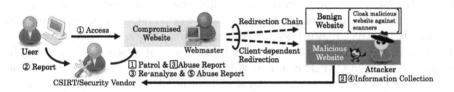

Fig. 1. Overview of compromised website response

and/or plugins are redirected to malicious websites, is beneficial for confirming the reproducibility of attacks. In addition, we can also accelerate security updates by warning users of the targeted client environments. Thus, we must mitigate cloaking techniques.

However, conventional methods are not sufficient for identifying the information stated above. Methods of detecting website compromises that compare original web content to compromised web content have been proposed [11,12]. Moreover, TripWire [13], widely known as a compromise detection tool, can detect file operations, such as modification and deletion, by monitoring files on a web server. However, these methods have limitations in terms of operation; for example, they require the original files and can detect only compromised web content on one's own web server.

Methods for constructing a redirection graph, in which the nodes represent accessed URLs and directed edges represent redirection methods, by using a `Referer` header or a `Location` header [14] and by leveraging some heuristics/features in addition to HTTP headers [15] have been proposed. However, in many cases, the `Referer` header is not set. Additionally, these methods cannot connect tricky links such as a redirection with an inconsistent `Referer` header. This *semantic gap* in the `Referer` header occurs when the redirection results from an external JavaScript.

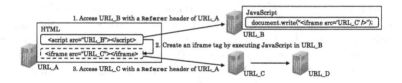

Fig. 2. Semantic gap between Referer header and JavaScript redirection

We now give more details on the semantic gap in a redirection graph using the website in Fig. 2. In this website, a web browser loads JavaScript of URL_B by using a `script` tag in URL_A accessed first. Next, the DOM API code in URL_B is executed. In this case, an `iframe` tag that points to URL_C is inserted into the HTML of URL_A. As a result, an HTTP request to URL_C is generated with the `Referer` header of URL_A. The `Referer` header indicates the base URL, i.e., URL_A, of the web content that is rendered on the web browser, not the external JavaScript URL, i.e., URL_B, that contains the redirection code. This semantic gap occurs due to the general behavior of web browsers and is frequently observed on legitimate websites. However, this gap results in a logically incorrect redirection graph without some edges, for example, an edge from URL_B to URL_C is not connected, which we call a *semantic gap edge*. In other words, when URL_D is a malicious URL, a conventional redirection graph cannot identify the `document.write` statement in URL_B as a redirection origin due to a semantic gap even if traversing backwards along the path from URL_D to URL_A.

3   Proposed Method and System

To identify the redirection origin, we propose a method of constructing a redirection graph with context, such as which content redirects to which malicious websites, by tracing the redirection and JavaScript execution processes. The combination of a redirection graph and a JavaScript execution graph, which we call a "redirection call graph" (RCG), can bridge semantic gap edges and contribute to identifying the precise position of redirection origins. We implemented a system with our method, as shown in Fig. 3. Our system accesses a website using a multi-client environment to identify targeted client environments while constructing RCGs. It detects the differences of accessed URLs among multiple analysis results while minimizing the number of environment profiles by designing them on the basis of known vulnerability information. We detail each system component in the following subsections.

3.1   Identifying Redirection Origin as Evidence of Compromise

Our method of identifying redirection origins is composed of a *monitoring behavior* phase, *constructing RCG* phase, *identifying malicious node* phase, and *extracting compromised content* phase (① in Fig. 3).

Monitoring Behavior. Our system accesses websites and collects redirection and JavaScript execution traces by monitoring behaviors during the process of interpreting fetched web content. We explain the behavioral information as follows.

- **HTTP transaction:** An HTTP response with the status code 3XX is captured in HTTP transactions for tracing HTTP redirections. When an HTTP server responds to this status code, the HTTP request URL, URL in the `Location` header, and HTTP status code are recorded as a redirection source URL, redirection destination URL, and redirection method, respectively.
- **HTML parsing:** Our system monitors HTML tags, e.g., `iframe`, `frame`, `script`, `meta`, `object`, `embed`, and `applet`, that redirect to a different URL

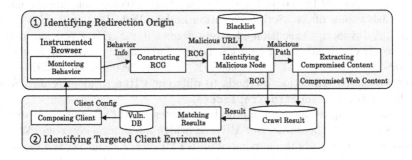

Fig. 3. System overview

during HTML parsing to trace redirections with HTML tags. When these HTML tags are parsed, the URL that contains the HTML tag, URL to which the HTML tag points, and HTML tag name are recorded as a redirection source URL, redirection destination URL, and redirection method, respectively.

– **JavaScript API hooking:** Our system monitors executed JavaScript code and JavaScript function calls, e.g., `eval()`, `setInterval()`, `setTimeout()`, function calls of `window`, `location`, `element`, `node`, and `document` objects, to construct a JavaScript execution graph and connects semantic gap edges. Then, to trace redirections with JavaScript, the JavaScript URL, URL to which the JavaScript points, and JavaScript function name are recorded as a redirection source URL, redirection destination URL, and redirection method, respectively.

Constructing Redirection Call Graph. This phase constructs a RCG based on recorded trace information. As a result, a directed graph with the following nodes and edges, such as in Fig. 4 on the left, is structured.

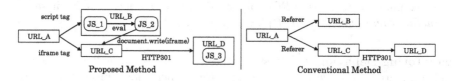

Fig. 4. Comparison of graphs constructed with proposed and conventional methods

– **Redirection node and edge:** A redirection node represents an accessed URL. A redirection edge represents a redirection method and connects redirection nodes. To construct these nodes and edges, we use information obtained from HTTP transaction and HTML parsing in the previous phase.
– **JavaScript execution node and edge:** A JavaScript execution node represents code executed by the JavaScript interpreter. We can identify which code is executed by tracing these code executions. This node is managed by the hash value of the code. Figure 4 shows that a redirection graph contains the hash values of JavaScript execution nodes (JS_1, JS_2, and JS_3 in this case). A JavaScript execution edge represents a JavaScript execution method and connects JavaScript execution nodes, for example, browser rendering, JavaScript events, `eval`, `setInterval`, and `setTimeout`. In addition, this edge contains redirection methods to different URLs to identify JavaScript redirections, e.g., `location.replace()`.
– **Semantic gap edge:** Our method associates an HTML tag generated by JavaScript with the JavaScript URL to bridge a semantic gap edge. When a redirection occurs via the parsing of an HTML tag, e.g., an `iframe` tag and a `script` tag, the source URL is identified from not only the base URL but also the associated JavaScript URL if the HTML tag is generated by JavaScript.

We explain a semantic gap edge using Fig. 2. When `document.write` is executed in URL_B, a pair of URL_B and the `iframe` tag generated by `document.write` is saved. Next, when the `iframe` tag inserted in URL_A is parsed, URL_B is uniquely identified from the pair information. Finally, when the redirection of the `iframe` tag occurs, an edge from URL_B to URL_C is connected. Then, the redirection method of the edge is set to the DOM API function and HTML tag name, "`document.write(iframe)`."

Figure 4 depicts a comparison of Fig. 2 between a RCG and a conventional redirection graph. Our method can identify an obfuscation process from JS_1 to JS_2 by `eval` and connect an edge from URL_B to URL_C by `document.write`. This information is necessary for incident responders to conduct efficient and effective website forensics, but conventional methods cannot identify it.

Identifying Malicious Node. This phase identifies malicious nodes in the RCG constructed in the previous phase using a blacklist of known malicious URLs. These known malicious URLs can be obtained from detection results by using conventional techniques such as a high-interaction honeyclient and anti-virus. In addition to matching exact malicious URLs, we detected suspicious URLs of the same domain name and the same number of path hierarchies or the same number of domain name hierarchies and the same path compared with the malicious URLs. This suspicious URL detection helps minimize the effects of URLs using random strings. This phase also extracts malicious paths from identified malicious nodes to the node of the landing URL.

Extracting Compromised Content. A redirection origin is extracted by traversing backwards along a malicious path, which is identified in the previous phase, from the leaf URL to the origin URL. We explain the extraction method in Fig. 4. If the redirection path from URL_A to URL_D is classified as malicious, e.g., JS_3 contains the exploit code, the `script` tag that points to URL_B in URL_A is extracted as a redirection origin. A redirection origin contains the origin/leaf URLs and the redirection method/destination URL. Moreover, to identify the precise position of redirection origins, this phase extracts DOM information, such as the DOM tree structure, in the case of an HTML-based compromise. In the case of a JavaScript-based compromise, the JavaScript execution information is extracted such as executed code.

It is important to note that redirection origin of the landing URL is not always compromised web content. For example, if JS_1 in Fig. 4 is compromised web content, the `script` tag in URL_A described above is a false positive. Therefore, this phase minimizes false positives by following a malicious path from the landing URL to the URL with a domain that is different from the source URL after traversing backwards. This means that we consider web content that generates such inter-domain edge as a redirection origin because the domain of compromised websites is different from that of malicious websites [6]. Specifically, JS_1 in URL_B is detected as a redirection origin by the difference between URL_B's domain and URL_C's domain.

Table 1. Matrix of CVEs and Flash Player versions

	2013-0634	2013-5329	2014-0497	2014-0502	2014-0515	2014-0556	2014-0569	2014-8440	2014-8439	2015-0310	2015-0311	2015-0313	2015-0336	2015-0359
10.1.102.64	✓													
11	✓	✓	✓	✓										
11.2.202.233	✓	✓	✓	✓	✓	✓	✓							
11.5.502.149		✓	✓	✓										
11.2.202.270		✓	✓	✓	✓	✓	✓							
11.7.700.169		✓	✓	✓	✓									
11.7.700.225				✓	✓									
11.7.700.252			✓	✓										
11.7.700.257			✓	✓	✓									
11.2.202.332			✓	✓	✓	✓	✓							
12.0.0.44					✓									
11.2.202.336					✓	✓	✓	✓						
11.7.700.269						✓								
11.2.202.341						✓	✓	✓						
13.0.0.206						✓	✓							
14.0.0.125						✓	✓			✓	✓	✓	✓	✓
14.0.0.179						✓	✓		✓	✓	✓	✓	✓	✓
14.0.0.176						✓	✓	✓		✓	✓	✓	✓	✓
13.0.0.244						✓								
15.0.0.152							✓			✓	✓	✓	✓	✓
13.0.0.250								✓						
15.0.0.189							✓			✓	✓	✓	✓	✓
11.2.202.423									✓					
15.0.0.239										✓	✓	✓	✓	✓
13.0.0.260								✓						
11.2.202.438											✓			
16.0.0.287											✓	✓	✓	✓
11.2.202.440											✓			
13.0.0.264												✓	✓	✓
16.0.0.305													✓	
17.0.0.134														✓

CVE version	2016-AAAA	2016-BBBB	2016-CCCC	2016-DDDD
Plugin 1.0.0	✓			
Plugin 1.0.1	✓			
Plugin 2.0.0		✓	✓	✓
Plugin 2.1.0			✓	✓

↓ Aggregate duplication

CVE version	2016-AAAA	2016-BBBB	2016-CCCC 2016-DDDD
Plugin 1.0.0 Plugin 1.0.1	✓		
Plugin 2.0.0		✓	✓
Plugin 2.1.0			✓

Fig. 5. Aggregation of duplicated CVEs and plugin versions

Table 2. Number of plugin versions

	JRE	PDF	Flash
Exploit kits from 2014–2015	14	1	31
Exploit kits from 2011–2013	37	23	32
Official installer	193	103	251

3.2 Identifying Targeted Client Environment as Impact of Compromise

To identify targeted client environments, our system analyzes a website in a multi-client environment that increases the possibility of changing the behavior of a website by browser fingerprinting, such as boundary testing. The analysis environment is composed of a *composing client* phase and a *matching results* phase (② in Fig. 3).

Composing Client. This phase decides on a client environment from a matrix of vulnerabilities and its affected client environments. Our method can decrease the number of client environments by aggregating the environment's duplications. If we can predict potential targeted vulnerabilities in websites, the number can be further decreased by filtering out the corresponding columns of the matrix (Fig. 5). For example, we show a matrix of the matching of known vulnerability information obtained from CVE Details[2] and affected versions of Adobe Flash Player in Table 1. We further decreased the elements of the matrix by utilizing the vulnerability information of exploit kits from 2014–2015 obtained from contagio[3]. In Table 1, the versions of Adobe Flash Player were aggregated from 251 to 31. Note that oldest version is selected from aggregated versions.

---

[2] CVE Details, http://www.cvedetails.com/.

[3] contagio, http://contagiodata.blogspot.jp/2014/12/exploit-kits-2014.html.

Matching Results. Our system compares crawl results of various environments and detects differences of accessed URLs among the results, i.e., it investigates whether each crawl result contains malicious URLs. From the matching results, we can identify which client environment is redirected to a malicious URL.

3.3 Implementation

To monitor fine-grained processes of HTML parsing and JavaScript execution and to configure various client environments, we need to be able to hook browser processes and modify the environment profiles. Therefore, we used a browser emulator, HtmlUnit[4], in our system and implemented the monitoring and configuration functions into it. In this paper, we focused on plugins, Java Runtime Environment (JRE), Adobe Reader (PDF), and Adobe Flash Player (Flash), for a multi-client environment because many recent exploit kits check for the presence of vulnerable versions of several plugins [7,9]. Therefore, we collected vulnerability information on these plugins from CVE Details and contagio. The numbers of aggregated versions of JRE, PDF, and Flash are listed in Table 2. The rows of Table 2 represent the number of plugins on the basis of vulnerability information of exploit kits from 2014–2015, exploit kits from 2011–2013, and the number of official installers we found manually. Table 2 shows that our method can dramatically reduce the number of environment profiles by utilizing known vulnerability information. It is important to note that our system can change environment profiles on the basis of not only plugins but also operating systems or browsers in the same way.

4   Experiment and Evaluation

We evaluated the effectiveness and performance of our system using the HTTP communication data of 2,058 compromised websites that were preliminarily detected during a four-year period (2011–2015). Although we can run our system to reveal malicious content and the functions of websites on the *live* Internet, online crawlings, especially with our multi-client environment, place a load on web servers and make it easy to detect inspections by server-side cloaking. Therefore, it is appropriate for utilizing our system in a local environment while leveraging forensic artifacts that have been already detected. In this experiment, we first investigated the impact of semantic gaps to evaluate the effectiveness of an RCG. More precisely, we evaluated whether a RCG can precisely connect more links than a conventional redirection graph. Next, we analyzed redirection origins extracted from malicious paths and investigated the statistical trend regarding website compromises. Finally, we evaluated whether our system can identify targeted client environments and the target range.

---

[4] Gargoyle Software Inc., http://htmlunit.sourceforge.net/.

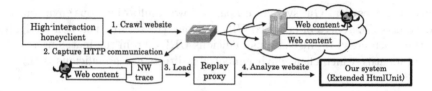

Fig. 6. Experimental environment

4.1   Experimental Environment

The experimental environment for our system was composed of a high-interaction honeyclient, a replay proxy, and our system, as shown in Fig. 6.

High-Interaction Honeyclient. We used the HTTP communication data of websites that were preliminary detected drive-by download attacks by a high-interaction honeyclient [16]. Exploit URLs and malware distribution URLs detected by the honeyclient were also used as a blacklist in the *identifying malicious node* phase.

Replay Proxy. A replay proxy responds to a HTTP request with web content on the basis of a URL using HTTP communication data. Thus, due to the dynamic nature of modern websites, some HTTP requests may not match any of the original data. This occurs when a URL using time-dependent or random parameters is included in the data. To compensate for dynamically generated URLs, we used an *approximate matching* approach, which was inspired from a method [17], during replay. This approach measures the similarity between a requested URL and URLs with the same domain and the same file path but different parameters in the HTTP communication data. To compute a similarity score, this approach calculates a Jaccard index of the set of parameter names. Finally, the proxy responds to a HTTP request with web content on the basis of a URL that has a score that is higher than a threshold. The threshold was set to a high score, e.g., 0.9, to prevent false positives, and no false positives were observed in this experiment. Note that the purpose of this study is to identify the evidence and impact of compromise, and not to propose a traffic replay method.

Our System. Our system, which is the extended HtmlUnit described in Sect. 3.3, analyzes web content and stores the results through accesses to the replay proxy. Then, to further reduce the analysis time, we used our multi-client environment for only websites that tried to use browser fingerprinting. Browser fingerprinting can be detected by monitoring the use of the name and version strings of the client environment in JavaScript function arguments and object properties. Therefore, we preliminarily detected browser fingerprinting by analyzing a website once. The results of preliminary crawls were also used for analyzing a website that does not use browser fingerprinting.

We obtained the experimental results presented in this section by using two servers, both running Ubuntu 12.01. Our replay proxy replayed the HTTP communication data on one server (2.93 GHz processor and 24 GB of RAM), and our system evaluated web content on the other server (3.16 GHz processor and 4 GB of RAM).

4.2   Evaluation of Redirection Call Graph and Redirection Origin

Constructing Redirection Graph. We evaluated how many nodes (URLs) can be connected with the proposed method compared with conventional methods. We computed the differences between the number of nodes on malicious paths identified by the proposed method (PRO) and the conventional methods. As the conventional methods, we implemented originally the referer-based method (REF) [14] and the heuristic-based method (HEU) [15]. As a result, the number of nodes identified by *only* PRO was 1,068 and 367 compared with REF and HEU, respectively. We found through manual inspection that these nodes were false negatives of the conventional methods caused by a redirection without a `Referer` header or with a semantic gap. The semantic gap edge was included in 16.6% of websites. In addition, the numbers of nodes identified by only the conventional methods were 0 and 9 compared with REF and HEU, respectively. However, these nodes were false positives (noise URLs) caused by linking a *likely* edge with the rule "Domain-in-URL" of HEU. We show in detail the differences of redirection graphs between the proposed method and the conventional methods in Appendix. These results show that the proposed method can accurately construct a redirection graph, and identify malicious redirection chains, but the conventional methods cannot.

In this evaluation, we found several redirection graphs without a malicious path. Therefore, we measured the analysis capabilities of our system by calculating its reachability to malicious URLs that the high-interaction honeyclient detected. As a result, our system identified malicious paths from 1,479 (71.9%) websites among the 2,058 websites. We give more details on the websites that could not reach malicious URLs in the next subsection, i.e., these websites correspond to unknown or false negatives.

Redirection Graph Without Malicious Path. We manually analyzed the causes of the *incomplete redirection graphs* that did not contain malicious URLs. Table 3 shows a breakdown of redirection graphs without a malicious path. The most common sophisticated browser fingerprinting in this breakdown changed behavior on the basis of the presence of a specific property of JavaScript or security vendor products. JavaScript properties exist in only Internet Explorer, e.g., `window.sidebar`, and is abused as an indirect browser fingerprint by attackers. Many methods of such browser fingerprinting are proposed and also known to affect the behavior of not only a browser emulator but also a real browser [18]. Attackers can also maliciously access a file system and check the presence of security vendor products through Internet Explorer by abusing an information

Table 3. Breakdown of redirection graph without malicious path

Category	#graph	Reason	Handling
Sophisticated browser fingerprinting	231	Anti-virus detection and browser-specific JavaScript property	Analyze it with a real browser
URLs with random strings and/or domains with DGA	165	Lack of approximate matching and suspicious URL detection ability	Improve accuracy of algorithm
Emulator evasion	122	Defect of DOM implementation in HtmlUnit	Fix it
Time-dependent redirection	57	Past crawl data	Analyze it immediately after detection
VBScript	4	Unsupported in HtmlUnit	Analyze it with real browser

disclosure vulnerability, i.e., CVE-2013-7331. Our browser emulator could not be redirected to malicious URLs because it did not execute the environment-specific code and exploit code. The emulator evasion in Table 3 was caused by a defect of DOM implementation in HtmlUnit. However, we can mitigate the evasion by improving the behavior emulation since a redirection graph could be accurately constructed by fixing this defect. The other causes were lack of approximate matching and suspicious URL detection ability, time-dependent redirections, and use of VBScript.

Extracting Compromised Web Content. To investigate the statistical trend regarding compromised web content and compromise methods, we analyzed redirection origins extracted from malicious paths. Compromise methods were 43% HTML-based compromises, 9% JavaScript-based compromises, and 47% DOM API code injections. Almost all HTML-based compromises injected automatic redirections to different URLs using `script` and `iframe` tags. The DOM API code also injected 98% `iframe` tags and 2% `script` tags. These injected HTML tags were written in strange positions such as outside the `html` tag or `body` tag

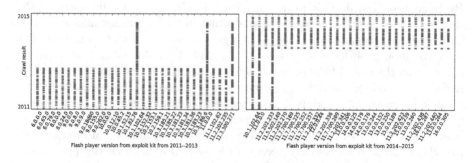

Fig. 7. Identification of target range of Flash Player version

Table 4. Analysis of client-dependent redirection with browser fingerprinting

Detected: Suspicious:Unknown	#crawls	Description
1:0:1	359	Client-dependent redirection with browser fingerprinting
0:1:1	117	Client-dependent redirection with browser fingerprinting
1:1:1	149	Client-dependent redirection with browser fingerprinting
0:0:1	209	Emulator evasion, time-dependent redirection, etc. (see Table 3)
1:1:0	226	Malicious websites with DGA-domain and/or random path
0:1:0	91	Malicious websites with DGA-domain and/or random path
1:0:0	370	Simple malicious websites

(5%) with in a small area (width < 15, height < 15 or area < 30; 20%) or outside the display (72%).

We also investigated redirection paths from compromised web content. As a result, the semantic gap edge was included in 33% of redirection paths, which made it difficult to analyze it. We will give two case studies of these semantic gap edges in Sect. 5.1.

4.3 Evaluation of Targeted Client Environments

We evaluated whether our system can identify which client environment is redirected to a malicious URL. The client environments emulated each plugin, as shown in Table 2, on the basis of the observation period of the websites and the browser fingerprint acquired by the websites. The crawl results per each *environment* were categorized into three groups: detected crawls that contain malicious URLs, suspicious crawls that contain suspicious URLs, and unknown crawls that contain neither. As a result of comparing crawl results per each *website*, we identified client-dependent redirections that contained detected and/or suspicious crawl results at the same time as unknown crawl results from 625 (30.4%) of the websites (Table 4). These websites changed the destination URL depending on the difference among the plugin versions. We plot these detected and/or suspicious crawl results in Fig. 7, in which the horizontal axis indicates versions of Flash (left is from exploit kits from 2011–2013, and right is from exploit kits from 2014–2015) and the vertical axis indicates crawl results on the order of the time scale. Figure 7 shows that some of the results were widely detected, and the others were detected by only specific versions. We found through manual inspection that these results were derived from the exploit kit periods of 2011–2013 and 2014–2015. This means that client environments based on information of

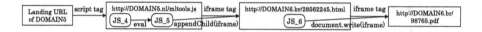

Fig. 8. Malicious path that contains obfuscated semantic gap edge

exploit kits from 2011–2013 were not redirected to malicious websites observed from 2014–2015 and vice versa. These results show that it is important to change a client environment for analysis depending on that attack trend of that time. Furthermore, as a result of analyzing websites of the same detection pattern, we found that these websites used the same browser fingerprinting code and redirection code. Using these multiple analysis results, we can categorize malicious infrastructures, such as vulnerabilities (see Sect. 5.2).

4.4   Performance Overhead

We evaluated the total time and the average time of analyzing 2,058 websites with our system. The results indicated that the time costs were 685,773 s and 333 s, respectively. Since 90% of benign website crawlings done by the high-interaction honeyclient that detected compromised websites used in this experiment finished within 154 s [16], the analysis time of our system took approximately twice as long. The performance of our system, however, clearly depends on the number of environment profiles. The analysis time per one environment was only 12 s on average. Therefore, our system is appropriate for frequent re-analysis of websites because the browser emulator does not require the rendering time of a website and the execution time of exploit code. In addition, since the browser emulator can be more easily deployable and parallelized compared with a high-interaction honeyclient that individually requires a real browser whenever the environment is changed, performance can be further improved.

5   Case Studies

We manually analyzed redirection origins, redirection paths, and client-dependent redirection code. Among these manual inspections, we now describe notable samples.

5.1   Redirection Call Graph with Semantic Gap

Obfuscated Semantic Gap Edge. We depict an example of malicious paths that contained dynamically generated code and a semantic gap in Fig. 8. The semantic gap was caused by DOM API code (JS_5) in obfuscated code (JS_4) injected by compromising. The conventional methods could not completely identify these malicious paths because the link to the URL of DOMAIN5 could not be connected due to the semantic gap and the destination URL of DOMAIN6 is concealed in the obfuscated code, i.e., JS_4.

Multiple Compromised Web Content. We show an example of a part of RCGs constructed from crawl results, which contain two or more differences in

Fig. 9. Malicious path that contains multiple semantic gap edges

Table 5. PDF version range detected by website analysis in multi-client environment

4.0.5	7.0.0	7.1.0	7.1.1	8.0.0	8.1.1	8.1.2	8.1.3	8.1.4	8.2.0	8.2.4	9.0.0	9.1.0	9.1.1	9.3.0	9.3.1	9.3.3	9.4.0	9.4.1	10.0.0	10.0.3	10.1.1
			✓	✓	✓	✓	✓	✓	✓	✓	✓	✓	✓	✓	✓	✓					

the number of identified URLs between PRO and REF/HEU in Sect. 4.2 (Fig. 9). Compromised web content in Fig. 9 was injected into multiple files such as an HTML file of the landing URL and JavaScript files referred from the landing URL. The conventional methods could not identify URLs of these JavaScript files because DOM API code were injected into all files and semantic gaps occurred on all of them. In other words, this means that JavaScript files remain compromised even if we deleted only the `iframe` tag of the landing URL identified by the conventional methods.

5.2 Client-Dependent Redirection with Browser Fingerprinting

The JS_6 contained in the redirection path of Fig. 8 changed the destination URL by executing the following browser fingerprinting code that gets the version of PDF plugin.

```
pdf_ver = PluginDetect.getVersion("AdobeReader");
pdf_ver = pdf_ver.split(",");
if ((pdf_ver[0] == 8 && pdf_ver[1] <= 2) || (pdf_ver[0] == 9 && pdf_ver[1] <= 3)) {
    document.write("<iframe width=10 height=10 src='http://DOMAIN6.br/98765.pdf'></iframe>");
}
```

We analyzed the above code using our system that emulated 23 individual versions of a PDF based on Table 2 because the code was observed in 2012. As a result, the versions shown in Table 5 reached malicious URLs and the behavior was along the condition of the above branch code. In addition, these code features and characteristic lexical features of URLs suggest that these malicious paths were built using RedKit, which is known to exploit a PDF's vulnerability (CVE-2010-0188) [19]. CVE-2010-0188 exists in Adobe Reader/Acrobat 8.X before 8.2.1 and 9.X before 9.3.1, and the above code has also been implemented to redirect to the URL of DOMAIN6 when a PDF version that has the vulnerability is used.

6 Discussion

Browser Emulator Limitations. The analysis of malicious websites with a browser emulator, such as our system, is known to have some limitations.

For example, a browser emulator is known not to be able to execute attack code that exploits the vulnerabilities of a web browser and/or its plugins. Our system also cannot execute exploit code as described in Sect. 4.2. In other words, our method cannot construct a complete redirection graph including a malware distribution URL because a malware distribution URL is accessed due to exploit code execution. Similarly, improving behavior emulation is challenging in browser fingerprinting and the diversity of browser implementations. The redirection graphs without malicious paths in Sect. 4.2 were also one of the factors preventing the construction of graphs. We admit all these issues can affect the performance of our system. However, these issues are not specific to our system and affect in some degree all real browsers and browser emulators. More importantly, our system could identify the evidence and impact of 71.9% of compromised websites under the limitations. To maximize the disclosure of malicious content and detect it, we must combine our system with other techniques, which we discuss in Sect. 7.

Evaluation of Compromised Content. In this study, we did not conduct a user study on how the evidence and impact information identified by our system can contribute to remedying compromised websites and preventing malware infections because we evaluated our system using past crawl data in our experiments. As future work, we will perform a user study on how much and how long this identified information can increase the response rate and the reduces response time required for clean-up done by webmasters, such as in an existing user study [5].

Instead of a user study on webmasters, we calculated the content reduction rate (CRR) and the URL reduction rate (URR) to evaluate how our system can contribute to the work of incident responders. The CRR is how much web content on compromised websites would not be analyzed by extracting compromised web content using our method. The URR is how many URLs our method can filter out by extracting malicious redirection paths from the entire redirection graph of each crawling. These rates were obtained with the following formulas.

$$\text{CRR} = 1 - \frac{1}{n}\sum_{k=1}^{n}\left(\frac{\#\text{ of bytes of } compromised\ content_k}{\#\text{ of bytes of } original\ content_k}\right),$$

$$\text{URR} = 1 - \frac{1}{n}\sum_{k=1}^{n}\left(\frac{\#\text{ of access URLs in } path_k}{\#\text{ of access URLs in } crawl_k}\right)$$

As a result, our method could reduce 99.2% of bytes on the basis of the value in a `Content-Length` header (16,568 bytes on average). Furthermore, the URR was 85.0% (23 URLs on average), i.e., the amount of web content and the number of URLs to be analyzed were sufficient for incident responders by 0.8% and 15.0%, respectively. The results show that our method can identify malicious websites both at a content-level and a URL-level. However, web content dynamically injected, for example, from database and a .htaccess file cannot be accurately identified. Although we must cooperate with webmasters to remove the root cause of compromise in the case of dynamic compromises, our method can still provide practical directions for prompt incident response.

Accuracy of Vulnerability Database. Our system chose a client environment for emulation on the basis of known vulnerability information. The vulnerability information in Table 1 showed a correlation that old versions have old vulnerabilities and new versions have new vulnerabilities but non-consecutively, e.g., CVE-2014-0497 exists in Adobe Flash Player before 11.7.700.261, but 11.7.700.225 is not checked in Table 1. We can infer that these are derived from the omission of information or untested plugin versions. Therefore, it is important to note that our analysis method using a multi-client environment cannot identify completely the target range of client environments on malicious websites. However, the target range clearly depends on the implementation of malicious websites, and even our method can get enough beneficial information, as described in Sect. 5.2.

7   Related Work

Detecting Compromised Websites. The methods of detecting website compromises are generally used for comparing original and compromised web content. For example, a comparison method [11] using HTML files as original content and a comparison method [12] using well known libraries and frameworks of JavaScript as original content have been proposed. Moreover, TripWire [13] can notify webmasters of changes on websites by e-mail when file operations are detected on a web server on which TripWire is installed. However, these methods have limitations in terms of method application. For example, original content is necessary for compromise detection, and these methods can detect only compromised web content on the web server under control. These limitations prevent websites using external content such as third-party libraries and advertisements from performing effectively. However, using these methods with compromised web content identified by our method can contribute to finding more malicious websites and detoxifying them.

Detecting Malicious Websites. Over the past few years, many researchers have proposed methods of detecting drive-by downloads. A high-interaction honeyclient [16,20] crawls websites with a vulnerable real browser and detects malware downloads by monitoring unintended processes and file system accesses, whereas a low-interaction honeyclient [21,22] crawls websites with a browser emulator and detects malicious behaviors by signature matching and machine learning. Many learning-based detection methods of malicious websites have also been proposed and leveraged features from HTML, JavaScript, URL, and social-reputation [23–25]. However, these methods cannot identify which web content is the redirection origin of a malicious path. In comparison, we can extract malicious paths more effectively using these research results because all methods can detect malicious websites with high accuracy.

Detecting Malicious Redirection. Many methods of detecting a redirection graph on malicious websites rather than for detecting exploit code and malware have also been proposed [15,26–28]. Graph-based methods [26,27] using the behavioral information of web browsers construct a redirection graph on the basis of redirection information collected from a number of honeyclients or a user's clients. These methods detect malicious websites by leveraging co-occurring URLs in graphs and a diverse dataset of graphs. Others [15,28] focus on HTTP redirections and executable file downloads on a network and apply a classifier to detect malicious redirection paths. However, these methods fail to construct a redirection graph of many malicious websites (see Sect. 4.2 and Appendix A) because of the coarse-grained redirection information. These methods can also identify malicious URLs but cannot identify malicious content as well as stated in the previous subsection.

8   Conclusion

To identify the evidence and impact of compromise, we proposed a method of constructing a fine-grained redirection graph. Our system with the proposed method analyzes a website in a multi-client environment while minimizing the number of environment profiles. The evidence and impact information includes which from web content does redirection originate, which URLs are associated with the attacks, and which client environment is exposed to threats. Our evaluation with compromised website data obtained during a four-year period showed that our system can successfully identify the precise position of compromised web content, malicious URL relations, and targeted client environments. We also showed that it can effectively identify an exploit kit and a vulnerability that has been used in malicious websites by leveraging the information. We believe that our system can contribute to improving the daily work of CSIRTs/security vendors and expediting compromised website clean-up done by webmasters.

A   Appendix: Difference Between Proposed Graph and Conventional Graph

We show redirection graph examples constructed with the referer-based method [14], the heuristic-based method [15], and the proposed method in Figs. 10, 11, and 12, respectively. Figure 10 depicts a graph smaller than the other graphs because a redirection without a `Referer` header was caused by a function of the `location` object. In this case, the referer-based method cannot connect the any of the following redirections. The heuristic-based method can connect all redirections. However, semantic gaps between `Referer` headers and JavaScript redirections occur. As a result, we cannot identify precise redirection origins, e.g., the web content of URL "http://DOMAIN10/gzcr?t=[a-zA-Z0-9]{118}," due to the gaps. Our method can connect all redirections and precisely identify all of their redirection origins.

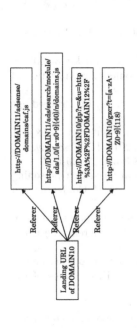

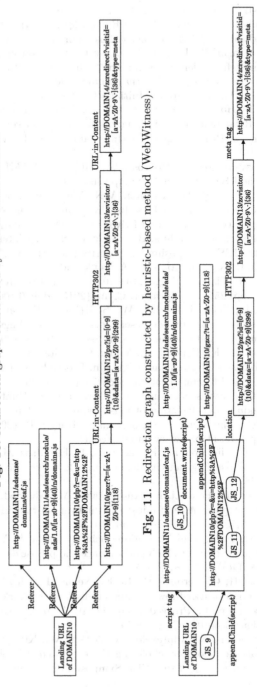

Fig. 10. Redirection graph constructed by referer-based method.

Fig. 11. Redirection graph constructed by heuristic-based method (WebWitness).

Fig. 12. Redirection graph constructed by proposed method (redirection call graph).

References

1. Symantec Corporation: Internet Security Threat Report 2014: Volume 19 (2014). http://www.symantec.com/content/en/us/enterprise/other_resources/b-istr_main_report_v19_21291018.en-us.pdf
2. Sophos Ltd.: Security Threat Report 2014 (2014). https://www.sophos.com/en-us/medialibrary/PDFs/other/sophos-security-threat-report-2014.pdf
3. Kobayashi, H., Uchiyama, T.: Keeping eyes on malicious websites - 'ChkDeface' against fraudulent sites. In: The 27th Annual FIRST Conference (2015)
4. Japan's Ministry of Internal Affairs and Communications: ACTIVE: Advanced Cyber Threats response InitiatiVE. http://www.active.go.jp/en/
5. Li, F., Ho, G., Kuan, E., Niu, Y., Ballard, L., Thomas, K., Bursztein, E., Paxson, V.: Remedying web hijacking: notification effectiveness and webmaster comprehension. In: Proceedings of the International World Wide Web Conference (WWW) (2016)
6. Mavrommatis, N., Monrose, M.: All your iFRAMEs point to us. In: Proceedings of the USENIX Security Symposium (2008)
7. Eshete, B., Venkatakrishnan, V.N.: WebWinnow: leveraging exploit kit workflows to detect malicious URLs. In: Proceedings of the ACM Conference on Data and Application Security and Privacy (CODASPY) (2014)
8. Kolbitsch, C., Livshits, B.: Rozzle: de-cloaking internet malware. In: Proceedings of the IEEE Symposium on Security and Privacy (SP) (2012)
9. Min, B., Varadharajan, V.: A simple and novel technique for counteracting exploit kits. In: Tian, J., Jing, J., Srivatsa, M. (eds.) SecureComm 2014. LNICSSITE, vol. 152, pp. 259–277. Springer, Cham (2015). doi:10.1007/978-3-319-23829-6_19
10. Lu, L., Perdisci, R., Lee, W.: SURF: detecting and measuring search poisoning categories and subject descriptors. In: Proceedings of the ACM Conference on Computer and Communications Security (CCS) (2011)
11. Borgolte, K., Kruegel, C., Vigna, G.: Delta: automatic identification of unknown web-based infection campaigns. In: Proceedings of the ACM Conference on Computer and Communications Security (CCS) (2013)
12. Li, Z., Alrwais, S., Wang, X., Alowaisheq, E.: Hunting the red fox online: understanding and detection of mass redirect-script injections. In: Proceedings of the IEEE Symposium on Security and Privacy (SP) (2014)
13. TripWire. http://www.tripwire.com/
14. Xie, G., Iliofotou, M., Karagiannis, T., Faloutsos, M., Jin, Y.: ReSurf: reconstructing web-surfing activity from network traffic. In: IFIP Networking Conference (2013)
15. Nelms, T., Perdisci, R., Antonakakis, M., Ahamad, M.: WebWitness: investigating, categorizing, and mitigating malware download paths. In: Proceedings of the USENIX Security Symposium (2015)
16. Akiyama, M., Yagi, T., Kadobayashi, Y., Hariu, T., Yamaguchi, S.: Client honeypot multiplication with high performance and precise detection. IEICE Trans. Inf. Syst. **E98–D**(4), 775–787 (2015)
17. Neasbitt, C., Perdisci, R., Li, K., Nelms, T.: ClickMiner: towards forensic reconstruction of user-browser interactions from network traces categories and subject descriptors. In: Proceedings of the ACM Conference on Computer and Communications Security (CCS) (2014)
18. Nikiforakis, N., Kapravelos, A., Joosen, W., Kruegel, C., Piessens, F., Vigna, G.: Cookieless monster: exploring the ecosystem of web-based device fingerprinting. In: Proceedings of the IEEE Symposium on Security and Privacy (SP) (2013)

19. Intel Security Inc.: Red kit an emerging exploit pack, January 2013. https://blogs. mcafee.com/mcafee-labs/red-kit-an-emrging-exploit-pack/

20. Lu, L., Yegneswaran, V., Porras, P., Lee, W.: BLADE: an attack-agnostic approach for preventing drive-by malware infections. In: Proceedings of the ACM Conference on Computer and Communications Security (CCS) (2010)

21. Cova, M., Kruegel, C., Vigna, G.: Detection and analysis of drive-by-download attack and javascript code. In: Proceedings of the International World Wide Web Conference (WWW) (2010)

22. Dell'Aera, A.: Thug. http://buffer.github.io/thug/

23. Curtsinger, C., Livshits, B., Zorn, B., Seifert, C.: ZOZZLE: fast and precise in-browser javascript malware detection. In: Proceedings of the USENIX Security Symposium (2011)

24. Canali, D., Cova, M., Vigna, G.: Prophiler: a fast filter for the large-scale detection of malicious web pages categories and subject descriptors. In: Proceedings of the International World Wide Web Conference (WWW) (2011)

25. Eshete, B., Villafiorita, A., Weldemariam, K.: BINSPECT: holistic analysis and detection. In: Proceedings of the International Conference on Security and Privacy in Communication Networks (SecureComm) (2013)

26. Zhang, J., Seifert, C., Stokes, J.W., Lee, W.: Arrow: generating signatures to detect drive-by downloads. In: Proceedings of the International World Wide Web Conference (WWW) (2011)

27. Stringhini, G., Kruegel, C., Vigna, G.: Shady paths: leveraging surfing crowds to detect malicious web pages categories and subject descriptors. In: Proceedings of the ACM Conference on Computer and Communications Security (CCS) (2013)

28. Mekky, H., Torres, R., Zhang, Z.L., Saha, S., Nucci, A.: Detecting malicious HTTP redirections using trees of user browsing activity. In: Proceedings of the IEEE International Conference on Computer Communications (INFOCOM) (2014)

SecWeb: Privacy-Preserving Web Browsing Monitoring with w-Event Differential Privacy

Qian Wang$^{1(\boxtimes)}$, Xiao Lu^1, Yan Zhang^1, Zhibo Wang^1, Zhan Qin^2, and Kui Ren^2

^{1} The State Key Lab of Software Engineering, School of CS,
Wuhan University, Wuhan, China
{qianwang,luxiao,stong,zbwang}@whu.edu.cn
^{2} Department of CSE, The State University of New York, Buffalo, USA
{zhanqin,kuiren}@buffalo.edu

Abstract. Nowadays aggregated web browsing histories of individual users have been collected and extensively used by Internet service providers as well as third-party researchers, due to their great value to data mining for in-depth understanding of important phenomena, such as suspicious behavior detection. While providing tremendous benefits, the release of private users' data to the public will pose a considerable threat to users' privacy. Sharing web browsing data with privacy preservation has so far received very limited research attention. In this paper, we investigate the problem of real-time privacy-preserving web browsing monitoring, and propose SecWeb, an online aggregated web browsing behavior monitoring scheme over infinite time with theoretical privacy guarantee. Specifically, we propose an adaptive sampling mechanism and an adaptive budget allocation mechanism to better allocate appropriate privacy budget to sampling points within any successive w time stamps. In addition, we propose a dynamic grouping mechanism that groups web pages with small visits together and adds Laplace noise to each group instead of single web page to eliminate the effects of perturbation error for the web pages. We prove that SecWeb satisfies w-event differential privacy and the experimental results on a real-world dataset show that SecWeb outperforms the state-of-the-art approaches.

Keywords: Web browsing · Privacy preservation · Real-time data publishing · Differential privacy · w-event privacy

1 Introduction

The Internet plays a more and more important role in people's daily life as the explosive growth of mobile devices. People can obtain their interested information by browsing various websites, while their browsing behaviors which can be characterized by browsing histories are also recorded by the host servers simultaneously. The servers may publish the browsing histories[1] to the public since

---

[1] In this paper, we interchangeably use "web browsing histories" and "web browsing data" throughout the paper without confusion.

© ICST Institute for Computer Sciences, Social Informatics and Telecommunications Engineering 2017
R. Deng et al. (Eds.): SecureComm 2016, LNICST 198, pp. 454–474, 2017.
DOI: 10.1007/978-3-319-59608-2_26

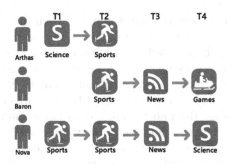

Fig. 1. An example of web browsing behaviors

Table 1. Statistics of web browsing behaviors

	News	Games	Sports	Science
T1	0	0	1	1
T2	0	0	3	0
T3	2	0	0	0
T4	0	1	0	1

these data is of great value for companies or third-party researchers in many data mining applications to analyze the browsing behavior of users. It is also strategic significance for understanding the users' habits in order to improve the user experience and websites performance, such as recommending web pages to users based on their browsing behavior, finding the current hot news, and watching the network traffic to detect anomaly [5].

However, there is always a risk in releasing this kind of private and sensitive data to the public. Studies have indicated that a user's web browsing history (i.e., a sequence of visited websites) can be regarded as a fingerprint which can be used to uniquely identify or track the user [21]. The AOL data release [4] is a representative privacy incident where a newspaper journalist quickly identified a user by the released anonymized search logs and consequently the sensitive information of this user was disclosed. This and other related findings indicate that the released private data must be carefully processed to protect the privacy of individuals [25].

Generally speaking, different people behave different web browsing patterns. Thus, people's sensitive information can be easily figured out by exploiting users' browsing histories. Even the identification information is hidden from the public, it is still possible to discover the browsing histories of users. For example, Fig. 1 illustrates the browsing behaviors of three people, e.g., Baron starts his browsing session at time stamp $T2$, visiting a sports news page, then he moves to a local news page and his session ends after browsing a web page about games. Table 1 shows the number of visits to each type of web page without any identification information. With background information, the adversary knows that Baron starts to browse the web page at time stamp $T2$. Then the adversary can easily obtain two browsing traces for Baron, i.e., *sports* → *news* → *games* or *sports* → *news* → *science*, from the released data. Suppose the adversary already knows that Baron is interested in playing games from the side channel information, e.g., the public tweet from Twitter. Then he can infer that *sports* → *news* → *games* is more likely to be the true browsing trace of Baron. Therefore, it is important and necessary to process the web browsing data before publishing so that the released data is not only useful but also privacy-preserved.

The technique of differential privacy (DP) [9] can ensure privacy protection for statistic data publishing with vigorous guarantee theoretically. Now it has become an appealing privacy model. In particular, DP does not need to make any assumption about the adversary's background information. That is, even the adversary has obtained a user's background information, it cannot derive any additional information about the user based on his/her published data.

Almost all of the existing differentially private protocols investigated either event-level privacy on infinite streams [6,7,11] or user-level privacy on finite streams [12,13]. The authors in [18] successfully bridged the gap between the user-level and the event-level over streams using the *w-event ε-differential privacy* model (i.e., *w*-event privacy) to make a good trade-off between the privacy and the utility, and thus it can protect any sequence of events existing within any time stamp window of length w.

In this paper, we investigate the real-time web browsing data publishing problem with privacy protection, e.g., securing the number of visits to different web pages at each time stamp. [12] took the first step to share web browsing data with differential privacy, which focused on real-time web browsing data release over a pre-specified finite time stamps. However, the continuous publication of web browsing data (called data streaming) may further reveal sensitive information of users, which motivates the research on privacy preserving real-time web browsing data publishing over infinite time. The *w*-event privacy model well suits for the infinite stream case, and it can provide a full protection of any user's browsing traces (e.g., a sequence of visited web pages) over any sequence of continuous time stamps of length w. We summarize the main contributions of this paper as follows.

- We design a novel privacy preserving scheme, called SecWeb, for real-time web browsing data publishing with strong privacy guarantee. We design a dynamic grouping mechanism which groups all web pages with a small number of visits, and Laplace noise is inserted to every group other than a single web page to eliminate the effects of perturbation error on web pages.
- We propose adaptive sampling and budget allocation schemes to better allocate appropriate budget of privacy to the sampling points within any sequence of continuous time stamps of length w. We further propose a pre-sampling mechanism to reduce the high query sensitivity and integrate it with SecWeb seamlessly.
- We theoretically prove that SecWeb satisfies the notion of w-event ϵ-differential privacy. SecWeb is evaluated with a real-world dataset,

and compare it with the state-of-the-art approaches. The results demonstrate that SecWeb outperforms the previous approaches and improves the utility or accuracy of real-time web browsing data publishing with a vigorous privacy guarantee.

The remaining parts of this paper are organized as the following sections. Section 2 introduces some preliminary knowledge, describes the problem formulation and briefly discuss the related works. We present SecWeb and analyze its privacy in Sect. 3. We evaluate the performance of SecWeb with extensive experiments in Sect. 4 and finally conclude the paper in Sect. 5.

2 Backgroud

2.1 Preliminaries and Problem Statement

In this section, we introduce some preliminary knowledge of differential privacy and w-event privacy, and present the problem to be studied in this paper.

Differential Privacy. Differential privacy has become a *de-facto* standard privacy model for statistics analysis with provable privacy guarantee. Intuitively, a mechanism satisfies differential privacy if its outputs are approximately unchanged even if a record in the dataset is removed, so that an adversary infers no more information about the record from the mechanism outputs.

Definition 1 (Differential Privacy [9]). *A privacy mechanism $\mathcal{M}$ gives ϵ-differential privacy, where $\epsilon > 0$, if for any datasets D and D' differing on at most one record, and for all sets $S \subseteq Range(\mathcal{M})$,*

$$\Pr[\mathcal{M}(D) \in S] \leq \exp(\epsilon) \cdot \Pr[\mathcal{M}(D') \in S], \tag{1}$$

where ϵ is the *privacy budget* representing the privacy level the mechanism provides. Generally speaking, a smaller ϵ guarantees a stronger privacy level.

Definition 2 (l_1-norm Sensitivity [10]). *For any function $f : \mathcal{D} \to \mathcal{R}^d$, the l_1-norm sensitivity of f w.r.t. $\mathcal{D}$ is*

$$\Delta(f) = \max_{D,D' \in \mathcal{D}} \|f(D) - f(D')\|_1 \tag{2}$$

for all D, D' differing on at most one record.

Laplace mechanism is commonly used to realize ϵ-differential privacy, which adds noise drawn from a Laplace distribution into the datasets to be published.

Theorem 1 (Laplace Mechanism [10]). *For any function $f : \mathcal{D} \to \mathcal{R}^d$, the Laplace Mechanism $\mathcal{M}$ for any dataset $D \in \mathcal{D}$*

$$\mathcal{M}(D) = f(D) + \langle Lap(\Delta(f)/\epsilon) \rangle^d \tag{3}$$

satisfies ϵ-differential privacy, where the noise $Lap(\Delta(f)/\epsilon)$ is drawn from a Laplace distribution with mean zero and scale $\Delta(f)/\epsilon$.

Intuitively, the noise is large if sensitivity $\Delta(f)$ is big or the budget ϵ is small.

w-**Event Privacy.** The notion of w-event ϵ-differential privacy (i.e., w-event privacy) was first proposed in [18]. This new privacy model can give provable privacy assurance for any sequence of events within successive time stamps of length w.

Before giving the formal definition of w-event privacy, we first introduce some necessary notions. Two data sets D_i, D_i' at time stamp i are neighboring if they have at most one different row. At time stamp t, we define the stream prefix of an infinite series $S = (D_1, D_2, ...)$ as $S_t = (D_1, D_2, ..., D_t)$.

Definition 3 (w-neighboring [18]). w is a positive integer, we say that S_t, S_t' are w-neighboring, if

1. For every $S_t[i]$, $S_t'[i]$ such that $i \in [t]$ and $S_t[i] \neq S_t'[i]$, it holds that $S_t[i]$, $S_t'[i]$ are neighboring, and
2. For every $S_t[i_1]$, $S_t[i_2]$, $S_t'[i_1]$, $S_t'[i_2]$ with $i_1 < i_2$, $S_t[i_1] \neq S_t'[i_1]$ and $S_t[i_2] \neq S_t'[i_2]$, it holds that $i_2 - i_1 + 1 \leq w$.

Simply put, if S_t, S_t' are w-neighboring, their elements are pairwise the same or neighboring, and the time interval of any two neighboring datasets will not exceed w time stamps.

Definition 4 (w-**Event Privacy** [18]). A mechanism $\mathcal{M}$ satisfies w-event ϵ-differential privacy, if for all sets $S \subseteq Range(\mathcal{M})$ and all w-neighboring stream prefixes S_t, S_t' and all t, it holds that

$$\Pr[\mathcal{M}(S_t) \in S] \leq exp(\epsilon) \cdot \Pr[\mathcal{M}(S_t') \in S]. \tag{4}$$

A mechanism satisfying w-event privacy will protect the sensitive information that may be disclosed from a sequence of some length w.

Theorem 2 ([18]). Let $\mathcal{M}$ be a mechanism that takes stream prefix S_t as input, where $S_t[i] = D_i \in \mathcal{D}$, and outputs $\boldsymbol{s} = (\boldsymbol{s}_1, ..., \boldsymbol{s}_t) \in Range(\mathcal{M})$. Suppose $\mathcal{M}$ can be decomposed into t mechanisms $\mathcal{M}_1, ..., \mathcal{M}_t$ such that $\mathcal{M}_i(D_i) = \boldsymbol{s}_i$, each $\mathcal{M}_i$ generates independent randomness and achieves ϵ_i-differential privacy. Then, $\mathcal{M}$ satisfies w-event privacy if

$$\forall i \in [t], \sum_{k=i-w+1}^{i} \epsilon_k \leq \epsilon. \tag{5}$$

This theorem enables us to view ϵ as the total available privacy budget in any sliding window of size w, and appropriately allocate portions of it across the time stamps.

Problem Statement. In this paper, we consider the application of continually publishing web browsing histories to the public in real-time manner and aim to realize w-event privacy for real-time web browsing data publishing. Here, a browsing history is defined as a sequence of web pages browsed at consecutive and discrete time stamps. A host server collects and records users' browsing data, and generates a database D as time goes. The objective is to continually make the data statistics calculated on D public in a real-time manner with the guarantee of w-event privacy. To achieve this goal, the host server will not release the real value of statistics, but apply a well-designed privacy protection scheme to publish a sanitised version of the original statistics.

The server gathers the users' browsing logs throughout the time, and at time stamp i obtains a two-dimensional database/matrix D_i, where the columns correspond to the web pages and the rows correspond to the users. $D_i[m][n]$ is set to 1 if the user m has visited the web page n at time stamp i(during time stamp $i-1$ and i), and 0 otherwise. Note that each row of D_i may contains several 1 s since a user may visit more than one web page for a period of time in reality. The server then publishes the statistics of the visits for each page at time stamps i. Here, we define the statistic of the visits for each web page as a query function Q on D_i, $Q(D_i) = X_i = (x_i^1, x_i^2, \cdots, x_i^d)$, where d denotes the total number of pages and x_i^j denotes the number of visits of page j. Since each user can visit several web pages for each time stamp, the sensitivity $\Delta(Q)$ may be large and consequently leads to a huge injected noise.

Instead of directly releasing x_i^j with high privacy leakage, the server publishes a sanitized version of x_i^j, denoted by r_i^j. At time stamp i, based on the statistics X_i, we denote its corresponding sanitized version by $R_i = (r_i^1, r_i^2, \cdots, r_i^d)$. Therefore, the goal of this paper is to design a privacy protection mechanism to generate and publish the sanitized version R_i in real-time and guarantee that the subsequent releases $\mathbf{R} = \{R_1, R_2, ..., R_i, ...\}$ is satisfying w-event privacy.

Here, we briefly explain several important notions to be used throughout the paper.

Utility. The utility of the published data measures how valid the data is used for subsequent analysis or mining tasks. In this paper, we evaluate the utility with the following metrics: Mean Absolute Error (MAE), Mean Relative Error (MRE), and Top-K mining precision.

Sampling Point and Non-Sampling Point. A sampling point is a selected time stamp where the raw statistic is queried and perturbed. The statistic at a non-sampling point will not be queried but instead will be approximated by the perturbed data at last sampling point.

2.2 Related Work

In [4,21], it has been shown that there exist severe privacy risks when users' data is released, and many privacy-assured data publishing schemes have been designed accordingly.

To publish search logs or web browsing data, many schemes were proposed to achieve k-anonymity [2,16]. However, it was shown in [15] that the existing solutions always assume the attackers have no background knowledge, and this is not true in practice. In comparison, the notion of differential privacy proposed in [9] can ensure much stronger privacy guarantee, where a user's privacy can be well protected even if the attackers have obtained the others' information in the database. Following the differential privacy model, [10] proposed the first differentially private scheme called Laplace mechanism. On top of that, many schemes have been presented for achieving differentially private data publishing in the past years.

In [8,20,24], several mechanisms were proposed for the release of statistical data computed based on the static database. Until recently, researchers began to consider releasing time series data. One direction is to study the off-line data release [1,23] while the other direction is to investigate the real-time data publishing [7,11]. The key difference between these two direction is that the solutions for the off-line data release deal with the whole time series data at one time, but the solutions for the real-time data publishing deal with the data streamingly.

In [7,11], the authors proposed differentially private solutions for continual counting queries over time series data, and the techniques can be used for real-time monitoring. Their limitation is that only *event-level* privacy guarantee is provided. That is, only one's presence at a single time stamp is fully protected over the whole data stream.

In [12,13,18], the proposed solutions considered differentially private release of real-time time series. Different from [7,11,13] established a new framework called FAST. FAST consists of sampling and filtering operations with the appealing property of providing *user-level* privacy. That is, the presence of a user over the whole time series is protected. But FAST has the limitation of pre-assigning the maximum times of publications, so it is only suitable for finite-time data publishing. To fill the gap between *event-level* privacy and *user-level* privacy, Kellaris et al. [18] proposed *w-event ϵ-differential privacy*, and it can protect any sequence of events existing in any continuous time stamps of length w over infinite time. Due to its nice property, in this paper we use it to protect users' web browsing traces within any window of w continuous time stamps.

Fan and Xiong [12] took the first step towards sharing web browsing data with differential privacy. They proposed two algorithms based on FAST. The first algorithm slightly changes FAST to the web browsing scenario, which is called univariate Kalman filter (U-KF). The second algorithm, called multivariate Kalman filter (M-KF), establishes a multivariate model and utilizes the Markov property of web browsing behavior. M-KF uses Markov chain to improve accuracy of the prediction step in Kalman filter and have a more accurate result than U-KF. However, the Markov model must be learned by an appropriate training set in advance and the multiple steps of matrix operations in M-KF extremely reduce its efficiency, which is especially vital for a real-time algorithm.

Competitors. We identify three competitors. The first is an application of LPA [10] on w-event privacy, which is also called UNIFORM in [18]. UNIFORM assigns $\frac{\epsilon}{w}$ to every time stamp, where ϵ is the total budget. And then UNIFORM straightforwardly applies LPA at each time stamp. Obviously, the budget for each time stamp will be very small if w is large, which leads to a very bad utility.

The last two competitors are U-KF and M-KF. Since U-KF and M-KF are not w-event private, we slightly change them to satisfy w-event privacy according to [18] and name the new schemes as U-KF$_w$ and M-KF$_w$. To be precise, we make an instantiation of the two methods which consist of sub mechanisms, each operating on a disjoint w time stamps. In order to guarantee that the total budget allocated in any w successive time stamps is less than ϵ, for each sub mechanism, we allocate budget $\epsilon/2$ to satisfy w-event privacy.

3 SecWeb: Real-Time Web Browsing Data Publishing with Privacy Preservation

In this section, we present our SecWeb design to achieve real-time web browsing data publishing with privacy preservation. In order to realize this purpose, we propose a framework for SecWeb, as shown in Fig. 2, which is mainly composed of five components: *adaptive sampling, dynamic grouping, adaptive budget allocation, grouping based perturbation, filtering* and *pre-sampling*.

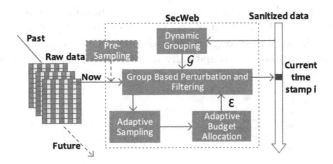

Fig. 2. The framework of SecWeb

Specifically, the *adaptive sampling* component can adjust the sampling rate based on dynamic data, and it enables SecWeb to perturb statistics at selected sampling time stamps while approximating the non-sampled statistics with perturbed statistics at the last sampling time stamp. The *adaptive budget allocation* component can dynamically allocate appropriate budget for each sampling page according to the changing trend of each web page. For the sampling pages at each time stamp, the *dynamic grouping* component can group sampling pages with similar features together, and the *group based perturbation* component can inject Laplace noise to the groups other than individual web pages with the allocated budget to reduce the perturbation error to each web page. Moreover, following FAST, the *filtering* component is used to further enhance the utility of published sanitized data. Finally, the server publishes the sanitized data after filtering and chooses the new sampling interval for the sampling pages using the *adaptive sampling* component. After presenting SecWeb, we further propose a pre-sampling method to reduce the high query sensitivity, and this method can be integrating with SecWeb seamlessly.

3.1   Adaptive Sampling

Every noisy data release comes at the cost of budget consumption while the entire budget ϵ is a constant. Thus, publishing noisy data at every time stamp will introduce large magnitude of noise when the window size w is large. An efficient way to overcome this problem is to use a sampling mechanism which queries and perturbs statistics at selected time stamps and approximates the non-sampled statistics with perturbed sampled statistics. Consequently, non-sampled statistics can be approximated without any budget allocation, and more budget can be allocated to sampling points within any successive w time stamps given a fixed ϵ.

Figure 3 shows the general idea of the *adaptive sampling* mechanism. The blue line with markers represents the raw data series, the red line denotes the released data and the dashed green lines denote the sampling points. Note that here we inject Laplace noise at each sampling point with value of zero for simplicity. As shown in Fig. 3, the *adaptive sampling* mechanism only samples three points through time stamp 1 to 10, since the raw series change gently and the non-sampled statistics could be roughly approximated. The sampling rate increases when the raw data changes dramatically through time stamp 10 to 20 in order to avoid large error introduced by approximation.

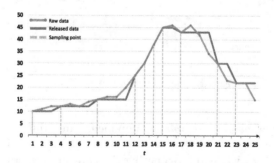

Fig. 3. An illustration of adaptive sampling (Color figure online)

In this paper, we consider both the data dynamics and the remaining budget to design an adaptive sampling mechanism. Specifically, the proportional-integral-derivative (PID) control is utilized to characterize the dynamic data. At the next time stamp, we then choose the next sampling interval for every page with the PID error and the remaining budget. In comparison to FAST [13], here a new *feedback error* measure is used to compute the PID error. This is because FAST's *feedback error* can be too sensitive to data dynamics, and the adaptive sampling performance would be affected when we have small data values.

Let k_n and k_{n-1} be the current and the last sampling points, respectively. For page j, we have the *feedback error*:

$$E^j_{k_n} = |r^j_{k_n} - r^j_{k_{n-1}}|.$$

It is actually the error of the released data values between the current and the last sampling points. The PID error δ^j for statistics on the jth column of D_{k_n} (i.e., page j) is computed as

$$\delta^j = K_p E^j_{k_n} + K_i \frac{\sum^n_{o=n-\pi-1} E^j_{k_o}}{\pi} + K_d \frac{E^j_{k_n}}{k_n - k_{n-1}}, \qquad (6)$$

where K_p, K_i, and K_d denote the standard PID scale factors, which respectively represents the proportional gain, the integral gain and the derivative gain. The first term $K_p E^j_{k_n}$ is the proportional error standing for the present error; the second term $K_i \frac{\sum^n_{o=n-\pi-1} E^j_{k_o}}{\pi}$ is the integral error standing for the accumulation of past errors, and π is how many recent errors are taken for the integral error; the third term $K_d \frac{E^j_{k_n}}{k_n-k_{n-1}}$ denotes the derivative error used to predict the future error. In our experiments, for the PID controller we choose $\pi = 3$, $K_p = 0.9$, $K_i = 0.1$, and $K_d = 0$.

It may seem that we should choose a small sampling interval if the data rapidly changes. However, this is not always the case. When we have a very small remaining budget, sampling and perturbing statistics at the next time stamp may incur quite high perturbation error. So, a better choice is to adopt a relatively large sampling interval, then the previously-allocated budget can be used again, and it will approximate the statistics at the next time stamp with the previous publication. We have the new sampling interval

$$I = \max\{1, I_l + \theta(1 - (\frac{\delta^j}{\lambda_r})^2)\}, \qquad (7)$$

where I and I_l respectively denotes the next and the last sampling intervals of page j. In our settings, $\lambda_r = 1/\epsilon_r$ is chosen to measure the scale of Laplace noise. Here ϵ_r denotes the remaining budget at the next time stamp, and θ denotes a pre-defined scale factor used to adjust the sampling interval. In our experiments, we set $\theta = 10$. In particular, the relative value of PID error δ^j and the scale of Laplace noise λ_r are used to determine the increase or decrease of the sampling interval. In fact, we increase the sampling interval when $\delta^j < \lambda_r$ and decrease it when $\delta^j > \lambda_r$.

3.2 Dynamic Grouping

Intuitively, directly injecting Laplace noise to each statistic is the simple and straightforward way to achieve differential privacy. However, this is not true.

For the web pages with small statistics, their utilities will be severely affected when the privacy level is satisfied, especially when the limited privacy budget should be allocated to multiple time stamps. Even a small noise may cause large relative error when the statistics of sampling pages are small.

Fan et al. [14] proposed a grouping mechanism to solve this kind of problems. The main idea is to aggregate the statistics of similar regions together and inject noise to each aggregated group, and then average the noisy count to each group member. Note that the proposed grouping mechanism in [14] is based on the assumption that the statistics of regions which are close in space have similar changing trend, and the grouping process is performed offline at one time. This assumption however does not hold for real-time web browsing data publishing since the statistics of web pages behave high dynamics and should not be grouped offline at one time.

Inspired by the grouping mechanism in [14], in this paper, we propose a dynamic grouping mechanism that aggregates the web pages with small statistics dynamically based on their real-time changing trend. The main idea is that web pages with small statistics can be grouped together if their statistics are close and the changing trends of statistics are similar.

To realize this objective, we use the released statistics at previous sampling points to predict the statistic at current sampling point as well as characterize the changing trends of statistics. Let $(r^j_{k_{i-\kappa}}, r^j_{k_{i-\kappa+1}}, \cdots, r^j_{k_{i-1}})$ denote the released statistics at previous κ sampling points, and $\bar{x}^j_{k_i}$ denote the predicted statistic at sampling point k_i for page j. We let $\bar{x}^j_{k_i} = \sum_{o=i-\kappa}^{i-1} r^j_{k_o}/\kappa$, and adopt Pearson Correlation Coefficient [22], the most commonly used measure of correlation in statistics, to measure the similarity of changing trend of statistics. Finally, pages with small statistics and high similarity are grouped together.

The pseudocode of the *dynamic grouping* mechanism is formally presented in Algorithm 1. Note that at each time stamp, dynamic grouping only considers the set of pages that need to be sampled, denoted by Ψ. Let $\mathcal{G}_{k_i}$ denote the group strategy at time stamp k_i. First, the mechanism predicts the statistic at k_i for each sampling page in Ψ. Let τ_1 denotes the noise resistance threshold that reflects whether the statistics of pages have sufficient capacity to resist noise. If $\bar{x}^j_{k_i} \geq \tau_1$, the page itself can be a group; otherwise, the page is encouraged to be grouped with other pages. Thus, in lines 2–7, the mechanism filters out the pages that can resist noise individually which do not need to be grouped with other pages together. These found pages are put into the group strategy $\mathcal{G}_{k_i}$ where each of them is an individual group.

Lines 8–20 describes how to group web pages with small statistics together. Generally speaking, two pages i and j can be grouped together if they have small error between $\bar{x}^i_{k_i}$ and $\bar{x}^j_{k_i}$, and also they have sufficient similarity of the changing trend. The similarity of two pages i and j at time stamp k_i can be calculated by the Pearson Correlation Coefficient of R^i_k and R^j_k. Let τ_2 denote the similarity threshold that decides whether two pages have similar changing trends of statistics. Thus, when the similarity of two pages is no less than τ_2, the two pages have sufficient similarity. Let τ_3 denote the error threshold that

---

Algorithm 1. Dynamic Grouping

Input: Ψ: the collection of sampling pages;

$R_k^j = (r_{k_{i-\kappa}}^j, r_{k_{i-\kappa+1}}^j, \cdots, r_{k_{i-1}}^j)$: the released statistics at previous κ sampling points for a sampling page j.

Output: Group strategy $\mathcal{G}_{k_i}$.

1: Calculate $\bar{x}_{k_i}^j = \sum_{o=i-\kappa}^{i-1} r_{k_o}^j / \kappa$ for each page j in Ψ
2: **for** each page in Ψ, say j **do**
3:   **if** $\bar{x}_{k_i}^j > \tau_1$ **then**
4:     Let the page j itself as a group and add it to $\mathcal{G}_{k_i}$
5:     Remove page j from Ψ
6:   **end if**
7: **end for**
8: Sort Ψ in increasing order according to $\bar{x}_{k_i}^j$
9: **while** $\Psi \neq \varnothing$ **do**
10:   Initialize a empty group g with the first page in Ψ
11:   Let $o = 2$
12:   **while** $o < \Psi.length$, $\bar{x}_{k_i}^o - \bar{x}_{k_i}^1 < \tau_2$ and the sum of $\bar{x}_{k_i}^j$ in $g < \tau_1$ **do**
13:     $pc \leftarrow$ calculate Pearson Correlation Coefficient between page o and page 1
14:     **if** $pc > \tau_3$ **then**
15:       Add page o to g
16:     **end if**
17:     $o = o + 1$
18:   **end while**
19:   Remove the pages in g from Ψ and add g to $\mathcal{G}_{k_i}$
20: **end while**
21: Return grouping strategy $\mathcal{G}_{k_i}$

---

decides whether two pages are close or not in terms of predicted statistics. Thus, when the error is less than τ_3 and the similarity is larger than τ_2, two pages are encouraged to be grouped together.

In line 8, the dynamic grouping mechanism first sorts the remaining web pages in Ψ in increasing order according to $\bar{x}_{k_i}^j$. In lines 9–20, the mechanism repeatedly forms groups by putting the pages in Ψ with small error and high similarity to the first page in Ψ, and puts the formed groups into the group strategy $\mathcal{G}_{k_i}$. The process terminates until there is no page in Ψ. Note that when forming a group, the grouping process checks the remaining pages one by one in Ψ and put qualified pages into a group. However, if the sum of predicted statistics of all pages put in the group is larger than τ_1, which means the group has sufficient capacity to resist noise, no more page need to be added to this group and a new grouping process can start.

3.3 Adaptive Budget Allocation

To achieve w-event differential privacy, we should make sure that the budget sum of any successive w time stamps is at most ϵ. Here, we propose an adaptive budget allocation mechanism based on the trend of data change to adaptively

---

Algorithm 2. Adaptive Budget Allocation

Input: Privacy budget ϵ, new sampling interval I, allocated budget for each time
    stamp $(\epsilon_1, ..., \epsilon_{i-1})$, and the maximum allocated budget at each sampling point
    ϵ_{max}. Note that $\epsilon_k = 0$ if time stamp k is not a sampling point.
Output: Budget allocation ϵ_i for the sampling time stamp i
1: Compute the remaining budget $\epsilon_r = \epsilon - \sum_{k=i-w+1}^{i-1} \epsilon_k$
2: Compute the portion $p = \min(\phi \cdot \ln(I+1), p_{max})$
3: Compute the allocated budget $\epsilon_i = \min(p \cdot \epsilon_r, \epsilon_{max})$

---

allocate appropriate budget at *each sampling point*. In our design, based on
the data change trend, we adjust the length of the sampling interval. In fact,
when data changes rapidly (slowly) the new sampling interval is small (large).
Thus, for the small sampling interval, we could infer that the data is changing
rapidly, so we have more sampling points within a time window of length w.
Then, we determine to put a small portion of the remaining budget to the next
sampling point. In this case, more available budget can be given to the (potential)
successive sampling points. When we have a large the sampling interval, we could
infer that the data is changing slowly, so we only have fewer sampling points
within the time window of length w. So, we determine to put a large portion of
the remaining budget to the next sampling point.

To achieve our goal, we propose to use the natural logarithm to link p (the
portion of the remaining budget) and I. So, we define $p = \phi \cdot \ln(I+1)$, where
the scale factor ϕ ranges in $(0,1]$. Because I has the minimum value 1, to avoid
the case that $p = 0$ we use $\ln(I+1)$ other than $\ln I$.

Algorithm 2 formally presents the adaptive budget allocation mechanism.
First, we compute the remaining budget ϵ_r in $[i-w+1, i]$. Here ϵ_r equals to ϵ
minus the budget sum allocated in $[i-w+1, i-1]$. Then we compute the portion
p to determine how much budget will be used for the current sampling point i. It
is worth noting that $p \leq p_{max}$ is set to avoid the case that we leave to the next
sampling point too few budget. Finally, we compute the budget allocated to the
current time stamp as $\epsilon_i = \min(p \cdot \epsilon_r, \epsilon_{max})$, where ϵ_{max} is the upperbound for
the budget allocated at each sampling point. The introduction of ϵ_{max} is due
to the fact that the utility enhancement is small when the allocated budget is
larger than ϵ_{max}, say $\epsilon_{max} = 0.2$ when $\epsilon = 1$.

3.4   Group-Based Perturbation and Filtering

At each time stamp, we apply Laplace mechanism to inject Laplace noise to
statistics at sampling pages to provide differential privacy guarantee. For each
non-sampling page, the publication is approximated by its last release. Here,
Laplace mechanism is applied to every group other than every page. Then we
compute the average of the perturbed statistic to each page. To guarantee that
the total budget assigned to every page at any successive w time stamps is less
than ϵ, the budget assigned to a group is the smallest budget assigned to pages
in the group.

Assume we have a group g of φ pages. Thus, g contains φ columns of D_i and $g \subseteq D_i$. We use $f(g)$ to denote the statistic function that accumulates all 1's in g. We use $\lambda(g)$ to denote the scale of Laplace noise injected to $f(g)$. The Laplace mechanism is applied to group g, and we have

$$\mathcal{M}(g) = f(g) + Lap(\lambda(g))$$
$$= \sum_{j=1}^{\varphi} \sum g[j] + Lap(\Delta(f)/\min(\epsilon_{g[j]})), \tag{8}$$

where $g[j]$ is the jth column of g and $\Delta(f)$ is decided by the database.

Then the perturbed statistic for each column/page at group g is calculated as the average of $\mathcal{M}(g)$. That is,

$$\mathcal{M}(g[j]) = \mathcal{M}(g)/\varphi, \quad \forall j = 1, \cdots, \varphi. \tag{9}$$

However, we would not release $\mathcal{M}(g[j])$ directly and further apply the Kalman filtering mechanism of FAST algorithm [13] to improve the utility of released statistics. The detail of the mechanism can be found in [13].

3.5   Pre-sampling to Reduce Sensitivity

We use dynamic grouping to diminish the perturbation error on small statistics, which greatly improves the data utility of pages with small counts. However, the high query sensitivity will still bring a huge injected noise, which may also have a bad influence on the utility of released data.

In [17], the authors proposed a sampling method to generate a small portion of the original database, which is used to calculate the grouping strategy. Inspired by their work, we consider whether we can further reduce the injected noise by cutting down the sensitivity $\Delta(Q)$ through a pre-sampling method.

Here, we propose a concise and effective pre-sampling method to generate the representative database D_i' at each sampling point i. Specifically, at each sampling point i, our method gets a new database D_i' by randomly sampling m 1s in each row in D_i(if there are only $n < m$ 1s in a row, preserve them all), and setting the remaining to 0. Consequently, there are at most m 1s in each row after pre-sampling, i.e., each user can visits at most m web pages per time stamp and the sensitivity $\Delta(Q(D_i')) = m$. We then use D_i' to replace the original database D_i, and the remaining procedures are just the same as the original SecWeb. The only difference is, for each group g, only $Lap(m/\min(\epsilon_g))$ of noise is needed to be injected, where m can be a user-defined parameter. Note that the pre-sampling method also cause a biased estimate error since D_i' is a selected portion of D_i. The error is heavily data-dependent which can not be rigorously analyzed, and consequently we cannot give a certain value of m to get the optimal performance without knowing the data distribution. Intuitively, the value of m should be close to the average counts of each page in the database, we will test the effectiveness of pre-sampling over different values of m in our experiments.

3.6   Privacy Analysis

Theorem 3. *SecWeb satisfies w-event ε-differential privacy.*

Proof. According to Axiom 2.1.1 in [19], post-processing the sanitized data maintains privacy as long as the post-processing algorithm does not use the sensitive information directly. In SecWeb, group-based perturbation is the only component processing the raw data directly, while other components process the sanitized data. Thus, we will first show that the group-based perturbation component achieves w-event ϵ-differential privacy, then it is easy to prove that SecWeb can achieve the same privacy guarantee.

Based on $\mathcal{G}$, D_i is separated to n disjoint groups $\{g_1, g_2, \ldots, g_n\}$, and every group contains some columns of D_i. Without any loss of generality, we consider g_1, and suppose g_1 consists of φ_1 columns. Based on Eq. 8, we have

$$\mathcal{M}(g_1) = f(g_1) + Lap(\lambda(g_1))$$
$$= \sum_{j=1}^{\varphi_1} \sum g_1[j] + Lap(\Delta(f)/\min(\epsilon_{g_1})).$$

Here, $g_1[j]$ denotes g_1's j-th column.

Based on Theorem 1, $\mathcal{M}(g_1)$ achieves $\min(\epsilon_{g_1})$-differential privacy. Based on Axiom 2.1.1 in [19], $\mathcal{M}(g_1[j])$ $(\forall j = 1, \cdots, \varphi)$ also achieves $\min(\epsilon_{g_1})$-differential privacy. Analogously, every group runs Laplace mechanism independently on a column/page in group g_k satisfying $\min(\epsilon_{g_k})$-differential privacy. We use $\hat{\epsilon}_k$ and ϵ_k to respectively denote the budget used for perturbation and the allocated budget (generated by the adaptive budget allocation component) for a page at time stamp k, then we have $\hat{\epsilon}_k \leq \epsilon_k$.

Based on Theorem 2, to show that the perturbation component for a page achieves w-event ϵ-differential privacy, we should show that for each t and $i \in [t]$, $\sum_{k=i-w+1}^{i} \hat{\epsilon}_k \leq \epsilon$ will hold. Because our adaptive budget allocation component guarantees that $\sum_{k=i-w+1}^{i} \epsilon_k \leq \epsilon$ for any w successive time stamps, and $\hat{\epsilon}_k \leq \epsilon_k$, then we have $\sum_{k=i-w+1}^{i} \hat{\epsilon}_k \leq \epsilon$. Hence, the perturbation component on each group achieves w-event ϵ-differential privacy. Hence, SecWeb can also achieve the same privacy guarantee.

Theorem 4. *SecWeb with pre-sampling(SecWeb-S for short) satisfies w-event ε-differential privacy.*

Proof. The only differences between SecWeb-S and SecWeb are the procedure of pre-sampling and the noise injected in group-based perturbation. Consider a possible D_i' derived from pre-sampling D_i, each row in D_i' contains at most m 1s. Therefore, the sensitivity of the query f on D_i' in proof Sect. 3.6 is $\Delta(f(D_i')) = m$. Recall that, for each group g we inject noise $Lap(m/\min(\epsilon_g))$, where $\min(\epsilon_g)$ is the minimum budget in g, thus we can derive that the pre-sampling and group-based perturbation in SecWeb-S satisfies $\min(\epsilon_g)$-differential privacy. Similar to proof Sect. 3.6, we can then conclude that SecWeb-S satisfies w-event ϵ-differential privacy.

4   Performance Evaluation

In this section, we used a real-world web dataset, WorldCup [3], as a source of the input stream to evaluate the performance of SecWeb. The entire dataset contains 1,352,804,107 web server logs collected by the FIFA 1998 World Cup Web site between April 30, 1998 and July 26, 1998. These logs are the requests made to 89,997 different URLs and each log consists of a client ID, a requested URL, a time stamp, etc. We randomly choose 1,500 URLs as the test set, create a stream from the set and publish the data per hour, which has a total of 1000 time stamps. The query sensitivity defined in Sect. 2.1 is 30, and the average count of each page per time stamp is 17.9.

We compare our schemes SecWeb and SecWeb-S with three competitors as introduced in Sect. 2.2, UNIFORM, U-KF$_w$ and M-KF$_w$, where the latter are the first two schemes proposed for web browsing monitoring with differential privacy [12]. All the mechanisms are fine-tuned and implemented in Python. We conduct all the experiments on a machine with Intel Core i5 CPU 2.9 GHz and 12 GB RAM, running Windows 10. We set $\phi = 0.2$ for the adaptive budget allocation, and let $\tau_1 = 50$, $\tau_2 = 0.5$ and $\tau_3 = 25$ for dynamic grouping.

We use Mean Absolute Error (MAE) and Mean Relative Error (MRE) as the utility metrics to evaluate the performance of the five mechanisms.

For any web page, let $\mathbf{x} = \{x_1, ..., x_n\}$ denote the raw time series and $\mathbf{r} = \{r_1, ..., r_n\}$ denote the sanitized time series. The MAE and MRE for this page are

$$\mathbf{MAE}(\mathbf{x}, \mathbf{r}) = \frac{1}{n} \sum_{i=1}^{n} |r_i - x_i| \tag{10}$$

$$\mathbf{MRE}(\mathbf{x}, \mathbf{r}) = \frac{1}{n} \sum_{i=1}^{n} \frac{|r_i - x_i|}{\max(\gamma, x_i)} \tag{11}$$

For the bound γ, we set its value to 0.1% of $\sum_{i=1}^{n} x_i$ to mitigate the effect of excessively small results. In experiments, we first calculate the MAE and MRE for each page and then figure out the average of all pages as the final results.

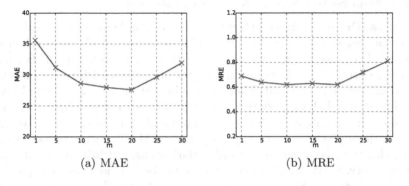

(a) MAE   (b) MRE

Fig. 4. Utility comparison when m changes ($w = 120, \epsilon = 1$)

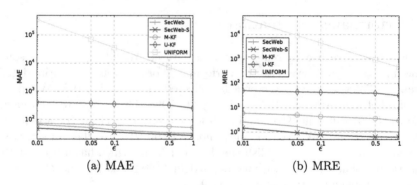

Fig. 5. Utility comparison when ϵ changes ($w = 120$)

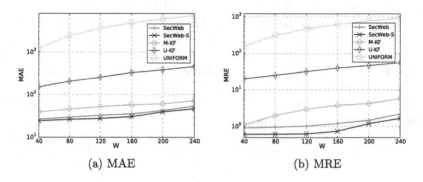

Fig. 6. Utility comparison when w changes ($\epsilon = 1$)

Varying parameter m. Figure 4 illustrates the different performances of SecWeb-S when changing the value of m. As we can see, the pre-sampling method can improve the data utility by reducing the query sensitivity, and SecWeb-S achieves the best performance in both MAE and MRE when $m = 20$. This results also verify our intuition that the value of m should be close to the average count of each page per time stamp(the average count is 17.9 in our dataset). We set $m = 20$ for SecWeb-S in the rest of our experiments.

Utility vs. Privacy. Figure 5 shows the relationship between data utility and privacy budget ϵ. As we can see, the MAE and MRE of all five mechanisms decrease when ϵ increases. This is because that lager ϵ requires smaller noise to preserve privacy, which results in a better utility. UNIFORM has the worst performance since it uniformly allocates the budget and simply adopts LPA at each time stamp. U-KF$_w$ performs much better compared to UNIFORM, since the posteriori estimate on each web page produced by Kalman Filter extremely improves the utility. While the improved method M-KF$_w$ performs better than U-KF$_w$ due to its adoption of fisrt-order Markov chain utilizing user pattern to improve utility. SecWeb and SecWeb-S have the best performance compared to other algorithms, and SecWeb-S performs a little better. The reason is that the well designed dynamic grouping strategy significantly improves the capacity of resisting Laplace noise for pages with small statistics by grouping them together, and the adaptive sampling mechanism also helps avoiding unnecessary noise. The pre-sampling method in SecWeb-S also helps reducing the injected noise.

Utility vs. w. Figure 6 shows the comparison of different utility metrics between the five schemes when window size w varies from 40 to 240. We can also observe that SecWeb and SecWeb-S outperforms other algorithms when w changes. The MAE and MRE of M-KF$_w$ and U-KF$_w$ increase when w becomes large. The reason is that the budget allocated to each time stamp becomes less when w increases since both of them allocate budget uniformly, which results in larger error. The MAE and MRE of our two schemes are much smaller than that of M-KF$_w$ and U-KF$_w$ and are robust to w changes, which is because that SecWeb takes the remaining budget into consideration to adaptively allocate budget on sampling points to reduce the error.

Effects of Dynamic Grouping. We evaluate the performance of our grouping method. Specifically, we calculate the average statistics of each page and pick out the half part of pages with smallest statistics being the test set to see the performance of dynamic grouping. Figure 7 shows the comparison of MAE and MRE between the five schemes on the pages with small statistics. We can observe that SecWeb achieves a much better utility on both MAE and MRE. The reason is that the grouping mechanism in SecWeb groups these pages together dynamically, injects noise to the whole group and averages the counts, which can extremely reduce the perturbation error compared to the schemes that inject noise to each page individually. Note that SecWeb-S also achieves a much better utility, but not always as good as SecWeb. That is because the pages that we select have small counts, where the selected portion of the original database produced by pre-sampling mechanism cannot represent them well since these pages have a less times to be selected than the pages with larger statistics.

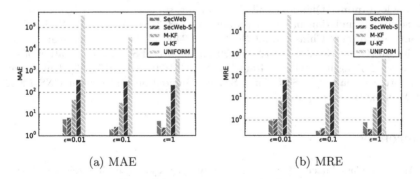

(a) MAE   (b) MRE

Fig. 7. Utility comparison on pages with small statistics($w = 120, \epsilon = 1$)

Running Time. Table 2 shows the comparison of time complexity of the five mechanisms. We can see that U-KF$_w$ and UNIFORM are the fastest mechanisms

Table 2. Comparison of running time

	UNIFORM	U-KF$_w$	M-KF$_w$	SecWeb	SecWeb-S
Time complexity	$\mathcal{O}(d)$	$\mathcal{O}(d)$	$\mathcal{O}(d^3)$	$\mathcal{O}(d^2)$	$\mathcal{O}(d^2)$
Running time (d = 1500)	0.4×10^{-5} s	0.4×10^{-5} s	1.2 s	0.4×10^{-2} s	0.45×10^{-2} s

with time complexity $\mathcal{O}(d)$, while M-KF$_w$ is the slowest mechanism with time complexity $\mathcal{O}(d^3)$, where d is the number of pages. SecWeb and SecWeb-S with the time complexity of $\mathcal{O}(d^2)$ are slower than U-KF$_w$ but much faster than M-KF$_w$. Note that although U-KF$_w$ and UNIFORM are the most fast schemes, they have the worst utility as seen from Figs. 5 and 6. Although the MAE and MRE of M-KF$_w$ are close to that of SecWeb, SecWeb is much faster than M-KF$_w$. Note that SecWeb-S is a little bit slower than SecWeb since it has a pre-sampling procedure. Overall, SecWeb and SecWeb-S achieve a well tradeoff between time efficiency and utility.

5   Conclusions

In this paper, we proposed SecWeb to enable continually publishing aggregated web browsing data for real-time monitoring purposes with w-event privacy guarantee. SecWeb is designed with five integrated components: *adaptive sampling, adaptive budget allocation, dynamic grouping, group-based perturbation* and *filtering*. We proved that SecWeb satisfies w-event ϵ-differential privacy. We further proposed a pre-sampling method to reduce the high query sensitivity and integrated it with SecWeb seamlessly (SecWeb-S). Extensive experiments on real-world dataset showed that SecWeb-S outperforms the existing methods and improves the utility of the released data with strong privacy guarantee.

Acknowledgment. Qian and Zhibo's research is supported in part by National Natural Science Foundation of China (Grant No. 61373167, 61502352), National Basic Research Program of China (Grant No. 2014CB340600), Wuhan Science and Technology Bureau (Grant No. 2015010101010020), and Natural Science Foundation of Hubei Province and Jiangsu Province (Grant No. 2015CFB203, BK20150383). Kui's research is supported in part by US National Science Foundation under grant CNS-1262277. Qian Wang is the corresponding author.

References

1. Acs, G., Castelluccia, C.: A case study: privacy preserving release of spatio-temporal density in Paris. In: Proceedings of ACM SIGKDD, pp. 1679–1688 (2014)
2. Adar, E.: User 4xxxxx9: Anonymizing query logs. In: Proceedings of Query Log Analysis Workshop, International Conference on World Wide Web (2007)
3. Arlitt, M., Jin, T.: Workload characterization of the 1998 world cup web site. Technical report, HPL-1999-35R1, HP (1999)

4. Barbaro, M., Zeller, T.: A face is exposed for AOL searcher no. 4417749. The New York Times (2006)
5. Canali, D., Balzarotti, D.: Behind the scenes of online attacks: an analysis of exploitation behaviors on the web. In: 20th Annual Network & Distributed System Security Symposium (NDSS 2013) (2013)
6. Chan, T.H.H., Li, M., Shi, E., Xu, W.: Differentially private continual monitoring of heavy hitters from distributed streams. In: Proceedings of Privacy Enhancing Technologies, pp. 140–159 (2012)
7. Chan, T.H.H., Shi, E., Song, D.: Private and continual release of statistics. ACM Trans. Inf. Syst. Secur. **14**(3), 26 (2011)
8. Cormode, G., Procopiuc, M., Srivastava, D., Tran, T.T.: Differentially private publication of sparse data. arXiv preprint arXiv:1103.0825 (2011)
9. Dwork, C.: Differential privacy. In: Bugliesi, M., Preneel, B., Sassone, V., Wegener, I. (eds.) ICALP 2006. LNCS, vol. 4052, pp. 1–12. Springer, Heidelberg (2006). doi:10.1007/11787006_1
10. Dwork, C., McSherry, F., Nissim, K., Smith, A.: Calibrating noise to sensitivity in private data analysis. In: Proceedings of Theory of Cryptography, pp. 265–284 (2006)
11. Dwork, C., Naor, M., Pitassi, T., Rothblum, G.N.: Differential privacy under continual observation. In: Proceedings of ACM STOC, pp. 715–724 (2010)
12. Fan, L., Bonomi, L., Xiong, L., Sunderam, V.: Monitoring web browsing behavior with differential privacy. In: Proceedings of ACM WWW, pp. 177–188 (2014)
13. Fan, L., Xiong, L.: An adaptive approach to real-time aggregate monitoring with differential privacy. IEEE Trans. Knowl. Data Eng. **26**(9), 2094–2106 (2014)
14. Fan, L., Xiong, L., Sunderam, V.: Differentially private multi-dimensional time series release for traffic monitoring. In: Proceedings of Data and Applications Security and Privacy, pp. 33–48 (2013)
15. Götz, M., Machanavajjhala, A., Wang, G., Xiao, X., Gehrke, J.: Publishing search logsa comparative study of privacy guarantees. IEEE Trans. Knowl. Data Eng. **24**(3), 520–532 (2012)
16. Hong, Y., He, X., Vaidya, J., Adam, N., Atluri, V.: Effective anonymization of query logs. In: Proceedings of the 18th ACM Conference on Information and Knowledge Management, pp. 1465–1468 (2009)
17. Kellaris, G., Papadopoulos, S.: Practical differential privacy via grouping and smoothing. In: Proceedings of the VLDB Endowment, vol. 6, pp. 301–312. VLDB Endowment (2013)
18. Kellaris, G., Papadopoulos, S., Xiao, X., Papadias, D.: Differentially private event sequences over infinite streams. Proc. VLDB Endowment **7**(12), 1155–1166 (2014)
19. Kifer, D., Lin, B.R.: Towards an axiomatization of statistical privacy and utility. In: Proceedings of ACM PODS, pp. 147–158 (2010)
20. Korolova, A., Kenthapadi, K., Mishra, N., Ntoulas, A.: Releasing search queries and clicks privately. In: Proceedings of the 18th International Conference on World Wide Web, pp. 171–180 (2009)
21. Olejnik, L., Castelluccia, C., Janc, A.: Why Johnny can't browse in peace: on the uniqueness of web browsing history patterns. In: 5th Workshop on Hot Topics in Privacy Enhancing Technologies (HotPETs 2012) (2012)
22. Pearson, K.: Note on regression and inheritance in the case of two parents. Proc. R. Soc. Lond. **58**, 240–242 (1895)
23. Rastogi, V., Nath, S.: Differentially private aggregation of distributed time-series with transformation and encryption. In: Proceedings of the 2010 ACM SIGMOD International Conference on Management of data, pp. 735–746 (2010)

24. Xu, J., Zhang, Z., Xiao, X., Yang, Y., Yu, G., Winslett, M.: Differentially private histogram publication. VLDB J. Int. J. Very Large Databases **22**(6), 797–822 (2013)
25. Zang, H., Bolot, J.: Anonymization of location data does not work: a large-scale measurement study. In: Proceedings of ACM MobiCom, pp. 145–156 (2011)

A Behavioral Biometrics Based Approach to Online Gender Classification

Nicolas Van Balen[1][(✉)], Christopher T. Ball[1], and Haining Wang[2]

[1] College of William and Mary, Williamsburg, VA 23187, USA
njvanbalen@email.wm.edu
[2] University of Delaware, Newark, DE 19716, USA

Abstract. Gender is one of the essential characteristics of personal identity but is often misused by online impostors for malicious purposes. However, men and women differ in their natural aiming movements of a hand held object in two-dimensional space due to anthropometric, biomechanical, and perceptual-motor control differences between the genders. Exploiting these natural gender differences, this paper proposes a naturalistic approach for gender classification based on mouse biometrics. Although some previous research has been done on gender classification using behavioral biometrics, most of them focuses on keystroke dynamics and, more importantly, none of them provides a comprehensive guideline for which metrics (features) of movements are actually relevant to gender classification. In this paper, we present a method for choosing metrics based on empirical evidence of natural difference in the genders. In particular, we develop a novel gender classification model and evaluate the model's accuracy based on the data collected from a group of 94 users. Temporal, spatial, and accuracy metrics are recorded from kinematic and spatial analyses of 256 mouse movements performed by each user. A mouse signature for each user is created using least-squares regression weights determined by the influence movement target parameters (size of the target, horizontal and vertical distances moved). The efficacy of our model is validated through the use of binary logistic regressions.

1 Introduction

The popularity of online social networks, online forums, and various online dating sites has significantly increased the visibility of online users' personal information. However, these online sites also allow a great deal of anonymity in the sense that a user's identity is tied to the user's account but not personally to the user. This anonymity has been exploited by impostors, such as sexual predators, who lie about their gender or age for malicious purposes, while a victim user has little way of verifying that the provided information is valid. To date, very little has been done to address this problem of fake online personal identity. A strict registration policy, such as providing legal documents, is just not feasible for regulating this problem.

© ICST Institute for Computer Sciences, Social Informatics and Telecommunications Engineering 2017
R. Deng et al. (Eds.): SecureComm 2016, LNICST 198, pp. 475–495, 2017.
DOI: 10.1007/978-3-319-59608-2_27

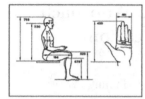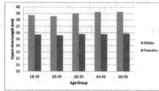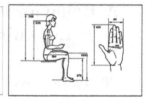

Fig. 1. Illustration of the major anatomical measurements relevant to using a computer mouse from a seated position. Graph of gender differences in upper limb length (data taken from Anthropometric Reference Data for Children and Adults: Unites States, 2007–2010; U.S. Department of Health and Human Services) [1].

One promising alternative involves the use of physical or behavioral biometrics, such as keystroke dynamics or mouse dynamics, to enhance user authentication. These biometrics are non-invasive and can be used actively as a confirmation step or passively through continuous re-authentication to determine the demographic characteristics of a user. However, previous soft biometric systems tend to take a very data driven approach based on simple aggregate measures (e.g., averages) of behavioral metrics. In this paper, we present a new naturalistic approach to using behavioral biometrics for verifying an online user's demographics. We will illustrate the advantages of this approach by applying mouse biometrics to discriminate a user's gender. Our approach takes advantage of intra-user variability in mouse movements, and has the potential to overcome generalizability issues when using mouse biometrics for user verification.

The proposed approach is mainly based on two important assumptions regarding naturally occurring mouse movements: (1) Gender differences naturally exist when performing two-dimensional aiming movements of a hand held device. The support for this assumption comes from a variety of basic and applied research domains, which include occupational health, physical therapy, public health, ergonomics, human anatomy, and perceptual-motor control theory. (2) The gender differences alluded to in the first assumption can be further elaborated by tracking the changes to naturally occurring mouse movements that are imposed by different target parameters. These target parameters are defined by the horizontal and vertical distances between the start and endpoint target locations, and by the size of the endpoint target. All three task parameters are known to affect aiming movements [11,25,28] while recent research in perceptual-motor control has highlighted that gender can also mediate these effects [4,23,24].

As a result of these two assumptions, this approach incorporates a much wider array of mouse movement metrics than those used in previous security applications of mouse biometrics. Consequently, the data analysis of these metrics required a different statistical approach from that used in traditional investigations of mouse biometrics. Twenty one different mouse movement metrics (temporal, spatial, and accuracy) were extracted from the movements recorded, and then each metric was expressed as a vector of four variables. The four variables correspond to the intercept and three unstandardized regression coefficients that are obtained from a multiple regression equation formulated to predict each metric using the three target parameters (vertical distance, horizontal distance, and target size). Binary logistic regressions were then employed to predict each participant's gender using an optimal subset of the multiple regression coefficients.

The proposed model was validated with mouse movement data collected from 94 participants (45 male and 49 female) who each performed 256 movement trials. Our user data collection has been filed and approved by the Institutional Review Board (IRB) to ensure participants are treated ethically. The model's accuracy was tested on both labeled and unlabeled data. The labeled data is used as a verification step to test our method's ability to accurately fit the model to the real data and identify a user that has uncommon mouse movement characteristics as an outlier, while the unlabeled data is used to test the ability to accurately classify a user who has not yet been sighted before. Based on the evaluation results in both labeled and unlabeled data, an analysis of the outliers' impact was further performed to test the impacts that outliers, i.e., those users with mouse movement characteristics greatly different from the average, would have on the model. The achieved maximum accuracy is 89.4% for the full labeled data set and 100% after removing outliers, while 72.4% for the unlabeled data set and 75.9% after removing outliers.

The remainder of the paper is structured as follows. Section 2 describes the logic behind the naturalistic approach, along with a summary of related work. Section 3 details the methodology used to collect data, filter data, and extract the metrics from the data to be used for gender classification. Section 4 presents the two analysis steps used in building the statistical models for predicting the gender of each participant. Section 5 reports the results of testing the statistical models. Section 6 reviews the findings and limitation of the study, as well as describing future directions for this naturalistic approach. Finally, Sect. 7 summarizes the paper.

2   Background

In this section, we first highlight the gender difference in anthropometrics, including its induced differences in movement behaviors and grip postures. We then present the background of using behavioral biometrics for user authentication.

2.1   Gender Difference in Anthropometrics

Men and women clearly differ in their physical dimensions as described by anthropometric data recorded in many countries for the purposes of monitoring public health and designing ergonomically sound work environments. Figure 1 illustrates the important anthropometric attributes of an individual working with a typical computer system. Maneuvering a computer mouse across a 2-Dimensional work space requires the complex coordination of the upper and lower arms in combination with the wrist and fingers. As shown in Fig. 1, the anthropometric data for the upper arm length (reported by the United States Health Department [1]) reveals large consistent gender differences in the physical dimensions of a key limb component for moving a mouse on a table top. Physical differences like these arguably underlie many of the movement and grip differences that will be described in the remainder of this section [17].

Moving a computer mouse is classified as an aiming movement by researchers in the field of motor behavior, and aiming movements are generally composed of consistent temporal and spatial characteristics. An aiming movement typically includes a ballistic component (single phase of acceleration followed by deceleration) that corresponds to the main movement of the hand into the general area of the target location. The ballistic component is followed by a sequence of sub-movements (multiple phases of acceleration and deceleration) that consist of small spatial corrections of the hand to reach the final target destination [20]. The field of motor behavior suggests that men and women differ in their aiming movements with men tending to move faster than women and with less accuracy [4,6,9,23,27]. It was also reported that the location of the target in relation to the hand being used affected the accuracy of movements made by men, but showed no significant effect on women's movements [23]. These results not only highlight gender differences in movement behavior again, but also stress the importance of incorporating target parameter effects when investigating these gender differences. Here the target parameters include target size, horizontal distance, and vertical distance.

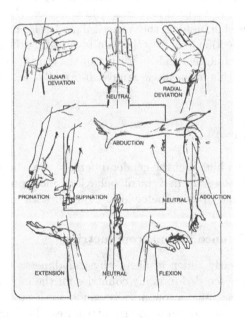

Fig. 2. Anatomical terms for motions of upper limb, wrist, and joints.

Research in physical therapy that has examined the effects of mouse use on wrist and arm pain in computer users has shown gender differences in hand and arm postures when performing movements with a mouse. A study on the finger postures of mouse users showed that men more frequently had a finger posture, in which the finger used for mouse clicking had a lifted finger posture where the middle portion of the finger was not in contact with the mouse [18]. Male participants in this study were also more likely to show an extended finger posture with a flexion angle of less than 15° when gripping the mouse (refer to Fig. 2 for an illustration of relevant movement terms). These different grip postures may not only affect mouse movement characteristics, but also influence mouse button presses that can also be an important component of mouse biometrics. Johnson et al. [16] found that women exerted more relative force on the mouse when gripping it, while Wahlstrom et al. [30] reported that women exerted more force on the mouse button while pressing it. Johnson and colleagues also revealed different wrist postures between men and women when moving the mouse with women showing higher wrist extensions, larger ulnar deviations (refer to Fig. 2), a larger range of motion in the wrist, and higher wrist velocities. A similar study by Yang and Cho [32] reported larger elbow flexion angles in men as well as different ulnar deviations, but in this study it was the men who exhibited the larger ulnar deviation angles. All of these different grip postures have the potential to affect mouse movement characteristics, including mouse button presses that can also be an important component of mouse biometrics. The results of these studies suggest that mouse biometrics should not only consider movement characteristics of aiming movements, but also consider movement characteristics unique to the physical manipulation of gripping a computer mouse.

2.2   Behavioral Biometrics

The use of biometrics is an attractive option for user authentication since it is inherently based on "who you are," and unlike other conventional methods cannot be lost, forgotten, or stolen. A large variety of user characteristics are used in biometric identification with some involving physiological recording, such as iris scanning, fingerprint scanning, facial recognition, and pulse recording [22][1]; and some involving behavioral recording, such as keystroke and mouse dynamics [26,31]. The behavioral biometric systems, however, have the distinct advantage of not requiring specialized hardware to record the user behaviors. Research interest in behavioral biometrics started in the 1990s with the study of keystroke dynamics [19] that eventually led to research involving keystroke dynamics combined with mouse dynamics [2].

Behavioral biometrics have been used in the past to predict the gender of a user, but these studies have primarily focused on keystroke dynamics. Fairhurst and Da Costa-Abreu [10] conducted a study using a multiclassifier system on the GREYC-keystroke database [12], and achieved an accuracy for gender prediction

---

[1] It records the response at the palm of the hand while sending a low voltage electrical current through the body from the other palm.

of 95%. Giot et al. [13] conducted a similar study using fixed-text input for gender prediction and reported an accuracy of 91%. They also reported that traditional keystroke authentication systems had an accuracy increase of 20% when combined with the user's gender prediction model. These studies achieve impressive accuracy for gender classification, but further research is required to determine if these results can be generalized to different sets of keyboard data that are not fixed, as well as to different types of keyboard interfaces. In addition, authentication systems based on keyboard dynamics may not be suited to new graphical password interfaces (see Biddle et al. for a survey of these interfaces [5]).

Mouse dynamics have been employed as a means of reauthentication to discriminate the identities of web browser users [21]. Ahmed et al. [3] used neural networks to learn a user's mouse dynamics in a specific environment while performing continuous identity authentication. Hamdy and Traore [14] combined mouse dynamics with cognitive measures of visual search capability and short term memory to create a static user verification system. These studies highlight the utility of using mouse biometrics in user re-authentication; however their findings are limited to identity authentication and have not been generalized to other purposes. To the best of our knowledge, no previous studies have reported the use of mouse biometrics to classify users' gender.

3   Methodology

This section describes the apparatus and method used for data collection. The data analysis procedures used to calculate and evaluate movement metrics are also described in this section.

3.1   Data Collection

There are 94 participants (45 men and 49 women) aged between 17 and 48 years participated in this study. The participants consist of students, faculty, and staff who were all experienced computer mouse users. The male and female participants did not differ statistically with respect to prior computer use experience or age.

All participants were seated in a static non-reclining chair in front of a computer monitor with the right hand resting comfortably on the same mouse and table surface used by all participants. Participants were instructed to find a seating location and arm posture in which moving the mouse would feel the most natural to them. They were requested to maintain this posture while conducting all experiment trials.

Raw mouse movement data were collected using an application implemented with the processing programing language. The same home (starting point) target was used on all trials and was displayed within an application window. Once a participant positioned the cursor on the home target and clicked the mouse button, this target was hidden and a new endpoint target was displayed. The screen position of the mouse was recorded at a rate of approximately 100 Hz with each data point consisting of a timestamp, the x screen coordinate, the y screen coordinate, and a tag that identified what type of a movement event was recorded. The movement events consisted of a standard movement event (mouse stationary or in motion without the left button being depressed), a target click event (left mouse button depressed while the mouse cursor is located inside the target area), a click event (left mouse button depressed while the cursor is outside of the target area), and a new target event (a new target displayed and the location and size of the target are recorded, instead of the mouse location).

Fig. 3. Illustration of screen target positions for movements of mouse cursor. Home target located in center of window. All endpoint target positions are displayed in this diagram. (Color figure online)

The display window consisted of a rectangular frame (1680 px $\times$ 1050 px) displayed on a 45×30 cm computer monitor. As Figure 3 shows, the home target consisted of a blue 30 px radius circle located in the center of the display window. All endpoint targets were displayed as red circles and consisted of one of two possible target sizes (30 px or 60 px radius) located at one of 16 possible locations. The endpoint target locations varied in their direction of approach and in their distance from the starting target position.

Each participant was instructed to move the mouse cursor from the home target to the endpoint target. Once the participants had located the cursor in the home target circle, they were requested to click the mouse button to start the trial. The participants were instructed to only pick up the mouse when readjusting the starting position of their hands on the table, during which they were moving the screen cursor back to the home target. Each participant conducted a sequence of 32 practice trials that consisted of all 32 possible combinations of target size, target distance, and angle of approach as describe above. After successfully completing the practice trials, each participant then performed four blocks of 64 movement trials with each block of trials consisting of a random sequence of two trials for each combination of the 16 target locations and 2 target sizes. The participants were allowed to take a short rest after completing each block of movement trials.

3.2 Movement Metrics

The profiles of distance and velocity were extracted from the raw data of each movement trial. These profiles were used to calculate ten temporal metrics that distinguish aiming movements and button presses. The spatial trace of each movement was smoothed, and then six spatial metrics were calculated to highlight differences in the trajectory of each movement. Five accuracy metrics were also calculated for each mouse movement. Following the naturalistic approach, the choices of these metrics were guided by previous empirical research on gender differences in aiming movements that have used the same or similar metrics [4,6,9,15,23,24,27]. For example, researchers have reported that men are quicker at perceiving object location, faster in their movements, rely less on visual guidance of the ballistic omponent of the movement, perform less visual corrections towards the endpoint of the movement, and are less accurate when they reach the endpoint of the movement. Some additional metrics were calculated, because prior empirical research would imply gender differences are possible for these mouse metrics even if they were not reported in the actual studies. For example, males and females differ in their grip postures of the mouse and positioning of the finger over the mouse button [16,18,32], implying that gender differences could exist for metrics influenced by these grip postures.

3.2.1 Profiles

The distance profile was calculated from the Euclidean distance traveled between consecutive movement events, and smoothed using a Kolmogorov-Zurbenko (KZ) filter. The KZ filter belongs to the low pass filter class, and is a series of k iterations of a moving average filter with a window size of m, where m is a positive odd integer. In other words, the KZ filter repeatedly runs a moving average filter with the initial input being the original data and the result of the previous run of the moving averages as the subsequent inputs. With this in mind, the first iteration of a KZ filter over a process $X(t)$ can be defined as:

$$KZ_{m,k=1}[X(t)] = \sum_{s=-2(m-1)/2}^{2(m-1)/2} X(t+s)\frac{1}{m},$$

the second iteration as:

$$KZ_{m,k=2}[X(t)] = \sum_{s=-2(m-1)/2}^{2(m-1)/2} KZ_{m,k=1}[X(t+s)]\frac{1}{m},$$

and so on. In this study, we set m to 11 and k to 3, respectively. The value of $m = 11$ was chosen such that the window over which the data is averaged would correspond to 100 ms or more. Thus, the window can cover a period of time with an intentional movement since smaller ones are likely to be just jitters. The value 11 was chosen, instead of 10, because the value of m needs to be odd. The value $k = 3$ was chosen because 3 was the smallest value that produced a smooth curve.

The velocity profile was then calculated from sets of pairs (t, v_t), where v_t is the average velocity in pixels per millisecond (px/ms) over the time interval between t and the time at which the previous data point was recorded.

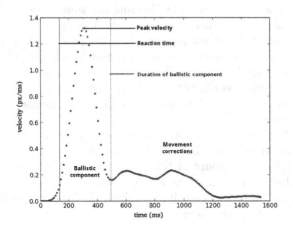

Fig. 4. Example of a velocity profile with various temporal metrics illustrated.

Aiming movements generally produce velocity profiles that are composed of one large peak (peak velocity) called the ballistic component that is followed by zero or more smaller peaks that reflect sub-movements used to position the cursor over the final target position (refer to Fig. 4). The velocity profile was used to calculate some of the 10 temporal features of the mouse dynamics recorded from each participant.

3.2.2 Temporal Movement and Button Press Metrics

- *Reaction time (RT):* the time interval from the moment the endpoint target appears on the screen until the participant initiates a movement towards it. The onset of the movement was determined to begin at the point when movement velocity exceeded 7% of the peak velocity for the ballistic component (refer to Fig. 4). Various methods were tested for determining the beginning point of movements, including measuring the slope of the velocity profile, pixels moved during consecutive time steps, and the percentage of peak velocity exceeded. All methods were tested using a visual inspection of a randomly selected group of trials and a set of known edge cases. Through this testing, we found that using the percentage of peak velocity exceeded with a value of 7% was the most effective solution.
- *Peak velocity (PV):* the maximum velocity value found for the ballistic component of the movement (refer to Fig. 4).
- *Time to peak velocity (TPV):* the time interval from the beginning of the movement until the peak velocity was reached (refer to Fig. 4).

– *Duration of ballistic component (DB):* the time interval from the beginning of the movement until the first local minima on the velocity profile following the peak velocity (refer to Fig. 4).
– *Shape of the velocity profile (SV):* a measure of the symmetry of the ballistic component, which is calculated by dividing the time to the peak velocity by the duration of the ballistic component (refer to Fig. 4).
– *Proportion of the ballistic component (PB):* the proportion of the movement time taken up by the ballistic component, which is calculated by dividing the ballistic component duration by the movement time (refer to Fig. 4).
– *Number of movement corrections (NC):* the total number of observed local maxima in the velocity profile after the ballistic component has been completed (refer to Fig. 4).
– *Time to click (TC):* the time interval between the arrival at the endpoint of the movement and the pressing of the mouse button.
– *Hold time (HT):* the amount of time the user held the mouse button down after the endpoint of the movement was reached.
– *Movement time (MT):* the time interval from the beginning of the movement until the endpoint of the movement.

Fig. 5. Example of a mouse trajectory to illustrate differences between three movement change metrics with task axis drawn in a dashed line.

3.2.3   Spatial Movement Metrics

These metrics are calculated from the spatial trajectory traveled by the mouse cursor for reaching the endpoint of the movement.

– *Path length (PL):* the total distance traveled by the mouse cursor during the trial. It is calculated as follows:

$$\sum_{t=1}^{T} \Delta d_t$$

where T is the total number of the trial, and Δd_t represents the distance traveled between time t and time $t-1$.

- *Path length to best path ratio (PLR):* the value of the path length divided by the length of the shortest path between the start and endpoints of the movement.
- *Task axis crossings (TXC):* the number of times that the movement path crossed the task axis. The task axis is defined as a straight line between the home target and the endpoint target (refer to Fig. 5).
- *Movement direction changes (MDC):* the number of times the movement changed direction perpendicular to the task axis (refer to Fig. 5).
- *Orthogonal movement changes (OMC):* the number of times the movement changed direction parallel to the task axis (refer to Fig. 5).
- *Movement variability (MV):* the standard deviation of the distance of the movement path to the task axis. This metric measures the spatial consistency of the movement path.

3.2.4 Movement Accuracy Metrics

These metrics represent how closely a participant came to clicking the center of the endpoint target.

- *Absolute error (AE):* absolute error corresponds to the Euclidean distance between the endpoint of the movement and the center of the endpoint target.
- *Horizontal error (HE):* the difference in the horizontal (x) coordinates between the endpoint of the movement and the center of the endpoint target. Negative errors reflect undershooting the target location whereas positive errors reflect overshooting the target location.
- *Vertical error (VE):* the difference in the vertical (y) coordinates between the endpoint of the movement and the center of the end position target. Negative errors reflect undershooting the target location whereas positive errors reflect overshooting the target location.
- *Absolute horizontal error (AHE):* the absolute value of the difference in the horizontal coordinates between the endpoint of the movement and the center of the endpoint target.
- *Absolute vertical error (AVE):* the absolute value of the difference in the vertical coordinates between the endpoint of the movement and the center of the endpoint target.

These defined errors are illustrated in Fig. 6, where an absolute error consists of Euclidean distance between the end of a movement and the center of an endpoint target. The horizontal error corresponds to the difference in the *x* coordinates of the movement endpoint and the center of the endpoint target. The vertical error corresponds to the difference in the *y* coordinates of the movement endpoint and the center of the endpoint target. In both cases, a negative value depicts undershooting and a positive value depicts overshooting.

3.3 Data Filtering

Before calculating the movement metrics for each participant as described above, the movement data were filtered to remove invalid trials where mouse movements

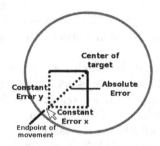

Fig. 6. Graphical depiction of movement accuracy metrics.

did not fall within the acceptable criteria for successful movement recording. The trials in which mouse movements clearly left the designated screen window were rejected, as well as the trials where the reaction times were less than 150 ms. This value of 150 ms was chosen, because the lower end of human reaction time is 100 ms. However, the method of determining the start of the movement is not perfect and causes some false positives. The same visual testing for determining the movement onset was used here, and we found that the value of 150 ms made a good balance between the false positive ratio and the false negative ratio while determining if the reaction time value was realistic. Only 4% of data points were rejected for these reasons across those more than 24,000 trials recorded.

4   Model Design

The gender classification model results from a two-step procedure of statistical analyses. The first step involves conducting least-squares multiple regressions to determine the effects of target parameters (target size, horizontal distance, and vertical distance) on movement metrics for each participant. The resulting unstandardized regression coefficients provide a movement signature for each participant, which will be used to distinguish the corresponding participant's gender. The second step involves conducting logistic regressions to select the statistical model that most accurately classifies participants by gender.

4.1   Mouse Signatures

Traditional analyses of mouse biometrics usually rely on a single aggregate indicator (e.g., average) for each metric. Unfortunately, previous studies have shown that this approach may be ineffective. For example, in the study conducted by Rohr [23], men were shown to have their accuracy reduced as a target was made smaller and placed further away, whereas women were more consistent with their accuracy. By simply taking the average accuracy, the gender difference would be diminished or lost since the lower values counteract the higher values. Thus, it is imperative to find a new way to produce features that capture not only the actual values observed in the data, but also the amount of changes caused by the target parameters. Our approach involves a more detailed analysis that incorporates the effects of target parameters on these mouse metrics. The effects of target parameters on the mouse metrics were quantified by unstandardized regression coefficients obtained from a multiple linear regression analysis with least squares fitting conducted for each metric. Multiple regression analyses predict the scores of a dependent variable y by fitting a straight line defined by a set of independent variables $\{x_1, x_2, x_3, ...\}$ to a set of known data points $(y_i, x_{1,i}, x_{2,i}, ...)$ such that it satisfies the equation:

$$y_i = a + b_1 x_{1,i} + b_2 x_{2,i} + ... + b_n x_{n,i} + \varepsilon_i,$$

where a and b_k are unknown constants that are estimated, and ε_i is the residual defined as the vertical deviation of the known data to the estimated line. If the estimated line is a perfect fit, all values of ε are zero.

The least squares fitting method estimates the values of a and b_k by reducing the squares of the residuals such that the following equation is minimized:

$$\sum_{i=1}^{r} \varepsilon_i^2 = \sum_{i=1}^{r} [y_i - (a + \beta_1 x_{1,i} + b_2 x_{2,i} + ... + b_n x_{n,i})]^2.$$

Three target parameters were chosen as predictor variables for these multiple regressions: the size of the endpoint target, the vertical distance between the home and endpoint targets, and the horizontal distance between the home and endpoint targets. The target distance was measured in separate horizontal and vertical components, because prior research suggests that these components should be the most influential on aiming movements rather than more complex combinations of the angle of approach and distance moved [29]. Absolute values were used for the distances traversed because previous research also suggests that the direction of movement (left vs. right and up vs. down) does not affect movement metrics as much as whether it is just a vertical movement or a horizontal movement [7,8]. Consequently, the size and sign of the regression coefficients for the distance variables simply represent how much of an effect, moving vertically or moving horizontally, had on the predictability of a metric.

For each metric recorded, three regression coefficients and the intercept value were provided to highlight the effect of these target parameters on the metric. For example, if the peak velocity (PV) was used as the dependent variable, four values were provided for this metric (intercept value PV_{const}, regression coefficient for horizontal distance moved PV_{horz}, regression coefficient for vertical distance moved PV_{vert}, and regression coefficient for target size PV_{size}). This results in a metric vector for the peak velocity that specifies the following equation:

$$PV = PV_{const} + PV_{size}(size) + PV_{vertD}(vertD) + PV_{horzD}(horzD).$$

It was expected that these regression variables would better reveal gender differences in the metrics. This assumption is supported by 4-way ANOVAs (gender × target size × distance × angle of approach) that were conducted for each metric. The significant results of these ANOVAs are summarized in Table 1. These results clearly show that many of the metrics revealed consistent target parameter effects, and these effects could be mediated by gender.

Table 1. Significant main effects and interactions found for 4-way ANOVAs (Gender × Distance × Angle of approach × Target size) conducted for each metric.

Variable	Significant effects
Reaction time	Gender, Distance, Size, Angle, Distance × Angle, Gender × Distance × Size × Angle
Movement time	Distance, Size, Angle
Hold time	Gender, Size, Angle
Time to peak V	Distance, Size, Angle, Distance × Angle, Gender × Size × Angle
Peak velocity	Distance, Size, Angle, Distance × Angle
T ballistic comp	Distance, Angle
Shape of velocity profile	Distance, Angle, Distance × Angle
Ballistic prop	Distance, Size, Angle, Gender × Size, Distance × Size, Distance × Angle, Size × Angle
N of corrections	Distance, Size, Angle, Distance × Size, Distance × Angle, Size × Angle
Time to press	Size, Angle
Path length	Distance, Size, Angle, Gender × Size, Distance × Angle, Gender × Size × Angle
Path L best ratio	Distance, Size, Angle, Size × Angle
Axis crossings	Distance, Angle, Distance × Angle
Direction changes	Distance, Size, Angle
Orthog changes	Distance, Size, Angle, Distance × Angle, Size × Angle
Movement var	Distance, Angle, Distance × Gender, Distance × Angle, Gender × Distance × Angle
Index of dIff	Distance, Size, Angle, Distance × Size, Distance × Angle, Size × Angle, Distance × Size × Angle
Index of performance	Distance, Size, Angle, Size × Angle
Horizontal error	Size, Angle, Size × Angle, Gender × Distance × Angle
Vertical error	Size, Angle, Size × Angle
Absolute error	Distance, Size, Angle, Size × Angle

4.2   Gender Prediction Model

The second step in developing a gender prediction model involves with the input of the metric variables obtained from each participant in a logistic regression to predict the gender of a participant. The logistic regression is often used for classification when dependent variables have binary values. The curve used in this type of regression is an S shaped curve asymptotically tapered between 0 and 1 and is derived from the following linear relation:

$$logit(P) = \alpha + \beta_1 x_1 + \beta_2 x_2 + ...,$$

where $logit(P)$ refers to the natural logarithm of the odds function defined as follows:

$$logit(p) = ln(odds) = ln\left(\frac{P}{1-P}\right).$$

This function can then be substituted into the original linear relation and be solved for P giving the formula:

$$P = \frac{e^{\alpha+\beta_1 x_1 + \beta_2 x_2 + \dots}}{1 + e^{\alpha+\beta_1 x_1 + \beta_2 x_2 + \dots}},$$

where P is the probability that the dependent variable has the outcome coded as 1 given the values of x_i.

The values of constant α and coefficients β_i are determined by maximizing the conditional probability of the observed data, given the parameters used as predictors. An initial model is constructed with arbitrary values for the coefficients, and the conditional probability is evaluated. The coefficients are then modified in order to increase this probability, and the procedure is repeated until the model converges or a maximum number of iterations are reached. A maximum of 20 iterations were allowed to determine the values of the coefficients, and the results lead to a threshold value of 0.5 (i.e., whose values above 0.5 were considered as male and whose values no larger than 0.5 were considered as female).

5   Evaluation

The accuracy of the proposed approach for classifying a user' gender was evaluated on both labeled and unlabeled data. The labeled data consisted of the full data set, while the unlabeled data test was performed with 70% of the participants used as the training set and the remaining 30% of participants used as the test set (Table 2).

Table 2. Accuracy of predicted results. Labeled set refers to the full data set used in Sect. 4.1. Labeled 70% and unlabeled 30% refer to the training set and test set used in Sect. 4.2, respectively.

Set	Full set			Outliers removed		
	Labeled	Labeled 70%	Unlabeled 30%	Labeled	Labeled 70%	Unlabeled 30%
Male	91.1%	83.9%	57.1%	100%	100%	71.4%
Female	87.8 %	91.2%	86.7%	100%	100%	80.0%
Total	89.4%	87.7%	72.4%	100%	100%	75.9%

5.1 Labeled Data Analysis

In this section, we verify how well a model may be fit the data and the accuracy of such a model on users who have been sighted before. We also use this step to identify any users with unusual characteristics as outliers. The logistic regression model was tested on all 94 participants, but given the very large number of predictor variables (21 metrics × 4 metric features = 84 predictor variables) only smaller sub-sets of predictor variables were actually tested. The first subset of predictor variables was determined by testing each metric separately. The four features of each metric were tested as a single group separate from the features of the other metrics. The statistical significances ($p < 0.05$) of each metric's variables for predicting gender determined if these variables were included in the first sub-set of predictor variables. The significant predictors included in this subset were: $\{HT_{const}, PV_{horz}, PB_{size}, TC_{const}, TC_{horz}, MDC_{const}, MDC_{horz}, MDC_{size}, AE_{const}\}$. To improve the overall accuracy of this model, additional predictor variables were included while providing a moderate level of statistical significance ($p < 0.1$) in predicting gender when each metric was tested separately. Two additional variables were included to this sub-set of predictor variables: PB_{const} and PLR_{vert}. The amount of explained variance in gender classification using these two subsets of variables was 0.532 according to the Nagelkerke pseudo r-squared measure, and the classification accuracy based on this model was 75.5%.

The first subset of predictor variables was reduced from a total number of 84 to 9 by examining each metric's predictive power one metric at a time. However, a better subset of predictors may be possible if multiple metrics are included in the initial logistic regression model. One way to reduce the number of tested metrics is to only include those metrics that can characterize significant gender effects from the previously conducted 4-way ANOVAs. These findings highlight the metrics that show consistent gender differences or interactions of gender with target parameters. We also included those metrics published by other researchers with significant gender effects. The logistic regression model was tested again with a new subset of predictors that included the four variables for each of these metrics: $\{RT, HT, TPV, PB, PL, MV, AE, HE, TC, PV, AHE, AVE, VE\}$. The 52 predictor variables in this subset were added to the original subset with a stepwise method, and the following 10 new variables were revealed as significant predictors: $\{RT_{size}, RT_{horz}, RT_{vert}, TPV_{vert}, MV_{const}, MV_{vert}, MV_{horz}, PV_{const}, PV_{vert}, VE_{const}\}$. The amount of explained variance after the addition of these variables to the final model was 0.676, and the resulting classification accuracy was 89.4%.

We now test the effects that outliers had on the model. Five users were identified as having scores that were more than two standard deviations away from the mean. These are likely users with mouse movement characteristics that do not entirely fit the average for their gender, since there can be an overlap of physical characteristics between the two populations and such an overlap affects the features being used. After the removal of these outliers, our model can discriminate the gender of the remaining 89 participants with an accuracy of

100%. It is difficult to uncover the actual causes for these outliers, and they can occur for a variety of reasons including, but not limited to, distraction or injury. In a real application, one would likely test for outliers at input time, and if an outlier is detected, the user would be asked to re-do the input trials in the case of a one time authentication. However, identifying the best methods to handle outliers is beyond the scope of this paper.

5.2 Unlabeled Data Analysis

To evaluate the accuracy of our approach on unlabeled data, the movement data from 65 randomly selected participants were used as the training set to create the logistic regression model. And the model was then tested on the movement data from the remaining 29 participants who comprised the test set. The same variable selection procedure was followed with the unlabeled data as the one used for the labeled data, except that substantially fewer participants were involved in these selections.

The statistically significant predictors determined for subset one were: HT_{const}, TC_{horz}, MDC_{const}, MDC_{size}, MDC_{horz}, AE_{const}, AHE_{const}, AHE_{horz}, RT_{const}, PB_{size}, and VE_{vert}. Six of these predictor variables were consistent with the selections based on the full data set (labeled data). The fit of this model was tested on the training set and accounted for 0.449 of the explained variance in predicting gender with a correct classification of 76.9% of the participants in the set. The second subset included the following predictor variables: $\{PV_{const}, PV_{vert}, PV_{horz}, MV_{vert}, RT_{size}, RT_{vert}, RT_{horz}\}$. All seven variables were included in the subset of the predictors obtained previously with the full data set (labeled data). This overlap shows that this feature selection method produces a set of features close to what is expected based on research in other fields. On the other hand, what can be observed over the entire set may still have sensitivity to the training set, which one should be careful of when fitting the model. The fitness of this model with the combined subsets was tested on the training set and accounted for 0.579 of the explained variance in predicting gender. This final model was tested on the test set and was able to achieve a gender classification accuracy of 72.4%. After removing the outliers identified previously in the labeled data analysis, the test set was then classified with a 75.9% accuracy. These results suggest that outliers have a visible effect on the classifier, but the negative impact is relatively small.

6 Discussion

Men and women differ naturally, both physically and psychologically. The development of computer security tools can take advantage of these natural differences by focusing authentication procedures on these differences. This study used the naturalistic approach to successfully classify male and female participants by measuring the temporal, spatial, and accuracy characteristics of their mouse movements while evaluating how these mouse metrics were affected by target parameters.

The measurement of one such metric, movement accuracy, will be used to exemplify this approach to the biometric analysis of mouse dynamics. Previous research with aiming movements has revealed gender differences in the spatial accuracy of these movements with women being on average more accurate than men [4,23]. However, this gender difference is actually more complicated than one suggested by simply comparing average errors, because target parameters (target size, distance moved, and direction of movement) can also differentially affect the movement accuracy of men and women [23]. In support of this premise, our study also found complex interaction effects of gender and target parameters on spatial error. Consequently, rather than just recording the mean accuracy of each participant's movements, a multiple regression analysis was conducted to predict spatial error using target parameters (size, horizontal distance, vertical distance) as predictor variables.

This novel approach to biometric analysis comes with some cost, because there are now four variables representing each metric's potential contribution to the prediction model. Given the relatively large number of movement features already required by our approach, a large number of predictor variables could be introduced to discriminate the gender of a participant using logistic regressions. Therefore, two criteria were followed to reduce the set of predictor variables for testing: (1) each metric was tested individually and only those variables that were significant predictors of gender in these tests were included in the first subset of predictors, (2) all the metrics that produced significant ANOVA gender effects and those with gender effects suggested in prior research were included in a second subset. Our logistic regressions produced correct classification of a participant's gender at a rate of 89.4–100% for the labeled data and 72.4–75.9% for the unlabeled data. These results are very promising given the limited range of values provided for each target parameter in this study.

The optimal classification accuracy was achieved after removing outliers from the labeled data set and from the training data set for the analysis of unlabeled data. It is unclear why a few participants had such discrepant mouse metrics, and further research is needed to rule out the possibility of introducing user behavioral outliers into data collection and evaluation. However, their effects on the unlabeled data were minor, indicating that they do not have a large impact on classifying previously unseen users.

Once the recording accuracies of the movement metrics have been established, the current procedure has very low computational overheads because it relies on simple statistical models for computing predictor variables and gender classification. A client machine can collect the raw movement data and then send it to a server for feature extraction and prediction of gender with minimal overhead, and relatively low latency for the client. Consequently, static and continuous authentications are viable options with this approach. In fact, real-life mouse movements that are not constrained to an experimental manipulation, as was the case in the current study, should provide a larger range of target parameters and therefore better predictive accuracy. A larger, more diverse data set of participants would also facilitate the testing of this approach, because the majority of the participants in the current study were highly educated undergraduate college students.

7   Future Work

A direct application of this method to be explored is the generalization of this method across computer platforms with different hardware. One major advantage of the naturalistic approach to biometric analysis is that predictive models based on natural differences are assumed to have a universal, biological basis, and therefore, should be more generalizable than traditional data driven approaches to biometrics analysis. Accordingly, the gender classification model formulated in the current paper should generalize to other populations of computer-users (e.g., other countries, different education backgrounds), and also, be somewhat independent of the computer-user environments where the mouse data are collected (e.g., table height, table surface, type of mouse etc.). A comparison of the classification success found in the current study for labeled and unlabeled data provides some support for this assumption. When participants were classified using a model based on another group's data (unlabeled data) there was still a reasonable rate of classification success (72.4–75.9%) albeit with some drop in performance from a completely labeled set of data (89.4–100%). Future research could examine this generalization prediction using different computer work stations and cross-cultural tests of classification success.

8   Conclusion

This paper proposes a naturalistic approach for gender classification of computer users based solely on their mouse movements. The design rationale of our approach lies in the observation that men and women differ naturally in how they make mouse movements. We defined a series of temporal, spatial, and accuracy metrics to quantify the mouse movement differences between male and female users. In particular, we identified the metrics related to peak velocity, length of the deceleration phase, target accuracy, finger posture, and reaction time are relevant to gender classification. There were 94 volunteers participated in this study, and a mouse signature was created for each participant. We evaluated the efficacy of our approach for gender classification by conducting binary logistic regression tests, and achieved promising results.

References

1. Anthropometric Reference Data for Children and Adults: United States, 2007–2010. Number 252 in 11. U.S. Department of Health (2012)
2. Ahmed, A., Traore, I.: Anomaly intrusion detection based on biometrics. In: Information Assurance Workshop, IAW 2005. Proceedings from the Sixth Annual IEEE SMC, pp. 452–453, June 2005
3. Ahmed, A., Traore, I.: A new biometric technology based on mouse dynamics. IEEE Trans. Dependable Secure Comput. 4(3), 165–179 (2007)
4. Barral, J., Bettina, D.: Aiming in adults: sex and laterality effects. Laterality 9(3), 299–312 (2004)
5. Biddle, R., Chiasson, S., Van Oorschot, P.: Graphical passwords: learning from the first twelve years. ACM Comput. Surv. 44(4), 19:1–19:41 (2012)
6. Buchman, A.S., Leurgans, S., Gottlieb, G.L., Chen, C.H., Almeida, G.L., Corcos, D.M.: Effect of age and gender in the control of elbow flexion movements. J. Mot. Behav. 32(4), 391–399 (2000)
7. Dounskaia, N.V., Ketcham, C.J., Stelmach, G.E.: Influence of biomechanical constraints on horizontal arm movements. Mot. Control 6(4), 366–387 (2002)
8. Dounskaia, N.V., Swinnen, S.P., Walter, C.B., Spaepen, A.J., Verschueren, S.M.: Hierarchical control of different elbow-wrist coordination patterns. Exp. Brain Res. 121(3), 239–254 (1998)
9. Jiménez-Jiménez, F.J., et al.: Influence of age, gender in motor performance in healthy subjects. J. Neurol. Sci. 302(12), 72–80 (2011)
10. Fairhurst, M., Da Costa-Abreu, M.: Using keystroke dynamics for gender identification in social network environment. In: 4th International Conference on Imaging for Crime Detection and Prevention 2011 (ICDP 2011), pp. 1–6, November 2011
11. Fitts, P.M.: The information capacity of the human motor system in controlling the amplitude of movement. J. Exp. PSychol. 74, 381–391 (1954)
12. Giot, R., El-Abed, M., Rosenberger, C.: Greyc keystroke: a benchmark for keystroke dynamics biometric systems. In: Proceedings of the 3rd IEEE International Conference on Biometrics: Theory, Applications and Systems, BTAS 2009, Piscataway, NJ, USA, pp. 419–424. IEEE Press (2009)
13. Giot, R., Rosenberger, C.: A new soft biometric approach for keystroke dynamics based on gender recognition. Int. J. Inf. Technol. Manage. 11(1/2), 35–49 (2012). Dec
14. Hamdy, O., Traoré, I.: Homogeneous physio-behavioral visual and mouse-based biometric. ACM Trans. Comput. Hum. Interact. 18(3), 12:1–12:30 (2011)
15. Hansen, S., Elliott, D.: Three-dimensional manual responses to unexpected target perturbations during rapid aiming. J. Mot. Behav. 41(1), 16–29 (2009)
16. Johnson, P.W., Hagberg, M., Hjelm, E.W., Rempel, D.: Measuring and characterizing force exposures during computer mouse use. Scand. J. Work Environ. Health 26(5), 398–405 (2000)
17. Karlqvist, L.K., Bernmark, E., Ekenvall, L., Hagberg, M., Isaksson, A., Rost, T.: Computer mouse position as a determinant of posture, muscular load and perceived exertion. Scand. J. Work Environ. Health 24, 62–73 (2012)
18. Lee, D.L., McLoone, H., Dennerlein, J.T.: Observed finger behaviour during computer mouse use. Appl. Ergon. 39(1), 107–113 (2008)
19. Monrose, F., Reiter, M.K., Wetzel, S.: Password hardening based on keystroke dynamics. In: Proceedings of the 6th ACM Conference on Computer and Communications Security, CCS 1999, New York, NY, USA, pp. 73–82. ACM (1999)

20. Phillips, J.G., Triggs, T.J.: Characteristics of cursor trajectories controlled by the computer mouse. Ergonomics **44**(5), 527–536 (2001)
21. Pusara, M., Brodley, C.E.: User re-authentication via mouse movements. In: Proceedings of the 2004 ACM Workshop on Visualization and Data Mining for Computer Security, VizSEC/DMSEC 2004, New York, NY, USA, pp. 1–8. ACM (2004)
22. Rasmussen, K.B., Roeschlin, M., Martinovic, I., Tsudik, G.: Authentication using pulse-response biometrics. In: The Network and Distributed System Security Symposium (NDSS), vol. 2 (2014)
23. Rohr, L.E.: Gender-specific movement strategies using a computer-pointing task. J. Mot. Behav. **38**(6), 431–437 (2006)
24. Rohr, L.E.: Upper and lower limb reciprocal tapping: evidence for gender biases. J. Mot. Behav. **38**(1), 15–17 (2006)
25. Soukoreff, R.W., MacKenzie, I.S.: Towards a standard for pointing device evaluation, perspectives on 27 years of fitts' law research in HCI. Int. J. Hum. Comput. Stud. **61**(6), 751–789 (2004)
26. Stefan, D., Shu, X., Yao, D.D.: Robustness of keystroke-dynamics based biometrics against synthetic forgeries. Comput. Secur. **31**(1), 109–121 (2012)
27. Teeken, J.C., Adam, J.J., Paas, F.G., van Boxtel, M.P., Houx, P.J., Jolles, J.: Effects of age and gender on discrete and reciprocal aiming movements. Psychol. Aging **11**(2), 195–198 (1996)
28. Thibbotuwawa, N., Hoffmann, E.R., Goonetilleke, R.S.: Open-loop and feedback-controlled mouse cursor movements in linear paths. Ergon. Int. J. Res. Pract. Hum. Factors Ergon. **55**, 476–488 (2012)
29. Thompson, S.G., McConnell, D.S., Slocum, J.S., Bohan, M.: Kinematic analysis of multiple constraints on a pointing task. Hum. Mov. Sci. **26**(1), 11–26 (2007)
30. Wahlstrm, J., Svensson, J., Hagberg, M., Johnson, P.W.: Differences between work methods and gender in computer mouse use. Scand. J. Work Environ. Health **26**(5), 390–397 (2000)
31. Yampolskiy, R.V., Govindaraju, V.: Behavioural biometrics: a survey and classification. Int. J. Biometrics **1**(1), 81–113 (2008)
32. Yang, J.-F., Cho, C.-Y.: Comparison of posture and muscle control pattern between male and female computer users with musculoskeletal symptoms. Appl. Ergon. **43**, 785–791 (2011)

Unique on the Road: Re-identification of Vehicular Location-Based Metadata

Zheng Xiao[1], Cheng Wang[1(✉)], Weili Han[2], and Changjun Jiang[1(✉)]

[1] Tongji University, Shanghai 201804, China
{cwang,cjjiang}@tongji.edu.cn
[2] Software School, Fudan University, Shanghai 201203, China
wlhan@fudan.edu.cn

Abstract. For digging individuals' information from anonymous metadata, usually the first step is to identify the entities in metadata and associate them with persons in the real world. If an entity in metadata is uniquely re-identified, its host is possibly confronting a serious privacy disclosure problem. In this paper, we study the privacy issue in VLBS (Vehicular Location-Based Service) by investigating the re-identification problem of vehicular location-based metadata in a VLBS server. We find that the trajectories of vehicles are highly unique after studying 131 millions mobility traces of taxis in Shenzhen and 1.1 billions of taxis in Shanghai. More specifically, with the help of the urban road maps, four spatio-temporal points are sufficient to uniquely identify vehicles, achieving an accuracy of 95.35%. This indicates that there is a high risk of privacy leakage when VLBS applications are widely deployed.

Keywords: Privacy · VLBS · Re-identification · Uniqueness · Trajectory

1 Introduction

With the increasing popularity of the LBS (Location-Based Service) in our daily life, massive applications are developed to help their users provide more personalized user experience. For example, we could use an online map application to find the restaurants nearby and their discount information, [1,2]. We can track our lost phones by a security-based application. Those applications are making our lives more convenient and comfortable based on GPS location-based queries. As GPS queries are highly associated with human mobility traces, sometimes LBS can bring serious threat to users' privacy,[3–5]. According to the classification by Shin [6], LBS-related privacy problems can be mainly divided into two types: The first one is whether users' private information (habits, location, etc.) can be inferred from their LBS queries. For example, the specific location where a driver always parks his/her car can be inferred with high certainty as his/her home. The second one is whether a user can be uniquely identified by malicious adversaries [7–9]. When an individual is identified, his/her precise locations for

© ICST Institute for Computer Sciences, Social Informatics and Telecommunications Engineering 2017
R. Deng et al. (Eds.): SecureComm 2016, LNICST 198, pp. 496–513, 2017.
DOI: 10.1007/978-3-319-59608-2_28

all LBS query time are exposed to adversaries. In this work, we limit our scope to the second type, i.e., the user's re-identification problem.

In an LBS system, LBS providers/servers are often regarded as non-trustworthy components that perhaps leak users' information to the third party deliberately or unintentionally. To improve their reliability, the servers usually anonymize the data to protect users' privacy, [10–12]. Under such anonymous protection, if an adversary hacks into an LBS server to get its trajectory meta-data, he/she usually can only obtain an anonymous trajectory dataset, and cannot infer an individual's trace from the anonymous data. As a result, a completely anonymous dataset is often presumed to be *slightly sensitive* when only several non-anonymous records of a specific user could be exposed to adversaries, [13]. The objective of our work is to probe the possibly "hidden" privacy leakage problem of user's re-identification in LBS.

More specifically, we intently investigate the user's re-identification problem for a special type of LBS, *Vehicular Location-Based Service* (VLBS). The reasons why we focus on VLBS are two-fold: Firstly, VLBS is becoming a promising type of location-based services, since more and more vehicles are able to access the Internet as mobile terminals, and then many LBS-related applications are devised to serve vehicles. For example, a transportation monitor application [14] collects real-time vehicle location information to predict road condition and generate suggestions to drivers. Secondly, a significant feature of VLBS, i.e., the mobility traces of vehicles are usually constrained by roads, draws us to figure out whether road information could improve the risk of user's re-identification. To the best of our knowledge, few researches distinguished the privacy issue of VLBS as an independent problem from the LBS privacy problem, [15–17].

In this paper, we utilize non-sensitive datasets to evaluate whether they can still cause privacy leakage problems (user's re-identification) in VLBS. To be specific, we extract a few non-anonymous trajectories from two datasets of taxi trajectory metadata, 131 millions mobility traces of taxis in Shenzhen and 1.1 billions of taxis in Shanghai, and compute the uniqueness of taxi trajectories. Surprisingly, we find that four spatio-temporal points are sufficient to identify vehicles even when anonymous protection strategies are adopted, achieving an accuracy of 95.35% for Shenzhen dataset and 96.75% for Shanghai dataset respectively. Experiment results show that vehicles trajectory privacy is inclined to be risky. We provide an intuitive explanation for this observation as follows: Compared with diverse human trajectories, vehicle traces are mostly binded by roads. The road information is possibly the underlying reason for user's re-identification only by four record points.

The rest of this paper is organized as follows: Sect. 2 introduces related work in LBSs and VLBSs privacy fields. Section 3 gives the main results of this work. In Sect. 4, we provide the analyzing procedure based on two real-life datasets. Section 5 makes a discussion on what insights can be obtained from the experimental results. Section 6 draws a conclusion and discusses about the future work.

2   Related Work

One of the classic privacy protection mechanisms is the k-anonymous algorithm [18–24]. In the model, a dataset must have k undistinguishable items on a specific property, where k infers the least risks that we can suffer when information is leaked. At the beginning, the algorithm was designed for databases like hospital and school for user privacy protection. Later, researchers found that k-anonymity can also work effectively in the LBS privacy protection.

To disclose the risk of user's re-identification in anonymous dataset, Montjoye et al. [25] studied the uniqueness of shopping mall metadata. The shopping mall metadata has four fields: anonymous ID, time, location and money spent by that customer. In their experiments, they applied different resolutions to all fields except ID to simulate basic privacy protection methods. The conclusion is that four purchase records are enough to uniquely re-identify 90% individuals. This result is achieved with metadata that has three dimensions (purchase time, shop, price). If an individual is re-identified, his/her mobility traces corresponding to purchase behaviors can be inferred by adversaries. To explain this result, an underlying reason is that the *relatively high dimension of metadata* could expose individuals' privacy with a high accuracy. Another similar work [26] studied the uniqueness of human traces associated with phone activities. They use anonymous mobile phone dataset for their experiments. When people use their phones (to make a call or send a message), the phone will communicate with the nearest antenna and the whole activity is recorded by telecommunication company. There are three fields in their dataset: anonymous ID, the beginning time and antenna used (location, one antenna covers a specific area). Similarly, they applied different resolutions to the time and location fields. The result shows that four phone activities are enough to uniquely identify 95% individuals. If an individual is re-identified using the dataset, his/her mobility traces corresponding to phone activities are exposed to adversaries. Compared to the shopping mall metadata which has three dimensions, this work just use a two-dimension metadata. It is noteworthy that a user's location information is indeed represented by the coverage area of corresponding antenna. In other words, adversaries are just aware of which antenna the individual has communicated with.

In our work, the taxi trajectory metadata are also of two dimensions, i.e., LBS query time and position on the road. Compared to the study in [26] where there is intuitively a greater diversity in the two-dimension trajectory metadata associated with phone activities, the re-identification in our scenario seems more difficult, then possibly leads to a less serious privacy problem. We aim at examining this intuition in this paper.

3   Main Results

In LBS, application server stores records of users, including ID, time and location information. We cannot infer one's real identity by ID, since ID is anonymously stored in the server. For example, when we use Google Maps [27] for navigation,

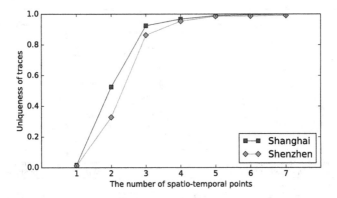

Fig. 1. The uniqueness of traces with a specific number of known non-anonymous spatial-temporal points. Given a 100 × 100 spatial resolution and 20 min temporal resolution, the uniqueness is up to 95.35% for Shenzhen taxis and 96.75% for Shanghai's, when the number comes to 4.

Google just uses our Google account as ID, so the application will never know our identities or the plates of our cars. Although this basic mechanism protects our privacy to some extent, the LBS servers are still considered unreliable.

In our attacker model, we assume that adversaries have full access to LBS servers, and that adversaries conduct attacks by collecting several spatio-temporal points of a user's car, [25, 26]. When these spatio-temporal points are collected, adversaries use them to match with the database on servers. If an unique match is found, adversaries can decide the identity of the user in the database, and know the precise position of the car at any moment. Generally, one spatio-temporal point is enough for re-identifying a target if its trajectory is without an anonymous protection. In our experiments, we attempt to figure out the risk of being re-identified with basic generalization protection methods. Generalization also helps to eliminate spatial and temporal error because the adversaries cannot record spatio-temporal points without any error. It is achieved by spatial and temporal resolution. The details will be explained in Sect. 4 later.

In our experiments, we have 6 levels (20, 30, 60, 80, 120, 240 min) of temporal resolutions and 11 levels (10 × 10, 20 × 20, . . . , 100 × 100 and 200 × 200 blocks) of spatial resolutions. Besides, 1 ∼ 7 spatio-temporal points are randomly sampled for our matching experiment respectively. The three mentioned parameters have 462 (6 × 11 × 7) combinations in all. For each combination, we obtain 150, 000 samples and for each sample we test its uniqueness. By this procedure, we can compute the proportion that a taxi can be uniquely identified. Figure 1 illustrates the uniqueness of traces when we set the temporal resolution to 20 min and spatial resolution to 100 × 100 square blocks. We can observe that the uniqueness grows rapidly as the number of known spatio-temporal points increases, and its value approximates 100% rapidly when the number is larger than 4. What's more, the uniqueness of Shanghai's grows slightly faster than that of Shenzhen's.

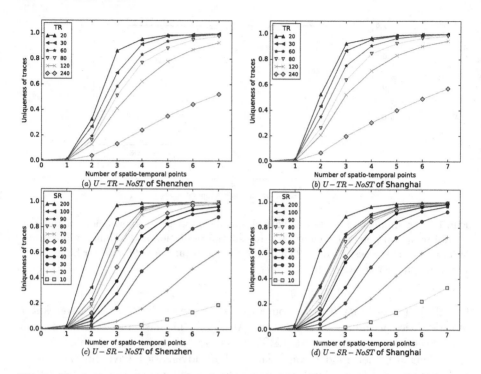

Fig. 2. The impacts of temporal and spatial resolutions on the uniqueness. (a) and (b) show how different levels of temporal resolutions affect the uniqueness. (c) and (d) show the effects of different spatial resolutions on the uniqueness. The notations U, TR, SR, $NoST$ stand for Uniqueness of traces, Temporal Resolution, Spatial Resolution, Number of Spatio-Temporal points, respectively.

By now, we can state that 4 spatio-temporal points are sufficient to re-identify a taxi's trajectory.

In order to find out the effects of the temporal and spatial resolution on the uniqueness of traces, we conduct experiments with different temporal and spatial resolutions. The results are shown in Fig. 2. By these, we can conclude that the uniqueness benefits from a larger number of spatio-temporal points, a shorter temporal resolution, and a bigger spatial resolution (i.e., a smaller block size). Furthermore, in Fig. 3, we plot the contour map according to the uniqueness of traces extracted from two cities with the given known points 2, 4 and 6.

For each given number of spatio-temporal points, we plot the uniqueness of two datasets in Figs. 4 and 5, corresponding to changing temporal and spatial resolutions. When the number of spatio-temporal points equals to 1 ($N = 1$, Figs. 4(c), 5(c)), the surface is nearly flat, which means that a single point is insufficient to re-identify a taxi, whatever the temporal and spatial resolutions are given. With the growing of N, the re-identified accuracy (uniqueness) is increasing rapidly. When N equals to 4 ($N = 4$, Figs. 4(b), 5(b)), moderate temporal and spatial resolutions can lead to a uniqueness over 90%. And the

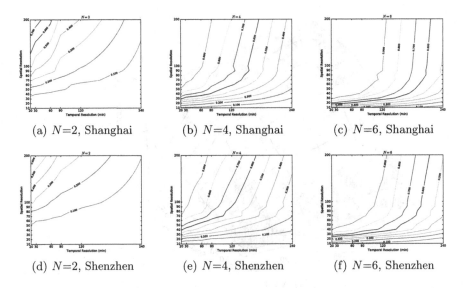

(a) N=2, Shanghai   (b) N=4, Shanghai   (c) N=6, Shanghai

(d) N=2, Shenzhen   (e) N=4, Shenzhen   (f) N=6, Shenzhen

Fig. 3. Contour map of uniqueness of traces of two cities.

uniqueness exceeds 90% for most temporal and spatial resolutions while N equals to 7 ($N = 7$, Figs. 4(g), 5(g)).

In both datasets, the trajectories cover square areas with a side length of 200 km, spreading over two degrees in longitude and latitude. If the spatial resolution is chosen to be 10×10, then we get 100 square blocks, with a 20-km side length for each. Such a block is much too huge for estimation. The appropriate and practical resolution is 100×100, which means that the side length of each block becomes only 2 km.

4 Investigating Procedure

In the experiments, we generalize the spatial and temporal dimensions to simulate the basic privacy protection methods. Our experiments can be divided into four steps: pre-processing, temporal generalization, spatial generalization and uniqueness calculation. During pre-processing, datasets are processed to satisfy the requirements of experiments. Temporal generalization applies a specific resolution to the time field. For adversaries, points within a resolution cannot be distinguished. Similarly, spatial generalization applies a resolution to the location field. After temporal and spatial generalization, the last step is to find out the possibilities that one taxi can be re-identified uniquely by adversaries given specific number of spatio-temporal points. When carrying out the experiment, we test different temporal and spatial resolutions with different number of spatio-temporal points.

The details of each step are shown in the following sections. We will give an overview of our datasets at the end.

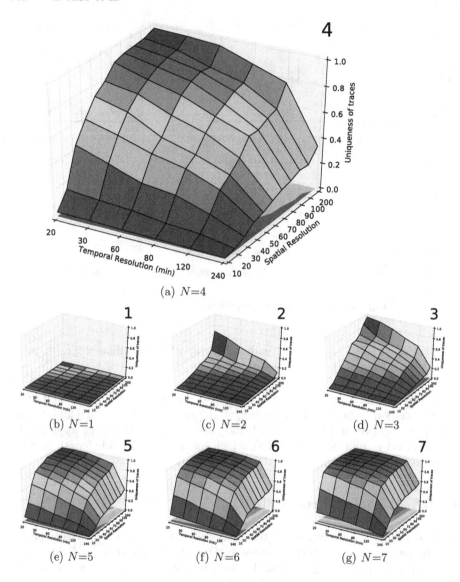

(a) $N=4$

(b) $N=1$ (c) $N=2$ (d) $N=3$

(e) $N=5$ (f) $N=6$ (g) $N=7$

Fig. 4. The result of Shanghai's Taxis.

4.1   Dataset Pre-processing

The two adopted datasets take about 60 GB disk storage in all. The data get a lot of redundances and mistakes when taxi companies record and store them. Before implementing the experiments, we have to do some pre-precessing work to clean the datasets.

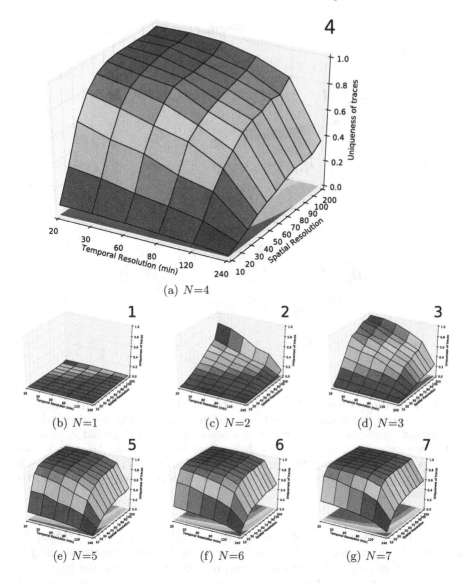

Fig. 5. The result of Shenzhen's Taxis.

In the first step of pre-processing, redundant fields are removed. Besides redundant data, logs can also have minor mistakes. The data contains broken records, such as those with temporal disorder and spatial misplace.

Records in datasets are expected to be temporally well organized, but some of them are chronological disordered. When such a temporal disorder takes place, uncorrelated points may occur in the chronological sequences (as is shown in Fig. 6(a)). All of the temporal uncorrelated points in the logs should be removed in this stage. Another temporal disorder case is that all the point sequences are

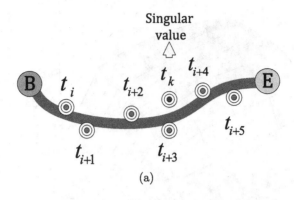

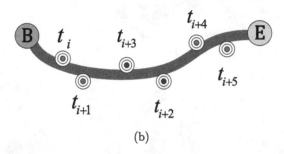

Fig. 6. Illustration of temporal disorder. In (a), on the road segment from B to E, there are several points among t_i and t_{i+5}, and t_k's temporal tag doesn't match the surrounding points' tags, which makes it a broken point. So t_k should be removed in the pre-precessing stage. In (b), t_3 shifts ahead t_2 (or t_2 shifts behind t_3). Two solutions are used for solving this temporal error. One is removing t_2 or t_3, the other is correcting t_2's or t_3's temporal tag. Both solutions need the average speed parameter as a reference.

correlated with each other, but some of them are shifted (as Fig. 6(b) shows). In general, GPS-measured time has a difference from GPS-received time, and the records on logs may shift over one or two records. By scanning the sequences, one point temporal disorder can be fixed easily. Given that one point temporal disorder is already a low possibility event, we do not concern the high-order points temporal disorder cases.

The last case is spatial displace. When taxis report their locations to the server, they upload their longitude and latitude information, and the server receives and stores this information into database. The whole process can not be done perfectly. The bits representing the longitude and latitude may be changed when the location information is being transmitted and stored, which leads to spatial displace. Spatial displace makes one point from the sequences shift away from others, as is shown in Fig. 7. After calculating the speed between points,

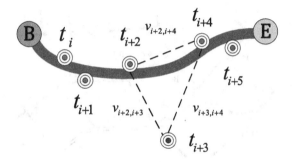

Fig. 7. Illustration of spatial misplace. t_{i+3} has a deflection from the main road, which can be tested by communication error between GPS devices and GPS servers. The average speed is calculated for finding the deflection points. In the figure, $v_{i+2,i+3}$ is the average speed between t_{i+2} and t_{i+3}, and so are $v_{i+3,i+4}$ and $v_{i+2,i+4}$. By comparison, $v_{i+2,i+3}$ and $v_{i+3,i+4}$ are much more larger than $v_{i+2,i+4}$. Frequently their values exceeds taxis' maximum speed. So we can consider t_{i+3} as an invalid point and remove it from logs.

a point spatial displace can be distinguished if its speed to adjacent points is extremely large. Spatial displaced points will be removed from the records.

In the end, some taxis have only a small number of records, so they are not suitable for the experiments. These cars are simply removed from logs.

4.2   Temporal Generalization

Take Shenzhen taxis data as an example, whose timeline covers 9 days. In temporal generalization step, different levels of temporal resolutions are tested in our experiments. A specific temporal resolution tr will divide the whole timeline (9 days, $12,960$ min) into $12,960/tr$ periods. In Fig. 8, the spatio-temporal points are mapped to each interval according to their temporal tags. By doing so, points nearby are classified to the same period. Thus, the adversaries can not tell the temporal differences among the points within the same period.

Actually, two time-related concepts are involved in our attacker model, say, the Adversary spying time (AST) and the Server recording time (SRT). AST is the time that adversaries record when following a car, while SRT is the time that the server records when a car starts a query to server. In fact, the adversary can not obtain the query start time (QST) easily and the QST also has a numerical difference from the AST. These two reasons make a unstable numerical difference between AST and SRT. In our experiments, we set temporal resolutions to simulate the situations that AST has a shift from SRT.

In the experiments, we try 6 levels of temporal resolutions: 20, 30, 60, 80, 120, and 240 min.

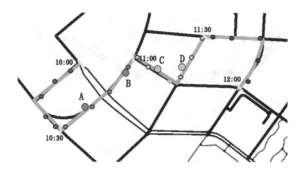

Fig. 8. Illustration of temporal generalization. The gray line is the trajectory of a car in timeline from 10:00 to 12:00. In temporal generalization process, we set the temporal resolution to half an hour, and the path is divided into 4 periods marked by different colors. Points in the same period are considered undistinguishable. For example, A and B, C and D are undistinguishable, while A and C, B and D are distinguishable. (Color figure online)

4.3   Spatial Generalization

The Shenzhen and Shanghai taxis' trajectories both cover an approximate square area that spreads over 2° in longitude and 2° in latitude. In this stage, we use a simple and direct way to generalize the spatial area. We draw lines with different densities along the longitude and latitude lines and divide the entire mobility spatial area into different blocks.

As shown in the Fig. 9, points in the same blocks are identical in their location when exposed to adversaries. This method of division can simulate k-anonymous algorithm to some extent, while pure k-anonymous division will create dynamic districts as time goes by. With the source dataset, we can not locate the precise position of all taxis at a specific time, which means that the pure k-anonymous algorithm is impractical. In our experiments, different division densities are set to replace different values of k's in k-anonymous algorithm. The more blocks are divided, the smaller each block is. We apply 11 different spatial resolutions in the experiments (10×10, 20×20, ..., 100×100, and 200×200).

4.4   Uniqueness Calculation

After pre-processing, temporal generalization and spatial generalization, we can calculate the uniqueness of a taxi's trajectory. Let U_s denote the uniqueness of a trace given several known spatio-temporal points. We also define uniqueness indicator ϵ, which indicates the possibility that a trace can be identified with a specific number of spatio-temporal points.

$$U_s = \begin{cases} 1 & \text{if a sample is unique,} \\ 0 & \text{otherwise.} \end{cases}$$

Fig. 9. Illustration of spatial generalization. The entire area is divided into 6×6 blocks bounded by yellow and gray dotted lines. After the spatial generalization, A and B are in different blocks, while C and D are in same block. So A and B are distinguishable, C and D are undistinguishable. We say that the 6×6 spatial resolution cannot tell C from D. When spatial resolution level is reduced to 3×3 (divided by yellow dotted line), B is mingled with C and D. (Color figure online)

In Fig. 10, when the number of known spatio-temporal points is 2 (points B and C here), the value of U_s is 0 according to the above formula. If 3 points are known (either A, B, C or B, C, D), then U_s equals 1.

Now that we can calculate the value of U_s given several spatio-temporal points, the last problem to solve is how to get enough samples of several spatio-temporal points. We use statistical approaches to sample from the taxis' records repeatedly, and match it with the entire dataset to calculate U_s. With enough samples, the uniqueness indicator ϵ can be inferred as in Eq. (1).

$$\epsilon = \frac{\sum_{s \in S} U_s}{|S|} \times 100\% \tag{1}$$

In our experiments, we mainly have 3 variables (the temporal resolution TR, the spatial resolution SR, and the number of known spatio-temporal points N). Please refer to the detailed results of our experiment and the relations between ϵ and the three variables can be found in Sect. 3.

Algorithm 1 gives the procedures of computing the uniqueness of users' traces.

4.5   Datasets overview

We adopt two datasets, the overview of which is shown in Table 1. Table 2 gives the main fields of the datasets. *ID* corresponds to taxi's identity, which is the

Fig. 10. Illustration of uniqueness judgement. The blue and red lines are trajectories of two taxis with a timeline from 10:00 to 12:00, A and E turned out to be in period 10:00 to 10:30 (similarly, B and F in period from 10:30 to 11:00; C and G in period from 11:00 to 11:30; D and H in period from 11:30 to 12:00). Given 2 spatio-temporal points, B and C, we cannot identify the blue line trajectories. But if additional points, A or D or both of them, are given, this trajectory can be uniquely identified. (Color figure online)

Table 1. Overview of datasets

Index	Date	#Taxis	#Records
Shenzhen	2011 04/18~04/26	13798	130,551,644
Shanghai	2015 04/01~04/10	13899	1,141,606,183

unique identification of taxis. *Time* is the time when the taxi reports its location to LBS server. *Longitude* and *Latitude* denote the location of a taxi. In our datesets, each taxi has plenty of records every day, and more records mean that a taxi has more trajectory data. Figure 11 gives the probability density distribution of the number of taxi trajectory records per day. We can see from the figure that the probability density of Shanghai dataset is increasing with the growing number of records while that of Shenzhen dataset is decreasing. Taxis in Shanghai tend to have more trajectory records per day than those in Shenzhen.

Actually, a larger number of records do not mean more trajectory information. For example, given the same number of trajectory records, those with larger time-span may contain more information. Figure 12 gives the interval length distribution of two adjoined records. As we use taxi trajectory data from taxi companies instead of private cars, and taxi companies often collect their taxis' location diligently, more than 95% interval length is within one hour. The rest

---

Algorithm 1. Computing Uniqueness of Traces

Input:

The entire original datasets, DS_o.

Output:

A list with result tuples which contain parameters and the value of uniqueness, R.

1: Clean the original dataset DS_o with methods in pre-preprocess stage, get DS_c.
2: Initialize R with an empty list.
3: Initialize $Count$ with 150,000.
4: **for** each $TR \in [20, 30, 60, 80, 120, 240]$ **do**
5:     **for** each $SR \in [10, 20, 30, 40, 50, 60, 70, 80, 90, 100, 200]$ **do**
6:         Divide the DS_c with TR, SR, get DS_d.
7:         **for** each $N \in [1, 2, 3, 4, 5, 6, 7]$ **do**
8:             $c = 0$
9:             $m = 0$
10:            **while** $c < Count$ **do**
11:                Sample N spatio-temporal points P_n from DS_c
12:                **if** len(matched(P_n, DS_d)) $== 1$ **then**
13:                    $m += 1$
14:                **end if**
15:                $c += 1$
16:            **end while**
17:            $\epsilon = m/Count$
18:            R.append((TR, SR, N, ϵ))
19:        **end for**
20:    **end for**
21: **end for**
22: **return** R

Table 2. Data sample from Shenzhen's Taxicab

ID	Time	Longitude	Latitude
B00T12	2011/04/18 00:00:18	113.984566	22.560133
B00T12	2011/04/18 00:01:14	113.994598	22.556467
...	...	...	...
B001B2	2011/04/20 00:01:55	113.881699	22.742943
B001B2	2011/04/20 00:02:55	113.880867	22.739964
...	...	...	...
B02S48	2011/04/23 19:54:42	114.262413	22.711182
B02S48	2011/04/23 19:55:22	114.261932	22.715206
B02S48	2011/04/23 19:56:39	114.261513	22.718210
...	...	...	...

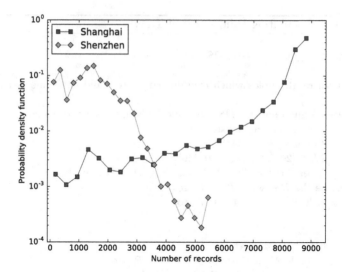

Fig. 11. Probability density function of the average number of a taxi trajectory records per day.

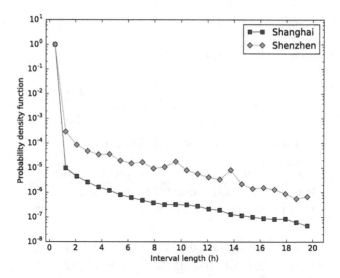

Fig. 12. The distribution of interval length of two adjoined records.

of the length of intervals is decreasing progressively. For records that are collected every ten seconds or less, the taxi location barely changes numerically on longitude and latitude, which means a high redundance in our data. We can vote one point on behalf of all the points within a specific threshold of time. For example, if we set the threshold to be 20 min, then the mobilities in 20 min can be summarized to one spatio-temporal point.

5   Discussion

The experimental result shows that 95.35% of uniqueness can be achieved if 4 spatio-temporal points are exposed to adversaries. With the growing of the number, the possibilities rapidly increase to 99%. Also, we find both spatial and temporal generalization methods help to protect the trajectory privacy and lower the possibilities of being re-identified. When the level of spatial and temporal resolution increases, the information contained in the data goes vague and the dataset becomes useless, which will end up with one spatio-temporal point standing for all taxis and none can be identified. Our result shows four spatio-temporal points are sufficient for re-identifying a taxi with a moderate level of spatial and temporal resolution, which suggests that the data after this level generalization be sufficiently useful for LBS providers.

If we focus on taxis that cannot be identified in our experiments, we find that several spatio-temporal points from those taxis trajectory can still match two or three taxis, which means those taxis' identities can be decided by making a choice from two or three entities. So adversaries can still identify those taxis with several attempts. In our experiments, we utilize trajectory data from taxis instead of private cars. Generally speaking, the trajectory of a taxi is less regular as compared to a private car. Under this observation, we can predict that private cars have even more serious privacy problems than taxis. Thereby, we can conclude that VLBS is confronted with a noteworthy privacy problem.

There may be a doubt that the vehicle quantity we have used in experiments is too little to support our conclusion. Nowadays, the number of VLBS applications are growing rapidly, such as Here Maps, Google Maps, Foursquare, etc. We assume that millions of vehicles are driven around in the city, only some of which are distributed in various VLBSs applications. For a single application, the number of vehicles that its server serves could be very small in the city. Hence, our datasets are enough for most cases.

We provide several suggestions for drivers and VLBS providers to reduce the risk of privacy leakage.

- *Advice 1*: Use VLBS applications only when it is necessary. Most LBS-related applications keep on uploading users' location data under specific frequency while running in backend. Most of drivers are familiar with the roads, but they may still keep using the application unintentionally when driving. Some of them may want to use the application for a second, for example, just in order to find POIs (Place Of Interests) nearby, but fail to turn it down.
- *Advice 2*: Do not reveal personal information to LBS-related applications. For example, when you register Google Maps account, you are not supposed to reveal unnecessary personal information.
- *Advice 3*: In principle, using different accounts and different applications is helpful for privacy protection.

Here are also several advices for the VLBS providers.

VLBS's Advice 1: Lower the information collection frequency if it dose not harm basic services.

VLBS's Advice 2: Adopt more advanced cryptographic algorithm and store less sensitive information on the server.

With the efforts of both drivers and VLBS providers, users' privacy can be protected better.

6   Conclusion and Future Work

Based on investigating two real world datasets of taxi traces, we found that with the help of urban road maps, four spatio-temporal points are sufficient to uniquely identify vehicles, achieving an accuracy over 95%. Then, we can draw a conclusion that in a VLBS environment, the privacy protect is a critical challenge even though the queries are sparse.

People may have different concerns about their privacy when using LBS-related applications. For our future work, we plan to provide customized privacy strategies with different privacy levels. In detail, we would turn to machine learning methods to automatically learn users' habits and preferences, which can aid in adaptable choice among different privacy levels.

Acknowledgements. The research of authors is partially supported by the National Natural Science Foundation of China (NSFC) under Grants 61571331, the Integrated Project for Major Research Plan of the National Natural Science Foundation of China under Grant 91218301, Fok Ying-Tong Education Foundation for Young Teachers in the Higher Education Institutions of China under Grant 151066, "Shuguang Program" from Shanghai Education Development Foundation under Grant 14SG20, the Shanghai Science and Technology Innovation Action Plan Project under Grant 16511100901, and the Shanghai Innovation Action Project under Grant 16DZ1100200. We thank all anonymous reviewers for their insightful comments.

References

1. Wang, C., Tang, S., Yang, L., Guo, Y., Li, F., Jiang, C.: Modeling data dissemination in online social networks: a geographical perspective on bounding network traffic load. In: Proceedings of ACM MobiHoc (2014)
2. Cheng Wang, L., Shao, Z.L., Yang, L., Li, X.-Y., Jiang, C.: Capacity scaling of wireless social networks. IEEE Trans. Parallel Distrib. Syst. **26**(7), 1839–1850 (2015)
3. Theodorakopoulos, G., Shokri, R., Troncoso, C., Hubaux, J.-P., Le Boudec, J.-Y.: Prolonging the hide-and-seek game: optimal trajectory privacy for location-based services. In: Proceedings of ACM WPES (2014)
4. Hwang, R.-H., Hsueh, Y.-L., Chung, H.-W.: A novel time-obfuscated algorithm for trajectory privacy protection. IEEE Trans. Serv. Comput. **7**(2), 126–139 (2014)
5. Guo, M., Jin, X., Pissinou, N., Zanlongo, S., Carbunar, B., Iyengar, S.S.: In-network trajectory privacy preservation. ACM Comput. Surv. (CSUR) **48**(2), 23 (2015)
6. Shin, K.G., Ju, X., Chen, Z., Chen, X.: Privacy protection for users of location-based services. IEEE Wirel. Commun. **19**(1), 30–39 (2012)
7. Pan, J., Zuo, Z., Zhanyi, X., Jin, Q.: Privacy protection for lbs in mobile environments. Int. J. Secur. Appl. **9**(1), 249–258 (2015)

8. Zhu, J., Kim, K.-H., Mohapatra, P., Congdon, P.: An adaptive privacy-preserving scheme for location tracking of a mobile user. In: Proceedings of IEEE SECON (2013)

9. Corser, G., Huirong, F., Shu, T., D'Errico, P., Ma, W.-J.: Endpoint protection zone (EPZ): protecting LBS user location privacy against deanonymization and collusion in vehicular networks. In: Proceedings of IEEE ICCVE (2013)

10. Gkoulalas-Divanis, A., Stephenson, M.: Method and system for anonymization in continuous location-based services. US Patent 9,135,452, September 15 2015

11. Song, D., Sim, J., Park, K., Song, M.: A privacy-preserving continuous location monitoring system for location-based services. Int. J. Distrib. Sens. Netw. **2015**, 14 (2015)

12. Montazeri, Z., Houmansadr, A., Pishro-Nik, H.: Defining perfect location privacy using anonymization. In: Proceedings of IEEE CISS (2016)

13. Feldman, D., Sugaya, A., Sung, C., Rus, D.: iDiary: from GPS signals to a text-searchable diary. In: Proceedings of ACM SenSys (2013)

14. Zhang, Y., Tan, C.C., Xu, F., Han, H., Li, Q.: Vproof: lightweight privacy-preserving vehicle location proofs. IEEE Trans. Veh. Technol. **64**(1), 378–385 (2015)

15. Rongxing, L., Li, X., Luan, T.H., Liang, X., Shen, X.: Pseudonym changing at social spots: an effective strategy for location privacy in vanets. IEEE Trans. Veh. Technol. **61**(1), 86–96 (2012)

16. Rongxing, L., Lin, X., Liang, X., Shen, X.: A dynamic privacy-preserving key management scheme for location-based services in vanets. IEEE Trans. Intell. Transp. Syst. **13**(1), 127–139 (2012)

17. Forster, D., Lohr, H., Kargl, F.: Decentralized enforcement of k-anonymity for location privacy using secret sharing. In: Proceedings of IEEE VNC (2015)

18. Sweeney, L.: k-anonymity: a model for protecting privacy. Int. J. Uncertainty Fuzziness Knowl.-Based Syst. **10**(05), 557–570 (2002)

19. Gruteser, M., Grunwald, D.: Anonymous usage of location-based services through spatial and temporal cloaking. In: Proceedings of ACM MobiSys (2003)

20. Beresford, A.R., Stajano, F.: Mix zones: user privacy in location-aware services. In: Proceedings of IEEE PerCom (2004)

21. Gedik, B., Liu, L.: Location privacy in mobile systems: a personalized anonymization model. In: Proceedings of IEEE ICDCS (2005)

22. Rebollo-Monedero, D., Forné, J., Pallarès, E., Parra-Arnau, J.: A modification of the lloyd algorithm for k-anonymous quantization. Inf. Sci. **222**, 185–202 (2013)

23. Qiu, F., Fan, W., Chen, G.: Slicer: a slicing-based k-anonymous privacy preserving scheme for participatory sensing. In: Proceedings of IEEE MAAS (2013)

24. Stokes, K., Farràs, O.: Linear spaces and transversal designs: k-anonymous combinatorial configurations for anonymous database search notes. Des. Codes Crypt. **71**(3), 503–524 (2014)

25. de Montjoye, Y.-A., Radaelli, L., Singh, V.K., et al.: Unique in the shopping mall: on the reidentifiability of credit card metadata. Science **347**(6221), 536–539 (2015)

26. de Montjoye, Y.-A., Hidalgo, C.A., Verleysen, M., Blondel, V.D.: Unique in the crowd: the privacy bounds of human mobility. Sci. Rep. **3** (2013)

27. Google Maps. https://www.google.com/maps

System Security

BinDNN: Resilient Function Matching Using Deep Learning

Nathaniel Lageman[1]([✉]), Eric D. Kilmer[1], Robert J.Walls[2],
and Patrick D. McDaniel[1]

[1] Pennsylvania State University, University Park, PA, USA
{njl5114,ekilmer,mcdaniel}@cse.psu.edu
[2] Worcester Polytechnic Institute, Worcester, MA, USA
rjwalls@wpi.edu

Abstract. Determining if two functions taken from different compiled binaries originate from the same function in the source code has many applications to malware reverse engineering. Namely, this process allows an analyst to filter large swaths of code, removing functions that have been previously observed or those that originate in shared or trusted libraries. However, this task is challenging due to the myriad factors that influence the translation between source code and assembly instructions—the instruction stream created by a compiler is heavily influenced by a number of factors including optimizations, target platforms, and runtime constraints. In this paper, we seek to advance methods for reliably testing the equivalence of functions found in different executables. By leveraging advances in deep learning and natural language processing, we design and evaluate a novel algorithm, BinDNN, that is resilient to variations in compiler, compiler optimization level, and architecture. We show that BinDNN is effective both in isolation or in conjunction with existing approaches. In the case of the latter, we boost performance by 109% when combining BinDNN with BinDiff to compare functions across architectures. This result—an improvement of 32% for BinDNN and 185% for BinDiff—demonstrates the utility of employing multiple orthogonal approaches to function matching.

Keywords: Reverse engineering · Malware · Deep learning

1 Introduction

Understanding the behavior and structure of malware is critical to developing and improving our defenses against malicious code. However, the practitioners tasked with this analysis rarely have access to the malware's source code. As a result, the binary has to be disassembled and manually reverse-engineered in a time-consuming and expensive process. An important consideration, therefore, is deciding how to prioritize the analyst's limited resources. In other words, the analyst must determine which parts of the malware deserve their initial focus. Fortunately, malware authors commonly reuse code (e.g., libraries used for

© ICST Institute for Computer Sciences, Social Informatics and Telecommunications Engineering 2017
R. Deng et al. (Eds.): SecureComm 2016, LNICST 198, pp. 517–537, 2017.
DOI: 10.1007/978-3-319-59608-2_29

command and control) and thus a new piece of malware may significantly overlap with previously examined binaries. If the investigator can identify functions that have been analyzed before, they can leverage those existing results to increase the speed and accuracy of the reverse engineering. Such identification is key to reducing the cost of performing analysis.

The challenge in identifying these functions is that the same source code may have multiple equivalent byte code representations. The reason for this discrepancy is straightforward. When compiling the binary, high-level language features—such as control flow operations while, for, if, case, etc.—must be reduced and translated to the processor's instruction set. This translation depends on myriad factors including the choice of compiler, performance optimizations, and target architecture. While some researchers have proposed using control flow structure to match functions across binaries [3,6,9], such approaches often make the simplifying assumption that functions come from the same compiler, architecture, and optimization level. Consequently, these methods are insufficient for many practical scenarios.

The core of the challenge of identifying different compilations of the same code in different environments (target platforms, optimization levels) is an example of a *variant recognition problem*. More broadly, this is a common classification problem in which some base artifact is perturbed into a class sample. Later, a *classifier* uses an algorithm to identify the sample as belonging to the class. Note that machine learning has been extremely successful at building classifiers. For example, machine learning has been used to accurately detect malware and network intrusion [15,18,21,24], identify objects in images [4,7,19], and a host of other applications. In this paper, we build a machine learning classifier that identifies function variants created by compilation. We use large collections of sample functions executables to train a deep learning network. Later, the network is used to compare pairs of functions for their equivalence—that they were compiled from the same original source code.

In this paper, we introduce an orthogonal approach to function matching for malware analysis. Our algorithm, BINDNN, leverages recent advances in deep neural networks to build a model robust to changes in compiler or architecture. At its core, BINDNN uses a Long Short-Term Memory (LSTM) neural network to develop temporal relationships between assembly code instructions. These relationships enable BINDNN to approximate mappings from the assembly instructions back to the source code functions. Further, BINDNN incorporates a belief threshold that allows an analysis to dynamically adjust the sensitivity of the model. In short, we make the following contributions.

- We design a novel approach, BINDNN, for prioritizing functions during malware analysis. Based on deep learning, our approach matches function representations across different compilers, architectures, and optimizations.
- We evaluate BINDNN on a set of more than 70,000 binary function representations compiled from 2,598 unique functions. We find BINDNN classifies function matches with extremely high confidence, creating score distributions

strongly weighted towards their respective classes, with median values of 0.99 for true matches and 0.0 for non-matches.

– Finally, we show that BINDNN compliments existing approaches. By using BINDNN in conjunction with BinDiff, we boost the performance by 109% when comparing functions across architectures and optimization level. This represents an average improvement of 32% for BINDNN and 185% for BinDiff.

We begin by more formally defining the function recognition problem and building a classifier for it using a deep learning network.

2   Problem Definition

The fundamental challenge of our work is identifying whether two distinct instruction sequences were compiled from the same source code. This proves to be a formidable task as even a single function may have multiple equivalent representations depending on the choice of compiler, the target architecture, and other factors. To illustrate, let us examine the impact of one such factor, optimization level.

Compiler optimizations are intended to make the code faster or more memory efficient. Consider the two instruction sequences in Fig. 1. Both sequences were compiled from the same source code function (Fig. 2) with the same compiler (gcc), but with different optimization levels. The assembly on the left was compiled with no optimizations (O0), whereas the assembly on the right was compiled with optimization O2. The primary difference lies in how O2 eliminates the need to set up the stack. First, lines 1 and 2 are removed. Next, at lines 3 and 4 the O0 code grabs the "o" pointer argument using the base stack pointer and compares it to 0 (to check for NULL). But in the O2 code we see it transfers the "o" pointer argument to register eax and perform the test operation to set the flags register. Then, at line 6, the O0 code moves the "o" pointer argument to the eax register, and the O2 code dereferences the "o" pointer argument and stores it back in the eax register. On line 7 we see the O0 code jumps

```
1   0804 A9A2   push   ebp                          1
2   0804 A9A3   mov    ebp, esp                     2
3   0804 A9A5   cmp    ss:[ebp+o], b1 0             3   0804 B850   mov    eax, ss:[esp+o]
4                                                   4   0804 B854   test   eax, eax
5   0804 A9A9   jz     0x804A9B0                    5   0804 B856   jz     0x804B860
6   0804 A9AB   mov    eax, ss:[ebp+o]              6   0804 B858   mov    eax, ds:[eax]
7   0804 A9AE   jmp    0x804A9B5                    7   0804 B85A   retn
8                                                   8
9   0804 A8B0   mov                                 9   0804 B860   mov
    eax, default_quoting_options                        eax, default_quoting_options
10  0804 A9B5   mov    eax, ds:[eax]                10  0804 B865   mov    eax, ds:[eax]
11  0804 A9B7   pop    ebp                          11
12  0804 A9B8   retn                                12  0804 B867   retn
```

(a) Assembly of x86 with optimization O0.   (b) Assembly of x86 with optimization O2.

Fig. 1.

```
1 /* Get the value of O's quoting style.  If O is null, use the default.  */
2 enum quoting_style
3 get_quoting_style (struct quoting_options const *o)
4 {
5   return (o ? o : &default_quoting_options)->style;
6 }
```

Fig. 2. The source code for the assembly instructions seen in Figs. 1 and 3.

to line 10 to perform the same dereference the O2 code already performed while the O2 code returns. If we took the jump on line 5, we see that O0 has to restore the stack base pointer on line 11 whereas the O2 code does not as it never set up the stack.

Even for our simple example function, optimization level had a significant impact on the compiled assembly. We can quantify this impact, in general, by using the edit distance between equivalent function representations. For example, on a large sample set of binaries compiled under various optimization levels, we calculated an average edit distance of 26.63 instructions.[1] Given that the average instruction length for a function was just over 50, these results mean that approximately 53% of each function changed based on choice of optimization level alone.

As mentioned previously, optimization level is just one factor affecting the translation between source code and binary. Another factor, architecture, has an even greater impact on the resulting binary. For example, the ARM-based assembly in Fig. 3, does not share any instructions with the equivalent x86 from Fig. 1. This, in combination with the factors discussed above, can make it extraordinarily difficult to match functional equivalences across program binaries by simple comparison.

```
1    00013110    STR    R11, ![SP,0xFFFFFFFC]
2    00013114    ADD    R11, SP, 0
3    00013118    SUB    SP, SP, 0xC
4    0001311C    STR    R0, [R11,0xFFFFFFF8]
5    00013120    LDR    R3, [R11,0xFFFFFFF8]
6    00013124    CMP    R3, 0
7    00013128    BEQ    b2 loc_13134
8    0001312C    LDR    R3, [R11,0xFFFFFFF8]
9    00013130    B      b2 loc_13138
10   00013134    LDR    R3, [off_1314C]
11   00013138    LDR    R3, [R3]
12   0001313C    MOV    R0, R3
13   00013140    SUB    SP, R11, 0
14   00013144    LDR    R11, [SP,4]
15   00013148    BX     LR
```

Fig. 3. Assembly of ARM with optimization O0.

---

[1] We paired functions representations from gcc -O0 against gcc O1, O2, and O3. See Sect. 4.1 for a description of the data set.

We identify the main difficulty in this problem to be determining if two particular assembly instructions map back to the same source code function. Specifically, the goal of our method will be to devise a model that is able to classify a pair of instruction sequences as either a function match or non-match, regardless of the input factors that cause these sequences to change. From this classification, we can compare functions across binaries and look for previously examined functions in scenarios akin to the ones above.

2.1   Previous Methods

BinDiff [26] is the current state-of-the-art tool for comparing binary files to find similarities. BinDiff takes two input binaries, finds functions in the binaries, and then performs graph isomorphism detection on pairs of functions from the two binaries. This technique works well when two semantically equivalent binaries have similar control flow graphs. However, when they have different control flow graphs, such as when the binaries are compiled with different optimization levels, this approach loses its effectiveness [8].

Several others have proposed related techniques for detecting similarities. BinHunt [9] and BinSlayer [3] are two such examples. BinHunt uses graph isomorphism detection similar to BinDiff; however, BinHunt finds maximum subgraph isomorphism while BinDiff utilizes a greedy method for performance. BinHunt's algorithm works best when the graphs generated from the binary files are similar. Hence, they suggest using a different graph isomorphism technique when the differences are large. BinSlayer creates a polynomial time algorithm for calculating differences between two binaries by combining BinDiff's algorithm with the Hungarian algorithm for bi-partite graph matching [3]. We choose not to use either of these techniques in our analysis, as BinSlayer relies on BinDiff's structural comparison algorithm and shares many of the same weaknesses, and BinHunt loses effectiveness when analyzing binaries that produce largely different graphs.

unstrip [13] uses system calls in the form of semantic-descriptors to identify GNU C Library wrapper functions such as read and write in 32-bit binaries. The purpose of this tool is to mitigate the effort that analysts must spend in order to parse stripped binaries. The unstrip tool is used to label wrapper functions for *system calls* in Linux binaries. Their matching system uses a database of semantic descriptors and fingerprints to identify functions. While the identification of wrapper functions is important, our tool is more generalized and can detect both wrapper functions and functions that do not contain system calls.

When looking at methods for function identification within binaries, we see there has been some focus in using machine learning methods. Two of these methods are ByteWeight [1] and experiments with RNNs [23]. ByteWeight uses weighted prefix trees to classify the beginnings and ends of functions [1]. In [23], Shin et al. train a Recurrent Neural Network to classify the beginnings and ends of functions, and their method is able to outperform other methods [23]. However, it should be noted that finding function boundaries is related, but it is a different problem than function matching.

Finally, BLEX, created by Egele et al. is a tool for function matching that introduces a new method called blanket execution. This method executes functions in a controlled environment to analyze its behavior. This method performs better than most other methods for cross compiler (or cross optimization level) function identification, obtaining accuracy of 55%, and 64% when used as a search engine [8]. However, BLEX does not currently consider target architecture changes—something our method aims to consider.

3   Function Matching with Deep Learning

We propose BINDNN, a new approach to function matching inspired by recent deep learning approaches for Natural Language Processing (NLP). BINDNN is based on the following intuition: By representing assembly instructions as words, and their orderings as sentences, we can equate function matching to the problem of finding sentences with the same meaning. Framing function matching as an NLP problem allows us to leverage a wealth of past research as the starting point for our model.

In particular, BINDNN utilizes three types of neural network models: Convolutional neural networks (CNN) [16], Long Short-Term Memory recurrent neural networks (LSTM) [10,12,25], and regular fully connected feed-forward neural networks (DNN). We layer these models to construct an architecture similar to the design proposed by Sainath et al. for speech recognition [22]. This design takes advantage of the LSTM, allowing BINDNN to infer the temporal relationships necessary for function matching. In addition, our approach employs an embedding layer to make the model more effective at representing different inputs which have similar meaning [5,17].

Approach Overview. BINDNN uses a three step process to find function matches, as depicted in Fig. 4. Upon receiving binaries to analyze, BINDNN first needs to find and represent the functions in assembly code. This involves leveraging preexisting techniques for function boundary detection, and then performing feature extraction to translate the assembly code functions representations into a more appropriate format for the neural network. Next, we generate samples that the neural network uses to learn the structure of a function match. Finally, we can use the neural network to determine if the assembly code functions originate from the same source code.

3.1   Binary to Feature Vector Translation

Identifying Function Boundaries. The first step of BINDNN begins the process that translates the binaries into a classifiable object that the neural network will be able to understand. This first requires finding the function boundaries in the input binaries. On an unstripped binary (one compiled with the debug flag on) this process is trivial, however, as our method is designed to work on unstripped binaries, we must have a method that can still find these function boundaries. This is a difficult task for which has seen recent research [20,23].

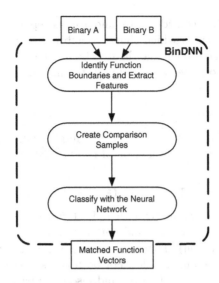

Fig. 4. Method overview of BINDNN. BINDNN uses a three step process. In the first step it has to find the function boundaries, so it can extract the features for each function. Next, it uses these feature function representation to create comparison samples before finally classifying these sample with a deep neural network.

However, IDA Pro [11] is still one of the best performing tools, and is commercially available. We choose to use IDA for finding function boundaries.

After the system has function boundaries, it can start to convert the functions from assembly to instruction sequences. In order for the comparison component of BINDNN to be able to perform the comparison, we need a way to represent the functions so our neural network is able to deduce discriminatory pieces from the functions that exist cross compiler, architecture, and optimization level. We designed our system to use an ordered set of the assembly instructions that make up the function with their arguments removed. This highlights the temporal relationship between the instructions, which the neural network is able to employ to aid in classifying the functions.

Feature Extraction. Our approach is similar to what is seen in the taxonomy of deep learning for natural language processing [5]. BINDNN uses a global vocabulary of instructions that could appear in a function.

```
[aaa, aad, aam, aas, adc, ..., XTN, XTN2, YIELD, ZIP1, ZIP2]
[0,   1,   2,   3,   4,   ..., 1940, 1941, 1942, 1943, 1944]
```

Specifically, it holds the instructions available for the architectures for which this model will be (or has been) trained to handle. In our experiments, we trained BINDNN to support binaries from two architectures, x_86 and arm. Therefore, its global vocabulary contains the instruction sets for both architectures. Notably for these two architectures, the model saw no shared assembly instructions, as arm instructions were represented as uppercase and x86 were represented in lowercase, e.g. BINDNN considers MOV and mov as separate instructions. Additionally, given architectures which share assembly instructions syntactically, it would likely be beneficial to change them to be unique when storing them in the vocabulary; in order to prevent confusion in the neural network.

3.2   Sample Creation

In BINDNN's second step, it constructs the sample that is passed to the neural network. A sample is the concatenation of two function representations, as seen below.

```
[push, mov, ..., retn] + [BARRIER] + [push, mov, ..., retn]
```

A sample can represent a match (where both function representations belong to the same source code function) and non-matches (the representations do not belong to the same function). There are two types of samples we need to create, training samples and testing samples. For both types of samples, it is must pair instructions sequences with each other and insert the barrier index. However in training, it must also contain the size discrepancy between the true match and false match samples sets, so the network can train on a balanced dataset. During classification, there is no such constraint.

A single sample that is provided to the neural network is the representations of two functions concatenated on either side of a barrier index. The barrier index is also stored in the global vocabulary like an assembly instruction. Each sample represents a pair of function representations that are either a matching pair (they represent two instruction sequences originating from the same source code function) or non-matching (they originate for two separate source code functions). We add the barrier index to provide an indicator that the neural network can use to distinguish where one function representations ends and the other begins. The index becomes the length of our global instruction dictionary. Our current global vocabulary consists of 1945 total instructions, i.e. our barrier index is 1945. Additionally, we do not create samples including functions that are less than 5 instructions, or greater than 150 instructions.

Constructing the Training Dataset. Consider the construction of the samples used in the training the phase of our tool, we only cover the generation of the training set because it is analogous to the generation of the test step. The only difference is that the test set generation uses a smaller set of functions. Let X be the set of functions in the training data, and k be a function in X. Then X_k is the list of representations for function k. To construct a "true match" sample for the training set, we find the indices of two representations, (i, j), such that $i \neq j$, from X_k and pair them together. This provides us with $\binom{|X_i|}{2}$ possible true matches for function i. To construct the "false match" samples we need another variable, $\bar{X}_k$, defined as follows.

$$\bar{X}_k := \{x \in X_m | \forall m \in X \text{ s.t. } m \neq k\} \tag{1}$$

Then the false match sample can be constructed as the pairs between each $i \in X_k$ and $\forall j \in \bar{X}_k$. However, using this method directly creates an unmanageable total of false samples causing the model to take far too long in the learning phase, and creating an unbalance in the number of true and false comparison samples. Specifically, the total number of true samples created is,

$$\text{Number of true samples} = \binom{|X_k|}{2} \tag{2}$$

and the number of false samples is,

$$\text{Number of false samples} = \sum_{i=0}^{|X_k|} |\bar{X}_k| \tag{3}$$

for function k. With over 10,000 unique functions, this quickly balloons the training set to an unmanageable size. To address this problem we used a cap, α, when constructing the true matches, so that we create $\min(|X_k|, \alpha)$ samples for function k. Then we also create an approximately equal number of false match samples.

3.3 Using the Neural Network

The third and final phase of our method is using the deep neural network to classify the samples. It is an 8 layer network, we describe the model's architecture in detail in Appendix A. The network takes a comparison structure as input, and returns the confidence score indicating the likelihood that it is made of two matching function representations. That is, they represent instruction sequences compiled from the same source code function. BINDNN tests all of the comparison structures created in the previous step for each function. It then returns a list of all functions that could be matches, based on the threshold value, along with there associated confidence scores.

Before we can use our tool, we have to train it on the large sample set we constructed. With a network this size, this can take a substantial amount of time. The model does not have to be retrained for the ability to classify new functions that it has not previously seen. However, it does have to be retrained when expanding the number of architectures it can classify across. In preparation for our experiments, we train the network using the dataset constructed from Sect. 3.2. We train the network using 10 epochs, i.e. 10 pass through the entire dataset. Our loss function uses binary cross-entropy following the implementation in theano.[2] Following their notation the loss function is calculated elementwise as,

$$\text{Loss} = -(t * log(o) + (1 - t) * log(1 - 0)) \tag{4}$$

---

[2] http://deeplearning.net/software/theano/library/tensor/nnet/nnet.html#tensor. nnet.binary_crossentropy.

where t is the target value (the actual value), and o is the output value (the predicted value). The optimization function is what the network is trying to minimize during training. There are many optimization methods to approximate the gradient descent, as purely calculating it is not efficient enough. We use an optimization method called, "Adam" [14], which utilizes an adaptive learning rate allowing it to naturally perform a form of step size annealing. After training the network, BINDNN is ready for use.

When classifying, the network receives a set of samples for a particular function in a binary. Specifically, the set will hold the set of samples for that function versus every other function in the other binary. The network generates a confidence score for each of the samples indicating its belief that the two function representations are instruction sequences from the same source code function. BINDNN then compares these confidence scores to the threshold value that it was given, and returns a list of the comparisons that scored higher than the threshold. These represent the instruction sequences that the network believes to be from the same source code function.

4   Evaluation and Discussion

Our evaluation focuses on determining how the system would perform in the real world. We analyze the system's ability to detect instruction sequences originating from the same source code functions. This evaluation allows us to understand how well the system can improve an analyst's efficiency when analyzing malware. We compare our system, BINDNN, to a state-of-the-art tool, BinDiff. We test both system's abilities to detect function matches across real binaries compiled with different settings.

4.1   Data Set

We choose our dataset to represent real world programs. So, we used real programs that are often used on UNIX systems. Additionally, we want our results to be easily compared to other previous works. Specifically, ByteWeight [1] and their dataset of compiled programs. This dataset consists of the popular binutils, findutils, and coreutils toolsets. Each toolset was compiled for both x86 and x86-64 with gcc (version 4.7.2) and icc (version 14.0.1) using optimization levels ranging from -O0 (none) to -O3 for gcc. This dataset presented us with 2,064 binaries to include in our dataset.

However, this set of binaries only provides us with variations in compilers and compiler optimizations levels. We also need to expand the dataset to include binaries from multiple architectures, so we compiled multiple versions and implementations of libc for Linux. In particular, we tested Embedded GLIBC, eglibc, (version 2.19) and glibc (versions 2.22, 2.21, 2.20). We used the eglibc implementation because it is the default implementation installed on Ubuntu 14.04 LTS. Additionally, we also used 3 recent versions of GLIBC, which is included on Fedora, OpenSuSe, CentOS, and later versions of Ubuntu.

We trained BINDNN on this dataset in order to identify C library functions in programs that were compiled statically and stripped. Each C library implementation was compiled with default CFLAGS and optimizations. Ideally, we would have liked to extract C library implementations that came by default in popular Linux distributions, however those libraries are already stripped of debugging information and are unusable for training purposes.

We compiled the binaries with the debug flag so that the function names would be included in the assembly code. This allowed us to establish ground truth for our training experiments. However, during testing, both systems were only provided with stripped binaries to make their decision on function matches. Specifically, the systems were attempting to match functions from one stripped binary to a second stripped binary[3]. Our analysis did not require matching functions from the dynamically linked libraries. Specifically, we analyze the ability of our method in matching functions that were directly contained in the source code. Our final dataset contained multiple instruction sequences for 12,993 unique functions.

4.2   Classifying Function Comparisons

In measuring the performance of BINDNN, we focus on two questions: (1) How many function pairs were correctly identified (true positives) out of the total number of identifiable pairs? (2) How many function pairs did the system identify that do not originate from the same source code function (false positives)? Since there will be such a large number of function comparisons, even in relatively small binaries (e.g. 1,000,000 comparisons for 2 binaries with 1,000 functions each), it is ever more important to correctly classify as many as possible. For instance, in our neural network testing phase, we generated the results seen in Table 1. This table represents the raw number of function comparisons the neural network of BINDNN was able to classify from a set of functions not previously disclosed to the system. We see that although it was able to correctly classify over 93% of the 2,166,126 function comparisons, it still ends up misclassifying 146,976 comparisons. This number of misclassifications severely reduces the ability of the system to aid an analyst in reverse engineering. For instance, if we incorrectly say that two functions are the same, the analyst may not see important information. If we incorrectly say that the same two functions are different, then we waste their time.

To better understand how we can improve these misclassifications, we analyze the distribution of the confidence scores assigned to the comparisons by the neural network. In Fig. 5, we see the distribution of confidence scores the network

---

[3] This complicates the process of deciding when BinDiff has correctly or incorrectly identified a function. Our process for making this decision required that we first provide BinDiff with unstripped binaries, where is would successfully match all functions via name hashing, then save the effective address of the two functions it matched. Using these effective addresses, we were then able to verify matches made by BinDiff on the stripped binaries.

Table 1. Confusion matrix for the LSTM.

	Predicted NO	Predicted YES
Actual NO	1097555	52393
Actual YES	94583	921595

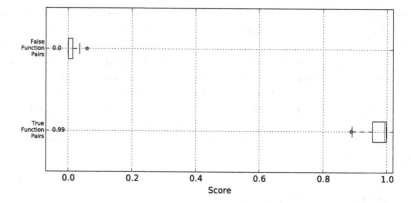

Fig. 5. Score distribution by class. The score distribution is very highly weighted for its respective class. This indicates that when the network correctly classifies a function comparison, it does so with extremely high belief.

gives when provided with a true pair of matching instruction sequences and a false pair. We see that confidence scores given to true pairs are extraordinarily high, with a median of 0.99. Likewise, the score for the false pairs are very low, with a median of 0.0. This indicates that if the network is given two instruction sequences for the same source code function, and if it successfully identifies them as a match, then it will do so with extremely high belief. This indication leads us to believe that varying the threshold for detecting functions is an important part of our system.

Configuring the Confidence Threshold. The confidence threshold (introduced in Sect. 3.3) allows an analyst to adjust the sensitivity of BINDNN when detecting function matches. This is useful in setting the number of acceptable false matches that may occur when comparing the functions from two different binaries. If the threshold is set too high, we may miss a large number of detectable function matches, and if it is set too low, there may be too many false matches for the results to be useful. We found that, for our system, the optimal threshold value changes according to the compiler, compiler optimization level, and architecture. Hence, the threshold value should remain as a tunable parameter in BINDNN. To determine the optimal threshold values for our tests, we looked at the relationship between this threshold and the average number of functions identified for both true matches and false matches.

We studied this relationship for 3 configurations of the program binaries, as seen in Figs. 6, 7, and 8. We see that with an increase in threshold, the number

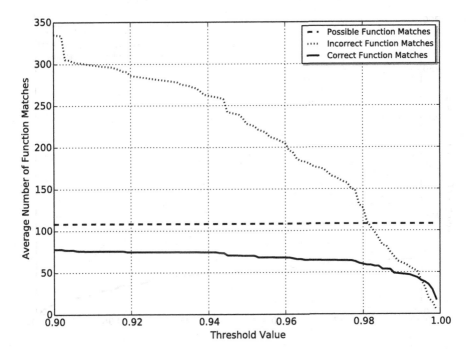

Fig. 6. Threshold analysis for compiler optimization level variations. Although a threshold value of 0.94 gives us (on average) the best coverage of the matchable functions, it still causes the system to incorrectly identify function matches at over 2 times the rate of correct matches. There are some situations where this might be acceptable, however, in our evaluation we chose a threshold that would provide similar results to BinDiff.

of false matches decreases at a much higher rate than the true matches. We saw indication of this in Fig. 5, as the median and mean of the network's scores for true matches was very close to 1. As such, it appears that when the network correctly classifies a pair of instruction sequences as from the same source code function, it does so with very high belief. This allows us to increase the threshold to even out the true matches and false matches. Increasing the threshold does reduce the total number of true matches found by BINDNN, but it greatly increases the confidence for the matches it does find. In our tests, we choose to use threshold values that will allow approximately one false match for every true match, as this provides the most comparable results to BinDiff.

Test Environment. The machine we used to train, test, and ran the tool on used Ubuntu 14.04. It has an Intel Xeon E5-2630 clocked at 2.30 GHz and 32 GB of memory. We installed an EVGA GeForce GTX TITAN X graphic card to be used by the network model into the computer. It has 12 GB of memory clocked at 7010 MHz and has 3072 CUDA Cores clocked at 1127 MHz.

On this machine, when training the network we saw it average approximately 65000 s (18 h) per epoch. This means 10 epochs took a little over 1 week. When

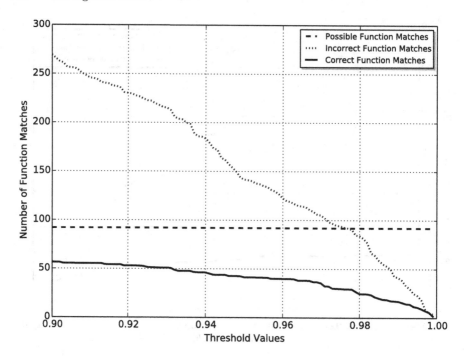

Fig. 7. Threshold analysis for architecture changes. We see the best correct function matches coverage without unnecessarily increasing incorrect matches at a threshold value of 0.92. This time we notice that also at this value the number of incorrect matches starts to decrease at a significantly higher rate than the true matches. Hence, we find we are able to hold a very low false positive rate at a high threshold.

actually using the network after it has been trained in the tool, we only have to consider how long on average it takes to process 1 sample and how many control function representations are in our control set. On average we saw each sample take less than a second, and about 10 s for 2500 samples. This means if we were analyzing two binaries with a 1,000 functions each, we would expect BINDNN to complete its process in approximately an hour.

4.3   Resilience to Optimization Differences

We perform a case study to test the ability of both systems when matching functions from binaries compiled with the same compiler, but different compiler optimization levels. Specifically, we use binaries that were compiled with gcc on x86 using optimization levels O2 and O3. In Fig. 9, we see the number of correct and incorrect function matches for both BINDNN and BinDiff for the shortest (by function count) 80 binaries in our test set. We chose the 80 shortest binaries for the sake of presentations; generally the results were comparable across the entire data set. The two systems have similar results, however, BinDiff generally outperforms BINDNN in this test. We also see that both methods produce low

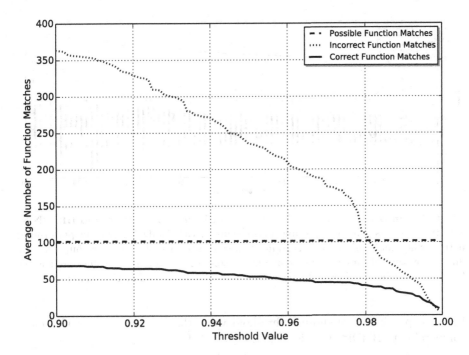

Fig. 8. Threshold analysis for compiler and compiler optimization level changes. This time again we see optimal coverage around 0.92, however, the average number of incorrect matches is still rather high. Although, this time there is a substantial increase in the rate at which the incorrect matches start to fall off around 0.975.

false positive rates, and the union of their correct matches provides a significant increase in correct matches. Specifically, we see an average increase of 45.7% for BinDiff and 66.3% for BINDNN. This indicates that using the two methods together creates an even more effective solution.

We can infer from the results, that although there is change in the assembly code structure, it still has parts similar enough for BinDiff to successfully match the functions. Although BINDNN could detect as many or more function matches as BinDiff from these two binaries, it cannot do this without increasing the number of false matches by a substantial amount. For instance, recall the relationship between the threshold and true and false positive rates, in Fig. 6. We see that a threshold value of 0.94 will match, on average, approximately 70% of all possible function matches. However, it will also increase the number of false positives by a substantial amount. Even so, there are situations in which this would be acceptable practice. For instance, if an analyst was looking for shared functions between two malware applications compiled with different optimization levels, a number of false matches would still be acceptable, as that will still be better for the analyst than manually comparing each function to each other.

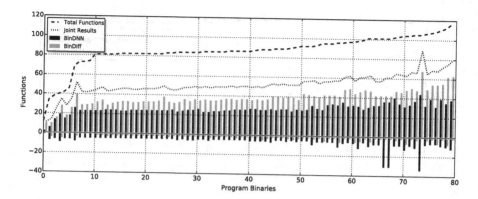

Fig. 9. Optimization level resilience comparison with BinDiff and BinDNN.
The two systems have comparable performance (with BinDiff generally performing better) when matching functions from binaries compiled with the same compiler, but different optimization levels, i.e. gcc -O2 and gcc -O3. The positive values are correct functions matches; whereas, the negative values are incorrect function matches.

In our experiment, we chose a threshold value that provides the results most comparable to BinDiff. In this case, that was 0.993.

4.4 Resilience to Architecture and Optimization Differences

We create another configuration of program binaries to determine the effectiveness at which BinDNN and BinDiff are able to match functions from binaries compiled for different architectures. The binaries we used in this experiment were compiled with gcc -O0 for x86 and with gcc -O3 for arm. When determining the threshold BinDNN should use, we consult the relationship between the threshold and the classification rates, as seen in Fig. 7. Notably, we could choose a value close to 0.92 to obtain the most coverage of the entire binary without unnecessarily increasing the false positives. However, in order to generate comparable results with BinDiff and across experiments, we again choose a high threshold value. This time we use 0.991.

In Fig. 10, we see a comparison of the number of correct and incorrect function matches for BinDNN and BinDiff on the programs compiled across architectures. Again, we only show the results for the 80 shortest (by function count) binaries for presentation reasons, and the results for the longer programs are comparable. This time we see that BinDNN was still able to successfully match a number of functions across the programs, whereas BinDiff does not perform as well.

These results show the weakness of systems like BinDiff, which rely on graph isomorphic methods. Since the structure of assembly code for the two programs is substantially different, the control graphs end up being different, causing these methods to fail. Even though BinDNN uses instruction sequences, and these binaries use different instructions (as they are on different architectures), our

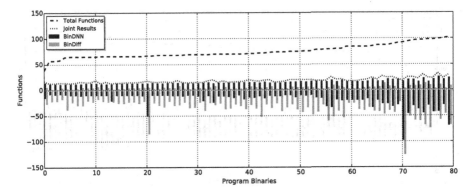

Fig. 10. Architecture resilience comparison with BinDiff and BINDNN. When matching functions from binaries compiled across architectures, BINDNN vastly outperforms BinDiff. These binaries were compiled with different optimization levels (O0 and O3), and on two different architectures (arm and x86). The positive values are correct functions matches; whereas, the negative values are incorrect function matches.

system can still find function matches. This is due to the nature of the deep neural network. It was able to develop approximation functions during the training phase that can map instruction sequences across architectures to the same source code function. Additionally, by reducing the threshold, BINDNN can find more true function matches at the cost of adding in additional false matches, as was the case with the previous optimization level experiment. Additionally, we see that the union of both method's results increases BINDNN's results by 26% on average (and BinDiff's by nearly 190%). However, this would also increase BINDNN's false positive rate by substantial amount. Hence, in this use case, it is actually detrimental to combine the results of both methods, and is instead better to only use BINDNN's classifications.

4.5   Resilience to Compiler and Optimization Differences

We use a different configuration to analyze the ability of BINDNN and BinDiff to detect function matches in program compiled with both a different compiler and different compiler optimization levels. Specifically, we use programs compiled for x86 with icc -O2 and gcc -O3. In Fig. 8, we see the relationship between the threshold and classification rate. As with the multiple architecture experiment, we see that BINDNN provides the best coverage around 0.92, without increasing the number of false positives an excessive amount. However, there are still an average of approximately 330 incorrectly matched functions with this threshold. We see an increase in the rate at which the incorrect matches fall off as the threshold value approaches and passes 0.98. Therefore, it is beneficial to select a threshold value greater than 0.99, we find an appropriate value to be 0.997.

Figure 11 shows the comparison of function matches for BINDNN and BinDiff. Once again, we only show the results for the shortest 80 functions to make

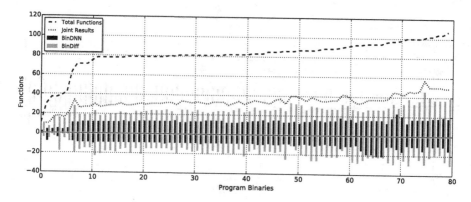

Fig. 11. Compiler and compiler optimization level resilience comparison.
Both BINDNN and BinDiff struggle to keep their incorrect matches low when working
on programs compiled on `icc -02` and `gcc -03`. However, we do see that BINDNN is
able to a number of function matches, whereas BinDiff cannot. The positive values are
correct functions matches, and the negative values are incorrect function matches.

presentation more clear. The results were comparable across the entire data set.
In this experiment, we see that both BINDNN and BinDiff struggle to maintain
a low number of incorrect matches. We see that generally BinDiff has a higher
true positive and false positive rate than BINDNN. However, we see that the
union of both method's results provides an overall increase for both systems.
Once again indicating that an ensemble use between these or similar methods
may be effective.

4.6   Network Limitations

We can further improve the classification rate of the network—currently at
93%—by tuning the architecture, feature vectors, and hyperparameters. However, tuning alone is insufficient as some of the network's inaccuracy is due to
missing information. For example, we currently remove the arguments for each
of the instructions when constructing the feature vectors. We do this because
our network represents functions as sequences of indices into a global vocabulary.
If we were to naively include each of the instructions along with their possible
arguments, the size of the vocabulary would quickly become intractably large.
While this makes our approach more tractable, it also reduces the fidelity of
the function representations passed to the network. We plan to explore this area
more in future work.

5   Conclusions

In this paper we proposed and evaluated BINDNN, a new method for determining if two assembly instruction sequences originate from the same source code.

Our method allows an analyst to prioritize their limited resources by filtering large swaths of code, removing functions that have been previously analyzed, and locating functions present in other malicious programs. We overcome the challenges posed by differences in compiler, compiler optimization level, and target architecture by framing the problem as natural language processing. This framing enables us to leverage deep learning as the foundation for resilient function matching. Our evaluation shows BINDNN is more effective than current state-of-the-art tools (e.g., BinDiff) when matching functions across binaries compiled for different architectures.

BINDNN's greatest strength is its ability to augment, not supplant, existing approaches. Indeed, we show that when BINDNN is combined with BinDiff we boost performance for both methods. For example, we saw an improvement of 46% over using BinDiff alone when comparing functions compiled at different optimization levels. While such ensemble methods are effective, we must consider the relative strengths and weaknesses of each method. Take the cross-architecture results for example; combining BINDNN and BinDiff had little effect as BinDiff's false positive rate was too high.

As the demand for binary analysis rises so too will the need for triage techniques. Put simply, there are more malicious binaries introduced every month than analysts can reverse engineer. However, no technique is a panacea. BINDNN represents an important step in addressing the limitations of previous approaches and provides analysts with another tool in their fight against malware.

Acknowledgments. Research was sponsored by the Army Research Laboratory and was accomplished under Cooperative Agreement Number W911NF-13-2-0045 (ARL Cyber Security CRA). The views and conclusions contained in this document are those of the authors and should not be interpreted as representing the official policies, either expressed or implied, of the Army Research Laboratory or the U.S. Government. The U.S. Government is authorized to reproduce and distribute reprints for Government purposes notwithstanding any copyright notation here on.

Additionally, this material is based upon work supported by the National Science Foundation under Grant Nos. CNS-1228700 and CNS-1064900. Any opinions, findings, and conclusions or recommendations expressed in this material are those of the author(s) and do not necessarily reflect the views of the National Science Foundation.

A   Network Architecture

We design what is essentially an 8 layer network. The first layer is an embedding layer, this layer learns mappings for global vocabulary indexes into dense vectors. This layer is especially important for our first goal, the ability to recognize similar instructions that have different names. This layer allows the model to more easily map instructions that appear to have similar meaning to real values that are close.

Next, we pass the output from the embedding layer to two 1 dimensional convolutional layers. The convolutional layers each use 64 kernels with filter size 3. These layers allows the model to learn small groups of instructions. This allows the model to classify not only on the exact sequence of instructions that makes up the function representation, but also the sequence of meaningful instruction subsequences. From the convolutional layers we downscale by a factor of 2 by using Max Pooling.

Next, we use two long-short term memory (LSTM) layers with 70 cells each. These layers are the heart of the model. They learn the temporal relationships between instructions. By using LSTM layers, we are better able to overcome the vanishing or exploding gradient problem associated with standard RNNs [2], which in turn allows us to more easily learn long-term dependencies within the functions.

Lastly, we incorporate dropout throughout the model to help it resist overfitting. Specifically, we include 25% dropout in-between the two convolutional layers, and we include 50% dropout between the final two dense layers. The model also uses a sigmoid activation function. We provide a diagram of the network architecture in Fig. 12.

Fig. 12. Network architecture. We use an 8 layer deep learning model. It is primarily built around the LSTM layers, which develop the temporal relationships between instructions. The CNN layers vastly increase the stability of the model while also aiding in preventing it from overfitting. The DNN layers at the end bring everything from the previous layers together in a classification value stating if it was given matching function representations

References

1. Bao, T., Burket, J., Woo, M., Turner, R., Brumley, D.: Byteweight: learning to recognize functions in binary code. In: USENIX Security Symposium (2014)
2. Bengio, Y., Simard, P., Frasconi, P.: Learning long-term dependencies with gradient descent is difficult. IEEE Trans. Neural Netw. **5**(2), 157–166 (1994)
3. Bourquin, M., King, A., Robbins, E.: Binslayer: accurate comparison of binary executables. In: Proceedings of the 2nd ACM SIGPLAN Program Protection and Reverse Engineering Workshop, p. 4. ACM (2013)
4. Ciregan, D., Meier, U., Schmidhuber, J.: Multi-column deep neural networks for image classification. In: 2012 IEEE Conference on Computer Vision and Pattern Recognition (CVPR), pp. 3642–3649. IEEE (2012)
5. Collobert, R., Weston, J.: A unified architecture for natural language processing: deep neural networks with multitask learning. In: Proceedings of the 25th International Conference on Machine Learning, pp. 160–167. ACM (2008)
6. Dullien, T., Rolles, R.: Graph-based comparison of executable objects (English version). SSTIC **5**, 1–3 (2005)
7. Duygulu, P., Barnard, K., Freitas, J.F.G., Forsyth, D.A.: Object recognition as machine translation: learning a lexicon for a fixed image vocabulary. In: Heyden, A., Sparr, G., Nielsen, M., Johansen, P. (eds.) ECCV 2002. LNCS, vol. 2353, pp. 97–112. Springer, Heidelberg (2002). doi:10.1007/3-540-47979-1_7

8. Egele, M., Woo, M., Chapman, P., Brumley, D.: Blanket execution: dynamic similarity testing for program binaries and components. In: USENIX Security Symposium (2014)

9. Gao, D., Reiter, M.K., Song, D.: BinHunt: automatically finding semantic differences in binary programs. In: Chen, L., Ryan, M.D., Wang, G. (eds.) ICICS 2008. LNCS, vol. 5308, pp. 238–255. Springer, Heidelberg (2008). doi:10.1007/978-3-540-88625-9_16

10. Gers, F.A., Schmidhuber, J., Cummins, F.: Learning to forget: continual prediction with lstm. Neural Comput. **12**(10), 2451–2471 (2000)

11. Hex-Rays. Hex-rays: IDA pro disassembler and debugger (2016). https://www.hex-rays.com/products/ida/

12. Hochreiter, S., Schmidhuber, J.: Long short-term memory. Neural Comput. **9**(8), 1735–1780 (1997)

13. Jacobson, E.R., Rosenblum, N., Miller, B.P.: Labeling library functions in stripped binaries. In: Proceedings of the 10th ACM SIGPLAN-SIGSOFT Workshop on Program Analysis for Software Tools, pp. 1–8. ACM (2011)

14. Kingma, D., Ba, J.: Adam: a method for stochastic optimization (2014). arXiv preprint arXiv:1412.6980

15. Lageman, N., Lindsey, M., Glodek, W.: Detecting malicious android applications from runtime behavior. In: Military Communications Conference, MILCOM 2015–2015 IEEE, pp. 324–329. IEEE (2015)

16. LeCun, Y., Bottou, L., Bengio, Y., Haffner, P.: Gradient-based learning applied to document recognition. Proc. IEEE **86**(11), 2278–2324 (1998)

17. Mikolov, T., Yih, W.-T., Zweig, G.: Linguistic regularities in continuous space word representations. In: HLT-NAACL, pp. 746–751 (2013)

18. Mukkamala, S., Janoski, G., Sung, A.: Intrusion detection using neural networks and support vector machines. In: Proceedings of the 2002 International Joint Conference on Neural Networks, IJCNN 2002, vol. 2, pp. 1702–1707. IEEE (2002)

19. Pontil, M., Verri, A.: Support vector machines for 3D object recognition. IEEE Trans. Pattern Anal. Mach. Intell. **20**(6), 637–646 (1998)

20. Rosenblum, N.E., Zhu, X., Miller, B.P., Hunt, K.: Learning to analyze binary computer code. In: AAAI, pp. 798–804 (2008)

21. Saad, S., Traore, I., Ghorbani, A., Sayed, B., Zhao, D., Lu, W., Felix, J., Hakimian, P.: Detecting P2P botnets through network behavior analysis and machine learning. In: 2011 Ninth Annual International Conference on Privacy, Security and Trust (PST), pp. 174–180. IEEE (2011)

22. Sainath, T.N., Vinyals, O., Senior, A., Sak, H.: Convolutional, long short-term memory, fully connected deep neural networks. In: 2015 IEEE International Conference on Acoustics, Speech and Signal Processing (ICASSP), pp. 4580–4584. IEEE (2015)

23. Shin, E.C.R., Song, D., Moazzezi, R.: Recognizing functions in binaries with neural networks. In: 24th USENIX Conference on Security Symposium (SEC). USENIX Association, Washington, DC (2015)

24. Sinclair, C., Pierce, L., Matzner, S.: An application of machine learning to network intrusion detection. In: Proceedings of 15th Annual Computer Security Applications Conference (ACSAC 1999), pp. 371–377. IEEE (1999)

25. Werbos, P.J.: Backpropagation through time: what it does and how to do it. Proc. IEEE **78**(10), 1550–1560 (1990)

26. Zynamics: zynamics BinDiff (2016). https://www.zynamics.com/bindiff.html

TZ-SSAP: Security-Sensitive Application Protection on Hardware-Assisted Isolated Environment

Yanhong He[1,2(✉)], Xianyi Zheng[1,2], Ziyuan Zhu[1,2], and Gang Shi[1,2]

[1] Institute of Information Engineering,
Chinese Academy of Sciences, Beijing, China
{heyanhong,zhengxianyi,zhuziyuan,shigang}@iie.ac.cn
[2] University of Chinese Academy of Sciences, Beijing, China

Abstract. In the current operating systems (OS), the kernel has complete access to and control over all system sources. However, there are many secure vulnerabilities in kernel because it has the large code base and attack surfaces. Thus, an attacker can attack sensitive applications running on OS by exploiting kernel vulnerabilities. Unfortunately, there are various shortcomings for the existing applications protection mechanisms, such as ignoring the integrity of kernel code, relying on special compiler and et al. In this paper, we have proposed a security-sensitive application (*SSApp*) protection mechanism called *TZ-SSAP* on TrustZone enabled platforms. *TZ-SSAP* introduces four protection modules altogether to provide a safe executable environment for *SSApp* during the system is running. The first one is the *SSApp* protection module which takes advantage of the existing page table mechanism to protect the integrity of code executed by *SSApp* as well as the confidentiality and integrity of *SSApp*'s data. The second is the security arrangement which prevents an attacker from compromising *SSApp* protection module by depriving the kernel authority of the *ROS* (Rich OS). The third is the page table update verification module in *TOS* (Trusted OS) which traps the update of page table in *ROS* and handles with it based on the predefined security policies. The last one is the security policies module which prevents an attacker from tampering the code and data of *SSApp*. At the same time, it keeps the memory of *SSApp* from an attacker to guarantee the confidentiality of critical data. We have evaluated our prototype on a simulation environment by using ARM FastModel and presented our implementation on a real development by using ARM CoreTile Express A9x4. Our security analysis and experimental results show that *TZ-SSAP* can ensure the *SSApp* execute as expected even if the kernel is compromised.

Keywords: Security-sensitive application · *TZ-SSAP* · TrustZone

1 Introduction

As is known to all, applications are managed by OS (operating system), which always use large monolithic kernels that have complete access to and control over all system resources, including memory management, process scheduling and communication,

© ICST Institute for Computer Sciences, Social Informatics and Telecommunications Engineering 2017
R. Deng et al. (Eds.): SecureComm 2016, LNICST 198, pp. 538–556, 2017.
DOI: 10.1007/978-3-319-59608-2_30

device management, file management and so on [1]. A large amount of security defense systems are implemented based on the view that the OS is the trusted root.

However, there is no denying that there are many secure vulnerabilities [2–4] due to the large attack surfaces existed in the current OS kernel. This leads to the result that the application running on the OS is no longer safe since an attacker can exploit kernel vulnerabilities to escalate privilege or execute a rootshell. For example, attacker can tamper the kernel code or insert some malicious code through the data segment via PTMA [5] attack which can modify the attribute of physical pages by modifying the content in page table entry. Once the kernel is compromised, attacker can control the kernel to compromise applications. For example, it can manipulate the return value of system services to attack applications, which is named Iago attack [6]. Furthermore, attackers can freely acquire all the sensitive information belonging to security-sensitive applications by accessing main memory or intercepting the control or data flow of the applications, which can be achieved by the address mapping manipulation attacks [7], such as mapping overlap attack, double mapping attack, mapping reorder and mapping release attack. Even worse, the kernel has become an equally attractive attacked target in the recent years. It is in urgent need of protection mechanism to make security-sensitive application remain safe even if the OS is compromised.

Previous research about application protection mechanism widely relies on hypervisor [14, 15, 17, 18]. Most of them use extended page table to provide an isolated environment for sensitive applications. When the application interacts with the OS, hypervisor has to verify the legitimacy of the operation. However, they ignore the integrity of kernel code. Despite the fact that Virtual Ghost [19] interposes a thin hardware abstraction layer to intercept instruction of kernel which can prevent unauthorized code from executing, it still have drawbacks. For example, it depends on new instruction set and compiler and all operating system software has to be compiled again.

In this paper, we have proposed a secure framework named *TZ-SSAP* based on hardware-assisted environment provided by TrustZone technology. It provides a strong protection mechanism for security-sensitive applications (*SSApps*). Unlike previous protection mechanisms which need to establish an external page table to protect sensitive applications, our prototype does not modify the existing page table and our design is suitable to the current commercial OSes. *TZ-SSAP* traps all updates of the page table in the *ROS* (Rich OS). The result is that the *ROS* has no right to tamper the page table limited to its write protection mechanism. And each update of page table all follow those rules: Firstly, physical pages of code and static data in kernel space is mapped read only; and the rest of data pages is mapped non-executable forever. Second, the physical pages belonging to *SSApp*'s user space will never be mapped to the normal applications, vice versa. In the end, kernel stack of *SSApps* will be mapped read only when their state switches from running to other during process scheduling.

To summarize, we make the following contributions:

- We enforce our security policies based on the existing page table mechanism in the current OSes without extending page table, which has little modification to the *ROS*. Therefore, our prototype is suitable to the existing commercial OSes.

- We secure the execution environment for *SSApps*. Our design framework ensure the integrity of all the code and the kernel static data used by *SSApp*. In other words, the *SSApp* will always remain safe even if the *ROS* is compromised or even crashed. Furthermore, *TZ-SSAP* can guarantee the confidentiality of *SSApp*'s data because it prevents malicious process from accessing the memory of *SSApp*.
- *TZ-SSAP* does not need to encrypt and hash any application pages which is accessed when the *ROS* is running. And it also does not need to validate the legitimacy of the parameter when it interacts with the *ROS*.
- *TZ-SSAP* is safer than previous work which relies on hypervisor. It has been implemented in the hardware-assisted isolated environment, so it is enough safe to defense these attacks from the malicious *ROS*.

In the next section, we introduce something about application and our experiment platform. Section 3 gives our threat model and some assumptions of *TZ-SSAP*. Then Sect. 4 describes the *TZ-SSAP* design while Sect. 5 presents its implementation mode. Section 6 discusses the security and performance of *TZ-SSAP*. Finally, we also describe the related works at present in Sect. 7 and give a conclusion in Sect. 8.

2   Background

2.1   Application Analysis

There is no doubt that applications are made up of codes and data, which is illustrated in Fig. 1. The first one states the implementation of the functionality it absolutely needs while the last one is the carrier of sensitive information and the direction of control flow. Therefore, it can ensure the security of applications if we can guarantee the safe of its codes and data.

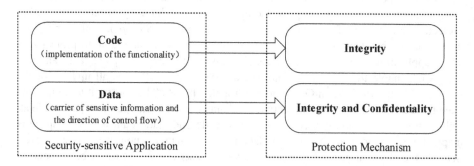

Fig. 1. Application architecture

Each application's code consists of three parts: basic code written by developer, the standard library code and the kernel code when it is in kernel mode. It is clear that the basic code is private and the kernel code must be shared with other applications. As for standard library code, it will be shared with other applications when compiled dynamically, and will be private like basic code while compiled statically.

For application's data, it consists of two parts: the kernel data and the user data. The kernel data contains the dynamic data in application's kernel stack and the static data. Meanwhile, the static data is initialized when the OS starts and shared with other applications, such as the system call table and the exception vectors table. Despite the fact that each process has unique kernel stack to store dynamic data produced by application during the run time, the data in kernel stack still can be accessed by other processes because all processes share the same kernel page tables. Moreover, the user data belonging to application is private as the basic code of application since they are stored in the user space which is separated from other applications normally by OS.

2.2 ARM TrustZone

ARM TrustZone [10, 11] technology is a set of security extensions first added to ARMv6 processors. Its architecture is illustrated in Fig. 2. Based on hardware logic present in AMBA bus fabric, peripherals and processors, it partitions the computing platform into two execution domains: *SW* (the Secure World) and *NW* (the Normal World) and partitions system resources into two parts: the non-secure resources and the secure resources. The OS running in *NW* is named *ROS* while *TOS* is running in *SW*. *ROS* can only access non-secure resources whereas *TOS* can see all resources. *TZ-SSAP* uses this feature to manage the page table mechanism in *ROS*.

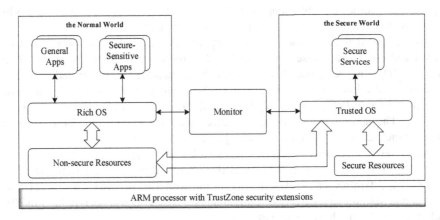

Fig. 2. TrustZone architecture

To control the context switch between the two worlds, a special processor mode, known as the monitor mode, is added by TrustZone. The monitor mode resides in *SW*, and maintains the processor state during the world switch. To trigger the entry to monitor mode, *ROS* or *TOS* can execute a Secure Monitor Call (*SMC*) instruction. Therefore, *TZ-SSAP* can switch between *ROS* and *TOS* through *SMC* instruction. Monitor can acquire the current context of the domain through the Non-secure (NS) bit from the Secure Configuration Register (SCR). That's to say, monitor can access *NW* if the NS bit is set. *TZ-SSAP* takes advantage of this to save the coprocessor CP15 of *NW* when it acquires the context of data abort exception.

Our software is the OV [13], which is the first open source and free implementation for ARM TrustZone. When the system is power on, it starts from BootROM security. Once the *TOS* is running, it will establish security perimeter and perform key operations such as decrypting *NW* OS images. And before activating *NW* bootloader, keys, media and other assets are fully protected.

3   Threat Model and Assumption

We briefly describe our threat model and assumption in this section. Our goal is to protect *SSApps* by guaranteeing the integrity of *SSApps'* code and data as well as the confidentiality of *SSApps'* data. We assume the *SSApp* has strong sense to protect its derived data using encryption techniques, for example, it can encrypt the file contents before writing to disk, and use existing secure I/O path schemes like [8, 9] to protect I/O data which used by peripheral devices, such as the fingerprint reader and keyboard. Thus, attacks against the *SSApp* itself are not in our consideration. We assume that *SSApp's* base code is bug-free, thus to say, it will be carefully designed and tested in order to achieve high confidence in its own security.

Besides, we also assume that *SSApp* is static-compiled. In other words, *SSApp* will not share the standard library code with other processes, which can avoid malicious applications attacking it by tampering the standard library code. And the LKM (Loadable Kernel Module) is outside the scope of the current work.

We assume that the hardware implements the TrustZone extensions, and can be trusted with no Trojan-Horse circuits and no bus traffic interception and so on. Both *ROS* and *TOS* have been loaded securely which is guaranteed by the trusted boot. The worst thing of all is that it cannot guarantee the security of *ROS* during its run time since the kernel in *ROS* is vulnerable because of those discovered vulnerabilities, such as [5–7]. The attacker may use existing attack methods to damage *SSApp*, such as PTMA attack, Iago attack and address mapping manipulation attacks.

Moreover, the security-sensitive feature varies with the user. In this paper, we assume that the user has established a whitelist about *SSApps* that should be protected by *TZ-SSAP*. To prevent attacker modifying the whitelist, the user uses the *TOS* to encrypt and hash it in a relatively safe environment. And *TOS* will decrypt the whitelist and check the hash whenever it starts.

4   TZ-SSAP Design

TZ-SSAP is implemented on TrustZone which provides a hardware-assisted isolation environment. According to application analysis in background, we can know that *SSApp* consists of code and data. In the following, we put forward the *SSApp* protection module in accordance with the characteristics of *SSApp's* code and data. Then we present the security arrangement including page table update and process schedule in *ROS*. Afterwards, we propose how *TZ-SSAP* traps all updates of the page table and the

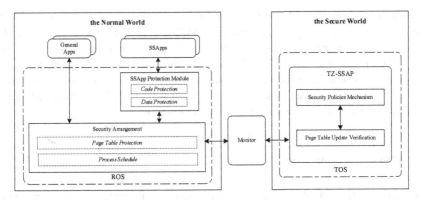

Fig. 3. TZ-SSAP system architecture

security policies mechanism that *TZ-SSAP* uses them to verify the operation of the kernel in *ROS*. *TZ-SSAP* prototype as illustrated in Fig. 3.

4.1 SSApp Protection Module

Code Protection. *SSApp* is static-compiled according to assumption. Thus, it only contain the private code and the kernel code. The private code will not be changed since it has become an executable file through compiling and linking. However, it is different for the kernel code. In Linux, administrator may load LKM due to some special requirements. In that case, additional code will be injected into the kernel at run time. For convenience, we do not take LKM into consideration. Therefore, the kernel code will remain unchanged during the system operation as well as the private code.

In order to protect integrity of the code executed by *SSApp*, *TZ-SSAP* maps all physical pages of code to read-only. Meanwhile, it must make sure that there won't be any writable map of them to prevent attacker tampering them. Those can be achieved through the page table management mechanism, which defines the virtual to physical address mapping and the access permissions of virtual memory in *ROS*. That's to say, *TZ-SSAP* modifies the access permissions of those physical pages so that they are write-protected and traps all updates of page table to avoid writable mapping of them.

Data Protection. According to application analysis, the user data is private in the whole operation period. Therefore, the integrity and confidentiality of the user data can be guaranteed as long as *TZ-SSAP* prevents malicious process from accessing them. We know that the memory can be accessed by OS only if it is mapped to the virtual address space. Therefore, *TZ-SSAP* can keep the *SSApp*'s user data from attacker by preventing double mapping the memory holding *SSApp*'s user data to general applications.

TZ-SSAP takes different measures to protect the integrity and security of *SSApp*'s kernel data. For static data, *TZ-SSAP* protects it by mapping its physical pages to read-only as the kernel code. And for dynamic data in kernel stack, it cannot be write-protected since it may be changed when *SSApp*'s process is running. Similarly, it cannot prevent other process accessing them because they share the same kernel page tables. For those reasons, *TZ-SSAP* makes the *SSApp*'s kernel stack to be write-protected when the process's state switches from running to other during process scheduling. As a result, other process cannot tamper it via kernel page table, which can ensure the integrity of *SSApp*'s control flow in kernel mode.

4.2 Security Arrangement

Page Table Protection. As mentioned above, both code protection and data protection of *SSApp* are based on the page table management mechanism which is managed by the kernel in OS. When a new process is created, kernel establishes a new set of page tables for it. And after that, the kernel always keep updating it whenever process wants to change its map, such as applying for new physical pages, releasing old physical pages or modifying the attribute in page table entry. Unfortunately, because of the kernel ability to manage page table management, attacker can make *SSApp* protection module be out of control by attacking kernel through privilege escalation or PTMA attack.

To guarantee the security of *SSApp* protection module, we have to protect the page table management mechanism. Moreover, page tables are also in the form of physical pages in kernel. The updates of page table are normal memory writes which can be controlled by memory access permissions like code protection. And as described in background, *TOS* is capable of accessing the non-secure physical memory in *NW*. As a result, we replace kernel with *TZ-SSAP* to control the update of page tables. This can be achieved by modifying the access permissions of page tables to be read only in *ROS*. Besides, a great part of *TZ-SSAP* is realized in *SW*. Details are as follows.

In order to deprive the kernel's ability to update page tables, *TZ-SSAP* makes page tables of every process read-only once the process is scheduled into the *ROS* at the first time. Then *TZ-SSAP* intercepts the update of page tables through data abort whenever the kernel attempts to modify them. At that point, *TZ-SSAP* acquires the intention of kernel by decoding the instruction that generates the data abort exception in *ROS*. Furthermore, *TZ-SSAP* verifies the legitimacy of the instruction on the basis of the security policies. If it goes against any point of them, it will be rejected. On the opposite, *TZ-SSAP* will write the value to the corresponding address in *SW*.

Process Schedule. Trapping the update of page tables is critical to *TZ-SSAP*. Since *TZ-SSAP* completely makes page tables write-protected, the attacker can bypass *TZ-SSAP* through one possible method which is forging the whole page tables of process. In other words, attacker can forge a whole page table via rootkit and then set the base physical address of it to *TTBR0* (translation table base register 0) which stores the base address of page table in ARM Linux. On this occasion, *TZ-SSAP* will lose the ability to trap the update of fake page table since it not be write-protected by *TZ-SSAP*. As a result, attacker can steal the sensitive information and tamper the critical data structure or code of *SSApp* by double mapping *SSApp*'s physical page into fake page table.

To prevent these attack, *TZ-SSAP* must make sure that the value in *TTBR0* keep the same with which transferred to *TZ-SSAP* at the first time. *TZ-SSAP* enforces this policy by depriving the kernel from its own ability to set the value of *TTBR0* during the process scheduling. Once the kernel tries to schedule process, it must request *TZ-SSAP* for changing the value in *TTBR0*. In that case, *TZ-SSAP* can use this opportunity to verify the legitimacy of kernel operation in *ROS*.

4.3   Page Table Update Verification

TZ-SSAP gets the ability to update all page table of process running in the *ROS* since the physical pages of page table are write-protected. In order to verify the legitimacy of kernel operation, *TZ-SSAP* must get the content of the instruction that caused the fault. Then, *TZ-SSAP* decodes this instruction and retrieve it on the basis of the data abort exception context. Finally, *TZ-SSAP* takes action based on the result whether it goes against security policies mechanism. Security policies mechanism is described in Sect. 4.4 and implementation is described in Sect. 5.

4.4   Security Policies Mechanism

TZ-SSAP enforces the following policies for protecting the *SSApp* whenever the kernel attempts to update page table or schedule process.

- Write-protection. The access permissions of all process's page tables play an important role in *TZ-SSAP*. Not only physical pages of code and static data in kernel mode should be write-protected, but also all page tables should be non-writable in *ROS* at run time. Any writable maps of write-protected pages or operations changing the read only attribute of kernel space into writable should be prohibited.
- Double-mapping. It's important to make sure that any physical page of *SSApp* does not exist double-mapping to general applications. When the *SSApp* tries to map a new physical page to its address space, *TZ-SSAP* must guarantee that it does not exist virtual to physical mapping. In this way, we can easily keep security-sensitive data from attacker, which ensures the integrity and confidentiality of those data.
- Executable attribute. In order to prevent attacker from inserting some malicious code through its data area and then making it executable by attacks such as PTMA, operations that change those non-executable attribute to executable should be prohibited.
- Inherited attribute. It's clear that child process which is created by parent process belonging to *SSApp* is also security-sensitive, and the same with normal process. Any protection mechanism for parent process is still suitable for its child process.
- Share property. All *SSApp*s can share protected physical pages with each other. However, it should be rejected between *SSApp*s and general applications since it may damage protection mechanism.
- Zero clearing. Whenever *SSApp* requests physical page frames from the *ROS*, it's necessary to verify that all virtual to physical mappings for this frames have been removed. Afterwards, it cannot be neglected to clear the frame's contents since

malicious applications may have injected some threat thing. Moreover, *TZ-SSAP* also zero out the physical frame's contents when it's no longer needed by *SSApp*s.

5 Implementation

We have implemented *TZ-SSAP* on the ARM platform which supports TrustZone hardware extensions. In order to facilitate debugging, we used Fastmodel to emulate ARM Cotex-A15 in the beginning. Finally, we presented *TZ-SSAP* on a TrustZone-enabled development board ARM CoreTile Express A9x4 [12]. Our software experimental environment is Open Virtualization [13], which is the first open source and free implementation for ARM TrustZone.

5.1 Foundation Work of TZ-SSAP

Splitting Section Mapping. According to Sect. 4, we learn that *TZ-SSAP*'s design idea is mainly concentrated on write-protection method to deprive the kernel from its ability to update the page tables. Only under such circumstance can *TZ-SSAP* prevent malicious process from accessing the private physical pages of *SSApp* and tampering the share content in kernel space via damaging the page table mechanism. Unfortunately, the kernel space is mapped in section, which just use the first-level table and each entry of it consists of 1 MB blocks of memory in ARM-Linux OS. However, the user space is converted to small page mapping through the second-level table. In other words, the first-level descriptors contains the pointers to a second-level table for a small page, which consists of 4 KB blocks of memory, instead of the base address and translation properties for a section. Meanwhile, the page tables allocated by kernel are page-aligned small page, and the physical page of page tables must be mapped in kernel space to prevent unauthorized tampering with the user. Therefore, if *TZ-SSAP* makes the memory area where the page table information is stored read only through translation properties in first-level table, the 1 MB blocks of memory mapped by the entry will all become read-only. The trouble is that we cannot make sure the content stored in the 1 MB blocks of memory are page table information since all small pages are allocated dynamically. It may cause the system to crash if there are some dynamic data.

That problems described above can be solved by either one of two ways. First, we can aggregate the small page belonging to page tables of all process so that they are in a 1 MB blocks of memory. Only in this way can we make the 1 MB blocks of memory read-only through first-level descriptors. Second, we can change the section map into small page map in kernel space by modifying the kernel initialization code. In order to facilitate subsequent operation, *TZ-SSAP* directly change the map mode into small page and map the kernel code and static data to read only at the same time.

TZ-SSAP Interaction Between the ROS and TOS. In our implementation, *TZ-SSAP* uses *SMC* instruction to switch between *ROS* and *TOS* and passes parameters through general-purpose register. Specific implementation details are as follows. When switching from the *ROS* to *TOS*, *TZ-SSAP* uses ARM core register R0 to transfer the variable corresponding to the *SMC* handler while register R1 transfers the parameters that required by *SMC* handler. Examples as below.

```
register u32 r0 asm("r0") = CALL_TRUSTZONE_FAULT;
register u32 r1 asm("r1") = param;
```

The content CALL_TRUSTZONE_FAULT in register R0 indicates that *TOS* will invoke the function corresponding to CALL_TRUSTZONE_FAULT after monitor mode switch to *SW*. The content param in register R1 indicates the parameters that *SMC* handler in *TZ-SSAP* requires. When the number of parameters is greater than one, we can transfer the parameters via memory since *TOS* is able to access all physical memory including the source in *NW*. In other words, *TZ-SSAP* in *ROS* declares a parameter structure, and uses register R1 to transfer the physical base address of this structure. *TZ-SSAP* in *TOS* can acquire those parameters through mapping these physical address to its virtual address space.

The same goes with *TOS* switch to *ROS* when *TZ-SSAP* completed *SMC* handler.

Getting the Context of Data Abort Exception. It will generate a data abort exception whenever the kernel of *ROS* tries to update the page tables since they are read only. Next, the kernel saves the context of data abort exception and jumps to exception handler which has been set in the exception vector table. As a result, it will execute *SMC* instruction which has been added in the __do_kernel_fault() by *TZ-SSAP* to enter to monitor mode. Then the monitor saves the context of the *ROS* and restores the context of the *TOS*. Finally, *TZ-SSAP* invokes the *SMC* handler related to the parameters transferred by the *ROS*.

The context of the *ROS* does not contain the coprocessor CP15 because most of the CP15 register are banked in *NW* and *SW*. It's necessary for *TZ-SSAP* to access the coprocessor CP15 of *NW*. On one hand, *TZ-SSAP* has to get the value in *TTBR0* of *NW* to traverse the page table in *ROS*. On the other hand, *TZ-SSAP* has to set the value in *TTBR0* of *NW* due to it removes the ability to set *TTBR0* from kernel in *ROS* to prevent attacker from forging page tables. This can be achieved in monitor mode because monitor can access the coprocessor CP15 of *NW* when the *NS* bit in *SCR* is set. Pseudocode is as follows.

```
scr_nsbit_set        // set ns bit, NW
save_cp15_context
scr_nsbit_clear      // clear ns bit, SW
```

The procedures above proves that *TZ-SSAP* gets the context of *ROS* is the context of *SMC* exception instead of the context of the data abort exception. Therefore, we must transfer them to the *TOS* in the form of parameter relating to *SMC* exception in order to get the specific content of the instruction which generated the data abort.

In ARMv7, OS will invoke __dabt_svc assemble function when it generates data abort in kernel mode. Moreover, the __dabt_svc calls the svc_entry assemble function to save the context of data abort exception in stack in the form of global structure pt_regs in kernel firstly. As a result, *TZ-SSAP* introduces a global variable svc_dabt_sp to store the base address of the context in stack. *TZ-SSAP* in *TOS* can acquire the context of data abort exception in *ROS* by mapping svc_dabt_sp into its virtual address space. In order to get the instruction that has generated the data abort exception, *TZ-SSAP* must get the address of the instruction. Besides, the register *LR* is a special register which holds return link information. However, in ARMv7 architecture, the *LR* register is banked in supervisor mode and abort mode, which of them are named lr_svc and lr_abt. Despite the fact that the monitor has saved both lr_svc and lr_abt, the value in lr_abt is no longer the address to be restored since it has been used as a general register in abort mode after kernel saved it in abort stack. To solve this problem, *TZ-SSAP* in *ROS* changes the *CPSR* (the current program status register) mode field into abort mode through *CPS* (change processor state) instruction and then recovers lr_abt from the stack in __do_kernel_fault(). After doing it, *TZ-SSAP* changes the *ROS* mode into supervisor and executes *SMC* instruction to enter monitor mode.

5.2   Security Policies Implementation

It's obvious that our main work is to ensure page tables all write-protected and secure update at the same time. In our implementation, we built an array named ns_phy to store the information of physical pages in *ROS*, which is similar to physmap in TZ-RKP [21]. Each entry of ns_phy corresponds to a 4 KB physical page of *ROS*. The value of the entry is a 32 bits integrity that indicates the state of this physical page. Besides, ns_phy is initialized to zero by *TZ-SSAP* at beginning.

TZ-SSAP divides the physical pages into four types by using a flag which is the bits [1:0] in the value. The value format as illustrated in Fig. 4.

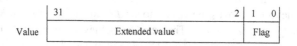

Fig. 4. Value format

– 0b00: Unmapped. The physical page is unmapped. The extended value is invalid.
– 0b01: Normal. The physical page is mapped by general applications and the extended value represents how many virtual page mappings the physical page has.

– 0b10: Protected. The physical page is mapped by *SSApps* or used by the code or static data of kernel. The extended value is the same with 0b01.
– 0b11: Page table. The physical page is mapped as the page table of each process. In this case, the front 20 bits of extended value marks the base address of its first-level page table.

Process Schedule. To prevent attacker from forging the whole page table, *TZ-SSAP* must guarantee that the value wrote to *TTBR0* is authorized during process schedule in *ROS*. And when the security-sensitive process is scheduled to go out, in other words, its state is switched from running to other, *TZ-SSAP* must map the kernel stack of *SSApp* read only to avoid being tampered by malicious process.

In *TOS*, *TZ-SSAP* establishes a read-black tree structure process_info to store critical information of running process in *ROS*.

```
struct process_info{
    struct rb_node rb_node;
    Type process_task;
    Type process_ttbr0;
    Type process_thread;
    ...
}
```

Variable process_task represents the base address of the data structure task_struct in *ROS*, which is the process descriptor in Linux system. Variable process_ttbr0 represents the base address of the process's first-level page table in *ROS*. There are four small pages as the first-level page table for each process owing to the size of each process virtual address space is four Gigabytes. What counts is the four physical pages of first-level page tables are continuous. It's capable of *TZ-SSAP* in *TOS* to get the physical address of the process's first-level page tables in *ROS* according to the base address and size of each page. As pages are aligned, *TZ-SSAP* uses the last bit of process_ttbr0 as flag to indicate whether the process is security-sensitive. Variable process_thread represents the virtual base address of the process's thread_union, which contains the process's kernel stack in *ROS*.

In *ROS*, the kernel will invoke switch_mm() function to complete the switch of process's address space by writing the physical base address of the first-level page table, belonging to the process to be executed, into *TTBR0*. The MMU (memory management unit) will convert the virtual address to physical address according to the value in *TTBR0*. To prevent attacker from forging the page table, *TZ-SSAP* inserts *SMC* instruction during the process is scheduled in *ROS*. Namely, *TZ-SSAP* updates *TTBR0* of *NW* instead of the kernel in *ROS*. When kernel invokes switch_mm() function, it will execute the *SMC* instruction and then the processor will switch to *SW*.

Algorithm 1. Process schdule

Input: *SMC parameter (process_task_n, process_ttbr0_n, process_task_pre ...)*
1: *NodeN = FindInProcess_info(process_task_n)*
2: **if** *NodeN != NULL* **then**
3:      *NodeNInfo = GetNodeInfo(NodeN)*
4:      *UnEqual0 = Compare(process_ttbr0_n, NodeNInfo.process_ttbr)*
5:      *UnEqual1 = Compare(process_ttbr0_n, NodeNInfo.process_thread)*
6:      **if** *UnEqual0 or UnEqual1* **then**
7:          *Record and Recover(NodeNInfo.process_ttbr, NodeNInfo.process_thread)*
8: **else**
9:      *InsertNodeInProcess_info*
10:      *PageTableWalk(process_ttbr0_n) and SetValueInNs_phy*
11:      *MakeReadOnly(page table)*
12:      *SetTTBR0(process_ttbr0_n)*
13: **endif**
14: *NodeP = FindInProcess_info(process_task_pre)*
15: **if** *NodeP ∈ SSApps*
16:      *MakeReadOnly(kernel stack)*
17: **endif**

Algorithm 1 is the *SMC* handler in *TZ-SSAP* when the process is scheduled by kernel in *ROS*. The `process_task_pre` is represented the process whose state will be non-running while the `process_task_n` will be scheduled to run in *ROS*.

Page Table Update. In ARM Linux, a data abort exception will be generated if the OS tries to access memory that it has no right to access it. As a result, the kernel will generate a data abort exception when it attempts to update page tables which is write-protected. To solve this exception, the kernel in *ROS* will call the corresponding exception handling function named `do_page_fault()`. The last function to be executed is `__do_kernel_fault()` because the virtual address that caused the data abort exception are in kernel space. In order to update the page table, *TZ-SSAP* inserts *SMC* instruction in the `__do_kernel_fault()` function of *ROS*. When the processor switches to *TZ-SSAP* through *SMC* instruction, it will invoke the *SMC* handler.

Algorithm 2. Page table update

Input: *SMC parameter (phy_base_addr....)*
1: *ttbr0 = GetTTBR0*
2: *context = GetContextOfDataAbort(phy_base_addr)*
3: *content = Decode(fault instruction)*
4: *Node = FindInProcess_info(ttbr0)*
5: *GetNodeInfo(Node)*
6: *Pa = VaToPa(GetDFAR)*
7: **if** *Pa* ∈ *FirstLevelPageTable* **then**
8:      *contentP = GetContent(Pa)*
9:      **if** *content is invalid* **then**
10:         *SetValueInNs_phy*
11:         *SetValueInPa(content)*
12:      **else**
13:         *VerifyWithSecurityPolicies(content, contentP)*
14:         **if** *authorized* **then**
15:            *SetValueInPa(content)*
16:         **else**
17:            *Record and Reject*
18:         **endif**
19:      **endif**
20: **else**
21:      *PaInfo = GetInfoInNs_phy(Pa)*
22:      **if** *(PaInfo* ∈ *page table) and (Pa* ∈ *CurrentProcess)*
23:         *VerifyWithSecurityPolicies(content, PaInfo)*
24:         **if** *authorized*
25:            *SetValueInPa(content)*
26:         **else**
27:            *Record and Reject*
28:         **endif**
29:      **endif**
30: **endif**

Algorithm 2 is the *SMC* handler in *TZ-SSAP* when kernel tries to update page table in *ROS*. The phy_base_addr is the base physical address of pt_regs which stores the context of data abort exception in *ROS*. When kernel tries to unmap a physical page, *TZ-SSAP* must change the value in ns_phy array to maintain consistency.

5.3   Performance Enhancement

One method that can improve performance is locality principle. During the process running, it may generate data abort exception successional because of page fault interrupt. Under this circumstances, it will always update page table entry located in one physical page. So *TZ-SSAP* can apply a variable `fault_addr_latest` to record the latest address which generated the data abort exception and mark its attribute to indicate the address belongs to the second-level page table in *ROS* or not. When the data abort exception is generated again next time, *TZ-SSAP* will compare the `fault_addr_latest` with the content in *DFAR* (the Data Fault Address Register). It will reduce some operations to get the content in `ns_phy` array if the `fault_addr_latest` and the value in *DFAR* are in the same physical page.

6 Evaluation

TZ-SSAP provides a safe execution environment for *SSApp* to ensure it executes as expected even if the kernel is compromised. It achieves that by protecting the integrity of *SSApp*'s control flow and data flow. During runtime, *TZ-SSAP* keeps the *SSApp*'s memory from attacker through inserting *SMC* instruction and depriving the kernel of *ROS* from its own ability to set *TTBR0* and update page table in *NW*. In that case, *TZ-SSAP* can enforce our security policies mechanism whenever it traps *SMC* exception from the kernel. As a result, *TZ-SSAP* can prevent the attacker from tampering the code executed by *SSApp* and stealing critical information of *SSApp*.

TZ-SSAP can keep *SSApp* from the PTMA attack because the update of page tables must obey the security policies. For example, when the attacker attempts to change the read only attribute into writable in page table entry via PTMA attack, *TZ-SSAP* will intercept and verify it on the basis of security policies. It's clear that it will be rejected due to write protection in security policies, and the same with executable attribute in page table entry. As a result, *TZ-SSAP* can prevent attacker from tampering kernel code directly because of write protection. Besides, *TZ-SSAP* also prevent attacker from executing unauthorized code which is inserted into kernel space through malicious process's data segment since it is non-executable.

TZ-SSAP can defense the Iago attack. There is no doubt that *TZ-SSAP* can prevent attacker from modifying the kernel code and the static data in kernel as well as the data in kernel stack of the *SSApps*. If the attacker tries to tamper those, it will generate a data abort exception. According to our implementation, *TZ-SSAP* will handle with this exception. At the beginning of the *SMC* hander in *TZ-SSAP*, it will verify whether the address generated the data abort exception belongs to the address range of current process's page table in *ROS*. *TZ-SSAP* will refuse to modify the content in the fault address if the operation is unauthorized.

What's more, *TZ-SSAP* can keep *SSApp* from the address mapping manipulation attacks. When *SSApp* requests physical page frames from *ROS*, *TZ-SSAP* will verify that there is not any virtual to physical mapping for this physical pages and zero out the content of this physical page. In additional, when general applications attempt to map new physical page, *TZ-SSAP* guarantees that the new physical page has not been mapped by *SSApp* or used as page table. Moreover, *TZ-SSAP* zeroes the physical page's content when changes its attribute as non-protected page.

To evaluate the security of *TZ-SSAP*, we built a malicious LKM that attempts to attack the TEST application which is designed as *SSApp* in our platform. The LKM tries to directly tamper the code and static data in kernel space, such as sys_-call_table. Also, LKM takes advantage of its privilege to write a fake value into *TTBR0*. Moreover, it also tries to double map the protected physical page into its virtual space. Firstly, we can get the base address of physical page in TEST through traversing its page table. Then, we change the source code of LKM to map the physical page to its virtual address. Our experimental results show that *TZ-SSAP* can prevent those attacks effectively.

And for performance evaluation, we define the consuming time in *ROS* from invoking the *SMC* instruction to backing from *SW*. Details as Table 1.

Table 1. Consuming time

Operations	Switching time	Traversing page tables	Update page table	Find page table entry
Consuming time	8us	257ms	345us	754us

According to Table 1, traversing page tables costs the most time. But it only take 6.7% for *SSApp*s whose executed time is only one minute. This percentage will be smaller and smaller as the executed time increases. Therefore, *TZ-SSAP* will not cause too much time loss for *SSApp*s.

7 Related Work

In recent years, there are several systems attempt to protect security-sensitive application code and data. We divide them into two classes in term of the way used to protect applications. One is the whole application protection which regards all the application code and data as a whole. The other is the split application protection achieved by protecting the critical part of the application instead of the whole.

7.1 Whole Application Protection

InkTag [14] is a virtualization-based architecture that uses a trusted hypervisor to isolate the *HAP* (high-assurance process) from OS which is achieved by the *EPT* (extended page tables). InkTag uses two separate *EPT*: the trusted *EPT* is installed for *HAP* execution while the untrusted *EPT* is used for OS and other applications. *HAP* updates the trusted *EPT* through hypercall. InkTag can defend again Iago attacks because of its paraverification to ease verifying of OS. Also it protects the confidentiality of secure page via encryption technology and detects corruption of the secure page through digital signing. However, it cannot keep the encrypted pages from reading and modifying by OS as well as Overshadow [15, 16] system which also need complex encryption and decryption technologies to protect the whole application execution. In addition, Overshadow cannot prevent the address mapping manipulation attacks.

Sego [17] is similar with InkTag for the *EPT*. But it is faster than InkTag since it does not need encryption technology. All secure data stays in plain text which is protected by hardware memory protection to ensure OS cannot access them. AppShield [7] is a hypervisor-based approach that reliably safeguards code, data and execution integrity of a critical application. It consists of two parts: a transit module in kernel space mediating control flow between the *CAP* (critical application) and OS, and a trusted shim in user space assisting the data flows between *CAP* and shared buffer. It can defense the address mapping manipulation attacks since the hypervisor and shim code jointly to protect the address space of *CAP* when OS updates the page tables. What is worse is that both of them cannot guarantee the integrity of kernel code.

7.2   Split Application Protection

SeCage [18] retrofits commodity hardware virtualization extensions to support efficient isolation of sensitive code manipulating critical secrets from the remaining code. It decomposes the applications into two parts. One is the secret compartment which contains a set of secrets defined by user as well as its corresponding code. Another is the main compartment that deals with the rest of the application logic. Firstly, it uses an analysis framework CI to discover potential functions related to secrets statically. And then it combines the `mprotect` and debug exception together to dynamic analysis with different workloads. Once the analysis result comes to a fixed point, SeCage decomposes the application to secret and main compartments on the basis of them. It also use the extended page tables to guarantee two compartments isolation. Despite the fact that SeCage can keep applications from many attacks, such as PTMA attack and the address mapping manipulation attacks, there are still some weaknesses. The closure related to secrets may be not complete since designers cannot be exhaustive of all possible input about applications. Besides, it also cannot guarantee the effectiveness of non-secret data accessed by secret functions due to no protection against them.

Virtual Ghost [19] is different with the above systems. It protects secret data and code with the ghost memory instead of *EPT*. The ghost memory is achieved by adding a compiler-based virtual machine (VM) between OS and hardware. All system software is compiled to the virtual instruction set based on the LLVM compiler intermediate representation [20]. Therefore, Virtual Ghost can prevent OS accessing the ghost memory since those virtual instruction set are implemented by VM and need to be validity verification, which can defense the address mapping manipulation attacks and prevent repurposing existing instruction sequences because of its control flow integrity enforcement. However, it depends on the virtual instruction set and compiler which are not always practical for current infrastructures.

8   Conclusion

In this paper, we have presents *TZ-SSAP*, which provides a safe execution environment for security-sensitive applications in the face of the OS may be compromised because of the kernel vulnerability. *TZ-SSAP* is implemented based on the hardware-assisted isolated environment TrustZone. The general OS is installed in *NW* while *TZ-SSAP* is mainly located in *SW*. *TZ-SSAP* takes advantage of the page table mechanism instead of the extended page tables. *TZ-SSAP* makes *SSApp* perform as expected since it can guarantee the integrity of both the code and its control flow during run time. In addition, it also guarantee the confidentiality of *SSApps'* data through preventing attacker from double mapping the *SSApp's* physical page, which leads to keep the security-sensitive information of *SSApps* from attacker.

In future work, we can add safeguard to protect the code of standard library and LKM in *TZ-SSAP*. For example, we can verify the integrity of the library file or LKM module before it is loaded into memory, and make them write-protected once they are authorized and loaded into physical page.

Acknowledgments. This work is supported by the National High-tech R&D Program (863 Program) of China under Grant No. 2012AA01A401 and National Science and Technology Major Project of China under Grant No. 2013ZX01029003-001.

References

1. Bovet, D.P., Cesati, M.: Understanding the Linux Kernel. O'Reilly Media, Sebastopol (2005)
2. https://www.exploit-db.com/
3. http://www.security-database.com/
4. http://www.securityfocus.com/
5. Lee, J.S., Ham, H.M., Kim, I.H., et al.: POSTER: page table manipulation attack. In: Proceedings of the 22nd ACM SIGSAC Conference on Computer and Communications Security, pp. 1644–1646. ACM (2015)
6. Checkoway, S., Shacham, H.: Lago attacks: Why the system call api is a bad untrusted rpc interface. ACM (2013)
7. Cheng, Y., Ding, X., Deng, R.H.: Efficient virtualization-based application protection against untrusted operating system. In: Proceedings of the 10th ACM Symposium on Information, Computer and Communications Security, pp. 345–356. ACM (2015)
8. Cheng, Y., Ding, X., Deng, R.H.: DriverGuard: a fine-grained protection on I/O flows. In: Atluri, V., Diaz, C. (eds.) ESORICS 2011. LNCS, vol. 6879, pp. 227–244. Springer, Heidelberg (2011). doi:10.1007/978-3-642-23822-2_13
9. Zhou, Z., Gligor, V.D., Newsome, J., et al.: Building verifiable trusted path on commodity x86 computers. In: 2012 IEEE Symposium on Security and Privacy (SP), pp. 616–630. IEEE (2012)
10. ARM A R M.: Security Technology Building a Secure System Using TrustZone Technology (white paper). ARM Limited (2009)
11. ARM: TrustZone Introduction. http://www.arm.com/zh/products/processors/technologies/trustzone/index.php
12. ARM Limited: ARM CoreTile Express A9X4 Cotex-A9 MPCore (V2P-CA9) Technical Reference Manual (2014)
13. Sierraware: Open Virtualization Build and Boot Guide for ARM V7 and ARM V8 (2014)
14. Hofmann, O.S., Kim, S., Dunn, A.M., et al.: Inktag: secureapplications on an untrusted operating system. ACM SIGARCH Comput. Archit. News ACM **41**(1), 265–278 (2013)

15. Chen, X., Garfinkel, T., Lewis, E.C., et al.: Overshadow: a virtualization-based approach to retrofitting protection in commodity operating systems. ACM SIGARCH Comput. Archit. News ACM **36**(1), 2–13 (2008)
16. Ports, D.R.K., Garfinkel, T.: Towards application security on untrusted operating systems. In: HotSec (2008)
17. Kwon, Y., Dunn, A.M., Lee, M.Z., et al.: Sego: pervasive trusted metadata for efficiently verified untrusted system services. In: Proceedings of the Twenty-First International Conference on Architectural Support for Programming Languages and Operating Systems, pp. 277–290. ACM (2016)
18. Liu, Y., Zhou, T., Chen, K., et al.: Thwarting memory disclosure with efficient hypervisor-enforced intra-domain isolation. In: Proceedings of the 22nd ACM SIGSAC Conference on Computer and Communications Security, pp. 1607–1619. ACM (2015)
19. Criswell, J., Dautenhahn, N., Adve, V.: Virtual Ghost: Protecting applications from hostile operating systems. ACM SIGARCH Comput. Archit. News **42**(1), 81–96 (2014)
20. Lattner, C., Adve, V.: LLVM: a compilation framework for lifelong program analysis & transformation. In: International Symposium on Code Generation and Optimization, 2004 (CGO 2004), pp. 75–86. IEEE (2004)
21. Azab, A.M., Ning, P., Shah, J., et al.: Hypervision across worlds: real-time kernel protection from the arm trustzone secure world. In: Proceedings of the 2014 ACM SIGSAC Conference on Computer and Communications Security, pp. 90–102. ACM (2014)

SQLite Forensic Analysis Based on WAL

Yao Liu[1], Ming Xu[1(✉)], Jian Xu[1], Ning Zheng[1], and Xiaodong Lin[2]

[1] Internet and Network Security Laboratory, School of Computer Science and
Technology, Hangzhou Dianzi University, Hangzhou, China
{141050061,mxu,jian.xu,nzheng}@hdu.edu.cn
[2] Faculty of Business and Information Technology,
University of Ontario Institute of Technology,
Oshawa, Canada
xiaodong.lin@uoit.ca

Abstract. SQLite database is an important source of evidence in forensic investigations. Write-Ahead Logging (WAL) was introduced to ensure
data integrity and improve performance in SQLite databases. However,
few attentions have been paid to utilizing it for forensic purposes, particularly in deleted record recovery. Without using WAL, prior recovery methods have been ineffective. This paper addresses techniques for
SQLite forensic analysis based on WAL. Specifically, based on the storage
mechanisms of SQLite and the structure of the WAL, both the original
SQLite database and WAL are first constructed by extracting and analyzing all valid pages. SQLite history versions are then produced by using
two reconstructed files above. Deleted records can then be recovered and
tampered behaviors can be detected by comparing different versions of
the reconstructed history file. Experimental results show that the proposed method can reconstruct history versions, recover deleted records
and detect tampered behaviors effectively.

Keywords: Digital forensics · SQLite · Reconstruction · History
versions · Recovery · Tamper detect

1 Introduction

SQLite is an open source, embedded relational database. Originally released in
2000, it was designed to provide a convenient means for applications to manage
data. In addition to it's widely used in embedded devices, various communication
applications and mobile Apps use SQLite (e.g., SMS, Contacts, Call History,
E-mail Client, and third-party apps). It is estimated that several millions devices
currently use this standard [1].

It is not surprising that the data stored in the SQLite database has grown
from simple contacts lists ten years ago to several gigabytes of potentially sensitive and personally identifiable information (PII) today. Thus, forensic analysis
of SQLite database has become essential and critical to investigating authorities, where recovery of deleted records is the most common task. Specifically, it

© ICST Institute for Computer Sciences, Social Informatics and Telecommunications Engineering 2017
R. Deng et al. (Eds.): SecureComm 2016, LNICST 198, pp. 557–574, 2017.
DOI: 10.1007/978-3-319-59608-2_31

is very common to extract deleted records from the unallocated space (e.g., free space and free block) of database files during an investigation.

Flash memory capacity has increased considerably. To improve the performance of the SQLite database, a new WAL (Write-ahead Log) option is used in place of a rollback journal when SQLite is operating in WAL mode. This was made available in version 3.7.0 and later [2–5]. While some operations (e.g., insert, delete, update, etc.) are performed, original content is retained in the database file. The changes append to a separate WAL. Before a commit condition (i.e., checkpoint [3–5]) occurs, all operations are not committed immediately and the changes are not made to the actual data in the database. Therefore, it is difficult to recover recently deleted records from the database file until a checkpoint is made.

Our current work gives a detailed illustration of the procedure to reconstruct SQLite history versions through the original database file and WAL. The proposed method features two main utilities through the analysis of reconstructed history versions. The first is to restore deleted records, and the second is to detect tampered behaviors. Both are achieved by comparing different versions of the history file.

The remainder of this paper is outlined as follows: Sect. 2 introduces the background information concerning SQLite database and WAL. The methods to reconstruct SQLite history versions are given in Sect. 3. Section 4 evaluates the experiment and demonstrates the utility of our proposed method using two case studies. Sections 5 and 6 discusses some practical issues and related work. The paper ends with the discussion of the future work and conclusions in Sect. 7.

2   Background

SQLite is a SQL database engine widely used in embedded devices. It is especially popular in the applications of mobile devices where it is the de facto database to manage user data. This database utilizes either a rollback journal or a WAL to ensure the atomic operations. The behavior of the synchronous WAL and database is called checkpoint, which is automatically executed by SQLite. This section describes SQLite database features associated WAL and checkpoint mechanisms.

2.1   SQLite Database

Structure of SQLite. Typically, each SQLite database consists of fixed-size pages. These can be either table B-tree page, index B-tree page, free page or overflow page. The page size is defined in the first 100 bytes of the database file. All pages are of the same size and are comprised of multi-byte fields. The most significant fields are magic header string(aka file signature), text encoding, parameters of Btree structures, and incremental-vacuum settings. These important fields are stored in big-endian format as shown in Fig. 1.

Magic header string is used to effectively identify SQLite database files. Every valid SQLite database file begins with the following 16 bytes (in hex): 53 51 4c 69 74 65 20 66 6f 72 6d 61 74 20 33 00. This byte sequence corresponds to the UTF-8 string "SQLite format 3\0" including the null terminator character at the end.

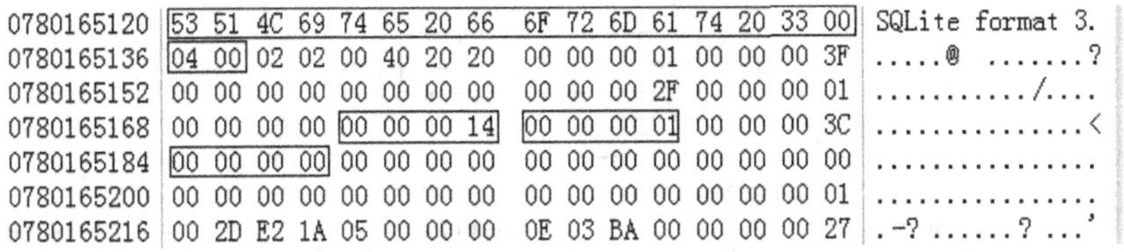

```
0780165120 53 51 4C 69 74 65 20 66  6F 72 6D 61 74 20 33 00  SQLite format 3.
0780165136 04 00 02 02 00 40 20 20  00 00 00 01 00 00 00 3F  .....@ .......?
0780165152 00 00 00 00 00 00 00 00  00 00 00 2F 00 00 00 01  .........../....
0780165168 00 00 00 00 00 00 00 14  00 00 00 01 00 00 00 3C  ...............<
0780165184 00 00 00 00 00 00 00 00  00 00 00 00 00 00 00 00  ................
0780165200 00 00 00 00 00 00 00 00  00 00 00 00 00 00 00 01  ................
0780165216 00 2D E2 1A 05 00 00 00  0E 03 BA 00 00 00 00 27  .-?......?...'
```

Fig. 1. Main fields of SQLite database file header

For database in auto-vacuum mode or incremental-vacuum mode, there is another significant page called pointer bitmap page. Pointer bitmap pages are extra pages inserted into the database to make operations of auto-vacuum and incremental-vacuum more efficient. The decision to use pointer bitmap page depends on a non-zero largest root B-tree page value. This is located at byte offset 52 in the database header.

SQLite Master Table. The SQLite master table (or SQLite temp master table in the case of a TEMP database) is a system table that contains information about all tables, views, indexes, and triggers in the database. It stores the complete database schema [6]. The structure of the SQLite master table can be created using the following SQL statement: CREATE TABLE sqlite master (type TEXT, name TEXT, tbl name TEXT, rootpage INTEGER, sql TEXT), the value of each filed is described in Table 1.

Table 1. SQLite master fields

No	Field	Value
1	type	Table, index, trigger or view
2	name	Table name for a table
3	tbl_name	Same to second filed (for table or view), or related to table name (for index or trigger)
4	rootpage	0 (for trigger or view), or rootpage number (for table or index)
5	SQL	Creating sentence for specific type of objects

B-tree Structure. SQLite databases are stored in segments, called pages. A SQLite database is composed of multiple B-trees, with each B-tree occupying a minimum of one page. One B-tree is needed for each table and index. These are referred to as table B-trees and index B-trees. Each table or index in a SQLite database has a rootpage which defines the location of its first page. The root pages for all indexes and tables are kept in the SQLite master table [6].

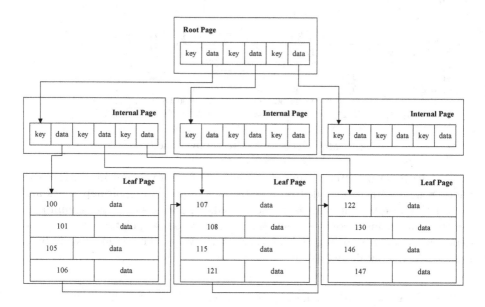

Fig. 2. Table B-tree structure of SQLite database (Owens, 2010)

A B-tree page is either an internal page or a leaf page. In the case of a table B-tree as shown in Fig. 2 (Owens, 2010), a leaf page contains keys and each key has associated data. An internal page contains K keys together with K pointers to child B-tree pages. A pointer in an internal B-tree page is just the 31-bit integer page number of the child page. Whereas for index B-tree, its structure is almost identical with table B-tree. The most obvious difference is that the internal pages contain not only keys but also index records. Furthermore, an internal page contains K keys together with K+1 pointers to child B-tree pages.

In an internal B-tree page, pointers and keys logically alternate. All keys within the same page are unique and are logically organized in ascending order from left to right. The ordering is logical, not physical. The actual location of keys within the page is arbitrary. For any key X, pointers to the left of X refer to B-tree pages on which all keys are less than or equal to X. Pointers to the right of X refer to pages where all keys are greater than X. Taking Fig. 2 as an example, the first data in the first internal page have referred to a leaf page, all keys in this leaf page are less than or equal to 106.

Within an internal B-tree page, each key and pointer to its immediate left are grouped into a structure called a cell [4]. The cell is the basic element to organize data within a B-tree page. The right-most pointer is held separately.

A leaf B-tree page has no pointers. It however, uses the cell structure to hold keys for index B-trees or both keys and contents for table B-trees. Data is also contained in the cell.

Cells are placed from bottom to top of the page. Since sizes are unfixed, the offset of its first byte is also recorded. These offset values are placed from top to bottom of a page. This bi-growing design makes it easy to add new record without defragmentation.

2.2 Write-Ahead Log

Beginning in version 3.7.0, SQLite introduced the option of using WAL mode to implement atomic commit and rollback. In this mode, the original content is preserved in the database and changes are appended into a separate WAL. A commit occurs when a special record indicating a commit is appended to the WAL. Thus a commit can occur without writing to the original database. This allows readers to work with unaltered original databases while changes are simultaneously being committed into the WAL. Multiple transactions can be appended to the end of a single WAL.

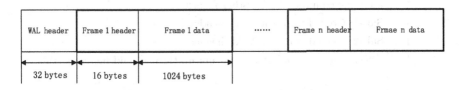

Fig. 3. WAL file structure

The logical structure of the WAL is provided in Fig. 3. It consists of a file header and several frames. The number of frames can be ranged from 0 to a lot, indicated in bold black box. Each frame is divided into a frame header and frame data. When checkpoint (is) triggered, valid data stored in WAL would be transformed into the database. WAL can be reused with new frames overwriting prior frames after checkpoints. WAL always grows from the beginning to the end of the sequence. The checksum and counter appended to each frame indicate that whether the frame is effective or not.

WAL has a 32-byte length header which includes eight 32-bit big-endian unsigned integers as shown in Table 2. Among them, the database page size corresponds with that of the database. Salt-1 is a random number that increases by 1 after a checkpoint. Salt-2 is a random number which is replaced by another random number after a checkpoint.

Frames trail after WAL file headers. Each frame consists of 24-byte frame header and frame data. Frame headers consist of six 32-bit big-endian unsigned integers as shown in Table 3. Page Number indicates which page of the database is recorded here. Salt-1 & 2 may match or differ to the corresponding value in the file header, and determine whether data in this frame is effective or not.

Table 2. WAL file header structure

Offset	Size	Description
0	4	Magic number: 0x377f0682 or 0x377f0683
4	4	Format version: Currently 3110100
8	4	Page size: Default size is 1024 bytes
12	4	Checkpoint number
16	4	Salt-1: Random integer incremented with each checkpoint
20	4	Salt-2: A different random number for each checkpoint
24	4	Checksum-1: First part of a checksum on the first 24 bytes of header
28	4	Checksum-2: Second part of the checksum on the first 24 bytes of header

Table 3. WAL frame header structure

Offset	Size	Description
0	4	Page number: Logical page number from database file
4	4	File size: For commit records, the size of the database files in pages after the commit. For all other records, zero
8	4	Salt-1: Copied from the WAL header
12	4	Salt-2: Copied from the WAL header
16	4	Checksum-1: Cumulative checksum up through and including this page
20	4	Checksum-2: Second half of the cumulative checksum

2.3   Checkpoint Mechanism

Similar to several mainstream databases (e.g., SQL Server, MySQL, Oracle, etc.), SQLite supports atomic transaction commit when reading and writing records. Transactions define boundaries around a group of SQL commands such that they either all successfully execute together or not at all.

By default, SQLite does a checkpoint automatically when the WAL reaches a threshold size of one thousand pages or more in size, or when the last database connection on a database file close. That is to say, the occurrence of a checkpoint means to transfer all the transactions that are appended in the WAL back into the original database.

With the use of checkpoints in WAL, all committed atomic transactions are appended into the WAL and will not be transformed into the database immediately. The transactions submitted at different times constitute different operation states. Taking each committed atomic transaction as granularity, several histroy versions can be achieved from WAL.

3   Methodology

In this section, a method is proposed to reconstruct SQLite history versions from Android devices. Figure 4 shows the framework for our reconstruction approach. The method consists of four main parts: Reconstructing SQLite database, extracting correspond WAL, combining original SQLite database with corresponding WAL to recreate SQLite history versions and forensic analysis for deleted record recovery and tamper detection.

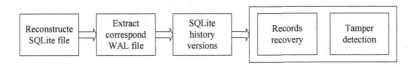

Fig. 4. Framework of reconstruct approach

3.1   Reconstructing SQLite Database

Pre-processing. Pre-Processing is intended to extract the real master table from phone image. Based on the storage mechanism of SQLite, only the tables and indexes have actual storage space. Thus, these information are the main consideration when analyzing SQLite master table. In addition to SQL fields, other fields are also the focus of our consideration. Prior to this, we define a candidate set for the SQLite master table. Considering various Android devices are designed according to the Goggle's official source code. There is a slight discrepancy between different mobile phones. We obtained the master table structure from Android source code as the initial candidate set [7]. For those customized mobile phones, we need to adjust candidate sets on an individual basis. Using short message databases as an example, Fig. 5 shows a typical master table structures.

```
00000130  00 00 00 00 00 00 00 00  81 21 15 07 17 21 21 01  .........!...!!.
00000140  82 0D 74 61 62 6C 65 6D  79 63 68 61 6E 6E 65 6C  ..tablemychannel
00000150  73 6D 79 63 68 61 6E 6E  65 6C 73 17 43 52 45 41  smychannels.CREA
00000160  54 45 20 54 41 42 4C 45  20 6D 79 63 68 61 6E 6E  TE TABLE mychann
00000170  65 6C 73 20 28 5F 69 64  20 49 4E 54 45 47 45 52  els (_id INTEGER
00000180  20 50 52 49 4D 41 52 59  20 4B 45 59 20 41 55 54  PRIMARY KEY AUT
00000190  4F 49 4E 43 52 45 4D 45  4E 54 2C 63 68 61 6E 6E  OINCREMENT,chann
000001A0  65 6C 5F 69 64 20 49 4E  54 45 47 45 52 2C 63 68  el_id INTEGER,ch
000001B0  61 6E 6E 65 6C 5F 6E 61  6D 65 20 54 45 58 54 20  annel_name TEXT
000001C0  4E 4F 54 20 4E 55 4C 4C  2C 69 73 5F 63 68 65 63  NOT NULL,is_chec
000001D0  6B 65 64 20 49 4E 54 45  47 45 52 29 62 14 06 17  ked INTEGER)b...
```

Fig. 5. Example of master table structure

Algorithm 1. Extracting and Analyzing Master Pages Algorithm

Input: image file, candidate master table records
Output: result1 = {offset, sql, field type order}
1: /*default page size is 1024bytes*/
2: **for** $block \in image\ file$ **do**
3:     $page[\ ] \leftarrow block$
4: **end for**
5: **if** $page[0] = 0x0D$ or $page[0 - 15] = magic\ number$ **then**
6:     /*recognize B-tree pages*/
7:     **if** $data\ block \in table\ name\ from\ candidate\ master\ table$ **then**
8:        **while** $i < total\ records\ in\ each\ page$ **do**
9:           extract all fields within pages and store in database
10:          $i + +$
11:       **end while**
12:    **end if**
13: **end if**
14: $offset \leftarrow offset + page\ size$
15: **for** $extracted\ page \in image\ file$ **do**
16:    extract sql and analysis field type order f1
17: **end for**
18: **return** $result1$

Several steps are necessary to retrieve a true master table. First, a phone's image and candidate master table are taken as an input. Second, the image is then traversed to recognize all pages belonging to a true master table. Third, pages are analyzed to extract all SQL statements and field types of tables and indexes. The simplified algorithm is presented in Algorithm 1.

Among them, set $result1$ contains three fields, which are used to describe the internal information of a master page. Each field is explained as follows:

$$(offset, sql, field\ type\ order)$$

where:

- $offset$ is the address of a specific page belonging to a master table;
- sql is the creating sentence for specific types of objects;
- $field\ type\ order$ is a string which contains all filed types within a specific page;

Extracting and Analyzing Pages. For a given phone image and a real master table, we can get all the B-tree pages that belong to the specified database. This stage of the algorithm is shown in Algorithm 2.

In the extracting phase, the purpose is to acquire pages that match the given conditions. These conditions are used to determine whether a page belongs to a specified table. As described in Algorithm 2, two main match conditions are used: The first is to confirm the basic structure of the database pages (e.g., if we locate a data page when traversing the image, it must begin with 0x0D. Additionally, cell sums should not exceed the page size defined in first 100 bytes of the database

Algorithm 2. Extracting All Pages Algorithm

Input: result1, image file
Output: result2 = {offset, table name, row head, row tail}
1: /*default page size is 1024 bytes*/
2: **if** $page[0] = 0x0D$ or $page[0] = 0x05$ or $page[0] = 0x0A$ or $page[0] = 0x02$ **then**
3:   /* recognize four type of pages*/
4:   **if** *the fix offset value conform to page structure* **then**
5:     for each page locate one record and acquire field type order f2
6:   **end if**
7: **end if**
8: **if** $f1$ *page* $\in f2$ **then**
9:   offset, table name, row head, row tail
10: **end if**
11: $offset \leftarrow offset + page\ size$
12: **return** $result2$

file). The second match condition is to compare field types extracted above with pages use d for analysis from the image.

Among them, set $result2$ contains four fields, which are used to describe the internal information of a page. Each field is explained as follows:

$$(offset, table\ name, row\ head, row\ tail)$$

where:

- *offset* is the address of a specific page within the image file;
- *table name* is the page belonging to;
- *row head* is the minimum value of the row id within a specific page;
- *row tail* is the maximum value of the row id within a specific page;

Due to the fact that the field types only have three values in SQLite database tables, this causes more pages to be located than previously expected which hinders analysis. This is addressed in the processing phase by using B-trees. B-tree assists in maintaining unique keys which are sorted in order for sequential traversing. Besides, taking into account the allocation mechanism of Ext file system and the use of WAL, we can make further filter out of extracted pages. The processing algorithm is presented in pseudo-code shown in Algorithm 3.

Among them, the set $result3$ contains three fields, which are used to describe additional information on the page. Each field is described as follows:

$$(validate\ list, root\ page\ list, offset\ list)$$

where:

- *offset* is the address of pages extracted in Algorithm 2;
- *validate list* is the list to mark valid pages;
- *root page list* is the list to mark root page;

Algorithm 3. Processing Extracted Pages Algorithm

Input: result2, image file
Output: result3 = {offset, validate list, root page list}
 1: **for** *table name* ∈ *result2* **do**
 2:     get row head list, row tail list and offset list by table name
 3:     **for** *row head value* ∈ *row head list* **do**
 4:         **if** *value* = 1 **then**
 5:             *result3* ← *offset, validate* = 1
 6:             *id* ← *the first id when value* = 1
 7:         **end if**
 8:     **end for**
 9: **end for**
10: **for** *row head value* ∈ *row head list* **do**
11:     *i* = 0
12:     **if** *i* < *id* **then**
13:         *result3* ← *offset, validate* = 0
14:     **end if**
15:     **if** *i* > *id* **then**
16:         **if** *value* = 1 **then**
17:             *break*
18:         **else**
19:             compare two adjacent row head values
20:         **end if**
21:         **if** *row head*[*i*] = *row head*[*i* − 1] **then**
22:             *result3* ← *offset, validate* = 1, *rootpagelist* = 1
23:         **else**
24:             *result3* ← *offset, validate* = 0, *rootpagelist* = 0
25:         **end if**
26:     **end if**
27: **end for**
28: **return** *result3*

Reorganizing Pages. After completing the previous two steps, we now have a series of valid table pages with the range of records and index pages with leaf order and key order. With this information, the size of a database file and the logical number of each page can be easily determined.

When analyzing extracted pages, we found that some tables within the database were empty. This was previously unconsidered during extraction and analysis. We filled empty table pages to reorganize the file. The main reorganization steps are described commonly as follows:

- Comparing rootpage number from master table pages and leaf order from interior pages (include tables and indexes) to obtain the most right leaf number. This is also the total page number of the database file.
- Creating an empty file which contains the total number of pages. Each known page is duplicated in at a corresponding location in the new file. Remaining

pages will be filled with empty data pages or index pages according to the master table.
- Inserting pointer map pages if they exist.

3.2 Extracting WAL File

Recovering WAL is based on the data blocks reorganize method. A data block represents a data frame as previously described. A frame is considered valid if and only if the following conditions are true [4]: First, the salt-1 and salt-2 values in the frame-header match salt values in the wal-header. Second, the checksum values in the final 8 bytes of the frame-header exactly match the checksum computed consecutively on the first 24 bytes of the WAL header and the first 8 bytes and the content of all frames up to and including the current frame. The main recovery steps are described as follows:

- Finding the WAL file header by magic bytes, saving all the 4-byte random value in a given set.
- Traversing the set, searching for a random value which belongs to the current WAL file using the field type characteristics of a specific table. For example, an SMS table. Pointer map pages are inserted if they exist.
- Finding the each frame of the WAL file. Locating and saving the offsets of the 4-byte random value in frames which matches the value previously mentioned.
- Reorganizing the frames by the constant size of data frame, which belongs to the current WAL file.

3.3 Reconstructing SQLite History Versions

Previous studies on the reconstruction of the SQLite history versions mainly discussed in [22, 23]. They proposed a recovery method using YAFFS2 metadata. However, this method cannot be applied to newer devices with extensive use of ext4 file system.

Our method for reconstructing the SQLite history versions is closely related to the methods proposed in Sects. 3.1 and 3.2. As mentioned above, we have reconstructed the SQLite database and its corresponding WAL. Each frame header shows the page number of its related database file and whether the transaction was committed. The details can be seen in Sect. 3.

The occurrence of a transaction operation may affect multiple data pages. Each operation is not immediately written back to the database. Thus, we aim to locate which frame blocks contain commit markers. By individually considering each marker we can obtain a number of history versions of SQLite database.

4   Experiment and Evaluation

The following experimentation tests the method proposed in Sect. 3. All experiments were conducted on Android smartphones with WAL. SMS is one of the most common applications that have adopted SQLite for storage and management of data. Furthermore, it also has a substantial amount of important user information which is of interest for forensic investigations [8]. In this paper, we attempt to recover deleted SMS messages as a case study for the proposed method.

The first stage of the experiment involved conducting a series of predefined activities on the device. This stage is divided into two experimental scenarios, in the first scenario, some activities are conducted as follows: restore the phone to the factory settings, add 150 records, delete 50 records and update 10 records. Similar to the first scenario, the second is just different in that the number of records used in add and delete operations are 250 and 100, respectively.

4.1   Collection of Data Image

There are two main methods to obtain data image: physical method and logical method [9,10]. In this paper, we focus on user data partition for acquiring data.

Rooting mobile devices for the purpose of data acquisition is often discussed in literature. While we believe it should generally be avoided [11], we have decided to root this device for expediency of data collection. We utilized the dd tool to acquire storage images for analysis:

- Put the mobile device in developer mode and connect it with the computer.
- Establish TCP communication between the device and computer using the *adbforward* command.
- View the partition information using the *adbcatpartitions* command.
- Copy and transfer the image from the device to computer using the *dd* and *nc* commands [12].

In order to support *dd* and *nc* commands, the BusyBox [13] tool is required. It can be installed on the system partition to protect the integrity of the data partition. As a result, the image of data partition can be obtained bit-by-bit that is important for the next step in our investigation.

4.2   Reconstruction of SQLite History Versions

The aim of the experiments is to test the proposed method for reconstructing the history versions of SQLite database. Prior to this point, we have to reconstruct SQLite database and corresponded WAL, and evaluate the effectiveness of the two reconstructed files.

A common method in the literature to compare whether two files are identical is through their hash values [14]. The two original files are acquired from the image file using dd tool and their hash values are calculated separately (Only calculate the effective part for WAL). Then, these two files are reconstructed with the method described in Sect. 3. The hash values of these files are subsequently calculated by comparing the original files with reconstructed files, we

Table 4. The comparison results of SQLite and WAL

Case Num	Original valid file	Reconstructed file	Compared result
1	554f7e0b621c4b9c2c1d8df7d3faf5d4(SQLite)		√
	0cfdfcf0252254760a01620154b9036e(WAL)		√
2	c03ca026d59987f97a79af90747b7c47(SQLite)		√
	a076bb47b198b2b932c966c8f2bf51cf(WAL)		√

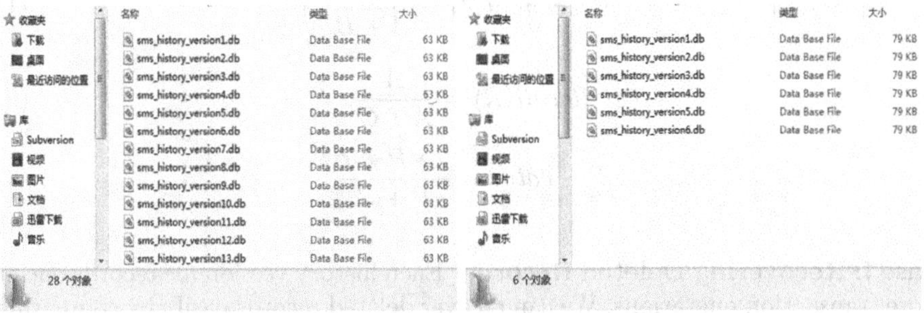

(a) Case I   (b) Case II

Fig. 6. The result of reconstruct history files in two cases

can determine whether the experimental result was effective or not. The comparison results of the two files are displayed in Table 4. It can be observed that two files are reconstructed correctly.

In our research, we found the factors that affected the result of the experiments is checkpoint mechanism. We will discuss two situations according to whether the checkpoint is triggered.

The experimental results of the reconstructed history versions are displayed in Fig. 6. For the sake of simplicity, we named file based on the incremental version number. Situation I indicate that the checkpoint is not triggered, in contrast, situation II means the checkpoint is triggered. As a result, 28 history versions and 6 history versions are found respectively from the situation I and situation II. In situation II, a part of the records in WAL were transformed into database and are marked as invalid pages, and we reconstructed those as valid history versions.

4.3 Case Studies Using Reconstructed Files

As some common database operations (e.g., insert, delete, update, etc.) occurred in WAL and are transferred back into the database file when checkpoint conditions is reached. History version files contain valuable evidences, especially on operation of deleted and updated records. Through the comparison of different history version files, we can discern each operation about a database. Two case studies are discussed below.

Evaluation Criterion. The precision rate (define as Eq. (1)) and recall rate (define as Eq. (2)) are adopted as the criterions to evaluate the proposed method, and the F-value (define as Eq. (3)) is used to evaluate the quality of the recovery approach. In the below equations, the A refers t o the number of recovered records belonging to the SMS database; the B refers to the number of records that do not belong to the SMS database; and the C refers to the number of records which belong to the SMS database but were not recovered from the image file.

$$Precision(P) = \frac{A}{A+B}. \tag{1}$$

$$Recall(R) = \frac{A}{A+C}. \tag{2}$$

$$F - value = \frac{2*P*R}{P+R}. \tag{3}$$

Case I: Recovering Deleted Records. Each history version file records one or more transaction operations. We can recover deleted records easily by comparing two different version files. As shown in Table 5, we recovered all deleted records in situation I and approximately 75% in situation II. The value of precision, recall, and F-value indicates that the proposed method can recover recently deleted records effectively

Table 5. The result of delete operation

No	Image size (KB)	Total records	Deleted records	Recover records	Precision	Recall	F-value
1	3251200	150	50	50	1	1	1
2	3251200	250	100	76	1	0.76	0.86

To confirm the effectiveness of our approach, we compare it to results of similarly proposed schemes in [18]. Since the compared recovery method restores records from the SQLite database file, the file of SMS database was first retrieved from two images. The result is described in Fig. 7. In situation I, there are no records being restored by Sangjun's method. Moreover, 17 records were restored from situation II. The P is 1, the R is 0.068, and the F-value is 0.127. It is clear that our proposed method has an improvement over the precision rate, recall rate and F-value.

Case II: Detecting Tampered Behaviors. Consider a scenario where a suspect commits a crime. Incriminating evidence was transmitted somehow, perhaps via SMS. To avoid incarceration the criminal attempts to destroy all electronic evidence. Fortunately, we can recover deleted records to retrieve evidence if the

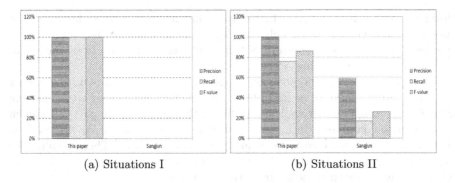

(a) Situations I   (b) Situations II

Fig. 7. The result of recover deleted records in two situations

suspect simply delete SMS messages using built-in SMS deletion functionality. Knowing this, the suspect may simply tamper with the content of evidence and do not delete records. In this case, traditional recovery method will not work effectively. However, we can detect these tamper behaviors by comparing two different version files.

The compared results of tamper operation are shown in Table 6. As we can see, these results are similar to those when recovering deleted records in case I. For all 10 tampered records, we can detect 10 records in situation I and 8 records in situation II. The value of precision, recall and F-value indicate that the proposed method can detect tampered behaviors effectively.

Table 6. The result of tamper operation

No	Image size (KB)	Total records	Tamper records	Detect records	Precision	Recall	F-value
1	3251200	150	10	10	1	1	1
2	3251200	250	10	8	1	0.8	0.89

5   Discussion

In this section, we discuss some practice issues and considerations related to our method to reconstruct original SQLite database and WAL.

For expediency in the collection of data for this research, we decided to gain root privileges and utilize the *dd* tool to acquire storage images for analysis. In practical cases, however, the physical acquisition method is recommended to ensure data integrity.

If the metadata of the file system allows normal to access, we may be able to retrieve the directory structure of the file system and extract two files directly through existing tools [15,16]. In the case that a file system is damaged, the above method will not work well (e.g., system crash, human factors, etc.). In this case, we need to reconstruct SQLite database and WAL from the whole physical image as Sect. 3 has described.

When we extracting and analyzing pages to reconstruct the SQLite database file, there are a number of pages to filter out which do not belong to the current database. Through further analysis, we found that this is due in part to frequent deletion of the databases during several different cases studies. We also verified that the restore factory settings created the same problem. These results also prove that the restore factory settings do not erase all data, we are still able to recover some potential evidence from the image file.

6   Related Work

Although there are previous works on the recovery of SQLite records and history versions, substantial research on forensic analysis of SQLite based on WAL is limited. This section will review the existing researches on the analysis of SQLite.

The earliest research of database records recovery can trace back to 1983. Haerder [17] suggested a method that restored the deleted records using the transaction file. This method can be applied to traditional database on the PC when the information of deleted records is included in the transaction file.

Sangjeon [18] explained the management mechanism of the SQLite database when records were deleted. Sangjeon later proposed a method to recover deleted records from free blocks. However, the approach can only restore the deleted records from unallocated space within the page.

A year later, Lamine [19] presented a new tool to recover deleted records from SQLite databases based on a low-level analysis. In order to perform further shrink of the candidate page sets, they used pointer map page [4] to keep only pages that are part of a table B-tree and pages in overflow chains.

Other publications deal with the recovery of deleted records, which are not in the database file itself, but in the unallocated disk space. Pereira [20] researched the forensic analysis of SQLite databases of Mozilla Firefox. In contrast to other applications, no expired data remain in the Firefox database file. Therefore Pereira proposed a carving method for single records.

Shu, Zheng, and Xu [21] presented a new recovery method for Firefox history records based on the SQLite WAL file. An effective algorithm was proposed to reconstruct the whole data frame in WAL file from the unallocated space based on its structure, and the history records are extracted from the data frames according to the content of the records.

Xu, Yang, Wu, et al. [22,23] proposed a method to recover files, reconstruct the file system, and their previous history versions (Taking the SQLite database as a case study) using YAFFS2 metadata. However, since ext4 file system is widely used in android phones and Linux systems, this method cannot be applied to newer devices.

Generally, most of these works focus on recovering deleted records from the database file or carving single records from unallocated disk space. This paper details the reconstruction of SQLite history versions using the original database and WAL, and analyses two case studies using reconstructed history versions.

7 Conclusion

SQLite database is widely used to store messages, call history, browser history and much more, both on desktop computers as well as mobile devices. Therefore, it has tremendous forensic potential data and drawn more attention to digital forensic investigators and analysts.

When a SQLite database is in WAL mode, these potential forensic data will first present in WAL, and then be written to the database periodically. That is, WAL is also the source of evidence that we should study.

In this paper, we first reconstructed the original SQLite database and WAL. Then a method based on the original database and WAL to reconstruct SQLite history versions was proposed. The experimental results show that the proposed method can reconstruct history versions correctly.

Based on reconstructed files, we also demonstrated the utility of our proposed method. Our proposed method is capable of recovering deleted records and detecting tampered behaviors. It is evident that our method can recover recently deleted records and detect tampered behaviors effectively.

The widely use of large capacity flash memory provides us several opportunities and challenges. Large capacity will store more useful information. However much more effort is required to recover data and perform forensic analysis. Our future research will look at creating tools to ease forensic analysis on large capacity data storage.

Acknowledgment. This work is support by Natural Science Foundation of China under Grant Nos. 61070212 and 61572165, the State Key Program of Zhejiang Province Natural Science Foundation of China under Grant No. LZ15F020003.

References

1. Most widely deployed SQL Database. http://www.sqlite.org/mostdeployed.html
2. Rollback Journals. https://www.sqlite.org/tempfiles.html#rollb-ackjrnl
3. Write-Ahead Logging. https://www.sqlite.org/wal.html
4. The SQLite Database File Format. https://www.sqlite.org/filefo-rmat2.html
5. SQLite Source Code. https://www.sqlite.org/download.html
6. Xu, M., Yao, Y., Ren, Y.Z., Xu, J., Zhang, H.P., Zheng, N., Ling, S.: A reconstructing android user behavior approach based on YAFFS2 and SQLite. J. Comput. **9**(10), 2294–2302 (2014)
7. Master Table Structure. https://github.com/android/platform_packages_providers_telephonyprovider
8. Short Message Service. https://en.wikipedia.org/wiki/Short_Message_Service

9. Hoog, A.: Android Forensics: Investigation, Analysis and Mobile Security for Google Android, 1st edn. Syngress Publishing, Waltham (2011)
10. Breeuwsma, M.I.: Forensic imaging of embedded systems using JTAG (boundary-scan). Digit. Invest. 3(1), 32–42 (2006)
11. Martini, B., Do, Q., Choo, R.K.-K.: Conceptual evidence collection and analysis methodology for Android devices. ArXiv e-prints, June 2015
12. Netcat(windows). http://www.securityfocus.com/tools/139
13. BusyBox. https://play.google.com/store/apps/details?id=stericson.busybox
14. DFRWS Challenge Report. http://sandbox.dfrws.org/2006/garfinkel/part1.txt
15. Proposed Methodology for victim android forensics. https://viaforensics.com/viaforensics-articles/viaforensicsaflgical-tool-android-forensic-investigations.html
16. ViaForensics. https://viaforensics.com/products/viaextract
17. Theo, H., Andreas, R.: Principles of transaction-oriented database recovery. ACM Comput. Surv. 15(4), 287–317 (1983)
18. Jeon, S., Bang, J., Byun, K., et al.: A recovery method of deleted record for SQLite database. Pers. Ubiquit. Comput. 16(6), 707–715 (2011)
19. Aouad, L.M., Kechadi, T.M., Russo, R.: ANTS ROAD: a new tool for SQLite data recovery on android devices. In: Rogers, M., Seigfried-Spellar, K.C. (eds.) ICDF2C 2012. LNICST, vol. 114, pp. 253–263. Springer, Heidelberg (2013). doi:10.1007/978-3-642-39891-9_16
20. Pereira, T.M.: Forensic analysis of the firefox 3 internet history and recovery of deleted SQLite records. Digit. Invest. 5(3–4), 93–103 (2009)
21. Xu, M., Shu, W.X., Zheng, N.: A history records recovering method based on WAL file of firefox. J. Comput. Inf. Syst. 10(20), 8973–8982 (2014)
22. Xu, M., Yang, X., Wu, B.B., Yao, Y., Zhang, H.P., Xu, J., Zheng, N.: A metadata-based method for recovering files and file traces from YAFFS2. Digit. Invest. 10(1), 62–72 (2013)
23. Wu, B., Xu, M., Zhang, H., Xu, J., Ren, Y., Zheng, N.: A recovery approach for SQLite history recorders from YAFFS2. In: Mustofa, K., Neuhold, E.J., Tjoa, A.M., Weippl, E., You, I. (eds.) ICT-EurAsia 2013. LNCS, vol. 7804, pp. 295–299. Springer, Heidelberg (2013). doi:10.1007/978-3-642-36818-9_30

Impact of Environment on Branch Transfer of Software

Jianming Fu[1,2(✉)], Yan Lin[1,2], and Xu Zhang[1,2]

[1] State Key Laboratory of Aerospace Information Security and Trusted Computing of the Ministry of Education, Wuhan 430072, China
jmfu@whu.edu.cn
[2] Computer School, Wuhan University, Wuhan 430072, China

Abstract. Current intrusion detection approaches based on control flow integrity (CFI) can detect the majority of control flow hijacking attacks, but few of them take into account the impact of environment on CFI, so there may exist false alarms. In this paper, we have investigated systematically the impact of environment on branch transfer from time, space and mechanisms of Linux operating system. Moreover, we have presented finite state automata (FSA) to describe difference patterns caused by these environmental factors, and have exploited FSA-Stack model to detect these impacts. Finally, for some common applications (gzip, grep, tesseract, bzip2 etc.), we have leveraged a dynamic binary instrumentation tool Pin to record direct and indirect branch transfers produced by them and the shared libraries they depend on. The experimental results demonstrate that impact of environment on branch transfer exists universally and normally among usual applications, and the difference patterns of impacts can be beneficial to understand and mitigate the false alarms of CFI.

Keywords: Intrusion detection · Control flow integrity · Environmental factors · Finite state automata · Dynamic binary instrumentation

1 Introduction

Software (Program) behavior is a sequence of states or state transitions, which can be described by the low-level machine code or the high-level program statements, functions and system calls. Generally, software behavior is used in intrusion detection [1], but, it is dependent on the running environment and may be prone to be bypassed by attackers. Many existing intrusion detection techniques rely on monitoring the sequence of system calls a program invoked [1,2], or the arguments of system calls [3], or both [4] to detect malicious behaviors. However, if the attacker does not use the monitored system calls to achieve his goal, this kind of detection can be bypassed easily. For example, code-reuse attack [5,6] leverages existing code to form malicious gadgets, instead of using existing functions or system calls to achieve the attack.

© ICST Institute for Computer Sciences, Social Informatics and Telecommunications Engineering 2017
R. Deng et al. (Eds.): SecureComm 2016, LNICST 198, pp. 575–593, 2017.
DOI: 10.1007/978-3-319-59608-2_32

In order to counter this kind of low-level control flow hijacking attack, control flow integrity (CFI) [7,8] is proposed, which marks the valid targets of indirect control flow transfers with unique identifiers(IDs), and then inserts ID-checks before each indirect branch transfers. CFIMon [9], CFIGuard [10] and ROPecker [11] collect all possible indirect transfers or potential gadgets, then leverage Branch Trace Store (BTS) or Last Branch Record (LBR) [12] to capture control flow transfers when the program is running. Not only the shellcode but also some environmental factors will affect the control flow. For instance, in Linux, the Global Offset Table and LD_PRELOAD environment variable will have an impact on branch transfer.

According to Zhong [13], software behavior not only depends upon the program itself, but also depends on the running environment, including time, event, space, shared libraries, OS kernel, device driver, Hypervisor, garbage collector, compiler and so on. In this paper, we study the impact of environment on branch transfer of software from time, space and mechanisms of Linux operating system. In the meantime, we have confirmed these impacts based on a dynamic binary instrumentation tool Pin, and analyzed how these factors affect a program's branch transfer. Finally, we have used finite state automata (FSA) to describe difference patterns of branch transfers resulted from these environmental factors. These FSAs can be used to mitigate false alarms in CFIMon and ROPecker, and to distinguish what factors will cause the difference. In general, these FSAs are helpful to detect and counter shellcode.

In summary, this paper makes the following contributions:

- We have investigated systematically impacts of environment on branch transfers from time, space and mechanisms in Linux systems, and have discovered interested observations to understand the false alarms of CFI.
- We have presented a model of Finite State Automata(FSA) to capture these impacts, and have exploited FSA-Stack model to detect these impacts.
- We have designed the convinced experiment to validate impact patterns of different environmental factors, and its results are beneficial to reduce the false alarms of CFI.

The rest of this paper is structured as follows. Section 2 summarizes and discusses related work on intrusion detection based on control flow integrity. Section 3 analyzes environmental factors affecting branch transfer in detail. Section 4 introduces our approach which leverages a dynamic binary instrumentation tool Pin to record all branch transfers. Meanwhile, we give all FSAs that describe the difference patterns of branch transfers caused by environmental factors. Section 5 outlines the experimental results. Section 6 makes some concluding remarks and discusses the limitations of our work.

2   Related Work

Software behavior integrity detection has a long history, from the detection based on audit data and log information [14,15] to the detection based on system call [1–4,17,18], now it has been extended to control flow integrity detection. The purpose of the extension is to detect attacks that try to divert the program's control flow.

Some of these proposals mark the valid targets of indirect branch transfers with unique identifiers (IDs), and then inserts ID-checks into the program before each indirect branch transfer [7,8,20–23]. For example, Abadi et al. [7,8] introduced the term CFI and they suggested using a single identifier for all indirect branch transfers. Bin-CFI [21] used two IDs for all indirect branch transfers, one for ret and indirect jump instructions, another for indirect call instructions. And all indirect branches are instrumented by means of a jump to a CFI validation routine. But it does not validate the integrity of addresses in the global offset table (GOT), this leaves it be vulnerable to the so-called GOT overwriting attacks. CCFIR [20] implemented a 3-IDs approach, which extended the 2-IDs approach by further separating returns to sensitive and non-sensitive functions. In CCFIR, all targets for indirect branches are collected and randomly allocated on a so-called springboard section, and indirect branches are only allowed to use control flow targets contained in the springboard section. However, memory disclosure can reveal the content of the entire springboard section, which can be leveraged by attackers. DynCFI [23] used a dynamic code optimization tool to enforce CFI detection, which has the same problem with Bin-CFI, as it does not validate the integrity of GOT.

Others often leverages available hardware support for branch recording in commercial processors to collect the sets of control transfers when the program is running, and then compare them with the valid targets collected beforehand [9–11,24]. For instance, CFIMon [9] made use of static analysis and online training to get all valid targets of indirect branch transfers. It leverages BTS mechanism supported by hardware to collect in-flight control transfers and once the BTS buffer is nearly full, a monitor process will start to compare them with the valid targets to decide whether there exists an attack. But the variance of environment variable may cause some indirect jump instructions have different target addresses, which will produce false alarms. Similar CFI polices are also enforced by ROPecker [11]. It collects all potential gadgets beforehand, then leverages LBR mechanism to record all source addresses and target addresses of branches to decide whether there are gadgets. However, it does not take into account the signal mechanism in Linux. Due to the signal handler is in the process address space, ROPecker also will record the branch transfer when it is running, but these records are not in the potential gadgets database gained beforehand.

All these work mentioned above does not take into account environment may have an impact on the control flow integrity. Although Zhao et al. [25] introduced many factors (memory state, operating system kernel, system time etc.) would affect the control flow, but they did not analyze why these factors have impacts on the control flow, and what branch transfers may be affected. In this paper, we introduce some factors that will affect the control flow, and analyze why they have impacts on control flow, and construct branch patterns produced by these factors. There is little work related to environment, we list them in Table 1.

Table 1. Researches related to environment

Approach	Description
Giffin et al. [19]	Take configuration files, command-line parameters, and environment variables into intrusion detection
Mytkowicz et al. [16]	Introduce UNIX environment size and link order have an effect on performance analysis
Zhao et al. [25]	Introduce many factors (memory state, operating system kernel, system time et al.) will affect the program's control flow
This paper	Introduces environmental factors that will impact on the control flow from a fine-grained perspective (branch transfers), and analyzes why they have impacts on the control flow, and gets difference patterns produced by these factors

3   Impact of Environment on Branch Transfer

Ideally, with the same input, the control flow of a program will be the same too. However, the experimental results show that even with a simple program, its control flow may be different in different environments. The difference is the number of branch transfers is nearly the same, but branch transfers are different greatly. In this section, we give definitions related to control flow and factors impacting on branch transfers.

Definition 1. A **basic block** is a sequence of consecutive instructions, without any branches except at end of the sequence. For an arbitrary basic block b, $b = i_1, i_2, \ldots, i_k$, if instruction i_j is executed at step n, then instruction i_{j+1} must be executed at step $n + 1 (1 \leq j < k)$.

Definition 2. **Branch transfer** can be represented as $I = <From, To>$, where $From$ is the address of the last branch instruction in a basic block. To is the address of the first instruction in consecutive basic block.

Definition 3. Control flow transfer depends on the branch instructions in the program. A program's **control flow** can be represented as: $S_0 \xrightarrow{I_0} S_1 \xrightarrow{I_1} S_2 \ldots \xrightarrow{I_k} S_k \ldots \xrightarrow{I_n} S_n$. Where I_k is a branch instruction, whose address is $From$ in I defined in Definition 2, the targets of the branch instruction is To, S_k is the state of the program. Due to environment will affect the control flow, there is $S_i \times E \rightarrow S_j$, E is the environmental factor.

3.1   Impact of Time

System time will affect the behavior of programs. For example, the dynamic linker will invoke rdtsc (Read Time Stamp Counter) to decide whether to jump. The experimental result shows that the number of a branch transfer will change. This branch transfer is located in function HP_TIMING_DIFF_INIT in _dl_start_final(), and it is a direct branch transfer. This branch transfer is the 13th line in HP_TIMING_DIFF_INIT shown in Listing 1. When the time difference between __t2 and __t1 is less than the threshold dl_hp_timing_overhead, this branch transfer will take happen.

Listing 1. HP_TIMING_DIFF_INIT

```
1    /* Use two 'rdtsc' instructions in a row to find out how long it takes. */
2    #define HP_TIMING_DIFF_INIT() \
3    do { \
4        if (GLRO(dl_hp_timing_overhead) == 0) \
5        { \
6          int __cnt = 5; \
7          GLRO(dl_hp_timing_overhead) = ~0ull; \
8          do \
9          { \
10           hp_timing_t __t1, __t2; \
11           HP_TIMING_NOW (__t1); \  // Gets the current time
12           HP_TIMING_NOW (__t2); \  // Gets the current time
13           if (__t2 - __t1 < GLRO(dl_hp_timing_overhead)) \
14             GLRO(dl_hp_timing_overhead) = __t2 - __t1; \
15          } \
16          while (--__cnt > 0); \
17        } \
18      } while (0)
```

3.2 Impact of Space

Branch transfer is closely related to the program's memory layout. In Linux, a program's memory layout is illustrated in Fig. 1, the stack area includes the command line, environment variables and the context of function calls, dynamically allocated memory area is located in the heap. For example, when the program allocates memory using malloc or new, the reserved area is protected and not allowed to access. The stack area has a great impact on the branch transfer, which we will introduce in detail later.

Address Space Layout Randomization (ASLR). In Linux, addresses of stack, heap, and shared libraries are randomized using ASLR [26]. In the 32-bit operating system, the 4–23 bit of the stack base address is randomized, the 12–27 bit of the heap and shared libraries base addresses are randomized. As we know, local variables are located in stack, so the address of the local variables may be not the same every time as the program is loaded. However, In some applications, many branches are conducted in accordance with the last 8-bit or 12-bit addresses of local variables, which will cause the targets of the branch transfers become different.

580   J. Fu et al.

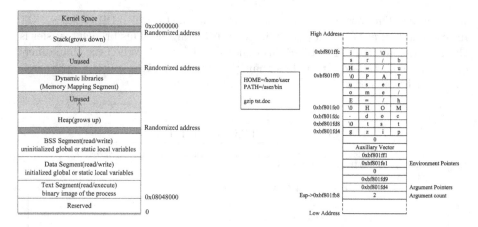

Fig. 1. A process's virtual memory layout in Linux

Fig. 2. Initial stack of a process

Environment Variables and Command Lines. The operating system must know something about the running environment before the program starts to run. Such as environment variables and arguments of the process, the operating system will save related information into the stack.

Assume the environment variables and the command-line are as the left side of Fig. 2, and the value of register Esp is 0xbf801ffc, then after the program is loaded, the content of the stack is shown as the right side in Fig. 2. Now Esp points to the count of the arguments, and the next are pointers linking to arguments and environment variables. Auxiliary Vector saves some auxiliary information needed by the dynamic linker, for instance, AT_ENTRY and AT_BASE respectively represents the entry address of the executable and the loaded address of the dynamic linker.

When the CPU processes memory-related operations (mainly located in shared libraries), it will check whether the address is memory boundary alignment. For example, In the 32-bit operating system, the processor will check whether the address is 4 byte boundary alignment, there will be different operations for different alignment. As shown in Listing 2, in function strrchr(), it will check whether the address of the string is 4 byte boundary alignment (testl $3,%esi), if it is, then executes it in sequence, otherwise jumps to L(19).

Listing 2. strrchr function

```
1   ENTRY (strrchr)
2       ......
3       testl 0x3, %esi              /* correctly aligned ? */
4       jz L(19)                     /* yes => begin loop */
5       movb (%esi), %dl
6       ......
7   L(19):movl (%esi), %edx /* get word (= 4 bytes) */
8       movl 0xfefefeff, %edi
9       addl %edx, %edi
```

It shows that the memory address boundary alignment has a significant impact on branch transfer. Usually, the memory address boundary alignment are impacted by the length of environment variables and command-line.

3.3   Mechanisms in Linux

There are many mechanisms in Linux, such as signals, the management of shared libraries, Global Offset Table (GOT), and all of them will have impacts on branch transfers. In this section, we will introduce these impacts in detail.

Searching for Shared Libraries. Linux uses a called SO-NAME (retaining only the shared library's major version number) naming mechanism to record shared library dependencies, meanwhile a symbolic link is created in each shared library's directory which has the same name with its "SO-NAME". And the directories of shared libraries a program depends on are saved in the section of dynamic.

In Linux, there is a procedure called ldconfig, which is responsible for creating, deleting, and updating the symbolic linking, and then collecting these symbolic linking into a file called /etc/ld.so.cache, which has a special structure. And the dynamic linker will directly search for shared libraries from this file. When a new application installs shared libraries into the system, ldconfig is invoked automatically to update the content of /etc/ld.so.cache, thus, the branch transfers that the dynamic linker searches for the shared libraries will change too.

Signal in Linux. Signal is an asynchronous communication mechanism in Linux, which notifies the process what event occurs. When a process P2 sends a signal to a process P1, the kernel will receive this signal, and put it into the signal queue of P1. When the process P1 traps into the kernel, the kernel will check its signal queue and invoke the signal handler according to the corresponding signal number.

Global Offset Table (GOT). In Linux, cross-module access is achieved according to Procedure Linkage Table (PLT) and GOT. The former contains a series of jump entries, and the latter contains the absolute addresses of library functions. For dynamic linking programs, there are many function calls between modules, ELF makes use of an approach named Lazy Binding to accelerate the speed of the dynamic linking.

As shown in Fig. 3(a), when the program first invokes `printf()`, it will jump to `printf@plt` to execute instruction jmp *0x804a000, which links to the address of the instruction push 0x0, 0 is the reference index in the relocation table .rel.plt for symbol printf, then it will invoke function _dl_runtime_resolve to achieve symbol resolution and relocation, and then patch the address of `printf` into GOT. When the program calls `printf` function again, its procedure

is shown as Fig. 3(b), also it will jump to `printf@plt` to execute instruction jmp
*0x804a000, but now the pointer *0x804a000 points to the address of `printf`,
it will call `printf` directly. In this procedure, the number of branch transfers
this time is two times less than the first time. Also this mechanism leaves it be
vulnerable to so-called GOT-overwriting attacks.

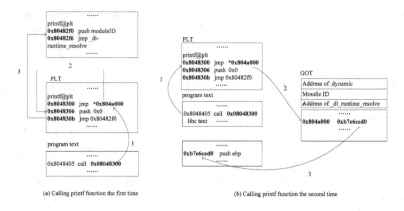

Fig. 3. Process of calling shared library function in Linux

Configuration of Environment Variables. In Linux, many environment
variables can be used by attackers, such as attackers can leverage LD_PRELOAD
to load shared libraries that they defined. The file specified in LD_PRELOAD will
be loaded before the dynamic linker searches for shared libraries in accordance
with fixed rules. And as a result of the existence of global symbol mechanism,
global symbols specified in the shared libraries through LD_PRELOAD will cover
the same global symbols specified in the normal shared libraries, which makes it
easy to modify the functions in standard libraries. Meanwhile attackers also can
modify the configuration file /etc/ld.so.preload to load the target files.

4   Software Behavior Analysis

We have recorded all direct and indirect branch transfers in the program and
shared libraries it depends on based on the dynamic binary instrumentation
tool Pin [27] on x86 32-bit version of Ubuntu 12.04, and compared the difference
between the branches to get the behavior patterns caused by factors mentioned
above, these patterns are described using Finite State Automata.

4.1   Environment and Branch Transfer

In Sect. 3, we have introduced many environmental factors that will impact on
branch transfers. In this section, we will introduce how these factors affect the
direct and indirect branch transfers of the program and the shared libraries, the
results are shown in Table 2.

Table 2. Impact of environmental factors on branch behavior

Factor	Item	Shared library		Program	
		Direct branch	Indirect branch	Direct branch	Indirect branch
Time	Time	Y			
Space	ASLR	Y	Y		
	Environment variable length	Y	Y		
	Command line length	Y	Y	Y	
Mechanims of Linux	GOT	Y	Y	Y	Y
	Searching for shared libraries	Y			
	Linux singal	Y	Y	Y	Y
	LD_PRELOAD	Y	Y		

Same Input for Same Program. All factors mentioned in Sect. 3 will affect the direct branch transfers in shared libraries even with the same input. These direct branches mainly belong to jump instructions and call instructions in the same function. There is an observation in these differences of branches: just the last bits of the source address (relative address) are different, and the target address is the same. Moreover, the indirect instructions affected mainly are ret instructions and jmp instructions in the same function, but the difference is the source address is the same, the target addresses are different. The branch transfer of the program itself is all the same when the input is the same. When the input is the same but the length of the directory that the input file is located in are different, the branch transfer of the program itself will be different on direct branches, and there is no impact on indirect branches in program itself.

Different Inputs for Same Program. When the inputs are different, there will be a great differences on branch transfers, especially for direct branches in shared libraries. We do not take into account the impact on direct branch transfers when the inputs are different, also because the most majority of attacks just leverage indirect branches to achieve their goals.

The difference on indirect branches are mainly indirect call instructions and fast system call instructions, that is to say different inputs will lead to different function calls and system calls.

4.2   Representation of Differences

We use the dynamic binary instrumentation tool Pin to record all branch transfers, and then compare them using the tool diff in Linux. For example, we run the program graphicsmagic to convert the format of a picture two times, and get the branch transfers in libc.so, the difference is shown in Fig. 4. These two hexadecimal number are the source and target addresses respectively, the number in the last column is the version number of the shared library, the differences

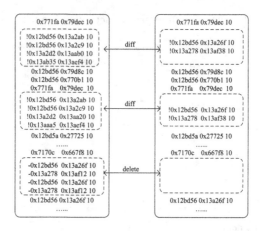

Fig. 4. Comparison of branch record

are shown in the dotted box, where '!' denotes they are different, '-' denotes these branch transfers should be deleted.

Definition 4 (Concepts of FSA). Difference pattern can be described as a sequence of addresses $<addr_0, (*), addr_1, ..., (*), addr_n>$, where $addr_k$ is the source address, $0 < k < n$, $addr_0$ and $addr_n$ can be the source or the target address, $(*)$ represents there may be other source addresses that do not equal to $addr_{i+1}$ between $addr_i$ and $addr_{i+1}$. For instance, the sequence of $<0x12bd56, 0x13a278>$ represents that the difference pattern is the source address of a branch is 0x12bd56, and the next branch's source address is 0x13a278.

Definition 5. Finite State Automata (FSA) includes five parts (Σ, S, S_0, T, F), and the meaning of each part is as follows:

1. Σ is the input symbol set. In this paper, it is the set of source and target addresses.
2. S is the state set. In this paper, it is a set of number from 0 to n.
3. S_0 is the initial state.
4. T is the state transition function, which gives the subsequent state according to the state in S and the symbol in Σ.
5. F is the accepted state.

Representation of Difference Patterns Using FSA. We leverage FSA to describe the impact of environment on branch transfers. The test programs are shown in Table 3, which were run on an Intel Core i7 processor with 32-bit Ubuntu 12.04 system.

Input is the same. When the input is the same, the differences are mainly located in the shared library libc.so. In this section, we mainly discuss differences produced by libc.so for programs in Table 3.

Table 3. Test programs

Application	Size	Experiment
gzip	806 KB	Compress multiple files
grep	153.7 KB	Search regular expression in multiple files
bzip2	30.2 KB	Compress multiple files
bubblesort	7.3 KB	Sort different inputs
cat	46.8 KB	Connect two files
diff	112.3 KB	Compare two files
tesseract	236.9 KB	Recognize multiple license plates
graphicsmagic	5.4 MB	Connect two pictures, convert pictures into different forms
bunzip2	30.2 KB	Uncompress multiple files
hmmer	617.2 KB	Search sequence databases for homologs of protein sequence

The difference pattern of indirect branch transfers is the sequence started with a source address 0x12bd56 and ended with a source address 0x13a278 or 0x13a288. It can be described as the FSA in Fig. 5(a), where 0 is the started state, state 2 is the accepted state, '||' represents *or* operation.

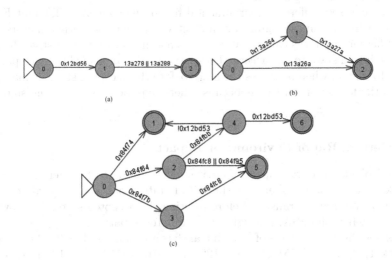

Fig. 5. Difference patterns produced by libc.so

The difference patterns of direct branch transfers in libc.so are shown as Fig. 5(b) and (c). In Fig. 5(b), all addresses are source addresses. In Fig. 5(c) all addresses are source addresses except address 0x12bd53. When the source address of a branch is 0x84f64, and the source address of the next branch is 0x84fbb, there is a need to decide whether the target address of another branch is 0x12bd53, if it is, then the difference patterns is $<0x84f64, 0x84ffb>$, otherwise, the difference pattern is $<0x84f74>$.

Same input but different length of command-line. Although the input is the same, the different length of the input file name will have an impact on branch transfer too. Since the program itself has variability, this section also discusses the difference patterns produced by shared library libc.so. The difference patterns of indirect branch transfers are shown in Fig. 6(a), (b). We can find the differences are mainly the return address of __i686_get_pc_thunk_bx and __i686_get_pc_thunk_dx. The difference patterns of direct branch transfers are shown in Fig. 6(c), (d), (e) and (f), & means *and* operation.

Linux signals. The difference pattern caused by Linux signals is described as Fig. 7. The procedure of the OS to execute the signal handler will produce branch transfers between targets 0x414 and source address 0x427.

Procedure of searching for shared libraries. When there are other shared libraries installed, the procedure of searching for shared libraries will have an impact on branch transfers, and these difference patterns can be described as Fig. 8 and all addresses are source addresses.

In order to accelerate the speed of pattern matching, for these FSAs, we allocate a 1-bit flag for every state except for the accepted state to distinguish the source address and target address. If flag equals 0, it is the source address, otherwise, it is the target address.

As we can see, different environmental factors will generate different FSAs, and space has the most significant impact compared with other factors. For most difference patterns caused by space, its feature is that they just go through from the initial state to the accepted state straightly, and the difference pattern caused by signal, when it arrives the state before the accepted state, it may goes back to the former state, this is because there may be more than one signal at a time.

4.3   Getting Rid of Environment Impact

In order to get rid of the impact of environment on branch transfer, we allocate a stack for every state except for the initial state. Each stack records the row number of the branch transfers before meeting the accepted state. As shown in Fig. 9, the left is the FSA, the right is the difference pattern.

Assume the row numbers of branch transfers are shown in Fig. 9. The contents of stack 1, 2, 3 are (12513, 12514, 12515, 12516, 12517), (12518, 12519) and (12520) respectively. When it meets the accepted state, outputs these contents to a file until all branch transfers have been recorded, then we can delete these branch transfers according to the row number.

The time overhead of getting rid of environment impact depends on the number of states and state transitions a FSA have. The space overhead will be $O(M * N)$, where M is the number of states in the FSA and N is the average number of transitions for every state. If we use **Bloom filter**, the time overhead can be a constant.

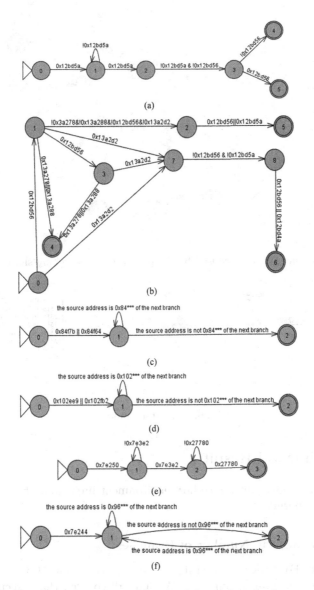

Fig. 6. Difference patterns caused by the different length of command-line

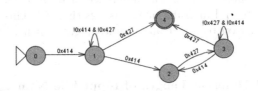

Fig. 7. Difference pattern caused by Linux signals

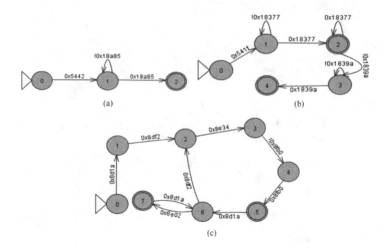

Fig. 8. Difference patterns caused by the procedure of searching shared libraries

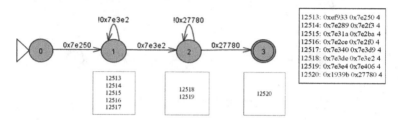

Fig. 9. FSA-Stack model

5   Experimental Result

In this section, we will introduce how environment impacts on branch transfers through our experiments.

5.1   Comparing the Number of Branches

Same Input. For programs in Table 3, we have run them 50 times to get the difference between branch numbers. We have discovered that except tesseract and graohicsmagic, the difference of branch number in other programs is very small, which is no more than 3. The difference of branch number in tesseract is no more than 300, and in grahicsmagic is less than 80. This is because space has a greater impact on tesseract and grahicsmagic, which will be discussed in Sect. 5.3.

Same Input but Different Length of Input File Name. For programs in Table 3, we change the length of the input file's name (close ASLR) and then observe the difference of the branch number. We can find that for most programs, the difference of branch number is mainly located in direct branches produced by shared libraries. The number of direct branches of program itself will increase as the length of the input file's name increases in gzip and graphicsmagic. And we can get that the number of indirect branches for program itself is always the same.

Different Inputs. For programs gzip, bzip2, grep, and tesseract, we change their input (types of input file include doc, pdf, txt, ppt, and tif) to observe their branch number. We get that the difference of branch number is great when inputs are different. These differences are mainly located in direct branch transfers of the program itself.

5.2 Impact of Time

We have tested the impact of time on branch transfer for programs in Table 3. As described in Sect. 3, the impact of time on branch transfer is focused on branch transfer $<0x00004e80, 0x00004e86>$. Table 4 records the number this branch occurs, we can find this branch occurs no more than four times. There are 4 occurrences of this branch for 38 out of 50 runs in gzip. And it is related to the CPU, the faster the CPU runs, the more this branch transfer number is.

Table 4. The number of branch transfer $<0x00004e80, 0x00004e86>$

Application	Number				Total
	4	3	2	1	
gzip	38	8	3	1	50
grep	39	10	1	0	50
bzip2	37	9	4	0	50
bubblesort	38	10	2	0	50
cat	38	8	2	2	50
diff	38	6	5	1	50
tesseract	33	13	4	0	50
graphicsmagic	41	8	1	0	50
bunzip2	38	7	5	0	50
hmmer	38	10	2	0	50

5.3 Impact of Space

User Input. For programs in Table 3, we find that as the input is the same, only the control flow of gzip, tesseract, and graphicsmagic are different(excluding the impact of time), and these differences are located in shared library. Functions that these differences are located in are shown in Table 5.

Table 5. Impact of input on software behavior

Application	Function name	Library
gzip	`strlen_sse2_bsf`	libc.so
tesseract	`strrchr_ia32`	
	`strlen_sse2_bsf`	
	`memcpy_sse3_rep`	
graphicsmagic	`strlen_sse2_bsf`	
	`strrchr_sse2_bsf`	
	`memcpy_sse3_rep`	

As shown, when the input is the same, the differences of branch transfers are located in functions related to string operation in shared library libc.so. For string handling functions, in order to accelerate the processing speed, the address of the string will be checked to determine whether it is 4-byte boundary alignment or 16-byte boundary alignment (Streaming SIMD Extension (SSE) instruction). These differences cover direct call branches, direct jump branches, ret branches, and indirect jump branches.

From experimental result, we find that these differences are caused by the ALSR for stack, which leads to the temporary variables' 16-byte boundary alignment change. In order to determine the impact of ASLR on software behavior, we close ASLR mechanism in Linux, and run programs in Table 5, get that there is no difference on branch transfer for all programs.

Meanwhile, we change the directory of the input file to observe the change of the control flow. The experimental results show that when the length of the input file's directory is not changed, the control flow still is not different. But if the length of the input file has been changed, the control flow will produce great differences. This is because in Linux many operations are related to the input, such as getting the length of the command-line, copying parameters of the command line, and getting the name of the program.

Environment Variables. We change the length of the environment variables (close ASLR) to observe its impact on branch transfer. We find that these functions almost are the same with Table 5, and the reason is the same as user input.

5.4 Impact of Signal

In order to determine the impact of signals on software behavior, we add a signal SIGINT into the program bubblesort. When it receives ^C, the signal will be triggered. We have found that when there is a signal, the number of branch transfers will be more than without signal. The pattern is $(0x414, ..., 0x427)$, the control flow will be transferred to the signal handler, and then return to 0x427 to continue the normal control flow. Due to the signal handler is located in user space, so we can record its branch transfers using Pin.

5.5   Impact of Searching for Shared Libraries

When we install r-base on the testing system, it will install other shared libraries into the system, we compare the contents of /etc/ld.so.cache, and find its contents are modified, the difference of the content is shown in Fig. 10.

```
101a102
> libpcrecpp.so.0 -> libpcrecpp.so.0.0.0
123a125
> libgfortran.so.3 -> libgfortran.so.3.0.0
195a198
> libodbc.so.1 -> libodbc.so.1.0.0
226a230
> libodbcinst.so.1 -> libodbcinst.so.1.0.0
......
```

Fig. 10. Difference of /etc/ld.so.cache

In Fig. 10, many other shared libraries are written into /etc/ld.so.cache. For example, 101a102 represents that now there is a new symbolic linking libpcrecpp.so.0 → libpcrecpp.so.0.0.0 in the file, and 'a' means *add*.

6   Discussion and Conclusion

Software behavior is affected by environmental factors, especially for branch transfers. In this paper, we study the impact of environment on branch transfer of software from time, space (memory boundary alignment) and mechanisms of the Linux operating system (the procedure of searching for shared libraries, signals, GOT/PLT, and the configuration of the environment variable LD_PRELOAD). At the same time, we leverage Finite State Automata (FSA) to describe the difference patterns of branch transfers caused by environmental factors. These difference patterns can be used to control flow integrity detection that the testing and validation code is independent on the program to mitigate the false alarms. Meanwhile they can be used to CIMB [28] to reduce the impact of environmental factors on computation integrity measurement.

In future work, we will focus on attacks caused by these environmental factors as these factors are ignored by CFI.

Also, there are some limitations in our work. For instance, we just investigate environmental factors from time, space and mechanisms in Linux, there may be some other factors, such as compiler optimization and the upgrade of operating systems. And we do not investigate the impact of environment on the branch transfer of kernel code.

Acknowledgements. Supported by the National Natural Science Foundation of China (61373168), and Doctoral Fund of Ministry of Education of China (20120141110002).

References

1. Forrest, S., Hofmeyr, S., Somayaji, A.: The evolution of system-call monitoring. In: Proceeding of the 24th Annual Computer Security Applications Conference, California, USA, pp. 418–430 (2008)
2. Wee, K., Moon, B.: Automatic generation of finite state automata for detecting intrusions using system call sequences. In: Gorodetsky, V., Popyack, L., Skormin, V. (eds.) MMM-ACNS 2003. LNCS, vol. 2776, pp. 206–216. Springer, Heidelberg (2003). doi:10.1007/978-3-540-45215-7_17
3. Kruegel, C., Mutz, D., Valeur, F., Vigna, G.: On the detection of anomalous system call arguments. In: Snekkenes, E., Gollmann, D. (eds.) ESORICS 2003. LNCS, vol. 2808, pp. 326–343. Springer, Heidelberg (2003). doi:10.1007/978-3-540-39650-5_19
4. Maggi, F., Matteucci, M., Zanero, S.: Detecting intrusions through system call sequence and argument analysis. IEEE Trans. Dependable Secure Comput. **7**(4), 381–395 (2010)
5. Shacham, H.: The geometry of innocent flesh on the bone: return-into-libc without function calls (on the x86). In: Proceeding of the 14th ACM Conference on Computer and Communications Security, Alexandria, USA, pp. 552–561. ACM (2007)
6. Bletsch, T., Jiang, X., Freeh, V.W., Liang, Z.: Jump-oriented programming: a new class of code-reuse attack. In: Proceeding of the 6th ACM Symposium on Information, Computer and Communications Security, Hong Kong, China, pp. 30–40. ACM (2011)
7. Abadi, M., Budiu, M., Erlingsson, U., Ligatti, J.: Control-flow integrity. In: Proceeding of the 12th ACM Conference on Computer and Communications Security, Alexandria, USA, pp. 340–353. ACM (2005)
8. Abadi, M., Budiu, M., Erlingsson, U., Ligatti, J.: Control-flow integrity principles, implementations, and applications. J. ACM Trans. Inf. Syst. Secur. **13**(1), 1–41 (2009)
9. Xia, Y., Liu, Y., Chen, H., Zang, B.: CFIMon: detecting violation of control flow integrity using performance counters. In: IEEE/IFIP International Conference on Dependable Systems and Networks, Boston, USA, pp. 1–12. IEEE/IFTP (2012)
10. Yuan, P., Zeng, Q., Ding, X.: Hardware-assisted fine-grained code-reuse attack detection. In: Bos, H., Monrose, F., Blanc, G. (eds.) RAID 2015. LNCS, vol. 9404, pp. 66–85. Springer, Cham (2015). doi:10.1007/978-3-319-26362-5_4
11. Cheng, Y., Zhou, Z., Yu, M., Ding, X., Deng, R.H.: ROPecker: a generic and practical approach for defending against ROP attacks. In: Proceeding of Symposium on Network and Distributed System Security, San Diego, USA. ISOC (2014)
12. Intel Manual. Intel 64 and IA-32 architecture software developers manual, vol. 3
13. Zhong, S.: Certified software. Commun. ACM **53**(12), 56–66 (2010)
14. Murali A, Rao M. A survey on intrusion detection approaches. In: Proceeding of the First International Conference on Information and Communication Technologies, Karachi, Pakistan, pp. 233–240. IEEE (2005)
15. Garcia-Teodoro, P., Diaz-Verdejo, J., Maci-Fernndez, G., Vazque, Z.: Anomaly-based network intrusion detection: techniques, systems and challenges. Comput. Secur. **28**(1), 18–28 (2009). Elsevier
16. Mytkowicz, T., Diwan, A., Hauswirth, M., Sweenry, P.F.: Producing wrong data without doing anything obviously wrong! ACM Sigplan Not. **44**(3), 265–276 (2009)
17. Yeung, D.Y., Ding, Y.: Host-based intrusion detection using dynamic and static behavioral models. Pattern Recogn. **36**(1), 229–243 (2003). Elsevier

18. Li, P., Park, H., Gao, D., Fu, J.: Bridging the gap between data-flow and control-flow analysis for anomaly detection. In: Proceeding of the 24th Annual Computer Security Application Conference, California, USA. IEEE (2008)

19. Giffin, J.T., Dagon, D., Jha, S., Lee, W., Miller, B.P.: Environment-sensitive intrusion detection. In: Proceeding of Recent Advances in Intrusion Detection, Hamburg, Germany, pp. 185–206. Springer (2006)

20. Zhang, C., Wei, T., Chen, Z,, Duan, L.: Practical control flow integrity and randomization for binary executables. In: Proceeding of IEEE Symposium on Security and Privacy, San Francisco, USA, pp. 559–573. IEEE (2013)

21. Zhang, M., Sekar, R.: Control flow integrity for COTS binaries. In: Proceeding of the 22nd USENIX Security Symposium, pp. 337–352. IEEE, Washington, D.C. (2013)

22. Wang, M., Yin, H., Bhaskar, A.V., Continent, B.C., et al.: Finer-grained control flow integrity for stripped binaries. In: Proceedings of the 31st Annual Computer Security Applications Conference, Los Angeles, USA, pp. 331–340. IEEE (2015)

23. Lin, Y., Tang, X., Gao, D., Fu, J.: Control flow integrity enforcement with dynamic code optimization. In: Bishop, M., Nascimento, A.C.A. (eds.) ISC 2016. LNCS, vol. 9866, pp. 366–385. Springer, Cham (2016). doi:10.1007/978-3-319-45871-7_22

24. Pappas, V.: kBouncer: efficient and transparent ROP mitigation. Technical report, Columbia University (2012)

25. Zhao, T., Tang, Y., Xu, W., Fu, G., Qi, S., Jia, X., et al.: Exactly reproducible program execution and its application in computer architecture simulation. Chin. J. Comput. **34**(11), 2073–2083 (2011)

26. Shacham, H., Page, M., Pfaff, B.: On the effectiveness of address-space randomization. In: Proceeding of the 11th ACM Conference on Computer and Communications Security 2004, pp. 298–307 (2004)

27. Luk, C.K., Cohn, R., Muth, R., Patil, H., Klauser, A., Lowney, G., et al.: Pin: building customized program analysis tools with dynamic instrumentation. ACM Sigplan Not. **40**(6), 190–200 (2005)

28. Fu, J., Lin, Y., Zhang, X., Li, P.: Computation integrity measurement based on branch transfer. In: Proceeding of the 13th International Conference on Trust, Security and Privacy in Computing and Communications, Beijing, China, pp. 590–597. IEEE (2014)

Mobile Security II

DroidClassifier: Efficient Adaptive Mining of Application-Layer Header for Classifying Android Malware

Zhiqiang Li[1(✉)], Lichao Sun[1], Qiben Yan[1], Witawas Srisa-an[1],
and Zhenxiang Chen[2]

[1] University of Nebraska–Lincoln, Lincoln, NE 68588, USA
{zli,lsun,qyan,witty}@cse.unl.edu
[2] University of Jinan, Jinan 250022, Shandong, China
czx.ujn@gmail.com

Abstract. A recent report has shown that there are more than 5,000 malicious applications created for Android devices each day. This creates a need for researchers to develop effective and efficient malware classification and detection approaches. To address this need, we introduce DroidClassifier: a systematic framework for classifying network traffic generated by mobile malware. Our approach utilizes network traffic analysis to construct multiple models in an automated fashion using a supervised method over a set of labeled malware network traffic (the training dataset). Each model is built by extracting common identifiers from multiple HTTP header fields. Adaptive thresholds are designed to capture the disparate characteristics of different malware families. Clustering is then used to improve the classification efficiency. Finally, we aggregate the multiple models to construct a holistic model to conduct cluster-level malware classification. We then perform a comprehensive evaluation of DroidClassifier by using 706 malware samples as the training set and 657 malware samples and 5,215 benign apps as the testing set. Collectively, these malicious and benign apps generate 17,949 network flows. The results show that DroidClassifier successfully identifies over 90% of different families of malware with more than 90% accuracy with accessible computational cost. Thus, DroidClassifier can facilitate network management in a large network, and enable unobtrusive detection of mobile malware. By focusing on analyzing network behaviors, we expect DroidClassifier to work with reasonable accuracy for other mobile platforms such as iOS and Windows Mobile as well.

Keywords: Mobile security · Android malware detection · Malware classification · HTTP network traffic

1 Introduction

Android is currently the most popular smart-mobile device operating system in the world, holding about 80% of world-wide market share. Due to their popularity and platform openness, Android devices, unfortunately, have also been subjected to a marked increase in the number of malware and vulnerability exploits targeting them.

© ICST Institute for Computer Sciences, Social Informatics and Telecommunications Engineering 2017
R. Deng et al. (Eds.): SecureComm 2016, LNICST 198, pp. 597–616, 2017.
DOI: 10.1007/978-3-319-59608-2_33

According to a recent study from F-Secure Labs, there are at least 275 new families (or new variants of known families) of malware that currently target Android [8]. On the contrary, only one new threat family on iOS was reported.

As smart-mobile devices gradually become the preferred end-hosts for accessing the Internet, network traffic of mobile apps has been utilized to identify mobile applications to facilitate network management tasks [33]. However, the methods of identifying benign mobile applications fall short when dealing with mobile malware, due to the unique traffic characteristics of malicious applications. From our observation, malicious attacks by mobile malware often involve network connectivity. Network connection has been utilized to launch attack activities or steal sensitive personal information. As a result, studying network traffic going into or coming out of Android devices can yield unique insights about the attack origination and patterns.

In this paper, we present DroidClassifier, a systematic framework for classifying and detecting malicious network traffic produced by Android malicious apps. Our work attempts to aggregate additional application traffic header information (e.g., method, user agent, referrer, cookies and protocol) to derive at more meaningful and accurate malware analysis results. As such, DroidClassifier has been designed and constructed to consider multiple dimensions of malicious traffic information to establish malicious network patterns. First, it uses the traffic information to create clusters of applications. It then analyzes these application clusters (i) to identify whether the apps in each cluster are malicious or benign and (ii) to classify which family the malicious apps belong to.

DroidClassifier is designed to be efficient and lightweight, and it can be integrated into network IDS/IPS to perform mobile malware classification and detection in a large network. We evaluate DroidClassifier using more than six thousand Android benign apps and malware samples; each with the corresponding collected network traffic. In total, these malicious and benign apps generate 17,949 traffic flows. We then use DroidClassifier to identify the malicious portions of the network traffic, and to extract the multi-field contents of the HTTP headers generated by the mobile malware to build extensive and concrete identifiers for classifying different types of mobile malware. Our results show that DroidClassifier can accurately classify malicious traffic and distinguish malicious traffic from benign traffic using HTTP header information. Experiments indicate that our framework can achieve more than 90% classification rate and detection accuracy while it is also more efficient than a state-of-the-art malware classification and detection approach [2].

In summary, the contributions of our work are mainly two-fold. First, we develop DroidClassifier, which considers multiple dimensions of mobile traffic information from different families of mobile malware to establish distinguishable malicious patterns. Second, we design a novel weighted score-based metric for malware classification, and we further optimize the performance of our classifier using a novel combination of supervised learning (score-based classification) and unsupervised learning (malware clustering). The clustering step makes our detection phase more efficient than prior efforts, since the subsequent malware classification can be performed over clustered malware requests instead of individual requests from malware samples.

The rest of this paper is organized as follows. Section 2 explains why we consider multidimensional network information to build our framework. Section 3 provides overview of prior work related to the proposed DroidClassifier. Section 4 discusses the approach used in the design of DroidClassifier, and the tuning of important parameters in the system. DroidClassifier is evaluated in Sect. 5. Section 6 discusses limitations and future work, followed by the conclusion in Sect. 7.

2 Motivation

A recent report indicates that close to 5,000 Android malicious apps are created each day [6]. The majority of these apps also use various forms of obfuscation to avoid detection by security analysts. However, a recent report by Symantec indicates that Android malware authors tend to improve upon existing malware instead of creating new ones. In fact, the study finds that more than three quarters of all Android malware reported during the first three months of 2014 can be categorized into just 10 families [26]. As such, while malware samples belonging to a family appear to be different in terms of source code and program structures due to obfuscation, they tend to exhibit similar runtime behaviors.

This observation motivates the adoption of network traffic analysis to detect malware [2, 5, 20, 31]. The initial approach is to match requested URIs or hostnames with known malicious URIs or hostnames. However, as malware authors increase malware complexities (e.g., making subtle changes to the behaviors or using multiple servers as destinations to send sensitive information), the results produced by hostname analysis tend to be inaccurate.

To overcome these subtle changes made by malware authors to avoid detection, Aresu et al. [2] apply clustering as part of network traffic analysis to determine malware families. Once these clusters have been identified, they extract features from these clusters and use the extracted information to detect malware [2]. Their experimental results indicate that their approach can yield 60% to 100% malware detection rate. The main benefit of this approach is that it handles these subtle changing malware behaviors as part of training by clustering the malware traffic. However, the detection is done by analyzing each request to identify network signatures and then matching signatures. This can be inefficient when dealing with a large traffic amount. In addition, as these changes attempted by malware authors occur frequently, the training process may also need to be performed frequently. As will be shown in Sect. 5, this training process, which includes clustering, can be very costly.

We see an opportunity to deal with these changes effectively while streamlining the classification and detection process to make it more efficient than the approach introduced by Aresu et al. [2]. Our proposed approach, DroidClassifier, relies on two important insights. First, most newly created malware belongs to previously known families. Second, clustering, as shown by Aresu et al., can effectively deal with subtle changes made by malware authors to avoid detection. We construct DroidClassifier to exploit previously known information about a malware sample and the family it belongs to. This information can be easily obtained from existing security reports as well as malware classifications provided by various malware research archives including Android Malware Genome Project [36]. Our approach uses this information to perform training by analyzing traffic generated by malware samples belonging to the same family to extract most relevant features.

To deal with variations within a malware family and to improve testing efficiency, we perform clustering of the testing traffic data and compare features of each resulting cluster to those of each family as part of classification and detection process. Note that the purpose of our clustering mechanism is different from the clustering mechanism used by Aresu et al. [2], in which they apply clustering to extract useful malware signatures. Our approach does not rely on the clustering mechanism to extract malware traffic features. Instead, we apply clustering in the detection phase to improve the detection efficiency by classifying and detecting malware at the cluster granularity instead of at each individual request granularity, resulting in much less classification and detection efforts. By relying on previously known and precise classification information, we only extract the most relevant features from each family. This allows us to use fewer features than the prior approach [2]. As will be shown in Sect. 5, DroidClassifier is both effective and efficient in malware classification and detection.

3 Related Work

Network Traffic Analysis has been used to monitor runtime behaviors by exercising targeted applications to observe app activities and collect relevant data to help with analysis of runtime behaviors [9, 15, 22, 28, 35]. Information can be gathered at ISP level or by employing proxy servers and emulators. Our approach also collects network traffic by executing apps in device emulators. The collected traffic information can be analyzed for leakage of sensitive information [7, 10], used for classification based on network behaviors [20], or exploited to automatically detect malware [3, 5, 31].

Supervised and unsupervised learning approaches are then used to help with detecting [14, 30, 34] and classifying desktop malware [17, 20] based on collected network traffic. Recently, there have been several efforts that use network traffic analysis and machine learning to detect mobile malware. Shabtai et al. [25] present a Host-based Android machine learning malware detection system to target the repackaging attacks. They conclude that deviations of some benign behaviors can be regarded as malicious ones. Narudin et al. [18] come up with a TCP/HTTP based malware detection system. They extracted basic information, (e.g. IP address), content based, time based and connection based features to build the detection system. Their approach can only determine if an app is malicious or not, and they cannot classify malware to different families.

FIRMA [21] is a tool that clusters unlabeled malware samples according to network traces. It produces network signatures for each malware family for detection. Anshul et al. [3] propose a malware detection system using network traffic. They extract statistical features of malware traffic, and select decision trees as a classifier to build their system. Their system can only judge whether an app is malicious or not. Our system, however, can identify the family of malware.

Aresu et al. [2] create malware clusters using traffic and extract signatures from clusters to detect malware. Our work is different from their approach in that we extract malware patterns from existing families by analyzing HTTP traffic and determining scores to help with malware classification and detection. To make our system more efficient, we then form clusters of testing traffics to reduce the number of test cases (each cluster is a test case) that must be evaluated. This allows our approach to be more efficient than the prior effort that analyzes each testing traffic trace.

4 Introducing DroidClassifier

Our proposed system, DroidClassifier, is designed to achieve two objectives: (i) to distinguish between benign and malicious traffic; and (ii) to automatically classify malware into families based on HTTP traffic information. To accomplish these objectivesthe system employs three major components: *training module*, *clustering module*, and *malware classification* and *detection module*.

The *training module* has three major functions: feature extraction, malware database construction, and family threshold decision based on scores. After extracting features from a collection of HTTP network traffic of malicious apps inside the training set, the module produces a database of network patterns per family and the z_{score} threshold that can be used to evaluate the maliciousness of the network traffic from malware samples and classify them into corresponding malware families. To address subtle behavioral changes among malware samples and to improve detection efficiency, the *clustering module* is followed to collect a set of network traffic and gather similar HTTP traffic into the same group so as to classify network traffic as groups.

Finally, the *malware classification and detection module* computes the scores and the corresponding z_{score} based on HTTP traffic information of a particular traffic cluster. If this absolute value of z_{score} is less than the threshold of one family, our system classifies the HTTP traffic into the malware family. It then evaluates whether the HTTP traffic requests are from a certain malware family or from benign apps, the strategy of which is similar to that of the classification module. Our Training and Scoring mechanisms provide a quantitative measurement for malware classification and detection. Next, we describe the training, traffic clustering, malware classification, and malware detection process in details.

4.1 Model Training

The training process requires four steps as shown in Fig. 1. The first step is collecting network traffic information of applications that can be used for training, classification, and detection. With respect to training, the network traffic data set that we focus on is collected from malicious apps. The second step is extracting relevant features that can be used for training and testing. The third step is building malware database. Lastly, we compute the scores that can be used for classification and detection. Next, we describe each of these steps in turn.

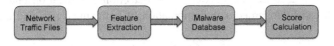

Fig. 1. Steps taken by DroidClassifier to perform training

Collecting Network Traffic. To collect network traffic, we locate malware samples that *have already been classified into families*. We use the real-world malware samples provided by Android Malware Genome Project [36] and Drebin [4] project, which classify 1,363 malware samples, making a total of 2,689 HTTP requests, into 10 families. We randomly choose 706 samples to build the training model, and the remaining 657 samples as malware evaluation set. We also use 5,215 benign apps, generating 15,260 HTTP requests, to evaluate the detection phase. These benign apps are from the Google Play store.

The first step of traffic collection is installing samples belonging to a family into an Android device or a device emulator (as used in this study). We use 50% of malware samples for training; i.e., 30% for database building and 20% for threshold calculation. We also use 20% of benign apps for threshold calculation.

To exercise these samples, we use *Monkey* to randomly generate event sequences to run each of these samples for 5 min to generate network traffic. We choose this duration because a prior work by Chen et al. [5] shows that most malware would generate malicious traffic in the first 5 min.

In the third step, we use *Wireshark* or *tcpdump*, a network protocol analyzer, to collect the network traffic information. In the last step, we generate the network traffic traces as PCAP files. After we have collected the network traffic information from a family of malware, we repeat the process for the next family. It is worth noting that our dataset contains several repackaged Android malware samples. Though most of the traffic patterns generated by repackaged malware apps and carrier apps are similar, we find that these repackaged malware samples do generate malicious traffic. Furthermore, our samples also generate some common ad-library traffic, and the traffic can also bring noise to our training phase. In our implementation, we establish a "white-list" request library containing requests sending to benign URLs and common ad-libraries. We filter out white-listed requests and use only the remaining potential malicious traffic to train the model and perform the detection.

Extracting Features for Model Building. We limit our investigation to HTTP traffic because it is a commonly used protocol for network communication. There are four types of HTTP message headers: General Header, Request Header, Response Header and Entity Header. Collectively, these four types of header result in 80 header fields [27]. However, we also observe that fewer than 12 fields are regularly used in the generated traffic. We manually analyze these header fields and choose five of them as our features. Note that we do not rank them. If more useful headers can be obtained from a different dataset, we may need to retrain the system.

Also note that we utilize these features differently from the prior work [20]. In the training phase, we make use of multiple fields, and come up with a new weighted score-based mechanism to classify HTTP traffic. Perdisci et al. [20], on the other hand, use clustering to generate malware signatures. In our approach, clustering is used as an optimization to reduce the complexity of the detection/classification phase. As such, our approach can be regarded as a combination of both supervised and unsupervised learning.

By using different fields of HTTP traffic information, we, in effect, increase the dimension of our training and testing datasets. If one of these fields is inadequate in determining malware family, e.g., malware authors deliberately tamper one or more fields to avoid analysis, other fields can often be used to help determine malware family, leading to better clustering/classification results. Next, we discuss the rationale of selecting these features and the relative importance of them.

Table 1. Features extracted

Field name	Description
Host	This field specifies the Internet host and port number of the resource
Referer	This field contains URL of a page from which HTTP request originated
Request-URI	The URI from the request source
User-Agent	This field contains information about the user agent originating the request
Content-Type	This field indicates the media type of the entity-body sent to the recipient

- *Host* can be effective in detecting and classifying certain types of malware with clear and relatively stabilized hostname fields in their HTTP traffic. Based on our observation, most of the malware families generate HTTP traffic with only a small number of disparate host fields.
- *Referrer* identifies the origination of a request. This information can introduce privacy concerns as IMEI, SDK version and device model, device brand can be sent through this field as demonstrated by *DroidKungFu* and *FakeInstaller* families.
- *Request-URI* can also leak sensitive information. We observe that *Gappusin* family can use this field to leak device information, such as IMEI, IMSI, and OS Version.
- *User-Agent* contains a text sequence containing information such as device manufacturer, version, plugins, and toolbars installed on the browser. We observe that malware can use this field to send information to the Command & Control (C&C) server.
- *Content-Type* can be unique for some malware families. For example, *Opfake* has a unique "multipart/form-data; boundary=AaB03x" Content-Type field, which can also be included to elevate the successful rate of malware detection.

Request-URI and Referrer are the two most important features because they contain rich contextual information. Host and User-Agent serve as additional discernible features to identify certain types of malware. Content-Type is the least important in terms of identifiable capability; however, we also observe that this feature is capable of recognizing some specific families of malware.

Although dedicated adversaries can dynamically tamper these fields to evade the detection, such adaptive behaviors may incur additional operational costs, which we suspect is the reason why the level of adaptation is low, according to our experiments. We defer the investigation of malware's adaptive behaviors to future work. In addition, employing multiple hosts can possibly evade our detection at a cost of higher maintenance expenses. In our current dataset, we have seen that some families use multiple hosts to receive information and we are still able to detect and classify them by using multiple network features.

We also notice that these malware samples utilize C&C servers to receive leaked information and control malicious actions. In our data set, many C&C servers are still fully or partially functional. For fully functional servers, we observe their responses. We notice that these responses are mainly simple acknowledgments (e.g., "200 OK"). For the partially functional servers, we can still observe information sent by malware sample to these servers.

Building Malware Database. Once we have identified relevant features, we extract values for each field in each request. As an example, to build a database for the *DroidKungFu* malware family, we search all traffic trace files (PCAPs) of the all samples belonging to this family (100 samples in this case), extract all values or common longest substring patterns, in the case of Request-URI fields, of the five relevant features, put them into lists with no duplicated values, and build a map between each key and its values.

Scoring of Malware Traffic Requests. In the training process, we assign scores to malware traffic requests to compute the classification/detection threshold, which we termed as *training z_{score} computation*. We need to calculate the malware z_{score} range for each malware family. We use traffic from 20% of malware samples belonging to each family for training z_{score} computation. For each malware family, we assign a weight to each HTTP field to quantify different contributions of each field according to the number of patterns the field entails, since the number of patterns of a field indicates the uncertainty of extracted patterns. For example, the field with a single pattern is deemed as a unique field, thus it is considered to be a field with high contributions. In contrast, the field with a number of patterns would be weighted lower. As such, we compute the total number of patterns of each field from the malware databases to determine the weight. The following formula illustrates the weight computation for each field: $w_i = \frac{1}{t_i} \times 100$, where w_i stands for the weight for ith field, and t_i is the number of patterns for the ith field for each family in malware databases. For instance, there are 30 patterns for field User-Agent of one malware family in malware databases, so the weight of User-Agent is $\frac{1}{30} \times 100$.

In terms of the Request URI field, we use a different strategy because this filed usually contains a long string. We use the Levenshtein distance [16] to calculate the similarity between the testing URI and each pattern. Levenshtein distance measures the minimum number of substitutions required to change one string into the other. After comparing with each pattern, we choose the greatest similarity as a target value, for example, if the similarity value is 0.76, the weight will be 0.76×100 or 76 for the URI field. The score can be calculated using the following equation: $Score = \frac{1}{N}\sum_{i=1}^{N} w_i \times m_i$, where w_i is weight for i_{th} field, and m_i indicates whether there is a pattern in the database that matches the field value. If there is, m_i is 1, otherwise, it is 0. Note that m_i is always 1 for the URI field.

Algorithm 1: Calculating Request Scores From One PCAP

1: dataBase[ ] ← Database built from the previous phrase
2: pcapFile ← Each PCAP file from 20% of malware families
3: fieldNames[ ] ← Name list for all the extracted fields
4: tempScore ← 0
5: sumScore ← 0
6: avgScore ← 0
7: **for** each httpRequest in pcapFile **do**
8:     **for** each name in fieldNames **do**
9:         **if** httpRequest.name /= NULL **then**
10:            **if** name /= "requestURI" **then**
11:                **if** httpRequest.name in dataBase(name) **then**
12:                    tempScore ← 100 {The default weight is 100}
13:                **else**
14:                    tempScore ← 0
15:                **end if**
16:            **else**
17:                similarity ←
                   similarityFunction(httpRequest.requestURI, dataBase("requestURI"))
18:                tempScore ← 100 × similarity
19:            **end if**
20:        **end if**
21:        sumScore ← sumScore + tempScore
22:    **end for**
23:    avgScore ← sumScore ÷ Size of fieldNames
24:    record avgScore as the original score of each httpRequest
25: **end for**

After obtaining all the field values and calculating the summation of these values, we then divide it by the total number of fields (i.e., 5 in this case). The result is the original score of this HTTP request.

Then we need to calculate the malware z_{score} range for each family. we calculate the average score and standard derivation of those original scores which are mentioned above. Next, we calculate the absolute value of the z_{score}, which represents the distance between the original score (x) and the mean score ($\bar{x}$) divided by the standard deviation (s) for each request: $|z_{score}| = \left|\frac{x-\bar{x}}{s}\right|$.

Once we get the range of absolute value of z_{score} from all malware training requests of each family, it is used to determine the threshold for classification and detection. We will illustrate the threshold decision process in the following section. Algorithm 1 outlines the steps of calculating original scores from PCAP files. Note that in the testing process, the same z_{score} computation is conducted to evaluate the scores of the testing traffic requests, which we termed as *testing z_{score} computation* to avoid confusion.

4.2 Malware Clustering During Testing

We automatically apply clustering analysis to all of our testing requests. We use hierarchical clustering [24], which can build either a top-down or bottom-up tree to determine malware clusters. The advantage of hierarchical clustering is that it is flexible on the proximity measure, and is able to visualize the clustering results using dendrogram that can be used to choose the optimal number of clusters.

In our framework, we use the single-linkage [24] clustering, which is an agglomerative or bottom-up approach. According to Perdisci et al. [20], singlelinkage hierarchical clustering has the best performance compared to X-means [19] and complete-linkage [12] hierarchical clustering.

Feature Extraction for Clustering. First, we need to compute distance measures to represent similarities among HTTP requests. We extract features from URLs and define a distance between two requests according to an algorithm proposed in [20], except that we reduce the number of features to make our algorithm much more efficient. In the end, we extract three types of features to perform clustering: domain name and port number, path to the file, and Jaccard's distance [11] between parameter keys. As an example, consider the following request:

http://www.example.com:80/path/to/myfile.html?key1=value1&key2=value2

The field, www.example.com:80, represents the first feature. The field,/path/to/ myfile.html, represents the second feature. The field, key1=value1&key2=value2, represents the parameters, each is a key-value pair, of this request. To compute the third feature, we calculate the Jaccard's distance [11] between the keys. We do not use the parameter values here because these values can be very long, and the comparison between a large number of long strings will consume a large amount of time.

Note that in work by Perdisci et al. [20], they also use the same three features with an addition of the fourth with is the concatenation of parameter values to calculate the similarity of requests for desktop applications. According to [2], the length of URL is larger for the Android malware than the desktop malware, and from our tests, we find the time to calculate the similarity using the fourth feature is much longer than with just three features. We also find that we can get comparable clustering accuracy with just using the three features. As such, we exclude the fourth feature to make our system more efficient but without sacrificing accuracy. In Sect. 5, we show that our system is as effective as using four features [2], but is also significantly faster.

Recall that we extract five HTTP features (see Table 1) to perform training. Since these features are strings, we use the Levenshtein Distance [16] between two strings to measure their similarity. For parameter keys, Jaccard's distance [11] is applied to measure the similarity. Suppose the number of HTTP requests is N, we can get three $N \times N$ matrices based on three clustering feature sets. We calculate the average value of the three matrices, and regard this average matrix as the similarity matrix used by the clustering algorithm.

After the clustering, we calculate the average of the $|z_{score}|$ of each cluster. We consider requests from the same cluster as one group and use the average value to classify this cluster.

4.3   Malware Classification

We use the remaining 50% of malware samples in each family as the testing set. In order to determine the threshold for classification, we include traffic from 20% benign apps and 20% malware samples. We use the same method as depicted in the previous section to calculate the original score of each benign request. However, when we calculate the z_{score} range of benign apps, we use the mean score ($\bar{x}$) and standard derivation(s) of the 20% malware family we have in previous sections (i.e. $|z_{score}| = \left|\frac{x-\bar{x}(malware)}{S(malware)}\right|$). Then we use the malware z_{score} range and benign z_{score} range to determine the threshold for each malware family in an adaptive manner.

For instance, in the *BaseBridge* family, the absolute range of z_{score} varies from 1.0 to 1.3 using malicious traffic from 20% malware samples. Meanwhile, this value ranges from 1.5 to 10 for the 20% benign apps using the *BaseBridge* database. As a result, we can then set the threshold to be 1.4, which is computed by (1.3 + 1.5)/2. For the testing traffic, if the absolute value of z_{score} derived by testing z_{score} computation is less than the threshold, the app will be classified into this BaseBridge family.

4.4 Malware Detection

This detection process is very similar to the clustering process. However, the testing set has been expanded to include traffic from both malicious apps and 5,215 benign apps. The detection phase proceeds like the classification phase. We use BaseBridge family as an example. After extracting each HTTP request from PCAP files, we calculate the score based on BaseBridge training database, similar to classification phase, if the traffic's absolute value of z_{score} is greater than the BaseBridge threshold, we believe this traffic comes from BaseBridge family, and the traffic request is classified as malicious. Otherwise, the traffic does not belong to the BaseBridge family. In the end, if the traffic request is not assigned to any malware families, this request is deemed as benign.

Next, we illustrate how to calculate the detection accuracy for each malware family through an example using the BaseBridge family. If a request is from a BaseBridge family app, and it is also identified as belonging to it, then this is true positive (TP). Otherwise, it is false negative (FN). If the request is not from BaseBridge family app, but it is identified as belonging to it, then it is false positive (FP); otherwise, it is true negative (TN). We then calculate the *detection accuracy* (*Detection Accuracy* $= \frac{TP+TN}{TP+TN+FN+FP}$) and *malware detection rate* (*Malware Detection Rate* $= \frac{SUM(TP)}{SUM(FN)+SUM(TP)}$) of each family.

5 Evaluation

We evaluate the malware classification performance of DroidClassifier. We use 30% of the malware samples for database building, 20% of both malware and benign apps for threshold calculation. We set up the testing set to use the remaining 50% of the malware samples and 80% of benign apps. Specifically, we evaluate the following performance aspects of DroidClassifier system.

1. We evaluate *classification effectiveness* of DroidClassifier to classify malicious apps into different families of malware. We present the performance in terms of detection accuracy, TPR (True Positive Rate), TNR (True Negative Rate) and F-Measure. Our evaluation experiments with using different numbers of clusters to determine which one yields the most accurate classification result.
2. We evaluate the *malware detection effectiveness* of DroidClassifier using only malware samples as the training and testing sets. We only focus on how well DroidClassifier correctly detects malware. The detection performance is represented by detection accuracy.
3. We evaluate the *influence of clustering on malware detection effectiveness* by comparing the detection rates between the best case in DroidClassifier when the number of cluster is 1000, and DroidClassifier without clustering process.
4. We *compare our classification effectiveness with results of other approaches*. We also compare the efficiency of DroidClassifier with a similar clustering system [2].

Our dataset consists of 1,363 malicious apps, and our benign apps are downloaded from multiple popular app markets by app crawler. Each app downloaded from app market is sent to VirusTotal for initial screening. The app is added to our normal app set only if the test result is benign. Eventually, we get a normal app set of 5,215 samples belonging to 24 families. A large amount of traffic data are collected by an automatic mobile traffic collection system, similar to the system described in [5], in order to evaluate the classification/detection performance of DroidClassifier. In the end, we get 500.4 MB of network traffic data generated by malware samples in total, out of which we extract 18.1 MB of malicious behavior traffic for training purpose. In a similar manner, we collect 2.15 GB of data generated by normal apps for model training and testing.

5.1 Malware Classification Effectiveness Across Different Cluster Numbers

In our experiment, we perform an evaluation to investigate the sensitivity of our approach to the number of clusters. Therefore, we strategically adjust the number of clusters to find the optimal number that is used to classify malware in the testing data. To do so, we evaluate 13 different numbers of clusters for the whole dataset, ranging from 200 to 7000 clusters. Table 5 shows the classification results using 13 different numbers of clusters. When we increase the number of clusters from 200 to 1000, the detection accuracy also improves from 46.95% to 94.66%, respectively. However, using more than 1000 clusters does not improve accuracy. As such, using 1000 clusters is optimal for our dataset. In this setting but without using *DroidKungfu* and *Gappusin*, the two families previously known to be hard to detect and classify [4], DroidClassifier achieves TPR of 92.39% and TNR of 94.80%, respectively. With these two families, our TPR and TNR still yield 89.90% and 87.60%, respectively (Table 2).

Table 2. Classification result with different number of clusters (TPR = TP/(TP + FN); TNR = TN/(TN + FP); F measure = 2 * (TPR * TNR)/(TPR + TNR))

Number of clusters	TPR	TNR	Detection accuracy	F measure
200	73.90%	46.59%	46.95%	57.15%
400	60.70%	66.45%	66.34%	63.44%
600	60.70%	66.61%	66.52%	63.52%
800	70.24%	91.39%	91.12%	79.43%
1000	92.39%	94.80%	94.66%	93.58%
1200	90.70%	94.45%	94.30%	92.54%
1400	90.76%	94.42%	94.28%	92.55%
2000	90.76%	93.79%	93.64%	92.25%
3000	89.08%	93.15%	93.01%	91.07%
4000	89.08%	93.11%	92.97%	91.05%
5000	89.08%	93.06%	92.92%	91.03%
6000	88.75%	92.45%	92.30%	90.56%
7000	88.12%	93.02%	92.79%	90.50%

Table 3. Malware classification performance with 1000 clusters

Family name	TP	FN	TN	FP	TPR (%)	TNR (%)	Detection accuracy (%)	F measure (%)
BaseBridge	351	104	11994	44	77.14	99.63	98.82	86.96
DroidKungFu	286	74	7306	4827	79.44	60.22	60.77	68.51
FakeDoc	229	1	12263	0	99.57	100.00	99.99	99.78
FakeInstaller	73	1	11968	451	98.65	96.37	96.38	97.50
FakeRun	70	6	11890	527	92.11	95.76	95.73	93.90
Gappusin	66	16	7170	5241	80.49	57.77	57.92	67.26
Iconosys	17	4	8465	4007	80.95	67.87	67.89	73.84
MobileTx	227	1	12265	0	99.56	100.00	99.99	99.78
Opfake	93	4	12396	0	95.88	100.00	99.97	97.89
Plankton	1025	51	11279	138	95.26	98.79	98.49	96.99
AVG results					89.90	87.64	87.60	88.76
AVG results w/o DroidKungFu & Gappusin					92.39	94.80	94.66	93.58

5.2 Detection Effectiveness Per Family

Next, we further decompose our analysis to determine the effectiveness of DroidClassifier by evaluating our effectiveness metrics per malware family. As shown in Table 3, in six out of ten families, our system can achieve more than 90% in F-Measure, meaning that it can accurately classify malicious family as it detects more true positives and true negatives than false positives and false negatives. As the table reports, our system yields accurate classification results in BaseBridge, FakeDoc, FakeInstaller, FakeRun, MobileTx, Opfake, and Plankton. Specifically, FakeDoc and

MobileTx shows above 99% in F-measure, which means it almost detect everything correctly in these two families. However, DroidKungFu, Gappusin and Iconosys shows less than 80% F-measure.

Discussion. Our system cannot accurately classify these three families (i.e. Droid-KungFu, Gappusin and Iconosys) due to two main reasons. First, the amounts of the network traffic for these families are too small. For example, we only have 38 applications in Iconosys family and among these, only 19 applications produce network traffic information. We plan to extend the traffic collection time to address this issue in future works.

Second, the malware samples in DroidKungFu and Gappusin families produce a large amount of traffic information that shares similar patterns with that of other families. This leads to ambiguity. We also cross-reference our results with those reported by Drebin [4]. Their results also confirm our observation as their approach can only achieve less than 50% detection accuracy, which is even lower than that achieved by our system. This is the main reason why we report our result in Table 5 by excluding DroidKungFu and Gappusin.

Table 4. Classification performance without clustering procedure

Family name	TP	FN	TN	FP	TPR (%)	TNR (%)	Detection accuracy (%)	F measure (%)
BaseBridge	437	18	12038	0	96.04	100.00	99.86	97.98
DroidKungFu	286	74	2195	9938	79.44	18.09	19.86	29.47
FakeDoc	229	1	12263	0	99.57	100.00	99.99	99.78
FakeInstaller	73	1	12419	0	98.65	100.00	99.99	99.32
FakeRun	75	1	11876	541	98.68	95.64	95.66	97.14
Gappusin	66	16	2914	9497	80.49	23.48	23.85	36.35
Iconosys	20	1	11304	1168	95.24	90.64	90.64	92.88
MobileTx	227	1	12265	0	99.56	100.00	99.99	99.78
Opfake	84	13	12396	0	86.60	100.00	99.90	92.82
Plankton	1049	27	11302	115	97.49	98.99	98.86	98.24
AVG results					93.18	82.68	82.86	87.62
AVG results w/o DroidKung Fu & Gappusin					96.48	98.16	98.11	97.31

5.3 Comparing Detection Effectiveness of Clustering Versus Non-clustering

In Table 4, we report the detection results when clustering is not performed (i.e., we configure our system to have a cluster for each request). As shown in the table, the detection accuracy without clustering are significantly worse than those with clustering for DroidKungFu and Gappusin. In DroidKungFu family, the detection accuracy decreases from 60.77% to 19.86% by eliminating clustering procedure. In Gappusin family, the detection accuracy decreases from 57.92% to 23.85%. However, after removing these two families, it shows better average detection accuracy than DroidClassifier with clustering procedure. The detection accuracy of the Iconosys family increases from 67.89% to 90.64% by removing the clustering procedure.

Discussion. Upon further investigation of the network traffic information, we uncover that the network traffic generated by many benign applications and that of the Iconosys family are very similar. As such, many benign network traffic flows are included with malicious traffic flows as part of the clustering process. However, the overall detection rate including two worst cases (i.e. AVG results in Tables 3 and 4) shows that DroidClassifier with clustering is more accurate than DroidClassifier without clustering. In addition, the clustering mechanism enables the cluster-level classification, which classifies malware as a group, while the mechanism without clustering classifies malware individually. This makes DroidClassifier with clustering much more efficient than the mechanism without clustering, in terms of system processing time.

5.4   Comparing Performance with Other Mobile Malware Detectors

In this section, we compare our detection results with other malware detection approaches, including Drebin, PermissionClassifier, Aresu et al. [2], and Afonso et al. [1].

- Drebin [4] is an approach that detects malware by combining static analysis of permissions and APIs with machine learning. It utilizes Support Vector Machine (SVM) algorithm to classify malware data set.
- PermissionClassifier, on the other hand, uses only permission as the features to perform malware detection. During the implementation, we use the same malicious applications used to evaluate Drebin. Then we use Apktool [29] to find the permissions called by each application. We randomly separate the data set as training and testing set. SVM classification approach is employed to perform malware classification.
- Aresu et al. [2] extract malware signatures by clustering HTTP traffic, and they use these signatures to detect malware. We implement their clustering method, and compare the result with that produced by our system.
- Afonso et al. [1] develop a machine learning system that detects Android malicious apps by using the dynamic information from system calls and Android API functions. They employ a different dynamic way to detect malware and also use Android Malware Genome Project [36] as the dataset.

Table 5 reports the results of our evaluation. Drebin uses more features than PermissionClassifier, including API calls and network addresses. As a result, Drebin outperforms PermissionClassifier in detection accuracy. We also compare the results of our system against those of 10 existing anti-virus scanners [4]: AntiVir, AVG, BitDefender, ClamAV, ESET, F-Secure, Kaspersky, McAfee, Panda, Sophos. We report the minimum, maximum, and average detection rate of these 10 virus scanner in columns 5 to 7 (AV1 – AV10).

Table 5. Detection rates of DroidClassfier and ten anti-virus scanners

Method	Droid classifier	Permission classifier	Drebin	Aresu et al.	Afonso et al.	AV1 – AV10		
						Min	Max	Avg.
Full dataset	94.33%	89.30%	93.90%	60–100%	96.82%	3.99%	96.41%	61.25%

The most time consuming part of the hierarchical clustering is the calculation of the similarity matrix. Aresu et al. [2] use one more feature, the aggregation of values in Request-URI field, to build their clustering system. We implement their method and evaluate the time to compute the similarity matrix. We then compare their time consumption for matrix computation of each malware family with that of DroidClassifier and report the result in Table 6. For BaseBridge, DroidKungFu, FakeDoc and Gappusin, our approach incurs 60% to 100% less time than their approach while yielding over 94% detection rate. For other families, the time is about the same. This is due to the fact that those families do not generate traffic with Request-URI field.

Table 6. Time comparison of matrix calculation (Experiments run on Apple MacBook Pro with 2.8 GHz Intel Core i7 and 16G memory)

Family name	Number of requests	DroidClassifier (seconds)	Aresu et al. (seconds)
Plankton	1075	361	361
BaseBridge	454	**37**	**10230**
DroidKungFu	359	**86**	**3520**
FakeDoc	229	**9**	**820**
Opfake	96	8	8
FakeInstaller	73	9	9
FakeRun	75	10	10
Gappusin	81	**11**	**264**
MobileTx	227	61	61
Iconosys	20	9	9

Drebin and PermissionClassifier are the state-of-the-art malware detection system with high detection accuracy. Our approach is dynamic-analysis based approach. In the literature, as far as we know, there is a lack of comparative work using dynamic analysis on a large malware dataset to evaluate malware detection accuracy. Therefore, though Drebin and PermissionClassifier use static analysis features, we compare with them in terms of malware detection rate to prove the detection accuracy of DroidClassifier. As our proposed classifier is networktraffic based classifier, the main advantage of our classifier is that we can deploy our system on gateway routers instead on end user devices.

Work by Aresu et al. uses clustering to extract signatures to detect malware. We have emphasized the difference between our work and Aresu before. In terms of comparison, we compare the detection rate and time cost with them. Our work can achieve over 90% detection rate. Even though the purpose of our clustering is different, we can still compare the clustering efficiency. For BaseBridge, DroidKungFu, FakeDoc and Gappusin, our approach, in terms of clustering time, is more efficient than their approach by 60% to 100%.

Work by Afonso et al. [1] can achieve the average detection accuracy of 96.82%. So far, the preliminary investigation of detection effectiveness already indicates that our system can achieve nearly the same accuracy. Unlike their approach, our system can also classify samples into different families, which is important, as repackaging is a common form to develop malware. Their approach still requires that a malware sample executes completely. In the case that it does not (e.g., interrupted connection with a C&C server or premature termination due to detection of malware analysis environments), their system cannot perform detection. However, our network traffic-based system can handle partial execution as long as the malware attempts to send sensitive information. The presence of our system is also harder to detect as it captures the traffic on the router side, preventing certain malware samples from prematurely terminating execution to avoid analysis.

6 Limitations and Future Work

In this paper, we use HTTP header information to help classify and detect malware. However, our current implementation does not handle encrypted requests through HTTPS protocol. To handle such type of requests in the future, we may need to work closely with runtime systems to capture information prior to encryption, or use on-device software such as Haystack [23] to decrypt HTTPs traffic.

Our system also expects a sufficient number of requests in the training set. As shown in families such as Iconosys, insufficient data used during training can cause the system to incorrectly classify malware and benign samples. Furthermore, to generate network traffic information, our approach, similar to work by Afonso et al. [1], relies on Monkey to generate sufficient traffic. However, events triggered by Monkey tool are random, and therefore, may not replicate realworld events especially in the case that complex event sequences are needed to trigger malicious behaviors. In such scenarios, malicious network traffic may not be generated. Creating complex event sequences is still a major research challenge in the area of testing GUI- and event-based applications. To address this issue in the future, we plan to use more sophisticated event sequence generation approaches to including GUI ripping and symbolic or concolic execution [13]. We will also evaluate the minimum number of traffic requests that are required to induce good classification performance in future works.

Currently, our framework can only detect new samples from known families if they happen to share previously modeled behaviors. For sample requests from totally unknown malware samples, our framework can put all these similar requests into a cluster. This can help analysts to isolate these samples and simplify the manual analysis process. We also plan to extract other features beyond application-layer header information. For example, we may want to focus on the packet's payload that may contain more interesting information such as C&C instructions and sensitive data. We can also combine the network traffic information with other unique features including permission and program structures such as data-flow and control-flow information.

Similar to existing approaches, our approach can still fail against determined adversaries who try to avoid our classification approach. For example, an adversary can develop advanced techniques to dynamically change their features without affecting their malicious behaviors. Currently, machine-learning based detection systems suffer from this problem [32]. We need to consider how adversaries may adapt to our classifiers and develop better mobile malware classification and detection strategies.

We are in the process of collecting newer malware samples to further evaluate our system. We anticipate that newer malware samples may utilize more complex interactions with C&C servers. In this case, we expect more meaningful network behaviors that our system can exploit to detect and classify these emerging malware samples.

Lastly, our system is lightweight because it can be installed on the router to automatically detect malicious apps. The system is efficient because our approach classifies and detects malware at the cluster granularity instead of at each individual request granularity, resulting in much less classification and detection efforts. As future work, we will experiment with deployments of DroidClassifier in a real-world setting.

7 Conclusion

In this paper, we introduce DroidClassifier, a malware classification and detection approach that utilizes multidimensional application-layer data from network traffic information. An integrated clustering and classification framework is developed to take into account disparate and unique characteristics of different mobile malware families. Our study includes over 1,300 malware samples and 5,000 benign apps. We find that DroidClassifier successfully identifies over 90% of different families of malware with 94.33% accuracy on average. Meanwhile, it is also more efficient than state-of-the-art approaches to perform Android malware classification and detection based on network traffic. We envision DroidClassifier to be applied in network management to control mobile malware infections in a large network.

Acknowledgment. We thank the anonymous reviewers and our shepherd, Aziz Mohaisen, for their insightful feedback on our work. This work is supported in part by NSF grant CNS-1566388. This work is also based on research sponsored by DARPA and Maryland Procurement Office under agreement numbers FA8750-14-2-0053 and H98230-14-C-0140, respectively. Any opinions, findings, conclusions, or recommendations expressed here are those of the authors and do not necessarily reflect the views of the funding agencies or the U.S. Government.

References

1. Afonso, V.M., de Amorim, M.F., Grégio, A.R.A., Junquera, G.B., de Geus, P.L.: Identifying android malware using dynamically obtained features. J. Comput. Virol. Hacking Tech. **11**(1), 9–17 (2015)
2. Aresu, M., Ariu, D., Ahmadi, M., Maiorca, D., Giacinto, G.: Clustering android malware families by http traffic. In: 10th International Conference on Malicious and Unwanted Software (MALWARE). IEEE (2015)

3. Arora, A., Garg, S., Peddoju, S.K.: Malware detection using network traffic analysis in android based mobile devices. In: 2014 Eighth International Conference on Next Generation Mobile Apps, Services and Technologies (NGMAST), pp. 66–71. IEEE (2014)
4. Arp, D., Spreitzenbarth, M., Hübner, M., Gascon, H., Rieck, K., Siemens, C.: Drebin: effective and explainable detection of android malware in your pocket. In: Annual Symposium on Network and Distributed System Security (NDSS) (2014)
5. Chen, Z., Han, H., Yan, Q., Yang, B., Peng, L., Zhang, L., Li, J.: A first look at android malware traffic in first few minutes. In: IEEE TrustCom 2015 (Aug. 2015)
6. G Data. GData mobile malware report, July 2015. https://public.gdatasoftware.com/Presse/Publikationen/Malware_Reports/G_DATA_MobileMWR_Q2_2015_EN.pdf
7. Enck, W., Gilbert, P., Han, S., Tendulkar, V., Chun, B.-G., Cox, L.P., Jung, J., Mc-Daniel, P., Sheth, A.N.: Taintdroid: an information-flow tracking system for realtime privacy monitoring on smartphones. ACM Trans. Comput. Syst. (TOCS) 32(2), 5 (2014)
8. F-Secure. F-secure mobile threat report, March, 2014. https://www.f-secure.com/documents/996508/1030743/Mobile_Threat_Report_Q1_2014.pdf
9. Gill, P., Erramilli, V., Chaintreau, A., Krishnamurthy, B., Papagiannaki, K., Rodriguez, P.: Best paper–follow the money: understanding economics of online aggregation and advertising. In: Conference on Internet Measurement Conference, pp. 141–148. ACM (2013)
10. Hornyack, P., Han, S., Jung, J., Schechter, S., Wetherall, D.: These aren't the droids you're looking for: retrofitting android to protect data from imperious applications. In: ACM Conference on Computer and Communications Security, pp. 639–652. ACM (2011)
11. Jaccard, P.: Etude comparative de la distribution florale dans une portion des Alpes et du Jura. Impr, Corbaz (1901)
12. Jain, A.K., Murty, M.N., Flynn, P.J.: Data clustering: a review. ACM Comput. Surv. (CSUR) 31(3), 264–323 (1999)
13. Jensen, C.S., Prasad, M.R., Møller, A.: Automated testing with targeted event sequence generation. In: International Symposium on Software Testing and Analysis, ISSTA 2013, Lugano, Switzerland, pp. 67–77 (2013)
14. Kheir, N.: Analyzing HTTP user agent anomalies for malware detection. In: Pietro, R., Herranz, J., Damiani, E., State, R. (eds.) DPM/SETOP -2012. LNCS, vol. 7731, pp. 187–200. Springer, Heidelberg (2013). doi:10.1007/978-3-642-35890-6_14
15. Le, A., Varmarken, J., Langhoff, S., Shuba, A., Gjoka, M., Markopoulou, A.: Antmonitor: a system for monitoring from mobile devices. In: SIGCOMM Workshop on Crowdsourcing and Crowdsharing of Big (Internet) Data, pp. 15–20. ACM (2015)
16. Levenshtein, V.I.: Binary codes capable of correcting deletions, insertions, and reversals. Forschungsbericht, 707–710 S (1966)
17. Nari, S., Ghorbani, A.A.: Automated malware classification based on network behavior. In: 2013 International Conference on Computing, Networking and Communications (ICNC), pp. 642–647. IEEE (2013)
18. Narudin, F.A., Feizollah, A., Anuar, N.B., Gani, A.: Evaluation of machine learning classifiers for mobile malware detection. Soft. Comput. 20(1), 343–357 (2016)
19. Pelleg, D., Moore, A.W., et al.: X-means: extending k-means with efficient estimation of the number of clusters. In: ICML, vol. 1, 2000
20. Perdisci, R., Lee, W., Feamster, N.: Behavioral clustering of http-based malware and signature generation using malicious network traces. In: NSDI, pp. 391–404 (2010)
21. Rafique, M.Z., Caballero, Juan: FIRMA: malware clustering and network signature generation with mixed network behaviors. In: Stolfo, S.J., Stavrou, Angelos, Wright, C.V. (eds.) RAID 2013. LNCS, vol. 8145, pp. 144–163. Springer, Heidelberg (2013). doi:10.1007/978-3-642-41284-4_8

22. Rao, A., Sherry, J., Legout, A., Krishnamurthy, A., Dabbous, W., Choffnes, D.: Meddle: middleboxes for increased transparency and control of mobile traffic. In: ACM Conference on CoNEXT Student Workshop, pp. 65–66. ACM (2012)

23. Razaghpanah, A., Vallina-Rodriguez, N., Sundaresan, S., Kreibich, C., Gill, P., Allman, M., Paxson, V.: Haystack: In situ mobile traffic analysis in user space. In arXiv preprint arXiv: 1510.01419 (2015)

24. Rokach, L., Maimon, O.: Clustering methods. In: Maimon, O., Rokach, L. (eds.) Data Mining and Knowledge Discovery Handbook, pp. 321–352. Springer, USA (2005)

25. Shabtai, A., Kanonov, U., Elovici, Y., Glezer, C., Weiss, Y.: andromaly: a behavioral malware detection framework for android devices. J. Intell. Inf. Syst. 38(1), 161–190 (2012)

26. Symantec Corporation. Internet Security Threat Report 2014. http://www.symantec.com/content/en/us/enterprise/other_resources/b-istr_main_report_v19_21291018.en-us.pdf. Accessed 21 June 2016

27. Tutorialspoint. HTTP header. http://www.tutorialspoint.com/http/http_header_fields.htm. Accessed 21 June 2016

28. Vallina-Rodriguez, N., Shah, J., Finamore, A., Grunenberger, Y., Papagiannaki, K., Haddadi, H., Crowcroft, J.: Breaking for commercials: characterizing mobile advertising. In: ACM Conference on Internet Measurement Conference, pp. 343–356. ACM (2012)

29. Winsniewski, R.: Android–apktool: a tool for reverse engineering android apk files. http://ibotpeaches.github.io/Apktool/, Accessed 21 June 2016

30. Wurzinger, P., Bilge, L., Holz, T., Goebel, J., Kruegel, C., Kirda, E.: Automatically generating models for botnet detection. In: Backes, M., Ning, P. (eds.) ESORICS 2009. LNCS, vol. 5789, pp. 232–249. Springer, Heidelberg (2009). doi:10.1007/978-3-642-04444-1_15

31. Xu, Q., Liao, Y., Miskovic, S., Mao, Z.M., Baldi, M., Nucci, A., Andrews, T.: Automatic generation of mobile app signatures from traffic observations. In: IEEE INFOCOM, April 2015

32. Xu, W., Qi, Y., Evans, D.: Automatically evading classifiers, a case study on pdf malware classifiers. In: Annual Symposium on Network and Distributed System Security (NDSS) (2016)

33. Yao, H., Ranjan, G., Tongaonkar, A., Liao, Y., Mao, Z.M.: Samples: self adaptive mining of persistent lexical snippets for classifying mobile application traffic. In: Annual International Conference on Mobile Computing and Networking (2015)

34. Zhang, J., Saha, S., Gu, G., Lee, S.-J., Mellia, M.: Systematic mining of associated server herds for malware campaign discovery. In: 2015 IEEE 35th International Conference on Distributed Computing Systems (ICDCS), pp. 630–641. IEEE (2015)

35. Zhang, Y., Yang, M., Xu, B., Yang, Z., Gu, G., Ning, P., Wang, X.S., Zang, B.: Vetting undesirable behaviors in android apps with permission use analysis. In: ACM SIGSAC Conference on Computer & Communications Security, pp. 611–622. ACM (2013)

36. Zhou, Y., Jiang, X.: Dissecting android malware: characterization and evolution In: 2012 IEEE Symposium on Security and Privacy (SP), pp. 95–109. IEEE (2012)

GreatEatlon: Fast, Static Detection of Mobile Ransomware

Chengyu Zheng[(✉)], Nicola Dellarocca, Niccolò Andronio, Stefano Zanero, and Federico Maggi

DEIB, Politecnico di Milano, Milan, Italy
{chengyu.zheng,nicola.dellarocca,niccolo.andronio,
stefano.zanero,federico.maggi}@polimi.it

Abstract. Ransomware is a class of malware that aim at preventing victims from accessing valuable data, typically via data encryption or device locking, and ask for a payment to release the target. In the past year, instances of ransomware attacks have been spotted on mobile devices too. However, despite their relatively low infection rate, we noticed that the techniques used by mobile ransomware are quite sophisticated, and different from those used by ransomware against traditional computers.

Through an in-depth analysis of about 100 samples of currently active ransomware apps, we concluded that most of them pass undetected by state-of-the-art tools, which are unable to recognize the abuse of benign features for malicious purposes. The main reason is that such tools rely on an inadequate and incomplete set of features. The most notable examples are the abuse of reflection and device-administration APIs, appearing in modern ransomware to evade analysis and detection, and to elevate their privileges (e.g., to lock or wipe the device). Moreover, current solutions introduce several false positives in the naïve way they detect cryptographic-APIs abuse, flagging goodware apps as ransomware merely because they rely on cryptographic libraries. Last but not least, the performance overhead of current approaches is unacceptable for appstore-scale workloads.

In this work, we tackle the aforementioned limitations and propose GreatEatlon, a next-generation mobile ransomware detector. We foresee GreatEatlon deployed on the appstore side, as a preventive countermeasure. At its core, GreatEatlon uses static program-analysis techniques to "resolve" reflection-based, anti-analysis attempts, to recognize abuses of the device administration API, and extract accurate data-flow information required to detect truly malicious uses of cryptographic APIs. Given the significant resources utilized by GreatEatlon, we prepend to its core a fast pre-filter that quickly discards obvious goodware, in order to avoid wasting computer cycles.

We tested GreatEatlon on thousands of samples of goodware, generic malware and ransomware applications, and showed that it surpasses current approaches both in speed and detection capabilities, while keeping the false negative rate below 1.3%.

© ICST Institute for Computer Sciences, Social Informatics and Telecommunications Engineering 2017
R. Deng et al. (Eds.): SecureComm 2016, LNICST 198, pp. 617–636, 2017.
DOI: 10.1007/978-3-319-59608-2_34

1   Introduction

Nowadays there are approximately 1.9 billion smartphone and tablet users worldwide [1], using 3.7 billion devices, a number that is expected to grow to 6.75 billion by 2021 [2]. This widespread diffusion of mobile devices makes the attack surface substantial and the tendency to store sensitive data on mobile devices makes them an attractive target for malware authors.

According to GData [3], in the first half of 2015 more than 1 million infections on Android devices occurred, which means 6,100 newly infected devices every day, a 25% increase since 2014. Out of these infections, a few more than a half are financially motivated. More specifically, in 2015 the most dangerous threats were ransomware, whose number of families doubled in only one year and infected nearly 100,000 distinct users, a five-fold increase since 2014 [4].

Even though there are tools [5] that aim at post-infection recovery, they are effective only against some (known) ransomware families. Moreover, the state-of-the-art approach [6] is imprecise since it is only partially able to recognize certain feature of modern mobile ransomware. HelDroid works by analyzing three main characteristics that belongs to a ransomware, composed by a text, encryption, and locking analyzer. In this paper, we propose how to enhance HelDroid to overcome the limitations that we noticed after about one year of operation on modern ransomware families. More in detail, we modified the static taint analysis tool, on which the encryption detector is based. For instance, preventing decryption flows from being erroneously considered as malicious, lowering the number of false positives. Furthermore, we identified a different set of sources and sinks that allows the detector to identify encryption flows independently of the particular folder that contains the target files and augmented HelDroid for detecting the abuse of admin APIs, which are used by modern ransomware to urge victims to effectively lock the device. In addition to that, we propose a heuristic to statically resolve the method invoked via the most common reflection patterns, even in the presence of lightweight method name obfuscation. Finally, we implemented a pre-filter that aims to reduce the overhead of HelDroid by recognizing goodware.

We tested the resulting system, named GreatEatlon, on thousands of samples including ransomware, generic malware and goodware, using HelDroid as a benchmark.

In summary, the main contributions of this work are:

- a novel encryption-detection approach that can recognize, with good precision, malicious encryption flows, thanks to a generic set of sources and sinks, and by taking into account the nature of the encryption operation (*i.e.*, encryption vs. decryption initiated by the user via UI);
- a static technique, to discover device administration APIs abuse, which is widely used by modern ransomware families;
- a heuristic to detect the most common patterns used by malware to call methods via reflection;
- a lightweight and fast pre-filter able to discard goodware from the analysis;

2   Motivation

In this section, we introduce the problem in more detail, together with some solutions proposed by other researchers along with their limitations, and finally set the goals for this work.

2.1   Ransomware

A ransomware is a particular kind of malware which business model is to extort money from the victims. In order to force the user to pay the ransom, ransomware usually performs actions that limit the ability for the victim to use her device such as screen locking, or encrypting personal files. Mobile ransomware represents a concrete threat that is increasing by about 14.8% per year [7]. Mobile ransomware started with SimpleLocker [8], which is the first family of mobile ransomware that encrypts user's data with a unique key embedded in the binary and subsequently ask for money. In 2015 a more advanced version of Simple-Locker [9] appeared, instead of using a unique key able to decrypt and encrypt, it uses a per-device key.

It is important to note that by default Android's security model does not allow applications to do all kinds of operations. In particular, there are many APIs that are considered as potentially dangerous. In order to let an application to use these APIs, Android requires that, at install time, the user explicitly grants an application all the permissions it needs. Moreover, if an application needs to use the so-called Device Administration APIs (Sect. 3.2), then an additional run-time permission grant dialog is shown to the user, listing the administration policies the application requires, together with a brief message about the associated risk. Since the decision of whether to grant or deny these permissions is made by the user, it is very important that she understands the danger associated with the permission. Unfortunately, in [10] researchers have demonstrated that 84% of the users either do not pay attention to the permissions they grant or do not even know about the existence of them, and only 20% of all participants demonstrated "awareness of permissions and reasonable rates of understanding," choosing at least 70% of right answers to the survey they took. In fact, malware authors exploit this lack of attention to massively obtain permissions and use them to perform malicious actions and to spread quickly.

2.2   State of the Art

Being mobile ransomware a recent problem there are currently two kinds of tools available: commercial removal/cleanup utilities (*e.g.,* Avast Ransomware Removal [5]) and a research prototype that we prosecuted in [6], which offer a more generic approach, mainly based on static analysis.

Ransomware removal/cleanup utilities are specific to each ransomware family, thus it requires a certain effort keep them up to date with the development of new families. Additionally, these utilities are mobile applications that, like any Android app, are restricted by the security model of Android, hence they have limited functionalities. Therefore, their detection approach is not possible to do anything more than signature checking [11]. Moreover, certain ransomware families exploit high privileges (*e.g.,* device admin API) to kill those processes that are typically associated to common AVs.

The second approach *HelDroid*, proposes a *feature-based* detection mechanism using advanced static-analyses techniques directly on the bytecode extracted from APK files. We envisioned HelDroid deployed on the app-store side to scan submitted application's code and resources in order to discover whether they exhibit one or more characteristics that belong to a ransomware-distinguishing feature set.

The quality of the outcome strongly depends both on the set of extracted features and on the ability of HelDroid to extract them correctly. *HelDroid* recognizes three main characterizing actions than can be used to distinguish ransomware from other kinds of malware or goodware. Namely, it detects whether the app is (1) displaying threatening message, (2) locking the device, and (3) encrypt personal files. Clearly, since HelDroid is based on static analysis, what it actually detects is the presence of code dedicated to implement these features. Such code may or may not be executed at runtime, depending on factors that fall outside the scope of analysis of HelDroid.

After about one year of experience with running[1] HelDroid on thousands of mobile ransomware samples, taken from the VirusTotal daily feed, we concluded that this set of features is good to characterize ransomware, it does not take into account some new features introduced by the most recent families, such as the ability to use highly privileged APIs. For this reason, we augmented the original HelDroid it with new detectors, which will be explained in detail in the following sections.

Moreover, we found that some of the features detectors were not precise enough to detect all possible ways for a ransomware to perform a malicious action. In particular, we refer to the encryption detector, which can easily be circumvented by using the encryption API in a slight different way than the expected one, and to the text detector, which does not take into account the possibility to convey the threatening text through pictures instead of plain text.

2.3   Goals and Challenges

The goal of this work is to improve the ability of some detectors to correctly identify those features that make ransomware distinguishable from other malware and goodware, providing at the same time new ones capable of finding new characteristics. In this way, the updated system will be able to increase the reliability of the outcomes.

The main challenge is to create a solution that is generic enough to be effective even with new samples.

---

[1] http://ransom.mobi/scans.

3   Approach

In this section, we introduce, at a high level, the novel detectors, postponing the implementation details to Sect. 4. Recall that the process unit of GreatEatlon is the APK file. Therefore, the detectors described in the rest of this section are run on each APK file—in addition to the detectors already present in HelDroid. Each APK file contains three kinds of files: a manifest file (`AndroidManifest.xml`), source code files, and resource files. We used Apktool [12] to decode APK files, but the same information can be extracted in other ways.

As in HelDroid [6], the final output of GreatEatlon is a combination of the detectors. However, the focus of this paper is not how the detectors are combined, but rather on how we improved the original ones.

3.1   Encryption Detector

Ransomware encrypts personal files of a victim, which can be stored in any paths, typically under the SD card tree. These paths can be retrieved (by the malware) in several ways. Therefore, a path- or folder-dependent detection can easily be circumvented. Our solution, instead, is based on the impossibility of the attacker to know the location of the target files in advance. As a result, ransomware will perform at least one folder/file-listing operation, mediated by the OS, to know which files are within inside a specific folder. Therefore, we take advantage of a static taint analysis to track all code flows originating in a "query" (a request sent to the OS to get the list of files contained inside a folder) and ending in one of the encryption-related APIs that Android offers to developers. The OS offers only a few ways to perform such query: a couple of methods from the `File` class and a low-level query that relies on the underlying shell. For this reason, if we are able to detect that there is an information flow starting from one of these methods and ending in a bulk file encryption, then we can reasonably assume that relevant encryption-related operations are made to user's files.

We minimize the chances of false positives by focusing only in those flows that actually perform encryption (and not decryption) because the latter is harmless, and can be performed by a wide variety of benign applications. To this end, we implemented the notion of **conditional flows**. A conditional flow is considered by the taint-analysis engine only if there exists at least one path between the source(s) and the sink(s) that satisfies all the given conditions. In our proof-of-concept prototype, we support conditions on function arguments because this is the minimum requirement for implementing our detection logic, but the concept can be extended further.

The ability for an encryption-related flow to either encrypt or decrypt depends on the value with which the `Cipher` (i.e., the Java class responsible for performing encryption and decryption) is initialized. Therefore, we are interested in defining conditions that based on this value. In particular, the `init()` method (and all its overloads) currently supports only two values: `ENCRYPT_MODE` (i.e., `0x1`) and `DECRYPT_MODE` (i.e., `0x2`). Given that these values are numeric constants, and that both the compiler for the Dalvik virtual machine and the taint-analysis tool are able to perform constant propagation, we can adopt static conditions to make sure that a given tainted flow is an encryption or decryption one. To satisfy such a condition, an instruction like `cipher.init(ENCRYPT_MODE, ...)` must be called before a sink is reached.

3.2 Device Administration APIs Misuse Detector

Android's security model requires each application using Device Administration APIs to declare a specific set of permissions and components in the manifest file. Ransomware is obviously not exempted from doing so, allowing us discover the misuse of these APIs. More specifically, an app that needs to use device-admin policies must:

- Declare a class extending `DeviceAdminReceiver`, which is a component in charge of receiving and processing specific broadcast messages sent by the system whenever particular events happen (*e.g.*, when the user grants or revokes the privileges to the app).
- Declare a so-called *policy meta-data* XML file containing the list of all security policies that the app wants to use.
- Associate the XML file with the `Receiver` through a `<meta-data>` XML element.

Given these strict requirements, we created a detector that parses the `AndroidManifest` file, looking for the declaration of the appropriate `Receiver`. If found, and if the related meta-data contains dangerous policies (e.g., the ability to change the device unlock password and/or to remotely wipe the device), then it proceeds to analyze the source code.

Whenever the manifest and policy meta-data file analyses are completed and return a positive result, the detector processes the application source code. In this phase, we are interested in discovering if there exists at least a call to one of the potentially harmful methods of `DevicePolicyManager`, the main class that implements the Device Administrator APIs. In particular, the methods of interest are `wipeData()` and `resetPassword()`. To check whether the application calls one of these methods, we inspect the CFG to perform reachability analysis.

Interestingly, in an effort to hinder abuse of such APIs for permanent screen locking, the upcoming major release of Android (7.0, code-named "Nougat") eliminates [13] the possibility of creating device-admin policies to (programmatically) change the pass-code (e.g., PIN, pattern) without user intervention. This will certainly help in the future, but a short-time countermeasure—such as the detector presented in this section—is still required until mass adoption of Android Nougat.

3.3 Reflection Heuristic

Given the static nature of our analyses, all ransomware samples that make use of reflection or other dynamic techniques would not be detected by HelDroid, causing the detector to produce a wrong outcome. Therefore, we implemented a heuristic that resolves the most common reflective calls and includes them in the CFG. For efficiency, this heuristic is invoked only if the statically built CFG does not trigger any of the GreatEatlon detectors. In particular, GreatEatlon perform a series of forward and backward analyses that recognize the usage of reflection (*i.e.,* method calls like `method.invoke()`) and reconstruct which are the target class and method in case they are obfuscated.

Although far from being general and exhaustive, we our heuristic traces back to the origin of the string that holds the method name, including string-obfuscating transformations—if any (e.g., the original string is "`lockNow`" but the malware author obfuscated it by inserting random chars in between each couple of chars). Since we noticed that the de-obfuscating process typically involves only methods from the `String` class (such as `replace` or `substring`), our detector re-applies any method found along the backward path on the target string. This method is clearly not generic, and can certainly be improved. However, string de-obfuscation is a wide research topic, falling outside the scope of this paper, which *leverages* such program-analysis techniques rather than proposing new ones.

3.4 Text Detector

In its original form implemented in HelDroid [6], this component is responsible for analyzing any ASCII string extracted from the sample (both statically and dynamically), guessing the language, and determining whether the phrases form a threatening message—typical of any ransomware scheme.

In GreatEatlon, we pre-pended a lightweight image-processing phase to this component in order extract text from images, so to make the overall system resilient to evasion (e.g., text rendered into images). In particular, we added an image scanner that inspects all image files shipped in the application resource directories and applies a set of transformations to optimize them for optical character recognition (OCR).

The extracted text is then automatically corrected by a standard spell checker, to remove the obvious errors that may occur during OCR. The resulting, corrected text is then processed with the original text analyzer of HelDroid, which queries a classifier that returns a score indicating the amount of "threatening" sentiment found. If higher than an empirically determined threshold, then the text is considered as threatening, indicating that the sample is likely to be ransomware.

3.5 Lightweight Pre-filtering

To quickly decide whether an application is suspicious, and thus worth spending computing resources to analyze it, we adopt a supervised-learning classification approach. When tackling a classification task it is crucial to design features that best discriminate between goodware and all the rest. A great amount of research work has been done in the area, proposing several static and dynamic features that characterize malware vs. goodware [14–20]. However, if the goal is malware detection, errors are very costly in either sense (*i.e.,* false positives and negatives).

Instead, we make use of (some of the) features identified by previous work and relax some of these constraints by working on the dual problem (*i.e.,* detecting goodware). Since the pre-filtering is followed by the ransomware-detection pipeline, the cost of a few benign samples mis-classified as suspicious is negligible, because they will be eventually recognized as non ransomware. In other words, we can allow a slight penalty in the pre-filter accuracy in favor of almost perfect precision. We detail the choice of the classification algorithms and the features that we selected in Sect. 4.4. Since we need this phase to be fast, features that can be only extracted at runtime are unsuitable because the extraction would be prohibitively time consuming. Therefore, we focus on features that can be extracted efficiently by parsing the APK files. The output of this phase is a binary decision: "goodware" or "suspicious".

4   Implementation Details

In this section, we explain the technical details of GreatEatlon.

4.1   Encryption Detector

To implement our encryption detection approach, we extended FlowDroid [21] (the state-of-art static taint-analysis tool for Android) to allow the taint-propagation engine to track information flows through files (*e.g.,* a function writes to a file, another function reads such file, and passes the reference to function). Note that FlowDroid can be configured to ignore flows that originate from the user interface, effectively eliminating many false positives due to benign, user-initiate encryption. In particular, we modified FlowDroid to track information flows between (1) `InputStream` (and related classes) linked to the victim files and (2) `Cipher` objects in charge of encrypting them. Ransomware usually reads the original file through a loop, placing the bytes read in one of the parameters passed to the `read()` method, which is usually an array. Given that this parameter is not tainted directly by the ransomware, but it is manipulated internally by the `InputStream`, FlowDroid would not be able to detect this information flow. Luckily, the component that is in charge of deciding whether a particular instruction is involved in taint propagation (namely, one of the "taint wrapper" classes) can be easily extended to override the default taint propagation rules. Hence, we created a custom `TaintWrapper` that taints the parameter that will receive the file's bytes if the underlying `InputStream` is tainted in turn. In this way GreatEatlon is able to taint also the `Cipher` objects that receive the same tainted parameter, and that will eventually perform the encryption.

Conditional Flows. We designed conditional flows to be as generic as possible, in order to allow adding, removing and modifying conditions in a simple way in the future. In particular, we created a module that "injects" conditions in FlowDroid by reading them from a text file formatted as follows:

```
NUMBER -> <CLASS: RET_TYPE METHOD(PARAMS)>
```

where:

- NUMBER is the index for the condition.
- CLASS is the fully-qualified class name for the class that declares the method on which we want to check the condition.
- RET_TYPE is the method return type.
- METHOD is the method name.
- PARAMS is the (possibly empty) list of comma-separated method's parameters.

The NUMBER token can take any non-negative integer value (typically a sequential number starting from 0 or 1) and is not part of the method signature, but instead it is used by GreatEatlon to decide whether the condition should be considered as an alternative or standalone. In fact, it is possible to specify an *alternative condition* (*i.e.,* a condition composed by two or more sub-conditions that is valid if at least one of the sub-conditions is valid) by using the same value for two or more conditions. In other words, the parser evaluates all conditions with the same index as logical disjunctions and conditions with different indexes as logical conjunctions. Alternative conditions can be useful to specify requirements on a method that has overloads or on multiple different methods.

The PARAMS token represents the list of actual parameters used in a method call. Currently, the only allowed values are Java primitive types, that are numbers (both integers and floating-point decimals), Boolean values, and characters, plus null, and a custom type indicated by "_". This custom type is essentially a "don't care", meaning that the i-th parameter can take any value (including reference types).

Condition Verification. In general, we could check for condition satisfaction either while performing the taint propagation, or after the taint analysis is completed. These two approaches have different impacts on performance and resource usage. The latter needs to store all the potential source-to-sink paths resulting from the taint analysis to perform the subsequent check. This number can explode if the sample is complex. Moreover, given that FlowDroid does not return the full path, but just a summary (*i.e.,* a path that typically contains only the source, the sink and the intermediate nodes involved in branch decisions), it would be necessary to manually reconstruct the full source-to-sink path to check whether there are some nodes that satisfy the conditions. This implies performing an additional control-flow graph analysis. In the worst case, all the potential paths are reconstructed and visited twice: the first time to perform the taint propagation, and the second time to check for conditions verification. This solution, however, does not require any modification to the taint analysis tool, so it might be helpful to implement the analysis this way if taint analysis is performed by a proprietary or immutable tool.

Instead, when conditions are checked while performing the taint analysis, the control-flow graph is examined only once, by the taint-analysis tool, which would also be in charge of verifying the conditions. This approach is undoubtedly faster than the previous one, but it requires to modify the taint analysis tool source code. Thanks to its open-source nature, we were able to extend InfoFlow, the FlowDroid sub-component that computes the taint analysis, to perform it this way, by modifying the objects that are responsible for taint tracking in order to make them deal with conditions sets. In particular, for each node visited during the taint propagation, we check whether it contributes in satisfying the conditions set. This information is then stored inside the object responsible for containing all data related to the taint, which is propagated to all children of a node when the CFG is explored. We finally modified the `TaintPropagationResults` class, which is responsible for adding paths to the set of results, to allow conditions verification: In this way, whenever a sink node is reached, this component adds the source-to-sink path to the set of results only if the associated condition set has been verified by a previous node.

4.2   Device Administration APIs Misuse Detector

In order to detect misuses of the device-admin APIs, we created a component that starts by analyzing the `AndroidManifest`. Subsequently, we take advantage of FlowDroid for generating CFG and entry-points, because it is designed to deal with this kind of applications and it can be configured to consider or ignore specific callbacks that can be invoked during the application life-cycle. For instance, two interesting entry-points are the `onEnable()` and `onDisable()` methods from class `DeviceAdminReceiver`, which are called by the OS whenever the user grants or revokes device administration rights to the application.

After these setup operations, the tool is ready to analyze the CFG. Since we are interested only in knowing if some methods are called by the sample but not in knowing the exact path, we can perform a simple reachability analysis, which allows us to quickly discover such a method call, if it exists. In particular, we decided to explore the CFG in a breadth-first fashion (BFS), because since the step costs are uniform (*i.e.*, we can assume that visiting a child node has a unitary cost) it can provide the optimal solution, reaching the target node (if it exists) by traversing as few edges as possible. Moreover, we avoid visiting the same node twice. This serves both as an optimization (when a target node is present in the CFG) and to avoid entering an infinite loop it the CFG is not acyclic. A never-terminating analysis, for instance, could occur if a sample contains a suspicious `AndroidManifest`, but it does not actually use any of the potentially dangerous methods, which often happens with (usually benign) applications that require more permissions than needed, or when the target nodes cannot be recognized by the detector, which happens when the sample uses reflection or other kinds of obfuscation.

4.3   Reflection Heuristic

Thanks to manual analyses, we observed that many ransomware applications exploit reflection to call device administration-related methods, which we cannot detect through the above-described procedure. For this reason, we decided to implement a heuristic to detect some common cases, in order to reduce the number of false negatives. In this step, we reuse the CFG generated in Section 4.2 to perform a series of forward and backward analyses in order to discover whether reflection is used and, if this is the case, to try to figure out which method is executed. In particular, we perform a first forward analysis from the application entry-points trying to reach a reflection call, that is an instruction like method.invoke(...), where method is an object from class Method and represents a Java-callable method. If we find at least one instruction of this kind, it means that the application dynamically calls a method. Unfortunately, this information is not enough to prove that the sample is performing something malicious because we do not know the invoked method yet. To obtain this additional information, we perform a backward analysis whose target is to reach the method variable assignment, which usually involves hard-coded strings (because the attacker already knows which is the method to call).

Unluckily we discovered that in a few cases this procedure is not enough because in several samples the hard-coded method name was obfuscated, in order to circumvent those AVs that perform strings analysis. In particular, we observed that attackers manipulate these strings by adding some extra characters to the method name, for instance by transforming the string "resetPassword" to "resLetXPassVUwgXord". Given that the string de-obfuscation is performed by applying some transformations on the string, such as String.replace, we, in turn, take advantage of reflection to apply the same modifications to the original string to try to clean it.

4.4   Lightweight Pre-filtering

The design of the filter revolves around the design of the classification features, the automatic feature-selection algorithm, and the choice of the classifier.

Feature Set. Our features can be extracted via simple static analysis. Although some of them are inspired by previous work (e.g., [15,21]), we propose novel features. In particular, features that capture the app behavior, package name heuristics, file types and count, obfuscation, domain name "well-formedness" and reachability, and commands executed through Runtime.exec(). To keep the filter lightweight, the majority of our features are either binary (i.e., presence vs. absence) or numeric. The behavioral features (namely, Called APIs and Lightweight Behavioral Features) express runtime behavior of an app, although we match them statically, at the price of a few more false positives, which are perfectly acceptable given the problem setting.

Permission Features (Binary). Android applications are sandboxed within Linux processes, plus an additional layer of permissions that regulate inter-process communication. Permissions [22,23] are known to be abused by malware to escape the sandbox. Indeed, previous research showed that permissions are distributed differently among goodware vs. malware [19,24], and can certainly be used to recognize goodware from "suspicious" applications.

Lightweight Behavioral Features (Binary, Novel). We developed simple reachability heuristics that determine, statically (from the Smali code) whether the application sends SMS at startup (*i.e.,* onStartup), reads phone data at startup, sends data when receiving an SMS, sends SMS to short numbers used in premium services, calls built in utilities (*e.g.,* su, ls, grep, root, chmod), and so forth. Clearly, these features alone are by no means complete nor perfect for malware detection. However, combined with the others, they help in finding suspicious samples.

Other Binary Features (Novel). We calculate some aggregated features from package names, URLs and use of obfuscation. For example, one feature is whether the package name is composed by only one part, whether the domain of the main package name is valid, the presence of URLs whose domain does not match the main package name, whether ProGuard has obfuscated the source code, and so on. We designed this diverse but simple set of features by manually inspecting several malicious and benign samples.

Numerical Features (Novel). We include numeric features such as the number of files in an APK, its size, number of permissions, activities and services, the average class size, the total number of packages and the number of classes contained only in the main package.

Feature Selection. We ended up with a collection of more than 220 attributes. GreatEatlon automatically selects the first 120 most significant features by gain ratio ranking [25]. The choice of gain ratio as information measure is driven by the use of decision trees and random forests as suitable classifier models, as explained in the next section.

Classifier Model and Training. We tested several classification techniques, including decision trees (J48), random forests, support vector machine (SVM), stochastic gradient descent (SGD), decision tables (DT), and rule learners (JRip, FURIA, LAC, RIDOR). We found that the best trade off between time, accuracy and precision is an ensemble classifier that performs majority voting [26] among a J48 decision tree, a random forest and a decision table. Essentially, it chooses the prediction on which most classifiers agree. A relevant aspect of our design is that we incorporate a cost-sensitive wrapper around each classifier to make false positives (non-goodware mis-classified as goodware) count more than false negatives [27]. This is crucial to give more importance to precision. By empirical tests, we found that the cost to assign to mis-classifications of such type in order to obtain reasonably high accuracy and very high precision ranges between 16 and 20 times the default mis-classification cost.

5 Experimental Evaluation

In this section, we present the experiments that we performed to evaluate GreatEatlon as well as the dataset we used to test it.

5.1 Experiments

We conducted four experiments to evaluate the ability of GreatEatlon to detect file-encrypting ransomware apps, and three experiments to evaluate the performance of the pre-filter. More precisely, **Experiment 1** evaluates the detection precision between GreatEatlon and the state of the art on dataset of manually vetted ransomware apps known to encrypt files. **Experiment 2** is similar to **Experiment 1**, but on a larger dataset, containing *potential* file-encrypting ransomware. **Experiment 3** evaluates the number of false positives on a dataset of benign apps and generic malware samples. **Experiment 4** evaluates the quality of the image scanner. **Experiment 5** and **6** evaluate the precision and speed of the pre-filter, and **Experiment 7** evaluates the impact of the pre-filter on a large-scale scenario.

5.2 Dataset

We have built 5 distinct data sets to evaluate the various characteristics of GreatEatlon:

- The **Ransomware1** dataset, composed by 75 ransomware samples of which 5 were obtained from "Contagio Mobile" dataset [28] and the rest from Virus-Total Intelligence [29]. We manually vetted these samples to ensure that they actually try to surreptitiously encrypt files.
- The **Ransomware2** dataset, composed by samples downloaded from Virus-Total based on the AV labels. In particular, we queried the database for samples with labels containing the most common ransomware family names, or the generic ``crypto'' keyworkd, filtering out samples with less than 5 positive detections. We expect the dataset to contain both the kind of ransomware we want to analyze and other kinds of malware samples, due to the intrinsic imperfection of AVs.
- The **Malware** dataset, composed by 153,982 malware samples, of which 147,145 obtained from the AndRadar project [30] and 6,837 from the Andro-Total repository [31] (having at least 5 positive detections). This dataset contain malware that we used to test precision and speed of the pre-filter.
- The **ThreateningPicture** dataset, which contains screenshots of threatening messages displayed by real ransomware samples, in English and Russian language. In this dataset we included uncommon font faces with handwritten style, so as to test the capabilities of the Tesseract OCR decoder.

- The **Generic** dataset, composed by 1,239 goodware and generic malware samples gathered both from the Google Play store and alternative markets.
- The **AppScale** dataset, taken from AndRadar, MalGenome, Contagio-Minidump, and the top 1,000 APKs submitted to VirusTotal in between Dec 2014 and Jan 2015.

5.3   Experiment 1: GreatEatlon vs. State of the Art (Benchmark)

We compared the precision of the new encryption detectors of GreatEatlon against those implemented in HelDroid using the **Ransomware1** dataset. Hel-Droid detected only 35 out of 75 ransomware samples, whereas GreatEatlon detected 74 samples. GreatEatlon is able to detect more samples thanks to the customized taint analysis engine. For instance, many samples create target file paths by combining dynamically obtained strings (e.g., file names as a result of a directory listing operation) with hard-coded ones (e.g., default directory names), or by using only hard-coded names. HelDroid is not able to taint fully hard-coded paths. Consequently, even if the malware composes the target path using a mix of hard-coded and dynamically obtained paths, the resulting path will not be tainted because the composition itself would cancel any existing taint. Conversely, GreatEatlon can detect this data flow because the taint is generated only when the application retrieves files in bulk, and not when it obtains a reference to one particular folder.

The false negative was caused by the fact that `MainActivity`, which contain flow sources, is placed as a public inner class of the device-admin class. Unfortunately FlowDroid does not support nested classes, and therefore it is unable to detect flow sources originating from them. Clearly, this is a simple technical limitation of FlowDroid, by no means affecting the conceptual validity of our approach.

5.4   Experiment 2: GreatEatlon vs. State of the Art

We found 11 positives out of 547 analyzed samples. However, only 54 of them were positive to the text detector. If we consider only these 54 samples, we notice that only 43 of them have the `WRITE_EXTERNAL_STORAGE` permission—to write on the SD card (all the aforementioned 11 positives belong to this set). This means that the remaining 504 samples are certainly not file-encrypting ransomware apps. We manually analyzed 10 samples, randomly chosen among the remaining 32 samples confirming that they were true negatives.

5.5   Experiment 3: False Positive Rate

We analyzed the **Generic** dataset to test the false positives rate of GreatEatlon. The results show that our improved detectors do not confuse generic malware with ransomware.

5.6   Experiment 4: Image Scanner Quality

We tested the image scanner on the **ThreateningPicture** dataset. GreatEatlon was able to extract text and classify it as threatening from all the original pictures (*i.e.*, the ones with original font). Instead, if we consider only the images we created by using uncommon font faces, the detector was able to correctly extract the ones with simple symbols, but failed in recognizing the others (e.g., handwritten style). However, we consider thin, handwritten or other fonts of the like more difficult to read for victims, too, hence our assumptions on the reading and understanding ease for threatening text would be no longer satisfied.

Table 1. Precision, accuracy, and area under the ROC curve of different classifiers.

Classifier(s)	Accuracy	Precision	AUC
J48	93.74%	99.4%	0.979
SGD	90.90%	98.9%	0.916
Decision table	91.83%	99.5%	0.986
Random forests	87.18%	99.6%	0.991
J48 + DT + RF	92.75%	99.6%	0.934
J49 + DT + SGD	93.75%	99.6%	0.956
SGD + DT + RF	91.29%	99.6%	0.941

5.7   Experiment 5: Pre-filtering Precision

We evaluated the pre-filter on **Malware** dataset using the standard 10-fold cross-validation approach. We split the dataset in 10 random sub-samples (9 for training, 1 for validation) and repeated this procedure using each sub-sample exactly once per validation. Table 1 shows that the classification capabilities of our pre-filter are very encouraging, especially considering that the training dataset is not homogeneous (*e.g.*, samples from diverse sources and time frames). Notice that the filter alone should not be used as a malware detector! Since our scope is ransomware detection, as opposed to generic malware detection, misclassified innocuous applications would have been analyzed anyways. The goal of our filter is to reduce their amount vastly, and quickly, as showed in the next experiment.

5.8   Experiment 6: Pre-filtering Speed

As training is performed offline, we are interested in measuring the speed of the actual classification. Each APK goes through unpacking, feature extraction, and then the actual classification. Using the **Malware** dataset, we measured that the actual classification has a negligible impact (milliseconds), and unpacking takes 2.484 seconds on average (median 1.922, 3rd quantile 2.814). The feature-extraction step is the core of the pre-filter. Thus, we measured the execution time

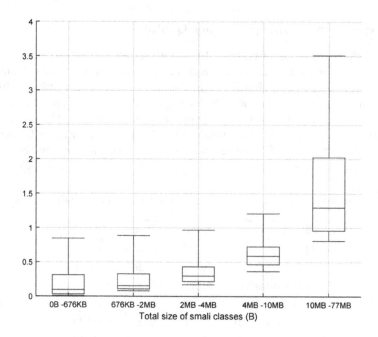

Fig. 1. Pre-filter execution time.

while varying the total size of Smali classes, total Smali classes count, and total files count, and APK size. We found out that time is mainly influenced by the total size of the Smali classes. Therefore, we plot this dependency in Fig. 1. In the worst cases encountered in our large dataset, the feature extraction takes less than 1.5s. Even considering the unpacking, in less than 4 seconds our pre-filter produces an answer.

5.9   Experiment 7: Impact of the Pre-filter on Large Scale Analysis

We measured the response time of HelDroid with and without the pre-filter on 50 distinct random splits of 1,000 samples each from the **AppScale** dataset. Under this scenario, with the pre-filter we pay a small precision penalty but we gain 1.5 to 2.0× on the overall processing time, on average.

6   Limitations

Despite the good performance, GreatEatlon has some limitations, which are described in this section.

6.1   Native Code

GreatEatlon assumes that ransomware will use the Android APIs. Despite the effectiveness of GreatEatlon on the majority of the samples that we analyzed, it is unable to deal with native machine code, which could be used by malware authors to evade static analyses. Nevertheless, it is possible to discover if a certain sample makes use of native code, or by inspecting the Smali code looking for methods containing the `native` modifier. In this case, it would be appropriate to use an external, dedicated tool to perform the consequent analysis. Therefore, this limitation is not conceptual, but simply technical.

6.2   Conditional Flows

Conditional flows are evaluated while performing the taint analysis. Although in this way we save time and resources, we cannot specify complex conditions, such as conditions related to object fields, or on values known only at runtime. Therefore, if a sample bases its decision of whether to encrypt or decrypt a file on a value that is computed at runtime, GreatEatlon would not be able to detect it. Unluckily, there is no easy solution to both solve this problem with pure static analysis, because the only way to precisely know the value stored inside a certain variable is to watch such variable at runtime.

6.3   Reflection Heuristic

In Sect. 3.3, we anticipated that we designed this heuristic to detect the most common approaches used by ransomware samples. Malware authors could evade it by encrypting strings or other hard-coded values and decrypt them at runtime, as soon as the application needs them. In this scenario, the only way to retrieve those values would be to decrypt them (which requires to know the encryption key), to retrieve the memory dump from a dynamic analysis or to use dynamic techniques such as Harvester (see Sect. 7). Generally, the ultimate solution would be to use a fully dynamic-analysis approach, because it would allow to know with certainty which is the exact signature of the methods that the sample calls, despite of the calling technique.

6.4   Image Scanner

Our image scanner assumes that each threatening text unit is contained inside a single picture. In the future, though, ransomware samples could split the threatening text in multiple images, rendering them in a sort of grid at runtime and composing the complete message in a sort of "mosaic picture," or an animated sequence. In this scenario, GreatEatlon would probably be not able to extract an amount of text significant enough to trigger the text analyzer, specially if the complete threatening message is split in a great number of "tiles".

In order to allow the image scanner to extract meaningful text, we would need to pre-process the layout and Java files to an additional component that is capable of deciding whether a given APK contains such "mosaic" pictures, if that is the case, to reconstruct the final picture. Whenever the resulting image is reconstructed, it can be submitted to our image scanner, that would treat it as a traditional picture and extract any text it contains.

7   Related Work

Ransomware Detection. HelDroid represents the state of the art in the field of static ransomware detection and is the ground on which GreatEatlon is based. HelDroid mainly contributed with three techniques: the text analyzer, which is in charge of deciding whether a given string should be considered as threatening or not, the lock detector, which is able to detect active action made by ransomware that are trying to lock the user out of his phone, and the encryption detector, which is able to detect whether an application is trying to do an unsolicited encryption operations. In particular, we improved the encryption detection system and we added a lightweight pre-filter that is able to recognize goodwares, and discard it from the analysis queue.

Runtime Values Extraction. Harvester [32] is a new system intended to dynamically extract runtime values. Since it is based on a cyclical combination of slicing and code execution, it can extract values regardless of any possible encryption, obfuscation or other anti-analysis techniques applied to them. Given its extraction capabilities, we think that this tool could be integrated into GreatEatlon to replace the heuristic we developed, in order to improve both the device administrator abuse and the encryption detectors as well as FlowDroid's recall (as demonstrated by paper authors, Harvester improved FlowDroid detection by roughly three times).

8   Conclusions

Ransomware is a real threat for mobile devices and is expected to grow in the next years. As a countermeasure against this threat, we propose an approach for detecting encryption-capable apps based on a customized static taint analysis tool, allowing it to accept or discard taint flows based on a set of static conditions. We also designed and developed a new component to detect device administration API abuse, a feature that is present in the newest ransomware families as well as in other recent, non-ransomware malware families.

Our experiments show that GreatEatlon can identify more encryption-capable apps than the state of the art, while maintaining a low false positive rate. Moreover, the new device administration API abuse detector allow us to identify modern ransomware families with better precision. In particular, in the experiment relative to the pre-filter show that is possible to detect goodware with around 99% accuracy.

We believe that merging these new components with the (already good) text analyzer and lock detector of HelDroid can lead to improved and fast detection of modern mobile ransomware families, making GreatEatlon the most advanced mobile ransomware detection tools. If we could also include some external tools such as Harvester or other runtime values extractor, then we would be able to deal with obfuscated, encrypted or other kinds of evasive samples, too.

Finally, we provide a publicly accessible website, which allows other security researchers or end users to submit their samples, to focus on prevention and fight the mobile ransomware threat.

References

1. Statista: Number of smartphone users worldwide from 2014 to 2019, August 2015. http://www.statista.com/
2. Ericcson: Mobility report, February 2016. http://www.ericsson.com/
3. G Data: G data mobile malware report (2015). https://www.gdatasoftware.com/
4. K Lab: The volume of new mobile malware tripled in 2015, February 2016. http://www.kaspersky.com/
5. Avast Software: Avast ransomware removal, June·2014. https://play.google.com/
6. Andronio, N., Zanero, S., Maggi, F.: HELDROID: dissecting and detecting mobile ransomware. In: Bos, H., Monrose, F., Blanc, G. (eds.) RAID 2015. LNCS, vol. 9404, pp. 382–404. Springer, Cham (2015). doi:10.1007/978-3-319-26362-5_18
7. Spreitzenbarth Mobile Security and Forensics: Summary of the year 2015, January 2016. http://forensics.spreitzenbarth.de/
8. Symantec: Simplocker: first confirmed file-encrypting ransomware for android, June 2014. http://www.symantec.com/
9. Avast: Mobile crypto-ransomware simplocker now on steroids, February 2015. http://www.symantec.com/
10. Felt, A.P., Ha, E., Egelman, S., Haney, A., Chin, E., Wagner, D.: Android permissions: user attention, comprehension, and behavior. In: SOUP'S 2012 Proceedings of the Eighth Symposium on Usable Privacy and Security, no. 3 (2012)
11. ESET: Eset simplocker decryptor, August 2014. http://www.eset.com/
12. Apktool v2.0.3. https://github.com/iBotPeaches/Apktool
13. Venkatesan, D.: Android nougat prevents ransomware from resetting device passwords, July 2016. http://www.symantec.com/connect/blogs/android-nougat-prevents-ransomware-resetting-device-passwords
14. Zhou, Y., Wang, Z., Zhou, W., Jiang, X.: Hey, you, get off of my market: detecting malicious apps in official and alternative android markets. NDSS 25(4), 50–52 (2012)
15. Arp, D., Spreitzenbarth, M., Hubner, M., Gascon, H., Rieck, K.: Drebin: effective and explainable detection of android malware in your pocket. In: NDSS (2014)
16. Chakradeo, S., Reaves, B., Traynor, P., Enck, W.: Mast: triage for market-scale mobile malware analysis. In: Proceedings of the Sixth ACM Conference on Security and Privacy in Wireless and Mobile Networks, pp. 13–24. ACM (2013)
17. Shabtai, A., Kanonov, U., Elovici, Y., Glezer, C., Weiss, Y.: Andromaly: a behavioral malware detection framework for android devices. J. Intell. Inf. Syst. 38(1), 161–190 (2012)
18. Apvrille, L., Apvrille, A.: Pre-filtering mobile malware with heuristic techniques. In: Proceedings of GreHack (2013)
19. Zhou, Y., Jiang, X.: Dissecting android malware: characterization and evolution. In: IEEE Symposium on Security and Privacy (SP) 2012, pp. 95–109. IEEE (2012)
20. Lindorfer, M., Neugschwandtner, M., Weichselbaum, L., Fratantonio, Y., Van Der Veen, V., Platzer, C.: Andrubis-1,000,000 apps later: a view on current android malware behaviors. In: Proceedings of the 3rd International Workshop on Building Analysis Datasets and Gathering Experience Returns for Security (BADGERS) (2014)
21. Arzt, S., Rasthofer, S., Fritz, C., Bodden, E., Bartel, A., Klein, J., Le Traon, Y., Octeau, D., McDaniel, P.: Flowdroid: precise context, flow, field, object-sensitive and lifecycle-aware taint analysis for android apps. In: Proceedings of the 35th ACM SIGPLAN Conference on Programming Language Design and Implementation, PLDI 2014, pp. 259–269 (2014)

22. Felt, A.P., Chin, E., Hanna, S., Song, D., Wagner, D.: Android permissions demystified. In: Proceedings of the 18th ACM Conference on Computer and Communications Security, pp. 627–638. ACM (2011)

23. Felt, A.P., Ha, E., Egelman, S., Haney, A., Chin, E., Wagner, D.: Android permissions: user attention, comprehension, and behavior. In: Proceedings of the Eighth Symposium on Usable Privacy and Security, p. 3. ACM (2012)

24. Andrubin. https://anubis.iseclab.org

25. Han, J., Kamber, M., Pei, J.: Data Mining: Concepts and Techniques. Elsevier, Amsterdam (2011)

26. Jarvis, K.: Cryptolocker ransomware. Viitattu **20**, 2014 (2013)

27. Domingos, P.: Metacost: a general method for making classifiers cost-sensitive. In: Proceedings of the Fifth ACM SIGKDD International Conference on Knowledge Discovery and Data Mining, pp. 155–164. ACM (1999)

28. Contagio mobile. http://contagiominidump.blogspot.it/

29. Virustotal. https://virustotal.com/

30. Lindorfer, M., Volanis, S., Sisto, A., Neugschwandtner, M., Athanasopoulos, E., Maggi, F., Platzer, C., Zanero, S., Ioannidis, S.: AndRadar: fast discovery of android applications in alternative markets. In: Dietrich, S. (ed.) DIMVA 2014. LNCS, vol. 8550, pp. 51–71. Springer, Cham (2014). doi:10.1007/978-3-319-08509-8_4

31. Maggi, F., Valdi, A., Zanero, S.: Andrototal: a flexible, scalable toolbox and service for testing mobile malware detectors. In: Proceedings of the 3rd Annual ACM CCS Workshop on Security and Privacy in Smartphones and Mobile Devices (SPSM). ACM, November 2013

32. Rasthofer, S., Arzt, S., Miltenberger, M., Bodden, E.: Harvesting runtime values in android applications that feature anti-analysis techniques. In: Proceedings of the Annual Symposium on Network and Distributed System Security (NDSS) (2016)

Data Flow Analysis on Android Platform with Fragment Lifecycle Modeling

Yongfeng Li[1]([✉]), Jinbin Ouyang[1], Shanqing Guo[2], and Bing Mao[1]

[1] State Key Laboratory for Novel Software Technology,
Department of Computer Science and Technology,
Nanjing University, Nanjing, China
jsliyongfeng@gmail.com, oyjb1992@gmail.com, maobing@nju.edu.cn
[2] School of Computer Science and Technology, Shandong University, Jinan, China
guoshanqing@sdu.edu.cn

Abstract. Smartphones carry a large quantity of sensitive information to satisfy people's various requirements, but the way of using information is important to keep the security of users' privacy. There are two kinds of misuses of sensitive information for apps. On the one hand, careless programmers may leak the data by accident. On the other hand, the attackers develop malware to collect sensitive data intentionally. Many researchers apply data flow analysis to detect data leakages of an app. However, data flow analysis on Android platform is quite different from the programs on desktop. Many researchers have solved some problems of data flow analysis on Android platform, like Activity lifecycle, callback methods, inter-component communication. We find that Fragment's lifecycle also has an effect on the data flow analysis of Android apps. Some data will be leaked if we don't take Fragment's lifecycle into consideration when performing data flow analysis in Android apps. So in this paper, we propose an approach to model Fragment's lifecycle and its relationship with Activity's lifecycle, then introduce a tool called Frag-Droid based on FlowDroid [7]. We conduct some experiments to evaluate the effectiveness of our tool and the results show that there are 8% of apps in our data set using Fragment. In particular, for popular apps, the result is 50.8%. We also evaluate the performance of using FragDroid to analyze Android apps, the result shows the average overhead is 17%.

Keywords: Data flow · Fragment · Android · Program analysis

1 Introduction

With the progress of technology, smartphones have pervaded into all aspects of human life, and have become an indispensable part of daily life. Compared with the traditional PC devices, smartphones carry more user privacy data, such as location information, contact information, fingerprint information, text message records, which brings endless attacks against smartphones. The security protection of smartphones has become a problem which needs to be solved urgently.

© ICST Institute for Computer Sciences, Social Informatics and Telecommunications Engineering 2017
R. Deng et al. (Eds.): SecureComm 2016, LNICST 198, pp. 637–654, 2017.
DOI: 10.1007/978-3-319-59608-2_35

According to the recent report [1], in the current smartphone markets, Android platform market share has been far more than the iOS platform. This means protecting the privacy of Android users is very important.

On Android platform, there is a variety of malware. In the research of Jiang's team [2], they classify the malware based on behavior. In their malware classification, there are many kinds of malware which collect users' privacy information and leak it out. Sometimes, privacy information is not leaked by malware intentionally. Developers always use some third-party libraries to develop an Android app conveniently, which is hard for developers to know the details of data flow in the libraries. And when they pass privacy information to the library procedure, information may be leaked. The library itself can also lead to information leakage.

To protect the privacy information, there is a kind of technology called taint analysis, whose main task is to record the data flow relationship among some specific objects. In taint analysis, before propagating the data flow, some nodes called sources (in data leakage, these are sensitive APIs which get information like GPS, location, etc.) should be specified. During the data flow propagation, taint analysis will check if the data flow reach nodes called sinks (APIs which send messages). Through taint analysis, privacy information leakage which violate predefined rules will be found. There are two approaches to perform taint analysis on Android platform: dynamic analysis and static analysis. Some dynamic analysis techniques like TaintDroid [3], Droidscope [4] have been proposed. These approaches all are suffering from the code coverage problem, that is, when running an app, some code may not be executed. Moreover, as mentioned in [5], malware can use the runtime information to decide whether it is running on a monitor or not. Then, it can decide whether to trigger malicious behaviors or not.

Static analysis is performed with scanning the apps instead of executing programs, which avoids the problems mentioned above. However, it demands to emulate the runtime state of an app approximately. Previous researchers [6–11] have proposed some approaches to solve the problems in static analysis on Android platform. Chex [6] is a static analysis system designed to solve the component hijacking problems of Android apps. To handle the multiple entry points, Chex conducts data flow analysis for code reachable from each entry point, and then combines these results to find data flow between code splits. FlowDroid [7,8] models the taint-analysis problem within the IFDS [12] framework for inter-procedural distributive subset problems. FlowDroid generates a dummy main method for each app to model the control flow transfers between component lifecycle methods. FlowDroid also models the control flow of callback methods in a dummy main method. Amandroid [9] and IccTA [10] handle the inter-component communication when performing data flow analysis. Amandroid calculates all objects' points to information, while IccTA handles the situation when Activity is not the target of ICC based on FlowDroid. EdgeMiner [11] conducts a deep study of callback methods in Android system. EdgeMiner proposes an automatic approach to extract callback methods and their corresponding registration methods in Android system. FlowDroid can apply EdgeMiner's result to get more precise data flow information.

The fragment introduced in Android 3.0(API level 11) is mainly to support a more dynamic and flexible UI design for the large screen(such as tablet PC). Because of the much larger screen of tablets' compared with that of smartphones, more space can be used to combine and exchange UI components. On account of the Activity layout divided into fragments, you can modify its appearance and keep the changes in return stack which is managed by Activity itself. Fragments is part of the behavior or the user interface of Activity. We can use multiple fragments combination in an Activity to build multiple pane UI, and reuse a fragment in multiple Activities. We can put the fragment as a modular part of the Activity, which has its own lifecycle and can receive their own input events. Moreover, we can dynamically add, replace, and remove some fragments. None of the previous researchers have described Fragment's lifecycle has an effect on data flow analysis. When performing data flow analysis, some data flow will be missed without taking Fragment's lifecycle into consideration, which will lead to false negative when analyzing data leakage in apps. Moreover, malware can also adopt Fragment's lifecycle to evade the detection method based on data flow and control flow analysis. Moreover, Fragment's lifecycle is not independent as it depends on Activity's lifecycle. So we also model the interaction between Activity and Fragment. Malware is out of the scope of this paper, so we don't discuss it in this paper.

To summarize, this paper makes the following contributions:

- We find that Fragment's lifecycle has an effect on data flow analysis on Android apps. And we do some research to reveal the relationship between Fragment's lifecycle and Activity's lifecycle.
- We model all the Fragments' and Activities' lifecycle control flow transfers in a control flow graph, then we make an extension on Flowdroid [7]. All of the lifecycle methods are contained in a dummy main method. With using the extended tool, we can perform information leakage detection without false negative caused by Fragment's lifecycle.
- We make an in-depth evaluation of the extended tool. The experiments' result include the statistics of the Fragment usage in Android apps and the runtime performance after modeling the Fragment's lifecycle.

2 Background and Motivation

2.1 Background

In Android, an application's execution is driven by system events. When an event occurs, Android system invokes the predefined method which implemented by developers. Android adopts a component-based mechanism to simplify the development of apps. There are four kinds of application components: Activity, Service, Content Provider, Broadcast Receiver. Each app is composed of many application components, and the components' execution is controlled by system according to events. When performing data flow analysis in Android apps, components' lifecycle must be taken into consideration. Previous researchers [7–10] have modeled the lifecycle of four main application components. But in 3.0, Android introduces Fragment to support more dynamic and flexible UI designs on large screens, such as tablets. In Android apps, Fragment is always included in an Activity which has its own lifecycle, so does the Fragment. The lifecycle of Fragment and its relationship with Activity's lifecycle are described in Fig. 1.

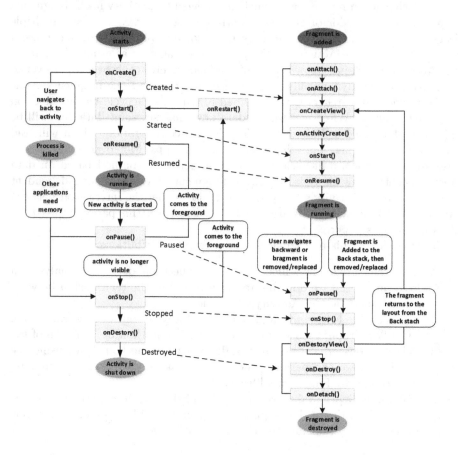

Fig. 1. Fragment lifecycle

As is depicted in Fig. 1, when a Fragment starts, onAttach(), onCreate(), onCreateView(), onActivityCreated(), onStart() and onResume() will be invoked by Android system one by one. When the app is paused, for example, Fragment's onPause() method will be invoked if the user presses the home button. When the memory is low, Android system will recycle some memory, so the onStop() method will be invoked. When the user navigates back to the app, Fragment's onStart() and onResume() method will be invoked to restore the Fragment. When the user kills the app, onDestroyView(), onDestroy(), onDetach() will be invoked. Moreover, the Fragment's lifecycle depends on Activity's lifecycle.

Thus we can't use Fragment alone. Activity's lifecycle dominates Fragment's lifecycle. So the Activity starts and pauses before Fragment, while stops and destroys after Fragment. Thus, Activity's onCreate(), onStart(), onResume() will be invoked before Fragment's onCreate(), onStart() and onResume(). And Activity's onPause(), onStop(), onDestroy() will be invoked after Fragment's onPause(), onStop(), onDestroy().

2.2   Motivation

In this section, we demonstrate our motivation by introducing some code snippets. As is depicted in Fig. 2, there is an Activity named "LifecycleActivity" and a Fragment named "LifecycleFragment". "LifecycleActivity" overrides two lifecycle methods onCreate() and onPause(), "NativePhoneNumber" is a field in this class. "LifecycleFragment" overrides three lifecycle methods onAttach(), onResume() and onPause(). "LifecycleFragment" also has two fields named "NativePhoneNumber" and "attachedActivity". The first one stores string value, while the second one stores the reference of Activity this Fragment attached to. In "LifecycleActivity", onCreate() method invokes replace() method to attach a "LifecycleFragment" to this Activity. onPause() method invokes getLine1Number() and stores the phone number to field "NativePhoneNumber". In "LifecycleFragment", onAttach() method stores attached Activity's reference to field "attachedActivity". onResume() method passes the the field "NativePhoneNumber" of "attachedActivity" to its field "NativePhoneNumber". onPause() method invokes sendTextMessage() and sends out the value stored in "NativePhoneNumber".

FlowDroid models the application components' lifecycle in a dummy main method, but the Fragment's lifecycle is not in this dummy main method. So if we use FlowDroid [7] to detect data leakage in this app, it will report nothing. FlowDroid has generated control flow graph before data flow analysis and the Fragment's lifecycle methods are not in this graph, so data flow will not propagate out of these lifecycle methods. But actually, this app leaks the phone number through sending text message. AmanDroid [9] also can't detect this data leakage, because it doesn't consider Fragment's lifecycle as well.

From Fig. 1, we know that when "LifecycleActivity" starts, the system invokes onCreate() method, then the "LifecycleFragment" is attached to this Activity. At the same time, Android system invokes the lifecycle method onAttach() of "LifecycleFragment". In this method, the reference of "LifecycleActivity" is passed to "attachedActivity". When "LifecycleActivity" is activated, the onResume() method of "LifecycleFragment" is invoked, so the string value in "NativePhoneNumber" of "LifecycleFragment" is "default". At this moment, if user leaves "LifecycleActivity" Activity, the lifecycle method onPause() of "LifecycleFragment" will be invoked. It sends the value of "NativePhoneNumber" which is "default". It means the information leakage has not happened so far. Then the lifecycle method onPause() of "LifecycleActivity" will be invoked, so the string value in "NativePhoneNumber" of "LifecycleActivity" will be the phone number. When user navigates back to "LifecycleActivity", lifecycle

```
public class LifecycleActivity extends Activity
{
    public String NativePhoneNumber = "default";
    public void onCreate (Bundle savedInstanceState)
    {
        super. onCreate (savedInstanceState);
        setContentView (R. layout. main);
        LifecycleFragment fragment = new LifecycleFragment ();
        getFragmentManager (). beginTransaction ()
                           . replace (R. id. container, fragment). commit ();
    }
    protected void onPause () {
        super. onPause ();
        NativePhoneNumber = telephonyManager. getLine1Number ();
    }

}

public class LifecycleFragment extends Fragment
{
    private String NativePhoneNumber = "default";
    private LifecycleActivity attachedActivity;
    @Override
    public void onAttach (Activity activity)
    {
        super. onAttach (activity);
        attachedActivity = (FragmentLifecycle) activity;
    }
    public void onResume ()
    {
        super. onResume ();
        NativePhoneNumber = attachedActivity. NativePhoneNumber;
    }
    public void onPause ()
    {
        super. onPause ();
        SmsManager sms = SmsManager. getDefault ();
        sms. sendTextMessage ("134444", null, NativePhoneNumber, null, null);
    }
}
```

Fig. 2. Motivation example

method onResume() of "LifecycleFragment" will be invoked, and the value of "NativePhoneNumber" in "LifecycleFragment" will be the phone number. If the user leave "LifecycleActivity" again, the lifecycle method onPause() of "LifecycleFragment" will be invoked, and the phone number will be leaked through text message this time.

From the description above, we can learn that this app gets phone number through the lifecycle method onPause() of "LifecycleActivity", and sends a text message with the phone number in the lifecycle method onPause() of "Lifecycle-Fragment". During this process, the Activity's state changes many times. Some data flows will be lost if we don't model the control flow transfers between lifecycle methods when state changes, which will make malware evade detection with some state-of-art static analysis tools like FlowDroid and Amandroid. Besides control flow, some data dependencies between parameters of lifecycle methods also need to be handled carefully. For example, in lifecycle method onAttach() of "LifecycleFragment", its parameter, which is passed by Android system, is the Activity it attached to. When performing data flow analysis, we should take this data dependence into consideration.

2.3 Goals and Assumption

In this paper, we focus on Fragment's lifecycle and its effects on data flow analysis. We propose an approach to model Fragment's lifecycle and implement a tool named FragDroid. FragDroid is based on FlowDroid [7], so its data flow analysis has the same limits as FlowDroid. It can't deal with native code and decide the target objects or methods for java reflection.

3 System Design

We demonstrate FragDroid's work flow in Fig. 3. As is depicted in this figure, FragDroid takes six steps to analyze an app. First of all, it parses the manifest file and then the app's entry points like Activity, Service will be obtained. Then, FragDroid scans the Activity's lifecycle methods to find Fragment registrations. At the same time, FragDroid gets the Activity's layout xml file. Next, FragDroid parses the layout file to find the Fragment registration because Fragment can be attached in layout file as well. And then, Fragment gets some Fragments, but Fragment can also be declared in callback methods. So in the callback methods, some Fragments can be attached to Activity dynamically. The work flow will go back to step two unless no new fragments and callback methods can be found. At last, FragDroid generates a dummy main method to model the control flow transfer between the lifecycle methods of Fragment and Activity. A demo of dummy main method's control flow is shown in Fig. 4. After the dummy main method has generated, FragDroid builds the call graph and perform taint analysis just as FlowDroid does.

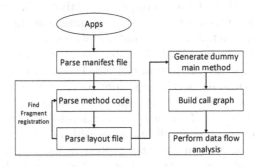

Fig. 3. System architecture

4 Implementation

4.1 Identify Fragments Which Attached to Activity

In order to model the Fragment's lifecycle, we must find all Fragments what an app's Activities contain at first. In an Android application, Fragments can be

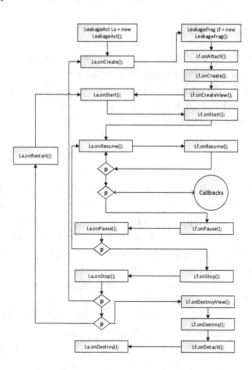

Fig. 4. Dummy main method control flow

attached to an Activity through two approaches. Firstly, developers can attach a Fragment to an Activity by declaring in the Activity's layout file. This file is an xml file, in which Fragment is declared by 'fragment' tag. For this kind of registration, we can scan the Activity's onCreate() method and get its layout file, then the fragment can be identified. Secondly, developers can attach Fragment to an Activity through some registration methods like FragmentTransaction.add() or FragmentTransaction.replace(). It is more complex here to find this kind of Fragment registration than in the first approach because these registration methods can be invoked during Activity's lifecycle. Moreover, users can change the Activity's user interface dynamically through callback methods like onClickListener(). Fragment registration can also happen in these callback methods. In order to find this kind of registration, we scan all lifecycle methods of the Activity implements. Then, we scan the Fragments' lifecycle methods and callback methods until no new Fragments' lifecycle and callback methods can be found.

4.2   Deal with Data Flow Between Activity and Fragment

In an Android app, Activity and Fragment have not only control flow relationships, but also some data flow dependencies. For example, as is shown in Fig. 2, the parameter of lifecycle method onAttach() in LifecyceFragment is passed by Android system. We need to handle this situation, otherwise some data flows will be lost. To solve this problem, we can modify the code of Fragment because we just need to maintain the data flow relationship instead of running the app. We create a new private field 'attachedActivity' in the class for Fragment's onAttach() and getActivity() method. When generating dummy main method, for each Fragment, we pass the related Activity to Fragment's onAttach() method. And then, in onAttach() method, the passed Activity is stored in 'attachedActivity'. To get the correct Activity, we rewrite the getActivity() method whose return value is 'attachedActivity'.

4.3 Create Dummy Main Method

After getting all Fragments each Activity contains, we need to generate a dummy main method to model the control flow transfers between lifecycle methods of Fragment and Activity. Figure 4 shows us the dummy main method's control flow when an Activity only contains one fragment. If an Activity contains multiple Fragments, the situation will be more complex. We will describe how to solve it in the next section. In order to create a dummy main method whose control flow is like Fig. 4, we use a conditional jump instruction to model the control flow transfer among lifecycle methods.

```
public static void dummyMainMethod()
{
    int $i0 = 0; LifecycleActivity$r1; LifecycleFragment $r2;
    label01:
        if $i0 == 1 goto label07;
        $r1.<LifecycleActivity: void onCreate()>();
    label02:
        if $i0 == 2 goto label03;
        $r2.<LifecycleFragment: void onAttach(Activity)>($r1);
    label03:
        if $i0 == 3 goto label04;
        $r2.<LifecycleFragment: void onResume()>();
    label04:
        if $i0 == 4 goto label05;
        $r2.<LifecycleFragment: void onPause()>();
    label05:
        $r1.<LifecycleActivity: void onPause()>();
        if $i0 == 5 goto label03;
    label07:
        return;
}
```

Fig. 5. Dummy main method IR code of motivation sample

We use the motivation example to demonstrate the creation of the dummy main method as is shown in Fig. 5. In this figure, at first, conditional value 'i0', Activity 'r1' and Fragment 'r2' is declared. In lable01, it creates a conditional jump whose target is label07 because this Activity may not be executed. If the condition is not met, 'r1' will invoke onCreate() method. In label02, the fragment's onAttach() method is invoked depending on the conditional jump. Although we can get the Fragments which can be attached to an Activity, but we don't know which Fragments are attached to the Activity at an exact moment. We don't implement the Activity's onStart() and onResume() methods, so in label03, Fragment's onResume() is invoked. When the Activity is paused, the Fragment's onPause() method has been invoked before Activity's onPause() method. So in label04, Fragment's onPause() is invoked. And in label05, Activity's onPause() is invoked. The Activity's state can be resumed, so in label05 there is a conditional jump going to label03. In label07 the app is terminated.

4.4   Handle One Activity Carried with Multiple Fragments

In the last section, we have described how to create a dummy main method when an Activity only contains one Fragment. Actually, multiple Fragments can be attached to an Activity. Sometimes it is required to modify the entire page, but creating a new Activity is unnecessary. It can be efficient to use an Activity to manage multiple Fragments. News application, for example, can use a fragment to display article list on the left and another fragment to display the article on the right. Therefore, users do not need to use an Activity to select articles and use another Activity to read the article, but can choose articles within an Activity. In this section, we will show how to deal with this situation. If multiple Fragments are attached to an Activity, the lifecycle methods of Fragments are invoked according to the order of attaching these Fragments. Take an Activity with two fragments as an example, when the lifecycle methods of Fragments are invoked, as is shown in Fig. 4, the first attached Fragment's onAttach() to onActivityCreated() will be invoked after Activity's onCreate(). As there are two Fragments, the second attached Fragment's onAttach() to onActivityCreated() will be invoked after the first Fragment's. Fragments' onStart(), onResume(), onPause(), onStop() are also invoked in the Fragments' attached order. And the first Fragments' onDestroyView(), onDestroy(), onDetach() has been invoked before the second Fragment's. However, as is described in Sect. 4.1, Fragments in an Activity can be dynamically added or replaced by callback methods. Thus

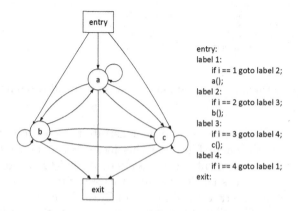

Fig. 6. Control flow sequence of lifecycle methods when there are multiple fragments

we can't exactly know the order of how Fragments are added. In this paper, we assume the Fragments are attached in any order.

We show this kind of control flow transfer in Fig. 6. In this Figure, we assume there are three Fragments in an Activity. The vertexes labeled as a, b, c, have the same lifecycle method like onResume() of each Fragment. For the process from onAttach() to onActivityCreated(), we use an intermediate method to invoke them one by one. To make the dummy main method generate the control flow transfer as is shown in Fig. 6, we can generate the code shown in this figure. In the code, we use a conditional jump statement to model the execution. The lifecycle methods can be executed in any order by emulating different conditions.

5   Evaluation

5.1   Dataset and Experiment Setup

We collect 19342 apps from three popular Android markets (Baidu [17], Xiaomi [18] and Anzhi [19]). In order to measure the amount of Fragments in the most popular apps, we also select 887 apps from baidu market according to their downloads. To test the efficiency of FragDroid, we develop some test apps based on lifecycle methods of Fragment and Activity which override different lifecycle methods.

We conduct experiments on a computer equipped with Intel(R) Core(TM) i7-4770k CPU(3.5 GHz) and 16 GB of physical memory. The operation system is Windows 7.

5.2   Summary of Fragment Usage in App

The experiment results of Fragment usage of apps in the two data sets mentioned in the last section are shown in Figs. 7 and 8. In the first app data set, 1557 apps in 19342 cases use Fragment. This means, for an ordinary app, the probability of using Fragment is 8%. In the second app data set, 451 apps in 887 cases use Fragment, the probability is 50.8%. We also give the statistic result for multiple fragments can be attached to one activity in Fig. 9. According to these figures, we conclude that the more popular the app is, the higher its possibility of using Fragment is.

Figure 7 lists the distribution of the number of Fragments in the first app data set. From the figure, we find that 45.8% of apps which use Fragment only have one kind of Fragment, and Activities share the same user interface provided by this Fragment. Most of apps (91.9%) have less than 10 kinds of Fragments. Figure 8 shows the result of the second app data set, we can see that more kinds of Fragments are contained in one app, 28.3% apps have more than 10 kinds of Fragment classes.

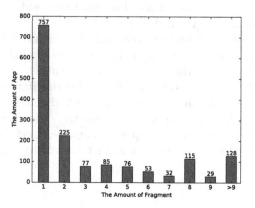

Fig. 7. Distribution of the number of fragments

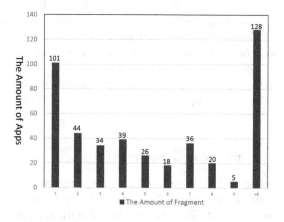

Fig. 8. Distribution of the number of fragments for popular apps

	Number of apps using fragment	Number of activities carried with multiple Fragments
First dataset	1557	9941
Second dataset	451	2916

Fig. 9. Distribution of the number of activities carried with multiple fragments

5.3   Data Leakage Results

The result of data leakage in the second app data set is shown in Fig. 10. This figure contains the results of analyzing and do not analyzing Fragment. In this figure, we find that when we don't consider Fragment lifecycle, 47.4% of apps report more than 150 source to-sink pairs. After Fragment's lifecycle is modelled, 57.3% of apps report more than 150 source-to sink pairs. The amount of source-to sink pairs has an average increase of 18 in an app. In this experiment, we demonstrate that Fragment's lifecycle has an effect on the data leakage detection result.

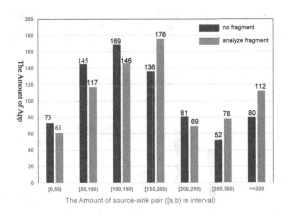

Fig. 10. Distribution of source-sink pairs

5.4   Runtime Performance

The runtime performance of FragDroid is shown in Figs. 11 and 12. The experiment result of the first app data set is depicted in Fig. 11. As is shown in this figure, when we do not analyze Fragment, 90% of the apps can be finished in 20 s and the average time is 12 s. After analyzing Fragment, 80% of the apps can be finished in 20s and the average time is 14 s. It means that after we modelled the Fragment's lifecycle, the average overhead is 17%. The experiment result for popular app data set is shown in Fig. 12. After Fragment analysis, the overhead is 114%. The run time of analysis is highly depended on the amount of Fragments this app using.

6   Discussion

Current data flow analysis techniques on Android platform are not perfect. In this paper, we focus on fragment's lifecycle, and get a more complete control flow which is the prerequisite for data flow analysis. We have no in-depth analysis of native code and java reflection, so the data flow may be not precise enough. In addition, there exists a large number of callback methods in Android system,

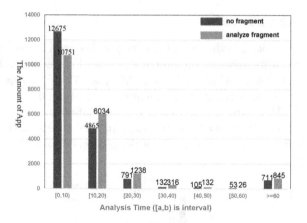

Fig. 11. Distribution of analysis time

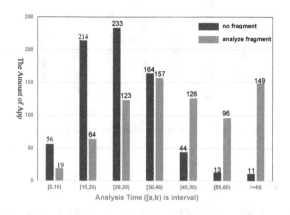

Fig. 12. Distribution of analysis time for popular apps

which can be rewritten to add malicious behavior. Thus, we just consider the control flow among callback methods. Actually, it is not complete, because these callback methods may have data dependencies. For example, in AsyncTask, the return value of doInBackground() is passed to onPostExecute() as the first parameter. But in our tool, we don't consider this. Malware can hide sensitive data flows through these dependencies. In the future, we can analyze the data dependence between callback methods' return values and parameters, and integrate these into data flow analysis procedure.

7   Related Work

Previous researchers have proposed some approaches to solve problems in static analysis on Android platform. We summarize the differences of existing static analysis tools in Fig. 13. CHEX [6], FlowDroid [7], AmanDroid [9] are three tools which perform static data flow analysis on Android platform. CHEX [6] is designed to detect the component hijacking problems in Android apps. When performing data flow analysis, CHEX analyzes each program split which includes code reachable from a single entry point at first. Cross split data flow are analyzed based on those system dependence graphs [24] which will be generated for every program split. FlowDroid [7] is aimed at detecting data leakages in Android apps. It models data flow analysis problem within the IFDS [25] framework for inter-procedural distributive subset problems. It also models the Activity's lifecycle in a dummy main method. AmanDroid [9] is an Android data flow analysis framework. It computes an inter-component data flow graph (IDFG) which contains all objects points-to information in both flow and context-sensitive way. IccTA [10] makes a more complete analysis on Android inter-component communication. It can decide the implicit intents' target, which can be Activity or Service. EdgeMiner [11] focuses on Android's callback. EdgeMiner designs an automatic approach to find callback methods on Android platform. These callback methods can be adopted to complement other data flow analysis tools like FlowDroid. None of the tools above considers Fragment's lifecycle, which may lead to the overlook of some data flows. Thus, in this paper we model the Fragment's lifecycle.

Tool	Goal	Modeling fragment's lifecycle
CHEX	Component Hijacking	No
IccTA	Inter-component privacy leaks	No
FlowDroid	Data Leakages	No
AmanDroid	Compute IDFG	No
EdgeMiner	Callback Methods	No
FragDroid	Data Leakages	Yes

Fig. 13. Comparison of different taint analysis tools

There are also some tools analyzing apps dynamically. TaintDroid [3] is one of them to modify the Dalvik virtual machine. Every instruction is interpreted by Dalvik, so TaintDroid can record the data flow relationship between objects. DroidScope [4] is an emulation based Android malware analysis engine that can be used to analyze Java and native components of Android Applications. It performs taint analysis on native instruction and dalvik instruction, so it's more precise than TaintDroid. SMV-HUNTER [13] is a tool designed to identify apps which is vulnerable to SSL/TLS Man-in-the-Middle attacks. AppAudit [14] is an efficient program analysis tool that detects data leakages in mobile applications. It combines static and dynamic analysis to overcome the shortcomings of each individual analysis.

Malware detection is an important topic in Android security research. RiskRanker [15], TriggerMetric [28] and DroidRanger [16] are heuristic-based malware detection tools. RiskRanker determines a malicious app according to risk behavior is performing in the app. TriggerMetric captures the static dependence relations between user inputs and sensitive operations providing critical system functions in programs. DroidRanger analyzes the permissions that malware and benign apps apply, then it identifies the combination of permissions which are frequently used in malware and rarely used by benign apps. Drebin [21], DroidAPIMiner [26], DroidMiner [22], DroidSIFT [23] and DR-Droid [27] identify malware based on machine learning algorithm. Drebin and DroidAPIMiner extract permissions and security APIs an app using to construct feature vector. DroidMiner uses control flow, while DroidSIFT uses data dependence. DR-Droid proposed a new Android repackaged malware detection technique based on code heterogeneity analysis, and the features in DR-Droid are extracted from each dependence region to profile both benign and malicious dependence region behaviors.

8 Conclusion

In this paper, we describe how Fragment's lifecycle can influence the data flow analysis result and propose an approach to model Fragment's lifecycle. To model the Fragment's lifecycle and its relationship with Activity's lifecycle, we design a tool FragDroid to generate a dummy main method which can model the control flow transfer between Fragment's and Activity's lifecycle methods. Our tool is built based on FlowDroid [7]. We perform some experiments using apps crawled from some alternative app markets. Experiments show that 8% of the selected apps use Fragment, and for most popular apps, the probability is 50.8%. We also evaluate our tool with the same data sets, the result shows the average overhead is 17%.

Acknowledgments. We would like to thank the anonymous reviewers for their comments. This work was supported in part by grants from the Chinese National Natural Science Foundation (61272078, 61073027, 90818022, and 61321491), and the Chinese National 863 High-Tech Program (2011AA01A202).

References

1. iOS and Android capture combined 98.4% share of smartphone market. http://www.macrumors.com/2016/02/18/ios-android-market-share-q4-15-gartner/
2. Zhou, Y., Jiang, X.: Dissecting android malware: characterization and evolution. In: 2012 IEEE Symposium on Security and Privacy (SP), pp. 95–109. IEEE, May 2012
3. Enck, W., Gilbert, P., Han, S., Tendulkar, V., Chun, B.G., Cox, L.P., Jung, J., McDaniel, P., Sheth, A.N.: TaintDroid: an information-flow tracking system for realtime privacy monitoring on smartphones. ACM Trans. Comput. Syst. (TOCS) **32**(2), 5 (2014)

4. Yan, L.K., Yin, H.: Droidscope: seamlessly reconstructing the OS and Dalvik semantic views for dynamic Android malware analysis. Presented as Part of the 21st USENIX Security Symposium (USENIX Security 2012), pp. 569–584 (2012)
5. Vidas, T., Christin, N.: Evading Android runtime analysis via sandbox detection. In: Proceedings of the 9th ACM Symposium on Information, Computer and Communications Security, pp. 447–458. ACM, June 2014
6. Lu, L., Li, Z., Wu, Z., Lee, W., Jiang, G.: Chex: statically vetting Android apps for component hijacking vulnerabilities. In: Proceedings of the 2012 ACM Conference on Computer and Communications Security, pp. 229–240. ACM, October 2012
7. Arzt, S., Rasthofer, S., Fritz, C., Bodden, E., Bartel, A., Klein, J., Le Traon, Y., Octeau, D., McDaniel, P.: Flowdroid: precise context, flow, field, object-sensitive and lifecycle-aware taint analysis for Android apps. In: Proceedings of the 35th ACM SIGPLAN Conference on Programming Language Design and Implementation, p. 29. ACM, June 2014
8. Fritz, C., Arzt, S., Rasthofer, S., Bodden, E., Bartel, A., Klein, J., Le Traon, Y., Octeau, D., McDaniel, P.: Highly precise taint analysis for Android applications. EC SPRIDE, TU Darmstadt, Technical report (2013)
9. Wei, F., Roy, S., Ou, X.: Amandroid: a precise and general inter-component data flow analysis framework for security vetting of Android apps. In: Proceedings of the 2014 ACM SIGSAC Conference on Computer and Communications Security, pp. 1329–1341. ACM, November 2014
10. Li, L., Bartel, A., Bissyand, T.F., Klein, J., Le Traon, Y., Arzt, S., Rasthofer, S., Bodden, E., Octeau, D., McDaniel, P.: IccTA: detecting inter-component privacy leaks in Android apps. In: Proceedings of the 37th International Conference on Software Engineering, vol. 1, pp. 280–291. IEEE Press, May 2015
11. Cao, Y., Fratantonio, Y., Bianchi, A., Egele, M., Kruegel, C., Vigna, G., Chen, Y.: Automatically detecting implicit control flow transitions through the Android framework. In: NDSS (2015)
12. Reps, T., Horwitz, S., Sagiv, M.: Precise interprocedural dataflow analysis via graph reachability. In: POPL 1995, pp. 49–61 (1995)
13. Sounthiraraj, D., Sahs, J., Greenwood, G., Lin, Z., Khan, L.: Large scale, automated detection of SSL/TLS man-in-the-middle vulnerabilities in Android apps. In: Proceedings of the 21st Annual Network and Distributed System Security Symposium (NDSS 2014) (2014)
14. Xia, M., Gong, L., Lyu, Y., Qi, Z., Liu, X.: Effective real-time Android application auditing. In: 2015 IEEE Symposium on Security and Privacy (SP), pp. 899–914. IEEE, May 2015
15. Grace, M., Zhou, Y., Zhang, Q., Zou, S., Jiang, X.: Riskranker: scalable and accurate zero-day android malware detection. In: Proceedings of the 10th International Conference on Mobile Systems, Applications, and Services, pp. 281–294. ACM, June 2012
16. Liang, S., Du, X.: Permission-combination-based scheme for Android mobile malware detection. In: 2014 IEEE International Conference on Communications (ICC), pp. 2301–2306. IEEE, June 2014
17. Baidu Android market. http://shouji.baidu.com/software/
18. Xiaomi Android market. http://app.mi.com/
19. Anzhi Android market. http://www.anzhi.com/
20. Android malware genome project. http://www.malgenomeproject.org/
21. Arp, D., Spreitzenbarth, M., Hbner, M., Gascon, H., Rieck, K., Siemens, C.E.R.T.: Drebin: effective and explainable detection of Android malware in your pocket. In: Proceedings of NDSS, February 2014

22. Yang, C., Xu, Z., Gu, G., Yegneswaran, V., Porras, P.: DroidMiner: automated mining and characterization of fine-grained malicious behaviors in Android applications. In: Kutyłowski, M., Vaidya, J. (eds.) ESORICS 2014. LNCS, vol. 8712, pp. 163–182. Springer, Cham (2014). doi:10.1007/978-3-319-11203-9_10

23. Zhang, M., Duan, Y., Yin, H., Zhao, Z.: Semantics-aware Android malware classification using weighted contextual API dependency graphs. In: Proceedings of the 2014 ACM SIGSAC Conference on Computer and Communications Security, pp. 1105–1116. ACM, November 2014

24. Horwitz, S., Reps, T., Binkley, D.: Interprocedural slicing using dependence graphs. ACM Trans. Program. Lang. Syst. (TOPLAS) 12(1), 26–60 (1990)

25. Reps, T., Horwitz, S., Sagiv, M.: Precise interprocedural dataflow analysis via graph reachability. In: Proceedings of the 22nd ACM SIGPLAN-SIGACT Symposium on Principles of Programming Languages, pp. 49–61. ACM, January 1995

26. Aafer, Y., Du, W., Yin, H.: DroidAPIMiner: mining API-level features for robust malware detection in Android. In: Zia, T., Zomaya, A., Varadharajan, V., Mao, M. (eds.) SecureComm 2013. LNICSSITE, vol. 127, pp. 86–103. Springer, Cham (2013). doi:10.1007/978-3-319-04283-1_6

27. Elish, K.O., Shu, X., Yao, D., Ryder, B., Jiang, X.: Profiling user-trigger dependence for Android malware detection. Comput. Secur. (C&S) 49, 255–273 (2015)

28. Tian, K., Yao, D., Ryder, B., Tan, G.: Analysis of code heterogeneity for high-precision classification of repackaged malware. In: Proceedings of Mobile Security Technologies (MoST), in Conjunction with the IEEE Symposium on Security and Privacy, San Jose, CA, May 2016

Alde: Privacy Risk Analysis of Analytics Libraries in the Android Ecosystem

Xing Liu[1], Sencun Zhu[2,3], Wei Wang[1(✉)], and Jiqiang Liu[1]

[1] School of Computer and Information Technology,
Beijing Jiaotong University, Beijing, China
{xingliu,wangwei1,jqliu}@bjtu.edu.cn
[2] Department of Computer Science and Engineering,
The Pennsylvania State University, State College, PA 16801, USA
szhu@cse.psu.edu
[3] College of Information Sciences and Technology,
The Pennsylvania State University, State College, PA 16801, USA

Abstract. While much effort has been made to detect and measure the privacy leakage caused by the advertising (ad) libraries integrated in mobile applications (i.e., apps), analytics libraries, which are also widely used in mobile apps have not been systematically studied for their privacy risks. Different from ad libraries, the main function of analytics libraries is to collect users' in-app actions. Hence, by design, analytics libraries are more likely to leak users' private information.

In this work, we study what information is collected by the analytics libraries integrated in popular Android apps. We design and implement a tool called "Alde". Given an app, Alde employs both static analysis and dynamic analysis to detect the data collected by analytics libraries. We also study what private information can be leaked by the apps that use the same analytics library. Moreover, we analyze apps' privacy policies to see whether app developers have notified the users that their in-app action information is collected by analytics libraries. Finally, we select 8 widely used analytics libraries to study and apply our method on 300 apps downloaded from both Chinese app markets and Google play. Our experimental results request the emerging need for better regulating the use of analytics libraries in Android apps.

Keywords: Android · Analytics libraries · Privacy leakage

1 Introduction

According to the statistical result from AppBrain [6], the number of apps in Google Play has reached 2.1 millions. The sheer number of apps that are in the Google Play and the number of new ones added daily only show that the mobile app ecosystem has become a gigantic marketplace that is still expanding. It is thus becoming more and more difficult for app developers to make their apps stand out. Hence, it is increasingly important for developers to understand their users and make their apps better for the users.

© ICST Institute for Computer Sciences, Social Informatics and Telecommunications Engineering 2017
R. Deng et al. (Eds.): SecureComm 2016, LNICST 198, pp. 655–672, 2017.
DOI: 10.1007/978-3-319-59608-2_36

Collecting and analyzing the interactions between users and apps help developers to get insights about their users' in-app actions[1] and learn more about their users' behavior. With the analysis results, developers study the actions their users have taken and understand how the users use their apps. They can find out what problems their users are experiencing, and then work out solutions to fix the problems. This process of collecting and analysis is very important to developers for enhancing the users' experience. Hence, almost every popular app contains code snippets to collect and analyze users' in-app actions. Some developers implement the collecting and analysis functions by themselves, while others implement these functions with the help of some third-party libraries. We call a third-party library that is used to collect and analyze the users' in-app actions as "analytics library".

Analytics libraries are similar to ad libraries in some aspects. For example, they both are integrated with the host app. Host app and the library share privileges and resources. They have the same Linux file access control permissions and Android permissions. Both analytics library and ad library require some permissions that may not be needed by the host app. Therefore, analytics libraries may cause security and privacy issues similar to that caused by ad libraries [12,15]. However, ad libraries do not require developers to do many settings. Take AdMob's banner Ads [1] as an example, developers only need to add an ad view in their apps and set up the corresponding ad unit ID [2]. Then the ad library will automatically request ads and displays them in the ad view. Developers do not care so much about the ads' content. Though ad libraries have provided some ad control APIs, many developers do not use them [9,21]. In contrast, when developers use analytics libraries to collect users' in-app actions, developers need to invoke some tracking APIs provided by the analytics libraries at locations they want [14]. For example, developers may invoke the tracking APIs to collect user's payment action after the user touches a payment button. In other words, what information to collect is set by developers. The more a developer wants to profile his users, the more tracking points he will set in his app.

After collecting users' in-app action data, analytics libraries send it to the analytics companies, which analyze the data and present some results to developers. Now, curiosities are aroused on what private information is leaked to analytics companies and to app developers through this data. This problem is exacerbated because analytics libraries may collect unique device information (IMEI, MAC, etc.) that can be used to link the information collected by different apps together to get a more comprehensive record of users' activities. However, previous studies only concern the information protected by Android permissions or information input by users (e.g., account number, password), therefore, they cannot answer this question. As a first step in the direction of answering this question, we explore the users' in-app actions collected by the analytics libraries

---

[1] "users' in-app actions" means the users' behaviors when they are using an app, such as opening the app, browsing different pages in the app, pressing a button in the app, etc.

integrated in the popular apps. To fulfill this goal, we design and implement a tool called "Alde" (Analytics libraries data explorer) which employs both static analysis and dynamic analysis to discover the users' in-app actions collected by analytics libraries. In the static analysis process, Alde performs a backward trace analysis based on the app's smali codes [17]. This backward trace analysis aims to find out what information is sent to these APIs. In the dynamic analysis process, we hook the tracking APIs to explore what information is sent to these APIs at the app's running time. After obtaining the users' in-app actions collected by the analytics libraries, we manually review this data to determine what personal information is leaked to the analytics companies. We also manually review the popular apps' privacy policies to check whether they notify the users about such data collection. We select 8 widely used analytics libraries for study and apply our method on 300 apps downloaded from both Wandoujia (a Chinese app market) and Google Play. The experimental results show that (i) analytics libraries can be exploited by malicious developers to collect users' personal information directly; (ii) some apps indeed leak users' personal information to analytics companies even though their genuine purposes of using analytics libraries are legal; (iii) users will be deeply profiled if analytics companies link the information collected from different apps, especially in China; (iv) developers seldom describe the use of analytics libraries in their apps' privacy policies even though they are asked to do so. In a summary, we make the following contributions in this paper:

- To the best of our knowledge, our work is the first research focusing on understanding information leakage caused by the users' in-app actions collected by analytics libraries.
- We design and implement a tool named "Alde" that is used to discover the users' in-app actions collected by analytics libraries.
- We apply our method on 300 apps downloaded from both Wandoujia and Google Play and reveal the data collected by the analytics libraries integrated in these apps.

The remainder of this paper is organized as follows. Section 2 describes the background of Android analytics libraries. Section 3 gives our system design and implementation. Section 4 describes the dataset that we use in this study. Experimental results and related work are given in Sects. 5 and 6, respectively. Section 7 concludes our work.

2   Background

2.1   Analytics Libraries

Analytics libraries are important tools that mobile app developers commonly employ in their apps. Through them, analytics companies provide mobile app developers well analyzed data that shows how the users are using their apps. To understand how an analytics library is embedded into an Android app, next we provide a simplified structural overview of the mobile analytics library through Fig. 1.

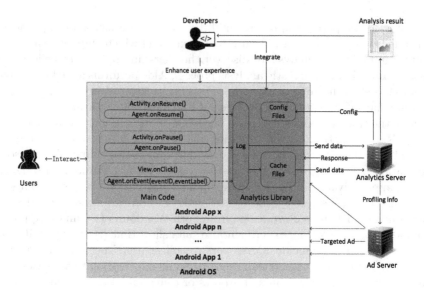

Fig. 1. Structural overview of a mobile third-party analytics library

Take Umeng [26], the most popular analytics library in China, as an example. In order to integrate this library into their apps and obtain the analysis results, developers need to take the following steps:

1. Register an account at the analytics company and log in. Then, a developer are required to set up the basic information (name, category, etc.) of the app that he wants to track. After the setup for the app, the analytics company will generate a unique AppKey. This AppKey will be utilized to track the app.
2. Add the SDK provided by the analytics company into the app's build path. Then, edit the app's AndroidManifest file and add the unique AppKey into the app's metadata. Moreover, the developer is required to add the permissions required by the analytics library into the AndroidManifest file.
3. Initialize the analytics library. Commonly, a developer needs to invoke the initialization method provided by the analytics library to initialize the library when the app is launched.
4. Invoke the tracking APIs provided by the analytics library to collect users' in-app action information. For example, with Umeng library, a developer can invoke *MobclickAgent.onResume()* and *MobclickAgent.onPause()* in each Activity's *onResume()* and *onPause()* methods to collect each Activity's start time and end time. He can invoke *MobclickAgent.onEvent(...)* to collect the users' in-app actions of his interest. For instance, if the developer wants to know how many users are interested in movies in a video app he developed, he can invoke this method (triggered when users press the "movies" button) and set the parameter *eventID* as "movies". Developers can also set up the

analytics library to automatically collect the run-time errors occurred in the app.

5. Upload the app to Android app market(s). When users download and enjoy this app, the analytics company will receive users' in-app actions data, analyze it and present the analysis results to the app's developer through a web interface.

The steps described above are the common procedures that developers need to follow if they want to use analytics library. Although most analytics libraries can be used successfully like this, different analytics libraries are different in implementation details. Hence, the processes of integrating different analytics libraries into the apps are not totally the same. Additionally, some new analytics libraries (such as *Appsee* [7] and *UXCam* [27]) use a totally different method to collect users' in-app actions. They do not require developers to invoke tracking APIs to collect users' actions. Instead, they collect all the interactions between users and apps as videos and show the videos to the developers directly. We do not consider this kind of analytics library in this paper.

2.2 What Information Is Presented to the Developers

When users play with apps, their in-app actions data is collected by analytics libraries and sent to the analytics servers. It is analyzed automatically in the analytics servers, which presents the analysis results to developers (See Fig. 2).

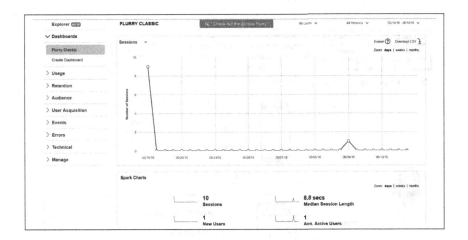

Fig. 2. Snapshot of flurry analytics

In Table 1, we list the information that developers can see. Besides the basic information shown in this list, analytics companies also present some statistical information, such as *User growth rate*, *User retention*, *User loyalty*, *Event conversion rate*, etc. This statistical information can be presented in different time

Table 1. The information that developers obtain about their apps

Categories	Details
Users	Total users, New users, Returning users, Active users, Launch times, Launch frequency, Duration of once use, Activity path, App versions
Terminals	Devices, Resolutions, OS versions, Carriers, Area, Languages
Events	Event IDs, Event labels, Event times, Event values
Errors	Error summary, Error times, First appearance time, Last appearance time

periods, by day, by week, by month, or by year, which helps developers learn whether their apps are popular or not in a period, or whether the new functions they added in the apps attract more users. Data presented to the developers is the statistical analysis results based on *all* users. In principle, developers cannot access the raw data of an individual user's in-app actions.

3   System Design and Implementation

To understand what private information can be leaked by the analytics libraries integrated with the popular apps, we develop "Alde", a tool for this purpose. Alde uses both static analysis and dynamic analysis to discover the values of the tracking APIs' parameters, which are the users' in-app actions collected by these tracking APIs. The overview of Alde is illustrated in Fig. 3.

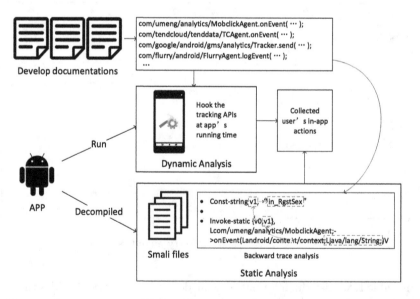

Fig. 3. Overview of Alde

3.1 Documentation Analysis

As we described in Sect. 2.1, developers need to invoke the tracking APIs provided by analytics libraries to collect users' in-app actions. Hence, our first step is to determine the tracking APIs provided by each analytics library. We obtain this information by analyzing the development documentations provided by each analytics library. However, some analytics libraries only give a brief description of the tracking APIs in their development documentations. The complete class names (including class package names) of the tracking APIs that are needed in the following processes are not given. To address this problem, we download some apps that contain these analytics libraries, decompile them with Apktool [5], and find out the complete class names of the tracking APIs in the decompiled codes.

3.2 Static Analysis

Some information collected by the tracking APIs is written in the app's source code, such as some buttons' names. Static analysis aims to discover the users' in-app actions defined in the app's source code. Alde performs a static backward trace analysis to find out the values of the tracking APIs' parameters based on the app's smali code. As shown in Fig. 3, given an app, Alde carries out the following analysis.

First, Alde decompiles the app into smali code files with Apktool. Second, Alde finds out the corresponding smali codes of the tracking APIs and identifies the registers that store the values of the tracking APIs' parameters. For instance, in Fig. 3, the second parameter of the *onEvent* method is the parameter that we need to trace. The corresponding register that stores the value of this parameter is $v1$. Third, Alde searches the smali code in the reverse order to find the value of $v1$. Alde decides what value is assigned to $v1$ based on the syntax of Dalvik bytecode [3]. If another register assigns its value to $v1$, that register will be traced instead of $v1$. This trace process will not stop until Alde finds a constant value is assigned to the traced register or Alde traces into a method that cannot be analyzed by Alde. Last, the final constant value and the trace path are reported. As shown in Fig. 3, the final constant value of $v1$ is "in_RgstSex".

The code snippet shown in Fig. 3 appeared in a fitness app. When users go to *Gender Setting* page, this code snippet will run and collect this in-app action.

3.3 Dynamic Analysis

Though the above static analysis can explore the in-app actions defined in app's source code, some information is generated at app's running time, so it cannot be captured by static analysis. Hence, Alde also performs a dynamic analysis on the app.

In the dynamic analysis process, Alde runs the app for 5 min with the help of AndroidViewClient [19]. Developed with python, AndroidViewClient is a test

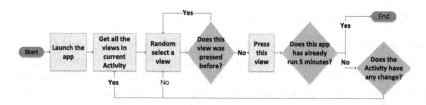

Fig. 4. Flowchart of the Alde's dynamic app running. The "views" in this figure include various elements in an Activity, such as buttons, text-areas, pictures, etc.

framework for Android apps and is more powerful than monkeyrunner [4]. We write a python script based on AndroidViewClient to automatically run Android apps. Given an app, Alde runs it according to the process described in Fig. 4. At the same time, the tracking APIs are hooked by Alde with the help of Cydia Substrate [22]. Cydia Substrate is an app running on rooted Android devices. It provides an easy way to hook the other apps running on the same phone. We develop an extension for Cydia Substrate to hook the tracking APIs. When the app under analysis invokes a tracking API, the values of the API's parameters will be captured by Cydia Substrate and stored in the files located in the phone's external sdcard. When the app stops running, we pull these files from the phone. Through this method, we get the users' in-app actions that are collected by the analytics libraries at the app's running time.

For the apps that ask the users to register an account, we register the account manually and then analyze it with Alde. After the entire analysis processes of an app are finished, we merge the analysis results from both static analysis and dynamic analysis to get the final analysis results (as shown in Fig. 5).

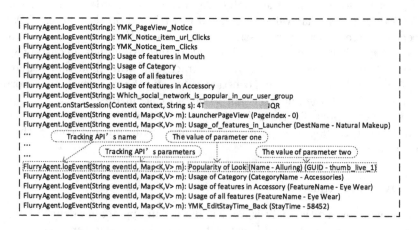

Fig. 5. Parts of the analysis result of app "YouCamMakeUp". If the parameter's type is *map*, the value of the parameter is presented as "(key - value)".

4   Dataset

In this section, we describe the dataset that we use in this study.

4.1   Analytics Libraries

In this paper, we focus on 8 widely used analytics libraries, shown in Table 2. To select these widely used analytics libraries, we search the Internet for analytics libraries and also learn from previous studies [20]. After this, we get a list of 25 analytics libraries. Then, we search these analytics libraries' class names in the smali code that is decompiled from the apps we downloaded. If an analytics library's class names appear in an app, we consider that this app uses this library. Finally, we select 8 most widely used analytics libraries in our app dataset (the rest of the analytics libraries in the list are seldom used in our app dataset). Four of them are mainly used by the apps in the Chinese app market and the other four of them are mainly used by the apps in Google Play. In the rest of this paper, we call them analytics libraries from Chinese app market and analytics libraries from Google Play, respectively.

Table 2. Analytics libraries' required permissions and optional permissions. "✔" means required permission and "●" means optional permission.

	Umeng	Talking data	Tencent analytics	Baidu analytics	Flurry	Adjust	Localytics	Google analytics
INTERNET	✔	✔	✔	✔	✔	✔	✔	✔
ACCESS_WIFI_STATE	✔	✔	✔	✔		●		
ACCESS_NETWORK_STATE	✔	✔	✔	✔	●			✔
READ_PHONE_STATE	✔	✔	✔	✔				
WRITE_EXTERNAL_STORAGE		✔	✔	✔				
WRITE_SETTINGS				✔				
GET_TASKS		●		✔				
READ_EXTERNAL_STORAGE				✔				
MOUNT_UNMOUNT_FILESYSTEMS				✔				
ACCESS_FINE_LOCATION		●		●	●			
ACCESS_COARSE_LOCATION		●			●			
BLUETOOTH				●				
WAKE_LOCK							✔	

Table 2 also shows the permissions required by these 8 analytics libraries as well as their optional permissions. Analytics libraries from Chinese app market commonly require more permissions. This is because they need the device information (IMEI, MAC, etc.) to generate the ID that is used to identify the individual device. And they also need to know the network state and WIFI state in order to adjust the interval of sending collected data to their servers. They may also need to store some cache files in the external storage. Meanwhile, analytics libraries from Google Play can do the similar things with the help of Google Play Service which is not available in China. However, these permissions also give the analytics libraries from Chinese app market the abilities to collect more information than they need.

4.2   Apps

We download 200 apps from a Chinese app market[2] and 100 apps from Google Play. All these apps are popular and free apps. As described in Sect. 3, our method needs to know where the tracking APIs are invoked. If an app obfuscates the tracking APIs it used, we cannot apply our method on it. Hence, we run an API search (i.e., searching the tracking APIs' names in apps' smali code) to filter out the apps we can analyze. If a tracking API provided by an analytics library appears in an app's main package, we consider this app uses this analytics library and can be analyzed by our method. To understand how many apps are missed by our method, we carry out another file search process to determine the analytics libraries used by each app. In this file search process, we launch each app on a device and determine what analytics libraries it uses based on the files generated at the app's running time. This is because different analytics libraries will generate different files (such as database files, cache files, Shared_prefs files) at their running time. The generated files' names are not influenced by code obfuscation. We present the filtering result in Fig. 6.

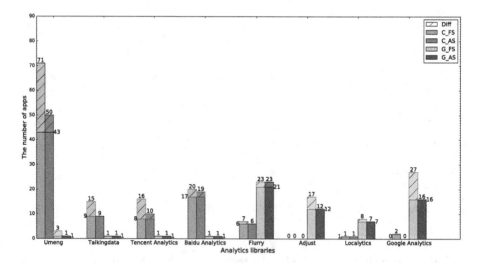

Fig. 6. The number of popular apps containing each of the analytics libraries. "Diff" means the apps on which these two kinds of search process generate different result. "C_FS" and "C_AS" means file search result and API search result of apps from Chinese app market. "G_FS" and "G_AS" means file search result and API search result of apps from Google play.

---

[2] We download Chinese apps from "Wandoujia" market. "Wandoujia" is a famous Android app market in China.

Figure 6 shows that our method can analyze most of the apps. We manually review the apps that obtain different results in these two kinds of search processes. We find that the apps not found in API search but found in file search indeed obfuscate the code of analytics libraries. More discussion on obfuscation will be presented in Sect. 5.3. Meanwhile, since dynamic running cannot cover all the code in an app, some apps do not generate the corresponding files at running time even they contain the tracking APIs. For such apps, we only consider their static analysis results in the following analysis. Finally, we select 81 popular apps from Chinese app market and 50 popular apps from Google play to analyze.

5   Experimental Results and Discussions

5.1   Experimental Results

We analyze the selected popular apps with our proposed method and then review the analysis results manually. Based on the information collected by the analytics libraries, we classify the apps into three levels: App level, Activity level and User level (See Table 3).

Table 3. The number of apps in each level of information collection

	Umeng	Talking data	Tencent analytics	Baidu analytics	Flurry	Adjust	Localytics	Google analytics
App level	8	1	4	4	9	5	2	4
Activity level	33	8	3	14	14	6	3	10
User level	9	1	4	2	6	1	3	2

In Table 3, "App level" means the app only uses analytics libraries to collect the information that reflects the running status of the whole app, such as what Activities are visited by the users. "Activity level" means the app uses analytics libraries to collect the running status of each Activity in an app, such as which "view" in the Activity is pressed by the users. A "view" means an element in an Activity, such as buttons, text-areas, pictures, etc. "User level" means the app uses analytics libraries to collect the data generated by the users. For instance, how long time a user spends on a song in a music app. Table 3 shows most apps belong to the Activity level.

In order to detail the results we found in our analysis, we organize them as the answers to the following four questions.

Q1: Do analytics libraries leak users' personal information to app developers?

As the developers cannot get the raw data of the collected information, it is hard for them to profile individual users. However, developers can exploit the vulnerabilities in these analytics libraries to collect users' private data directly.

For example, *Wo Mailbox* is a mailbox app that helps users manage their emails. It was developed by China Unicom and has more than 2.6 million active users in February 2016 [13]. Our tool finds that this app automatically records senders' email addresses, recipients' email addresses, email addresses of CCed recipients, emails' subjects and users' IP addresses through the analytics library.

We also find the analytics libraries do not check the information collected by the developers. They only perform some statistical analysis and present the analysis results to the developers. This makes it possible for developers to collect users' sensitive information through these analytics libraries. To test and verify this vulnerability, we developed two apps with Umeng and Talkingdata [25], respectively. We may disguise these two apps as communication apps, so it is reasonable for them to require READ_CONTACTS permission. When users open their contacts book with our apps, these apps read their contacts and show to them. Besides, these apps secretly collect their contacts through analytics libraries by invoking *MobclickAgent.onEvent(Context ctx, String eventId, Map eventValue)* for Umeng and *TCAgent.onEvent(Context ctx, String eventId, String eventValue)* for Talkingdata. Both Umeng and Talkingdata successfully collect users' contact information and present them to us through the servers' web interfaces (See Fig. 7 for the case of Umeng), although the tracking APIs we invoked are designed to collect user's in-app actions. Although we have not found real-world apps that have the similar behaviors, this vulnerability could be exploited for very stealthy information stealing.

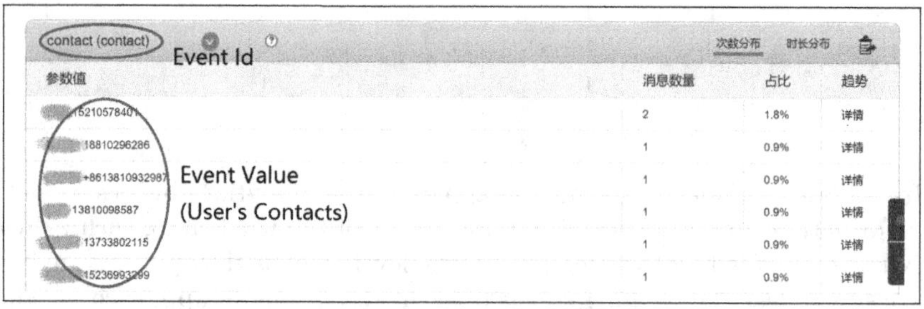

Fig. 7. User's contacts were successfully collected by Umeng

Q2: Do analytics libraries leak users' personal information to analytics companies?

Since analytics companies own the raw data of the collected information, compared with the information leaked to the developers, information leaked to the analytics companies is much more serious.

For example, *com.culiukeji.huanletao*[3] is a shopping app and *com.tadu. android* is a reading app. These two apps ask users to select their gender before using and collect user's gender information via Umeng. Their developers intend to understand the popularity of their apps in female or male users. They can get the percentage of female users and male users from Umeng. However, Umeng gets each app user's gender information through this way. Since Umeng collects the user's device identifier (IMEI, MAC, etc.) at the same time, it gets to know each device user's gender directly. *com.autohome.usedcar* is a used car trade app. It leaks user's fine location to Umeng. Apps in Google play also have similar behaviors. *Skype* sends call ended time and message sent time to Flurry. *Text Free* sends user's fine location, the rough number of the user's contacts and the rough length of every message to Flurry and sends the device's IMEI to Adjust. *The Weather Channel* leaks user's location to Localytics. Due to the space limit, we do not list all the apps that have the similar behaviors here.

Besides, some analytics libraries collect users' data secretly. Talkingdata is a well-known analytics library in China. We find that this analytics library reads the smartphone's sensors data without any notice to users and not even to developers. When developers invoke the tracking APIs provided by this analytics library to collect users' in-app actions, this analytics library will read the sensors' data (including ambient temperature sensor, relative humidity sensor, rotation vector sensor, pressure Sensor, light sensor and magnetic field sensor) and send the data to the analytics server. The collected sensor data will not be presented to the developers, and Talkingdata does not describe this behavior in their development documentation. Hence, neither the developers nor the users know about this. This is not a direct privacy risk, but this data indeed can be used to infer users' surrounding environment and sensitive information such as user touchscreen input [24,28]. During the course of our paper writing, Talkingdata released a special version of its SDK for Google Play, which has removed the code snippet for collecting sensor data.

Q3: What will analytics companies know about the users if they link the information collected from different apps?

As we mentioned before, the privacy risk caused by analytics libraries is exacerbated if analytics companies link the data collected from different apps together to profile the users. Analytics companies can do this work easily because they collect the device identifier together with the users' in-app actions. They know which apps are installed in the same device and used by the same user. The more popular an analytics library is, the more information it can collect. Take Umeng as an example, it is the most widely used analytics library in China. Apps integrating Umeng cover almost all the app categories (See Table 4). As these apps are popular apps, it is very possible that multiple of them are installed in the same phone.

---

[3] Some Chinese apps do not have corresponding English names, so we use their package names instead.

Table 4. App categories that Umeng collects data from

Category	Number of apps	Category	Number of apps
Health & fitness	1	Lifestyle	4
Photography	1	Tools	6
Weather	3	Music & audio	3
Media & video	10	News & magazines	1
Entertainment	2	Books & reference	3
Personalization	2	Finance	1
Travel & local	1	Communication	4
Education	4	Shopping	4

We review the information that is collected through Umeng to see what user's personal information may be inferred by Umeng if the user installs these apps. First, Umeng knows what apps that have integrated it are installed in the same phone. According to the previous study [12], this app install pattern will leak some user's information to Umeng. If the app is developed for particular users, more information will be leaked to Umeng. For example, *com.xtuone.android.syllabus* is developed for undergraduate students, *cn.haoyunbang* is developed for pregnant woman and new mother, and so on. Second, data sent to Umeng often has clear semantics. Umeng can learn user's gender and reading habits from a reading app; learn user's location and approximate income level from a used car trade app; learn user's video watching habits from a video app and learn user's health condition from a health app, etc. If Umeng analyzes and links all types of collected data, it can characterize the users in various aspects.

Q4: Do users know their in-app actions are collected by third-party analytics companies?

According to a previous study [16], 90% users care if apps share their personal data with third parties and 45% users believe the apps should never share their personal data with third parties without their explicit confirmation. This inspires us to see whether users know their in-app actions are collected by third-party analytics companies. Hence, we review these analytics libraries' privacy policies manually to discover what information they have claimed to collect. In these analytics libraries' privacy policies, we find that some analytics companies have listed what information they will collect and ask the developers to show the use of analytics libraries as well as the information collected by analytics libraries in their apps' privacy policies. However, after we review the privacy policies of the apps we selected, we find only a handful of apps follow this rule. In the 81 apps from the Chinese app market, only two apps clearly describe the using of third-party analytics services in their privacy policies, and only one of them gives the name of the analytics library it uses. In the 50 apps from Google Play, only

16 apps clearly describe the using of third-party analytics services and 4 apps give the names of the analytics libraries they uses. Hence, we believe most users do not know their in-app actions are collected by third-party analytics libraries.

5.2 Discussions

Our study shows the privacy risks stemmed from the analytics libraries. We think it might be caused by the following reasons.

First, in today's Android devices, users' private information is not limited to the information protected by Android permissions. Due to the lack of a clear definition on what information is users' personal information, developers might have difficulty in deciding what information should not be collected. Second, most developers disregard the end users' privacy, which can be known from the apps' privacy policies. Only a few apps describe the use of analytics libraries in their privacy policies. Third, some analytics companies do not provide privacy policies specifically for mobile analytics, which makes mobile app developers hard to understand the privacy risk caused by analytics libraries.

To protect users' privacy in this situation, we think the first thing is to let the users know what information is leaked through the analytics libraries in each app. Then they can choose to use the app or use another similar app. We believe that the app market should play the most important role. App markets can ask the developers to write clear descriptions about the using of analytics libraries and the information collected by analytics libraries in their apps' privacy policies. Our tool can be used by both users and app markets to explore the information collected by analytics libraries.

5.3 Limitations

In the static analysis process, Alde uses the methods provided by Apktool to decompile Android apps. Hence, we cannot analyze the apps that cannot be decompiled by Apktool. In the dynamic analysis process, we cannot cover all the execution paths. This is a common shortcoming of dynamic analysis. The most important shortcoming of our approach is that we cannot analyze the apps that obfuscate the tracking APIs they used. These limitations, however, may be overcome by our approach in the future. We can compare all the APIs in an app with the tracking APIs provided by each analytics library based on their instructions and call graphs rather than their names. In this way, we can identify which API is the tracking API even the API's name is obfuscated. Then we can use the obfuscated API name instead of the original API name in the following analysis.

6 Related Work

Privacy and Mobile Advertising. There are many studies focusing on the privacy issues associated with the advertising libraries in mobile apps. Grace *et* *al.* [15] studied potential privacy and security risks caused by in-app ad libraries. They analyzed 100000 Android apps and found that most existing ad libraries collected private information. Book *et al.* [9] studied how app developers used the APIs through which a host app can send private information about the users to ad server. They found that although most apps did not make use of these privacy-related APIs, the number of apps that used these APIs is not negligible. The information collected by these APIs can be simply identified by the APIs' names. They [10] also studied mobile ad targeting using simulated user profiles and found that a large portion of mobile ads are targeted based on app, location, time, and profiles built around actual users. Nath [21] studied what targeting information was sent to ad networks by mobile apps and how effectively the information was used by ad networks to target users. Demetriou *et al.* [12] developed a tool called "Pluto" that can be used to analyze apps and discover whether they leak targeted user data. They also studied what ad networks can learn from the list of apps installed in a phone. Meng *et al.* [18] studied what ad networks know about the user's interest and demographic information. They also studied whether the host apps could conversely use the targeted ads to infer some of the user information collected by the ad network. Different from this studies, our study focuses on the analytics libraries.

Privacy and Mobile Analytics Service. Han *et al.* [16] studied how real-world users were tracked by the apps running on their Android smartphones. They employed dynamic information flow tracking to monitor when sensitive information was sent off the device. They recruited 20 volunteers to participate in this study. They found advertising and analytics were embedded in 57% of the apps and every participant in their study was tracked multiple times. However, they only studied the information protected by Android permissions. Chen *et al.* [11] studied the leakage of user's sensitive information through the vulnerabilities in mobile analytics services. They also studied how the ads served to users can be influenced by modifying the user profiles generated by these analytics services. Their experiments, conducted on Google Mobile Analytics and Flurry, validated the information leakage problem they described. They focus on the user profiles generated by analytics libraries and we focus on the tracking APIs.

Privacy and Mobile App's Privacy Policy. Slavin *et al.* [23] proposed a semi-automated framework to detect privacy policy violations in Android apps. They constructed a policy terminology-API map that linked policy phrases to API functions. Then they used this map to find the APIs and perform information flow analysis. They analyzed 501 top Android apps and discovered 63 potential privacy policy violations. But, they did not consider the information collected through tracking APIs. Yu *et al.* [29] developed a tool called "AutoPPG" that can be used to automatically construct correct and readable descriptions about the collection of user's private information. AutoPPG is able to generate the descriptions of third-party libraries used in apps; however, the information it focuses on is limited to the information protected by Android permissions. Balebako *et al.* [8] studied how app developers make decisions about privacy and security. They interviewed 13 app developers to get information about privacy and security decision-making. And they test what they found with 228 app developers online. One important thing they found was that although third-party ads and analytics services are pervasive, developers aren't aware of the data collected by these tools.

7   Conclusion

In this paper, we studied the information leakage caused by analytics libraries that collect users' in-app action information. We developed a tool named "Alde" to explore the users' in-app actions. Through experiments on 8 popular analytics libraries and 300 apps downloaded from both Chinese app market and Google play, we found that some apps leaked users personal information to analytics libraries without notifying users. We also found that popular analytics companies have the capability to characterize and profile users. In the future work, we plan to improve our tool by making it more automated and more suitable for large-scale analysis. Then we will make it an online service to help users and app markets understand the information collected by analytics libraries.

Acknowledgment. We thank the anonymous reviewers for their insightful comments. This work was supported in part by the Scientific Research Foundation through the Returned Overseas Chinese Scholars, Ministry of Education of China, under Grant K14C300020, in part by Shanghai Key Laboratory of Integrated Administration Technologies for Information Security, and in part by the 111 Project under Grant B14005. The work of Sencun Zhu was partially supported by NSF CCF-1320605 and CNS-1618684.

References

1. Admob: Admob by Google (2016). https://www.google.com/admob/
2. Admob: Admob quick start (2016). https://developers.google.com/admob/android/quick-start?hl=en
3. Android: Dalvik bytecode (2016). https://source.android.com/devices/tech/dalvik/dalvik-bytecode.html
4. Android: Monkey runner (2016). https://developer.android.com/studio/test/monkeyrunner/index.html
5. Apktool: Apktool (2016). http://ibotpeaches.github.io/Apktool/
6. Appbrain: Appbrain stats, May 2016. http://www.appbrain.com/stats
7. Appsee: Appsee, 09 March 2016. https://www.appsee.com
8. Balebako, R., Marsh, A., Lin, J., Hong, J.I., Cranor, L.F.: The privacy and security behaviors of smartphone app developers (2014)
9. Book, T., Wallach, D.S.: A case of collusion: a study of the interface between ad libraries and their apps. In: Proceedings of the Third ACM Workshop on Security and Privacy in Smartphones & Mobile Devices, pp. 79–86. ACM (2013)
10. Book, T., Wallach, D.S.: An empirical study of mobile ad targeting. arXiv preprint arXiv:1502.06577 (2015)
11. Chen, T., Ullah, I., Ali Kaafar, M., Boreli, R.: Information leakage through mobile analytics services. In: Proceedings of the 15th Workshop on Mobile Computing Systems and Applications, p. 15. ACM (2014)

12. Demetriou, S., Merrill, W., Yang, W., Zhang, A., Gunter, C.A.: Free for all! Assessing user data exposure to advertising libraries on android. In: NDSS 2016 (2016)
13. Eguan: Eguan mobile apps top list, March 2016. http://qianfan.analysys.cn/user-radar/view/ranking/topRanking.html
14. Flurry: Custom events with flurry analytics for Android (2016). https://developer.yahoo.com/flurry/docs/analytics/gettingstarted/events/android/
15. Grace, M.C., Zhou, W., Jiang, X., Sadeghi, A.-R.: Unsafe exposure analysis of mobile in-app advertisements. In: Proceedings of the Fifth ACM Conference on Security and Privacy in Wireless and Mobile Networks, pp. 101–112. ACM (2012)
16. Han, S., Jung, J., Wetherall, D.: A study of third-party tracking by mobile apps in the wild. Technical report, University of Washington (2012)
17. JesusFreke: Smali (2016). https://github.com/JesusFreke/smali
18. Meng, W., Ding, R., Chung, S.P., Han, S., Lee, W.: The price of free: privacy leakage in personalized mobile in-app ads. In: NDSS Symposium 2016 (2016)
19. Milano, D.T.: Androidviewclient (2016). https://github.com/dtmilano/AndroidViewClient
20. Mobyaffiliates: The best app analytics tools list (2015). http://www.mobyaffiliates.com/guides/best-app-analytics-tools-list/
21. Nath, S.: Madscope: characterizing mobile in-app targeted ads. In: Proceedings of the 13th Annual International Conference on Mobile Systems, Applications, and Services, pp. 59–73. ACM (2015)
22. LLC SaurikIT: Cydia substrate: the powerful code modification platform behind cydia (2016). http://www.cydiasubstrate.com/
23. Slavin, R., Wang, X., Hosseini, M.B., Hester, J., Krishnan, R., Bhatia, J., Breaux, T.D., Niu, J.: Toward a framework for detecting privacy policy violations in Android application code. In: Proceedings of the 38th International Conference on Software Engineering, pp. 25–36. ACM (2016)
24. Spreitzer, R.: Pin skimming: exploiting the ambient-light sensor in mobile devices. In: Proceedings of the 4th ACM Workshop on Security and Privacy in Smartphones & Mobile Devices, pp. 51–62. ACM (2014)
25. Talkingdata: Talkingdata (2016). https://www.talkingdata.com/
26. Umeng: Umeng (2016). https://www.umeng.com/
27. UxCam: Uxcam, 09 March 2016. https://uxcam.com
28. Xu, Z., Bai, K., Zhu, S.: Taplogger: inferring user inputs on smartphone touchscreens using on-board motion sensors. In: Proceedings of the Fifth ACM Conference on Security and Privacy in Wireless and Mobile Networks, pp. 113–124. ACM (2012)
29. Yu, L., Zhang, T., Luo, X., Xue, L.: Autoppg: towards automatic generation of privacy policy for Android applications. In: Proceedings of the 5th Annual ACM CCS Workshop on Security and Privacy in Smartphones and Mobile Devices, pp. 39–50. ACM (2015)

Hardware Security

FROPUF: How to Extract More Entropy from Two Ring Oscillators in FPGA-Based PUFs

Qinglong Zhang[1,2,3], Zongbin Liu[1,2], Cunqing Ma[1,2], Changting Li[1,2,3],
and Lingchen Zhang[1,2(✉)]

[1] Data Assurance and Communication Security Research Center, Beijing, China
[2] State Key Laboratory of Information Security,
Institute of Information Engineering, CAS, Beijing, China
{qlzhang,zbliu,limiao12,jixiang,jing}@lois.cn
[3] University of Chinese Academy of Sciences, Beijing, China

Abstract. Ring oscillator (RO) based physically unclonable function (PUF) on FPGAs is popular for its nice properties and easy implementation. The conventional compensated measurement though proved to be particularly effective in extracting entropy of manufacturing features, only one bit entropy can be extracted from two ROs, which implies enormous consumption of hardware resources. Motivated by this, we propose an elegant and efficient method to extract at least 31 bits entropy from two ROs by utilizing the fine control of programmable delay lines of look up table (LUT), and denominate this new construction as Further ROPUF. We will elaborate how to take advantage of the underlying manufacturing variations of LUTs and display how deeper variations are extracted by the second order difference calculation method. Additionally, we reveal the consistency between the evaluation results on Xilinx FPGAs and by simulations, and the responds' low bit-error-rate of 1.85% manifests the proposed FROPUF maintains considerable reliability.

Keywords: PUFs · Ring Oscillator · Entropy · FPGA

1 Introduction

With flourishing development of embedded devices in modern age, cryptographic algorithms are easily implemented on FPGA for FPGA's reconfigurable nature. An indispensable premise for the security of cryptographic primitives is the competence to securely generate, store and retrieve secret keys. In general, it rests upon a protected memory which stores the private information reliably and shields it completely from unauthorized parties. Whereas this requirement is non-trivial to achieve in practice [1]. Recently, physically unclonable function (PUF)

L. Zhang—The work is supported by a grant from the National Natural Science Foundation of China (No.61402470).

© ICST Institute for Computer Sciences, Social Informatics and Telecommunications Engineering 2017
R. Deng et al. (Eds.): SecureComm 2016, LNICST 198, pp. 675–693, 2017.
DOI: 10.1007/978-3-319-59608-2_37

has attracted wider attention as a technique to provide physical roots of trust in embedded systems [2–4]. Due to the submicron random variation during manufacturing, nominally identical logic circuit turns out to have individual physical features. The main idea of PUF is to utilize these intrinsic random manufacturing features to extract a unique electronic fingerprint, therefore providing an approach to issues such as cryptographic key generation [5], intellectual property (IP) protection [6,7], device authentication [8–10] and trusted computing etc.

Up to now, a variety of electronic PUFs have been proposed, such as SRAM PUF [11], Butterfly PUF [12], Glitch PUF [13], Flip-Flop PUF [14], Ring Oscillator PUF [15] and so on. However, some of them are not suitable for FPGAs. In the state of the art commercial FPGAs of Xilinx and Altera, the start-up values of SRAM are reset to a certain value according to the manufacturer's design, which leads to the failure of deploying SRAM PUF on these FPGAs. Moreover, many other PUF designs like Butterfly PUF and Arbiter PUF demand a careful routing symmetry, which is also difficult to implement on FPGAs. Especially for Butterfly PUF, even the fundamental element, a latch with a preset signal and a clear signal, is not provided on Xilinx's latest 6-series and 7-series FPGAs. RO PUF which is first proposed by Suh and Devadas [15] has been widely used due to its sensitivity to manufacturing variations, and particularly the hard-macro design technique simplifies the implementation of identical ROs on FPGA. However, besides these advantages, Maiti [16] pointed out that some factors like the systematic or correlated manufacturing variations and the regional environmental noise would degrade the uniqueness and reliability of RO PUF.

A lot of researches [15–21] have been done in order to strengthen the properties of RO PUF. In DAC 2007, Suh and Devadas [15] applied a post-processing technique called 1-*out-of-k* masking and greatly enhanced the reliability of the PUF's response, but resulted in a relatively large resource overhead. In J.Cryptol.2011, Maiti et al. [16] proposed a configurable RO technique to produce nearly 100% error-free PUF outputs over varying environmental condition without post-processing. This technique is quite effective to resolve PUF reliability issues on FPGAs. However, two configurable ROs generate only one bit response in making a tradeoff between reliability and the length of response sequence, and the calculation cost is relatively high.

To serve as a physical root of trust, it is vital for a PUF design to provide sufficient entropy in its response. Nevertheless, the most commonly used fuzzy extraction technics in PUFs always cause entropy loss [22,23]. As a result, the amount of extractable entropy of a PUF becomes another essential evaluation index. Given this, Habib et al. [24] proposed an FPGA PUF base on programmable LUT delays to acquire more entropy from two ROs. According to his research, when the logically unrelated inputs of LUT vary from '000' to '111', the RO's frequency changes irregularly. While in CHES 2011 [25,26], it stated that the loop delays of input '111' were on average about 10 picoseconds larger than the delay values of input '000'. Habib et al. pointed out this disagreement is caused by employing different devices (in [24] is Spartan-3E, while in [25,26] are Virtex-5 series). However, if the frequency varies regularly as the LUT inputs change, the method used in [24] would be invalid.

In this paper, by utilizing the fine adjustment of LUT's propagation path on FPGAs [25], we propose a comprehensive scheme to extract more available manufacturing features and through a second order difference calculation way, we are able to achieve at least 31-bit entropy from two ROs. Furthermore, this difference calculation method can efficiently reduce the effect of the systematic manufacturing variation and the regional environmental noise. To make it more persuasive, the evaluation results obtained from our experiments and simulations demonstrate that the proposed PUF construction possesses excellent reliability and uniqueness under varied temperatures.

Although RO PUF is threatened by modeling attacks, a secure one-way hash over the PUF's outputs, so called a Controlled PUF [27], is an efficient solution. The staple of this paper is how to extract more entropy from ROs, rather than a secure access to the response of PUFs.

In summary, our contributions in this paper are as follows:

- We propose an elegant method to extract more subtle manufacturing variations by second order difference calculation, which can efficiently reduce the impact of systematic variation and regional environmental noise to guarantee the PUF's reliability.
- We design a new construction named Further RO PUF (FROPUF), which can extract at least 31-bit entropy from only two ROs on FPGAs.
- We conduct both simulation and practical experiments to demonstrate that our new proposed PUF has a bit-error-rate of 1.85% at 27 °C and an average inter-distance of 49.32%.

The rest of the paper is organized as follows. Section 2 presents preliminaries for our paper. Section 3 describes our model for RO PUFs with fine control of LUT's inputs and proposes our new construction with second order difference calculation. Section 4 evaluates the performance of our PUF from simulations and practical experiments. Finally, we conclude this paper in Sect. 5.

2   Preliminaries

A typical example of RO based PUF is shown in Fig. 1. It consists of n identically laid-out ROs, RO_1 to RO_n, with frequencies f_1 to f_n respectively. In general, the challenge (i, j) is applied to the multiplexers to select a pair of ROs, RO_i and RO_j $(i \neq j)$. Due to intrinsic manufacturing variations, f_i and f_j actually differs from each other. Based on the compensated measurement proposed by Gassend et al. [2], a response bit r_{ij} can be generated by the comparison expression as follows:

$$r_{ij} = \begin{cases} 1 & if \ \ f_i > f_j, \\ 0 & otherwise. \end{cases} \tag{1}$$

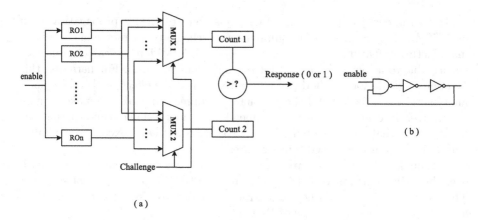

Fig. 1. (a) A typical example of RO PUF. (b) A three-stage ring oscillator

2.1   Evaluation Scheme of RO PUF

The evaluation scheme of a PUF is usually divided into three basic aspects, uniqueness, reliability and security [16].

- Uniqueness estimates how uniquely a PUF entity can be distinguished from others according to its responses.
- Reliability evaluates how stable the responses are with environmental factors (such as temperature, supply voltage) vary.
- Security is a PUF's ability in preventing adversaries from predicting the PUFs response.

Uniqueness can be measured by inter-distance. As defined in [28], when apply a particular challenge to the PUF's two different instances, the inter-distance is the hamming distance (HD) between their current responses. We estimate the uniqueness of a PUF base on the average inter-distance over a group of chips. With two PUF instantiations, denoted as i and j $(i \neq j)$, both having a n-bit response, R_i and R_j respectively, the average inter-distance μ_{inter} among k chips is calculated as

$$\mu_{inter} = \frac{2}{k(k-1)} \sum_{i=1}^{k-1} \sum_{j=i+1}^{k} \frac{HD(R_i, R_j)}{n} \times 100\% \tag{2}$$

Reliability can be evaluated through intra-distance. It is the hamming distance between different evaluation values of the same response on the same PUF instance. Due to environmental factors, such as temperature variation, supply voltage fluctuation and circuit noise, PUF's responses are not perfectly reproducible. To evaluate the reliability of a PUF's response, we achieve n-bit response $m+1$ times from the PUF instance i at some environmental condition and select the first n-bit response as the reference response R_i and the other responses as $R_{i,j}$ $(1 \leq j \leq m)$. The average intra-distance μ_{intra} can be calculated as follows:

$$\mu_{intra} = \frac{1}{m} \sum_{j=1}^{m} \frac{HD(R_i, R_{i,j})}{n} \times 100\% \tag{3}$$

2.2 Systematic Variation

In J.Cryptol.2011, Maiti et al. [16] pointed out that the total delay in a RO loop can be modeled as follows:

$$d_{LOOP} = d_{AVG} + d_{RAND} + d_{SYST} \tag{4}$$

where d_{AVG} = the nominal delay which is the same for all the identical ROs; d_{RAND} = delay variation due to manufacturing variation; d_{SYST} = delay variation due to the systematic variation. Then the difference between two ROs, a and b, can be calculated as follows:

$$\begin{aligned} \Delta d_{LOOP} &= (d_{AVG} + d_{RAND_a} + d_{SYST_a}) - (d_{AVG} + d_{RAND_b} + d_{SYST_b}) \\ &= \Delta d_{RAND} + \Delta d_{SYST} \end{aligned} \tag{5}$$

According to formula (5), a single response bit r_{ab} of these two ROs is not only decided by the random manufacturing variation, but also by the systematic variation. Maiti et al. noted that the systematic manufacturing variation could lead to a gradual change in the RO's loop delay as a function of the physical location, and its existence hazards RO PUF's uniqueness. In [16] a solution is given. Because two closely located ROs will have similar d_{SYST} in (4), their d_{SYST} can be counteracted by difference calculation.

2.3 Programmable Delay Lines

LUT is the main programmable delay logic unit of FPGA, and the construction of a 3-input LUT is shown in Fig. 2. The LUT is composed of a set of SRAM cells and a tree-like structure of multiplexers (MUXs). The former stores the intended functionality and the latter enables selection of each individual SRAM cell content. A LUT can be configured as an inverter, whose output (O) is always an inversion of its first input (A_1), and the inputs (A_2 and A_3) are logically irrelevant with A_1 and O. In CHES 2011, Majzoobi et al. [25] proposed a novel technique to adjust the propagation path in minute increments /decrements by using only a single LUT on reconfigurable FPGA platform. The mechanism changes the propagation path inside the LUT by altering the logically irrelevant inputs. Although the inputs A_2 and A_3 have no influence on the inverters logic, their values affect the signal propagation path from input A_1 to output O. Majzoobi et al. pointed that when $A_2A_3 = 00$ and $A_2A_3 = 11$, the propagation path from A_1 to O is the shortest and the longest respectively as shown in Fig. 2. The latest Xilinx series products, Virtex-5,6,7 and Spartan 6, adopt 6-input LUTs. Therefore, as the method proposed by Majzoobi, a programmable delay inverter can be implemented with at most $2^5 = 32$ discrete levels for controlling the propagation delay. For example, it is an example of this

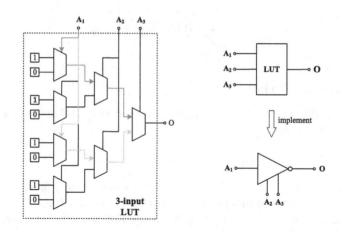

Fig. 2. Programmable delay lines using an LUT

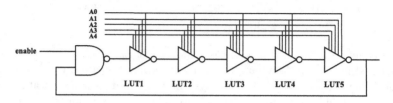

Fig. 3. An example of this fine control for 5-stage ROs

fine control for 5-stage ROs and the LUTs are 6-input in Fig. 3. Five of these inputs are configured as delay control.

Based on the multiple control of the LUT's propagation delay, Habib et al. [24] managed to extract more entropy from a pair of RO. According to their experiment results, the frequency varies significantly with the LUT's input sequence and the frequency's changing pattern is irregular. Based on this, Habib et al. were able to extract more entropy by comparing two RO's frequencies under all configurations from '000' to '111' correspondingly. However, the experiment results of Majzoobi et al. [25], demonstrates that the propagation delays of input '11111' are on average about 10 picoseconds larger than the corresponding delays of input '00000'. Habib et al. explained that the reason might be the Spartan 3E devices they used were based on 90 nm technology, while Majzoobi et al. employed Virtex-5 devices which were 65 nm technology. Therefore, if the frequency varies in a rough order depending on the LUT's input sequence, the result of the proposed method in [24] will lose efficiency on Virtex-5 devices.

3   Our Proposed Further ROPUF

Based on the propagation delay model proposed by Majzoobi et al. [25], we present a model which is involved with the subtle manufacturing variation of different LUT's inputs. Consider a RO l consisting of 6-input LUTs, its loop delay can be modeled as follows:

$$d_{LOOP(l,j)} = d_{AVG} + d_{RAND(l,j)} + d_{SYST(l,j)} \quad (1 \le j \le 32) \quad (6)$$

where d_{AVG} is the nominal delay which is the same for all the identical ROs; $d_{RAND(l,j)}$ represents the delay variation due to the random manufacturing variation when LUTs are driven by the jth input; $d_{SYST(l,j)}$ denotes the delay variation due to the systematic variation. The variables $d_{RAND(l,j)}$ and $d_{SYST(l,j)}$ could be positive and negative. For a RO with different LUT inputs, in_{j_1} and in_{j_2}, these two $d_{SYST(l,j_1)}$ and $d_{SYST(l,j_2)}$ are extremely close as shown in [16]. Therefore, in formula (6), the subscript of $d_{SYST(l,j_1)}$ and $d_{SYST(l,j_2)}$ can be modified to $d_{SYST(l)}$, where l is only related to the RO's location. And formula (6) will change into formula (7) as follows:

$$d_{LOOP(l,j)} = d_{AVG} + d_{RAND(l,j)} + d_{SYST(l)} \quad (1 \le j \le 32) \quad (7)$$

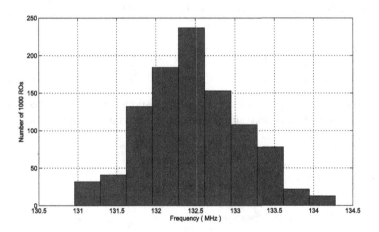

Fig. 4. The histogram distribution of 1000 ROs' frequencies

Moreover, when apply the same LUT input in_j on a group of L ROs, L variable values $d_{RAND(1,j)}, d_{RAND(2,j)}, \cdots, d_{RAND(L,j)}$ are acquired. According to ReConFig 2008 [29] and HOST 2011 [30], these values are almost complying with Gaussian distribution. Figure 4 shows the distribution of our experimental data, and it also seems like a normal distribution. Therefore, we assume that these L values are normally distributed. Apply this assumption to other LUT input configurations and we can achieve 32 normal distributions as follows:

$$(d_{RAND(1,j)}, d_{RAND(2,j)}, \cdots, d_{RAND(L,j)}) \sim N(\mu_j, \sigma_j^2) \quad (1 \le j \le 32) \quad (8)$$

Which indicates the random variable $d_{RAND(j)}$ is a normal distribution with mean μ_j and standard deviation σ_j.

3.1   Second Order Difference Calculation

On the basis of the above description, for a group of L ROs, by varying the LUT's input from '00000' to '11111', we can obtain $32 * L$ different $d_{LOOP(l,j)}$ which are in the same form of formula (9). Then we generate responses by second order difference calculation.

According to the above description, for a group of L ring oscillators, by varying the LUT's input from '00000' to '11111', we can get $32 * L$ different $d_{LOOP(l,j)}$ which has the similar form in formula (9). We propose an elegant method to generate responses based on second order difference calculation.

$$d_{LOOP(l,j)} = d_{AVG} + d_{RAND(l,j)} + d_{SYST(l)} \quad (1 \leq j \leq 32, 1 \leq l \leq L) \quad (9)$$

Our proposed method can be divided into two steps and here we present a neat example to illustrate our method.

1. For a RO l, select $d_{LOOP(l,j)}$ and $d_{LOOP(l,j+1)}$, then calculate the difference value $\Delta d_{LOOP(l,j)}$, $1 \leq j \leq 31$.
2. For two ROs l_1 and l_2, generate one bit $r_{l_1,l_2,j}$ $(1 \leq l_1 \neq l_2 \leq L, 1 \leq j \leq 31)$ as follows.

$$r_{l_1,l_2,j} = \begin{cases} 1 & if \ \ \Delta d_{LOOP(l_1,j)} > \Delta d_{LOOP(l_2,j)}, \\ 0 & otherwise. \end{cases} \quad (10)$$

Through these two steps, we will get a 31-bit response from two of these L ROs, thus $31*(L-1)$ bits can be extracted. Based on formula (9), $\Delta d_{LOOP(l,j)}$ can be calculated as follows:

$$\begin{aligned} \Delta d_{LOOP(l,j)} &= d_{LOOP(l,j)} - d_{LOOP(l,j+1)} \\ &= (d_{AVG} + d_{RAND(l,j)} + d_{SYST(l)}) - (d_{AVG} + d_{RAND(l,j+1)} + d_{SYST(l)}) \\ &= d_{RAND(l,j)} - d_{RAND(l,j+1)} \end{aligned} \quad (11)$$

Observing formula (11), we note that the systematic variation is neatly removed by this first order difference calculation. According to the assumption condition (8) that both $d_{RAND(j)}$ and $d_{RAND(j+1)}$ are normally distributed, we can get the distribution of the random variable $\Delta d_{LOOP(j)}$ as follows:

$$\Delta d_{LOOP(j)} \sim N(\mu_j - \mu_{j+1}, \sigma_j^2 + \sigma_{j+1}^2 - 2 * r_j * \sigma_j^2 * \sigma_{j+1}^2) \quad (1 \leq j \leq 31) \quad (12)$$

where r_j is the correlation coefficient between these two random variables. Let $\mu_{LOOP(j)}$ and $\sigma_{LOOP(j)}$ represent $\mu_j - \mu_{j+1}$ and $\sigma_j^2 + \sigma_{j+1}^2 - 2 * r_j * \sigma_j^2 * \sigma_{j+1}^2$ respectively. Through the second step of second order difference calculation, we can calculate the distribution of the random variable $R_{l_1,l_2,j}$ as follows:

$$R_{l_1,l_2,j} \sim N(0, 2 * \sigma_{LOOP(j)}^2) \quad (1 \leq j \leq 31) \quad (13)$$

For the mean of $R_{l_1,l_2,j}$'s distribution is zero, as the result of our second order difference calculation method, probabilities for $r_{l_1,l_2,j}$ equals '0' and '1' are the same. Theoretically, every response bit has 50% probability to be '0' or '1' and if these 31 bits have no correlation, it can be stated that 31-bit entropy is extracted from these two ROs.

In order to evaluate the randomness and entropy of responses, we will carry out NIST test suits on the responses generated by FROPUF in Sect. 4.4.

3.2   Analysis of the Second Order Difference Calculation

The key point to extract more entropy from two ROs is to extract more manufacturing features whose magnitude may be close to that of noise. Therefore we should suppress or eliminate the noise to the greatest extent.

In the conventional architecture of RO PUF, every RO has unique signal propagation path. While in programmable delay line model, the fine control of LUT's logically irrelevant inputs leads to different propagation paths. Habib et al. [24] have tried to extract more responses by utilizing this character. However, these propagation paths have a rough order on Xilinx Virtex-5, 6, 7 series devices. In that case, although the direct comparison between the corresponding delays of two ROs can acquire a 32-bit response sequence, the correlation between these bits may give rise to a large amount of entropy loss.

In our proposed scheme, we take advantage of the similarity of adjacent ROs' systematic variations and effectively eliminate the influence of systematic factors by the first order difference calculation between loop delays of the same RO. Follow the second step, we obtain the second order difference as formula (14) shows. This result is affected by the combination of two ROs' manufacturing features. As described in Sect. 3.1, the value of each response bit is decided by the sign of formula (14).

$$(d_{LOOP(l,j)} - d_{LOOP(l,j+1)}) - (d_{LOOP(l+1,j)} - d_{LOOP(l+1,j+1)}) \qquad (14)$$

Rewrite formula (14) we get:

$$(d_{LOOP(l,j)} - d_{LOOP(l+1,j)}) - (d_{LOOP(l,j+1)} - d_{LOOP(l+1,j+1)}) \qquad (15)$$

Observing formula (15), you will see the most important difference between Habib et al. and us is that we compare the relative magnitude of two ROs' corresponding loop delays. And also because of this, our scheme is able to extract more subtle manufacturing features.

Furthermore, the second order difference calculation method maintains the primary idea presented by Gassend et al. [2] which alleviates the impact of environmental fluctuations by comparing two ROs' frequencies to generate one bit response. To sum up, the second order difference calculation involves two difference functions which reduce both influence of the systematic variation and of the environmental fluctuations.

3.3 Simulation of Second Order Difference Calculation

To prove the effectiveness and correctness of our proposed model through simulation, some necessary parameters needs to be collected from experimental data on FPGA. In order to reflect individual differences, manufacturing variation and environmental change should be considered during simulation. Manufacturing variation is generally divided into systematic variation and random variation. Systematic variation is mainly affected by the ROs location on the wafer or chip. There is a research pointing out that systematic variation dominates the frequencies of ROs in one region are average larger than those in another region [16]. On the contrary, random variation has no relationship with components' spatial location. Therefore, we assume the parameters are as follows:

- Systematic delay d_{SYST} affected by spatial location: $\sim N(0,\sigma_{syst}^2)$.
- Component delay d_{RAND} affected by random variation: $\sim N(\mu_j,\sigma_j^2)$, where j represents the jth input for LUTs.

According to the parameters defined above, the delay value for different LUT inputs of different ROs can be generated by simulation, and we can also calculate every response bit following Algorithm 1, where sampling y from a distribution $N(\mu,\sigma^2)$ is denoted as $y \longleftarrow N(\mu,\sigma^2)$.

Algorithm 1. Simulation Algorithm of Second Order Difference Calculation

Settings: $\cdot MAX_{NumRO}$ is the number of ring oscillators.

$\cdot MAX_{NumIn}$ is the number of different LUT's inputs.

Output: $r_{l,j}$, $0 \le l \le MAX_{NumRO} - 1$, $0 \le j \le MAX_{NumIn} - 1$

```
 1: for l = 1 to MAX_NumRO do
 2:     d_SYST(l) ← N(0,σ²_syst)
 3:     for j = 1 to MAX_NumIn do
 4:         d_RAND(l,j) ← N(μ_l,σ²_l)
 5:     end for
 6: end for
 7: for l = 1 to MAX_NumRO − 1 do
 8:     for j = 1 to MAX_NumIn − 1 do
 9:         Δ_LOOP(l,j) ← (d_AVG + d_RAND(l,j) + d_SYST(l)) − (d_AVG + d_RAND(l,j+1) + d_SYST(l))
10:         Δ_LOOP(l+1,j) ← (d_AVG + d_RAND(l+1,j) + d_SYST(l+1)) − (d_AVG + d_RAND(l+1,j+1) + d_SYST(l+1))
11:         if Δ_LOOP(l,j) ≥ Δ_LOOP(l+1,j) then
12:             r_l,j ← 1
13:         else
14:             r_l,j ← 0
15:         end if
16:     end for
17: end for
```

4   Evaluation

In this section, we present the evaluation result of our FROPUF on 15 Virtex-5 XC5VLX110T-1FF1136 FPGAs, 10 Virtex-6 XC6VLX240T-1FF1156 FPGAs and 5 Kintex-7 XC7K325T-2FFG900 FPGAs. On the basis of practical measurements, we firstly acquire parameters for simulation. Then by comparing experimental and simulative results, we reveal the consistency of our simulation model and the practical architecture.

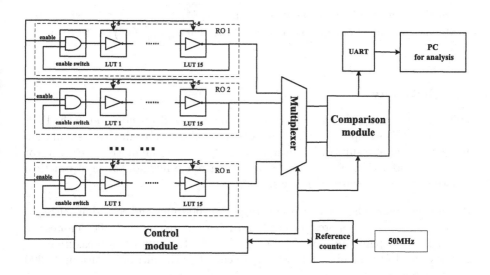

Fig. 5. The experimental evaluation system

Figure 5 shows our experimental evaluation system on Virtex-5 FPGA. A 50-MHz clock signal generated by an on-board oscillator and is applied to the reference counter. In Fig. 5, we place 200 ring oscillators and each of them is composed of 16 LUTs. 15 LUTs are instantiated as inverters with 5 configuration inputs and the last one serves as an enable switch. All the 16 LUTs are deployed in four adjacent slices, which means every RO occupies 4 slices of FPGA. Hard Macro technique is adopted to guarantee identical layout of these 200 ROs. The whole system is mainly controlled by the control module, which is responsible for the inverters' configuration inputs and control signals of multiplexer and reference counter. In order to evaluate the responses generated by our FROPUF, we utilize UART interface to transmit these responses to PC for analysis.

As high frequency makes RO instable, we select 15-stage RO whose frequency is about 132 MHz. To demonstrate the validity of our design, the configuration inputs for all LUTs are the same, i.e. the configuration input space is 2^5. In our evaluation system, there are 200 ROs which consume 800 slices. The other control module and the UART module have 213 and 126 slices separately.

In normal environmental condition, we perform a basic experiment on delay characteristics described in Sect. 3 and extract the parameter required by simulation. The obtained parameters are shown in Table 1. Based on these parameters and our simulation model, we can calculate the *intra-distance* and *inter-distance* to evaluate the reliability and uniqueness of FROPUF.

Table 1. Parameters for simulation in normal environmental condition

Parameter	Value
Standard deviation of systematic delay $\sigma_{d_{SYST}}$ $(\%^2)$	3.5336
Standard deviation of component random variation $\sigma_{d_{RAND}}$ $(\%^2)$	4.7636

4.1 Reliability

Reliability is mainly evaluated by intra-distance and reflects how stably the PUF can reproduce its responses. Figure 6 plots the evaluation results from simulation and experimental results of our evaluation systems. The simulative average error rate is around 1.25%. Steps to calculate the average intra-distance of practical experiments are depicted as follows:

1. Let every two ROs generate 31-bit response 200 times and record as $\text{RES}_{l,k,t}$. Where $1 \leq l \leq 15$ denotes the index of FPGA boards, $1 \leq k \leq 100$ denotes the index of RO pairs and $1 \leq t \leq 200$ denotes the the number of measurement.
2. For every RO pair, obey formula (3) to calculate the intra-distance of its 200 responses.
3. Average all the RO pairs intra-distance.

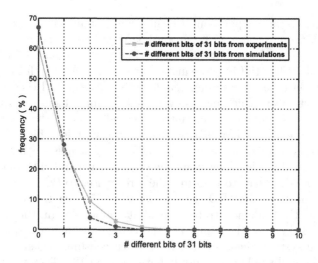

Fig. 6. The intra-distance evaluation from practical experiments and simulations

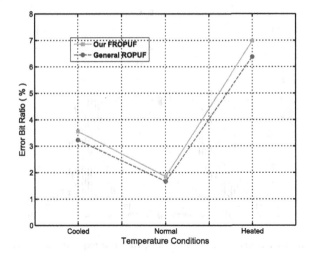

Fig. 7. The error bit ratio under different temperature conditions

The measurement is carried out at normal temperature (27 °C) on 15 Virtex-5 XC5VLX110T- 1FF1136 FPGAs. The experimental average error rate is around 1.85%, which is comparable to other RO PUF designs [5,18]. In addition, Fig. 6 indicates that the behavior of experimental error rate can be assessed by simulation with high accuracy.

The change of temperature is a major disturbance for RO based PUF, therefore we conduct experiments under different temperatures to investigate the FROPUF's property. Figure 7 shows that as the temperature rising (up to about 70 °C), the intra-distance continues to increase until 6.98%, which is about the half of 15% assumed in [31]. According to Figure 7, FROPUF achieves almost the same error bit rate as the general ROPUF.

4.2   Uniqueness

Uniqueness is mainly evaluated by inter-distance and Fig. 8(a) is a histogram of hamming distances between different PUF instances' responses in practice. Every instance consists of two ROs and produces a 31-bit response. We totally deploy 1500 instances on 15 Virtex-5 FPGAs. The result shows that the average inter-distance is about 49.32%, which indicates that FROPUF instances possess enough uniqueness to be identified from each other. Figure 8(b) shows the result of the same evaluation by simulation. Through Fig. 8(a) and (b), we conclude that the simulation is able to evaluate the uniqueness of responses generated by PUF instances.

4.3   The Randomness Evaluation

NIST test suites are carried out to evaluate the randomness of the responses generated by FROPUF. The length of the response generated by each instantiation

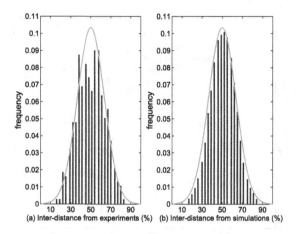

Fig. 8. The inter-distance evaluation from practical experiments and simulations

is 31 bits and we get totally 46500 bits responses. For the limitation of the length of response, we conduct 9 basic NIST tests and the result is shown in Table 2. The *Frequency* test manifests that the response bit has nearly 50% to be '1' and 50% to be '0' and this practical result is similar to the theoretical analysis in Sect. 3.1.

Table 2. The result of NIST for FROPUF's responses

Statistical test	P-value	Proportion
Frequency	0.350485	10/10
Blockfrequency	0.911413	10/10
Cumulativesums(forward)	0.739918	10/10
Cumulativesums(backward)	0.035174	10/10
Runs	0.534146	10/10
Longestruns	0.628713	10/10
Rank	0.122325	10/10
FFT	0.523478	10/10
Serial(∇^1)	0.712378	10/10
Serial(∇^2)	0.328793	10/10
Linearcomplexity	0.189283	10/10

In Table 3, we list some designs extracting responses from ROs and make comparisons of the variable *Bits per Ring*. The result shows that in our architecture, we can extract 16.5 bits entropy per ring, which is 7 times larger than that of Habib et al. [24], and moreover it is 31 times larger than that of the general RO PUF.

Table 3. Comparison of the entropy extracted from two ROs

	Our work	General RO PUF	Habib et al. [24]	Maiti et al. [16]
Number of ring oscillators	2	2	130	512
Average independent response bits	31	1	318	511
Bits per ring	16.5	0.5	2.44	≈ 1

4.4 The Evaluation Result on Other FPGAs

The above reliability and uniqueness are tested on Xilinx Virtex-5 FPGAs. We also conduct experiments on Xilinx Virtex-6 and Kintex-7 FPGAs. The results show that the intra-distance and inter-distance is 1.68% and 49.12% on Virtex-6 FPGAs, and is 1.62% and 48.95% respectively on Kintex-7 FPGAs. Therefore, our new proposed FROPUF is also available on these new fashioned FPGA products.

5 Further Discussion

In Sect. 3, our proposed second order difference calculation just generates a 31-bit response. However, follow Algorithm 2, we can get a 496-bit response from two ROs. Obviously, the Shanon entropy of this 496-bit response is less than 496 bits. On the observation of Sect. 3, a lower bound entropy of this 496-bit response is 31 bits. Based on the model proposed in Sect. 3, we can calculate the Shanon entropy of this 496-bit response as follows.

Based on the model proposed in Sect. 3, we have the formula (16) as follows because we assume no prior information about the response when only the manufacturing variation is present.

$$Prob(r_i = 1) = Prob(r_i = 0) = 0.5 \quad (1 \leq i \leq 496) \tag{16}$$

However, because of the existence of correlations, if we know some bits' value, some other bits' information leaks out. For example, if r_1 and r_2 are known, the value of r_{32} distributes as follows.

$$Prob(r_{32} = 0) = \begin{cases} 1 & if \ r_1 = 1 \ and \ r_2 = 0, \\ 0.5 & if \ r_1 = 1 \ and \ r_2 = 1, \\ 0.5 & if \ r_1 = 0 \ and \ r_2 = 0, \\ 0 & if \ r_1 = 0 \ and \ r_2 = 1. \end{cases} \tag{17}$$

Figure 9 shows the correlation between these 496 bits response. Based on formula (16) and Fig. 9, we can calculate the Shanon entropy of the 496-bit response as follows. The 31 bits in the first row of Fig. 9 have 31 bits Shanon entropy, and the 30 bits in second row have 15 bits Shanon entropy and so on. We can acquire that the responses in the ith row have $\frac{1}{2^{i-1}}(32 - i)$ bits Shanon entropy. As a result, the Shanon Entropy of this 496-bit response is $\sum_{i=1}^{31} \frac{1}{2^{i-1}}(32 - i) = 60$ bits.

Algorithm 2. Simulation Algorithm of Second Order Difference Calculation

---

Settings: · There are two ROs, A and B.
    · Both A and B have 5-bit configuration inputs.
    · According to 32 different inputs, there will be $Counter_{A_j}$ and
      $Counter_{B_j}$, $1 \leq j \leq 32$
Output: · Response r_i, $1 \leq i \leq 496$
 1: $i \longleftarrow 0$
 2: **for** m = 1 to 32 **do**
 3:    **for** n = m+1 to 32 **do**
 4:        $i \longleftarrow i + 1$
 5:        $\Delta Counter_{A(m,n)} \longleftarrow Counter_{A_m} - Counter_{A_n}$
 6:        $\Delta Counter_{B(m,n)} \longleftarrow Counter_{B_m} - Counter_{B_n}$
 7:        **if** $\Delta Counter_{A(m,n)} \geq \Delta Counter_{B(m,n)}$ **then**
 8:            $r_i \leftarrow 1$
 9:        **else**
10:            $r_i \leftarrow 0$
11:        **end if**
12:    **end for**
13: **end for**

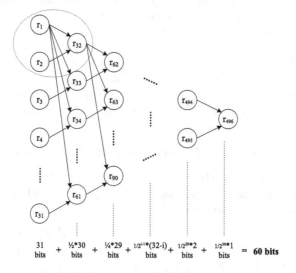

$$\underset{\text{bits}}{31} + \underset{\text{bits}}{\frac{1}{2}*30} + \underset{\text{bits}}{\frac{1}{4}*29} + \underset{\text{bits}}{1/2^{i-1}*(32-i)} + \underset{\text{bits}}{1/2^{29}*2} + \underset{\text{bits}}{1/2^{30}*1} = \mathbf{60\ bits}$$

Fig. 9. The Shanon Entropy of the 496-bit response

6   Conclusion

In this paper, we propose a new architecture called Further RO PUF, which takes advantage of LUT's fine control to achieve more random manufacturing variations. Through the second order difference calculation, we on one hand extract more subtle features from RO pairs, and on the other hand, neatly reduce the influence of systematic variation and environmental fluctuation to strengthen the reliability. The key point of FROPUF is that we can extract at least 31 bits entropy from only two ROs and according to our analysis, the Shanon Entropy of the response reaches 60 bits. By conducting simulation and practical experiments, we found the intra-distance of FROPUF is only 1.85% at 27 °C and never exceed 10% with drastic temperature changes, and the inter-distance is about 49.32%, which guarantees the uniqueness of different PUF instances.

References

1. Ruhrmair, U., Holcomb, D.E.: PUFs at a glance. In: Design, Automation and Test in Europe Conference and Exhibition (DATE), pp. 1–6 (2014)
2. Gassend, B., Clarke, D., Van Dijk, M., Devadas, S.: Silicon physical random functions. In: Proceedings of the 9th ACM Conference on Computer and Communications Security, pp. 148–160 (2002)
3. Katzenbeisser, S., Kocabaş, Ü., Rožić, V., Sadeghi, A.-R., Verbauwhede, I., Wachsmann, C.: PUFs: myth, fact or busted? a security evaluation of physically unclonable functions (PUFs) cast in silicon. In: Prouff, E., Schaumont, P. (eds.) CHES 2012. LNCS, vol. 7428, pp. 283–301. Springer, Heidelberg (2012). doi:10.1007/978-3-642-33027-8_17
4. Ravikanth, P., Recht, B., Taylor, J., Gershenfeld, N.: Physical One-Way Functions, vol. 297. American Association for the Advancement of Science, Washington, DC (2002). pp. 2026–2030
5. Maes, R., Van Herrewege, A., Verbauwhede, I.: PUFKY: a fully functional PUF-based cryptographic key generator. In: Prouff, E., Schaumont, P. (eds.) CHES 2012. LNCS, vol. 7428, pp. 302–319. Springer, Heidelberg (2012). doi:10.1007/978-3-642-33027-8_18
6. Guajardo, J., Kumar, S.S., Schrijen, G.-J., Tuyls, P.: FPGA intrinsic PUFs and their use for IP protection. In: Paillier, P., Verbauwhede, I. (eds.) CHES 2007. LNCS, vol. 4727, pp. 63–80. Springer, Heidelberg (2007). doi:10.1007/978-3-540-74735-2_5
7. Roy, J.A., Koushanfar, F., Markov, I.L.: EPIC: Ending piracy of integrated circuits. In: Proceedings of the Conference on Design, Automation and Test in Europe, pp. 1069–1074 (2008)
8. Koeberl, P., Li, J., Maes, R., Rajan, A., Vishik, C., Wójcik, M.: Evaluation of a PUF device authentication scheme on a discrete 0.13 um SRAM. In: Chen, L., Yung, M., Zhu, L. (eds.) INTRUST 2011. LNCS, vol. 7222, pp. 271–288. Springer, Heidelberg (2012). doi:10.1007/978-3-642-32298-3_18
9. Devadas, S., Suh, E., Paral, S., Sowell, R., Ziola, T., Khandelwal, V.: Design and implementation of PUF-based unclonable RFID ICs for anti-counterfeiting and security applications. In: 2008 IEEE International Conference on RFID, pp. 58–64 (2008)
10. Tuyls, P., Škorić, B.: Strong authentication with physical unclonable functions. In: Petković, M., Jonker, W. (eds.) Security, Privacy, and Trust in Modern Data Management. Data-Centric Systems and Applications, pp. 133–148. Springer, Heidelberg (2007)
11. Holcomb, D.E., Fu, K.: Bitline PUF: building native challenge-response PUF capability into any SRAM. In: Batina, L., Robshaw, M. (eds.) CHES 2014. LNCS, vol. 8731, pp. 510–526. Springer, Heidelberg (2014). doi:10.1007/978-3-662-44709-3_28

12. Kumar, S.S., Guajardo, J., Maes, R., Schrijen, G-J., Tuyls, P.: Extended abstract: the butterfly PUF protecting IP on every FPGA. In: IEEE International Workshop on Hardware-Oriented Security and Trust, HOST 2008, pp. 67–70 (2008)

13. Suzuki, D., Shimizu, K.: The glitch PUF: a new delay-PUF architecture exploiting glitch shapes. In: Mangard, S., Standaert, F.-X. (eds.) CHES 2010. LNCS, vol. 6225, pp. 366–382. Springer, Heidelberg (2010). doi:10.1007/978-3-642-15031-9_25

14. Maes, R., Tuyls, P., Verbauwhede, I.: Intrinsic PUFs from flip-flops on reconfigurable devices. In: 3rd Benelux Workshop on Information and System Security (WISSec 2008) (2008)

15. Suh, G.E., Devadas, S.: Physical unclonable functions for device authentication and secret key generation. In: Proceedings of the 44th Annual Design Automation Conference, pp. 9–14 (2007)

16. Maiti, A., Schaumont, P.: Improved ring oscillator PUF: an FPGA-friendly secure primitive. J. Cryptology 2, 375–397 (2011)

17. Gao, M., Lai, K., Qu, G.: A highly flexible ring oscillator PUF. In: Proceedings of the 51st Annual Design Automation Conference on Design Automation Conference. ACM (2014)

18. Rahman, T., Forte, D., Fahrny, J., Tehranipoor, M.: ARO-PUF: an aging-resistant ring oscillator PUF design. In: Proceedings of the Conference on Design, Automation & Test in Europe (2014)

19. Cherkaoui, A., Fischer, V., Aubert, A., Fesquet, L.: Comparison of self-timed ring and inverter ring oscillators as entropy sources in FPGAs. In: Design, Automation & Test in Europe Conference & Exhibition (DATE), pp. 1325–1330. IEEE (2012)

20. Yin, C-E., Qu, G., Zhou, Q.: Design and implementation of a group-based RO PUF. In: Proceedings of the Conference on Design, Automation and Test in Europe, pp. 416–421. EDA Consortium (2013)

21. Dominik, M., Heyszl, J., Heinz, B., Schuster, D., Stumpf, F., Sigl, G.: Localized electromagnetic analysis of RO PUFs. In: 2013 IEEE International Symposium on Hardware-Oriented Security and Trust (HOST), pp. 19–24. IEEE (2013)

22. Dodis, Y., Reyzin, L., Smith, A.: Fuzzy extractors: how to generate strong keys from biometrics and other noisy data. In: Cachin, C., Camenisch, J.L. (eds.) EUROCRYPT 2004. LNCS, vol. 3027, pp. 523–540. Springer, Heidelberg (2004). doi:10.1007/978-3-540-24676-3_31

23. Bösch, C., Guajardo, J., Sadeghi, A.-R., Shokrollahi, J., Tuyls, P.: Efficient helper data key extractor on FPGAs. In: Oswald, E., Rohatgi, P. (eds.) CHES 2008. LNCS, vol. 5154, pp. 181–197. Springer, Heidelberg (2008). doi:10.1007/978-3-540-85053-3_12

24. Habib, B., Kris, G., Kaps, J-P.: FPGA PUF based on programmable LUT delays. In: 2013 Euromicro Conference on Digital System Design (DSD). IEEE (2013)

25. Majzoobi, M., Koushanfar, F., Devadas, S.: FPGA-based true random number generation using circuit metastability with adaptive feedback control. In: Preneel, B., Takagi, T. (eds.) CHES 2011. LNCS, vol. 6917, pp. 17–32. Springer, Heidelberg (2011). doi:10.1007/978-3-642-23951-9_2

26. Majzoobi, M., Koushanfar, F., Devadas, S.: FPGA PUF using programmable delay lines. In: 2010 IEEE International Workshop on Information Forensics and Security (WIFS) (2010)

27. Rührmair, U., Sehnke, F., Sölter, J., Dror, G., Devadas, S., Schmidhuber, J.: Modeling attacks on physical unclonable functions, pp. 237–249 (2010)

28. Maes, R., Verbauwhede, I.: Physically unclonable functions: a study on the state of the art and future research directions. In: Sadeghi, A.-R., Naccache, D. (eds.) Towards Hardware-Intrinsic Security. Information Security and Cryptography, pp. 3–37. Springer, Heidelberg (2010)

29. Wold, K., Tan, C.H.: Analysis and enhancement of random number generator in FPGA based on oscillator rings. In: Proceedings of the 2008 International Conference on Reconfigurable Computing and FPGAs, pp. 385–390. IEEE Computer Society (2008)

30. Maiti, A., Casarona, J., McHale, L.: A large scale characterization of RO-PUF. In: IEEE International Symposium on Hardware-Oriented Security and Trust (HOST), pp. 94–99. IEEE (2010)

31. Maes, R., Tuyls, P., Verbauwhede, I.: Low-overhead implementation of a soft decision helper data algorithm for SRAM PUFs. In: Clavier, C., Gaj, K. (eds.) CHES 2009. LNCS, vol. 5747, pp. 332–347. Springer, Heidelberg (2009). doi:10.1007/978-3-642-04138-9_24

Extracting More Entropy for TRNGs Based on Coherent Sampling

Jing Yang[1,2,3], Yuan Ma[1,2]([✉]), Tianyu Chen[1,2,3], Jingqiang Lin[1,2],
and Jiwu Jing[1,2]

[1] Data Assurance and Communication Security Research Center,
Chinese Academy of Sciences, Beijing, China
{yangjing,yma,tychen,linjq,jing}@is.ac.cn
[2] State Key Laboratory of Information Security,
Institute of Information Engineering,
Chinese Academy of Sciences, Beijing, China
[3] University of Chinese Academy of Sciences, Beijing, China

Abstract. True Random Number Generators (TRNGs) are essential
for cryptographic systems and communication security. According to the
published standards, sufficient entropy derived from the stochastic model
is required for TRNGs. Compared with the directly sampling jittery oscillating signal, the coherent sampling is a more efficient entropy extraction
technique. In this paper, under the premise that the entropy per bit is
sufficient, we focus on how to extract the entropy as much as possible from the coherent sampling in order to enhance the throughput of
TRNGs. We provide a parameter adjustment method to maximize the
generated entropy rate, and this method is based on our proposed stochastic model. According to the method, we design a TRNG architecture
and implement it in Field Programmable Gate Arrays (FPGAs). In the
experiment, the improved generation speed is up to 4 Mbps, and the
output sequence is able to pass NIST SP 800-22 statistical tests without postprocessing. Compared to the basic coherent sampling, the bit
generation rate is improved to 12 times.

Keywords: True Random Number Generators · Coherent sampling ·
FPGA · Stochastic model · Entropy extraction

1 Introduction

Random Number Generators (RNGs) play an important role in many cryptographic applications, such as the session key generation in communications, digital signature generation and key exchange. The property of generated random
numbers determines the security of cryptographic systems. Generally speaking,
RNGs are separated into two categories: Pseudo Random Number Generators
(PRNGs) and True Random Number Generators (TRNGs). PRNGs extend the
seed to extremely long sequence by using deterministic algorithms, so the PRNG
security is based on the unpredictability of the seed. TRNGs collect randomness from physical phenomena such as temperature, noises, radiation, which are

© ICST Institute for Computer Sciences, Social Informatics and Telecommunications Engineering 2017
R. Deng et al. (Eds.): SecureComm 2016, LNICST 198, pp. 694–709, 2017.
DOI: 10.1007/978-3-319-59608-2_38

assumed to contain unpredictable random components. In addition, the TRNG output usually serves for the seeds of PRNGs, so it is important to design security TRNGs with sufficient entropy.

Entropy is used as the measurement of the unpredictability, and also quantifies the true randomness of a TRNG output. The standards ISO 18031 [6] and AIS 31 [7] recommend to use the entropy derived from stochastic model to assess the security of a TRNG. Several works provided different modeling and entropy calculation methods for different types of TRNGs. For example, the entropy of oscillator-based TRNGs was calculated in [1,8,10], and Cherkaoui et al. [3] analyzed the behavior of self-timed ring (STR) and estimated the entropy of a STR based TRNG.

In addition to the entropy, the speed (i.e., the generation rate) is another important factor for a TRNG. Although the traditional method of sampling jittery oscillating signals has been well studied in the aspect of entropy estimation [1,10], the amount and the utilization rate of the randomness are both very low, yielding that the bit generation speed is very slow. Hence, the improvements either on refining the oscillator structure (such as [3,17]) or on improving the probability of capturing jitter (such as [12,14]) have been presented in literature.

Coherent sampling is one of the improvement techniques, where an oscillating signal is sampled by another with a similar frequency. The principle of this method utilizes the tiny difference between the two close frequencies of the signals to distinguish the jitter accumulation. In the traditional sampling, the accumulation of jitter within one sampling interval is required to be large than half or even one period of the sampled signal, thus the sampling interval has to be significantly large to guarantee the sufficiency of entropy. While, in coherent sampling, the required jitter accumulation is approximated to be the period difference between the two signals, thus the accumulation time can be much shortened to acquire a much higher generation speed. In general, the sampling result is called *beat* signal, and its period is equal to an integer times of the period of sampling signal. Actually, this integer times is random due to the accumulation of jitter. Hence, an intuitive method is counting the number edges of sampling signal within the period of *beat* signal, and using the Least Significant Bit (LSB) as the outputted random bit.

The TRNG based on coherent sampling was first presented in [9], and the random bit sequence was generated at a speed of up to 0.5 Mbps with good statistical properties in Field Programmable Gate Arrays (FPGAs). For the model of a Phase Locked Loop (PLL) based TRNG structure [4], Bernard et al. [2] proposed a mathematical model using two oscillating signals with rationally related frequencies, and then estimated the entropy per bit. An enhancement of this type of a TRNG was presented in [16] which employed the mutual sampling principle, and the improved speed up to 4 times compared to the basic coherent sampling.

In this paper, on the premise that the entropy per bit is sufficient, we focus on how to extract more entropy from the coherent sampling to enhance the speed of TRNGs. Our key insight is that the counting edge number in the *beat* signal contains more entropy which is more than 1 bit in the basic [9] or 2 bits in the enhanced [16]. Therefore, we provide a parameter adjustment method to maximize the generated entropy rate, and this method is based on our proposed stochastic model. According to the method, we design a TRNG architecture and implement it in FPGAs. In the experiment, the improved generation speed is up to 4 Mbps, and the output sequence is able to pass NIST SP 800-22 statistical test suite [13]. Compared to the basic coherent sampling, the bit generation rate is improved to 12 times.

In summary, we make the following contributions.

- We establish an equivalent model for coherent sampling from the aspect of the bias of two frequencies rather than the ratio, thus the model has a wider applicability.
- Based on the model, we propose a parameter adjustment method to maximize the generated entropy rate, and design the TRNG architecture to acquire a higher bit generation speed.
- We provide the simulation results to validate the correctness of the equivalent model, and implement the TRNG architecture in Xilinx Virtex-5 FPGA. In the experimental results, the generated bit sequence passes NIST SP800-22 statistical tests without postprocessing at a speed of 4 Mbps. The improvement factor is 12 compared to the speed of the basic coherent sampling.

The rest of paper is organized as follows. In Sect. 2, we mainly establish an equivalent model to evaluate entropy per bit. Next, we propose an architecture of TRNGs, which is based on an improved method to extract more entropy in Sect. 3. In Sect. 4, we give the simulation and implementation results to verify the effectiveness of the architecture, and compare with other related work. We conclude the paper in Sect. 5.

2   Equivalent Stochastic Model

In this section, we first introduce the principle of the traditional sampling and the coherent sampling. Then, we propose an equivalent model to transfer the coherent sampling process to the traditional sampling process. Finally, based on the equivalent model, we evaluate the bit-rate entropy and give the required condition to acquire sufficient entropy.

2.1   Principle of Traditional and Coherent Sampling Methods

The traditional sampling is defined that a stable slow clock signal (such as crystal clock signal) samples an unstable fast oscillating signal to generate bit sequences [1,10]. Relatively, the coherent sampling is defined that an oscillating signal S_{ro_1} is sampled using a D flip-flop by another oscillating signal S_{ro_2} with a similar period of S_{ro_1} [9]. The basic components of the coherent sampling are shown as Fig. 1. The signal on the output of the D flip-flop is called a *beat* signal S_{beat} and it is a low-frequency signal depending on the period difference between S_{ro_1}

and S_{ro_2}. Figure 2 shows the principle of the basic coherent sampling. The period of *beat* signal is always equal to an integer period number of S_{ro_2}. Since the S_{ro_1} and S_{ro_2} are unstable due to the jitter, the number is random. Therefore, the period number of S_{ro_2} during the period of *beat* signal can be counted as the random output.

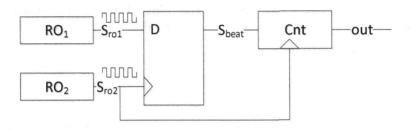

Fig. 1. Basic components of the coherent sampling

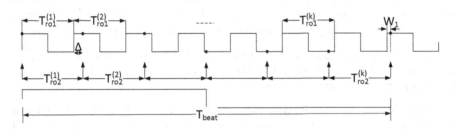

Fig. 2. Principle of the coherent sampling

2.2 Proposed Equivalent Model

Bernard et al. [2] proposed a mathematical model for the case of two oscillating signals with rationally related frequencies. Their model is efficient for the signals with known relationship (i.e., integer ratio), e.g., for the signals generated from two PLLs [4]. However, for two free-oscillating signals, the ratio could not be exactly the ratio of two (small) integers, thus the model is not applicable for this case. Therefore, we provide a more general model from the aspect of the bias of two frequencies rather than the ratio, and we succeed in transferring the coherent sampling process to the traditional sampling process, whose model and entropy have been well studied in literature [1,8,10].

Definition. The important notations are shown in Fig. 2, where the periods $T_{ro_1}^{(k)}$ and $T_{ro_2}^{(k)}$ are the time intervals between two adjacent rising edges of signal S_{ro_1} and S_{ro_2}, respectively. In this paper, we assume that $T_{ro_1}^{(k)}$ and $T_{ro_2}^{(k)}$ are independent and identically distributed (i.i.d.), and T_{ro_1} and T_{ro_2} are independent of each other. The time span between the rising edge of the signal S_{beat} and the previous rising edge of the signal S_{ro_1} is denoted as W_i. The rising edge number of signal S_{ro_2} from time zero to ith T_{beat} is denoted as N_i. Hence, N_i is represented as $N_i = min\{k|Y_k > X_{k+i}\}$, where $X_k = T_{ro_1}^{(1)} + T_{ro_1}^{(2)} + \cdots + T_{ro_1}^{(k)}$, $Y_k = T_{ro_2}^{(1)} + T_{ro_2}^{(2)} + \cdots + T_{ro_2}^{(k)}$, meaning N_i is the first increasing k ensuring that the signal S_{ro_1} has more i rising edges than the signal S_{ro_2}.

Then we denote $R_i = N_i - N_{i-1}$ as the rising edge number of signal S_{ro_2} within the ith T_{beat}, which is employed as the random output. Then we have

$$R_i = min\{k|Y_k > X_{k+i}\} - min\{k|Y_k > X_{k+i-1}\}$$

$$= min\{k| \sum_{j=N_{i-1}+1}^{N_{i-1}+k} (T_{ro_2}^{(j)} - T_{ro_1}^{(j+i-1)}) + W_{i-1} > T_{ro_1}^{(N_{i-1}+k+i)}\} \quad (1)$$

Let $\{\Delta_n\} = \{T_{ro_2}^{(1)} - T_{ro_1}^{(1)}, T_{ro_2}^{(2)} - T_{ro_1}^{(2)}, \cdots T_{ro_2}^{(N_{i-1}+1)} - T_{ro_1}^{(N_{i-1}+i)}, \cdots T_{ro_2}^{(N_i)} - T_{ro_1}^{(N_i+i-1)}, T_{ro_2}^{(N_i+1)} - T_{ro_1}^{(N_i+i+1)}, \cdots\}$, where $\{\Delta_n\}$ is a sequence of random variable Δ. The mean and variance of Δ are denoted as μ_Δ and σ_Δ^2, respectively. Let $\{S_n\} = \{T_{ro_1}^{(N_1+1)}, T_{ro_1}^{(N_2+2)}, \cdots T_{ro_1}^{(N_i+i)}, \cdots\}$, where $\{S_n\}$ is a sequence of random variable S. The mean and variance of S are denoted as μ_S and σ_S^2, respectively. Under the above assumptions about the two oscillating signals, we conclude

(1) Δ_n are i.i.d. and Δ is subject to the same distribution with $T_{ro_2} - T_{ro_1}$;
(2) S_n are i.i.d. and S is subject to the same distribution with T_{ro_1};
(3) Δ and S are mutually independent.

According to Eq. (1), R_i also means the number of Δ within the interval S. We ignore the jitter of S because jitter accumulation rate of which is much slower than Δ (i.e., $\frac{\sigma_\Delta^2}{\mu_\Delta} \gg \frac{\sigma_S^2}{\mu_S}$). The time span W_i corresponds to the waiting time in paper [10]. Therefore, we can declare that the coherent sampling process (called the coherent sampling model) is approximated to the following sampling process (called the traditional sampling model) as Fig. 3.

- The half-periods of the unstable fast oscillating signal is Δ;
- The sampling period of the stable slow oscillating signal is $\mu_S(= \mu_{T_{ro_1}})$.

Next, we only consider the case of injecting independent Gaussian jitter to both oscillating signals in order to obtain the distribution of various random variables. Let us assume the two oscillating signals are derived from two Ring Oscillators (ROs), and let $\mu_{T_{ro_1}}$ and $\mu_{T_{ro_2}}$ be the two ideal jitter-free periods. Hence, the periods of two oscillating signals T_{ro_1} and T_{ro_2} are assumed to be Gaussian distributions

$$T_{ro_1} \sim N(\mu_{T_{ro_1}}, \sigma_{T_{ro_1}}^2), \quad (2)$$

$$T_{ro_2} \sim N(\mu_{T_{ro_2}}, \sigma_{T_{ro_2}}^2), \quad (3)$$

where $N(0, \sigma^2)$ denotes a zero-mean normal distribution with standard variance σ. The values $\sigma_{T_{ro_1}}^2$ and $\sigma_{T_{ro_2}}^2$ denote the variances of T_{ro_1} and T_{ro_2}, respectively.

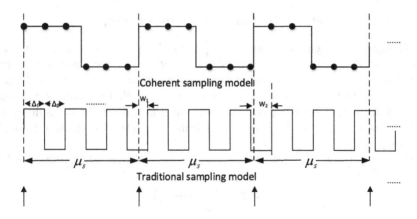

Fig. 3. The description of equivalence between two models

Assuming $\mu_{T_{ro_2}} > \mu_{T_{ro_1}}$ without loss of generality, we express the distribution of the variable Δ as

$$\Delta \sim N(\mu_\Delta, \sigma_\Delta^2), \tag{4}$$

where $\mu_\Delta = \mu_{T_{ro_2}} - \mu_{T_{ro_1}}$, $\sigma_\Delta = \sqrt{\sigma_{T_{ro_1}}^2 + \sigma_{T_{ro_2}}^2}$.

Remark. In order to simplify the model, we assume only independent random jitter exists in oscillating signals. Just as [5,10], the correlated noise also exists in oscillating signals. However, research and analysis based on correlated noise behavior are too complex to model. It is noticed as long as the amount of independent random jitter is enough, the generated bits entropy is sufficient. Therefore, we do not consider the influence of correlated noise in our model.

2.3   Entropy Evaluation

Ma et al. [10] presented a stochastic model to evaluate the entropy of oscillator-based TRNGs, and used the typical example that a stable slow clock signal samples an unstable fast oscillating signal to generate random bits which is the same as proposed equivalent model (traditional sampling model). Hence, the traditional sampling model can be employed to calculate the bit-rate entropy. We use the conclusion in this paper that in the worst case, when the standard variance of the counting results σ_R is larger than 1, the bit-rate entropy is sufficient. According to the conclusion from [15], we can express σ_R by

$$\sigma_R = \sqrt{\frac{\mu_{T_{ro1}}}{\mu_\Delta}} \cdot \frac{\sigma_\Delta}{\mu_\Delta}. \tag{5}$$

3   Proposed Architecture

In this section, based on the analysis in previous section, we first propose an improved method for extracting more entropy. Then, we propose an achievable circuit architecture for the implementation.

3.1   Improved Method for Extracting More Entropy

Key insight. Through the results of [15] and our experimental results, we have noticed that the standard variances of the counting result σ_R are significantly larger than 1. While, the condition of sufficient entropy derived from the proposed equivalent model is just $\sigma_R \geq 1$, which suggests that more entropy is contained in individual counting process, not only the LSB of the counting result R. Hence, our method is designed to maximize the extracted entropy from the counting process.

According to the principle of coherent sampling, the bit generation speed F_s is expressed as

$$F_s = 1/(\frac{\mu_{T_{ro_1}}}{\mu_\Delta} \cdot \mu_{T_{ro_2}}). \tag{6}$$

In order to enhance throughput under the status of sufficient entropy, our aim is to increase F_s and meanwhile guarantee $\sigma_R^2 \geq 1$. If $\sigma_R^2 > 1$, we can reduce the sampling period μ_S in the above equivalent model. According to Eqs. (5) and (6), when the value of σ_R^2 drops to 1, the value of F_s would be increased to σ_R^2 times. Therefore, the bit generation speed can be increased up to σ_R^2 times in theory. If we can further adjust the period difference μ_Δ to improve the sensitivity to jitter accumulation, the bit generation speed would be improved to more than σ_R^2 times.

Our approach for maximizing the extracted entropy is listed as the following Steps.

1. Minimize the period difference between two oscillating signals for increasing the sensitivity to jitter accumulation (i.e., reduce μ_Δ);
2. Use the signal S_{beat} to generate the m-multiple-frequency signal S'_{beat}, where m is the largest value to guarantee the variance of the counting numbers of T_{ro_2} is greater than 1.
3. Count the number of periods T_{ro_2} during the half-period of S'_{beat}, and use the LSB as the random bit.

It is observed that the approach also agrees with the proposed equivalent model. In the approach, we reduce μ_Δ (i.e., the half-periods of the unstable fast oscillating signal in equivalent model) and reduce μ_S (i.e., the sampling period in equivalent model), so the efficiency of extracting entropy is improved. When the period difference μ_Δ has been adjusted to an expected value in Step 1, we obtain

$$\sigma_{R'}^2 = \frac{1}{2m} \cdot \sigma_R^2 \quad (F'_s = 2m \cdot F_s), \tag{7}$$

where $\sigma_{R'}^2$ and F'_s denote the variance of counting results and bit generation speed based on the improved method, respectively. The values σ_R^2 and F_s denote the variance of counting results and bit generation speed based on the basic coherent sampling, respectively. It means that the bit generation speed is increased to 2 m times when the variance of counting results is decreased to 2 m times.

3.2   Circuit Architecture

Challenges. We have described the improved approach, but it do not involve the implementation methods. In practice, there are two challenges.

- For Step 1, how to perform a fine-grained adjustment to minimize the period difference between two oscillating signals.
- In Step 2, employing a PLL is common to generate multiple-frequency signal, but such an analog device is too heavy for a lightweight TRNG design. How to use the existing digital components to complete the same function of Step 2 is a challenging task, especially to dynamically adjust the frequency multiple.

Carry-Chain Primitive. In FPGAs, we employ the carry-chain primitives to address the above implementation problems. In Xilinx FPGAs, the circuit as shown in Fig. 4 represents the fast carry logic in a Slice. The carry chain consists of a series of four MUXes and four XORs that connect to the other logic in the Slice via dedicated routes to form more complex function [18]. If we set the port "CI" or "CYINIT" as the input port and the port "CO" as the output port, the signal is just propagated through the four MUXes (called single delay elements). It is found that the delay of a single delay element in a carry chain is much smaller than a Look Up Table (LUT).

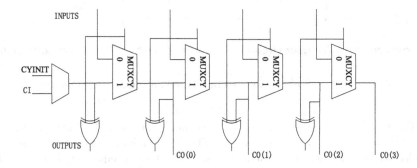

Fig. 4. Carry-chain primitives

Due to the much smaller delay and the property of cascade connection, carry chains in FPGAs have two primary uses to implement our approach:

- Finely adjusting to the period difference μ_Δ between the two oscillating signals;
- Leading out more delayed sampled signals with the smaller delay Δt of adjacent delayed sampled signals.

Architecture. By employing the carry chains, we propose the circuit architecture to implement the improved method, as shown in Fig. 5, which consists of an entropy source, a sampler circuit, a counter circuit and a bit generation circuit.

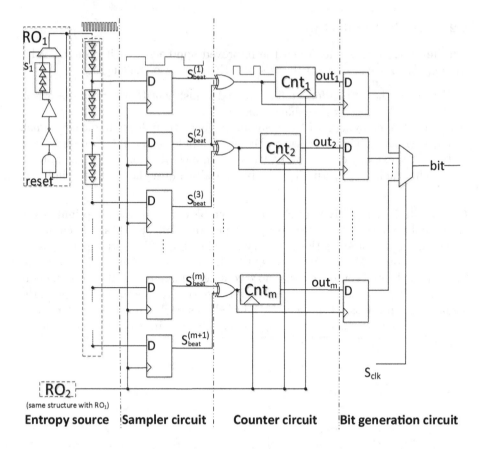

Fig. 5. Proposed circuit architecture based on the improved method

The entropy source is composed of two independent and identically configured ROs and a fast, tapped delay line. The frequency of two oscillating signals is selected to be closest but not identical. One of the oscillating signals as the sampled signal is propagated through the fast, tapped delay line to produce $m + 1$ delayed sampled signals. The sampler unit uses another oscillating signal to sample all the delayed sampled signals and produces $m + 1$ beat signals with low-frequency. XORing the adjacent beat signals produces m XORed signals and the lengths of these XORed signals lasting in high level are counted in counter circuit. The bit generation circuit uses the XORed signals produced by counter circuit to sample the LSB of the counting results, and then uses the random bit clock signal S_{clk} which should has 2m periods during $T_{beat}^{(i)}$ as the clock signal to combine multiple-channel random bits. Next, we introduce various components in details.

Entropy Source. Our ROs consist of a NAND gate, even inverters, some faster delay elements and a multiplexer. The faster delay elements and the multiplexer are used to slightly alternate propagation delay of RO to adjust the period difference μ_Δ, in which we choose the smallest period difference μ_Δ for improving the sensitivity to jitter accumulation. Then, the sampled signal in our architecture is propagated through a fast, tapped line to generate more delayed sampled signals.

Sampler Circuit. The sampler unit in our design uses the sampling signal to sample all delayed sampled signals respectively and produces m *beat* signals $S_{beat}^{(i)}$ with period $T_{beat}^{(i)}$. The signal after XORing these signals can be treated as the multiple-frequency signal, i.e., S_{clk} in the bit generation circuit.

Counter Circuit. In order to acquire the length of the delay between two adjacent *beat* signals, the adjacent *beat* signals are XORed (i.e., $S_{xor}^{(i)} = S_{beat}^{(i)} \oplus S_{beat}^{(i+1)}$) as enable terminal of respective counter and the lengths of these XORed signals lasting in high level are counted in counter unit. Only the two adjacent *beat* signals rather than all *beat* signals are XORed because it can be easier to ensure smaller impact caused by the difference of placement and routing.

An example of the counting process (without jitter) in the counter circuit is illustrated in Fig. 6, when $m = 3$. The shaded part is counting process, and the blank part denotes halting process. We can see that the counting results are all sampled at the halting process where these results are stable.

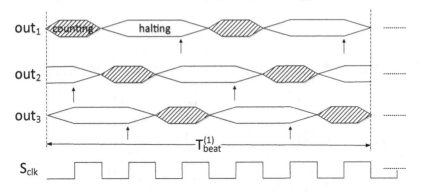

Fig. 6. Wave diagrams for the counter circuit ($m = 3$)

Bit Generation Circuit. There are m channels counting results from counter circuit ($out_1, out_2, ...out_m$). In order to acquire the random bit, the following measures are taken. At first, the bit generation unit uses all signals $S_{xor}^{(i)}$ as clock signal to sample corresponding LSB of out_i to obtain m channels random bit. The constant counting results are sampled through this way for acquiring more accurate counting values. Then, we use the random bit clock signal S_{clk} as the clock signal to combine the multiple-channel random bits.

4   Simulation and Implementation

In this section, we simulate these processes using Matlab to verify the proposed equivalent model and the improved method. Furthermore, we implement our proposed method in FPGAs and use statistical tests to test the output quality of the generator. Finally, we evaluate the speed of the implementation, and provide a comparison with related work.

4.1   Simulation Results in Matlab

We first use Matlab simulation to validate that the coherent sampling model is approximated to the traditional sampling model, where the environment is assumed to be ideal as the above mentioned. In the simulation, the period of sampled signal T_{ro_1} is set to be a normal distribution $N(5 \times 10^{-9}, 5 \times 10^{-12})$, i.e., $\mu_{T_{ro_1}} = 5000\,ps$ (200 MHz), $\sigma_{T_{ro_1}} = 5\,ps$. And the period of sampling signal T_{ro_2} is set to be $N(5.04 \times 10^{-9}, 5 \times 10^{-12})$, i.e., $\mu_{T_{ro_2}} = 5040\,ps$, $\sigma_{T_{ro_2}} = 5\,ps$. Then the period difference Δ is set to be $N(40 \times 10^{-12}, 5\sqrt{2} \times 10^{-12})$, i.e., $\mu_\Delta = 40\,ps$, $\sigma_\Delta = \sqrt{5^2 + 5^2}\,ps$. Then, we simulate the following two sampling processes to verify the correctness of the equivalent model.

- **Process 1:** Coherent sampling the sampled signal S_{ro_1} using the sampling signal S_{ro_2};
- **Process 2:** Traditional sampling the period difference Δ with the interval of $\mu_{T_{ro_1}}$.

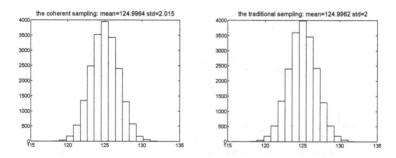

Fig. 7. Histogram of the simulated R_{coh} vs. R_{tra}

Figure 7 presents the results of counter based on the coherent sampling R_{coh} (the left), and which of the traditional sampling R_{tra} (the right). Obviously, both of the distributions are normal, and the deviation of corresponding statistics (including the expectation and variance) for these two distributions is negligible, i.e., satisfying the same distribution, which agrees with our theoretical proof mentioned above.

In order to verify the relationship predicted by the theory (Eq. (7)), we calculate the variances of counting results in term of the adjustable parameter m using Matlab numerical calculation and plot the shape of $\sigma_{R'}^2$ as a function of m with simulation data (shown in Fig. 8). The variances of counting results and the bit generation speeds for different m from 2 to 7 are listed in Table 1. The $\mu_{T_{ro_1}}$ and $\mu_{T_{ro_2}}$ are set to be 5000 ps (200 MHz) and 5040 ps respectively. The variables T_{ro_1} and T_{ro_2} are injected the same random jitter $10\sqrt{2}$ ps, i.e., $\sigma_{T_{ro_1}} = \sigma_{T_{ro_1}} \approx 14.1$ ps. We can see that the expression of fitting curve is $\sigma_{R'}^2 = 16.8355/m \approx \sigma_R^2/2\,m$, and the results indicate that the change of fitting curve is coordinated with the change of Eq. (7).

Table 1. The variances and bit generation speeds for different m.

	Basic	$m = 2$	$m = 3$	$m = 4$	$m = 5$	$m = 6$	$m = 7$
$\sigma_{R'}^2$	31.6131	8.0996	5.5265	4.1949	3.3225	2.8601	2.4413
$F_{s'}[Mbps]$	1.587	6.347	9.520	12.695	15.870	19.041	22.216

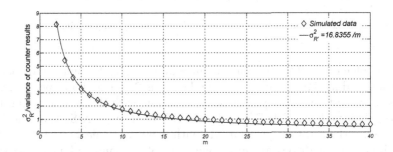

Fig. 8. The shape of $\sigma_{R'}^2$ as a function of m

4.2 Implementation Results in FPGA

We implement the circuit on Xilinx Virtex-5 FPGA. The two ROs producing oscillating signals consist of a single NAND gate, 8 inverters, 4 faster delay elements and a multiplexer, where the single NAND gate, these inverters and the multiplexer are implemented by LUTs, the faster delay elements are implemented by a stage carry chain. In order to guarantee the period difference between the two oscillating signals as small as possible, we should handle the placement and routing manually and further adjust the two multiplexers. The frequency of one RO producing sampled signal is about 146.22 MHz, The other RO producing sampling signal is about 145.88 MHz. A fast, tapped delay line is implemented by 54-stages carry chains ($54 \cdot 4 = 216$ single delay elements). We obtain $\mu_\Delta \simeq 16$ ps and $T_{beat}^{(1)} \simeq T_{beat}^{(2)} \ldots \simeq 0.34$ MHz.

An example of some key signals captured on oscilloscope is given in Fig. 9 with the case of $m = 3$. The upper signal is $S_{xor}^{(1)}$, the out_1 is counting process in high level of which. The middle signal is $S_{xor}^{(2)}$, similarly, the out_2 is counting process in high level of which. the bottom signal is the random bit clock signal S_{clk} in bit generation unit.

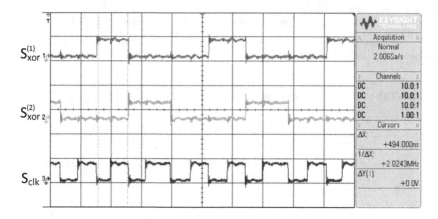

Fig. 9. Experimental $S_{xor}^{(1)}$, $S_{xor}^{(2)}$ and S_{clk} signals example with $m = 3$.

We implement a TRNG that can manually select the number of delayed sampled signal m. The parameter m can be set as 2, 3, 6 and 9 respectively. For all cases, we test the quality of generator output with different m using both the FIPS 140-2 [11] and NIST [13] statistical tests. For the NIST statistical test suite, we use the software (version 2.1) with default significance level $\alpha = 0.01$ and collect a set of 1000 consecutive sequences of 10^6 random bits for each case of m.

Table 2. Statistical tests and output bit-rate results for different m.

Throughput	Basic	$m = 2$	$m = 3$	$m = 6$	$m = 9$
	0.34 Mbps	1.36 Mbps	2.04 Mbps	4.08 Mbps	6.12 Mbps
FIPS 140-2	Pass	Pass	Pass	Pass	Pass
NIST	Pass	Pass	Pass	Pass	Fail

Table 2 shows the results of both statistical tests and output bit-rate results for different parameters m. We can see that all the cases successfully pass the FIPS tests. However, the case for $m = 9$ does not pass the NIST test. Hence, we draw the conclusion that a larger m implies a higher throughput, but also a lower quality of the random bits due to the fact that the jitter accumulation

Table 3. Results of the NIST test suite with $m = 6$ and $m = 9$.

Statistical test	$m = 6$		$m = 9$	
	P-value	Passing Rate	P-value	Passing Rate
Frequency	0.366918	990/1000	0.452173	994/1000
BlockFrequency	0.000136	983/1000	0.000000	941/1000
CumulativeSums	0.266235	990/1000	0.967382	991/1000
Runs	0.777265	991/1000	0.729870	989/1000
LongestRun	0.851383	986/1000	0.325206	9085/1000
Rank	0.858002	985/1000	0.368587	994/1000
FFT	0.861264	990/1000	0.426272	987/1000
NonOverlappingTemplate	0.329850	997/1000	0.522100	995/1000
OverlappingTemplate	0.534146	989/1000	0.969588	990/1000
Universal	0.699313	987/1000	0.189625	987/1000
ApproximateEntropy	0.000126	981/1000	0.000000	976/1000
RandomExcursions	0.739918	638/642	0.620056	612/615
RandomExcursionsVariant	0.785760	639/642	0.979761	610/615
Serial	0.380407	986/1000	0.695200	988/1000
LinearComplexity	0.363593	992/1000	0.645448	987/1000

Table 4. Comparison with related work.

Work	Platform	Resources	Throughput
This work	Virtex 5	109 Slices	4.08 Mbps
[9]	SLAAC-1 V	Not reported	0.5 Mbps
[16]	Actel	14 tiles,1 PLL	2 Mbps
[3]	Cyclone 3	> 511 LUTs	133 Mbps
	Virtex 5	> 511 LUTs	100 Mbps
[17]	Spartan 3E	Not reported	0.25 Mbps
[14]	Not reported	Not reported	2.5 Mbps
[12]	Spartan 6	67 Slices	14.3 Mbps

time is shortened. In addition, Table 3 shows the results of running the NIST suite for cases $m = 6$ and $m = 9$, respectively. As the trade-off between the security and speed, the output with the case $m = 6$ passes all of the tests, while the BlockFrequency and the ApproximateEntropy are failed for $m = 9$.

The comparison with related work is summarized in Table 4. Our design achieves higher throughput than all TRNGs based on coherent sampling [9,16]. As for other implementation, Our design achieves higher throughput than [14, 17]. However, the TRNG in [3] uses more than 511 LUTs. The generated data of TRNG in [12] are compressed using XOR postprocessing. Our entropy source are a dual ROs which consumes 109 Slices. In addition, the circuit design can adjust the period difference of two ROs and select various bit generation speeds to serve different cryptographic applications.

5 Conclusion and Future Work

Under this premise of sufficient entropy, the throughput is an indispensable factor for TRNG designs, such as for the application of session key generation in high-speed communication systems. In this paper, we design and implement a coherent sampling-based TRNG which can extract entropy as much as possible to enhance the bit generation speed. We first provide a parameter adjustment method to maximize the generated entropy rate, and this method is based on our proposed stochastic model. According to the method, we design a TRNG architecture and implement it in FPGAs. In the experiment, the improved generation speed is up to 4 Mbps, and the output sequences pass NIST SP 800-22 statistical tests successfully without postprocessing. Compared to the basic coherent sampling, the bit generation rate is improved to 12 times. In future work, we will further design the embedded module for the health test or online test of the TRNG.

Acknowledgments. This work was partially supported by National Basic Research Program of China (973 Program No. 2013CB338001), Strategy Pilot Project of Chinese Academy of Sciences (No. XDA06010702) and National Natural Science Foundation of China (No. 61602476, No. 61402470).

References

1. Baudet, M., Lubicz, D., Micolod, J., Tassiaux, A.: On the security of oscillator-based random number generators. J. Cryptology **24**(2), 398–425 (2011)
2. Bernard, F., Fischer, V., Valtchanov, B.: Mathematical model of physical RNGs based on coherent sampling. Tatra Mountains Math. Publ. **45**(1), 1–14 (2010)
3. Cherkaoui, A., Fischer, V., Fesquet, L., Aubert, A.: A very high speed true random number generator with entropy assessment. In: Bertoni, G., Coron, J.-S. (eds.) CHES 2013. LNCS, vol. 8086, pp. 179–196. Springer, Heidelberg (2013). doi:10.1007/978-3-642-40349-1_11
4. Fischer, V., Drutarovský, M.: True random number generator embedded in reconfigurable hardware. In: Kaliski, B.S., Koç, K., Paar, C. (eds.) CHES 2002. LNCS, vol. 2523, pp. 415–430. Springer, Heidelberg (2003). doi:10.1007/3-540-36400-5_30
5. Haddad, P., Teglia, Y., Bernard, F., Fischer, V.: On the assumption of mutual independence of jitter realizations in P-TRNG stochastic models. In: Design, Automation & Test in Europe Conference & Exhibition, DATE 2014, Dresden, Germany, 24–28 March 2014, pp. 1–6 (2014)
6. ISO/IEC JTC 1/SC 27, Berlin, Germany: ISO/IEC 18031: Information technology - Security techniques - Random bit generation (2011)
7. Killmann, W., Schindler, W.: AIS 31: Functionality Classes and Evaluation Methodology for True (Physical) Random Number Generators. Version 3.1. T-Systems GEI GmbH and Bundesamt fr Sicherheit in der Informationstechnik (BSI), Bonn, Germany (2001)

8. Killmann, W., Schindler, W.: A design for a physical RNG with robust entropy estimators. In: Oswald, E., Rohatgi, P. (eds.) CHES 2008. LNCS, vol. 5154, pp. 146–163. Springer, Heidelberg (2008). doi:10.1007/978-3-540-85053-3_10

9. Kohlbrenner, P., Gaj, K.: An embedded true random number generator for FPGAs. In: Proceedings of the ACM/SIGDA 12th International Symposium on Field Programmable Gate Arrays, FPGA 2004, Monterey, California, USA, 22–24 February 2004, pp. 71–78 (2004)

10. Ma, Y., Lin, J., Chen, T., Xu, C., Liu, Z., Jing, J.: Entropy evaluation for oscillator-based true random number generators. In: Batina, L., Robshaw, M. (eds.) CHES 2014. LNCS, vol. 8731, pp. 544–561. Springer, Heidelberg (2014). doi:10.1007/978-3-662-44709-3_30

11. PUB, N.F.: 140-2: Security Requirements for Cryptographic Modules, Washington, DC, USA, May 2001

12. Rozic, V., Yang, B., Dehaene, W., Verbauwhede, I.: Highly efficient entropy extraction for true random number generators on FPGAs. In: Proceedings of the 52nd Annual Design Automation Conference, San Francisco, CA, USA, 7–11 June 2015, pp. 116: 1–116: 6 (2015)

13. Rukhin, A., Soto, J., Nechvatal, J., Smid, M., Barker, E., Leigh, S., Levenson, M., Vangel, M., Banks, D., Heckert, A., et al.: A Statistical Test Suite for the Validation of Random Number Generators and Pseudo Random Number Generators for Cryptographic Applications, pp. 800–822. NIST special publication, USA (2001)

14. Sunar, B., Martin, W.J., Stinson, D.R.: A provably secure true random number generator with built-in tolerance to active attacks. IEEE Trans. Comput. **56**(1), 109–119 (2007)

15. Valtchanov, B., Fischer, V., Aubert, A.: A coherent sampling-based method for estimating the jitter used as entropy source for true random number generators. In: SAMPTA 2009, pp. Special-session (2009)

16. Valtchanov, B., Fischer, V., Aubert, A.: Enhanced TRNG based on the coherent sampling. In: International Conference on Signals, Circuits and Systems (SCS) (2009)

17. Varchola, M., Drutarovsky, M.: New high entropy element for FPGA based true random number generators. In: Mangard, S., Standaert, F.-X. (eds.) CHES 2010. LNCS, vol. 6225, pp. 351–365. Springer, Heidelberg (2010). doi:10.1007/978-3-642-15031-9_24

18. Xilinx: Virtex-5 Libraries Guide for HDL Designs (2012). http://www.xilinx.com/support/documentation/sw_manuals/xilinx14_1/virtex5_hdl.pdf

A Very Compact Masked S-Box
for High-Performance Implementation of SM4
Based on Composite Field

Hailiang Fu[1], Guoqiang Bai[1,2(✉)], and Xingjun Wu[1]

[1] Institute of Microelectronics, Tsinghua University, Beijing, China
fhl14@mails.tsinghua.edu.cn, baigq@mail.tsinghua.edu.cn
[2] Tsinghua National Laboratory for Information Science and Technology,
Beijing, China

Abstract. Implementations of the SM4 algorithm, including different hardware applications with limited resources, are vulnerable to Side-Channel Attacks. This paper presents a countermeasure against such attacks by adding a random "mask" to the input plaintext and protect all variables through the whole encryption process. As is known to all, the unique nonlinear step in each round of SM4 algorithm is the "S-Box" and the previous works using lookup-table method to implement the S-Box always incur large area and high power. Here we give the compact design of masked S-Box using the normal basis in the composite field (consisting of a Galois inversion and several affine transformations). Then we compute the different masks diffused to all the steps in the SM4 algorithm process. The proposed design results in ultra-low cost of hardware and capability to resist first-order differential power analysis (DPA), which is suitable for the resource constrained devices. The synthesis result of masked S-Box shows that the area under the SMIC 0.13 μm is only about 978-gates, 46.8% fewer than the other works. Further, we apply the pipeline technique to our proposed "masked S-Box", thereby to the whole masked SM4 algorithm. The results of FPGA implementation present that our works have achieved an ultra-high speed with frequency nearly 551 MHz and the throughput over 70 Gbps.

Keywords: SM4 · S-Box · Mask · Pipeline · Composite field

1 Introduction

With the rapid development of the computer science and internet technology in the modern world, the information and data security have become more and more important. Thus, preventing the significant information from attacking by any other unauthorized parts is a challenging and essential task. There is no doubt that the security of hardware is the basis for data transmission, especially in the Wireless Local Area Network (WLAN). For this reason, plenty of methods about hardware cryptography (e.g. hiding, masking, etc.) have been come up with to

© ICST Institute for Computer Sciences, Social Informatics and Telecommunications Engineering 2017
R. Deng et al. (Eds.): SecureComm 2016, LNICST 198, pp. 710–721, 2017.
DOI: 10.1007/978-3-319-59608-2_39

protect the sensitive data and applied in different domains, such as embedded systems, wireless handsets and smart cards. In January 2006, the Office of State Commercial Cipher Administration of China (OSCCA) announced a specific encryption standard named SM4 block cipher, the purpose of which is to form the Wireless LAN Authentication and Privacy Infrastructure (WAPI) standard for our country [1]. Since then, there have been a large variety of researches focusing on improving the performance and security of SM4. On the other hand, some researchers try to seek the weakness of SM4 algorithm and do attacks on the specific hardware implementations. For example, smart cards may be vulnerable to first order side-channel attacks such as differential power analysis, which takes advantages of the leakage of information to do the physical analysis such as power consumption, electromagnetic radiation and so on, then to deduce the real secret key of the algorithm.

Due to the potential attacks above, this paper proposes a countermeasure against the first order side-channel attacks, applying the masking strategy to the nonlinear S-Box as well as the data path in the SM4 algorithm based on the composite field introduced by the previous work [2]. Compared to the other method to achieve the masking, this protection saves 46.8% area for the whole circuit. However, it incurs some other parts which slow down the encryption process. Thus we make use of the pipeline technique to accelerate the calculation, resulting in an ultra-high clock frequency up to 551 MHz and throughput over 70 Gbps for the masked SM4 algorithm.

The organization of this paper is as follows. In Sect. 2, we describe the SM4 block cipher and the algebraic description of S-Box very briefly. Section 3 shows the detailed masking strategy for S-Box, including masking the inversion and the affine transformation, and the reutilization of the masks. Section 4 presents the implementation of the SM4 algorithm using the masked S-Box. Also, the architecture of pipelined masked SM4 is designed and implemented in this part. Then we state the low-cost results of area using masking strategy and the high speed in pipeline scheme for SM4 in Sect. 5. At last, Sect. 6 concludes the paper.

2 Algebraic Description for S-Box

SM4 block cipher is a 32-round iterative algorithm with 128-bit input plaintext, secret key and output ciphertext. The input plaintext is first divided into four words and each word consists of 32 bits. Before encryption, the key for each round (rk_i) will be generated through the key expansion arithmetic, which is nearly identical with the encryption process, and the only difference between them is the linear part—round shifting left. With the rk_i, a new word, i.e. X_{i+4} will be produced in the i-th round of the encryption process by doing XOR, nonlinear substitution and round shifting left operations $(X_{i+4} = X_i \oplus T(X_{i+1} \oplus X_{i+2} \oplus X_{i+3} \oplus rk_i)(i = 0, ..., 31))$, shown in Fig. 1. Finally, the order of the last four words will be reversed to form the output ciphertext. The XOR and round shifting left operations are linear with respect to the data block, so it provides "diffusion"; While the S-Box is the only nonlinear step that provides "confusion".

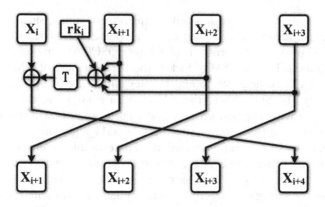

Fig. 1. SM4 round arithmetic

The S-Box can be implemented using the lookup tables, which occupies the majority of the cost in devices. In 2007, Liu et al. [3] gave the algebraic structure for SM4 algorithm, comprising two substeps: (i) regarding the byte as an element in the Galois Field $GF(2^8)$, get its inversion in this field (Note that the zero byte has no inversion, so it keeps unchanged); (ii) regarding the result of the inversion as a vector of bits in $GF(2^8)$, then multiply it by a given bit matrix and add a constant row vector, that is the procedure of an affine transformation. The inversion and affine transformation are shown below in Eq. (1):

$$S(\mathbf{X}) = I(\mathbf{X} \cdot A + \mathbf{C}) \cdot A + \mathbf{C}, \qquad (1)$$

where the input of S-Box (S) is a 8-bit row vector $\mathbf{X} = \mathbf{X}_{7-0}$, and the cyclic matrix A in the algebraic expression is

$$A = \begin{pmatrix} 1\,1\,1\,0\,0\,1\,0\,1 \\ 1\,1\,1\,1\,0\,0\,1\,0 \\ 0\,1\,1\,1\,1\,0\,0\,1 \\ 1\,0\,1\,1\,1\,1\,0\,0 \\ 0\,1\,0\,1\,1\,1\,1\,0 \\ 0\,0\,1\,0\,1\,1\,1\,1 \\ 1\,0\,0\,1\,0\,1\,1\,1 \\ 1\,1\,0\,0\,1\,0\,1\,1 \end{pmatrix},$$

and the row vector C is

$$\mathbf{C} = \mathbf{C}_{7-0} = [1,1,0,1,0,0,1,1].$$

For SM4 in the specific Galois Field, a byte represents a polynomial where the bits are coefficients of corresponding powers of x, and multiplication is modulo the irreducible primitive polynomial:

$$f(x) = x^8 + x^7 + x^6 + x^5 + x^4 + x^2 + 1.$$

We could consider the root of this polynomial as θ, then $f(\theta) = 0$ in $GF(2^8)$. Thus the bits of a byte could be related to the coefficients of powers of θ, e.g., $3 = \theta, 4 = \theta + 1, 9 = \theta^2$, etc. Therefore the bits make up a vector with respect to what is known as polynomial basis. However, we can change the representation of the polynomial basis in $GF(2^8)$ to a different one, named normal basis in composite field [4]. Instead of a vector of dimension 8 in $GF(2)$, we regard a byte as a vector of dimension 2 in $GF(2^4)$, where each 4-bit element is in turn a vector of dimension 2 in $GF(2^2)$, and each 2-bit element is a vector of dimension 2 in $GF(2)$. For each of these subfields, it has been introduced in details, referring to [5].

3   Masking Strategy

To convert the standard polynomial representation to the composite field representation, we need to choose the appropriate basis and build an isomorphic matrix. For more detailed information, please refer to [4]. In this paper, we try to add an additive mask to all the steps during the inversion, which will described below.

3.1   Inversion Without Masking

Now we apply the following convention: upper-case bold symbols stand for elements in the main field (e.g. $\mathbf{A} \in GF(2^8)$); upper-case italic symbols represent elements in the subfield (e.g. $A \in GF(2^4)$); lower-case bold symbols are for the sub-subfield (e.g. $\mathbf{a} \in GF(2^2)$); and lower-case italic symbols are used for single bits (e.g. $a \in GF(2)$).

To begin with, we don't concern about the mask. So the inversion in $GF(2^8)/GF(2^4)$ (this expresses the representation of $GF(2^8)$ as vectors in $GF(2^4)$ using a normal basis $[\mathbf{Y}^{16}, \mathbf{Y}]$), where $\mathbf{Y}^{16}$ and $\mathbf{Y}$ are the roots of $\mathbf{Y}^2 + \mathbf{Y} + N$ and $N \in GF(2^4)$ is the norm ($N = Y^{16} \cdot Y$), is given as [4]:

$$\mathbf{A} = A_h \mathbf{Y}^{16} + A_l \mathbf{Y}(\text{known}), \tag{2}$$

$$B = N \otimes (A_h \oplus A_l)^2 \oplus A_h \otimes A_l, \tag{3}$$

$$\mathbf{A}^{-1} = (A_l \otimes B^{-1})\mathbf{Y}^{16} + (A_h \otimes B^{-1})\mathbf{Y}(\text{result}). \tag{4}$$

Here we make a agreement on the meaning of the operators above: $\oplus$ and $\otimes$ denote addition and multiplication in Galois Field, respectively. The expression $A_h \mathbf{Y}^{16} + A_l \mathbf{Y}$ is an algebraic method using the normal basis to denote the vector $[A_h, A_l]$ (i.e. $[A_h, A_l] = [\mathbf{A}_{7-4}, \mathbf{A}_{3-0}]$). To achieve the inversion in $GF(2^8)$, it requires the inversion, addition, multiplication and the combined square-scaling operation ($N \otimes A^2$) in the subfield $GF(2^4)$. In the same way, the inversion in $GF(2^4)/GF(2^2)$ which uses a normal basis $[X^4, X]$, where the X^4 and X are the roots of $X^2 + X + \mathbf{n}$ (and $\mathbf{n} \in GF(2^2)$ is the norm ($\mathbf{n} = X^4 \cdot X$)), is given as:

$$B = \mathbf{b}_h X^4 + \mathbf{b}_l X (\texttt{known}), \tag{5}$$

$$\mathbf{c} = \mathbf{n} \otimes (\mathbf{b}_h \oplus \mathbf{b}_l)^2 \oplus \mathbf{b}_h \otimes \mathbf{b}_l, \tag{6}$$

$$B^{-1} = (\mathbf{b}_l \otimes \mathbf{c}^{-1}) X^4 + (\mathbf{b}_h \otimes \mathbf{c}^{-1}) X (\texttt{result}). \tag{7}$$

However, finding the inversion in the sub-subfield $GF(2^2)$, using the normal basis $[\mathbf{w}^2, \mathbf{w}]$, where $\mathbf{w}^2$ and $\mathbf{w}$ are the roots of $\mathbf{w}^2 + \mathbf{w} + 1$ (and here we define the norm as 1), is very easy. It is equivalent to the squaring operation, shown as a bit swap:

$$\mathbf{c} = c_h \mathbf{w}^2 + c_l \mathbf{w} (\texttt{known}), \tag{8}$$

$$\mathbf{c}^{-1} = c_l \mathbf{w}^2 + c_h \mathbf{w} (\texttt{result}). \tag{9}$$

All the steps above are used to obtain the inversion in $GF(2^8)$ without masking. In the following, we will detail the steps about how to mask the inversion.

3.2 Masking the Inversion

As is mentioned above, additive mask becomes our preference due to its resistance to zero-value attacks. It has been analyzed in [2] that the statistical distribution of masks is uniform over the field by adding a random mask. Therefore the operands appear randomly, uncorrelated to either the input plaintext or the secret key. Thus the data leaked from the side channel is independent of the chosen input plaintext, might regarded as noise, and the key in this way will be protected against first-order differential power attacks. To ensure the correct process from the input mask to the output mask, we apply the masking strategy as follows.

In $GF(2^8)$, we express the masked byte with a tilde (i.e. $\tilde{\mathbf{A}}$), and similarly for the other masked variables. Now we use the mask $(\mathbf{M})$ to mask the input plaintext.

$$\mathbf{M} = M_h \mathbf{Y}^{16} + M_l \mathbf{Y}; \tag{10}$$

$$\tilde{\mathbf{A}} = \mathbf{A} \oplus \mathbf{M} = \tilde{\mathbf{A}}_h \mathbf{Y}^{16} + \tilde{\mathbf{A}}_l \mathbf{Y} \tag{11}$$

Then let

$$\tilde{B} = N \otimes (\tilde{\mathbf{A}}_h \oplus \tilde{\mathbf{A}}_l)^2 \oplus \tilde{\mathbf{A}}_h \otimes \tilde{\mathbf{A}}_l \oplus \tilde{\mathbf{A}}_h \otimes M_l \oplus \tilde{\mathbf{A}}_l \otimes M_h \oplus M_h \otimes M_l, \tag{12}$$

$$M_2 = N \otimes (M_h \oplus M_l)^2, \tag{13}$$

Here the result $\tilde{B}$ is B above in Eq. (3) masked by M_2 (i.e. $\tilde{B} = B \oplus M_2$). Note that the products in Eq. (12) must be added in turn to make all the intermediate results uniformly distributed and masked, so that the information about the original data will not be leaked out.

For the inversion in $GF(2^4)$, say $\tilde{B} = \tilde{\mathbf{b}}_h X^4 + \tilde{\mathbf{b}}_l X$ and $M_2 = \mathbf{m}_h X^4 + \mathbf{m}_l X$, then let

$$\tilde{\mathbf{c}} = \mathbf{n} \otimes (\tilde{\mathbf{b}}_h \oplus \tilde{\mathbf{b}}_l)^2 \oplus \tilde{\mathbf{b}}_h \otimes \tilde{\mathbf{b}}_l \oplus \tilde{\mathbf{b}}_h \otimes \mathbf{m}_l \oplus \tilde{\mathbf{b}}_l \otimes \mathbf{m}_h \oplus \mathbf{m}_h \otimes \mathbf{m}_l, \tag{14}$$

$$\mathbf{p} = \mathbf{n} \otimes (\mathbf{m}_h \oplus \mathbf{m}_l)^2, \tag{15}$$

and $\tilde{c}$ is c above in Eq. (6), masked by p (say $p = p_h w^2 + p_l w$, and let $q = p^2 = n^2 \otimes (m_h \oplus m_l) = p_l w^2 + p_h w$). Above we employ the convention of the inversion as squaring in the sub-subfield $GF(2^2)$, so

$$\tilde{c}^{-1} = (c \oplus p)^{-1} = (c \oplus p)^2 = c^2 \oplus p^2 = c^{-1} \oplus q, \tag{16}$$

Therefore $\tilde{c}^{-1}$ (say $\tilde{c}^{-1} = \tilde{c}_l W^2 + \tilde{c}_h W$) is c^{-1} above in Eq. (9) masked by another mask q.

Now we introduce a new 4-bit mask $S = s_h X^4 + s_l X$, and let

$$\begin{aligned}
\tilde{b}_h^{-1} &= s_h \oplus b_h^{-1} = s_h \oplus (b_l \otimes c^{-1}), \\
&= s_h \oplus [(\tilde{b}_l \oplus m_l) \otimes (\tilde{c}^{-1} \oplus q)], \\
&= s_h \oplus \tilde{b}_l \otimes \tilde{c}^{-1} \oplus \tilde{b}_l \otimes q \oplus m_l \otimes \tilde{c}^{-1} \oplus m_l \otimes q, \tag{17} \\
\tilde{b}_l^{-1} &= s_l \oplus b_l^{-1} = s_l \oplus (b_h \otimes c^{-1}) \\
&= s_l \oplus [(\tilde{b}_h \oplus m_h) \otimes (\tilde{c}^{-1} \oplus q)] \\
&= s_l \oplus \tilde{b}_h \otimes \tilde{c}^{-1} \oplus \tilde{b}_h \otimes q \oplus m_h \otimes \tilde{c}^{-1} \oplus m_h \otimes q, \tag{18}
\end{aligned}$$

thus the result $\tilde{B}^{-1} = \tilde{b}_h^{-1} X^4 + \tilde{b}_l^{-1} X$ is B^{-1} above in Eq. (7) masked by S.

Similarly, apply the output 8-bit mask $T = T_h Y^{16} + T_l Y$ to the output A^{-1}, and let:

$$\tilde{A}_h^{-1} = T_h \oplus \tilde{A}_l \otimes \tilde{B}^{-1} \oplus \tilde{A}_l \otimes S \oplus M_l \otimes \tilde{B}^{-1} \oplus M_l \otimes S, \tag{19}$$

$$\tilde{A}_l^{-1} = T_l \oplus \tilde{A}_h \otimes \tilde{B}^{-1} \oplus \tilde{A}_h \otimes S \oplus M_h \otimes \tilde{B}^{-1} \oplus M_h \otimes S \tag{20}$$

So the result $\tilde{A}^{-1} = \tilde{A}_h^{-1} Y^{16} + \tilde{A}_l^{-1} Y$ is the original inversion A^{-1} above in Eq. (4) masked by the output mask T:

$$\tilde{A}^{-1} = A^{-1} \oplus T. \tag{21}$$

3.3 Reutilization of Masks

Canright and Batina [2] shows the re-using of the masks to make the implementation more vulnerable to the higher-order differential side channel attacks and save the cost of the same operations. Firstly, by replacing the mask q by m_l or m_h, we can modify the expression as follows:

$$\tilde{c}^{-1} = (\tilde{c}_l w^2 + \tilde{c}_h w) \oplus m_h \oplus q \quad (\text{masked by } m_h), \tag{22}$$

$$\tilde{b}_h^{-1} = m_{1h} \oplus \tilde{b}_l \otimes \tilde{c}^{-1} \oplus \underline{\tilde{b}_l \otimes m_h} \oplus m_l \otimes \tilde{c}^{-1} \oplus \underline{m_l \otimes m_h}, \tag{23}$$

$$\tilde{c}_2^{-1} = \tilde{c}^{-1} \oplus (m_l \oplus m_h) \quad (\text{masked by } m_l), \tag{24}$$

$$\tilde{b}_l^{-1} = m_{1l} \oplus \tilde{b}_h \otimes \tilde{c}_2^{-1} \oplus \underline{\tilde{b}_h \otimes m_l} \oplus m_h \otimes \tilde{c}_2^{-1} \oplus \underline{m_h \otimes m_l}, \tag{25}$$

where the underlined products had already been calculated in Eq. (14), so here we can re-use these results. Now the result $\tilde{B}^{-1} = \tilde{b}_h^{-1} X^4 + \tilde{b}_l^{-1} X$ is B^{-1} above, but here masked by $M_h = \mathbf{m}_{1h}X^4 + \mathbf{m}_{1l}X$, which is the upper nibble of the input mask $\mathbf{M}$. In the same way, we get the updated masked $\mathbf{A}^{-1}$ in the following:

$$\tilde{A}_h^{-1} = T_h \oplus \tilde{A}_l \otimes \tilde{B}^{-1} \oplus \underline{\tilde{A}_l \otimes M_h} \oplus M_l \otimes \tilde{B}^{-1} \oplus \underline{M_l \otimes M_h}, \tag{26}$$

$$\tilde{B}_2^{-1} = \tilde{B}^{-1} \oplus M_l \oplus M_h \quad (\text{masked by } M_l), \tag{27}$$

$$\tilde{A}_l^{-1} = T_l \oplus \tilde{A}_h \otimes \tilde{B}_2^{-1} \oplus \underline{\tilde{A}_h \otimes M_l} \oplus M_h \otimes \tilde{B}_2^{-1} \oplus \underline{M_h \otimes M_l}, \tag{28}$$

the underlined products are re-used and the output $\tilde{\mathbf{A}}^{-1}$ is still $\mathbf{A}^{-1}$ above masked by output mask $\mathbf{T}$ (which might be same with the input mask $\mathbf{M}$ or not):

$$\tilde{\mathbf{A}}^{-1} = \mathbf{A}^{-1} \oplus \mathbf{T}. \tag{29}$$

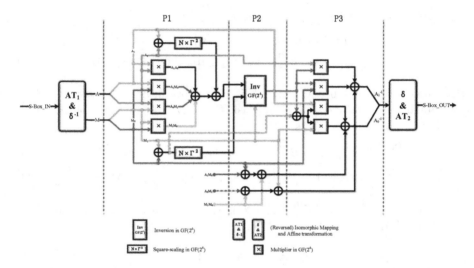

Fig. 2. Architecture of masked S-Box: (a) Single cycle (without the red dash line); (b) Pipeline (the red dash line is the pipeline registers) (Color figure online)

3.4   Mask Transformation

Equation (1) shows the algebraic expression of unmasked S-Box. Here we make some changes to the mathematical relationship and deduce the correct mask transformation from input to output, where the function I stands for inversion process in $GF(2^8)$ and the function Inv represents inversion process in the "tower field", i.e. $GF(((2^2)^2)^2)$. Note the matrix δ is the isomorphic mapping from the normal basis in composite field to the standard polynomial basis (and δ^{-1} is the reversed mapping).

$$S(\mathbf{X} + \mathbf{M}) = I[(\mathbf{X} + \mathbf{M}) \cdot A + \mathbf{C}] \cdot A + \mathbf{C} \tag{30}$$
$$= A^T \cdot I[A^T \cdot (\mathbf{X} + \mathbf{M}) + \mathbf{C}^T] + \mathbf{C}^T$$
$$= A^T \cdot I[(A^T\mathbf{X} + C^T) + A^T\mathbf{M}] + \mathbf{C}^T$$
$$= A^T\delta \cdot Inv[\delta^{-1}(A^T\mathbf{X} + \mathbf{C}^T) + \delta^{-1}A^T\mathbf{M}] + \mathbf{C}^T \tag{31}$$

where A^T is the transposition of A (also similar with $\mathbf{C}^T$). Here we can learn from Eq. (29) that $Inv(\hat{\mathbf{A}} + \hat{\mathbf{M}}) = Inv(\hat{\mathbf{A}}) + \hat{\mathbf{M}}$ only if the output mask is equal to the input mask: $\mathbf{S} = \mathbf{M}$ (this is the conclusion in $GF(((2^2)^2)^2)$. With this assumption, Eq. (31) in $GF(2^8)$ could be modified as follows:

$$S(\mathbf{X} + \mathbf{M}) = (31)$$
$$= A^T \cdot I(A^T\mathbf{X} + \mathbf{C}^T) + \mathbf{C}^T + A^TA^T\mathbf{M}$$
$$= S(\mathbf{X}) + A^TA^T\mathbf{M} \tag{32}$$

If the input mask of S-Box is $\mathbf{M}$, the Eq. (32) shows the correct output mask of S-Box in $GF(2^8)$, i.e. $A^TA^T\mathbf{M}$, which is the "confusion" of the mask. Until now, we have achieved the masking process using the normal basis in composite field. Figure 2 gives the complete hardware implementation of the masked S-Box, depending on all the mathematical computing above.

4   Implementation of Masked SM4

In this section, we apply our "masked S-Box" to the encryption process and illustrate the architecture of the SM4 round arithmetic in two different directions: (i) use the iterative architecture and make all the steps of SM4 secure, the purpose of which is to decrease the cost of the area; (ii) insert some registers inside the S-Box appropriately to increase the clock frequency and improve the throughput, which will be very useful in high-speed applications.

4.1   Iterative Architecture of Masked SM4

In Fig. 3. The rk_i is well prepared in RAM or it can be produced by the iterative architecture presented in [4] before each round. Here the latter is our preference and we just concentrate on the masked encryption. For instance, we choose a 32-bit mask $\mathbf{M}$ for our design. Before the first round of encryption, the mask is produced and extended to 128 bits (e.g. $\{4\{\mathbf{M}\}\}$), which is XORed to the input 128-bit plaintext to obtain the masked input $\underline{\mathbf{X}} = (\underline{X}_0, \underline{X}_1, \underline{X}_2, \underline{X}_3)$ for the first round. It is obvious that all the variables before the function "Masked S-Box" are masked by $\mathbf{M}$. As is shown above, the outputs of the "Masked S-Box" are masked by $A^TA^T\mathbf{M}$. So we do the same round shifting left to $A^TA^T\mathbf{M}$, then add the outputs together and XOR the $\underline{X}_0$ simultaneously. Thus the mask $A^TA^T\mathbf{M}$ is eliminated and the output $\underline{X}_4$ has been already masked by $\mathbf{M}$, which is diffused from $\underline{X}_0$. In this way, we redo the arithmetic for 32 rounds, then reverse the last four words and finally XOR the output with $\{4\{\mathbf{M}\}\}$, we can certainly get the right result of ciphertext.

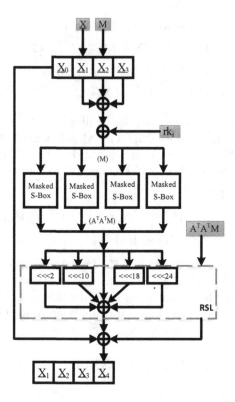

Fig. 3. Architecture of masked SM4 round arithmetic using the single cycle "Masked S-Box" (the underlined elements in this picture are masked variables and (·) in the architecture shows the transient mask at that step. The red dash rectangle is the round shifting left function) (Coloe figure online)

4.2   Pipelined Architecture of Masked SM4

For the pipeline scheme, we use the synchronous technique to adjust the structure of the round arithmetic of SM4. However, one key problem is to balance the pipeline stages. So we divide the round arithmetic into several periods to achieve one round encryption in order to ensure the approximate executing time for each part, which means to decrease the time of the critical-path. The registers being inserted into the S-Box are shown as red dash line in Fig. 2. Although the pipelined S-Box is well designed, the SM4 round arithmetic needs to be seriously considered according to the linear parts execution. Here we present the optimized architecture for pipelined masked SM4, given as Fig. 4. To keep the variables of each period secure, we add the random mask to all the input elements and transfer them to their corresponding buffers in each pipeline stage (shown as the yellow registers in Fig. 4). In this way, all the elements in the round encryption are securely masked and can be parallel implemented.

Figure 4 is just one round encryption for the SM4 algorithm, which contains five levels for the pipeline. As we expect, we implement 32 same structures and finally do the reversion function. The right results are realized and it will be shown in next section.

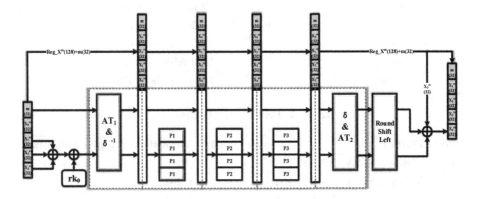

Fig. 4. Pipelined round arithmetic of masked SM4 (the red dash rectangle is pipelined masked S-Box described above in Fig. 2, similarly with the modules P1, P2 and P3) (Color figure online)

5 Results

The proposed SM4 algorithm implemented in two different ways based on "Masked S-Box" in composite field has been realized by Verilog HDL and simulated in Modelsim software. All the input plaintexts have achieved correct output ciphertexts.

Besides, the area reports of the masked S-Box under the SMIC $0.13\,\mu m$ in the Synopsys Design Compiler indicate that the equivalent amount of gates is 978, at least 46.8% fewer than 1,840 in [6] (where the area has been divided by 9.79, which is the area of one NAND2X1 cell under the SMIC $0.18\,\mu m$). We firmly believe that our compact masked S-Box has occupied the lowest area and it certainly contributes to the low-cost iterative masked SM4 algorithm very much.

In addition, comparing to the other designs, we implement it in different FPGA boards and show the results in Table 1. Because of the large cost for masking, our design has reached a very suitable and satisfying resource usage and it is still much lower than some other works without anti-attack methods (Table 2).

Furthermore, by employing the pipelined masked S-Box to the SM4 algorithm, the pipeline SM4 round arithmetic shown in Fig. 4 achieve the ultra-high clock frequency up to $551\,MHz$ under Xilinx FPGAs, resulting in the ultra-high throughput over $70\,Gbps$. To our knowledge, this is the highest speed and throughput to date.

Table 1. Resources comparison

Work	FPGA devices	Area	Anti-attack
[4]	Cyclone-II EP2C35F672C6	1657 LEs	NO
[7]		3406 LEs	NO
Ours		**2255** LEs	**YES**
[4]	Stratix-II EP2S15F484C3	535 ALMs	NO
[8]		1150 ALMs	NO
[9]		1552 ALMs	NO
Ours		**1321** ALMs	**YES**

Table 2. Performance comparison

Work	Platform	Frequency (MHz)	Throughput (Gbps)	Anti-attack
[10]	Virtex-6 XC6VLX240T	253	0.253	NO
	Virtex-5 XC5VLX110T	203	0.203	
	Virtex-4 XC4VLX100	211	0.211	
Ours	Virtex-6 XC6VLX240T	**551**	**70.5**	**YES**
	Virtex-5 XC5VLX110T	**462**	**59.1**	
	Virtex-4 XC4VLX100	**368**	**47.1**	

6   Conclusion

In this paper, the process to design a very compact "Masked S-Box" has been described clearly using normal basis in composite field at first. Second, we analyze the "diffusion" and "confusion" of the mask through the whole SM4 algorithm, and make sure every variable during encryption has been securely masked. Third, we implement the masked S-Box in two architecture: iteration and pipeline. Then we simulate all the designs and get the correctly inspiring results. The synthesis results in different devices have been compared with other works. As far as we know, our proposed work has reached the lowest area of masked S-Box, which leads to the lowest cost for masked SM4 implementation. What's more, the proposed pipelined S-Box has been implemented to construct a pipelined masked SM4 architecture, which achieves the highest speed to date. We believe this work has developed a good countermeasure to the side-channel attacks and will be widely used in resource constrained devices and speed demanded area in the future.

Acknowledgment. This work was supported by the National Natural Science Foundation of China (Grants 61472208), and by the National Key Basic Research Program of China (Grant 2013CB338004).

References

1. Office of State Commercial Cipher Administration of China. Block Cipher for WLAN products-SMS4 (2006). http://www.oscca.gov.cn/UpFile/200621016423197990.pdf
2. Canright, D., Batina, L.: A Very Compact Perfectly Masked S-Box for AES. Springer, Berlin (2008)
3. Liu, F., Ji, W., Hu, L., Ding, J., Lv, S., Pyshkin, A., Weinmann, R.-P.: Analysis of the SMS4 block cipher. In: Pieprzyk, J., Ghodosi, H., Dawson, E. (eds.) ACISP 2007. LNCS, vol. 4586, pp. 158–170. Springer, Heidelberg (2007). doi:10.1007/978-3-540-73458-1_13
4. Fu, H., Bai, G., Wu, X.: Low-cost hardware implementation of SM4 based on composite field. In: IEEE Information Technology, Networking, Electronic and Automation Control Conference, pp. 260–264. IEEE (2016)
5. Canright, D.: A very compact Rijndael S-box (2004)
6. Niu, Y., Jiang, A.: The low power design of SM4 cipher with resistance to differential power analysis. In: 2015 16th International Symposium on Quality Electronic Design (ISQED) (2015)
7. Yuan-Yang, Z.: Area-efficient IP core design of block cipher SMS4. Electr. Technol. Appl. **23**, 127–129 (2007)
8. Husen, W., Shuguo, L.: High performance FPGA implementation for SMS4. In: Wu, Y. (ed.) ICHCC 2011. CCIS, vol. 163, pp. 469–475. Springer, Heidelberg (2011). doi:10.1007/978-3-642-25002-6_66
9. Gao, X., Lu, E., Xian, L., Chen, H.: FPGA implementation of the SMS4 block cipher in the Chinese WAPI standard. In: International Conference on Embedded Software and Systems Symposia, ICESS Symposia 2008, pp. 104–106. IEEE (2008)
10. Shang, M., Zhang, Q., Liu, Z., Xiang, J.: An ultra-compact hardware implementation of SMS4. In: 2014 IIAI 3rd International Conference on Advanced Applied Informatics (IIAIAAI), pp. 86–90 (2014)

Security Analysis of Vendor Customized Code in Firmware of Embedded Device

Muqing Liu[⊠], Yuanyuan Zhang, Juanru Li, Junliang Shu,
and Dawu Gu

Lab of Cryptology and Computer Security,
Shanghai Jiao Tong University, Shanghai, China
liumuqing@sjtu.edu.cn

Abstract. Despite the increased concerning about embedded system security, the security assessment of commodity embedded devices is far from being adequate. The lack of assessment is mainly due to the tedious, time-consuming, and the very ad hoc reverse engineering procedure of the embedded device firmware. To simplify this procedure, we argue that only a particular part of the entire embedded device's firmware, as we called vendor customized code, should be thoroughly analyzed. Vendor customized code is usually developed to deal with external inputs and is especially sensitive to attacks compared to other parts of the system. Moreover, vendor customized code is often highly specific and proprietary, which lacks security implementation guidelines. Therefore, the security demands of analyzing this kind of code is urgent.

In this paper, we present empirical security analysis of vendor customized code on commodity embedded devices. We first survey the feasibility and limitations of state-of-the-art analysis tools. We focus on investigating typical program analysis tools used for classical security assessment and check their usability on conducting practical embedded devices' firmware reverse engineering. Then, we propose a methodology of vendor customized code analysis corresponding to both the feature of embedded devices and the usability of current analysis tools. It first locates the vendor customized code part of the firmware through black-box testing and firmware unpacking, and focuses on assessing typical aspects of common weakness of embedded devices in the particularly featured code part.

Based on our analysis methodology, we assess five popular embedded devices and find critical vulnerabilities. Our results show that: (a) the workload of assessing embedded devices could be significantly reduced according to our analysis methodology and only a small portion of programs on the device are needed to be assessed; (b) the vendor customized code is often more error-prone and thus vulnerable to attacks; (c) using existing tools to conduct automated analysis for many embedded devices is still infeasible, and manual intervention is essential to fulfil an effective assessment.

Keywords: Security assessment · Vendor customized code · Embedded device

This work was partially supported by the Major Program of Shanghai Science and Technology Commission (Grants No.: 15511103002).

© ICST Institute for Computer Sciences, Social Informatics and Telecommunications Engineering 2017
R. Deng et al. (Eds.): SecureComm 2016, LNICST 198, pp. 722–739, 2017.
DOI: 10.1007/978-3-319-59608-2_40

1 Introduction

Embedded devices are nowadays widely deployed in not only industrial environment but also in personal residences. While the embedded devices are becoming more and more prevailing, their functionalities are becoming more sophisticated. Smart embedded devices are used to perform home network routing, TV signal receiving and decoding, real-time camera monitoring and security altering, etc. As a result, the code base of current embedded device is much larger compared to previous one, and will become even more complex with the evolvement of smart homes and related Internet-connected devices

Security issues often compose severe threats to embedded devices and applications being deployed. Unfortunately, many embedded devices are designed and implemented without a clear and well-defined security goal. An observation is that the development of embedded device tends to repeat the mistakes once occurred on developing desktop computer systems. However, while manufacturers and researchers invest time and money in testing and securing them, the status of security assessment for those embedded devices is far from well-developed since the assessment tool is insufficient. Since a profusion of embedded devices have been developed by various manufacturers and been used in different environments. this inherent diversity makes the universality of security analysis a very difficult goal to be achieved. Although a multitude of research works have been proposed, less developed tool is universal to different devices. Although a large portion of research works aim to develop novel and automated analysis techniques suitable for embedded device, to the best of our knowledge, most of those techniques are only suitable for a small range of device models. Due to the lack of proper tool, security assessment of embedded device is well-known as a highly skilled procedure and requires expertise, which is still not systematic and practical. Hence, to help developers testing the security of embedded devices, not only should we transit the experience and best practice of security analysis for classical computer systems to the analysis of embedded device, but also should we consider the restriction of tools and formulate proper security assessment procedure that is practical and universal.

To employ effective and in-depth analysis, manual effort is still essential. However, since the manual analysis (e.g., reverse engineering of the firmware of the embedded device) is often time-consuming, the scalability must be effectively controlled to make such analysis feasible. An important aspect of reducing the amount of analyzing work is to elaborately filter out unnecessary targets. Particularly, it is necessary to extract and analyze only those executables related to possible attack surface of the embedded device. Thus the problem is how to locate such executables. The vendor of the embedded device often provides a firmware containing both operating system and the applications. A common observation is that most of the code in the firmware is reused (e.g., OS and standard libraries) and is publicly certificated, and it is often laborious and unnecessary to verify every part of the firmware. Therefore, focusing on the code related to high level operations of the device (e.g., network communication, user interaction) is more likely to find potentially vulnerability.

The target of this paper is to illustrate the security analysis methodology of vendor customized code assessment. Vendor customized code (VCC) denotes to the code fulfilling specific functionalities of the device. For instance, a wireless router may contain particular code to fulfil the authentication of the user. That code usually performs a proprietary authentication implemented by the vendor and is therefore not publicly known. This kind of code is often not fully evaluated by professional security analyst and is error-prone. Our security assessment thus focuses on such vendor customized code trying to find security flaws. In detail, our security assessment focuses on four typical aspects: *protocol cryptographic misuse, identity authentication, firmware integrity tampering*, and *incorrect patching of known vulnerability*. This helps us concentrate the analysis task and conduct practical operations.

To employ the assessment, we first summarize to what extend could the prevailing commodity program analysis techniques and automated security assessment tools be applied to existing embedded device systems. The issues of analysis of embedded devices are concluded and we propose some solutions to address them practically. The next goal is to find vendor customized code and analyze it. To this end, we present a systematic security assessment procedure to help conduct firmware reverse engineering and vendor customized code searching. We expect our proposed procedure to dispel misconceptions and mystifications of embedded devices' security assessment, and further promote the analysis efficiency of typical embedded devices. Notice that our assessment is not trying to answer questions like "are there any security flaws in the device" or "are some functionalities of this device is secure". Instead, our methodology is to answer the questions that how a vendor feature is implemented, and whether the implementation (vendor customized code) violates some expectations for the feature.

To evaluate the effectiveness of our methodology, we demonstrate the experimental results using five embedded devices including two wireless routers, one smart camera, one modem, and a smart CDN device. By adopting our methodology, vendor customized code can be located accurately and the amount of code needed to analyze is reduced significantly for each device. What's more, the extraction of vendor customized code allows us to employ in-depth security assessment, which reveals critical security flaws among those devices that are not discovered before.

2   Issues of Firmware Analysis

In this section we briefly review the state-of-the-art tools and techniques proposed for embedded devices' firmware analysis, and discuss their deficiencies. Although many classical security analysis techniques are applicable for embedded device's code, corresponding analysis tools may not, or at least not fully, adapted. We summarize major issues of current analyses in the following.

2.1   Firmware Acquiring

Unlike commodity personal computer, the executable code of operating system and applications of embedded device are not easily accessed. Obtaining firmware of the device is usually the most direct and the only way of analyzing target programs. To obtain the firmware of a device, two aspects should be concerned: the updating process of firmware, and the storage format of the device. Both of them are the frequently utilized sources to help acquire complete or part of the firmware.

The most common way for users to update their embedded devices is to uploading an firmware image provided by the vendor via a specific interface (an upgrade page for web management in most routers, upgrade utilities for Apple Airport, HP Printer, etc.) Thus analyst has the chance to intercept this process and extract the firmware image. Although previous studies often utilize the accessed URL of the update process and use crawler to download firmware packages from vendor's website, especially for large scale analysis [1], many devices often perform automatic and silent update checking to upgrade firmware. For those upgrade routines in which firmware packages are not direct accessible to users, manual analysis is still required to trace the upgrading agents and network traffic (and obtain the firmware).

Another major source of firmware is the storage medium of devices. For most embedded devices, softwares and configurations are stored in their local storage, such as ROM and flash. Thus analysts can manually dump stored content for further unpacking. This technique for device repairing and memory forensics has been widely applied to firmware analysis [2] with the growing concern of embedded security. To hamper firmware dumping, SoCs of some vendor may encrypt the firmware in ROM. In this case, although advanced dumping methods such as half-blind attack [3] can be applied, much manual intervention are required and sometimes the analyst may make use of known vulnerability (e.g., memory corruption) to help dump data.

2.2 Firmware Unpacking

In most cases, the obtained firmware is a single image that requires to be separated into different parts according to it's original layout organization. State-of-the-art tools such as Binwalk [4], FRAK [5], and BAT [6] provide functionalities for standard format firmware unpacking. By scanning signatures of common file systems and file formats in firmware images, individual files or a whole file system will be identified and extracted automatically and recursively. If the header of a common file system is identified, it is used as the identifier to split the image, and the cut out filesystem part is able to be mounted on another normal Linux system. After that, files inside the image are available to access.

In our practice, however, although those unpacking tools are sufficient for most Linux based firmwares, which contains a common file system (*squashfs*, *jffs2*, etc.), there are still many so-called monolithic firmware images of Real- Time Operating System (RTOS), which are packed with proprietary formats. For those images, universal tools often fail to identify and unpack them.

Another situation is that the acquired firmware is only a raw image of storage dump instead of a well formatted package, and there often does not exist the concept of file in such image. In this case, manual effort on determining the entry point of the raw bootloader becomes the last resort to recover possible system kernels and software applications, even if it is very complicated and tedious.

2.3   Code Debugging

Debugging code on embedded device is inconvenient and often impossible. A commercial off-the-shelf embedded device is rarely enabled debugging functionality of its main board. Comparing with a development board, a released device has no debugging peripherals to monitor the running state of the CPU and memory. Meanwhile, a full debugging solution including technique documents and debugger softwares is not provided either. Thus, it is usually impossible to directly debug a device like what developers do.

To implement the task of debugging, analysts utilize alternative measures. For instance, when using GDB stub [7] to debug, the device should execute a piece of stub code to build a remote debugging tunnel before booting. Then, the stub downloads and executes the original firmware. Also, if the system of the device is an embedded Linux System, analyst could attach debug server to specific running process and debug it. But to implement those functionalities inevitably involves manual intervening. As the vendors are not likely to provide the debugging privilege to normal user, analyst should either insert such a stub before booting process or gain a root privilege of the devices, which are both not easy to achieve.

2.4   Code Emulation

Emulation is a promising alternative way to achieve dynamic code analysis and inspect any run-time information. State-of-the-art emulators support most architectures (MIPS, ARM) that embedded devices are adopting. The overhead for emulation is also acceptable (four times slower than the execution of native code according to [8]). But a main restriction for emulation is that it often requires a full system emulation to execute the code correctly. For an embedded system image, it is not emulated as easy as desktop systems. Desktop operating system only requires few I/O devices (hard drive, screen, etc.) to boot up. Those I/O devices work with a clear protocol to emulate. For a embedded device, on the contrary, because neither peripherals details nor board support package of a devices are easily known for an analyst, full or approximate system level emulation is usually impossible.

Previous works [9] try to address this issue by utilizing process-level emulation or run an ELF executable file in another emulated Linux environment. Unfortunately, this technique is not always effective since a large portion of embedded software access NVRAM to load/store the configurations, which is essential to the execution but hard to be accurately emulated.

3   Vendor Customized Code Analysis

3.1   Target

As a complex combination of tightly connected softwares, an embedded system consists of many parts and components such as bootloader, operating system, daemon software, shared libraries, etc. Among them, most are auxiliary components. For example, DHCP daemon in a router, decompression libraries in bootloader are used to be implemented using open-source code base or mature solution, which are vetted beforehand and rarely have vulnerabilities. So, for a specific embedded device, we should focus on those **vendor features** which are implemented by the vendor self, and only specific for one or a series of device. The code to implement those features is often the particular part of the system that accepts user's input, which means the attack surface is restricted to this part of code. We denote this part of code as the **vendor customized code**. In a word, in the firmware of an embedded device, vendor customized code indicates to those proprietary code which are implemented for some vendor features.

In the following sections, we will demonstrate our security concern about vendor features and our methodology to locate and assess vendor customized code. In detail, we try to answer the following investigative questions of common functionalities related:

- **Q1**: *Is the protocol properly protecting private data transferring on the Internet?*
  Since the "Never roll your own cryptography" principle is not familiar to non-expert developers, many home-brewed cryptographic procedures are used in an embedded device. Meanwhile, due to the inherent complexity of cryptographic libraries, cryptographic misuse becomes another critical problem [10]. Thus any proprietary protocol should be assessed to find potential cryptographic flaws.
- **Q2**: *Can the device properly authenticate a granted user accessing this device?*
  Nowadays many embedded devices utilize an HTTP management interface for user to set up device configurations. Vendor may exclude unnecessary session modules, which are commonly used in current web authentication application from the web server program of the device. This introduces new authentication factors and potentially causes various security problems. Another common problem in embedded devices is that vendor may intentionally leave some backdoors to access the device conveniently [11, 12]. This often tends to be a serious security threat and leads to security breach to the device.
- **Q3**: *Could the integrity of firmware in this device self be preserved?*
  Modification attacks against firmware [5] often inject malicious code into a device, and the final user turns to be the specific victim. Since consumers are usually not able to distinguish a refurbished device and will not know if the software in a device has been modified, attacker could modify the original executables on the device before it is sent to the end-user to fulfil the attack. Meanwhile, attacker could also intercept the firmware update process of the device and inject malicious image if the integrity checking is missing. For these reasons, we should consider whether the device adopts a robust code integrity checking scheme to protect the system against any unauthorized code's execution.
- **Q4**: *Have previous vulnerabilities been correctly patched?*
  Some failed patches [13, 14] for PC software or mobile software has been witnessed in recent years. This would also happen to embedded devices, and thus additional assessment on a patched code is still essential.

3.2   Searching Vendor Customized Code

Black-Box Behavior Analysis. Part of vendor features are obvious such as video capturing for a smart camera, while much more of those are hidden. For example, automatic upgrading of a device may not be acknowledged by the users, but clues of this behavior can be found in the network record.

It is what we concerned of to discover vendor features in this stage of analysis. In one hand, we test any functionalities of target device, by feeding data normal or abnormal and recording the response. In the other hand, during the blackbox analysis, the network traffic is captured which reveal the corresponding host, port and protocol for any network connection.

Executable Retrieving. In this section, we will show how we derive binary code, which enable our white-box analysis for target devices.

We derive the code from two major sources, one is a running device, and the other one is device firmware package for device upgrading or recovering.

We can obtain software code of a running device, if we can access the console of this device. Possible methods are, utilizing previous vulnerability to get a shell, manufacturing a malicious upgrading firmware package to get a backdoor, connecting to the console of device via UART interface directly, etc. If any of those attempts succeed, we can easily collect binary codes, executable files and runtime information.

The other method is to decompose the firmware package. *file* utility and *binwalk* [4] are used to identify known format for file and data blob. If the steps above failed, which usually happens to a monolithic operating system, we try to find the correct base address of the image, and then get a more precise disassembly code.

Vendor Customized Code Locating. The final step of our searching is to locate some code snippets which are responsible for the vendor features we concern about.

This step plays an important role on minimizing the range of code analysis by restricting it into few small pieces.

In detail, two code locating schemes can be followed depending on whether we can access to the running device, respectively. If we are able to access to the running device, listening port/alive connection can be used to infer the responsible process. For example, we can execute 'lsof -i TCP:80 -n' or 'netstat-ln' command to get the process ID for the web server running in the devices. Although such utilities may not installed in the devices, we can upload a static linked utility to the device, since we have root privilege. Some devices adopt tailoring embedded Linux system, which have no required utilities ('nc', 'wget', 'chmod', etc.), to upload a executable file directly. In this case, we first copy an existing file which already have 'X' permission, and then overwrite the copy by 'echo' arbitrary bytes into this copy. As far as we known, since all the shell for Linux enable 'cp' and 'echo' command, this method is universal for all devices which adopt Linux operating system. We are also able to obtain the corresponding program binary by following the symbolic link, which is located at '/proc/PID/exe'. Any shared libraries which are loaded in the process can be also found in '/proc/self/map files/' or '/proc/self/maps'. To confirm whether a process is related to some features, we kill the running process, and observe whether the vendor features are still working.

The other scheme is a static string analysis based. We perform keyword string searching for every extracted executable from the whole firmware image. For a specific feature, some critical keyword should be used by the code. For example, if the target feature is a HTTP server running in the device, *GET*, *POST*, *HTTP*, *Host* can be a set of keywords. If we find an executable contains specific keywords, we choose it as the candidate executable for the following security assessment.

3.3   Security Assessment of Vendor Customized Code

Our assessment is to recovery any details of vendor customized code. As the analysis scope has been minimized and restricted, coarse-grained manual static assessment is feasible in an acceptable period of time, to understand the basic behavior for the VCC. But there are also many pieces of code are complicated, and also not easy as well as necessary to understand. For example, some encoding/decoding functions may be significant for protocol analysis, which only contains encoding algorithm. We do not have to be aware of the details of this implementation, but only need obtain some output for some specific input. In this case, We try to debug, or emulate the piece of code. Some executable files depend no peripherals, thus we run and debug it in an QEMU emulated Linux system for the corresponding architecture. We also emulate those routines by unicorn engine, if no unknown initialized global variables or I/O will be accessed during the execution of those routines. We may also need to derive the input for specific output. In this situation, we utilize angr to perform a dynamic symbolic execution. To achieve this, we feeding the routine a symbolic input, and explore the path satisfying the constraints for output data at exit point of the routine.

4   Experimental Evaluation

In this section, we investigate five commodity embedded devices in Chinese market including two wireless routers, one modem, one smart Content Delivery Network (CDN) device, and a smart camera. We first report our analyzing results of firmware and vendor customized code of these devices. Then we discuss the security assessment of vendor customized code focusing on the issues mentioned in Sect. 3.3, and report the discovered vulnerabilities.

4.1   General Analysis

The five devices we choose to assess are:

- *TP-LINK WR740nv5:* a wireless router produced by TP-LINK, the world largest WLAN device manufacturer.
- *TOTOLINK A850R*: a wireless router produced by TOTOLINK, a networking equipment vendor in Korea.

- *HUAQIN HGU421:* a fiber optic modem used by *China Telecom*, the major ISP in China.
- *Thunder Money Maker:* a smart CDN device manufactured by Thunder Corporation.
- *Yi Smart Webcam*, a smart camera released by Xiaomi Inc., one of the leading Chinese consuming electronics cooperations.

For each device, we test every functionality of it, try to observe how the device behaves and record any network event as mentioned in Sect. 3.2. After that we figure out some vendor features for each devices:

- Different from many other routers of TP-LINK that adopt embedded Linux system, *TP-LINK WR740nv5* is based on VxWorks, which is a prevailing RTOS. We find that this device will check if a user uploaded firmware package is valid or not.
- As a tiny CDN node, *Thunder Money Maker* shares customer's bandwidth to Thunder CDN Network, and earns commission from Thunder Corporation according to the amount of uploaded data. It will automatically download upgrade package via HTTP protocol. Moreoover, we observed the device frequently prompt SSL request to the URL *kjapi.peiluyou.com.*
- *TOTOLINK A850R* is a Linux based wireless router. Common features for home router are provided via an HTTP based interface. During our test, we found that no cookie is used to authenticate web users (the response contains no 'Set-Cookies' header for a successful login request), which suggests that device uses an uncommon way for authentication.
- *Yi Smart Webcam* allows users to bind their mobile phones to the camera, then the real-time captured video can be watched in a corresponding app on user's phone. The format of video stream tansfered via Internet is unkonwn. Thus we guess the data is encrypted or some-kind proessed. Also we notice that the device listens on a strange TCP port, and response a magic string when a client connects to it.
- *HUAQIN HGU421* allow users to login to configure the device via a WEB interface. But only a low-privileged account is given to user.

4.2   Firmware Analysis

We first try to gain access to each device, as mentioned in Sect. 3.2. We find four of them disclose an access terminal via different ways.

- For *WR740* and *HGU421*, we direct access them via TTL.
- For *A850R*, a known PoC of remote command execution vulnerability is used.
- For *Thunder*, we replace the upgrading package during the auto-upgrading process, and implant a backdoor.

We also scan for any known-formated blob for those device with firmware package provided. The results are listed in Table 1.

After the primary analysis, we show that it is able to retrieve executable files (ELF files) for four Linux based devices (from known format file system image, or download

Table 1. Firmware format and content analysis

Device	Firmware format	File carving result
Thunder	Zip file	None
WR740	Unknown	Some zlib compress image
A850R	Unknown	A standard squashfs file system
WebCam	Unknown	A jffs2 file system
HGU421	–	–

from a running device). The only device whose executables are not able to be extracted is *TPLINK WR740*. To address, we utilize the memory dumping functionality provide by UART console to directly retrieved the application code. Since no UART pin is provided on the mainboard of *WR740*, we distinguish the corresponding pins of AR9331 microcontroller according to its datasheet [15], and directly welded two jumper wires to lead them out (as depicted in Fig. 1). Finally we conduct memory dumping to obtain a raw image of the memory. After the dumping, we obtain the memory image containing kernel and application.

We also decompress all compressed blob in the firmware package, list all the strings appearing in those images using *strings* utility. Some strings such as *"auto-booting..."*, *"I'm booting now......"*, and *"Press Ctrl + C or Shift + C to stop auto-boot..."* indicate the existence of the bootloader. To determine the base address of the bootloader, we find a piece of code of switch statement by searching the switching jump instruction ($jr \ \$v0$). Before swiching jump instruction, few instructions (*sltiu $v0, $v1, 9; beqz $v0, default; nop;..; li $v0, 0x8046FE70; addu $v0, $v1; lw $v0, 0($v0); jr $v0*) reveals the virtual address (0x8046FE70) and size (9) of the jump table. It's also able to find the starts of most case blocks, because case blocks are usually after the end (a jump instruction to the end of swich statement) of another case block. Since all the case blocks should has a corresponding pointer in the jump table, we can easily deduce the bootloader is loaded to the address of 0x80400000. Once the base address is determined, this image can correctly disassembled and most of the binary code is readable.

4.3 Vendor Customized Code Searching

To locate the vendor customized code out of all the retrieved executable code, various criteria are applied to five devices as mentioned in Sect. 3.2. In the following, we demonstrate how we locate the corresponding vendor customized code for each vendor feature, and show the amount of assessment is significantly reduced after it (Table 2).

- As *TP-LINK WR740nv5* has a fully unknown formated firmware, we firstly found the bootloader has a recovery functionality interacting with users on the serial port. After loading the bootloader in IDA, some prompt strings such as *Usage error, please try %s-help* lead us to the code for the recovery mode. During the analysis of firmware recovering routines, we confirmed that the entire operating system compressed in a special region of flash is also a piece of the firmware package. Therefore, the decompressed operating system as well as applications were

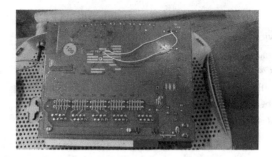

Fig. 1. Jumper Wires connect to UART pins of AR9331

Table 2. Vendor feature and size of customized code for each device.

Device	Feature	Unpacked firmware size	Vendor customized code
WR740	Firmware verification	2.4M (3868 functions)	83 functions
WR740	Packet forwarding	2.4M (3868 functions)	46 functions
Thunder	Upload statistic reporting	54.6M	3.9M shared library
A850R	User authentication	29.1M	476K executable file
WebCam	Video encryption	33.3M	272K executable file
HGU421	User authentication	No firmware package obtained	836K executable file

obtained. Then, we tried to figure out whether the device is able to verify the validity of an uploaded firmware package. We locate this feature by searching the URL for upgrading page in the HTTP. This helped us pinpoint the logic of upgrading and confirmed the missing of firmware integrity check.

- For *Thunder*, we focused on the implementation of its unique upload statistic reporting functionality, which is directly related to user's reward. We found a *dcdn client* process is listening to one particular port (4693), and more than 10 different IP addresses are connected to that port. We also found in this process a library *libdcdn client.so* is loaded. Searching for meaningful names in symbol tables, five potential relevant functions were located.

- For *TOTOLINK A850R*, we aimed to find executables related to user authentication. We first statically disassembled every binary code file on the device to determine which one is the web server. After the code reverse engineering, we identify the file with name 'boa' as the device's web server. Therefore, the following in-depth analysis could concentrate on this executable.

- Our black-box analysis indicated that the *Yi Smart Webcam* encrypts the data before sending it to the user's mobile application. The very particular vendor feature we concerned about is how the data is encrypted. The corresponding process was first identified according to the network connection information. Then we obtained the executable of the process and further searched for functions responsible for data encryption. We found symbols for AES encryption function in wolfSSL library occurred in the executable. This helped us narrow the assessment scope of executable code to only one function.

– As mentioned before, the *HGU421* modem sets a restricted privilege to its normal user. The assessment of this device is therefore trying to find how the device authenticate an user. Similar to the feature locating of *TOTOLINK A850R*, we used the URL for login page as the indicator to search every executable. We found the executable *uhttpd* as the corresponding file, and we could focus on analyzing the handler for requesting to that page in this executable.

4.4   Security Assessment

In this section, we will demonstrate our concrete secure assessment for each device.

Device Modification. Among the five devices we analyzed, we found TP-LINK WR740nv5 and Thunder Money Maker fail to check the integrity of the code. We detail the vulnerability and related attack as follows.

TP-LINK We manually analyzed the routine for firmware verification in *TPLINK* and obtained the exact format of firmware. According to our analysis, an MD5 checksum is contained in the header of the firmware package, the uploaded package will be accepted only if the checksum of remaining data corresponds to the one in the header. So the attacker can easily modify the package to inject some malicious code into the firmware and then repack it. We also emulated the MD5 hash function in the *unicorn* engine [16], and the emulated code also executes correctly with correct result returned. This means even if the checksum function is proprietary, the attacker can simply reuse it to re-create a valid firmware package.

To demonstrate the effectiveness of the modification, we inject code into the firmware's packet forwarding routine to duplicate any packet to a specific host. This malicious firmware leads the device to send the entire network traffic to a malicious server, which proves the threat of the firmware modification attack.

Thunder. As the major functionality of this device, the file uploading and its corresponding CDN protocol of Thunder Money Maker is very complex, and the communication between account server and the device is encrypted by an unknown encryption algorithm. However, we conduct a device firmware modification attack to circumvent the encryption. We directly reverse engineer the 'libdcdn client.so' file, which is responsible for D-CDN function in this device. By searching for meaningful names in exported symbols, we can locate five potential relevant functions. After a manual analysis, how each function returns statistical data (i.e., in return value, arguments or global variables) is understood. Then we modify each function to report a tampered statistical data, uploaded it to the server to replace the original one and check whether the uploading speed shown in the mobile application is changed. Through this testing we pinpoint the specific function for accounting. By maliciously adjusting the upload speed of this function, we can cheat the server to earn much more money than what we should deserve.

Corrupted Authentication

A850R We extract the binary file of the web server, *Boa*, in the *squashfs* filesystem of A850R. The handle for login request is located by searching login path 'boafrm/formLogin'. The handle contains only 172 assembly instructions, so it's easy to recover its logic. Instead of keeping sessions for login users, *Boa* stores the user's IP into the management information base (MIB) as an item 'LoginIP'. Different from normal session management, this mechanism in web server has two problems:

1. Any clients behind a NAT box in LAN will share same address connecting to the router, which means privilege will be leaked to the whole subnet if one user logins to the HTTP interface.
2. An attacker in LAN may simply discover and gain the authorized IP address by ARP spoofing.

List 1.1 Authentication Code in A850R

```
bool check_login(input_user, input_pass)
{
  char user[16], pass[16];
  char user0[16], pass0[16];
  load_from_mib(USERNAME, user);
  load_from_mib(PASSWORD, pass);
  //load_from_mib(SUPER_USER, user0);
  //load_from_mib(SUPER_PASS, pass0);
  if (0==strcmp(input_user, user) && 0==strcmp(input_pass,
      pass))
  {
    return true;
  }
  if (0==strcmp(input_user, user0) && 0==strcmp(input_pass,
      pass0))
  {
    return true;
  }
  return false;
}
```

We find that, request not from "loginIP" will also be allow to access the management interface, if correct username and password are provided in 'Authentication' header of HTTP request. There is another vulnerability in the routine to check 'Authentication' header which is shown in List 1.1. To check the validity of 'Authentication' header, the web server allocates two pairs of username and password on the stack. One is filled with the actual user's information, which is loaded from MIB, while the other is left to be uninitialized. Then the server compares the user's input with these two pairs of information, authorizing the user if either of the information is matched. Since both of the uninitialized stack strings may be empty, it is possible for attacker to bypass the authentication with an empty username and password. What make things worse is that the CPU of A850R is a big-endian architecture. The most significant byte of a word is often zero, if the word is a small interger, pointer to static array, or return address to some position to the code section. This makes the success rate of the attack much higher, comparing with same attack against little-endian architecture. To figure out the success rate of an attacker, we employ 10 malicious attempts, and all of them succeed.

To further derive how this issue has been introduced, we intended to also compare an old version of the firmware for A850R. We found no old version firmware of A850R on the Internet, so we take an old version of N301RT to compare. We find that the authentication process is very similar to that of AR850, but the uninitialized variables are initialized as *SUPERUSER* and *SUPERPASS* in MIB.

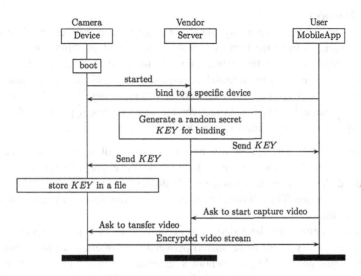

Fig. 2. Xiaoyi key agreement

Thus, we can confirm that it is the incomplete patching procedure that causes this issue.

HGU421 Our analysis of the *uhttpd* executable suggests a DoS vulnerability in this device. The vendor implements the parser (shown in List 1.2) for HTTP header of basic access authentication [17], which separates the username and password with a colon in a base64-encoded HTTP header. After a call to *strchr(header, ':')*, the web server does not check whether the return value is NULL or not (i.e., whether a colon exists). Then the server uses the return value to separate the authentication info. As a consequence, an attacker may send a crafted request to crash the web server.

List 1.2 Authentication Code in HGU421

```
bool check_auth_header(char * header)
{
  char *user, *pass;
  base64decode(header);
  user = header;
  pass = strchr(header, ':');
  pass[0] = '\0';
  pass ++;
  return check_user_info(user, pass);
}
```

Insecure Protocol

Yi Smart WebCam We search any file that contains keywords 'encrypt' in the jffs2 filesystem extracted from the firmware image. The executable binary named 'remote' has been noticed since it's the only executable file containing AES related symbols from WolfSSL. We confirm 'remote' is responsible for video capture and transfer, because we also find symbols for video codec in this binary. Since this executable is not large, we manual analyse it to recover the key agreement protocol (Fig. 2). Our future analysis discovers at least two issues in *Yi Smart Camera*:

1. The vendor only encryption the first two blocks of each video stream using AES-128 with ECB mode. It seems that to make the encrypt/decrypt faster on a tiny embedded device as well as on a mobile device, the vendor abandons a standard encrypt procedure. This allows a Man-In-The-Middle attack to decode most of the video stream.
2. The key agreement of the video transmission protocol contains serious problem. Since a secret key needs to be shared between the camera and mobile application, the key is first generated by the vendor's server and is transferred to both the mobile application and the device after a binding operation. However, the camera launches a special daemon service that listens to a TCP port (38888), and echoes this session key if received arbitrary request. Then any attacker captured the encrypted stream can also get the secret key via this TCP port. It seems that this port is used to debug, but the vendor forgets to remove before releasing the device.

5 Related Work

5.1 Static Binary Code Analysis

Disassembler is required for most binary code analyses. Due to the complexity and diversity of different instruction sets, many disassembly engines (udis86, diStorm3, etc.) can only support i386/x86-64 architecture and is not feasible for embedded system analysis. IDA is the state-of-the-art universal disassembler for most of processors. Many previous cross-architecture works [18, 19] are based IDA's disassembly result.

However, to acquire a precise analysis result, the disassembling of IDA involves many interactive processes, which requires the participation of expertise. Capstone is another multi-platform, multi-architecture disassembly framework that supports ARM, ARM64, MIPS etc. But some frequently used instruction sets such as MSP430, 8051 and AVR, are still not supported.

5.2 Dynamic Binary Code Analysis

To perform dynamic analysis, analyst may execute programs in a firmware with an emulated environment. As common emulators contain no peripheral details, previous works [20–22] try to fully or approximately emulate those peripherals. Those solutions face different problems such as short of documentation or misbehavior of the emulated code. Avatar [23] is another platform that is able to connect emulated code with physical device to achieve a fully emulated environment, but until now it's not publicly released. For Linux-based firmware, although full system emulation is not possible, the file system in the firmware can be mounted and programs could be emulated. Cui et al. [9] run startup script in an alternative Linux system to emulate a running system. Meanwhile, executing an emulated process in QEMU user mode is also an alternative way. Those techniques are suitable for Linux based firmware in our practice. Even though, missing MTD devcie in file system, User Defined Instructions in MIPS, or any differences between emulated and real environment may also cause problems.

5.3 Heavyweight Program Analysis

Dynamic taint analysis and dynamic symbolic execution are prevalent dynamic analysis techniques for program analysis of desktop or mobile platform. However, most tainting and symbolic execution engines aiming for x86, ARM or JVM cannot be adapted to MIPS or other instruction sets used by embedded devices. Also, those emulating based engines are limited by the restriction of emulators, which we have mentioned before. The gap between concrete values needed by those engines and incompleteness of emulation or debugging environment is still unbridgeable now.

Static taint analysis and symbolic execution benefit from the property of not relying on runtime concrete value, and make significant uses in firmware analysis. Nevertheless, large scale taint analysis and symbolic execution encounters many issues such as path explosion, low speed of constraint solvers, difficulties for pointer identification. Project angr [24] fulfill the requirements that solving a combination of path and input data from a start point to trigger some target, or collecting possible behaviors for further manual analysis starting from a critical point. But its usage scenarios are very limited because of the overhead.

5.4 Automatic Firmware Analysis

Many works have been done on automatic firmware analyzing. Some work are scalable but perform no in-deepth analysis. A. Costin [1] scan in thousands of firmware images for specific artifacts with known problems. FIRMADYNE [25] run startup script of the firmware filesystem, in a emulated Linux system with NVRAM shared-library replaced. FIRMADYNE also find known by executing exploits from Metaspolit Framework. There are some automatic techniques have been presented to discover unknown vulnerabilities. Firmalice [26] utilizes a symbolic model of authentication bypass flaws to determine the required inputs to perform privileged operations. FIE [27] developed a symbolic engine to find memory-safety bugs in MSP430 open-source softwares.

6 Conclusion

As the embedded devices are becoming more and more complex, state-of-the-art security analysis techniques and tools are not adequate to address real-world analysis tasks. In this paper we systematically study the limitation of embedded device analyzing tools and inefficiency of automatic analysis for embedded devices. We argue that current techniques and tools are still not universal for automatic security assessment, and currently we should still acknowledge the necessity of manual intervention for an effective assessment. We then suggest a practical and comprehend security assessment procedure that focuses on common weak points of embedded design and implementation. Guide by this assessment procedure, we reveal critical security flaws in five real-world devices.

References

1. Costin, A., Zaddach, J. Francillon, A., Balzarotti, D., Antipolis, S.: A large scale analysis of the security of embedded firmwares. USENIX Security. USENIX Association (2014)
2. Cui, A., Stolfo, S.: Print me if you dare: firmware modification attacks and the rise of printer malware (2011)
3. Goodspeed, T., Francillon, A.: Half-blind attacks: mask rom bootloaders are dangerous. In: Proceedings of the 3rd USENIX Conference on Offensive Technologies, p. 6. USENIX Association (2009)
4. Heffner, C.: Binwalk-firmware analysis tool. https://code.google.com/p/binwalk/
5. Cui, A., Costello, M., Stolfo, S.J.: When firmware modifications attack: a case study of embedded exploitation. In: NDSS (2013)
6. Hemel, A., Kalleberg, K.T., Vermaas, R., Dolstra, E.: Finding software license violations through binary code clone detection. In: Proceedings of the 8th Working Conference on Mining Software Repositories, pp. 63–72. ACM (2011)
7. Ji, J.-H., Woo, G., Park, H.-B., Park, J.-S.: Design and implementation of retargetable software debugger based on gdb. In: Third International Conference on Convergence and Hybrid Information Technology, ICCIT 2008, vol. 1, pp. 737–740. IEEE (2008)
8. Bellard, F.: Qemu, a fast and portable dynamic translator. In: USENIX Annual Technical Conference, FREENIX Track, pp. 41–46 (2005)
9. Costin, A., Zarras, A., Francillon, A.: Automated dynamic firmware analysis at scale: a case study on embedded web interfaces. arXiv preprint arXiv:1511.03609 (2015)

10. Egele, M., Brumley, D., Fratantonio, Y., Kruegel, C.: An empirical study of cryptographic misuse in android applications. In: Proceedings of the 2013 ACM SIGSAC Conference on Computer & Communications Security, pp. 73–84. ACM (2013)
11. A vulnerability and a hidden admin account all inside sitel ds114w routers! https://rootatnasro.wordpress.com/2015/01/04/a-vulnerability-anda-hidden-admin-account-all-inside-sitel-ds114-w-routers/
12. More than 60 undisclosed vulnerabilities affect 22 soho routers. http://seclists.org/fulldisclosure/2015/May/129
13. Cve-2015-3864. https://cve.mitre.org/cgi-bin/cvename.cgi?name=CVE-2015-3864
14. Cve-2014-7169. https://cve.mitre.org/cgi-bin/cvename.cgi?name=CVE-2014-7169
15. Ar9331 highly-integrated and cost effective ieee 802.11n 1x1 2.4 ghz soc for ap and router platforms. https://www.openhacks.com/uploadsproductos/ar9331datasheet.pdf
16. Quynh, N.A., Dang, H.-V.: Unicorn: next generation cpu emulator frame-work. In: BlackHat (2015)
17. Franks, J., Hallam-Baker, P., Hostetler, J., Lawrence, S., Leach, P., Luotonen, A., Stewart, L.: Rfc 2617: Http authentication: basic and digest access authentication. Internet RFCs (1999)
18. Pewny, J., Garmany, B., Gawlik, R., Rossow, C., Holz, T.: Cross-architecture bug search in binary executables (2015)
19. Bao, T., Burket, J., Woo, M., Turner, R., Brumley, D.: Byteweight: learning to recognize functions in binary code. In: USENIX Security Symposium (2014)
20. Chipounov, V., Candea, G.: Reverse engineering of binary device drivers with revnic. In: Proceedings of the 5th European Conference on Computer Systems, pp. 167–180. ACM (2010)
21. Kuznetsov, V., Chipounov, V., Candea, G.: Testing closed-source binary device drivers with ddt. In: USENIX Annual Technical Conference, no. EPFL-CONF- 147243 (2010)
22. Schlich, B.: Model checking of software for microcontrollers. ACM Trans. Embed. Comput. Syst. (TECS) 9(4), 36 (2010)
23. Zaddach, J., Bruno, L., Francillon, A., Balzarotti, D.: Avatar: a framework to support dynamic security analysis of embedded systems firmwares. In: Symposium on Network and Distributed System Security (NDSS) (2014)
24. Shoshitaishvili, Y., Wang, R., Salls, C., Stephens, N., Polino, M., Dutcher, A., Grosen, J., Feng, S., Hauser, C., Kruegel, C., Vigna, G.: SoK: (State of) the art of war: offensive techniques in binary analysis. In: IEEE Symposium on Security and Privacy (2016)
25. Chen, D.D., Egele, M., Woo, M., Brumley, D.: Towards automated dynamic analysis for linux-based embedded firmware. In: ISOC Network and Distributed System Security Symposium (NDSS) (2016)
26. Shoshitaishvili, Y., Wang, R., Hauser, C., Kruegel, C., Vigna, G.: Firmalice- automatic detection of authentication bypass vulnerabilities in binary firmware. In: NDSS (2015)
27. Davidson, D., Moench, B., Ristenpart, T., Jha, S.: Fie on firmware: finding vulnerabilities in embedded systems using symbolic execution. Presented as part of the 22nd USENIX Security Symposium (USENIX Security 2013), pp. 463–478 (2013)

Poster Session

POSTER: Security Analysis of Personal Unmanned Aerial Vehicles

Peng Chen[✉] and Hao Chen

ShanghaiTech University, Shanghai, China
{chenpeng,chenhao}@shanghaitech.edu.cn

Abstract. Personal unmanned aerial vehicles (UAVs) have become popular in recent years. While their extreme mobility enables exciting new applications, they also raise security concerns. However, currently we understand little about UAV's vulnerabilities, feasible attacks, and defense options. Toward securing UAVs, we analyzed two of the most popular personal UAVs. We discovered a series of vulnerabilities, including insecure communication channels and misuse of cryptography. By exploiting these vulnerabilities, an attacker can eavesdrop on the data acquired or transmitted by the aircraft, impersonate the aircraft to send bogus data to the user's mobile device, hijack the camera on the aircraft or the aircraft itself, and prevent the aircraft from communicating with the user's mobile device.

Keywords: Unmanned aerial vehicles · Security vulnerabilities · DJI

1 Introduction

Personal UAVs have become popular in recent years. As they can fly to areas where human access is infeasible, dangerous, expensive, or inconvenient, they have many applications in photography, delivery, and wildlife protection. Unfortunately, security has not been a priority for personal UAVs manufacturers. In the current fast growing market for personal UAVs, manufacturers care more about functions, cost, and applications. In the research community, there is no comprehensive study on UAV's vulnerabilities, feasible attacks, and defense options. To make progress toward securing UAVs, we conducted an empirical security analysis of the DJI series of quadcopters, which are among the most popular personal UAVs.

A UAV consists of an aircraft, a hardware remote controller, a commodity mobile device (e.g., an Android-powered device or iPhone) running a mobile app for the UAV. In this paper, we examined two representative DJI UAVs: *Phantom 2 Vision+* [3], *Phantom 3 Professional* [4].

2 Phantom 2

Phantom 2 Vision+ is a quadcopter consisting of an aircraft, remote controller, and range extender. The aircraft has a WiFi module, video module, receiver,

© ICST Institute for Computer Sciences, Social Informatics and Telecommunications Engineering 2017
R. Deng et al. (Eds.): SecureComm 2016, LNICST 198, pp. 743–746, 2017.
DOI: 10.1007/978-3-319-59608-2_41

NAZA V2 controller, gimbal, and camera. The aircraft communicates independently with the remote controller and the mobile app DJI Vision, where the remote controller controls the flight and the mobile app controls the camera.

2.1 Vulnerabilities

Phantom 2 Vision+ fails to provide secure networks, and its servers fail to authenticate clients. Since neither of the WiFi APs in the UAV is encrypted, any one can connect to them. Neither the users manual nor DJI Vision allows the user to enable encryption on these networks. Any DJI Vision app can connect to the UAV without authentication, after which the app can control the camera, ground station etc. However, the TCP server created by *ser2net* [7] in the WiFi module accepts at most one connection at any time. The UAV designer might have intended to use this mechanism to protect the UAV owner, because her app will likely connect to the UAV first after she powers on the UAV.

2.2 Hijack Aircraft Communication

The goal of this attack is to hijack the communication between the aircraft and victim DJI Vision app. Since *ser2net* allows only one TCP connection at any time, we must close the existing TCP connection between the WiFi module and victim app before we could connect to the WiFi module. We achieved this by the TCP reset attack [5,8]. The requiresite parameters for the attack (IPs, ports, and sequence numbers) can be sniffed in the packets transmitted between the app and the aircraft. After the TCP reset attack closed the existing connection between the WiFi module and the victim app, we connected to the WiFi module. This connection allowed us to prevent victim app from acquiring live video, to exfiltrate photos and videos from aircraft, to control aircraft's camera and hijack aircraft (Sect. 2.4).

2.3 Attack on Video Module

By reverse engineering the video module, we found that it uses a modified version of UDP-based data transfer (UDT) [6] for communicating with the app and H.264 for video codec. Similar to the TCP reset attack described in Sect. 2.2, we can sniffed the IPs, ports and sequence numbers of the UDT packets transmitted from the aircraft to the app. Then we created our UDT packets using these parameters and sent them to the victim app from our malicious device. Our attack caused the following damages: we sent packets containing our bogus video and verified that the app indeed was playing our video; after receiving some crafted UDT packets for a while, DJI Vision crashed; we sent UDT packets to DJI Vision as fast as we could and observed the communication between aircraft and app was disabled.

2.4 Ground Station

Ground station allows the user to create flight tasks via DJI Vision. After we reverse engineered the protocol for controlling ground station. we were able to hijack the aircraft by sending upload job, upload point, and joystick commands. We were also able to exfiltrate existing job and waypoints on the aircraft. This would be useful for forensic analysis or reconnaissance.

3 Phantom 3 Professional

In Phantom 3, the mobile device connects via a USB cable to the remote controller, which connects to the aircraft via a DJI-proprietary wireless system. The DJI Pilot app on the mobile device connects to the remote controller via Android debug bridge (ADB) [1]. DJI Pilot creates a TCP server at the host 0.0.0.0 and the port 22345. Once the remote controller powers on, it runs a TCP client to connect to the server via ADB port forwarding.

3.1 Insecure Server

A vulnerability in the TCP server created by DJI Pilot is that it listens to 0.0.0.0, which the official Android security tips advise against [2], since this allows any host that can address the mobile device (e.g., an attacker on the same wireless LAN) to connect to this server. To fix this vulnerability, the server should listen to localhost (or 127.0.0.1), because ADB forwards the remote controller's connection request from localhost. This way, the server will reject any connection request that originates outside the mobile device.

3.2 Hijack Aircraft

The TCP server created by Pilot does not authenticate clients. However, it accepts at most one connection at any time, so no other program can connect to this server if the remote controller has already connected to it. The Pilot developers might have intended to use this mechanism to protect the Pilot and aircraft, but we found three attacks to circumvent it.

Win Race Against Remote Controller. As soon as Pilot starts, the remote controller requests connection. However, we found that if our malware app also requested connection repeatedly when Pilot started, our malware almost always won the race against the remote controller, after which the remote controller could never connect. Now that our malware impersonated the remote controller (and transitively, the aircraft), it was able to send bogus data, such as fake photos or videos, to Pilot, and Pilot could no longer communicate with the aircraft.

Kill and Impersonate Pilot. If the remote controller is already connected to Pilot's TCP server when our malware starts, the malware must close the existing connection. One way to achieve this is to push Pilot into the background and then invoke the *killBackgroundProcesses* method in the *ActivityManager* class[1]. The malware can send an attractive bogus notification to trick the user to click it. The click brings the malware to the foreground and pushes Pilot to the background. After killing Pilot, the malware creates a TCP server to impersonate Pilot to communicate with the remote controller.

4   Conclusion

We studied the risks of UAVs and conducted an empirical analysis of three popular DJI UAVs. We discovered a series of vulnerabilities, including insecure communication channels and misuse of cryptography. We have demonstrated that, by exploiting these vulnerabilities, an attacker can eavesdrop on the data acquired or transmitted by the aircraft, impersonate the aircraft to send bogus data to the user's mobile device, hijack the camera on the aircraft or the aircraft itself, and prevent the aircraft from communicating with the user's mobile device.

5   Other Works and Responsible Disclosure

We also analysed DJI Matrice 100, DJI's mobile and onboard SDKs, founding that the steps of UAV activation and developer authorization are insecure.

We notified DJI of all the discovered vulnerabilities and verified attacks between June and August of 2015. DJI was confident that they would be able to fix the vulnerabilities by the time of this conference.

References

1. Android Debug Bridge. http://developer.android.com/tools/help/adb.html
2. Android Security Tips. http://developer.android.com/training/articles/security-tips.html
3. DJI Phantom 2 Vision+. http://www.dji.com/product/phantom-2-vision-plus
4. DJI Phantom 3 Professional. http://www.dji.com/product/phantom-3
5. Floyd, S.: Inappropriate TCP Resets Considered Harmful. RFC, United States (2002). 3360
6. Gu, Y., Grossman, R.L.: UDT: UDP-based data transfer for high-speed wide area networks. Comput. Netw. **51**(7), 1777–1799 (2007)
7. ser2net. http://ser2net.sourceforge.net/
8. Watson, P.: Slipping in the Window: TCP Reset attacks (2004)

---

[1] Our malware needs the KILL_BACKGROUND_PROCESSES permission to invoke this operation.

Modeling User Browsing Activity
for Application Layer DDoS Attack Detection

TungNgai Miu[1], Chenxu Wang[2,3(✉)], Daniel Xiapu Luo[3], and Jinhe Wang[2]

[1] NexusGuard Limited, Hong Kong, China
[2] Xi'an Jiaotong University, Xi'an, Shaanxi, China
cxwang@mail.xjtu.edu.cn
[3] The Hong Kong Polytechnic University, Hong Kong, China

Abstract. Application layer distributed denial of service (App-layer DDoS) attacks are becoming a severe threat to the security of web servers. In this paper, we model user browsing activity in order to detect abnormal requests. User access patterns are analyzed to detect anomaly at the session level. The likelihood of a browsing session is then calculated to distinguish abnormal behaviors from normal ones. We evaluate our methods based on a real dataset collected from a commercial website that suffered from actual DDoS attacks. The experimental results validate the effectiveness of the proposed methods.

Keywords: DDoS attack · Browsing activity · User access pattern

1 Introduction

Application layer DDoS attacks attempt to disrupt legitimate users' services by exhausting the resources of the victims [1]. Since such attacks masquerade as flash crowds (a large number of normal users access to a web server simultaneously) by generating legitimate traffic [2], conventional signature-based intrusion detection systems (IDS) become ineffective to them. Moreover, compared with the botnet-induced volumetric attacks that generate a significant amount of traffic, low-volume DDoS attacks are even more pernicious and problematic from a defensive standpoint since attacks generally consume less bandwidth and are stealthier in nature [3].

The eventual criterion to distinguish illegitimate users from legitimate ones is the intentions of visiting users [4], which could be well inferred from the browsing activity. In this paper, we propose a Markov model to profile users' browsing activity. The model well characterizes user's access patterns in HTTP sessions. Then the likelihood of a user's browsing activity is calculated based on the access patterns to detect abnormal sessions. The proposed method affiliates the detection of stealthy DDoS attacks, thus reducing the false positive rate. Finally, we evaluate the performance of the detection method based on a real DDoS attack dataset collected from a busy e-commercial web server.

© ICST Institute for Computer Sciences, Social Informatics and Telecommunications Engineering 2017
R. Deng et al. (Eds.): SecureComm 2016, LNICST 198, pp. 747–750, 2017.
DOI: 10.1007/978-3-319-59608-2_42

2   Detection Schemes

In an HTTP session, the user browses the website by jumping from one web page to another. We assume that in a single session the next page a user will browse only depends on the current browsing page, and employ the Markov Chain Model to describe user access patterns. The Markov property of user access patterns has been validated in [5]. We further use a directed weighted graph to represent the Markov Chain, where each node representing a main page and the weights of the edge representing the transition probabilities from one page to another. Formally, the transition probability from page i to page j is defined as

$$p(i|j) = \frac{n_{ij}}{\sum_{j=1}^{N} n_{ij}}, \tag{1}$$

where n_{ij} is the number of observations that page i is followed by page j in a single session; N is the total number of pages. Denote a session as $\{MP_1, MP_2, \ldots, MP_n\}$, where n is the length of the session representing the number of main pages. Then, the log likelihood of the session is defined as

$$\ln L = \ln p(MP_1) + \sum_{i=1}^{n-1} \ln p(MP_i|MP_{i+1}) \tag{2}$$

where $p(MP_1)$ is the probability of page MP_1, and $p(MP_i|MP_{i+1})$ is the transition probability from the i_{th} to $(i+1)_{\text{th}}$ page.

3   Experiments

We conduct the experiments based on real data collected from a commercial web server. Table 1 lists a brief summary of the dataset.

Table 1. Summary of the dataset

Date	Requests	Users	Max. RR[1]	Min. RR[1]	Suspected IPs
2015/12/29	30,933,159	30,242	283	20	845
2015/12/30	32,202,986	32,886	290	18	1023
2015/12/31	30,850,731	31,063	341	19	1139
Total	93,986,876	74,773	-	-	1270

[1] RR is the abbreviate of request rate with a time unit of second.

The website has a total of 8464 pages and 14036 objects. The access patterns are closely related to the web structure, which exhibits hierarchical clusters. The transition matrix of the top 80 most accessed pages are shown in Fig. 1. These pages dominates 90% of the total requests. Then, we use the transition matrix to calculate the likelihood of all sessions and the results versus the session

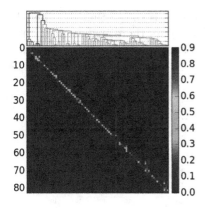

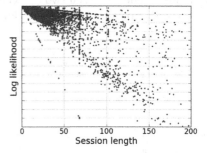

Fig. 1. Transition matrix of web pages

Fig. 2. Session likelihoods v.s. length

length are shown in Fig. 2. It is clearly shown that there are some outliers for different session lengths. This demonstrates that our methods can distinguish the abnormal sessions from the normal ones.

Testing and validation of a detection method is complicated due to the lack of adequate datasets that clearly identify attack behaviors and legitimate human users particularly flash crowd. Following we conducted statistical experiments to evaluate the effectiveness of our method [6].

Denote n_t as the number of requests received by the server in a time unit, and the request rate is plotted versus the time in Fig. 3(a). It is observed that the server suffered from periodic DDoS attacks which result in the comb-shape. Figure 3(b) shows the request rate after filtering the attacking traffic based on the detection results of the combined method. The comparison indicates that the detection method is effective to reduce the burden of the server. In addition, it is noticeable that the request rate varies periodically, suggesting that detection methods should avoid the impacts of fluctuations raised by such periodicity.

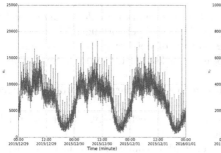

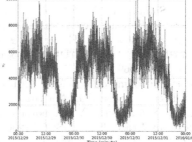

(a) Original request rate

(b) Filtered request rate

Fig. 3. The request rate versus the time

Figure 4 compare the access frequency of pages. It is shown that the filtered activity follows the Zipf distribution. Figure 5 presents the distribution of the inter-request times between two consecutive accessed pages. It is shown that the filtered data follows Pareto distribution.

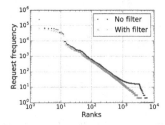

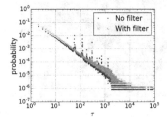

Fig. 4. Page frequency distributions   **Fig. 5.** Time interval distributions

4   Conclusion

We propose a new mechanism to detect application layer DDoS attacks. Based on the access log at the sever end, we propose a Markov model to describe the browsing activity of a user in an HTTP session. Then, the likelihood of a session is calculated and the results are used to distinguish the attack behaviors from the normal ones. We use a real dataset to evaluate the effectiveness of our method.

Acknowledgments. We thank the anonymous reviewers for their quality reviews and suggestions. This work is supported in part by the Hong Kong ITF (No. UIM/285) and Shenzhen City Science and Technology R&D Fund (No. JCYJ20150630115257892).

References

1. Xie, Y., Shun-Zheng, Y.: A large-scale hidden semi-markov model for anomaly detection on user browsing behaviors. IEEE/ACM Trans. Networking **17**(1), 54–65 (2009)
2. Zargar, S.T., Joshi, J., Tipper, D.: A survey of defense mechanisms against distributed denial of service (DDoS) flooding attacks. IEEE Commun. Surv. Tutorials **15**(4), 2046–2069 (2013)
3. DARPA. Extreme ddos defense (2015). http://www.darpa.mil/program/extreme-ddos-defense. Accessed 17 Apr 2016
4. Xie, Y., Shun-Zheng, Y.: A novel model for detecting application layer DDoS attacks. In: Proceedings IMSCCS (2006)
5. Li, Z., Tian, J.: Testing the suitability of markov chains as web usage models. In: Proceedings COMPSAC (2003)
6. Sivabalan, S., Radcliffe, P.J.: A novel framework to detect and block DDoS attack at the application layer. In: Proceedings IEEE TENCON (2013)

POSTER: A Framework for IoT Reprogramming

Nian Xue[1,2], Lulu Liang[3], Jie Zhang[1,2], and Xin Huang[1(✉)]

[1] Department of Computer Science and Software Engineering,
Xi'an Jiaotong-Liverpool University, Suzhou, China
Nian.Xue15@student.xjtlu.edu.cn, Xin.Huang@xjtlu.edu.cn
[2] School of Electrical Engineering and Electronics and Computer Science,
University of Liverpool, Liverpool, UK
Jie.Zhang3@liverpool.ac.uk
[3] China Information Technology Security Evaluation Center, Beijing, China
lianglulu@secemail.cn

Abstract. The OpenFlow protocol, as a fundamental element for Software Defined Networking (SDN) architecture, only supports for packet forwarding across switches in general networks. In this paper, the authors propose Software-Defined Function (SDF) which entitles administrators to manage the Internet of Things (IoT) devices and services through abstraction of the underlying infrastructure. The authors further present OpenFunction, a secure communications protocol stemmed from OpenFlow, which enables the IoT devices to be upgraded or reprogrammed remotely and securely. Finally, the authors implement a preliminary SDF system and evaluate its performance. The experimental results demonstrate that the SDF and OpenFunction can grant programmability, flexibility, centralization and security to the IoT.

Keywords: OpenFunction · Security · IoT · Software Defined Function

1 Introduction

The recent burgeoning of the Internet of Things (IoT) has been attracting an increasing number of researchers and experts with great attentions due to its significant economic and social values [1]. However, in the wake of the incremental number of the IoT devices, it is more and more difficult to manage and maintain so many devices efficiently [4,5]. In the meantime, as current IoT devices become considerably intelligent and heterogeneous [6], people thus expect more capabilities and features from these devices. According to [2], there is a tendency that the IoT nodes will receive software updates more frequently due to the growingly dynamic and changeful requirements and services from users and enterprises. Thereupon, how to reprogram or update the remote IoT devices securely and timely is another ongoing challenge.

In order to address the problems mentioned above, this paper proposes Software Defined Function (SDF) that utilizes an SDF controller in the control layer, via a function station situated in the physical infrastructure layer, to reprogram

© ICST Institute for Computer Sciences, Social Informatics and Telecommunications Engineering 2017
R. Deng et al. (Eds.): SecureComm 2016, LNICST 198, pp. 751–754, 2017.
DOI: 10.1007/978-3-319-59608-2_43

the corresponding IoT end device through OpenFunction protocol derivated from OpenFlow [3]. In particular, two specific security protocols of OpenFunction are designed to assure the secure communication between an SDF controller and a Function Station. Lastly, a demo system is realized and performance is evaluated in the archetypal SDF system.

2 System Design Overview

In our proposed framework, it comprises three kinds of components: *SDF Controller*, *Function Station* and *IoT Device*. The controller and the function station are usually connected by the Internet or LAN, while the IoT devices are often connected to the function station through short range wireless or wire manners such as WiFi, Bluetooth, Zigbee, serial line and so on. Below is the system design.

- **IoT device.** IoT devices in our framework are low-price and low-energy ones, mainly responsible for collecting or sending data. They consist of various smart entities, for example, temperature sensor, noise sensor, PM 2.5 sensor, etc.
- **Function station.** A function station connects to IoT devices and a controller simultaneously in the middle, responsible for upgrading or reprogramming the IoT devices according to the instruction from the controller.
- **SDF controller.** An SDF controller plays a pivotal role in the SDF framework, similar to the function of a human brain. Since it is able to remotely upgrade or reprogram the functions in IoT devices via a function station, it is unnecessary to deploy the controller near those IoT end devices.
- **Protocol I: OpenFunction Authenticated Handshake.** The primary aim is to provide authentication between a controller and function stations. In the first two steps, IDs and nonces are exchanged. Then the function station and the controller negotiate a session key using the pre-distributed public key with an SSL (Secure Socket Layer)-like procedure.
- **Protocol II: OpenFunction Messaging.** It is used to transmit the Open-Function reprogramming messages. Messages are encrypted using the session key; and its authenticity is guaranteed with a message authentication code. After the above processes, the function station can reprogramme the IoT device according to the message content. Figure 1 below shows the whole process.

3 Evaluation and Implementation

A function station has stored beforehand a series of functions like a function warehouse. After receiving the update instructions from the authenticated controller, the function station will reprogramme the specified smart device through Avrdude, a program used to burn a hexadecimal coding into a firmware. In our experiment, one IoT device was originally preprogrammed as a temperature sensor, as shown in Fig. 3(a). After the experiment, its function has been

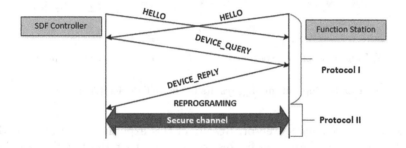

Fig. 1. Process of OpenFunction.

```
PMK 89272774
b1f8e6048ea2c7287ae4f49f32053bb76fcd2d3b998215d0d9075a2aab14e1c5
success
OpenFunction Reprogramming
key_1: 2693a337e3921b0d8f3a89aba15795866d8800361a74a8fce0db013ee9753350
key_2: 7fb7cb408db0413adb415c24fae3933ca29e2e206cb107ab6ba987804301ebdd
HESHEXCODE: e5fe7872c8f1cc63ff8ab89380f9d246
REPROGRAMMING MAC
60a7db4cf68453f759fcf17011ba0aa1f3bf17d426cb9733ef9f055ede0bca7b
```

(a) Experiment result on controller

```
success
PMK: 89272774
skey: b1f8e6048ea2c7287ae4f49f32053bb76fcd2d3b998215d0d9075a2aab14e1c5
OpenFunction REPROGRAMMING
key_1: 2693a337e3921b0d8f3a89aba15795866d8800361a74a8fce0db013ee9753350
key_2: 7fb7cb408db0413adb415c24fae3933ca29e2e206cb107ab6ba987804301ebdd
REPROGRAMMING MAC
60a7db4cf68453f759fcf17011ba0aa1f3bf17d426cb9733ef9f055ede0bca7b

avrdude: AVR device initialized and ready to accept instructions

Reading | ################################################## | 100% 0.00s

avrdude: Device signature = 0x1e950f
avrdude: NOTE: "flash" memory has been specified, an erase cycle will be performed
         To disable this feature, specify the -D option.
avrdude: erasing chip
avrdude: reading input file "ss.hex"
avrdude: writing flash (5868 bytes):

Writing | ################################################## | 100% 0.98s

avrdude: 5868 bytes of flash written
avrdude: verifying flash memory against ss.hex:
avrdude: load data flash data from input file ss.hex:
avrdude: input file ss.hex contains 5868 bytes
avrdude: reading on-chip flash data:

Reading | ################################################## | 100% 0.79s

avrdude: verifying ...
avrdude: 5868 bytes of flash verified

avrdude: safemode: Fuses OK (E:00, H:00, L:00)

avrdude done.  Thank you.
```

(b) Experiment result on function station

Fig. 2. Implementing results of OpenFunction

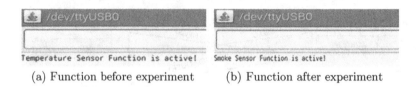

(a) Function before experiment   (b) Function after experiment

Fig. 3. Reprogramming results of the IoT device (Arduino)

reprogrammed to a smoke sensor. Results of this experiment are illustrated in Figs. 2(a) and 3(b). From the figures we can find that the function has been changed. The average runtime for Protocol I is 35.01 ms, and for Protocol II is 31.33 ms. The overhead costs are acceptable.

4 Conclusion

In this paper, we have proposed and implemented SDF, a secure framework for reprogramming IoT devices. Two protocols are designed to guarantee the security during the reprogramming process. Test result indicates OpenFunction can be used to support IoT devices, as well as obtaining flexibility and security.

Acknowledgments. This work has been supported by the XJTLU research development fund projects RDF140243, as well as by the Suzhou Science and Technology Development Plan under grant SYG201516, and Jiangsu Province National Science Foundation under grant BK20150376. This work has been supported in part by the Natural Science Foundation of China under Grant No. 61401517, in part by the National High Technology Research and Development Program ("863" Program) of China under Grant No. 2015AA016001.

References

1. Gubbi, J., Buyya, R., Marusic, S., Palaniswami, M.: Internet of Things (IoT) a vision, architectural elements, and future directions. Future Gener. Comput. Syst. **29**(7), 1645–1660 (2013)
2. Huth, C., Duplys, P., GNeysu, T.: Secure software update and IP protection for untrusted devices in the Internet of Things via physically unclonable functions. In: 2016 IEEE International Conference on Pervasive Computing and Communication Workshops (PerCom Workshops) (2016)
3. Mckeown, N., Anderson, T., Balakrishnan, H., Parulkar, G., Peterson, L., Rexford, J., Shenker, S., Turner, J.: OpenFlow: enabling innovation in campus networks. ACM SIGCOMM Comput. Commun. Rev. **38**(2), 69–74 (2008)
4. Xu, R., Huang, X., Zhang, J., Lu, Y., Wu, G., Yan, Z.: Software defined intelligent building. Int. J. Inf. Secur. Priv. (IJISP) **9**(3), 84–99 (2015)
5. Xue, N., Huang, X., Zhang, J.: S^{2}Net: a security framework for software defined intelligent building networks. In: The IEEE International Conference on Trust, Security and Privacy in Computing and Communications (2016)
6. Wang, D., Lo, D., Bhimani, J., Sugiura, K.: AnyControl - IoT based home appliances monitoring and controlling. In: IEEE Computer Software and Applications Conference (2015)

Privacy Preserving Data Classification Using Inner Product Encryption

Damien Ligier[1]([✉]), Sergiu Carpov[1], Caroline Fontaine[2], and Renaud Sirdey[1]

[1] CEA LIST, Point Courrier 172, 91191 Gif-sur-Yvette Cedex, France
{damien.ligier,sergiu.carpov,renaud.sirdey}@cea.fr
[2] CNRS/Lab-STICC and Telecom Bretagne and UEB,
Technopôle Brest-Iroise, France
caroline.fontaine@telecom-bretagne.eu

Abstract. In the context of data outsourcing more and more concerns raise about the privacy of user's data. One solution is to outsource the data in encrypted form. Meanwhile obtaining a service based on machine learning predictions on user data remains very important in real-life situations.

This paper presents ways to combine machine learning algorithms and IPE in order to perform classification on encrypted data. The proposed privacy preserving classification schemes allow to keep user's data encrypted but at the same time revealing to a server classification results on this data. We study the performance of such classification schemes and their information leakage.

Keywords: Functional encryption · Inner-product encryption · Classification · Linear classification

1 Introduction

With the generalization of data outsourcing, more and more concerns raise about the privacy and the security of the outsourced data. In this context, machine learning methods have to be conceived and deployed by keeping in mind and assuring the user's privacy.

In a privacy preserving data classification process, one has to be able to extract knowledge (e.g. in the case of a classifier, deduct the class label of an individual without compromising his private data) by assuring the protection of the sensitive data and, if possible, by hiding data access patterns from which useful properties could be inferred.

In this work we propose a privacy preserving classification algorithm based on functional encryption, in particular the inner product encryption. The performance of the classification algorithm is evaluated on the MNIST database [3].

An inner product encryption scheme is a functional encryption one that enables the evaluation of inner products. In those public encryption schemes vectors are encrypted and each secret key is associated with one vector.

© ICST Institute for Computer Sciences, Social Informatics and Telecommunications Engineering 2017
R. Deng et al. (Eds.): SecureComm 2016, LNICST 198, pp. 755–757, 2017.
DOI: 10.1007/978-3-319-59608-2_44

For example if c_v is an encryption of the vector v and sk_w is a secret key associated with the vector w, when one decrypts c_v with sk_w he gets $\langle v, w \rangle$. Note that secret keys are generated with the master secret key by the authority.

In the use case we focus in the paper, there is an entity called *server* that has performed a training step of a linear classifier. Thus he has a set of linear classification coefficients and he wants to keep them secret. There are many *users* that have informations that they want to keep secret as well but they also want to release classification results to the server (for example for obtaining a service). We introduce a third party that both of the server and the users can trust and we call it *authority*. His goal is in a first time to check that the server's coefficients are not dishonest and in a second time, to generate an instance of an inner product encryption to perform the classification over the encrypted inputs.

2   Privacy Preserving Classification

A linear classification algorithm makes a decision on the membership of an input data object, based on a linear combination of its features (characteristics). For example, in an image classification algorithm the input object is an image and the features can be image pixels. In a binary classification, the decision is made as a function of a threshold overrun by the dot product between object features and linear classifier coefficients.

In this work we propose a privacy preserving data classification method. Input data is encrypted using an inner product encryption scheme. In the context of ML algorithms, the inner product encryption can be seen as a linear binary classifier. In order to perform a multi-class linear classification, we need to compute several inner products on the same input data. Usually, linear classifiers provide worse results when compared to other more elaborate classification methods. At the same time, only a linear classifier is able to provide a prediction for data encrypted using the inner product encryption.

In order to fill this gap we propose a combined classification method, in which a linear classifier is applied to encrypted data and is followed by a more complex classification algorithm (for example an ensemble method in our case but not limited to). For each piece of input encrypted data, several inner products are computed. These products are then used as input features for a second, more elaborate, classifier. In this way, we are able to perform classification of encrypted data with increased performance in terms of an evaluation metric (e.g. error rate).

3   Performance

We use our implementation (in C++ using FLINT library [2]) of the functional encryption for inner product scheme of Agrawal *et al.* [1] which provides full security under the DDH assumption. We work in a group $\mathbb{F}_p^*$ such that p is a safe prime of approximatively 2048-bits.

We try our construction with the MNIST database [3] which is a collection of handwritten digit images (28×28 pixels with 256 levels of grey). So in this use case, the classifier has 10 output classes (digits from 0 to 9).

The experiments were performed on a regular laptop computer with an Intel Core i7-4650U CPU and 8 GB of RAM. A plaintext and a secret key have size about one kB and a ciphertext has a size about 200 kB.

The algorithm to generate a secret key associated with a vector and the encryption algorithm take less than a second to be computed. The decryption algorithm takes about 23 s to be computed.

We get 14% of error rate with a single linear classifier, and 7% using a second classifier after the first one which does not take significant time to perform.

4 Classification Security

We emphasize that the use case of a such construction can be unsecure even if the cryptographic scheme is secure. An attacker gets a system of diophantine equations. The easiness of solving it and the precision of the description of the inputs increase the ability to compute which vector has been encrypted.

5 Conclusion and Future Work

In this work we have used an instantiation of an inner product encryption in order to perform classification over encrypted data. The learning process is kept secret as only linear classifiers coefficients are public. In the use-case we study, we have a trusted authority, a server computing the classification and the users who encrypt their data. Obtained execution times are reasonably small (a prediction is made in approximatively 69 s without any parallelization) as well as the size of the ciphertexts. We have studied a method to ensure that we cannot find original image from the inner product values. In perspective, we consider to study more deeply the leakage of inner product encryption schemes and to propose methods to lower it.

References

1. Agrawal, S., Libert, B., Stehle, D.: Fully Secure Functional Encryption for Inner Products, from Standard Assumptions (2015)
2. Hart, W., Johansson, F., Pancratz, S.: FLINT: Fast Library for Number Theory, Version 2.4.0 (2013). http://flintlib.org
3. LeCun, Y., Cortes, C., Burges, C.J.: The MNIST Database. http://yann.lecun.com/exdb/mnist/

POSTER: Location Privacy Using Homomorphic Encryption

Peizhao Hu$^{(\boxtimes)}$ and Siyu Zhu

Department of Computer Science, Rochester Institute of Technology,
Rochester, USA
ph@cs.rit.edu

Users' location data has become important contextual information that is used by many popular geosocial applications (such as Facebook) to notify users when a friend is within specified vicinity, to recommend like-minded users who are within a given geographic proximity, or to deliver targeted ads. While service providers want "noise-free" location data to enable value-added social features or targeted ads, and need solutions that offer provable data security, users want robust control during or after releasing location data. There are various categories of techniques in preserving location privacy [13], but many existing solutions fall short in achieving the needs of robust and dynamic control from the user and preserving high data granularity [1]. As an example, one type of solutions focuses on masking users' coordinates using *spatial cloaking* [6], anonymity or obfuscation. These techniques typically require a trusted server that will see all location data. Also, since data is not encrypted these solutions fail to protect users' private data in situations like security breaches or insider attacks, which are more than just occasional incidents [11].

This paper investigates solutions that (i) meet the needs of users and service providers discussed above, (ii) can benefit from the trend of computation outsourcing to support resource constrained mobile devices, and (iii) offer measurable security protection to users' private data. Specifically, we investigate a mix of spatial cloaking that offers flexible control of location masking, and Homomorphic Encryption (HE) that provides the ability for service providers to perform computations on encrypted location data without decryption [5]. Many HE schemes base their security on the *Learning-With-Errors* (LWE) problems that can be reduced to the *average-case* lattice-based cryptography problems, such as *Shortest Vector Problem* (SVP) [12]. A quantum reduction from LWE to standard SVP problem was constructed [12], which suggests that it is unlikely that we can efficiently solve the LWE problem in polynomial time [8,10]. This property offers promising post-quantum cryptographic assurance to users' location data. Regarding the encryption scheme, our prototype implementation used the NLV2011 [9] Somewhat HE (SWHE) scheme. NLV2011 is a practical construction of a well studied SWHE scheme—BV2011 [2]. An SWHE scheme supports a limited number of computations before the ciphertexts become too noisy for decryption.

To compute proximity information securely, the common first attempt is to construct homomorphic operations to evaluate a distance function, such as

© ICST Institute for Computer Sciences, Social Informatics and Telecommunications Engineering 2017
R. Deng et al. (Eds.): SecureComm 2016, LNICST 198, pp. 758–761, 2017.
DOI: 10.1007/978-3-319-59608-2_45

Euclidean distance. Due to the complexity of implementing the *haversine* function in HE schemes, our earlier attempt [7] focused on projecting the WGS84 coordinates onto the Cartesian coordinates, such as the Universal Transverse Mercator coordinate system, and developing homomorphic functions to calculate the Euclidean distance. However, the transformation between coordinate systems introduce undesirable noise, which increases as two points become further apart. Thus, this approach limits user's ability to control the granularity of location data. Also, given a point if we can calculate the extract distance to another point, then we know the other point must be on circumference. By triangulation technique, we can easily determine the location of a point. Hence, this approach leads to serious privacy issues. Instead, we focus on the idea of spatial cloaking, which dynamically compute an appropriate region that encloses the two given points. The size of this region (or level of details) can be controlled by the user. Due to space limitation, two approaches for homomorphic proximity computation will be discussed below. Interested readers can refer to additional papers[1] [7].

Spatial Cloaking using User Preferences. Usually, spatial cloaking solutions mask coordinates with multidimensional data access methods [4], such as *Z-order* or *Hilbert* curve. These geohashing techniques reduce the dimensionality of coordinate data while preserving locality of points. We used the *Z-order* curve to geo-hash the two dimensional coordinates into an array of concatenated indexing keys. Each key represents the position of the point at a particular level of detail. The indexing keys are represented in base 4, hence *quad-key*. Every time we increase one level of detail, we divide each bounding box into four equal subboxes, with each assigned a new quad-key appended to the existing quad-key string, as illustrated. Essentially, in this representation the longer the common prefix between the quad-keys of two points, the closer they are. Also, the longer the indexing key provides a more precise reference to the original coordinates.

Given GPS coordinates in WGS84 encoding, we can compute quad-keys. As an example, given the coordinates (43.584474, −77.675472) the quad-keys at level 5 is 03023. We transform the quad-keys into binary-keys, as 0011001011. Due to space constraints, we only show the indexing keys at a limited level. The maximum level of detail in the form of quad-key is 22 (or 44 level in binary-keys), which corresponds to the exact GPS coordinates. Ideally, users will share the complete quad-keys with a server and update it periodically, rather than sending different versions of the masked keys to reduce communication overhead. Users specify the privacy preferences as a list of prefix masks to control the granularity of location data depending on the friendship with another user. By applying different masks, the server can generate different masked areas for the different requesters; hence achieving the level of privacy as desired by users. However, because we can invert the binary-keys to coordinates, a trusted server is required.

To avoid using a trusted server, we encrypt both the binary-keys and the masks, and construct homomorphic operations to select an appropriate mask

---

[1] http://cs.rit.edu/~ph/research.

and apply it to the binary-keys. Using homomorphic encryption, users can share periodic updates of their coordinates in full level of detail while preserving privacy. We encrypt each element in the binary-keys as a separate ciphertext. Hence, the encryption of Alice's binary-keys yields a vector of ciphertexts. This is common in many existing works [3] to simplify the prototype implementation. When a user B or a third-party application requests another user A's location, the server performs coordinate-wise homomorphic multiplications using the appropriate masks, $Enc(A) \otimes Enc(M_B)$ or $Enc(A) \otimes Enc(M_\#)$, yielding the encrypted results that are sent back to the corresponding information requesters. In this cases, since we only need homomorphic multiplications with depth one, no noise reduction step is needed; hence this approach should be relatively efficient, as shown in our results.

Computing Common Prefix of Two Geo-hashing Codes. With homomorphic encryption we can achieve spatial cloaking with untrusted servers. Extending from the simple masking operation, we explore the possibility of computing the appropriate proximity information in the form of a common prefix (CP), if given $Enc(A)$ and $Enc(B)$. The server will apply the corresponding masks as defined in user's preference before computing the common prefix, because individual users' privacy preferences have higher priority. To simplify the discussion, we assume users are happy with using the location data in full level of detail to compute the common prefix. The resulting encrypted common prefix can then be used to compute a bounding box that contains the location of Alice and Bob. Since the maximum distance between any two points in the bounding box is the length of the diagonal, we know the upper bound of how far apart the two points are without giving away their exact locations. In addition, we can use this property to hide users' mobility trajectories within an area; hence, this approach does not only preserve the privacy of coordinates but also the mobility patterns of users.

To find the common prefix, we apply homomorphic operations to compute a common prefix mask of two binary-keys. The logical way is to implement a homomorphic equality operator which compares the encrypted vectors and figures out the matching bits. However, because HE schemes are nondeterministic due to the use of random noise in every encryption, different encryptions of the same value generate ciphertexts that are different. It is difficult to implement an equality operator that compares the ciphertexts. In literature, the equality operator [3] for vectors $X = (x_1, ..., x_n)$ and $Y = (y_1, ..., y_n)$ is implemented as arithmetic circuits, $EQU(X, Y) = \wedge_{i=1}^{n}(1 \oplus x_i \oplus y_i)$, where $\wedge$ and $\oplus$ are bitwise AND and XOR. However, this operation can only tell whether the two vectors are identical but cannot dynamically compute the common prefix with an appropriate level of detail. In this regard, this approach is similar to the work on private proximity test [13].

In this paper, we construct a special arithmetic circuit to compute the common prefix. Given two encrypted binary vectors A and B, we first apply a coordinate-wise XNOR, which returns encryption of 1, if the corresponding bit values in the encrypted coordinates are the same, otherwise it will return encryption of 0. We then perform a prefix mask *purification* step in which bit value after the left most 0 is reset to 0. This process requires consecutive homomorphic multiplications which increase the multiplicative depth. Due to the use of multiple levels of homomorphic multiplications, the relinearization step is required to reduce the size of the ciphertext. We study the characteristics of this algorithm and compare it to other homomorphic operations, such as the equality operator *EQU* [3]. We found that they share similar computation time profile because they both rely on consecutive homomorphic multiplications.

References

1. Bettini, C., Riboni, D.: Privacy protection in pervasive systems: state of the art and technical challenges. Pervasive Mob. Comput. Part B **17**, 159–174 (2015)
2. Brakerski, Z., Vaikuntanathan, V.: Efficient fully homomorphic encryption from (Standard) LWE. In: Proceedings of FOCS 2011, pp. 97–106. IEEE Computer Society, Washington, DC, USA (2011)
3. Cheon, J.H., Kim, M., Lauter, K.: Homomorphic computation of edit distance. In: Workshop on Encrypted Computing and Applied Homomorphic Cryptography, Isla Verde, Puerto Rico, ACM, January 2015
4. Gaede, V., Günther, O.: Multidimensional access methods. ACM Comput. Surv. **30**(2), 170–231 (1998)
5. Gentry, C.: Computing arbitrary functions of encrypted data. Commun. ACM **53**(3), 97–105 (2010)
6. Hashem, T., Kulik, L.: "Don't trust anyone": privacy protection for location-based services. Pervasive Mob. Comput. **7**(1), 44–59 (2011)
7. Hu, P., Mukherjee, T., Valliappan, A., Radziszowski, S.: Homomorphic proximity computation in geosocial networks. In: Proceeding of BigSecurity 2016, An INFO-COM 2016 Workshop, San Francisco, CA, USA, April 2016
8. Micciancio, D., Regev, O.: Lattice-based cryptography. In: Bernstein, D.J., Buchmann, J., Dahmen, E. (eds.) Post-Quantum Cryptography, pp. 147–191. Springer, Heidelberg (2009)
9. Naehrig, M., Lauter, K., Vaikuntanathan, V.: Can homomorphic encryption be practical? In: Proceedings of CCSW 2011, pp. 113–124, Chicago, IL, USA (2011)
10. Peikert, C.: A decade of lattice cryptography. IACR Cryptology ePrint Archive (2015/939), p. 939 (2015)
11. Popa, R.A., Zeldovich, N.: How to compute with data you can't see. In: IEEE Spectrum, July 2015
12. Regev, O.: The learning with errors problem (invited survey). In: Proceedings of CCC 2010, pp. 191–204, Cambridge, MA, June 2010
13. Saldamli, G., Chow, R., Jin, H., Knijnenburg, B.: Private proximity testing with an untrusted server. In: Proceedings of WiSec 2013, Budapest, Hungary, ACM, April 2013

SDNGuardian: Secure Your REST NBIs with API-Grained Permission Checking System

Kailei Ren[1,2(✉)], Qiang Wei[1,2], Zehui Wu[1,2], and Qingxian Wang[1,2]

[1] State Key Laboratory of Mathematical Engineering and Advanced Computing,
Zhengzhou 450001, China
eric_ren0418@sina.com, xdweiqiang@163.com,
wangqingxian2015@163.com, wuzehui2010@foxmail.com
[2] China National Digital Switching System Engineering and Technological
Research Center, Zhengzhou 450001, China

Abstract. REST NBI (REST Northbound API) is the mainstream NBI implementation method of current SDN controllers, but none of them has achieved authorization management, which leads to serious privilege abuse problems. In this paper, we propose *SDNGuardian*, an API-grained permission checking method based SDN REST NBI security defense system that achieves API level REST NBI authorization and effectively solves the problem of privilege abuse. Comparing with current authorization enhanced SDN controllers, our system is able to defend against attacks via REST NBIs within the same permission group.

Keywords: SDN · Privilege abuse · Authorization · REST NBI · API-grained permission checking

1 Introduction

REST NBI is not only easy to be implemented, but also introduces small overhead [1]. As a result, it is supported by all mainstream SDN controllers. However, REST NBI of most mainstream controllers is implemented with the lack of encryption, authentication and authorization management, which can lead to serious potential security problems. By exploiting vulnerabilities of REST NBI, attackers can interact with core resources of SDN network, and obtain the same level of control as the controller. All mainstream controllers, like Floodlight [2], OpenDaylight [3], Ryu [4], Open Mul [5] and ONOS [6], have not even implemented all basic REST NBI security mechanisms (encryption, authentication and authorization management), and in particular, none of them supports authorization. That is to say, any application is able to call REST NBI without restrictions as long as it has access to the controller's IP address and port. As a result, SDN network is vulnerable to attacks launched via REST NBI by malicious applications, for example, flow hijacking attacks launched by tampering with flow tables via REST NBI, information leakage attacks via querying type REST NBIs.

© ICST Institute for Computer Sciences, Social Informatics and Telecommunications Engineering 2017
R. Deng et al. (Eds.): SecureComm 2016, LNICST 198, pp. 762–765, 2017.
DOI: 10.1007/978-3-319-59608-2_46

Motivated by the lack of authorization management problem of REST NBI, we present *SDNGuardian*, an API-grained REST NBI permission checking system that prevents the privilege of REST NBI from being abused and achieves a more secure SDN controller.

2 System Design

2.1 Overview

In this paper, we propose *SDNGuardian*, an API-grained REST NBI authorization management system that overcomes the weaknesses of current permission based authorization management systems. An overview of *SDNGuardian* architecture is shown in Fig. 1.

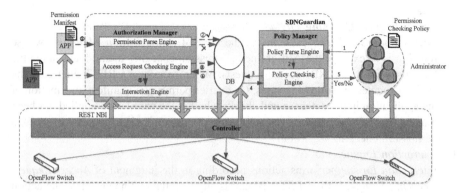

Fig. 1. *SDNGuardian* overview

SDNGuardian is composed of *Authorization Manager*, *Policy Manager* and the database, and it is built as an extension of the controller. Our system plays the role of a protection barrier between third-party applications and SDN networks, which checks the legitimacy of every REST NBI call of third-party applications by executing API-grained permission checking method. Third-party applications complete their registrations, submit their permission manifest files and send their access requests of REST NBI via *Authorization Manager*, while *Policy Manager* is the management center of permission checking policies, via which administrators insert, delete and update permission policies. The database stores all the registration information, permission manifest information, permission checking policy information, REST NBI information and all user information.

2.2 Authorization Manager

We divide *Authorization Manager* into three parts, including *Permission Parse Engine*, *Access Request Checking Engine* and *Interaction Engine*, which are shown in Fig. 1.

Authorization Manager is the mediation between third-party applications and the controller. By adding *Authorization Manager*, third-party applications can no longer directly interact with controllers and call REST NBI without restrictions. All applications must complete registrations and submit their permission manifest files before requesting REST NBI, which ensures the legitimacy and safety of each REST NBI call.

A. *Permission Parse Engine*

Permission Parse Engine receives and parses the permission manifest file and complete registration. In the permission manifest file, application developers manifest the permissions they need to apply to correctly execute the application and basic information of both applications and users. *Permission Parse Engine* extracts the parameters of permission manifest file, and generates data structures of applied permission set and basic information set. The engine checks the legitimacy of user identification, and the result determines whether the application can be registered and whether the applied permissions can be granted and inserted into the database.

B. *Access Request Checking Engine*

Access Request Checking Engine is the core of *Authorization Manager*, whose function is to execute the API-grained permission checking method and judge the legitimacy of REST NBI access requests. When receiving a REST NBI call, the engine executes the following steps: (1) queries permission manifest information of the application in the database and checks whether the permission applied has been granted by *SDNGuardian* (if yes, go to step (2), or stop); (2) executes API-grained permission checking algorithm.

C. *Interaction Engine*

Interaction Engine performs actions according to the judgment of *Access Request Checking Engine*. If the REST NBI call is allowed, the engine performs the action applied and directly interacts with the controller, and returns the execution result to the application.

2.3 Policy Manager

Policy Manager is made up of *Policy Parse Engine* and *Policy Checking Engine*, and it plays the role of permission checking policy management center and provides the administrators with an interface to insert, delete and update permission checking policies.

A. *Policy Parse Engine*

Policy Parse Engine receives and parses the permission checking policy file and generates formatted permission checking policies. In the permission checking policy file, administrators regulate the permission checking scheme and manifest the permission checking policies they want to execute in the SDN network. *Policy Parse Engine* extracts the parameters of the file, and generates data structures of permission checking policies.

B. *Policy Checking Engine*

The function of *Policy Checking Engine* includes three parts: (1) judging the legitimacy of permission checking policies; (2) judging the conflicts of policies; (3) labeling priorities to the policies. When receiving the formatted permission checking policies, the engine executes the policy checking algorithm (discussed in detail in Sect. 5), the result of which tells the legitimacy of the policies and whether they cause conflicts with the existing policies in the database. If the policies are allowed to insert into the database, the engine labels priorities to the policies and performs the action of insertion.

In conclusion, the working procedure of *SDNGuardian* is shown in Fig. 2. The left part is the working procedure of *Authorization Manager* when a REST NBI access request arrives, while the right part is that of *Policy Manager* when an administrator inserts a permission checking policy.

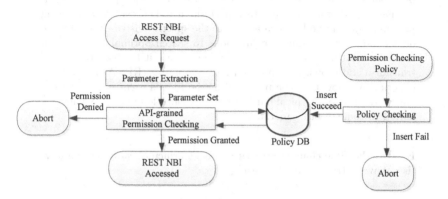

Fig. 2. Working procedure of *SDNGuardian*

References

1. Zhou, W., Li, L., Luo, M., et al.: REST API design patterns for SDN northbound API. In: 2014 28th International Conference on Advanced Information Networking and Applications Workshops (WAINA), pp. 358–365. IEEE (2014)
2. FIOODLIGHT. http://floodlight.openflowhub.org/
3. OPENDAYLIGHT. http://www.opendaylight.org/
4. RYU. http://osrg.github.io/ryu/
5. OPEN MUL. http://www.openmul.org/
6. ONOS. http://onosproject.org/

POSTER: A Novel Wavelet Denoising Method Based on Robust Principal Component Analysis in Side Channel Attacks

Juan Ai[1,2], Zhu Wang[1(✉)], Xinping Zhou[1,2], and Changhai Ou[1,2]

[1] Institute of Information Engineering, Chinese Academy of Sciences,
Beijing, People's Republic of China
{aijuan,wangzhu,zhouxinping,ouchanghai}@iie.ac.cn
[2] University of Chinese Academy of Sciences, Beijing, People's Republic of China

Abstract. In the context of side channel attacks (SCA), multiple pre-processing methods proposed are used to improve the quality of measurements and enhance the attack performance. Different from existing preprocessing methods which accord to the spectral distribution of noise or depend on some objective functions to search optimal linear transform, we treat noise as an ensemble and separate it by discrete wavelet transform and robust principal component analysis (RPCA) blindly. All experiments show that the proposed method has a great impact on the noise reduction of a typical hardware implementation of AES when comparing to some existing methods.

Keywords: Side channel attacks · Robust principal component analysis · Wavelet transform · Denoising

1 Introduction

Noise in side channel attacks (SCA) has been a hot topic since the threat is posed. Not only the multiple kinds of noise affect the analysis performance but also can be difficult to deal with efficiently. Actually, measurements from the device under target (DUT) are contaminated by different noise.

One solution to noise reduction is based on signal processing tools, including but not limited to wavelet transform (WT) [6], empirical mode decomposition (EMD) [4], least squares [3]. The majority of them consider that the leakage concentrates on specific frequencies. However, the commonly used threshold for filtering out interference frequencies limits the denoising efficiency. The other one is the method related to linear transform. For example, a known technique for dimension reduction, i.e., principal component analysis (PCA), is used to preprocess raw measurements [5] in SCA. The biggest challenge of PCA is that the principal components may not contain the most useful leakages, which results that less confidential data can be retrieved eventually.

In this paper, we propose a novel denoising method that combine the discrete wavelet transform and robust principal component analysis before performing

© ICST Institute for Computer Sciences, Social Informatics and Telecommunications Engineering 2017
R. Deng et al. (Eds.): SecureComm 2016, LNICST 198, pp. 766–769, 2017.
DOI: 10.1007/978-3-319-59608-2_47

correlation power analysis (CPA). A comparison is made between the proposed method and some existing methods on a typical hardware implementation of AES. The proposed method outperforms other denoising methods significantly.

2   Background

2.1   Robust Principal Component Analysis

For a data matrix $X \in \Re^{m \times n}$ composed of a low-rank matrix L and a sparse matrix S, for the purpose of separation, the problem can be formulated by

$$\min_{L,S \in \Re^{m \times n}} \quad rank(L) + \lambda \| S \|_0$$

$$s.t. \quad X = L + S, \tag{1}$$

where $rank(\cdot)$ is the rank of a matrix, $\| \cdot \|_0$ is the number of non-zero elements in a matrix, λ represents the parameter to balance two object functions. The problem can be solved by augmented Lagrange multiplier algorithm (ALM) for guaranteeing good accuracy and convergence as suggested by [2].

3   Proposed Denoising Method

Since wavelet transform has the advantage of transforming a signal into such a representation with only several sparse coefficients, we first transform a single trace into the wavelet domain and construct a trajectory matrix on these approximation coefficients. Then, reconstructed approximation coefficients are obtained such as follows.

Separation. For a measurement l of length T, a Hankel matrix is constructed by a window with width of N, such as

$$X_{N \times K} = \begin{pmatrix} l_0 & l_1 & l_2 & \cdots & l_{K-1} \\ l_1 & l_2 & l_3 & \cdots & l_K \\ l_2 & l_3 & l_4 & \cdots & l_K+1 \\ \vdots & \vdots & \vdots & \ddots & \vdots \\ l_{N-1} & l_N & l_N+1 & \cdots & l_{T-1} \end{pmatrix}, \tag{2}$$

where $K = T - N + 1$.

Reconstruction. A new measurement y can be obtained by averaging along cross-diagonals of the sparse matrix S, such as

$$y_t = \begin{cases} \frac{1}{t+1} \sum_{k=1}^{t+1} s_{k,t-k+2}^* & 0 \leq t \leq N^* - 1, \\ \frac{1}{L^*} \sum_{k=1}^{L^*} s_{k,t-k+2}^* & N^* - 1 \leq t \leq K^*, \\ \frac{1}{T-t} \sum_{k=t-K^*+2}^{T-K^*+1} s_{k,t-k+2}^* & K^* \leq t \leq T, \end{cases} \tag{3}$$

where s^* is the element of S, and $N^* = min\{N, K\}$, $K^* = max\{N, K\}$. The denoising method is summarized in Algorithm 1.

Algorithm 1. RPCA based denoising (RPCA-D)

Input: l, N (1 represent a single trace, N reprents the window width)
Output: y (represent the reconstructed approximation coefficients)
1: Transform l into the wavelet domain to obtain approximation coefficients APP
2: Construct a Hankel matrix $X_{N \times K}$ on coefficients APP
3: Perform RPCA on X to obtain a sparse matrix S
4: Reconstruct y by averaging along cross-diagonals of the matrix S
5: **return** y

---

4 Experiment

In this section, a series of experiments on hardware implementation of AES are performed, and the actual power traces are from the second stage of DPA Contest [1]. CPA can be performed either in the wavelet domain after the proposed denoising method or in the time domain by inverse wavelet transform after the proposed one. Firstly, two analysis methods will be compared to some existing methods, including unprocessed condition, wavelet transform from [6], empirical mode decomposition from [4], trend removing from [3] and combination method from [4], and corresponding attacks are named as Unprocessed-CPA, WT-CPA, EMD-IIT-CPA, TR-CPA, EMD-IIT-TR-CPA. Success rate (SR) will be used to evaluate the analysis efficiency proposed in [7], which is widely used in the cryptographic implementation evaluation. The comparison result is shown in Fig. 1. Secondly, the proposed analysis methods will be used to preprocess the traces with different level of signal to noise ratio (SNR). It can interpret the robustness of the proposed method in denoising. The result is shown in Fig. 2.

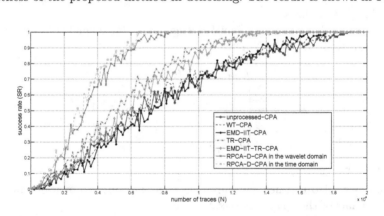

Fig. 1. Success rate of CPA by using different denoising methods

The results showed that the proposed method improves the success rate of CPA significantly both in the time domain and wavelet domain. Especially, even in the condition of low SNR, the proposed method shows excellent denoising performance.

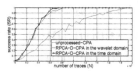

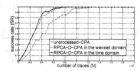

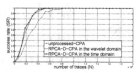

(a) Traces with a low level of SNR

(b) Traces with a middle level of SNR

(c) Traces with a high level of SNR

Fig. 2. Success rate of CPA in different level of SNR by using the proposed denoising method

5 Conclusion

In this paper, we presented a novel denoising method that using robust principal component analysis to separate approximation coefficients in the wavelet domain. Different from the methods proposed in the open literatures, the proposed denoising method has no restriction on the type of noise or the number of power traces for parameters setting. The proposed method outperforms some existing methods significantly and has great robustness ability in denoising.

Acknowledgments. This research is supported by the Nation Natural Science Foundation of China(No.61372062).

References

1. http://www.dpacontest.org/home/
2. Candès, E.J., Li, X., Ma, Y., Wright, J.: Robust principal component analysis? J. ACM **58**(3), 11 (2011)
3. Cao, Y., Zhou, Y., Yu, Z.: On the negative effects of trend noise and its applications in side-channel cryptanalysis. Chinese J. Electron. **23**(CJE–2), 366–370 (2014). http://eprint.iacr.org/2013/102.pdf
4. Feng, M., Zhou, Y., Yu, Z.: EMD-based denoising for side-channel attacks and relationships between the noises extracted with different denoising methods. In: Qing, S., Zhou, J., Liu, D. (eds.) ICICS 2013. LNCS, vol. 8233, pp. 259–274. Springer, Cham (2013). doi:10.1007/978-3-319-02726-5_19
5. Hogenboom, J., Batina, L.: Principal component analysis and side-channel attacks-master. Thesis (2010)
6. Souissi, Y., Elaabid, M.A., Debande, N., Guilley, S., Danger, J.L.: Novel applications of wavelet transforms based side-channel analysis. In: Non-Invasive Attack Testing Workshop. Citeseer (2011)
7. Standaert, F.-X., Malkin, T.G., Yung, M.: A unified framework for the analysis of side-channel key recovery attacks. In: Joux, A. (ed.) EUROCRYPT 2009. LNCS, vol. 5479, pp. 443–461. Springer, Heidelberg (2009). doi:10.1007/978-3-642-01001-9_26

Exploitation of NetEm Utility for Non-payload-based Obfuscation Techniques Improving Network Anomaly Detection

Ivan Homoliak[✉], Martin Teknos, Maros Barabas, and Petr Hanacek

Faculty of Information Technology, Brno University of Technology,
Bozetechova 1/2, 612 66 Brno, Czech Republic
ihomoliak@fit.vutbr.cz
http://www.fit.vutbr.cz/~ihomoliak/.en

Keywords: NetEm · Network anomaly detection · Intrusion detection ·
Obfuscation · Evasion · ADS · NBAD · Naive Bayes

1 Introduction

The impact of a successfully performed intrusion can be very crucial. There exists a lot of space which needs research in order to improve detection capabilities of various types of intrusions. Therefore, many researchers and developers are encouraged to design new methods and approaches for detection of known and unknown (zero-day) network attacks. These facts are the most important reasons why Anomaly Detection Systems (ADS) intended for intrusion detection arose. Network ADS (further ADS) approaches attack detection by utilizing packets' headers and communication behavior, not the content of the packets. Thus, basic principles of ADS open possibilities of an attacker to evade ADS detection by obfuscation techniques.

The goal of our work is to train the ADS detection engine to be aware of the behavior of obfuscated attacks, and thus correctly predict other similar obfuscated attacks. The obfuscation techniques leveraged in our current research are based on non-payload-based modifications of connection-oriented communications. Our work instantiates ADS features by *Advanced Security Network Metrics* (ASNM) [5], which are aimed at offline intrusion detection. In our previous work, experiments showed interesting intrusion detection capabilities on CDX 2009 dataset. But the possibility of evading an intrusion detection employing such features still exists, which is the subject of our current research.

2 Related Work

Although non-payload-based evasions of network attacks in the area of intrusion detection were considered as an actual research subject of more than one and a half decades ago [3,6,7], it revealed to be actual a few years ago as well [2].

© ICST Institute for Computer Sciences, Social Informatics and Telecommunications Engineering 2017
R. Deng et al. (Eds.): SecureComm 2016, LNICST 198, pp. 770–773, 2017.
DOI: 10.1007/978-3-319-59608-2_48

There exist several related works considering non-payload-based evasions of network attacks for payload-based intrusion detection, however, there is a lack of works performing investigations into non-payload-based network behavior anomaly detection and this kind of evasion.

3   Obfuscation Tool

We designed and implemented a tool for automatic exploitation of network services which is able to perform various obfuscation techniques based on NetEm utility and *ifconfig* Linux command. Execution of direct attacks (non-obfuscated ones) is also supported by the tool as well as capturing network traffic.

The most suggested obfuscations are performed by *tc* utility and its extension NetEm [4], respectively. NetEm enables us to add latency of packets, loss of packets, duplication of packets, reordering of packets and other outgoing traffic characteristics of the selected network interface. The modification of MTU is performed by the linux utility *ifconfig*. Table 1 presents instances of these techniques and contains appropriate empirically recognized parameters.

4   Data Mining Experiments

All experiments were performed in Rapid Miner Studio [1] using a 5-fold cross validation and conditional probability based Naive Bayes classifier.

Forward Feature Selection Experiment

For the purpose of finding the best subset of ASNM features [5], we performed the forward feature selection (FFS) method. The experiment considered two class prediction – the first for legitimate traffic and the second for intrusive traffic.

The experiment consisted of two executions of the FFS. The first took as input just legitimate traffic and direct attack entries (denoted as FFS DL), and represented the case where ADS was trained without knowledge about obfuscated attacks. The second execution took as input the whole dataset of network traffic – consisting of legitimate traffic, direct attacks as well as obfuscated ones (denoted as FFS DOL), and thus, represented the case where ADS was aware of obfuscated attacks.

Binary Classification Experiment

A 5-fold cross validation was performed using direct attacks with legitimate traffic considering FFS DOL features. The classifier achieved average recall of 99.35%, while it correctly predicted 98.71% of direct attacks. The classifier trained on all direct attacks and legitimate traffic instances was then applied in the prediction of the whole dataset (including obfuscated attacks) and it correctly predicted 71.25% of obfuscated attacks and 78.26% of all attacks respectively. The achieved result proclaimed the existence of some successful obfuscations of attacks which were predicted as legitimate traffic.

Table 1. Experimental obfuscation techniques with parameters

Technique	Instance	ID
Spread out packets in time	• Constant delay: 1 s	(a)
	• Constant delay: 8 s	(b)
	• Normal distribution of delay with 5 s mean 2.5 s standard deviation (25% correlation)	(c)
Packets' loss	• 25% of packets	(d)
Unreliable network channel simulation	• 25% of packets damaged	(e)
	• 35% of packets damaged	(f)
	• 35% of packets damaged with 25% correlation	(g)
Packets' duplication	• 5% of packets	(h)
Packets' order modification	• Reordering of 25% packets; reordered packets are sent with 10 ms delay and 50% correlation	(i)
	• Reordering of 50% packets; reordered packets are sent with 10 ms delay and 50% correlation	(j)
Fragmentation	• MTU 1000	(k)
	• MTU 750	(l)
	• MTU 500	(m)
	• MTU 250	(n)
Combinations	• Normal distribution delay ($\mu = 10\,ms$, $\sigma = 20\,ms$) and 25% correlation; loss: 23% of packets; corrupt: 23% of packets; reorder: 23% of packets	(o)
	• Normal distribution delay ($\mu = 7750\,ms$, $\sigma = 150\,ms$) and 25% correlation; loss: 0.1% of packets; corrupt: 0.1% of packets; duplication: 0.1% of packets; reorder: 0.1% of packets	(p)
	• Normal distribution delay ($\mu = 6800\,ms$, $\sigma = 150\,ms$) and 25% correlation; loss: 1% of packets; corrupt: 1% of packets; duplication: 1% of packets; reorder 1% of packets	(q)

In the next part of the current binary classification experiment, we performed 5-fold cross validation of the whole dataset including obfuscated attacks. The classifier achieved average recall of 99.63%, while it correctly predicted 99.37% of all attacks. Therefore, we confirmed the assumption that a classifier trained with knowledge about some obfuscated attacks is able to detect the same or similar obfuscated attacks later.

Comparing the results of the current experiment reproduced with the FFS DL feature set, we concluded that the model using FFS DL features had achieved slightly better results in learning direct attacks and legitimate traffic characteristics than the case of the first model (using DOL features), but on the other hand, it resulted in more misclassified cases of obfuscated attacks than the first one (i.e. 155:138) as well as it achieved worse results in cross validation of the whole dataset.

5 Summary of the Obfuscation Techniques

The results presented in the section originate from a binary classification experiment in which the classifier is trained without obfuscated attack knowledge and validated on the whole dataset. The obfuscations are considered successful if they are predicted as legitimate traffic, and therefore the situation represents the ADS evasion case. The most successful obfuscations use combinations of more techniques (i.e. o, q, p), damaging of packets (i.e. f, e) and spreading out packets in time with delays specified by normal distribution (i.e. c). From the MTU modification techniques, (n) appear to be the most successful.

(Non) Exigency of a Network Normalizer

If we would assume existence of an optimal network normalizer for ADS which would be able to completely eliminate the impact of proposed non-payload based obfuscation techniques, then these obfuscation techniques would be useless. If such optimal network normalizer would exists, then it would still be prone to state holding and CPU overload attacks.

Contrary, if we would not assume network normalizer as part of ADS system, then non-payload-based obfuscation techniques might be employed as training data driven approximation of network normalizer, which would not be prone to previously mentioned issues and attacks.

Acknowledgments. This article was created within the project Reliability and Security in IT (FIT-S-14-2486) and supported by The Ministry of Education, Youth and Sports from the National Programme of Sustainability (NPU II); project IT4Innovations excellence in science – LQ1602.

References

1. RapidMiner: RapidMiner Studio. https://rapidminer.com/products/studio/
2. Boltz, M., Jalava, M., Walsh, J.: New Methods and Combinatorics for Bypassing Intrusion Prevention Technologies. Technical report Stonesoft (2010)
3. Handley, M., Paxson, V., Kreibich, C.: Network Intrusion Detection: Evasion, Traffic Normalization, and End-to-End Protocol Semantics. In: 10th USENIX Security Symposium, pp. 115–131 (2001)
4. Hemminger, S., et al.: Network Emulation with NetEm. In: Australia's 6th National Linux Conference, pp. 18–23. Citeseer (2005)
5. Homoliak, I., Barabas, M., Chmelar, P., Drozd, M., Hanacek, P.: ASNM: Advanced Security Network Metrics for Attack Vector Description. In: Proceedings of the International Conference on Security and Management (SAM), pp. 350–358 (2013)
6. Ptacek, T.H., Newsham, T.N.: Insertion, Evasion, and Denial of Service: Eluding Network Intrusion Detection. Technical report, DTIC Document (1998)
7. Puppy, R.F.: A look at Whisker's Anti-IDS Tactics (1999). http://www.ussrback.com/docs/papers/IDS/whiskerids.html

POSTER: Non-intrusive Face Spoofing Detection Based on Guided Filtering and Image Quality Analysis

Fei Peng[1(✉)], Le Qin[1], and Min Long[2]

[1] College of Computer Science and Electronic Engineering,
Hunan University, Changsha 410082, China
eepengf@gmail.com, qinle@hnu.edu.cn
[2] College of Computer and Communication Engineering,
Changsha University of Science and Technology, Changsha 410014, China
caslongm@gmail.com

Abstract. Aiming to counterstrike the spoofing attacks in face recognition system, a non-intrusive face spoofing detection method based on guided filtering and image quality analysis is proposed. Guided image filtering (GIF) is first implemented for the enhancement of texture component of facial image, and then the local texture features are extracted by calculating local binary patterns (LBP). Meanwhile, the global facial image quality features are obtained from image quality measures. With these features, the spoofing detection is accomplished by using support vector machine (SVM) classifier. Experiments results indicate its effectiveness and it has great potential to be applied for the authenticity verification in face recognition system.

Keywords: Face anti-spoofing · Guided filtering · Image quality

1 Introduction

As an important identity authentication means, biometric identification technologies have been widely used in door control system, criminal investigation and security inspection equipment. Among them, face recognition has attracted extensive attention due to its high security, good stability and easy operation. However, with the development of information technologies, images or videos containing a target's face can be easily acquired from social network. If they are abused by malicious attackers, it is possible to launch spoofing attacks to face recognition systems [1].

Currently, the researches of face recognition are mainly concentrated on the accurate discrimination of different individuals' faces in complex scenes, while few works have been done to the authenticity forensics of human faces. This situation leads to the vulnerability of spoofing attacks, such as photo attacks, video attacks and mask attacks.

To counterstrike image printing and video replaying attacks in face recognition systems and improve the detection performance, a non-intrusive face spoofing

© ICST Institute for Computer Sciences, Social Informatics and Telecommunications Engineering 2017
R. Deng et al. (Eds.): SecureComm 2016, LNICST 198, pp. 774–777, 2017.
DOI: 10.1007/978-3-319-59608-2_49

detection method based on guided image filtering (GIF) [2] and image quality analysis is proposed in this paper, the rationale and motivation are as follows:

- Guided image filtering has been successfully used in previous works for forgery detection in small-size image. To a certain extent, many spoofing attacks can be regarded as a type of image forgery or manipulation, and they can be effectively detected by using guided image filtering.
- Guided image filtering can enhance the useful texture component of facial image, and local binary patterns (LBP) operator [3] can extract more powerful texture feature from an enhanced texture space, which has less redundancy information compared with the original facial image.
- Spoofing faces in photo or video are recaptured by device, and they tend to be more seriously distorted by reproduction process. Classical image quality assessments have potential of analyzing the image quality, and their limitation of sensitivity can be compensated by integrating them with texture features.

In summary, the contributions of this paper are:

(1) A face spoofing detection method based on hybrid features is proposed.
(2) A new feature space of texture enhancement for face spoofing detection is provided by guided image filtering.

2   The Proposed Method

Based on guided filter [2] and image quality assessment [7], a framework of the face spoofing detection method is presented in Fig. 1. For an input frame (image), it is first normalized to an image with a size of 64×64 to decrease the computation complexity and avoid the influence of different size of the input frame. After that, local binary pattern (LBP) features are obtained from the image after guided filtering, and image quality features are calculated from the image and the counterpart after Gaussian filtering. Finally, these features are fed to a support vector machine (SVM) classifier [4], and the output score value describes whether there is a live person or a fake one in front of the camera.

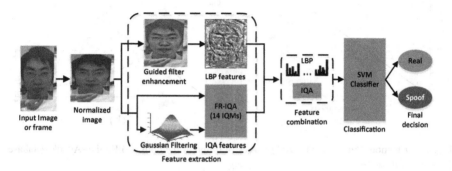

Fig. 1. Framework of the proposed face spoofing detection scheme

Extraction of Guided Filtering Features. For the normalized facial image, guided filter is implemented for the texture enhancement of R, G, B channels, respectively. Then, LBP operator [3] with $P = 8$, $R = 1$ is used for calculating guided LBP facial image. With a guided LBP facial image, a sliding window B with a size of 32×32 is used to make a statistics of the LBP coding with the uniform mode. The sliding step is $s = 16$. Thus, the dimension of the guided filtering features is $59 \times 9 = 531$.

Extraction of Image Quality Features. For the normalized facial image, it is first transformed into a grayscale image G, and then a Gaussian low-pass filter ($\sigma = 0.5$, size 3×3) is used for it. After that, the corresponding distorted image G' is obtained. In this way, full-reference image quality measures [7] can be calculated from G and G'. Thus, 14 dimensions of image quality features is obtained.

3 Experimental Results and Analysis

Here, the performance of the methods in [5–8] are compared with that of the proposed method using Replay-Attack database [9] and CASIA database [6]. The results are shown in Table 1 and Fig. 2.

Table 1. Performance comparison using the frame based evaluation

Methods	Replay-Attack database			CASIA database		
	EER%	HTER%	Accuracy%	EER%	HTER%	Accuracy%
MLBP [5]	**0.33**	**1.08**	**98.21**	20.89	20.67	87.91
DoG [6]	17.25	17.45	77.17	33.52	25.92	82.69
IQA [7]	24.50	29.06	77.48	25.36	25.91	83.57
LSP [8]	6.00	6.20	93.50	25.15	25.80	86.10
GIF + IQA	1.02	1.31	97.81	**18.70**	**11.54**	**92.98**

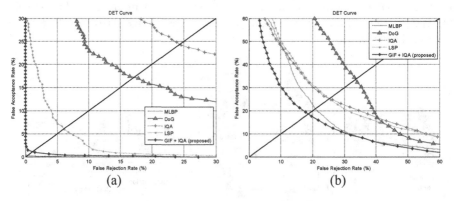

Fig. 2. Detection error tradeoff (DET) curves of different methods. (a) Replay-Attack database. (b) CASIA database

As seen from Table 1 and Fig. 2, the results show that extracting LBP features after guided filtering is able to achieve stable performance across two databases. It also can be found that the fusion of the guided filtering features and image quality features can remedy the weakness of a single kind of features. The average processing time for the test set of the Replay-attack database and CASIA database is 27.80 ms per frame.

4 Conclusions

A face spoofing detection method based on guided filtering and image quality analysis is proposed. The proposed non-intrusive method extracted useful texture features and image quality features from a single facial image, it is fast response and does not require any specific user cooperation. Thus, it can be applied to real-time detection scene.

Acknowledgements. This work was supported in part by project supported by National Natural Science Foundation of China (Grant No. 61572182, 61370225), project supported by Hunan Provincial Natural Science Foundation of China (Grant No. 15JJ2007), and supported by the Scientific Research Plan of Hunan Provincial Science and Technology Department of China (2014FJ4161). The authors would like to thank the Idiap and CASIA institutes for sharing their face spoofing databases.

References

1. Hadid, A., Evans, N., Marcel, S., Fierrez, J.: Biometrics systems under spoofing attack: an evaluation methodology and lessons learned. IEEE Signal Process. Mag. **32**(5), 20–30 (2015)
2. He, K., Sun, J., Tang, X.: Guided image filtering. IEEE Trans. Pattern Anal. Mach. Intell. **35**(6), 1397–1409 (2013)
3. Ojala, T., Pietikäinen, M., Mäenpää, T.: Multiresolution gray-scale and rotation invariant texture classification with local binary patterns. IEEE Trans. Pattern Anal. Mach. Intell. **24**(7), 971–987 (2002)
4. Chang, C.C., Lin, C.J.: LIBSVM: a library for support vector machines. ACM Trans. Intell. Syst. Technol. **2**(3), 27 (2011)
5. Määttä, J., Hadid, A., Pietikainen, M.: Face spoofing detection from single images using micro-texture analysis. In: IEEE International Joint Conference on Biometrics (IJCB), pp. 1–7 (2011)
6. Zhang, Z., Yan, J., Liu, S., Lei, Z., Yi, D., Li, S. Z.: A face antispoofing database with diverse attacks. In: IAPR International Conference on Biometrics (ICB), pp. 26–31 (2012)
7. Galbally, J., Marcel, S.: Face anti-spoofing based on general image quality assessment. In: IEEE International Conference on Pattern Recognition (ICPR), pp. 1173–1178 (2014)
8. Kim, W., Suh, S., Han, J.J.: Face liveness detection from a single image via diffusion speed model. IEEE Trans. Image Process. **24**(8), 2456–2465 (2015)
9. Chingovska, I., Anjos, A., Marcel, S.: On the effectiveness of local binary patterns in face anti-spoofing. In: IEEE International Conference of the Biometrics Special Interest Group (BioSIG), pp. 1–7 (2012)

Author Index

Printed in the United States
By Bookmasters